American Casebook Series
Hornbook Series and Basic Legal Texts
Nutshell Series

of

WEST PUBLISHING COMPANY
P.O. Box 64526
St. Paul, Minnesota 55164–0526

ACCOUNTING

Faris' Accounting and Law in a Nutshell, 377 pages, 1984 (Text)

Fiflis, Kripke and Foster's Teaching Materials on Accounting for Business Lawyers, 3rd Ed., 838 pages, 1984 (Casebook)

Siegel and Siegel's Accounting and Financial Disclosure: A Guide to Basic Concepts, 259 pages, 1983 (Text)

ADMINISTRATIVE LAW

Davis' Cases, Text and Problems on Administrative Law, 6th Ed., 683 pages, 1977 (Casebook)

Gellhorn and Boyer's Administrative Law and Process in a Nutshell, 2nd Ed., 445 pages, 1981 (Text)

Mashaw and Merrill's Cases and Materials on Administrative Law–The American Public Law System, 2nd Ed., 976 pages, 1985 (Casebook)

Robinson, Gellhorn and Bruff's The Administrative Process, 3rd Ed., 978 pages, 1986 (Casebook)

ADMIRALTY

Healy and Sharpe's Cases and Materials on Admiralty, 2nd Ed., 876 pages, 1986 (Casebook)

Maraist's Admiralty in a Nutshell, 390 pages, 1983 (Text)

Schoenbaum's Hornbook on Admiralty and Maritime Law, Student Ed., about 550 pages, 1987 (Text)

Sohn and Gustafson's Law of the Sea in a Nutshell, 264 pages, 1984 (Text)

AGENCY—PARTNERSHIP

Fessler's Alternatives to Incorporation for Persons in Quest of Profit, 2nd Ed., 326 pages, 1986 (Casebook)

AGENCY—PARTNERSHIP—Cont'd

Henn's Cases and Materials on Agency, Partnership and Other Unincorporated Business Enterprises, 2nd Ed., 733 pages, 1985 (Casebook)

Reuschlein and Gregory's Hornbook on the Law of Agency and Partnership, 625 pages, 1979, with 1981 pocket part (Text)

Seavey, Reuschlein and Hall's Cases on Agency and Partnership, 599 pages, 1962 (Casebook)

Selected Corporation and Partnership Statutes and Forms, 555 pages, 1985

Steffen and Kerr's Cases and Materials on Agency-Partnership, 4th Ed., 859 pages, 1980 (Casebook)

Steffen's Agency-Partnership in a Nutshell, 364 pages, 1977 (Text)

AGRICULTURAL LAW

Meyer, Pedersen, Thorson and Davidson's Agricultural Law: Cases and Materials, 931 pages, 1985 (Casebook)

ALTERNATIVE DISPUTE RESOLUTION

Kanowitz' Cases and Materials on Alternative Dispute Resolution, 1024 pages, 1986 (Casebook)

Riskin and Westbrook's Dispute Resolution and Lawyer's, about 300 pages, 1987 (Coursebook)

Teple and Moberly's Arbitration and Conflict Resolution, (The Labor Law Group), 614 pages, 1979 (Casebook)

AMERICAN INDIAN LAW

Canby's American Indian Law in a Nutshell, 288 pages, 1981 (Text)

Getches and Wilkinson's Cases on Federal Indian Law, 2nd Ed., 880 pages, 1986 (Casebook)

List current as of February, 1987

T7202—1g

I

LAW SCHOOL PUBLICATIONS—Continued

ANTITRUST LAW

Gellhorn's Antitrust Law and Economics in a Nutshell, 3rd Ed., 472 pages, 1986 (Text)

Gifford and Raskind's Cases and Materials on Antitrust, 694 pages, 1983 with 1985 Supplement (Casebook)

Hovenkamp's Hornbook on Economics and Federal Antitrust Law, Student Ed., 414 pages, 1985 (Text)

Oppenheim, Weston and McCarthy's Cases and Comments on Federal Antitrust Laws, 4th Ed., 1168 pages, 1981 with 1985 Supplement (Casebook)

Posner and Easterbrook's Cases and Economic Notes on Antitrust, 2nd Ed., 1077 pages, 1981, with 1984–85 Supplement (Casebook)

Sullivan's Hornbook of the Law of Antitrust, 886 pages, 1977 (Text)

See also Regulated Industries, Trade Regulation

ART LAW

DuBoff's Art Law in a Nutshell, 335 pages, 1984 (Text)

BANKING LAW

Lovett's Banking and Financial Institutions in a Nutshell, 409 pages, 1984 (Text)

Symons and White's Teaching Materials on Banking Law, 2nd Ed., 993 pages, 1984 (Casebook)

BUSINESS PLANNING

Painter's Problems and Materials in Business Planning, 2nd Ed., 1008 pages, 1984 with 1987 Supplement (Casebook)

Selected Securities and Business Planning Statutes, Rules and Forms, 470 pages, 1985

CIVIL PROCEDURE

Casad's Res Judicata in a Nutshell, 310 pages, 1976 (text)

Cound, Friedenthal, Miller and Sexton's Cases and Materials on Civil Procedure, 4th Ed., 1202 pages, 1985 with 1985 Supplement (Casebook)

Ehrenzweig, Louisell and Hazard's Jurisdiction in a Nutshell, 4th Ed., 232 pages, 1980 (Text)

Federal Rules of Civil-Appellate Procedure—West Law School Edition, 607 pages, 1986

Friedenthal, Kane and Miller's Hornbook on Civil Procedure, 876 pages, 1985 (Text)

Kane's Civil Procedure in a Nutshell, 2nd Ed., 306 pages, 1986 (Text)

Koffler and Reppy's Hornbook on Common Law Pleading, 663 pages, 1969 (Text)

Marcus and Sherman's Complex Litigation—Cases and Materials on Advanced Civil Procedure, 846 pages, 1985 (Casebook)

CIVIL PROCEDURE—Cont'd

Park's Computer-Aided Exercises on Civil Procedure, 2nd Ed., 167 pages, 1983 (Coursebook)

Siegel's Hornbook on New York Practice, 1011 pages, 1978 with 1985 Pocket Part (Text)

See also Federal Jurisdiction and Procedure

CIVIL RIGHTS

Abernathy's Cases and Materials on Civil Rights, 660 pages, 1980 (Casebook)

Cohen's Cases on the Law of Deprivation of Liberty: A Study in Social Control, 755 pages, 1980 (Casebook)

Lockhart, Kamisar, Choper and Shiffrin's Cases on Constitutional Rights and Liberties, 6th Ed., 1266 pages, 1986 with 1986 Supplement (Casebook)—reprint from Lockhart, et al. Cases on Constitutional Law, 6th Ed., 1986

Vieira's Civil Rights in a Nutshell, 279 pages, 1978 (Text)

COMMERCIAL LAW

Bailey's Secured Transactions in a Nutshell, 2nd Ed., 391 pages, 1981 (Text)

Epstein and Martin's Basic Uniform Commercial Code Teaching Materials, 2nd Ed., 667 pages, 1983 (Casebook)

Henson's Hornbook on Secured Transactions Under the U.C.C., 2nd Ed., 504 pages, 1979 with 1979 P.P. (Text)

Murray's Commercial Law, Problems and Materials, 366 pages, 1975 (Coursebook)

Nickles, Matheson and Dolan's Materials for Understanding Credit and Payment Systems, 923 pages, 1987 (Casebook)

Nordstrom and Clovis' Problems and Materials on Commercial Paper, 458 pages, 1972 (Casebook)

Nordstrom, Murray and Clovis' Problems and Materials on Sales, 515 pages, 1982 (Casebook)

Nordstrom, Murray and Clovis' Problems and Materials on Secured Transactions, 594 pages, 1987 (Casebook)

Selected Commercial Statutes, 1389 pages, 1985

Speidel, Summers and White's Teaching Materials on Commercial and Consumer Law, 4th Ed., about 1400 pages, 1987 (Casebook)

Stockton's Sales in a Nutshell, 2nd Ed., 370 pages, 1981 (Text)

Stone's Uniform Commercial Code in a Nutshell, 2nd Ed., 516 pages, 1984 (Text)

Uniform Commercial Code, Official Text with Comments, 994 pages, 1978

UCC Article 9, Reprint from 1962 Code, 128 pages, 1976

UCC Article 9, 1972 Amendments, 304 pages, 1978

LAW SCHOOL PUBLICATIONS—Continued

COMMERCIAL LAW—Cont'd

Weber and Speidel's Commercial Paper in a Nutshell, 3rd Ed., 404 pages, 1982 (Text)

White and Summers' Hornbook on the Uniform Commercial Code, 2nd Ed., 1250 pages, 1980 (Text)

COMMUNITY PROPERTY

Mennell's Community Property in a Nutshell, 447 pages, 1982 (Text)

Verrall and Bird's Cases and Materials on California Community Property, 4th Ed., 549 pages, 1983 (Casebook)

COMPARATIVE LAW

Barton, Gibbs, Li and Merryman's Law in Radically Different Cultures, 960 pages, 1983 (Casebook)

Glendon, Gordon and Osakive's Comparative Legal Traditions: Text, Materials and Cases on the Civil Law, Common Law, and Socialist Law Traditions, 1091 pages, 1985 (Casebook)

Glendon, Gordon, and Osakwe's Comparative Legal Traditions in a Nutshell, 402 pages, 1982 (Text)

Langbein's Comparative Criminal Procedure: Germany, 172 pages, 1977 (Casebook)

COMPUTERS AND LAW

Maggs and Sprowl's Computer Applications in the Law, 316 pages, 1987 (Coursebook)

Mason's An Introduction to the Use of Computers in Law, 223 pages, 1984 (Text)

CONFLICT OF LAWS

Cramton, Currie and Kay's Cases-Comments-Questions on Conflict of Laws, 4th Ed., about 925 pages, 1987 (Casebook)

Scoles and Hay's Hornbook on Conflict of Laws, Student Ed., 1085 pages, 1982 with 1986 P.P. (Text)

Scoles and Weintraub's Cases and Materials on Conflict of Laws, 2nd Ed., 966 pages, 1972, with 1978 Supplement (Casebook)

Siegel's Conflicts in a Nutshell, 469 pages, 1982 (Text)

CONSTITUTIONAL LAW

Barron and Dienes' Constitutional Law in a Nutshell, 389 pages, 1986 (Text)

Engdahl's Constitutional Federalism in a Nutshell, 2nd Ed., about 360 pages, 1987 (Text)

Lockhart, Kamisar, Choper and Shiffrin's Cases-Comments-Questions on Constitutional Law, 6th Ed., 1601 pages, 1986 with 1986 Supplement (Casebook)

CONSTITUTIONAL LAW—Cont'd

Lockhart, Kamisar, Choper and Shiffrin's Cases-Comments-Questions on the American Constitution, 6th Ed., 1260 pages, 1986 with 1986 Supplement (Casebook)—abridgment of Lockhart, et al. Cases on Constitutional Law, 6th Ed., 1986

Manning's The Law of Church-State Relations in a Nutshell, 305 pages, 1981 (Text)

Miller's Presidential Power in a Nutshell, 328 pages, 1977 (Text)

Nowak, Rotunda and Young's Hornbook on Constitutional Law, 3rd Ed., Student Ed., 1191 pages, 1986 (Text)

Rotunda's Modern Constitutional Law: Cases and Notes, 2nd Ed., 1004 pages, 1985, with 1986 Supplement (Casebook)

Williams' Constitutional Analysis in a Nutshell, 388 pages, 1979 (Text)

See also Civil Rights

CONSUMER LAW

Epstein and Nickles' Consumer Law in a Nutshell, 2nd Ed., 418 pages, 1981 (Text)

Selected Commercial Statutes, 1389 pages, 1985

Spanogle and Rohner's Cases and Materials on Consumer Law, 693 pages, 1979, with 1982 Supplement (Casebook)

See also Commercial Law

CONTRACTS

Calamari & Perillo's Cases and Problems on Contracts, 1061 pages, 1978 (Casebook)

Calamari and Perillo's Hornbook on Contracts, 3rd Ed., about 900 pages, 1987 (Text)

Corbin's Text on Contracts, One Volume Student Edition, 1224 pages, 1952 (Text)

Fessler and Loiseaux's Cases and Materials on Contracts, 837 pages, 1982 (Casebook)

Friedman's Contract Remedies in a Nutshell, 323 pages, 1981 (Text)

Fuller and Eisenberg's Cases on Basic Contract Law, 4th Ed., 1203 pages, 1981 (Casebook)

Hamilton, Rau and Weintraub's Cases and Materials on Contracts, 830 pages, 1984 (Casebook)

Jackson and Bollinger's Cases on Contract Law in Modern Society, 2nd Ed., 1329 pages, 1980 (Casebook)

Keyes' Government Contracts in a Nutshell, 423 pages, 1979 (Text)

Schaber and Rohwer's Contracts in a Nutshell, 2nd Ed., 425 pages, 1984 (Text)

Summers and Hillman's Contract and Related Obligation: Theory, Doctrine and Practice, about 1060 pages, 1987 (Casebook)

COPYRIGHT

See Patent and Copyright Law

CORPORATIONS

Hamilton's Cases on Corporations—Including Partnerships and Limited Partnerships, 3rd Ed., 1213 pages, 1986 with 1986 Statutory Supplement (Casebook)

Hamilton's Law of Corporations in a Nutshell, 2nd Ed., 515 pages, 1987 (Text)

Henn's Teaching Materials on Corporations, 2nd Ed., 1204 pages, 1986 (Casebook)

Henn and Alexander's Hornbook on Corporations, 3rd Ed., Student Ed., 1371 pages, 1983 with 1986 P.P. (Text)

Jennings and Buxbaum's Cases and Materials on Corporations, 5th Ed., 1180 pages, 1979 (Casebook)

Selected Corporation and Partnership Statutes, Regulations and Forms, 555 pages, 1985

Solomon, Stevenson and Schwartz' Materials and Problems on Corporations: Law and Policy, 1172 pages, 1982 with 1986 Supplement (Casebook)

CORPORATE FINANCE

Hamilton's Cases and Materials on Corporate Finance, 895 pages, 1984 with 1986 Supplement (Casebook)

CORRECTIONS

Krantz's Cases and Materials on the Law of Corrections and Prisoners' Rights, 3rd Ed., 855 pages, 1986 (Casebook)

Krantz's Law of Corrections and Prisoners' Rights in a Nutshell, 2nd Ed., 386 pages, 1983 (Text)

Popper's Post-Conviction Remedies in a Nutshell, 360 pages, 1978 (Text)

Robbins' Cases and Materials on Post Conviction Remedies, 506 pages, 1982 (Casebook)

CREDITOR'S RIGHTS

Bankruptcy Code, Rules and Forms, Law School Ed., 838 pages, 1986

Epstein's Debtor-Creditor Law in a Nutshell, 3rd Ed., 383 pages, 1986 (Text)

Epstein, Landers and Nickles' Debtors and Creditors: Cases and Materials, 3rd Ed., about 700 pages, 1987 (Casebook)

LoPucki's Player's Manual for the Debtor-Creditor Game, 123 pages, 1985 (Coursebook)

Riesenfeld's Cases and Materials on Creditors' Remedies and Debtors' Protection, 4th Ed., 914 pages, 1987 (Casebook)

White's Bankruptcy and Creditor's Rights: Cases and Materials, 812 pages, 1985 (Casebook)

CRIMINAL LAW AND CRIMINAL PROCEDURE

Abrams', Federal Criminal Law and its Enforcement, 882 pages, 1986 (Casebook)

Carlson's Adjudication of Criminal Justice, Problems and References, 130 pages, 1986 (Casebook)

Dix and Sharlot's Cases and Materials on Criminal Law, 3rd Ed., about 835 pages, 1987 (Casebook)

Federal Rules of Criminal Procedure—West Law School Edition, 463 pages, 1986

Grano's Problems in Criminal Procedure, 2nd Ed., 176 pages, 1981 (Problem book)

Israel and LaFave's Criminal Procedure in a Nutshell, 3rd Ed., 438 pages, 1980 (Text)

Johnson's Cases, Materials and Text on Criminal Law, 3rd Ed., 783 pages, 1985 (Casebook)

Kamisar, LaFave and Israel's Cases, Comments and Questions on Modern Criminal Procedure, 6th Ed., 1558 pages, 1986 with 1986 Supplement (Casebook)

Kamisar, LaFave and Israel's Cases, Comments and Questions on Basic Criminal Procedure, 6th Ed., 860 pages, 1986 with 1986 Supplement (Casebook)—reprint from Kamisar, et al. Modern Criminal Procedure, 6th ed., 1986

LaFave's Modern Criminal Law: Cases, Comments and Questions, 789 pages, 1978 (Casebook)

LaFave and Israel's Hornbook on Criminal Procedure, Student Ed., 1142 pages, 1985 with 1986 P.P. (Text)

LaFave and Scott's Hornbook on Criminal Law, 2nd Ed., Student Ed., 918 pages, 1986 (Text)

Langbein's Comparative Criminal Procedure: Germany, 172 pages, 1977 (Casebook)

Loewy's Criminal Law in a Nutshell, 2nd Ed., about 350 pages, 1987 (Text)

Saltzburg's American Criminal Procedure, Cases and Commentary, 2nd Ed., 1193 pages, 1985 with 1986 Supplement (Casebook)

Uviller's The Processes of Criminal Justice: Investigation and Adjudication, 2nd Ed., 1384 pages, 1979 with 1979 Statutory Supplement and 1986 Update (Casebook)

Uviller's The Processes of Criminal Justice: Adjudication, 2nd Ed., 730 pages, 1979. Soft-cover reprint from Uviller's The Processes of Criminal Justice: Investigation and Adjudication, 2nd Ed. (Casebook)

Uviller's The Processes of Criminal Justice: Investigation, 2nd Ed., 655 pages, 1979. Soft-cover reprint from Uviller's The Processes of Criminal Justice: Investigation and Adjudication, 2nd Ed. (Casebook)

CRIMINAL LAW AND CRIMINAL PROCEDURE—Cont'd

Vorenberg's Cases on Criminal Law and Procedure, 2nd Ed., 1088 pages, 1981 with 1985 Supplement (Casebook)

See also Corrections, Juvenile Justice

DECEDENTS ESTATES

See Trusts and Estates

DOMESTIC RELATIONS

Clark's Cases and Problems on Domestic Relations, 3rd Ed., 1153 pages, 1980 (Casebook)

Clark's Hornbook on Domestic Relations, 754 pages, 1968 (Text)

Krause's Cases and Materials on Family Law, 2nd Ed., 1221 pages, 1983 with 1986 Supplement (Casebook)

Krause's Family Law in a Nutshell, 2nd Ed., 444 pages, 1986 (Text)

Krauskopf's Cases on Property Division at Marriage Dissolution, 250 pages, 1984 (Casebook)

ECONOMICS, LAW AND

Goetz' Cases and Materials on Law and Economics, 547 pages, 1984 (Casebook)

See also Antitrust, Regulated Industries

EDUCATION LAW

Alexander and Alexander's The Law of Schools, Students and Teachers in a Nutshell, 409 pages, 1984 (Text)

Morris' The Constitution and American Education, 2nd Ed., 992 pages, 1980 (Casebook)

EMPLOYMENT DISCRIMINATION

Jones, Murphy and Belton's Cases on Discrimination in Employment, 1116 pages, 1987 (Casebook)

Player's Cases and Materials on Employment Discrimination Law, 2nd Ed., 782 pages, 1984 (Casebook)

Player's Federal Law of Employment Discrimination in a Nutshell, 2nd Ed., 402 pages, 1981 (Text)

See also Women and the Law

ENERGY AND NATURAL RESOURCES LAW

Laitos' Cases and Materials on Natural Resources Law, 938 pages, 1985 (Casebook)

Rodgers' Cases and Materials on Energy and Natural Resources Law, 2nd Ed., 877 pages, 1983 (Casebook)

Selected Environmental Law Statutes, 965 pages, 1986

Tomain's Energy Law in a Nutshell, 338 pages, 1981 (Text)

See also Environmental Law, Oil and Gas, Water Law

ENVIRONMENTAL LAW

Bonine and McGarity's Cases and Materials on the Law of Environment and Pollution, 1076 pages, 1984 (Casebook)

Findley and Farber's Cases and Materials on Environmental Law, 2nd Ed., 813 pages, 1985 (Casebook)

Findley and Farber's Environmental Law in a Nutshell, 343 pages, 1983 (Text)

Rodgers' Hornbook on Environmental Law, 956 pages, 1977 with 1984 pocket part (Text)

Selected Environmental Law Statutes, 965 pages, 1986

See also Energy Law, Natural Resources Law, Water Law

EQUITY

See Remedies

ESTATES

See Trusts and Estates

ESTATE PLANNING

Kurtz' Cases, Materials and Problems on Family Estate Planning, 853 pages, 1983 (Casebook)

Lynn's Introduction to Estate Planning, in a Nutshell, 3rd Ed., 370 pages, 1983 (Text)

See also Taxation

EVIDENCE

Broun and Meisenholder's Problems in Evidence, 2nd Ed., 304 pages, 1981 (Problem book)

Cleary and Strong's Cases, Materials and Problems on Evidence, 3rd Ed., 1143 pages, 1981 (Casebook)

Federal Rules of Evidence for United States Courts and Magistrates, 337 pages, 1984

Graham's Federal Rules of Evidence in a Nutshell, 2nd Ed., 473 pages, 1987 (Text)

Kimball's Programmed Materials on Problems in Evidence, 380 pages, 1978 (Problem book)

Lempert and Saltzburg's A Modern Approach to Evidence: Text, Problems, Transcripts and Cases, 2nd Ed., 1232 pages, 1983 (Casebook)

Lilly's Introduction to the Law of Evidence, 490 pages, 1978 (Text)

McCormick, Sutton and Wellborn's Cases and Materials on Evidence, 6th Ed., 1067 pages, 1987 (Casebook)

McCormick's Hornbook on Evidence, 3rd Ed., Student Ed., 1156 pages, 1984 with 1987 P.P. (Text)

Rothstein's Evidence, State and Federal Rules in a Nutshell, 2nd Ed., 514 pages, 1981 (Text)

Saltzburg's Evidence Supplement: Rules, Statutes, Commentary, 245 pages, 1980 (Casebook Supplement)

LAW SCHOOL PUBLICATIONS—Continued

FEDERAL JURISDICTION AND PROCEDURE

Currie's Cases and Materials on Federal Courts, 3rd Ed., 1042 pages, 1982 with 1985 Supplement (Casebook)

Currie's Federal Jurisdiction in a Nutshell, 2nd Ed., 258 pages, 1981 (Text)

Federal Rules of Civil-Appellate Procedure—West Law School Edition, 607 pages, 1986

Forrester and Moye's Cases and Materials on Federal Jurisdiction and Procedure, 3rd Ed., 917 pages, 1977 with 1985 Supplement (Casebook)

Redish's Cases, Comments and Questions on Federal Courts, 878 pages, 1983 with 1986 Supplement (Casebook)

Vetri and Merrill's Federal Courts, Problems and Materials, 2nd Ed., 232 pages, 1984 (Problem Book)

Wright's Hornbook on Federal Courts, 4th Ed., Student Ed., 870 pages, 1983 (Text)

FUTURE INTERESTS

See Trusts and Estates

HEALTH LAW

See Medicine, Law and

IMMIGRATION LAW

Aleinikoff and Martin's Immigration Process and Policy, 1042 pages, 1985 (Casebook)

Weissbrodt's Immigration Law and Procedure in a Nutshell, 345 pages, 1984 (Text)

INDIAN LAW

See American Indian Law

INSURANCE

Dobbyn's Insurance Law in a Nutshell, 281 pages, 1981 (Text)

Keeton's Cases on Basic Insurance Law, 2nd Ed., 1086 pages, 1977

Keeton's Basic Text on Insurance Law, 712 pages, 1971 (Text)

Keeton's Case Supplement to Keeton's Basic Text on Insurance Law, 334 pages, 1978 (Casebook)

York and Whelan's Cases, Materials and Problems on Insurance Law, 715 pages, 1982, with 1985 Supplement (Casebook)

INTERNATIONAL LAW

Buergenthal and Maier's Public International Law in a Nutshell, 262 pages, 1985 (Text)

Folsom, Gordon and Spanogle's International Business Transactions – a Problem-Oriented Coursebook, 1160 pages, 1986 (Casebook)

INTERNATIONAL LAW—Cont'd

Frank and Glennon's United States Foreign Relations Law: Cases, Materials and Simulations, about 875 pages, 1987 (Casebook)

Henkin, Pugh, Schachter and Smit's Cases and Materials on International Law, 2nd Ed., 1517 pages, 1987 with Documents Supplement (Casebook)

Jackson and Davey's Legal Problems of International Economic Relations, 2nd Ed., 1269 pages, 1986, with Documents Supplement (Casebook)

Kirgis' International Organizations in Their Legal Setting, 1016 pages, 1977, with 1981 Supplement (Casebook)

Weston, Falk and D'Amato's International Law and World Order—A Problem Oriented Coursebook, 1195 pages, 1980, with Documents Supplement (Casebook)

Wilson's International Business Transactions in a Nutshell, 2nd Ed., 476 pages, 1984 (Text)

INTERVIEWING AND COUNSELING

Binder and Price's Interviewing and Counseling, 232 pages, 1977 (Text)

Shaffer and Elkins' Interviewing and Counseling in a Nutshell, 2nd Ed., about 472 pages, 1987 (Text)

INTRODUCTION TO LAW STUDY

Dobbyn's So You Want to go to Law School, Revised First Edition, 206 pages, 1976 (Text)

Hegland's Introduction to the Study and Practice of Law in a Nutshell, 418 pages, 1983 (Text)

Kinyon's Introduction to Law Study and Law Examinations in a Nutshell, 389 pages, 1971 (Text)

See also Legal Method and Legal System

JUDICIAL ADMINISTRATION

Nelson's Cases and Materials on Judicial Administration and the Administration of Justice, 1032 pages, 1974 (Casebook)

JURISPRUDENCE

Christie's Text and Readings on Jurisprudence—The Philosophy of Law, 1056 pages, 1973 (Casebook)

JUVENILE JUSTICE

Fox's Cases and Materials on Modern Juvenile Justice, 2nd Ed., 960 pages, 1981 (Casebook)

Fox's Juvenile Courts in a Nutshell, 3rd Ed., 291 pages, 1984 (Text)

LAW SCHOOL PUBLICATIONS—Continued

LABOR LAW

Atleson, Rabin, Schatzki, Sherman and Silverstein's Collective Bargaining in Private Employment, 2nd Ed., (The Labor Law Group), 856 pages, 1984 (Casebook)

Gorman's Basic Text on Labor Law—Unionization and Collective Bargaining, 914 pages, 1976 (Text)

Grodin, Wollett and Alleyne's Collective Bargaining in Public Employment, 3rd Ed., (the Labor Law Group), 430 pages, 1979 (Casebook)

Leslie's Labor Law in a Nutshell, 2nd Ed., 397 pages, 1986 (Text)

Nolan's Labor Arbitration Law and Practice in a Nutshell, 358 pages, 1979 (Text)

Oberer, Hanslowe, Andersen and Heinsz' Cases and Materials on Labor Law—Collective Bargaining in a Free Society, 3rd Ed., 1163 pages, 1986 with Statutory Supplement (Casebook)

See also Employment Discrimination, Social Legislation

LAND FINANCE

See Real Estate Transactions

LAND USE

Callies and Freilich's Cases and Materials on Land Use, 1233 pages, 1986 (Casebook)

Hagman's Cases on Public Planning and Control of Urban and Land Development, 2nd Ed., 1301 pages, 1980 (Casebook)

Hagman and Juergensmeyer's Hornbook on Urban Planning and Land Development Control Law, 2nd Ed., Student Edition, 680 pages, 1986 (Text)

Wright and Gitelman's Cases and Materials on Land Use, 3rd Ed., 1300 pages, 1982, with 1987 Supplement (Casebook)

Wright and Wright's Land Use in a Nutshell, 2nd Ed., 356 pages, 1985 (Text)

LEGAL HISTORY

Presser and Zainaldin's Cases on Law and American History, 855 pages, 1980 (Casebook)

See also Legal Method and Legal System

LEGAL METHOD AND LEGAL SYSTEM

Aldisert's Readings, Materials and Cases in the Judicial Process, 948 pages, 1976 (Casebook)

Berch and Berch's Introduction to Legal Method and Process, 550 pages, 1985 (Casebook)

Bodenheimer, Oakley and Love's Readings and Cases on an Introduction to the Anglo-American Legal System, 161 pages, 1980 (Casebook)

Davies and Lawry's Institutions and Methods of the Law—Introductory Teaching Materials, 547 pages, 1982 (Casebook)

LEGAL METHOD AND LEGAL SYSTEM—Cont'd

Dvorkin, Himmelstein and Lesnick's Becoming a Lawyer: A Humanistic Perspective on Legal Education and Professionalism, 211 pages, 1981 (Text)

Greenberg's Judicial Process and Social Change, 666 pages, 1977 (Casebook)

Kelso and Kelso's Studying Law: An Introduction, 587 pages, 1984 (Coursebook)

Kempin's Historical Introduction to Anglo-American Law in a Nutshell, 2nd Ed., 280 pages, 1973 (Text)

Kimball's Historical Introduction to the Legal System, 610 pages, 1966 (Casebook)

Murphy's Cases and Materials on Introduction to Law—Legal Process and Procedure, 772 pages, 1977 (Casebook)

Reynolds' Judicial Process in a Nutshell, 292 pages, 1980 (Text)

See also Legal Research and Writing

LEGAL PROFESSION

Aronson, Devine and Fisch's Problems, Cases and Materials on Professional Responsibility, 745 pages, 1985 (Casebook)

Aronson and Weckstein's Professional Responsibility in a Nutshell, 399 pages, 1980 (Text)

Mellinkoff's The Conscience of a Lawyer, 304 pages, 1973 (Text)

Mellinkoff's Lawyers and the System of Justice, 983 pages, 1976 (Casebook)

Pirsig and Kirwin's Cases and Materials on Professional Responsibility, 4th Ed., 603 pages, 1984 (Casebook)

Schwartz and Wydick's Problems in Legal Ethics, 285 pages, 1983 (Casebook)

Selected Statutes, Rules and Standards on the Legal Profession, 276 pages, Revised 1984

Smith's Preventing Legal Malpractice, 142 pages, 1981 (Text)

Wolfram's Hornbook on Modern Legal Ethics, Student Edition, 1120 pages, 1986 (Text)

LEGAL RESEARCH AND WRITING

Cohen's Legal Research in a Nutshell, 4th Ed., 450 pages, 1985 (Text)

Cohen and Berring's How to Find the Law, 8th Ed., 790 pages, 1983. Problem book by Foster, Johnson and Kelly available (Casebook)

Cohen and Berring's Finding the Law, 8th Ed., Abridged Ed., 556 pages, 1984 (Casebook)

Dickerson's Materials on Legal Drafting, 425 pages, 1981 (Casebook)

Felsenfeld and Siegel's Writing Contracts in Plain English, 290 pages, 1981 (Text)

Gopen's Writing From a Legal Perspective, 225 pages, 1981 (Text)

LAW SCHOOL PUBLICATIONS—Continued

LEGAL RESEARCH AND WRITING—Cont'd

Mellinkoff's Legal Writing—Sense and Nonsense, 242 pages, 1982 (Text)

Ray and Ramsfield's Legal Writing: Getting It Right and Getting It Written, 250 pages, 1987 (Text)

Rombauer's Legal Problem Solving—Analysis, Research and Writing, 4th Ed., 424 pages, 1983 (Coursebook)

Squires and Rombauer's Legal Writing in a Nutshell, 294 pages, 1982 (Text)

Statsky's Legal Research and Writing, 3rd Ed., 257 pages, 1986 (Coursebook)

Statsky and Wernet's Case Analysis and Fundamentals of Legal Writing, 2nd Ed., 441 pages, 1984 (Text)

Teply's Programmed Materials on Legal Research and Citation, 2nd Ed., 358 pages, 1986. Student Library Exercises available (Coursebook)

Weihofen's Legal Writing Style, 2nd Ed., 332 pages, 1980 (Text)

LEGISLATION

Davies' Legislative Law and Process in a Nutshell, 2nd Ed., 346 pages, 1986 (Text)

Nutting and Dickerson's Cases and Materials on Legislation, 5th Ed., 744 pages, 1978 (Casebook)

Statsky's Legislative Analysis and Drafting, 2nd Ed., 217 pages, 1984 (Text)

LOCAL GOVERNMENT

McCarthy's Local Government Law in a Nutshell, 2nd Ed., 404 pages, 1983 (Text)

Reynolds' Hornbook on Local Government Law, 860 pages, 1982 (Text)

Valente's Cases and Materials on Local Government Law, 3rd Ed., 1010 pages, 1987 (Casebook)

MASS COMMUNICATION LAW

Gillmor and Barron's Cases and Comment on Mass Communication Law, 4th Ed., 1076 pages, 1984 (Casebook)

Ginsburg's Regulation of Broadcasting: Law and Policy Towards Radio, Television and Cable Communications, 741 pages, 1979, with 1983 Supplement (Casebook)

Zuckman and Gayne's Mass Communications Law in a Nutshell, 2nd Ed., 473 pages, 1983 (Text)

MEDICINE, LAW AND

Furrow, Johnson, Jost and Schwartz' Health Law: Cases, Materials and Problems, about 1090 pages, 1987 (Casebook)

King's The Law of Medical Malpractice in a Nutshell, 2nd Ed., 342 pages, 1986 (Text)

Shapiro and Spece's Problems, Cases and Materials on Bioethics and Law, 892 pages, 1981 (Casebook)

MEDICINE, LAW AND—Cont'd

Sharpe, Fiscina and Head's Cases on Law and Medicine, 882 pages, 1978 (Casebook)

MILITARY LAW

Shanor and Terrell's Military Law in a Nutshell, 378 pages, 1980 (Text)

MORTGAGES

See Real Estate Transactions

NATURAL RESOURCES LAW

See Energy and Natural Resources Law

NEGOTIATION

Edwards and White's Problems, Readings and Materials on the Lawyer as a Negotiator, 484 pages, 1977 (Casebook)

Peck's Cases and Materials on Negotiation, 2nd Ed., (The Labor Law Group), 280 pages, 1980 (Casebook)

Williams' Legal Negotiation and Settlement, 207 pages, 1983 (Coursebook)

OFFICE PRACTICE

Hegland's Trial and Practice Skills in a Nutshell, 346 pages, 1978 (Text)

Strong and Clark's Law Office Management, 424 pages, 1974 (Casebook)

See also Computers and Law, Interviewing and Counseling, Negotiation

OIL AND GAS

Hemingway's Hornbook on Oil and Gas, 2nd Ed., Student Ed., 543 pages, 1983 with 1986 P.P. (Text)

Kuntz, Lowe, Anderson and Smith's Cases and Materials on Oil and Gas Law, 857 pages, 1986, with Forms Manual (Casebook)

Lowe's Oil and Gas Law in a Nutshell, 443 pages, 1983 (Text)

See also Energy and Natural Resources Law

PARTNERSHIP

See Agency—Partnership

PATENT AND COPYRIGHT LAW

Choate and Francis' Cases and Materials on Patent Law, 2nd Ed., 1110 pages, 1981 (Casebook)

Miller and Davis' Intellectual Property—Patents, Trademarks and Copyright in a Nutshell, 428 pages, 1983 (Text)

Nimmer's Cases on Copyright and Other Aspects of Entertainment Litigation, 3rd Ed., 1025 pages, 1985 (Casebook)

PRODUCTS LIABILITY

Noel and Phillips' Cases on Products Liability, 2nd Ed., 821 pages, 1982 (Casebook)

Noel and Phillips' Products Liability in a Nutshell, 2nd Ed., 341 pages, 1981 (Text)

LAW SCHOOL PUBLICATIONS—Continued

PROPERTY

Bernhardt's Real Property in a Nutshell, 2nd Ed., 448 pages, 1981 (Text)

Boyer's Survey of the Law of Property, 766 pages, 1981 (Text)

Browder, Cunningham and Smith's Cases on Basic Property Law, 4th Ed., 1431 pages, 1984 (Casebook)

Bruce, Ely and Bostick's Cases and Materials on Modern Property Law, 1004 pages, 1984 (Casebook)

Burke's Personal Property in a Nutshell, 322 pages, 1983 (Text)

Cunningham, Stoebuck and Whitman's Hornbook on the Law of Property, Student Ed., 916 pages, 1984, with 1987 P.P. (Text)

Donahue, Kauper and Martin's Cases on Property, 2nd Ed., 1362 pages, 1983 (Casebook)

Hill's Landlord and Tenant Law in a Nutshell, 2nd Ed., 311 pages, 1986 (Text)

Kurtz and Hovenkamp's Cases and Materials on American Property Law, 1296 pages, 1987 (Casebook)

Moynihan's Introduction to Real Property, 254 pages, 1962 (Text)

Uniform Land Transactions Act, Uniform Simplification of Land Transfers Act, Uniform Condominium Act, 1977 Official Text with Comments, 462 pages, 1978

See also Real Estate Transactions, Land Use

PSYCHIATRY, LAW AND

Reisner's Law and the Mental Health System, Civil and Criminal Aspects, 696 pages, 1985 (Casebooks)

REAL ESTATE TRANSACTIONS

Bruce's Real Estate Finance in a Nutshell, 2nd Ed., 262 pages, 1985 (Text)

Maxwell, Riesenfeld, Hetland and Warren's Cases on California Security Transactions in Land, 3rd Ed., 728 pages, 1984 (Casebook)

Nelson and Whitman's Cases on Real Estate Transfer, Finance and Development, 3rd Ed., about 1200 pages, 1987 (Casebook)

Nelson and Whitman's Hornbook on Real Estate Finance Law, 2nd Ed., Student Ed., 941 pages, 1985 (Text)

Osborne's Cases and Materials on Secured Transactions, 559 pages, 1967 (Casebook)

REGULATED INDUSTRIES

Gellhorn and Pierce's Regulated Industries in a Nutshell, 2nd Ed., 389 pages, 1987 (Text)

Morgan, Harrison and Verkuil's Cases and Materials on Economic Regulation of Business, 2nd Ed., 666 pages, 1985 (Casebook)

REGULATED INDUSTRIES—Cont'd

See also Mass Communication Law, Banking Law

REMEDIES

Dobbs' Hornbook on Remedies, 1067 pages, 1973 (Text)

Dobbs' Problems in Remedies, 137 pages, 1974 (Problem book)

Dobbyn's Injunctions in a Nutshell, 264 pages, 1974 (Text)

Friedman's Contract Remedies in a Nutshell, 323 pages, 1981 (Text)

Leavell, Love and Nelson's Cases and Materials on Equitable Remedies and Restitution, 4th Ed., 1111 pages, 1986 (Casebook)

McCormick's Hornbook on Damages, 811 pages, 1935 (Text)

O'Connell's Remedies in a Nutshell, 2nd Ed., 320 pages, 1985 (Text)

York, Bauman and Rendleman's Cases and Materials on Remedies, 4th Ed., 1029 pages, 1985 (Casebook)

REVIEW MATERIALS

Ballantine's Problems

Black Letter Series

Smith's Review Series

West's Review Covering Multistate Subjects

SECURITIES REGULATION

Hazen's Hornbook on The Law of Securities Regulation, Student Ed., 739 pages, 1985, with 1987 P.P. (Text)

Ratner's Securities Regulation: Materials for a Basic Course, 3rd Ed., 1000 pages, 1986 (Casebook)

Ratner's Securities Regulation in a Nutshell, 2nd Ed., 322 pages, 1982 (Text)

Selected Securities and Business Planning Statutes, Rules and Forms, 470 pages, 1985

SOCIAL LEGISLATION

Hood and Hardy's Workers' Compensation and Employee Protection Laws in a Nutshell, 274 pages, 1984 (Text)

LaFrance's Welfare Law: Structure and Entitlement in a Nutshell, 455 pages, 1979 (Text)

Malone, Plant and Little's Cases on Workers' Compensation and Employment Rights, 2nd Ed., 951 pages, 1980 (Casebook)

SPORTS LAW

Schubert, Smith and Trentadue's Sports Law, 395 pages, 1986 (Text)

TAXATION

Dodge's Cases and Materials on Federal Income Taxation, 820 pages, 1985 (Casebook)

LAW SCHOOL PUBLICATIONS—Continued

TAXATION—Cont'd

Dodge's Federal Taxation of Estates, Trusts and Gifts: Principles and Planning, 771 pages, 1981 with 1982 Supplement (Casebook)

Garbis, Struntz and Rubin's Cases and Materials on Tax Procedure and Tax Fraud, 2nd Ed., about 700 pages, 1987 (Casebook)

Gelfand and Salsich's State and Local Taxation and Finance in a Nutshell, 309 pages, 1986 (Text)

Gunn's Cases and Materials on Federal Income Taxation of Individuals, 785 pages, 1981 with 1985 Supplement (Casebook)

Hellerstein and Hellerstein's Cases on State and Local Taxation, 4th Ed., 1041 pages, 1978 with 1982 Supplement (Casebook)

Kahn and Gann's Corporate Taxation and Taxation of Partnerships and Partners, 2nd Ed., 1204 pages, 1985 (Casebook)

Kragen and McNulty's Cases and Materials on Federal Income Taxation: Individuals, Corporations, Partnerships, 4th Ed., 1287 pages, 1985 (Casebook)

McNulty's Federal Estate and Gift Taxation in a Nutshell, 3rd Ed., 509 pages, 1983 (Text)

McNulty's Federal Income Taxation of Individuals in a Nutshell, 3rd Ed., 487 pages, 1983 (Text)

Pennell's Cases and Materials on Income Taxation of Trusts, Estates, Grantors and Beneficiaries, about 300 pages, 1987 (Casebook)

Posin's Hornbook on Federal Income Taxation of Individuals, Student Ed., 491 pages, 1983 with 1985 pocket part (Text)

Selected Federal Taxation Statutes and Regulations, 1576 pages, 1987

Solomon and Hesch's Cases on Federal Income Taxation of Individuals, about 1075 pages, 1987 (Casebook)

Sobeloff and Weidenbruch's Federal Income Taxation of Corporations and Stockholders in a Nutshell, 362 pages, 1981 (Text)

TORTS

Christie's Cases and Materials on the Law of Torts, 1264 pages, 1983 (Casebook)

Dobbs' Torts and Compensation—Personal Accountability and Social Responsibility for Injury, 955 pages, 1985 (Casebook)

Green, Pedrick, Rahl, Thode, Hawkins, Smith, and Treece's Advanced Torts: Injuries to Business, Political and Family Interests, 2nd Ed., 544 pages, 1977 (Casebook)

Keeton, Keeton, Sargentich and Steiner's Cases and Materials on Torts, and Accident Law, 1360 pages, 1983 (Casebook)

Kionka's Torts in a Nutshell: Injuries to Persons and Property, 434 pages, 1977 (Text)

TORTS—Cont'd

Malone's Torts in a Nutshell: Injuries to Family, Social and Trade Relations, 358 pages, 1979 (Text)

Prosser and Keeton's Hornbook on Torts, 5th Ed., Student Ed., 1286 pages, 1984 (Text)

See also Products Liability

TRADE REGULATION

McManis' Unfair Trade Practices in a Nutshell, 444 pages, 1982 (Text)

Oppenheim, Weston, Maggs and Schechter's Cases and Materials on Unfair Trade Practices and Consumer Protection, 4th Ed., 1038 pages, 1983 with 1986 Supplement (Casebook)

See also Antitrust, Regulated Industries

TRIAL AND APPELLATE ADVOCACY

Appellate Advocacy, Handbook of, 2nd Ed., 182 pages, 1986 (Text)

Bergman's Trial Advocacy in a Nutshell, 402 pages, 1979 (Text)

Binder and Bergman's Fact Investigation: From Hypothesis to Proof, 354 pages, 1984 (Coursebook)

Goldberg's The First Trial (Where Do I Sit?, What Do I Say?) in a Nutshell, 396 pages, 1982 (Text)

Haydock, Herr and Stempel's, Fundamentals of Pre-Trial Litigation, 768 pages, 1985 (Casebook)

Hegland's Trial and Practice Skills in a Nutshell, 346 pages, 1978 (Text)

Hornstein's Appellate Advocacy in a Nutshell, 325 pages, 1984 (Text)

Jeans' Handbook on Trial Advocacy, Student Ed., 473 pages, 1975 (Text)

Martineau's Cases and Materials on Appellate Practice and Procedure, about 550 pages, 1987 (Casebook)

McElhaney's Effective Litigation, 457 pages, 1974 (Casebook)

Nolan's Cases and Materials on Trial Practice, 518 pages, 1981 (Casebook)

Parnell and Shellhaas' Cases, Exercises and Problems for Trial Advocacy, 171 pages, 1982 (Coursebook)

Sonsteng, Haydock and Boyd's The Trialbook: A Total System for Preparation and Presentation of a Case, Student Ed., 404 pages, 1984 (Coursebook)

TRUSTS AND ESTATES

Atkinson's Hornbook on Wills, 2nd Ed., 975 pages, 1953 (Text)

Averill's Uniform Probate Code in a Nutshell, 2nd Ed., about 418 pages, 1987 (Text)

Bogert's Hornbook on Trusts, 6th Ed., Student Ed., about 800 pages, 1987 (Text)

Clark, Lusky and Murphy's Cases and Materials on Gratuitous Transfers, 3rd Ed., 970 pages, 1985 (Casebook)

LAW SCHOOL PUBLICATIONS—Continued

TRUSTS AND ESTATES—Cont'd

Gulliver's Cases and Materials on Future Interests, 624 pages, 1959 (Casebook)

Gulliver's Introduction to the Law of Future Interests, 87 pages, 1959 (Casebook)—reprint from Gulliver's Cases and Materials on Future Interests, 1959

McGovern's Cases and Materials on Wills, Trusts and Future Interests: An Introduction to Estate Planning, 750 pages, 1983 (Casebook)

Mennell's Wills and Trusts in a Nutshell, 392 pages, 1979 (Text)

Simes' Hornbook on Future Interests, 2nd Ed., 355 pages, 1966 (Text)

Turano and Radigan's Hornbook on New York Estate Administration, 676 pages, 1986 (Text)

Uniform Probate Code, 5th Ed., Official Text With Comments, 384 pages, 1977

Waggoner's Future Interests in a Nutshell, 361 pages, 1981 (Text)

Waterbury's Materials on Trusts and Estates, 1039 pages, 1986 (Casebook)

WATER LAW

Getches' Water Law in a Nutshell, 439 pages, 1984 (Text)

WATER LAW—Cont'd

Sax and Abram's Cases and Materials on Legal Control of Water Resources in the United States, 941 pages, 1986 (Casebook)

Trelease and Gould's Cases and Materials on Water Law, 4th Ed., 816 pages, 1986 (Casebook)

See also Energy and Natural Resources Law, Environmental Law

WILLS

See Trusts and Estates

WOMEN AND THE LAW

Kay's Text, Cases and Materials on Sex-Based Discrimination, 2nd Ed., 1045 pages, 1981, with 1986 Supplement (Casebook)

Thomas' Sex Discrimination in a Nutshell, 399 pages, 1982 (Text)

See also Employment Discrimination

WORKERS' COMPENSATION

See Social Legislation

PROBLEMS, CASES AND MATERIALS ON

FEDERAL INCOME TAXATION

By

Lewis D. Solomon
Professor of Law
George Washington University

Jerome M. Hesch
Professor of Law
University of Miami

AMERICAN CASEBOOK SERIES

WEST PUBLISHING CO.
ST. PAUL, MINN., 1987

Library of Congress Cataloging-in-Publication Data

Solomon, Lewis D.
  Problems, cases and materials on federal income taxation.

  (American casebook series)

  Includes index.
  1. Income tax—Law and legislation—United States—Cases. I. Hesch, Jerome M., 1944–
II. Title. III. Series.

KF6368.S65 1987   343.7305'2   86–10974
                     347.30352

ISBN 0–314–98584–0

Fed'l Inc. Tax (S. & H.) ACB

∞

Dedication

In memory of my mother

LDS

In memory of Philip E. Heckerling

JMH

*

Preface

Our principal reason for adding another casebook to an already well-populated field is that we have become firmly convinced that the most effective pedagogical approach to the basic income tax course is the so-called "problem method." We set out, therefore, to create a set of materials specifically designed to facilitate the use of the problem method. We feel strongly the need to present a comprehensive doctrinal framework and believe it can best be achieved by forcing students to apply a variety of legal materials to the solution of problems. In addition to the problems, we have included questions in the materials. These questions are generally designed to be covered in the context of the problems instead of being discussed separately.

While the problem method has been both the reason for undertaking this project and its theme, we are aware that not all teachers will want to use the materials in the same way and have, therefore, arranged them in such a way as to allow the maximum flexibility in the use, or nonuse, of the problems. It should be possible to use the book in a conventional manner making little or no reference to the problems.

We believe there are advantages to the problem method in a basic income tax course. First, by the second year law students are convinced (although not always correctly) that they have learned all there is to know about reading cases. Students tend to be bored by a pedagogical approach that emphasizes analyzing and extracting legal rules from cases.

Second, during the first year of the typical law school curriculum, students learn to "make the arguments" on both sides of every issue, but are all too seldom given much exercise in developing the all-important qualities of judgment that distinguish the good lawyer from the merely adequate attorney. The problems in this book are designed to make the student confront the hard task of deciding what course of action to recommend in the face of a variety of legal materials. In dealing with the problems, the student is called to go beyond the abstract exercise of reading cases and extracting and applying holdings to hypothetical appellate litigation questions. Instead, the student is encouraged to use primary tax materials, including the Code, legislative histories, administrative materials, and cases as a practicing lawyer would: as tools to assist in resolving a concrete problem. Indeed, that is how lawyers, and surely how tax lawyers, spend most of their time.

Third, the conventional law school course often gives too little attention to developing skills other than case analysis. This is particu-

larly unfortunate in a basic income tax course in which the bulk of the
practice is planning and counselling rather than litigation. We have,
therefore, attempted to design problems to afford the teacher convenient opportunities to give the students exercises in planning, counselling, negotiating, drafting, litigation, statutory construction, and policy
making.

This book is not limited to the application in a problem context of
the "law" as it is. Conceptual and policy questions have a place (if not
a significant place) in a basic income tax course. The Internal Revenue
Code is an important policy instrument. Students should reflect on the
consequences of and uses to which the income tax system is put. The
policy making approach is presented in the form of carefully focused
problems, a technique that helps avoid the fuzzy open-endedness that
too often characterizes a discussion of conceptual and policy issues.
Divergent viewpoints are generally presented thereby helping students
discuss each policy making problem.

While the bulk of the material will be familiar to the experienced
teacher of the basic income tax course, we have endeavored also to
present material in several areas that are ignored or only touched
lightly in most casebooks in the field. The treatment of the ethical and
professional responsibility problems that often confront the tax lawyer
is, for example, quite specific.

This book integrates basic income tax concepts including basis,
timing, realization, and character of gain from the beginning of the
book. The problems and materials in Chapter 1 are designed to
introduce most of the fundamental principles of income taxation and
provide students with a basic understanding of the structure of the
income tax system. This technique also enables the instructor to
mention with some familiarity the basic income tax concepts as the
course unfolds.

One of the chief difficulties in teaching a basic income tax course is
that the majority of students are totally innocent of any understanding
of the business world. They encounter difficulties in understanding the
traditional appellate cases and, therefore, approach the course with
trepidation. Students may also view the course as a branch of accounting or mathematics. The struggle of fine arts and French literature
majors, among others, in wrestling with traditional income tax materials has been kept in mind. Computational complexities are generally
de-emphasized. Textual materials are extensively used as a means to
put the Code, administrative and judicial materials in a comprehensible
context and lessen the amount of time devoted to explaining basic
business and tax concepts.

We have placed a great deal of emphasis throughout the book on
the construction and use of the Internal Revenue Code and administrative materials, wherever possible referring the student to particular
provisions and materials that appear relevant to a given problem. The

book is designed to be supplemented by the West Publishing Company's Selected Federal Taxation Statutes and Regulations.

As to editorial details, citations in cases and other materials, as well as the footnotes of courts and commentators, have been omitted without so specifying. The footnotes of decisions and excerpts from books and articles have been renumbered; those of the authors are indicated by a notation to that effect.

A teacher's manual is available from the publisher. It contains further details and suggestions as to how the book and the problems might be used.

We wish to express our gratitude to the numerous secretaries who labored with us as the book underwent numerous drafts. We also wish to acknowledge the work done by our student research assistants at the University of Miami, Michael Kosnitzky, Marian Schweiger and Richard Alayon. We are particularly indebted to Professor Elliott Manning of the University of Miami School of Law for the many useful suggestions from which we profited enormously. We wish to thank our students—both those that inspired us to write this book and those who served as guinea pigs on whom we tried out the many draft editions and whose reactions and constructive criticism added much to the final product.

LEWIS D. SOLOMON
JEROME M. HESCH

February, 1987

*

Acknowledgements

The following copyright holders have graciously consented to the reprinting of excerpts from their works:

American Bar Association, Model Rules of Professional Conduct, Rules (and comments) 1.2, 1.5, 1.6, 1.16, 2.1 and 6.4. Excerpted from the Model Rules of Professional Conduct, copyright August, 1983. All rights reserved. Reprinted with permission.

Billman and Cunningham, Nonbusiness State and Local Taxes: The Case for Deductibility, 28 Tax Notes 1107, 1107–1120 (1985).

Davenport, Tax Expenditure Analysis as a Tool for Policymakers, 11 Tax Notes 1051, 1052–1053.

Goode, The Individual Income Tax, 80, 83–87, 126–127, 129–133, 180, 182–191, 194–201, 203–211 (Rev. ed. 1976).

Marsh, Taxation of Imprinted Income, 58 Political Science Quarterly 514, 514–521 (1943). Reprinted with permission from Political Science Quarterly (December 1943): 514–21.

Paul, The Lawyer as a Tax Advisor, 25 Rocky Mountain Law Review 412, 412–421, 433–434 (1953).

*

Summary of Contents

Table of Contents

*

Table of Internal Revenue Code Sections

*

Table of Treasury Regulations

Table of Cases

References are to pages

Table of Revenue Rulings

Table of Revenue Procedures

——————

*

Table of Letter Rulings

*

PROBLEMS, CASES AND MATERIALS ON
FEDERAL INCOME TAXATION

*

Chapter 1

INTRODUCTION TO FEDERAL
INCOME TAXATION

Our study will be initiated by a very brief look at the Federal income tax today, the history of and constitutional framework for the Federal income tax, the significance and coverage of the Federal income tax, the sources of Federal income tax law, and the operation of the tax system.

A. OVERVIEW OF THE FEDERAL INCOME TAX TODAY

The Federal income tax is imposed annually on the taxable income of every individual who is a resident or citizen of the United States. Taxable income, that is, gross income as defined, minus certain allowable deductions is, beginning in 1988, subject to a two bracket structure with rates of 15 percent and 28 percent. Examine the tax rate tables for individuals contained in § 1 of the Internal Revenue Code. Beginning in 1988 the benefit of the 15 percent bracket is phased out for individual taxpayers having taxable income exceeding specified levels. Read § 1(g). Thus, the income tax liability of such taxpayers is increased by 5 percent of their taxable income within specified ranges. For example, the phase-out occurs for a married couple with taxable income between $71,900 and $149,250. If the maximum phase-out has occurred, the 28 percent rate applies to all of the taxpayer's taxable income. With the two bracket rate structure and the 5 percent surcharge, the question of timing (in what year is an item includible in gross income?) is significant.

For taxable years beginning on or after July 1, 1987, corporate income is taxed at 15 percent on the first $50,000 of taxable income and 25 percent on the next $25,000.[1] Taxable income in excess of $75,000 is taxed at 34 percent. See § 11(b). The benefits of these low brackets

1. The effective rate of taxation for the first $75,000 of corporate taxable income is 18.33%.

1

for corporations are phased out for corporations with taxable income of more than $100,000. A tax of an additional 5 percent is placed on taxable income between $100,000 and $335,000. § 11(b). Therefore, corporations with taxable income in excess of $335,000, in effect, pay a flat tax at a 34 percent rate.

B. HISTORY OF AND CONSTITUTIONAL FRAMEWORK FOR THE FEDERAL INCOME TAX

Constitutional Power to Tax Income. The constitutional power of Congress to tax income does not begin or end with the Sixteenth Amendment to the Constitution. The taxing power of Congress, which "is exhaustive and embraces every conceivable power of taxation," [2] is based on Article I, Section 8, clause 1 of the Constitution which provides that:

> Congress shall have Power to Lay and Collect Taxes, Duties, Imposts, and Excises, to pay the Debts and provide for the common Defense and general Welfare of the United States; but all Duties, Imposts, and Excises shall be uniform throughout the United States.

Under Article I, Sections 2 (clause 3) and 9 (clause 4) of the Constitution, direct Federal taxes, such as a real estate tax, must be apportioned among the states according to population, a requirement that makes them totally impractical. Apportionment requires a different rate for each state to insure that the total amount paid by each state is proportional to its population. Only if a tax is direct is it necessary to refer to the Sixteenth Amendment. Without relying on the Sixteenth Amendment, Congress, however, has the power to levy an indirect tax on certain items, such as salaries and other receipts not derived from property, without the tax being regarded as a direct tax under Article I of the Constitution. An indirect tax is subject to a standard of geographical uniformity.

Early Income Tax Statutes. Before the Civil War, the Federal Government basically relied upon customs revenues to finance its activities. During the Civil War, however, customs revenues were insufficient, and in 1861, the Federal Government first undertook to tax income.[3] The 1861 statute, however, is of little significance because it was not put into effect and was superseded by the Act of 1862,[4] the Act of 1864 [5] and finally by the Act of 1870.[6] This Federal income tax expired in 1872.

---

2. Brushaber v. Union Pacific Railroad Co., 240 U.S. 1, 12, 36 S.Ct. 236, 239, 60 L.Ed. 493, 499 (1916).

3. Act of August 5, 1861, c. 45, 12 Stat. 292, § 49.

4. Act of July 1, 1862, c. 119, 12 Stat. 432, § 90.

5. Act of June 30, 1864, c. 173, 13 Stat. 223, § 116 amended by Act of March 3, 1865, c. 78, 13 Stat. 469.

6. Act of July 14, 1870, c. 255, 16 Stat. 256, § 6.

The Act of 1864 was the first income tax statute to come under constitutional challenge. In Springer v. U.S.,[7] the Supreme Court upheld the constitutionality of the law against the allegation that the tax was invalid because it was a direct tax which was not apportioned. The Court viewed the Federal income tax imposed by the Act of 1864 as an indirect tax.

The 1894 Act and the Pollock Decision. The Federal income tax was reinstated in 1894. The Federal income tax law of 1894 imposed an annual tax of 2 percent on individual incomes in excess of $4,000.[8]

Evidencing its hostility to the concept of an income tax, the Supreme Court, in Pollock v. Farmers' Loan & Trust Co.,[9] held the Act of 1894 unconstitutional. In considering whether the income tax was a direct or an indirect tax, the Court looked to the source of the income in question. The income tax, being unapportioned, was found invalid. The Court reasoned that the tax on income from real estate was a tax on real estate and thus a direct tax which had to be apportioned.

On rehearing, the Supreme Court reaffirmed its previous holding with respect to real estate. The Court also held that the tax on the income from personal property was an invalid, direct tax. The tax on income from investments in personalty constituted a direct burden on income-producing property itself. Because the invalid provisions were considered as part of one tax scheme the Court declared the entire act unconstitutional. The Court did not, however, question the power of Congress to tax income.

The 1909 Act. In 1909, a corporation excise tax measured by income became effective. The measure of tax liability was one percent of net income over five thousand dollars.[10]

The Supreme Court held that the 1909 corporation income tax was constitutional in Flint v. Stone Tracy Co.[11] The Court concluded that the levy was a tax on the privilege of doing business, not a direct tax that had to be apportioned by population.

The Sixteenth Amendment and the 1913 Act. The Sixteenth Amendment became part of the United States Constitution in 1913. The Amendment grants Congress the power "to lay and collect taxes on incomes, from whatever source derived, without apportionment among the several States, and without regard to any census or enumeration." Thus Congress is freed from the need for a per capita apportionment when levying taxes "on incomes, from whatever source derived." Responding to the Sixteenth Amendment, Congress quickly passed the

7. 102 U.S. (12 Otto) 586, 25 L.Ed. 253 (1880).

8. Act of August 27, 1894, c. 349, 28 Stat. 509, § 27.

9. 157 U.S. 429, 15 S.Ct. 673, 39 L.Ed. 759 (1895), on rehearing 158 U.S. 601, 15 S.Ct. 912, 39 L.Ed. 1108 (1895).

10. Act of August 5, 1909, c. 6, 36 Stat. 11, § 38.

11. 220 U.S. 107, 31 S.Ct. 342, 55 L.Ed. 389 (1911).

Revenue Act of 1913.[12] Shortly thereafter, the Supreme Court, in Brushaber v. Union Pacific Railroad Co.,[13] held this income tax valid.

C. SIGNIFICANCE AND COVERAGE OF THE FEDERAL INCOME TAX

Income taxes predominate as a source of Federal revenue,[14] providing the Federal government with approximately two-thirds of all budget receipts. The individual income tax raises over four times more revenue than the corporate income tax. Employment taxes bring in one quarter of Federal Government revenues. Increases in Social Security payroll taxes will augment the future importance of employment taxes. A variety of other taxes, including estate and gift taxes, alcohol, tobacco and other excise taxes, bring in the remainder of Federal collections.

The income tax has only relatively recently become a preminent source of revenue. Although the income tax was imposed during the Civil War (and expired in 1872), throughout the nineteenth century customs receipts and excise taxes on tobacco and liquor comprised the major sources of Federal revenues.

As previously noted, after the ratification of the Sixteenth Amendment to the Constitution in 1913, Congress passed the Revenue Act of 1913 which levied an income tax on individual and corporate incomes. The income tax became a major revenue source in World War I and the predominant source during and after World War II.

In addition to its preeminence as a revenue source, the income tax is imposed on the most people. About three-quarters of the population either file tax returns or are claimed as dependents on returns. Prior to World War II (with the exception of 1918–1920) only about 5 percent of the population was required to file tax returns. Most of the revenue generated by the individual income tax is, however, derived from middle income persons taxed at relatively modest tax rates.

D. SOURCES OF FEDERAL INCOME TAX LAW AND OPERATION OF THE TAX SYSTEM

We now turn to an examination of the three primary sources of the Federal income tax law: (1) legislative; (2) administrative; and (3) judicial materials. The administrative and judicial functions in the operation of the tax system are also discussed.

Legislative Materials. The Federal income tax is a statutory creature—the Internal Revenue Code of 1986. Under Article I, Section 8 of

12. Act of October 3, 1913, ch. 16, 38 Stat. 166, § 2.

13. 240 U.S. 1, 36 S.Ct. 236, 60 L.Ed. 493 (1916).

14. U.S. Bureau of the Census, Statistical Abstract of the United States 1982–1983, 254 (table 430) (1982).

the Constitution, the taxing power of the Federal government is vested in Congress. Congress has exercised its power by enacting legislation. From 1913 to 1938 numerous revenue acts were passed, usually every other year. In 1939, the then operative internal revenue laws (scattered throughout the many volumes of the Statutes at Large) were codified as the Internal Revenue Code of 1939. The next major recodification, the Internal Revenue Code of 1954, involved a substantial rewriting and rearranging of the existing law but it was amended many times since 1954. In light of the scope of the reforms enacted by the Tax Reform Act of 1986, the tax laws as amended were enacted as the Internal Revenue Code of 1986. The 1986 Code consists of the provisions of the 1954 Code (as in effect immediately prior to the enactment of the Tax Reform Act of 1986) together with the amendments made by the Tax Reform Act of 1986. Congress usually amends a number of Code provisions in one act rather than enacting separate acts to change individual Code sections. The Code constitutes the basic, and often the only relevant, statutory document.

Legislative history includes bills, hearings held before House and Senate committees, the reports of the House Ways and Means and Senate Finance Committees. Conference committee reports and Congressional floor debates may also illuminate the tax law as enacted. One of the more frequent judicial gambits in statutory interpretation is to assert that the conclusion reached by a court accords with the intention of Congress. This becomes less of a bootstrap operation if comments made in the reports of House and Senate committees or by the members in charge of the bill on its way through Congress point to the result. Consequently, such statements have long been used as an aid in the construction of tax statutes. Quotations from the committee and conference reports will be frequent throughout this work.

In recent years, the staff of the Joint Committee on Taxation has published explanations (sometimes referred to as the blue book) after the enactment of major tax acts. The weight accorded these explanations is unclear because they are published after the passage of the bill.

Administrative Materials. The administrative materials are basically divided into Treasury Regulations, Revenue Rulings and Revenue Procedures. The Regulations, promulgated by the Treasury Department, constitute the most formal and authoritative administrative interpretation of the Internal Revenue Code. Under § 7805(a) the Secretary of the Treasury is authorized to "prescribe all needful rules and regulations for the enforcement * * *" of the internal revenue laws. The Regulations interpret the Code for the guidance of taxpayers and the staff of the Internal Revenue Service.

Interpretative regulations enjoy a presumption of correctness. The extent to which interpretative regulations are binding on the courts obviously depends on the circumstances of each case. The effectiveness of a regulation may turn on the length of time a regulation has been in force and the consistency with which a regulation has been maintained.

A court may declare an interpretative regulation invalid if the regulation is not consistent with statutory language or if no statutory provision supports the regulation.

Congress may also carve out areas in which the Treasury may make, rather than merely interpret, the rules. Certain acts expressly delegate to the Treasury the task of resolving important items Congress omitted from the statute. These are known as rule-making regulations. Examine § 274(o). A court may declare a rule-making regulation involved only if it is beyond the scope Congress intended.

The Internal Revenue Service, a unit of the Treasury Department, issues private letter rulings, technical advices, revenue rulings, and revenue procedures. A private letter ruling is a written statement issued to a taxpayer or his authorized representative by the National Office of the Internal Revenue Service interpreting and applying the tax laws to the taxpayer's specific set of facts. A technical advice is an interpretation of the proper application of the tax laws and regulations furnished by the National Office of the Internal Revenue Service on the request of a District office of the Internal Revenue Service in connection with an examination of a taxpayer's claim for refund or credit.

Private letter rulings and technical advices must be distinguished from published revenue rulings which are official interpretations of tax law by the Internal Revenue Service. The Service publishes revenue rulings (as well as revenue procedures) in the weekly Internal Revenue Bulletin. The Service publishes the accumulated weekly bulletins semi-annually in a bound volume called the Cumulative Bulletin.

Revenue rulings have precedential value for taxpayers in substantially similar situations, although the Service has authority to amend or revoke a revenue ruling. In contrast a private letter ruling or a technical advice has no precedential effect and may only be relied on by the taxpayer who requested the ruling (or advice). The validity of a private letter ruling also depends on the taxpayer accurately stating all material facts in the ruling request and the law remaining unchanged after the Service gives the ruling.

With the increased exposure of tax advisors and tax return preparers to penalties, it is probable that taxpayers will seek (and tax advisors and tax return preparers will insist on) a private letter ruling before undertaking a speculative transaction or before filing a return on a completed transaction. However, the Service will not always respond to a request for a private letter ruling. With respect to certain specific issues, the Service will not issue a ruling or will not ordinarily issue a ruling. The Service also refuses to give rulings on "inherently factual" matters prior to a taxpayer filing a return. See Rev.Proc. 86–1, 1986–1 I.R.B. 6, and Rev.Proc. 86–3, 1986–1 I.R.B. 26.

A revenue procedure is a statement of procedure affecting the rights or duties of taxpayers or other members of the public under the tax laws that should be a matter of public knowledge even though it does not affect a particular taxpayer's rights and duties.

Treatment of Tax Returns. Before describing the judicial function and judicial materials, we must consider the administrative treatment given tax returns. When an income tax return, which must be filed annually (§ 6072), has been submitted by the taxpayer to a District office of Internal Revenue Service, it may or may not be audited. If it is audited, the examining officer may find a deficiency (too little tax paid) or an overassessment (too much tax paid). A claimed deficiency in an income tax return must be made by the Service within three years after the return is filed, except in cases where the taxpayer omitted from gross income more than 25% of the amount reported on a return, failed to file a return, or filed a false or fraudulent return. § 6501(a), (c) and (e)(1). If the taxpayer and the examining agent cannot reach an agreement on the alleged deficiency, the taxpayer has an administrative appeal to the Regional Appeals Office of the Internal Revenue Service. If the one-level administrative appeal procedure does not produce an agreement, the controversy may go into litigation. Three different courts, the United States Tax Court, Federal district courts, and the United States Claims Court, perform trial functions with respect to tax controversies. The failure to exhaust administrative remedies provides a basis for the Tax Court imposing a discretionary penalty. § 6673.

The Judicial Function and Judicial Materials. A taxpayer who refuses to pay a notice of deficiency may file a petition in the United States Tax Court seeking a redetermination of the proposed deficiency within a prescribed time period. §§ 6211(a), 6212(a) and 6213(a). This involves, in most respects, an adversary litigation between the taxpayer and the Service as in the case of the usual civil trial. A Tax Court case is tried without a jury before one of the judges of the Tax Court. Although there is only one Tax Court, the judges serving on the Tax Court sit in a number of cities throughout the United States. For taxpayers with small proposed tax deficiencies (the amount of the tax deficiency is $10,000 or less for any one taxable year) the Tax Court offers informal procedures designed to expedite the resolution of and reduce the expense of tax litigation. If a taxpayer elects this informal small case procedure, the outcome of the case cannot be appealed by either taxpayer or the Service. § 7463(a) and (b). In general, a taxpayer cannot be required to pay the proposed deficiency while the case is pending before the Tax Court (§ 6213(a)). However, interest accrues on the unpaid deficiency from the due date of the return if the Tax Court upholds the deficiency. § 6601(a). A practical advantage of litigating in the Tax Court is that a taxpayer does not have to pay the proposed deficiency while the case is pending before the Tax Court.

Should a taxpayer fail to file a petition with the Tax Court within the time permitted (§ 6213(c)) (or lose in the Tax Court), various collection procedures are available to the Internal Revenue Service.

These include distraint (seizure and sale of a taxpayer's personal and real property) and the imposition of liens. If the Service believes that the collection of a deficiency may be jeopardized by delay, it may demand immediate payment of a tax without reference to the time limitations and restrictions generally in effect.

Instead of litigating in the Tax Court, the taxpayer may pay the full amount of the tax and file an administrative claim for a refund for the overpayment of taxes. If there is administrative inaction for a specified time period or if there is an administrative disallowance of the refund claim, the taxpayer may file a suit for a refund in a Federal district court in the district in which he resides. The taxpayer (or the government) may demand a jury trial in a Federal district court proceeding.

The United States Claims Court also has jurisdiction over claims asserted by taxpayers that the Federal government has improperly collected internal revenue taxes. A Claims Court case is tried without a jury. The taxpayer may sue for a refund in the Claims Court only if he has paid the full amount of a deficiency.

In litigation the decision of the Internal Revenue Service is generally presumed correct for purposes of determining who has the burden of proof, except in cases where fraud is alleged.

A word should be added about the scope of appeals. Decisions by the Tax Court (except small claims procedures) or a Federal district court are appealable by right by either party to a United States Court of Appeals for the appropriate circuit. Decisions in the Claims Court are appealable by right by either party to the United States Court of Appeals for the Federal Circuit. The United States Supreme Court occasionally (but not often) ventures into the tax field to review decisions of an appellate court.

Interest at an adjustable rate (§ 6621) is payable with respect to deficiencies (§ 6601(a)) or overpayments (§ 6611(a)). This interest rate is keyed to market rates. The interest rate taxpayers pay to the Government on deficiencies equals the rate on short-term Treasury bonds (i.e., the average market yield on outstanding marketable obligations of the United States with a maturity of three years or less) plus three percentage points. The interest rate the Government pays taxpayers on overpayments equals the rate on short-term Treasury bonds plus two percentage points. § 6621(a). Additional penalties are assessed for late filing (§ 6651(a)(1)), failure to file a return (§ 6651(a) (1)), failure to pay a tax shown (§ 6651(a)(2)), and for negligence or fraud (§ 6653). Criminal prosecution may also be instituted for, among other offenses, fraud or a willful failure to file a return.

Nonacquiescence in Decisions. It may startle some students to learn that when the taxpayer wins a case in the Tax Court which the Internal Revenue Service believes to be based on an erroneous legal concept, the Service may announce, whether or not it appeals the decision, that it does not acquiesce in the decision. Nonacquiescence puts other taxpayers on notice of a disputed issue and indicates that the Service may litigate the same issue when it arises again. The decision, unless reversed on appeal, is binding as to the Service in the case itself. On the other hand, by acquiescing in a determination adverse to the government, the Service indicates that it will not continue to contest the issue when it arises in other cases. The Internal Revenue Service in its published revenue rulings may also announce whether or not it will follow a decision of the United States Claims Court, a Federal district court or a court of appeals.

The acquiescences and nonacquiescences indicate the viewpoint of the Service. They are not given great weight and may be repudiated by a court. Sometimes the Service will announce that it has substituted one for the other.

Problem

Able, an accountant, has performed various bookkeeping and financial counseling services without charge for his father over a twenty year period. His father now decides that Able is the most deserving of his children, by reason of his devotion and assistance, so he transfers a boat worth $10,000 to Able.

Able does not report the receipt of the boat as income on his Federal income tax return. The Internal Revenue Service proposes to assess a deficiency for taxes on $10,000 of additional income. Able does not agree to the finding of a deficiency. Able engages you as counsel after receiving the so-called "90 day letter" from the Internal Revenue Service which advises him that unless he files a petition with the Tax Court within 90 days, the deficiency will be assessed and collected by the Service. §§ 6212(a) and 6213(a) and (c).

The question is whether the boat represents gross income, subject to taxation, under § 61(a) or a nontaxable gift under § 102(a). You should read these sections of the Code. Under the facts, this question is assumed to be open, but, you are asked:

(a) What alternative courses of action are open to Able to obtain a judicial adjudication of his claim on the merits?

(b) As a matter of strategy, do you believe Able would be better advised to refuse to pay the alleged deficiency or to pay and sue for a refund? What other factors would you consider in making a recommendation with respect to a litigation forum?

(c) What do you think will be the probable outcome of your recommended course of action, taking into account the various sources of tax law? Start by examining §§ 61(a) and 102 as well as Reg. § 1.102–1(a). Consider the effect courts give to each of these items. What else should you examine?

E. INTRODUCTION TO TAX TERMS
AND TAX CONCEPTS

This section provides an introduction to some of the key terms used in the Internal Revenue Code and the basic concepts underlying the income tax system. It also gives you an idea of how the Federal income tax is computed.

Because the Federal tax law uses terms which are unfamiliar to the uninitiated, it is helpful to explain some of this terminology. The touchstone of the income tax is *gross income*. Section 61 defines the term "gross income" broadly as "all income from whatever source derived." There is no definition of income anywhere in the Internal Revenue Code. Although § 61 includes a general list of items which are included in gross income, this enumeration is not exclusive. Other sections (§§ 71–86) specifically include other items in gross income. However, certain benefits received by a taxpayer are not included in gross income and, therefore, are never taxed. Many of thse items are specifically excluded by §§ 101 to 132 (and are thus called *exclusions*). Exclusions narrow the statutory concept of gross income and do not enter into the computation of tax. For a fuller understanding of the gross income concept, the relevant judicial and administrative materials must be analyzed.

A taxpayer includes certain items of income in gross income only if they are both *realized* and *recognized* for tax purposes. The concepts of realization and recognition constitute essential prerequisites to the taxation of an item or event. The realization concept differentiates between items or events which create mere economic income and those items or events which trigger potential tax consequences to the income recipient. Economic income may take many forms including an increase in the value of property owned by an individual. But the mere appreciation in the value of property and the resulting increase in the taxpayer's net worth produces no tax consequences for the owner. For realization to occur, a benefit must be in hand. The Federal tax system imposes an income tax on transactions, not on the enrichment of a property owner. Under § 61(a)(3) gross income includes "[g]ains derived from dealings in property" thereby implying that unrealized gain is not taxable. The moment of realization, according to § 1001(a), is the time of "the sale or other disposition of property."

Recognized gain (or loss) is the amount of the realized gain (or loss) included in a taxpayer's gross income. As a general rule, the entire realized gain (or loss) is recognized for tax purposes. § 1001(c). However, the Internal Revenue Code provides a number of exceptions to this general rule which permit taxpayers to postpone, but not permanently exclude, the reporting of gain (or loss) to a later date. Many of these so-called non-recognition provisions are grounded on the concept that the taxpayer has not changed his economic position and, therefore, has not, in substance, terminated his interest in a particular investment. However, these non-recognition provisions are narrowly defined and constitute the exception rather than the general rule.

Basis is a fundamental tax concept. In its simplest form, the basis of property is usually the cost of the property. § 1012. Cost is the amount paid for or invested in the property in cash or other property. Instead of a cost basis, a taxpayer may have a carryover basis which is established by referring to someone else's basis. A multitude of situations having tax significance, discussed elsewhere in this book, affect the basis of property. The additions to or subtractions from the taxpayer's original basis in the property constitute the adjusted basis of the property.

The measurement of *gain* or *loss* for tax purposes involves a comparison of the *amount realized* by a taxpayer from the sale of property with the *adjusted basis* of the property. Read § 1001(a). Under § 1001(b) the amount realized from the sale of property equals "the sum of any money received plus the fair market value of the property (other than money) received." The concept of basis thus permits a taxpayer to receive a taxfree return of capital. This is necessary because the Internal Revenue Code is a tax on income, not on gross receipts.

Just as gains derived from dealing in property are included in the taxpayer's gross income under § 61(a)(3), losses sustained by the taxpayer are generally deductible under § 165(a) unless the loss sustained by an individual taxpayer is unconnected with a business or a transaction entered into for profit. § 165(c)(1) and (c)(2), but see § 165(c)(3). On the disposition of business or investment property, if the amount realized is less than the adjusted basis, the taxpayer has a deductible loss.

After the taxpayer determines whether or not he has realized a gain (or loss) on the disposition of property and whether or not the gain (or loss) is recognized, the character of the gain or loss must be considered. A gain or loss is either *capital* or *ordinary*. Prior to 1988, taxpayers preferred to characterize gains as capital gains because of the preferential treatment capital gains received. Beginning in 1988, capital gains are taxed at the same rates as ordinary income. Taxpayers do not want to characterize a loss as a capital loss because of the limited deductibility of capital losses. Each year, capital losses are deductible to the extent of an individual taxpayer's capital gains plus $3,000 of other income. § 1211(b). In brief, the character of gain (or loss) turns on the nature of the asset and whether the taxpayer disposed of an asset in a sale or exchange transaction.

Not all expenditures give rise to a *deduction* for tax purposes. Personal, living, or family expenses are generally nondeductible under § 262. Certain personal deductions, such as medical expenses, interest, and alimony are deductible by statutory exceptions to the general rule of § 262. The taxpayer need not engage in a business or a profit-making transaction to qualify for these statutory personal deductions.

There are several Code sections which permit deductions arising out of a taxpayer's trade or business or a taxpayer's transactions for profit. Section 162 permits deductions for the "ordinary and necessary" expenses of carrying on a "trade or business." For individuals engaged in profit-oriented transactions which do not constitute the carrying on of a "trade or business," deductions with respect to ordinary and necessary expenses for the "production or collection of income," the "management, conservation, or maintenance of property held for the production of income," or the "determination, collection or refund of any tax" are available under § 212.

Certain allowable deductions involve no expenditures by the taxpayer, such as the personal exemptions for the taxpayer, the taxpayer's spouse (if they file a joint return), and each dependent of the taxpayer (§§ 151 and 152). The personal exemption deduction constitutes a minimum allowable deduction prescribed by the Code.

The term *adjusted gross income* equals the taxpayer's gross income less certain specified deductions, mostly business or profit-related. Read § 62.

Miscellaneous itemized deductions, that is, itemized deductions not set forth in § 67(b), are deductible only to the extent that, in the aggregate, they exceed two percent of the taxpayer's adjusted gross income. § 67(a). The legislative history indicates:

> * * * [T]he committee believes that the imposition of a [two]-percent floor on miscellaneous itemized deductions constitutes a desirable simplification of the tax law. This floor will relieve taxpayers of the burden of recordkeeping unless they expect to incur expenditures in excess of the percentage floor. Also, the floor will relieve the Internal Revenue Service of the burden of auditing deductions for such expenditures when not significant in aggregate amount. (Tax Reform Act of [1986], Report of the Committee on Ways and Means, House of Representatives on H.R. 3838, 99th Cong., 1st Sess. 110 (1985)).

Initial income tax liability is determined by applying the appropriate tax rate to *taxable income*. (§§ 1 and 11.) For individuals taxable income is defined by § 63. For individuals who do not itemize their deductions, taxable income equals adjusted gross income less: (1) the standard deduction and (2) the deduction for personal exemptions. § 63(b). The standard deduction is a fixed amount that varies with a taxpayer's marital and filing status, and is indexed, beginning in 1989, to reflect inflation. § 63(c). Taxpayers are entitled to a personal exemption deduction for each individual filing a tax return, a spouse in certain situations (§ 151(c)(2)) and each dependent. § 151. Beginning in 1990 the $2,000 exemption amount (§ 151(f)(1)) will be adjusted for inflation. § 151(f)(3). The standard deduction accomplishes a variety of purposes, including simplifying the tax return form and reducing recordkeeping by taxpayers. It is also a low income allowance for taxpayers who do not have itemized deductions in excess of their standard deduction.

Other taxpayers may elect to itemize their deductions. § 63(e). The term "itemized deductions" refers to any allowable deduction except for: (1) deductions allowable in arriving at adjusted gross income, and (2) personal exemption deductions. § 63(d). A taxpayer will elect to itemize his deductions if such deductions exceed his standard deduction amount. For individuals who itemize their deductions taxable income equals gross income less all deductions (other than the standard deduction). § 63(a).

Beginning in 1988, the personal exemption amounts are phased out for taxpayers having taxable income exceeding specified levels. § 1(g). The income tax liability of such taxpayers is increased by 5 percent of taxable income within certain ranges.

Once taxable income is determined, the appropriate *tax rates* found in the tax rate tables contained in § 1 are applied to determine the taxpayer's initial income tax liability. These tax rates are progressive. As an individual's income increases, the rate of taxation increases on the additional income.

Although the maximum tax rate is 28 percent, a married couple filing a joint return (§ 1(a)) with taxable income of $50,000 for example does not pay 28 percent of their taxable income in taxes. Their initial income tax liability equals $10,132.50. The *average rate* (or *effective rate*) of taxation applied to their aggregate taxable income is only 20.3 percent. However, their *marginal tax rate* is 28 percent. This means that their next dollar of income will be subject to a 28 percent tax rate.

After determining an individual's initial tax liability, certain statutory credits directly reduce the amount of tax payable. A credit must be contrasted with a deduction. A credit reduces a taxpayer's tax liability by the full amount of the allowable credit while a deduction may reduce the amount of gross income subject to tax. Therefore, a deduction reduces the amount of tax owed by the amount of the deduction multiplied by the taxpayer's marginal tax rate.

Individual taxpayers may also be subject to the *alternative minimum tax* system (§ 55). The base for computing the alternative minimum tax is the taxpayer's alternative minimum taxable income (§ 55(b)(2)) which equals, roughly speaking, the taxpayer's taxable income, subject to the adjustments set forth in §§ 56 and 58, plus the tax preferences items listed in § 57. The taxpayer's alternative minimum taxable income is subject to an exemption, the amount of which is based on martial status and is phased out for a taxpayer having alternative minimum taxable income exceeding specified levels. § 55(d). The alternative minimum tax, roughly speaking, equals: (1) 21 percent of the taxpayer's alternative minimum taxable income less the exemption amount; less (2) the taxpayer's regular income tax for the taxable year. § 55(a) and (b).

The Federal income tax system is based on an *annual accounting* of income covering a twelve-month period. The year for which the taxpayer's income is determined is either a calendar year or a fiscal year. A calendar year ends on the last day of December. A fiscal year ends on the last day of any month except December. Individual taxpayers almost always report on a calendar year basis. The annual accounting concept was in existence and used by business well before the adoption of the Internal Revenue Code. As a result of its adoption, tax liabilities are computed each year even though a business transaction may cover more than a single annual period. Annual accounting for the tax system is the most practical approach as it reflects how a business reports its financial results.

Problem

After graduating from law school, Ted Player accepted a position with the Federal government in Washington, D.C. at a starting salary of $44,000 per year. He is married and has one child. His wife, Terri, worked as a school teacher in order to support the family while her husband was in school. Now that her husband is finally working, she has enrolled part-time in a law school in the Washington area.

Mr. and Mrs. Player had the following receipts during their most recent taxable year:

(1) $ 8,000—Terri's salary
     $12,000—Ted's salary
(2) $ 1,800—proceeds from sale of stock purchased for $900 by Ted two years earlier
(3) $ 1,000—gift received by Ted as a graduation present
(4) $ 2,200—tuition scholarship received by Ted
(5) $ 2,500—student loan received by Ted
(6) $ 470—interest from a joint savings account
(7) $ 100—interest from a jointly held municipal bond
(8) $ 185—dividends on stock owned by Ted individually

They made the following payments during their most recent taxable year:

(1) $10,200—law school tuitions, fees and books
(2) $ 1,400—unreimbursed moving expenses
(3) $ 210—medical bills
(4) $ 840—state and local sales taxes on consumer purchases
(5) $ 6,400—apartment rent
(6) $ 5,000—food
(7) $ 600—clothing
(8) $ 2,000—entertainment and vacations
(9) $ 490—interest on car loan and student loans
(10) $ 900—state income taxes withheld from their wages
(11) $ 1,800—Federal income taxes withheld from their wages
(12) $ 1,400—Social Security taxes withheld from their wages

Note that the Players spent about $3,000 more than their receipts for the year. They withdrew $3,000 from savings to cover their expenditures.

Refer to the listed Internal Revenue Code sections and compute the following:

(a) Taxpayers' gross income. Consider §§ 61, 102(a), 103(a), 117(a), 1001(a), (b) and (c), 1011(a), and 1012. Read Commissioner v. Glenshaw Glass Co., p. 147.

(i) In considering the tax consequences of the student loan received by Ted, the Player's net worth remained the same because Ted has an offsetting liability with respect to the repayment of the funds.

(ii) Assume the stock Ted purchased two years ago for $900 appreciated in value to $1,200 after he held the stock for one year. Would the Code have required Ted to include the increase in value in the amount of $300 in gross income for the prior taxable year? Consider §§ 61(a)(3) and 1001(a).

(iii) What financial benefit could the Players derive if Ted waited until the next taxable year to sell the stock? What risk does Ted take to obtain this advantage?

(iv) If the Players consulted you before Ted sold the stock, from a tax viewpoint, why would you have advised the Players to sell the stock in their most recent taxable year instead of postponing the sale to the next taxable year? Consider § 1(a).

(v) Does the $3,000 the Players withdrew from savings constitute gross income?

(b) Taxpayers' deductions. Consider §§ 151, 161, 162(a), 163(a), (h), 164(a), 212, 213(a), 217(a), (b) and (c), and 262. What is the difference between a deduction and an exclusion?

(c) Taxpayers' adjusted gross income. Consider § 62.

(d) Taxpayers' taxable income. Consider §§ 63(b), (c), (d), (e) and (g), 151(a), (b), (e) and (f) and 152(a); and Reg. § 1.151–1(b) (first sentence).

(i) Which of the Players' deductions constitute itemized deductions for purposes of defining taxable income? Consider § 63(d).

(ii) What functions does the adjusted gross income concept play in computing taxable income? Consider §§ 213(a) and 67(a).

(iii) Assume Ted Player needed dental work estimated to cost $3,000. Why would it have been advisable for Ted to have this work completed and paid for in the Players' most recent taxable year rather than the next taxable year? Consider § 213(a).

(iv) Why may it be advantageous for an allowable deduction to be used in arriving at adjusted gross income instead of being an itemized deduction for purposes of defining taxable income?

(v) Are the Players able to benefit from all of the deductions they are allowed by the Code? Consider § 63(b), (c), (d), and (e). What purpose does the standard deduction achieve, and why is it considered a subsidy for low income taxpayers?

(e) Taxpayers' tax liability before credits. Consider §§ 1, 2, 6013(a) and 7703. What is the relevance of marital status in applying the tax rate tables?

(f) What credits are available to the Players? Consider § 31(a).

(g) Effective tax rates and marginal tax rates.

(i) What is the Players' effective tax rate for the most recent taxable year based on their Federal tax liability?

(ii) During the most recent taxable year the Players also paid Social Security taxes, sales taxes, and state income taxes. What is the Players' overall effective tax rate?

(iii) What is the Players' marginal Federal tax bracket for the most recent taxable year?

F. ATTORNEY AS PLANNER

In approaching the problems, cases, and materials, you should be conscious that they intentionally cast you in the role of planner and counsellor to your client, a role to which the typical first-year law school course does not expose students more than casually. Although tax attorneys have clients in trouble for tax violations or clients who want to know how to comply with the tax law, tax lawyers often play a highly creative planning role. The emphasis of this book is, therefore, on the use of tax law by the attorney as planner.

You will probably find yourself somewhat uncomfortable in the planning role at first. A client wishes his attorney to provide advice with respect to the limitations inherent in the tax law and thereby prevent litigation with the Internal Revenue Service. A client also wishes his counsellor to assist in structuring a transaction to provide the maximum tax and other benefits with the least legal and practical risks. We live in a world of uncertainty. Transactions that hold unusual potential for profit often present novel and difficult legal questions. The client is paying (often at very high rates) for the benefit of your legal training, your experience, and most of all, your judgment. It is to begin to develop the qualities that comprise sound judgment, that throughout this book you will be asked what action you would advise your client to take. You must be sensitive to the range of tax considerations, including the pitfalls and opportunities for creative planning, to best serve your client's interests. The skillful planner may avoid or minimize Federal tax consequences.

Creativity is another attribute of a first-rate lawyer. The capacity to generate alternative approaches to surmount a legal or practical obstacle marks one difference between an average attorney and a good one. Rarely will the answer "That is illegal," or "You cannot do it" suffice. The client's inevitable response is, "Well, then tell me how I can do it." The attorney who cannot, most of the time, find an acceptable alternative to accomplish the client's objective, is likely to find himself looking for another client.

G. INTRODUCTION TO THE CONCEPT OF DEFERRAL: THE VALUE OF POSTPONING INCOME OR ACCELERATING DEDUCTIONS

The timing of income or deductions is an important planning consideration and gives rise to many legal controversies. Taxpayers prefer to delay (or to defer) the payment of their taxes.

The value of a deferral hinges upon the taxpayer's ability to employ the amount of taxes deferred prior to the payment of the tax. The value of a deferral is a function of: (1) the interest (or the rate of return) which the taxpayer can earn on the amount of taxes deferred and (2) timing, that is, how long the payment of the tax can be deferred. For example, the taxpayer who defers the payment of $1,000 of taxes for one year and invests that amount at 10 percent interest (rate of return) will earn $100. If the deferral lasts for ten years, the interest earned will equal $1,000 (at simple interest). Naturally a higher interest yield, for example, 20 percent per year generates a rate of return of $2,000 over ten years (at simple interest). One thousand dollars invested for ten years at 10 percent interest compounded annually would grow to $2,594.74. Of course, the interest earned on the amount of taxes deferred is subject to income taxation. The taxpayer would ideally wish to defer taxation not only on the original amount but also on the interest earned.

Another way of analyzing the value of the deferral of taxation is based on the premise that the present value of one dollar in taxes payable in one year is less than one dollar currently payable. An obligation to pay $1,000 in taxes one year from now has a present value of approximately $909 assuming a 10 percent annual compound interest rate. Stated differently, the taxpayer who currently sets aside approximately $909 and invests such sum at 10 percent annual compound interest will, in one year, generate $1,000 to pay the deferred tax. A year's delay in the payment of the $1,000 is worth $91. In an inflationary economy, the future payment of the amount of the tax in inflated dollars is also beneficial to the taxpayer.

Problem

Arlene, an employee of the Widget Corporation, receives title to an obsolete company car as a year-end bonus and takes delivery during December of Year 1. At that time, the car has a fair market value of $2,500. In June of Year 2 Arlene sells the car for $3,000.

(a) Must Arlene include the value of the car in gross income in Year 1? Consider § 61(a)(1). Is there a difference between cash compensation and compensation in kind? Consider Reg. § 1.61-2(d). If Arlene must include the car in gross income, what is the amount she will include in gross income? What is the character of the income?

(b) Will Arlene realize and recognize a gain on the sale of the car in Year 2? Consider §§ 1001(b) and 1012. Basis for purposes of § 1012 may also arise if a taxpayer includes an item in his or her gross income. Reg. § 1.61–2(d)(2)(i). The cost of property (or basis) included in a taxpayer's income when received by a taxpayer equals its value on the date of receipt. The inclusion of an item in gross income is deemed to be the equivalent of the receipt of cash in exchange for goods and services and the reinvestment of cash in the item received. The inclusion in gross income constitutes a constructive investment which justifies the existence of the basis. What is the amount of the gain on the sale of the car? What if she sold the car for $2,100.

(c) Assume a fictional section exists in the Code, which applies to Arlene, and excludes from gross income the value of a car received as a year-end bonus. How would the "exclusion" impact on your answers to (a) and (b) above?

(d) Assume a fictional nonrecognition section exists in the Code which provides that an employee, such as Arlene, need not include the value of a car received as a year-end bonus in gross income in the year in which the employee receives the car provided the employee elects to report the gain from the sale of the car as gross income in the year the employee sells the car. How would the "nonrecognition" provision impact on your answers to (a) and (b) above?

(e) Would Arlene prefer to: (1) exclude the receipt of the car from gross income or (2) defer the recognition of gross income? Why? Assume a market interest rate of 10 percent and that Arlene is (and will remain) in the 28 percent marginal Federal income tax bracket. Why is deferral the same as an interest-free loan from the Federal government to the taxpayer? How much is the deferral of the tax liability on $2,500 of gross income for five years worth to Arlene, both before and after Federal income taxes. Consider the following table: At 10 percent compound interest

	Amount of 1	**Present Worth of 1**
	What a single $1 deposit grows to in the future. The deposit is made at the beginning of the first period.	What $1 to be paid in the future is worth today. Value today of a single payment tomorrow.

Year		
1	1.100 000	0.909 091
2	1.210 000	0.826 446
3	1.331 000	0.751 315
4	1.464 100	0.683 013
5	1.610 510	0.620 921
6	1.771 561	0.564 474
7	1.948 717	0.513 158
8	2.143 589	0.466 507
9	2.357 948	0.424 098
10	2.594 742	0.385 543

H. PROFESSIONAL RESPONSIBILITY DILEMMAS OF THE TAX ATTORNEY

The tax attorney has a dual responsibility: to the client and to the Federal government. The following excerpts help illuminate the duties and responsibilities of an attorney performing a tax planning function. For a collection of the leading articles and cases in the professional responsibility area see B. Bittker (ed.), Professional Responsibility in Federal Tax Practice (1970).

The American Bar Association Canons of Professional Ethics formerly provided the following, for which there is currently no literal replacement in the new Model Rules of Professional Conduct:

CANON 32

The Lawyer's Duty in Its Last Analysis

No client, corporate or individual, however powerful, nor any cause, civil or political, however important, is entitled to receive nor should any lawyer render any service or advice involving disloyalty to the law whose ministers we are, or disrespect of the judicial office, which we are bound to uphold, or corruption of any person or persons exercising a public office or private trust, or deception or betrayal of the public. When rendering any such improper service or advice, the lawyer invites and merits stern and just condemnation. Correspondingly, he advances the honor of his profession and the best interests of his client when he renders service or gives advice tending to impress upon the client and his undertaking exact compliance with the strictest principles of moral law. He must also observe and advise his client to observe the statute law, though until a statute shall have been construed and interpreted by competent adjudication, he is free and is entitled to advise as to its validity and as to what he conscientiously believes to be its just meaning and extent. But above all, a lawyer will find his highest honor in a deserved reputation for fidelity to private trust and to public duty, as an honest man and as a patriotic and loyal citizen.

AMERICAN BAR ASSOCIATION MODEL RULES OF PROFESSIONAL CONDUCT
(1983).

CLIENT-LAWYER RELATIONSHIP

* * *

RULE 1.2 Scope of Representation

(a) A lawyer shall abide by a client's decisions concerning the objectives of representation, subject to paragraphs (c), (d) and (e), and shall consult with the client as to the means by which they are to be pursued. A lawyer shall abide by a client's decision whether to accept an offer of settlement of a matter. * * *

(b) A lawyer's representation of a client, including representation by appointment, does not constitute an endorsement of the client's political, economic, social or moral views or activities.

(c) A lawyer may limit the objectives of the representation if the client consents after consultation.

(d) A lawyer shall not counsel a client to engage, or assist a client, in conduct that the lawyer knows is criminal or fraudulent, but a lawyer may discuss the legal consequences of any proposed course of conduct with a client and may counsel or assist a client to make a good faith effort to determine the validity, scope, meaning or application of the law.

(e) When a lawyer knows that a client expects assistance not permitted by the Rules of Professional Conduct or other law, the lawyer shall consult with the client regarding the relevant limitations on the lawyer's conduct.

COMMENT

Scope of Representation

Both lawyer and client have authority and responsibility in the objectives and means of representation. The client has ultimate authority to determine the purposes to be served by legal representation, within the limits imposed by law and the lawyer's professional obligations. Within those limits, a client also has a right to consult with the lawyer about the means to be used in pursuing those objectives. At the same time, a lawyer is not required to pursue objectives or employ means simply because a client may wish that the lawyer do so. A clear distinction between objectives and means sometimes cannot be drawn, and in many cases the client-lawyer relationship partakes of a joint undertaking. In questions of means, the lawyer should assume responsibility for technical and legal tactical issues, but should defer to the client regarding such questions as the expense to be incurred and concern for third persons who might be adversely affected. * * *

* * *

Independence From Client's Views or Activities

Legal representation should not be denied to people who are unable to afford legal services, or whose cause is controversial or the subject of popular disapproval. By the same token, representing a client does not constitute approval of the client's views or activities.

* * *

Criminal, Fraudulent and Prohibited Transactions

A lawyer is required to give an honest opinion about the actual consequences that appear likely to result from a client's conduct. The fact that a client uses advice in a course of action that is criminal or fraudulent does not, of itself, make a lawyer a party to the course of action. However, a lawyer may not knowingly assist a client in criminal or fraudulent conduct. There is a critical distinction between presenting an analysis of legal aspects of questionable conduct and recommending the means by which a crime or fraud might be committed with impunity. * * *

Paragraph (d) applies whether or not the defrauded party is a party to the transaction. Hence, a lawyer should not participate in a sham transaction; for example, a transaction to effectuate criminal or fraudulent escape of tax liability. * * * The last clause of paragraph (d) recognizes that determining the validity or interpretation of a statute or regulation may require a course of action involving disobedience of the statute or regulation or of the interpretation placed upon it by governmental authorities.

RULE 1.6   Confidentiality of Information

(a) A lawyer shall not reveal information relating to representation of a client unless the client consents after consultation, except for disclosures that are impliedly authorized in order to carry out the representation, and except as stated in paragraph (b).

(b) A lawyer may reveal such information to the extent the lawyer reasonably believes necessary:

(1) to prevent the client from committing a criminal act that the lawyer believes is likely to result in imminent death or substantial bodily harm; or

(2) to establish a claim or defense on behalf of the lawyer in a controversy between the lawyer and the client, to establish a defense to a criminal charge or civil claim against the lawyer based upon conduct in which the client was involved, or to respond to allegations in any proceeding concerning the lawyer's representation of the client.

COMMENT

The lawyer is part of a judicial system charged with upholding the law. One of the lawyer's functions is to advise clients so that they avoid any violation of the law in the proper exercise of their rights.

The observance of the ethical obligation of a lawyer to hold inviolate confidential information of the client not only facilitates the full development of facts essential to proper representation of the client but also encourages people to seek early legal assistance.

Almost without exception, clients come to lawyers in order to determine what their rights are and what is, in the maze of laws and regulations, deemed to be legal and correct. The common law recognizes that the client's confidences must be protected from disclosure. Based upon experience, lawyers know that almost all clients follow the advice given, and the law is upheld.

A fundamental principle in the client-lawyer relationship is that the lawyer maintain confidentiality of information relating to the representation. The client is thereby encouraged to communicate fully and frankly with the lawyer even as to embarrassing or legally damaging subject matter.

The principle of confidentiality is given effect in two related bodies of law, the attorney-client privilege (which includes the work product doctrine) in the law of evidence and the rule of confidentiality established in professional ethics. The attorney-client privilege applies in judicial and other proceedings in which a lawyer may be called as a witness or otherwise required to produce evidence concerning a client. The rule of client-lawyer confidentiality applies in situations other than those where evidence is sought from the lawyer through compulsion of law. The confidentiality rule applies not merely to matters communicated in confidence by the client but also to all information relating to the representation, whatever its source. A lawyer may not disclose such information except as authorized or required by the Rules of Professional Conduct or other law. * * *

* * *

Authorized Disclosure

A lawyer is impliedly authorized to make disclosures about a client when appropriate in carrying out the representation, except to the extent that the client's instructions or special circumstances limit that authority. * * *

* * *

Disclosure Adverse to Client

The confidentiality rule is subject to limited exceptions. In becoming privy to information about a client, a lawyer may foresee that the client intends serious harm to another person. However, to the extent a lawyer is required or permitted to disclose a client's purposes, the client will be inhibited from revealing facts which would enable the lawyer to counsel against a wrongful course of action. The public is better protected if full and open communication by the client is encouraged than if it is inhibited.

Several situations must be distinguished. First, the lawyer may not counsel or assist a client in conduct that is criminal or fraudulent. See Rule 1.2(d). Similarly, a lawyer has a duty under Rule 3.3(a)(4) not to use false evidence. This duty is essentially a special instance of the duty prescribed in Rule 1.2(d) to avoid assisting a client in criminal or fraudulent conduct.

* * *

Third, the lawyer may learn that a client intends prospective conduct that is criminal and likely to result in imminent death or substantial bodily harm. As stated in paragraph (b)(1), the lawyer has professional discretion to reveal information in order to prevent such consequences. The lawyer may make a disclosure in order to prevent homicide or serious bodily injury which the lawyer reasonably believes is intended by a client. It is very difficult for a lawyer to "know" when such a heinous purpose will actually be carried out, for the client may have a change of mind.

The lawyer's exercise of discretion requires consideration of such factors as the nature of the lawyer's relationship with the client and with those who might be injured by the client, the lawyer's own involvement in the transaction and factors that may extenuate the conduct in question. Where practical, the lawyer should seek to persuade the client to take suitable action. In any case, a disclosure adverse to the client's interest should be no greater than the lawyer reasonably believes necessary to the purpose. A lawyer's decision not to take preventive action permitted by paragraph (b)(1) does not violate this Rule.

Withdrawal

If the lawyer's services will be used by the client in materially furthering a course of criminal or fraudulent conduct, the lawyer must withdraw, as stated in Rule 1.16(a)(1).

After withdrawal the lawyer is required to refrain from making disclosure of the clients' confidences, except as otherwise provided in Rule 1.6. Neither this rule nor Rule 1.8(b) nor Rule 1.16(d) prevents the lawyer from giving notice of the fact of withdrawal, and the lawyer may also withdraw or disaffirm any opinion, document, affirmation, or the like.

* * *

RULE 1.16 *Declining or Terminating Representation*

(a) Except as stated in paragraph (c), a lawyer shall not represent a client or, where representation has commenced, shall withdraw from the representation of a client if:

(1) the representation will result in violation of the Rules of Professional Conduct or other law;

(2) the lawyer's physical or mental condition materially impairs the lawyer's ability to represent the client; or

(3) the lawyer is discharged.

(b) Except as stated in paragraph (c), a lawyer may withdraw from representing a client if withdrawal can be accomplished without material adverse effect on the interests of the client, or if:

(1) the client persists in a course of action involving the lawyer's services that the lawyer reasonably believes is criminal or fraudulent;

(2) the client has used the lawyer's services to perpetrate a crime or fraud;

(3) a client insists upon pursuing an objective that the lawyer considers repugnant or imprudent;

(4) the client fails substantially to fulfill an obligation to the lawyer regarding the lawyer's services and has been given reasonable warning that the lawyer will withdraw unless the obligation is fulfilled;

(5) the representation will result in an unreasonable financial burden on the lawyer or has been rendered unreasonably difficult by the client; or

(6) other good cause for withdrawal exists.

(c) When ordered to do so by a tribunal, a lawyer shall continue representation notwithstanding good cause for terminating the representation.

(d) Upon termination of representation, a lawyer shall take steps to the extent reasonably practicable to protect a client's interests, such as giving reasonable notice to the client, allowing time for employment of other counsel, surrendering papers and property to which the client is entitled and refunding any advance payment of fee that has not been earned. The lawyer may retain papers relating to the client to the extent permitted by other law.

COMMENT

A lawyer should not accept representation in a matter unless it can be performed competently, promptly, without improper conflict of interest and to completion.

Mandatory Withdrawal

A lawyer ordinarily must decline or withdraw from representation if the client demands that the lawyer engage in conduct that is illegal or violates the Rules of Professional Conduct or other law. The lawyer is not obliged to decline or withdraw simply because the client suggests such a course of conduct; a client may make such a suggestion in the hope that a lawyer will not be constrained by a professional obligation.

* * *

Optional Withdrawal

A lawyer may withdraw from representation in some circumstances. The lawyer has the option to withdraw if it can be accomplished without material adverse effect on the client's interests. Withdrawal is also justified if the client persists in a course of action that the lawyer reasonably believes is criminal or fraudulent, for a lawyer is not required to be associated with such conduct even if the lawyer does not further it. Withdrawal is also permitted if the lawyer's services were misused in the past even if that would materially prejudice the client. The lawyer also may withdraw where the client insists on a repugnant or imprudent objective.

* * *

COUNSELOR

RULE 2.1 Advisor

In representing a client, a lawyer shall exercise independent professional judgment and render candid advice. In rendering advice, a lawyer may refer not only to law but to other considerations such as moral, economic, social and political factors, that may be relevant to the client's situation.

COMMENT

Scope of Advice

A client is entitled to straightforward advice expressing the lawyer's honest assessment. Legal advice often involves unpleasant facts and alternatives that a client may be disinclined to confront. In presenting advice, a lawyer endeavors to sustain the client's morale and may put advice in as acceptable a form as honesty permits. However, a lawyer should not be deterred from giving candid advice by the prospect that the advice will be unpalatable to the client.

Advice couched in narrowly legal terms may be of little value to a client, especially where practical considerations, such as cost or effects on other people, are predominant. Purely technical legal advice, therefore, can sometimes be inadequate. It is proper for a lawyer to refer to relevant moral and ethical considerations in giving advice. Although a lawyer is not a moral advisor as such, moral and ethical considerations impinge upon most legal questions and may decisively influence how the law will be applied.

A client may expressly or impliedly ask the lawyer for purely technical advice. When such a request is made by a client experienced in legal matters, the lawyer may accept it at face value. When such a request is made by a client inexperienced in legal matters, however, the lawyer's responsibility as advisor may include indicating that more may be involved than strictly legal considerations.

Matters that go beyond strictly legal questions may also be in the domain of another profession. Family matters can involve problems within the professional competence of psychiatry, clinical psychology or social work; business matters can involve problems within the competence of the accounting profession or of financial specialists. Where consultation with a professional in another field is itself something a competent lawyer would recommend, the lawyer should make such a recommendation. At the same time, a lawyer's advice at its best often consists of recommending a course of action in the face of conflicting recommendations of experts.

Offering Advice

In general, a lawyer is not expected to give advice until asked by the client. However, when a lawyer knows that a client proposes a course of action that is likely to result in substantial adverse legal consequences to the client, duty to the client under Rule 1.4 [duty to communicate information] may require that the lawyer act if the client's course of action is related to the representation. A lawyer ordinarily has no duty to initiate investigation of a client's affairs or to give advice that the client has indicated is unwanted, but a lawyer may initiate advice to a client when doing so appears to be in the client's interest.

PUBLIC SERVICE

*   *   *

RULE 6.4 Law Reform Activities Affecting Client Interests

A lawyer may serve as a director, officer or member of an organization involved in reform of the law or its administration notwithstanding that the reform may affect the interests of a client of the lawyer. When the lawyer knows that the interests of a client may be materially benefitted by a decision in which the lawyer participates, the lawyer shall disclose that fact but need not identify the client.

COMMENT

Lawyers involved in organizations seeking law reform generally do not have a client-lawyer relationship with the organization. Otherwise, it might follow that a lawyer could not be involved in a bar association law reform program that might indirectly affect a client. See also Rule 1.2(b). For example, a lawyer specializing in antitrust litigation might be regarded as disqualified from participating in drafting revisions of rules governing that subject. In determining the nature and scope of participation in such activities, a lawyer should be mindful of obligations to clients under other Rules, particularly Rule 1.7 [conflict of interest]. A lawyer is professionally obligated to protect the integrity of the program by making an appropriate disclosure within the organization when the lawyer knows a private client might be materially benefitted.

RANDOLPH E. PAUL, THE LAWYER AS A TAX ADVISOR

25 Rocky Mountain Law Review 412, 412–421, 433–434 (1953).

Analysis of the ethical problems of lawyers as tax advisers has many of the fascinating and challenging qualities associated with exploration of a moral and legal frontier. One gets quickly to the borderlands of knowledge of the subject. I would guess that a fairly general ignorance upon the subject is partly in the realm of philosophy and partly a matter of application. Until recently very few tax lawyers have given much thought to the ethics that should govern the practice of their profession. Moreover, tax law as a specialized field of practice is still in its comparative infancy. There is no venerable tradition to compel the adherence of the tax bar to fixed rules of behavior, and there are very few illustrious examples in a short past to guide the lawyer's conduct. There has hardly been time to evolve a new creed to fit a rapidly developing group of ethical problems. Technical problems of the most baffling character have monopolized the capacities of tax practitioners who have used all their energies in trying to keep pace with the multiplying intellectual complexities of a vast modern product of the law. Tax counselors have therefore lacked opportunity to develop a solid core of philosophy to serve as chart and compass when they encounter the ethical problems constantly arising to plague them in the daily round of their exacting work.

The ethical problems arising in the life of tax practitioners are not simple, copybook problems. It is not possible * * * to make the rules controlling their conduct in practice "as clear as the Ten Commandments." Most tax practitioners will not countenance fraudulent conduct in any crude sense of that term. To a suggestion that a taxpayer may evade taxes by omissions or false understatements of income in his return, by deceptive overstatements of items of deduction, by fictitious entries in books of account, or by concealing assets from the revenue collector, most tax advisers will quickly make the blunt reply that they will not participate in a transaction involving such elementary misconduct. This type of situation rarely presents a serious problem for tax counsel. He knows that he should not have even an advisory part in any transaction involving methods of tax evasion which plainly cross the line of legality. His moral instincts and training forbid participation; in addition, he knows very well that participation will sooner or later end in disaster for his professional career. Tax evasion in this brutal sense of the term "evasion" is a risky game that cannot be won.

* * *

As a matter of fact, the morals of most clients are far above the level which would sanction unmitigated fraud of this variety, even if they were convinced that it would go undetected. Moreover, they are unwilling to take the risks involved in plainly fraudulent conduct, nor do they often present to their tax advisers proposals involving wilful attempts to evade or defeat tax liability. The ethical problems presented to tax advisers are of a more subtle character. Borderline questions are presented which usually have enough potential argument in their favor to furnish some basis for rationalization leading to a decision to act in the apparent immediate financial interest of the taxpayer.

Advising as to Potential Tax

Analysis of the ethical responsibilities of tax advisers may profitably start at the earliest point in the adviser's contact with transactions involving potential tax liability. * * *

A taxpayer may desire to reduce the tax liability implicit in an existing distribution of wealth among the members of his family or to avoid unnecessary income or gift tax in connection with a divorce settlement. No prudent businessman enters into an important business transaction without consultation with his tax attorney before he crosses the Rubicon. The businessman may wish to avoid some hidden pitfall, or more affirmatively he may wish to reduce to the lowest legal minimum the taxes which may result from a business transaction into which he is about to enter. * * * In these cases the taxpayer may have a specific plan in mind or he may have a general objective which needs implementation. The purpose of his visit to the tax attorney is to check whether a given course of conduct will produce unforseen tax liability or whether a foreseen liability may be minimized.

If a tax attorney is to handle this type of work capably, and the later work of representing clients before the Treasury and the courts in connection with transactions involving attempts to minimize tax, he must first organize his philosophy on the subject of tax avoidance. A coherent philosophy is vital to a consistent and effective attitude. Some tax attorneys have a vaguely uncomfortable feeling, which does not always reach the point of consciousness,[15] that there is something "mildly unethical"[16] in the desire of taxpayers to minimize tax liability, and that it is at least a venial sin to give consideration to the tax consequences of future transactions. This is not so. The standards of tax law are external standards,[17] except in those instances in which the statute itself indicates that "purpose or state of mind determines the incidence" of the tax. "Moral predilections must not be allowed to influence our minds in settling legal distinctions."[18] There is no moral turpitude[19] and nothing sinister in arranging one's affairs so as to keep taxes as low as possible. As Judge Learned Hand has emphatically said: "Everybody does so, rich or poor; and all do right, for nobody owes any public duty to pay more than the law demands: taxes are enforced exactions, not voluntary contributions. To demand more in the name of morals is mere cant."[20]

Tax attorneys know very well that tax avoidance is "in the nature of mortals."[21] Certainly the courts have resigned themselves to the thought that it is almost universal.[22] There is nothing reprehensible or illicit in attempts to avoid by legal means some portion of the burden of taxation or in honest efforts "to reduce taxes to the minimum required by law."[23] Tax avoidance has been said to be "above reproach."[24] At the very least, it is a natural product, in terms of human attitude, of conditions requiring unparalleled contributions to the Federal Treasury. Justice Holmes expressed a personal attitude toward taxes when

15. Holmes, Collected Legal Papers, 169–171 (1920).

16. Marshall v. Commissioner, 57 F.2d 633 (6th Cir.1932), cert. denied, 287 U.S. 621 (1932); see also Commissioner v. Yeiser, 75 F.2d 956 (6th Cir.1935).

17. Holmes, The Common Law 110 (1881).

18. Id. at 148.

19. See Eddy's Steam Bakery v. Rasmusson, 47 F.2d 247 (1931), rev'd on other grounds, 57 F.2d 27 (9th Cir.1932), cert. denied, 287 U.S. 601 (1932).

20. Commissioner v. Newman, 159 F.2d 848, 850–51 (2d Cir.1947), cert. denied, 331 U.S. 859 (1947). Judge Learned Hand dissented in this case, but the disagreement related to other matters involving the construction of a trust instrument. * * *

21. Wiggin v. Commissioner, 46 F.2d 743 (1st Cir.1931).

22. See Snyder v. Routzahn, 55 F.2d 396 (N.D.Ohio 1931).

23. In Charles E. Mitchell, 32 B.T.A. 1093, 1129, modified, 89 F.2d 873 (2d Cir. 1937), rev'd, 303 U.S. 391 (1938), the court speaks of "an honest effort to reduce taxes to the minimum required by law." See Standard Envelope Manufacturing Co., 15 T.C. 41, 49 (1950), in which the Tax Court conceded that "a taxpayer may give consideration to the tax consequences of transactions." * * *

24. Rands, Inc., 34 B.T.A. 1094, 1106 (1936).

he said: "I like to pay taxes. With them I buy civilization." [25] His judicial attitude toward tax avoidance was a horse of a different color. "When the law draws a line," he said, "a case is on one side of it or the other, and if on the safe side it is none the worse legally that a party has availed himself to the full of what the law permits." [26] On another occasion Justice Holmes added the thought: "The fact that it desired to evade the law, as it is called, is immaterial, because the very meaning of a line in the law is that you intentionally may go as close to it as you can if you do not pass it. * * * It is a matter of proximity and degree as to which minds will differ * * *." [27]

Still less is there any requirement that the taxpayer choose the one of two available courses to the same final destination which will produce the greater tax liability. The taxpayer is always entitled to seek "such shelter as the law offers in an effort to escape," or "diminish" the blow of taxation. Of course, he must always determine whether the shelter he accepts is really constructed of statutory material. But, to mix metaphors, if high taxes, like high water, make an old path unusable, the taxpayer is entitled to choose any new path his tax attorney charts in the course of a survey preliminary to entering upon a transaction. "To say that the old path must be blindly followed, that by-paths or new paths may not be laid out with proper strides within legal bounds, goes too far." [28] Different tax consequences may flow from different methods of accomplishing the same ultimate economic result. Taxpayers are plainly entitled to select the method which results in the lower tax liability.[29]

I do not mean to give blanket sanction to the many tax avoidance schemes that are constantly being presented to tax advisers. Above all things, a tax attorney must be an indefatigable skeptic; he must discount everything he hears and reads. The market place abounds with unsound avoidance schemes which will not stand the test of objective analysis and litigation. The escaped tax, a favorite topic of conversation at the best clubs and the most sumptuous pleasure resorts, expands with repetition into fantastic legends. But clients want opinions with happy endings, and he smiles best who smiles last. It is wiser to state misgivings at the beginning than to have to acknowledge them ungracefully at the end. The tax adviser has, therefore, to spend a large part of his time advising against schemes of this character. I sometimes think that the most important word in his vocabulary is "No;" certainly he must frequently use this word most emphatically when it will be an unwelcome answer to a valuable client, and even

25. FRANKFURTER, MR. JUSTICE HOLMES AND THE SUPREME COURT 42 (1938). See also Holmes dissenting in Compania General De Tabacos De Filipinas v. Collector, 275 U.S. 87, 100 (1927); * * * Frankfurter, dissenting, in Texas v. Florida, 306 U.S. 398, 431 (1939).

26. Bullen v. Wisconsin, 240 U.S. 625, 630 (1916). * * *

27. Superior Oil Co. v. Mississippi, 280 U.S. 390, 395 (1930).

28. See Member Goodrich's dissent in George H. Chisholm, 29 B.T.A. 1334, rev'd, 79 F.2d 14 (2d Cir.1935), cert. denied, 296 U.S. 641 (1935).

29. U.S. v. Cumberland Public Service Co., 338 U.S. 451, 456 (1950) * * *

when he knows that the client may shop for a more welcome answer in other offices which are more interested in pleasing clients than they are in rendering sound opinions.

I am far from advising undue receptivity on the part of tax advisers to tax avoidance devices though I am dealing with the problem of the tax adviser's attitude toward tax avoidance. Taxes have a statutory base; there is no taxation without legislation. Every tax asserted by the Commissioner must be "authorized by Congress." [30] The question for the tax adviser is not what the law ought to be, but what it is or will become. My point is that in deciding that question the tax adviser must put aside his personal notions of tax policy and make his most intelligent guess as to the meaning of a statute passed by Congress.

True, the tax practitioner must be careful not to put undue trust in the letter of the law; the policy of tax statutes is not always to be found in the literal meaning of the language employed by Congress.[31] The tax adviser must accept interstitial judicial legislation as one of the realities of life.[32] Legislative words are not inert, but derive vitality from the obvious purpose at which they are aimed.[33] But sometimes the words of a statute are too clear to be escaped; there is no room for construction; and there is nothing for the courts to do but to bow their heads and obey.[34] At any rate, the tax adviser need not worry about his moral position. It is not his function to improve men's hearts.[35] As Judge Frank has observed, the task of a lawyer is to win specific cases and guide clients to pleasant destinations.[36]

To accomplish this result, the tax counselor must divorce from his thinking all "mental prepossessions" [37] and think in terms of things, not words.[38] It is sufficient that his advice puts his client on the safe side of the line drawn by the statute. Indeed, it is his positive duty to show the client how to avail himself to the full of what the law permits. He is not the keeper of the Congressional conscience. In representing his client in a particular case the tax lawyer must take the law as he finds it. He is functioning as an adviser with respect to the meaning of a statute the policy of which has been or will be determined by properly

---

30. Helvering v. Griffiths, 318 U.S. 371, 394 (1943).

31. See Cardozo, The Nature of the Judicial Process 103, 113 (1921).

32. Id. at 29. Courts do and must legislate, but "they can do so only interstitially; they are confined from molar to molecular motions." Holmes, dissenting in Southern Pacific Co. v. Jensen, 244 U.S. 205, 221 (1917).

33. Griffiths v. Commissioner, 308 U.S. 355–58 (1939).

34. See Morse Drydock Company v. Northern Star, 271 U.S. 552, 555 (1926) * * *.

35. Holmes, The Common Law 144, 148 (1881).

36. Frank, Law and the Modern Mind (1930) *passim;* Frank, What Courts Do in Fact, 26 Ill.L.Rev. 645 (1932); Frank, Are Judges Human?, 80 U. of Pa.L.Rev. 233 (1931); Frank, Mr. Justice Holmes and Non-Euclidean Legal Thinking, 17 Cornell L.Q. 568 (1932).

37. Cf. Brandeis, The Living Law, 10 Ill. L.Rev. 467 (1911).

38. Holmes, Collected Legal Papers 238, 282 (1920); Dixon, The Human Situation 60, 65 (1937). * * *

constituted authority, and he is entitled—in fact, he is obliged—to help his client in the case he is handling.

At times he will be wise to discard some arguments, and he should exercise discretion to emphasize the arguments which in his judgment are most likely to be persuasive. But this process involves legal judgment rather than moral attitudes. The tax lawyer should put aside private disagreements with Congressional and Treasury policies. His own notions of policy, and his personal view of what the law should be, are irrelevant. The job entrusted to him by his client is to use all his learning and ability to protect his client's rights, not to help in the process of promoting a better tax system. The tax lawyer need not accept his client's economic and social opinions, but the client is paying for technical attention and undivided concentration upon his affairs. He is equally entitled to performance unfettered by his attorney's economic and social predilections.

It may be added that in tax cases the protection of a client's rights is a sufficient job for most lawyers. It is not always easy to determine the policy of tax statutes, and the private views of the lawyer may be at variance with Congressional policy. Even though the tax adviser is in violent disagreement, the client is entitled to an objective expression of views as to that policy.

These are the principles which guide me when I discuss with clients tax questions involving the minimization of tax liability. I do not hesitate to advise the client fully and frankly in choosing among "the oddities in tax consequences" [39] that emerge from different methods of accomplishing the same ultimate result. I will do all I can to help the client reduce his tax liability to the lowest possible legal level or save him from a greater tax liability than his transaction needs to carry. This sometimes requires a substantial modification of an originally proposed transaction and a consideration by the client of the question whether the modified transaction will sufficiently serve his business purposes. Modifications must have substance,[40] and the client may decide that the price he has to pay is more than the projected tax saving is worth. On the other hand, he may be willing to do what is required to place the transaction on the safe side of the line drawn by the statute. He is entitled to counsel which makes the outlines of his choice clear to him.

These problems frequently arise in the lives of tax attorneys when their clients seek to take advantage of the capital gain rate of tax, or when their purpose is to minimize the impact of taxation upon the family by a bona fide distribution of property to wife and children. When this happens to me, I take, as I see it, a statute the policy of which I do not personally favor; I even accept the policy of statutes

39. U.S. v. Cumberland Public Service Co., 338 U.S. 451, 455 (1950).

40. See Commissioner v. Court Holding Co., 324 U.S. 331, 334 (1945). Cf. United States v. Cumberland Public Service Co., 338 U.S. 451, 454 (1950).

which I have opposed. This is true, for example, of the stock option provision [§§ 421 and 422A], the family partnership provision [§ 704(e)], and the percentage depletion provision [§ 613]. In advising in connection with provisions of this kind, I try to be strictly on guard against over-interpreting relief provisions; but I see no reason why in my role as tax adviser I should set myself up against Congress as the arbiter of tax policy. My assignment is simply to be careful that the client does not overstep the line of policy drawn in the statute as Congress has passed it and as the Treasury and the courts have refined that line in their interpretive regulations and decisions.

Guided by these principles I feel that I am justified in recommending to a client that he transfer some of his property to a trust for the benefit of members of his family with the object of minimizing the family tax burden. The client may express a natural desire to retain as much control over the property as he can without sacrifice of the objective of shifting the tax on the income from the transferred property. As I see it, my task is to help the client without letting him venture any further than necessary into unsafe territory. In doing so I will feel no moral qualms. The problem does not involve ethical issues. My client's objective is legitimate. I often resolve some legal doubts in favor of the Government so that the client has a reasonable margin of safety. This too is my duty, but I would be derelict in the performance of my responsibility if I failed, because of moral scruples or because of disagreement with the policy of the statute, to guide the client as far as he can safely go in the direction of his desire.

Keeping to the concrete, I may sanction a plan under which a corporation with a history of recent losses acquires a profitable business so that the profits and losses of the two businesses will offset one another. When I am consulted in such a matter, my assignment is to appraise conservatively the effect of [§ 269] which deals with this subject, but which may not apply to the particular facts of the case presented to me. In advising with respect to the transaction my sole concern should be whether the desired result can be safely achieved. It does not concern me that as a matter of policy it might have been better if Congress had passed a more comprehensive statute eliminating this tax saving opportunity. I frequently have to make a calculation of the risks involved in going forward with a proposed business deal. If I am not prepared to devote my undivided loyalty to the objective of gaining for the client every advantage offered by the law as it is written, I should tell him at the outset to go to some other lawyer whose allegiance to his interest will be less fractional.

Of course there are limits as to how far a tax attorney may honorably go in advising clients as to the tax effect of future transactions. He should not yield to a temptation sometimes presented when his client consults him with respect to the tax effect of a desired course of action. The suggestion may be that the contracts and other papers expressing the transaction disguise its real character so that a revenue agent will miss its tax impact when it is later presented as a consummated transaction. I hope that it is almost superfluous for me to express a lack of sympathy with all techniques designed to camouflage contemplated transactions in such a way as to conceal those parts of them which may provide the basis for an assertion of tax liability. The Government is a silent partner in all business transactions and is entitled to a fair view of those transactions so that it may assert its claim of interest. One may go further by saying unequivocally that attempts at misrepresentation border on fraudulent conduct. At least it is conduct unbecoming a tax attorney.

It is easy to give illustrations of prevailing techniques of misrepresentation. One favorite device is to put a transaction into two contracts, one of which is to be shown to the Government's representatives, and the other of which is to be kept secret. This happened once in my experience in connection with a sale of stock to a buyer for about $5 million. Since the buyer had an option on the stock of about $3 million, it was obvious that $2 million was being paid for an agreement not to compete. A payment for this covenant would have been ordinary income and not capital gain. The seller insisted that this transaction be put in two documents, one which would recite the sale of stock for $5 million, and the other of which would provide against competition without mentioning any consideration. I felt obliged to refuse to be an adviser in this transaction. As a result, my client, who had reluctantly agreed because of anxiety to procure the stock, went to another attorney who was willing to let the client do what the seller wished. The client never came to me with his subsequent problems.

The ingenuity of fertile-minded clients and fringe tax advisers has devised many dubious methods of tax avoidance. The president of a family corporation may ask his lawyer if it is all right to minimize corporate tax liability by making his wife vice-president of the corporation and paying her a substantial salary, even though she performs no services whatever for the corporation. Some businessmen, in an attempt to become members of what Life calls "the expense account aristocracy," may seek arrangements under which they receive a substantial fixed allowance for miscellaneous entertainment and promotional expenses greatly exceeding the amount they expect to spend for those expenses. The argument is usually made that others in the same business engage in similar practices. It is hardly necessary to say that this is no argument at all, yet it is one which appeals to some clients.

* * *

REPRESENTING BROADER INTERESTS

As I come to the end of this inconclusive discussion of the ethics of tax advocacy, I find myself wanting to be sure that the reader does not misunderstand my attitude upon one point. I have argued that a tax lawyer should be careful not to let his private notions of fiscal policy intrude into work for a client on a tax case except as his knowledge of policy considerations may help him the more intelligently to represent the client. But I do not want anyone to infer from this discussion that I object to participation by tax advisers in efforts looking to the improvement of tax law. I feel strongly to the contrary. To me it is one of the tragedies of the time that tax advisers do not use more generally for their Government, as well as for their clients, the special knowledge their education and experience have bestowed upon them. I think that they should use this knowledge actively, affirmatively, and even aggressively. The country most sorely needs the contribution they are so well qualified to make to the serious problems the Government faces at home * * *.

The tax adviser is not disqualified from activity on this front because he represents taxpayers. The shoe is on the other foot. The representation of taxpayers gives to tax advisers the experience that theory always needs if it is to ripen into maturity. It teaches them what will work in practice, as distinguished from what looks good on paper. It enriches the whole outlook of tax advisers, and makes their advice to their Government more realistic and dependable. It makes them all the more qualified to express a constructive opinion about what is wrong with tax law and what should be done to improve the tax system. On the other hand, it is necessary to be on guard against a tendency to assume that what is best for clients is best for the United States. Much representation of clients sometimes makes lawyers captives of their clients' opinions, and an analysis of many tax betterment proposals from tax lawyers quickly reveals that the lawyers are promoting the special interests of their clients. A tax lawyer needs to preserve an independence of outlook, unclouded by prejudices acquired from his clients. His clients do not always know what is good for them, and there is a sense in which what is good for the United States is good for clients.

No doubt some tax lawyers feel constrained to abstain from activities on behalf of a better tax system because they think that their clients may object. Clients have no right to object if the tax adviser handles their affairs competently and faithfully and independently of his private views as to tax policy. They buy his expert services, not his private opinions or his silence on issues that gravely affect the public interest.

I suspect that the thinking of some tax advisers exaggerates the objections clients have to activities on behalf of improvement in the tax system. It is true, as Adams once observed,[41] that taxation is "a group contest in which powerful interests vigorously endeavor to rid themselves of present or proposed tax burdens," and that "class politics" is of its essence. But more and more in recent years there has developed in businessmen, and that wealthier segment of the population which furnishes tax clients, a realization of the need of more expert attention

---

41. Adams, Ideals and Idealism in Taxation, 18 Am.Econ.Rev. 1 (1928). Cf. Griswold, The Blessings of Taxation: Recent Trends in the Law of Federal Taxation, 36 A.B.A.J. 999, 1002, 1057 (1950).

to the tax problems than can come from persons within the Government. It is one encouraging sign of the times that taxes have captured the interest of a wide public. Sometimes that interest expresses itself in pressure politics and propaganda, and attempts to advance the cause of the few at the expense of the many. But objectivity is also spreading its more wholesome influence. At least, it is no longer a mark of condemnation of a tax adviser that he serves his country on the tax front.

Problems

1. (a) Are you satisfied with Randolph Paul's comments on the attorney's role as tax planner and the objective of minimizing the client's tax liability? Why or why not? Consider ABA Canons of Professional Ethics, Canon 32 and ABA Model Rules of Professional Conduct, Rule 2.1.

(b) Next year Ted and Terri Player expect to be in a higher tax bracket. Ted holds stock which has appreciated in value. Ted indicates to you he wants to sell the stock sometime during the next twelve months. Would you advise him to sell the shares now instead of next year and thereby minimize the tax consequences?

2. Alex comes to you on January 10 of Year 2 and informs you that he would like to sell his boat to a friend. Alex will realize and recognize a gain on the sale. If the sale had occurred in Year 1, the gain could have been offset by a loss carryover from a prior year which will expire at the end of Year 1, thereby reducing Alex's tax liability in Year 1. Alex suggests that the document be predated to December 28 of Year 1 so that the gain might be reported on his tax return for Year 1 and the loss carryover used as an offset. How would you advise Alex? From the client's standpoint consider §§ 6653(b) and 7201. From an attorney's viewpoint what professional responsibility problems do you see? Consider ABA Model Rules of Professional Conduct, Rules 1.2, 1.6 and 1.16. Consider also the practical professional problems. If you think you would tell the client "No," how should the matter be handled so you will not lose Alex as a client? Do you (and should you) have a professional responsibility to notify the Internal Revenue Service if Alex proceeds as he wishes. Consider ABA Model Rules of Professional Conduct, Rule 1.6.

3. A citizens group asks you to sign a petition urging Congress to reform a tax law which you believe to be needed but which, if adopted, would adversely affect some of your firm's clients.

(a) Assume you are a partner in a law firm. What would you do? Would you remain silent if you felt you would get into difficulty with one or more of your firm's clients? Consider ABA Model Rules of Professional Conduct, Rule 6.4.

(b) Assume you are an associate in a law firm. What would you do? Would you remain silent if you felt the firm's partners would frown on your expressing your views?

I. INTRODUCTION TO TAX POLICY AND TAX REFORM

1. PROGRESSIVE TAX CONCEPT

Although the current Federal income tax structure can still be called progressive in that higher incomes are taxed at higher marginal rates, it is considerably less progressive than in prior years. The maximum marginal rate was, in 1954, as high as 91 percent on taxable income in excess of $300,000 on a separate return and $400,000 on a joint return. The maximum rate was reduced to 70 percent in 1965, to 50 percent in 1981 and to 28 percent in 1988. See § 1.

Most taxing schemes are not progressive. For example, sales taxes, property taxes and excise taxes are proportional, not progressive, in nature. These proportional taxes are keyed to the value of the property or to the number of units purchased, i.e. the greater the value or the greater the quantity of units purchased, the greater the tax. A sales tax is in reality a tax on consumption. The rationale for a non-progressive income tax is that if the tax on the first widget is no more than the tax on the ten thousandth widget then the tax on the first dollar of income should be no greater than the tax on the ten thousandth dollar of income.

Theoretically, at least, there are sound political and economic justifications for either the progressive or proportional approach.[42] Discounting, however, the appealing political attractions for either school, a system which taxes each increasingly higher income bracket at a progressively higher tax rate most often finds justification in the basic premise that those with the greater ability to pay taxes should do so even if it means that they are paying to some extent the tax burdens of others in society.

Scholars and politicians alike have criticized the concept of a progressive income tax. Critics argue that the progressive tax is in reality a tax on the successful in society and constitutes an anti-capitalist technique to redistribute wealth and reduce risk taking.

As a practical matter, however, those individuals in the 28 percent marginal tax bracket will seek to reduce their average tax rates to more acceptable levels by investments in items which create lower levels of taxable income. For example, higher marginal tax bracket individuals invest in tax exempt municipal bonds the income from which is not subject to tax.

Questions

1. What is the difference between a progressive tax and a proportional (regressive) tax? How would you classify the Social Security tax? Is

42. For an overview see Blum, Revisiting the Uneasy Case for Progressive Taxation, 60 Taxes 16 (1982) and Blum and Kalven, The Uneasy Case for Progressive Taxation, 19 U.Chi.L.R. 417 (1952).

progression justified? Is progression effective or does the higher income taxpayer pay a lower "effective rate" of tax than someone who earns less?

2. What impact does inflation have on the progressive rate structure? Consider the materials on indexing for inflation set forth below.

3. Do you favor replacing the graduated rate structure with a single percentage flat rate, for example, 20 percent, coupled with the elimination of a wide variety of exclusions, deductions, and credits? How would you determine the rate of taxation to use? Would you favor a modified flat rate tax using a progressive rate structure of 15, 25, and 35 percent? Consider the following excerpt:

> Office of the Secretary, Department of the Treasury, Tax Reform for Fairness, Simplicity, and Economic Growth, vol. 1, 21, 23 (1984).

> A single, totally flat rate, * * * would involve a substantial shift of tax burden from those in the highest income brackets to low- or middle-income taxpayers. Under [prior] law families with less than $20,000 of income pay 5.5 percent of the individual income tax, although they receive 13.7 percent of the income. A pure flat tax—even one with liberalized personal exemptions and [standard deduction] amounts designed to eliminate tax for families at or below the poverty level—would raise the share of taxes paid by families with less than $20,000 of income to 9.5 percent of the total. This pure flat tax would sharply reduce the share of individual taxes paid by those with incomes over $50,000 from 59.9 percent under current law to 48.9 percent. Stated differently, taxpayers with incomes above $50,000, would pay about 18 percent less under a revenue-neutral flat-rate tax than under current law. Conversely, those with incomes between $20,000 and $50,000 would pay one-fifth more tax than under [prior] law.

2. INDEXING FOR INFLATION

A progressive rate structure has the effect of taxing individuals on increases in income which reflect only gains due to inflation, not "real" earning power. This phenomenon, known as "bracket creep," produces automatic tax increases without any legislative action.

Bracket creep may be illustrated by the following example. Assume the following progressive rate table:

Taxable Income	Rate
$0 to 10,000	15%
$10,000 to 20,000	20%

If a taxpayer has $10,000 of taxable income, the income tax will be $1,500, leaving $8,500 available for consumption. Assuming an inflation rate of 10%, the taxpayer who receives a 10% pay raise, will earn $11,000 the second year. On an $11,000 taxable income, the income tax will equal $1,700, leaving $9,300 for consumption. However, $8,500 worth of goods and services from the previous year will now cost 10% more or $9,350. Therefore, taxpayer's standard of living has decreased by $50. The bracket creep occurs because the raise taxpayer receives, which is intended to keep his salary up with inflation, is taxed at the higher rate of the next marginal tax bracket. In this manner, the rate of the individual's income taxed has increased.

Indexing the rate table for the 10% rate of inflation results in an increase of the 15% tax bracket to $11,000. The tax on $11,000 of taxable income will be $1,650, leaving $9,350 after taxes and eliminating the bracket creep.

In the past, Congress responded to inflationary pressures by providing frequent tax cuts. Until recently, legislators refused to follow the lead of some countries and certain states and adopt a system of automatic adjustments which would periodically remove the effects of inflation. Apparently, the prevailing view was that a system of automatic adjustments which would reduce tax brackets in periods of inflation implicitly acknowledged that inflation would never be overcome.

The Economic Recovery Tax Act of 1981, followed by the Tax Reform Act of 1986, enacted a narrowly focused system of indexing for individuals. Beginning in 1989, the taxable income amounts at which the 28 percent rate starts, as well as the standard deduction amounts, will increase or decrease with changes in the Consumer Price Index. Read § 1(f). Beginning in 1990, the personal exemption amount will be adjusted for inflation. The following excerpt summarizes the Congressional objectives:

> Inflation erodes the value of the fixed dollar amounts utilized to determine tax liability. As a result, when incomes rise by (say) ten percent, income taxes rise by approximately 16 percent. This is an increase in the real tax burden of approximately six percent and occurs even though the increase in real incomes may be much less than ten percent (or even zero).
>
> The Congress believed that "automatic" tax increases resulting from the effects of inflation were unfair to taxpayers, since their tax burden as a percentage of income could increase during intervals between tax reduction legislation, with an adverse effect on incentives to work and invest. In addition, the Federal Government was provided with an automatic increase in its aggregate revenue, which in turn created pressure for further spending.
>
> [I]ndexing will prevent inflation from increasing that percentage and thus will avoid the past pattern of inequitable, unlegislated tax increases and induced spending.

Staff of Joint Committee on Taxation, General Explanation of the Economic Recovery Tax Act of 1981, 38 (1981).

Some of the arguments for and against indexing are as follows: [43]

43. Adapted from American Institute of Certified Public Accountants, Indexation of the Tax Laws for Inflation 6–9 (1980). For a summary of the major arguments for and against indexing see Congressional Budget Office, Indexing the Individual Income Tax for Inflation 13–27 (1980) reprinted in M. McIntyre, F. Sander, D. Westfall, Readings in Federal Taxation 108–120 (2d ed. 1983). See also Yoran & Shimer, Adjusting Taxes

Arguments for Indexation

1. Indexation is fair to all taxpayers. Indexation ends "bracket creep," a nonlegislated tax increase. Indexing may be the best (perhaps the only) way to keep the proportion of individual income taken by the Government from constantly rising.

2. Indexation does not imply a willingness to live with inflation. It removes the inflation-generated tax revenue bonus and tends to reduce the rate of growth in Federal government spending.

3. If Congress wants to increase Government spending, it should vote to raise taxes to finance the increased spending. Keeping taxes from rising may force Congress to limit outlays.

4. Tax increases caused by inflation fuel further inflation because no astute business executive or labor negotiator fails to consider the progressive tax burdens. The labor negotiator seeks an increase in take-home pay; the business executive sets prices to increase after tax profits. Similarly, lenders seek higher interest to cover both inflation and their marginal rates of taxation.

5. Automatic tax increases without Congressional action do not stabilize the economy. Contrary to traditional economic theories, severe inflation may occur during recessions characterized by high levels of unemployment. The removal of purchasing power from the economy under those conditions can be a destabilizer that aggravates economic downturns.

Arguments Against Indexation

1. Limiting tax increases reduces flexibility in setting budget policy. It may also lead to bigger budget deficits if Federal spending is not held in check. Because a large portion of Federal spending consists of entitlement programs that increase with inflation, denying the government automatic revenue increases institutionalizes the imbalance between spending programs and the money needed to fund such programs.

2. Congress periodically responded to the increase in taxes resulting from inflation by reducing taxes. As a result, the individual income tax fluctuated between 9.2 and 11.6 percent of personal income from 1951 to the late 1970's.

3. Indexation may imply a willingness to live with inflation. Automatic tax increases caused taxpayers to seek relief and generated the political pressure necessary to pass anti-inflationary legislation. Protecting taxpayers against inflation by indexing may weaken their already feeble will to resist inflation.

4. The rates of return established for financial instruments in negotiations between lender and borrower take both anticipated inflation and levels of taxation into account.

for Inflation: The Impact of the Economic
Recovery Act, 23 Bos.Col.L.R. 1257 (1982).

5. Inflation may create a need for tax increases which serve to reduce the demand for goods and services. Holding down tax increases automatically limits Congress' ability to use tax cuts for policy purposes.

3. TAX POLICY CRITERIA

Introduction. The primary determinant of the necessary level of taxation is the necessary level of government expenditures. Although this relationship is not "direct" in that government need not wait to finance an expenditure by the receipt of taxes, the relationship does affect the overall inflationary level of the nation's economy. Accordingly, the financing of government expenditures remains the primary function of our system of taxation.

Beyond its role as a revenue raising device, many provisions of the Internal Revenue Code may be viewed as, either direct or indirect, incentives or disincentives which, respectively, serve to encourage or discourage specific conduct or transactions. Tax incentives are designed to stimulate conduct which society views as beneficial. The Code provides both economic and non-economic incentives. By promoting certain types of profit-making activities the tax system shifts all or part of the cost of these activities from the so-called "players" to the government. The tax system is also used to promote certain socially desirable conduct. Tax disincentives, conversely, are designed to discourage conduct thought to be harmful or inappropriate.

The tax law changes enacted as the Tax Reform Act of 1986 are, in part, premised on the assumption that the tax system should play less of a role in shaping society and its economic foundations. The changes are designed to diminish the Code's incentives to steer investments to certain activities and let individuals keep more of their income which they could feed with the economy as they wish. As you go through this book consider whether, under the Code as revised in 1986, spending decisions are still (and should they be) based on incentives provided by the market place?

Criteria for Analyzing Current and Proposed Federal Income Tax Provisions. A voluminous literature has developed analyzing the current incentive-disincentive structure of the Federal income tax system. Critics maintain that this incentive-disincentive structure can and should be more systematically rationalized.[44] The following criteria,[45] redistribution, equity, efficiency, neutrality, economic growth, revenue

44. Surrey, Tax Incentives as a Device for Implementing Government Policy: A Comparison with Direct Government Expenditures, 83 Harv.L.R. 705 (1970); S. Surrey, Pathways to Tax Reform (1973).

45. Judge Sneed used the following seven criteria to measure the income tax structure: (1) supply adequate revenue, (2) achieve a practical and workable income tax system, (3) impose equal taxes on those who enjoy equal incomes, (4) assist in achieving economic stability, (5) reduce economic inequality, (6) avoid impairment of the operation of a market-oriented economy, and (7) accomplish a high degree of harmony between the income tax and the political order. Sneed, The Criteria of Federal Income Tax Policy, 17 Stan.L.Rev. 567, 568–597 (1965).

impact, simplicity and administrative convenience, will help you assess the impact of a tax provision or proposal:

Redistribution of Income and Reduction of Economic Inequality. A tax provision may be analyzed in terms of its demonstrated or supposed effect on the goal of reducing economic disparities between classes of individuals. The goal of reducing economic inequality and redistributing income and wealth from some segment of the population to another group emphasizes the progressivity of the rate structure. Theorists intent on redistributing income to the more economically disadvantaged segments of society oppose tax provisions which principally benefit more affluent individuals. Thus, redistributive theorists favor tax advantages in the form of tax credits which are available to less affluent persons as well as to other taxpayers. The fact that rich and poor taxpayers are equally entitled to lower their taxes through tax credits pleases redistributive critics. Equity criteria are also frequently emphasized by those who wish to lessen economic disparity among taxpayers.

Equity. The goal of an equitable, progressive tax system is founded on an ability to pay premise. More specifically, two types of "equity" exist: (a) "horizontal equity" which demands that taxpayers with the same income should pay the same tax and (b) "vertical equity" which demands that an income tax provision make an appropriate differentiation among "unequals," i.e., tax-payers with higher incomes should bear a higher tax burden.

The following example illustrates a classic violation of the "horizontal equity" criterion. A and B are taxpayers in the 28% marginal tax bracket. Each receives $1000 annually in additional gross income derived from bond interest payments. A pays an individual income tax of $280 and retains $720 of after tax, disposable income because A invested in corporate bonds whose interest was taxable. B, being more alert to the Federal income tax consequences, invested in equally secure municipal bonds whose annual interest return is tax-exempt to the bondholder. The $1000 which B realizes annually from the municipal bond investment is free from any federal income tax exactions. In this example, "horizontal equity" is violated because A should not be compelled to invest in municipal bonds which he might not desire to purchase, and which he should not have to purchase simply to gain the same tax advantages as B.

Efficiency. In recent times, the system of exclusions, deductions, and credits has been subject to criticism on the grounds of a lack of "efficiency." Efficiency-minded critics ask whether tax structure promotes or inhibits the efficient allocation of resources. If "equity" theorists condemn those tax allowances which impose variant tax burdens on taxpayers with equal economic incomes, "efficiency" theorists condemn tax allowances which cause and perpetuate a misallocation of resources. "Efficiency" commentators evaluate tax provisions with respect to their ability to attract capital, which, of necessity, flows from non-tax favored activities to tax-favored activities.

Of course, the allocation of resources in our mixed "private-public" economy responds to a variety of factors apart from tax policy and the provisions of the Internal Revenue Code. No generalizations concerning the impact of the tax system on resource allocation should be made without realizing that other forces, such as aggregate income, savings, consumption, the rate of inflation-deflation ("stagflation") and other forms of governmental regulation, often determine the price of goods and services and the origin, direction, rate, volume, and destination of capital movements.

Neutrality. Another goal of the tax system is neutrality. Tax laws should not produce an advantage for one of two similarly situated individuals. One form of investment should not produce a tax advantage over another investment. The tax structure, theoretically, should not influence taxpayers' economic decisions; otherwise resources may be misallocated. However, tax incentives are designed to impact on economic choices and reach socially desirable results.

Economic Growth and Capital Formation. Many maintain that the tax structure should encourage economic growth in the context of a market allocation of resources. These commentators favor tax provisions to raise the levels of savings and investment and reduce the relative benefits of leisure and consumption.[46] Increased savings and investment, it is felt, will lead to higher productivity, a greater supply of goods and services, and strengthen our economic base. The impact of the tax structure on human motivation, however, remains illusive. The encouragement of economic growth is intertwined with a variety of facts which make it impossible to isolate tax from other incentives.

Revenue Considerations. A tax provision may also be evaluated in terms of its impact on Federal revenues. Commentators emphasize the need for the government to generate adequate revenues to effectuate its mandated programs and commitments and to keep budgetary deficits within manageable proportions. To the extent that a tax proposal permits or would allow "large" amounts of revenue to escape taxation, the "revenue loss" school of tax policy would oppose such legislation.

Simplicity and Administrative Convenience. Many advocate "simplification" of the current Federal income tax. Little progress in the war on complexity is discernible. Complexity arises from many factors: our complex society, the impact of special interests, the impact of tax reformers, and the use of the Internal Revenue Code as a policy instrument. The problem must be seen in the context of tracing a line, particularly for complex transactions, between conduct which furthers or retards the other tax goals sought to be achieved. Moreover, our desire to achieve an equitable tax structure based on ability to pay criteria leads to a complex tax structure in our attempt to draw the line between the deserving and the undeserving.

The criterion of simplicity and structural coherence for the tax system remains a significant topic. As a tax provision increases in complexity, transactional costs increase because taxpayers allocate

46. See generally, G. Gilder, Wealth and Poverty (1981).

more time and money in the field of tax avoidance, particularly, structuring transactions to minimize tax consequences. Also, a "simplified" tax structure would help promote the goal of administrative ease from the standpoint of tax assessment and collection. Revenue should be raised with low administrative and compliance expenses.

Criticism of Tax Incentives. Numerous criticisms have been levelled at the tax incentives-disincentives which abound in the Internal Revenue Code. As we go through the course, you should reflect on whether the following are generally applicable:

(1) *Tax Incentives Provide Windfalls for Taxpayers to Engage in Specified Economic Conduct in Which They Would Participate Without the Stimulus Provided by the Tax Incentive.* Critics contend that tax incentives compel the Treasury to forego needed revenue because these incentives are made available to taxpayers to induce them to engage in economic transactions which they would have consummated without the tax incentive. Taxpayers receive an unexpected windfall while no further economic activity is generated. In short, the tax incentives are wasteful and deprive the government of tax revenues. You should consider whether it is possible to devise a tax incentive, whether in the form of an exclusion, a deduction, or a credit, which will be free from this basic objection.

(2) *Tax Incentives Frequently Provide Assistance to the Wrong Class of Taxpayers.* Tax incentives designed to assist "middle class, middle income" taxpayers, who frequently need tax relief, are difficult to devise. The majority of middle bracket taxpayers lack sufficient investment capital to make most tax incentives meaningful to them. Of course, tax incentives are also meaningless to individuals who have either a meager income near the poverty level or those individuals who have no income and are dependent upon some sort of Federal, state or local assistance.

(3) *Tax Incentives Embedded in the Internal Revenue Code Frequently are Developed in a Haphazard Fashion and Are Difficult to Eliminate Because of Special Interest Group Pressure and Generalized Public Inattentiveness.* Tax incentive provisions found in the Internal Revenue Code are not subject to high visibility. Generalized public inattention to specific tax incentives benefitting higher bracket taxpayers translates into a continuing failure to effectuate any systematic or meaningful alteration of the tax structure.

Problem

A homeowner's mortgage interest on his principal residence is deductible in computing taxable income pursuant to § 163(a) and (h). Assume A and B are homeowners. A and B each pay $100 in home mortgage interest. A is in the 28 percent marginal tax bracket, B is in the 15 percent marginal tax bracket.

(a) How much is the mortgage interest deduction worth in tax savings to A and B, respectively? What will be the after tax cost of the mortgage interest expenditure for A and B, respectively? Why is a portion of A's and B's interest expense borne by the Federal government? Does the home mortgage interest deduction violate any tax goal (or goals)? Should a dollar ceiling be placed on the home mortgage interest deduction?

(b) Would you favor changing the deduction for home mortgage interest to a credit against each taxpayer's tax liability equal to 10 percent of the interest paid on a mortgage for his principal residence? A credit for home mortgage interest would promote which tax goal (or goals)? Consider the impact on the value of homes of switching from a deduction to a credit for home mortgage interest. How would you handle the situation of a homeowner who pays no Federal income taxes?

4. TAX EXPENDITURE ANALYSIS

Critics use the tax expenditure concept as an analytical and policymaking tool to evaluate a tax provision or proposal in terms of redistribution, equity, efficiency, and administrative ease. The Congressional Budget Act of 1974 defines a "tax expenditure" as "revenue losses attributable to provisions of the Federal tax laws which allow a special exclusion, exemption, or deduction from gross income or which provide a special credit, a preferential rate of tax or a deferral of liability * * *." P.L. 93–344, 88 Stat. 297, 299 (1974). The tax expenditure concept focuses on selective, as opposed to, general tax reductions. The tax expenditure budget estimates the revenue loss from a list of certain deductions, exclusions, and other provisions. The items are broken down into various categories. In theory, the tax expenditure budget facilitates a comparison of these expenditures with direct Federal government expenditures in these same categories. The following excerpts discuss the tax expenditure concept:

CHARLES DAVENPORT, TAX EXPENDITURE ANALYSIS AS A TOOL FOR POLICYMAKERS
11 Tax Notes 1051, 1052–1053 (1980).

* * * [I]t sometimes is helpful to invite policymakers to consider tax expenditures and to evaluate them in terms of equity, efficiency, administration, and need. These seem to me to be issues about which policymakers, primarily legislators, should be concerned.

Tax equity might be better described as "fairness that is consistent with the underlying nature of the tax." Our income tax is a progressive tax on net income. It is fair if two people with the same income bear the same tax or if one taxpayer with higher income pays a higher proportion of income in tax. A tax expenditure budget is a catalog of provisions that offend this fairness principle. Such a budget will assist in the debate over fairness. Clearly, our citizenry believes the income tax is unfair—perhaps in large measure because it is too high—but also because some people have preferred income and thus the fairness principle is violated.

A listing of tax preferences with their approximate revenue losses should certainly raise the question of efficiency. If a tax expenditure costs $1 million, but if the same purpose can be achieved by $600,000 if done by a direct government outlay, it should be clear that the tax expenditure is inefficient. Without the tax expenditure budget, this kind of question will probably not be asked. Existence of the tax expenditure budget does not assure a testing of efficiency, but it does make it more likely.

A tax expenditure budget will also show the wide and disparate kind of assistance programs that are run through the tax system. It should then force legislators to ask themselves whether the revenue arm of the executive branch is likely to have the expertise and under-standing necessary for proper administration. * * * [I]t also raises questions as to whether tax committees have the time and expertise to deal with these problems properly.

BRINGING RATIONALITY TO THE DEBATE

If a full list of tax expenditures is made up, the question whether any or all of these activities need assistance through special tax relief must surely be presented. The alternative to all these special tax breaks is general tax relief. Thanks to the tax expenditure budget, heat can be kept on legislators to justify the special relief at the price of general relief. Without a tax expenditure budget, the justification for tax expenditures is less likely to be thought through. Furthermore, if zero based budgeting or sunsetting of government programs is em-ployed, a tax expenditure budget is necessary so that all government intervention will be considered similarly. A tax expenditure budget is also necessary if spending limitations are enacted.

In short, the concept of tax expenditures and the existence of a tax expenditure budget improves the quality of debate about selective tax cuts. In an era when a good part of the public seems to believe that any tax cut is a good tax cut, the tax expenditure budget is useful in bringing rationality to the debate and emphasizing that some tax cuts may be better than others.

WEAKNESSES AND DISADVANTAGES

* * *

There are weaknesses in tax expenditure budgets. * * * The major weakness lies in the measurement of tax expenditures. There are some similar problems in estimating direct outlays.

* * *

For example, in theory the total for all investment credits allowed [in a given tax year] can be determined. The revenue lost from a deduction or exclusion is not, however, so easily determined, either in theory or in practice. The amount of a deduction can be determined, but frequently an exclusion must be estimated. After the amount of either is ascertained, then the tax rate that would have applied to it must also be established before the tax loss can be estimated. * * *

As to projections or estimates of future numbers, estimation of outlays is quite similar to estimation of tax expenditures. They are both based on past experience and on assumptions about future economic activity and future human behavior. There are obvious weaknesses in numbers based on such vagaries. But, as with outlay estimates, questions about accuracy do not diminish either the need for or the usefulness of the numbers.

* * *

JOINT COMMITTEE ON TAXATION

Estimates of Federal Tax Expenditures for Fiscal Years
1987–1991, 7–17 (1986).

* * *

II. MEASUREMENT OF TAX EXPENDITURES

Estimates of tax expenditures as revenue losses are subject to important limitations. Each tax expenditure is measured in isolation. The amount of a deduction is added back into taxable income, which raises its level. The difference between the estimates of tax liabilities under present law, which provides for the deduction, and the higher level of tax liabilities under the assumption that the provision does not exist is the amount of the tax expenditure. For this computation, it is assumed that nothing else changes.

If two or more items were to be eliminated simultaneously, the result of the combination of changes might produce a lesser or greater revenue effect than the sum of the amounts shown for each item separately. This means that the addition of the amounts of various tax expenditure items is of quite limited usefulness * * *.

If a tax expenditure item were to be eliminated, it is possible that Congress would deal with the underlying reason for enacting the tax expenditure in another way, rather than simply terminating federal assistance of any kind. To the extent that a replacement program would be adopted, the higher revenues received as a result of the elimination of a tax expenditure might not represent a net budget gain. The nature of any alternative program cannot be anticipated: it could involve direct expenditures, direct loans, or loan guarantees; or it could involve a different form of a tax expenditure, or a general reduction in tax rates. If any of these provisions would be repealed, adjustments might be made through fiscal or monetary policy to offset the effects of higher tax liabilities on the economy, but the estimates of tax expenditures do not anticipate such policy responses.

Year-to-year differences in the estimates for each tax expenditure may be explained by change in tax law, e.g., the indexing provision enacted in the Economic Recovery Tax Act of 1981, which affect the estimates for successive years. Some of the estimates for this tax expenditure budget may differ from estimates made in previous years because of inflation, changed economic conditions, the availability of better data, and improved estimating techniques. Similar differences also occur in the budget estimates for direct outlays.

———

For a further defense of the tax expenditure concept and an analysis of its uses see Surrey and McDaniel, The Tax Expenditure Concept: Current Developments and Emerging Issues, 20 Bost.Col.L.R. 225 (1979). See also McIntyre, A Solution to the Problem of Defining a Tax Expenditure, 14 U.C. Davis L.R. 79 (1980). A critique of the tax expenditure concept is found in Bittker, Accounting for Federal Subsidies in the National Budget, 22 Nat.Tax J. 244 (1971).

Question

Are tax expenditures less desirable than direct expenditures in all situations?

Chapter 2

GROSS INCOME—BENEFIT RECEIVED

A. DEFINITION OF GROSS INCOME

1. JUDICIAL INTERPRETATION OF GROSS INCOME

Section 61 contains the definition of "gross income." It begins with the catch-all clause "gross income means all income from whatever source derived" and then enumerates fifteen common items which constitute "gross income" such as salaries, fringe benefits, business profits, interest, rents and dividends. The parenthetical clause "but not limited to" indicates that "gross income" is not limited to the items enumerated. Any item not named specifically in paragraphs (1) to (15) of § 61(a) may still constitute "gross income" if it falls within the definition of "gross income." The catch-all clause, which is intended to supplement the enumeration, circularly defines gross income as all income.

According to the legislative history of § 61 contained in S.Rep. No. 1622, 83rd Cong., 2d Sess. 168 (1954), "[T]he word 'income' is used in section [61 of the Internal Revenue Code of 1954, as amended] in its constitutional sense. It [was] not intended [in § 61 of the 1954 Code] to change the concept of income that obtains under § 22(a) [of the 1939 Code]. Therefore, although the § 22(a) [of the 1939 Code] phrase 'in whatever form paid' has been eliminated, statutory gross income will continue to include gross income realized in any form." In short, although you would expect Congress to have provided some guidance as to the definition of the terms "gross income" or "income", authoritative statements cannot be found in Congressional hearings or the committee reports. What then is the judicial interpretation of "income"?

Is the phrase "all income" found in § 61 as broad and encompassing as a literal application would make it? Or are some forms of benefits a taxpayer receives excluded? The inquiry is a difficult one. Early on the Supreme Court attempted to formulate a workable definition of gross income. In Eisner v. Macomber, 252 U.S. 189, 207, 40

S.Ct. 189, 193, 64 L.Ed. 521, 529 (1920), the Supreme Court stated: " '[I]ncome may be defined as the gain derived from labor, from capital, or from both combined,' provided it be understood to include profit gained through a sale or conversion of capital assets * * *." This definition, or really a generalization, would force courts to dissect narrowly the term "labor" or "capital." The Supreme Court soon had the opportunity to see if its newly-formulated definition of income would be satisfactory in a situation where a corporation paid an executive's Federal and state income taxes on his salary.

OLD COLONY TRUST CO. v. COMMISSIONER

Supreme Court of the United States, 1929.
279 U.S. 716, 49 S.Ct. 499, 73 L.Ed. 918.

MR. CHIEF JUSTICE TAFT delivered the opinion of the Court.

* * *

The facts certified to us are substantially as follows:

William M. Wood was president of the American Woolen Company during the years 1918, 1919, and 1920. In 1918 he received as salary and commissions from the company $978,725, which he included in his federal income tax return for 1918. In 1919 he received as salary and commissions from the company $548,132.87, which he included in his return for 1919.

August 3, 1916, the American Woolen Company had adopted the following resolution, which was in effect in 1919 and 1920:

> "Voted: That this company pay any and all income taxes, State and Federal, that may hereafter become due and payable upon the salaries of all the officers of the company, including the president, William M. Wood; the comptroller, Parry C. Wiggin; the auditor, George R. Lawton; and the following members of the staff, to wit: Frank H. Carpenter, Edwin L. Heath, Samuel R. Haines, and William M. Lasbury, to the end that said persons and officers shall receive their salaries or other compensation in full without deduction on account of income taxes, State or Federal, which taxes are to be paid out of the treasury of this corporation."

This resolution was amended on March 25, 1918, as follows:

> "Voted: That, referring to the vote passed by this board on August 3, 1916, in reference to income taxes, State and Federal, payable upon the salaries or compensation of the officers and certain employees of this company, the method of computing said taxes shall be as follows, viz.:
>
> > " 'The difference between what the total amount of his tax would be, including his income from all sources, and the amount of his tax when computed upon his income excluding such compensation or salaries paid by this company.' "

Pursuant to these resolutions, the American Woolen Company paid to the collector of internal revenue Mr. Wood's federal income and surtaxes due to salary and commissions paid him by the company, as follows:

Taxes for 1918 paid in 1919 .... $681,169 88
Taxes for 1919 paid in 1920 .... 351,179 27

The decision of the Board of Tax Appeals here sought to be reviewed was that the income taxes of $681.169.88 and $351,179.27 paid by the American Woolen Company for Mr. Wood were additional income to him for the years 1919 and 1920.

The question certified by the Circuit Court of Appeals for answer by this Court is:

"Did the payment by the employer of the income taxes assessable against the employee constitute additional taxable income to such employee?"

* * *

* * * Coming now to the merits of this case, we think the question presented is whether a taxpayer, having induced a third person to pay his income tax or having acquiesced in such payment as made in discharge of an obligation to him, may avoid the making of a return thereof and the payment of a corresponding tax. We think he may not do so. The payment of the tax by the employers was in consideration of the services rendered by the employee, and was again derived by the employee from his labor. The form of the payment is expressly declared to make no difference. Section 213, Revenue Act of 1918, c. 18, 40 Stat. 1065. It is therefore immaterial that the taxes were directly paid over to the government. The discharge by a third person of an obligation to him is equivalent to receipt by the person taxed. The certificate shows that the taxes were imposed upon the employee, that the taxes were actually paid by the employer, and that the employee entered upon his duties in the years in question under the express agreement that his income taxes would be paid by his employer. This is evidenced by the terms of the resolution passed August 3, 1916, more than one year prior to the year in which the taxes were imposed. The taxes were paid upon a valuable consideration, namely, the services rendered by the employee and as part of the compensation therefor. We think, therefore, that the payment constituted income to the employee.

* * *

Nor can it be argued that the payment of the tax * * * was a gift. The payment for services, even though entirely voluntary, was nevertheless compensation within the statute. This is shown by the case of Noel v. Parrott (C.C.A.) 15 F.(2d) 669. There it was resolved that a gratuitous appropriation equal in amount to $3 per share on the outstanding stock of the company be set aside out of the assets for distribution to certain officers and employees of the company, and that the executive committee be authorized to make such distribution as they deemed wise and proper. The executive committee gave $35,000 to be paid to the plaintiff taxpayer. The court said [page 672 of 15 F.(2d)]:

> "In no view of the evidence, therefore, can the $35,000 be regarded as a gift. It was either compensation for services rendered or a gain or profit derived from the sale of the stock of the corporation, or both; and, in any view, it was taxable as income."

It is next argued against the payment of this tax that, if these payments by the employer constitute income to the employee, the employee will be called upon to pay the tax imposed upon this additional income, and that the payment of the additional tax will create further income which will in turn be subject to tax, with the result that there would be a tax upon a tax. This, it is urged, is the result of the government's theory, when carried to its logical conclusion, and results in an absurdity which Congress could not have contemplated.

In the first place, no attempt has been made by the Treasury to collect further taxes, upon the theory that the payment of the additional taxes creates further income, and the question of a tax upon a tax was not before the Circuit Court of Appeals, and has not been certified to this Court. We can settle questions of that sort when an attempt to impose a tax upon a tax is undertaken, but not now. United States v. Sullivan, 274 U.S. 259, 264, 47 S.Ct. 607, 71 L.Ed. 1037; Yazoo & Mississippi Valley R. Co. v. Jackson Vinegar Co., 226 U.S. 217, 219, 33 S.Ct. 40, 57 L.Ed. 193. It is not, therefore, necessary to answer the argument based upon an algebraic formula to reach the amount of taxes due. The question in this case is, "Did the payment by the employer of the income taxes assessable against the employee constitute additional taxable income to such employee?" The answer must be "Yes."

Separate opinion of MR. JUSTICE MCREYNOLDS is omitted.

Questions

1. Should difficulty or inability to place a numerical value on a benefit received preclude that benefit from being reported as income in the year received?

2. What is the "tax upon a tax" argument referred to in the Old Colony case? Although a tax reimbursement agreement can have a pyramiding effect, the amounts to be reimbursed will decrease with each succeeding reimbursement and eventually reach a miniscule figure. Consequently, a cumulative amount to be included in gross income can be algebraically determined by the use of the following formula:

$$\text{gross income} = \frac{1}{1-x}$$

where x = the taxpayer's marginal rate of taxation. For an employee in the 28% bracket the payment by the employer of $1.00 in salary and any Federal income taxes on this compensation would result in the employee reporting $1.39 in gross income. Another way of looking at this is to ask what result would occur if the employee received $1.39 of salary and no tax reimbursement provision existed? The employee would be left with $1.00 after taxes.

3. Should the Commissioner in Old Colony have included a larger amount as gross income? Also consider the effect of the Old Colony decision on §§ 164 and 275. Why would it be inefficient to allow a deduction for a taxpayer's payment of Federal income taxes?

———

If the Eisner v. Macomber definition is taken literally, any benefit a taxpayer received which did not derive from labor or capital would not be encompassed in the definition of income. The Supreme Court in Commissioner v. Wilcox, 327 U.S. 404, 407, 66 S.Ct. 546, 549, 90 L.Ed. 752, 755 (1946), announced: "In fact, no single, conclusive criterion has yet been found to determine in all situations what is a significant gain to support the imposition of an income tax. No more can be said in general than that all relevant facts and circumstances must be considered."

In 1955 the Supreme Court attempted to clarify the uncertainty which its earlier attempts at a definition had caused by finally abandoning its rigid labor-capital formulation in favor of a much broader and simpler concept of "income." In Commissioner v. Glenshaw Glass Co., 348 U.S. 426, 75 S.Ct. 473, 99 L.Ed. 483 (1955), rehearing denied 349 U.S. 925, 75 S.Ct. 657, 99 L.Ed. 1256 (1955) (at p. 147), the taxpayers received treble damage awards under the Federal antitrust laws. The taxpayers argued that the punitive damage portion of the awards, which they characterized as a "windfall" flowing from penalties imposed on wrongdoers for violating Federal antitrust laws, did not constitute gross income. In holding the award taxable in the entirety, the Supreme Court stated:

> Here we have instances of undeniable accessions to wealth, clearly realized, and over which the taxpayers have complete dominion. The mere fact that the payments were extracted from the wrongdoers as punishment for unlawful conduct cannot detract from their character as taxable income to the [taxpayers]. (348 U.S. at 431, 75 S.Ct. at 477, 99 L.Ed. at 490).

In addressing the question of what constitutes gross income, the Supreme Court has stated that the starting point "begins with the basic premise that the purpose of Congress was to use the full measure of its taxing power." James v. United States, 366 U.S. 213, 218, 81 S.Ct. 1052, 1055, 6 L.Ed.2d 246, 253 (1961). In holding that the embezzler in the James case must include embezzled funds in gross income in the year in which the funds are taken, the Supreme Court reiterated that it "was the intention of Congress to tax all gains except those specifically exempted."

By adopting an enrichment standard in the Glenshaw Glass case as the test for gross income, the Supreme Court raised at least two further questions: (1) has a particular event resulted in the taxpayer obtaining the necessary "accession to wealth," or stated differently, is there a gain (a change in the taxpayer's personal wealth) and in what amount? (2) when is the income "clearly realized," that is, sufficiently "in hand" to be taxable?

It must be remembered that no matter how broad and flexible the income tax definition of gross income, not all benefits received are included in gross income under § 61. For example, although the Supreme Court in United States v. Kirby Lumber (p. 236) stated that the language in the Code "was used by Congress to exert in this field the full measure of its taxing power," such a generalized statement was (and is) far too broad. Clearly, Congress did not intend to tax all benefits received. Reconsider the gross income part of the problem on p. 14 and examine briefly §§ 101 to 134.

As commentators have noted, "The courts have given a wide scope to the income tax, but have recognized that the borderline content of 'income' must be determined case by case. Essentially, the concept of income is a flexible one, with the result in a particular case being determined by the interplay of common usage, accounting concepts, administrative goals, and finally, judicial reaction to these forces * * *." Surrey and Warren, The Income Tax Project of the American Law Institute: Gross Income, Deductions, Accounting, Gains and Losses, Cancellation of Indebtedness, 66 Harvard Law Review 761, 770 (1953).

Questions

1. How has the Supreme Court dealt with the definition of gross income? Is this solution satisfactory?

2. As a method of statutory construction how will a court construe § 61 in deciding whether an item constitutes gross income for purposes of being included in the tax base? Should the Regulations under § 61 attempt to set forth an exhaustive list of every type of benefit included in gross income and if new items appear just add them to that administrative list?

3. If a court construes an item as within the definition of gross income, but Congress does not wish that item to be included in the tax base, what remedy does Congress prescribe?

2. THE VIEW OF ECONOMISTS

Economists have developed broad-based definitions of income encompassing many more items than are currently treated as gross income for Federal income tax purposes. One prominent economist early defined income as the money value of the net accretion to one's economic power between two points of time.[1]

1. Haig, The Concept of Income in the Federal Income Tax, 7 (1921).

The most widely accepted and often quoted definition of economic income today is a refinement of the Haig definition referred to as the Haig-Simons definition of income:

> Personal income may be defined as the algebraic sum of (1) the market value of rights exercised in consumption and (2) the change in the value of the store of property rights between the beginning and end of the period in question. In other words, it is merely the result obtained by adding consumption during the period to "wealth" at the beginning. The sine qua non of income is gain, as our courts have recognized in their more lucid moments, and gain to someone during a specified time interval. Moreover, this gain may be measured and defined most easily by positing a dual objective or purpose, consumption, and accumulation, each of which may be estimated in a common unit by appeal to market prices.[2]

Questions

1. For Federal income tax purposes, should any item which increases a taxpayer's net worth constitute gross income? Why is the economists' definition of income not satisfactory for Federal income tax purposes.

2. Could the present definition of gross income contained in § 61 be interpreted as broadly as the Haig-Simons definition?

3. COMPREHENSIVE TAX BASE AND THE FLAT RATE TAX

The economist's view of "what is income," as the Haig-Simons definition suggests, is an extremely broad and all inclusive standard. Advocates of a Comprehensive Tax Base (CTB) utilize this standard as a benchmark in their analysis of recommendations for tax policy.[3] The CTB proponents argue that our current tax system is replete with exceptions, preferences, loopholes and leakages which favor some taxpayers over others and thus destroy the notion of tax equity. A prime example is the exemption of interest from municipal and state obligations (§ 103).

Proponents of the CTB also assert that although good reasons can be offered for certain so-called preferences, equally good reasons can be used to support almost any proposed preference. A further argument in favor of the CTB is the suggestion that tax preferences are a less efficient and a less democratic way of distributing government largess.

Adoption of the CTB, and therefore, the Haig-Simons definition of income, would logically result in the elimination of all preferences. The imposition of tax on the resulting broader base would permit a reduction in rates thereby mitigating the effect of the lost preferences.

The CTB approach may be illustrated using the following fact pattern: Assume the taxpayer on January 1 of Year 1 has a portfolio of

2. Simons, Personal Income Taxation, 50 (1938).

3. J. Pechman (ed.), Comprehensive Income Taxation, 1–36 (1977). For a critique, see Bittker, A "Comprehensive Tax Base" as A Goal of Income Tax Reform, 80 Harv.L.R. 925 (1967).

securities worth $100. Assume further that the taxpayer uses $50 for the purchase of consumable items, such as food, and liquidates his securities investments to purchase a going business for $50. If the business generates $20 in profits during the year, but otherwise does not increase in value, the taxpayer would have economic income under the Haig-Simons definition of $20 determined as follows:

Consumption during Year 1		$50.00
Net worth on December 31 of Year 1	$70.00	
Less: Net worth on January 1 of Year 1	100.00	(30.00)
		$20.00

Although in theory the CTB approach may be appealing, even proponents admit that adjustments would be required to the tax base in order to adjust for items, such as unrealized appreciation and imputed income. Without such adjustments valuation and administrative problems would be overwhelming.

The problem is further compounded by the lack of a generally accepted definition of property rights for purposes of applying the Haig-Simons definition. For example, if a taxpayer receives the benefit of using a public park or library does he have an increase in wealth? In the economic sense he may well have an increase in wealth but to tax him on such increases would be administratively impossible. Consider also non-pecuniary benefits associated with certain jobs, such as a flexible schedule, the authority to manage people or the ability to be creative, all which can be considered as increasing an individual's psychic income yet the thought of taxing these benefits is unpalatable.

The fairness (or the apparent fairness) of the tax system is essential because the success of the self-assessment system ultimately depends on public confidence. For any system of taxation to survive this confidence level must be maintained. Therefore, the issue really boils down to the public's perception of what is fair. Although no empirical study supports the proposition, the public would apparently not demand that someone pay income tax for the use of a public park or for closer proximity to a public hospital. However, the public seems to demand that those receiving inordinate "tax benefits" from tax shelters or fringe benefits contribute their equitable share to government revenues.

Questions

1. Does the current Federal income tax system use a comprehensive tax base (CTB)? If not, point to examples in the Internal Revenue Code which reveal the lack of a CTB. Indicate those statutory changes which would make the tax base more comprehensive.

2. Why would lower and middle income taxpayers favor a more comprehensive tax base?

Other, and closely related, attempts to simplify the income tax system and improve its fairness are proposals for a "flat rate tax." Unlike the CTB approach, which merely considers the broadening of the tax base by utilizing an economic concept of income that focuses on a taxpayer's increase in wealth, the flat rate tax does not necessarily adopt an economic approach to income. Flat rate tax proponents advocate both the broadening of the tax base and a corresponding reduction of so-called preferences, but their focus is more closely related to the fixing of a single rate of tax (e.g., 20 percent) as a substitute for the current progressive rate structure. The flat rate tax is related to the CTB approach in that the adoption of either may necessitate a reevaluation and an ultimate broadening of the concept of gross income. Consider the following excerpt from a Treasury Department study advocating a broadened tax base, elimination of most deductions, and a modified flat rate tax (a progressive rate structure of 15, 25, and 35 percent).

OFFICE OF THE SECRETARY, DEPARTMENT OF THE TREASURY, TAX REFORM FOR FAIRNESS, SIMPLICITY AND ECONOMIC GROWTH
Vol. 1, 21–29 (1984).

I. The Pure Flat Tax

Most pure "flat tax" proposals share two characteristics: a much more comprehensive tax base than under current law and a *single* low tax rate. * * * In the most extreme proposals there are virtually no deviations from a comprehensive definition of income or consumption, except for personal exemptions.

A. Advantages of the Flat Tax

A pure flat tax would have major advantages over current law, because of the breadth of the tax base and the low tax rate made possible by the comprehensive base. Such a tax would reduce the inequality of tax treatment of families with equal incomes, the distortions of economic decisions, the disincentives to growth, and some of the complexities that plague the current tax system. Because the present system contains many exclusions, exemptions, deductions, and credits not required for the accurate measurement of income, it requires higher tax rates than would be necessary under a pure flat tax. In addition, a uniform tax rate lessens problems inherent in steeply graduated rates, such as the bunching of income, discrimination between single persons and married couples, and incentives to shift income artificially to family members subject to lower tax rates.

* * *

II. Reconciliation: The Modified Flat Tax

In order to simplify and reform the existing income tax, but avoid the massive redistribution of tax liabilities of a pure flat tax, the

Treasury Department proposes that a modified flat tax on income be enacted. The proposal is broadly consistent with several modified flat tax proposals advanced by members of Congress, but it goes beyond them in the scope of its recommendations for simplification and reform.

Many believe that conflict between the goal of distributional equity, on the one hand, and the goals of simplicity, economic neutrality, encouragement of growth, and equal tax treatment of equals (horizontal equity), on the other, is inherent in any flat tax proposal, whether pure or modified. In fact, this conflict is more apparent than real. Most of the advantages commonly attributed to pure flat tax proposals result primarily from the inclusion of all income (or consumption) in the tax base and have relatively little to do with whether tax rates are flat or graduated. Conversely, the redistribution of the tax burden from high- to middle-income taxpayers that would result from application of a flat rate cannot be traced to implementation of a comprehensive definition of the tax base. It results entirely from the substitution of a flat rate for graduated rates.

Because the effects produced by a totally flat rate are quite distinct from those resulting from base-broadening, it is possible to achieve most of the base-broadening advantages of a pure flat tax without the shift in tax burdens among income classes a pure flat rate would entail. This is, in effect, the approach taken in proposals for a modified flat tax. By combining a more comprehensive definition of income than under [prior] law with modestly graduated low rates, modified flat tax proposals are able to achieve gains in simplicity, economic neutrality, equal tax treatment of families with equal incomes, and economic growth, without sacrificing distributional equity.

A modified flat tax that includes only two or three tax rates covering a wide range of low to middle income would be indistinguishable from a pure flat tax for most taxpayers. (Of course, low-income taxpayers would pay lower rates under a modified flat tax than under a pure flat tax.) The use of flat rates over wide ranges of incomes minimizes marriage penalties and bonuses, as well as problems caused by bunching of income in one year.

A. Questions Common to Income and Consumed Income Taxes

The term "modified flat tax" could be applied to an expanded income tax base or to a consumption tax base. The only inherent difference between these two tax bases involves the treatment of saving. Under a tax on consumed income, a deduction is allowed for net saving, whereas under an ordinary income tax it is not. * * * Under either approach many of the issues that must be answered in defining the tax base are the same. Should fringe benefits provided by employers be taxed, or should they be exempt? How are business assets to be distinguished from private assets? Should housing receive preferential treatment? Should charitable contributions be favored? Should activities of state and local governments be subsidized through the tax system? ＊ ＊ ＊ The remainder of this section focuses on questions such as these, on suggested modifications of the present taxation of capital and business income, and on proposed deviations from the pure income tax model.

B. Advantages of a Comprehensive Measure of Income

A comprehensive definition of taxable income or consumption is generally conducive to simplicity and to equal treatment of equally situated taxpayers, while retreat from a comprehensive base generally involves complexity and horizontal inequity. A comprehensive tax base is also necessary for economic neutrality, since high tax rates and discrimination between various ways of earning and spending income distort economic decisions.

Omissions from the tax base generally also result in a distribution of tax liability between families with different income levels that is at least somewhat different—and frequently markedly different—from what the schedule of marginal tax rates suggests. Finally, any deviations from a comprehensive definition of income, unless based on widely-held views of tax equity and other generally accepted economic objectives, are likely to reduce the perceived fairness of the tax system and therefore undermine taxpayer morale.

Erosion of the tax base also has a heavy political cost. If one special interest group is allowed a deduction or credit not required for the accurate measurement of income, it becomes more difficult to resist others. Ultimately, the only way to maintain a fair tax base—one without the many loopholes in the present tax code—is to resist requests for special treatment. For all those reasons, the tax base should be defined as broadly as possible.

C. Distributional Neutrality

Modification of the uniform rate contained in flat-tax proposals also involves difficult trade-offs. Fairness suggests that a single flat tax rate should not be levied at all income levels. And yet tax equity and due regard for the disincentive effects of high marginal tax rates dictate that the top marginal tax rates should not be excessive. By-and-large, the rate structure proposed by the Treasury Department, when applied to an expanded definition of taxable income, is designed to approximate the distribution of tax liabilities that prevails under current law. The primary exception is at the bottom of the income scale. Increased personal exemptions and [standard deduction] amounts will ensure that most taxpayers with incomes below the poverty line will be exempt from income tax altogether.

An important feature of modified flat tax proposals is a reduction in the number of tax rates. Because rates would be constant over much wider ranges of incomes than under [prior] law, a modified flat tax system would resemble a flat-rate system for most taxpayers. Of course, for marginal tax rates to be reduced significantly, without sacrificing revenue, it would be necessary to define the tax base much more comprehensively than under [prior] law.

D. Issues in Income Measurement

At a conceptual level, the proper tax treatment of many currently untaxed sources and uses of income is clear. Fringe benefits provided by employers and payments that represent wage replacement should be included in income subject to tax. Only in a few cases do problems of valuation make this ideal unattainable, as in the case of small hard-to-value fringe benefits recently determined to be tax-exempt in the 1984 Deficit Reduction Act. Taxpayers should not be allowed business deductions for what are really personal expenses, and they should not be allowed artificially to shift income between family members to reduce taxes. Preferential treatment of above-average amounts of charitable contributions is desirable, in order to maintain incentives for contributions; moreover, taxpayers making extraordinary contributions may be considered to have less taxpaying ability than others with similar incomes. The deduction of state and local taxes should be phased out, both because it is unnecessary for the measurement of income and because there is no compelling reason for the deduction. The Federal Government, through the tax system, in effect pays part of the cost of expenditures by state and local governments. Only real income should be taxed; capital gains and nominal profits that only represent inflation should not be taxed.

Special credits and deductions that are not required to measure income accurately should be repealed. These include depreciation allowances that are greater than real economic depreciation, percentage depletion allowances in excess of cost depletion, intangible drilling expenses, and various forms of preferential treatment currently accorded certain financial institutions. Particularly important is the need to deal with inconsistencies in the tax law that give rise to tax shelters. Tax shelters and the complexities, inequities, and distortions they create can be eliminated only by repealing the tax preferences that make them possible. * * *

* * *

F. Simplification

Simplifying the income tax for most individual taxpayers has been an important objective of the Treasury Department study. Simplification would result from several general approaches. First, increasing the personal exemptions and [standard deduction] amounts will eliminate many poor Americans from the income tax rolls. Second, several itemized deductions will be eliminated or subjected to floors. Like the floor under the current deduction for medical expenses, these floors will reduce the need for so many to keep records of deductible expenditures for extended periods of time. With the expanded [standard deduction] amount and fewer deductions, about one-third fewer taxpayers will find it advantageous to itemize deductions. Third, most tax credits would simply be eliminated. The Treasury Department believes that most Americans would rather pay low taxes on all of their income than pay high taxes on part of it; doing so is simpler, as well as fairer and more neutral toward economic behavior.

Questions

1. What types of problems would exist if a flat tax rate (or a modified flat tax rate) were applied to a comprehensive tax base? Could effective and fair transitional rules be implemented?

2. What groups would oppose proposals to eliminate various exclusions and deductions?

B. THE UNDERGROUND ECONOMY

1. INTRODUCTION

Millions of individuals contribute to America's underground economy—a network of unreported and thus untaxed transactions estimated to annually total between two hundred and eight hundred billion dollars. The underground economy consists of a growing variety of activities, including cash transactions, payments in kind, organized barter, and illegal drug smuggling and gambling. The opportunity to evade taxes is greatest for those who provide services, such as professionals and laborers, and those who own their own business. In fact, anyone who receives cash in a business transaction has the opportunity of joining, and many do. Bartering, which involves the swapping of services or payment in kind, has caught on throughout the United States. Organized, franchised bartering associations supplement the more traditional and informal mode of swapping between individuals. A barter club enables an individual to contribute goods and services at fair market value for trade credits which may be used to buy goods and services from other club members. Because of the government's inability to collect taxes on cash and barter transactions the underground economy is of major concern. The following is one of the administrative responses to the problem of barter transactions.

REV.RUL. 80–52
1980–1 C.B. 100.

ISSUE

What is the amount includible in gross income as a result of the bartering transactions described below, and when is the amount includible in gross income?

FACTS

A and *B* are both members of a barter club. The barter club operates as a vehicle for the exchange of property and services among the members. The club uses "credit units" as a medium of exchange and makes available to members information concerning property and services other members are offering for exchange. The club debits or credits members' accounts for goods or services received from or rendered to other members. Exchanges are made on the basis that one credit unit equals one dollar of value. The rules of the club require that the value placed on goods or services exchanged be equal to the member seller's normal retail price. The transfer of credit units between members is accomplished by various source documents, such as invoices, and the club charges the member purchaser a 10 percent commission payable in cash on barter purchases. Any barter transaction between members is reflected in the form of bookkeeping entries on the books and records of the club. The club does not guarantee that a member will be able to use all of that member's credit units and does not pay a member cash for any credit units not used. However, a member's credit units can be used immediately to purchase goods or services offered by other members of the club, and the member may transfer or sell the member's credit units to another member of the club.

Situation 1. Both *A* and *B* use the cash receipts and disbursements method of accounting.[4] Through the club, *A* bartered to *B* for 200 credit units services that *A* would normally perform for $200. During the same taxable year, *B* bartered to *A* for 200 credit units services that *B* would normally perform for $200.

* * *

LAW AND ANALYSIS

Section 61 of the Internal Revenue Code and regulations thereunder provide that, except as otherwise provided by law, gross income means all income from whatever source derived.

Section 1.61–1 of the Income Tax Regulations provides, in part, that gross income includes income realized in any form, whether in money, property, or services.

Section 1.61–2(d)(1) of the regulations provides that, if services are paid for other than in money, the fair market value of the property or services taken in payment must be included in income as compensation.

* * *

Section 451 of the Code provides that the amount of any item of gross income is includible in the gross income for the taxable year in which received by the taxpayer, unless, under the method of accounting used in computing taxable income, such amount is to be properly accounted for as of a different period.

Section 1.451–1(a) of the regulations provides that income is includible in gross income for the taxable year in which it is actually or

---

4. Under the cash method, a taxpayer realizes and recognizes items of income and deduction in the year actually (or constructively) received or made. Accounting method concepts are considered in detail in Chapter 4.—Eds.

constructively received by the taxpayer, unless it is includible in a different year in accordance with the taxpayer's method of accounting.

* * *

In this case A [and] B * * * received income in the form of a valuable right represented by credit units that can be used immediately to purchase goods or services offered by other members of the barter club. There are no restrictions on their use of the credit units because [they] are free to use the credit units to purchase goods or services when the credit units are credited to their accounts.

HOLDINGS

Situation 1. A and B must include $200 in their gross incomes for the taxable year in which the credit units are credited to their accounts. * * *

* * *

Questions

1. What test does the Service use for gross income in Rev.Rul. 80–52?

2. Why did taxpayers realize and recognize income in the year they earned the barter club units instead of when they used the units to purchase goods or services?

3. What is the justification in this ruling for valuing the amount of income at $200?

* * *

For an analysis of direct barter transactions in which one taxpayer swaps goods or services with a second taxpayer and indirect barter transactions accomplished through barter clubs see Keller, The Taxation of Barter Transactions, 67 Minn.L.R. 441 (1982); Newman, A Response to Robert Keller's The Taxation of Barter Transactions, 68 Minn.L.R. 711 (1984).

2. LEGISLATIVE RESPONSES TO THE UNDERGROUND ECONOMY

In the Tax Equity and Fiscal Responsibility Act of 1982 Congress recognized that many forms of income were not being reported. Congress concluded that taxing unreported income would increase revenue collection without raising tax rates. Consequently, Congress enacted several provisions designed to compel taxpayers to report certain types of previously unreported income.

Employees overwhelmingly report their wages and salaries on their tax returns because their employers report the amount of compensation to the Internal Revenue Service. Employers also withhold a portion of employees' pay and directly remit the withheld amounts to the government.

Prior to the Tax Equity and Fiscal Responsibility Act of 1982, the Internal Revenue Code required payers of most types of interest and dividends to file an information return (Form 1099), but did not require withholding on such payments.   However, no information reporting was required for interest payments on bearer bonds.[5]   The Internal Revenue Service estimated that taxpayers did not report 15 percent of dividend income and 11 percent of interest income.   In contrast, 99 percent of wage income was reported.   Congress determined that the difference in compliance resulted in large part from the withholding requirement.   Congress concluded that withholding would improve voluntary compliance.   Consequently, the 1982 Act provided for a system of withholding on dividends and interest at a rate of 10 percent, effective for payments made after June 30, 1983.   Congress also required the registration of bonds thereby reducing the ability of bond holders to conceal income by cashing negotiable coupons in bearer form.   § 163(f).   The 1982 Act eliminated the issuance of most types of bearer bonds after December 31, 1982.   This change did not affect bonds already issued in bearer form.

The banking industry vehemently opposed the withholding requirement and lobbied extensively for its repeal.   Banks claimed that the increased paperwork costs incurred in implementing the withholding requirement would impair their ability to pay the highest possible interest rates to depositors.

In 1983 Congress repealed the withholding requirement.   Congress decided to wait five years to ascertain if other compliance techniques, such as increased computer matching of the information returns (Form 1099) with individual returns, would effectively close the compliance gap.   In place of the withholding requirement, Congress substituted a system of backup withholding on dividends and interest.   Starting in 1984, payors must withhold 20% of taxable dividends and interest if the payee fails to furnish the payor the correct taxpayer identification number.   For most taxpayers this is his Social Security number.

Any employee who receives tips in the course of his employment must treat all such tips as compensation and must report the amount of tips to his employer each month.   The compliance rate in 1981 with respect to tip income was estimated at approximately 16 percent.   The only type of income with a lower compliance rate was illegal income (5 percent).   Congress believed that the low compliance rate on tip income was fundamentally unfair to wage earners and other taxpayers with substantially higher levels of voluntary compliance.   Therefore, Congress sought to achieve expanded information reporting on tip income. Under the 1982 Act all restaurants and bars normally employing 10 or more persons must file annual information returns indicating gross food and beverage sales receipts and the tip income of all of their

5.   Bearer bonds are bonds issued in bearer form with the interest and principal payable to the person who holds the bonds at the time the obligations to pay the interest and redeem the bond becomes due. Bearer bonds could be transferred by delivery of the instrument to the purchaser. Registered bonds, on the other hand, are issued in the name of the owner; the interest on these bonds is payable to the holder of record on the issuer's books.

employees. Most employees who receive tips are required to report the amount of tips to their employers on a regular basis. At the end of the year, the W–2 form issued by the employer lists the tips as taxable income. Congress determined that the average tip for restaurant or bar employees who receive tips is 8 percent. (Think about the kind of service a patron can expect if he tips only 8 percent). The new rules come into play if the total tips reported by an employee to an employer amount to less than 8 percent of the employer's annual gross receipts. When that happens, each restaurant or bar must allocate among the employees an amount equal to the excess of 8 percent of its gross sales receipts over the amount of tip income reported by the employees to the employer. § 6053(c)(3)(A). The allocation is not required if the employees voluntarily report aggregate tips in an amount equal to or greater than the minimum 8 percent figure. As amended by the Tax Reform Act of 1984, the employer or a majority of the employees may petition for a reduction of the tip allocation from 8 percent of the gross sales receipts to a percentage not lower than 2 percent. § 6053(c)(3)(C). Restaurant or bar employees who receive tips are also on notice that their tax returns will be identified for audit unless the 8 percent (or the lesser percentage) tip reporting requirement is satisfied.

As part of the 1982 Act, Congress added other provisions designed to improve taxpayer compliance, relating mostly to improved information reporting. Congress believed that inadequate information reporting constituted a substantial factor in the underreporting of income. In many cases, persons required to make information reports did not do so. Accordingly, Congress greatly expanded the category of information returns subject to a failure to file penalty and increased the amount of the penalty for failing to file the required information returns.

Question

Will the combination of a more comprehensive tax base with a modified flat rate tax or would a comprehensive tax base or a flat rate tax alleviate the compliance problems inherent in the current tax system?

C. IMPUTED INCOME

Income is not imputed (assumed) from labor an individual performs for himself or from the rental value of a residence occupied by the taxpayer-homeowner. The court in Morris v. Commissioner, 9 B.T.A. 1273, 1278 (1928) (Acq. VII–2 C.B. 75) stated:

> Products of a farm consumed by the operator thereof and his family do not appear to come within any of the categories of income enumerated in the taxing statutes and administrative regulations of the Commissioner. To include the value of such products * * * as compensation would automatically subject such amounts to normal tax and in effect include in income something which Congress did not intend should be so regarded. If products of a farm consumed thereon are income to the producer, it would seem to follow that the rental

value of the farmer's home, the gratuitous services of his wife and children, and the value of the power derived from draft animals owned by the farmer and used without cost should also be so considered. It is obvious that such items are comparable to the rental value of a private residence, which has never been regarded as income or as a factor in the determination of tax liability.

Question

Can you find any Internal Revenue Code section allowing an exclusion for imputed income?

_____

DONALD B. MARSH, THE TAXATION OF IMPUTED INCOME
58 Pol.Sci.Q. 514, 514–521 (1943).

I

Imputed income may be defined provisionally as a flow of satisfactions from durable goods owned and used by the taxpayer, or from goods and services arising out of the personal exertions of the taxpayers on his own behalf.

Imputed income is non-cash income or income in kind. But all non-cash income, or income in kind, is not included in the category of imputed income. For example, where income in kind is received in return for services rendered, we have an ordinary market transaction without a transfer of cash but with a direct monetary valuation implied. Or, again, we may have income in kind arising from ownership which, for similar reasons, is not imputed income. Such is the case where the landlord receives rent in the form of produce.

Imputed income is, therefore, a species of the genus *income in kind*, and its distinguishing characteristic is that it arises outside the ordinary processes of the market.

Examples of imputed income may be given which correspond to the various types of income payments by distributive shares (paid to the classical "factors of production"). Thus we have *imputed rent*, which consists of the net value of the services rendered by a house to its owner (and occupier), for which he would otherwise pay cash rent to a landlord. The category may be widened to include the rental value of other owned durable goods such as automobiles, aeroplanes, refrigerators and the like. But where comparable cash rentals do not exist, it may be more accurate to think of imputed income here as a form of *imputed interest* on an investment in durable goods. *Imputed wages and profits* arise from services rendered by one's family or oneself, such as housework or tending the lawn (wages), and subsistence farming (wages and profits).

All income arising in the market, whether in cash or in kind, is theoretically subject to income tax. Exceptions arise where receipts, which are generally recognized to be income, are not taxed as they accrue for administrative reasons having to do mainly with the difficulty of taxing "unrealized" income: and again where border-line receipts, especially receipts in kind, are declared not to be income by judicial decree while the economists split into two (or more!) camps. But in general anything which looks like income and which arises in the ordinary processes of the market may be presumed to be taxable in the absence of some specific regulation or statute to the contrary.

On the other hand, imputed gain with the clearest logical claim to be designated income is not subject to tax. Realization, separation, and every other subsidiary *criterion*, except the cash form (which is not decisive in other cases), may be met, but the anomalous status of imputed income is allowed to continue.

Income in kind in the form of imputed income is in no way different so far as the individual is concerned. His power to consume and to accumulate is increased by its existence. A taxpayer who has acquired the sum of $20,000 (after payment of income tax) has the choice (among other, but similar, alternatives) of (1) investing the sum in, say, five per cent bonds, collecting $1,000 and spending the interest income left, after payment of income tax, on house rent; or (2) investing the $20,000 in a house, in which case he receives his rental services directly. If the tax is a flat 20 per cent with no exemptions, the first alternative leaves $800 for rent. The second alternative would yield rental services to the full value of $1,000 yearly, since the homeowner pays, under our statute, no tax upon his imputed income.

Another major source of imputed income is the tedious and unrequited labor of housewives. Pigou has immortalized the innocent man who reduced the national income by marrying his housekeeper. Under our statute he would be able also to reduce his income tax liability, since he could maintain the same level of comfort with a smaller cash income than before. The imputed wages of his wife should be at least as great as the cash wages of his housekeeper. But the former do not appear in the taxpayer's accounts, and he receives tax free the excess of her imputed wages over the cost of her subsistence.

In the real world, decisions to marry or not to marry are unlikely to be much influenced by the possibilities of tax avoidance. But the alternatives may appear in another form. Thus, a man and wife may have to consider whether the wife ought to continue her former occupation, using part of her earnings, after paying income taxes, to pay for household service; or whether the wife should herself keep house, earning imputed wages instead of cash and paying no income tax. Let us suppose that she is a competent school teacher, but an indifferent housekeeper. It may nevertheless be impossible for her to earn sufficient money, after taxes, to pay for household service as good as she could herself provide if she stayed at home. In this case, as in most other cases of imputed income from services, our tax laws tend to penalize specialization.

Another example among the numberless possibilities of imputed income from service would be that of a suburban dweller who has to decide whether to hire a gardener to care for his lawn, or whether to do the job himself. If he chooses to hire a gardener, he may have to work harder at his own profession in order to earn additional income on which he pays income tax, and the balance of which after taxes he pays to the gardener for his service. On the other hand, he may earn imputed wages by tending his own lawn, thereby making it possible to maintain the same degree of tidiness with a smaller cash income and therefore a smaller income tax liability.

In all these examples we have assumed that imputed income can in fact be measured by the money value of analogous services in the market. Thus, imputed house rent is determined by what an identical house would bring if rented for cash; the imputed wages of a man who fires his own furnace may be measured by comparing the going wages of janitors; and so on. It is clear, therefore, that in relating imputed income to a workable concept of taxable income we must amend our provisional definition. Ideally, perhaps, imputed income, like taxable income in general, should be defined as a flow of satisfactions, but in practice we must leave such imponderables out of our definition and concentrate on analogous market payments, the satisfaction involved in every case being presumptive only.

This is not to argue that the definition of income in terms of a flow of satisfactions is philosophically unsound. It is perhaps the soundest criterion of all in a purely logical context. But it involves un-measurable quantities not only in the form of psychic income derived from imputed wages, interest, profit and rent, but in the form of satisfactions derived from the receipt of analogous payments of cash income, as well as in the form of subjective valuations placed on the enjoyment of leisure, which is, of all satisfactions, the least susceptible of measurement in monetary terms.

A tax on leisure might take the form of a tax on the individual's excess productive capacity. But clearly any such tax administratively possible could be only a very clumsy instrument, even if the end were considered desirable. One man's work is another man's leisure; and it is probable that the exemption of some forms of imputed income is not an unmixed evil from the point of view of equity in taxation. If we were to tax a man on his imputed income from trimming his lawn (which we may assume he does as a hobby), why should we exempt the man who neglects his lawn because he likes tall grass and the leisure to contemplate it? If we were to tax *all* forms of imputed income we should put a premium on idleness as a way of employing leisure time. It is probable, therefore, that a considerable amount of imputed income should remain exempt from tax because it tends to balance the exemption of leisure income and thus to restore in a measure the balance between work and leisure as alternative ways of using one's time.

There is little danger, however, that the taxation of imputed income will become too broad for equity, because other factors set fairly narrow limits to any proposed imputed income tax base. In the first place, the imputed income from a multitude of activities cannot be assessed properly, or, when assessed, it amounts to so little that it is not worth the administrative trouble and expense. For example, shaving oneself instead of going to a barber yields imputed income; so does the use of personal goods such as furniture, clothes, crockery, etc. But, with the possible exception of the larger pieces of furniture, it is unlikely that a tax on imputed income from these items would be worth the trouble, from the point of view either of revenue or of correcting existing inequities. Finally, some rather large items of imputed income may properly be left out of the tax base because most of the recipients are below the exemption level under the income tax even with imputed income added. This would be true in the main of imputed wages from housework. And this category of imputed income is especially competitive with leisure income, so that there is further reason on equity grounds for leaving it alone.

With regard to the eligibility of imputed income for a place in the concept of income proper, we may conclude, then, that all imputed income should be contemplated in an ideal concept, along with income, from leisure: but that the necessary exclusion of the latter from any practical concept of taxable income makes the exclusion of some types of imputed income less objectionable on equity grounds. This leaves, for purposes of taxation, imputed rent from owner-occupied urban and rural homes, and from owner-used automobiles, aeroplanes, radios, electrical appliances and furniture. * * *

For a further analysis of the concept of imputed income see R. Goode, The Individual Income Tax, 117–125, 139–143 (rev. ed. 1976); Halperin, Business Deduction for Personal Living Expenses; A Uniform Approach to an Unsolved Problem, 122 U.Pa.L.R. 859, 880–885 (1974).

Problems

1. (a) Roe, an attorney, usually prepares her own tax return. Does Roe have income?

(b) This year, Doe, an accountant, prepares Roe's tax return for which Doe would normally charge $50. In return Roe prepares Doe's will for which Roe would normally charge $50. Do Doe and Roe have income? If so, in what amount? When? See Reg. § 1.61–1(a), –2(a), –2(d). Consider Rev.Rul. 80–52.

(c) Boe, a middle-aged physician, relinquishes his $300,000 per year medical practice in order to enter full-time medical teaching at a salary of $75,000 per year. Is Boe utilizing his time in a fashion which would make him taxable on the $225,000 difference between what he earned ($300,000) and what he earns after relinquishing his medical practice ($75,000)? Does Boe have any imputed income? Should Boe be taxed on $225,000 of imputed income for each year he continues his full-time teaching?

2. (a) A and B are married. A and B both work outside their home. In addition, A prepares the meals at home and B cleans the house and A and B take turns, on alternate weekends, mowing their lawn. Do A and B have gross income from these domestic activities? Consider the practical difficulties of calculation. Reconsider Rev.Rul. 80–52.

(b) What if A and B consume $100 worth of vegetables grown in their home garden? What if A and B give C, a neighbor, $100 worth of vegetables grown in their home garden in exchange for watching their home while they are on vacation? What if A owns a grocery store and A takes home groceries which A and B consume?

(c) Why will a couple where both spouses work usually have more out-of-pocket expenses than a couple where one spouse is a full-time homemaker?

3. Compare the situations of Renter and Homeowner (1) with respect to advising an individual to rent or purchase a residence and (2) from a policy-making perspective. Although a homeowner incurs costs, some of which are non-deductible, remember that a homeowner can deduct real estate taxes and mortgage interest on his principal residence (§§ 163 (especially § 163(h)(2)(D) and (h)(5)(A)(i)) and 164); a renter cannot deduct even the portion of the rent the landlord pays in taxes and interest.

(a) Renter invests $50,000 in securities from which Renter derives a return of $5,000. Does Renter have gross income from the return on the securities? § 61(a)(4) and (7). Renter uses the interest to pay the rent on a home identical to the house Homeowner purchased. Assume Renter is in the 28% marginal tax bracket.

(b) Homeowner buys, for cash, a personal residence for $50,000. Homeowner obtains no revenue from the residence. Assume the annual rental value of the residence is $5,000. The imputed annual rental value of Homeowner's residence is not included in Homeowner's gross income. Should the value of the imputed rent be included in the definition of gross income? Should the Homeowner be viewed as an investor in an asset (the residence) which yields a return in the form of housing services which could be converted into cash if the owner moved out and rented the residence? What difficulties do you see?

(c) Should imputed income from an owner's equity in personal property, such as an automobile or a yacht, be taxable?

(d) What income level of taxpayers receive the most benefit from the exclusion of various forms of imputed income from gross income under § 61?

D. FRINGE BENEFITS

Problems

1. (a) Ted Player had two job offers in Washington, D.C. One was with a private law firm for an annual salary of $30,000. The other was with a government agency for $24,000. The office of the private firm was not air-conditioned. Remembering how hot and humid Washington can be in the summer, Ted Player accepted the lower-paying job because all government offices are air-conditioned. Is this benefit taxable to Ted? Consider § 132(a)(3) and (d). Should this benefit be taxable to Ted? What would be the result for the individual who did not care about an air-conditioned office?

(b) While Richard Nixon was President, the General Services Administration paid for and installed a permanent electric forced-air heating system in his San Clemente residence. When President Nixon left public office, the government had no intention of dismantling the heating system because the dismantling cost far exceeded the salvage value of the system. Two-thirds of the value of the heating system was held to constitute gross income to former President Nixon. Both former President Nixon and Ted Player were provided with heating or air conditioning in their working environment. How would you justify the difference in tax treatment? Why did only two-thirds, not 100 percent, of the value of the heating system constitute gross income to former President Nixon? Would there be a different result under § 132(a)(3) and (d)?

2. (a) Ted Player discovered that there was no bus service from his home to his office. Furthermore, he learned that to find a parking space near his place of employment, he had to leave his home at least two hours prior to the commencement of his work day. The loss of the extra sleep each morning reduced his efficiency on the job. To alleviate this situation, his government employer allowed Ted to park in a government parking lot next to his office building. Is the fair rental value of this parking space gross income to Ted? Consider § 132(a)(3), (d), and (h)(4). Should the fair rental value of the parking space constitute gross income to Ted?

(b) Assume Ted's employer paid for parking space in a commercial parking lot near Ted's office, rather than giving Ted a raise? What are the tax consequences to Ted?

(c) Would the result be different if Ted's employer raised his salary by the amount it would cost Ted to rent a parking space?

3. Linda, a computer sales representative, is given a car by her employer to use in performing her job. She is allowed to take the car home with her and use it for personal purposes. Is the personal use of the car taxable to Linda? Consider § 132(a)(3), (d), (e)(1), and (h)(3). Should the personal use of the car be taxable to Linda?

4. Assume the government sent Ted to Tulsa, Oklahoma to try a case. Ted's boss placated him by allowing him to fly first class. Does the cost of the first class fare in excess of the coach fare constitute gross income to Ted? Assume the government paid all of Ted's travel expenses. Consider

§ 132(a)(3) and (d). Is the nondiscriminatory rule applicable? Consider § 132(h)(1).

5. Are any of the following items included in an employee's gross income? Consider § 132(a)(3), (d) and (h)(5). Should any of the following items be included in an employee's gross income?

(a) A company provides its employees with a company gym located in its main building. The gym contains a swimming pool, sauna, hot tub and exercise equipment. In addition, there is a running track laid out on the perimeter of the front lawn. All employees are entitled to use these facilities during the weekdays.

(b) In addition, all employees and their families are allowed to use these facilities on weekends.

(c) Instead of building its own facilities, the company pays the dues for its employees to use the facilities of a commercial health club across the street from its plant during weekdays. Does § 132(h)(5) favor large employers over small employers?

6. Airline employees are allowed to fly at no charge on regularly scheduled flights if the seats are unsold at flight time. Is flying on a space available basis gross income to an airline employee? Consider § 132(a)(1), (b), and (h)(1). Should the value of free or discounted flights be included in an airline employee's gross income? Is the value of a free flight to an airline employee's immediate family includable in gross income? Consider § 132(f)(2). Assume an airline employee's mother takes a free flight. Is the value of the flight included in gross income? Consider § 132(f)(3).

7. (a) Terri Player obtained a part-time job in an appliance store. Her employer gives all employees a 25 percent employee discount. Terri purchases a color television set for 25 percent off the retail price. Does this employee discount constitute gross income to Terri? Assume Terri's employer had aggregate sales of $1,000,000 during its latest taxable year and a cost of goods sold of $600,000. Consider § 132(a)(2) and (c). Is the non-discrimination rule applicable? Consider § 132(h)(1). Should an employee discount constitute gross income? Consider Reg. § 1.61–2(d)(2)(i).

(b) Assume Terri goes to another store and finds that they have a sale on television sets for 30 percent off the retail price. If she purchases a set at this store, does this discount constitute gross income? Instead of a discount, the other store offers to sell her a set for list price, but will give her, at no extra cost, a television stand that normally sells for $50. Is the value of the stand gross income?

8. All sales clerks at a local department store are entitled to a 20 percent discount on the purchase of all store merchandise. Assume the store had aggregate sales of $10 million and a cost of goods sold of $7 million during its latest taxable year. Can the employees exclude their discounts from gross income under § 132(a)(2) and (c) in each of the following situations:

(a) Robert purchases several small items during the year with a total retail value of $400, receiving aggregate discounts of $80.

(b) Jean purchases only one item during the year, an oriental rug retailing for $4000, receiving an $800 discount.

1. ADMINISTRATIVE AND JUDICIAL TREATMENT OF FRINGE BENEFITS

Employers use fringe benefits such as free parking space, use of employer provided automobiles or atheletic facilities, special fares for airline employees, and merchandise discounts for store employees to provide additional tax-free compensation to employees. For years prior to 1985, the tax treatment of fringe benefits had been uncertain because there were no guidelines as to the taxability of fringe benefits in either the Code or the Regulations.

Section 61 broadly defines gross income and Reg. § 1.61–1(a) states that gross income includes compensation in kind for services. The Supreme Court has stated that § 61 is broad enough to include in gross income "any economic or financial benefit conferred on the employee as compensation, whatever the form or mode by which it is effected." Commissioner v. Smith, 324 U.S. 177, 181, 65 S.Ct. 591, 593, 89 L.Ed. 830, 834 (1945). See also Reg. § 1.61–2(d).

Within the broad spectrum of employee fringe benefits, the treatment of bargain or discount purchases of goods and services was often litigated. Under Reg. § 1.61–2(d)(1)(i) if an employee acquires property from his employer for less than its fair market value, he must include the "spread" in gross income. Reconsider the problem at page 17.

In Commissioner v. Minzer, 279 F.2d 338, (5th Cir.1960), an insurance agent was taxable when he purchased a life insurance policy on his own life from one of the companies he represented, whether he sent the full premium to the company and received the company's check for the amount of his usual commission or simply deducted the commission when he remitted the premium. The court stated (279 F.2d at 340):

> The taxpayer obtained insurance which the companies were prohibited by law from selling to him at any discount. * * * It cannot be said that the insurance had a value less than the amount of the premiums. It must then be said that a benefit inured to the taxpayer to the extent of his commissions. The benefit is neither diminished nor eliminated by referring, as does the Tax Court, to the word "commission" as a verbal trap. The commissions were, we conclude, compensation for services and as such were income within the meaning of § 61(a)(1).

In Commissioner v. Daehler, 281 F.2d 823 (5th Cir.1960) a real estate salesman purchased for himself real estate listed with a second broker who divided the commission with the first salesman's employer. The first salesman's employer gave his portion of the commission to the salesman who did not include it in gross income. The court held that the payment was compensation for services rather than a reduction of the purchase price. Similarly in Kobernat v. Commissioner, 31 T.C.M. (CCH) 593 (1972), a stockbroker had to treat as income commissions paid to him on purchases and sales made for his own and his wife's account.

But the partner-partnership relationship should be distinguished from the employee-employer relationship. Assume the taxpayer who engaged in personal transactions in securities markets conducts them through a brokerage firm in which he is a partner. The partner pays the brokerage commission to the firm; at the end of the year the firm pays the partner $X as the individual's share of partnership income, including commissions on transactions for the partner's own account. It has been held that the partner did not receive income from his own transactions because "what one pays to one's self cannot be part of one's income." Benjamin v. Hoey, 139 F.2d 945, 946 (2d Cir.1944).

Each time you analyze whether a fringe benefit is income consider not only is it income, but also (1) to whom is it income and (2) what is the value of the benefit?

The following excerpt considers some executive fringe benefits, such as the use of aircraft.

STAFF OF THE JOINT COMMITTEE ON TAXATION, EXAMINATION OF PRESIDENT NIXON'S TAX RETURNS FOR 1969 THROUGH 1972. PART VI

Personal Use of Government Aircraft by the President's Family and Friends.
157–168 (1974).

SCOPE OF EXAMINATION

Since the President took office in 1969, members of his family and their friends, unaccompanied by him in many instances, have travelled extensively in the United States on Government aircraft. It appears that some of these flights were in connection with the performance of official duties, such as standing in for the President in his absence. This seems to be particularly true for many of the trips by Mrs. Nixon.

A question has been raised whether, for flights which were not primarily official business and, therefore, personal, the cost of such unreimbursed Government-furnished transportation should be considered additional income to the President.

Flights that appear to be personal are particularly those taken by Julie and Tricia to join either David Eisenhower or Edward Cox while the latter were either students or stationed in various cities other than Washington D.C. On several occasions both Edward Cox and David Eisenhower joined Julie and Tricia on flights to and from these same cities and to and from the President's homes in either Key Biscayne, Florida, or San Clemente, California. Occasionally, members of the President's family took along friends or guests on these flights.

*   *   *

Based upon the flight manifests supplied, the staff has computed the value, based upon first class air fare, of air travel by the President's family that did not appear to be primarily official and, therefore, appears to be personal travel.

* * *

ANALYSIS OF TAX TREATMENT

Economic Benefit to the President

This aspect of the examination involves two basic questions. The first is whether the free use of Government transportation by the President's family and friends created income subject to Federal tax. If the answer to the first question is in the affirmative, it is necessary to determine to whom the income should properly be taxed.

* * *

The apparent proliferation in the use of corporate-owned assets for the personal use of employees and shareholders as a device to provide tax-free fringe benefits or constructive dividends has received increased attention by the Service in recent years. However, there is not presently an announced uniform official policy on the general issue, probably because of the diverse types of benefits available, contrasting applicable tax theories, and the enforcement problems inherent in this area.

In the early history of the Federal income tax it was the apparent policy of the Internal Revenue Service and the courts to consider that an employee or shareholder realized income from the free or bargain rate use of corporate assets or services only where there was a measurable direct economic benefit arising from the employment or shareholder relationship.

* * *

More recently the Internal Revenue Service has contended successfully that a shareholder's use of a wide range of corporate assets resulted in income to the shareholder. The courts have held that constructive dividends were realized from the shareholder's personal use of a corporate yacht, an automobile, supplies and materials, and a lake house. Constructive dividends have also been found to result to the shareholder by corporation payments of the shareholder's home expenses, club expenses, life insurance policy premiums, and travel expenses.

The court decisions have not been confined to constructive dividend results, but have also found that compensation income resulted from the personal use of corporate facilities or from corporate payments for personal purposes of the individual taxpayer. In Rodgers Dairy Co. v. Commissioner, 14 T.C. 66 (1950), an officer's use of a corporate automobile was taxed to the officer as compensation. * * * In Silverman v. Commissioner, 253 F.2d 849 (8th Cir.1958), a corporation's payment of travel expenses for the wife of an employee, who accompanied the employee on a business trip, was also found to result in additional compensation to the employee. In Dean v. Commissioner, 9 T.C. 256 (1947), and Chandler v. Commissioner, 41 B.T.A. 165 (1940), affirmed 119 F.2d 623 (3d Cir.1941), officers or shareholders were found to have realized additional compensation from the personal use by them and their families of a residence and a lodge owned by the corporation.

In addition to the cases set forth above, there are a number of other cases holding that taxable income was created, without identifying the income as to whether it was a constructive dividend or compensation.

There is also the question of whether taxable income can be attributed to an employee for the use of the employer's facilities or services by his friends or family members. This question in a sense involves the doctrine of constructive receipt, but not in the traditional sense, since we are not concerned with the question of who should be taxed on the economic benefit.

With respect to this issue, the authorities recognize it is not necessary that the individual taxpayer himself receive the direct benefit of the use of the facility or the payment of the expenses by the employer. For example, the Internal Revenue Service has held in Rev. Rul. 69–104, 1969–1 Cum.Bull. 33, that where payments are made to dependents of a corporation's former employees who are in the U.S. Armed Forces, the payments are taxable as constructively received by the former employees. In the context of travel expenses, in the *Silverman* case, cited supra, the Tax Court remarked:

> It is also well settled that where funds of a corporation are disbursed for the personal use or economic benefit of a stockholder or his immediate family, there being no intention of repayment, the amounts so disbursed are either the equivalent of corporate distributions or additional compensation for services (depending upon the facts and circumstances), especially in the case of dealings between closely held corporations and their stockholders. 28 T.C. at 1064.

Here the payments for the transportation expenses of the spouse were considered to be income to the husband. * * * In United States v. Gotcher, 401 F.2d 118 (5th Cir.1968), the taxpayer was held to have realized income through a supplier's payment of his wife's travel expenses on a trip to tour the supplier's plant. The basis for the attribution of income to the taxpayer was that the supplier's payments had relieved him of the financial responsibility for the wife's expenses.

It is, of course, obvious that if a taxpayer entertains or benefits his friends by use of his employer's property, this does not change the result that the use is income to the taxpayer, any more than the taxpayer would be entitled to a deduction if he took part of his salary and rented comparable facilities for the benefit of his friends.

The rules set forth in the *Silverman* case have recently been applied by the Tax Court to include economic benefits received by individuals who were not family members of the taxpayer. In Bauer v. Commissioner, 32 T.C.M. 496 (1973), the employer's payment of air fare to Japan for the taxpayer's woman companion and her two children was held to be compensation income to the taxpayer. The court reasoned that when the air fare was paid by the employer it "was done because of the employment relationship" and the taxpayer was "relieved of what would otherwise have been a personal expense." The court concluded that "it is of no consequence that those provided with air fare were not members of his household" and therefore that the "fair market value" of the air fare was includible in the taxpayer's income.

It is apparent that Mrs. Nixon, the President's daughters, and the friends of the Nixon family have enjoyed the personal use of the Presidential aircraft only because of the employment relationship between the President and the United States. It is, therefore, the belief of the staff that the President has realized taxable income where members of his family or his friends had free use of Government transportation for personal excursions or where it has not been established that they were on Government business. The staff also considers this to be equally applicable where the President's family and/or friends accompanied him on trips which for him were in performance of the official duties of the President, but for which there is no evidence that the family and/or friends performed any official functions.

Measure of Income

Where it is determined that an employee has received compensation other than in money, "the fair market value of property or services taken in payment must be included in income." Reg. § 1.61–2(d). Generally, where compensation is paid by allowing the taxpayer to enjoy the use of property, courts look to the rental value of the property to determine the amount of the compensation. (See e.g., Dole v. Commissioner, 43 T.C. 697 (1965)).

It is the staff's understanding that the present position of the Internal Revenue Service, where the personal nonbusiness use of corporate aircraft is involved, is to consider that the benefit is measured by the ratio of miles traveled for the personal benefit of the employee to the total miles the corporate aircraft traveled during the taxable year, multiplied by all costs (both operating and fixed) arising from the employer's ownership of the aircraft. * * *

If the fair rental value of the Government aircraft were to be used here to measure the income to the President, it would result in a significantly higher figure than the first class commercial fare basis which has been used by the President in reimbursing the Government for part of the personal excursion flights of his family. For example, the staff has been informed that the present charter rates for a Jet Star executive jet aircraft are generally in the range of $1.70 per mile or $1,000 per flight hour. If current Service practice is followed and operating and fixed expenses are used, a slightly lower figure will result, about $1.50 per mile or $900 per flight hour for the typical annual hours of use for such aircraft. This compares to current costs of approximately 11 to 17 cents per passenger mile for first class commercial airfare, depending on the trip.

It is the staff's belief, however, that in order to reach a reasonable and equitable measure of the benefit to the President, it is necessary to consider the reason Government aircraft were used to transport the President's family and friends. Because of security precautions, such as the risk of hijacking, the Secret Service recommends that these individuals not travel on commercial scheduled airlines. But for those considerations the family and friends could have travelled on commercial airlines. In recognition of these circumstances, the staff believes that the appropriate measure of the President's economic benefit is the cost of first class commercial fares for the trips provided by Government aircraft, rather than charter rates or the costs of the use of the aircraft.

Question

Under § 132 would the personal use of government aircraft by former President Nixon's daughters be income? To whom? Consider § 132(a)(1), (b), (d), (f)(2) and (h)(1). Should former President Nixon be taxed in this situation?

2. STATUTORY TREATMENT OF FRINGE BENEFITS

Although all fringe benefits could be treated as gross income, Congress has chosen to exempt by statute certain benefits, for example, certain employer-provided meals and lodging (§ 119) (pp. 308–331), accident and health plans (§ 106), wage continuation plans (§ 105) group term life insurance (§ 79), and group legal service plans (§ 120) (pp. 349–354). Many other benefits made available to employees have, for one reason or another, been excluded from gross income by prior administrative practice or rulings, instead of by specific statutory exclusion.

Understandably, in the past Congress had been reluctant to confront these bastions of taxpayer freedom from taxation. Nevertheless, as a matter of tax policy, we must face the following question: Should a taxpayer include all benefits received from his employer in gross income? If this question is answered in the affirmative, then Congress may exclude, by statute, certain fringe benefits just as the Code already excludes some.

Many commentators maintain that the tax treatment of fringe benefits should result from a reasoned legislative judgment. With the tremendous growth in employer provided fringe benefits, the problems can only become worse if the current haphazard and arbitrary treatment continued. A recent study showed that employee benefits as a share of total payroll equalled 32.5 percent in 1982 as compared with 26 percent in 1971 and only 3 percent in 1929. The Chamber of Commerce of the United States, Employee Benefits 1982, 27–28 (1984). Congress and the Treasury preceived a need for either legislation or regulations because of this dramatic increase in employee fringe benefits. Although several attempts were made to deal with this problem, they were highlighted by the inability of Congress and the Service to reach a compromise in dealing with the treatment of fringe benefits.

In September, 1975, the Treasury Department published a discussion draft of proposed regulations which set forth specific rules for determining whether various nonstatutory fringe benefits constituted gross income. 40 Fed.Reg. 41118 (Sept. 5, 1975). The 1975 proposal was widely criticized, especially by representatives of groups receiving tax-free fringe benefits. The discussion draft was later withdrawn. 41 Fed.Reg. 56334 (Dec. 28, 1976). In 1978 Congress passed a moratorium on the promulgation by the Treasury of any new regulations affecting fringe benefits. Congress extended the moratorium several times. The last moratorium expired on December 31, 1983.

In 1979, a Task Force of the House Ways and Means Committee issued a Discussion Draft Bill and Report on Employee Fringe Benefits in an attempt to provide a basis for the legislative treatment of fringe benefits. [1979] 5 P–H Fed. Taxes ¶ 59,505. The proposal was lost in the shuffle of other tax legislation which apparently had a higher priority. Shortly before the Carter Administration left office, the Treasury Department, in January, 1981, issued a Fringe Benefit Discussion Draft for proposed fringe benefit regulations. Finally, in 1983, a bipartisan Congressional group introduced a fringe benefit bill as a starting point for the formulation of legislation in this area. The basic purpose of this bill, which was embraced by Congress as part of the Tax Reform Act of 1984, was aptly stated by Rep. Barber B. Conable, one of the Congressmen who introduced it:

> The importance of providing a uniform set of rules for the taxation of fringe benefits should not be understated and, in fact, becomes greater with each passing year. A number of factors support this conclusion.

> First, a continued lack of guidance with respect to the taxation of fringe benefits will permit a continued erosion of the tax base as more and more employers provide non-cash forms of compensation in the hope of avoiding includability in taxable income. * * *

> Second, the absence of a uniform set of rules for taxing fringe benefits imposes serious inequities within the system as taxpayers in different parts of the country are treated in a discriminatory manner with respect to identical or comparable forms of fringe benefit compensation. * * *

> Third, the untaxed status of fringe benefits encourages employers to provide non-cash forms of compensation, thus restricting the employees' freedom of choice as to what their compensation may be used to purchase. * * *

Fourth, the nontaxed status of certain fringe benefits creates inequities among various taxpayers because not all employers will provide comparable compensation packages. * * *

Cong. Record (July 12, 1983) at H5059–H5060.

Section 132, the most comprehensive statutory treatment of fringe benefits, largely excludes from gross income most noncash benefits emanating from long-established practices which taxpayers had already perceived as being tax-free and which the Service had administratively been treating as tax-free. Congress wanted to codify the exclusion for existing practices so that new practices could not arise which would also escape taxation. This was accomplished by adding the phrase "fringe benefits" to § 61(a)(1), thereby reaffirming the broad scope of § 61. The legislative history emphasized that any form of compensation not specifically exempted by the Code is intended to be taxable. More importantly, Congress in providing clear and meaningful guidelines to be used in judging the taxability of a fringe benefit, wanted to alleviate the inequities, confusion and administrative difficulties existing in the past.

The following excerpt identifies the objectives achieved by codifying the tax treatment of employee fringe benefits:

JOINT COMMITTEE ON TAXATION, GENERAL EXPLANATION OF THE REVENUE PROVISIONS OF THE DEFICIT REDUCTION ACT OF 1984
838–844 (1984).

C. Tax Treatment of Fringe Benefits

Prior Law

General rules

The Internal Revenue Code defines gross income for purposes of the Federal income tax as meaning "all income from whatever source derived," and specifies that it includes "compensation for services" (sec. 61). Treasury regulations provide that gross income includes compensation for services paid other than in money (Reg. sec. 1.61–1(a)). Further, the U.S. Supreme Court has stated that Code section 61 "is broad enough to include in taxable income any economic or financial benefit conferred on the employee as compensation, whatever the form or mode by which it is effected."[6]

6. Comm'r v. Smith, 324 U.S. 177, 181 (1945); see also, Comm'r v. Kowalski, 434 U.S. 77 (1977). Similarly, the Court has stated: "Congress applied no limitations as to the source of taxable receipts, nor restrictive labels as to their nature. And the Court has given a liberal construction to this broad phraseology in recognition of the intention of Congress to tax all gains except those specifically exempted" (Comm'r v. Glenshaw Glass Co., 348 U.S. 426, 429–30 (1955)). The many types of employee benefits that have been held includible in gross income under this sweeping definition include, among others, commuting or other personal use of company aircraft (e.g., Ireland v. U.S., 621 F.2d 731 (5th Cir.1980)); personal use by an employee of an employer-provided automobile (e.g., Est. of Runnels v. Comm'r, 54 T.C.

* * *

Reasons for Change

In providing statutory rules for exclusion of certain fringe benefits for income and payroll tax purposes, the Congress struck a balance between two competing objectives.

First, the Congress was aware that in many industries, employees may receive, either free or at a discount, goods and services which the employer sells to the general public. In many cases, these practices are long established, and generally have been treated by employers, employees, and the Internal Revenue Service as not giving rise to taxable income.

Although employees receive an economic benefit from the availability of these free or discounted goods or services, employers often have valid business reasons, other than simply providing compensation, for encouraging employees to avail themselves of the products which those employees sell to the public. For example, a retail clothing business will want its salespersons to wear, when they deal with customers, the clothing which it seeks to sell to the public, rather than clothing sold by its competitors. In addition, where an employer has only one line of business, the fact that the selection of goods and services offered in that line of business may be limited in scope makes it appropriate to provide a limited exclusion, when such discounts are generally made available to employees, for the income employees realize from obtaining free or reduced-cost goods or services. By contrast, allowing tax-free discounts for all lines of business of a conglomerate organization, where the employee might have unlimited choices among many products and services which individuals normally consume or use on a regular basis, would be indistinguishable in economic effect from allowing tax-free compensation in the form of cash or gift certificates. Also, the noncompensatory element involved in providing discounts on the particular products or services that the employee sells to the public may be marginal or absent where an employer offers discounts across all lines of business.

The Congress believed, therefore, that many present practices under which employers may provide to a broad group of employees, either free or at a discount, the products and services which the employer sells or provides to the public do not serve merely to replace cash compensation. These reasons support the decision to codify the

762 (1970); Dole v. Comm'r, 43 T.C. 697, aff'd per curiam, 351 F.2d 3081 (1st Cir. 1965); Long Chevrolet Co. v. Comm'r, 26 CCH Tax Ct. Mem. 1054 (1967)); personal use of a company yacht (Nicholls, North, Buse Co. v. Comm'r, 56 T.C. 1225 (1971)); reimbursement of lunches for employees engaged in nonovernight travel (Central Ill. Public Service Co. v. U.S., 435 U.S. 21 (1978)); employer payment or reimburse-ment of expenses for convention trip not primarily for business purposes (e.g., Patterson v. Thomas, 289 F.2d 108 (5th Cir.), cert. denied, 368 U.S. 837 (1961)); reimbursement of new employee's expenses or economic loss on sale of former residence (e.g., Bradley v. U.S., 324 F.2d 610 (4th Cir. 1963)); and employer-furnished suits worn by employees (Rev.Rul. 80–322, 1980–2 C.B. 36).

ability of employers to continue many of these practices without imposition of income or payroll taxes.

The second objective of the new statutory rules is to set forth clear boundaries for the provision of tax-free benefits. Because of the moratorium on the issuance of fringe benefit regulations, the Treasury Department has been precluded from clarifying the tax treatment of many of the forms of noncash compensation commonly in use. As a result, the administrators of the tax law have not had clear guidelines in this area, and hence taxpayers in identical or comparable situations have been treated differently. The inequities, confusion, and administrative difficulties for businesses, employees, and the Internal Revenue Service resulting from this situation have increased substantially in recent years. The Congress believed that it would be unacceptable to allow these conditions—which had existed since 1978—to continue.

In addition, the Congress was concerned that without any well-defined limits on the ability of employers to compensate their employees tax-free by providing noncash benefits having economic value to the employee, new practices will emerge that could shrink the income tax base significantly. This erosion of the income tax base results because the preferential tax treatment of fringe benefits serves as a strong motivation to employers to substitute more and more types of benefits for cash compensation. A similar shrinkage of the base of the social security payroll tax could also pose a threat to the viability of the social security system above and beyond the adverse projections which the Congress addressed in the Social Security Amendments of 1983. In addition, continuation of the dramatic growth in noncash forms of compensation in recent years—at a rate exceeding the growth in cash compensation—could further shift a disproportionate tax burden to those individuals whose compensation is in the form of cash.

Finally, an unrestrained expansion of noncash compensation would increase inequities among employees in different types of businesses, because not all employers can or will provide comparable compensation packages. For example, consumer-goods retail stores can offer their employees discounts on clothing, hardware, etc.; by contrast, a manufacturer of aircraft engines cannot give its workers compensation in the form of tax-free discounts on its products. Similarly, an unlimited exclusion for noncash benefits discriminates among employers. For example, if tax-free discounts were allowed across all lines of business of an employer, a large employer with many types of businesses (e.g., department store, hotel, airline, etc.) would be given a favorable edge by the tax system in competing for employees as compared with a small firm having one line of business (e.g., a specialty clothing store). Also, a failure to put any limits on the untaxed status of fringe benefits would encourage employers to provide further noncash forms of compensation and thus, in effect, restrict the employees' freedom of choice over how to spend or save their compensation.

Accordingly, the Congress determined that specific rules of exclusion should be set forth in the Code, with limitations on the availability, applicability, and scope of these statutory exclusions. These general limitations include a nondiscrimination rule, the line of business limitation, and the limitation on exclusions to benefits provided to the employee and the employee's spouse and dependent children. In addition, specific limitations apply to particular types of benefits.

The nondiscrimination rule is an important common thread among the types of fringe benefits which are excluded under the Act from income and employment taxes. Under the Act, most fringe benefits may be made available tax-free to officers, owners, or highly compensated employees only if the benefits are also provided on substantially equal terms to other employees. The Congress believed that it would be fundamentally unfair to provide tax-free treatment for economic benefits that are furnished only to highly paid executives. Further, where benefits are limited to the highly paid, it is more likely that the benefit is being provided so that those who control the business can receive compensation in a nontaxable form; in that situation, the reasons stated above for allowing tax-free treatment would not be applicable. Also, if highly paid executives could receive free from taxation economic benefits that are denied to lower-paid employees, while the latter are compensated only in fully taxable cash, the Congress was concerned that this situation would exacerbate problems of noncompliance among taxpayers. In this regard, some commentators argued that the prior-law situation—in which the lack of clear rules for the tax treatment of nonstatutory fringe benefits encouraged the nonreporting of many types of compensatory benefits—led to nonreporting of types of cash income which are clearly taxable under present-law rules, such as interest and dividends.

In addition to enacting specific statutory exclusions covering many fringe benefit practices, the tax treatment of which had been uncertain under prior law, the Congress provided amendments in the Act to Code section 61, defining gross income, and to comparable employment tax provisions. These amendments made clear that any fringe benefit that does not qualify for exclusion under a specific Code provision is includible in the recipient's gross income, and in wages for withholding and other employment tax purposes, at the excess of the fair market value of the benefit over any amount paid by the recipient for the benefit.

The Congress recognized that the inclusion of taxable fringe benefits at fair market value raises valuation issues. However, the problem has been ameliorated because the Act exempts from any taxation a significant portion of benefits made available under existing practices. In addition, the Congress has directed the Treasury to issue regulations, to the extent feasible, setting forth appropriate and helpful rules for the valuation of taxable fringe benefits, to assist both employers, employees, and the Internal Revenue Service.

Also, the Congress understood that valuation issues inherently arise whenever compensation is paid in the form of noncash benefits. For example, both under prior law and the Act, the personal use by an employee (including use by members of the employee's family) of an employer-provided car or plane is includible in income, thereby necessitating a determination of the fair market value of the personal use. While it is understood that as a matter of practice, some taxpayers have not been reporting the full fair market value of such benefits, and that the Internal Revenue Service may not have been actively pursuing the matter on audit, the Congress anticipated that with the enactment in the Act of statutory rules delineating exclusions for fringe benefits, the Internal Revenue Service will be more effective in assuring that all sources of income and wages are properly reported on employer and employee tax returns. The Congress believed that this will help achieve a greater fairness in the tax law, by treating alike employees having equivalent economic income.

In summary, the Congress believed that by providing rules which essentially codify many present practices under which employers provide their own products or services tax-free to a broad group of employees whose work involves those products or services, and by ending the uncertainties arising from a moratorium on the Treasury Department's ability to clarify the tax treatment of these benefits, the Act substantially improves the equity and administration of the tax system.

* * *

Explanation of Provisions

a. *Overview*

* * *

The excluded fringe benefits are those benefits that qualify under one of the following [four] categories as defined in the Act: (1) a no-additional-cost service, (2) a qualified employee discount, (3) a working condition fringe, (4) a de minimis fringe, * * *. Special rules apply with respect to certain parking and subsidized eating facilities provided to employees, on-premises athletic facilities provided by an employer to employees, and demonstration use of cars by full-time auto salespersons. Some of the exclusions under the Act apply to benefits provided to the spouse and dependent children of a current employee, to former employees who separated from service because of retirement or disability (and their spouses and dependent children), and to the widow(er) of a deceased employee (and the dependent children of deceased employees).

In the case of a no-additional-cost service, a qualified employee discount, subsidized eating facilities, or a qualified tuition reduction, the exclusion applies with respect to benefits provided to officers, owners, or highly compensated employees only if the benefit is made available to employees on a basis which does not discriminate in favor of officers, owners, or highly compensated employees.

Although § 132 significantly clarifies the tax treatment of many fringe benefits, several areas of uncertainty and ambiguity remain. A cornerstone of § 132 is the nondiscrimination requirement. However, § 132(h)(1) provides for a nondiscrimination test based on a "reasonable classification." Classifications based on factors, such as seniority, full-time employment or job descriptions, may pass the test, if the effect is not discriminatory. Certain classes of employees may be excluded for purposes of applying the nondiscrimination rules. Reg. § 1.132–8T(b)(3). Compare the eligibility and benefit requirements for nondiscriminatory statutory employee benefit plans, namely, group-term life insurance and accident and health plans. § 89(i), (d), and (e). Why did not the Tax Reform Act of 1986 bring no-additional-cost and qualified employee discount fringe benefits within the definition of a statutory employee benefit plan for purposes of the nondiscrimination rules?

In addition, the Code excludes a de minimus fringe benefit when accounting for it is unreasonable or administratively impractical. § 132(e)(1). Regulations § 1.132–6T attempt to provide some guidelines as to what this means.

Finally, § 132 does not address the valuation quandary. According to Reg. § 1.61–2T(b)(2), the fair market value of a fringe benefit is determined on the facts and circumstances. "Specifically, the fair market value of a fringe benefit is that amount a hypothetical person would have to pay a hypothetical third party to obtain (i.e., purchase or lease) the particular fringe benefit." Reg. § 1.61–2T(b)(2). Furthermore, fair market value is not determined by the cost to the employer to provide the benefit. Reg. § 1.61–2T(b)(2). Special rules are provided to determine the fair market value of certain fringe benefits, such as, the use of a car or an airplane. Reg. § 1.61–2T(b)(4) and (5).

Question

What is the purpose of the nondiscriminatory rule under § 132(h)(1)? Must it be satisfied for all fringe benefits excludable from gross income under § 132(a)? If a fringe benefit, which is subject to the anti-discrimination rules, is provided on a discriminatory basis, who is subject to taxation? Consider § 132(h)(1).

3. POLICY PERSPECTIVES ON THE TREATMENT OF FRINGE BENEFITS

a. *Problems Created by Untaxed Fringe Benefits*

Despite the statutory basis for the inclusion of fringe benefits in gross income, the failure to tax fringe benefits causes many problems, including the erosion of the tax base, inequity among and within various classes of taxpayers, and allocative inefficiency of economic resources.

i. *Erosion of the Tax Base.* The statutory exclusion of certain fringe benefits from gross income results in an erosion in the tax base.

Taxing fringe benefits could raise revenues and possibly lead to a reduction in tax rates.

ii. *Equity Among Taxpayers.* Not all employees receive equivalent fringe benefits. Some taxpayers, in fact, receive none. Exempting certain fringe benefits from tax or valuing them at less than their real value creates substantial tax inequities among taxpayers. Fairness in a tax system requires the minimization of differences in the taxation of persons with similar incomes. Compensation received in kind may be just as valuable as compensation received in cash. When certain fringe benefits are exempted from tax, taxpayers with equal incomes do not pay equal taxes.

iii. *Allocative Inefficiency of Economic Resources.* Inefficiency in the allocation of economic resources results if some forms of economic benefits go untaxed because the aftertax value of such benefits does not reflect their true relative value to society. When certain fringe benefits are exempted from tax, employees will demand and employers will provide a greater amount of compensation in the form of these fringe benefits than they would if such benefits were taxed. The resulting shift in demand caused by the tax laws interferes with allocation of economic resources by the marketplace producing economic distortion. Taxed goods will be underconsumed, while untaxed goods will be overconsumed. Also, the exclusion or undertaxation of certain fringe benefits may even cause a shift of the labor force towards industries and occupations which are more likely to provide these fringe benefits.

b. *Roadblocks to the Taxation of Fringe Benefits*

More comprehensive taxation of fringe benefits faces two significant roadblocks, namely, valuation problems and administrative difficulties.

i. *Valuation Problems.* The difficulty in valuing fringe benefits provided in kind constitutes a major obstacle to their taxation. Regulation § 1.61–2(d)(1)(i) requires the recipient of noncash compensation to include in income the "fair market value" of such compensation. In addition, § 83(a) requires that any property transferred in connection with the performance of services be included in the gross income of the recipient, subject to certain qualifications considered later in the chapter, to the extent that the fair market value of the property received exceeds the amount the recipient paid for the property.

The valuation problem arises in defining the term "fair market value" and in justifying the use of the fair market value standard. "Fair market value" is usually defined as the price paid for a benefit in an informed marketplace and in a willing, arms-length transaction. See e.g. Reg. § 1.170A–1(c)(2). It is not at all certain that the price charged by the employer to customers for the same product or service, if publicly offered or the retail price commonly charged for similar products or services, is the value of the benefit realized by an employee.

A fringe benefit restricts an employee's choice and, therefore, the employee is not a willing buyer.

Another possible basis on which to value fringe benefits would be the reduction in cash compensation which an employee would be willing to accept in return for the provision of the benefit. This value would never exceed the market cost of a benefit. Such a subjective measurement of income, while perhaps ideal, would be impossible to administer. Our system of self-assessment would cease to function effectively if gross income were subjectively determined on a case-by-case basis. The concept of "psychic income" (the cash valuation of satisfaction received from the performance of one's job) would also be impossible to value and administer and, therefore, should be ignored in computing taxable income.

The incremental cost to the employer is another valuation possibility. This method, while more easily ascertainable and more objective than some other possibilities, would not accomplish the objective of taxing fringe benefits. For example, an airline that provides free flights to its employees might incur little or no incremental cost to fly an extra passenger on a plane that is not full, but certainly the flight has some measurable value to the employee.

Even if "fair market value" is accepted as the standard of measurement, it is still an uneasy standard. Is the fair market price a sale price, a price at a "full service store", or a price at a discount store? The 1979 Discussion Draft Bill and Report on Employee Fringe Benefits issued by the staff of the House Ways and Means Committee Task Force on Employee Fringe Benefits defined "fair market value" as the lowest price at which the employee might reasonably have obtained a comparable benefit in the same geographical area within a reasonable period of time (e.g., 90 days before or after the benefit was received). The burden of substantiation with respect to this "lowest price available" test would have been placed on the employee. This standard, while not perfect, does limit subjectivity.

ii. *Administrative Difficulties.* The taxation of fringe benefits is fraught with administrative difficulties. Some sort of exception is needed to prevent the administrative costs to the employer and the tax collection costs to the government from exceeding the revenue realized by taxing fringe benefits. Such a rule might apply on an item by item as well as a cumulative basis. For example, a discount on employee purchases would be excluded only if a single purchase did not exceed a certain dollar amount and if total discounts received by the employee for the year did not exceed a specified level. However, the need to aggregate items requires the keeping of records with respect to each employee's discount purchases.

For additional background see Wasserman, Principles in Taxation of Nonstatutory Fringe Benefits, 32 Tax Lawyer 137 (1978); Popkin,

The Taxation of Employee Fringe Benefits, 22 B.C.L.Rev. 439 (1981); Note, Federal Income Taxation of Employee Fringe Benefits, 89 Harv.L. Rev. 1141 (1976); Kies, Analysis of the New Rules Governing the Taxation of Fringe Benefits, 24 Tax Notes 981 (1984).

E. STOCK OPTIONS AND RESTRICTED STOCK

1. THE QUALIFIED STOCK OPTION: DEFERRAL OF TAX CONSEQUENCES OF EARNINGS AND CONVERSION OF ORDINARY INCOME INTO CAPITAL GAINS

Dual Purposes of the Stock Option Device: To Defer Income and Obtain Capital Gains. Two objectives frequently sought by taxpayers are closely related. One objective is reflected in the attempts by taxpayers to perform services during one tax period but postpone the payment for the services until a later tax period. There is also a second objective: to transform ordinary income from personal earnings into capital gains which prior to 1988 received preferential tax treatment. The obvious purpose of the attempts to create capital gains was to reduce income taxes. The stock option device seeks to accomplish: (1) the deferring of the realization and recognition of income until the sale or other disposition of the stock and (2) the obtaining of capital gains.

The Rule That Payment in Kind Creates Income. The best way to show how the stock option works is to consider some of its primitive forerunners. Here is an example:

> X Company employs T at a salary of $40,000 per year. Company officials desire to increase T's compensation. If they give him a $20,000 addition in salary, it will be received by T at ordinary income rates. They desire to avoid this result. Consequently they give T $20,000 worth of X Company's stock.

This strategy will not save taxes. The stock will be included in the income of the employee just as though the employee had received it in cash. Payments in kind—whether stock, potatoes, typewriters, or others—are measured by their fair market value at the time they are received and are includible in the recipient's gross income. Reg. § 1.61–2(d)(1).

The same result would follow if X Company sold employee T stock at a bargain price. The Regulations require that where services are paid for "other than in money," the "fair market value of the property or services taken in payment must be included in income." Consequently a bargain sale of stock to T would be treated as ordinary income to the extent of the bargain to Reg. § 1.61–2(d)(2).

The Defeat of Early Stock Option Arrangements in the Smith Case. Failure of the above devices made it obvious that some other method had to be found to obtain capital gains treatment for individuals providing personal services. Consequently, corporations gave their employees options to purchase stock at a future time. Note that the grant of a stock option does not involve the immediate ownership of stock. The hope was that tax consequences would not arise when the option was given, or when the stock was purchased on the exercise of the option, but only when the employee sold the stock. At which time, the employee would report capital gains equal to the difference between the purchase price of the stock on the exercise of the option and the price of the stock at the time of sale. However, this hope was dashed when the Supreme Court held that because such an option to acquire shares was in fact given as compensation for services, the excess of the fair market value of the shares over the employee's option price, when the option was exercised, represented compensation taxable as ordinary income. Commissioner v. Smith, 324 U.S. 177, 65 S.Ct. 591, 89 L.Ed. 830 (1945).

How Statutory Scheme Operates: Advantages and Disadvantages of Qualified Stock Option Plans. The restrictive doctrines of the *Smith* case were discarded by Congress in 1950. Stock options meeting statutory requirements, so-called qualified stock options, had the following advantages and disadvantages under §§ 421–422:

   a. An employee does not realize income when his employer gives him an option to purchase stock;

   b. The employee does not receive income when he exercises the option;

   c. When he sells the stock, the employee realizes and recognizes capital gains in the amount by which the sale price exceeds his purchase price, with qualifications to be hereafter mentioned;

   d. The employing corporation cannot get a deduction under § 162 for compensation paid to the employee, with respect to either the grant of a qualified stock option or the transfer of stock to the employee when he exercises a qualified option.

The principal advantages of a qualified stock option plan to the employee have been stated: (1) it permitted, prior to 1988, an employee to treat payment for services as preferential capital gains rather than as ordinary income and (2) the realization and recognition of that gain is postponed until the employee sells stock which he has purchased by virtue of the stock option.

The business advantage of stock option arrangements to the employer are substantial, particularly where the employer is anxious to retain the services of an employee who does not have an equity interest in the enterprise, or for other reasons wishes to expand the equity interest of the employee in the enterprise.

The stock option constitutes a highly desirable method of attracting or retaining exceptional administrative and creative talent. Because no payment is made in cash, the credit position of the company will not be endangered by the use of qualified stock option plans.

A major disadvantage of qualified stock option plans to the employer is that while the executives of the business are enriched, the corporate employer does not receive any deduction arising from the increment obtained by the executives through the exercise of the stock options or even with respect to the grant of the options. It must also be kept in mind that every stock option issued to an employee will, when exercised, adversely affect the previous stockholders. That is, if an employee is permitted to buy stock at an option price of $10 per share when the stock is worth $20 per share, people who already hold stock worth $20 per share will suffer a dilution in the value of their stock by reason of the bargain arrangement given to the executive. In this sense, all the shareholders pay for stock options given to executives. On the other hand, if the stock option truly represents an inducement to the executive to increase the value of the enterprise, the other shareholders are protected on the theory that the executive will create enough value in the enterprise by reason of his services to make up for the dilution.

The Tax Reform Act of 1976 removed the favorable tax treatment accorded qualified stock options. In explaining the reasons for the change in tax treatment the Staff of the Joint Committee on Taxation, General Explanation of the Tax Reform Act of 1976, 94th Cong. 1st Sess. 152–153 (1976), stated:

> The principal reason for the [pre-1976] tax treatment of qualified stock options was said to be that such treatment allowed corporate employers to provide "incentives" to key employees by enabling these employees to obtain an equity interest in the corporation. However, it seems doubtful whether a qualified stock option gives key employees more incentive than does any other form of compensation, especially since the value of compensation in the form of a qualified option is subject to the uncertainties of the stock market. Moreover, even to the extent a qualified option is an incentive, it still represents compensation and Congress believes that as such it should be subject to tax in much the same manner as other compensation. Moreover, to the extent that there is an incentive effect resulting from stock options, it could be argued that [pre-1976] law discriminates in favor of corporations (which are the only kind of employers who can grant qualified options) as opposed to all other forms of business organization.

Incentive Stock Options. Incentive stock options (§ 422A) are the latest embodiment of the qualified stock option concept. Report of the Senate Finance Committee, Report No. 97–144, Economic Recovery Tax Act of 1981, 97th Cong., 1st Sess. 98–99 (1981) states:

> The Committee believes that reinstitution of a stock option provision will provide an important incentive device for corporations to attract new management and to retain the service of executives who might otherwise leave, by providing an opportunity to acquire an interest in the business. Encouraging the management of business to have a proprietary interest in its successful operation will provide an important incentive to expand and improve the profit position of the

companies involved. The committee bill is designed to encourage the use of stock options for key employees without reinstituting the alleged abuses which arose with the restricted stock option provisions of prior law.

———

The requirements for incentive stock options are detailed in § 422A(b). Major corporate requirements include the following: (1) shareholder approval is required; (2) the option must be exercisable within ten years after the date of grant; (3) the option price must equal or exceed the fair market value of the stock when the option is granted; (4) the option is non-transferable by the employee except at death; (5) the option cannot be granted to a person who owns more than 10 percent of the employer corporation or its parent or subsidiary, unless the exercise price is at least 110 percent of the fair market value of the stock when the option is granted and the option expires within five years from the date of grant; (6) the employer may not, in the aggregate, grant an employee incentive stock options that are first exercisable during any one calendar year to the extent the aggregate fair market value of the stock (determined at the time the options are granted) exceeds $100,000.

At the employee level, three requirements exist. First, the employee, after exercising the option, must hold the acquired stock for at least one year. Second, the employee cannot dispose of the acquired stock within two years after the grant of the option. § 422A(a)(1). Third, the employee must have been in the continuous employ of the corporation granting the option (or a parent or subsidiary of that corporation) for the period beginning with the grant of the option and ending three months prior to the exercise of the option (unless the employee is disabled). § 422A(a)(2) and (c)(9).

If a stock option qualifies as an incentive stock option, the option recipient realizes and recognizes no income on the grant or the exercise of the option. § 421(a)(1). The entire gain (or loss) on the subsequent sale of the stock acquired on the exercise of the option is characterized as capital gain (or capital loss). However, after 1987 capital gains are taxed as ordinary income. The employer will receive no business expense deduction, as compensation to the employee, for the benefits which the employee receives through the grant or the exercise of the option. § 421(a)(2).

Problems

1. Barry, an employee of Production Corp., receives an incentive stock option from Production Corp. that meets the requirements of § 422A(a) and (b). The option price is set at $5 per share which equals the fair market value of stock when the option is granted. The option will expire in ten years. Assume further that three years after the option is granted, Barry exercises the option, and the stock is then trading at $7 per share. After

holding the acquired stock for two years, Barry sells the stock for $10 per share. What are the tax consequences to:

(a) Barry on:

i. the receipt of the option. Consider § 421(a).

ii. the exercise of the option. Consider § 421(a)(1).

iii. the sale of the stock. What is the amount of Barry's gain and can Barry treat the compensatory element of the option as capital gain? Consider §§ 422A(a)(1), 1001(a), 1001(c), 1221 and 1222.

(b) Production Corporation. Consider §§ 118(a) and 421(a)(2).

2. Should the incentive stock option provisions be repealed? Consider the advantages and disadvantages of incentive stock options. Apart from favorable tax treatment, are incentive stock options more attractive to key employees than cash or other forms of compensation? Consider the taxation of capital gains as ordinary income after 1987. Why should the recipients of incentive stock options be permitted to defer their income for tax purposes? Is the incentive stock option "equitable"? Would you favor recasting the incentive stock option provisions in the form of a direct budgetary expenditure? Reconsider pp. 44–47. Would you favor retaining the incentive stock option provisions, but subjecting such options to anti-discrimination requirements?

2. RESTRICTED STOCK: TAX CONSEQUENCES WHERE AN EMPLOYEE RECEIVES STOCK SUBJECT TO SUBSTANTIAL RESTRICTIONS

Corporations soon began to seek devices to get even greater benefits from the use of stock to compensate employees. Consider the corporate employer which—through use of an option or even without an option—sells its stock to an employee but places substantial restrictions on the employee's disposition of the stock. For example, the employee-purchaser is required to resell the stock to the corporation at his cost unless the employee remains employed by the corporation for five years. The employee, moreover, cannot transfer the stock for five years. Suppose an employee buys the stock at $1 per share and works for the corporation for five years until the stock is worth $20 per share. The employee now has absolute title to the stock and sells the stock for $20 per share hoping to get preferential capital gains treatment with respect to the transaction. However, after 1987 capital gains are taxed as ordinary income.

Questions respecting the success of this device were resolved in the Tax Reform Act of 1969 by adding § 83 and by amending §§ 402(b) and 403(c). Under § 83(a) if a person receives property in connection with the performance of services for less than its fair market value, such a person will generally be taxed at the time of the receipt of the property unless the property is both non-transferable and subject to a substantial risk of forfeiture. If the property is either transferable or not subject to a substantial risk of forfeiture, the person who performed the services in connection with the transfer of property realizes income in the year in which he received the property. The amount the recipient includes in gross income is the spread, that is, the excess of the fair market value of the property over the amount, if any, paid for the property. § 83(a). This amount is ordinary income. Section 83(c)(1) generally defines a substantial risk of forfeiture to mean that the "rights to full enjoyment of such property are conditioned upon the future performance of substantial services by any individual." Read Reg. § 1.83–3(c)(1). Examples of substantial risks of forfeiture are provided in Reg. § 1.83–3(c)(2). Property is considered transferable if it can be transferred to a third party who will hold the property free of the substantial risk of forfeiture. Read § 83(c)(2) and Reg. § 1.83–3(d). If the property transferred in connection with the performance of services is subject to a substantial risk of forfeiture and is non-transferable, the recipient need not include any amount in gross income until the property is no longer subject to a substantial risk of forfeiture or the property becomes transferable, whichever occurs first. The impact of § 83 on restricted stock is explained in the following Congressional reports.

REPORT OF SENATE FINANCE COMMITTEE, TAX REFORM ACT OF 1969

91st Cong. 1st Sess.
119–121 (1969).

PRESENT LAW

Present law does not contain any specific rules governing the tax treatment of deferred compensation arrangements known as restricted stock plans.

A restricted stock plan, generally, is an arrangement under which an employer transfers stock to one or more of his employees (often without the payment of any consideration), where the stock is subject to certain restrictions which affect its value. A restricted stock plan may cover only one employee or it may cover a number of employees. The stock transferred under a plan may be stock in the employer corporation, stock of another company—often an unrelated growth company—or even shares of a mutual fund.

The restrictions which are imposed on the stock are of various types. One type of restriction often imposed requires the employee to return the stock to the employer if he does not complete a specified additional period of employment and prohibits the employee from selling the stock in the interim. Another common type of restriction provides that the employee may not sell the stock for a specified period of time, such as a 5-year period, or until he retires.

The existing [pre-1969] Treasury regulations generally provide that no tax is imposed when the employee receives the restricted stock. Tax is deferred until the time the restrictions lapse; at that time, only the value of the stock when it was transferred to the employee (determined without regard to restrictions) is treated as compensation, provided the stock has increased in value. If the stock has decreased in value in the interim, then the lower value at the time the restrictions lapse is considered the amount of compensation. Thus, under existing regulations there is a deferral of tax with respect to this type of compensation, and any increase in the value of the stock between the time it is granted and the time when the restrictions lapse is not treated as compensation.

The existing [pre-1969] Treasury Regulations also provide that the employer is entitled to deduct compensation at the time and in the same amount as the employee is considered to have realized income.

* * *

General Reasons for Change

The [pre-1969] tax treatment of restricted stock plans is significantly more generous than the treatment specifically provided in the law for other types of similarly funded deferred compensation arrangements. An example of this disparity can be seen by comparing the situation where stock is placed in a nonexempt employees' trust rather than given directly to the employee subject to restrictions. If an employer transfers stock to a trust for an employee and the trust provides that the employee will receive the stock at the end of 5 years if he is alive at that time, the employee is treated as receiving and is taxed on the value of the stock at the time of the transfer. However, if the employer, instead of contributing the stock to the trust, gives the stock directly to the employee subject to the restriction that it cannot be sold for 5 years, then the employee's tax is deferred until the end of the 5-year period. In the latter situation, the employee actually possesses the stock, can vote it, and receives the dividends, yet his tax is deferred. In the case of the trust, he may have none of these benefits, yet he is taxed at the time the stock is transferred to the trust.

* * *

To the extent that a restricted stock plan can be considered a means of giving employees a stake in the business, the committee believes the present tax treatment of these plans is inconsistent with the specific rules provided by Congress in the case of qualified stock options, which were considered by Congress as the appropriate means by which an employee could be given a shareholder's interest in the business.

STAFF OF THE JOINT COMMITTEE ON TAXATION, GENERAL EXPLANATION OF THE TAX REFORM ACT OF 1969

91st Cong. 2d Sess.
110–112 (1970).

Explanation of [§ 83]

The Act provides that a person who receives a beneficial interest in property, such as stock, by reason of his performance of services must report as income in the taxable period in which received, the value of the property unless his interest in the property is subject to a substantial risk of forfeiture and is nontransferable. The amount included in income is the excess of the fair market value of the property over the amount paid for it. The fair market value of the property is determined without regard to any restrictions, except a restriction which by its terms will never lapse.

If the property is subject to a substantial risk of forfeiture and is nontransferable, the employee is not required to recognize any income with respect to the property until his interest in the property either becomes transferable or no longer is subject to such risk. A substantial risk of forfeiture is considered to exist where the recipient's rights to the full enjoyment of the property are conditioned upon his future performance of substantial services. The question of whether there is a substantial risk of forfeiture depends upon the facts and circumstances. An interest in property is considered to be transferable only if the rights of the transferee are not subject to any substantial risk of forfeiture. However, a property would not be considered to be subject to a substantial degree of forfeiture, for example, where the employee receives a forfeitable interest in stock, but the fact of forfeitability is not indicated on the stock certificate, and a transferee would have no notice of it.

An employee is not taxed, either when he receives forfeitable property or when he gives it to another person, if it remains subject to forfeitability in the hands of the donee. However, the employee (and not the donee) is taxable at the time the donee's rights become nonforfeitable. If the employee who has a forfeitable interest in property sells the property in an arm's length transaction, the employee is treated as realizing income at that time.

When a person is allowed to sell property only at a price determined by formula, under a provision which will never lapse, this restriction is taken into account in valuing the property. The Act provides that the formula price is deemed to be the fair market value of the property, unless established to the contrary by the Secretary or his delegate.

* * *

To add flexibility, the Act allows employees the option of treating restricted property as compensation in the year it is received, even though it is nontransferable and subject to a substantial risk of forfeiture. If this election is made, the restricted property rules do not apply, and later appreciation in the value of the property is not treated as compensation. However, if the property is later forfeited, no deduction is allowed with respect to the forfeiture. The employee must make this election not later than 30 days after the date of transfer * * *. The election may not be revoked except with the consent of the Secretary of the Treasury or his delegate.

The holding period of restricted property is deemed to begin at the first time the taxpayer's rights in the property are transferable or are not subject to a substantial risk of forfeiture, whichever occurs earlier (i.e., the time he is deemed to receive compensation).

The restricted property rules do not apply to: (1) a transaction which involves a stock option to which § 421 applies; * * * (4) the transfer of an option without a readily ascertainable fair market value; or (5) the transfer of property pursuant to the exercise of an option with a readily ascertainable fair market value at date of grant.

* * *

The Act allows the employer a deduction equal to the amount which the employee is required to recognize as income. The deduction is allowed in the employer's taxable year which includes the close of the taxable year in which the employee recognizes the income.

* * *

Problems

1. Beth, an employee of the Widget Corporation, receives 100 shares of Widget stock as a year-end bonus. The stock is publicly traded at $10 per share. The stock (1) cannot be sold or otherwise transferred (except at death) for a period of five years after receipt and (2) if Beth leaves the employ of the corporation during this five-year period, she must return the stock to the corporation. Assume that five years after the stock is transferred, it is worth $17 per share. Assume further that seven years after the stock is transferred, Beth sells the stock for $25 per share.

(a) Is § 83 applicable to this transaction? Is property transferred in connection with the performance of services? Consider § 83(a), Reg. § 1.83–3(a), (e), and (f). Is there a substantial risk of forfeiture? Consider § 83(c)(1) and Reg. § 1.83–3(c)(1), (2), and (4) Ex. 1. Is the stock nontransferable? Consider § 83(c)(2) and Reg. § 1.83–3(d). What are the tax consequences of this arrangement to Beth in the year she receives the stock, in the year the restrictions expire, and in the year she sells the stock? Consider §§ 83(a), 83(b), 1001(a) and (c), 1221, and 1222. Determine the year when Beth realizes income (or gain), the amount of income (or gain), and the character of the income (or gain)?

(b) What are the advantages and disadvantages of an election by Beth under § 83(b) to include the fair market value of the stock in gross income in the year she first receives the stock? Analyze the tax consequences to Beth in the year in which she makes the election, the year in which the restrictions expire, and the year in which she sells the stock. When does Beth realize income (or gain), what is the amount of the income (or gain), and what is the character of the income (or gain)? Consider §§ 83(b), 1001(a) and (c), 1221, and 1222. Note that under Reg. § 1.83–2(a) the basis of the stock subject to the election equals the amount, if any, paid for it, increased by the amount included in gross income on the receipt of the stock.

(c) Assume Beth elected under § 83(b). What if Beth took another job three years after receipt of the stock and returned the stock to the corporation. Can Beth take a deduction when she returns the stock to the corporation? Consider § 83(b)(1) and Reg. § 1.83–2(a).

(d) Assume the stock given to Beth was only subject to the restriction that it could not be sold for five years. Would this change Beth's tax consequences? Consider § 83(c)(2).

(e) What are the tax consequences to the Widget Corporation in each of the above situations? Consider § 83(h) and Reg. § 1.83–6(a). The deduction is allowed under § 162 if it meets the requirements of that section.

(f) What advantages and disadvantages does a transfer of restricted stock offer in comparison with the grant of an incentive stock option?

2. The Widget Corporation buys a house and transfers it to Susan, a vice president of the corporation. By contract, only Susan and her immediate family can live in the house. The corporation also prohibits Susan from selling the house and if Susan leaves the employ of the company, for any reason, including death or retirement, the house must be returned to the corporation and the corporation will pay no consideration. Although the property is subject to a substantial risk of forfeiture, is § 83 applicable? Consider Reg. § 1.83–3(a)(3).

3. Elliott was given the opportunity to buy 100 shares of stock in his company at a discount of $2 per share. The stock was then selling for $10 per share on the market. He immediately gave his employer $800 for the 100 shares of stock. The stock he acquired was subject to the restriction that it could not be sold for five years after the date of purchase and if the employee left the company for any reason (except death or disability), prior to the expiration of five years from the date he acquired the stock, he must resell the stock to the company for the same amcunt as he originally paid for the stock. Elliott elected under § 83(b) to include $200 in gross income in the year he acquired the stock, and the company deducted $200 under § 83(h). Unfortunately, Elliott was fired two years later and returned the stock to the company, receiving only the $800 he originally paid for the stock.

(a) What is the amount of Elliott's deduction, if any? Consider § 83(b)(1) and Reg. § 1.83–2(a).

(b) What happens to the deduction previously taken by the company? Consider § 1032(a) and Reg. § 1.83–6(c).

(c) Assume that on the forfeiture of the stock, Elliott did not receive the $800 he originally paid. What are the tax consequences to Elliott and the company? Consider Reg. §§ 1.83–2(a) and –6(c).

3. NONQUALIFIED STOCK OPTIONS: ADVERSE TAX CONSEQUENCES

Judicial Treatment of Nonqualified Stock Options. Stock options which do not meet the qualified stock option requirements are called nonqualified stock options. Numerous cases have arisen over a period of time involving arguments by employers that nonqualified stock options were issued solely to bind the employees to the company. Employers and employee option holders asserted that under these circumstances the stock option was not intended as compensation and consequently could not constitute ordinary income to the recipient. If this argument proved unsuccessful, litigants tried to obtain a prompt termination to the compensation aspect of the transaction and commencement of the investment portion of the transaction so that the appreciation in the value of the stock gave rise, prior to 1988, to maximum amount of preferential capital gains treatment. In large part, the timing question turns on whether a nonqualified stock option has an ascertainable market value at the date of grant.

COMMISSIONER v. LoBUE

Supreme Court of the United States, 1956.
351 U.S. 243, 76 S.Ct. 800, 100 L.Ed. 1142.

MR. JUSTICE BLACK delivered the opinion of the Court.

∗ ∗ ∗ From 1941 to 1947 LoBue was manager of the New York Sales Division of the Michigan Chemical Corporation, a producer and distributor of chemical supplies. In 1944 the company adopted a stock option plan making 10,000 shares of its common stock available for distribution to key employees at $5 per share over a 3-year period. LoBue and a number of other employees were notified that they had been tentatively chosen to be recipients of nontransferable stock options contingent upon their continued employment. LoBue's notice told him: "You may be assigned a greater or less amount of stock based entirely upon your individual results and that of the entire organization." About 6 months later he was notified that he had been definitely awarded an option to buy 150 shares of stock in recognition of his "contribution and efforts in making the operation of the Company successful." As to future allotments he was told "It is up to you to justify your participation in the plan during the next two years."

LoBue's work was so satisfactory that the company in the course of 3 years delivered to him 3 stock options covering 340 shares. He exercised all these $5 per share options in 1946 and in 1947, paying the company only $1,700 for stock having a market value when delivered of $9,930. Thus, at the end of these transactions, LoBue's employer was worth $8,230 less to its stockholders and LoBue was worth $8,230 more than before. The company deducted this sum as an expense in its 1946 and 1947 tax returns but LoBue did not report any part of it as income. Viewing the gain to LoBue as compensation for personal services the Commissioner levied a deficiency assessment against him, relying on § [61(a)]. ∗ ∗ ∗

LoBue petitioned the Tax Court to redetermine the deficiency, urging that "The said options were not intended by the Corporation or the petitioner to constitute additional compensation but were granted to permit the petitioner to acquire a proprietary interest in the Corporation and to provide him with the interest in the successful operation of the Corporation deriving from an ownership interest." The Tax Court held that LoBue had a taxable gain if the options were intended as compensation but not if the options were designed to provide him with "a proprietary interest in the business." Finding after hearings that the options were granted to give LoBue "a proprietary interest in the corporation, and not as compensation for services" the Tax Court held for LoBue. 22 T.C. 440, 443. Relying on this finding the Court of Appeals affirmed, saying: "This was a factual issue which it was the peculiar responsibility of the Tax Court to resolve. From our examination of the evidence we cannot say that its finding was clearly erroneous." 3 Cir., 223 F.2d 367, 371. * * *

We have repeatedly held that in defining "gross income" as broadly as it did in § [61(2)] Congress intended to "tax all gains except those specifically exempted." See, e.g., Commissioner of Internal Revenue v. Glenshaw Glass Co., 348 U.S. 426, 429–430, 75 S.Ct. 473, 476, 99 L.Ed. 483. The only exemption Congress provided from this very comprehensive definition of taxable income that could possibly have application here is the gift exemption of § [102(a)]. But there was not the slightest indication of the kind of detached and disinterested generosity which might evidence a "gift" in the statutory sense. These transfers of stock bore none of the earmarks of a gift. They were made by a company engaged in operating a business for profit, and the Tax Court found that the stock option plan was designed to achieve more profitable operations by providing the employees "with an incentive to promote the growth of the company by permitting them to participate in its success." 22 T.C. at page 445. Under these circumstances the Tax Court and the Court of Appeals properly refrained from treating this transfer as a gift. The company was not giving something away for nothing.

Since the employer's transfer of stock to its employee LoBue for much less than the stock's value was not a gift, it seems impossible to say that it was not compensation. The Tax Court held there was no taxable income, however, on the ground that one purpose of the employer was to confer a "proprietary interest." [7] But there is not a word in § [61(a)] which indicates that its broad coverage should be narrowed because of an employer's intention to enlist more efficient service from his employees by making them part proprietors of his business. In our view there is no statutory basis for the test established by the courts below. When assets are transferred by an employer to an employee to secure better services they are plainly compensation. It makes no difference that the compensation is paid in stock rather than in money. Section [61(a)] taxes income derived from compensation "in whatever form paid." And in another stock option case we said that § [61(a)] "is broad enough to include in taxable income any economic or financial benefit conferred on the employee as compensation, whatever the form or mode by which it is effected." Commissioner of Internal

---

7. The Tax Court noted "that in practically all such cases as the one before us, both the element of additional compensation and the granting of a proprietary interest are present." 22 T.C. at page 445. See also Geeseman v. Commissioner of Internal Revenue, 38 B.T.A. 258, 263.

Revenue v. Smith, 324 U.S. 177, 181, 65 S.Ct. 591, 593, 89 L.Ed. 830. LoBue received a very substantial economic and financial benefit from his employer prompted by the employer's desire to get better work from him. This is "compensation for personal service" within the meaning of § [61(a)].

LoBue nonetheless argues that we should treat this transaction as a mere purchase of a proprietary interest on which no taxable gain was "realized" in the year of purchase. It is true that our taxing system has ordinarily treated an arm's length purchase of property even at a bargain price as giving rise to no taxable gain in the year of purchase. See Palmer v. Commissioner of Internal Revenue, 302 U.S. 63, 69, 58 S.Ct. 67, 69, 82 L.Ed. 50. But that is not to say that when a transfer which is in reality compensation is given the form of a purchase the Government cannot tax the gain under § [61(a)]. The transaction here was unlike a mere purchase. It was not an arm's length transaction between strangers. Instead it was an arrangement by which an employer transferred valuable property to his employees in recognition of their services. We hold that LoBue realized taxable gain when he purchased the stock.

A question remains as to the time when the gain on the shares should be measured. LoBue gave his employer promissory notes for the option price of the first 300 shares but the shares were not delivered until the notes were paid in cash. The market value of the shares was lower when the notes were given than when the cash was paid. The Commissioner measured the taxable gain by the market value of the shares when the cash was paid. LoBue contends that this was wrong, and that the gain should be measured either when the options were granted or when the notes were given.

It is of course possible for the recipient of a stock option to realize an immediate taxable gain. See Commissioner of Internal Revenue v. Smith, 324 U.S. 177, 181–182, 65 S.Ct. 591, 593, 89 L.Ed. 830. The option might have a readily ascertainable market value and the recipient might be free to sell his option. But this is not such a case. These three options were not transferable and LoBue's right to buy stock under them was contingent upon his remaining an employee of the company until they were exercised. Moreover, the uniform Treasury practice since 1923 has been to measure the compensation to employees given stock options subject to contingencies of this sort by the difference between the option price and the market value of the shares at the time the option is exercised. We relied in part upon this practice in Commissioner of Internal Revenue v. Smith, 324 U.S. 177, 65 S.Ct. 591, 89 L.Ed. 830; Id., 324 U.S. 695, 65 S.Ct. 891, 89 L.Ed. 1295. And in its 1950 Act affording limited tax benefits for "restricted stock option plans" Congress adopted the same kind of standard for measurement of gains. § 130A, Internal Revenue Code of 1939 * * *. And see § 421 * * *. Under these circumstances there is no reason for departing from the Treasury practice. The taxable gain to LoBue should be measured as of the time the options were exercised and not the time they were granted.

It is possible that a bona fide delivery of a binding promissory note could mark the completion of the stock purchase and that gain should be measured as of that date. Since neither the Tax Court nor the Court of Appeals passed on this question the judgment is reversed and the case is remanded to the Court of Appeals with instructions to remand the case to the Tax Court for further proceedings.

Reversed and remanded.[8]

[MR. JUSTICE FRANKFURTER and MR. JUSTICE CLARK, concurred].

MR. JUSTICE HARLAN, whom MR. JUSTICE BURTON joins, concurring in part and dissenting in part.

In my view, the taxable event was the grant of each option, not its exercise. When the respondent received an unconditional option to buy stock at less than the market price, he received an asset of substantial and immediately realizable value, at least equal to the then-existing spread between the option price and the market price. It was at that time that the corporation conferred a benefit upon him. At the exercise of the option, the corporation "gave" the respondent nothing; it simply satisfied a previously-created legal obligation. That transaction, by which the respondent merely converted his asset from an option into stock, should be of no consequence for tax purposes. The option should be taxable as income when given, and any subsequent gain through appreciation of the stock, whether realized by sale of the option, if transferable, or by sale of the stock acquired by its exercise, is attributable to the sale of a capital asset and, if the other requirements are satisfied, should be taxed as a [preferential] capital gain.[9] Any other result makes the division of the total gains between ordinary income (compensation) and capital gain (sale of an asset) dependent

8. On remand, the Tax Court held that the income was realized when the taxpayer gave his notes, rather than when he paid them. LoBue v. Commr., 28 T.C. 1317 (1957).—Eds.

9. Commissioner of Internal Revenue v. Smith, 324 U.S. 177, 65 S.Ct. 591, 89 L.Ed. 830; Id., 324 U.S. 695, 65 S.Ct. 891, 89 L.Ed. 1295, does not require an opposite result. In that case Smith's employer, Western, had undertaken the management of a reorganized corporation, Hawley, under a contract by which Western was to receive as compensation for its managerial services a specified amount of stock in Hawley if it was successful in reducing Hawley's indebtedness by a stated amount. Western, in turn, gave Smith, who was active in the Hawley reorganization, an option to buy, at the then-existing market price, a fixed share of any Hawley stock received under the management contract. The management contract was successfully performed, and a part of the Hawley stock received by Western—the value of which was of course substantially enhanced by the performance of the contract—was sold to Smith at the option price. Under the peculiar facts of that case—more analogous to an assignment to an employee of a share in the anticipated proceeds of a contract than to the usual employee stock option plan—the Tax Court's finding that the gain that would accrue to Smith upon the successful performance of the management contract was intended as "compensation" to him for his services was no doubt amply justified. But as the Court expressly stated in upholding that finding: "It of course does not follow that in other circumstances not here present the option itself, rather than the proceeds of its exercise, could not be found to be the only intended compensation." Id., 324 U.S. at page 182, 65 S.Ct. at page 593.

solely upon the fortuitous circumstance of when the employee exercises his option.[10]

The last two options granted to respondent were unconditional and immediately exercisable, and thus present no further problems. The first option, however, was granted under somewhat different circumstances. Respondent was notified in January 1945 that 150 shares had been "allotted" to him, but he was given no right to purchase them until June 30, 1945, and his right to do so then was expressly made contingent upon his still being employed at that date. His right to purchase the first allotment of stock was thus not vested until he satisfied the stated condition, and it was not until then that he could be said to have received income, the measure of which should be the value of the option on that date.

Accordingly, while I concur in the reversal of the judgment below and in the remand to the Tax Court, I would hold the granting of the options to be the taxable events and would measure the income by the value of the options when granted.

Current Treatment of Nonqualified Stock Options: Valuation and Timing Questions. The following summarizes the current statutory tax treatment of nonqualified stock options:

STAFF OF THE JOINT COMMITTEE ON TAXATION, GENERAL EXPLANATION OF THE TAX REFORM ACT OF 1976

94th Cong. 2d Sess.
153–154 (1976).

[Under § 83] if an employee receives [a nonqualified stock] option which has a readily ascertainable fair market value at the time it is granted, this value (less the price paid for the option, if any) constitutes ordinary income to the employee at that time.[11]

On the other hand, if the option does not have a readily ascertainable fair market value at the time it is granted, the value of the option does not constitute income to the employee at that time, but would be taxable to the employee when the option is exercised. The ordinary income recognized at that time is the spread between the option price and the value of the stock (unless the stock is nontransferable and subject to a substantial risk of forfeiture).

10. Suppose two employees are given unconditional options to buy stock at $5, the current market value. The first exercises the option immediately and sells the stock a year later at $15. The second holds the option for a year, exercises it, and sells the stock immediately at $15. Admittedly the $10 gain would be taxed to the first as capital gain; under the Court's view, it would be taxed to the second as ordinary income because it is "compensation" for services. I fail to see how the gain can be any more "compensation" to one than it is to the other.

11. However, if the option is nontransferable and is also subject to a substantial risk of forfeiture, recognition of income would be postponed until one or both of these encumbrances is removed.

* * *

To illustrate these rules, consider the case of a[n] * * * option granted to a corporate executive to buy 100 shares at $10 per share. The employee exercises the option in full when the shares are selling at $15 per share in the open market. Under the act, this transaction would be treated (under § 83) as follows:

(a) At the time that the company grants the option to the executive, if the option as such has a readily ascertainable fair market value, the value of the option (less any amount which he may have paid for it) is taxable to the executive as ordinary income.

(b) If the option itself does not have a readily ascertainable market value, the executive will be subject to tax when he exercises the option and acquires the shares under option to him. In this example, the employee will be taxable on the $5 per share bargain element (or a total of $500) at the time he exercises his option. This income will be treated as compensation taxable at ordinary income rates.[12]

* * *

(c) After the executive pays tax at ordinary income rates on the compensation portion of the transaction, he would be entitled to add the amount of ordinary income recognized to his basis in the shares. Any further gain (realized when the employee sells the shares) would generally be taxable as a [preferential] capital gain.

(d) The employer corporation is entitled to a deduction (under § 83) in an amount equal to the ordinary income realized by an employee under the above rules. The employer's deduction accrues at the time that the employee is considered to have realized compensation income.

The Congress intends that in applying these rules for the future, the Service will make every reasonable effort to determine a fair market value for an option (i.e., in cases where similar property would be valued for estate tax purposes) where the employee irrevocably elects (by reporting the option as income on his tax return or in some other manner to be specified in regulations) to have the option valued at the time it is granted (particularly in the case of an option granted for a new business venture). The Congress intends that the Service will promulgate regulations and rulings setting forth as specifically as possible the criteria which will be weighed in valuing an option which the employee elects to value at the time it is granted.

---

12. As indicated above, recognition of income could be postponed if the stock is not transferable and if it is subject to a substantial risk of forfeiture. In this case, the tax is imposed (at ordinary income rates) at the time when either of these two restrictions is removed and the tax base is the excess of the fair market value of the shares at the time when either of these two restrictions is removed over the amount which the employee originally paid for the property. However, under section 83, an employee who receives stock (or other property) in his employer corporation burdened by restrictions which would free him from paying a tax at that time may, nevertheless, elect to pay tax on the bargain element existing at that time. If the employee makes this election and pays tax when he exercises the option, any later increase in value of the shares will generally be taxable to him as [preferential] capital gain (rather than compensation income) when he disposes of the shares.

Of course, merely because the option is difficult to value does not mean that the option has no value. The Congress intends that under these rules, the value of an option would be determined under all the facts and circumstances of a particular case. Among other factors that would be taken into account would be the value of the stock underlying the option (to the extent that this could be [ascertained]), the length of the option period (the longer the period, the greater the chance the underlying stock might increase in value), the earnings potential of the corporation, and the success (or lack of success) of similar ventures. Corporate assets, including patents, trade secrets and know-how would also have to be taken into account.

The Congress anticipates that under the Service's rules, certain options, such as those traded publicly, would be treated as having a readily ascertainable fair market value, regardless of whether the employee makes an election. However, the regulations could provide that in certain other cases the option would ordinarily not be valued at the time it is granted unless the employee so elects.

Problems

1. Joan, an employee of Service Corporation, receives an unrestricted and nonforfeitable option to purchase 100 shares of the publicly traded stock of the corporation. The option will expire in six months. Assume that similar options were publicly traded at $4.50 each when Joan was granted the option. The stock is currently selling for $9 per share. The option price is $5 per share. Two months after receiving the option, Joan exercises the option when the stock is trading at $13 per share. Joan sells the stock, after having held it for 3 years, for $20 per share. What are the tax consequences to Joan and the corporation on the grant of the option, the exercise of the option, and the sale of the stock? When does Joan realize income (or gain), what is the amount of the income (or gain), and what is the character of the income (or gain)? Consider § 83(e)(4); Reg. § 1.83–7(b); §§ 83(a) and (f), 1001(a) and (c), 1221, 1222, and 83(h). What if Joan sold the stock in 3 years for $7 per share?

2. Burt, an executive of Manufacturing Corporation, is allowed to purchase shares in this company at substantially under the market price. During Year 1, Burt receives an option to purchase 100 shares of the corporation's stock for $6 per share at a time when the stock has a fair market value of $10 per share. The option will expire if it is not exercised within the next five years. The option can only be exercised by the employee who was granted the option and that person must be an employee of the corporation at the time of exercise of the option. If the employee leaves the company for any reason, he forfeits the option. The stock purchased on the exercise of this option is non-forfeitable and subject to no restrictions. Assume that four years after he was granted the option, Burt exercised the option and paid $6 per share. The stock had a fair market value at the time of exercise of $17 per share. Six years after he was granted the option, Burt sells the stock for $25 per share.

(a) Assume that the option has no readily ascertainable fair market value because of the various restrictions. Read Reg. § 1.83–7(b)(2). What are the tax consequences to Burt and the corporation on the grant of the option, the exercise of the option, and the sale of the stock? Consider § 83(e)(3) which provides that the transfer of options without a readily ascertainable fair market value when granted are not subject to § 83. Read Reg. § 1.83–7(a). Consider also the LoBue case, §§ 83(a) and (f), 1001(a) and (c), 1221, 1222, and 83(h).

(b) Is an election under § 83(b) available for the year the option is granted?

Chapter 3

RECOVERY OF CAPITAL

A. THE REALIZATION REQUIREMENT

1. INTRODUCTION

Although the Supreme Court in the next case, Eisner v. Macomber, attempted to formulate a workable definition of gross income, this case is important today for its discussion of the realization concept. Fundamental to our tax system is the notion that tax consequences turn on the realization of gain or loss. The stockholder who continues to hold shares of stock which have appreciated in value is not taxed on the gain until the sale or other disposition of the shares. Similar to the individual who has sold his appreciated shares and realized gain, the taxpayer with unsold shares, which have appreciated in value, has increased his wealth. However, the Federal tax system imposes an income tax only on transactions, such as the sale of property, not on the mere enrichment of a property owner.

The realization requirement constitutes a deferral of taxation as unrealized appreciation from a prior year will be taxed in the year of sale or other disposition of the property. In addition, the deferral may be continued or transformed into a total exemption from taxation, if for example, a non-recognition provision applies on the sale of the property or the basis of the property is stepped up on the taxpayer's death (§ 1014(a)). In addition, the gain, when realized and recognized on the sale of the property, may be taxed at preferential capital gains rates (if the 1986 code is subsequently amended to restore capital gains) or in a year in which the owner is in a lower marginal tax bracket because he has less income (or in which tax rates have been reduced). If the property is transferred by gift to a donee, the gain, when realized and recognized by the donee, may be taxed at the donee's lower marginal tax rate. § 1015(a). Even if the gain is ultimately taxed to the original owner at ordinary income rates, the taxpayer receives something of value as a result of the deferral of tax. Reconsider the explanation of the concept of deferral at p. 17.

EISNER v. MACOMBER

Supreme Court of the United States, 1920.
252 U.S. 189, 40 S.Ct. 189, 64 L.Ed. 521.

MR. JUSTICE PITNEY delivered the opinion of the Court.

This case presents the question whether, by virtue of the Sixteenth Amendment, Congress has the power to tax, as income of the stockholder and without apportionment, a stock dividend made lawfully and in good faith against profits accumulated by the corporation since March 1, 1913.

It arises under the Revenue Act of September 8, 1916 (39 Stat. 756 et seq., c. 463), which, in our opinion (notwithstanding a contention of the government that will be noticed), plainly evinces the purpose of Congress to tax stock dividends as income.

The facts, in outline, are as follows:

On January 1, 1916, the Standard Oil Company of California, a corporation of that state, out of an authorized capital stock of $100,000,000, had shares of stock outstanding, par value $100 each, amounting in round figures to $50,000,000. In addition, it had surplus and undivided profits invested in plant, property, and business and required for the purposes of the corporation, amounting to about $45,000,000, of which about $20,000,000 had been earned prior to March 1, 1913, the balance thereafter. In January, 1916, in order to readjust the capitalization, the board of directors decided to issue additional shares sufficient to constitute a stock dividend of 50 per cent. of the outstanding stock, and to transfer from surplus account to capital stock account an amount equivalent to such issue. Appropriate resolutions were adopted, an amount equivalent to the par value of the proposed new stock was transferred accordingly, and the new stock duly issued against it and divided among the stockholders.

Defendant in error, being the owner of 2,200 shares of the old stock, received certificates for 1,100 additional shares, of which 18.07 per cent., or 198.77 shares, par value $19,877, were treated as representing surplus earned between March 1, 1913, and January 1, 1916. She was called upon to pay, and did pay under protest, a tax imposed under the Revenue Act of 1916, based upon a supposed income of $19,877 because of the new shares; and an appeal to the Commissioner of Internal Revenue having been disallowed, she brought action against the Collector to recover the tax. In her complaint she alleged the above facts, and contended that in imposing such a tax the Revenue Act of 1916 violated article 1, § 2, cl. 3, and article 1, § 9, cl. 4, of the Constitution of the United States, requiring direct taxes to be apportioned according to population, and that the stock dividend was not income within the meaning of the Sixteenth Amendment. * * *

* * *

The Sixteenth Amendment must be construed in connection with the taxing clauses of the original Constitution and the effect attributed to them before the amendment was adopted. In Pollock v. Farmers' Loan & Trust Co., 158 U.S. 601, 15 Sup.Ct. 912, 39 L.Ed. 1108, under the Act of August 27, 1894 (28 Stat. 509, 553, c. 349, § 27), it was held that taxes upon rents and profits of real estate and upon returns from investments of personal property were in effect direct taxes upon the property from which such income arose, imposed by reason of owner- ship; and that Congress could not impose such taxes without apportion- ing them among the states according to population, as required by article 1, § 2, cl. 3, and section 9, cl. 4, of the original Constitution.

Afterwards, and evidently in recognition of the limitation upon the taxing power of Congress thus determined, the Sixteenth Amendment was adopted, in words lucidly expressing the object to be accomplished:

"The Congress shall have power to lay and collect taxes on in- comes, from whatever source derived, without apportionment among the several states, and without regard to any census or enumeration."

As repeatedly held, this did not extend the taxing power to new subjects, but merely removed the necessity which otherwise might exist for an apportionment among the states of taxes laid on income. Brus- haber v. Union Pacific R.R. Co., 240 U.S. 1, 17–19, 36 Sup.Ct. 236, 60 L.Ed. 493; Stanton v. Baltic Mining Co., 240 U.S. 103, 112 et seq., 36 Sup.Ct. 278, 60 L.Ed. 546.

* * *

In order, therefore, that the clauses cited from article 1 of the Constitution may have proper force and effect, save only as modified by the amendment, and that the latter also may have proper effect, it becomes essential to distinguish between what is and what is not "income," as the term is there used, and to apply the distinction, as cases arise, according to truth and substance, without regard to form. Congress cannot by any definition it may adopt conclude the matter, since it cannot by legislation alter the Constitution, from which alone it derives its power to legislate, and within whose limitations alone that power can be lawfully exercised.

The fundamental relation of "capital" to "income" has been much discussed by economists, the former being likened to the tree or the land, the latter to the fruit or the crop; the former depicted as a reservoir supplied from springs, the latter as the outlet stream, to be measured by its flow during a period of time. For the present purpose we require only a clear definition of the term "in come," as used in common speech, in order to determine its meaning in the amendment, and, having formed also a correct judgment as to the nature of a stock dividend, we shall find it easy to decide the matter at issue.

After examining dictionaries in common use (Bouv.L.D.; Century Dict.), we find little to add to the succinct definition adopted in two cases arising under the Corporation Tax Act of 1909 (Stratton's Inde- pendence v. Howbert, 231 U.S. 399, 415, 34 Sup.Ct. 136, 140 [58 L.Ed.

285]; Doyle v. Mitchell Bros. Co., 247 U.S. 179, 185, 38 Sup.Ct. 467, 469 [62 L.Ed. 1054]), "Income may be defined as the gain derived from capital, from labor, or from both combined," provided it be understood to include profit gained through a sale or conversion of capital assets, to which it was applied in the Doyle Case, 247 U.S. 183, 185, 38 Sup.Ct. 467, 469 (62 L.Ed. 1054).

Brief as it is, it indicates the characteristic and distinguishing attribute of income essential for a correct solution of the present controversy. The government, although basing its argument upon the definition as quoted, placed chief emphasis upon the word "gain," which was extended to include a variety of meanings; while the significance of the next three words was either overlooked or misconceived. *"Derived—from—capital"*; "the *gain—derived—from—capital,"* etc. Here we have the essential matter: *not* a gain *accruing to* capital; not a *growth* or *increment* of value *in* the investment; but a gain, a profit, something of exchangeable value, *proceeding from* the property, *severed from* the capital, however invested or employed, and *coming in,* being *"derived"*—that is, *received* or *drawn by* the recipient (the taxpayer) for his *separate* use, benefit and disposal—*that* is income derived from property. Nothing else answers the description.

The same fundamental conception is clearly set forth in the Sixteenth Amendment—"incomes, *from* whatever *source derived"*—the essential thought being expressed with a conciseness and lucidity entirely in harmony with the form and style of the Constitution.

Can a stock dividend, considering its essential character, be brought within the definition? To answer this, regard must be had to the nature of a corporation and the stockholder's relation to it. We refer, of course, to a corporation such as the one in the case at bar, organized for profit, and having a capital stock divided into shares to which a nominal or par value is attributed.

*   *   *

For bookkeeping purposes, the company acknowledges a liability in form to the stockholders equivalent to the aggregate par value of their stock, evidenced by a "capital stock account." If profits have been made and not divided they create additional bookkeeping liabilities under the head of "profit and loss," "undivided profits," "surplus account," or the like. None of these, however, gives to the stockholders as a body, much less to any one of them, either a claim against the going concern for any particular sum of money, or a right to any particular portion of the assets or any share in them unless or until the directors conclude that dividends shall be made and a part of the company's assets segregated from the common fund for the purpose. The dividend normally is payable in money, under exceptional circumstances in some other divisible property; and when so paid, then only (excluding, of course, a possible advantageous sale of his stock or winding-up of the company) does the stockholder realize a profit or gain which becomes his separate property, and thus derive income from the capital that he or his predecessor has invested.

* * *

[A stock dividend] however, is merely bookkeeping that does not affect the aggregate assets of the corporation or its outstanding liabilities; it affects only the form, not the essence, of the "liability" acknowledged by the corporation to its own shareholders, and this through a readjustment of accounts on one side of the balance sheet only, increasing "capital stock" at the expense of "surplus"; it does not alter the pre-existing proportionate interest of any stockholder or increase the intrinsic value of his holding or of the aggregate holdings of the other stockholders as they stood before. The new certificates simply increase the number of the shares, with consequent dilution of the value of each share.

A "stock dividend" shows that the company's accumulated profits have been capitalized, instead of distributed to the stockholders or retained as surplus available for distribution in money or in kind should opportunity offer. Far from being a realization of profits of the stockholder, it tends rather to postpone such realization, in that the fund represented by the new stock has been transferred from surplus to capital, and no longer is available for actual distribution.

The essential and controlling fact is that the stockholder has received nothing out of the company's assets for his separate use and benefit; on the contrary, every dollar of his original investment, together with whatever accretions and accumulations have resulted from employment of his money and that of the other stockholders in the business of the company, still remains the property of the company, and subject to business risks which may result in wiping out the entire investment. Having regard to the very truth of the matter, to substance and not to form, he has received nothing that answers the definition of income within the meaning of the Sixteenth Amendment.

* * *

We are clear that not only does a stock dividend really take nothing from the property of the corporation and add nothing to that of the shareholder, but that the antecedent accumulation of profits evidenced thereby, while indicating that the shareholder is the richer because of an increase of his capital, at the same time shows he has not realized or received any income in the transaction.

It is said that a stockholder may sell the new shares acquired in the stock dividend; and so he may, if he can find a buyer. It is equally true that if he does sell, and in doing so realizes a profit, such profit, like any other, is income, and so far as it may have arisen since the Sixteenth Amendment is taxable by Congress without apportionment. The same would be true were he to sell some of his original shares at a profit. But if a shareholder sells dividend stock he necessarily disposes of a part of his capital interest, just as if he should sell a part of his old stock, either before or after the dividend. What he retains no longer entitles him to the same proportion of future dividends as before the sale. His part in the control of the company likewise is diminished. Thus, if one holding $60,000 out of a total $100,000 of the capital stock of a corporation should receive in common with other stockholders a 50 per cent. stock dividend, and should sell his part, he thereby would be reduced from a majority to a minority stockholder, having six-fifteenths instead of six-tenths of the total stock outstanding. A corresponding and proportionate decrease in capital interest and in voting power would befall a minority holder should he sell dividend stock; it being in the nature of things impossible for one to dispose of any part of such an issue without a proportionate disturbance of the distribution of the entire capital stock, and a like diminution of the seller's comparative voting power—that "right preservative of rights" in the control of a corporation. Yet, without selling, the shareholder, unless possessed of other resources, has not the wherewithal to pay an income tax upon the dividend stock. Nothing could more clearly show that to tax a stock dividend is to tax a capital increase, and not income, than this demonstration that in the nature of things it requires conversion of capital in order to pay the tax.

* * *

Conceding that the mere issue of a stock dividend makes the recipient no richer than before, the government nevertheless contends that the new certificates measure the extent to which the gains accumulated by the corporation have made him the richer. There are two insuperable difficulties with this: In the first place, it would depend upon how long he had held the stock whether the stock dividend indicated the extent to which he had been enriched by the operations of the company; unless he had held it throughout such operations the measure would not hold true. Secondly, and more important for present purposes, enrichment through increase in value of capital investment is not income in any proper meaning of the term.

* * *

It is said there is no difference in principle between a simple stock dividend and a case where stockholders use money received as cash dividends to purchase additional stock contemporaneously issued by the corporation. But an actual cash dividend, with a real option to the stockholder either to keep the money for his own or to reinvest it in new shares, would be as far removed as possible from a true stock dividend, such as the one we have under consideration, where nothing of value is taken from the company's assets and transferred to the individual ownership of the several stockholders and thereby subjected to their disposal.

The government's reliance upon the supposed analogy between a dividend of the corporation's own shares and one made by distributing shares owned by it in the stock of another company, calls for no comment beyond the statement that the latter distributes assets of the company among the shareholders while the former does not, and for no citation of authority except Peabody v. Eisner, 247 U.S. 347, 349, 350, 38 Sup.Ct. 546, 62 L.Ed. 1152.

* * *

Thus, from every point of view we are brought irresistibly to the conclusion that neither under the Sixteenth Amendment nor otherwise has Congress power to tax without apportionment a true stock dividend made lawfully and in good faith, or the accumulated profits behind it, as income of the stockholder. The Revenue Act of 1916, in so far as it imposes a tax upon the stockholder because of such dividend, contravenes the provisions of article 1, § 2, cl. 3, and article 1, § 9, cl. 4, of the Constitution, and to this extent is invalid, notwithstanding the Sixteenth Amendment.

Judgment affirmed.

MR. JUSTICE HOLMES, dissenting.

I think that Towne v. Eisner, 245 U.S. 418, 38 Sup.Ct. 158, 62 L.Ed. 372, was right in its reasoning and result and that on sound principles the stock dividend was not income. But it was clearly intimated in that case that the construction of the statute then before the Court might be different from that of the Constitution. 245 U.S. 425, 38 Sup.Ct. 158, 62 L.Ed. 372. I think that the word "incomes" in the Sixteenth Amendment should be read in "a sense most obvious to the common understanding at the time of its adoption." Bishop v. State, 149 Ind. 223, 230, 48 N.E. 1038, 1040; State v. Butler, 70 Fla. 102, 133, 69 South. 771. For it was for public adoption that it was proposed. McCulloch v. Maryland, 4 Wheat. 316, 407, 4 L.Ed. 579. The known purpose of this Amendment was to get rid of nice questions as to what might be direct taxes, and I cannot doubt that most people not lawyers would suppose when they voted for it that they put a question like the present to rest. I am of opinion that the Amendment justifies the tax. See Tax Commissioner v. Putnam, 227 Mass. 522, 532, 533, 116 N.E. 904.

MR. JUSTICE DAY concurs in this opinion.

MR. JUSTICE BRANDEIS delivered the following [dissenting] opinion:

Financiers, with the aid of lawyers, devised long ago two different methods by which a corporation can, without increasing its indebtedness, keep for corporate purposes accumulated profits, and yet, in effect, distribute these profits among its stockholders. One method is a simple one. The capital stock is increased; the new stock is paid up with the accumulated profits; and the new shares of paid-up stock are then distributed among the stockholders pro rata as a dividend. If the stockholder prefers ready money to increasing his holding of the stock in the company, he sells the new stock received as a dividend. The other method is slightly more complicated. Arrangements are made for an increase of stock to be offered to stockholders pro rata at par, and, at the same time, for the payment of a cash dividend equal to the amount which the stockholder will be required to pay to the company, if he avails himself of the right to subscribe for his pro rata of the new

stock. If the stockholder takes the new stock, as is expected, he may
endorse the dividend check received to the corporation and thus pay for
the new stock. In order to ensure that all the new stock so offered will
be taken, the price at which it is offered is fixed far below what it is
believed will be its market value. If the stockholder prefers ready
money to an increase of his holdings of stock, he may sell his right to
take new stock pro rata, which is evidenced by an assignable instrument. In that event the purchaser of the rights repays to the corporation, as the subscription price of the new stock, an amount equal to that
which it had paid as a cash dividend to the stockholder.

Both of these methods of retaining accumulated profits while in
effect distributing them as a dividend had been in common use in the
United States for many years prior to the adoption of the Sixteenth
Amendment. They were recognized equivalents. Whether a particular
corporation employed one or the other method was determined sometimes by requirements of the law under which the corporation was
organized; sometimes it was determined by preferences of the individual officials of the corporation; and sometimes by stock market conditions. Whichever method was employed the resultant distribution of
the new stock was commonly referred to as a stock dividend. * * *

* * *

Hitherto powers conferred upon Congress by the Constitution have
been liberally construed, and have been held to extend to every means
appropriate to attain the end sought. In determining the scope of the
power the substance of the transaction, not its form has been regarded.
Martin v. Hunter, 1 Wheat. 304, 326, 4 L.Ed. 97; McCulloch v. Maryland, 4 Wheat. 316, 407, 415, 4 L.Ed. 579; Brown v. Maryland, 12
Wheat. 419, 446, 6 L.Ed. 678. Is there anything in the phraseology of
the Sixteenth Amendment or in the nature of corporate dividends
which should lead to a departure from these rules of construction and
compel this court to hold, that Congress is powerless to prevent a result
so extraordinary as that here contended for by the stockholder?

First. The term "income," when applied to the investment of the
stockholder in a corporation, had, before the adoption of the Sixteenth
Amendment, been commonly understood to mean the returns from
time to time received by the stockholder from gains or earnings of the
corporation. A dividend received by a stockholder from a corporation
may be either in distribution of capital assets or in distribution of
profits. Whether it is the one or the other is in no way affected by the
medium in which it is paid, nor by the method or means through which
the particular thing distributed as a dividend was procured. If the
dividend is declared payable in cash, the money with which to pay it is
ordinarily taken from surplus cash in the treasury. But (if there are
profits legally available for distribution and the law under which the
company was incorporated so permits) the company may raise the
money by discounting negotiable paper; or by selling bonds, scrip or
stock of another corporation then in the treasury; or by selling its own

bonds, scrip or stock then in the treasury; or by selling its own bonds, scrip or stock issued expressly for that purpose. How the money shall be raised is wholly a matter of financial management. The manner in which it is raised in no way affects the question whether the dividend received by the stockholder is income or capital; nor can it conceivably affect the question whether it is taxable as income.

Likewise whether a dividend declared payable from profits shall be paid in cash or in some other medium is also wholly a matter of financial management. If some other medium is decided upon, it is also wholly a question of financial management whether the distribution shall be, for instance, in bonds, scrip or stock of another corporation or in issues of its own. And if the dividend is paid in its own issues, why should there be a difference in result dependent upon whether the distribution was made from such securities then in the treasury or from others to be created and issued by the company expressly for that purpose? So far as the distribution may be made from its own issues of bonds, or preferred stock created expressly for the purpose, it clearly would make no difference in the decision of the question whether the dividend was a distribution of profits, that the securities had to be created expressly for the purpose of distribution. If a dividend paid in securities of that nature represents a distribution of profits Congress may, of course, tax it as income of the stockholder. Is the result different where the security distributed is common stock?

Suppose that a corporation having power to buy and sell its own stock, purchases, in the interval between its regular dividend dates, with moneys derived from current profits, some of its own common stock as a temporary investment, intending at the time of purchase to sell it before the next dividend date and to use the proceeds in paying dividends, but later, deeming it inadvisable either to sell this stock or to raise by borrowing the money necessary to pay the regular dividend in cash, declares a dividend payable in this stock; can any one doubt that in such a case the dividend in common stock would be income of the stockholder and constitutionally taxable as such? See Green v. Bissell, 79 Conn. 547, 65 Atl. 1056. And would it not likewise be income of the stockholder subject to taxation if the purpose of the company in buying the stock so distributed had been from the beginning to take it off the market and distribute it among the stockholders as a dividend, and the company actually did so? And proceeding a short step further: Suppose that a corporation decided to capitalize some of its accumulated profits by creating additional common stock and selling the same to raise working capital, but after the stock has been issued and certificates therefor are delivered to the bankers for sale, general financial conditions make it undesirable to market the stock and the company concludes that it is wiser to husband, for working capital, the cash which it had intended to use in paying stockholders a dividend, and, instead, to pay the dividend in the common stock which it had planned to sell; would not the stock so distributed be a distribution of profits—

and hence, when received, be income of the stockholder and taxable as such? If this be conceded, why should it not be equally income of the stockholder, and taxable as such, if the common stock created by capitalizing profits, had been originally created for the express purpose of being distributed as a dividend to the stockholder who afterwards received it?

Second. It has been said that a dividend payable in bonds or preferred stock created for the purpose of distributing profits may be income and taxable as such, but that the case is different where the distribution is in common stock created for that purpose. Various reasons are assigned for making this distinction. One is that the proportion of the stockholder's ownership to the aggregate number of the shares of the company is not changed by the distribution. But that is equally true where the dividend is paid in its bonds or in its preferred stock. Furthermore, neither maintenance nor change in the proportionate ownership of a stockholder in a corporation has any bearing upon the question here involved. Another reason assigned is that the value of the old stock held is reduced approximately by the value of the new stock received, so that the stockholder after receipt of the stock dividend has no more than he had before it was paid. That is equally true whether the dividend be paid in cash or in other property, for instance, bonds, scrip or preferred stock of the company. The payment from profits of a large cash dividend, and even a small one, customarily lowers the then market value of stock because the undivided property represented by each share has been correspondingly reduced. The argument which appears to be most strongly urged for the stockholders is, that when a stock dividend is made, no portion of the assets of the company is thereby segregated for the stockholder. But does the issue of new bonds or of preferred stock created for use as a dividend result in any segregation of assets for the stockholder? In each case he receives a piece of paper which entitles him to certain rights in the undivided property. Clearly segregation of assets in a physical sense is not an essential of income. The year's gains of a partner is taxable as income, although there, likewise, no segregation of his share in the gains from that of his partners is had.

* * *

Sixth. If stock dividends representing profits are held exempt from taxation under the Sixteenth Amendment, the owners of the most successful businesses in America will, as the facts in this case illustrate, be able to escape taxation on a large part of what is actually their income. So far as their profits are represented by stock received as dividends they will pay these taxes not upon their income but only upon the income of their income. That such a result was intended by the people of the United States when adopting the Sixteenth Amendment is inconceivable. Our sole duty is to ascertain their intent as therein expressed. In terse, comprehensive language befitting the Constitution, they empowered Congress "to lay and collect taxes on incomes from whatever source derived." They intended to include thereby everything which by reasonable understanding can fairly be regarded as income. That stock dividends representing profits are so regarded, not only by the plain people, but by investors and financiers, and by most of the courts of the country, is shown beyond peradventure, by their acts and by their utterances. It seems to me clear, therefore, that Congress possesses the power which it exercised to make dividends representing profits, taxable as income, whether the medium in which the dividend is paid be cash or stock, and that it may define, as it has done, what dividends representing profits shall be deemed income. It surely is not clear that the enactment exceeds the power granted by the Sixteenth Amendment. * * *

MR. JUSTICE CLARKE concurs in this opinion.

The Supreme Court failed in Eisner v. Macomber to explain why gain must be severed from capital. Subsequent cases have eroded the severance requirement. Other appropriate points in time, as illustrated by Helvering v. Bruun, (p. 118) can be used to include the gain in gross income. The strict severance interpretation was further eroded when the Supreme Court in Helvering v. Horst (p. 713) described it as a rule "founded on administrative convenience." This is quite a change from Justice Pitney's view that severance was a constitutional mandate. The following excerpt sums up the impact of the realization concept discussed in Eisner v. Macomber:

> The cornerstone was laid, but the Court proceeded no further with its task of building upon it a concept of income. Each succeeding opinion paid its respects to the principle of realization which was the core of the Court's pronouncement in Eisner v. Macomber, but went on to a result which never matched the rigor of that pronouncement.[1]

You should be aware that subsequent cases (e.g. United States v. Davis, p. 632 and Farid-es-Sultanah v. Commissioner, p. 282) found a realization in situations not normally perceived as giving rise to a benefit in hand. As you proceed through these materials consider, as one commentator suggested, "whether income exists in a particular case should turn on a much simpler question, specifically, whether there exists an occasion on which it is just and socially desirable to impose liability for an income tax * * *."[2]

Questions

1. Compare and contrast the differences between the definition of income in Eisner v. Macomber and the Haig-Simons definition (p. 54). How are realization and the source of income treated?

2. Does Eisner v. Macomber stand for the proposition that Congress could not constitutionally tax unrealized appreciation? If Congress were to

---

1. Surrey, The Supreme Court and the Federal Income Tax: Some Implications of the Recent Decisions, 35 Ill.L.Rev. 779, 782 (1941).

2. Lowndes, Current Conceptions of Taxable Income, 25 Ohio St.L.J. 151, 182 (1964).

tax unrealized appreciation, could all increases in value be taxed? Assume a share of stock increases in value not only because of additional retained earnings, but also because of a projected rise in the corporation's future earnings?

Problems

1. (a) On January 1 of Year 1, A and B each invest $5,000 in a newly-formed corporation and each receives a one-half interest in the corporation, each one-half interest represented by 100 shares of stock. Should the contribution of capital by the shareholders result in income to the corporation? The corporation exchanges a capital interest and a share of potential earnings for the capital it receives. Consider § 118(a).

(b) During Year 1, the corporation generates taxable income of $2,000 and pays $300 in Federal income taxes on this income. See § 11. At the end of Year 1, the value of the corporation's assets equals $11,700. Determine the income tax consequences to the shareholders in each of the following situations:

(i) On January 1 of Year 2, the corporation distributes $850 cash to each shareholder as a dividend (§ 316(a)). How does the payment of $1,700 in dividends affect the value of the 200 shares of stock? Is the dividend included in the gross income of the shareholders? Consider §§ 301(c)(1) and 61(a)(7). Can any portion of the cash dividend be treated as a return of a shareholder's basis in his stock? Does § 1001(a) apply to the payment of a cash dividend? Why are the $2,000 in corporate earnings taxed twice?

(ii) The corporation does not pay a cash dividend. Instead, the corporation retains the $1,700 in earnings to purchase additional assets for expansion. The shareholder intends to sell his entire interest in the corporation in Year 2. How much could the shareholder sell each share of stock for? Assume he sells his stock in Year 2. What are the tax consequences to the selling shareholder? When is gain realized? What is the amount of the gain? What is the character of the gain? What are the advantages of a corporation retaining its earnings rather than paying out its earnings as a dividend? If a shareholder gives stock to his child as a gift, is it possible for increases in the value of the shares, when sold and eventually taxed, to be taxed at his child's lower rates? Consider § 1015(a). Can this deferral of unrealized appreciation become an eventual exclusion from taxation? Consider § 1014(a).

(iii) The corporation does not pay a cash dividend. Instead, the corporation declares a stock dividend on January 1 of Year 2 and each shareholder receives an additional 17 shares of stock. What is the value of a single share of stock both before and after the stock dividend? What is the value of each shareholder's one-half interest both before and after the stock dividend? What are the tax consequences of the payment of the stock dividend to each shareholder. Consider the opinion in Eisner v. Macomber, §§ 305(a) and 1001(a). Should a stock dividend be regarded as a cash dividend followed by the reinvestment of the cash in additional shares?

What are the tax consequences if each shareholder sells during Year 2:

  (a) only the 17 shares received as a stock dividend; or

  (b) only the original 100 shares; or

  (c) all 117 shares in the corporation.

In each situation what is the amount of the gain? What is the character of the gain?

Consider §§ 1001(a), 1001(b), 1012, 307(a), 1221, 1222 and 1223(5). What are the tax consequences of a shareholder having a basis in the stock received as a dividend? Is § 307(a), which requires that a portion of the basis of the old stock be allocated to the basis of the new stock, consistent with Eisner v. Macomber? Is § 1223(5), which allows the shareholder to tack (add on) the holding period of the old stock, consistent with Eisner v. Macomber?

  (iv) The corporation does not pay a cash dividend. Instead, the corporation declares a stock dividend on January 1 of Year 2 and each shareholder receives an additional 17 shares of stock during Year 2. Each shareholder now holds an aggregate of 117 shares. On January 1 of Year 3, the corporation purchases 17 shares from each shareholder for $850 in cash. Should the shareholders be able to cast this sale of their stock (otherwise known as a redemption) under § 1001(a) and thereby obtain a return of basis (capital)? What is the purpose of § 302(a) and (b)?

2. What are the differences between unrealized appreciation on an asset and imputed income, for example, the imputed rental value of an owner-occupied residence? Assume an individual's residence appreciates in value thereby increasing its imputed rental value. Are any of these increases in value ever subject to taxation? Reconsider Problem on p. 14 and Problem 3 at p. 69.

3. If the corporation had not declared a stock dividend, it is clear that Eisner v. Macomber would not require a shareholder to report any increase in the value of his shares as gross income. Should the unrealized gain on an asset (the change in value between the beginning and the end of a taxable year) be taxed as income on an annual basis? Should unrealized gains on the marketable shares of publicly held corporations be taxed, periodically, for example, once every year? Consider the advantage of better resource allocation. What are the disadvantages? Is it practical to make annual valuations of nonmarketable securities and real estate? Would the taxation of unrealized gains on the marketable shares of publicly held corporations deter a company from going public or force publicly held corporations to "go private"? Consider the impact on a controlling shareholder who might be forced to sell shares to pay the tax. How significant is the absence of cash to pay the tax on unrealized appreciation?

2. AMPLIFICATION OF THE REALIZATION REQUIREMENT: LEASEHOLD TERMINATION

HELVERING v. BRUUN

Supreme Court of the United States, 1940.
309 U.S. 461, 60 S.Ct. 631, 84 L.Ed. 864.

MR. JUSTICE ROBERTS delivered the opinion of the Court.

The controversy had its origin in the petitioner's assertion that the respondent realized taxable gain from the forfeiture of a leasehold, the tenant having erected a new building upon the premises. The court below held that no income had been realized. Inconsistency of the decisions on the subject led us to grant certiorari.

The Board of Tax Appeals made no independent findings. The cause was submitted upon a stipulation of facts. From this it appears that on July 1, 1915, the respondent, as owner, leased a lot of land and the building thereon for a term of ninety-nine years.

The lease provided that the lessee might, at any time, upon giving bond to secure rentals accruing in the two ensuing years, remove or tear down any building on the land, provided that no building should be removed or torn down after the lease became forfeited, or during the last three and one-half years of the term. The lessee was to surrender the land, upon termination of the lease, with all buildings and improvements thereon.

In 1929 the tenant demolished and removed the existing building and constructed a new one which had a useful life of not more than fifty years. July 1, 1933, the lease was cancelled for default in payment of rent and taxes and the respondent regained possession of the land and building.

The parties stipulated "that as at said date, July 1, 1933, the building which had been erected upon said premises by the lessee had a fair market value of $64,245.68 and that the unamortized cost of the old building, which was removed from the premises in 1929 to make way for the new building, was $12,811.43, thus leaving a net fair market value as at July 1, 1933, of $51,434.25, for the aforesaid new building erected upon the premises by the lessee."

On the basis of these facts, the petitioner determined that in 1933 the respondent realized a net gain of $51,434.25. The Board overruled his determination and the Circuit Court of Appeals affirmed the Board's decision.

The course of administrative practice and judicial decision in respect of the question presented has not been uniform. In 1917 the Treasury ruled that the adjusted value of improvements installed upon leased premises is income to the lessor upon the termination of the lease. The ruling was incorporated in two succeeding editions of the Treasury Regulations. In 1919 the Circuit Court of Appeals for the Ninth Circuit held in Miller v. Gearin, 258 F. 225, that the regulation was invalid as the gain, if taxable at all, must be taxed as of the year when the improvements were completed.

The regulations were accordingly amended to impose a tax upon the gain in the year of completion of the improvements, measured by their anticipated value at the termination of the lease and discounted for the duration of the lease. Subsequently the regulations permitted the lessor to spread the depreciated value of the improvements over the remaining life of the lease, reporting an aliquot part each year, with provision that, upon premature termination, a tax should be imposed upon the excess of the then value of the improvements over the amount theretofore returned.

In 1935 the Circuit Court of Appeals for the Second Circuit decided in Hewitt Realty Co. v. Commissioner, 76 F.2d 880, that a landlord received no taxable income in a year, during the term of the lease, in which his tenant erected a building on the leased land. The court, while recognizing that the lessor need not receive money to be taxable, based its decision that no taxable gain was realized in that case on the fact that the improvement was not portable or detachable from the land, and if removed would be worthless except as bricks, iron, and mortar. It said, 76 F.2d at page 884: "The question as we view it is whether the value received is embodied in something separately disposable, or whether it is so merged in the land as to become financially a part of it, something which, though it increases its value, has no value of its own when torn away."

This decision invalidated the regulations then in force.

In 1938 this court decided M.E. Blatt Co. v. United States, 305 U.S. 267, 59 S.Ct. 186, 83 L.Ed. 167. There, in connection with the execution of a lease, landlord and tenant mutually agreed that each should make certain improvements to the demised premises and that those made by the tenant should become and remain the property of the landlord. The Commissioner valued the improvements as of the date they were made, allowed depreciation thereon to the termination of the leasehold, divided the depreciated value by the number of years the lease had to run, and found the landlord taxable for each year's aliquot portion thereof. His action was sustained by the Court of Claims. The judgment was reversed on the ground that the added value could not be considered rental accruing over the period of the lease; that the facts found by the Court of Claims did not support the conclusion of the Commissioner as to the value to be attributed to the improvements after a use throughout the term of the lease; and that, in the circumstances disclosed, any enhancement in the value of the realty in the tax year was not income realized by the lessor within the Revenue Act.

The circumstances of the instant case differentiate it from the Blatt and Hewitt cases; but the petitioner's contention that gain was realized when the respondent, through forfeiture of the lease, obtained untrammeled title, possession and control of the premises, with the added increment of value added by the new building, runs counter to the decision in the Miller case and to the reasoning in the Hewitt case.

The respondent insists that the realty,—a capital asset at the date of the execution of the lease,—remained such throughout the term and after its expiration; that improvements affixed to the soil became part of the realty indistinguishably blended in the capital asset; that such improvements cannot be separately valued or treated as received in exchange for the improvements which were on the land at the date of the execution of the lease; that they are, therefore, in the same category as improvements added by the respondent to his land, or accruals of value due to extraneous and adventitious circumstances. Such added value, it is argued, can be considered capital gain only upon the owner's disposition of the asset. The position is that the economic gain consequent upon the enhanced value of the recaptured asset is not gain derived from capital or realized within the meaning of the Sixteenth Amendment and may not, therefore, be taxed without apportionment.

We hold that the petitioner was right in assessing the gain as realized in 1933.

We might rest our decision upon the narrow issue presented by the terms of the stipulation. It does not appear what kind of a building was erected by the tenant or whether the building was readily removable from the land. It is not stated whether the difference in the value between the building removed and that erected in its place accurately reflects an increase in the value of land and building considered as a single estate in land. On the facts stipulated, without more, we should not be warranted in holding that the presumption of the correctness of the Commissioner's determination has been overborne.

The respondent insists, however, that the stipulation was intended to assert that the sum of $51,434.25 was the measure of the resulting enhancement in value of the real estate at the date of the cancellation of the lease. The petitioner seems not to contest this view. Even upon this assumption we think that gain in the amount named was realized by the respondent in the year of repossession.

The respondent can not successfully contend that the definition of gross income in [§ 61(a)] is not broad enough to embrace the gain in question. That definition follows closely the Sixteenth Amendment. Essentially the respondent's position is that the Amendment does not permit the taxation of such gain without apportionment amongst the states. He relies upon what was said in Hewitt Realty Co. v. Commissioner, supra, and upon expressions found in the decisions of this court dealing with the taxability of stock dividends to the effect that gain derived from capital must be something of exchangeable value proceeding from property, severed from the capital, however invested or employed, and received by the recipient for his separate use, benefit, and disposal.[3] He emphasizes the necessity that the gain be separate from the capital and separately disposable. These expressions, however, were used to clarify the distinction between an ordinary dividend and a stock dividend. They were meant to show that in the case of a stock dividend, the stockholder's interest in the corporate assets after receipt of the dividend was the same as and inseverable from that which he owned before the dividend was declared. We think they are not controlling here.

While it is true that economic gain is not always taxable as income, it is settled that the realization of gain need not be in cash derived from the sale of an asset. Gain may occur as a result of exchange of property, payment of the taxpayer's indebtedness, relief from a liability, or other profit realized from the completion of a transaction. The fact that the gain is a portion of the value of property received by the taxpayer in the transaction does not negative its realization.

Here, as a result of a business transaction, the respondent received back his land with a new building on it, which added an ascertainable amount to its value. It is not necessary to recognition of taxable gain that he should be able to sever the improvement begetting the gain from his original capital. If that were necessary, no income could arise from the exchange of property; whereas such gain has always been recognized as realized taxable gain.

Judgment reversed.

THE CHIEF JUSTICE concurs in the result in view of the terms of the stipulation of facts.

Question

Before cancelling the lease for nonpayment of rent and taxes, what result if the taxpayer-lessor in Bruun, in order to avoid a default on the lease, reduced or postponed the rentals?

To overcome the problem of telescoping a large amount of income into one year and the payment of an amount of tax that might require the sale, for example, of the land and the building on the land, Congress reversed the result in Helvering v. Bruun. Section 109, a nonrecognition provision, excludes from the income of the lessor of real property on the termination of a lease, the value of the leasehold improvements made by the lessee, unless the improvements constitute a payment in kind of lease rentals. As a corollary, § 1019 excludes from the lessor's basis the amount of income which is realized, but not recognized, on the termination of the lease under § 109. As a result of the nonrecognition and basis exclusion provisions, the lessor's depreciation (or accelerated cost recovery) deductions [4] for the building or other improvements made

3. See Eisner v. Macomber, 252 U.S. 189, 207, 40 S.Ct. 189, 193, 64 L.Ed. 521 * * *.

4. Depreciation is a deduction from gross income under § 167 reflecting the cost to the taxpayer of using, over a period

by the lessee would, therefore, be lower than if the value of the building or the improvements had been included in the lessor's gross income and added to the lessor's adjusted basis. The recognition of the income from the leasehold improvement occurs when the lessor sells or otherwise disposes of the property.

If a tenant is required to make improvements which are a substitute for rent he would otherwise pay, the parenthetical phrase "(other than rent)" found in § 109 requires that the landlord report the present value of the improvement as income in the year the improvement is made even though the landlord does not come into possession until a subsequent point in time. Reg. § 1.61–8(c) states that this is a question of the intent of the parties based on the surrounding circumstances or the lease terms.

Problems

1. Larry purchased land in Year 1 for $10,000. He rents the land for three years to Tom, who built a $3,000 leasehold improvement on the land. When the lease expired in Year 4, the land was worth $10,000 and the improvement was worth $2,000. In Year 6, Larry sells the property for $11,000, allocating $10,000 to the land and $1,000 to the improvement.

    (a) What are the tax consequences to Larry under the Bruun case in Years 1, 4, and 6?

    (b) What are the tax consequences to Larry under §§ 109 and 1019 in Year 1, 4, and 6? What are the advantages and disadvantages to Larry of the present statutory arrangement in contrast to the result achieved by the Supreme Court in Bruun? Does the taxation of the lessee's improvements on the lessor's property concern the exemption from or the deferral of taxation? If Larry died in Year 5, what is the impact of § 1014(a)?

    (c) What are the tax consequences to the tenant, Tom, of the leasehold improvement he paid for? Is it deductible? Consider § 162(a). When is it deductible? Consider § 263.

2. Linda owns unimproved land and leases it to Todd who uses it for business purposes.

    (a) What are the tax consequences to Linda and Todd if, as part of the lease, Todd pays Linda an annual rental of $5,000 and pays $1,000 to the town, representing the yearly property taxes on the property? Consider Reg. §§ 1.61–8(c), 1.162–11(a) and §§ 162(a), 164(a). Reconsider the Old Colony case (p. 49).

    (b) Assume Todd uses the vacant land as a parking lot. The lease, which will terminate in five years, provides that (1) the tenant will bear the cost of any improvements and (2) on the termination of the

of years, an asset in his trade or business or for the production of income. The Accelerated Cost Recovery System (§ 168) generates a deduction to permit the accelerated recovery of the cost of a taxable asset subject to the allowance for depreciation which is used in the taxpayer's trade or business or held for the production of year. Depreciation and the Accelerated Cost Recovery System are considered in detail in Chapter 9.

lease, any improvements become the property of the landlord. Todd constructs and places in service a parking ramp on the land during year 1 at a cost of $31,500. (Note: The present discounted value of the right to receive a $31,500 leasehold improvement in five years is $19,559, using the 10 percent tables.) Todd estimates that over the next five years the ramp will increase parking revenues by $15,000 per year. Consider the tax consequences of the rental payment and the leasehold improvement to both Linda and Tom in the following situations:

i. Todd continues to pay the $6,000 annual rental during the lease term. Consider §§ 109, 1019, 162, and 263. (Note: If an improvement does not constitute a rent substitute, a lessee will be able to recover the cost of the improvement through equal, annual deductions of $1,000 over 31.5 years. § 168(i)(8). On the termination of the lease the lessee computes his loss by reference to the $26,500 adjusted basis of the improvement at that time.

ii. Linda reduces the annual rental to $1,000. Will the leasehold improvement be included in Linda's income? Reg. § 1.109–1(a) provides that the exclusion under § 109 does not apply to lessee improvements intended to be in lieu of rent. If the leasehold improvement is includible in Linda's income, what amount is includible in income and when is it includible in income? Is the amount included the cost of the improvement ($31,500) or the present discounted value of the improvement ($19,559, assuming a 10 percent interest rate)? Consider § 1.61–8(c). If the leasehold improvement is includible in Linda's income, what is the impact on Linda's basis for the property? Consider §§ 1019 and 1016(a)(1). Is the leasehold improvement deductible by Todd? Consider § 168(i)(8). What amount is deductible? When is it deductible?

B. RECOVERY OF DAMAGES FOR PERSONAL INJURY

1. STATUTORY EXCLUSION

Under § 104(a)(2), a taxpayer excludes from gross income any damages received, whether by suit or agreement, as compensation for personal injuries or sickness caused by another's tortious conduct, except if those amounts have been deducted in prior years under § 213. A Tax Court case concluded that a recovery founded on the defamation of personal character was a "personal injury" excludable from gross income under § 104(a)(2). Seay v. Commissioner, 58 T.C. 32 (1972) (Acq. 1972–2 C.B. 3). In short, § 104(a)(2) encompasses nonphysical as well as physical personal injuries. See Reg. § 1.104–1(c).

Although awards under § 104 (as well as a judicially developed exemption for damage recoveries for personal injuries, including nonphysical injuries), among other things, replace lost earnings which would have been taxed when received, the exclusion under § 104 is seemingly premised on: (1) the involuntary nature of the transaction, and (2) the concept that the money received constitutes a return of capital. The statutory exclusion may also represent "* * * the feeling that the taxation of recoveries carved from pain and suffering is offensive, and the victim is more to be pitied rather than taxed." [5] If this rationale suffices to explain the exclusion of a recovery for pain and suffering, it seemingly does not justify an exclusion for damage recoveries in situations which may not likely involve personal anguish, e.g. defamation of personal character or damages for fraud and deceit. In Rev.Rul. 85–97, 1985–2 C.B. 50, the entire amount received by an individual in settlement of a suit for personal injury, including the amount allocable to the claim for lost wages, was excluded from gross income under § 104(a)(2).

In United States v. Garber, 589 F.2d 843 (5th Cir.1979), remanded on rehearing 607 F.2d 92 (5th Cir.1979), the court held that the proceeds from the sale, on a regular basis, of the taxpayer's own rare type of blood was not excluded from gross income under § 104(a)(2). The court stated (589 F.2d at 847–848):

> The essential element of an exclusion under section 104(a)(2) is that the income involved must derive from some sort of tort claim against the payor. The regulations promulgated with respect to section 104(a)(2) specify that "the term 'damages received (whether by suit or agreement)' means an amount received (other than workmen's compensation) through prosecution of a legal suit or action based upon tort or tort type rights, or through a settlement agreement entered into in lieu of such prosecution." [Reg. § 1.1C4–1(c)] The regulation's emphasis on the tortious aspect of the claim is consistent with judicial construction of the section. In applying section 104(a)(2) courts have uniformly assumed that the exclusion applies only to payments resulting from the prosecution or settlement of a tort claim. See, e.g., Starrels v. Commissioner, 304 F.2d 574 (9th Cir.1962). This interpretation accords with the underlying purpose of section 104(a)(2). Where damages are paid as compensation for wrongful loss there has been no economic gain or accession to wealth by the taxpayer, but merely a restoration to the position he occupied prior to the loss. He has been made whole, not enriched. Starrells, 304 F.2d at 576.

> In the instant case, there has been no suggestion nor it seems could there have been, that the payments to appellant by the laboratories to which she sold plasma were either intended or understood as a settlement of some sort of tort liability. The record contains no indication that the laboratories' action with respect to [taxpayer] were in any sense tortious or that they or she ever believed that a tort claim existed. Undoubtedly appellant suffered pain and discomfort as the necessary and inevitable corollary of the means by which she chose to make her living; the mere presence of pain and discomfort, however, does not give rise to a cause of action in tort. Appellant was fully

5. Harnett, Torts and Taxes, 27 N.Y.
U.L.Rev. 614, 626 (1952).

cognizant of the side effects involved with the sale of her plasma; she negotiated her contracts with this in mind and was significantly remunerated for her trouble.

Absent any suggestion that the payments to [taxpayer] were in settlement of a possible tort liability, these payments could not as a matter of law fall within the exclusion of section 104(a)(2). There is no disputed issue of fact whose resolution would alter this conclusion. This is not a case where there exists some factual question as to whether payments were intended as a settlement of a tort claim or where made for some other purpose. In such a case, the applicability of the section 104(a)(2) would depend on the characterization of the payments. Where the relevant facts are not in dispute and the decision regarding an issue hinges solely on an interpretation of the applicable law, the responsibility for resolving that issue lies uniquely within the province of the court.

Question

In Garber did the taxpayer have a basis in her blood? Given that she was required to report the income, would the costs of her special diet be deductible? What was the character of the income realized in Garber?

2. PUNITIVE DAMAGES

The Glenshaw Glass Co. decision (p. 147) held that punitive damages constitute taxable income to the recipient because such damages were "undeniable accessions to wealth, clearly realized, and over which the taxpayers have complete dominion." 348 U.S. 426 at 431, 75 S.Ct. 473 at 477, 99 L.Ed. 483 at 490. The Treasury embodied the Glenshaw Glass Co. decision in Reg. § 1.61–14(a) which provides:

"In addition to the items enumerated in section 61(a), there are many other kinds of gross income. For example, punitive damages * * * are gross income."

However, Rev.Rul. 75–45, 1975–1 C.B. 47, appeared to revive the issue of excludability of punitive damage awards from gross income of the recipient in a personal injury situation. The ruling considered the treatment of payments made under an aircraft liability insurance policy which contained a full release of all claims against the insurer, including wrongful death. A series of state court decisions characterized the payments made under the applicable wrongful death statute as punitive in nature. The ruling, in excluding the entire payment under § 104(a)(2), held:

Section 104(a)(2) excludes from gross income "the amount of *any* damages received (whether by suit or agreement) *on account* of personal injuries or sickness" (emphasis added). Therefore, under § 104(a)(2), any damages, whether compensatory or punitive, received on account of personal injuries or sickness are excludable from gross income.

The Service cut back on this overly generous concession in the following revenue ruling:

REV.RUL. 84–108
1984–2 C.B. 32.

ISSUE

Are the amounts received from an insurance company by a decedent's surviving spouse and child, under the circumstances described below, excludable from their respective gross incomes?

FACTS

Situation 1. The decedent, *A*, was killed while a passenger in an airplane owned by *A*'s corporate employer. Under the terms of an aircraft liability insurance policy held by *A*'s employer, the insurer had agreed to pay 10*x* dollars to the personal representative of a person killed in the corporation's airplane, regardless of whether the insured was legally liable for such death, provided the decedent's personal representative executed a full release of any claim for wrongful death. Under the applicable wrongful death act, that of Virginia, the amount recoverable is limited to the amount necessary to compensate the survivors eligible to receive the damages for their actual loss sustained by reason of the wrongful death. No punitive damages are recoverable. See Wilson v. Whittaker, 154 S.E.2d 124 (Va.1967). The estate of the decedent has no interest in the wrongful death recovery, and the amounts recovered are required to be distributed in accordance with the express terms of the act. *A* was survived by *A*'s spouse and one child. The personal representative executed the release and immediately distributed 7.5*x* dollars to the surviving spouse and 2.5*x* dollars to the child.

Situation 2. The facts are the same as in *Situation 1* except that the applicable wrongful death act is that of Alabama, which provides exclusively for payment of punitive damages. That is, the amount of damages is determined exclusively on the basis of the degree of fault on the part of the party found liable for the wrongful death, rather than on the basis of the loss sustained by the survivors eligible to receive the damages. See Alabama Power Co. v. Irwin, 72 So.2d 300, (Ala.1954); Painter v. Tennessee Valley Authority, 476 F.2d 943, 944 (5th Cir.1973). Evidence of the amount of such loss is inadmissible. Smith v. Birmingham Ry., Light and Power Co., 41 So. 307, 310 (Ala.1906); Louisville and N.R. Co. v. Tegnor, 28 So. 510, 512 (Ala.1900).

LAW AND ANALYSIS

Section 61 of the Internal Revenue Code defines gross income as all income from whatever source derived, except as otherwise provided by law.

Section 1.61–14(a) of the Income Tax Regulations provides that gross income includes punitive damages such as treble damages under the antitrust laws and exemplary damages for fraud.

Section 101(a)(1) of the Code provides that gross income does not include amounts received (whether in a single sum or otherwise) under a life insurance contract, if such amounts are paid by reason of the death of the insured.

Section 1.101–1(a) of the regulations provides that the exclusion under section 101 of the Code embraces death benefit payments "having the characteristics of life insurance proceeds payable by reason of death under contracts, such as workmen's compensation insurance contracts, endowment contracts, or accident and health insurance contracts * * *".

Section 101(b) of the Code provides that the beneficiaries of a deceased employee may exclude from gross income certain death benefits paid by an employer by reason of the employee's death, up to an aggregate amount of $5000.

Section 1.101–2(a)(1) of the regulations provides that the exclusion from gross income applies whether the payment is made to the estate of the employee or to any beneficiary (individual, corporation, or partnership), whether it is made directly or in trust, and whether or not it is made pursuant to a contractual obligation of the employer.

Section 104(a)(2) of the Code provides that gross income does not include the amount of any damages received (whether by suit or agreement and whether as a lump sum or as periodic payments) on account of personal injuries or sickness.

Section 1.104–1(c) of the regulations defines the term "damages received (whether by suit or agreement)" as an amount received (other than workmen's compensation) through prosecution of a legal suit or action based upon tort or tort type rights, or through a settlement agreement entered into in lieu of such prosecution.

Although the amounts received in *Situation 1* and *Situation 2* are paid pursuant to a contract between *A*'s employer and an insurance company, the amounts are not life insurance proceeds excludable under section 101(a) of the Code because, unlike life insurance, no fixed sum is guaranteed or solely contingent upon the death of the employee. Instead, payment is contingent upon the personal representative's release of any claim under the applicable wrongful death act. An amount received in settlement does not become classifiable as insurance on the life of the passenger-employee merely because it is payable in settlement without requiring proof of the insured's legal liability. See Rev. Rul. 57–54, 1957–1 C.B. 298.

Similarly, the exclusion provided by section 101(b) of the Code also applies only to amounts paid "by reason of the death of the employee." Accordingly, an amount received in consideration of the execution of a release for liability under the wrongful death act also does not qualify for the $5000 exclusion under section 101(b).

The facts in this case indicate that the personal representative in *Situation 1* or *Situation 2* may elect to accept the payments provided for under the policy. However, if the election is made, the personal representative must execute a release relieving the insured from liability for any claim for damages. The intended effect of this requirement is that the acceptance of settlement payments under the policy shall be in lieu of prosecution of a suit for damages. Payments under such an arrangement constitute damages received. See section 1.104–1(c) of the regulations.

In *Situation 1*, payments made under the wrongful death act are limited to the amount necessary to compensate the survivors eligible to receive the damages for their actual loss sustained by reason of the wrongful death.

In *Situation 2*, payments made under the wrongful death act are punitive in nature. In Commissioner v. Glenshaw Glass Co., 348 U.S. 426 (1955), 1955–1 C.B. 207, the Supreme Court held that punitive damages received in an antitrust case and punitive damages received in a fraud case are includible in gross income. In arriving at this decision, the Court examined the nature of these damages and concluded that punitive damages are not a substitute for any amounts lost by the plaintiff or a substitute for any injury to the plaintiff or plaintiff's property, but are extracted from the wrongdoer as punishment for unlawful conduct. The Court held that these damages represent accessions to wealth and are includible in gross income.

In Starrels v. Commissioner, 304 F.2d 574 (9th Cir.1962), aff'g 35 T.C. 646 (1961), the United States Court of Appeals for the Ninth Circuit held that damages paid for personal injuries are excluded from gross income under section 104(a)(2) of the Code because, in effect, they restore a loss of capital. An award of punitive damages, however, does not compensate a taxpayer for a loss but adds to the taxpayer's wealth. Furthermore, punitive damages are awarded not "on account of personal injury," as required by section 104(a)(2), but are determined with reference to the defendant's degree of fault.

HOLDING

In *Situation 1*, the amounts received by *A*'s surviving spouse and child in consideration of the release from liability under the applicable wrongful death act are excludable from their gross incomes under section 104(a)(2) of the Code.

In *Situation 2*, the amounts received by *A*'s surviving spouse and child in consideration of the release from liability under a wrongful death act, which provided exclusively for payment of punitive damages, are includible in the gross incomes of the wife and child respectively.

EFFECT ON OTHER REVENUE RULINGS

Rev.Rul. 75–45, 1975–1 C.B. 47, is revoked.

PROSPECTIVE APPLICATION

Pursuant to the authority contained in section 7805(b) of the Code, the conclusion of the revenue ruling will be applied without retroactive effect to taxpayers who receive payments in consideration of a release from liability under a wrongful death act that provides exclusively for the payment of punitive damages, if the release was signed before July 16, 1984, the date of publication of this revenue ruling in the Internal Revenue Bulletin.

Questions

1. Read § 104(a)(2) carefully. Does the literal wording of this statute support the Commissioner's interpretation in Rev.Rul. 75–45? Is this a necessary or desirable reading of § 104(a)(2)? Is Revenue Ruling 75–45 necessarily inconsistent with the Glenshaw Glass decision which held that punitive damages must be included in gross income "in recognition of the intention of Congress to tax all gains except those specifically exempted"? 348 U.S. at 430, 75 S.Ct. at 476, 99 L.Ed. at 489. Consider that from a non-tax standpoint punitive damages are designed to penalize and deter wrong-doing and compensatory damages are in the nature of a substitute for something a taxpayer previously had. What is the effect of Rev.Rul. 84–108? Are taxpayers in Alabama being discriminated against?

2. You represent Charlie who has filed a complaint seeking compensatory and punitive damages in a personal injury action. Settlement negotiations are underway. How should the settlement be structured to obtain an exclusion from taxation for all or part of any payment?

———

Consider the Tax Court's treatment of compensatory and punitive damages for libel in the Roemer case which follows.

ROEMER v. COMMISSIONER

Tax Court of the United States, 1982.
79 T.C. 398.

DAWSON, JUDGE: * * * The issues presented for decision are:

1. Whether petitioner Paul F. Roemer, Jr., is entitled under section 104(a)(2) to exclude from his gross income for 1975 compensatory damages of $40,000 received as a result of a favorable jury verdict in a libel suit.

2. Whether punitive damages of $250,000 in the same libel suit are likewise excludable from petitioner's gross income as having been received on account of personal injuries.

3. If the compensatory and punitive damages are includable in petitioner's gross income, whether they should be treated, in whole or in part, as ordinary income or capital gain.

* * *

FINDINGS OF FACT

* * *

Petitioner is, and has been since 1941, an independent insurance broker. In 1952, he started his own insurance business in the area of Oakland, Calif., where he had lived all of his life. * * *

By the mid-1960's petitioner, then doing business as Paul F. Roemer, Jr., Inc., enjoyed an excellent reputation in the community, both personally and professionally. His gross income at that time had risen to approximately $300,000 (about one-half of which represented his net income).

Until 1965, petitioner sold primarily casualty insurance, but at that time he had an opportunity to expand into the field of selling life insurance. Gordon Maxson, an expert in the life insurance business and both a business associate and friend of petitioner's, persuaded petitioner to seek authorization from the Penn Mutual Life Insurance Co. (hereinafter Penn Mutual) so that they could form a partnership for the sale of casualty and life insurance and work on certain insurance matters. Petitioner applied for an agency license from Penn Mutual to sell life insurance. In the course of reviewing that application, a credit report was sought from Retail Credit Co. (hereinafter Retail Credit). Retail Credit subsequently prepared such a report and sent it to Penn Mutual and other insurance companies. The report on petitioner was grossly defamatory in nature. It falsely stated, among other things, that petitioner was ignorant in insurance matters, neglected his clients' affairs, was recently fired from his position as president of an insurance firm, and intentionally defaced property belonging to others. The report also questioned petitioner's honesty, implying that he misappropriated funds belonging to others for his personal benefit.

Upon learning of the defamatory report, petitioner demanded that Retail Credit issue a retraction. Thereupon, Retail Credit distributed to those companies which had received the original publication a letter and purported retraction which in fact contained further false and defamatory innuendos regarding petitioner's general business and personal character and his fitness as an insurance agent.

As a result of Retail Credit's report, petitioner was denied agency licenses to sell life insurance by Penn Mutual and other insurance companies. Furthermore, his then-existing business relationships were damaged, as well as his ability to attract new clients. This was due in part to the nature of his business because most of his friends were also his clients, and vice versa. Retail Credit's report thus caused his insurance profits to diminish and his business reputation to be damaged.

On May 14, 1965, petitioner filed a complaint for damages against Retail Credit in the Superior Court for Alameda County, Calif. He alleged that the publication of the Retail Credit report damaged his good reputation as a licensed insurance broker, and it caused him "to lose insurance business from Penn Mutual Life Insurance Company" and to lose "further profits from similar business with other insurance companies." He sought general damages of $50,000. In an amended complaint filed in November 1967, the petitioner alleged that the securing of insurance customers and credit was dependent upon his "business reputation, credit standing and financial responsibility."

* * *

In paragraph VIII of the amended complaint, it is alleged that the publication by Retail Credit was done "with intent to damage his reputation, and to injure him in his business profession and occupation" and that he was generally damaged in the total sum of $136,000. Punitive damages were claimed in the amount of $840,000.

* * * He told the jury that he lost income as a direct result of the false report. He described in detail to the jury how the defamatory report affected his business relations, but said little, if anything, about how it affected his personal affairs. The evidence presented through many witnesses in the trial of the libel suit was primarily directed at how the petitioner's business relationships and planned business ventures were harmed by the false report of Retail Credit. There was no testimony by the petitioner or others in the libel suit that the libelous report was published anywhere outside of the insurance industry.

* * *

Petitioner's counsel did not argue to the jury that separate amounts should be awarded for damages to petitioner's business reputation and to his personal reputation. Nor did counsel request a verdict dividing the "compensatory" damages between those which were "general" (personal injuries) and "special" (loss of business profits and reputation) in accordance with California Civil Code section 48a.4.(a) and (b).

* * *

* * * On February 14, 1971, a jury verdict was entered in favor of the petitioner, awarding compensatory damages of $40,000 and punitive damages of $250,000, together with costs.[6] The jury gave no indication of the basis upon which they arrived at such amounts.

* * *

In his notice of deficiency, respondent determined that the entire judgment received by petitioner should be included in his gross income, and that all costs and attorneys' fees should be allowed as a deduction.

OPINION

Petitioner contends that the damages, both compensatory and punitive, awarded to him by the jury were "on account of personal injuries" to his personal and professional reputation and are thus

6. The jury verdict was unsuccessfully appealed on the basis, inter alia, that it was excessive in amount. Roemer v. Retail Credit Co., 44 Cal.App.3d 926, 119 Cal. Rptr. 82 (1975). Petitioner received his damage award in 1975. His total net recovery was $147,140, calculated as follows:

Compensatory damages	$40,000
Punitive damages	250,000
Interest and costs	85,601
	$375,601
Less:	
Attorneys' fees	220,710
Costs	7,751
	228,461
Net to Petitioner	147,140

excludable from his gross income under section 104(a)(2). Alternatively, he argues that if the damages are includable in his gross income, they must be, at least in part, treated as [preferential] long-term capital gain because of the loss caused to his goodwill and going-concern value by the defamatory report.

Respondent, on the other hand, contends that the compensatory damages are includable in petitioner's gross income under section 61 since they were awarded *primarily* to compensate him for lost income, past and future. He argues that the petitioner has not brought himself within the exclusion of section 104(a)(2) because the amounts were awarded to compensate him for damages to his business and professional reputation, as distinguished from his personal reputation. With respect to the punitive damages, respondent contends that they are includable in petitioner's gross income "as a matter of law" and that, in any event, they were not paid on account of personal injuries and therefore are not excludable under section 104(a)(2). * * *

1. *Compensatory Damages*

Section 61 provides that, except as otherwise provided, gross income means "all income from whatever source derived." Section 104(a)(2) excludes from gross income "the amount of any damages received (whether by suit or agreement) on account of personal injuries or sickness." Section 1.104–1(c), Income Tax Regs., states in part that damages received means an amount received from an action based on tort or tort-type rights, thus making no distinction between physical and mental or emotional injuries. Seay v. Commissioner, 58 T.C. 32, 40 (1972). The law is settled that the tax consequences of an award for damages depend on the nature of the litigation and on the origin and character of the claims adjudicated, but not the validity of such claims. Woodward v. Commissioner, 397 U.S. 572 (1970); United States v. Gilmore, 372 U.S. 39 (1963); Seay v. Commissioner, supra. The proper inquiry is in lieu of what were the damages awarded.

The threshold question raised by the parties is whether a distinction should be drawn between personal reputation and business or professional reputation for purposes of determining excludability under section 104(a)(2) where, as here, the jury award of damages makes no apportionment in that respect. Although the petitioner acknowledges that he suffered injury to his professional reputation, and in essence admits that it is difficult, if not impossible, to determine what portion of the damages was on account of personal injury, he nevertheless argues that when there is an inextricable combination of damages to both professional and personal reputation, the entire award comes within the exclusion of section 104(a)(2). To the contrary, respondent asserts that since the petitioner's injury was *predominantly* to his business and professional reputation, the exclusion of section 104(a)(2) is unavailable to him.

In our opinion, a distinction must be made. We think the taxation of damages received pursuant to a court judgment in a suit for injury to a person's reputation, caused by defamatory statements constituting libel, depends on whether or not such defamation results in injury to the personal reputation of an individual, as distinguished from libel that injures his business or professional reputation, to the extent it has affected or may affect his income. In light of this principle, petitioner must bring himself squarely within the exclusion from tax upon which he bases his case, i.e., that the amounts for damages resulted from injury to his *personal reputation*. We think he has failed to do so.

To ascertain the nature of the damages received, it is necessary to examine the allegations contained in petitioner's first and amended complaints filed in the California libel suit and the issues and evidence before the State court. It is our view that a realistic consideration and analysis of the petitioner's pleadings, testimony, and other evidence in the libel suit lead to the conclusion that the predominant nature of his claims involved damages to his business and professional reputation as an insurance broker. This conclusion is supported by pertinent allegations in petitioner's complaints which are set out in our findings. It is also supported by his testimony at the libel trial about how he lost the insurance account which depended on the Penn Mutual license and about how his proposed partnership with Gordon Maxson failed to materialize. He described the instances where specific licenses were denied by other insurance companies because of the false qualification report circulated within the insurance industry by Retail Credit. His lawyer told the jury in his closing statement that the evidence they heard proved that the petitioner lost $136,000 in prospective income, which was the amount sought in the amended complaint. This was the main thrust of the evidence the jury had to consider in reaching its verdict of $40,000 in compensatory damages.

Accordingly, we hold that the petitioner has failed to establish that the amount of compensatory damages was on account of personal injury and excludable under section 104(a)(2).

2. *Punitive Damages*

We must next consider whether the punitive damages of $250,000 received by petitioner are includable or excludable from his gross income.

* * *

In Rev.Rul. 58–418, 1958–2 C.B. 18, the Internal Revenue Service ruled that an amount received in settlement of a libel suit, for both compensatory and exemplary (punitive) damages for injury to personal reputation, constitutes income to the recipient to the extent that such amount represents satisfaction of exemplary damages. This ruling does not relate to the specific exclusion from gross income of section 104(a)(2). However, several years later the Commissioner revived the question of excludability of punitive damages. In Rev.Rul. 75–45, 1975– 1 C.B. 47, the specific issue considered was whether an amount received by the estate of a deceased employee under his employer's aircraft liability policy could be excluded from gross income. The policy payment was contingent upon a full release from all claims which were considered punitive. The ruling focused on section 104(a)(2) and concluded that *any* damages, whether compensatory or punitive, received "on account of personal injuries or sickness" are excludable from gross income. Since his interpretation *arguably* comes within the language of section 104(a)(4), the Commissioner, in his administrative discretion, has chosen to allow punitive damages to be excluded from gross income in the same manner as compensatory damages *provided they arise out of a personal injury.* Otherwise, an award for punitive damages in a libel suit must be included in gross income and taxed like other gain. Rev.Rul. 58–418, supra.

Here we have found, factually, that the compensatory damages were intended to reimburse the petitioner for lost profits resulting from damage to his business reputation, rather than to his personal reputation. It therefore follows that the punitive damages were not awarded "on account of personal injuries" to the petitioner. This is consistent with the Supreme Court's decision in Commissioner v. Glenshaw Glass Co., 348 U.S. 426 (1955), and the Commissioner's ruling positions in Rev.Rul. 58–418, supra, and Rev.Rul. 75–45, supra. Accordingly, we hold that the punitive damages are includable in petitioner's gross income.

3. Ordinary Income or Capital Gain

As previously indicated, the taxability of the proceeds of a lawsuit depends upon the nature of the claim and the actual basis of recovery. If the recovery represents damages for lost profits, it is taxable as ordinary income. However, if it represents a replacement of capital destroyed or injured, the money received, to the extent it does not exceed the basis, is a return of capital and not taxable. See Sager Glove Corp. v. Commissioner, 36 T.C. 1173, 1180 (1961), affd. 311 F.2d 210 (7th Cir.1962), and the cases cited therein. To the extent that the money received exceeds the basis in the capital asset destroyed, i.e., goodwill, the gain therefrom may be taxable as a capital gain under section 1231(a).

* * *

The evidence in the libel suit indicates strongly to us that the amount of $40,000 received as compensatory damages was for lost profits, past and future. In that suit, no claim for loss of goodwill was alleged or considered or valued by the jury. There was no evidence regarding the loss of confidence by petitioner's insurance clients, only that he was unable to expand his business to cover the sale of life insurance as he had planned. The jury did not allocate any portion of the award for any damages to the loss of goodwill. It is also significant that later, when he filed his Federal income tax return for 1975, the petitioner made no claim that any portion of the award represented a reimbursement for loss of capital. We think that since the petitioner's anticipated profits would have been taxable as ordinary income, so must the jury award for compensatory damages. Consequently, upon consideration of the entire record, we conclude that the petitioner has not met his burden of proving that any portion of the amount received as compensatory damages was paid as compensation for injury to goodwill or any other capital item. The allegations of the complaints, the evidence as a whole, and the jury award simply do not provide any basis for making an allocation of the recovery, and finding that all or any part represented a return of capital. Under these circumstances the petitioner's claim for loss of goodwill appears to us to be nothing more than a tax-motivated afterthought.

Punitive damages, to the extent they are taxable, constitute ordinary income rather than [preferential] capital gain. In Commissioner v. Glenshaw Glass Co., 348 U.S. 426, 432 (1955), the Supreme Court stated that punitive damages, following injury to property, "cannot be considered a restoration of capital for taxation purposes."

* * *

Decision will be entered for the respondent.

Reviewed by the Court.

FORRESTER, J., dissenting: * * *.

At this point, the majority opines that a distinction must be made between defamatory injury to personal reputation vis-a-vis defamatory injury to business or professional reputation "to the extent it has or may affect * * * income."

At this point, I must depart the company of the majority for in my view no such distinction is possible in the factual posture here presented.

The term business or professional reputation does not refer to some intangible other than reputation, generally (or personal reputation). It does refer to the *manifestation* of that intangible in the context of one's career, as opposed to one's family and social life.

This is particularly evident in the instant case. Petitioner built an extremely successful insurance practice by making as many social friends and acquaintances as possible (through memberships in social and civic clubs and organizations) and then cultivating them into business clients. The net result was that almost all of his personal friends were also his business clients, and vice versa. The personal and professional sides of his reputation were so intertwined as to be inseparable and indistinguishable.

The test, therefore, of excludability under section 104(a)(2) is not one of injury to personal versus business reputation, as in either case, the injury is to reputation—a personal injury—and therefore excludable. Instead, I believe the proper inquiry is whether the injury sought to be redressed is one to reputation, at all, or only to one's occupation; as, for an example, an automobile dealer who has for years increased his volume of new car sales on the strength of his reputation for maintaining and operating an excellent service department. This operation is maliciously slandered by a competitor and tortious damage results. The slander obviously has nothing to do with the personal reputation (character, honesty, etc.) of the dealer, and the award of damages to him would be wholly business-related and outside the scope of section 104(a)(2).

I am well aware that the determination of whether the true nature of the claim in a given situation is injury to reputation or injury to occupation will not always be an easy one. This is especially true where a libel or slander is the impetus for the action. * * *

Care must be taken when considering arguments and evidence presented to the jury to determine whether facts concerning professional injury and lost profits are the injury sought to be compensated, *or are merely to show the collateral effects of injury to reputation in an effort to prove the extent or severity of the damages.* See generally State Fish Corp. v. Commissioner, 48 T.C. 465 (1967).

Applying these factors to the instant case, I would hold that the damages awarded to petitioner were for injury to his reputation and not to his occupation. Clearly, his profession suffered ill effects as a result of the libel, but the predominant wrong sought to be redressed by petitioner was injury to his personal reputation. The occupational damage and evidence regarding it were merely *manifestations* of that injury.

Consider how this petitioner could have convinced the jury of the enormity of the damage done to him. He could have said he was very, very very humiliated and hurt; or he could have showed them, as he did, that his personal service business, built upon trust, confidence, and honesty, was financially wounded and nearly destroyed.

I would hold that the compensatory damages received by petitioner are excludable under section 104(a)(2).

I agree with the reasoning of the majority regarding the punitive damages but, of course, would conclude that they were awarded on account of personal injuries and therefore excludable.

* * *

KÖRNER, J., agrees with this dissent.

WILBUR, J., I respectfully dissent. * * *

Either a physical injury or a defamation of character may inflict damages that include lost wages, reduced earning power, or diminished economic opportunity. Indeed, these elements very often comprise virtually all of the damages. In neither of these actions is a self-employed individual appropriately taxable at ordinary income tax rates in 1 year on damages replacing economic opportunities that—without the injury—would produce earnings over the period of his productive life.

* * *

A young surgeon who loses a finger will recover damages that for the most part replace future earnings otherwise taxable, but the loss is not bifurcated into its economic and personal components, thereby subjecting the former to taxation. Neither should damages for defamation of character, since defamation is by definition personal to the plaintiff. In both cases, section 104 excludes the damages from income—both the economic and personal components—from income.

However, the law is clear that punitive or exemplary damages must be included in gross income, and I would so hold. Commissioner v. Glenshaw Glass Co., 348 U.S. 426 (1955). Punitive damages are certainly not intended to compensate petitioner for a loss within the purview of section 104. I realize respondent has a revenue ruling that suggests a contrary result. Rev.Rul. 75–45, 1975–1 C.B. 47. Under appropriate circumstances, respondent may be precluded from taking one position in a ruling with respect to taxpayers in general, and a different position in regard to a taxpayer before the Court. Nevertheless, the facts in Rev.Rul. 75–45, supra, are sufficiently different from those herein to permit the surprising but general language of the ruling to be disregarded for now.

————

The Roemer case was reversed on appeal, 716 F.2d 693 (9th Cir. 1983). The Ninth Circuit focused on the fact that the nature of any defamation of an individual, whether business or personal, is an action for personal injury under California law. Because state law labeled the tort action of defamation a personal injury, the Ninth Circuit concluded that the damages were received on account of a personal injury under § 104(a)(2). Thus, the entire damage award, both compensatory and punitive, was excludable from gross income. In excluding the punitive damages, the following excerpt indicates that the court relied on the Service's interpretation in Rev.Rul. 75–45.

> Normally, an amount awarded for punitive damages is includable in gross income as ordinary income. Commissioner v. Glenshaw Glass Co. * * * Nevertheless, the Commissioner liberally interprets § 104(a)(2) to exclude punitive damages as well as all compensatory damages where there has been a personal injury. Rev.Rul. 75–45, 1975–1 C.B. 47. Therefore according to the Commissioner's own interpretation, the punitive damages received by Roemer on account of his § 104(a)(2) personal injury (the defamation) are excludable from gross income. Roemer, 716 F.2d at 698.

Consider the impact of Rev.Rul. 84–108 on the Ninth Circuit's decision. In Rev.Rul. 85–98, 1985–2 C.B. 51, the amount received by an individual in settlement of a libel suit for injury to personal reputation was included in gross income to the extent such amount represents the satisfaction of punitive damages. The Service allocated the settlement between compensatory and punitive damages as follows:

> In this case, the best evidence available to determine a proper allocation is the taxpayer's complaint, since the amount of punitive damages

relative to compensatory damages requested bore a reasonable relationship to what a jury might be expected to award. The taxpayer received a lump-sum settlement amount of 24X dollars. The taxpayer's complaint, however asked for compensatory damages of 15X dollars and punitive damages of 45X dollars. Thus, the amount of compensatory damages asked equaled 25 percent and the amount of punitive damages asked equaled 75 percent of the total 60X dollars damages asked.

Questions

Was the Ninth Circuit in Roemer correct in focusing on the state law determination of the classification of the injury rather than the nature of the rights the damages represented? Consider the application of the Ninth Circuit's analysis to a business wishing to be treated as a partnership for Federal income tax purposes. Assume the business possesses the corporate characteristics of limited liability, continuity of life, centralized management, and free transferability of interests. Yet, under the state law, the business is organized and registered with the state as a partnership. Can this business be taxable as a corporation for Federal income tax purposes even though state law treats it as a partnership? Read Reg. § 301.7701–1(b) and (c), –2(a)(1). What is the significance of the last two sentences in Reg. § 301.7701–1(c)? In Rev.Rul. 85–143, 1985–2 C.B. 55, the Service announced that it will follow the decision of the Tax Court in Roemer, giving the following reason:

> The Service continues to believe the decision of the Tax Court is correct. Whether a libel in a particular situation is a personal injury should depend on the nature of the libel. In factual situations similar to *Roemer*, where the libelous statements were directed primarily to the individual in the individual's business capacity, with the result that the primary harm suffered by the individual was loss of business income, the individual has not suffered a personal injury for purposes of section 104(a)(2) of the Code. The characterization of the lawsuit brought by the individual under the law of the particular state where suit was filed should not determine the characterization of the damages received for federal income tax purposes.

> It is true that where a taxpayer suffers a physical personal injury, all compensatory damages received therefore are excludable from gross income under section 104(a)(2) of the Code, including any damages received to compensate the taxpayer for income lost while the taxpayer was disabled by the injury [which was caused when the taxpayer was struck by a bus]. See Rev.Rul. 85–97, 1985–2 C.B. 50. Although damages may be measured, at least in part, by the amount of lost income, they nevertheless are attributable to a personal injury, as required by the statute. In the present case, however, the Tax Court found that the taxpayer's claims for which the state court awarded him a recovery were predominantly for injury to his business and professional reputation as an insurance broker, and that the main thrust of the evidence he presented to the jury was of lost business income. 79 T.C. at 406. If a taxpayer operates a business, whether as a proprietor-

ship or a corporation, a defamatory statement that is directed at the business and causes loss of business income is an injury to the business as distinguished from a personal injury. * * *

3. JUDICIAL AND ADMINISTRATIVE EXCLUSIONS

Apart from § 104, judicial and administrative exclusions exist for damage recoveries for personal injuries. Personal injury recoveries may be viewed as a return of capital, more specifically, human capital, because an individual's reputation or body are arguably forms of capital. In Hawkins v. Commissioner, 6 B.T.A. 1023, 1025 (1927), the court held that damages for personal defamation (libel and slander to personal reputation) were not taxable because such damages lack the element of gain and attempt to "make the plaintiff whole as before the injury." Stated differently, where the wrongdoer pays damages as compensation for wrongful loss, the argument, in support of the exclusion, asserts there has been no accession to wealth by the taxpayer, only a restoration of the position the taxpayer occupied prior to the loss. The taxpayer has been made whole; he has not been enriched. See e.g. Starrells v. Commissioner, 304 F.2d 574 (9th Cir.1962). Likewise, damage recoveries for wrongful death actions have been excluded. Rev.Rul. 54–19, 1954–1 C.B. 179. The difficulty with this rationale is that, apart from legal fees incurred in collecting the recovery, the taxpayer has not made an investment in the damaged interest. The victim lacks a basis (i.e. tax cost) in his personal rights.

Damages for lost earnings while a person was disabled, received as part of a personal injury action, are within the § 104(a)(2) exclusion. Rev.Rul. 85–97, 1985–2 C.B. 50. Does the argument that an individual's reputation is a type of capital explain why personal injury damages clearly allocable to loss of earnings are nontaxable? Should the excess of the taxpayer's recovery over his basis in human capital be taxable? The difficulty of assigning a basis to human capital might result in the taxation of the entire recovery.

Another rationale for the exclusion is based on the premise that "damages intended to compensate for losses that the taxpayer would have enjoyed tax-free should also be tax-free." [7] The non-taxability is premised on the assumption that such personal rights, absent the invasion, would not have been exercised to generate gross income. For example, damages paid as compensation for defamation of character are excludable because a taxpayer enjoys his reputation tax free. Because maintaining one's privacy is not a taxable event, damages for invasion of privacy are not generally taxable. Rev.Rul. 74–77, 1974–1 C.B. 33, concluded that damages for alienation of affection are not income as they " * * * relate to personal or family rights, not property rights * * *."

7. Yorio, The Taxation of Damages: Tax and Non-Tax Policy Considerations, 62 Cornell L.Rev. 701, 713 (1977).

Payments for anticipated harm prior to any infringement of a personal right (e.g. a release of right of privacy) are, however, includable in gross income. See e.g. Miller v. Commissioner, 299 F.2d 706 (2d Cir.1962), cert. denied 370 U.S. 923, 82 S.Ct. 1564, 8 L.Ed.2d 503 (1962). In these situations, the taxpayer voluntarily contracts away his personal rights. Thus, the payments received in advance for giving up one's privacy are not damages received on account of personal injuries under § 104(a)(2). This rationale, unlike the human capital argument, eliminates the problem of computing the basis of human capital, but it also fails to explain the exclusion for damages based on loss of earnings.

Should damages computed by reference to lost earnings be taxable? In an employment context, it is hard to distinguish the payment of compensation from the payment of damages. In Rev.Rul. 72–341, 1972–2 C.B. 32, the Service held taxable payments received by employees in settlement of an action brought by the Federal Government under the Civil Rights Act of 1964 based on discrimination by an employer. The damages were based on a formula which considered the differences between each employee's actual earnings and what his earnings would have been absent the discrimination. See also Watkins v. United States, 223 Ct.Cl. 731, 650 F.2d 286 (1980) and Hodge v. Commissioner, 64 T.C. 616 (1975). In these cases, the controversy centered around the respective employment rights of the parties. The courts held that the respective taxpayers recovered a compensation substitute. This conclusion is reinforced when the recovery is based on and measured by lost earnings. It seems that, just as it is more difficult to receive a tax free gift in a commercial context (Commissioner v. Duberstein, p. 267), it may be hard to justify a nonstatutory exclusion from gross income of damages based solely on lost earnings.

Problems

1. (a) Paula was injured in an automobile accident. She sued Darlene, the negligent driver, and received a $25,000 judgment paid by Darlene's insurance company. The judgment allocated the damages as follows:

> damage to sports car (which had a basis of $10,000), $2,000;
>
> reimbursement of medical costs, $4,000;
>
> lost earnings while hospitalized, $6,000;
>
> damage for scar on arm, $3,000;
>
> pain and suffering, $10,000.

Assume Paula's insurance policy paid all of her medical costs and that she turned over $4,000 of the award to her insurance carrier.

(i) Does § 104(a)(2) exclude the entire damage award?

(ii) If the Code did not contain § 104(a)(2), how would Paula treat each portion of the damage award?

(b) Assume Paula was a model and the scar on her arm hindered her modeling career. Assume further she also received $50,000 for permanent loss of earning power for the remainder of her career. Must Paula include this additional amount in gross income? Consider § 104(a)(2) and Rev.Rul. 85–97.

(c) Assume Paula is not married and did not carry any medical insurance. Assume that in the year of the accident, after the application of the 7.5 percent floor on medical expenses, Paula's medical deduction equalled $3,000. § 213(a). During the next year, Paula is reimbursed $4,000 as part of the damage award. Why is only $3,000 included in Paula's gross income? Why does § 104(a) only exclude certain reimbursements for medical costs? Consider Reg. § 1.213–1(g).

(d) Assume neither Paula nor Darlene carried insurance covering the accident. Paula settled her case against Darlene for $8,000. Darlene satisfied the settlement by transferring to Paula, in the same year as the accident occurred, shares of stock in a publicly traded corporation having a basis to Darlene of $6,500 and a value of $8,000. Darlene had purchased the stock five years prior to the transfer. Two years after the transfer of the shares, Paula sold the stock for $9,000. When do Paula and Darlene realize and recognize their gains? What is the amount of their respective gains? Consider §§ 1001(a), (b), and 1012. What is Paula's basis in the shares? What is the character of their respective gains? Consider §§ 1221 and 1222.

(e) Assume Paula was 16 years old when the accident occurred and when she received the damage award. The court ordered that $21,000 of the damage award in part "a" above be placed in a custodial savings account for her. Assume further that when Paula reached age 21 she withdrew the $24,000 then in the account. Does Paula have gross income? How much income must she report? What is the character of the income?

2. Carol was killed in an auto accident. Her husband, Curt received a $200,000 damage award covering Carol's medical expenses, Carol's pain and suffering while she lingered in the hospital, loss of consortium, and loss of support. Can Curt exclude all the elements of this damage award? Consider § 104(a)(2).

3. Bob and Susan, a married couple, were injured in an auto accident. They incurred $5,000 in medical costs. Bob's medical insurance paid these medical expenses. Susan's medical insurance carrier sent her a $4,000 check to reimburse her for her medical expenses. The negligent party settled the case and his insurance carrier gave Bob and Susan $5,000 to cover their medical bills. Bob and Susan never reimbursed either of their insurance companies. Why do Bob and Susan have income?

4. Should juries in personal injury cases be told that damage awards for lost earnings are not taxable? If juries received this instruction, would it effect the size of the award? Is there any justification for not telling the jury the tax status of an award?

C. RECOVERY OF DAMAGES FOR BUSINESS INJURY

1. RETURN OF CAPITAL

The Code strives to tax gain, rather than gross receipts. For example, in an early case, Doyle v. Mitchell Brothers Co., 247 U.S. 179, 38 S.Ct. 467, 62 L.Ed. 1054 (1918), the Supreme Court allowed the taxpayer, a lumber company, to deduct the cost of timber from its gross receipts in order to compute its gross income. The Supreme Court indicated:

> There is no express provision that even allows a merchant to deduct the cost of the goods that he sells.

> Yet, it is plain, we think, that by the true intent and meaning of the act the entire proceeds of a mere conversion of capital assets were not to be treated as income. * * * In order to determine whether there has been gain or loss, and the amount of the gain, if any, we must withdraw from the gross proceeds an amount sufficient to restore the capital value that existed at the commencement of the period under consideration. * * * [T]he object is to distinguish capital previously existing from income taxable under the act. (247 U.S. at 184, 185, 188, 38 S.Ct. at 469, 470, 64 L.Ed. at 1059, 1061).

2. BUSINESS REPUTATION

While damages for personal defamation are excludable from gross income, the recipient of an award for defamation of business reputation must include such payments in gross income. Thus, the settlement paid to a doctor in a libel and slander suit against his former employer constituted gross income where the evidence showed that the doctor wanted to restore his professional reputation in the research field. Wolfson v. Commissioner, 651 F.2d 1228 (6th Cir.1981); see also Glynn v. Commissioner, 76 T.C. 116 (1981). If the injured party can establish the basis for his business reputation, no gain results if the recovery does not exceed the taxpayer's basis; gain results to the extent that the recovery exceeds the taxpayer's basis.

Why should the tax system favor personal reputations over business reputations? If the exclusion for awards for personal reputation is found on sympathy for the victim, an injury to business reputation may be as emotionally upsetting as damage to a personal reputation. Some individuals may prize their business reputation as much as, or more than, their personal reputation. Furthermore, the destruction of both business and personal reputations may be involuntary.

3. TANGIBLE AND INTANGIBLE PROPERTY AND LOSS OF PROFITS

Compensatory damages to reimburse the taxpayer for damage to tangible property (for example, equipment) are included in the taxpayer's gross income to the extent that the recovery exceeds the taxpayer's basis in the damaged property. If the recovery equals the taxpayer's basis in the property, no gain results. If the gain is realized, the gain will be recognized unless a statutory nonrecognition provision, such as § 1033, is applicable. A nonrecognition provision postpones recognition of the gain and requires the taxpayer to carry over the adjusted basis of the old property to the newly acquired property of similar function.

Intangible business property may be damaged by tortious conduct. For example, a defamatory statement concerning a product or service of a business may damage the goodwill of a business. Goodwill is the excess earning capacity of a business and is measured by the worth of a business above its tangible assets. Goodwill includes the reputation, location, and established clientele of a business. Only that portion of the compensatory award for damages to intangible assets which exceeds the taxpayer's basis in his goodwill is taxable. Damages representing reimbursement for lost profits caused by another's wrongful action constitute gross income. But as the value of goodwill relates to its income generating attributes, the line between compensation for goodwill and for lost profits is unclear.

Because both lost income and injury to goodwill are measured in terms of lost profits, it is also necessary to identify and allocate the portions of a recovery attributable to each to obtain the most favorable tax treatment. Durkee v. Commissioner, 162 F.2d 184 (6th Cir.1947); Commissioner v. Sporck, 37 T.C.M. (CCH) 378 (1978) (taxpayer did not prove any cost basis for goodwill); Ad Visor, Inc., v. Commissioner, 37 T.C.M. (CCH) 606 (1978) (antitrust award allocated between loss of goodwill and loss of profits).

RAYTHEON PRODUCTION CORP. v. COMMISSIONER

United States Court of Appeals, First Circuit, 1944.
144 F.2d 110, cert. denied 323 U.S. 779, 65 S.Ct. 192, 89 L.Ed. 622 (1944).

Before MAGRUDER, MAHONEY, and WOODBURY, CIRCUIT JUDGES.

MAHONEY, CIRCUIT JUDGE.

This case presents the question whether an amount received by the taxpayer in compromise settlement of a suit for damages under the Federal Anti-Trust Laws, 15 U.S.C.A. § 1 et seq., is a non-taxable return of capital or income. * * *

* * * The original Raytheon Company was a pioneer manufacturer of a rectifying tube which made possible the operation of a radio receiving set on alternating current instead of on batteries. In 1926 its profits were about $450,000; in 1927 about $150,000; and in 1928, $10,000. The Radio Corporation of America had many patents covering radio circuits and claimed control over almost all of the practical circuits. Cross-licensing agreements had been made among several companies including R.C.A., General Electric Company, Westinghouse,

and American Telephone & Telegraph Company. R.C.A. had developed a competitive tube which produced the same type of rectification as the Raytheon tube. Early in 1927, R.C.A. began to license manufacturers of radio sets and in the license agreement it incorporated "Clause 9", which provided that the licensee was required to buy its tubes from R.C.A. In 1928 practically all manufacturers were operating under R.C.A. licenses. As a consequence of this restriction, Raytheon was left with only replacement sales, which soon disappeared. * * * Raytheon [brought] suit against R.C.A. * * * alleging that the plaintiff had by 1926 created and then possessed a large and valuable good will in interstate commerce in rectifying tubes for radios and had a large and profitable established business therein so that the net profit for the year 1926 was $454,935; that the business had an established prospect of large increases and that the business and good will thereof was of a value of exceeding $3,000,000; that by the beginning of 1927 the plaintiff was doing approximately 80% of the business of rectifying tubes of the entire United States; that the defendant conspired to destroy the business of the plaintiff and others by a monopoly of such business and did suppress and destroy the existing companies; that the manufacturers of radio sets and others ceased to purchase tubes from the plaintiffs; that by the end of 1927 the conspiracy had completely destroyed the profitable business and that by the early part of 1928 the tube business of the plaintiff and its property and good will had been totally destroyed at a time when it had a present value in excess of $3,000,000, and thereby the plaintiff was injured in its business and property in a sum in excess of $3,000,000. * * *

* * * R.C.A. and the petitioner finally agreed on the payment by R.C.A. of $410,000 in settlement of the anti trust action. * * *

Damages recovered in an antitrust action are not necessarily nontaxable as a return of capital. As in other types of tort damage suits, recoveries which represent a reimbursement for lost profits are income. Swastika Oil & Gas Co. v. Commissioner, 6 Cir., 1941, 123 F.2d 382, certiorari denied 1943, 317 U.S. 639, 63 S.Ct. 30, 87 L.Ed. 515. The reasoning is that since the profits would be taxable income, the proceeds of litigation which are their substitute are taxable in like manner.

Damages for violation of the anti-trust acts are treated as ordinary income where they represent compensation for loss of profits.

The test is not whether the action was one in tort or contract but rather the question to be asked is "In lieu of what were the damages awarded?" Farmers' & Merchants' Bank v. Commissioner, 6 Cir., 1932, 59 F.2d 912, Plumb, "Income Tax on Gains and Losses in Litigation" (1940) 25 Cornell L.Q. 221. Where the suit is not to recover lost profits but is for injury to good will, the recovery represents a return of capital and, with certain limitations to be set forth below, is not taxable. Farmers' & Merchants' Bank v. Commissioner, supra. Plumb, supra, 25 Cornell L.Q. 221, 225. "Care must certainly be taken in such cases to avoid taxing recoveries for injuries to good will or loss of capital". 1 Paul and Mertens Law of Federal Income Taxation § 6.48.

Upon examination of Raytheon's declaration in its anti-trust suit we find nothing to indicate that the suit was for the recovery of lost profits. The allegations were that the illegal conduct of R.C.A. "completely destroyed the profitable interstate and foreign commerce of the plaintiff and thereby, by the early part of 1928, the said tube business of the plaintiff and the property good will of the plaintiff therein had been totally destroyed at a time when it then had a present value in excess of three million dollars and thereby the plaintiff was then injured in its business and property in a sum in excess of three million dollars." This was not the sort of antitrust suit where the plaintiff's business still exists and where the injury was merely for loss of profits. The allegations and evidence as to the amount of profits were necessary in order to establish the value of the good will and business since that is derived by a capitalization of profits. A somewhat similar idea was expressed in Farmers' & Merchants' Bank v. Commissioner, supra, 59 F.2d at page 913. "Profits were one of the chief indications of the worth of the business; but the usual earnings before the injury, as compared with those afterward, were only an evidential factor in determining actual loss and not an independent basis for recovery." Since the suit was to recover damages for the destruction of the business and good will, the recovery represents a return of capital. Nor does the fact that the suit ended in a compromise settlement change the nature of the recovery; "the determining factor is the nature of the basic claim from which the compromised amount was realized." Paul Selected Studies in Federal Taxation, Second Series, pp. 328–9, footnote 76.

But, to say that the recovery represents a return of capital in that it takes the place of the business good will is not to conclude that it may not contain a taxable benefit. Although the injured party may not be deriving a profit as a result of the damage suit itself, the conversion thereby of his property into cash is a realization of any gain made over the cost or other basis of the good will prior to the illegal interference. Thus A buys Blackacre for $5,000. It appreciates in value to $50,000. B tortiously destroys it by fire. A sues and recovers $50,000 tort damages from B. Although no gain was derived by A from the suit, his prior gain due to the appreciation in value of Blackacre is realized when it is turned into cash by the money damages.

Compensation for the loss of Raytheon's good will in excess of its cost is gross income. See Magill Taxable Income, p. 339. 1 Mertens, Law of Federal Income Taxation, § 5.21, footnote 82. Plumb, supra, 25 Cornell L.Q. 225, 6.

* * * As the Tax Court pointed out, the record is devoid of evidence as to the amount of that basis and "in the absence of evidence of the basis of the business and good will of Raytheon, the amount of any nontaxable capital recovery cannot be ascertained." 1 T.C. 952.

Where the cost basis that may be assigned to property has been wholly speculative, the gain has been held to be entirely conjectural and not taxable. In Strother v. Commissioner, 4 Cir., 1932, 55 F.2d 626, affirmed on other grounds, 1932, 287 U.S. 308, 53 S.Ct. 150, 77 L.Ed. 325, a trespasser had taken coal and then destroyed the entries so that the amount of coal taken could not be determined. Since there was no way of knowing whether the recovery was greater than the basis for the coal taken, the gain was purely conjectural and not taxed. Magill explains the result as follows: "as the amount of coal removed could not be determined until a final disposition of the property, the computation of gain or loss on the damages must await that disposition." Taxable Income, pp. 339–340. The same explanation may be applied to Farmers' & Merchants' Bank v. Commissioner, supra, which relied on the Strother case in finding no gain. The recovery in that case had been to compensate for the injury to good will and business reputation of the plaintiff bank inflicted by defendant reserve banks' wrongful conduct in collecting checks drawn on the plaintiff bank by employing "agents who would appear daily at the bank with checks and demand payment thereof in cash in such a manner as to attract unfavorable public comment". Since the plaintiff bank's business was not destroyed but only injured and since it continued in business, it would have been difficult to require the taxpayer to prove what part of the basis of its good will should be attributed to the recovery. In the case at bar, on the contrary, the entire business and good will were destroyed so that to require the taxpayer to prove the cost of the good will is no more impractical than if the business had been sold.[8]

* * *

The decision of the Tax Court is affirmed.

Reading the Raytheon case with the excerpt from Doyle v. Mitchell Brothers Co., in which the Supreme Court held that a return of capital was nontaxable, it is apparent that damages received to compensate the taxpayer for the destruction of all or a portion of the goodwill of a business are nontaxable except to the extent that the damages recovered exceed the taxpayer's provable basis in the destroyed goodwill. It is often difficult, but not impossible, to establish the basis for the goodwill of a business. In the Farmers' and Merchants' Bank case, cited in Raytheon, the court held nontaxable a recovery of $13,000 even though it represented a recovery for damages to goodwill. Presumably, the bank was able to establish a basis in the goodwill equal at least to the amount of the recovery. For an analysis of the allocation for basis, see Inaja Land Co. v. Commissioner, p. 763.

8. Since the plant and other physical assets of the taxpayer were not destroyed but were used by it in the new tube business under licenses from R.C.A., the recovery was only for the destruction of business good will and not the physical assets. Hence the cost basis that the taxpayer could deduct from the recovery would only be that attributable to the good will, including the cost of development of its rectifier tube.

Although the compensatory damage payments in the Raytheon case represented the proceeds from a forced sale of the company's goodwill (the court relied on the complaint to hold that the suit was for damage to goodwill), a realization, although involuntary, occurred. Gain was computed under § 1001(a) just as in any voluntary realization. If a taxpayer uses the proceeds from forced sale to replace the destroyed property, taxing the gain would produce a rather harsh result. Congress enacted § 1033 to alleviate the potential hardship resulting from a taxpayer, after payment of the tax, lacking sufficient funds to replace the destroyed property. Section 1033 provides that a taxpayer need not report realized gain if the taxpayer reinvests the proceeds from an involuntary conversion, within a specified time period, in business property of a similar character.

Question

Why might a taxpayer, for example Raytheon, encounter difficulty in using § 1033?

4. PUNITIVE DAMAGES

COMMISSIONER v. GLENSHAW GLASS CO.

Supreme Court of the United States, 1955.
348 U.S. 426, 75 S.Ct. 473, 99 L.Ed. 483.

MR. CHIEF JUSTICE WARREN delivered the opinion of the Court.

This litigation involves two cases with independent factual backgrounds yet presenting the identical issue. The two cases [which] were consolidated for argument before the Court of Appeals for the Third Circuit and were heard *en banc*. The common question is whether money received as exemplary damages for fraud or as the punitive two-thirds portion of a treble-damage antitrust recovery must be reported by a taxpayer as gross income under § 22(a) of the Internal Revenue Code of 1939 [§ 61(a)]. In a single opinion, 211 F.2d 928, the Court of Appeals affirmed the Tax Court's separate rulings in favor of the taxpayers. 18 T.C. 860; 19 T.C. 637. Because of the frequent recurrence of the question and differing interpretations by the lower courts of this Court's decisions bearing upon the problem, we granted the Commissioner of Internal Revenue's ensuing petition for certiorari. 348 U.S. 813, 75 S.Ct. 50.

The facts of the cases were largely stipulated and are not in dispute. So far as pertinent they are as follows:

Commissioner v. Glenshaw Glass Co.—The Glenshaw Glass Company, a Pennsylvania corporation, manufactures glass bottles and containers. It was engaged in protracted litigation with the Hartford-Empire Company, which manufactures machinery of a character used by Glenshaw. Among the claims advanced by Glenshaw were demands for exemplary damages for fraud and treble damages for injury to its business by reason of Hartford's violation of the federal antitrust laws.

In December, 1947, the parties concluded a settlement of all pending litigation, by which Hartford paid Glenshaw approximately $800,000. Through a method of allocation which was approved by the Tax Court, 18 T.C. 860, 870–872, and which is no longer in issue, it was ultimately determined that, of the total settlement, $324,529.94 represented payment of punitive damages for fraud and antitrust violations. Glenshaw did not report this portion of the settlement as income for the tax year involved. The Commissioner determined a deficiency claiming as taxable the entire sum less only deductible legal fees. As previously noted, the Tax Court and the Court of Appeals upheld the taxpayer.

Commissioner v. William Goldman Theatres, Inc.—William Goldman Theatres, Inc., a Delaware corporation operating motion picture houses in Pennsylvania, sued Loew's, Inc., alleging a violation of the federal antitrust laws and seeking treble damages. After a holding that a violation had occurred, William Goldman Theatres, Inc., v. Loew's Inc., 3 Cir., 150 F.2d 738, the case was remanded to the trial court for a determination of damages. It was found that Goldman had suffered a loss of profits equal to $125,000 and was entitled to treble damages in the sum of $375,000. William Goldman Theatres, Inc., v. Loew's, Inc., D.C., 69 F.Supp. 103, affirmed 3 Cir., 164 F.2d 1021, certiorari denied 334 U.S. 811, 68 S.Ct. 1016, 92 L.Ed. 1742. Goldman reported only $125,000 of the recovery as gross income and claimed that the $250,000 balance constituted punitive damages and as such was not taxable. The Tax Court agreed, 19 T.C. 637, and the Court of Appeals, hearing this with the Glenshaw case, affirmed. 211 F.2d 928.

It is conceded by the respondents that there is no constitutional barrier to the imposition of a tax on punitive damages. Our question is one of statutory construction: are these payments comprehended by § 22(a) [of the 1939 Code; § 61(a) of the 1986 Code]?

The sweeping scope of the controverted statute is readily apparent:

"§ 22. Gross income

"(a) General definition. 'Gross income' includes gains, profits, and income derived from salaries, wages, or compensation for personal service * * * of whatever kind and in whatever form paid, or from professions, vocations, trades, businesses, commerce, or sales, or dealings in property, whether real or personal, growing out of the ownership or use of or interest in such property; also from interest, rent, dividends, securities, or the transaction of any business carried on for gain or profit, *or gains or profits and income derived from any source whatever.* * * * " (Emphasis added.)

This Court has frequently stated that this language was used by Congress to exert in this field "the full measure of its taxing power." Helvering v. Clifford, 309 U.S. 331, 334, 60 S.Ct. 554, 556, 84 L.Ed. 788. Respondents contend that punitive damages, characterized as "windfalls" flowing from the culpable conduct of third parties, are not within the scope of the section. But Congress applied no limitations as to the source of taxable receipts, nor restrictive labels as to their nature. And the Court has given a liberal construction to this broad phraseology in recognition of the intention of Congress to tax all gains except those specifically exempted. Commissioner v. Jacobson, 336 U.S. 28, 49, 69 S.Ct. 358, 369, 93 L.Ed. 477; Helvering v. Stockholms Enskilda Bank, 293 U.S. 84, 87–91, 55 S.Ct. 50, 51–53, 79 L.Ed. 211. Thus, the fortuitous gain accruing to a lessor by reason of the forfeiture of a lessee's improvements on the rented property was taxed in Helvering v. Bruun, 309 U.S. 461, 60 S.Ct. 631, 84 L.Ed. 864. Such decisions demonstrate that we cannot but ascribe content to the catchall provision of § [61(a)], "gains or profits and income derived from any source whatever." The importance of that phrase has been too frequently recognized since its first appearance in the Revenue Act of 1913 to say now that it adds nothing to the meaning of "gross income."

Nor can we accept respondents' contention that a narrower reading of § [61(a)] is required by the Court's characterization of income in Eisner v. Macomber, 252 U.S. 189, 207, 40 S.Ct. 189, 193, 64 L.Ed. 521, as " 'the gain derived from capital, from labor, or from both combined.' " [9] The Court was there endeavoring to determine whether the distribution of a corporate stock dividend constituted a realized gain to the shareholder, or changed "only the form, not the essence," of his capital investment. Id., 252 U.S. at page 210, 40 S.Ct. at page 194. It was held that the taxpayer had "received nothing out of the company's assets for his separate use and benefit." Id., 252 U.S. at page 211, 40 S.Ct. at page 194. The distribution, therefore, was held not a taxable event. In that context—distinguishing gain from capital—the definition served a useful purpose. But it was not meant to provide a touchstone to all future gross income questions. Helvering v. Bruun, supra, 309 U.S. at pages 468–469, 60 S.Ct. at page 634; United States v. Kirby Lumber Co., supra, 284 U.S. at page 3, 52 S.Ct. 4.

Here we have instances of undeniable accessions to wealth, clearly realized, and over which the taxpayers have complete dominion. The mere fact that the payments were extracted from the wrongdoers as punishment for unlawful conduct cannot detract from their character as taxable income to the recipients. Respondents concede, as they must, that the recoveries are taxable to the extent that they compensate for damages actually incurred. It would be an anomaly that could not be justified in the absence of clear congressional intent to say that a recovery for actual damages is taxable but not the additional amount

9. The phrase was derived from Stratton's Independence, Ltd. v. Howbert, 231 U.S. 399, 415, 34 S.Ct. 136, 140, 58 L.Ed. 285, and Doyle v. Mitchell Bros. Co., 247 U.S. 179, 185, 38 S.Ct. 467, 469, 62 L.Ed. 1054, two cases construing the Revenue Act of 1909, 36 Stat. 11, 112. Both taxpayers were "wasting asset" corporations, one being engaged in mining, the other in lumbering operations. The definition was applied by the Court to demonstrate a distinction between a return on capital and "a mere conversion of capital assets." Doyle v. Mitchell Bros. Co., supra, 247 U.S. at page 184, 38 S.Ct. at page 469. The question raised by the instant case is clearly distinguishable.

extracted as punishment for the same conduct which caused the injury. And we find no such evidence of intent to exempt these payments.

It is urged that re-enactment of § [61(a)] without change since the Board of Tax Appeals held punitive damages nontaxable in Highland Farms Corp., 42 B.T.A. 1314, indicates congressional satisfaction with that holding. Re-enactment—particularly without the slightest affirmative indication that Congress ever had the Highland Farms decision before it—is an unreliable indicium at best. Helvering v. Wilshire Oil Co., 308 U.S. 90, 100–101, 60 S.Ct. 18, 24, 84 L.Ed. 101; Koshland v. Helvering, 298 U.S. 441, 447, 56 S.Ct. 767, 770, 80 L.Ed. 1268. Moreover, the Commissioner promptly published his non-acquiescence in this portion of the Highland Farms holding and has, before and since, consistently maintained the position that these receipts are taxable.[10] It therefore cannot be said with certitude that Congress intended to carve an exception out of § [61(a)'s] pervasive coverage. Nor does the 1954 Code's legislative history, with its reiteration of the proposition that statutory gross income is "all-inclusive," give support to respondents' position. The definition of gross income has been simplified, but no effect upon its present broad scope was intended.[11] Certainly punitive damages cannot reasonably be classified as gifts, cf. Commissioner v. Jacobson, 336 U.S. 28, 47–52, 69 S.Ct. 358, 368–370, 93 L.Ed. 477, nor do they come under any other exemption provision in the Code. We would do violence to the plain meaning of the statute and restrict a clear legislative attempt to bring the taxing power to bear upon all receipts constitutionally taxable were we to say that the payments in question here are not gross income. See Helvering v. Midland Mutual Life Ins. Co., supra, 300 U.S. at page 223, 57 S.Ct. at page 425, 81 L.Ed. 612.

Reversed.

MR. JUSTICE DOUGLAS dissents.

MR. JUSTICE HARLAN took no part in the consideration or decision of this case.

---

10. The long history of departmental rulings holding personal injury recoveries non-taxable on the theory that they roughly correspond to a return of capital cannot support exemption of punitive damages following injury to property. See 2 Cum.Bull. 71; I–1 Cum.Bull. 92, 93; VII–2 Cum.Bull. 123; 1954–1 Cum.Bull. 179, 180. Damages for personal injury are by definition compensatory only. Punitive damages, on the other hand, cannot be considered a restoration of capital for taxation purposes.

11. In discussing § 61(a) of the 1954 Code, the House Report states:

"This section corresponds to section 22(a) of the 1939 Code. While the language in existing section 22(a) has been simplified, the all-inclusive nature of statutory gross income has not been affected thereby. Section 61(a) is as broad in scope as section 22(a).

"Section 61(a) provides that gross income includes 'all income from whatever source derived.' This definition is based upon the 16th Amendment and the word 'income' is used in its constitutional sense." H.R.Rep. No.1337, supra, note 10, at A18.

A virtually identical statement appears in S.Rep.No.1622, supra, note 10, at 168.

For a further analysis of the taxation of damages see Yorio, The Taxation of Damages: Tax and Non-Tax Policy Considerations, 62 Cornell L.Rev. 701 (1977); Stephan, Federal Taxation and Human Capital, 70 Va.L.Rev. 1357 (1984).

Problems

1. Big Mac Food Services Corporation purchased the Schultz Grocery Store from Papa Schultz, paying $150,000 for the entire business. The value of the tangible assets, including the land, building, fixtures and inventory, equalled $100,000. Everyone in the neighborhood knew that he carried the best bagels in town. Big Mac Food Services Corporation intends to keep the Schultz name on the store and continue to sell the same bagels.

Immediately after the purchase, a competing grocery store spread an unfounded rumor that the Schultz bagels contained carcinogens. The following year the profits generated by the Schultz store dropped to $6,000. Big Mac Food Services Corporation initiated a defamation action against the competitor and obtained a $90,000 judgment.

How should the corporation treat the receipt of $90,000? Consider the Raytheon case. How do you think the trier of fact arrived at the $90,000 damage figure? Why did the Food Services Corporation pay $50,000 in excess of the value of the tangible assets for Papa Schultz' business? How was the $50,000 excess arrived at? Did the corporation have a basis in the self-generated goodwill of Papa Schultz?

2. In March of Year 1, Dr. Caspar Smith was notified in writing that he had been appointed to the faculty of the Medical School of Metro University, with the rank of associate professor, effective September 1 of that year. In June, at a hearing before a Congressional committee, Dr. Smith declined to answer a question by the committee counsel concerning his association with certain so-called peace groups during his student days at State University. Dr. Smith "took" the Fifth Amendment. Following the hearings, Metro University revoked the appointment and refused to honor the contract. In addition, the Dean of the Medical School sent a letter to the local medical society explaining the Medical School's failure to go through with the appointment of Dr. Smith. In the letter the Dean stated, among other things, that Dr. Smith was a "liar", "communist sympathizer", and "butcher boy". Shortly after these events, Dr. Smith sued the University for breach of contract and the Dean for libel. In his suit against the University, Dr. Smith recovered an aggregate of $100,000 in damages. Compensatory damages for loss of salary and punitive damages for the aggravated nature of the University's conduct each represented $50,000 of the judgment. In the action against the Dean, Dr. Smith recovered compensatory damages of $60,000 plus punitive damages of $120,000. Both judgments were paid in Year 3.

a. Must Dr. Smith include the entire $100,000 received from the University in gross income in Year 3? Consider § 104(a)(2) and the Glenshaw Glass case.

b. Can Dr. Smith exclude from gross income the entire $180,000 received from the Dean in Year 3? Consider § 104(a)(2), Reg. § 1.104–1(c), Rev.Rul. 84–108, and the Roemer Case. Why would you argue that the Dean's letter exposed Dr. Smith to contempt and ridicule and that he suffered embarrassment, humiliation, and mental agony?

c. Are any of Dr. Smith's legal expenses deductible? Consider § 162(a).

3. How would you structure and draft the complaint of the owner of a business contemplating a defamation suit against a competitor? Remember that the recovery for lost profits usually will be included in the income of the plaintiff. If the case is tried, what type of evidence should be presented at trial? What type of finding as to damages should the jury be required to make? Consider the Roemer case and § 104(a)(2).

D. ANNUITIES

1. TAX DEFERRAL MECHANISM AND ALLOCATION OF ANNUITY PAYMENTS

Instead of receiving a replacement of capital in a single payment, such as a damage recovery, the taxpayer may recover his capital in a series of payments. We next examine the return of capital concept applicable to annuities.

Suppose that an individual, age 50, wishes to provide a steady source of income for his retirement years. The individual buys an annuity contract, generally from an insurance company, and pays one lump sum premium or a series of premiums. The amount of the premium is determined by the individual's life expectancy and the return the company expects to receive from investing the premium. In return for the present consideration, the insurance company invests the premium and promises to make specified future payments, for example, monthly payments to the individual commencing at age 65 and continuing for the individual's life. The number of payments is based on a contingency, usually the life of the annuitant.

How are the payments received under the annuity contract treated, especially the return of capital (the premiums paid by a taxpayer) and the income element (the interest earned by the company on the taxpayer's investment), and when is income realized and recognized? Section 72 defers taxation of the interest on the capital invested until the payments are received. This means that any interest income earned on the money on deposit with the insurance company is not included in gross income prior to the annuity starting date. Unlike a savings account, an annuity defers the tax consequences on the interest income. After the annuity starting date, the payments received are allocated between income and the return of capital. Through detailed Regulations, § 72, with an important exception noted below, enables an individual to recover his investment in an annuity contract pro rata over his projected life expectancy. For example, the taxpayer purchases an annuity contract for $9,000 which provides for annual payments of $1,000 for the rest of his life, payments to begin in one year. If the annuitant's life expectancy is 27 years, the expected return from the annuity over the annuitant's life is $27,000 and the exclusion ratio is 33.3%. Examine the life expectancy table in Reg. § 1.72–9. The exclusion ratio (§ 72(b)(1) and Reg. § 1.72–4(a)) is determined by dividing the $9,000 investment in the contract (§ 72(c) and Reg. § 1.72–6(a)) by the $27,000 expected return (§ 72(c) and Reg. § 1.72–5(a)) under the contract. Therefore, 33.3% of each annual payment of $1,000 would be excluded from the annuitant's gross income up to the amount of the annuitant's unrecovered investment in the contract. § 72(b)(2). If this individual lives for exactly 27 years, then $9,000 of the total annuity payments are excluded from gross income.

If the annuitant lives longer than the date of his projected life expectancy, he realizes more on the annuity contract than expected. After the annuitant's basis has been recovered, for individuals whose annuity starting date (as defined in § 72(c)(4)) is after December 31, 1986, subsequent annuity payments are fully taxable. § 72(b)(2).

The annuitant may die before his projected life expectancy. If so, he will not recover all of his basis. The Tax Reform Act of 1986 provides that if, after the annuity starting date (as defined in § 72(c)(4)) payments under an annuity stop because of the annuitant's death, the annuitant is allowed to deduct his unrecovered investment in the contract (as defined in § 72(b)(4)) in his last taxable year. § 72(b)(3). However, if the annuitant dies prior to the annuity starting date, no loss is deductible. This is known as a mortality loss. § 72(b)(3)(A).

Presumably, the deferral feature inherent in the present treatment of annuities is based on the policy of helping people provide for their old age and retirement. S.Rep. No. 1622, 83d Cong., 2d Sess. 11 (1954). The deferral aspect allows the retired person to report the interest element at lower tax rates after the individual's peak earning years.

Other possible alternatives exist for the tax treatment of annuities:

a. The annuitant could receive payments tax free until the individual had recovered his investment in the contract; thereafter, all further payments would be fully taxable. This method delays the government's collection of revenue and reduces, after several years, the annuitant's after-tax stream of income. It also fails to consider that there is an income element in every annuity payment. Prior to 1934, the tax law allowed the complete recovery of capital before requiring the reporting of income for all annuities.

b. Gross income derived from each payment under an annuity contract could equal a fixed percentage (for instance, 3%) of the cost of the contract. The balance of each payment (97%) could be excluded from gross income as a return of capital until an individual had recovered his capital; thereafter, the entire amount received would be taxable. The fixed percentage rule was used between 1934 and 1954.

However, the fixed percentage rule may not reasonably allow an annuitant to recover his investment.

c. The excluded portion of each payment under the contract could remain fixed even though the annuitant dies after the date of his projected life expectancy. If the annuitant lives longer than the date of his projected life expectancy, he realizes more on the annuity contract than anticipated. Although all of the annuitant's capital would be recovered, subsequent annuity payments continue to be divided into a taxable and an excludable portion and the annuitant's after-tax stream of income remains constant. This is known as a mortality gain. Conversely, if the taxpayer dies before his projected life expectancy, he fails to recover all of his capital. No loss is deductible even though the annuitant is taxed on amounts prior to the full recovery of his capital. This is known as a mortality loss. For annuities with a starting date between January 1, 1955 and December 31, 1986, the Code divided each payment into three components: (1) interest income; (2) return of capital; and (3) mortality gain or loss. The Treasury came out about even as the lost tax revenues attributable to mortality gains offset the increased tax revenues from the mortality losses. The mortality gain assured an individual a constant aftertax income during retirement. Thus, a retired person who lived past his life expectancy would not find that his increased tax burden forced a downward adjustment in his standard of living.

d. Gross income derived from each payment under an annuity contract could be set on a sliding scale; for example, more of the payments could be included in the annuitant's gross income in the earlier years of the payouts on the contract. Taxing more income in the earlier payout years more accurately reflects the apportionment between income and return of capital. Obviously, the greater the amount of capital on deposit with an insurance company, the more interest it will earn.

Annuities are an excellent tax deferral device because the income earned on the investment is not taxed until the annuity starting date. § 72(c)(4). Under prior law, any withdrawals of funds prior to the annuity starting date were first treated as a withdrawal of capital and were taxable only after the entire investment in the contract had been recovered. Insurance companies began marketing annuities providing investment yields competitive with other investments that did not enjoy the same deferral advantage. The benefits of the deferral of taxation to the annuity starting date and the return of capital treatment for partial withdrawals allowed insurance companies to market these annuities as tax shelters. In 1982, § 72(e) was amended to provide that amounts received under annuity contracts prior to the annuity starting date are first treated as withdrawals of the income already earned on the investment. Such withdrawals constitute a return of capital only after all the income already accumulated has been reported. § 72(e)(2) and (3). For example, X purchases a single premium annuity contract for $50,000. Ten years later, but prior to the annuity starting date, when the policy has a cash value of $125,000,

X withdraws $100,000. Under prior law, X could treat $50,000 as a return of capital. Now X must include in gross income $75,000, the portion of the withdrawal allocated to income already earned. The remaining $25,000 withdrawn is a return of capital. Afterwards, X has an investment in the contract of only $25,000. This change was prospective in effect. Investments in annuity contracts purchased prior to August 14, 1982 are exempt from the new provisions of § 72(e).

During the accumulation phase (i.e. prior to the annuity starting date) the interest earned on the annuitant's investment is not taxable. This deferral was previously available to all holders of annuity contracts. The Tax Reform Act of 1986 sought to prevent employers from using deferred annuity contracts, i.e. those under which the periodic payments are to begin after a specified period of time elapses after the purchase of the annuity contract, "to fund, on a tax-favored basis, significant amounts of deferred compensation for employees." Tax Reform Act of [1986], Report of the Committee on Ways and Means House of Representatives on H.R. 3838, 99th Cong., 1st Sess. 703 (1985). Any annuity contract held by a person who is not a natural person (for example, a corporation) is not treated as an annuity contract for Federal income tax purposes. § 72(u). As a result, the income on the contract (as defined in § 72(u)(2)(A)) is treated as ordinary income received by the contract holder during the taxable year it is earned. § 72(u)(1)(B). Certain exceptions are provided in § 72(u)(3).

Section 72(q) imposes a penalty tax on certain early distributions from any annuity in an attempt to discourage the use of an annuity as a short-term investment. Certain distributions are exempt from this penalty. § 72(q)(2).

Problems

1. After working for the Federal government for four years, Ted Player joined a Miami law firm. The firm has no formal retirement plan. Instead of giving Ted a $5,000 year-end bonus, the firm purchased, in Ted's name, a single payment annuity contract from an insurance company at a cost of $5,000. Assume that Ted holds the annuity contract so that § 72(u) is not applicable.

(a) Under the terms of the annuity contract, Ted, who is 28 years old, will receive payments of $100 per month for life, commencing when Ted reaches age 60. The contract contains no refund feature and Ted loses all rights to any monies on his death.

(i) What are the tax consequences of this arrangement to Ted? Note that under § 72(f)(1) in computing Ted's investment in the contract (§ 72(c)(1)) amounts contributed by Ted's employer, which are includible in Ted's gross income, are treated as paid by Ted. Consider the Drescher case (p. 160) and reconsider Problem at p. 17. Specifically, does Ted realize gross income? If so, when does he realize income, and what is the amount of income? Can he characterize any portion of the income as capital gain? Consider § 72(a), (b), (c)(1), (3) and (4), Regs. § 1.72–1(a), –4(a), –5(a)(1), –6(a), –9(Table I).

(ii) Can Ted still use the exclusion ratio if he lives beyond his life expectancy? Consider § 72(b)(2).

(iii) Can a loss be deducted under § 165(a) and (c) if Ted dies at age 40 (or at age 66)? Consider § 72(b)(3). Assume Ted's employer entered into the contract with the primary purpose of providing economic security for Ted in his retirement.

(iv) Assume Ted's annuity was subject to a substantial risk of forfeiture (§ 83(c)(1)) which expired on his retirement and the annuity was non-transferrable (§ 83(c)(2)) until Ted's retirement. What would be the tax consequences of the payment of the bonus and the purchase of the annuity for Ted and his employer? When does he realize income and what is the amount of income? Consider § 403(c). Reconsider Problem 1 at p. 95.

(b) Assume that under the terms of the annuity contract, Ted will receive payments of $100 per month for a period of 20 years, payments to commence when Ted reaches age 60. The payments are guaranteed to Ted or his designated beneficiary for a period of 20 years. Note that under § 72(c)(2) and Reg. § 1.72–7(a) and (b) the value of the guaranteed payments must be subtracted from the cost of the contract in figuring the exclusion ratio. What are the tax consequences of this arrangement to Ted? Consider Reg. § 1.72–7(a) and (b) and § 72(c)(2).

2. Connie invests $10,000 in a savings account at a local bank paying interest at 10%. Chris invests $10,000 in an annuity paying interest at 10%. Payments from the annuity will commence in five years. At the end of five years Connie and Chris each have accumulated $16,105.10. Commencing in Year 6, each starts to withdraw monies from their respective accounts. Compare the tax results for Connie and Chris. What tax advantage exists if an individual uses an annuity as a savings vehicle?

3. Conrad, age 60, purchases a single premium annuity contract for $50,000 with a $5,000 annual annuity payment starting at age 61. The insurance company guarantees a 10% rate of return during the first five years and a rate of return indexed to Treasury bills thereafter. Conrad has the right to withdraw all monies, including accumulated interest, at any time. Assume Conrad receives $5,000 at the end of each year so that the net value of the annuity remains constant. Can he apply the exclusion ratio? Are § 72(e)(2) and (3) effective in this situation to deal with the perceived abuse of the annuity provisions?

2. STRUCTURED SETTLEMENTS

Individuals recovering damages in personal injury actions are often reluctant to accept a lump sum damage payment because of a desire to provide for a guaranteed future cash flow without having to rely upon their ability to manage a large lump sum amount. They are often worried about providing for future medical and rehabilitation costs, replacing lost income, and providing for future living expenses. A viable alternative is known as the structured settlement. Such a settlement typically provides that the injured person will receive guaranteed fixed amounts for a term certain or for the rest of his life by means of the purchase of an annuity from an insurance company. A properly designed structured settlement can result in the entire amount of each annuity payment being excluded from gross income under § 104(a)(2) even though a portion of each annuity payment represents what would otherwise be taxable interest under § 72. The amount to be received under the annuity contract is generally based upon the lump sum payment that would otherwise be made. Typically, the negligent party uses the lump sum amount to fund the purchase of an annuity. As to the exclusion from taxation of the amount received by the assignee insurance company for agreeing to assume the defendant's liability, see § 130.

If an injured person receives a lump sum payment, fully excludable under § 104(a)(2), and invests the money in a savings account or uses the money to purchase an annuity himself, the interest earnings are fully taxable, immediately in the case of a savings account or during the payout in the case of an annuity. However, this interest element can be excluded from gross income if the injured person allows the negligent party (or his casualty insurance company) to provide him with the annuity instead of obtaining it himself.

REV.RUL. 79–220
1979–2 C.B. 74.

ISSUE

Does the exclusion from gross income provided by section 104(a)(2) of the Internal Revenue Code of 1954 apply to the full amount of monthly payments received in settlement of a damage suit or only to the discounted present value of such payments?

FACTS

A, an individual, sued B for damages for personal injuries. B is insured by M, an insurance company. Before trial, A accepted M's offer to settle the suit for a lump-sum payment of $8,000 and M's agreement to provide A with the discounted present value of the monthly payments of $250 for A's lifetime or 20 years, whichever is longer, the payments to be made to A's estate after A's death if A should die before the end of 20 years. A had no right to which, at date of settlement, was less than the total monthly payments to be provided) or to control the investment of that amount.

To provide the monthly payments for A, M purchased a single premium annuity contract from O, another insurance company. M advised O to make payments directly to A. However, M is the owner of the annuity contract and has all rights of ownership, including the right to change the beneficiary. A can rely on only the general credit of M for collection of the monthly payments.

LAW AND ANALYSIS

Section 61(a) of the Code and the Income Tax Regulations thereunder provide that, except as otherwise provided by law, gross income means all income from whatever source derived.

Section 104(a)(2) of the Code provides that except in the case of amounts attributable to (and not in excess of) deductions allowed under section 213 (relating to medical and dental expenses) for any prior taxable year, gross income does not include the amount of any damages received (whether by suit or agreement) on account of personal injuries or sickness.

Section 1.104–1(c) of the regulations provides, in part, that the term "damages received (whether by suit or agreement)" means an amount received (other than workmen's compensation) through prosecution of a legal suit or action based upon tort or tort type rights, or through a settlement agreement entered into in lieu of such prosecution.

However, if a lump-sum damage payment is invested for the benefit of a claimant who has actual or constructive receipt or the economic benefit of the lump-sum payment, only the lump-sum payment is received as damages within the meaning of section 104(a)(2) of the Code, and none of the income from the investment of such payment is excludable under section 104. See Rev.Rul. 65–29, 1965–1 C.B. 59, relating to damages awarded a claimant for tortious injuries in a lump-sum payment of $416x$ dollars over which claimant had unfettered control. The $416x$ dollars represented the discounted value of $520x$ dollars, which was found to be the reasonable cost of care, medicine, and medical attention for the injured person over a 10-year period. Rev.Rul. 65–29 holds that only the lump-sum payment, $416x$ dollars, is received as damages within the meaning of section 104(a)(2). See also Rev.Rul. 76–133, 1976–1 C.B. 34, which reaches a similar conclusion with regard to a court approved settlement awarded a minor and transmitted by the clerk of the court, in the name of the minor, to a savings and loan association for deposit in certificates of deposit.

In the instant case, there is a continuing obligation by M to pay $250 per month to A for the agreed period. M's purchase of a single premium annuity contract from the other insurance company was merely an investment by M to provide a source of funds for M to satisfy its obligation to A. See Rev.Rul. 72–25, 1972–1 C.B. 127, which relates to a similar arrangement made by an employer to provide for payment of deferred compensation to an employee. In Rev.Rul. 72–25, as here, the arrangement was merely a matter of convenience to the obligor and did not give the recipient any right in the annuity itself.

HOLDINGS

The exclusion from gross income provided by section 104(a)(2) of the Code applies to the full amount of the monthly payments received by A in settlement of the damage suit because A had a right to receive only the monthly payments and did not have the actual or constructive receipt or the economic benefit of the lump-sum amount that was invested to yield that monthly payment. If *A* should die before the end of 20 years, the payments made to *A* 's estate under the settlement agreement are also excludable from income under section 104.

———

In recognition of the position taken in Rev.Rul. 79–220 Congress amended the language in § 104(a)(2) in 1983, adding the words "and whether as a lump sum or as periodic payments."

Structured settlements have become increasingly popular in recent years as a method of settling personal injury claims. The tax advantages are undoubtedly a major factor in their growth. The tax windfall available to the injured party can result in reduced costs to the negligent party (and his insurance company) as the injured person may agree to settle the damage claims for an annuity with a present discounted value less than the amount a of lump sum payment. That is, the cost of funding a fully tax free annuity would be less than the lump sum settlement.

If a negligent party is permitted to currently deduct the cost of a damage claim, a structured settlement (prior to the Tax Reform Act of 1984) resulted in a tax windfall to him as well. The deduction for tort liabilities is discussed at p. 231.

E. DEFERRED COMPENSATION PLANS

1. INTRODUCTION

Formal deferred compensation plans may either be qualified or nonqualified. If an individual's employer has a qualified deferred compensation plan, the employee can postpone tax consequences on the income attributable to his employer's contributions to the plan. The earnings on the contributions are also not taxed until retirement. From the employer's standpoint, contributions to a qualified plan are deductible when made even though the employee postpones the inclusion in gross income. § 404(a)(1), (2) and (3). The requirements for qualified deferred compensation plans are set forth in §§ 401–415.

If an employer does not have a qualified plan, the tax consequences of a nonqualified plan are subject to general tax principles. Normally, an employee must currently include the present value of the retirement benefits in gross income as illustrated in the Drescher case which follows. However, if an employee's rights in the plan are subject to § 83, then the inclusion in the employee's gross income would be postponed § 83(a), and the employer's deduction would be deferred under § 83(h).

Informal deferred compensation plans are considered at p. 243.

UNITED STATES v. DRESCHER

United States Court of Appeals, Second Circuit, 1950.
179 F.2d 863 cert. denied 340 U.S. 821, 71 S.Ct. 60, 95 L.Ed. 603 (1950).

SWAN, CIRCUIT JUDGE.

* * * [Plaintiff] was an officer and director of Bausch & Lomb Optical Company, and in each of the taxable years the Company purchased from an insurance company at a cost of $5,000 a single premium annuity contract naming him as the annuitant. The taxes in dispute resulted from the Commissioner's including such cost as additional compensation received by the plaintiff in the year when the annuity contract was purchased. The district court awarded the plaintiff judgment for overpayments in the aggregate amount of $5,924.22, ruling that he received no income in 1939 or 1940 attributable to the purchase of the annuity contracts. The correctness of this ruling is presented by the appeal.

The facts are not in dispute. In 1936 the Optical Company inaugurated a plan to provide for the voluntary retirement at the age of 65 of its principal officers then under that age. There were five such, of whom Mr. Drescher was one. He was born April 28, 1894. Pursuant to this plan and in "recognition of prior services rendered," the Company purchased on December 28, 1939, and on the same date in 1940, a single premium, non-forfeitable annuity contract which named Mr. Drescher as the annuitant. Each policy was issued by Connecticut General Life Insurance Company and was delivered to the Optical Company which retained possession of it. It was the Company's intention, and so understood by the annuitant, that possession of the policy should be retained until the annuitant should reach the age of 65. The premium paid for each policy was $5,000. The amount of such payment was deducted by the Company in its tax return for the year of payment as part of the compensation paid to Mr. Drescher during that year. His salary as an officer was not reduced because of the purchase of the annuity contract, and he was not given the option to receive in cash the amounts expended by the Company for the premium payments. In filing income tax returns Mr. Drescher reported on the cash basis; the Optical Company on the accrual basis.

By the terms of the policy the Insurance Company agrees to pay the annuitant, commencing on December 28, 1958, a life income of $54.70 monthly under the 1939 policy and $44.80 monthly under the 1940 policy, with a minimum of 120 monthly payments. If the annuitant dies before receiving 120 monthly payments, the rest of them are payable to the beneficiary named in the policy. Each policy gives the annuitant an option to accelerate the date when monthly payments shall commence, but this option must be exercised by the annuitant in writing and endorsed on the policy. Consequently so long as the Optical Company retains possession of the policy the annuitant cannot exercise the option. If the annuitant dies before December 28, 1958, or before the acceleration date if he has exercised the option to accelerate monthly income payments, a death benefit is payable to the beneficiary designated by him (his wife). The policy reserves to him the right to change the beneficiary. The policy declares that "Neither this contract nor any payment hereunder may be assigned, and the contract and all payments shall be free from the claims of all creditors to the fullest extent permitted by law." The policy has no cash surrender, salable, or loan value, and does not entitle the annuitant to a distribution of surplus.

This case is governed by the provisions of the Internal Revenue Code as they existed in 1939 and 1940. The appellant contends that the contracts are taxable to the annuitant in the year of purchase by the employer because [§ 61(a), 26 U.S.C.A., sweeps into gross income "compensation for personal service, of whatever kind and in whatever form paid, * * * and income derived from any source whatever." * * * [The taxpayer] cites Treasury rulings to the effect that retirement annuity contracts purchased for an employee gave rise to taxable income only as the annuitant received payments under the contract; and that the entire amount of each annuity payment was includible in gross income for the year of its receipt if he had made no contribution toward the purchase of the annuity * * *.

Whether we should construe the statute in accord with these Treasury rulings if the matter were *res integra,* we need not say. In this court the question of construction is not *res integra,* because of our decision in Ward v. Commissioner, 2 Cir., 159 F.2d 502. That case involved a single premium annuity contract delivered to the annuitant and assignable by him. We there held that "the petitioner became taxable in 1941 upon whatever value was, by the delivery of the policy to him in that year, then unconditionally placed at his disposal. * * * This was the then assignable value of the policy." 159 F.2d page 504. We then considered whether it was error to value the policy in the amount of the premium paid for it. We recognized that the assignable value of the policy in 1941 might be less than the single premium paid for it, but as the purchaser had offered no proof that it was we held that the Tax Court was right in treating "cost to the purchaser as the assignable value of the policy when received by the taxpayer." 159 F.2d page 505.

As we shall not overrule the Ward case, the question is narrowed to determining whether the present case is distinguishable because the plaintiff's policies are non-assignable and were retained in the possession of the employer. We do not think these facts are sufficient to distinguish the cases with respect to taxability of the contracts, although they may affect the value of the rights the respective annuitants acquired. It cannot be doubted that in 1939 the plaintiff received as compensation for prior services something of economic benefit which he had not previously had, namely, the obligation of the insurance company to pay money in the future to him or his designated beneficiaries on the terms stated in the policy. That obligation he acquired in 1939 notwithstanding the employer's retention of possession of the policy and notwithstanding its non-assignability. The perplexing problem is how to measure the value of the annuitant's rights at the date he acquired them. The taxpayer contends that they then had no present value, while the appellant argues that their value was equal to the premium paid by the employer. We are unable to accept either contention.

The prohibition against assignment does not prove complete absence of present value. The right to receive income payments which accrued to the plaintiff when the Optical Company received each contract represented a present economic benefit to him. It may not have been worth to him the amount his employer paid for it; but it cannot be doubted that there is a figure, greater than zero although less than the premium cost, which it would have cost him to acquire identical rights. Likewise, the assurance that any beneficiary named by him at the time the contract was executed, or substituted by him at a later date, would in the event of his death receive the cost of each contract, plus interest after a few years, conferred a present economic benefit on him. Whatever present value the life insurance feature had to him is clearly taxable. Another element of value inheres in the possibility that the annuitant could realize cash by contracting with a putative third person to hold in trust for him any payments to be received under the annuity contract. True, the promisee would run the risk that the annuitant might die before becoming entitled to any payments, in which event they would be payable to the beneficiary designated in the policy, but by exercising the reserved power to change the beneficiary the annuitant could designate his promisee. The power to make such a contract based on the policy may well have had some present value. No proof was offered as to this. On the other hand, it seems clear that the policy was worth less to the annuitant than the premium paid because the employer's retention of possession precluded him from exercising the privilege of accelerating the date of annuity payments since the insurance company's approval had to be endorsed upon the policy. The granting of this privilege must have been one of the factors taken into account in fixing the premium—at least, we may so assume in the absence of evidence. Hence deprivation of ability to exercise the privilege would decrease the value of the policy to the annuitant below its cost to the employer.

None of the authorities relied on by the parties is precisely in point on the issue of valuation. In Hackett v. Commissioner, 1 Cir., 159 F.2d 121 although the policy was non-assignable, the value to the annuitant was measured by the cost of the premium. As already stated, that basis is inapplicable here, for retention of the policy by the employer cut off the acceleration privilege. The same distinction exists with respect to the partially assignable policy involved in Oberwinder v. Commissioner, 8 Cir., 147 F.2d 255. And the tax treatment of the assignable policy in that case, as well as of those involved in the Ward case affords little guidance to a correct valuation here. Likewise, the cases holding free from taxation a non-assignable promise to pay money at a future date do not assist us, since they rest decision on taxibility—here concluded by the Ward case—rather than on valuation. But it is unnecessary on the present appeal to determine the precise valuation of the policies.

* * * [T]he burden of proving by how much he was overtaxed was on the plaintiff. * * * He relied upon the terms of the contract to prove that it had no present value whatever. But for reasons already stated we are satisfied that the 1939 policy had some present value and since he did not prove that such value was less than $5,000, the judgment in his favor cannot stand.

* * *

Judgment reversed and cause remanded.

CLARK, CIRCUIT JUDGE (dissenting in part).

I agree that the judgment must be reversed, but do not share in the view that some amount less than the $5,000 expended by the employer for this taxpayer in each of the years in question may be found to be the value of the annuity and hence the amount of additional compensation for which he is to be taxed. For the contrary seems to me well supported in reason and well established by the authorities cited in the opinion, some directly in point and some with, I suggest, immaterial variations of fact. In the light of modern conditions of life, the satisfying of the highly natural and indeed burning desire of most men of middle age to obtain security for their old age and for their widows at death seems so clearly an economic benefit that I wonder it has been questioned as much as it has. Nor do I see the need to support this conclusion by looking for some highly theoretical possibility of turning this benefit into immediate dollars and cents any more than in the case where an employee is furnished living quarters or meals. Just as the latter are valued as additional compensation, though not assigned or assignable, so I think this highly valuable security is a purchased benefit for these company executives. Consequently the making of nice distinctions in either taxability or the amount thereof between assignable or accelerable annuities or their delivery or retention by the company—after careful forethought and advice of its attorneys with naturally an eye on both pension and tax possibilities—seems to me improper, when the general purpose to make adequate retirement provisions for these employees was made so clear.

Hence for any issues here involved I do not think it is important to discover what reasons impelled the employer to make the slightly differing provisions from those before this court in Ward v. Commissioner, 2 Cir., 159 F.2d 502, 505. Perhaps the employer may have had the prescience to foresee these tax problems which are troubling my brothers and did trouble the court below * * *. Perhaps, rather, the employer was providing only for a surer provision "free from the claims of all creditors to the fullest extent permitted by law" for this taxpayer and his wife. So in retaining possession of the policies and cherishing the present intent not to permit acceleration of the annuities, the employer may have had in mind a way of both securing the purchased services to the retirement age in normal cases and guarding against unusual situations due to disability or other special cause. In any event the fact is that the employer purchased at the going insurance rate those contracts which for the parties fulfilled the conditions desired.[12] Actually they would return to the annuitant, or to his widow, total amounts at least well in excess of the premiums paid and increasing yet more the longer he lived. The parties got just what they paid for in the insurance market, and its cost price is the additional compensation the executive received. The two features stressed in the opinion, namely, the nonassignability and the present nonaccelerability of the annuities, may add to their usability for the particular purpose, but would seem not to change the basis of value. Perhaps, indeed, they render the contracts more desirable not only to the employer, but also to the annuitant's wife, as making the security provisions less easily impaired, and thus have a special appeal to a husband solicitous of his wife's future. At least, I do not see what basis we have for thinking they adversely affect values of provisions for a particular purpose, viz., security. If, in fact, these conditions do affect the amount of the premium, as the opinion rather naturally assumes, then all the more is the bargain of the parties to be respected as made; even the annuitant would doubtless be interested in a maximum return though it be strictly limited to himself or his wife. It seems to me that there is being set up some premise, not found in any of the precedents, of a fictitious partly-impaired transferability which is now somehow to be given a value in place of the wholly practical values set upon these contracts in the insurance market itself.

Hence unless these benefits are now taxed, this small group of top executives will be given a tax advantage not accruing to less fortunate or less well-advised persons. Such taxation should not be confused or rendered abortive by directions for valuation impossible of execution in any realistic way.

Questions

1. Is Drescher consistent with Glenshaw Glass (p. 147)? What facts in Drescher support taxpayer's position?

2. Would Mr. Drescher, a cash method taxpayer, have preferred to have postponed the reporting of gross income to the year he received the cash and could actually spend the benefit?

12. This was a tightly controlled corporation, so much so that the executives receiving the annuities and their families owned approximately 35 per cent of the voting stock, while the older officers and directors owned approximately 57 per cent. Hence there was never a sharp divergency of interest between these executives and their employer.

(a) Upon retirement what are the tax consequences to Mr. Drescher, if the earlier premium payments, contrary to the Drescher case, were not included in gross income.

(b) Upon retirement what are the tax consequences to Mr. Drescher if the earlier premium payments were included in gross income in 1939 and 1940?

3. Is Drescher consistent with LoBue (p. 97)? Which is the better reasoned decision? How did each court deal with the valuation problem?

4. What is the significance of the fact that Mr. Drescher's employer deducted the cost of the annuity contracts in 1939 and 1940? Under § 404(a)(5), if a deferred compensation arrangement is not a qualified plan, the employer only receives a deduction in the year the employee includes the employer's contribution in gross income.

2. QUALIFIED EMPLOYEE BENEFIT PLANS

Advantages of Qualified Employee Benefit Plans. Most taxpayers would agree that a natural objective of a working individual is to accumulate wealth during high income years of employment to provide for those years when the taxpayer has either ceased work entirely or has done so to a substantial degree. A taxpayer can, of course, take a portion of his salary and invest it in income-producing property in anticipation of the leaner years ahead. Qualified pension, profit-sharing and similar plans [13] present a deviation from the standard income realization rules of §§ 61 and 83 and, therefore, may facilitate taxpayers' saving objectives. A standard retirement savings scenario may take one of three forms. These forms will be labeled, for purposes of illustration, as the deduction-income model, the no deduction-no income model, and the deduction-no income model.

In the "deduction-income" model, the employer pays the employee's entire compensation to the employee's account. The employer receives a deduction when the amount is either paid or accrued which depends on the employer's method of accounting. The employee, who has unrestricted control over the earned funds, is taxed in the year the funds are made available to him and generally subject to his control. Any earnings on the invested compensation in the form of interest or dividends is likewise taxed in the year it is credited to the employee's account.

The "no deduction-no income" model (or the § 83 model) results where the employer immediately pays a portion of the employee's earnings but to vest sometime in the future or subjects the earnings to two conditions: a substantial risk of forfeiture and non-transferability.

---

13. The principal difference between a pension plan and a profit-sharing plan is that in a pension plan the benefits which an employee will receive on retirement are predetermined. The contributions of the employer are tailored to meet the benefits set out in the original arrangement. A profit-sharing plan provides a formula to allocate employer contributions to employee-participants in the plan. The contributions are made from accumulated or current profits, or both, earned by the employer.

In such cases, the employee is not taxed and the employer cannot deduct the compensation until either the employee's rights become vested under the plan or are no longer subject to substantial risk of forfeiture (or are transferable). Any earnings on the invested compensation are taxed to the employer. The employer receives a deduction when the employee's rights become vested or are no longer subject to a substantial risk of forfeiture (or are transferable). The employee also takes the earnings into income at that time.

The "deduction-no income" (or qualified plan model) permits an employer to take a deduction in the year amounts are either: (1) paid into a qualified trust or (2) accrued and paid into the trust when the company's tax return is filed, which is usually within 2½ months of the company's year end. The employee neither includes the amounts in gross income at the time of the contribution to the trust, nor does he (as in the no deduction-no income model) include amounts in income when they are vested or no longer subject to substantial risk of forfeiture (or are transferrable). Rather, the amounts are included in income when actually paid out to the employee in later years. The earnings on the invested compensation are not taxed to the employee (or the employer, for that matter) until the shield of the qualified plan is lifted and the employee receives distributions. Finally, the trust is also exempt from income taxation.

The utilization of a qualified plan mechanism, therefore, provides numerous benefits to both the employer and the employee. The employer receives a current deduction. The employee pays no tax either on contributions into the trust or on the earnings on such contributions. Such earnings can grow without reduction for taxes at a much more rapid rate than if taxes were exacted on a yearly basis. The effect is more than a mere deferral of tax. The deferral must be considered in light of the compounding effect on the invested compensation and earnings which ultimately result in significantly greater after-tax dollars on distribution.

As is true in numerous other areas of the tax law, benefits are not without their restrictions. In order to take advantage of the preferential qualified plan mechanization, the employer must adhere to a series of extremely complex Internal Revenue Code provisions and Regulations as well as equally convoluted labor law provisions. These rules are so complex that this entire area of law has evolved into a speciality in its own right. Few practitioners who do not make qualified plan work a major part of their practice find it cost effective to engage in such work on an infrequent basis.

Types of Plans. The attorney must also assist the client in his choice of the type of plan best suited for his particular business. Although there are numerous types of plans, most practitioners will consider two basic types more frequently than any others, namely, defined benefit plans and defined contribution plans. The first broad category consists of the defined benefit type plans. These plans utilize actuarial computations to determine the amount which must be funded to pay a stated benefit at some future time. Since these plans tend to favor older employees who are near retirement (larger contributions are needed to fund an older employee's future stated benefit), closely-held corporations, whose employees are also shareholders, often take advantage of this type of plan. The other major category of qualified plans is the defined contribution plan. These plans do not utilize actuarial computations. Rather, contributions are made to a trust for the benefit of employee-participants based on a predetermined formula or possibly, if a profit sharing type of defined contribution plan is selected, at the discretion of the employer's board of directors. Unlike defined benefit plans, defined contribution plans provide an individual account for each participant. The benefits under a defined contribution plan depend on the length of service of each employee-participant and the investment results of the plan.

To achieve the tax benefits offered to employee-participants and employers, a plan (whether a defined contribution plan or a defined contribution plan) must be qualified. Limits exist on the benefits under and the contributions to qualified plans. The maximum annual benefit provided to a participant in a defined benefit plan generally is the lesser of $90,000 or 100% of the participant's average compensation for the participant's three consecutive highest paid years. § 415(b)(1). The annual additions for each participant under a defined contribution plan cannot exceed the lesser of $30,000 (or if greater, one-quarter of the dollar limitation for defined benefit plans) or 25% of the participant's compensation. § 415(c)(1). A $200,000 annual compensation limit applies for purposes of computing the allowable deductions as well as for purposes of defining the qualified status of a plan. §§ 404(a)(1) and 401(a)(17). Cost of living adjustments will be made to the defined benefit plan dollar limit beginning in 1988; however, no cost of living adjustments will be made to the defined contribution plan dollar limit until the $30,000 limit equals 25 percent of the defined benefit dollar limit. § 415(d). The $200,000 annual compensation limit is also indexed for inflation. § 401(a)(17).

Nondiscrimination Requirements. Qualification also requires minimum participation and vesting standards. §§ 410 and 411. Although a plan need not cover every employee, a specified minimum number of employees must be covered. §§ 401(a)(3) and 410(b). The Code provides general coverage rules to determine if the coverage of the plan is discriminatory and benefits only officers, shareholders, and highly compensated employees. A plan is not qualified unless it meets one of three coverage requirements: (1) a percentage test (§ 410(b)(1)(A)); (2) a ratio test (§ 410(b)(1)(B)); or (3) an average benefits test (§ 410(b)(1)(C) and (b)(2)). Furthermore, a plan may not involve discriminatory contributions or benefits. § 401(a)(4). These requirements guard against officers or highly compensated employees obtaining excessive benefits under a qualified plan. In addition, employee benefits must vest within specified time periods prior to retirement. §§ 401(a)(7) and 411.

3. INDIVIDUAL RETIREMENT ACCOUNTS

From 1982 through 1986 individuals who were participants in qualified plans or self-employed (Keogh) plans (as well as taxpayers who were not active participants in qualified plans or Keogh plans) could fund their own retirement benefits through an individual retirement account (IRA). Each year an individual could contribute and deduct up to the lesser of: (1) 100% of his compensation or (2) $2,000 (or $2,250 for an individual with a nonworking spouse). §§ 408(a)(1) and (b), 219(b)(1) and (c)(2).

Beginning in 1987, taxpayers may make deductible or nondeductible contributions to IRAs. A taxpayer and his spouse who are not covered under other retirement plans, by a qualified plan, may take the IRA deductions described in the preceding paragraph. If a taxpayer or his spouse is covered by (or is eligible to participate in) a qualified plan, he may make deductible IRA contributions provided his adjusted gross income, as defined in § 219(g)(3), falls below certain limits depending on marital status. § 219(g)(2) and (3). At that specified amount and higher, the IRA deduction is phased out. Single taxpayers lose the deduction for IRAs when their adjusted gross incomes reach $35,000; married couples lose it when their incomes reach $50,000. If one spouse is covered by a qualified plan and the other is not and the married couple has adjusted gross income of $50,000 or more, no IRA deduction is allowed even for the spouse without a plan. § 219(g)(1). Finally, other taxpayers may make nondeductible contributions to an IRA. § 408(o). The nondeductible contributions are limited to the amount of deductible contributions described in the preceding paragraph.

All IRAs, whether funded by deductible or nondeductible contributions, receive the favorable tax deferral on earnings with its associated compounding effect until funds are withdrawn.

In expanding the availability of IRAs, the legislative history (S.Rep. No. 97–144, 97th Cong., 1st Sess. 112–113 (1981)) indicates:

> The committee is concerned that the resources available to individuals who retire are often not adequate to avoid a substantial decrease from preretirement living standards. The committee believes that retirement savings by individuals can make an important contribution toward maintaining preretirement living standards and that the present level of individual savings is too often inadequate for this purpose. The committee understands that personal savings of individuals have recently declined in relation to personal disposable income (i.e., personal income after personal tax payments). During the years 1973 through 1975, the personal saving rate was no more than 8.6 percent. It declined to 5.2 percent in 1978 and 1979 and rose only slightly in 1980 to 5.6 percent. (These savings estimates include employer payments to private pension funds * * *).

The committee bill is designed to promote greater retirement security by increasing the amount which individuals can set aside for retirement in an IRA and by extending IRA eligibility to individuals who participate in employer-sponsored plans. * * *

To limit investments in collectibles, defined as a work of art, rug, antique, metal, gem, stamp, or alcoholic beverage, amounts invested in collectibles are treated as taxable distributions for income tax purposes. § 408(m). This provision reflects the concern of Congress that "collectibles divert retirement savings from thrift institutions and other traditional investment media and that investments in collectibles do not contribute to productive capital formation." House Report No. 97–201, 97th Cong., 1st Sess. 143 (1981). Beginning in 1987, IRAs may, however, invest in certain gold or silver coins. § 403(m)(3).

Reference: Note, Costs and Consequences of Tax Incentives: The Individual Retirement Account, 94 Harv.L.R. 864 (1981).

Problems

1. Clare is an employee of Production Corporation which has a qualified pension plan under § 401 for Clare, among other employees. The Corporation contributes on behalf of Clare $1,000 annually to a trust established under the plan.

(a) What are the tax consequences to Clare of such contributions and the earnings of such amounts contributed to the trust? Consider §§ 402(a)(1) and 501(a).

(b) What are the tax consequences to Clare when the payments from the trust are received in the form of an annuity? Consider § 402(a)(1). Can any portion of the annuity payments be deemed a return of capital? Does Clare have an investment in the annuity contract? Consider § 72(b) and (c).

(c) What are the consequences to the Corporation of such contributions? Consider § 404(a).

2. Compare and contrast the tax consequences to an executive and to a corporation of the following: Incentive stock option (Problem, p. 90), restricted stock (Problem, p. 95), and a qualified pension plan.

3. Do qualified employee benefit plans and individual retirement accounts present serious "loopholes" in the income tax system? Reconsider the materials on Tax Policy criteria (p. 40). Consider the following excerpt.

OFFICE OF THE SECRETARY, DEPARTMENT OF THE TREASURY, TAX REFORM FOR FAIRNESS, SIMPLICITY AND ECONOMIC GROWTH

Vol. 2, 337–338 (1984).

REASONS FOR CHANGE

The tax benefits applicable to IRAs are intended to encourage individuals to make adequate provision for their retirement security. Savings for this purpose also contribute to the formation of investment capital needed for economic growth. For many individuals, including individuals who are covered by employer-maintained retirement plans, IRAs are an important element in an overall strategy to provide for retirement security. The use of IRAs for retirement saving should thus not only be encouraged, but made available on a broad and consistent basis.

The existing limitations on IRA contributions are illogical and inequitable as applied to married couples. The relatively minor allowances for a spousal IRA fail to recognize the important economic contributions made by nonearning spouses. Moreover, they are inconsistent with other rules of current law under which married couples are treated as an economic and taxpaying unit. Thus, a husband and wife that each earn $10,000 can make aggregate IRA contributions of $4,000 under current law. A couple with the same joint income of $20,000, all of it earned by one spouse, can make aggregate IRA contributions of only $2,250. A third couple, also with $20,000 of joint income, but with one spouse earning only $200, is limited even further to a $2,200 aggregate IRA contribution. These disparate results are inconsistent with both the retirement savings policy reflected in IRAs and with general tax principles requiring similar treatment of similarly situated taxpayers.

PROPOSALS

The dollar limit on the deductible IRA contributions that may be made by an individual would be increased from $2,000 to $2,500.

A married individual filing a joint return, including an individual with no annual compensation, would be permitted to take into account his or her spouse's compensation (less the deductible IRA contribution made by such spouse) in determining the deduction limit for such individual. Thus, married couples with aggregate compensation of $5,000 or more would be entitled to the same $5,000 aggregate IRA contribution ($2,500 apiece) regardless of how much of the aggregate compensation was generated by either spouse.

* * *

ANALYSIS

Increasing the IRA deduction limits would encourage taxpayers to set aside additional amounts in long-term savings. This would not only enhance individual retirement security, but should also contribute to increased capital formation and productivity.

Chapter 4

GROSS INCOME—OTHER FORMS

A. CLAIM OF RIGHT

1. ANNUAL ACCOUNTING CONCEPT

A taxpayer computes taxable income for each annual accounting period as required by § 441. Although almost all individuals use the calendar year, some companies use fiscal years which generally conform to their normal business cycle. For example, a ski resort would not end its taxable year on December 31, in the middle of the winter season. Instead of dividing the ski season between two reporting periods, it would be more appropriate to measure the degree of success for a ski resort by viewing the taxable year as ending in April or May, after the snow melted. Regardless of the taxable year chosen, taxable income or loss is determined for a twelve-month period. Accordingly, a taxpayer reports all receipts and expenditures occurring during each twelve-month period on the income tax return for that taxable year.

Focusing only upon each taxable year can result in distortions if all of the events associated with a particular transaction take place over several annual accounting periods. For example, assume an investor enters into a business deal to buy and improve a parcel of land and then sell it at a profit. Assume the investment produces a net loss of $2,000 in the first year and a net loss of $1,000 in the second year. During the third year the property is sold, producing a net gain that year of $7,000 in the third year. Although this investment has generated a $4,000 profit, dividing the single transaction into yearly segments distorts the true financial results of that single transaction. Despite the fact that the distortion caused by the application of the annual accounting concept can have adverse income tax consequences, the Supreme Court, in the following case, upheld the integrity and application of the annual accounting concept in our income tax system.

BURNET v. SANFORD & BROOKS CO.

Supreme Court of the United States, 1931.
282 U.S. 359, 51 S.Ct. 150, 75 L.Ed. 383.

MR. JUSTICE STONE delivered the opinion of the Court.

* * *

From 1913 to 1915, inclusive, respondent, a Delaware corporation engaged in business for profit, was acting for the Atlantic Dredging Company in carrying out a contract for dredging the Delaware River, entered into by that company with the United States. In making its income tax returns for the years 1913 to 1916, respondent added to gross income for each year the payments made under the contract that year, and deducted its expenses paid that year in performing the contract. The total expenses exceeded the payments received by $176,271.88. The tax returns for 1913, 1915, and 1916 showed net losses. That for 1914 showed net income.

In 1915 work under the contract was abandoned, and in 1916 suit was brought in the Court of Claims to recover for a breach of warranty of the character of the material to be dredged. Judgment for the claimant, 53 Ct.Cl. 490, was affirmed by this Court in 1920. United States v. Atlantic Dredging Co., 253 U.S. 1, 40 S.Ct. 423, 425, 64 L.Ed. 735. It held that the recovery was upon the contract and was "compensatory of the cost of the work, of which the government got the benefit." From the total recovery, petitioner received in that year the sum of $192,577.59, which included the $176,271.88 by which its expenses under the contract had exceeded receipts from it, and accrued interest amounting to $16,305.71. Respondent having failed to include these amounts as gross income in its tax returns for 1920, the Commissioner made the deficiency assessment here involved, based on the addition of both items to gross income for that year.

The Court of Appeals ruled that only the item of interest was properly included, holding, erroneously as the government contends, that the item of $176,271.88 was a return of losses suffered by respondent in earlier years and hence was wrongly assessed as income. Notwithstanding this conclusion, its judgment of reversal and the consequent elimination of this item from gross income for 1920 were made contingent upon the filing by respondent of amended returns for the years 1913 to 1916, from which were to be omitted the deductions of the related items of expenses paid in those years. Respondent insists that as the Sixteenth Amendment and the Revenue Act of 1918, which was in force in 1920, plainly contemplate a tax only on net income or profits, any application of the statute which operates to impose a tax with respect to the present transaction, from which respondent received no profit, cannot be upheld.

If respondent's contention that only gain or profit may be taxed under the Sixteenth Amendment be accepted without qualification, see Eisner v. Macomber, 252 U.S. 189, 40 S.Ct. 189, 64 L.Ed. 521, 9 A.L.R.

1570; Doyle v. Mitchell Brothers Co., 247 U.S. 179, 38 S.Ct. 467, 62 L.Ed. 1054, the question remains whether the gain or profit which is the subject of the tax may be ascertained, as here, on the basis of fixed accounting periods, or whether, as is pressed upon us, it can only be net profit ascertained on the basis of particular transactions of the taxpayer when they are brought to a conclusion.

All the revenue acts which have been enacted since the adoption of the Sixteenth Amendment have uniformly assessed the tax on the basis of annual returns showing the net result of all the taxpayer's transactions during a fixed accounting period, either the calendar year, or, at the option of the taxpayer, the particular fiscal year which he may adopt. * * *

That the recovery made by respondent in 1920 was gross income for that year * * * cannot, we think, be doubted. The money received was derived from a contract entered into in the course of respondent's business operations for profit. While it equalled, and in a loose sense was a return of, expenditures made in performing the contract, still, as the Board of Tax Appeals found, the expenditures were made in defraying the expenses incurred in the prosecution of the work under the contract, for the purpose of earning profits. They were not capital investments, the cost of which, if converted, must first be restored from the proceeds before there is a capital gain taxable as income. See Doyle v. Mitchell Brothers Co., supra, page 185 of 247 U.S., 38 S.Ct. 467.

That such receipts from the conduct of a business enterprise are to be included in the taxpayer's return as a part of gross income, regardless of whether the particular transaction results in net profit, sufficiently appears from the quoted words of Section [61](a) and from the character of the deductions allowed. Only by including these items of gross income in the 1920 return would it have been possible to ascertain respondent's net income for the period covered by the return, which is what the statute taxes. The excess of gross income over deductions did not any the less constitute net income for the taxable period because respondent, in an earlier period, suffered net losses in the conduct of its business which were in some measure attributable to expenditures made to produce the net income of the later period.

Bowers v. Kerbaugh-Empire Co., 271 U.S. 170, 46 S.Ct. 449, 70 L.Ed. 886, on which respondent relies, does not support its position. In that case the taxpayer, which had lost, in business, borrowed money, which was to be repaid in German marks, and which was later repaid in depreciated currency, had neither made a profit on the transaction, nor received any money or property which could have been made subject to the tax.

But respondent insists that if the sum which it recovered is the income defined by the statute, still it is not income, taxation of which without apportionment is permitted by the Sixteenth Amendment, since the particular transaction from which it was derived did not

result in any net gain or profit. But we do not think the amendment is
to be so narrowly construed. A taxpayer may be in receipt of net
income in one year and not in another. The net result of the two years,
if combined in a single taxable period, might still be a loss; but it has
never been supposed that that fact would relieve him from a tax on the
first, or that it affords any reason for postponing the assessment of the
tax until the end of a lifetime, or for some other indefinite period, to
ascertain more precisely whether the final outcome of the period, or of
a given transaction, will be a gain or a loss.

The Sixteenth Amendment was adopted to enable the government
to raise revenue by taxation. It is the essence of any system of taxation
that it should produce revenue ascertainable, and payable to the
government, at regular intervals. Only by such a system is it practicable to produce a regular flow of income and apply methods of accounting, assessment, and collection capable of practical operation. It is not
suggested that there has ever been any general scheme for taxing
income on any other basis. The computation of income annually as the
net result of all transactions within the year was a familiar practice,
and taxes upon income so arrived at were not unknown, before the
Sixteenth Amendment. It is not to be supposed that the amendment
did not contemplate that Congress might make income so ascertained
the basis of a scheme of taxation such as had been in actual operation
within the United States before its adoption. While, conceivably, a
different system might be devised by which the tax could be assessed,
wholly or in part, on the basis of the finally ascertained results of
particular transactions, Congress is not required by the amendment to
adopt such a system in preference to the more familiar method, even if
it were practicable. It would not necessarily obviate the kind of
inequalities of which respondent complains. If losses from particular
transactions were to be set off against gains in others, there would still
be the practical necessity of computing the tax on the basis of annual or
other fixed taxable periods, which might result in the taxpayer being
required to pay a tax on income in one period exceeded by net losses in
another.

* * *

The assessment was properly made under the statutes. Relief from
their alleged burdensome operation which may not be secured under
these provisions, can be afforded only by legislation, not by the courts.

Reversed.

————

Congress alleviated the problem in Sanford & Brooks by enacting
the predecessor of § 172 which permits net operating losses to be
carried back to a specified number of prior taxable years, § 172(b)(1)(A),
and carried forward to a specified number of subsequent taxable years,
§ 172(b)(1)(B). This means that certain deductions which are of no tax
benefit in the year incurred may be used to offset income in other
taxable years. However, unused personal deductions and the depen-

dency exemptions may not be carried over to other years. § 172(d)(3) and (4).

2. IS THE RECEIPT TAXABLE WHEN RECEIVED?

When the taxpayer receives a payment, is the receipt always taxable? Where property is given to an individual as collateral for a loan or monies are deposited with an individual for the performance of obligations on a lease, the recipient does not realize gross income, unless or until the property or monies are forfeited. The property or funds are received subject to restrictions as to their disposition.

Another situation where it may be inappropriate to immediately report income is where a dealer sells a product and has net income of a certain sum. There is always a chance the buyer will claim that the item is not what he ordered. Should the dealer be able to postpone paying tax on the income now or take a deduction later if he has to make a refund to the buyer? Is it relevant that the dealer has the use of the funds received from the buyer?

A first step in analyzing how the problem is handled consists of examining a case where there existed a possibility that the taxpayer might have to return income earned in a previous year.

NORTH AMERICAN OIL CONSOLIDATED v. BURNET

Supreme Court of the United States, 1932.
286 U.S. 417, 52 S.Ct. 613, 76 L.Ed. 1197.

MR. JUSTICE BRANDEIS delivered the opinion of the Court.

The question for decision is whether the sum of $171,979.22, received by the North American Oil Consolidated in 1917, was taxable to it as income of that year.

The money was paid to the company under the following circumstances: Among many properties operated by it in 1916 was a section of oil land, the legal title to which stood in the name of the United States. Prior to that year, the government, claiming also the beneficial ownership, had instituted a suit to oust the company from possession; and on February 2, 1916, it secured the appointment of a receiver to operate the property, or supervise its operations, and to hold the net income thereof. The money paid to the company in 1917 represented the net profits which had been earned from that property in 1916 during the receivership. The money was paid to the receiver as earned. After entry by the District Court in 1917 of the final decree dismissing the bill, the money was paid, in that year, by the receiver to the company. United States v. North American Oil Consolidated, 242 F. 723. The government took an appeal (without supersedeas) to the Circuit Court of Appeals. In 1920, that court affirmed the decree. 264 F. 336. In 1922, a further appeal to this Court was dismissed by stipulation. 258 U.S. 633, 42 S.Ct. 315, 66 L.Ed. 802.

The income earned from the property in 1916 had been entered on the books of the company as its income. It had not been included in its original return of income for 1916; but it was included in an amended return for that year which was filed in 1918. Upon auditing the company's income and profits tax returns for 1917, the Commissioner of Internal Revenue determined a deficiency based on other items. The company appealed to the Board of Tax Appeals. There, in 1927, the Commissioner prayed that the deficiency already claimed should be increased so as to include a tax on the amount paid by the receiver to the company in 1917. The Board held that the profits were taxable to the receiver as income of 1916; and hence made no finding whether the company's accounts were kept on the cash receipts and disbursements basis or on the accrual basis. 12 B.T.A. 68. The Circuit Court of Appeals held that the profits were taxable to the company as income of 1917, regardless of whether the company's returns were made on the cash or on the accrual basis. 50 F.(2d) 752. This Court granted a writ of certiorari. 284 U.S. 614, 52 S.Ct. 208, 76 L.Ed. 524.

It is conceded that the net profits earned by the property during the receivership constituted income. The company contends that they should have been reported by the receiver for taxation in 1916; that, if not returnable by him, they should have been returned by the company for 1916, because they constitute income of the company accrued in that year; and that, if not taxable as income of the company for 1916, they were taxable to it as income for 1922, since the litigation was not finally terminated in its favor until 1922.

First. The income earned in 1916 and impounded by the receiver in that year was not taxable to him, because he was the receiver of only a part of the properties operated by the company. Under section 13(c) of the Revenue Act of 1916,[1] receivers who "are operating the property or business of corporations" were obliged to make returns "of net income as and for such corporations," and "any income tax due" was to be "assessed and collected in the same manner as if assessed directly against the organizations of whose businesses or properties they have custody and control." The phraseology of this section was adopted without change in the Revenue Act of 1918, 40 Stat. 1057, 1081, c. 18, § 239. The regulations of the Treasury Department have consistently construed these statutes as applying only to receivers in charge of the entire property or business of a corporation; and in all other cases have required the corporations themselves to report their income. Treas. Regs. 33, arts. 26, 209; Treas.Regs. 45, arts. 424, 622. That construction is clearly correct. The language of the section contemplates a

---

1. Act of September 8, 1916, 39 Stat. 756, 771, c. 463: "In cases wherein receivers, trustees in bankruptcy, or assignees are operating the property or business of corporations * * * subject to tax imposed by this title, such receivers, trustees, or assignees shall make returns of net income as and for such corporations * * * in the same manner and form as such organiza- tions are hereinbefore required to make returns, and any income tax due on the basis of such returns made by receivers, trustees, or assignees shall be assessed and collected in the same manner as if assessed directly against the organizations of whose businesses or properties they have custody and control."

substitution of the receiver for the corporation; and there can be such substitution only when the receiver is in complete control of the properties and business of the corporation. Moreover, there is no provision for the consolidation of the return of a receiver of part of a corporation's property or business with the return of the corporation itself. It may not be assumed that Congress intended to require the filing of two separate returns for the same year, each covering only a part of the corporate income, without making provision for consolidation so that the tax could be based upon the income as a whole.

Second. The net profits were not taxable to the company as income of 1916. For the company was not required in 1916 to report as income an amount which it might never receive. See Burnet v. Logan, 283 U.S. 404, 413, 51 S.Ct. 550, 75 L.Ed. 1143. Compare Lucas v. American Code Co., 280 U.S. 445, 452, 50 S.Ct. 202, 74 L.Ed. 538; Burnet v. Sanford & Brooks Co., 282 U.S. 359, 363, 51 S.Ct. 150, 75 L.Ed. 383. There was no constructive receipt of the profits by the company in that year, because at no time during the year was there a right in the company to demand that the receiver pay over the money. Throughout 1916 it was uncertain who would be declared entitled to the profits. It was not until 1917, when the District Court entered a final decree vacating the receivership and dismissing the bill, that the company became entitled to receive the money. Nor is it material, for the purposes of this case, whether the company's return was filed on the cash receipts and disbursements basis, or on the accrual basis. In neither event was it taxable in 1916 on account of income which it had not yet received and which it might never receive.

Third. The net profits earned by the property in 1916 were not income of the year 1922—the year in which the litigation with the government was finally terminated. They became income of the company in 1917, when it first became entitled to them and when it actually received them. If a taxpayer receives earnings under a claim of right and without restriction as to its disposition, he has received income which he is required to return, even though it may still be claimed that he is not entitled to retain the money, and even though he may still be adjudged liable to restore its equivalent. See Board v. Commissioner of Internal Revenue, 51 F.(2d) 73, 75, 76. Compare United States v. S.S. White Dental Manufacturing Co., 274 U.S. 398, 403, 47 S.Ct. 598, 71 L.Ed. 1120. If in 1922 the government had prevailed, and the company had been obliged to refund the profits received in 1917, it would have been entitled to a deduction from the profits of 1922, not from those of any earlier year. Compare Lucas v. American Code Co., supra.

Affirmed.

3. TREATMENT OF PAYMENT RECEIVED BY MISTAKE

The so-called "claim of right" doctrine expounded in the North American Oil Consolidated case has been applied in situations where the taxpayer has received a sum of money by mistake in one tax year and must pay it back in another tax year. The situation could arise if, to pursue the North American Oil Consolidated case further, the contingencies were finally resolved against the taxpayer. This could be handled in either of two ways:

     a. The transaction would be considered a "wash" with no income in the year when received and no deduction in the year when paid, or

     b. The amount would be considered taxable when received and deductible in the year when paid, that is, the receipt and deduction would be reflected in separate tax years.

Consider how the next case dealt with the return of a payment previously reported as gross income.

UNITED STATES v. LEWIS

Supreme Court of the United States, 1951.
340 U.S. 590, 71 S.Ct. 522, 95 L.Ed. 560.

Mr. Justice Black delivered the opinion of the Court.

Respondent Lewis brought this action in the Court of Claims seeking a refund of an alleged overpayment of his 1944 income tax. The facts found by the Court of Claims are: In his 1944 income tax return, respondent reported about $22,000 which he had received that year as an employee's bonus. As a result of subsequent litigation in a state court, however, it was decided that respondent's bonus had been improperly computed; under compulsion of the state court's judgment he returned approximately $11,000 to his employer. Until payment of the judgment in 1946, respondent had at all times claimed and used the full $22,000 unconditionally as his own, in the good faith though "mistaken" belief that he was entitled to the whole bonus.

On the foregoing facts the Government's position is that respondent's 1944 tax should not be recomputed, but that respondent should have deducted the $11,000 as a loss in his 1946 tax return. See G.C.M. 16730, XV-1 Cum.Bull. 179 (1936). The Court of Claims, however, relying on its own case, Greenwald v. United States, 57 F.Supp. 569, 102 Ct.Cl. 272, held that the excess bonus received "under a mistake of fact" was not income in 1944 and ordered a refund based on a recalculation of that year's tax. 91 F.Supp. 1017, 1022, 117 Ct.Cl. 336. We granted certiorari, 340 U.S. 903, 71 S.Ct. 279, because this holding conflicted with many decisions of the courts of appeals, see, e.g., Haberkorn v. United States, 6 Cir., 173 F.2d 587, and with principles announced in North American Oil Consolidated v. Burnet, 286 U.S. 417, 52 S.Ct. 613, 76 L.Ed. 1197.

In the North American Oil case we said: "If a taxpayer receives earnings under a claim of right and without restriction as to its disposition, he has received income which he is required to return, even though it may still be claimed that he is not entitled to retain the money, and even though he may still be adjudged liable to restore its equivalent." 286 U.S. at 424, 52 S.Ct. at page 615, 76 L.Ed. 1197.

Nothing in this language permits an exception merely because a taxpayer is "mistaken" as to the validity of his claim. * * *

Income taxes must be paid on income received (or accrued) during an annual accounting period. Cf. I.R.C. §§ [441, 451(a), 446(a)]; and see Burnet v. Sanford & Brooks Co., 282 U.S. 359, 363, 51 S.Ct. 150, 151, 75 L.Ed. 383. The "claim of right" interpretation of the tax laws has long been used to give finality to that period, and is now deeply rooted in the federal tax system. See cases collected in 2 Mertens, Law of Federal Income Taxation, § 12.103. We see no reason why the Court should depart from this well-settled interpretation merely because it results in an advantage or disadvantage to a taxpayer.[2]

Reversed.

MR. JUSTICE DOUGLAS (dissenting).

The question in this case is not whether the bonus had to be included in 1944 income for purposes of the tax. Plainly it should have been because the taxpayer claimed it as of right. Some years later, however, it was judicially determined that he had no claim to the bonus. The question is whether he may then get back the tax which he paid on the money.

Many inequities are inherent in the income tax. We multiply them needlessly by nice distinctions which have no place in the practical administration of the law. If the refund were allowed, the integrity of the taxable year would not be violated. The tax would be paid when due; but the government would not be permitted to maintain the unconscionable position that it can keep the tax after it is shown that payment was made on money which was not income to the taxpayer.

———

Although it may be more equitable for a taxpayer to adopt a wait and see approach, administrative practicality justifies the results in the North American Oil and Lewis cases. The Service would face a difficult task to constantly determine subtle questions regarding the certainty of right to income. If a taxpayer was allowed to postpone the reporting of income in a situation where the rights to the income were disputed at the outset, would this also mean that a claim for repayment arising in a subsequent year should also relate back? What about a claim that was not bona fide or one that was not seriously pursued? What if a bona fide claim for repayment is subsequently abandoned? Given the adoption of the annual accounting concept the judicial decisions allow for a practical administration of the tax laws. The difficult problems presented by these situations are often avoided by looking only at actual receipt and return in the years they occur.

2. It has been suggested that it would be more "equitable" to reopen respondent's 1944 tax return. While the suggestion might work to the advantage of this tax-payer, it could not be adopted as a general solution because, in many cases, the three-year statute of limitations would preclude recovery. I.R.C. § [6511(a)].

The claim of right doctrine requires the inclusion of an item of income in the year of receipt. This doctrine, as illustrated in the North American Oil Consolidated case, only determines when an item of income subject to a possible risk of return must be reported.

As a response to the inequity caused by the inclusion of the income in the year of receipt in the Lewis case, Congress enacted § 1341. Section 1341 does not change the claim of right doctrine. The enactment of § 1341 in 1954 only ameliorates the harshness of applying the annual accounting principle.

Section 1341 puts the taxpayer in no worse a position than if an item had never been included in income in the year of receipt. Section 1341 does not affect the year of receipt. Instead, under § 1341, qualifying taxpayers have the option of reducing the tax in the year of repayment "by either the tax attributable to the deduction or the decrease in the tax for the prior year attributable to the removal of the item, whichever is greater." S.Rep. No. 1622, 83d Cong.2d Sess. 451 (1954). Simply stated, a taxpayer may, in the year of repayment, either take a deduction for the year of repayment or reduce the taxes owed for the year of repayment by the amount of taxes caused by the inclusion for the year the amount was received. Carefully read § 1341(a). The legislative history further indicates, "In the case of a cash-basis taxpayer, in order to be entitled to a deduction in the later year, the amount must be repaid. However, in the case of an accrual-basis taxpayer, if the item was accrued but never received, the section [1341] applies when the deduction accrues in the later year although there is, of course, no amount to be repaid. Where an accrual-basis taxpayer has received the item, the time of accrual of the deduction again determines when the section comes into operation." S.Rep. No. 1622, 83d Cong.2d Sess. 451, 452 (1954). Note also that a deduction under § 1341 is exempt from the two percent floor on miscellaneous itemized deductions. § 67(b)(10).

Reference: Wootton, The Claim of Right Doctrine and Section 1341, 34 Tax Lawyer 297 (1981); Emanuel, The Scope of Section 1341, 53 Taxes 644 (1975). Dubroff, The Claim of Right Doctrine, 40 Tax.L. Rev. 729 (1985).

Problems

1. David, a cash method taxpayer, received, by mistake, a bonus of $10,000 from his employer in a tax year when his marginal tax rate was 28%. He repaid the sum in the following year, when his marginal bracket was 15%.

    (a) What would be the most advantageous treatment of the transaction sought by David?

    (b) What would be the most profitable claim for the Service?

    (c) What result would follow from the North American Oil and Lewis cases?

(d) What is the result if § 1341 is elected? Under what circumstances would a taxpayer elect § 1341?

(e) Why does a taxpayer consider the application of the annual accounting concept a harsh burden? Consider the Burnet v. Sanford & Brooks case. Can a taxpayer ever be better off by segregating income and a related deduction over different years?

2. When an embezzler repays his employer in a later year he cannot use § 1341. Why? See p. 195. Is this sound tax policy if the victim cannot recover all of the embezzled funds?

3. Donna, an investment banker, received a $10,000 fee from a client for working on a deal that was never consummated. If she voluntarily returns all or a portion of the fee in a later year, may Donna use § 1341?

4. Should the language of § 1341 be broadened to cover situations presently ineligible for special treatment?

B. CONTROL

1. ILLEGAL ACTIVITIES

Judicial attempts to provide bright-line definitions of gross income have proved notably unsuccessful. However, these decisions have indicated some of the attributes of gross income, such as benefit received. It is apparent that a court will not treat an individual who borrows money as having gross income because of the borrower's accompanying obligation to repay. The obligation to repay offsets the benefit of receiving the loan proceeds so that no increase occurs in the borrower's net worth. However, what happens if the borrower has no intention of repaying the loan? Or what if the lender is not aware that he has made the loan, such as an embezzlement? How are we to distinguish between bona fide loans and illegal appropriations?

It was once thought that money illegally obtained from another did not represent gross income where the recipient was bound to return it. Thus, in Commissioner v. Wilcox, 327 U.S. 404, 66 S.Ct. 546, 90 L.Ed. 752 (1946), the Supreme Court held that embezzled money did not constitute gross income to the embezzler. The court emphasized that because the embezzler had a legal obligation to return the money, he had no actual legal claim to it. To use a term borrowed from another context, the taxpayer did not hold the money under a "claim of right" and, therefore, the money could not represent gross income.

However, in Rutkin v. United States, 343 U.S. 130, 72 S.Ct. 571, 96 L.Ed. 833 (1952), the Supreme Court distinguished the gain of an extortionist from that of an embezzler on the ground that an extortionist is less likely to be asked for repayment. In holding that the funds obtained as a result of extortion constituted gross income in the year received although the recipient was, of course, obligated to return them, the Supreme Court stated: "An unlawful gain, as well as a lawful one, constitutes taxable income when its recipient has such control over it that, as a practical matter, he derives readily realizable economic value from it." (343 U.S. at 137, 72 S.Ct. at 575, 96 L.Ed. at 838). The Supreme Court declined to overrule the Wilcox case, stating "we limit that case to its facts." Most students of the issue then concluded, with the four dissenting judges in Rutkin, that the Wilcox case represented the law only in cases involving embezzlement by persons named Wilcox.

The Wilcox decision was in fact finally overruled in the James case which holds that illegal gains are gross income despite the legal obligation to repay.

JAMES v. UNITED STATES
Supreme Court of the United States, 1961.
366 U.S. 213, 81 S.Ct. 1052, 6 L.Ed.2d 246.

MR. CHIEF JUSTICE WARREN announced the judgment of the Court and an opinion in which MR. JUSTICE BRENNAN, and MR. JUSTICE STEWART concur.

The issue before us in this case is whether embezzled funds are to be included in the "gross income" of the embezzler in the year in which the funds are misappropriated under * * * § 61(a) of the Internal Revenue Code of [1986].

* * * The petitioner is a union official who, with another person, embezzled in excess of $738,000 during the years 1951 through 1954 from his employer union and from an insurance company with which the union was doing business. Petitioner failed to report these amounts in his gross income in those years and was convicted for willfully attempting to evade the federal income tax due for each of the years 1951 through 1954 in violation of * * * § 7201 of the Internal Revenue Code of [1986]. He was sentenced to a total of three years' imprisonment. The Court of Appeals affirmed. 273 F.2d 5. Because of a conflict with this Court's decision in Commissioner of Internal Revenue v. Wilcox, 327 U.S. 404, 66 S.Ct. 546, 90 L.Ed. 752, a case whose relevant facts are concededly the same as those in the case now before us, we granted certiorari. 362 U.S. 974, 80 S.Ct. 1059, 4 L.Ed.2d 1009.

In Wilcox, the Court held that embezzled money does not constitute taxable income to the embezzler in the year of the embezzlement under § [61(a)]. Six years later, this Court held, in Rutkin v. United States, 343 U.S. 130, 72 S.Ct. 571, 96 L.Ed. 833, that extorted money does constitute taxable income to the extortionist in the year that the money is received under § [61(a)]. In Rutkin, the Court did not overrule Wilcox, but stated:

"We do not reach in this case the factual situation involved in Commissioner of Internal Revenue v. Wilcox, 327 U.S. 404, 66 S.Ct. 546, 90 L.Ed. 752. We limit that case to its facts. There embezzled funds were held not to constitute taxable income to the embezzler under § [61(a)]." Id., 343 U.S. at page 138, 72 S.Ct. at page 576.

However, examination of the reasoning used in Rutkin leads us inescapably to the conclusion that Wilcox was thoroughly devitalized.

The basis for the Wilcox decision was "that a taxable gain is conditioned upon (1) the presence of a claim of right to the alleged gain and (2) the absence of a definite, unconditional obligation to repay or return that which would otherwise constitute a gain. Without some bona fide legal or equitable claim, even though it be contingent or contested in nature, the taxpayer cannot be said to have received any gain or profit within the reach of Section [61(a)]." Commissioner of Internal Revenue v. Wilcox, supra, 327 U.S. at page 408, 66 S.Ct. at page 549. Since Wilcox embezzled the money, held it "without any semblance of a bona fide claim of right," ibid., and therefore "was at all times under an unqualified duty and obligation to repay the money to his employer," ibid., the Court found that the money embezzled was not includible within "gross income." But, Rutkin's legal claim was no greater than that of Wilcox. It was specifically found "that petitioner had no basis for his claim * * * and that he obtained it by extortion." Rutkin v. United States, supra, 343 U.S. at page 135, 72 S.Ct. at page 574. Both Wilcox and Rutkin obtained the money by means of a criminal act; neither had a bona fide claim of right to the funds. Nor was Rutkin's obligation to repay the extorted money to the victim any less than that of Wilcox. The victim of an extortion, like the victim of an embezzlement, has a right to restitution. Furthermore, it is inconsequential that an embezzler may lack title to the sums he appropriates while an extortionist may gain a voidable title. Questions of federal income taxation are not determined by such "attenuated subtleties." Lucas v. Earl, 281 U.S. 111, 114, 50 S.Ct. 241, 74 L.Ed. 731; Corliss v. Bowers, 281 U.S. 376, 378, 50 S.Ct. 336, 337, 74 L.Ed. 916. Thus, the fact that Rutkin secured the money with the consent of his victim * * * is irrelevant. Likewise unimportant is the fact that the sufferer of an extortion is less likely to seek restitution than one whose funds are embezzled. What is important is that the right to recoupment exists in both situations.

Examination of the relevant cases in the courts of appeals lends credence to our conclusion that the Wilcox rationale was effectively vitiated by this Court's decision in Rutkin.[3] Although this case appears to be the first to arise that is "on all fours" with Wilcox, the lower federal courts, in deference to the undisturbed Wilcox holding, have earnestly endeavored to find distinguishing facts in the cases before

3. In Marienfeld v. United States, 214 F.2d 632, the Eighth Circuit stated, "We find it difficult to reconcile the Wilcox case with the later opinion of the Supreme Court in Rutkin * * *." Id., at page 636. The Second Circuit announced, in United States v. Bruswitz, 219 F.2d 59, "It is difficult to perceive what, if anything, is left of the Wilcox holding after Rutkin * * *." Id., at page 61. The Seventh Circuit's pri- or decision in Macias v. Commissioner, 255 F.2d 23, observed, "If this reasoning [of Rutkin] had been employed in Wilcox, we see no escape from the conclusion that the decision in that case would have been different. In our view, the Court in Rutkin repudiated its holding in Wilcox; certainly it repudiated the reasoning by which the result was reached in that case." Id., at page 26.

them which would enable them to include sundry unlawful gains within "gross income." [4]

It had been a well-established principle, long before either Rutkin or Wilcox, that unlawful, as well as lawful, gains are comprehended within the term "gross income." Section II B of the Income Tax Act of 1913 provided that "the net income of a taxable person shall include gains, profits, and income * * * from * * * the transaction of any *lawful* business carried on for gain or profit, or gains or profits and income derived from any source whatever * * *." (Emphasis supplied.) 38 Stat. 167. When the statute was amended in 1916, the one word "lawful" was omitted. This revealed, we think, the obvious intent of that Congress to tax income derived from both legal and illegal sources, to remove the incongruity of having the gains of the honest laborer taxed and the gains of the dishonest immune. Rutkin v. United States, supra, 343 U.S. at page 138, 72 S.Ct. at page 575; United States v. Sullivan, 274 U.S. 259, 263, 47 S.Ct. 607, 71 L.Ed. 1037. Thereafter, the Court held that gains from illicit traffic in liquor are includible within "gross income." Ibid. See also Johnson v. United States, 318 U.S. 189, 63 S.Ct. 549, 87 L.Ed. 704; United States v. Johnson, 319 U.S. 503, 63 S.Ct. 1233, 87 L.Ed. 1546. And, the Court has pointed out, with approval, that there "has been a widespread and settled administrative and judicial recognition of the taxability of unlawful gains of many kinds," Rutkin v. United States, supra, 343 U.S. at page 137, 72 S.Ct. at page 575. These include protection payments made to racketeers, ransom payments paid to kidnappers, bribes, money derived from the sale of unlawful insurance policies, graft, black market gains, funds obtained from the operation of lotteries, income from race track book-making and illegal prize fight pictures. Ibid.

The starting point in all cases dealing with the question of the scope of what is included in "gross income" begins with the basic premise that the purpose of Congress was "to use the full measure of its taxing power." Helvering v. Clifford, 309 U.S. 331, 334, 60 S.Ct. 554, 556, 84 L.Ed. 788. And the Court has given a liberal construction to the broad phraseology of the "gross income" definition statutes in recognition of the intention of Congress to tax all gains except those specifically exempted. Commissioner of Internal Revenue v. Jacobson, 336 U.S. 28, 49, 69 S.Ct. 358, 369, 93 L.Ed. 477; Helvering v. Stockholms Enskilda Bank, 293 U.S. 84, 87–91, 55 S.Ct. 50, 51–53, 79 L.Ed. 211. The * * * more simplified language of § 61(a) of the [1986] Code, "all income from whatever source derived," have been held to encompass all "accessions to wealth, clearly realized, and over which the taxpayers have complete dominion." Commissioner of Internal

4. For example, Kann v. Commissioner, 3 Cir., 210 F.2d 247, was differentiated on the following grounds: the taxpayer was never indicted or convicted of embezzlement; there was no adequate proof that the victim did not forgive the misappropriation; the taxpayer was financially able to both pay the income tax and make restitution; the taxpayer would have likely received most of the misappropriated money as dividends. * * *

Revenue v. Glenshaw Glass Co., 348 U.S. 426, 431, 75 S.Ct. 473, 477, 99 L.Ed. 483. A gain "constitutes taxable income when its recipient has such control over it that, as a practical matter, he derives readily realizable economic value from it." Rutkin v. United States, supra, 343 U.S. at page 137, 72 S.Ct. at page 575. Under these broad principles, we believe that petitioner's contention, that all unlawful gains are taxable except those resulting from embezzlement, should fail.

When a taxpayer acquires earnings, lawfully or unlawfully, without the consensual recognition, express or implied, of an obligation to repay and without restriction as to their disposition, "he has received income which he is required to return, even though it may still be claimed that he is not entitled to retain the money, and even though he may still be adjudged liable to restore its equivalent." North American Oil Consolidated v. Burnet, supra, 286 U.S. at page 424, 52 S.Ct. at page 615. In such case, the taxpayer has "actual command over the property taxed—the actual benefit for which the tax is paid," Corliss v. Bowers, supra [281 U.S. 376, 50 S.Ct. 336]. This standard brings wrongful appropriations within the broad sweep of "gross income"; it excludes loans. When a law-abiding taxpayer mistakenly receives income in one year, which receipt is assailed and found to be invalid in a subsequent year, the taxpayer must nonetheless report the amount as "gross income" in the year received. United States v. Lewis, supra; Healy v. Commissioner, supra. We do not believe that Congress intended to treat a law-breaking taxpayer differently. Just as the honest taxpayer may deduct any amount repaid in the year in which the repayment is made, the Government points out that, "If, when, and to the extent that the victim recovers back the misappropriated funds, there is of course a reduction in the embezzler's income." Brief for the United States, p. 24.

Petitioner contends that the Wilcox rule has been in existence since 1946; that if Congress had intended to change the rule, it would have done so; that there was a general revision of the income tax laws in 1954 without mention of the rule; that a bill to change it[5] was introduced in the Eighty-sixth Congress but was not acted upon; that, therefore, we may not change the rule now. But the fact that Congress has remained silent or has re-enacted a statute which we have construed, or that congressional attempts to amend a rule announced by this Court have failed, does not necessarily debar us from re-examining and correcting the Court's own errors. There may have been any number of reasons why Congress acted as it did. One of the reasons could well be our subsequent decision in Rutkin which has been thought by many to have repudiated Wilcox. Particularly might this be true in light of the decisions of the Courts of Appeals which have been riding a narrow rail between the two cases and further distinguishing them to the disparagement of Wilcox. * * *

5. H.R. 8854, 86th Cong., 1st Sess.

We believe that Wilcox was wrongly decided and we find nothing in congressional history since then to persuade us that Congress intended to legislate the rule. Thus, we believe that we should now correct the error and the confusion resulting from it, certainly if we do so in a manner that will not prejudice those who might have relied on it. We should not continue to confound confusion, particularly when the result would be to perpetuate the injustice of relieving embezzlers of the duty of paying income taxes on the money they enrich themselves with through theft while honest people pay their taxes on every conceivable type of income.

But, we are dealing here with a felony conviction under statutes which apply to any person who "willfully" fails to account for his tax or who "willfully" attempts to evade his obligation. In Spies v. United States, 317 U.S. 492, 499, 63 S.Ct. 364, 368, 87 L.Ed. 418, the Court said that § [7201] embodied "the gravest of offenses against the revenues," and stated that willfulness must therefore include an evil motive and want of justification in view of all the circumstances. Id., 317 U.S. at page 498, 63 S.Ct. at page 367. Willfulness "involves a specific intent which must be proven by independent evidence and which cannot be inferred from the mere understatement of income." Holland v. United States, 348 U.S. 121, 139, 75 S.Ct. 127, 137, 99 L.Ed. 150.

We believe that the element of willfulness could not be proven in a criminal prosecution for failing to include embezzled funds in gross income in the year of misappropriation so long as the statute contained the gloss placed upon it by Wilcox at the time the alleged crime was committed. Therefore, we feel that petitioner's conviction may not stand and that the indictment against him must be dismissed.

Since MR. JUSTICE HARLAN, MR. JUSTICE FRANKFURTER, and MR. JUSTICE CLARK agree with us concerning Wilcox that case is overruled. MR. JUSTICE BLACK, MR. JUSTICE DOUGLAS, and MR. JUSTICE WHITTAKER believe that petitioner's conviction must be reversed and the case dismissed for the reasons stated in their opinions.

Accordingly, the judgment of the Court of Appeals is reversed and the case is remanded to the District Court with directions to dismiss the indictment.

It is so ordered.

Reversed and remanded with directions.

MR. JUSTICE BLACK, whom MR. JUSTICE DOUGLAS joins, concurring in part and dissenting in part.

* * *

I.

We dissent from the way the majority of the Court overrules Wilcox. If the statutory interpretation of "taxable income" in Wilcox is wrong, then James is guilty of violating the tax evasion statute for the trial court's judgment establishes that he embezzled funds and wilfully refrained from reporting them as income. It appears to us that District

Courts are bound to be confused as to what they can do hereafter in tax-evasion cases involving "income" from embezzlements committed prior to this day. Three Justices vote to overrule Wilcox under what we believe to be a questionable formula, at least a new one in the annals of this Court, and say that although failure to report embezzled funds has, despite Wilcox, always been a crime under the statute, people who have violated this law in the past cannot be prosecuted but people who embezzle funds after this opinion is announced can be prosecuted for failing to report these funds as a "taxable gain." Three other Justices who vote to overrule Wilcox say that past embezzlers can be prosecuted for the crime of tax evasion although two of those Justices believe the Government must prove that the past embezzler did not commit his crime in reliance on Wilcox. Thus, although it was not the law yesterday, it will be the law tomorrow that funds embezzled hereafter are taxable income; and although past embezzlers could not have been prosecuted yesterday, maybe they can and maybe they cannot be prosecuted tomorrow for the crime of tax evasion. (The question of the civil tax liability of past embezzlers is left equally unclear.) We do not challenge the wisdom of those of our Brethren who refuse to make the Court's new tax evasion crime applicable to past conduct. This would be good governmental policy even though the *ex post facto* provision of the Constitution has not ordinarily been thought to apply to judicial legislation. Our trouble with this aspect of the Court's action is that it seems to us to indicate that the Court has passed beyond the interpretation of the tax statute and proceeded substantially to amend it.

We realize that there is a doctrine with wide support to the effect that under some circumstances courts should make their decisions as to what the law is apply only prospectively. Objections to such a judicial procedure, however, seem to us to have peculiar force in the field of criminal law. In the first place, a criminal statute that is so ambiguous in scope that an interpretation of it brings about totally unexpected results, thereby subjecting people to penalties and punishments for conduct which they could not know was criminal under existing law, raises serious questions of unconstitutional vagueness. Moreover, for a court to interpret a criminal statute in such a way as to make punishment for past conduct under it so unfair and unjust that the interpretation should be given only prospective application seems to us to be the creation of a judicial crime that Congress might not want to create. This country has never been sympathetic with judge-created crimes. * * *

In our judgment one of the great inherent restraints upon this Court's departure from the field of interpretation to enter that of lawmaking has been the fact that its judgments could not be limited to prospective application. This Court and in fact all departments of the Government have always heretofore realized that prospective lawmaking is the function of Congress rather than of the courts. We continue to think that this function should be exercised only by Congress under our constitutional system.

II.

We think Wilcox was right when it was decided and is right now. It announced no new, novel doctrine.   One need only look at the Government's briefs in this Court in the Wilcox case to see just how little past judicial support could then be mustered had the Government sought to send Wilcox to jail for his embezzlement under the guise of a tax evasion prosecution.   The Government did cite many cases from many courts saying that under the federal income tax law gains are no less taxable because they have been acquired by illegal methods.   This Court had properly held long before Wilcox that there is no "reason why the fact that a business is unlawful should exempt it from paying the taxes that if lawful it would have to pay."   We fully recognize the correctness of that holding in Wilcox:

> "Moral turpitude is not a touchstone of taxability.   The question, rather, is whether the taxpayer in fact received a statutory gain, profit or benefit.   That the taxpayer's motive may have been reprehensible or the mode of receipt illegal has no bearing upon the application of Section [61(a)]." [6]

The Court today by implication attributes quite a different meaning or consequence to the Wilcox opinion.   One opinion argues at length the "well-established principle * * * that unlawful, as well as lawful, gains are comprehended within the term 'gross income.'"   Wilcox did not deny that; we do not deny that.   This repeated theme of our Brethren is wholly irrelevant since the Wilcox holding in no way violates the sound principle of treating "gains" of honest and dishonest taxpayers alike.   The whole basis of the Wilcox opinion was that an embezzlement is not in itself "gain" or "income" to the embezzler within the tax sense, for the obvious reason that the embezzled property still belongs, and is known to belong, to the rightful owner.   It is thus a mistake to argue that petitioner's contention is "that all unlawful gains are taxable except those resulting from embezzlement."

* * * The whole picture can best be obtained from the court's opinion in McKnight v. Commissioner,[7] written by Judge Sibley, one of the ablest circuit judges of his time.   He recognized that the taxpayer could not rely upon the unlawfulness of his business to defeat taxation if he had made a "gain" in that business.   He pointed out, however, that the ordinary embezzler "got no title, void or voidable, to what he took.   He was still in possession as he was before, but with a changed purpose.   He still had no right nor color of right.   He claimed none." [8] Judge Sibley's opinion went on to point out that the "first takings [of an embezzler] are, indeed, nearly always with the intention of repaying, a sort of unauthorized borrowing.   It must be conceded that no gain is

6. 327 U.S. at page 408, 66 S.Ct. at page 549.

8. 127 F.2d at page 573.

7. 127 F.2d 572.—Eds.

realized by borrowing, because of the offsetting obligation." Approaching the matter from a practical standpoint, Judge Sibley also explained that subjecting the embezzled funds to a tax would amount to allowing the United States "a preferential claim for part of the dishonest gain, to the direct loss and detriment of those to whom it ought to be restored." [9] He was not willing to put the owner of funds that had been stolen in competition with the United States Treasury Department as to which one should have a preference to get those funds.

It seems to us that Judge Sibley's argument was then and is now unanswerable. The rightful owner who has entrusted his funds to an employee or agent has troubles enough when those funds are embezzled without having the Federal Government step in with its powerful claim that the embezzlement is a taxable event automatically subjecting part of those funds (still belonging to the owner) to the waiting hands of the Government's tax gatherer. We say part of the *owner's* funds because it is on the supposed "gain" from them that the embezzler is now held to be duty-bound to pay the tax and history probably records few instances of independently wealthy embezzlers who have had non-stolen assets available for payment of taxes.

There has been nothing shown to us on any of the occasions when we have considered this problem to indicate that Congress ever intended its income tax laws to be construed as imposing what is in effect a property or excise tax on the rightful owner's embezzled funds, for which the owner has already once paid income tax when he rightfully acquired them. * * * If Congress ever did manifest an intention to select the mere fact of embezzlement as the basis for imposing a double tax on the owner, we think a serious question of confiscation in violation of the Fifth Amendment would be raised. All of us know that with the strong lien provisions of the federal income tax law an owner of stolen funds would have a very rocky road to travel before he got back, without paying a good slice to the Federal Government, such funds as an embezzler who had not paid the tax might, perchance, not have dissipated. An illustration of what this could mean to a defrauded employer is shown in this very case by the employer's loss of some $700,000, upon which the Government claims a tax of $559,000.

It seems to be implied that one reason for overruling Wilcox is that a failure to hold embezzled funds taxable would somehow work havoc with the public revenue or discriminate against "honest" taxpayers and force them to pay more taxes. We believe it would be impossible to substantiate either claim. Embezzlers ordinarily are not rich people against whom judgments, even federal tax judgments, can be enforced. Judging from the meager settlements that those defrauded were apparently compelled to make with the embezzlers in this very case, it is hard to imagine that the Treasury will be able to collect the more than $500,000 it claims. * * *

9. 127 F.2d at page 574.

It follows that, except for the possible adverse effect on rightful owners, the only substantial result that one can foresee from today's holding is that the Federal Government will, under the guise of a tax evasion charge, prosecute people for a simple embezzlement. But the Constitution grants power to Congress to get revenue not to prosecute local crimes. And if there is any offense which under our dual system of government is a purely local one which the States should handle, it is embezzlement or theft.   *   *   *   It is very doubtful whether the further congestion of federal court dockets to try such local offenses is good for the Nation, the States or the people. Here the embezzler has already pleaded guilty to the crime of embezzlement in a state court, although the record does not show what punishment he has received. Were it not for the novel formula of applying the Court's new law prospectively, petitioner would have to serve three years in federal prison in addition to his state sentence. This graphically illustrates one of the great dangers of opening up the federal tax statutes, or any others, for use by federal prosecutors against defendants who not only can be but are tried for their crimes in local state courts and punished there. If the people of this country are to be subjected to such double jeopardy and double punishment, despite the constitutional command against double jeopardy, it seems to us it would be far wiser for this Court to wait and let Congress attempt to do it.

*   *   *

IV.

*   *   *

In departing from both the Wilcox and Rutkin decisions today, our Brethren offer no persuasive reasons to prove that their judgment in overruling Wilcox is better than that of the Justices who decided that case. It contributes nothing new to the analysis of this problem to say repeatedly that the dishonest man must be subject to taxation just as the honest. As already said, Chief Justice Stone and the others sitting with him on the Wilcox Court fully accepted that general principle and we do still. Applying it here, we would say the embezzler should be treated just like the law-abiding, honest borrower who has obtained the owner's consent to his use of the money.[10] It would be unthinkable to

---

10. The analogy between the borrower and the embezzler was lucidly analyzed by Judge Sibley in McKnight v. Commissioner, 5 Cir., 127 F.2d 572, 573–574.

The several cases relied on by the Court do not, in our judgment, justify imposing a tax upon embezzled money. Corliss v. Bowers, 281 U.S. 376, 50 S.Ct. 336, 74 L.Ed. 916, involved income accumulating in a trust fund belonging to the taxpayer and over which he retained control. North American Oil Consolidated v. Burnet, 286 U.S. 417, 52 S.Ct. 613, 76 L.Ed. 1197; United States v. Lewis, 340 U.S. 590, 71 S.Ct. 522, 95 L.Ed. 560; and Healy v. Commissioner, 345 U.S. 278, 73 S.Ct. 671, 97 L.Ed. 1007, were cases in which the taxpayer had asserted a bona fide, though mistaken, claim of right. In North American Oil, the taxpayer not only had a bona fide claim to the money taxed, but there had been an adjudication that he was entitled to it, and there was only the tenuous possibility that a competing claimant might later upset that adjudication. The Lewis and Healy cases involved a tax on payments made and received as a result of mutual mistake, and it was held that the administration of the tax laws on an annual basis need not be upset for the convenience of those who caused the mistaken payments to be made and reported as income. By contrast, the victims do not cause embezzlements, and the Government is not misled or inconve-

tax the borrower on his "gain" of the borrowed funds and thereby substantially impair the lender's chance of ever recovering the debt. The injury that the Government would inflict on the lender by making the borrower less able to repay the loan surely would not be adequately compensated by telling the lender that he can take a tax deduction for the loss, and it is equally small comfort to the embezzlement victim for the Government, after taking part of his property as a tax on the embezzler, to tell the victim that he can take a deduction for his loss if he has any income against which to offset the deduction. There is, of course, one outstanding distinction between a borrower and an embezzler, and that is that the embezzler uses the funds without the owner's consent. This distinction can be of no importance for purposes of taxability of the funds, however, because as a matter of common sense it suggests that there is, if anything, less reason to tax the embezzler than the borrower. But if this distinction is to be the reason why the embezzlement must be taxed just as "the gains of the honest laborer," then the use of this slogan in this case is laid bare as no more than a means of imposing a second punishment for the crime of embezzlement without regard to revenue considerations, the effect on the rightful owner, or the proper role of this Court when asked to overrule a criminal statutory precedent. The double jeopardy implications would seem obvious, and discussion of the serious inadvisability for other reasons of thus injecting the Federal Government into local law enforcement can be found in the dissenting opinion in Rutkin.

* * *

For the foregoing reasons, as well as the reasons stated in MR. JUSTICE WHITTAKER'S opinion, we would reaffirm our holding in Commissioner of Internal Revenue v. Wilcox, reverse this judgment and direct that the case be dismissed.

MR. JUSTICE CLARK, concurring in part and dissenting in part as to the opinion of THE CHIEF JUSTICE.

Although I join in the specific overruling of Commissioner of Internal Revenue v. Wilcox, 1946, 327 U.S. 404, 66 S.Ct. 546, 90 L.Ed. 752, in The Chief Justice's opinion, I would affirm this conviction on either of two grounds. I believe that the Court not only devitalized Wilcox, by limiting it to its facts in Rutkin v. United States, 1952, 343 U.S. 130, 72 S.Ct. 571, 96 L.Ed. 833, but that in effect the Court overruled that case *sub silentio* in Commissioner of Internal Revenue v. Glenshaw Glass Co., 1955, 348 U.S. 426, 75 S.Ct. 473, 99 L.Ed. 483. Even if that not be true, in my view the proof shows conclusively that petitioner, in willfully failing to correctly report his income, placed no bona fide reliance on Wilcox.

MR. JUSTICE HARLAN, whom MR. JUSTICE FRANKFURTER joins, concurring in part and dissenting in part as to the opinion of THE CHIEF JUSTICE.

nienced under Wilcox because the embezzler is always fully aware that the embezzled funds are not rightfully his and presumably will not report otherwise.

I fully agree with so much of The Chief Justice's opinion as dispatches Wilcox to a final demise. But as to the disposition of this case, I think that rather than an outright reversal, which his opinion proposes, the reversal should be for a new trial.

* * *

The proper disposition of this case, in my view, is to treat as plain error, Fed.Rules Crim.Proc. 52(b), 18 U.S.C.A., the failure of the trial court as trier of fact to consider whatever misapprehension may have existed in the mind of the petitioner as to the applicable law, in determining whether the Government had proved that petitioner's conduct had been willful as required by the statute. On that basis I would send the case back for a new trial.

MR. JUSTICE WHITTAKER, whom MR. JUSTICE BLACK and MR. JUSTICE DOUGLAS join, concurring in part and dissenting in part.

* * *

The Chief Justice's opinion, although it correctly recites Wilcox's holding that "embezzled money does not constitute taxable income to the embezzler *in the year of the embezzlement*" (emphasis added), fails to explain or to answer the true basis of that holding. Wilcox did not hold that embezzled funds may never constitute taxable income to the embezzler. To the contrary, it expressly recognized that an embezzler may realize a taxable gain to the full extent of the amount taken, if and when it ever becomes *his*. * * *

* * * Wilcox plainly stated that "if the unconditional indebtedness is cancelled or retired taxable income may adhere, under certain circumstances, to the taxpayer." 327 U.S. at page 408, 66 S.Ct. at page 549. More specifically, it recognized that had the embezzler's victim "condoned or forgiven any part of the [indebtedness], the [embezzler] might have been subject to tax liability to that extent," id., 327 U.S. at page 410, 66 S.Ct. at page 550, i.e., in the tax year of such forgiveness.

These statements reflect an understanding of, and regard for, substantive tax law concepts solidly entrenched in our prior decisions. Since our landmark case of United States v. Kirby Lumber Co., 284 U.S. 1, 52 S.Ct. 4, 76 L.Ed. 131, it has been settled that, upon a discharge of indebtedness by an event other than full repayment, the debtor realizes a taxable gain in the year of discharge to the extent of the indebtedness thus extinguished. Such gains are commonly referred to as ones realized through "bargain cancellations" of indebtedness, and it was in this area, and indeed, in Kirby Lumber Co. itself, that the "accession" theory or "economic gain" concept of taxable income, upon which The Chief Justice's opinion today mistakenly relies, found its genesis. * * *

* * * The Chief Justice's opinion quite understandably expresses much concern for "honest taxpayers," but it attempts neither to deny nor justify the manifest injury that its holding will inflict on those honest taxpayers, victimized by embezzlers, who will find their claims for recovery subordinated to federal tax liens. Statutory provisions, by which we are bound, clearly and unequivocally accord priority to federal tax liens over the claims of others, including "judgment creditors."

However, if it later happens that the debtor-creditor relationship between the embezzler and his victim is discharged by something other than full repayment, such as by the running of a Statute of Limitations against the victim's claim, or by a release given for less than the full amount owed, the embezzler at that time, but not before, will have made a clear taxable gain and realized "an accession to income" which he will be required under full penalty of the law to report in his federal income tax return for that year. No honest taxpayer could be harmed by this rule.

The inherent soundness of this rule could not be more clearly demonstrated than as applied to the facts of the case before us. Petitioner, a labor union official, concededly embezzled sums totaling more than $738,000 from the union's funds, over a period extending from 1951 to 1954. When the shortages were discovered in 1956, the union at once filed civil actions against petitioner to compel repayment. For reasons which need not be detailed here, petitioner effected a settlement agreement with the union on July 30, 1958, whereby, in exchange for releases fully discharging his indebtedness, he repaid to the union the sum of $13,568.50. Accordingly, at least so far as the present record discloses, petitioner clearly realized a taxable gain in the year the releases were executed, to the extent of the difference between the amount taken and the sum restored. However, the Government brought the present action against him, not for his failure to report this gain in his 1958 return, but for his failure to report that he had incurred "income" from—actually indebtedness to—the union in each of the years 1951 through 1954. It is true that the Government brought a criminal evasion prosecution rather than a civil deficiency proceeding against petitioner, but this can in no way alter the substantive tax law rules which alone are determinative of liability in either case.

* * *

The majority in James focused upon an acquisition "lawfully or unlawfully, without the consensual recognition, express or implied, of an obligation to repay * * *" Accordingly, in United States v. Rochelle, 384 F.2d 748 (5th Cir.1967), the court concluded that a swindler, who was lent money under false pretenses, realized gross income even though he received the money as a loan. In Buff v. Commissioner, 496 F.2d 847 (2d Cir.1974), reversing 58 T.C. 224 (1972), an embezzler confessed judgment and promised to make repayment in the same year he embezzled the money. Some payments were actually made that year, but the major portion had not been paid by the time the tax case was decided. The Tax Court found the transaction was converted into a loan which did not constitute gross income. The

Second Circuit reversed on the ground that the obligation to repay was of "no value" at the time it was given. It appears that a consensual obligation to repay in the year of the taking is irrelevant, unless a valid loan exists. Clearly, as in James, embezzlement does not rise to that level. However, consider Gilbert v. Commissioner, 552 F.2d 478 (2d Cir. 1977), where the corporate president had taken funds from the corporation without authorization for a use he believed was for the good of the corporation. The taxpayer established both his intention and ability to repay by the fact that he immediately executed promissory notes which were secured by his own assets with a value sufficient to cover the payments. Later, the corporation was unable to obtain payment on the notes. The court concluded from the taxpayer's intent that the taking was a loan. As a result, the taxpayer did not realize gross income at the time he took the money.

Although the embezzler must include the amount taken in gross income, a subsequent payment by the embezzler of the embezzled funds qualifies for a loss deduction under § 165(a) and (c)(2) in the taxable year in which he makes repayment. Rev.Rul. 65–254, 1965–2 C.B. 50.

Because embezzlement activities do not constitute a trade or business, an embezzler is not entitled to use the net operating loss carryback and carryforward provisions of § 172. McKinney v. United States, 76–2 USTC ¶ 9728 (W.D.Tex.1976), affirmed 574 F.2d 1240 (5th Cir.1978), cert. denied 439 U.S. 1072, 99 S.Ct. 843, 59 L.Ed.2d 38 (1979). And, because an embezzler has no claim of right to the embezzled funds, he cannot use the relief provided by § 1341. McKinney v. United States, supra. Since the embezzler can only deduct the repayment in the year of repayment, if he has insufficient income for that year, the deduction is of no tax benefit.

Reference: Bittker, Taxing Income From Unlawful Activities, 25 Case W.Res.L.Rev. 130 (1974).

Questions

1. Why did the victims in the James case settle their claims of over $738,000 in a later year for only $13,568?

2. Dodge steals $100,000 in a year he had legal income of $25,000. Two years later, the embezzlement is discovered. Dodge is willing to repay the stolen funds because he never spent any of it. In that year, Dodge also has other income of $30,000. Generally, Federal tax liens have priority over most other creditors. § 6323. Is this a sound policy? Should the victim's claim be given priority over the government's right to collect taxes?

2. FOUND PROPERTY

CESARINI v. UNITED STATES

United States District Court, Northern District of Ohio, 1969.
296 F.Supp. 3.
Affirmed per curiam 428 F.2d 812 (6th Cir.1970).

YOUNG, DISTRICT JUDGE.

This is an action by the plaintiffs as taxpayers for the recovery of income tax payments made in the calendar year 1964. Plaintiffs contend that the amount of $836.51 was erroneously overpaid by them in 1964, and that they are entitled to a refund in that amount, together with the statutory interest from October 13, 1965, the date which they made their claim upon the Internal Revenue Service for the refund.

Plaintiffs and the United States have stipulated to the material facts in the case, and the matter is before the Court for final decision. The facts necessary for a resolution of the issues raised should perhaps be briefly stated before the Court proceeds to a determination of the matter. Plaintiffs are husband and wife, and live within the jurisdiction of the United States District Court for the Northern District of Ohio. In 1957, the plaintiffs purchased a used piano at an auction sale for approximately $15.00, and the piano was used by their daughter for piano lessons. In 1964, while cleaning the piano, plaintiffs discovered the sum of $4,467.00 in old currency, and since have retained the piano instead of discarding it as previously planned. Being unable to ascertain who put the money there, plaintiffs exchanged the old currency for new at a bank, and reported the sum of $4,467.00 on their 1964 joint income tax return as ordinary income from other sources. On October 18, 1965, plaintiffs filed an amended return with the District Director of Internal Revenue in Cleveland, Ohio, this second return eliminating the sum of $4,467.00 from the gross income computation, and requesting a refund in the amount of $836.51, the amount allegedly overpaid as a result of the former inclusion of $4,467.00 in the original return for the calendar year of 1964. On January 18, 1966, the Commissioner of Internal Revenue rejected taxpayers' refund claim in its entirety, and plaintiffs filed the instant action in March of 1967.

Plaintiffs make three alternative contentions in support of their claim that the sum of $836.51 should be refunded to them. First, that the $4,467.00 found in the piano is not includable in gross income under Section 61 of the Internal Revenue Code. (26 U.S.C. § 61) Secondly, even if the retention of the cash constitutes a realization of ordinary income under Section 61, it was due and owing in the year the piano was purchased, 1957, and by 1964, the statute of limitations provided by 26 U.S.C. § 6501 had elapsed. And thirdly, that if the treasure trove money is gross income for the year 1964, it was entitled to capital gains treatment under Section 1221 of Title 26. The Government, by its answer and its trial brief, asserts that the amount found in the piano is includable in gross income under Section 61(a) of Title 26, U.S.C., that the money is taxable in the year it was actually found, 1964, and that the sum is properly taxable at ordinary income rates, not being entitled to capital gains treatment under 26 U.S.C. §§ 1201 et seq.

After a consideration of the pertinent provisions of the Internal Revenue Code, Treasury Regulations, Revenue Rulings, and decisional law in the area, this Court has concluded that the taxpayers are not entitled to a refund of the amount requested, nor are they entitled to capital gains treatment on the income item at issue.

The starting point in determining whether an item is to be included in gross income is, of course, Section 61(a) of Title 26 U.S.C., and that section provides in part:

> "Except as otherwise provided in this subtitle, *gross income means all income from whatever source derived,* including (but not limited to) the following items: * * *" (Emphasis added.)

Subsections (1) through (15) of Section 61(a) then go on to list fifteen items specifically included in the computation of the taxpayer's gross income, and Part II of Subchapter B of the [1986] Code (Sections 71 et seq.) deals with other items expressly included in gross income. While neither of these listings expressly includes the type of income which is at issue in the case at bar, Part III of Subchapter B (Sections 101 et seq.) deals with items specifically *excluded* from gross income, and found money is not listed in those sections either. This absence of express mention in any of the code sections necessitates a return to the "all income from whatever source" language of Section 61(a) of the code, and the express statement there that gross income is "not limited to" the following fifteen examples. Section 1.61–1(a) of the Treasury Regulations, the corresponding section to Section 61(a) in the [1986] Code, reiterates this broad construction of gross income, providing in part:

> "Gross income means all income from whatever source derived, unless excluded by law. *Gross income includes income realized in any form,* whether in money, property, or services. * * *" (Emphasis added.)

The decisions of the United States Supreme Court have frequently stated that this broad all-inclusive language was used by Congress to exert the full measure of its taxing power under the Sixteenth Amendment to the United States Constitution. Commissioner of Internal Revenue v. Glenshaw Glass Co., 348 U.S. 426, 429, 75 S.Ct. 473, 99 L.Ed. 483 (1955); Helvering v. Clifford, 309 U.S. 331, 334, 60 S.Ct. 554, 84 L.Ed. 788 (1940); Helvering v. Midland Mutual Life Ins. Co., 300 U.S. 216, 223, 57 S.Ct. 423, 81 L.Ed. 612 (1937); Douglas v. Willcuts, 296 U.S. 1, 9, 56 S.Ct. 59, 80 L.Ed. 3 (1935); Irwin v. Gavit, 268 U.S. 161, 166, 45 S.Ct. 475, 69 L.Ed. 897 (1925).

In addition, the Government in the instant case cites and relies upon an I.R.S. Revenue Ruling which is undeniably on point:

"The finder of treasure-trove is in receipt of taxable income, for Federal income tax purposes, to the extent of its value in United States currency, for the taxable year in which it is reduced to undisputed possession." Rev.Rul. 61, 1953–1, Cum.Bull. 17.

The plaintiffs argue that the above ruling does not control this case for two reasons. The first is that subsequent to the Ruling's pronouncement in 1953, Congress enacted Sections 74 and 102 of the [1986] Code, § 74 expressly *including* the value of prizes and awards in gross income in most cases, and § 102 specifically *exempting* the value of gifts received from gross income. From this, it is argued that Section 74 was added because prizes might otherwise be construed as non-taxable gifts, and since no such section was passed expressly taxing treasure-trove, it is therefore a gift which is non-taxable under Section 102. This line of reasoning overlooks the statutory scheme previously alluded to, whereby income from all sources is taxed unless the taxpayer can point to an express exemption. Not only have the taxpayers failed to list a specific exclusion in the instant case, but also the Government *has* pointed to express language covering the found money, even though it would not be required to do so under the broad language of Section 61(a) and the foregoing Supreme Court decisions interpreting it.

The second argument of the taxpayers in support of their contention that Rev.Rul. 61, 1953–1 should not be applied in this case is based upon the decision of Dougherty v. Commissioner, 10 T.C.M. 320, P–H Memo. T.C., ¶ 51,093 (1951). In that case the petitioner was an individual who had never filed an income tax return, and the Commissioner was attempting to determine his gross income by the so-called "net worth" method. Dougherty had a substantial increase in his net worth, and attempted to partially explain away his lack of reporting it by claiming that he had found $31,000.00 in cash inside a used chair he had purchased in 1947. The Tax Court's opinion deals primarily with the factual question of whether or not Dougherty actually *did* find this money in a chair, finally concluding that he did not, and from this petitioners in the instant case argue that if such found money is clearly gross income, the Tax Court would not have reached the fact question, but merely included the $31,000.00 as a matter of law. Petitioners argue that since the Tax Court did not include the sum in Dougherty's gross income until they had found as a fact that it *was not* treasure trove, then by implication such discovered money is not taxable. This argument must fail for two reasons. First, the *Dougherty* decision precedes Rev.Rul. 61, 1953–1 by two years, and thus was dealing with what then was an uncharted area of the gross income provisions of the Code. Secondly, the case cannot be read as authority for the proposition that treasure trove is not includable in gross income, even if the revenue ruling had not been issued two years later.[11]

---

11. The Dougherty Court, after carefully considering the evidence before it on the factual question of whether or not the taxpayer actually found the $31,000.00 as claimed, stated:

In partial summary, then, the arguments of the taxpayers which attempt to avoid the application of Rev.Rul. 61, 1953–1 are not well taken. The *Dougherty* case simply does not hold one way or another on the problem before this Court, and therefore petitioners' reliance upon it is misplaced. The other branch of their argument, that found money must be construed to be a gift under Section 102 of the [1986] Code since it is not expressly included as are prizes in Section 74 of the Code, would not even be effective were it being urged at a time prior to 1953, when the ruling had not yet been promulgated. In addition to the numerous cases in the Supreme Court which uphold the broad sweeping construction of Section 61(a) found in Treas.Reg. § 1.61–1(a), other courts and commentators writing at a point in time before the ruling came down took the position that windfalls, including found monies, were properly includable in gross income under Section 22(a) of the 1939 Code, the predecessor of Section 61(a) in the [1986] Code. See, for example, the decision in Park & Tilford Distillers Corp. v. United States, 107 F.Supp. 941, 123 Ct.Cl. 509 (1952); [12] and Comment, "Taxation of Found Property and Other Windfalls," 20 U.Chi.L.Rev. 748, 752 (1953).[13] While it is generally true that revenue rulings may be disregarded by the courts if in conflict with the code and the regulations, or with other judicial decisions, plaintiffs in the instant case have been unable to point to any inconsistency between the gross income sections of the code, the interpretation of them by the regulations and the courts, and the revenue ruling which they herein attack as inapplicable. On the other hand, the United States *has* shown a consistency in letter and spirit between the ruling and the code, regulations, and court decisions.

"In short, we do not believe the money was in the chair when the chair was acquired by the petitioner.

"Where the petitioner got the money which he later took from the chair and in what manner it was obtained by him, we do not know. It is accordingly impossible for us to conclude and hold the $31,000.00 here in question was not acquired by him in a manner such as would make it income to him within the meaning of the statute. Such being the case, *we do not reach the question whether money, if acquired in the manner claimed by the petitioner, is income under the statute.*" (Emphasis added.) 10 T.C.M. 320 at 323. (1951)

12. In this taxpayer's suit for a refund of corporation taxes, Judge Madden of the Court of Claims stated at pages 943–944: " * * * It is not, and we think could not rationally be, suggested that Congress lacks the power to tax windfalls as income. * * * A windfall may, of course, be a gift, and thus expressly exempt from in-

come tax. But if, as in the instant case, the windfall is clearly not a gift, but a payment required by a statute * * * we do not see how its exemption could be reconciled with the reiterated statements that Congress intended, by Section 22(a), to tax income to the extent of its constitutional power." 107 F.Supp. at 943, 944.

13. This article, after stating arguments both ways on the question, and thus suggesting by implication that the area was not clearly defined at that time, went on to state at page 752: "Perhaps a more appropriate interpretation of Section 22(a) would be to hold that all windfalls * * * are taxable income under its sweeping language. * * * Insofar as the policy of Section 22(a) is to impose similar tax burdens on persons in similar circumstances, there is no basis for distinguishing value received as windfall and * * * value received as salary." Footnote 50 of the Comment indicates that the article was in printing when Rev.Rul. 61–53–1 came out.

Although not cited by either party, and noticeably absent from the Government's brief, the following Treasury Regulation appears in the 1964 Regulations, the year of the return in dispute:

"§ 1.61–14   Miscellaneous items of gross income.

"(a) In general.   In addition to the items enumerated in section 61(a), there are many other kinds of gross income * * *. *Treasure trove, to the extent of its value in United States currency, constitutes gross income for the taxable year in which it is reduced to undisputed possession.*" (Emphasis added.)

Identical language appears in the 1968 Treasury Regulations, and is found in all previous years back to 1958. This language is the same in all material respects as that found in Rev.Rul. 61–53–1, Cum.Bull. 17, and is undoubtedly an attempt to codify that ruling into the Regulations which apply to the [1986] Code. This Court is of the opinion that Treas.Reg. § 1.61–14(a) is dispositive of the major issue in this case if the $4,467.00 found in the piano was "reduced to undisputed possession" in the year petitioners reported it, for this Regulation was applicable to returns filed in the calendar year of 1964.

This brings the Court to the second contention of the plaintiffs: that if any tax was due, it was in 1957 when the piano was purchased, and by 1964 the Government was blocked from collecting it by reason of the statute of limitations. Without reaching the question of whether the voluntary payment in 1964 constituted a *waiver* on the part of the taxpayers, this Court finds that the $4,467.00 sum was properly included in gross income for the calendar year of 1964. Problems of when title vests, or when possession is complete in the field of federal taxation, in the absence of definitive federal legislation on the subject, are ordinarily determined by reference to the law of the state in which the taxpayer resides, or where the property around which the dispute centers is located. Since both the taxpayers and the property in question are found within the State of Ohio, Ohio law must govern as to when the found money was "reduced to undisputed possession" within the meaning of Treas.Reg. § 1.61–14 and Rev.Rul. 61–53–1, Cum.Bull. 17.

In Ohio, there is no statute specifically dealing with the rights of owners and finders of treasure trove, and in the absence of such a statute the common-law rule of England applies, so that "title belongs to the finder as against all the world except the true owner." Niederlehner v. Weatherly, 78 Ohio App. 263, 69 N.E.2d 787 (1946), appeal dismissed, 146 Ohio St. 697, 67 N.E.2d 713 (1946). The *Niederlehner* case held, *inter alia*, that the owner of real estate upon which money is found does not have title as against the finder. Therefore, in the instant case if plaintiffs had resold the piano in 1958, not knowing of the money within it, they later would not be able to succeed in an action against the purchaser who *did* discover it. Under Ohio law, the plaintiffs must have actually *found* the money to have superior title over all but the true owner, and they did not discover the old currency until 1964. Unless there is present a specific state statute to the contrary,[14] the majority of jurisdictions are in accord with the Ohio rule.[15] Therefore, this Court finds that the $4,467.00 in old currency was not "reduced to undisputed possession" until its actual discovery in 1964, and thus the United States was not barred by the statute of limitations from collecting the $836.51 in tax during that year.

* * * Since it appears to the Court that the income tax on these taxpayers' gross income for the calendar year of 1964 has been properly assessed and paid, this taxpayers' suit for a refund in the amount of $836.51 must be dismissed, and judgment entered for the United States. An order will be entered accordingly.

Questions

1. Is Cesarini consistent with the consensual recognition principle in James?

2. What if in the Cesarini case the taxpayer reported the finding to the local authorities and attempted to locate the previous owner of the piano in order to return the money? Assume he gave up his search a year later and then spent the found money.

Problems

1. Don borrows money from a bank in a legitimate loan transaction. Don has no intention of ever repaying the loan. Is this appropriation of the bank's funds includible in Don's gross income? If so, when?

2. Lon embezzled $10,000. He took the money to pay for his son's operation with the honest intention of restoring the money to his company as soon as possible.

    (a) Does Lon realize gross income at the time of the embezzlement?

    (b) Can an honest intention to repay support a deduction in the year that intention is manifested, even though actual repayment takes place in a later year? What if Lon, in the year of the embezzlement, signed a note promising to repay?

    (c) What are the tax consequences if Lon returned the money in the year after the embezzlement? Consider §§ 165(c)(2) and 1341.

3. Ron embezzled $10,000, from his employer in Year 1. He never repaid the money. The theft was later discovered and he was convicted in Year 4. In Year 6, the Internal Revenue Service assessed a deficiency for failure to include the embezzled funds in income for Year 1. A 75% fraud penalty was also assessed. § 6653(b). Does the statute of limitations bar

14. See, for example, United States v. Peter, 178 F.Supp. 854 (E.D.La.1959) where it is held that under the Louisiana Civil Code and the Code D'Napolean the finder of treasure does not own it, and can only become the owner if no one else can prove that the treasure is his property.

15. See Weeks v. Hackett, 104 Me. 264, 71 A. 858, 860 (1908) for a review of the authorities in jurisdictions where the finder is the owner as against all but the true owner. Also, see Finding Lost Goods 36A C.J.S. § 5, p. 422 (1961).

the assessment of the deficiency and the fraud penalty? Consider § 6501(a) and (c).

4. In each of the following consider: (1) whether Ted and Terri Player must report each discovery as gross income and (2) if it is income, when is it income;

(a) Ted finds that the used piano they purchased is a genuine Steinway worth $15,000, far more than the $2,000 they paid for it.

(b) Terri finds a $50 bill buried in the sand at a public beach.

(c) Ted finds a gold coin buried in the sand at a public beach.

(d) The Players discover oil on their property.

(e) Terri finds a diamond in the used piano they recently purchased.

C. TAX BENEFIT CONCEPT

1. INTRODUCTION

Because the annual accounting concept requires that each taxable year be treated separately, a transactional approach cannot be used if more than one annual accounting period is covered. However, a strict application of the annual accounting approach may produce hardships for taxpayers. A transactional mechanism, developed by judicial interpretations and specific statutory provision, commonly referred to as the tax benefit theory, illustrates the harsh burdens sometimes imposed by the annual accounting concept. If a taxpayer takes a deduction in a prior year and recovers the amount giving rise to that deduction in a later year, he is required to report that recovery as income in the year of recovery. For example, assume a taxpayer takes a bad debt deduction for a loan he is unable to collect. If the loan is subsequently satisfied in a later year, the taxpayer must treat the loan payment as income in the year received. In effect, the taxpayer has recovered a prior deduction. However, an ameliorating effect of the tax benefit approach is found in § 111. Under § 111 and the accompanying Regulations, if the taxpayer deducted an item on his tax return but did not derive a tax savings from the entire amount of the deduction, the taxpayer's recovery, in a subsequent year, of all or any part of the recovery, is excluded from the taxpayer's income to the extent that the taxpayer did not enjoy a tax savings from the deduction in the year it was taken. For example, assume the taxpayer took a business bad debt deduction (§ 166(a)(1), (d)(2)) of $1,000 in a year but he gets no tax benefit from it because of the absence of other income. Later he collects the $1,000. Normally this sum would represent gross income, but it is excluded from gross income under § 111 because the earlier deduction provided no tax savings. In other words, a taxpayer excludes from income the recovery of any deduction taken in a prior year to the extent that the deduction did not reduce his income subject to taxation. Read § 111(a). If the taxpayer only enjoyed a tax benefit for part of the bad debt deduction in the prior year, the recovery on that debt in a subsequent year will not be included in the taxpayer's gross income to the extent that the prior deduction did not provide a tax benefit to the taxpayer. Conversely, if the taxpayer deducted an item on his tax return, thereby enjoying a tax benefit either directly or by increasing the amount of loss that was of tax benefit in another year, and in a subsequent year he recovered all or any part of that item, the taxpayer realizes and recognizes income in the year in which the previously deducted item is recovered. The objective of § 111 is to put the taxpayers in roughly the same position as if the "erroneous" deduction had never been taken.

The § 111 rule has been expanded to encompass diverse items which were previously deducted. For example, in Dobson v. Commissioner, 320 U.S. 489, 64 S.Ct. 239, 88 L.Ed. 248 (1943), rehearing denied 321 U.S. 231, 64 S.Ct. 495, 88 L.Ed. 691 (1944), the taxpayer sustained a loss with respect to the sale of certain stock in a year in which he failed to obtain a tax benefit because of the absence of taxable income. In a subsequent year, he recouped his losses from the sale by recovering damages from the person who had made fraudulent misrepresentations in connection with the sale of stock. The Supreme Court held that the receipts from the settlement were not "income" to the taxpayer who had derived no tax benefit from the loss deduction. Thus, the scope of the § 111 rule is very broad. See Reg. § 1.111–1(a)(1).

Can tax benefit principles be applied as a tax detriment theory? Assume in 1989 a single taxpayer reports a $1,000 fee in gross income and his adjusted gross income for the year is only $5,000. Since his taxable income is zero (his $5,000 adjusted gross income less the $3,000 standard deduction and a $2,000 personal exemption. § 63(b)), no tax liability resulted in the year he included the fee in gross income. Consider §§ 1(c), 63(b), (c), (d), and 151(b) and (f)(1). Should the taxpayer take a deduction in the year he later repays the fee? In United States v. Skelly Oil Co., 394 U.S. 678, 89 S.Ct. 1379, 22 L.Ed.2d 642 (1969), a taxpayer, which had reported income from the sale of natural gas, later refunded part of the sales proceeds to its customers. The taxpayer took a percentage depletion deduction (§ 611) on the sale proceeds. Because a portion of the taxpayer's income in the year of the sale was effectively excluded by the company, the Supreme Court ruled that the taxpayer could only deduct an equal percentage of the refund payment. Do you agree with the approach the Supreme Court took in Skelly Oil? An illustration of the Skelly Oil case is helpful. Assume a taxpayer has $10,000 of income for the sale of natural gas in Year 1. He is allowed to deduct $2,750 (27½%) as percentage depletion under § 611 in Year 1. The taxpayer refunds the $10,000 to customers in Year 2. The Supreme Court allowed the taxpayer to deduct only $7,250 in Year 2. Had he been allowed to deduct the entire $10,000 in Year 2, the taxpayer would have deducted $2,750 twice, in effect duplicating the depletion deduction taken in Year 1.

Consider also O'Meara v. Commissioner, 8 T.C. 622 (1947) (Acq. 1947–2 C.B. 3), in which the taxpayer reported $5,000 in royalties as income for 1937. He paid no taxes that year because losses from other activities far exceeded his income. In 1941, the taxpayer was compelled to return the $5,000 royalty payment. Although the taxpayer suffered no tax burden or detriment by including the $5,000 in income, the court allowed him to deduct the amount repaid. The court reasoned that including the royalty in income gave the taxpayer a basis and he must be granted the opportunity to recover that basis.

Must there be an actual recovery of the tangible asset or sum of money previously deducted to invoke the tax benefit theory? The Supreme Court considered this question in United States v. Bliss Dairy, Inc., 60 U.S. 370, 103 S.Ct. 1134, 75 L.Ed.2d 130 (1983), and concluded that no actual recovery is required. A corporation took a deduction for cattle feed paid for and received but not consumed. In the following year, the corporation distributed the unused feed to its shareholders pursuant to a plan of liquidation. The corporation was required to include the value of the distributed cattle feed in income. The Supreme Court concluded that the tax benefit theory may be used if a later event occurs which is "fundamentally inconsistent" with the assumptions made in the earlier year that served as the basis for the deduction. In other words, all that is needed is a subsequent event inconsistent with the prior deduction. See Tennessee-Carolina Transportation Inc. v. Commissioner, 582 F.2d 378 (6th Cir.1978), cert. denied 440 U.S. 909, 99 S.Ct. 1219, 59 L.Ed.2d 457 (1979); contra, Commissioner v. South Lake Farms, Inc., 324 F.2d 837 (9th Cir.1963).

Reference: White, An Essay on the Conceptual Foundations of The Tax Benefit Rule, 82 Mich.L.R. 486 (1984); A helpful discussion of the application of the tax benefit rule is contained in Del Cotto and Joyce, Double Benefits and Transactional Consistency Under the Tax Benefit Rule, 39 Tax.L.R. 473 (1984).

Questions

1. If Burnet v. Sanford and Brooks were decided today, would the tax benefit concept give the taxpayer the relief he sought? Consider the application of § 111(a), if § 172 is unavailable. Does the tax benefit rule eliminate the harshness of the annual accounting concept in this situation?

2. Section 186 deals with damage recoveries for breach of contract or fiduciary duties, antitrust violations and patent infringement. A taxpayer may reduce the damage recovery treated as income by those losses resulting from the injury which caused the recovery as long as taxpayer received no tax benefit from the losses. Would § 186 have provided relief for the taxpayer in Burnet v. Sanford and Brooks?

3. Why does the taxation of reimbursed medical expenses in § 104(a) and Reg. § 1.213–1(g)(1) follow a tax benefit approach? What result if the reimbursement was attributable to a previous year's medical expenses not deductible because of the 7.5% floor on medical expense deductions (§ 213(a)(1)) or that the taxpayer did not have itemized deductions in excess of the standard deduction amount (§ 63(b) and (c))?

Problem

In Year 1, Scott, a single taxpayer, had gross income of $25,000. During the Year 1 Scott paid $1,600 in state income taxes by having money withheld from his paycheck each week. Because he also had $4,400 in other itemized deductions (§ 63(d)) for the year, Scott deducted $6,000 in itemized deductions in arriving at his taxable income. § 63(d) and (e). The following January, in preparing his Year 1 state income tax return, Scott learned that his employer overwithheld state income taxes, and he is entitled to a $600 refund from the state. During Year 2, he received a $600 refund from the state.

(a) How much of the refund must Scott include in gross income for Year 2 or may he amend his Federal income tax return for Year 1 by reducing the deduction for state income taxes? See §§ 111 and 6501(a).

(b) Assume Scott's other itemized deductions for Year 1 totaled only $400 so that his itemized deductions were only $2,000 for Year 1. Will any portion of the $600 refund be taxed in Year 2? Consider §§ 63(b), (c), and (d) and 111.

(c) Assume that other itemized deductions for Year 2 totaled only $1,800 so that his itemized deductions totalled $3,400. Will the entire $600 refund be included in gross income in Year 2? Consider §§ 63(b), (c), (d) and 111.

2. TAX BENEFIT CONCEPT AND CHARITABLE CONTRIBUTIONS

Pursuant to § 170, individual taxpayers may deduct up to a specified portion of their charitable contribution base (roughly speaking, adjusted gross income) for gifts to certain charitable organizations. The charitable contribution deduction is considered in detail in Chapters 9 and 12.

A disposition of appreciated property by contribution to charity does not constitute a realization under § 1001(a), even though the amount of the taxpayer's charitable deduction generally equals the value of the property. This means that a taxpayer who contributes a capital asset, held for more than the long-term holding period, which has appreciated in value receives a tax benefit in the form of a deduction equal to the value of the contributed property without realizing a gain on the appreciation. Conversely, no loss is allowed on the contribution of property which has decreased in value. Accordingly, taxpayers find it advantageous to contribute appreciated capital assets to charity. If the property has decreased in value, a taxpayer should sell it in order to realize the loss and donate the sales proceeds to the charity.

Question

When is it advantageous for a taxpayer owning appreciated capital assets to contribute such assets to a charity? Assume an individual owns stock held for more than one year, worth $100 with a basis of $25. A charity needs $100 to support its activities. How much more can the individual give to the charity by contributing the property and having the charity sell it instead of selling it and contributing the net proceeds after taxes? Consider §§ 170(b)(1)(C)(i) and (iv) and 501(a) and (c)(3).

The next case considers whether a taxpayer realizes and recognizes income on the recovery of a previously deducted item and whether the recovery, if taxable, should be taxed at the same marginal tax rate applicable to the deduction.

ALICE PHELAN SULLIVAN CORP. v. UNITED STATES

United States Court of Claims (1967).
180 Ct.Cl. 659, 381 F.2d 399.

COLLINS, JUDGE.

Plaintiff, a California corporation, brings this action to recover an alleged overpayment in its 1957 income tax. During that year, there was returned to taxpayer two parcels of realty, each of which it had previously donated and claimed as a charitable contribution deduction. The first donation had been made in 1939; the second, in 1940. Under the then applicable corporate tax rates, the deductions claimed ($4,243.49 for 1939 and $4,463.44 for 1940) yielded plaintiff an aggregate tax benefit of $1,877.49.

Each conveyance had been made subject to the condition that the property be used either for a religious or for an educational purpose. In 1957, the donee decided not to use the gifts; they were therefore reconveyed to plaintiff. Upon audit of taxpayer's income tax return, it was found that the recovered property was not reflected in its 1957 gross income. The Commissioner of Internal Revenue disagreed with plaintiff's characterization of the recovery as a nontaxable return of capital. He viewed the transaction as giving rise to taxable income and therefore adjusted plaintiff's income by adding to it $8,706.93—the total of the charitable contribution deductions previously claimed and allowed. This addition to income, taxed at the 1957 corporate tax rate of 52 percent, resulted in a deficiency assessment of $4,527.60. After payment of the deficiency, plaintiff filed a claim for the refund of $2,650.11, asserting this amount as overpayment on the theory that a correct assessment could demand no more than the return of the tax benefit originally enjoyed, i.e., $1,877.49. The claim was disallowed.

This court has had prior occasion to consider the question which the present suit presents. In Perry v. United States, 160 F.Supp. 270, 142 Ct.Cl. 7 (1958) (Judges Madden and Laramore dissenting), it was recognized that a return to the donor of a prior charitable contribution gave rise to income to the extent of the deduction previously allowed. The court's point of division—which is likewise the division between the instant parties—was whether the "gain" attributable to the recovery was to be taxed at the rate applicable at the time the deduction was first claimed or whether the proper rate was that in effect at the time of recovery. The majority, concluding that the Government should be entitled to recoup no more than that which it lost, held that the tax liability arising upon the return of a charitable gift should equal the tax benefit experienced at time of donation. Taxpayer urges that the *Perry* rationale dictates that a like result be reached in this case.

* * *

A transaction which returns to a taxpayer his own property cannot be considered as giving rise to "income"—at least where that term is confined to its traditional sense of "gain derived from capital, from labor, or from both combined." Eisner v. Macomber, 252 U.S. 189, 207, 40 S.Ct. 189, 64 L.Ed. 521 (1920). Yet the principle is well engrained in our tax law that the return or recovery of property that was once the subject of an income tax deduction must be treated as income in the year of its recovery. Rothensies v. Electric Storage Battery Co., 329 U.S. 296, 67 S.Ct. 271, 91 L.Ed. 296 (1946); Estate of Block v. Commissioner, 39 B.T.A. 338 (1939), aff'd sub nom. Union Trust Co. v. Commissioner, 111 F.2d 60 (7th Cir.), cert. denied, 311 U.S. 658, 61 S.Ct. 12, 85 L.Ed. 421 (1940). The only limitation upon that principle is the so-called "tax-benefit rule." This rule permits exclusion of the recovered item from income so long as its initial use as a deduction did not provide a tax. But where full tax use of a deduction was made and a tax saving thereby obtained, then the extent of saving is considered immaterial. The recovery is viewed as income to the full extent of the deduction previously allowed.[16]

Formerly the exclusive province of judge-made law, the tax-benefit concept now finds expression both in statute and administrative regulations. * * *

Drawing our attention to the broad language of [Reg. 31.111–1], the Government insists that the present recovery must find its place within the scope of the regulation and, as such, should be taxed in a manner consistent with the treatment provided for like items of recovery, i.e., that it be taxed at the rate prevailing in the year of recovery. We are compelled to agree.

* * *

The regulation—being but the embodiment of that principle—is clearly adequate to embrace a recovered charitable contribution. But the regulation does not specify which tax rate is to be applied to the recouped deduction, and this consideration brings us to the matter here in issue.

---

16. The rationale which supports the principle, as well as its limitation, is that the property, having once served to offset taxable income (i.e., as a tax deduction) should be treated, upon its recoupment, as the recovery of that which had been previously deducted. See Plumb, The Tax Benefit Rule Today, 57 Harv.L.Rev. 129, 131 n. 10 (1943).

Ever since Burnet v. Sanford & Brooks Co., 282 U.S. 359, 51 S.Ct. 150, 75 L.Ed. 383 (1931), the concept of accounting for items of income and expense on an annual basis has been accepted as the basic principle upon which our tax laws are structured. "It is the essence of any system of taxation that it should produce revenue ascertainable, and payable to the government, at regular intervals. Only by such a system is it practicable to produce a regular flow of income and apply methods of accounting, assessment, and collection capable of practical operation." 282 U.S. at 365, 51 S.Ct. at 152. To insure the vitality of the single-year concept, it is essential not only that annual income be ascertained without reference to losses experienced in an earlier accounting period, but also that income be taxed without reference to earlier tax rates. And absent specific statutory authority sanctioning a departure from this principle, it may only be said of *Perry* that it achieved a result which was more equitably just than legally correct.[17]

Since taxpayer in this case did obtain full tax benefit from its earlier deductions, those deductions were properly classified as income upon recoupment and must be taxed as such. This can mean nothing less than the application of that tax rate which is in effect during the year in which the recovered item is recognized as a factor of income. We therefore sustain the Government's position and grant its motion for summary judgment. Perry v. United States, supra, is hereby overruled, and plaintiff's petition is dismissed.

Question

Why did the taxpayer in Alice Phelan Sullivan want to follow the result in Perry? Why did the Court of Claims disagree with its earlier Perry decision?

In Rosen v. Commissioner, 71 T.C. 226 (1978), affirmed 611 F.2d 942 (1st Cir.1980), taxpayers donated property to a charity and retained no reversionary interest as in the Alice Phelan Sullivan case. They donated property to the city in 1972 and claimed a charitable deduction equal to its $51,250 value at that time. In 1973, the city determined that it could not use the real estate and returned it to the taxpayers. They then donated all but a small part of it later in 1973 to a local hospital, which also concluded it could not use the property and transferred it back to the Rosens in 1974. The Rosens claimed a second

17. This opinion represents the views of the majority and complies with existing law and decisions. However, in the writer's personal opinion, it produces a harsh and inequitable result. Perhaps, it exemplifies a situation "where the letter of the law killeth; the spirit giveth life." The tax-benefit concept is an equitable doctrine which should be carried to an equitable conclusion. Since it is the declared public policy to encourage contributions to charitable and educational organizations, a donor, whose gift to such organizations is returned, should not be required to refund to the Government a greater amount than the tax benefit received when the deduction was made for the gift. Such a rule would avoid a penalty to the taxpayer and an unjust enrichment to the Government. However, the court cannot legislate and any change in the existing law rests within the wisdom and discretion of the Congress.

charitable deduction equal to its $48,000 value at the time of the second transfer in 1973. When the property was returned a second time in 1974 it was worth only $25,000. The Service contended that $51,250 must be included in income for 1973 and $25,000 for 1974. The Rosens maintained that both times the return of the property to them was a gift, excludable from gross income under § 102(a), and that the tax benefit rule did not apply to receipts by gift. The Tax Court concluded that the charities did not intend to make a gift by returning the property and deemed irrelevant the fact that the reconveyances were not required. The Tax Court required the taxpayers to treat the value of the returned property on the respective dates of return as income in the year returned.

Despite the application of the tax benefit theory, the Rosens obtained two advantages, the first being a deferral of their tax liabilities. The second benefit was that the Tax Court was bound by the Service's determination that the taxpayers need only include $25,000 in gross income when they received the returned property for the second time. As the Tax Court noted in a footnote:

> 16. We do not consider the possible contention that proper application of the tax benefit rule would require a complete reversal of the deduction in the earlier year by including in income of the later year the full amount previously deducted upon complete restoration of the identical property which gave rise to the deduction. * * * The Commissioner now seeks to include in income only the fair market value of the property when it was returned, an amount that is smaller than the amount previously deducted. * * * 71 T.C. at 234.

Although the next case was decided on the principle that a benefit received must be treated as gross income, the court applied tax benefit principles.

HAVERLY v. UNITED STATES

United States Court of Appeals, Seventh District, 1975.
513 F.2d 224, cert. denied 423 U.S. 912, 96 S.Ct. 216,
46 L.Ed.2d 140 (1975).

HASTINGS, SENIOR CIRCUIT JUDGE.

This case presents for resolution a single question of law which is of first impression: whether the value of unsolicited sample textbooks sent by publishers to a principal of a public elementary school, which he subsequently donated to the school's library and for which he claimed a charitable deduction, constitutes gross income to the principal within the meaning of Section 61 of the Internal Revenue Code of [1986], 26 U.S.C. § 61.

* * *

During the years 1967 and 1968 Charles N. Haverly was the principal of the Alice L. Barnard Elementary School in Chicago, Illinois. In each of these years publishers sent to the taxpayer unsolicited sample copies of textbooks which had a total fair market value at the time of receipt of $400. The samples were given to taxpayer for his personal retention or for whatever disposition he wished to make. The samples were provided, in the hope of receiving favorable consideration, to give taxpayer an opportunity to examine the books and determine whether they were suitable for the instructional unit for which he was responsible. The publishers did not intend that the books serve as compensation.

In 1968 taxpayer donated the books to the Alice L. Barnard Elementary School Library. The parties agreed that the donation entitled the taxpayer to a charitable deduction under 26 U.S.C. § 170, in the amount of $400, the value of the books at the time of the contribution.[18]

* * *

Taxpayer's report of his 1968 income did not include the value of the textbooks received, but it did include a charitable deduction for the value of the books donated to the school library. The Internal Revenue Service assessed a deficiency against the taxpayer representing income taxes on the value of the textbooks received. Taxpayer paid the amount of the deficiency, filed a claim for refund and subsequently instituted this action to recover that amount.[19]

The amount of income, if any, and the time of its receipt are not issues here since the parties stipulated that if the contested issue of law was decided in the taxpayer's favor, his taxable income for 1968 as determined by the Internal Revenue Service would be reduced by $400.00.

* * *

* * * The only question remaining is whether the value of the textbooks received is included within "all income from whatever source derived."

The Supreme Court has frequently reiterated that it was the intention of Congress "to use the full measure of its taxing power" and "to tax all gains except those specifically exempted." James v. United States, 366 U.S. 213, 218–219, 81 S.Ct. 1052, 1054–1055, 6 L.Ed.2d 246 (1961). The Supreme Court has also held that the language of Section 61(a) encompasses all "accessions to wealth, clearly realized, and over which the taxpayers have complete dominion." Id. at 219, 81 S.Ct. at 1055; Commissioner of Internal Revenue v. Glenshaw Glass Co., 348 U.S. 426, 431, 75 S.Ct. 473, 99 L.Ed. 483 (1955).

18. Since the tax year at issue in this litigation is 1968, the amount of the charitable deduction which could be taken was unaffected by 26 U.S.C. § 170(e)(1) which was added by the Tax Reform Act of 1969, Pub.L. No. 91–172, 83 Stat. 487.

19. Taxpayer originally sought a refund of $288.76 and sought to recover that amount in this action. This amount re-flected taxpayer's contentions that the books were not income and that he was entitled to a charitable deduction for $430 worth of books which had been given directly to the school by the publishers. In proceedings in the district court, taxpayer conceded that he was not entitled to a deduction for the books which the publishers had sent to the school.

There are no reported cases which have applied these definitions of income to the question of the receipt of unsolicited samples. * * * In view of the comprehensive conception of income embodied in the statutory language and the Supreme Court's interpretation of that language, we conclude that when the intent to exercise complete dominion over unsolicited samples is demonstrated by donating those samples to a charitable institution and taking a tax deduction therefor, the value of the samples received constitutes gross income.

The receipt of textbooks is unquestionably an "accession to wealth." Taxpayer recognized the value of the books when he donated them and took a $400 deduction therefor. Possession of the books increased the taxpayer's wealth. Taxpayer's receipt and possession of the books indicate that the income was "clearly realized." Taxpayer admitted that the books were given to him for his personal retention or whatever disposition he saw fit to make of them. Although the receipt of unsolicited samples may sometimes raise the question of whether the taxpayer manifested an intent to accept the property or exercised "complete dominion" over it, there is no question that this element is satisfied by the unequivocal act of taking a charitable deduction for donation of the property.

The district court recognized that the act of claiming a charitable deduction does manifest an intent to accept the property as one's own. It nevertheless declined to label receipt of the property as income because it considered such an act indistinguishable from other acts unrelated to the tax laws which also evidence an intent to accept property as one's own, such as a school principal donating his sample texts to the library *without* claiming a deduction. We need not resolve the question of the tax consequences of this and other hypothetical cases discussed by the district court and suggested by the taxpayer. To decide the case before us we need only hold, as we do, that when a tax deduction is taken for the donation of unsolicited samples the value of the samples received must be included in the taxpayer's gross income.

This conclusion is consistent with Revenue Ruling 70–498, 1970–2 Cum.Bull. 6, in which the Internal Revenue Service held that a newspaper's book reviewer must include in his gross income the value of unsolicited books received from publishers which are donated to a charitable organization and for which a charitable deduction is taken. This ruling was issued to supercede an earlier ruling, Rev.Rul. 70–330, 1970–1 Cum.Bull. 14, that mere retention of unsolicited books was sufficient to cause them to be gross income.

The Internal Revenue Service has apparently made an administrative decision to be concerned with the taxation of unsolicited samples only when failure to tax those samples would provide taxpayers with double tax benefits. It is not for the courts to quarrel with an agency's rational allocation of its administrative resources.

In light of the foregoing, the judgment appealed from is reversed and the case is remanded to the district court with directions to enter judgment for the United States.

Reversed.

Questions

1. How would the court have decided Haverly if he never took a charitable contribution deduction when he gave the books to the school library?

2. What result if the taxpayer in Haverly, instead of giving the books away, sold the books he received as complimentary copies?

Problem

Fifteen years ago Sheila purchased a parcel of vacant land in San Diego for $1,000. Ten years ago she donated this vacant land to the city on the condition that the city construct a library on the land within 10 years. At that time the land was worth $5,000 and Sheila properly deducted $5,000 on her tax return as a charitable contribution. (She received the full benefit from this deduction because she had sufficient other itemized deductions.) The city failed to build a library within the 10 year deadline, and this year returned the land to Sheila when its value was $7,000. Sheila was in the 15% marginal income tax bracket ten years ago. Today, she is in the 28% bracket.

(a) Assuming the charitable deduction was proper when taken, what are the tax consequences to Sheila of the return of the property? Consider § 111. Does Sheila realize and recognize income? If so, in what amount and what is the character of the income? What basis does Sheila take in the property on its return?

(b) Can Sheila elect to use § 1341?

D. METHODS OF ACCOUNTING

For tax purposes there are two basic methods of accounting—the cash method and the accrual method. The following material examines the cash and accrual methods and analyzes how a taxpayer may use the cash method to postpone the receipt of gross income.

1. THE CASH METHOD

Introduction. The cash method of accounting is used by almost all wage earners and employees. It is also used by taxpayers rendering personal services and other small-scale proprietorships in which inventories are not significant. Compared with the accrual method of accounting, which often requires that a taxpayer realize and recognize items of income (or deduct expenses) prior to receiving (or making) payment, the cash method has the merit of simplicity. Under the cash method the receipt and disbursement of cash controls the realization and recognition of items of income and deduction. Revenues and expenditures are realized and recognized at the time cash is actually (or constructively) received or paid out regardless of when the claims or obligations actually arose. Reg. § 1.446–1(c)(1)(i). The cash method minimizes bookkeeping and accounting duties; indeed, for most cash method taxpayers, all "accounting" is done in the family checkbook.

Receipts Taxable Though Not Cash: The Economic Benefit Doctrine: It is axiomatic that, if the taxpayer receives typewriters or potatoes as items of income, they are to be treated the same as the receipt of cash. This result follows as long as the items can be valued in terms of money. Reg. § 1.446–1(a)(3). It is difficult to conceive of cases where items received cannot be so valued because courts have been notably ambitious, and properly so, in weighing probabilities. For example, notes "received in payment for services constitute income in the amount of their fair market value at the time of the transfer." Reg. § 1.61–2(d)(4).

Consider how the following ruling applies the claim of right doctrine, discussed at pp. 175–180, and the cash method of accounting.

REV.RUL. 83–163
1983–2 C.B. 26.

ISSUE

Whether the value of services received by a member of a barter club is includible in the member's gross income in the year received.

FACTS

A, B, and *C,* individual taxpayers who use the cash receipts and disbursements method of accounting, are members of a barter club. Club members pay an initiation fee, annual dues, and agree to provide specific services to any member for a specified number of hours. Club membership entitles each member to have access to a directory that lists the members of the club and the variety of services available to each individual. There is no requirement that members provide services unless requested by another member. Members may use as many of the offered services as they wish without fee. However, members receiving services that include materials are required to reimburse the provider's cost only, in cash. The members contact each other directly and request services to be performed.

LAW AND ANALYSIS

Section 61 of the Internal Revenue Code provides that, except as otherwise provided by law, gross income means all income from whatever source derived.

Section 451 of the Code provides, in part, that the amount of any item of gross income is includible in the gross income for the taxable year in which received by the taxpayer.

Section 1.61–1 of the Income Tax Regulations provides, in part, that gross income includes income realized in any form, whether in money, property or services.

Section 1.61–2(d)(1) of the regulations provides that, if services are paid for in services, the fair market value of the services taken in payment must be included in income as compensation.

Rev.Rul. 79–24, 1979–1 C.B. 60, discusses a situation where members of a barter club utilize the club's directory to contact other members directly and negotiate the value of the services to be performed. Rev.Rul. 79–24 holds that the fair market value of the services received by the members is includible in their gross incomes under section 61 of the Code.

A, B, and C joined the barter club for the purpose of obtaining access to the services of other members. As a condition of membership, each member agrees to provide services to the other members at their request. Thus, while A, B, and C may anticipate receiving services from the other members, they must also anticipate providing their services to the other members.

If a taxpayer receives income under a claim of right and without restriction as to its disposition, the income is includible in gross income at time of receipt (even though a repayment of part or all of the income may be required at a later date). See North American Oil v. Burnet, 286 U.S. 417 (1932) [XI–1 C.B. 293 (1932)]. Thus, such income or services received in advance for services to be rendered in the future is taxable at the time of its receipt. See Schlude v. Commissioner, 372 U.S. 128 (1963) [1963–1 C.B. 99]; Brown v. Helvering, 291 U.S. 193 (1934) [XIII–1 C.B. 223 (1934)].

The situation of A, B, and C is similar to that of Rev.Rul. 79–24, although club members do not negotiate directly with each other at the time services are provided. A, B, and C receive services in exchange for their agreement to provide services to other club members on demand. The services are received without any restriction, contractual or otherwise, as to their disposition, use or enjoyment. Accordingly, the services received by A, B, and C represent advance compensation for A, B, and C's agreeing to provide future services to other club members, and the fair market value of these services is taxable to A, B, and C, pursuant to section 1.61–2(d)(1) of the regulations.

HOLDING

The fair market value of the services received by A, B, and C is includible in their gross incomes for the taxable year in which received. Furthermore, these exchanges are reportable by the barter club pursuant to section 6045 of the Code and the regulations thereunder.

Compare Rev.Rul. 83–163 to Rev.Rul. 80–52 at p. 60.

Tax Planning for Cash Method Taxpayer Limited by Doctrine of Constructive Receipt. The relation between the cash method of accounting and constructive receipt doctrine may be simply stated. In order to postpone receipt of income, cash method taxpayers sometimes make arrangements to have cash (or its equivalent) which is owing to them paid at some date later than it would normally be received if this is more suitable for their tax purposes. But the Commissioner desires to prevent the taxpayer from arranging his affairs to minimize tax liability without in substance changing his economic position. Consequently, the Commissioner has urged, and in many cases courts have supported the Commissioner, that the taxpayer on the cash method who may simply reach out and take income available to him is deemed to have done so for tax purposes. The doctrine of constructive receipt is based on the principle that income is received or realized by cash method taxpayers "when it is made subject to the will and control of the taxpayer and can be, except for his own action or inaction, reduced to actual possession." Loose v. United States, 74 F.2d 147, 150 (8th Cir. 1934). By failing to exercise the power to collect income, the taxpayer may not postpone the receipt of income otherwise available.

The problems raised by the constructive receipt doctrine may be illustrated by restating a familiar example:

Assume that Alice, an attorney, is on the cash method and has a calendar tax year. She sent her client, Cliff, a bill for $2,000 in December. If Alice discovers that her income for the year has been low, and she expects the income for the subsequent tax year to be higher, she will doubtless try to get this bill paid during December. If the contrary is true, she may attempt to have payment of the bill deferred until January. This would avoid the bunching of income in one year with consequent disadvantages arising from the progressive tax structure. It seems probable that this device will be successful. (Of course, counsel must remember that, if her bill were for a deductible expense (§ 162(a)), the client on the cash method might well desire to further his own tax purposes by paying it in the year suitable to him rather than a year designated by the attorney.)

There is nothing in the income tax law which requires a creditor to press or decline to press for payment of an obligation in a particular tax year. However, this device sometimes has been extended by taxpayers beyond limits which may fairly be considered proper. Thus, the taxpayer who is on a cash method and who receives a check in one tax accounting period may simply hold it until a subsequent tax accounting period. In such a case, the taxpayer may argue that, since he did not actually receive cash until the second accounting period, the check should not be treated as income to him until the second year. If this device were to remain unchallenged, a substantial loophole would be created with respect to the administration of the revenue laws. Consequently, the Commissioner has fought this type of tax avoidance with the frequent assistance of the courts. In addition, Reg. § 1.451–2(a) provides:

> Income although not actually reduced to a taxpayer's possession is
> constructively received by him in the taxable year during which it is
> credited to his account, set apart for him, or otherwise made available
> so that he may draw upon it at any time * * *. However, income is
> not constructively received if the taxpayer's control of its receipt is
> subject to substantial limitations or restrictions.

The key phrase is when is income "made available" to the taxpayer for
the purposes of the constructive receipt doctrine.

Payment by Check Sometimes Creates Constructive Receipt. The
time at which the receipt of payment in the form of a check is
attributed to the recipient must be considered. In Lavery v. Commissioner, 158 F.2d 859 (7th Cir.1946), the taxpayer received a check on
December 30 and cashed it on the succeeding January 2. It was held to
be income to him on December 30, the date of receipt, on the basis of a
predecessor regulation to Reg. § 1.451–2(a). The court held that the
receipt of a check was equivalent to the receipt of cash because the
taxpayer could have cashed the check on the day it was received by
him, or at least on December 31. There was no doubt about the
validity of the check or the solvency of the drawer. The Tax Court has
gone further and held that even where a check was received after
banking hours on December 31 it was income in the year the check was
received. Kahler v. Commissioner, 18 T.C. 31 (1952).

Moreover, it has been held that a dividend check represents income
on December 31 if the stockholder can pick it up at the corporation's
office but, instead, requests that it be mailed to him. Kunze v.
Commissioner, 19 T.C. 29 (1952), affirmed per curiam 203 F.2d 957 (2d
Cir.1953). On the other hand, if the payor's practice is to put checks in
the mail on December 31 and the taxpayer could not get the check in
any event until the next year, it has been held that the check is not
income to the taxpayer until it was received in the following year. Reg.
§ 1.451–2(b). The delay in receipt or the substantial limitation or
restriction was not of the taxpayer's own making. Avery v. Commissioner, 292 U.S. 210, 54 S.Ct. 674, 78 L.Ed. 1216 (1934); Sloper v.
Commissioner, 1 T.C. 746 (1943); but compare McEuen v. Commissioner, 196 F.2d 127 (5th Cir.1952).

Sale of Property, Constructive Receipt and Economic Benefit. In a
year when his income is high a taxpayer on the cash method can defer
income items simply by urging his debtors not to pay him until his next
accounting period. However, the cases are far from clear respecting
the circumstances under which income can be so deferred. This advice
has been upheld in some surprising situations, for example, where a
farmer followed a consistent practice of selling and delivering wheat in
Year 1, but receiving payment for it in Year 2 pursuant to a bona fide,
arm's-length oral arrangement whereby liability for the payment of the
purchase price arose only in January of Year 2. The Tax Court held
that under these circumstances the taxpayer had not constructively
received income in Year 1. Under the bona fide, arm's-length contract,

the taxpayer could not have demanded and received payment in Year 1. Amend v. Commissioner, 13 T.C. 178 (1949). In Rev.Rul. 58–162, 1958–1 C.B. 234, the Service followed the Amend decision and stated "the proceeds from the sale of wheat by a farmer, using the cash receipts and disbursements method of accounting, under a bona fide arm's-length contract calling for payment in the taxable year following that in which the wheat was delivered to the purchaser, are includable in his gross income for the taxable year in which payment is received." See also Schniers v. Commissioner, 69 T.C. 511 (1977).

On the other hand, it has been held that once the sale proceeds for goods are due and the purchaser is ready, willing and able to pay, but the seller requested the purchaser to postpone payment, then the seller obtained constructive receipt of the amount due. Frank v. Commissioner, 22 T.C. 945 (1954), affirmed per curiam 226 F.2d 600 (6th Cir.1955). In Williams v. United States, 219 F.2d 523 (5th Cir.1955), a portion of the money was placed in escrow with a third party who held the funds so that the seller was certain to get it at the expiration of the escrow period. An escrow imposed by the seller will not postpone the reporting of income.

Consider the court's interpretation of the constructive receipt and economic benefit doctrines to validate the escrow used in the following case.

REED v. COMMISSIONER

United States Court of Appeals, First Circuit, 1983.
723 F.2d 138.

FLOYD R. GIBSON, SENIOR CIRCUIT JUDGE.

John E. Reed appeals from the United States Tax Court's decision sustaining the Commissioner's determination of a $71,412.68 deficiency in Reed's 1973 federal income tax. On appeal to this court, Reed, a cash basis taxpayer, claims the Tax Court erred as a matter of law in ruling that he recognized a long-term capital gain from the sale of 80 shares of stock in 1973, when the stock purchaser deposited the stock sales proceeds into an escrow account, rather than in 1974, when the escrowee disbursed the sales proceeds to Reed. Reed urges that the escrow account was a valid income deferral device because: 1) the account was set up under a bona fide agreement between Reed and the stock purchaser providing for deferred payment of the sales proceeds; 2) Reed was not entitled to receive any incidental benefits from the escrow account in 1973; and 3) the escrowee was not Reed's agent. We agree with Reed's contentions and therefore reverse the Tax Court's assessment of the $71,412.68 deficiency.

* * *

II. DISCUSSION

The Commissioner argues that the Tax Court's ruling is supported by [two] separate doctrines: the constructive receipt doctrine, [and] the economic benefit doctrine * * *. Though these doctrines invariably overlap, as evidenced by the Tax Court's apparent reliance on a hybrid of the constructive receipt and economic benefit doctrines, we will address each separately.

A. *Constructive Receipt*

The Commissioner contends Reed constructively received the stock sales proceeds when they were deposited in the escrow account on December 27, 1973. A cash basis taxpayer such as Reed is required to recognize income from the sale of property in the taxable year in which he actually or constructively receives payment for the property. 26 U.S.C. § 451(a) [1986], Treas.Reg. § 1.451–1(a). Treasury Regulation § 1.451–2(a) explains the constructive receipt doctrine as follows:

> Income although not actually reduced to a taxpayer's possession is constructively received by him in the taxable year during which it is credited to his account, *set apart for him, or otherwise made available so that he may draw upon it at any time,* or so that he could have drawn upon it during the taxable year if notice of intention to withdraw had been given. *However, income is not constructively received if the taxpayer's control of its receipt is subject to substantial limitations or restrictions.*

(Emphasis added).

Thus, under the constructive receipt doctrine, a taxpayer recognizes taxable income when he has an unqualified, vested right to receive immediate payment. Ross v. Commissioner, 169 F.2d 483, 490 (1st Cir.1948); Amend v. Commissioner, 13 T.C. 178, 185 (1949); Metzer, Constructive Receipt, Economic Benefit and Assignment of Income: A Case Study in Deferred Compensation, 29 Tax L.Rev. 525, 531 (1974). However, a taxpayer-seller has the right to enter into an agreement with the buyer that he, the seller, will not be paid until the following year. Schniers v. Commissioner, 69 T.C. 511, 516 n. 2, 517–18 (1977). As long as the deferred payment agreement is binding between the parties and is made prior to the time when the taxpayer-seller has acquired an absolute and unconditional right to receive payment, then the cash basis taxpayer is not required to report the sales proceeds as income until he actually receives them. Id.; Oates v. Commissioner, 18 T.C. 570, 584–85 (1952); aff'd 207 F.2d 711 (7th Cir.1953); Glenn v. Penn, 250 F.2d 507, 508 (6th Cir.1958); Commissioner v. Tyler, 72 F.2d 950, 952 (3rd Cir.1934); Amend, 13 T.C. at 185.

Applying the language of Treasury Regulation § 1.451–2(a) quoted above, if the deferred payment agreement provides that the taxpayer-seller has no right to payment until the taxable year following the sale, then the income received from the sale is not "set apart for him, or otherwise made available so that he may draw upon it" in the year of the sale. See *Schniers*, 69 T.C. at 516. Alternatively stated, such a deferred payment agreement restricts the time of payment and therefore serves as a "substantial limitation" on the taxpayer control of the proceeds in the taxable year of the sale. See Tyler, 72 F.2d at 952.

Hence, as the parties agree and the Tax Court stated, courts have generally recognized that a cash basis taxpayer-seller may effectively postpone income recognition through the use of a bona fide arms-length agreement between the buyer and seller calling for deferred payment of the sales proceeds. See Busby v. United States, 679 F.2d 48, 49–50 (5th Cir.1982); Tyler, 72 F.2d at 952; Oates, 207 F.2d at 713; Kasper v. Banek, 214 F.2d 125, 127 (8th Cir.1954); Glenn, 250 F.2d at 508; Schniers, 69 T.C. at 516; Amend, 13 T.C. at 184–85. Compare Arnwine v. Commissioner, 696 F.2d 1102, 1111–12 (5th Cir.1983); Warren v. United States, 613 F.2d 591, 593 (5th Cir.1980) (agreement between seller and his agent for deferral of payment ineffective to defer income recognition).

Similarly, an existing agreement which has been amended or modified to provide for deferred payment of an amount not yet due serves to postpone income recognition. Oates, 18 T.C. at 585; 207 F.2d 712–14. Goldsmith v. United States, 586 F.2d 810, 817, 218 Ct.Cl. 387 (1978); Commissioner v. Olmstead, Inc., 304 F.2d 16, 21–2 (8th Cir. 1962). This is true even though: 1) the purchaser was initially willing to contract for immediate payment; and 2) the taxpayer's primary objective in entering into the deferred payment agreement was to minimize taxes. Goldsmith, 586 F.2d 819; Schniers, 69 T.C. 517–18; Cowden v. Commissioner, 289 F.2d 20, 23, 23 n. 1 (5th Cir.1959).[20] A deferred payment agreement is considered bona fide and hence given its full legal effect, if the parties intended to be bound by the agreement and were, in fact, legally bound. Oates, 18 T.C. at 585; Schniers, 69 T.C. at 516–18.

While recognizing these principles, the Commissioner claims the escrow modification providing for disbursement of the sales proceeds to Reed in 1974 was not a bona fide arms-length agreement between the [buyer] and Reed and, hence, did not "substantially limit" Reed's access to the sales proceeds deposited in escrow after the December 27, 1973 closing. Instead, the purported escrow modification was nothing more than Reed's self imposed limitation, designed to defer income recognition on proceeds he already had an unqualified, vested right to receive on December 27, 1973. The Commissioner claims the record reveals that Reed could have taken the sales proceeds immediately after the December 27, 1973 closing, had he so requested.

We agree with the Commissioner that a deferred escrow arrangement that is not part of a bona fide agreement between the buyer and the seller-taxpayer, but rather is a "self-imposed limitation" created by the seller-taxpayer, is legally ineffective to shift taxability on escrowed funds from one year to the next. See Williams v. United States, 219 F.2d 523, 527 (5th Cir.1953); Arnwine, 696 F.2d at 1107; Warren, 613

---

20. As Judge Learned Hand stated in Helvering v. Gregory, 69 F.2d 809, 810 (2nd Cir.1934) aff'd 293 U.S. 465, 55 S.Ct. 266, 79 L.Ed. 596 (1935): "Any one may so arrange his affairs that his taxes shall be as low as possible; he is not bound to choose that pattern which will best pay the Treasury; there is not even a patriotic duty to increase one's taxes".

F.2d at 593. However, in this case the escrow arrangement was the product of an arms-length, bona fide modification to the purchase sale agreement between Reed and [the buyer]; it was not Reed's self imposed limitation on the receipt of sales proceeds he had an unqualified, vested right to receive in 1973.

The modification setting up the escrow arrangement was orally agreed upon by the parties in early December, 1973, and, as the Tax Court found, was memorialized in the escrow agreement instruction letter executed prior to closing on December 27, 1973. Thus, the modification became effective prior to the time when Reed had an unqualified right to demand immediate payment under the then existing purchase agreement. As discussed above, an existing purchase-sale agreement can be modified to provide for deferred payment of an amount not already due under the existing agreement, provided the modification is considered by the parties to be legally binding. *Oates*, 18 T.C. at 585; 207 F.2d 712–19; *Goldsmith*, 586 F.2d at 817. * * *

The Commissioner relies heavily upon Williams v. United States, 219 F.2d 523 (5th Cir.1955) in support of its claim that the escrow arrangement here amounted to a "self-imposed", rather than "substantial", limitation on the taxpayer's access to the sales proceeds in 1973. However, the *Williams* case is clearly distinguishable and does not control here. In *Williams*, the seller-taxpayer entered into an agreement to sell timber to a lumber company for a cash price. After the sale contract was executed, the taxpayer-seller decided, for tax reasons, that he wanted to receive part of the purchase payment in four installments in later years. The taxpayer himself prepared an escrow agreement naming the bank as the escrow agent and the taxpayer personally secured the bank's approval of the arrangement. The *Williams* court, emphasizing that the escrow arrangement was unilaterally set up by the seller-taxpayer, concluded that under the terms of the purchase agreement, the entire purchase price became available to the taxpayer upon completion of the sale. Id. at 527.

Unlike in *Williams*, the escrow arrangement here was not unilaterally imposed by Reed, but rather was part of a bona fide modification to the purchase-sale agreement between Reed and [the buyer]. Under that agreement, as modified, the purchase price did not become available to Reed until the taxable year following the year of the sale.

The instant case is thus much closer to another Fifth Circuit case, Busby v. United States, 679 F.2d 48 (5th Cir.1982), involving a cotton farmer's use of an escrow device to defer income from the sale of a cotton crop until the year after it was harvested and delivered to the buyer. In *Busby*, the taxpayer-farmer emphasized the importance of a deferred payment and conditioned the sale upon it. Accordingly, the cotton gin, the buyer's purchasing agent, agreed to establish an irrevocable escrow account in a bank. Under the terms of purchase agreement, the buyer was to deposit the proceeds of the sale into the escrow account following the delivery of the cotton in 1973. The escrowee was to then pay the purchase price to the farmer in 1974. Once the purchase price had been deposited with the escrowee in 1973, there was no condition on the farmer's receipt of the funds other than the passage of time. The 5th Circuit in *Busby* concluded that there was an arms length agreement to defer payment which was effective to shift the farmer's tax on the proceeds until the year following the sale. Id. at 50.

The only notable distinction between *Busby* and this case is that the deferred payment arrangement in this case was part of a modification of the original purchase-sale agreement. However, as we discussed above, this distinction is not controlling where, as here, the modification was bona fide and became binding prior to the time when the taxpayer's right to immediate payment had vested.

Another case sanctioning the use of an escrow arrangement to defer income recognition is Commissioner v. Tyler, 72 F.2d 950 (3rd Cir. 1934). In *Tyler*, the taxpayer sold corporate stock under a deferred payment contract calling for the delivery of stock to the purchaser in December of 1927 and the payment of the purchase proceeds to the taxpayer in January, 1928. As provided under the agreement, in November, 1927, the taxpayer delivered stock to an escrowee. In December, 1927, the escrowee delivered the stock to the purchaser and the purchaser in turn deposited the purchase price with the escrowee. The escrowee then paid the purchase proceeds to the taxpayer in January of 1928. The *Tyler* court held that the taxpayer did not recognize income from the sale of stock in the taxable year 1927. The court held:

> The doctrine of constructive receipt is applicable only when there is *no substantial limitation or restriction as to the time of payment to the taxpayer. The deposit agreement, however, does limit and restrict the time of payment*, since it specifically provides that the depositing shareholders are not to receive any money until after January 1, 1928. They could neither demand their share nor control its disposition prior to that date. Under the agreement, the [taxpayers] could not and did not in fact or constructively receive the money for their shares until 1928. We are of the opinion, therefore, that the Board of Tax Appeals did not err in holding that the income was earned in 1928, and that the profit therefrom was taxable in that year.

72 F.2d at 952 (emphasis added).

Similarly, in the instant case, and in *Busby*, the taxpayer's right to demand payment of the escrowed purchase proceeds in the year of the sale was restricted by a binding agreement with the purchaser requiring that payments to the taxpayer be made the following year. See Harold W. Johnston v. Commissioner, 14 T.C. 560, 565 (1950) (sales proceeds held by escrowee under deferred payments agreement not subject to taxpayer's immediate demand and hence not constructively received by taxpayer). Under Treasury Regulation § 1.451–2(a), such an agreement, even though it restricts only the time of payment, serves as a "substantial limitation" on the taxpayer's right to demand payment of the escrowed purchase proceeds in the year of the sale. See McDonald, Deferred Compensation: Conceptual Astigmatism, 24 Tax L.Rev. 201, 204 (1969) ("[Section 1.451–2(a)] does not say that income is constructively received merely because its eventual payment is not subject to conditions of restrictions; the central consideration is whether the taxpayer's control of the time of its payment is subject to restrictions or limitations.")

Furthermore, as quoted above, Treasury Regulation § 1.451–2(a) also provides that income is recognized by a cash basis taxpayer "in the taxable year during which it is credited to his account, set apart for him, *or otherwise made available so that he may draw upon it at any time.*" (Emphasis added). Here, as in *Busby* and *Tyler*, the binding deferred payment agreement between the purchaser and seller prevented the taxpayer from "drawing" upon the escrowed funds in the year of the sale. See *Johnston*, 14 T.C. at 565.

B. Economic Benefit

The Commissioner next contends that in 1973 Reed received a taxable economic benefit by virtue of [the] deposit of the sales proceeds into the escrow account. The Commissioner argues that upon the December 27, 1973 closing, there were no open transactions remaining and Reed's right to future payment from the escrow account was irrevocable, being conditioned only upon the passage of time; hence, Reed received the "cash equivalent" of the sales proceeds deposited in the escrow account. The Commissioner points out that Reed could have assigned his irrevocable right to receive future payment of the escrow funds.

This argument, which was largely embraced by the Tax Court, is predicated upon a misapplication of various cases the Commissioner says espouse the economic benefit doctrine. See Kuehner v. Commissioner, 214 F.2d 437, 440–41 (1st Cir.1954); Williams v. United States, 219 F.2d 523, 527 (5th Cir.1955); Watson v. Commissioner, 613 F.2d 594, 597 (5th Cir.1980); Oden v. Commissioner, 56 T.C. 569, 575 (1971); Pozzi v. Commissioner, 49 T.C. 119 (1967). These cases held that escrow arrangements were ineffective to defer income tax because of the existence of one of two factors, not present in the instant case: (1) the taxpayer received some present, beneficial interest from the escrow account; see *Kuehner*, 214 F.2d at 440 (investment income); *Watson*, 613 F.2d at 597 (letter of credit); *Pozzi*, 49 T.C. at 127–28 (interest income); (2) the escrow arrangement was the product of the taxpayer's self-imposed limitation on funds the taxpayer had an unqualified, vested right to control. See *Williams*, 219 F.2d at 526–27 (escrow was self-imposed limitation); *Oden*, 56 T.C. at 577 (same).

Specifically, *Kuehner*, the First Circuit case upon which the Commissioner principally relies, held that a taxpayer recognized income when the purchase price was deposited with the escrowee because the

taxpayer's interest in the escrowed funds constituted a property interest equivalent to cash. The taxpayer's interest in the escrow fund was
so viewed because the taxpayer was entitled to investment income
earned while the funds were in escrow and hence enjoyed a complete
and present economic interest in the funds. As the court stated:

> Under the terms of the 1947 agreement the interest from the invested
> [escrow fund] was payable to the petitioner. The Trustee's duties were
> ministerial and the economic benefits of the [escrow] fund held by it
> belonged to the [taxpayer].

214 F.2d at 440.

By contrast, in this case Reed was not entitled to receive the
income earned from the investment of funds held by the escrowee, but
merely obtained an unconditional promise that he would ultimately be
paid on January 3, 1974 in accordance with the deferred payment
provision.

The Commissioner, however, seizes upon broad language in *Kuehner* as support for the proposition that one who has an unconditional
right to future payment from an irrevocable escrow account receives
taxable income in the year the escrow account was created.[21] There
are three reasons why we do not interpret *Kuehner* as supporting this
proposition. First, as the *Kuehner* court apparently recognized, the
deposited escrow funds could be characterized as "the equivalent of
cash" only if the taxpayer received a present beneficial interest in such
funds—e.g., investment income. The *Kuehner* court's discussion of the
taxpayer's present, beneficial interest in the escrow funds would have
been superfluous if it were holding that the taxpayer's unconditional
right to future payment of such funds was the equivalent of cash.
Hence, we believe it is reasonable to interpret the *Kuehner* court's
discussion of the unconditional nature of a right to future payment as
relating to the court's determination of the appropriate value of the
economic benefit conferred, the court having determined that the
taxpayer had received a present economic benefit.

Second, to apply the Commissioner's interpretation of *Kuehner* to
this case would be at odds with the well established principle that a
deferred payment arrangement is effective to defer income recognition
to a cash basis taxpayer, provided it is part of an arms-length agreement between the purchaser and seller. That the cash basis taxpayer's
right to receive future payment of the escrowed proceeds may be
characterized as unconditional or irrevocable does not render the contractually binding restriction on the time of payment any less substantial. See *Tyler*, 72 F.2d at 952; *Busby*, 679 F.2d at 50; *Johnston*, 14 T.C.
at 565; *Amend*, 13 T.C. at 184.

Third, to apply the Commissioner's interpretation of Kuehner here
would require an extension of the economic benefit doctrine that would

---

21. This proposition was rejected by the
Tax Court in Johnston, 14 T.C. at 565.

significantly erode the distinction between cash and accrual methods of accounting. The economic benefit doctrine, a nonstatutory doctrine emerging from and primarily related to the area of the employee deferred compensation, is based on the idea that an individual should be taxed on any economic benefit conferred upon him, to the extent that the benefit has an ascertainable fair market value. Metzer, Constructive Receipt, Economic Benefit and Assignment of Income: A Case Study in Deferred Compensation, 29 Tax L.Rev. 525, 550 (1974); see also Goldsmith, 586 F.2d at 820.[22] However, in applying the economic benefit doctrine to a cash basis taxpayer's contractual right to receive future payment, as we must do here, courts generally go beyond an inquiry into the fair market value of the contract right to ask the separate question of whether the contract right is the equivalent of cash. See *Johnston*, 14 T.C. at 565–66; Western Oakes Bldg. Corp. v. Commissioner, 49 T.C. 365, 376 (1968); Nina J. Ennis v. Commissioner, 17 T.C. 465, 469–70 (1951); see also Davies, A Model for Corporate Income Tax, 124 U.Pa.L.Rev. 299, 320–22 (1975). Without this separate inquiry, the economic benefit doctrine, as applied to a cash basis taxpayer, could be broadly construed to cover all deferred compensation and deferred payment contracts.[23]

In order to meet the cash equivalency requirement for income recognition, a cash basis taxpayer's contractual right to future payment must be reflected in a negotiable note, bond, or other evidence of indebtedness which, like money, commonly and readily changes hands in commerce. *Johnston*, 14 T.C. at 565–70; *Western Oaks*, 49 T.C. at 377; *Ennis*, 17 T.C. at 469–70; cf. Cowden v. Commissioner, 289 F.2d 20, 24 (5th Cir.1961) (contractual promise to pay must be "unconditional and assignable, not subject to set-offs, and * * * of a kind that is frequently transferred to lenders or investors at a discount not substantially greater than the generally prevailing premium for the use of money * * *.").[24] And, in addition to being readily transferrable, the evidence of indebtedness received by the taxpayer must be intended as present payment of the amount owed, rather than merely as evidence that payment will be forthcoming in the future. Davies, A Model for Corporate Income Tax, 124 U.Pa.L.Rev. 323–24; Schlemmer v. United States, 94 F.2d 77, 78 (2nd Cir.1938) (promissory note given by corporation to president in the amount of salary owed not intended as present

---

22. "[U]nlike constructive receipt, economic benefit requires the actual receipt of property or the actual receipt of a right to receive property in the future, at which point, the doctrine asks whether the property or the right confers a present economic benefit with an ascertainable fair market value." Metzer, Constructive Receipt, Economic Benefit, and Assignment of Income, 29 Tax L.Rev. at 551.

23. "Courts stress that unless the 'equivalent to cash' test is maintained separate from the 'ascertainable fair market value' test, the distinction between the cash and accrual methods will be eliminated." Davies, A Model for Corporate Income Tax, at 321 n. 7; see also Midgley, Federal Income Taxation of Private Annuitants, 406 Geo.Wash.L.Rev. 679, 689 (1972).

24. See Metzer, Constructive Receipt, Economic Benefit, and Assignment of Income, 29 Tax L.Rev. at 553–554; McDonald, Conceptual Astigmatism, 24 Tax L.Rev. at 225; Midgley, Federal Income Taxation of Private Annuitants, 406 Geo. Wash.L.Rev. 670, 688–89 (1972).

payment of salary and hence not equivalent to cash); Jay A. Williams v. Commissioner, 28 T.C. 1000, 1002 (1957); see also Metzer Constructive Receipt, Economic Benefit, and Assignment of Income, 29 Tax L.Rev. at 554.

In this case, it is difficult to conceive Reed's contractual right to future payment, even though unconditional and evidenced by an escrow account, as a right which commonly and readily changes hands in commerce. See *Johnston*, 14 T.C. at 565 (cash basis taxpayer's contractual right to future payment of purchase proceeds, evidenced by the deposit of such proceeds into an escrow account, not the equivalent of cash); see also Davies, A Model for Corporate Income Tax, 124 U.Pa.L. Rev. at 322. However, even assuming Reed's right to future payment of the escrowed proceeds was readily transferrable in commerce, the escrow account was not intended by the parties as present payment of the purchase price, but rather was intended to serve as an added assurance that payment would be made in the next year. As such, the escrow account cannot be characterized fairly as the equivalent of cash to Reed in 1973. We would have to ignore the distinction between cash and accrual methods of accounting to adopt a rule requiring immediate recognition of income by a cash basis taxpayer who has a contractual right to future payment from an escrow account, but who has received no present beneficial interest from that account. See *Johnston*, 14 T.C. at 565.

The Commissioner alternatively suggests that Reed received a present beneficial interest in the escrow funds in the sense that he could have assigned his right to receive payment under the agreement. This argument proves either too much or too little. It proves too much because any promisee under a contract for deferred payment could conceivably assign his right to receive future payment, provided the contract does not specifically include a non-assignment clause. Hence, to base the economic benefit rule on whether a taxpayer could have assigned his contractual right to future payment would eviscerate the well recognized rule that a taxpayer can defer income recognition pursuant to a bona fide deferred payment agreement. Furthermore, it proves too little in this case because Reed never attempted to make any assignment of his right to receive the escrow funds and thus did nothing to charge himself with any economic benefit to be derived from the funds. See Oates, 207 F.2d at 713 (taxpayer made no assignment of right to payment and hence received no economic benefit); compare Helvering v. Horst, 311 U.S. 112, 119–20, 61 S.Ct. 144, 148, 85 L.Ed. 75 (1940).

*   *   *

D. Conclusion

We therefore conclude that a purchase-sale contract calling for deferred payment of the purchase price through the use of an escrow arrangement is effective to shift income recognition by the seller until the taxable year when he actually receives payment of purchase price, rather than when the purchase price is deposited into escrow, provided the following three conditions exist: (1) the escrow arrangement is part of a bona fide, arms-length agreement between the purchaser and seller calling for deferred payment; (2) the seller receives no present beneficial interest (e.g., investment income) from the purchase funds while they are in escrow; and (3) the escrowee is not acting under the exclusive authority of the taxpayer. Because all three conditions exist here, we reverse the Tax Court's ruling assessing a $71,412.28 deficiency in Reed's 1973 federal income tax.

Judgment reversed.

Question

How sound is the court's interpretation of the economic benefit doctrine? Seemingly, the taxpayer's rights in the sales contract and the escrow were transferable. The taxpayer could have borrowed against the escrow funds or sold his rights. How realistic was the court's conclusion that the parties intended the escrow only to secure payment of the buyer's obligation under the contract when the terms of the escrow presumably provided that the escrow funds could be disbursed directly to the taxpayer on the termination of the escrow?

Rather than using an escrow, a cash method seller may simply rely on the general credit of the buyer. However, the seller does not have the benefit of the escrow. If the buyer does not pay, the seller may get nothing.

An alternative method of reducing the taxpayer's risk consists of a third party (e.g. an insurance company) guaranteeing the obligor's commitment. The third party's obligation is deemed a cash equivalent under the economic benefit test. Reconsider the Drescher case at p. 160 where the economic benefit test was used to find income when a third-party promise was received.

If the seller on the cash method took a negotiable note from the buyer for the purchase price, the seller would very probably be considered to have received income. Negotiable promissory notes are generally included in income (under the economic equivalent or cash equivalent test) at their fair market value when received. Reg. § 1.61–2(d)(4). If, however, the note is received as evidence of an underlying claim, the receipt of the note would not constitute income to the cash method taxpayer. Dial v. Commissioner, 24 T.C. 117, 122–23 (1955).

When is an Item Deductible by a Cash Method Taxpayer? As to the timing of the deduction of an item, the cash method taxpayer receives a deduction when he pays for the item. Assume a cash method taxpayer purchased office supplies on December 15 and paid for them on January 15. The taxpayer would have a deduction for the cost of the office supplies in January. Read Reg. § 1.461–1(a)(1).

2. THE ACCRUAL METHOD

Introduction. From an accountant's standpoint, the determination of periodic income involves the process of "timing" the recognition of revenue and "matching" against such revenue the expense items which are related thereto. The cash method makes no scientific effort either to "time" or to "match" because under the cash method the recognition of revenue and expense turns largely on the accidental factor of receipt or disbursement. Receivables and payables are recognized only when reduced to cash. While this simple method is suitable for individuals rendering personal services, for taxpayers engaging in the sale of merchandise, whether as manufacturers or distributors, and extending credit to their customers and receiving credit from their suppliers, a satisfactory determination of annual income requires a more refined technique. Almost all businesses of any substantial size, therefore, use the accrual method of accounting in respect to the recognition of revenues and expenses. Pursuant to § 448(a), most corporations and partnerships (where one of the partners is a C corporation) must use the accrual method. Excepted entities that can continue to use the cash method are: (1) farming businesses (as defined in § 263A(e)(4)); (2) qualified personal service corporations (as defined in § 448(d)(2)); and (3) entities with average annual gross receipts of $5 million or less. § 448(b). In addition, individual taxpayers engaged in the production or purchase and sale of goods are specifically required by Reg. § 1.471–1 to use opening and closing inventories in computing the cost of goods sold.

Briefly described, accrual involves the recognition of revenue items when earned not when the cash is received and the recognition of expense items when the liability for payment arises, not when paid. Thus, accounts receivable—amounts owed to the taxpayer by its customers—and accounts payable—amounts owed by the taxpayer to its suppliers—are both taken into account at the time the obligation becomes fixed, even though payment is not received or made until a later period.

Income Accrues When Amount and Fact of Liability is Fixed. Two elements are necessary in order to attribute income to the taxpayer on the accrual method: all the events must have occurred which fix the right to receive the income and it must be possible to determine the amount of the income with reasonable accuracy. Reg. § 1.446–1(c)(1)(ii). No question arises as to the propriety of these rules, though they are obviously uncertain in application.

Considerable leeway in the application of the accrual method is given to the taxpayer provided that the method he uses and its application " * * * accords with generally accepted accounting principles, is consistently used by the taxpayer from year to year, and is consistently with the Income Tax Regulations." Reg. § 1.446–1(c)(1)(ii). This Regulation is critical in tax planning, as may be illustrated by the provision in Reg. § 1.446–1(c)(1)(ii) that the taxpayer engaged in a manufacturing business may treat the sale of goods as having been made (thus accruing the item for tax purposes) either:

1. when the goods are shipped, or

2. when the product is delivered or accepted, or

3. when title to the goods passes to the customer, whether or not billed,

depending on the method regularly employed by the taxpayer in keeping his books.

However, an accrual method taxpayer need not accrue as income any portion of amounts billed for the performance of services, which, on the basis of experience, he will not collect. § 448(d)(5). This special rule does not apply if the taxpayer-service provider charges any interest or imposes a penalty for failure to make timely payment in connection with the amount billed.

How to Control Accrual Through Discretion in Setting Accrual Date: Judicial Approval. Regulations providing that the accrual taxpayer's practices may determine whether income was actually received have found vigorous judicial support. In one case, the taxpayer took orders for goods and billed customers without shipping instructions or without setting any goods aside to meet the specific buyer's requirements. The contract was considered valid and enforceable as of December 31 even though shipping orders were lacking. The goods were billed in one tax accounting period and taken out of the warehouse and shipped in a second accounting period; the taxpayer claimed the income had accrued in the first accounting period even though title remained with the taxpayer. The taxpayer had followed a practice of accruing income at the time of billing. In Pacific Grape Products Co. v. Commissioner, 219 F.2d 862 (9th Cir.1955), the court sustained the position of the taxpayer that its method of accounting accurately reflected its income. The court agreed with the dissenting opinion in the Tax Court:

* * * Methods of keeping records do not spring in glittering perfection from some unchangeable natural law but are devised to aid business men in maintaining sometimes intricate accounts. If reasonably adapted to that use they should not be condemned for some [abstruse] legal reason, but only when they fail to reflect income. There is no persuasive indication that such a condition exists here. On the contrary, a whole industry apparently had adopted the method used by [taxpayer]. (17 T.C. at 1110–1111).

How to Control Accrual: Amount Owed Must be Fixed With "Reasonable Accuracy." It has been noted that an amount will not be accrued as income to the taxpayer using the accrual method unless the fact of liability to the taxpayer and the amount are fixed. The requirement as to amount is phrased by the Regulations in terms of a recitation that it must be "determined with reasonable accuracy." Reg. § 1.446–1(c)(1)(ii).

In general, this rule affords substantial opportunities for tax planning. Assume that the taxpayer on the accrual method is selling services; if the billing for services is postponed from December to the following January, for a calendar year taxpayer, the sum cannot be said to accrue until January since the billing sets the amount owing in absence of a dispute. The same is true with respect to a sale of property where the price is not fixed. Postponement may also afford an incidental advantage in cases where no tax planning is intended but amounts are in dispute, such as cases involving litigation.

Use of an escrow for all or part of the sales price of property will not change the tax consequences for accrual method taxpayers who must include the sales price in gross income on the consummation of the sale. An exception exists if the funds are placed in escrow and the transaction is subject to the fulfillment of certain conditions. Until the conditions are satisfied, the events fixing the taxpayer's right to income have not occurred and income is not accrued. See e.g., Big Lake Oil Co. v. Commissioner, 95 F.2d 573 (3d Cir.1938), cert. denied 307 U.S. 638, 59 S.Ct. 1037, 83 L.Ed. 1520 (1939).

When is Amount Owed Said to Be Fixed? No single case can constitute a precedent for any other case when a concept as evanescent and dependent on facts as "reasonable accuracy" is involved. It has been suggested that an amount may be said to have accrued if it is known or could be fixed by the potential recipient on the basis of facts known to him. A leading case developing this concept is Continental Tie & Lumber Co. v. United States, 286 U.S. 290, 52 S.Ct. 529, 76 L.Ed. 1111 (1932), in which the taxpayer had a claim against the United States resulting from governmental operation of the taxpayer's railroad during the First World War. A statute authorizing compensation was passed in 1920; the taxpayer received the compensation in 1923. The delay arose because of the time required by the Interstate Commerce Commission to determine the amount to which the taxpayer was entitled. In holding that income from the claim for compensation arose in 1920, although there was uncertainty as to the amount, the Court stated that:

> The case does not fall within the principle that, where the liability is undetermined in any tax year, the taxpayer is not called upon to accrue any sum * * *, but presents the problem whether the taxpayer had in its own books and accounts data to which it could apply the calculations required by the statute and ascertain the quantum of the award within reasonable limits. (286 U.S. at 296, 52 S.Ct. at 531, 76 L.Ed. at 1113–1114).

The Continental Tie case favors the earlier inclusion of uncertain items. The subsequent cases have limited the scope of the Continental Tie decision. If a dispute exists only as to the amount, but not the basic liability, the amount is includible in income if a reasonably accurate estimate can be made. A dispute as to the underlying liability itself delays the inclusion into income, but uncertainty as to amount may not differ significantly from uncertainty as to liability.

How to Control Tax Liability Through Accrual Method: When is an Item Deductible? The accrual method taxpayer may deduct the expenses in the year in which all events occur creating an unconditional obligation to pay. Reg. § 1.461–1(a)(2). The problem of whether an item had accrued so as to be deductible under the "all events" test arose in United States v. Anderson, 269 U.S. 422, 46 S.Ct. 131, 70 L.Ed. 347 (1926). The Supreme Court held that a munitions tax was a proper item of deduction for the accrual method taxpayer with respect to munitions manufactured and sold during a tax year even though the tax had not been formally assessed, and in fact became due and was paid in the following tax year. Seeking to match expenses with associated revenues in the same taxable period, the Court applied the general doctrine of accrual in these circumstances: "In a technical legal sense it may be argued that a tax does not accrue until it has been assessed and becomes due; but it is also true that in advance of the assessment of a tax, all the events may occur which fix the amount of the tax and determine the liability of the taxpayer to pay it." 269 U.S. at 441, 46 S.Ct. at 134, 70 L.Ed. at 351.

In United States v. Hughes Properties, Inc., __ U.S. __, 106 S.Ct. 2092, 90 L.Ed.2d 569 (1986), the Supreme Court ruled that a gambling casino could deduct accrued but unpaid jackpots at the close of its tax year. The taxpayer's liability for the recorded amounts of the guaranteed jackpots was fixed and enforceable under state law even though no payment could be made until the jackpot was won. The casino's liability was not contingent. Although an extremely remote and speculative possibility existed that the jackpot would never be won, the casino was obligated under state law to pay the guaranteed jackpot amounts. Under state law, a guaranteed portion of the slot machine's intake was to be paid; although the exact time of payment and the winner's identity was unknown. No matter who the winner was, the casino was obligated to pay. In short, state law, not the identity of the winner, fixed the time of liability for purposes of the "all events" test.

However, in Mooney Aircraft, Inc. v. United States, 420 F.2d 400 (5th Cir. 1969), reproduced at p. 547, a current deduction for a liability satisfying the "all events" test under Reg. § 1.461–1(a)(2) was denied because the possible interval between the current accrual of the deduction and actual payment was too lengthy. The court reasoned that the likelihood of payment decreased as the time interval between accrual and payment increased. See, Gunn, Matching of Costs and Revenues As a Goal of Tax Accounting, 4 Va.Tax Rev. 1 (1984).

The "all events" test used by accrual method taxpayers is a windfall to them in that a current deduction for the entire amount of a future liability overstates the true financial cost of that future liability. This is attributable to the failure to take into account the time value of money. This can be illustrated by a taxpayer in the 28% marginal tax bracket who satisfies the all events test for a $10,000 expenditure to be made the following year. A $10,000 current deduction reduces his income taxes by $2,800. If he invests the taxes saved at 10% simple interest for one year, he will earn $280 and net $201.60 after payment of taxes on that interest income. Therefore, the true cost of the $10,000 expenditure to be made the following year is only $9,798.40. Congress was concerned about the revenue loss from these overstated deductions. Specifically,

> Congress believed that the rules relating to the time for accrual of a deduction by a taxpayer using the accrual method of accounting should be changed to take into account the time value of money and the time the deduction is economically incurred. Recent court decisions in some cases permitted accrual method taxpayers to deduct currently expenses that were not yet economically incurred (i.e., that were attributable to activities to be performed or amounts to be paid in the future). Allowing a taxpayer to take deductions currently for an amount to be paid in the future overstates the true cost of the expense to the extent that the time value of money is not taken into account; the deduction is overstated by the amount by which the face value exceeds the present value of the expense. The longer the period of time involved, the greater is the overstatement. Joint Committee on Taxation, General Explanation of the Revenue Provisions of the Deficit Reduction Tax Act of 1984, 260 (1985).

One alternative would have been to allow a current deduction in the year the "all events" test is satisfied for only the discounted present value of the future expenditure. However, Congress recognized that this approach would be complex and difficult to administer. Instead, Congress decided to postpone the deduction to a time closer to when payment is actually made. The 1984 Act added a new, additional test for an accrual method taxpayer to satisfy before the deduction is allowed. Under new § 461(h) no deduction is permitted until both the "all events" test is satisfied and "economic performance" has occurred. Simply stated, this means that a taxpayer who promises to pay for the future delivery of goods or the future performance of services cannot deduct the amount of the liability he incurs until delivery or performance. § 461(h)(2)(A). A taxpayer obligated to provide goods or services in the future cannot deduct the cost of providing those future goods or services until the delivery or performance takes place. § 461(h)(2)(B). A similar approach is applied to a taxpayer's obligation to provide workman's compensation benefits and meet tort liabilities. § 461(b)(2) (C). Where actual performance takes place over several taxable years, a taxpayer is not allowed a deduction for the entire amount in the year delivery or performance commences. Instead, the deduction is prorated and allowed only for that portion attributable to goods or services actually provided in that year.

Congress recognized that for many taxpayers the economic performance test would disrupt normal business and accounting practices and impose undue burdens, especially for recurring items and for those taxpayers who do not obtain the benefits of deferral beyond the next year. Accordingly, an exception was provided for certain recurring items. If the "all events" test and the four criteria contained in § 461(h)(3) are satisfied, a current deduction is allowed even though "economic performance" has not occurred.

As to items of contested liability, § 461(f) provides, in general, for the deduction of the contested items in the year in which they are paid into a trust or other escrow fund by the accrual method taxpayer even if, after payment, the taxpayer continues to contest the liability. To qualify for the deduction the accrual method taxpayer must meet two tests. First, that a deduction would be allowed for that year or an earlier year but for the contest and second, that the "economic perform-ance" test is satisfied. If the taxpayer's liability subsequently is less than the amount paid, the taxpayer takes the refund into gross income at that time (or in a earlier year if properly accruable) assuming the earlier deduction resulted in a tax benefit for the taxpayer. It should be noted that, with respect to workman's compensation and tort liabili-ties, economic performance occurs only as payments are made to a claimant. A payment to a trust under § 461(f) will not satisfy the "economic performance" test with respect to workman's compensation and tort liabilities. § 461(h)(2)(C).

Structured Settlements: When Deductible? As was discussed previ-ously at pp. 156–159, an injured person can exclude the entire amount received under a properly structured settlement of his claim for dam-ages. The question is whether an accrual method taxpayer can cur-rently deduct the amount he has agreed to pay in the future (either as an annuity or as a lump sum). Since the amount of the liability has been finally determined and there exists an unconditional obligation to make the payments in the future, the "all events" test under Reg. § 1.461–1(a)(2) has been satisfied and a current deduction should be allowed. Prior to the enactment of § 461(h) the Service might have attacked the deduction under § 446(b) as not clearly reflecting income or resulting from a tax avoidance motive, especially if the amount of the future liability had been inflated. See the Goldstein case at p. 661.

A structured settlement can be a tax windfall to the negligent party. Under the "all events" test, the accrual method taxpayer can currently deduct an amount for the obligation he has agreed to pay in the future. At a minimum he can deduct the present value of that future obligation. A literal reading of the "all events" test indicates that the entire amount of the future obligation can be currently deducted without discounting it to its present value. This can result in the anomolous situation of a taxpayer making money by losing money. For example, assume a taxpayer in the 28% marginal tax bracket is sued for $100,000 in a personal injury action. He agrees to settle this claim by paying $200,000 to the injured person at the end of 15 years. A current deduction for the entire $200,000 obligation would save the taxpayer $56,000 in taxes. If he then invested this $56,000 in tax free municipal bonds paying interest at 10% a year, he would have a fund totalling $233,925.88 at the end of 15 years. After using $200,000 to satisfy his obligation, taxpayer would have a $33,925.88 windfall. The taxpayer has in effect received a $56,000 interest free loan from the Government. And the injured party has the advantage of excluding the interest earned on the amount of his original claim under § 104(a) (2). See, McGowan, Structured Settlements: Deduct Now and Pay Later, 60 Taxes 251 (1982).

As with all things too good to be true, Congress brought structured settlements under the umbrella of the "economic performance" test contained in § 461(h). In the case of tort liabilities incurred by an accrual method taxpayer, economic performance occurs only when the payments are actually made to the injured person. § 461(h)(2)(C). A payment to a trust under § 461(f) is not treated as a payment and will not satisfy the economic performance test. A question remains as to when economic performance occurs if the taxpayer satisfies a tort claim by purchasing an annuity for the claimant. Does it occur at the time the annuity payments are received by the claimant or when the taxpayer purchases the annuity?

3. CHOICE OF ACCOUNTING METHODS: THE INDIVIDUAL TAXPAYER

Liberal Choice of Accounting Methods Available to the Individual Taxpayer. In general, the individual taxpayer is given a choice of several methods of accounting for income; that is, an individual may use the method under which he regularly computes his income in keeping his other books. § 446(a). Not only is the Code explicit but the administrative climate surrounding the Code is also significant. Particularly so is the observation in Reg. § 1.446–1(a)(2) that "[e]ach taxpayer shall adopt such forms and systems as are, in his judgment, best suited to his needs."

A method of accounting which is consistent with accepted conditions or practices in a trade or business of the taxpayer is normally regarded as clearly reflecting income if the treatment of the items is consistent over the years. Reg. § 1.446–1(a)(2), but see § 447(a). However, the Regulations also provide that no method of accounting is appropriate unless it clearly reflects income in the opinion of the Commissioner. Reg. § 1.446–1(b)(1). See also § 446(b). The taxpayer filing his first return may adopt any permissible method of accounting without clearance by the Internal Revenue Service. Reg. § 1.446–1(e).

Limitations on Selection of Accounting Method. There are some requirements which govern the selection of the individual taxpayer's accounting method; the choice is not without restrictions.

a. Subject to the limitations hereafter discussed, the individual taxpayer must use the same method of accounting for tax returns that he uses in regularly computing his income in keeping his books. § 446(a).

b. The method of accounting must clearly reflect income. If it does not, he will be required to compute his taxable income under "such methods as in the opinion of the Secretary or his delegate, does clearly reflect income." § 446(b).

c. In cases where it is necessary to use an inventory, the individual taxpayer cannot elect to use the cash method, but must use the accrual method with respect to purchases and sales unless the Commissioner permits a different system. Reg. § 1.446–1(c)(2)(i).

d. An accounting method is not acceptable unless items of gross profit and deductions are treated with consistency from year to year. Reg. § 1.446–1(c)(2)(ii). However, the Commissioner may authorize the individual taxpayer to adopt or to change to a method of accounting even though they are not specifically referred to either in the Code or Regulations provided that income is clearly reflected by use of the new method. Reg. § 1.446–1(c)(2)(ii).

e. If the individual taxpayer has been consistently using a method not specifically authorized by the Regulations, the Commissioner may authorize him to continue it as long as it clearly reflects his income. Reg. § 1.446–1(c)(2)(ii). (It should be noted that the Regulations do not recite that the Commissioner will, or has the power to, authorize the taxpayer to continue a method consistently used by him which contravenes the Regulations, even though income is clearly reflected thereby.)

f. The individual taxpayer who keeps no books or records is treated as though he were on the cash method of accounting. England v. Commissioner, 34 T.C. 617 (1960).

Alternative Accounting Systems: Other Methods. The Code specifically provides that the individual taxpayer may use (in addition to the cash and accrual methods) "any other method permitted by this chapter," or any combination of any of the methods permitted under the Regulations. § 446(c). Such a choice is available only under Regulations which require that the combination clearly reflect income and be consistently used. Reg. § 1.446–1(c)(1)(iv)(a). Moreover, in some cases, special items are given special accounting treatment under statutory authorization. See § 174, dealing with research and experimental expenditures, and § 175, relating to soil and water conservation expenditures.

Alternative Accounting Systems: Combination of Methods. Taxpayers should carefully consider the extent to which a combination of accounting methods may best serve their purposes. The legislative history and the Regulations with respect to § 446(c)(4) clarify several principles under which the taxpayer may prevent bunching of income and perhaps accelerate his annual allocation of deductions. Among the advantages of this section are that the taxpayer may use an accrual method of accounting with respect to purchases and sales of inventory and still use the cash method in computing all other items of income and expense. Reg. § 1.446–1(c)(1)(iv)(a). For example, a small retail store operated as a proprietorship may accrue such items as accounts payable and accounts receivable while deducting current expenses, such as rent, interest, clerks' salaries, insurance and similar items.

Different Accounting Methods May be Used by One Taxpayer for Personal and Business Purposes. An individual taxpayer is not required to maintain his personal affairs on the same accounting method as he uses for the conduct of his trade or business. Reg. § 1.446–1(c)(1)(iv)(b). Moreover, he may use one method with respect to one trade or business and adopt any other permissible method in connection with each other separate and distinct trade or business. § 446(d). Where income from the second business is reported for the first time, no consent need be obtained from the Commissioner to use such other method.

The Regulations make the very proper requirement that complete and separable books and records must be kept for each source of income where different accounting methods are used. Reg. § 1.446–1(d)(2). Moreover, if the taxpayer attempts to gain a tax advantage by creating or shifting profits or losses between his trades or businesses so that the income of the taxpayer will not be clearly reflected, the taxpayer's trades or businesses will not be considered as separate and distinct. Reg. § 1.446–1(d)(3); see also § 482.

Problems

1. Consider the tax treatment arising in the following situations, assuming the taxpayer uses a calendar year and the cash method:

(a) Derek, a dentist fixes the teeth of a patient on December 15. He bills the patient for $100 on December 20; the bill is paid on January 15. Is the receipt treated as income in December or January? Consider § 451(a).

(b) Derek rendered a bill and took a negotiable note in the sum of $100 as payment for services in December; it was paid in January. Consider § 451(a) and Regs. §§ 1.61–2(d)(4), 1.446–1(a)(3), 1.451–2(a).

(c) Derek takes a check from John Doe, for services rendered, in the sum of $100 on December 28. Doe is known to have an uncertain balance in his account at the end of the month, so Derek cashes the check on January 2. Doe in fact had no funds in the bank between December 28 and January 1, inclusive. Consider Reg. § 1.451–2(a).

(d) Derek sues X for breach of contract, alleging damages of $7000. Three years later, Derek is awarded a final judgment in the amount of $6500. In the fourth year, the judgment is paid in full.

2. What results would follow in "1" above if Derek were on the accrual method? Consider Reg. § 1.446–1(c)(1)(ii) and § 448(d)(5). What are the tax consequences to X in "1(d)" above if X is an accrual method taxpayer? Consider § 461(h) and Reg. § 1.461–2(a).

3. Venturesome, an accrual method taxpayer, purchased a mine from Seller. The mine was not as profitable as it was represented to be. In the same tax year, Seller admitted the misrepresentation and agreed to reim-

burse Venturesome, in cash, for his damages. If the amount of the damages is not agreed on in the tax year, can Venturesome accrue income in that year? What is the test? What more do you need to know? Consider Reg. § 1.446–1(c)(1)(ii) and the Continental Tie case at p. 228.

4. Margot is an attorney on the cash method who, for practical purposes, desires to set the amount of her fee with a client. Services will be rendered over the succeeding five years. The services will be deductible by the client under § 162. She proposes that in September of the tax year, she and her client will agree that the fee is to be $75,000 and that payment will be made in five equal annual installments of $15,000 over the next five years. The client will pledge securities worth $75,000 with a bank. As each payment is made, the bank will annually release to the client an equivalent amount of securities. If such payment is not made, the bank will release to Margot an equivalent amount of securities. The objective of this device is to spread the income over several years while insuring that payment will, in fact, be made to Margot by her client.

(a) Do you think Margot should take a negotiable note in the sum of $75,000? Will she receive an economic benefit? What if the note is intended as evidence of the debt? Consider Reg. § 1.61–2(d)(4).

(b) Do you think that, in the absence of a note, Margot runs some risk that the Service will assert she had income of $75,000 in September? Will the pledge of the securities be deemed an economic benefit or the constructive receipt of income? Consider Reg. § 1.451–2(a) and the Reed case at p. 216.

(c) Can you draft an agreement in such a fashion as to minimize the realization of income? How could you block the application of the doctrine of constructive receipt? Consider Reg. § 1.451–2(a).

(d) Would it be better just to execute a contract requiring further services and an annual payment of $15,000 for a period of five years contingent on the performance of future services? See Reg. § 1.451–2(a). Under what circumstances would you expect the client to be reluctant to go along with this device? What if the client is an accrual method taxpayer? Consider § 461(h). What if the client uses the cash method? Consider Reg. § 1.461–1(a)(1).

E.   CANCELLATION OF INDEBTEDNESS

1. GENERAL CODE PROVISIONS AND JUDICIAL AND ADMINISTRATIVE INTERPRETATIONS OF THE CANCELLATION OF INDEBTEDNESS CONCEPT

If the taxpayer borrows $1,000 for one year at a stated interest rate which the taxpayer repays in full, the taxpayer realized no income on either the borrowing or the repayment. Neither the borrowing nor the repayment changes the debtor's net worth. The debtor's obligation to repay the principal of the loan offsets the cash received on borrowing. On repayment, the termination of liability for the loan obligation is accompanied by the payment of cash to the creditor.

If, however, a solvent taxpayer pays off a debt for less than the amount owing, the amount of the assets thereby freed from the obligation to repay constitute income to the taxpayer ostensibly because his net worth has increased by the difference between the face amount of the debt and the amount paid to discharge the debt. Section 61(a)(12) requires that income from the discharge of indebtedness be included in the taxpayer's gross income. Consider the next case involving a solvent corporation that purchased its own bonds then selling at a discount.

UNITED STATES v. KIRBY LUMBER CO.

Supreme Court of the United States, 1931.
284 U.S. 1, 52 S.Ct. 4, 76 L.Ed. 131.

MR. JUSTICE HOLMES delivered the opinion of the court.

In July, 1923, the plaintiff, the Kirby Lumber Company, issued its own bonds for $12,126,800 for which it received their par value. Later in the same year it purchased in the open market some of the same bonds at less than par, the difference of price being $137,521.30. The question is whether this difference is a taxable gain or income of the plaintiff for the year 1923. By the Revenue Act of (November 23) 1921, c. 136, § 213(a), 42 Stat. 238, gross income includes "gains or profits and income derived from any source whatever," and by the Treasury Regulations * * * that have been in force through repeated re-enactments, "If the corporation purchases and retires any of such bonds at a price less than the issuing price or face value, the excess of the issuing price or face value over the purchase price is gain or income for the taxable year." * * * We see no reason why the Regulations should not be accepted as a correct statement of the law.

In Bowers v. Kerbaugh-Empire Co., 271 U.S. 170, 46 S.Ct. 449, 70 L.Ed. 886, the defendant in error owned the stock of another company that had borrowed money repayable in marks or their equivalent for an enterprise that failed. At the time of payment the marks had fallen in value, which so far as it went was a gain for the defendant in error, and it was contended by the plaintiff in error that the gain was taxable income. But the transaction as a whole was a loss, and the contention was denied. Here there was no shrinkage of assets and the taxpayer made a clear gain. As a result of its dealings it made available $137,521.30 assets previously offset by the obligation of bonds now extinct. We see nothing to be gained by the discussion of judicial definitions. The defendant in error has realized within the year an accession to income, if we take words in their plain popular meaning, as they should be taken here. Burnet v. Sanford & Brooks Co., 282 U.S. 359, 364, 51 S.Ct. 150, 75 L.Ed. 383.

Judgment reversed.

The "freeing of assets" rationable of Kirby Lumber is not satisfactory in all situations because it is possible that a taxpayer may be relieved of a debt without having "assets made available." It is not the freeing of assets or the cancellation of a debt which creates income. A taxpayer does not include loan proceeds as income because of the expectation that he will repay the loan. When the assumption of repayment proves erroneous, income results.

Assume an individual, with no assets, borrows $10,000 and loses most of the loan proceeds in a failed business venture. Assume he uses all of his remaining assets to repay part of the debt, and the creditor cancels the balance of the debt. No other assets are freed from the offsetting repayment obligation. A strict application of the Kirby Lumber principle would result in the debtor not realizing any income. However, is this result sound? A debtor who has his obligation to repay cancelled receives a benefit regardless of what assets he possesses after the cancellation. Also, when the debt is cancelled, should not the prior increase in the debtor's net worth on the original receipt of the loan result in gross income for the debtor in the year of the cancellation? For a further analysis of the rationale of the Kirby Lumber case see: Bittker and Thompson, Income from the Discharge of Indebtedness: The Progeny of United States v. Kirby Lumber Company, 66 Calif.L.Rev. 1159 (1978).

Questions

1. Why was the definition of income in Eisner v. Macomber (p. 106) an obstacle to treating the cancellation of a debt as income? Did the Supreme Court deal with this in Kirby Lumber?

2. Can the Kirby Lumber case be viewed as another application of the tax benefit principle?

3. What was the character of the income the taxpayer realized in Kirby Lumber?

4. A corporation borrows $10,000 by issuing a bond and uses the loan proceeds to invest in German marks. Later in the year, the corporation liquidates this position in German marks but is only able to realize $7,500 in United States currency because of fluctuations in the value of the German mark. At the end of the year, interest rate increases enable the corporation to retire the bond for $7,500. What are the consequences to the corporation under Bowers v. Kerbaugh-Empire referred to in Kirby Lumber? Note: Kerbaugh-Empire was decided before the Sanford & Brooks case. Would it make any difference if the corporation retired the loan in the following year?

———

Section 108, added to the Code by the Bankruptcy Tax Act of 1980, and amended in 1986, deals with the tax treatment of insolvent debtors with respect to the cancellation of indebtedness. We will first examine the treatment of solvent taxpayers and then consider the results to insolvent taxpayers.

Solvent Debtors.   For solvent taxpayers (i.e., taxpayers who are not insolvent or under the jurisdiction of a federal bankruptcy court), the cancellation or discharge of indebtedness results in the realization and recognition of gross income.   § 61(a)(12).

An important question for a solvent taxpayer is whether a transaction involves the discharge of indebtedness.   Consider the next Revenue Ruling.

REV.RUL. 84–176
1984–2 C.B. 34

ISSUE

Is the amount owed by a taxpayer, that is forgiven by a seller in return for a release of a contract counterclaim, income from discharge of indebtedness pursuant to section 61(a)(12) of the Internal Revenue Code * * *

FACTS

The taxpayer, a domestic corporation, is a wholesale distributor. In 1981, it entered into two contracts with an unrelated seller under which the taxpayer agreed to purchase various quantities of goods. The goods were to be shipped in six lots between March and August, 1982.   The seller subsequently shipped all of lot 1 and part of lot 2, and then refused to ship the rest of the order.   At the time of this refusal, the taxpayer had an outstanding account payable to the seller of 1,000x dollars for goods actually shipped.

After the seller failed to ship the remaining goods, the taxpayer refused to pay the 1,000x dollars already owed.   The seller then filed suit against the taxpayer in U.S. District Court for such payment.   The taxpayer later filed a counterclaim for breach of contract, claiming damages for lost profits.

In December, 1982, the parties settled the suit.   The taxpayer agreed to pay the seller 500x dollars of the 1,000x dollars outstanding indebtedness.   The remaining 500x dollars was "forgiven" by the seller in return for executing a release of the breach of contract counterclaim.

* * *

LAW AND ANALYSIS

Section 61(a) of the Code provides that gross income means gross income from whatever source derived.   Section 61(a)(12) provides that gross income includes income from discharge of indebtedness.   Section 1.61–12(a) of the Income Tax Regulations provides that a taxpayer may realize income by the payment of obligations at less than their face value.

* * *

The Supreme Court in United States v. Kirby Lumber Co., 284 U.S. 1 (1931), X–2 C.B. 356, established the principle that the gain or saving that is realized by a debtor upon the reduction or cancellation of the debtor's outstanding indebtedness for less than the amount due may be "income" for federal tax purposes. The taxpayer-corporation in *Kirby Lumber* had purchased its own bonds at a discount in the open market. Holding that the difference between the issue price and the price at which the bonds were subsequently acquired represented taxable income to the corporation, the Court said that as a result of these purchases, the taxpayer made available $137,521.30 of assets previously offset by the obligation of bonds now extinct. The taxpayer had realized within the year an accession to income.

Not every indebtedness that is cancelled results in gross income being realized by the debtor "by reason of" discharge of indebtedness within the meaning of section 108 of the Code. If a cancellation of indebtedness is simply the medium for payment of some other form of income, section 108 does not apply. For example, if an employee owes his employer $100 and renders $100 worth of services to the employer in return for cancellation of the debt, the employee has received personal services income, rather than income from cancellation of indebtedness within the meaning of section 108. In such a case, the full amount of the indebtedness is satisfied by the performance of services having a value equal to the debt. Since the debt cancellation is only the medium of paying the personal services income, section 108 is inapplicable. See Spartan Petroleum Co. v. United States, 437 F.Supp. 733 (D.S.C.1977). *See also* section 1.1017–1(b)(5) of the regulations (no reduction of basis of property is allowed under sections 108 and 1017 to the extent of the value of property transferred to a creditor in connection with a debt cancellation), and Rev.Rul. 83–60, 1983–1 C.B. 39.

The Senate Finance Committee Report regarding the amending of section 108 of the Code in the Bankruptcy Tax Act of 1980 [Pub.L. 96–589, 1980–2 C.B. 607], discusses the exceptions to the general rule of income realization when indebtedness is forgiven or otherwise cancelled. That report acknowledges the proposition set forth in *Spartan [P]etroleum* that income from cancellation of indebtedness does not automatically fall within the scope of the debt discharge rules. It states in a footnote that debt discharge that is only a medium for some other form of payment, such as a gift or salary, is treated as that form of payment rather than under the debt discharge rules. Footnote 6, S.Rep. No. 1035, 96th Cong., 2d Sess. 8 (1980), 1980–2 C.B. 624.

In this situation, the settlement should be analyzed as if the taxpayer actually received compensation for damages arising out of the seller's breach of contract and then paid the full amount of the account payable. There is no requirement that money be actually exchanged in order for taxation to result. The amount received by the taxpayer for the breach of contract is ordinary income because the facts demonstrate that the taxpayer was reimbursed for lost profits and income. Therefore, the 500x dollars not paid by the taxpayer to the seller was the medium through which income from the damages for breach of contract arose. This amount is to be treated as a payment for lost profits rather than a discharge of indebtedness.

HOLDING

The amount owed by the taxpayer that is forgiven by the seller in return for a release of a contract counterclaim is not income from discharge of indebtedness under section 61(a)(12) of the Code * * *.

Problems

1. The Widget Corporation borrows $10,000 from the public by issuing a $10,000 20-year bond with an obligation to pay $800 in annual interest. Two years later, market interest rates increase to 10%. Because of the rise in interest rates, the value of the bond decreases to $8,000.

(a) Why does a bond paying a fixed amount of interest each year fluctuate in value?

(b) Assume the bondholder sells the $10,000 bond to another individual for $8,000. How does the bondholder treat the sale of the bond? Consider § 165(a) and (c). If the bondholder can deduct the loss, what is the character of the loss? Does the corporation have $2,000 in cancellation of indebtedness income?

(c) Assume the bondholder sells the bond to the Widget Corporation, which is solvent, for $8,000. What are the tax consequences to the bondholder and the corporation? Consider the Kirby Lumber case and §§ 61(a)(12) and 166(a) and (b). If the bondholder can deduct the loss, what is the character of the loss?

2. X, Y and Z each owe their bank $8,000. Each incurred the indebtedness in connection with property used in their respective business. Although solvent, X has financial problems and is unable to pay his loan. The bank finally writes off X's loan as uncollectible and cancels it. Y owns stock held as a capital asset, which he acquired two years ago, worth $8,000 and with a basis of zero. Y transfers the stock to the bank in return for cancellation of the loan. Z is able to have the loan cancelled by performing $8,000 worth of services for the bank. In all three situations, the debtors have $8,000 of income.

Explain the three different principles involved in the finding of income. Although each individual will realize and recognize the same amount of gross income, why is it important to differentiate between the applicable tax principles. Consider § 61(a)(12), Reg. § 1.61–12(a), and Rev. Rul. 84–176.

3. The discharge of a debt does not automatically result in cancellation of indebtedness income for a solvent debtor. In each of the following consider other possible tax consequences of the cancellation.

(a) A's uncle lent him $6,500 for his law school tuition. After graduation, A receives a congratulatory letter from his uncle cancelling the loan. Consider § 102(a).

(b) B has a judgment of $15,000 rendered against him in a tort action. B agrees not to appeal and is able to settle his claim for $10,000. What was the amount of B's liability prior to the judgment?

(c) C pledges to give her church a $500 donation. C runs into unexpected financial difficulties and is allowed to reduce her pledge to $100. Will the $400 be characterized as a reduction in a charitable contribution or as a cancellation of indebtedness.

(d) D, who uses the cash basis method, received a bill from his doctor for $100 for a visit lasting only 15 minutes. D complains about the fee, and the doctor agrees to accept $50 as full payment.

(e) E owes money to a bank. Upon her mother's death, the estate pays E's debt pursuant to a provision in her mother's will. Consider § 102(a).

(f) F owes $500 in state income taxes which are paid by her employer. (Reconsider Old Colony Trust Co. case, p. 49).

(g) G buys a car from a used car dealer for $2,800. He pays $500 down and signs a note agreeing to pay the dealer the balance in monthly installments. After G paid $300 of the loan and spent $600 for a new transmission, the dealer reduced the $2,000 balance on the loan to $1,400. What is G's basis for the car?

4. Ted and Terri Player bought a house for $100,000, paying $20,000 in cash and borrowing $80,000 from a bank at 8½% interest, secured by a 30-year first mortgage. Ten years later the bank offers them a 10% discount if they prepay the remaining $70,000 principal balance on the loan. Assume the Players have $63,000 in certificates of deposit earning interest at a rate of 12%. They use their $63,000 in savings to pay off the loan.

(a) What are the tax consequences to the Players of prepaying the loan?

(b) Did the Players make a financial mistake in prepaying the mortgage even though they received a $7,000 discount?

(c) Assume the Player's basis for the house (after their purchase and just before the loan pay off) equals $100,000. (The Player's basis in their residence includes any cash paid and any monies borrowed under a mortgage loan. We will consider the rationale for this assumption in Chapter 9). After the loan cancellation, what basis do the Players have in the house?

(d) Can the bank take a deduction for the cancelled portion of the loan? Consider §§ 166(a) and 162.

5. In Year 1, Dennis leases a store for use in his business. Dennis runs into financial problems and is unable to pay the December rent of $1,000. The following year the landlord cancels the debt for the missed December rent payment. What are the tax consequences to Dennis if he uses:

(a) The cash method of accounting.

(b) The accrual method of accounting. When does an accrual method taxpayer deduct items of expense? Consider Reg. § 1.461–1(a)

(2) and § 461(h). Does the cancellation of the debt result in income for Dennis? Is the $1,000 of income reported by Dennis, an accrual method taxpayer, classified as cancellation of indebtedness income or income under the tax benefit theory? If Dennis had obtained no tax benefit from all or part of the deduction, then all or part of the cancelled debt will be excluded from income under § 111. Does the tax benefit theory override debt cancellation principles?

2. SPECIAL STATUTORY TREATMENT OF CANCELLATION OF INDEBTEDNESS: INSOLVENT TAXPAYERS

Prior to the amendment to § 108 in 1980, a debtor who was insolvent immediately after the discharge of the indebtedness, realized no income on such discharge.

Pursuant to § 108 the amount of indebtedness discharged when a taxpayer is insolvent (as defined in § 108(c)(3)) or as part of a bankruptcy proceeding in a Federal court continues to be excluded from the debtor's gross income. § 108(a)(1). The amount of discharge debt excluded from the debtor's gross income because of insolvency or bankruptcy reduces certain of the taxpayer's tax attributes. § 108(b)(1) and (2). The taxpayer disregards the excluded debt discharge income which cannot be absorbed by the taxpayer's tax attributes. In the alternative, the debtor may elect (under § 108(b) (5)(A)) to reduce the basis of his depreciable property [25] and realty held for sale to customers in the ordinary course of business. The provisions for making the basis reduction are contained in § 1017. The basis reduction technique defers the recognition of income until the subsequent sale or other disposition of the reduced-basis property. On the subsequent sale or other disposition, the taxpayer will realize and recognize a larger amount of income. To the extent the amount of the discharge of indebtedness exceeds the basis of the insolvent debtor's depreciable property, the electing debtor must include the excess in gross income.

Income arising from the discharge of indebtedness owed by a qualifying farmer to an unrelated lender is treated as income realized by an insolvent taxpayer, if the debt was incurred in the trade or business of farming. Examine § 108(g).

Assume the debt was not discharged in a bankruptcy proceeding in a Federal court. In this situation, a debtor who was insolvent (§ 108(c) (3)) before the discharge but who becomes solvent as a result of the discharge excludes the discharge of indebtedness from gross income to the extent of his insolvency (as defined in § 108(c)(3)). See § 108(a)(3).

---

25. Depreciation is a deduction from gross income under § 167 reflecting the cost to the taxpayer of using over a period of years, an asset in his trade or business or for the production of income. The Acceleration Cost Recovery System (§ 168) permits the accelerated recovery of the cost of a tangible asset subject to the allowance for depreciation which is used in the taxpayer's trade or business or held for the production of income. Depreciation and the Accelerated Cost Recovery System are considered in detail in Chapter 8.

The amount excluded reduces the insolvent debtor's tax attributes as above. The insolvent debtor also has the option of reducing the basis of his depreciable property. The insolvent debtor cannot exclude from gross income the amount of the debt which is greater than the amount by which the debtor is insolvent. § 108(a)(3).

Question

Is the statutory treatment of an insolvent taxpayer (whether insolvent when the indebtedness is discharged or insolvent before the discharge but rendered solvent by his discharge) consistent with the fresh start principle of bankruptcy law?

F. INFORMAL DEFERRED COMPENSATION

1. JUDICIAL AND ADMINISTRATIVE BASES FOR INFORMAL DEFERRAL OF INCOME

We next consider certain informal deferred compensation arrangements approved by the Commissioner and the courts. Recipients of deferred compensation plans obtain a deferral of taxation and the expectation that the benefits when received will be taxed at lower rates. This section sets forth administrative and judicial materials which supply the ground rules for the informal deferral of income. Consider the use of the constructive receipt and economic benefit doctrines in the following Revenue Ruling.

REV.RUL. 60–31
1960–1 C.B. 174.

Advice has been requested regarding the taxable year of inclusion in gross income of a taxpayer, using the cash receipts and disbursements method of accounting, of compensation for services received under the circumstances described below.

(1) On January 1, 1958, the taxpayer and corporation X executed an employment contract under which the taxpayer is to be employed by the corporation in an executive capacity for a period of five years. Under the contract, the taxpayer is entitled to a stated annual salary and to additional compensation of $10x$ dollars for each year. The additional compensation will be credited to a bookkeeping reserve account and will be deferred, accumulated, and paid in annual installments equal to one-fifth of the amount in the reserve as of the close of the year immediately preceding the year of first payment. The payments are to begin only upon (a) termination of the taxpayer's employment by the corporation; (b) the taxpayer's becoming a part-time employee of the corporation; or (c) the taxpayer's becoming partially or totally incapacitated. Under the terms of the agreement, corporation X is under a merely contractual obligation to make the payments when

due, and the parties did not intend that the amounts in the reserve be held by the corporation in trust for the taxpayer.

The contract further provides that if the taxpayer should fail or refuse to perform his duties, the corporation will be relieved of any obligation to make further credits to the reserve (but not of the obligation to distribute amounts previously contributed); but, if the taxpayer should become incapacitated from performing his duties, then credits to the reserve will continue for one year from the date of the incapacity, but not beyond the expiration of the five-year term of the contract. There is no specific provision in the contract for forfeiture by the taxpayer of his right to distribution, from the reserve; and, in the event he should die prior to his receipt in full of the balance in the account, the remaining balance is distributable to his personal representative at the rate of one-fifth per year for five years, beginning three months after his death.

(2) The taxpayer is an officer and director of corporation A, which has a plan for making future payments of additional compensation for current services to certain officers and key employees designated by its board of directors. This plan provides that a percentage of the annual net earnings (before Federal income taxes) in excess of 4,000x dollars is to be designated for division among the participants in proportion to their respective salaries. This amount is not currently paid to the participants; but, the corporation has set up on its books a separate account for each participant and each year it credits thereto the dollar amount of his participation for the year, reduced by a proportionate part of the corporation's income taxes attributable to the additional compensation. Each account is also credited with the net amount, if any, realized from investing any portion of the amount in the account.

Distributions are to be made from these accounts annually beginning when the employee (1) reaches age 60, (2) is no longer employed by the company, including cessation of employment due to death, or (3) becomes totally disabled to perform his duties, whichever occurs first. The annual distribution will equal a stated percentage of the balance in the employee's account at the close of the year immediately preceding the year of first payment, and distributions will continue until the account is exhausted. However, the corporation's liability to make these distributions is contingent upon the employee's (1) refraining from engaging in any business competitive to that of the corporation, (2) making himself available to the corporation for consultation and advice after retirement or termination of his services, unless disabled, and (3) retaining unencumbered any interest or benefit under the plan. In the event of his death, either before or after the beginning of payments, amounts in an employee's account are distributable in installments computed in the same way to his designated beneficiaries or heirs-at-law. Under the terms of the compensation plan, corporation A is under a merely contractual obligation to make the payments when due, and the parties did not intend that the amounts in each account be held by the corporation in trust for the participants.

(3) On October 1, 1957, the taxpayer, an author, and corporation Y, a publisher, executed an agreement under which the taxpayer granted to the publisher the exclusive right to print, publish and sell a book he had written. This agreement provides that the publisher will (1) pay the author specified royalties based on the actual cash received from the sale of the published work, (2) render semiannual statements of the sales, and (3) at the time of rendering each statement make settlement for the amount due. On the same day, another agreement was signed by the same parties, mutually agreeing that, in consideration of, and notwithstanding any contrary provisions contained in the first contract, the publisher shall not pay the taxpayer more than $100x$ dollars in any one calendar year. Under this supplemental contract, sums in excess of $100x$ dollars accruing in any one calendar year are to be carried over by the publisher into succeeding accounting periods; and the publisher shall not be required either to pay interest to the taxpayer on any such excess sums or to segregate any such sums in any manner.

(4) In June 1957, the taxpayer, a football player, entered into a two-year standard player's contract with a football club in which he agreed to play football and engage in activities related to football during the two-year term only for the club. In addition to a specified salary for the two-year term, it was mutually agreed that as an inducement for signing the contract the taxpayer would be paid a bonus of $150x$ dollars. The taxpayer could have demanded and received payment of this bonus at the time of signing the contract, but at his suggestion there was added to the standard contract form a paragraph providing substantially as follows:

> The player shall receive the sum of $150x$ dollars upon signing of this contract, contingent upon the payment of this $150x$ dollars to an escrow agent designated by him. The escrow agreement shall be subject to approval by the legal representatives of the player, the Club, and the escrow agent.

Pursuant to this added provision, an escrow agreement was executed on June 25, 1957, in which the club agreed to pay $150x$ dollars on that date to the Y bank, as escrow agent; and the escrow agent agreed to pay this amount, plus interest, to the taxpayer in installments over a period of five years. The escrow agreement also provides that the account established by the escrow agent is to bear the taxpayer's name; that payments from such account may be made only in accordance with the terms of the agreement; that the agreement is binding upon the parties thereto and their successors or assigns; and that in the event of the taxpayer's death during the escrow period the balance due will become part of his estate.

(5) The taxpayer, a boxer, entered into an agreement with a boxing club to fight a particular opponent at a specified time and place. The place of the fight agreed to was decided upon because of the insistence

of the taxpayer that it be held there. The agreement was on the standard form of contract required by the state athletic commission and provided, in part, that for his performance taxpayer was to receive 16x percent of the gross receipts derived from the match. Simultaneously, the same parties executed a separate agreement providing for payment of the taxpayer's share of the receipts from the match as follows: 25 percent thereof not later than two weeks after the bout, and 25 percent thereof during each of the three years following the year of the bout in equal semiannual installments. Such deferments are not customary in prize fighting contracts, and the supplemental agreement was executed at the demand of the taxpayer. Upon the taxpayer's insistence, the agreements also provided that any telecast of the fight must receive his prior consent and that he was to approve or disapprove all proposed sales of radio and motion picture rights.

Section 1.451–1(a) of the Income Tax Regulations provides in part as follows:

> Gains, profits, and income are to be included in gross income for the taxable year in which they are actually or constructively received by the taxpayer unless includible for a different year in accordance with the taxpayer's method of accounting. * * *

And, with respect to the cash receipts and disbursements method of accounting, section 1.446–1(c)(1)(i) provides in part—

> Generally, under the cash receipts and disbursements method in the computation of taxable income, all items which constitute gross income (whether in the form of cash, property, or services) are to be included for the taxable year in which actually or constructively received. * * *.

As previously stated, the individual concerned in each of the situations described above, employs the cash receipts and disbursements method of accounting. Under that method, as indicated by the above-quoted provisions of the regulations, he is required to include the compensation concerned in gross income only for the taxable year in which it is actually or constructively received. Consequently, the question for resolution is whether in each of the situations described the income in question was constructively received in a taxable year prior to the taxable year of actual receipt.

A mere promise to pay, not represented by notes or secured in any way, is not regarded as a receipt of income within the intendment of the cash receipts and disbursements method. See United States v. Christine Oil & Gas Co., 269 Fed. 458; William J. Jackson v. Smietanka, 272 Fed. 970, Ct.D. 5, C.B. 4, 96 (1921); and E.F. Cremin v. Commissioner, 5 B.T.A. 1164, acquiescence, C.B. VI–1, 2 (1927). Also C. Florian Zittel v. Commissioner, 12 B.T.A. 675, in which, holding a salary to be taxable when received, the Board said: "Taxpayers on a receipts and disbursements basis are required to report only income actually received no matter how binding any contracts they may have to receive more."

This should not be construed to mean that under the cash receipts and disbursements method income may be taxed only when realized in cash. For, under that method a taxpayer is required to include in income that which is received in cash or cash equivalent. W.P. Henritze v. Commissioner, 41 B.T.A. 505. And, as stated in the above-quoted provisions of the regulations, the "receipt" contemplated by the cash method may be actual or constructive.

With respect to the constructive receipt of income, section 1.451–2(a) of the Income Tax Regulations (which accords with prior regulations extending back to, and including, Article 53 of Regulations 45 under the Revenue Act of 1918) provides, in part, as follows:

> Income although not actually reduced to a taxpayer's possession is constructively received by him in the taxable year during which it is credited to his account or set apart for him so that he may draw upon it at any time. However, income is not constructively received if the taxpayer's control of its receipt is subject to substantial limitations or restrictions. Thus, if a corporation credits its employees with bonus stock, but the stock is not available to such employees until some future date, the mere crediting on the books of the corporation does not constitute receipt.

Thus, under the doctrine of constructive receipt, a taxpayer may not deliberately turn his back upon income and thereby select the year for which he will report it. The Hamilton National Bank of Chattanooga, as Administrator of the Estate of S. Strang Nicklin, Deceased, v. Commissioner, 29 B.T.A. 63. Nor may a taxpayer, by a private agreement, postpone receipt of income from one taxable year to another. James E. Lewis v. Commissioner, 30 B.T.A. 318.

However, the statute cannot be administered by speculating whether the payor would have been willing to agree to an earlier payment. See, for example, J.D. Amend, et ux., v. Commissioner, 13 T.C. 178, acquiescence, C.B. 1950–1, 1; and C.E. Gullett, et al., v. Commissioner, 31 B.T.A. 1067, in which the court, citing a number of authorities for its holding, stated:

> It is clear that the doctrine of constructive receipt is to be sparingly used; that amounts due from a corporation but unpaid, are not to be included in the income of an individual reporting his income on a cash receipts basis unless it appears that the money was available to him, that the corporation was able and ready to pay him, that his right to receive was not restricted, and that his failure to receive resulted from exercise of his own choice.

Consequently, it seems clear that in each case involving a deferral of compensation a determination of whether the doctrine of constructive receipt is applicable must be made upon the basis of the specific factual situation involved.

Applying the foregoing criteria to the situations described above, the following conclusions have been reached:

(1) The additional compensation to be received by the taxpayer under the employment contract concerned will be includible in his gross income only in the taxable years in which the taxpayer actually receives installment payments in cash or other property previously credited to his account. To hold otherwise would be contrary to the provisions of the regulations and the court decisions mentioned above.

(2) For the reasons in (1) above, it is held that the taxpayer here involved also will be required to include the deferred compensation concerned in his gross income only in the taxable years in which the taxpayer actually receives installment payments in cash or other property previously credited to his account.

In arriving at this conclusion and the conclusion reached in case "(1)," consideration has been given to section 1.402(b)–1 of the Income Tax Regulations and to Revenue Ruling 57–37, C.B. 1957–1, 18, as modified by Revenue Ruling 57–528, C.B. 1957–2, 263. Section 1.402(b)–1(a)(1) provides in part, with an exception not here relevant, that any contribution made by an employer on behalf of an employee to a trust during a taxable year of the employer which ends within or with a taxable year of the trust for which the trust is not exempt under section 501(a) of the Code, shall be included in income of the employee for his taxable year during which the contribution is made if his interest in the contribution is nonforfeitable at the time the contribution is made. Revenue Ruling 57–37, as modified by Revenue Ruling 57–528, held, *inter alia*, that certain contributions conveying fully vested and nonforfeitable interests made by an employer into separate independently controlled trusts for the purpose of furnishing unemployment and other benefits to its eligible employees constituted additional compensation to the employees includible, under section 402(b) of the Code and section 1.402(b)–1(a)(1) of the regulations, in their income for the taxable year in which such contributions were made. These Revenue Rulings are distinguishable from cases "(1)" and "(2)" in that, under all the facts and circumstances of these cases, no trusts for the benefit of the taxpayers were created and no contributions are to be made thereto. Consequently, section 402(b) of the Code and section 1.402(b)–1(a)(1) of the regulations are inapplicable.

(3) Here the principal agreement provided that the royalties were payable substantially as earned, and this agreement was supplemented by a further concurrent agreement which made the royalties payable over a period of years. This supplemental agreement, however, was made before the royalties were earned; in fact, it was made on the same day as the principal agreement and the two agreements were a part of the same transaction. Thus, for all practical purposes, the arrangement from the beginning is similar to that in (1) above. Therefore, it is also held that the author concerned will be required to include the royalties in his gross income only in the taxable years in which they are actually received in cash or other property.

(4) In arriving at a determination as to the includibility of the 150x dollars concerned in the gross income of the football player, under the circumstances described, in addition to the authorities cited above, consideration also has been given to Revenue Ruling 55–727, C.B. 1955–2, 25, and to the decision in E.T. Sproull v. Commissioner, 16 T.C. 244.

In Revenue Ruling 55–727, the taxpayer, a professional baseball player, entered into a contract in 1953 in which he agreed to render services for a baseball club and to refrain from playing baseball for any other club during the term of the contract. In addition to specified compensation, the contract provided for a bonus to the player or his estate, payable one-half in January 1954 and one-half in January 1955, whether or not he was able to render services. The primary question was whether the bonus was capital gain or ordinary income; and, in holding that the bonus payments constituted ordinary income, it was stated that they were taxable for the year in which received by the player. However, under the facts set forth in Revenue Ruling 55–727 there was no arrangement, as here, for placing the amount of the bonus in escrow. Consequently, the instant situation is distinguishable from that considered in Revenue Ruling 55–727.

In E.T. Sproull v. Commissioner, 16 T.C. 244, affirmed, 194 Fed.(2d) 541, the petitioner's employer in 1945 transferred in trust for the petitioner the amount of $10,500. The trustee was directed to pay out of principal to the petitioner the sum of $5,250 in 1946 and the balance, including income, in 1947. In the event of the petitioner's prior death, the amounts were to be paid to his administrator, executor, or heirs. The petitioner contended that the Commissioner erred in including the sum of $10,500 in his taxable income for 1945. In this connection, the court stated:

> * * * it is undoubtedly true that the amount which the Commissioner has included in petitioner's income for 1945 was used in that year for his benefit * * * in setting up the trust of which petitioner, or, in the event of his death then his estate, was the sole beneficiary * * *.
>
> The question then becomes * * * was "any economic or financial benefit conferred on the employee as compensation" in the taxable year. If so, it was taxable to him in that year. This question we must answer in the affirmative. The employer's part of the transaction terminated in 1945. It was then that the amount of the compensation was fixed at $10,500 and irrevocably paid out for petitioner's sole benefit. * * *."

Applying the principles stated in the *Sproull* decision to the facts here, it is concluded that the 150x-dollar bonus is includible in the gross income of the football player concerned in 1957, the year in which the club unconditionally paid such amount to the escrow agent.

(5) In this case, the taxpayer and the boxing club, as well as the opponent whom taxpayer had agreed to meet, are each acting in his or its own right, the proposed match is a joint venture by all of these participants, and the taxpayer is not an employee of the boxing club.

The taxpayer's share of the gross receipts from the match belong to him and never belonged to the boxing club. Thus, the taxpayer acquired all of the benefits of his share of the receipts except the right of immediate physical possession; and, although the club retained physical possession, it was by virtue of an arrangement with the taxpayer who, in substance and effect, authorized the boxing club to take possession and hold for him. The receipts, therefore, were income to the taxpayer at the time they were paid to and retained by the boxing club by his agreement and, in substance, at his direction, and are includible in his gross income in the taxable year in which so paid to the club. See the *Sproull* case, supra, and Lucas v. Earl, 281 U.S. 111 [p. 707].

As previously stated, in each case involving a deferral of compensation, a determination of whether the doctrine of constructive receipt is applicable must be made upon the basis of the specific factual situation involved.

Consistent with the foregoing, the nonacquiescence published in C.B. 1952–2, 5, with respect to the decision in Commissioner v. James F. Oates, 18 T.C. 570, affirmed, 207 Fed.(2d) 711, has been withdrawn and acquiescence substituted therefor at page 5 of this Bulletin.

With respect to deductions for payments made by an employer under a deferred compensation plan, see section 404(a)(5) of the 1954 Code and section 1.404(a)–12 of the Income Tax Regulations.

In the application of those sections to unfunded plans, no deduction is allowable for any compensation paid or accrued by an employer on account of any employee under such a plan except in the year when paid and then only to the extent allowable under section 404(a). Thus, under an unfunded plan, if compensation is paid by an employer directly to a former employee, such amounts are deductible under section 404(a)(5) when *actually* paid *in cash or other property to the employee,* provided that such amounts meet the requirements of section 162 or section 212.

Advance rulings will not be issued in specific cases involving deferred compensation arrangements.

A result apparently inconsistent with Example 5 was reached in Robinson v. Commissioner, 44 T.C. 20 (1965) (Acq. 1976–2 C.B. 2). The taxpayer, a boxing champion who was on the cash method, was approached by representatives of a corporation engaged in the presentation of entertainment events. Taxpayer, who owned no stock in the corporation, executed a contract with the corporation under which he agreed to box a designated opponent. Under the contract, the taxpayer was to receive 40% of his total compensation in the tax year and 20% in each of the succeeding three years. The compensation was not to be put in escrow. The taxpayer was an unsecured creditor. The Tax Court held that the taxpayer and the corporation did not enter into a joint venture as defined in § 7701(a)(2). The taxpayer did not constructively receive income; he could defer the realization and the recognition of the income until actual receipt. The Internal Revenue Service has substituted a new Example 5. See Rev.Rul. 70–435, 1970–2 C.B. 100.

Questions

1. Assume Mr. Drescher's employer promised to pay him the annuity on retirement, but did not fund it with the purchase of an annuity from an insurance company. Instead, the employer made an unfunded promise to pay in the future. Would this change the tax consequences to Mr. Drescher? What if Mr. Drescher's employer were IBM? Or a financially strapped airline? Reconsider the Drescher case at p. 160.

2. Assume, instead, Mr. Drescher's employer put the monies necessary to fund the annuity into an escrow account?

3. How would the Service view the contingencies attached to the payment of Mr. Drescher's annuity? What is the justification for the Service's position in Rev.Rul. 60–31?

COMMISSIONER v. OATES

United States Court of Appeals, Seventh Circuit, 1953.
207 F.2d 711.

[The taxpayer, an insurance agent, was entitled to receive renewal commissions collected on premiums over the nine-year period following his retirement. A retiring agent received relatively high commissions in the first year of retirement. The commissions would decrease in each of the eight subsequent years. Prior to the commencement of the retirement payments and before any amounts were due or owing from the insurance company to the taxpayer, the taxpayer and the insurance company revised the contract to provide that renewal commissions would be in fixed monthly payments of $1000 over 180 months. The court held that the payments were realized when received by the taxpayer.]

LINDLEY, CIRCUIT JUDGE.

* * *

The amended contract was in the nature of a novation, that is, a substitution of a new agreement or obligation for an old one which was thereby extinguished. To be valid of course, such a contract must be supported by a consideration. Here, the extinguishment of the original obligation was consideration for the new agreement and the new promise consideration for the release of the old, each being consideration for the other. Consequently the rights of the parties are to be determined entirely by the new contract. Under its terms the taxpayer was to receive commissions at the periods and in the fixed amounts stipulated. He was on a cash basis. He had no right to demand or to receive anything in addition to what he had agreed to accept, namely, $1000 per month.

The case is fully controlled, we think, by the reasoning in Massachusetts Mutual Life Insurance Co. v. United States, 288 U.S. 269, 53 S.Ct. 337, 339, 77 L.Ed. 739. There a policyholder permitted dividends and interest accumulating on his policies to remain on deposit with the company at interest. After observing that the regulation purported to require the policyholder to report interest credited to him and that the commissioner therefore contended that crediting the income constituted a "constructive payment," the court said: "This regulation has, however, not been applied in any case where income has been credited to another by a taxpayer employing the cash receipts and disbursements method of accounting; and specifically it has not been invoked to require policyholders to report as income the dividends or interest credited to them in cases such as this. No tax is demanded of them until actual receipt of the money. The constructive payment theory is, we think, untenable." * * *

* * * Here the parties were confronted by a situation where inconvenience and resulting dissatisfaction came to the retired agents by reason of the constantly decreasing payments made by the company under the original contract. To relieve the situation, the company and the taxpayer, after full and complete negotiations, before retirement of the agent, agreed to abrogate and annul the old contract, to substitute a new one and thus to improve the unsatisfactory posture of affairs. The taxpayer did not reduce to his immediate possession or to his present enjoyment anything that might thereafter accrue to him. He made no assignment; he took no dominion over the accrued commissions other than to agree to receive them in cash installments as they matured under the contract. He did nothing to charge himself with the economic benefit to be derived from the accruing commissions, but, on the contrary, let them accumulate under an agreement whereby the company was to pay the same amount every month rather than constantly decreasing amounts.

We think the Tax Court was right. Its decision is

Affirmed.

REV. PROC. 71–19

1971–1 C.B. 698.

SECTION 1. PURPOSE

The purpose of this Revenue Procedure is to set forth the conditions, or circumstances, under which the Internal Revenue Service will issue advance rulings concerning the application of the doctrine of constructive receipt to unfunded deferred compensation arrangements.

* * *

SEC. 3. REQUESTS FOR RULINGS

In each case involving a deferral of compensation, a determination of whether the doctrine of constructive receipt is applicable may be made only after consideration of the specific factual situation involved. A ruling letter will be issued concerning unfunded deferred compensation arrangements only if the plan meets the following requirements:

.01 If the plan provides for an election to defer payment of compensation, such election must be made before the beginning of the period of service for which the compensation is payable, regardless of the existence in the plan of forfeiture provisions.

.02 If any elections, other than the initial election referred to in .01 above, may be made by an employee subsequent to the beginning of the service period the plan must set forth substantial forfeiture provisions that must remain in effect throughout the entire period of the deferral. A substantial forfeiture provision will not be considered to exist unless its conditions impose upon the employee a significant limitation or duty which will require a meaningful effort on the part of the employee to fulfill and there is a definite possibility that the event which will cause the forfeiture could occur.

* * *

2. FAILURE TO INTEGRATE REVENUE RULING 60–31 WITH OTHER TYPES OF DEFERRED COMPENSATION ARRANGEMENTS

One critical factor which a student attempting to evaluate Rev.Rul. 60–31 must remember is that informal deferred compensation is only a part of the entire treatment of deferred compensation arrangements. With this in mind, it should be noted that the Ruling represents substantial concessions in legitimizing informal deferred compensation devices which formerly had been of dubious validity. It should also be noted at the outset that in the course of the Ruling the Commissioner acquiesced in the Oates case. Acq., 1960–1 C.B. 5. The student should consider the following:

1. Is it clear, as in the Oates case, that informal deferred compensation devices will be effective to postpone income until the sums to be paid are actually received by the employee, even in cases where receipt of such payment is not subject to conditions, such as that the employee will render consulting services or will not compete with the employer? Reread Rev.Proc. 71–19.

2. It seems clear that the mere fact that the employer might willingly have made an earlier payment is irrelevant. This had been thought to be the law previously; the Rev.Rul. 60–31 seems to confirm it.

3. In at least some cases (such as in Oates) deferred compensation arrangements may be made even after earlier arrangements calling for payment on a specific earlier date have been crystallized.

4. Deferred compensation arrangements with respect to income from royalties are approved. It is not possible to tell whether Rev.Rul. 60–31 will extend to deferral of rentals and interest. It is also impossible to tell the extent, if any, to which the Ruling will apply to

profits from the sale of property generally, although this field seems to be occupied by § 453, dealing with installment sales. See p. 817. It seems safe to assume that the Ruling was intended to be limited, but the scope of the Ruling is not clearly delineated.

5. An employer is not, in effect, permitted by means of informal deferred compensation arrangements to fund deferred compensation reserves on its books and invest the proceeds paid to the appropriate accounts in securities or other investments. These investments will attempt to provide protection against inflation. But if the employer sets aside the deferred amount under such an arrangement, does not this action indicate that the employer would be willing to pay that amount to the employee?

It may well be questioned whether this expansion of permissible devices for informal deferred compensation is wise in view of the tax advantages authorized for deferred compensation arrangements under statutory provisions for qualified employee benefit plans. Reconsider p. 159. The legislative history behind the Code sections dealing with qualified employee benefit plans reflect (though strained by statutory exceptions) the view that the benefits of deferral should be generally available to substantial segments of the employer's work force without discrimination among the members of such group. Should conditions similar to those required for qualified employee benefit plans apply to informal deferred compensation arrangements?

As distinguished from this statutory structure for qualified employee benefit plans, we now have a combination of judicial pronouncements and administrative rulings under which it seems probable that deferral of compensation is authorized in far different circumstances. In the plans now approved by the Rev.Rul. 60–31 an employer can select whoever it pleases to receive the benefits of deferred compensation; the employer can choose several persons and discriminate in any manner between them; the employer is not only not required, but is forbidden, to make payments into a trust fund or use a similar device so that the employee can rely on something more than the mere general credit of the employer. It is true that under informal deferred compensation arrangements, an employee who ultimately receives payments cannot obtain capital gains treatment for all or a portion of his deferred compensation and that a deduction by the employer under an informal plan is deferred until payment is actually made to the employee.

One final point. Limitations exist on the maximum annual amount which can be deferred under unfunded deferred compensation plans of state and local governments and tax-exempt organizations. § 457. Why should a limit exist on the amount of compensation that can be deferred under an arrangement with a public or tax-exempt employer, but not an arrangement maintained by a taxpaying employer?

Problems

1. Starstruck, an actor, is contemplating entering into an arrangement with Motion Pictures, Inc., under which the company will pay him

$100,000 in the tax year for his services in a motion picture. The company will agree to pay him an additional $25,000 per year for the next ten years as further compensation. Consider the tax consequences of the arrangement to Starstruck and Motion Pictures, Inc., under Rev.Rul. 60–31 and Rev.Proc. 71–19 if:

(a) Assume both are on the cash method. As to the time an employer can deduct the deferred compensation payments to an employee, consider § 404(a)(5). Note that § 404(d) subjects plans deferring the compensation of non-employees to the same rules as § 404(a)(5).

(b) Assume both are on the accrual method. Consider § 461(h) Reg. §§ 1.446–1(c)(1)(ii) and 1.461–1(a)(2).

(c) Assume Starstruck is on the cash method. Motion Pictures, Inc. uses the accrual method. Consider §§ 404(a)(5), 404(d) and 461(h). Reg. § 1.404(a)–1(c) provides, "deductions under section 404(a) are generally allowable only for the year in which the contribution compensation is paid, regardless of the fact that the [employer] may make his return on the accrual method of accounting."

(d) Is § 83 applicable to these arrangements? Consider Reg. § 1.83–3(e).

(e) Would you recommend a clause requiring the company to credit Starstruck's with interest at a specified annual rate? See Example 2 in Rev.Rul. 60–31.

(f) Assume that the corporation carries the funds in a special reserve account for Starstruck who is on the cash method. Would this change your conclusions? What if the funds were placed in escrow with a third party? What result? Are the economic benefit or constructive receipt doctrines applicable? Consider Rev.Rul. 60–31 and Reg. § 1.451–2(a). Is § 83 applicable to an obligation to pay deferred compensation guaranteed by a third party or funded by payments to a trust or an escrow agent? Has property been transferred under § 83? Consider Regs. § 1.83–3(a)(1), –3(a)(6), –3(e). What restrictions should be built into the arrangement?

2. Ruth, on the cash method, is an architect. By virtue of her contract with her firm she is entitled to continuing commissions for five years under a stated formula. The formula is based on work in process or completed during the previous five years, measured against a stated percentage of the firm's income for five years subsequent to her retirement. On the day before her retirement will become effective, the parties seek to renegotiate the agreement to provide for smaller continuing commissions to be paid over a ten-year period. Taxpayer will contribute no further services to the firm but will agree not to engage in her profession within a radius of fifty miles from the firm's location for ten years.

What are the tax consequences to the employee, considering, in particular, the renegotiation of the agreement and the covenant not to compete? Consider the following:

(a) The Oates case.

(b) Rev.Rul. 60–31.

(c) The constructive receipt doctrine. See Reg. § 1.451–2(a).

(d) The economic benefit doctrine. See the Sproull case referred to in Example 4 of Rev.Rul. 60–31 and the Reed case at p. 216.

(e) Rev.Proc. 71–19.

(f) Section 83 and Reg. § 1.83–3(c)(1).

Chapter 5

GROSS INCOME—EXCLUSIONS

A. PERSONAL CONTEXT

1. GIFTS AND BEQUESTS

Receipt of Gifts or Bequests. Section 102(a) excludes the receipt of a gift or bequest from the gross income of the donee or recipient. However, any income subsequently generated by the property received will be included in the donee's or recipient's gross income. § 102(b). The donor will generally not realize a gain (or a loss) on making a gift where the value of the donated property is different from the donor's basis in the property. § 1001(b).

Basis of Gifts in Kind. With respect to gifts in kind, § 1015 provides that for the purpose of determining gain on the sale of property acquired by gift, the donee's basis equals the donor's basis subject to adjustments which may occur during the time the donee holds the property. Under this carryover basis approach, the pre-gift appreciation is deferred and is taxed to the donee on the donee's sale or other disposition of the property.

Further, § 1015(a) provides that for the purpose of determining loss on the sale of property acquired by gift, the donee's basis is the lesser of: (1) the donor's basis at the time of transfer, or (2) the fair market value of the property at the time of the transfer. A loss realized on the sale of property acquired by gift may be deductible. § 165(a) and (c). However, the donee cannot deduct that portion of the loss attributable to any decline in value while property was held by the donor.

TAFT v. BOWERS

Supreme Court of the United States, 1929.
278 U.S. 470, 49 S.Ct. 199, 73 L.Ed. 460.

MR. JUSTICE MCREYNOLDS delivered the opinion of the Court.

Petitioners, who are donees of stocks, seek to recover income taxes exacted because of advancement in the market value of those stocks while owned by the donors. The facts are not in dispute. Both causes must turn upon the effect of [§ 1015(a)], which prescribes the basis for estimating taxable gain when one disposes of property which came to him by gift. * * *

During the calendar years 1921 and 1922 the father of petitioner, Elizabeth C. Taft, gave her certain shares of Nash Motors Company stock, then more valuable than when acquired by him. She sold them during 1923 for more than their market value when the gift was made.

The United States demanded an income tax reckoned upon the difference between cost to the donor and price received by the donee. She paid accordingly and sued to recover the portion imposed because of the advance in value while the donor owned the stock. The right to tax the increase in value after the gift is not denied.

Abstractly stated, this is the problem:

In 1916 A purchased 100 shares of stock for $1,000, which he held until 1923 when their fair market value had become $2,000. He then gave them to B who sold them during the year 1923 for $5,000. The United States claim that under the Revenue Act of 1921 B must pay income tax upon $4,000, as realized profits. B maintains that only $3,000—the appreciation during her ownership—can be regarded as income; that the increase during the donor's ownership is not income assessable against her within intendment of the Sixteenth Amendment.

The District Court ruled against the United States; the Circuit Court of Appeals held with them.

* * *

We think the manifest purpose of Congress expressed in [§ 1015] was to require the petitioner to pay the enacted tax.

The only question subject to serious controversy is whether Congress had power to authorize the exaction.

It is said that the gift became a capital asset of the donee to the extent of its value when received and, therefore, when disposed of by her no part of that value could be treated as taxable income in her hands.

The Sixteenth Amendment provides:

"The Congress shall have power to lay and collect taxes on incomes, from whatever source derived, without apportionment among the several states, and without regard to any census or enumeration."

Income is the thing which may be taxed—income from any source. The amendment does not attempt to define income or to designate how taxes may be laid thereon, or how they may be enforced.

Under former decisions here the settled doctrine is that the Sixteenth Amendment confers no power upon Congress to define and tax as income without apportionment something which theretofore could not have been properly regarded as income.

Also, this court has declared: " 'Income may be defined as the gain derived from capital, from labor, or from both combined,' provided it be understood to include profit gained through a sale or conversion of capital assets." Eisner v. Macomber, 252 U.S. 189, 207, 40 S.Ct. 189, 193 (64 L.Ed. 521, 9 A.L.R. 1570). The "gain derived from capital," within the definition, is "not a gain accruing to capital, nor a growth or increment of value in the investment, but a gain, a profit, something of exchangeable value proceeding from the property, severed from the capital however invested, and coming in, that is, received or drawn by the claimant for his separate use, benefit and disposal." United States v. Phellis, 257 U.S. 156, 169, 42 S.Ct. 63, 65 (66 L.Ed. 180).

If, instead of giving the stock to petitioner, the donor had sold it at market value, the excess over the capital he invested (cost) would have been income therefrom and subject to taxation under the Sixteenth Amendment. He would have been obliged to share the realized gain with the United States. He held the stock—the investment—subject to the right of the sovereign to take part of any increase in its value when separated through sale or conversion and reduced to his possession. Could he, contrary to the express will of Congress, by mere gift enable another to hold this stock free from such right, deprive the sovereign of the possibility of taxing the appreciation when actually severed, and convert the entire property into a capital asset of the donee, who invested nothing, as though the latter had purchased at the market price? And after a still further enhancement of the property, could the donee make a second gift with like effect, etc.? We think not.

In truth the stock represented only a single investment of capital— that made by the donor. And when through sale or conversion the increase was separated therefrom, it became income from that investment in the hands of the recipient subject to taxation according to the very words of the Sixteenth Amendment. By requiring the recipient of the entire increase to pay a part into the public treasury, Congress deprived her of no right and subjected her to no hardship. She accepted the gift with knowledge of the statute and, as to the property received, voluntarily assumed the position of her donor. When she sold the stock she actually got the original sum invested, plus the entire appreciation and out of the latter only was she called on to pay the tax demanded.

The provision of the statute under consideration seems entirely appropriate for enforcing a general scheme of lawful taxation. To accept the view urged in behalf of petitioner undoubtedly would defeat, to some extent, the purpose of Congress to take part of all gain derived from capital investments. To prevent that result and insure enforcement of its proper policy, Congress had power to require that for purposes of taxation the donee should accept the position of the donor in respect of the thing received. And in so doing, it acted neither unreasonably nor arbitrarily.

The power of Congress to require a succeeding owner, in respect of taxation, to assume the place of his predecessor is pointed out by United States v. Phellis, 257 U.S. 156, 171, 42 S.Ct. 63, 66 (66 L.Ed. 180):

"Where, as in this case, the dividend constitutes a distribution of profits accumulated during an extended period and bears a large proportion to the par value of the stock, if an investor happened to buy stock shortly before the dividend, paying a price enhanced by an estimate of the capital plus the surplus of the company, and after distribution of the surplus, with corresponding reduction in the intrinsic and market value of the shares, he were called upon to pay a tax upon the dividend received, it might look in his case like a tax upon his capital. But it is only apparently so. In buying at a price that reflected the accumulated profits, he of course acquired as a part of the valuable rights purchased the prospect of a dividend from the accumulations—bought 'dividend on,' as the phrase goes—and necessarily took subject to the burden of the income tax proper to be assessed against him by reason of the dividend if and when made. He simply stepped into the shoes, in this as in other respects, of the stockholder whose shares he acquired, and presumably the prospect of a dividend influenced the price paid, and was discounted by the prospect of an income tax to be paid thereon. In short, the question whether a dividend made out of company profits constitutes income of the stockholder is not affected by antecedent transfers of the stock from hand to hand."

There is nothing in the Constitution which lends support to the theory that gain actually resulting from the increased value of capital can be treated as taxable income in the hands of the recipient only so far as the increase occurred while he owned the property. And Irwin v. Gavit, 268 U.S. 161, 167, 45 S.Ct. 475, 69 L.Ed. 897, is to the contrary.

The judgment below is affirmed.

THE CHIEF JUSTICE took no part in the consideration or decision of these causes.

Questions

1. If the donee-taxpayer had prevailed in Taft v. Bowers and obtained a basis in the property equal to its fair market value at the time of the gift, would the Commissioner have required the donor to treat the making of a gift as a taxable event giving rise to a realized gain? Is the basis step-up allowed by § 1014(a) for property acquired by bequest consistent with the concept that the donor does not realize any gain on a transfer by gift? What statutory provision indicates Congressional intent not to treat a transfer by gift as a realization by the donor?

2. In Taft v. Bowers, the taxpayer argued that requiring the donee to carryover the donor's basis, would be unconstitutional because the donee would be forced to treat a portion of the gift as taxable income. Explain this position. Does the carry-over basis approach of § 1015 constitute a double tax?

Basis for Bequests. The basis for determining gain or loss from the sale of property passing or acquired from a decedent generally equals its fair market value on the date of the decedent's death or the alternative valuation date if the executor elects to use this date in valuing the estate for Federal estate tax purposes. § 1014(a). If property owned by a decedent appreciated in value after he acquired it, there is no income tax on the pre-death appreciation. Similarly, any pre-death decline in the value is non-deductible for income tax purposes.

Under the Tax Reform Act of 1976 the basis of property passing or acquired from a decedent dying after December 31, 1976, was to be carried over from the decedent, with specified adjustments, to the recipient of the property. The Revenue Act of 1978 deferred the application of the carryover basis rules until 1980. The Crude Oil Windfall Profit Tax Act of 1980 repealed the carryover basis approach.

The reasons in favor of the carryover basis approach are summarized in the following excerpt.

STAFF OF THE JOINT COMMITTEE ON TAXATION GENERAL EXPLANATION OF THE TAX REFORM ACT OF 1976
94th Cong.2d Sess. 552 (1976).

Prior law [step-up basis] resulted in an unwarranted discrimination against those persons who sell their property prior to death as compared with those whose property was not sold until after death. Where a person sells appreciated property before death, the resulting gain is subject to the income tax. However, if the sale of the property could be postponed until after the owner's death, all of the appreciation occurring before death would not be subject to the income tax.

This discrimination against sales occurring before death created a substantial "lock-in" effect. Persons in their later years who might otherwise sell property were effectively prevented from doing so because they realized that the appreciation in that asset would be taxed as income if they sold before death, but would not be subject to income tax if they held the asset until their death. The effect of this "lock-in" was often to distort the allocation of capital between competing sources.

In order to eliminate these problems, Congress believed that the basis of property acquired from or passing from a decedent should have the same basis in the hands of the recipient as it has in the hands of the decedent, i.e., a "carryover basis." This will have the effect of eliminating the unwarranted difference in treatment between lifetime and deathtime transfers.

The next excerpt sets forth the reasons for the repeal of the carryover basis provisions.

REPORT OF THE COMMITTEE ON FINANCE, UNITED STATES SENATE, CRUDE OIL WINDFALL PROFIT TAX ACT OF (1980)

96th Cong. 1st Sess. 122 (1979).

A number of administration problems concerning the carryover basis provisions have been brought to the attention of the committee. Administrators of estates have testified that compliance with the carryover basis provisions has caused a significant increase in the time required to administer an estate and has resulted in raising the overall cost of administration. The committee believes that the carryover basis provisions are unduly complicated.

An Exception to the Step Up (Step Down) Basis Approach. For decedents dying after December 31, 1981, § 1014(e) provides that the basis of appreciated property, as defined in § 1014(e)(2)(A), acquired by a decedent by a gift within one year of his death and returned to the donor of the property (or the donor's spouse) on the donee-decedent's death equals the decedent's adjusted basis in the property immediately prior to his death. For example, X transferred appreciated property with a basis of $10 and a fair market value of $100 to D. D died ten months later when the fair market value of the property equalled $200. If X receives the property from D's estate, X's basis in the property will be $10. In commenting on the reasons for this departure from the general step-up approach, the legislative history states:

REPORT, COMMITTEE ON WAYS AND MEANS, HOUSE OF REPRESENTATIVES, HOUSE REPORT NO. 97–201, [ECONOMIC RECOVERY TAX ACT OF 1981]

97th Cong., 1st Sess. (1981) 188.

Because an heir receives property from a decedent with a stepped-up basis, an heir can transfer appreciated property to a decedent immediately prior to death in the hope of receiving the property back at the decedent's death with a higher basis. The donor-heir might pay gift taxes on the fair market value of the gift (unless it qualified for the marital deduction or the amount of gift is less than the donor's annual exclusion or unified credit) but will pay no income tax on the appreciation. Then, upon the death of the donee-decedent, the donor-heir could receive back the property with a stepped-up basis equal to its fair market value. The stepped-up basis would permanently exempt the appreciation from income tax.

Because the committee bill provides an unlimited [gift and estate tax] marital deduction and substantially increases the unified [gift and estate tax] credit, the committee believes that there would be an even greater incentive to plan such deathbed transfers of appreciated property to a donee-decedent. Because the committee believes that allowing a stepped-up basis in this situation permits unintended and inappropriate tax benefits, the committee provides that the stepped-up basis rules should not apply with respect to appreciated property acquired by the decedent through gift within [one year] of death where such property passes from the decedent to the original donor or the donor's spouse.

Problems

1. D's basis for his stock equals $1,000. The stock, a capital asset, has a fair market value of $10,000 at the date of the gift. Assume the donor pays no Federal gift tax with respect to the transfer. The donee sells the shares one year later for:

    (1) $15,000

    (2) $5,000

    (3) $500

    (a) In each of the above, does the donee or the donor realize the gain (or loss)? When? Consider §§ 102(a) and 1001(a).

    (b) What is the amount of the gain (or loss)? Carefully read § 1015(a) (first sentence).

    (c) What income tax considerations should enter into a property owner's decision whether to transfer property which has appreciated in value? Why is it important to know whether the donor's marginal income tax rate is higher than the donee's?

2. What result upon the sale in each of the three situations in "1" above if D died when the stock was worth $10,000, and he left the stock as a bequest in his will? Consider §§ 102(a) and 1014(a).

3. D's basis for his stock is $10,000. The shares are worth $1,000 at the date of the gift. Assume D pays no Federal gift tax with respect to the transfer.

    (a) Does the donee realize gain (or loss) and in what amount, if the donee sells the shares for:

    (i) $15,000 (Is the basis for determining loss useful?)

    (ii) $500

    (iii) $5,000 (Consider Reg. § 1.1015–1(a)(1) and (2))

Consider § 1015. Can the donee take advantage of the pre-gift depreciation in the value of the property?

    (b) Would you recommend that an individual owning property with a basis in excess of the fair market value transfer the property by gift? What should the prospective donor do instead of making a gift of property which has declined in value?

4. (a) A father wants to give his son 100 shares of Corporation X stock currently worth $1,000 during his (the father's) lifetime and an additional 100 shares of Corporation X stock at his (the father's) death. He has 100 shares of Corporation X stock, bought 10 years ago, having a basis of $1 per share and a current value of $10 per share. He has another 100 shares of Corporation X stock, purchased 5 years ago, having a basis of $8 per share and the same $10 per share value. Should the father give the shares of

stock with a high basis compared to the fair market value and retain the shares of stock with a low basis compared to the fair market value? Why? Consider § 1014(a).

(b) X owns stock in Q Corporation, with a basis of $10,000, and a fair market value of $7,500. X is considering leaving this stock as a bequest. What advice would you give X to maximize his tax savings?

(c) Do you favor or oppose the step-up basis or carry-over basis approach for transfers at death? What is the rationale for different basis provisions for lifetime gifts and transfers at death? With respect to testamentary transfers, what is the impact of the step-up (or step-down) basis provision or the carryover basis approach on the "lock in" (a misallocation) of capital? Under the step-up (or step-down) basis provision do the beneficiaries of a decedent receiving appreciated property enjoy a tax advantage over the beneficiaries of a decedent whose estate has been accumulated out of currently taxed income? What kind of income is favored, income from services or from the appreciation in the value of property? What is the rationale in support of the step-up basis for testamentary transfers?

5. During a recent presidential election campaign, Steve contributed stock with a basis of $10 and a fair market value of $50 to a campaign committee. Can a donor ever realize a gain on a gift? Consider § 84.

Question

Why should gifts and bequests be excluded from the recipient's gross income? Is the exclusion based on the rationale that gifts and bequests, especially intra-family transfers, constitute a sharing (or a division) of wealth rather than the creation of new income? Should gifts and bequests constitute gross income to the recipient because the recipient's economic power is increased? Consider the problems of administration (especially numerous small gifts) and valuation. Should only gifts and bequests from sources not within the "family" be included in the recipient's gross income?

2. TRANSFERS IN TRUST

IRWIN v. GAVIT

Supreme Court of the United States, 1925.
268 U.S. 161, 45 S.Ct. 475, 69 L.Ed. 897.

Mr. Justice Holmes delivered the opinion of the Court.

* * *

The question is whether the sums received by the plaintiff under the will of Anthony N. Brady in 1913, 1914 and 1915, were income and taxed. The will, admitted to probate August 12, 1913, left the residue of the estate in trust to be divided into six equal parts, the income of one part to be applied so far as deemed proper by the trustees to the education and support of the testator's granddaughter, Marcia Ann Gavit, the balance to be divided into two equal parts and one of them to be paid to the testator's son-in-law, the plaintiff, in equal quarter-yearly payments during his life. But on the granddaughter's reaching the age of twenty-one or dying the fund went over, so that, the granddaughter then being six years old, it is said, the plaintiff's interest could not exceed fifteen years. (The Courts below held that the payments received were property acquired by bequest, were not income and were not subject to tax.)

The statute in Section 2, A, subdivision 1, provides that there shall be levied a tax "upon the entire net income arising or accruing from all sources in the preceding calendar year to every citizen of the United States." If these payments properly may be called income by the common understanding of that word and the statute has failed to hit them it has missed so much of the general purpose that it expresses at the start. Congress intended to use its power to the full extent. Eisner v. Macomber, 252 U.S. 189, 203, 40 S.Ct. 189, 64 L.Ed. 521. By B the net income is to include "gains or profits and income derived from any source whatever, including the income from but not not the value of property acquired by gift, bequest, devise or descent." By D trustees are to make "return of the net income of the person for whom they act, subject to this tax," and by D trustees and others, having the control or payment of fixed or determinable gains, etc., of another person who are required to render a return on behalf of another are "authorized to withhold enough to pay the normal tax." The language quoted leaves no doubt in our minds that if a fund were given to trustees for A for life with remainder over, the income received by the trustees and paid over to A would be income of A under the statute. It seems to us hardly less clear that even if there were a specific provision that A should have no interest in the corpus, the payments would be income none the less, within the meaning of the *statute* and the *Constitution,* and by *popular speech.* In the first case it is true that the bequest might be said to be of the corpus for life, in the second it might be said to be of the income. [But we think that the provision of the act that exempts bequests assumes the gift of a corpus and contrasts it with the income arising from it, but was not intended to exempt income property so-called simply because of a severance between it and the principal fund.] No such conclusion can be drawn from Eisner v. Macomber, 252 U.S. 189, 206, 207, 40 S.Ct. 189, 64 L.Ed. 521. The money was income in the hands of the trustees and we know of nothing in the law that prevented its being paid and received as income by the donee.

The courts below went on the ground that the gift to the plaintiff was a bequest and carried no interest in the corpus of the fund. We do not regard those considerations as conclusive, as we have said, but if it were material a gift of the income of a fund ordinarily is treated by equity as creating an interest in the fund. Apart from technicalities we can perceive no distinction relevant to the question before us between a gift of the fund for life and a gift of the income from it. The fund is appropriated to the production of the same result whichever form the gift takes. Neither are we troubled by the question where to draw the line. That is the question in pretty much everything worth arguing in the law. Hudson County Water Co. v. McCarter, 209 U.S. 349, 355, 28 S.Ct. 529, 52 L.Ed. 828. Day and night, youth and age are only types. But the distinction between the cases put of a gift from the corpus of the estate payable in instalments and the present seems to us not hard to draw, assuming that the gift supposed would not be income. This is a gift from the income of a very large fund, as income. It seems to us immaterial that the same amounts might receive a different color from their source. We are of opinion that quarterly payments, which it was hoped would last for fifteen years, from the income of an estate intended for the plaintiff's child, must be regarded as income within the meaning of the Constitution and the law. It is said that the tax laws should be construed favorably for the taxpayers. But that is not a reason for creating a doubt or for exaggerating one when it is no greater than we can bring ourselves to feel in this case.

Judgment reversed.

MR. JUSTICE SUTHERLAND (dissenting). By the plain terms of the Revenue Act of 1913, the value of property acquired by gift, bequest, devise, or descent is not to be included in net income. Only the income derived from such property is subject to the tax. The question, as it seems to me, is really a very simple one. Money, of course, is property. The money here sought to be taxed as income was paid to respondent under the express provisions of a will. It was a gift by will—a bequest. United States v. Merriam, 263 U.S. 179, 184, 44 S.Ct. 69, 68 L.Ed. 240. It, therefore, fell within the precise letter of the statute; and, under well settled principles, judicial inquiry may go no further. The taxpayer is entitled to the rigor of the law. There is no latitude in a taxing statute; you must adhere to the very words. United States v. Merriam, supra, pages 187, 188 (44 S.Ct. 69).

The property which respondent acquired being a bequest, there is no occasion to ask whether, before being handed over to him, it had been carved from the original corpus of, or from subsequent additions to, the estate. The corpus of the estate was not the legacy which respondent received, but merely the source which gave rise to it. The money here sought to be taxed was not the fruits of a legacy; it was the legacy itself. Matter of Stanfield, 135 N.Y. 292, 294, 31 N.E. 1013.

With the utmost respect for the judgment of my brethren to the contrary, the opinion just rendered, I think without warrant, searches the field of argument and inference for a meaning which should be found only in the strict letter of the statute.

MR. JUSTICE BUTLER concurs in this dissent.

Problem

A father transfers $100,000 in cash to T in trust with the direction that the income from the trust corpus be paid annually to his adult son for life and on his son's death the corpus of the trust be distributed to his only grandson who is now 15 years old. The trustee invests the money in a certificate of deposit paying 10% interest each year.

(a) Assuming the income distributed by the trust is not otherwise excluded, why is all of the income taxed to the life tenant? When is the income taxable to the life tenant? Consider Irwin v. Gavit, § 102(a) and (b)(2), and Reg. § 1.1014–5.

(b) Why does the entire benefit of the exclusion from gross income of the $100,000 go to the remainderman? What is the relation of §§ 273 and 1001(e) to § 102(b)(2)? What is the remainderman's basis for the trust property on the death of the life tenant?

(c) Why would the exclusion be greater if both the receipt of corpus and income were excluded from gross income? Compare this situation with one person receiving the entire $100,000 outright.

(d) Could (and should) the $100,000 exclusion be divided between the life tenant and the remainderman? Consider Reg. § 20.2031–7(f) Table A. Assume the son was age 50 at the time of the gift. If the $100,000 basis in the trust corpus was allocated between the life tenant and the remainderman, how would the life tenant handle the payments actually received and what would be the remainderman's basis in the transferred property when the life tenant died?

3. WHAT IS A GIFT?

Is a Commercial Transfer a Gift? As the following case illustrates, the line between a receipt included in gross income under § 61 and a gift excluded from gross income under § 102 may be hard to draw. Read § 102(c)(1).

COMMISSIONER v. DUBERSTEIN

Supreme Court of the United States, 1960.
363 U.S. 278, 80 S.Ct. 1190, 4 L.Ed.2d 1218.

Mr. Justice Brennan delivered the opinion of the Court.

These two cases concern the provision of the Internal Revenue Code which excludes from the gross income of an income taxpayer "the value of property acquired by gift." [1] They pose the frequently recurrent question whether a specific transfer to a taxpayer in fact amounted to a "gift" to him within the meaning of the statute. The importance to decision of the facts of the cases requires that we state them in some detail.

No. 376, Commissioner v. Duberstein. The taxpayer, Duberstein, was president of the Duberstein Iron & Metal Company, a corporation with headquarters in Dayton, Ohio. For some years the taxpayer's company had done business with Mohawk Metal Corporation, whose headquarters were in New York City. The president of Mohawk was one Berman. The taxpayer and Berman had generally used the telephone to transact their companies' business with each other, which consisted of buying and selling metals. The taxpayer testified, without

---

1. The operative provision in the cases at bar is § 22(b)(3) of the 1939 Internal Revenue Code, 26 U.S.C.A. § 22(b)(3). The corresponding provision of the present Code is § 102(a), 26 U.S.C.A. § 102(a).

elaboration, that he knew Berman "personally" and had known him for about seven years. From time to time in their telephone conversations, Berman would ask Duberstein whether the latter knew of potential customers for some of Mohawk's products in which Duberstein's company itself was not interested. Duberstein provided the names of potential customers for these items.

One day in 1951 Berman telephone Duberstein and said that the information Duberstein had given him had proved so helpful that he wanted to give the latter a present. Duberstein stated that Berman owed him nothing. Berman said that he had a Cadillac as a gift for Duberstein, and that the latter should send to New York for it; Berman insisted that Duberstein accept the car, and the latter finally did so, protesting however that he had not intended to be compensated for the information. At the time Duberstein already had a Cadillac and an Oldsmobile, and felt that he did not need another car. Duberstein testified that he did not think Berman would have sent him the Cadillac if he had not furnished him with information about the customers. It appeared that Mohawk later deducted the value of the Cadillac as a business expense on its corporate income tax return.

Duberstein did not include the value of the Cadillac in gross income for 1951, deeming it a gift. The Commissioner asserted a deficiency for the car's value against him, and in proceedings to review the deficiency the Tax Court affirmed the Commissioner's determination. It said that "The record is significantly barren of evidence revealing any intention on the part of the payor to make a gift. * * * The only justifiable inference is that the automobile was intended by the payor to be remuneration for services rendered to it by Duberstein." The Court of Appeals for the Sixth Circuit reversed. 265 F.2d 28, 30.

No. 546, Stanton v. United States. The taxpayer, Stanton, had been for approximately 10 years in the employ of Trinity Church in New York City. He was comptroller of the Church corporation, and president of a corporation, Trinity Operating Company, the church set up as a fully owned subsidiary to manage its real estate holdings, which were more extensive than simply the church property. His salary by the end of his employment there in 1942 amounted to $22,500 a year. Effective November 30, 1942, he resigned from both positions to go into business for himself. The Operating Company's directors, who seem to have included the rector and vestrymen of the church, passed the following resolution upon his resignation: "Be it resolved that in appreciation of the services rendered by Mr. Stanton * * * a gratuity is hereby awarded to him of Twenty Thousand Dollars, payable to him in equal instalments of Two Thousand Dollars at the end of each and every month commencing with the month of December, 1942; provided that, with the discontinuance of his services, the Corporation of Trinity Church is released from all rights and claims to pension and retirement benefits not already accrued up to November 30, 1942."

The Operating Company's action was later explained by one of its directors as based on the fact that, "Mr. Stanton was liked by all of the Vestry personally. He had a pleasing personality. He had come in when Trinity's affairs were in a difficult situation. He did a splendid piece of work, we felt. Besides that * * * he was liked by all of the members of the Vestry personally." And by another: "[W]e were all unanimous in wishing to make Mr. Stanton a gift. Mr. Stanton had loyally and faithfully served Trinity in a very difficult time. We thought of him in the highest regard. We understood that he was going in business for himself. We felt that he was entitled to that evidence of good will."

On the other hand, there was a suggestion of some ill-feeling between Stanton and the directors, arising out of the recent termination of the services of one Watkins, the Operating Company's treasurer, whose departure was evidently attended by some acrimony. At a special board meeting on October 28, 1942, Stanton had intervened on Watkins' side and asked reconsideration of the matter. The minutes reflect that "resentment was expressed as to the 'presumptuous' suggestion that the action of the Board, taken after long deliberation, should be changed." The Board adhered to its determination that Watkins be separated from employment, giving him an opportunity to resign rather than be discharged. At another special meeting two days later it was revealed that Watkins had not resigned; the previous resolution terminating his services was then viewed as effective; and the Board voted the payment of six months' salary to Watkins in a resolution similar to that quoted in regard to Stanton, but which did not use the term "gratuity." At the meeting, Stanton announced that in order to avoid any such embarrassment or question at any time as to his willingness to resign if the Board desired, he was tendering his resignation. It was tabled, though not without dissent. The next week, on November 5, at another special meeting, Stanton again tendered his resignation which this time was accepted.

The "gratuity" was duly paid. So was a smaller one to Stanton's (and the Operating Company's) secretary, under a similar resolution, upon her resignation at the same time. The two corporations shared the expense of the payments. There was undisputed testimony that there were in fact no enforceable rights or claims to pension and retirement benefits which had not accrued at the time of the taxpayer's resignation, and that the last proviso of the resolution was inserted simply out of an abundance of caution. The taxpayer received in cash a refund of his contributions to the retirement plans, and there is no suggestion that he was entitled to more. He was required to perform no further services for Trinity after his resignation.

The Commissioner asserted a deficiency against the taxpayer after the latter had failed to include the payments in question in gross income. After payment of the deficiency and administrative rejection of a refund claim, the taxpayer sued the United States for a refund in the District Court for the Eastern District of New York. 137 F.Supp. 803. The trial judge, sitting without a jury, made the simple finding that the payments were a "gift," and judgment was entered for the taxpayer. The Court of Appeals for the Second Circuit reversed. 268 F.2d 727.

The Government, urging that clarification of the problem typified by these two cases was necessary, and that the approaches taken by the Courts of Appeals for the Second and the Sixth Circuits were in conflict, petitioned for certiorari in No. 376, and acquiesced in the taxpayer's petition in No. 546. On this basis, and because of the importance of the question in the administration of the income tax laws, we granted certiorari in both cases. 361 U.S. 923, 80 S.Ct. 291, 4 L.Ed.2d 239.

The exclusion of property acquired by gift from gross income under the federal income tax laws was made in the first income tax statute passed under the authority of the Sixteenth Amendment, and has been a feature of the income tax statutes ever since. The meaning of the term "gift" as applied to particular transfers has always been a matter of contention. Specific and illuminating legislative history on the point does not appear to exist. Analogies and inferences drawn from other revenue provisions, such as the estate and gift taxes, are dubious. See Lockard v. Commissioner, 1 Cir., 166 F.2d 409. The meaning of the statutory term has been shaped largely by the decisional law. With this, we turn to the contentions made by the Government in these cases.

First. The Government suggests that we promulgate a new "test" in this area to serve as a standard to be applied by the lower courts and by the Tax Court in dealing with the numerous cases that arise.[2] We reject this invitation. We are of opinion that the governing principles are necessarily general and have already been spelled out in the opinions of this Court, and that the problem is one which, under the present statutory framework, does not lend itself to any more definitive statement that would produce a talisman for the solution of concrete cases. The cases at bar are fair examples of the settings in which the problem usually arises. They present situations in which payments have been made in a context with business overtones—an employer making a payment to a retiring employee; a businessman giving something of value to another businessman who has been of advantage to him in his business. In this context, we review the law as established by the prior cases here.

The course of decision here makes it plain that the statute does not use the term "gift" in the common-law sense, but in a more colloquial sense. This Court has indicated that a voluntarily executed transfer of his property by one to another, without any consideration or compensation therefor, though a common-law gift, is not necessarily a "gift" within the meaning of the statute. For the Court has shown that the

2. The Government's proposed test is stated: "Gifts should be defined as trans-fers of property made for personal as distinguished from business reasons."

mere absence of a legal or moral obligation to make such a payment does not establish that it is a gift. Old Colony Trust Co. v. Commissioner, 279 U.S. 716, 730, 49 S.Ct. 499, 504, 73 L.Ed. 918. And, importantly, if the payment proceeds primarily from "the constraining force of any moral or legal duty," or from "the incentive of anticipated benefit" of an economic nature, Bogardus v. Commissioner, 302 U.S. 34, 41, 58 S.Ct. 61, 65, 82 L.Ed. 32, it is not a gift. And, conversely, "[w]here the payment is in return for services rendered, it is irrelevant that the donor derives no economic benefit from it." Robertson v. United States, 343 U.S. 711, 714, 72 S.Ct. 994, 996, 96 L.Ed. 1237.[3] A gift in the statutory sense, on the other hand, proceeds from a "detached and disinterested generosity," Commissioner of Internal Revenue v. LoBue, 351 U.S. 243, 246, 76 S.Ct. 800, 803, 100 L.Ed. 1142; "out of affection, respect, admiration, charity or like impulses." Robertson v. United States, supra, 343 U.S. at page 714, 72 S.Ct. at page 996. And in this regard, the most critical consideration, as the Court was agreed in the leading case here, is the transferor's "intention." Bogardus v. Commissioner, 302 U.S. 34, 43, 58 S.Ct. 61, 65, 82 L.Ed. 32. "What controls is the intention with which payment, however voluntary, has been made." Id., 302 U.S. at page 45, 58 S.Ct. at page 66 (dissenting opinion).[4]

The Government says that this "intention" of the transferor cannot mean what the cases on the common-law concept of gift call "donative intent." With that we are in agreement, for our decisions fully support this. Moreover, the Bogardus case itself makes it plain that the donor's characterization of his action is not determinative—that there must be an objective inquiry as to whether what is called a gift amounts to it in reality. 302 U.S. at page 40, 58 S.Ct. at page 64. It scarcely needs adding that the parties' expectations or hopes as to the tax treatment of their conduct in themselves have nothing to do with the matter.

It is suggested that the Bogardus criterion would be more apt if rephrased in terms of "motive" rather than "intention." We must confess to some skepticism as to whether such a verbal mutation would be of any practical consequence. We take it that the proper criterion, established by decision here, is one that inquires what the basic reason for his conduct was in fact—the dominant reason that explains his action in making the transfer. Further than that we do not think it profitable to go.

3. The cases including "tips" in gross income are classic examples of this. See, e.g., Roberts v. Commissioner, 9 Cir., 176 F.2d 221.

4. The parts of the Bogardus opinion which we touch on here are the ones we take to be basic to its holding, and the ones that we read as stating those governing principles which it establishes. As to them we see little distinction between the views of the Court and those taken in dissent in Bogardus. The fear expressed by the dissent at 302 U.S. at page 44, 58 S.Ct. at page 66, that the prevailing opinion "seems" to hold "that every payment which in any aspect is a gift is * * * relieved of any tax" strikes us now as going beyond what the opinion of the Court held in fact. In any event, the Court's opinion in Bogardus does not seem to have been so interpreted afterwards. The principal difference, as we see it, between the Court's opinion and the dissent lies in the weight to be given the findings of the trier of fact.

Second. The Government's proposed "test," while apparently simple and precise in its formulation, depends frankly on a set of "principles" or "presumptions" derived from the decided cases, and concededly subject to various exceptions; and it involves various corollaries, which add to its detail. Were we to promulgate this test as a matter of law, and accept with it its various presuppositions and stated consequences, we would be passing far beyond the requirements of the cases before us, and would be painting on a large canvas with indeed a broad brush. The Government derives it test from such propositions as the following: That payments by an employer to an employee, even though voluntary, ought, by and large, to be taxable; that the concept of a gift is inconsistent with a payment's being a deductible business expense; that a gift involves "personal" elements; that a business corporation cannot properly make a gift of its assets. The Government admits that there are exceptions and qualifications to these propositions. We think, to the extent they are correct, that these propositions are not principles of law but rather maxims of experience that the tribunals which have tried the facts of cases in this area have enunciated in explaining their factual determinations. Some of them simply represent truisms: it doubtless is, statistically speaking, the exceptional payment by an employer to an employee that amounts to a gift. Others are overstatements of possible evidentiary inferences relevant to a factual determination on the totality of circumstances in the case: it is doubtless relevant to the over-all inference that the transferor treats a payment as a business deduction, or that the transferor is a corporate entity. But these inferences cannot be stated in absolute terms. Neither factor is a shibboleth. The taxing statute does not make nondeductibility by the transferor a condition on the "gift" exclusion; nor does it draw any distinction, in terms, between transfers by corporations and individuals, as to the availability of the "gift" exclusion to the transferee. The conclusion whether a transfer amounts to a "gift" is one that must be reached on consideration of all the factors.

Specifically, the trier of fact must be careful not to allow trial of the issue whether the receipt of a specific payment is a gift to turn into a trial of the tax liability, or of the propriety, as a matter of fiduciary or corporate law, attaching to the conduct of someone else. The major corollary to the Government's suggested "test" is that, as an ordinary matter, a payment by a corporation cannot be a gift, and, more specifically, there can be no such thing as a "gift" made by a corporation which would allow it to take a deduction for an ordinary and necessary business expense. As we have said, we find no basis for such a conclusion in the statute; and if it were applied as a determinative rule of "law," it would force the tribunals trying tax cases involving the donee's liability into elaborate inquiries into the local law of corporations or into the peripheral deductibility of payments as business expenses. The former issue might make the tax tribunals the most frequent investigators of an important and difficult issue of the laws of the several States, and the latter inquiry would summon one difficult and delicate problem of federal tax law as an aid to the solution of another.[5] Or perhaps there would be required a trial of the vexed issue whether there was a "constructive" distribution of corporate property, for income tax purposes, to the corporate agents who had sponsored the transfer. These considerations, also, reinforce us in our conclusion that while the principles urged by the Government may, in nonabsolute form as crystallizations of experience, prove persuasive to the trier of facts in a particular case, neither they, nor any more detailed statement than has been made, can be laid down as a matter of law.

Third. Decision of the issue presented in these cases must be based ultimately on the application of the factfinding tribunal's experience with the mainsprings of human conduct to the totality of the facts of each case. The nontechnical nature of the statutory standard, the close relationship of it to the data of practical human experience, and the multiplicity of relevant factual elements, with their various combinations, creating the necessity of ascribing the proper force to each, confirm us in our conclusion that primary weight in this area must be given to the conclusions of the trier of fact. Baker v. Texas & Pacific R. Co., 359 U.S. 227, 79 S.Ct. 664, 3 L.Ed.2d 756; Commissioner of Internal Revenue v. Heininger, 320 U.S. 467, 475, 64 S.Ct. 249, 254, 88 L.Ed. 171; United States v. Yellow Cab Co., 338 U.S. 338, 341, 70 S.Ct. 177, 179, 94 L.Ed. 150; Bogardus v. Commissioner, supra, 302 U.S. at page 45, 58 S.Ct. at page 66 (dissenting opinion).

This conclusion may not satisfy an academic desire for tidiness, symmetry and precision in this area, any more than a system based on the determinations of various fact-finders ordinarily does. But we see it as implicit in the present statutory treatment of the exclusion for gifts, and in the variety of forums in which federal income tax cases can be tried. If there is fear of undue uncertainty or over much litigation, Congress may make more precise its treatment of the matter by singling out certain factors and making them determinative of the matter, as it has done in one field of the "gift" exclusion's former application, that of prizes and awards.[6] Doubtless diversity of result will tend to be lessened somewhat since federal income tax decisions, even those in tribunals of first instance turning on issues of fact, tend

---

5. Justice Cardozo once described in memorable language the inquiry into whether an expense was an "ordinary and necessary" one of a business: "One struggles in vain for any verbal formula that will supply a ready touchstone. The standard set up by the statute is not a rule of law; it is rather a way of life. Life in all its fullness must supply the answer to the riddle." Welch v. Helvering, 290 U.S. 111, 115, 54 S.Ct. 8, 9, 78 L.Ed. 212. The same comment well fits the issue in the cases at bar.

6. I.R.C. § 74, 26 U.S.C.A. § 74, which is a provision new with the 1954 Code.

Previously, there had been holdings that such receipts as the "Pot O' Gold" radio giveaway, Washburn v. Commissioner, 5 T.C. 1333, and the Ross Essay Prize, McDermott v. Commissioner, 80 U.S.App.D.C. 176, 150 F.2d 585, were "gifts." Congress intended to obviate such rulings. S.Rep. No. 1622, 83d Cong., 2d Sess., p. 178. We imply no approval of those holdings under the general standard of the "gift" exclusion. Cf. Robertson v. United States, supra.

to be reported, and since there may be a natural tendency of professional triers of fact to follow one another's determinations, even as to factual matters. But the question here remains basically one of fact, for determination on a case-by-case basis.

One consequence of this is that appellate review of determinations in this field must be quite restricted. Where a jury has tried the matter upon correct instructions, the only inquiry is whether it cannot be said that reasonable men could reach differing conclusions on the issue. Baker v. Texas & Pacific R. Co., supra, 359 U.S. at page 228, 79 S.Ct. at page 665. Where the trial has been by a judge without a jury, the judge's findings must stand unless "clearly erroneous." Fed.Rules Civ.Proc. 52(a), 28 U.S.C.A. "A finding is 'clearly erroneous' when although there is evidence to support it, the reviewing court on the entire evidence is left with the definite and firm conviction that a mistake has been committed." United States v. United States Gypsum Co., 333 U.S. 364, 395, 68 S.Ct. 525, 542, 92 L.Ed. 746. The rule itself applies also to factual inferences from undisputed basic facts, id., 333 U.S. at page 394, 68 S.Ct. at page 541, as will on many occasions be presented in this area. Cf. Graver Tank & Mfg. Co. v. Linde Air Products Co., 339 U.S. 605, 609–610, 70 S.Ct. 854, 856, 857, 94 L.Ed. 1097. And Congress has in the most explicit terms attached the identical weight to the findings of the Tax Court. I.R.C. § 7482(a), 26 U.S.C.A. § 7482(a).

Fourth. A majority of the Court is in accord with the principles just outlined. And, applying them to the Duberstein case, we are in agreement, on the evidence we have set forth, that it cannot be said that the conclusion of the Tax Court was "clearly erroneous." It seems to us plain that as trier of the facts it was warranted in concluding that despite the characterization of the transfer of the Cadillac by the parties and the absence of any obligation, even of a moral nature, to make it, it was at bottom a recompense for Duberstein's past services, or an inducement for him to be of further service in the future. We cannot say with the Court of Appeals that such a conclusion was "mere suspicion" on the Tax Court's part. To us it appears based in the sort of informed experience with human affairs that fact-finding tribunals should bring to this task.

As to Stanton, we are in disagreement. To four of us, it is critical here that the District Court as trier of fact made only the simple and unelaborated finding that the transfer in question was a "gift." To be sure, conciseness is to be strived for, and prolixity avoided, in findings; but, to the four of us, there comes a point where findings become so sparse and conclusory as to give no revelation of what the District Court's concept of the determining facts and legal standard may be. See Matton Oil Transfer Corp. v. The Dynamic, 2 Cir., 123 F.2d 999, 1000–1001. Such conclusory, general findings do not constitute compliance with Rule 52's direction to "find the facts specially and state separately * * * conclusions of law thereon." While the standard of law in this area is not a complex one, we four think the unelaborated finding of ultimate fact here cannot stand as a fulfillment of these requirements. It affords the reviewing court not the semblance of an indication of the legal standard with which the trier of fact has approached his task. For all that appears, the District Court may have viewed the form of the resolution or the simple absence of legal consideration as conclusive. While the judgment of the Court of Appeals cannot stand, the four of us think there must be further proceedings in the District Court looking toward new and adequate findings of fact. In this, we are joined by MR. JUSTICE WHITTAKER, who agrees that the findings were inadequate, although he does not concur generally in this opinion.

Accordingly, in No. 376, the judgment of this Court is that the judgment of the Court of Appeals is reversed, and in No. 546, that the judgment of the Court of Appeals is vacated, and the case is remanded to the District Court for further proceedings not inconsistent with this opinion. It is so ordered.

Judgment of Court of Appeals in No. 376 reversed, and judgment of Court of Appeals in No. 546 vacated, and case remanded to District Court for further proceedings.

MR. JUSTICE HARLAN concurs in the result in No. 376. In No. 546, he would affirm the judgment of the Court of Appeals for the reasons stated by MR. JUSTICE FRANKFURTER.

MR. JUSTICE WHITTAKER, agreeing with Bogardus that whether a particular transfer is or is not a "gift" may involve "a mixed question of law and fact," 302 U.S., at page 39, 58 S.Ct. at page 64, concurs only in the result of this opinion.

MR. JUSTICE DOUGLAS dissents, since he is of the view that in each of these two cases there was a gift under the test which the Court fashioned nearly a quarter of a century ago in Bogardus v. Commissioner, 302 U.S. 34, 58 S.Ct. 61.

MR. JUSTICE BLACK, concurring and dissenting.

I agree with the Court that it was not clearly erroneous for the Tax Court to find as it did in No. 376 that the automobile transfer to Duberstein was not a gift, and so I agree with the Court's opinion and judgment reversing the judgment of the Court of Appeals in that case.

I dissent in No. 546, Stanton v. United States. The District Court found that the $20,000 transferred to Mr. Stanton by his former employer at the end of ten years' service was a gift and therefore exempt from taxation under [§ 102(a)]. I think the finding was not clearly erroneous and that the Court of Appeals was therefore wrong in reversing the District Court's judgment. * * *

MR. JUSTICE FRANKFURTER, concurring in the judgment in No. 376 and dissenting in No. 546.

* * *

On the remand of the Stanton case, the District Court, sitting without a jury, made detailed findings of fact to support its ultimate finding that the payment was a gift. Stanton v. United States, 186 F.Supp. 393 (E.D.N.Y.1960), affirmed on the ground that this finding was not clearly erroneous 287 F.2d 876 (2d Cir.1961).

The Supreme Court decided United States v. Kaiser, 363 U.S. 299, 80 S.Ct. 1204, 4 L.Ed.2d 1233 (1960), as part of the Duberstein and Stanton trilogy. In Kaiser it affirmed a jury finding that strike benefit payments received by a non-union employee from the union were gifts. Because the factual inferences to be drawn from the basic facts were for the jury to decide, the Court held that it was bound by the jury's finding. The dissent concluded that the payments were not made out of benevolence but were designed to achieve union objectives. The Commissioner announced that he will limit Kaiser strictly to its facts, indicating an intent to treat other strike benefit payments as compensation. Rev.Rul. 61–136, 1961–2 C.B. 20. Subsequent strike benefit cases have found the payments taxable. See e.g., Brown v. Commissioner, 398 F.2d 832 (6th Cir.1968). Why did the Supreme Court feel compelled to affirm the jury's finding in Kaiser? Why are most tax cases won or lost in the trial court?

In Olk v. United States, 536 F.2d 876 (9th Cir.1976), reversing 338 F.Supp. 1108 (D.Nev.1975), cert. denied 429 U.S. 920, 97 S.Ct. 317, 50 L.Ed.2d 287 (1976), tokes received by a craps dealer were treated as taxable despite the lower court's finding of a gift. The appellate court deemed it irrelevant that the dominant motive may have been superstition on the part of winning players. Was the Ninth Circuit in Olk, in exercising its appellate function, consistent with the Supreme Court in Kaiser? Administratively, how has the Internal Revenue Service dealt with taxpayers' contentions that tips are not taxable? Reconsider p. 63.

Questions

1. How did the Supreme Court in Duberstein resolve the question of what is a gift for income tax purposes? Does the fact that a wealth holder voluntarily transfers property or cash make it a tax free transfer? Does the absence of consideration received by the transferor necessarily result in an excludable gift? What if the donor's motives are mixed?

2. The Government argued in Duberstein, at footnote 2, that gifts can never be made in a business setting. How did the Supreme Court deal with the Government's proposed test? Was the Government consistent in its position? In Rev.Rul. 131, 1953–2 C.B. 112, the Commissioner concluded that amounts paid by a company for the rehabilitation of employees who suffered personal injury and property damage from a flood were not income to the employee. The Commissioner stressed that the payments were measured by employees' needs. In Rev.Rul. 59–58, 1959–1 C.B. 17, the Commissioner announced a pragmatic, no income rule for:

[T]he value of a turkey, ham, or other item of merchandise of similar nominal value distributed by an employer to an employee at Christmas, or a comparable holiday, as part of a general distribution to employees * * * In view of the small amounts involved, and since it may reasonably be contended * * * that such items constitute excludable gifts * * * the value of such an item of merchandise need not be treated as taxable income * * * The foregoing rules will not apply to distributions of cash * * * regardless of the amount involved.

Does this ruling set forth a valid distinction? Safe harbor rules exist for employee fringe benefits. § 132. How does § 132 handle the situation described in Rev.Rul. 59–58? Consider § 132(a)(4) and (e). Consider the impact of § 102(c) on § 132(a)(4). In narrowing the exclusion for employee gifts, the legislative history indicates:

[T]he committee wishes to clarify that the section 132(e) exclusion under present law for de minimis fringe benefits can apply to employee awards of low value * * *.

3. Although the Supreme Court in Duberstein refused to establish a judicial test for determining whether a gift was intended, by quoting from some of its previous decisions, it did lay down some guidelines for the trier of fact to follow. What were these guidelines? Why was the Supreme Court so reluctant to formulate a judicial definition of a gift?

4. How would Duberstein be decided under § 102(c)(1)? Can a gift to a customer of a business be excluded under § 102(a)? What about a gift to an independent contractor? In other words, how broadly do you interpret the word "employee" in § 102(c)? Does § 102(c) go as far as to adopt the Government's position in footnote 2 in the Duberstein case?

Problem

Hapless, a recent law school graduate, was unable to find a legal position on graduation. He now sells pencils for 10 cents each on the front steps of the law school. Each pencil costs him 2 cents. The same pencil sells for 6 cents in the bookstore. Does Hapless realize income? Consider Reg. § 1.1001–1(e). If you purchased a pencil from Hapless, what basis would you take in the pencil? Consider Reg. § 1.1015–4.

————

Deductibility of Business Gifts and Employees Awards. Section 274(b) provides that business "gifts," which, subject to certain exceptions, are defined as any item excludable from the recipient's gross income under § 102, but are not excludable under any other Code provision (e.g., a tuition scholarship (§ 117)) are deductible by the donor only to the extent of the aggregate of $25 per recipient per year. Business gifts in excess of $25 per year which are treated as a gift by the donee generally constitute a non-deductible business expense for the donor.

Question

What is the effect of §§ 102(c), 132(a)(4) and 274(b) on Rev.Rul. 131 and Rev.Rul. 59–58?

4. GIFTS IN THE CONTEXT OF TESTAMENTARY TRANSFERS

WOLDER v. COMMISSIONER

United States Court of Appeals, Second Circuit, 1974.
493 F.2d 608.

OAKES, CIRCUIT JUDGE:

These two cases, involving an appeal and cross-appeal in the individual taxpayers' case and an appeal by the Commissioner in the estate taxpayer's case, essentially turn on one question: whether an attorney contracting to and performing lifetime legal services for a client receives income when the client, pursuant to the contract, bequeaths a substantial sum to the attorney in lieu of the payment of fees during the client's lifetime. In the individual taxpayers' case, the Tax Court held that the fair market value of the stock and cash received under the client's will constituted taxable income under § 61, Int.Rev. Code of [1986], and was not exempt from taxation as a bequest under § 102 of the Code. From this ruling the individual taxpayers, Victor R. Wolder, the attorney, and his wife, who signed joint returns, appeal.

*   *   *

*   *   *

There is no basic disagreement as to the facts. On or about October 3, 1947, Victor R. Wolder, as attorney, and Marquerite K. Boyce, as client, entered into a written agreement which, after reciting Mr. Wolder's past services on her behalf in an action against her ex-husband for which he had made no charge, consisted of mutual promises, first on the part of Wolder to render to Mrs. Boyce "such legal services as she shall in her opinion personally require from time to time as long as both * * * shall live and not to bill her for such services," and second on the part of Mrs. Boyce to make a codicil to her last will and testament giving and bequeathing to Mr. Wolder or to his estate "my 500 shares of Class B common stock of White Laboratories, Inc." or "such other * * * securities" as might go to her in the event of a merger or consolidation of White Laboratories. Subsequently, in 1957, White Laboratories did merge into Schering Corp. and Mrs. Boyce received 750 shares of Schering common and 500 shares of Schering convertible preferred. In 1964 the convertible preferred was redeemed for $15,845. In a revised will dated April 23, 1965, Mrs. Boyce, true to the agreement with Mr. Wolder, bequeathed to him or his estate the sum of $15,845 and the 750 shares of common stock of Schering Corp. There is no dispute but that Victor R. Wolder had rendered legal services to Mrs. Boyce over her lifetime (though apparently these consisted largely of revising her will) and had not billed her therefor so that he was entitled to performance by her under the agreement, on which she had had a measure of independent legal advice. At least the New York Surrogate's Court (DiFalco, J.) ultimately so found in contested proceedings in which Mrs. Boyce's residuary legatees contended that the will merely provided for payment of a debt and took the position that Wolder was not entitled to payment until he proved the debt in accordance with § 212, New York Surrogate's Court Act.

* * *

* * *

Wolder argues that the legacy he received under Mrs. Boyce's will is specifically excluded from income by virtue of § 102(a), Int.Rev.Code of [1986], which provides that "Gross Income does not include the value of property acquired by gift, bequest, devise or inheritance * * *." See also Treas.Reg. 1.102–1(a). The individual taxpayer, as did dissenting Judge Quealy below, relies upon United States v. Merriam, 263 U.S. 179, 44 S.Ct. 69, 68 L.Ed. 240 (1923), and its progeny for the proposition that the term "bequest" in § 102(a) has not been restricted so as to exclude bequests made on account of some consideration flowing from the beneficiary to the decedent. In *Merriam* the testator made cash bequests to certain persons who were named executors of the estate, and these bequests were " 'in lieu of all compensation or commissions to which they would otherwise be entitled as executors or trustees.' " 263 U.S. at 184, 44 S.Ct. at 70. The Court held nevertheless that the legacies were exempt from taxation, drawing a distinction—which in a day and age when we look to substance and not to form strikes us as of doubtful utility—between cases where "compensation [is] fixed by will for services to be rendered by the executor and [where] a legacy [is paid] to one upon the implied condition that he shall clothe himself with the character of executor." 263 U.S. at 187, 44 S.Ct. at 71. In the former case, Mr. Justice Sutherland said, the executor "must perform the services to earn the compensation" while in the latter case "he need do no more than in good faith comply with the condition [that he be executor] in order to receive the bequest." The Court went on to take the view that the provision in the will that the bequest was in lieu of commissions was simply "an expression of the testator's will that the executor shall not receive statutory allowances for the services he may render." While the distinction drawn in the *Merriam* case hardly stands economic analysis, Bank of New York v. Helvering, 132 F.2d 773 (2d Cir.1943), follows it on the basis that it is controlling law.[7]

But we think that *Merriam* is inapplicable to the facts of this case, for here there is no dispute but that the parties did contract for services

---

7. One also doubts the present day validity of the underlying philosophical premise of Merriam, that "If the words are doubtful, the doubt must be resolved against the government and in favor of the taxpayer." 263 U.S. at 188, 44 S.Ct. at 71. In White v. United States, 305 U.S. 281, 292, 59 S.Ct. 179, 184, 83 L.Ed. 172 (1938), after noting for the majority that it was not "impressed" by this very argument, Mr. Justice Stone said, "It is the function and duty of courts to resolve doubts. We know of no reason why that function should be abdicated in a tax case more than in any other where the rights of suitors turn on the construction of a statute and it is our duty to decide what that construction fairly should be."

and—while the services were limited in nature—there was also no question but that they were actually rendered. Thus the provisions of Mrs. Boyce's will, at least for federal tax purposes, went to satisfy her obligation under the contract. The contract in effect was one for the postponed payment of legal services, i.e., by a legacy under the will for services rendered during the decedent's life.

Moreover, the Supreme Court itself has taken an entirely different viewpoint from *Merriam* when it comes to interpreting § 102(a), or its predecessor, § 22(b)(3), Int.Rev.Code of 1939, in reference to what are gifts. In Commissioner v. Duberstein, 363 U.S. 278, 80 S.Ct. 1190, 4 L.Ed.2d 1218 (1960), the Court held that the true test is whether in actuality the gift is a bona fide gift or simply a method for paying compensation. This question is resolved by an examination of the intent of the parties, the reasons for the transfer, and the parties' performance in accordance with their intentions—"what the basic reason for [the donor's] conduct was in fact—the dominant reason that explains his action in making the transfer." 363 U.S. at 286, 80 S.Ct. at 1197. See also Carrigan v. Commissioner, 197 F.2d 246 (2d Cir.1952); Fisher v. Commissioner, 59 F.2d 192 (2d Cir.1932). There are other cases holding testamentary transfers to be taxable compensation for services as opposed to tax-free bequests. Cotnam v. Commissioner, 263 F.2d 119 (5th Cir.1959); Mariani v. Commissioner, 54 T.C. 135 (1970); Cohen v. United States, 241 F.Supp. 740 (E.D.Mich.1965); Davies v. Commissioner, 23 T.C. 524 (1954). True, in each of these cases the testator did not fulfill his contractual obligation to provide in his will for payment of services rendered by the taxpayer, forcing the taxpayers to litigate the merits of their claims against the estates, whereas in the case at bar the terms of the contract were carried out. This is a distinction without a difference, and while we could decline to follow them in the case at bar, we see no reason to do so.

Indeed, it is to be recollected that § 102 is, after all, an exception to the basic provision in § 61(a) that "Except as otherwise provided in this subtitle, gross income means all income from whatever source derived, including * * * (1) Compensation for services, including fees, commissions and similar items * * *." The congressional purpose is to tax income comprehensively. Commissioner v. Jacobson, 336 U.S. 28, 49, 69 S.Ct. 358, 93 L.Ed. 477 (1949). A transfer in the form of a bequest was the method that the parties chose to compensate Mr. Wolder for his legal services, and that transfer is therefore subject to taxation, whatever its label whether by federal or by local law may be. See also Hort v. Commissioner, 313 U.S. 28, 31, 61 S.Ct. 757, 85 L.Ed. 1168 (1941).

Taxpayer's argument that he received the stock and cash as a "bequest" under New York law and the decisions of the surrogates is thus beside the point. New York law does, of course, control as to the extent of the taxpayer's legal rights to the property in question, but it does not control as to the characterization of the property for federal

income tax purposes.   United States v. Mitchell, 403 U.S. 190, 197, 91
S.Ct. 1763, 29 L.Ed.2d 406 (1971); Commissioner v. Duberstein, 363 U.S.
at 285, 44 S.Ct. at 69; Morgan v. Commissioner, 309 U.S. 78, 80–81, 60
S.Ct. 424, 84 L.Ed. 585 (1940); Higt v. United States, 256 F.2d 795, 800
(2d Cir.1958). New York law cannot be decisive on the question
whether any given transfer is income under § 61(a) or is exempt under
§ 102(a) of the Code. We repeat, we see no difference between the
transfer here made in the form of a bequest and the transfer under
Commissioner v. Duberstein, supra, which was made without consideration, with no legal or moral obligation, and which was indeed a
"common-law gift," but which was nevertheless held not to be a gift
excludable under § 102(a).

* * *

Judgment in the appeal of Victor R. Wolder and Marjorie Wolder
affirmed; judgment in the cross-appeal of the Commissioner reversed
and remanded for proceedings consistent with this opinion * * *.

Although the Wolder case is a situation where an attorney received
compensation for services in the form of a bequest in the client's will,
there are other situations where the facts are not so clear. For
example, an employee who received a bequest in her employer's will
was not taxable despite language in the will stating that the bequest
was "in appreciation of the many years of loyal service and faithful
care rendered me." McDonald v. Commissioner, 2 T.C. 840 (1943).
How should the employer's will have been drafted to avoid a tax
controversy? In Davies v. Commissioner, 23 T.C. 524 (1954), a wealth
holder promised to take care of an individual in his will in return for
that individual's services for the decedent. The payment received by
this individual from the estate in compromise of a claim against the
estate was treated as taxable income. Why was this individual effectively precluded from arguing he received a gift? See Rev.Rul. 67–375,
1967–2 C.B. 60. What about an executor of a decedent's estate who
renders administrative services for the estate without charge because a
bequest was made to the executor in lieu of compensation for these
services? In United States v. Merriam, 263 U.S. 179, 44 S.Ct. 69, 68
L.Ed. 240 (1923), a bequest was made to an executor in lieu of any
compensation or executor fees to which he would have been entitled.
The Supreme Court excluded from gross income the bequest which was
contingent only on the taxpayer's acceptance of the role of executor.
The Court framed the test as whether the beneficiary had to perform
the services to receive the bequest, not whether the bequest was for
services. How did the Second Circuit in Wolder view the Merriam
distinction?

In Lyeth v. Hoey, 305 U.S. 188, 59 S.Ct. 155, 83 L.Ed. 119 (1938),
the Court held that an heir not mentioned in his grandmother's will
could exclude an amount received in settlement of a will contest under
§ 102(a). The Court based its decision on the fact that the grandson

received the settlement "in lieu of" his rights of inheritance under state law. The Court observed that:

> Petitioner was concededly an heir of his grandmother under the Massachusetts statute. It was by virtue of that heirship that he opposed probate of her alleged will [as] * * * invalid because of want of testamentary capacity and undue influence. * * * It was in that situation, facing a trial of the issue of the validity of the will, that the compromise was made by which the heirs, including the petitioner, were to receive certain portions of the decedent's estate.

> * * *

> Respondent agrees that the word "inheritance" as used in the federal statute is not solely applicable to cases of complete intestacy. The portion of the decedent's property which petitioner obtained under the compromise did not come to him through the testator's will. That portion he obtained because of his heirship and to that extent he took in spite of the will and as in case of intestacy. The fact that petitioner received less than the amount of his claim did not alter its nature or the quality of its recognition through the distribution which he did receive. (305 U.S. at 195–196, 59 S.Ct. at 159, 83 L.Ed. at 125.)

Problems

1. Ellen is named as a beneficiary in a living person's will and sells that expectancy. Can she exclude the sales proceeds because they were "in lieu of" a bequest?

2. Can payments received in settlement of any will contest be treated as "in lieu of" an inheritance or a bequest and, therefore, be excludable under § 102(a)? Consider X who claims he is the long lost illegitimate son of the decedent and threatens a will contest because he was not mentioned in the will. If the executor pays him a small amount (as a nuisance settlement) to drop his claim, can X exclude the payment from gross income?

3. Decedent provides in her will that her nephew, Ralph, may purchase, on her death, the family ski chalet for $70,000. At the time of the execution of the will, the chalet was worth $80,000. At death, the chalet was valued at $100,000. Ralph exercises the option to purchase the chalet.

(a) Does the purchase of the chalet result in the realization of income by Ralph?

(b) What is Ralph's basis in the chalet? Consider § 1014.

5. IS AN ANTE–NUPTIAL TRANSFER A GIFT?

FARID–ES–SULTANEH v. COMMISSIONER

United States Court of Appeals, Second Circuit, 1947.
160 F.2d 812.

CHASE, CIRCUIT JUDGE.

The problem presented by this petition is to fix the cost basis to be used by the petitioner in determining the taxable gain on a sale she made in 1938 of shares of corporate stock. She contends that it is the adjusted value of the shares at the date she acquired them because her acquisition was by purchase. The Commissioner's position is that she must use the adjusted cost basis of her transferor because her acquisition was by gift. The Tax Court agreed with the Commissioner and redetermined the deficiency accordingly.

The pertinent facts are not in dispute and were found by the Tax Court as they were disclosed in the stipulation of the parties substantially as follows:

The petitioner is an American citizen who filed her income tax return for the calendar year 1938 with the Collector of Internal Revenue for the Third District of New York and in it reported sales during that year of 12,000 shares of the common stock of the S.S. Kresge Company at varying prices per share, for the total sum of $230,802.36 which admittedly was in excess of their cost to her. How much this excess amounted to for tax purposes depends upon the legal significance of the facts now to be stated.

In December 1923 when the petitioner, then unmarried, and S.S. Kresge, then married, were contemplating their future marriage, he delivered to her 700 shares of the common stock of the S.S. Kresge Company which then had a fair market value of $290 per share. The shares were all in street form and were to be held by the petitioner "for her benefit and protection in the event that the said Kresge should die prior to the contemplated marriage between the petitioner and said Kresge." The latter was divorced from his wife on January 9, 1924, and on or about January 23, 1924 he delivered to the petitioner 1800 additional common shares of S.S. Kresge Company which were also in street form and were to be held by the petitioner for the same purposes as were the first 700 shares he had delivered to her. On April 24, 1924, and when the petitioner still retained the possession of the stock so delivered to her, she and Mr. Kresge executed a written ante-nuptial agreement wherein she acknowledged the receipt of the shares "as a gift made by the said Sebastian S. Kresge, pursuant to this indenture, and as an ante-nuptial settlement, and in consideration of said gift and said ante-nuptial settlement, in consideration of the promise of said Sebastian S. Kresge to marry her, and in further consideration of the consummation of said promised marriage" she released all dower and other marital rights, including the right to her support to which she otherwise would have been entitled as a matter of law when she became his wife. They were married in New York immediately after the ante-nuptial agreement was executed and continued to be husband and wife until the petitioner obtained a final decree of absolute divorce from him on, or about, May 18, 1928. No alimony was claimed by, or awarded to, her.

The stock so obtained by the petitioner from Mr. Kresge had a fair market value of $315 per share on April 24, 1924, and of $330 per share on, or about May 6, 1924, when it was transferred to her on the books of the corporation. She held all of it for about three years, but how much she continued to hold thereafter is not disclosed except as that may be shown by her sales in 1938. Meanwhile her holdings had been increased by a stock dividend of 50 per cent, declared on April 1, 1925; one of 10 to 1 declared on January 19, 1926; and one of 50 per cent, declared on March 1, 1929. Her adjusted basis for the stock she sold in 1938 was $10.66⅔ per share computed on the basis of the fair market value of the shares which she obtained from Mr. Kresge at the time of her acquisition. His adjusted basis for the shares she sold in 1938 would have been $0.159091.

When the petitioner and Mr. Kresge were married he was 57 years old with a life expectancy of 16½ years. She was then 32 years of age with a life expectancy of 33¾ years. He was then worth approximately $375,000,000 and owned real estate of the approximate value of $100,000,000.

The Commissioner determined the deficiency on the ground that the petitioner's stock obtained as above stated was acquired by gift within the meaning of that word as used in § [1015], and, as the transfer to her was after December 31, 1920, used as the basis for determining the gain on her sale of it the basis it would have had in the hands of the donor. This was correct if the just mentioned statute is applicable, and the Tax Court held it was on the authority of Wemyss v. Commissioner, 324 U.S. 303, 65 S.Ct. 652, 89 L.Ed. 958, 156 A.L.R. 1022, and Merrill v. Fahs, 324 U.S. 308, 65 S.Ct. 655, 89 L.Ed. 963.

The issue here presented cannot, however, be adequately dealt with quite so summarily. The Wemyss case determined the taxability to the transferor as a gift, under §§ [2511(a) and 2512(b)], and the applicable regulations, of property transferred in trust for the benefit of the prospective wife of the transferor pursuant to the terms of an antenuptial agreement. It was held that the transfer, being solely in consideration of her promise of marriage, and to compensate her for loss of trust income which would cease upon her marriage, was not for an adequate and full consideration in money or money's worth within the meaning of § [2512(b)], the Tax Court having found that the transfer was not one at arm's length made in the ordinary course of business. But we find nothing in this decision to show that a transfer, taxable as a gift under the gift tax, is ipso facto to be treated as a gift in construing the income tax law.

In Merrill v. Fahs, supra, it was pointed out that the estate and gift tax statutes are in pari materia and are to be so construed. Estate of Sanford v. Commissioner of Internal Revenue, 308 U.S. 39, 44, 60 S.Ct. 51, 84 L.Ed. 20. The estate tax provisions in the Revenue Act of 1916 required the inclusion in a decedent's gross estate of transfers made in contemplation of death, or intended to take effect in possession and enjoyment at or after death except when a transfer was the result of "a bona fide sale for a fair consideration in money or money's worth." The first gift tax became effective in 1924, and provided inter alia, that where an exchange or sale of property was for less than a fair consideration in money or money's worth the excess should be taxed as a gift. Rev.Act of 1924, § 320, 43 Stat. 314, 26 U.S.C.A. Int.Rev.Acts, page 81. While both taxing statutes thus provided, it was held that a release of dower rights was a fair consideration in money or money's worth. Ferguson v. Dickson, 3 Cir., 300 F. 961, certiorari denied 266 U.S. 628, 45 S.Ct. 126, 69 L.Ed. 476; McCaughn v. Carver, 3 Cir., 19 F.2d 126. Following that, Congress in 1926 replaced the words "fair consideration" in the 1924 Act limiting the deductibility of claims against an estate with the words "adequate and full consideration in money or money's worth" and in 1932 the gift tax statute as enacted limited consideration in the same way. Rev.Act 1932, § 503. Although Congress in 1932 also expressly provided that the release of marital rights should not be treated as a consideration in money or money's worth in administering the estate tax law, Rev.Act of 1932, § 804, 26 U.S.C.A. Int.Rev.Acts, page 642, and failed to include such a provision in the gift tax statute, it was held that the gift tax law should be construed to the same effect. Merrill v. Fahs, supra.

We find in this decision no indication, however, that the term "gift" as used in the income tax statute should be construed to include a transfer which, if made when the gift tax were effective, would be taxable to the transferor as a gift merely because of the special provisions in the gift tax statute defining and restricting consideration for gift tax purposes. A fortiori, it would seem that limitations found in the estate tax law upon according the usual legal effect to proof that a transfer was made for a fair consideration should not be imported into the income tax law except by action of Congress.

In our opinion the income tax provisions are not to be construed as though they were in pari materia with either the estate tax law or the gift tax statutes. They are aimed at the gathering of revenue by taking for public use given percentages of what the statute fixes as net taxable income. Capital gains and losses are, to the required or permitted extent, factors in determining net taxable income. What is known as the basis for computing gain or loss on transfers of property is established by statute in those instances when the resulting gain or loss is recognized for income tax purposes and the basis for succeeding sales or exchanges will, theoretically at least, level off tax-wise any hills and valleys in the consideration passing either way on previous sales or exchanges. When Congress provided that gifts should not be treated as taxable income to the donee there was, without any correlative provisions fixing the basis of the gift to the donee, a loophole which enabled the donee to make a subsequent transfer of the property and take as the basis for computing gain or loss its value when the gift was made. Thus it was possible to exclude from taxation any increment in value during the donor's holding and the donee might take advantage of any shrinkage in such increment after the acquisition by gift in computing gain or loss upon a subsequent sale or exchange. It was to close this loophole that Congress provided that the donee should take the donor's basis when property was transferred by gift. Report of Ways and Means Committee (No. 350, P. 9, 67th Cong., 1st Sess.). This change in the statute affected only the statutory net taxable income. The altered statute prevented a transfer by gift from creating any change in the basis of the property in computing gain or loss on any future transfer. In any individual instance the change in the statute would but postpone taxation and presumably would have little effect on the total volume of income tax revenue derived over a long period of time and from many taxpayers. Because of this we think that a transfer which should be classed as a gift under the gift tax law is not necessarily to be treated as a gift income-tax-wise. Though such a consideration as this petitioner gave for the shares of stock she acquired from Mr. Kresge might not have relieved him from liability for a gift tax, had the present gift tax then been in effect, it was nevertheless a fair consideration which prevented her taking the shares as a gift under the income tax law since it precluded the existence of a donative intent.

Although the transfers of the stock made both in December 1923, and in the following January by Mr. Kresge to this taxpayer are called a gift in the ante-nuptial agreement later executed and were to be for the protection of his prospective bride if he died before the marriage was consummated, the "gift" was contingent upon his death before such marriage, an event that did not occur. Consequently, it would appear that no absolute gift was made before the ante-nuptial contract was executed and that she took title to the stock under its terms, viz: in consideration for her promise to marry him coupled with her promise to relinquish all rights in and to his property which she would otherwise acquire by the marriage. Her inchoate interest in the property of her affianced husband greatly exceeded the value of the stock transferred to her. It was a fair consideration under ordinary legal concepts of that term for the transfers of the stock by him. Ferguson v. Dickson, supra; McCaughn v. Carver, supra. She performed the contract under the terms of which the stock was transferred to her and held the shares not as a donee but as a purchaser for a fair consideration.

As the decisive issue is one of law only, the decision of the Tax Court interpreting the applicable statutory provisions has no peculiar finality and is reviewable. Bingham v. Commissioner, 325 U.S. 365, 65 S.Ct. 1232, 89 L.Ed. 1670.

Decision reversed.

CLARK, CIRCUIT JUDGE (dissenting).

The opinion accepts two assumptions, both necessary to the result. The first is that definitions of gift under the gift and estate tax statutes are not useful, in fact are directly opposed to, definitions of gift under the capital-gains provision of the income tax statute. The second is that the circumstances here of a transfer of the stock some months before the marriage showed, contrary to the conclusions of the Tax Court, a purchase of dower rights, rather than a gift. The first I regard as doubtful; the second, as untenable.

It is true that Commissioner of Internal Revenue v. Wemyss, 324 U.S. 303, 65 S.Ct. 652, 89 L.Ed. 958, and Merrill v. Fahs, 324 U.S. 308, 65 S.Ct. 655, 89 L.Ed. 963, which would require the transactions here to be considered a gift, dealt with estate and gift taxes. But no strong reason has been advanced why what is a gift under certain sections of the Revenue Code should not be a gift under yet another section. As a matter of fact these two cases indicate that the donative intent of the common law is not an essential ingredient of a gift for tax purposes. Conversely love, affection, and the promise of future marriage will not be consideration adequate to avoid the gift tax. If that is so, it would seem that these should not be sufficient to furnish new and higher cost bases for computing capital gains on ultimate sale. The Congressional purpose would seem substantially identical—to prevent a gap in the law whereby taxes on gifts or on capital gains could be avoided or reduced by judicious transfers within the family or intimate group.

But decision on that point might well be postponed, since, to my mind, the other point should be decisive. Kresge transferred the stock to petitioner more than three months before their marriage. Part was given when Kresge was married to another woman. At these times petitioner had no dower or other rights in his property. If Kresge died before the wedding, she could never secure dower rights in his lands. Yet she would nevertheless keep the stock. Indeed the specifically stated purpose of the transfer was to protect her against his death prior to marriage. It is therefore difficult to perceive how her not yet acquired rights could be consideration for the stock. Apparently the parties themselves shared this difficulty, for in their subsequent instrument releasing dower rights they referred to the stock transfer as a gift and an antenuptial settlement.

If the transfer be thus considered a sale, as the majority hold, it would seem to follow necessarily that this valuable consideration (equivalent to one-third for life in land valued at one hundred million dollars) should have yielded sizable taxable capital gains to Kresge, as well as a capital loss to petitioner when eventually she sold. I suggest these considerations as pointing to the unreality of holding as a sale what seems clearly only intended as a stimulating cause to eventual matrimony.

Since Judge Murdock in the Tax Court found this to be a gift, not a sale, and since this decision is based in part at least upon factual considerations, it would seem binding upon us. At any rate, it should be persuasive of the result we ought to reach.

Notes and Questions

1. Why did the government in Farid-Es-Sultaneh argue that Farid acquired the stock as a gift? Is the issue the deferral of the tax on the gain or the exclusion from taxation? Consider § 1015(a). If a deferral is involved, then who is taxed on the gain?

2. Because Farid did not receive the stock as a gift under § 102, the court concluded that she acquired the stock by purchase in exchange for her marital rights. Consequently, her basis as a purchaser would be her cost (equal to the fair market value of the stock received) under § 1012, and not a carryover basis under § 1015(a). Because Farid gave up her marital rights in exchange for the stock, did she have a gain in 1924 equal to the difference between the value of the stock received (her amount realized) and the basis in the property given up (her marital rights)? Consider the Davis case (p. 632) §§ 1041, 1015(e), and Rev.Rul. 67–221, 1967–2 C.B. 63 which states:

> Under the terms of a divorce decree and in accordance with a property settlement agreement, which was incorporated in the divorce decree, the husband transferred his interest in an apartment building to his former wife in consideration for and in discharge of her dower rights. The marital rights the former wife relinquished are equal in value to the value of the property she agreed to accept in exchange for those rights. *Held*, there is no gain or loss to the wife on the transfer and the basis of the property to the wife is its fair market value on the date of the transfer.

Does the basis of a wife's marital rights equal their value? How would a wife acquire this basis? Can the Commissioner's position be justified on the ground that a spouse is not taxable on support received while married or on property received by inheritance or bequest from a deceased spouse?

Problems

1. Eligible purchased, several years ago, stock for $10 per share. He gave 100 shares of this stock to Beautiful, his girl friend, in exchange for her signing an ante-nuptial agreement releasing the marital rights she would acquire in his estate on their marriage. At the time she received the stock, it had a market value of $100 per share. Shortly after the execution of the ante-nuptial agreement and the transfer of the stock, Eligible and Beautiful married. A few years later they were divorced. Beautiful, immediately after the divorce, sold the stock for $125 per share.

(a) Did the transfer of stock to Beautiful constitute a gift? Consider the Duberstein and Farid-Es-Sultaneh cases.

(b) Did Eligible realize a gain on the exchange? Should he have transferred high basis (in comparison to market value) or low basis stock? What is the character of the gain? Would Eligible have realized income if Beautiful merely released her marital rights without receiving any property in return?

(c) Did Beautiful realize income when she received the stock in the exchange? Recall the nontaxability of imputed income. By administrative practice a wife is not taxed on the acquisition of support rights on marriage or the support provided during marriage.

(d) What is Beautiful's basis in the stock? Consider § 1012. What is the amount of Beautiful's gain when she sold the stock for $125 per share? What is the character of the gain?

2. In terms of the transferee's basis and realization of gain or loss, why should a difference exist between:

(a) property transfers between spouses during marriage or to a former spouse if incident to a divorce and made after July 18, 1984. Such transfers are deemed a gift because of the intra-family division of wealth. A gift produces two income tax consequences: (1) the donor does not realize any gain; and (2) the donee carries over the donor's basis for the property. Consider § 1041, applying to transfers made after July 18, 1984, to a spouse or a former spouse, if incident to a divorce.

(b) property transfers between individuals in consideration of marriage.

6. LIFE INSURANCE

In General. A life insurance policy is a contract in which an insurance company (the insurer) promises to pay a specified amount (the face amount) to a designated person (the beneficiary) on the death of a named person (the insured) in consideration of payments (premiums) usually made by the person who owns the rights under the policy (the owner). Typically, the insured and the owner are the same person. The owner of a policy may assign his rights to another individual and, thereupon, the insured and the owner then are different persons.

Many different types of life insurance policies are written. We will consider two types: "term" and "ordinary" life insurance policies. A term policy insures against the death of the insured during a limited period of time. If the insured does not die during the policy term, the insurer retains the premiums. If the insured dies during the policy term, the insurer pays the beneficiary the face amount of the policy. In short, a term policy provides the insured with protection against his dependents being left without enough resources to provide for their economic needs. Since term insurance premiums reflect mortality rates, the amount of the annual premium increases with age.

An ordinary life insurance policy, which generally requires the payment of constant annual premiums, consists of three elements: pure insurance, savings, and mortality gain (or loss). A portion of the policy premiums on an ordinary life insurance policy are used to provide pure (term) insurance. The insurer invests the savings element of the policy premiums. The investment of the savings element produces earnings and thereby builds the cash value of the policy, that is, the amount for which the policy can be redeemed (or borrowed against) prior to the insured's death, at the maturity of the policy, or the conversion of the policy into a paid-up policy in which case no further policy premiums need be paid. If the insured dies while a loan against the policy is outstanding, the beneficiary receives the face amount of the policy less the unpaid loan balance. A beneficiary never receives the cash value and the face amount of the policy. The savings element also offsets the increasing cost of insurance as the insured gets older. A mortality gain (or loss) also enters into each policy.

Assume an insured takes out a $100,000 ordinary life insurance policy at age 45. The insured dies at age 65. The beneficiary receives the $100,000 face amount of the policy, but assume the insured paid net premiums equal to $60,000. The beneficiary thus receives a $40,000 "profit" on the policy. However, this approach is not accurate. By dying prematurely, the insured's beneficiary receives a mortality "gain" of $67,700 (which is taken from the mortality "losers," i.e., those individuals who live beyond their life expectancies) and $12,300 in interest earned on the $20,000 portion of the premiums invested as a savings element. (The cash surrender value of the policy is $32,300 at the time of death.)

Proceeds of a life insurance policy paid by reason of the death of the insured are generally excluded from the beneficiary's gross income. § 101(a)(1). The life insurance proceeds paid by reason of the insured's death are excluded regardless of the person or entity to whom paid or whether the payment is made directly or in trust. Reg. § 1.101–1(a)(1). Note that the proceeds paid on the death of an insured under an ordinary life policy includes interest carried on the portion of the premiums invested in the savings portion of the policy (or $12,300 in the above example), the amount put into the savings feature ($20,000), and a mortality gain ($67,700).

Higher bracket taxpayers may also purchase life insurance (so-called universal life insurance) with large savings and interest elements. In a typical universal life insurance policy, the amounts and frequency of the premium payments are determined by the policy holder and may be increased or decreased at any time. The policy holder may switch back and forth between ordinary life and term coverage and may increase or decrease the amount of coverage. To permit a variation in potential insurance plans, the policy accords the policy holder flexibility in determining the amount and frequency of premium payments as well as the ability to specify and change the policy's maturity date. The cash value of the policy, at any time, equals the sum of the net premium for the period in question (gross premium paid less expense charges), plus the cash value for the preceding period, increased by one period's interest for this combined sum, and reduced by the cost of insurance for the period. The insurance company guarantees a minimum rate of interest for the life of the policy. The company may increase this rate in advance of each policy year to provide excess interest. The company may also reduce the cost of term insurance in advance of each policy year.

A universal life insurance policy permits a policy holder to invest a substantial cash fund without increasing the amount of pure insurance protection offered by the contract. The increased cash fund, represented by the policy holder's account with the insurance company, earns interest for the policy holder, but the policy holder is not subject to tax consequences on any interest credited to his account. The interest may be used to fund future insurance costs on the policy or the policy holder may cash in the policy prior to maturity and withdraw the entire cash value at that time. In short, a universal life policy may be used as a vehicle for tax-deferred savings.

In response to the development of the universal life insurance policy Congress enacted § 101(f) in 1982 which provides guidelines a universal life insurance contract must meet if the policy is to be treated as life insurance for Federal income tax purposes. The guidelines contained in § 101(f) with respect to the proceeds of "flexible premium contracts" issued before January 1, 1985, payable by reason of death, and in § 7702 with respect to "life insurance contracts" issued after December 31, 1984, must be met both on the purchase of the policy and during the duration of the contract in order for the amounts received to be excluded from gross income. Congress designed the guidelines to prevent policies with extensive savings features and minimal pure (term) insurance protection from qualifying for the exclusion. By meeting the guidelines designed to ensure that a universal life insurance policy provides a minimum amount of term insurance protection at all times, a universal life insurance policy is treated as a life insurance contract with all the benefits flowing from such a designation.

Problems

1. Ellen, age 35, is considering the purchase of a 25-year endowment policy with an annual premium of $3,500, and a face amount of $100,000. The face amount of the policy is payable on the earlier of: (1) the insured's death prior to reaching age 60 or (2) the insured reaching age 60.

(a) What are the tax consequences for the policy beneficiary if the insured dies at age 50? Consider § 101(a).

(b) i. What are the tax consequences to the insured if she lives to age 60 and collects the face amount of $100,000 on the maturity of the policy? Consider § 101(a), § 72(e)(1)(A), (e)(5)(A), (C) and (E), and (e)(6) (A).

ii. Is § 72(e)(6) sound, in view of the fact that part of the premiums paid went to pay for the cost of the pure (term) insurance feature of the policy?

2. Ted Player is considering a certificate of deposit, an annuity, or the savings element of an ordinary life insurance policy as an investment vehicle. What tax and practical recommendations would you make among the three alternatives? Reconsider Problem 2 at page 156.

3. Infirm, 72 years old and in poor health, purchases a paid-up life insurance policy with a face amount of $100,000. He paid a $70,000 premium for this policy. At the same time, Infirm purchased a single payment annuity from the same insurance company for $30,000. The annuity will pay him $687.50 a month for the rest of his life, payments to commence immediately. Infirm named his grandson as the beneficiary

under the life insurance policy. Long-term Treasury bonds were yielding
8¼% at the time Infirm purchased both policies. Can the grandson
exclude the entire $100,000 of insurance proceeds? Can Infirm apply an
exclusion ratio under § 72 to exclude a portion of each annuity payment?
See Rev.Rul. 65–57, 1965–1 C.B. 56.

4. (a) Assume an insured purchased a term insurance policy. Should
the proceeds of that policy, less the premiums paid, be included in the gross
income of the beneficiary?

(b) Assume an insured purchased an ordinary life insurance policy.
Should the earnings on the savings element of an ordinary life policy be
allowed to accumulate without tax and eventually be paid tax free to the
beneficiary? What is the rationale for not taxing a beneficiary on the
accumulated savings element of an ordinary life insurance policy? Consider the following excerpt in deciding whether this exclusion is justified, and
reconsider the question at p. 264.

RICHARD GOODE, THE INDIVIDUAL INCOME TAX
126–127, 129–133 (Rev.Ed.1976).

* * *

Pure Insurance Proceeds

Pure life insurance proceeds are death benefits other than the
return of the policyholder's accumulated savings and the distribution of
interest income. These proceeds represent an increase in net worth of
the beneficiary and are income according to the Haig-Simons definition.[8] Life insurance is intended to replace part of the income that the
insured person would have earned if he had continued at work, and the
earned income would have been included in AGI [adjusted gross income].

An objection to including life insurance proceeds in taxable income
is that they resemble bequests, which are not included. Actually,
however, the close parallel is between a bequest and the return of the
insured person's own contribution, not between a bequest and pure
insurance proceeds. A bequest consists of property accumulated out of
income by the deceased or an earlier owner; when originally received it
was exposed to tax to the same degree as other income arising at that
time from the same source. The pure insurance proceeds, on the other
hand, are a new income item which partly replaces expected future
earnings.

Nevertheless, there are good reasons for the continued exclusion of
pure insurance proceeds from AGI. The death of the insured is often a
time of economic loss for the family and therefore an inconvenient
moment for paying an additional income tax. Application of graduated
income tax rates to lump-sum insurance settlements would be harsh
unless relief were granted, and the usual income-averaging plans might

8. The Haig-Simons definition of income is discussed at page 54.—Eds.

not be suitable for this purpose. There is, moreover, a social interest in encouraging individual efforts to provide for one's dependents. No close substitute exists for the pure insurance element of life insurance policies as a means for safeguarding dependents. In several countries, public approval of life insurance is expressed, not only by excluding pure insurance proceeds from taxable income, but also by allowing a deduction for a limited amount of insurance premiums.

INTEREST INCOME

Interest on personal savings built up through life insurance policies differs in an important respect from pure insurance proceeds. The interest income is related to the saving-investment features of insurance policies rather than their protective features.

* * *

The arguments that justify the exclusion of pure insurance proceeds from taxable income do not apply to interest on policy reserves. The interest income accrues as savings build up, not just at the time of family misfortune. Whereas no close substitutes for life insurance are available to an individual as a means of protecting his dependents against the risk of premature loss of his earning capacity, the saving provisions of insurance contracts are only one of a wide range of investment media. The benefit to a policyholder from the preferential treatment of interest on life insurance reserves depends on the extent to which he uses insurance as an investment rather than on the amount of pure insurance coverage for his dependents he carries.

* * *

The preferential tax treatment of interest earned on policy reserves makes possible a larger net yield on saving through life insurance than could be obtained if this interest were taxed in the same way as other investment income. Savers who wish to avail themselves of the tax shelter, however, must incur costs for insurance protection and loading charges. This may not be a disadvantage for those who desire life insurance for its own sake, especially since saving and insurance can be combined in widely different proportions. It may, however, diminish the attractiveness of the tax shelter to wealthy people, who have less need for life insurance protection than people who depend mainly on earned income. Among investors, moreover, the management skill and guaranteed minimum return associated with a life insurance policy are more attractive to people of moderate means than to those with large resources. For those in high tax brackets, municipal bonds offer tax exemption without the necessity of paying for life insurance company services. The net rate of interest earned by life insurance companies was higher than the yield of high-grade tax-exempt securities in 1950 and 1960, but in 1970 this relationship was reversed.

* * *

The case for ending the privileged tax status of savings through life insurance appears to be much more a matter of equity than of the desirability of correcting a distortion in the use of saving. Equal treatment of life insurance savings and fully taxable savings outlets would require that the accrued interest on life insurance policy reserves be allocated annually to policyholders and included in their AGI, even though the interest was not currently received in cash. The procedures necessary to carry out this revision would be bothersome for the government, insurance companies, and policyholders.

The insurance companies do not routinely allocate interest earnings to individual policies; their calculations relate to large classes of policies and policyholders. The companies would have to be required to make individual allocations. For participating policies, which are eligible to share in surplus earnings through dividends and which account for three-fifths of total life insurance, the allocation could appropriately be made by applying the actual earned interest rate to the average policy reserve. The interest rate would be net of investment expenses and company taxes. Policy dividends would be treated as a reduction of premium and excluded from AGI as they now are. For nonparticipating policies, the allocation would be made at the guaranteed rate provided in the policy.

An alternative procedure, which would be simpler but less satisfactory, would be to allocate to each policyholder an amount equal to the increase in the cash surrender value of his policy during the year, minus the premium paid. This procedure is similar to the rule now followed when the proceeds are paid for reasons other than death, with the important modification that the income would be reportable annually. As explained above, the cost of current insurance protection would, in effect, be charged against interest earnings, with the result that the greater part of this income would continue to escape tax.

Allocation of interest to individual policies and company reporting to policyholders and the Internal Revenue Service would not ensure that all of the income would appear on tax returns. Special collection procedures might be needed. For participating policies, the companies might be required to withhold tax from policy dividends, but this procedure would be inapplicable to nonparticipating policies and unsuitable for participating policies when interest earnings exceeded policy dividends. "Withholding" by the companies might have to take the form of collecting an addition to the annual premium which would be remitted to the Internal Revenue Service and credited to the policyholder.

Further study would be required to ascertain whether the inconvenience and expense for the insurance companies and the government would be as great as they at first appear to be. Consideration should be given to the possibilities of using automatic data processing, which has been installed by the large insurance companies and by the Internal Revenue Service. Consideration might also be given to an exemption from current reporting requirements for policies with small reserves, thus eliminating many small items.

An alternative approach would be to defer reporting and taxation of interest income until it is realized through loan, surrender or maturity of the policy, or death of the insured. This would allow tax deferral but would eliminate the permanent exclusion of a large part of interest on policy reserves. The approach would be subject to the same charge of harshness and inconvenience to taxpayers as mentioned in the comments on pure insurance proceeds. It might be acceptable, nevertheless, if applied only to new policies, inasmuch as the policy-holders would have been placed on notice about their future liabilities.

In light of the objections to the methods of taxing policyholders' interest income considered above, it is not clear what, if any, revision of the law should be adopted. The proven adaptability of the income tax to complex situations, however, encourages the hope that a way of improving the present situation can be discovered. The effectiveness of any plan for the taxation of policyholders' interest income would be enhanced if interest on state and local government securities were also taxed. Otherwise, savers could continue to avoid tax on interest income by switching from life insurance to tax-exempt bonds.

* * *

Distribution of Insurance Proceeds (Settlement Options). At death the distribution of the proceeds of a life insurance policy may be handled in one of four ways:

(1) lump sum payment to the primary or secondary beneficiary;

(2) lump sum payment to the insured's estate or executor;

(3) policy proceeds placed in trust by designating a trustee of a trust as the policy beneficiary. The trustee may hold and administer the policy proceeds under a testamentary or living (inter vivos) trust;

(4) policy settlement options. The proceeds may be left with the insurance company as money manager and paid out under one of several policy settlement options. The insured may, during his life-time designate the option, which designation may or may not be binding on the beneficiary. The settlement options consist of the following two major varieties:

(a) an interest option whereby the insurance company retains the proceeds and the beneficiary only receives the interest on the proceeds until the time agreed on for the payment of the fund in a lump sum; or

(b) a variety of installment options including:

(1) a fixed amount to be paid periodically until the pro-ceeds, with interest, are exhausted.

(2) a fixed amount to be paid periodically for a specified number of years with the amount of each installment to include interest and to liquidate the amount of the insurance proceeds at the end of the stated period; or

(3) an annuity to be purchased with the policy proceeds for the lifetime of the primary beneficiary, perhaps with a guaranteed minimum number of payments.

Problems

1. Goodlife, as part of his divorce settlement, transfers a $100,000 ordinary life insurance policy on his life to his wife in return for her promise to release all marital rights she has in his estate. He agrees to continue to pay the premiums on this policy. At the time of the transfer, the policy has a cash surrender value of $45,000. Goodlife died shortly thereafter, and his ex-wife collected the $100,000 insurance proceeds. Can any part of the proceeds be included in her gross income? Consider §§ 101(a)(2) and 1041.

2. Assume Goodlife names his son the beneficiary of the $100,000 ordinary life insurance policy. Goodlife executed a settlement option permitting the insurer to hold the proceeds intact, pay interest to the son in amount equal to $10,000 per year, and to pay over the $100,000 principal to the son (or his estate) in ten years. Can the son exclude from gross income the interest and the policy proceeds? Consider § 101(c) and (d).

7. PRIZES AND AWARDS

Prizes and awards were viewed as sufficiently unique to merit separate treatment from that accorded gifts.

In general. The Tax Reform Act of 1986 generally repeals the prior exclusion for prizes and awards. A prize or award may qualify for an exclusion under § 74(b) only if: (1) received for achievements in fields such as charity, sciences, or the arts; (2) the recipient has not specifically applied for the prize or award; (3) the recipient is not required to render substantial future services as a condition of receiving it; and (4) the recipient designates that the prize or award be transferred by the payor to a governmental unit or a tax-exempt organization contributions to which are deductible under §§ 170(c)(1) or 170(c)(2). If the conditions of § 74(b) are met, the prize or award is excluded from the winner's gross income and neither the winner nor the payor receives a charitable contribution deduction.

In sharply narrowing the exclusion for prizes and awards, the legislative history indicates:

> Prizes and awards generally increase an individual's net worth in the same manner as any other receipt of an equivalent amount adds to the individual's economic well-being. * * * Accordingly, the committee believes that prizes and awards should generally be includible in income even if received due to achievement in fields such as the arts and sciences.

> In addition, the committee is concerned about problems of complexity that have arisen as a result of the [prior] law exclusion * * *. The questions of what constitutes a qualifying form of achievement, whether an individual took action to enter a contest or proceeding, and

whether a prize or award involve rendering "substantial" services, have all caused some difficulty in this regard. * * * (Tax Reform Act of (1986), Report of the Committee on Ways and Means, House of Representatives on H.R. 3838, 99th Cong., 1st Sess. 104 (1985)).

Employee Achievement Awards. Pursuant to § 74(c), an exclusion exists, subject to specified dollar limitations considered in the next paragraph, for an employee achievement award, i.e., a length of service or safety award. § 274(j)(3)(A). A length of service award cannot qualify for the exclusion if it is received during the employee's first five years of employment for the employer making the award or if the employee received a length of service achievement award (except if excludable under § 132(e)(1)) from the employer during that year or any of the four previous years. § 274(j)(4)(B). An award for safety achievement cannot qualify for the exclusion made to an ineligible employee (as defined in § 274(j)(4)(C)(ii)) or if, during the year, employee awards for safety achievement were awarded by the employer to more than 10 percent of the employer's eligible employees (except if excludable under § 132(e)(1)).

The employer's deduction limit for employee achievement awards for length of service and safety provided to the same employee during the taxable year generally cannot exceed a cost to the employer of $400. § 274(j)(2)(A). The employer's deduction limitation for qualified plan awards, as defined in § 274(j)(3)(B), during the taxable year cannot exceed a cost to the employer of $1,600. § 274(j)(2)(B). The $400 and $1600 limitations cannot be added to allow deductions exceeding $1600 in the aggregate for employee achievement awards made to the same employee in a taxable year. § 274(j)(2)(B).

If the cost of an employee achievement award is fully deductible by an employer under § 274(j), then the fair market value of the award (not the cost of the award to the employer) is excludible from the employee's gross income. § 274(c)(1). If any part of the cost of an employee achievement award exceeds the amount allowable as a deduction by an employer as a result of the dollar limitations set forth in § 274(j), then the exclusion does not apply to the entire fair market value of the award. In such a case, the employee includes in gross income the greater of:

    1) an amount equal to the portion of the cost to the employer of the award that is not allowable as a deduction to the employer (but not an amount in excess of the fair market value of the award) or

    2) the amount by which the fair market value of the award exceeds the maximum dollar amount allowable as a deduction to the employer.

The remaining portion of the fair market value of the award is not included in the employee's gross income. § 74(c)(1)(B).

Except to the extent §§ 74(c) or 132(e) apply, the fair market value of an employee award is includible in the employee's gross income under § 61(a)(1) and is not excludible under § 102. The legislative history indicates:

> For purposes of sections 74 and 274 * * * an employee award that is excludable under section 132(e) is disregarded in applying the rules regarding how frequently an individual may receive a length of service award, or how many employees of an employer may receive a safety achievement award in the same taxable year. Under appropri-ate circumstances, however, the fact that an employer makes a prac-tice of giving to its employees length of service or safety achievement awards that qualify under section 74 and 274 may affect the question of whether other items given to such employees (particularly if given by reason of length of service or safety achievement) qualify as de minimis fringe benefits under section 132(e). * * * Moreover, in some cases the fact that a particular employee receives items having the maximum fair market value consistent, respectively, with the employee achievement award and the de minimis fringe benefit exclu-sions may suggest that the employer's practice is not de minimis. This is particularly so when employee awards and other items, purportedly within the scope of section 132(e), are provided to the same individual in the same year. Tax Reform Act of 1986, Senate Finance Committee Report on H.R. 3838, 99th Cong. 2d Sess. 53 (1986).

Problem

Cool Air Corporation, which manufactures air conditioners, wishes to give Zenia, a long-time employee, a gold watch on her retirement. The item has a cost to the corporation of $700 and a fair market value of $1000.

a. How should the transaction be structured so the value of the watch will not be included in Zenia's gross income? Consider §§ 102, 74(c), 274(j), and 132(e). What if the watch is not a qualified plan award as defined in § 274(j)(2)(B) and (j)(3)(B)? Consider § 74(c)(2).

b. What must the corporation do to receive a deduction under § 162(a) for the entire cost of the watch? Consider § 274(j).

Question

Should the exclusion for all employee awards be repealed? Consider the following excerpt:

OFFICE OF THE SECRETARY, DEPARTMENT OF THE TREASURY, TAX REFORM FOR FAIRNESS, SIM-PLICITY, AND ECONOMIC GROWTH
Vol. 2 at 45–46 (1984).

REASONS FOR CHANGE

A gift for tax purposes is a transfer of property or money attributa-ble to detached and disinterested generosity, motivated by affection, respect, admiration, or charity. The on-going business relationship between an employer and employee is generally inconsistent with the disinterest necessary to establish a gift for tax purposes. Moreover, in the unusual circumstances where an employee award truly has no business motivation, it cannot consistently be deducted as an ordinary and necessary expense of the employer's business.

Current law not only allows employee awards to be characterized as gifts but provides a tax incentive for such characterization. The amount of an employee award treated as a gift is excluded from the income of the employee, and the employer may nevertheless deduct the award to the extent it does not exceed certain dollar limits. Even to the extent an award exceeds those limits, gift characterization produces a net tax advantage if the employee's marginal tax rate exceeds that of the employer.

Current law also generates substantial administrative costs and complexity by requiring the characterization of employee awards to turn on the facts and circumstances of each particular case. The dedication of Internal Revenue Service and taxpayer resources to this issue is inappropriate, since relatively few employee awards represent true gifts and since the amounts involved are frequently not substantial.

PROPOSAL

Gift treatment would generally be denied for all employee awards of tangible personal property. Such awards would ordinarily be treated as taxable compensation, but in appropriate circumstances would also be subject to dividend or other non-gift characterization. It is anticipated that a de minimis award of tangible personal property would be excludable by the employee under rules of current law concerning de minimis fringe benefits.

* * *

ANALYSIS

Available data concerning employee awards of tangible personal property is incomplete. Surveys indicate that businesses made gifts to employees totalling approximately $400 million in 1983. It is unclear what portion of these gifts were in the form of tangible personal property; however, the majority of these gifts were less than $25 in value. Less than ten percent of all employees are covered by an employer plan for such benefits. Thus, the proposal would affect few employees and would promote horizontal equity.

8. QUALIFIED SCHOLARSHIPS

Section 117(a) excludes from gross income an amount received as a "qualified scholarship" by an individual who is a candidate for a degree (as defined in Reg. § 1.117–3(e)) at an educational organization (as defined in § 170(b)(1)(A)(ii)). The term "qualified scholarship" is a scholarship or fellowship grant that is received to be used, and is in fact used, for: (1) tuition and fees required for enrollment or attendence at an educational organization and (2) fees, books, supplies, and equipment required for courses at such educational organization. § 117(b). No exclusion is provided for nondegree candidates. Amounts designated or earmarked for other purposes, such as room and board, do not constitute an excludable scholarship or fellowship. Furthermore, any amount received as a scholarship or a tuition reduction representing payment for teaching, research, or other services by the student required as a condition of receiving a qualified scholarship is includible in gross income. § 117(c).

In narrowing the reach of the exclusion for scholarships and fellowships, the legislative history indicates:

> * * * The committee believes that the exclusion for scholarships should be targeted specifically for the purpose of educational benefits, and should not encompass other items which would otherwise constitute nondeductible personal expenses. * * * In addition, under the [Act], the committee has increased the income level at which individuals become subject to tax. Thus, grants of nonexcludable amounts based on financial need may not be subject to tax, if the amounts (together with other income) do not place the recipient above the taxable income threshold.

> Under [prior] law, controversies * * * [arose] over whether a particular stipend made in an educational setting [constituted] a scholarship or compensation for services. In particular, numerous court cases * * * involved resident physicians and graduate teaching fellows who [sought]—often notwithstanding substantial case authority to the contrary—to exclude income payments received for caring for hospitalized patients, for teaching undergraduate college students, or for doing research which insures to the benefit of the grantor. The limitation on the section 117 exclusion * * * and the repeal of the special rule relating to degree candidates who must perform services as a condition of receiving a degree, should lessen these problems. Tax Reform Act of [1986], Report of the Committee on Ways and Means, House of Representatives on H.R. 3838, 99th Cong., 1st Sess. 100–101 (1985).

BINGLER v. JOHNSON

Supreme Court of the United States, 1969.
394 U.S. 741, 89 S.Ct. 1439, 22 L.Ed.2d 695.

MR. JUSTICE STEWART delivered the opinion of the Court.

We are called upon in this case to examine for the first time § 117 of the Internal Revenue Code of [1986], which excludes from a taxpayer's gross income amounts received as "scholarships" and "fellowships." The question before us concerns the tax treatment of payments received by the respondents from their employer, the Westinghouse Electric Corporation, while they were on "educational leave" from their jobs with Westinghouse.

During the period here in question the respondents held engineering positions at the Bettis Atomic Power Laboratory in Pittsburgh, Pennsylvania, which Westinghouse operates under a "cost-plus" contract with the Atomic Energy Commission. Their employment status enabled them to participate in what is known as the Westinghouse Bettis Fellowship and Doctoral Program. That program, designed both to attract new employees seeking further education and to give advanced training to persons already employed at Bettis, offers a two-phase schedule of subsidized postgraduate study in engineering, physics, or mathematics.

Under the first, or "work-study," phase, a participating employee holds a regular job with Westinghouse and in addition pursues a course of study at either the University of Pittsburgh or Carnegie-Mellon University. The employee is paid for a 40-hour work week, but may receive up to eight hours of "release time" per week for the purpose of attending classes. "Tuition remuneration," as well as reimbursement for various incidental academic expenses, is provided by the company.

When an employee has completed all preliminary requirements for his doctorate, he may apply for an educational leave of absence, which constitutes the second phase of the Fellowship Program. He must submit a proposed dissertation topic for approval by Westinghouse and the AEC. Approval is based, *inter alia*, on a determination that the topic has at least some general relevance to the work done at Bettis. If the leave of absence is secured, the employee devotes his full attention for a period of at least several months, to fulfilling his dissertation requirement. During this period he receives a "stipend" from Westinghouse, in an amount based on a specified percentage (ranging from 70% to 90%) of his prior salary plus "adders," depending upon the size of his family. He also retains his seniority status and receives all employee benefits, such as insurance and stock option privileges. In return he not only must submit periodic progress reports, but under the written agreement that all participants in the program must sign, also is obligated to return to the employ of Westinghouse for a period of at least two years following completion of his leave. Upon return he is, according to the agreement, to "assume * * * duties commensurate with his education and experience," at a salary "commensurate with the duties assigned."

The respondents all took leaves under the Fellowship Program at varying times during the period 1960–1962, and eventually received their doctoral degrees in engineering. Respondents Johnson and Pomerantz took leaves of nine months and were paid $5,670 each, representing 80% of their prior salaries at Westinghouse. Respondent Wolfe, whose leave lasted for a year, received $9,698.90, or 90% of his previous salary. Each returned to Westinghouse for the required period of time following his educational leave.

Westinghouse, which under its own accounting system listed the amounts paid to the respondents as "indirect labor" expenses, withheld federal income tax from those amounts.[12] The respondents filed claims for refund, contending that the payments they had received were "scholarships," and hence were excludable from income under § 117 of the Code, * * *. When those claims were rejected, the respondents instituted this suit in the District Court for the Western District of Pennsylvania, against the District Director of Internal Revenue. After the basically undisputed evidence regarding the Bettis Program had been presented, the trial judge instructed the jury in accordance with Treas.Reg. on Income Tax ([1986] Code) § 1.117–4(c), 26 CFR § 1.117–4(c) which provides that amounts representing "compensation for past, present, or future employment services," and amounts "paid * * * to * * * an individual to enable him to pursue studies or research primarily for the benefit of the grantor," are not excludable as scholarships. The jury found that the amounts received by the respondents were taxable income. Respondents then sought review in the Court of Appeals for the Third Circuit, and that court reversed, holding that the Regulation referred to was invalid, that the jury instructions were therefore improper, and that on the essentially undisputed facts it was clear as a matter of law that the amounts received by the respondents were "scholarships" excludable under § 117. 396 F.2d 258.

The holding of the Court of Appeals with respect to Treas.Reg. § 1.117–4(c) was contrary to the decisions of several other circuits—most notably, that of the Fifth Circuit in Ussery v. United States, 296 F.2d 582, which explicitly sustained the Regulation against attack and held amounts received under an arrangement quite similar to the Bettis Program to be taxable income. Accordingly, upon the District Director's petition, we granted certiorari to resolve the conflict and to determine the proper scope of § 117 and Treas.Reg. § 1.117–4(c) with respect to payments such as those involved here. 393 U.S. 949, 89 S.Ct. 374, 21 L.Ed.2d 361.

In holding invalid the Regulation that limits the definitions of "scholarship" and "fellowship" so as to exclude amounts received as "compensation," the Court of Appeals emphasized that the statute itself expressly adverts to certain situations in which funds received by students may be thought of as remuneration. After the basic rule excluding scholarship funds from gross income is set out in § 117(a), for instance, subsection (b)(1) stipulates:

> "In the case of an individual who is a candidate for a degree at an educational institution * * *, subsection (a) shall not apply to that portion of any amount received which represents payment for teaching, research, or other services in the nature of part-time employment required as a condition to receiving the scholarship or the fellowship grant." [13]

---

12. Tuition and incidental fees were also paid by Westinghouse, but no withholding was made from those payments, and their tax status is not at issue in this case. Although conceptually includable in income, such sums presumably would be offset by educational expense deductions.

See Treas.Reg. on Income Tax ([1986] Code) § 1.162–5, 26 CFR § 1.162–5.

13. Subsection (b) goes on to except from that limitation situations in which "teaching, research, or other services are required of all candidates (whether or not recipients of scholarships or fellowship

In addition, subsection (b)(2) limits the exclusion from income with regard to nondegree candidates in two respects: first, the grantor must be a governmental agency, an international organization, or an organization exempt from tax under § 501(a), (c)(3) of the Code; and second, the maximum exclusion from income available to a nondegree candidate is $300 per month for not more than 36 months. Since these exceptions are expressly set out in the statute, the Court of Appeals, relying on the canon of construction that *expressio unius est exclusio alterius,* concluded that no additional restrictions may be put on the basic exclusion from income granted by subsection (a)—a conclusion forcefully pressed upon us by the respondents.

Congress' express reference to the limitations just referred to concededly lends some support to the respondents' position. The difficulty with that position, however, lies in its implicit assumption that those limitations are limitations on an exclusion of *all funds* received by students to support them during the course of their education. Section 117 provides, however, only that amounts received as "scholarships" or "fellowships" shall be excludable. And Congress never defined what it meant by the quoted terms. As the Tax Court has observed:

> "[A] proper reading of the statute requires that before the exclusion comes into play there must be a determination that the payment sought to be excluded has the normal characteristics associated with the term 'scholarship.'" Reese v. Commissioner, 45 T.C. 407, 413, aff'd, 373 F.2d 742.

The regulation here in question represents an effort by the Commissioner to supply the definitions that Congress omitted.[14] And it is fundamental, of course, that as "contemporaneous constructions by those charged with administration of" the Code, the Regulations "must be sustained unless unreasonable and plainly inconsistent with the revenue statutes," and "should not be overruled except for weighty reasons." Commissioner of Internal Revenue v. South Texas Lumber Co., 333 U.S. 496, 501, 68 S.Ct. 695, 698, 92 L.Ed. 831. In this respect our statement last Term in United States v. Correll, 389 U.S. 299, 88 S.Ct. 445, 19 L.Ed.2d 537, bears emphasis:

> "[W]e do not sit as a committee of revision to perfect the administration of the tax laws. Congress has delegated to the Commissioner, not to the courts, the task of describing 'all needful rules and regulations for the enforcement' of the Internal Revenue Code. 26 U.S.C. § 7805(a). In this area of limitless factual variations 'it is the province of Congress and the Commissioner, not the courts, to make the appropriate adjustments.'" Id., at 306–307, 88 S.Ct. at 449.

Here, the definitions supplied by the Regulation clearly are prima facie proper, comporting as they do with the ordinary understanding of

grants) for a particular degree as a condition to receiving such degree ＊ ＊ ＊." In those situations, scholarship or fellowship funds received for such services are nontaxable. See n. 10, supra.

14. See also Treas.Reg. on Income Tax ([1986] Code) §§ 1.117–3(a), (c), 26 CFR §§ 1.117–3(a), (c), which set out the "normal characteristics" associated with scholarships and fellowships ＊ ＊ ＊.

"scholarships" and "fellowships" as relatively disinterested, "no-strings" educational grants, with no requirement of any substantial *quid pro quo* from the recipients.

The implication of the respondents' *expressio unius* reasoning is that any amount paid for the purpose of supporting one pursuing a program of study or scholarly research should be excludable from gross income as a "scholarship" so long as it does not fall within the specific limitations of § 117(b). Pay received by a $30,000 per year engineer or executive on a leave of absence would, according to that reasoning, be excludable as long as the leave was granted so that the individual could perform work required for a doctoral degree. This result presumably would not be altered by the fact that the employee might be performing, in satisfaction of his degree requirements, precisely the same work which he was doing for his employer prior to his leave and which he would be doing after his return to "employment"—or by the fact that the fruits of that work were made directly available to and exploited by the employer. Such a result would be anomalous indeed, especially in view of the fact that under § 117 the comparatively modest sums received by part-time teaching assistants are clearly subject to taxation. Particularly in light of the principle that exemptions from taxation are to be construed narrowly, we decline to assume that Congress intended to sanction—indeed, as the respondents would have it, to compel—such an inequitable situation.

The legislative history underlying § 117 is, as the Court of Appeals recognized, "far from clear." We do not believe, however, that it precludes, as "plainly inconsistent" with the statute, a definition of "scholarship" that excludes from the reach of that term amounts received as compensation for services performed. The 1939 Internal Revenue Code, like predecessor Codes, contained no specific provision dealing with scholarship grants. Whether such grants were includable in gross income depended simply upon whether they fell within the broad provision excluding from income amounts received as "gifts." Thus case-by-case determinations regarding grantors' motives were necessary. The cases decided under this approach prior to 1954 generally involved two types of financial assistance: grants to research or teaching assistants—graduate students who perform research or teaching services in return for their stipends—and foundation grants to post-doctoral researchers. In cases decided shortly before the 1954 Code was enacted, the Tax Court, relying on the "gift" approach to scholarships and fellowships, held that amounts received by a research assistant were taxable income, but reached divergent results in situations involving grants to post-doctoral researchers.

In enacting § 117 of the 1954 Code, Congress indicated that it wished to eliminate the necessity for reliance on "case-by-case" determinations with respect to whether "scholarships" and "fellowships" were excludable as "gifts." Upon this premise the respondents hinge their argument that Congress laid down a standard under which all case-by-case determinations—such as those that may be made under Treas.Reg. § 1.117–4(c)—are unnecessary and improper. We have already indicated, however, our reluctance to believe that § 117 was designed to exclude from taxation all amounts, no matter how large or from what source, that are given for the support of one who happens to be a student. The sounder inference is that Congress was merely "recogni[zing] that scholarships and fellowships are sufficiently unique * * * to merit [tax] treatment separate from that accorded gifts," and attempting to provide that grants falling within those categories should be treated consistently—as in some instances, under the generic provisions of the 1939 Code, they arguably had not been. Delineation of the precise contours of those categories was left to the Commissioner.

Furthermore, a congressional intention that not all grants received by students were necessarily to be "scholarships" may reasonably be inferred from the legislative history. In explaining the basis for its version of § 117(b)(2), the House Ways and Means Committee stated that its purpose was to "tax those grants which are in effect merely payments of a salary during a period while the recipient is on leave from his regular job." This comment related, it is true, to a specific exception to the exclusion from income set out in subsection (a). But, in view of the fact that the statute left open the definitions of "scholarship" and "fellowship," it is not unreasonable to conclude that in adding subsection (b) to the statute Congress was merely dealing explicitly with those problems that had come explicitly to its attention—*viz.,* those involving research and teaching assistantships and post-doctoral research grants—without intending to forbid application to similar situations of the general principle underlying its treatment of those problems. One may justifiably suppose that the Congress that taxed funds received by "part-time" teaching assistants, presumably on the ground that the amounts received by such persons really represented compensation for services performed, would also deem proper a definition of "scholarship" under which comparable sorts of compensation—which often, as in the present case, are significantly greater in amount—are likewise taxable. In providing such a definition, the Commissioner has permissibly implemented an underlying congressional concern. We cannot say that the provision of Treas.Reg. § 1.117–4(c) that taxes amounts received as "compensation" is "unreasonable or plainly inconsistent with the * * * statut[e]."

Under that provision, as set out in the trial court's instructions,[15] the jury here properly found that the amounts received by the respon-

15. The instructions included, *inter alia,* the following passage:

"You are * * * instructed that, one, any amount of money paid to an individual to enable him to pursue studies or research, if such amount represents either compensation for past, present or future employment services, or represents payment for services which are subject to the direction or supervision of the grantor, * * * is not a scholarship or fellowship under the tax laws.

"Two, any amount of money paid to an individual to enable him to pursue studies or research which studies or research are primarily for the benefit of the grantor is not a scholarship under the tax laws."

dents were taxable "compensation" rather than excludable "scholarships." The employer-employee relationship involved is immediately suggestive, of course, as is the close relation between the respondents' prior salaries and the amount of their "stipends." In addition, employee benefits were continued. Topics were required to relate at least generally to the work of the Bettis Laboratory. Periodic work reports were to be submitted. And, most importantly, Westinghouse unquestionably extracted a *quid pro quo*. The respondents not only were required to hold positions with Westinghouse throughout the "work-study" phase of the program, but also were obligated to return to Westinghouse's employ for a substantial period of time after completion of their leave. The thrust of the provision dealing with compensation is that bargained-for payments, given only as a *"quo"* in return for the *quid* of services rendered—whether past, present, or future—should not be excludable from income as "scholarship" funds.[16] That provision clearly covers this case.

Accordingly, the judgment of the Court of Appeals is reversed, and that of the District Court reinstated.

It is so ordered.

Judgment of Court of Appeals reversed and judgment of District Court reinstated.

Questions

1. Should the exclusion for qualified scholarships apply to employees who receive such grants from their employers?

2. Should the exclusion for qualified scholarships be repealed and Federal funds used to provide additional scholarships or loan assistance? Will the exclusion under § 117 produce more revenue for the Federal government, over the long run, than the sums lost by the exclusion? Is the exclusion under § 117 justified in the context of other education assistance, for example, low tuition at state universities?

---

16. We accept the suggestion in the Government's brief that the second paragraph of Treas.Reg. § 1.117–4(c)—which excepts from the definition of "scholarship" any payments that are paid to an individual "to enable him to pursue studies or research primarily for the benefit of the grantor"—is merely an adjunct to the initial "compensation" provision:

"By this paragraph, the Treasury has supplemented the first in order to impose tax on bargained-for arrangements that do not create an employer-employee relation, as, for example, in the case of an independent contractor. But the general idea is the same: 'scholarship' or 'fellowship' does not include arrangements where the recipient receives money and in return provides a *quid pro quo*." Brief for Petitioner 22.

The respondents point out that the Internal Revenue Service is considering possible revisions of the Regulations under § 117. The Solicitor General informs us, however, that although revisions might "conform the Regulations to the results reached" in such cases as Wells v. Commissioner, 40 T.C. 40, no changes are contemplated with respect to situations such as that involved here. Reply Brief for Petitioner in support of certiorari 3, n. 2; see Rev.Rul. 65–59, 1965–1 Cum.Bull. 67.

References: Stuart, Tax Status of Scholarship and Fellowship Grants: Frustration of Legislative Purpose and Approaches to Obtain the Exclusion Granted by Congress, 25 Emory L.J. 357 (1976); Wolfman, Federal Tax Policy and the Support of Science, 114 U.Pa.L.Rev. 171 (1965).

B. BUSINESS CONTEXT

1. PLANNING FOR TAX FREE BENEFITS

A basic point to remember in connection with tax planning for employees is that where an employer gives so-called "fringe benefits" to an employee, the employer often seeks to arrange this transaction so that:

    a. The benefit received by the employee will not be taxed as income, or that the realization and recognition of income will be deferred until a later time.

    b. The employer will have a deduction for the amount so expended.

Assume that the taxpayer is in the 33 percent bracket and his employer gives him fringe benefits which are worth $5,000 a year, but which do not create income attributable to him for Federal income tax purposes. The employer deducts the $5,000 as an "ordinary and necessary" business expense (§ 162(a)) in the year in which such amount is expended. The employee, however, receives benefits which would be the equivalent of $7,500 paid to him in cash, because he would have had to earn $7,500 as salary to retain, after taxes, $5,000 to purchase the benefits.

Clearly, if a fringe benefit to the employee is shown by the employer to be intended as compensation, the expense ought to be deductible by the employer (§ 162(a)(2)). But, in that case, it should be income to the employee.

In a world emphasizing tax planning, it is desirable to list the major tax preference devices used where one person renders services to another. This is an area sometimes described as executive compensation, though some of the benefits are available to all. We have already considered the following techniques:

    (1) A broad array of fringe benefits under § 132 which an employee receives tax free and for which an employer gets an immediate deduction. Reconsider pp. 77–84.

    (2) Qualified employee benefit plans under which an employer gets an immediate deduction for funds set aside for an employee's pension but the employee does not realize and recognize income until the pension is received. Reconsider pp. 165–168.

    (3) Employee achievement awards previously discussed in this Chapter.

We next consider some further devices, including meals and lodging, employee death benefits, and other employee benefits excluded by statute from gross income. In the next chapter, we will analyze the deduction for travel and entertainment expenses.

2. CONVENIENCE OF THE EMPLOYER DOCTRINE

Judicial Exclusion for Meals and Lodging. The employer's convenience provided the basis for a judicial exclusion for meals and lodging from the broad reach of § 61. Consider the following case.

BENAGLIA v. COMMISSIONER

36 B.T.A. 838 (1937) (acq., 1940–1 C.B. 1).

The Commissioner determined a deficiency in the petitioners' joint income tax for 1933 of $856.68, and for 1934 of $1,001.61, and they contest the inclusion in gross income each year of the alleged fair market value of rooms and meals furnished by the husband's employer.

FINDINGS OF FACT

The petitioners are husband and wife, residing in Honolulu, Hawaii, where they filed joint income tax returns for 1933 and 1934.

The petitioner has, since 1926 and including the tax years in question, been employed as the manager in full charge of the several hotels in Honolulu owned and operated by Hawaiian Hotels, Ltd., a corporation of Hawaii, consisting of the Royal Hawaiian, the Moana and bungalows, and the Waialae Golf Club. These are large resort hotels, operating on the American plan. Petitioner was constantly on duty, and, for the proper performance of his duties and entirely for the convenience of his employer, he and his wife occupied a suite of rooms in the Royal Hawaiian Hotel and received their meals at and from the hotel.

Petitioner's salary has varied in different years, being in one year $25,000. In 1933 it was $9,625, and in 1934 it was $11,041.67. These amounts were fixed without reference to his meals and lodging, and neither petitioner nor his employer ever regarded the meals and lodging as part of his compensation or accounted for them.

OPINION

STERNHAGEN: The Commissioner has added $7,845 each year to the petitioner's gross income as "compensation received from Hawaiian Hotels, Ltd.", holding that this is "the fair market value of rooms and meals furnished by the employer." In the deficiency notice he cites article 52[53], Regulations 77, and holds inapplicable Jones v. United States, 60 Ct.Cls. 552; I.T. 2232; G.C.M. 14710; and G.C.M. 14836. The deficiency notice seems to hold that the rooms and meals were not in fact supplied "merely as a convenience to the hotels" of the employer.

From the evidence, there remains no room for doubt that the petitioner's residence at the hotel was not by way of compensation for his services, not for his personal convenience, comfort or pleasure, but solely because he could not otherwise perform the services required of him. The evidence of both the employer and employee shows in detail what petitioner's duties were and why his residence in the hotel was necessary. His duty was continuous and required his presence at a moment's call. He had a lifelong experience in hotel management and operation in the United States, Canada, and elsewhere, and testified that the functions of the manager could not have been performed by one living outside the hotel, especially a resort hotel such as this. The demands and requirements of guests are numerous, various, and unpredictable, and affect the meals, the rooms, the entertainment, and everything else about the hotel. The manager must be alert to all these things day and night. He would not consider undertaking the job and the owners of the hotel would not consider employing a manager unless he lived there. This was implicit throughout his employment, and when his compensation was changed from time to time no mention was ever made of it. Both took it for granted. The corporation's books carried no accounting for the petitioner's meals, rooms, or service.

Under such circumstances, the value of meals and lodging is not income to the employee, even though it may relieve him of an expense which he would otherwise bear. In *Jones v. United States*, supra, the subject was fully considered in determining that neither the value of quarters nor the amount received as commutation of quarters by an Army officer is included within his taxable income. There is also a full discussion in the English case of Tennant v. Smith, H.L. (1892) App.Cas. 150, III British Tax Cases 158. A bank employee was required to live in quarters located in the bank building, and it was held that the value of such lodging was not taxable income. The advantage to him was merely an incident of the performance of his duty, but its character for tax purposes was controlled by the dominant fact that the occupation of the premises was imposed upon him for the convenience of the employer. The Bureau of Internal Revenue has almost consistently applied the same doctrine in its published rulings.

The three cases cited by the respondent, Ralph Kitchen, 11 B.T.A. 855; Charles A. Frueauff, 30 B.T.A. 449; and Fontaine Fox, 30 B.T.A. 451, are distinguishable entirely upon the ground that what the taxpayer received was not shown to be primarily for the need or convenience of the employer. Of course, as in the *Kitchen* case, it can not be said as a categorical proposition of law that, where an employee is fed and lodged by his employer, no part of the value of such perquisite is income. If the Commissioner finds that it was received as compensation and holds it to be taxable income, the taxpayer contesting this before the Board must prove by evidence that it is not income. In the *Kitchen* case the Board held that the evidence did not establish that the food and lodging were given for the convenience of the employer. In the present case the evidence clearly establishes that fact, and it has been so found.

The determination of the Commissioner on the point in issue is reversed.

Reviewed by the Board.

Judgment will be entered under Rule 50.

MURDOCK concurs only in the result.

ARNOLD, dissenting: I disagree with the conclusions of fact that the suite of rooms and meals furnished petitioner and his wife at the Royal Hawaiian Hotel were entirely for the convenience of the employer and that the cash salary was fixed without reference thereto and was never regarded as part of his compensation.

Petitioner was employed by a hotel corporation operating two resort hotels in Honolulu—the Royal Hawaiian, containing 357 guest bed rooms, and the Moana, containing 261 guest bed rooms, and the bungalows and cottages in connection with the Moana containing 127 guest bed rooms, and the Waialae Golf Club. His employment was as general manager of both hotels and the golf club.

His original employment was in 1925, and in accepting the employment he wrote a letter to the party representing the employer, with whom he conducted the negotiations for employment, under date of September 10, 1925, in which he says:

> Confirming our meeting here today, it is understood that I will assume the position of general manager of both the Royal Waikiki Beach Hotel (now under construction) and the Moana Hotel in Honolulu, at a yearly salary of $10,000.00, payable monthly, together with living quarters, meals, etc., for myself and wife. In addition I am to receive $20.00 per day while travelling, this however, not to include any railroad or steamship fares, and I to submit vouchers monthly covering all such expenses.

While the cash salary was adjusted from time to time by agreement of the parties, depending on the amount of business done, it appears that the question of living quarters, meals, etc., was not given further consideration and was not thereafter changed. Petitioner and his wife have always occupied living quarters in the Royal Hawaiian Hotel and received their meals from the time he first accepted the employment down through the years before us. His wife performed no services for the hotel company.

This letter, in my opinion, constitutes the basic contract of employment and clearly shows that the living quarters, meals, etc., furnished petitioner and his wife were understood and intended to be compensation in addition to the cash salary paid him. Being compensation to petitioner in addition to the cash salary paid him, it follows that the reasonable value thereof to petitioner is taxable income. Cf. Ralph Kitchen, 11 B.T.A. 855; Charles A. Frueauff, 30 B.T.A. 449.

Conceding that petitioner was required to live at the hotel and that his living there was solely for the convenience of the employer, it does not follow that he was not benefited thereby to the extent of what such accommodations were reasonably worth to him. His employment was a matter of private contract. He was careful to specify in his letter accepting the employment that he was to be furnished with living quarters, meals, etc., for himself and wife, together with the cash salary, as compensation for his employment. Living quarters and meals are necessities which he would otherwise have had to procure at his own expense. His contract of employment relieved him to that extent. He has been enriched to the extent of what they are reasonably worth.

The majority opinion is based on the finding that petitioner's residence at the hotel was solely for the convenience of the employer and, therefore, not income. While it is no doubt convenient to have the manager reside in the hotel, I do not think the question here is one of convenience or of benefit to the employer. What the tax law is concerned with is whether or not petitioner was financially benefited by having living quarters furnished to himself and wife. He may have preferred to live elsewhere, but we are dealing with the financial aspect of petitioner's relation to his employer, not his preference. He says it would cost him $3,600 per year to live elsewhere.

It would seem that if his occupancy of quarters at the Royal Hawaiian was necessary and solely for the benefit of the employer, occupancy of premises at the Moana would be just as essential so far as the management of the Moana was concerned. He did not have living quarters or meals for himself and wife at the Moana and he was general manager of both and both were in operation during the years before us. Furthermore, it appears that petitioner was absent from Honolulu from March 24 to June 8 and from August 19 to November 2 in 1933, and from April 8 to May 24 and from September 3 to November 1 in 1934—about 5 months in 1933 and 3½ months in 1934. Whether he was away on official business or not we do not know. During his absence both hotels continued in operation. The $20 per day travel allowance in his letter of acceptance indicates his duties were not confined to managing the hotels in Honolulu, and the entire letter indicates he was to receive maintenance, whether in Honolulu or elsewhere, in addition to his cash salary.

At most the arrangement as to living quarters and meals was of mutual benefit, and to the extent it benefited petitioner it was compensation in addition to his cash salary, and taxable to him as income.

The Court of Claims in the case of *Jones v. United States,* relied on in the majority opinion, was dealing with a governmental organization regulated by military law where the compensation was fixed by law and not subject to private contract. The English case of *Tennant v. Smith,* involved the employment of a watchman or custodian for a bank whose presence at the bank was at all times a matter of necessity demanded by the employer as a condition of the employment.

The facts in both these cases are so at variance with the facts in this case that they are not controlling in my opinion.

SMITH, TURNER, and HARRON agree with this dissent.

In Van Rosen v. Commissioner, 17 T.C. 834, 838 (1951), the Tax Court stated:

> The better and more accurate statement of the reason for the exclusion from the employee's income of the value of subsistence and quarters furnished in kind is found, we think, in Arthur Benaglia, 36 B.T.A. 838, where it was pointed out that, on the facts, the subsistence and quarters were not supplied by the employer and received by the employee "for his personal convenience, comfort or pleasure, but solely because he could not otherwise perform the services required of him." In other words, though there was an element of gain to the employee, in that he received subsistence and quarters which otherwise he would have had to supply for himself, he had nothing he could take, appropriate, use and expend according to his own dictates, but rather, the ends of the employer's business dominated and controlled, just as in the furnishing of a place to work and in the supplying of the tools and machinery with which to work. The fact that certain personal wants and needs of the employee were satisfied was plainly secondary and incidental to the employment.

Question

Do you agree with the result in Benaglia? Did the dissent in Benaglia believe the taxpayer? Must Bengalia have lived in the hotel to do his job?

Problem

Assume that the President of the United States is an avid skier. A secret service agent assigned to protect the President must accompany the President to Vail, Colorado. Even though the agent detests winter sports, especially downhill skiing, as part of his job the agent must ski down the mountain with the President. The Federal government pays for the agent's lift tickets and ski equipment rentals. Compare the secret service agent's forced consumption to that of the taxpayer in the Benaglia case. Does the same element of compulsion exist in both instances?

Statutory Exclusion for Meals and Lodging. Under § 119, if certain requirements are met, the value of meals or lodging furnished to any employee by an employer is excluded from the income of the employee. The meals and lodging must be furnished for the convenience of the employer on the employer's business premises. In the case of lodging, the employee is also required to accept the lodging as a condition of employment. Even though the exclusion under § 119 may not be available, the employee has a second opportunity to exclude the benefits from gross income if § 132 is satisfied.

ADAMS v. UNITED STATES

United States Court of Appeals, Federal Circuit, 1978.
218 Ct.Cl. 322, 585 F.2d 1060.

* * *

[Adams was president of Mobil Sekiyu Kabushiki Kaisha ("Sekiyu"), a subsidiary of Mobil Oil Corporation. Under a policy designed to prevent its overseas employees from suffering a hardship from overseas service, Sekiyu furnished Adams with a house in Tokyo, with a rental value of $20,000 for 1970 and $20,599.90 for 1971. Sekiyu subtracted from Adams' salary the amounts of $4,439 for 1970 and $4,824 for 1971, its estimates of the average housing cost in the United States of a person "similarly situated" to Adams. Adams reported as income the amounts subtracted from his salary. The Government contended that the entire rental value of the house was includable in income.]

OPINION

Per Curiam:

The issue in this tax refund suit is whether the fair rental value of a Japanese residence furnished the plaintiffs by the employer of plaintiff Faneuil Adams, Jr., is excludable from their gross income under Section 119 of the Internal Revenue Code of [1986].

* * *

Plaintiff contends that the fair rental value of the residence supplied to him by Sekiyu in 1970 and 1971 is excludable from his gross income because of Section 119 of the [1986] Code. Alternatively, plaintiff asserts that the excess of the fair rental value of the residence over the U.S. Housing Element amount represented a benefit to his employer and not a benefit to him, and therefore is not gross income to him. Finally, plaintiff contends that even if the fair rental value of the residence is income to him, it should be measured by the amount plaintiff would have spent for housing in the United States, rather than the fair rental value in Japan. Because we hold that the conditions of Section 119 of the [1986] Code and the Regulations promulgated thereunder have been met, we do not address the other arguments of plaintiff.

Section 119 of the [1986] Code provides in part:

There shall be excluded from gross income of an employee the value of any meals or lodging furnished to him by his employer for the convenience of the employer, but only if—

* * *

(2) in the case of lodging, the employee is required to accept such lodging on the business premises of his employer as a condition of his employment.

Thus, in order to qualify for the exclusion of Section 119, each of three tests must be met:

(1) the employee must be required to accept the lodging as a condition of his employment;

(2) the lodging must be furnished for the convenience of the employer; and

(3) the lodging must be on the business premises of the employer. [Treas.Reg. § 1.119–1(b).]

The Regulations further provide that the first test is met where the employee is "required to accept the lodging in order to enable him properly to perform the duties of his employment." Id.

It is clear that the first requirement of the statute has been met because the plaintiff was explicitly required to accept the residence provided by Sekiyu as a condition of his employment as president of the company. Sekiyu's goal was twofold: first, it wanted to insure that its president resided in housing of sufficiently dignified surroundings to promote his effectiveness within the Japanese business community. Secondly, Sekiyu wished to provide its president with facilities which were sufficient for the conduct of certain necessary business activities at home. Since at least 1954 Sekiyu had required that its chief executive officer reside in the residence provided to plaintiff, as a condition to appointment as president.

With respect to this first test of Section 119, then, this case is as compelling as United States Junior Chamber of Commerce v. United States, 334 F.2d 660, 167 Ct.Cl. 392 (1964). In that case, the court found that it was not *necessary* for the taxpayer-president to reside in the Chamber's "White House" during his term of office so long as he lived in the Tulsa area. But, as a practical matter, for the convenience of his employer and as a condition of his tenure, the president was *required* to live there. Therefore, it was held that the "condition of employment" test was met. The court noted that the "condition of employment" test is met if

> due to the nature of the employer's business, a certain type of residence for the employee is required and that it would not be reasonable to suppose that the employee would normally have available such lodging for the use of his employer. 334 F.2d at 664, 167 Ct.Cl. at 399.

Here, because the size and style of one's residence had an important effect upon the Japanese business community, a certain type of residence was both required by Mobil and Sekiyu for the plaintiff and necessary for the proper discharge of his duties in Sekiyu's best interests.

In contrast, the Tax Court in James H. McDonald, 66 T.C. 223 (1976), found that the taxpayer was not expressly required to accept his accommodations as a condition of his employment in Tokyo. Moreover, the court noted that the apartment provided to the taxpayer was not integrally related to the various facets of the employee's position. In the present case, plaintiff was required to accept the housing, and the residence was directly related to plaintiff's position as president, both in terms of physical facilities and psychic significance. It is held, therefore, that plaintiff was required to accept the lodging in order to enable him properly to perform the duties of his employment.

As to the "for the convenience of the employer" test, in United States Junior Chamber of Commerce v. United States, 334 F.2d at 663, 167 Ct.Cl. at 397, the court stated,

"There does not appear to be any substantial difference between the * * * 'convenience of the employer' test and the 'required as a condition of his employment' test."

Since it has already been determined that the condition of employment test has been satisfied, on that basis alone it could be held that the convenience of the employer test has also been met.

In James H. McDonald, supra, 66 T.C. at 230, the court stated that the convenience of the employer test is satisfied where there is a direct nexus between the housing furnished the employee and the business interests of the employer served thereby. In *McDonald*, the taxpayer was a principal officer of Gulf who was furnished an apartment by his employer which totalled only about 1,500 square feet of living space. The taxpayer was not required to live in the apartment, and it was found that the only benefit Gulf received in maintaining the apartment was the flexibility it afforded Gulf in personnel transfers. There was no prestige consideration. The court held that there was an insufficient nexus between the apartment and the employer's business interests to meet the convenience of the employer test requirements. Moreover, the court further noted that:

While its practice of maintaining various leasehold interests for assignment to expatriate employees may have accorded Gulf a benefit in terms of flexibility in personnel transfers, that is not to conclude that the assignments of these lodgings to petitioners at a discount similarly served the interests of Gulf; that is, although convenience may have dictated the form in which the leasehold arrangements were structured, the convenience of Gulf did not require it to subsidize the assignments. 66 T.C. at 229.

Here there was a sufficiently direct relationship between the housing furnished the plaintiff by Sekiyu and Sekiyu's business interests to meet the convenience of the employer test. The lodging had been built and was owned by Sekiyu. It was specially identified with the business of Sekiyu, for the house had served as the home of its presidents since at least 1954. If Sekiyu's president had not resided in housing comparable to that supplied plaintiff, Sekiyu's business would have been adversely affected. The house had been designed for this purpose to accommodate substantial business activities, and therefore further served Sekiyu's business interests.

Moreover, the fact that Sekiyu subsidized plaintiff's use of the house was also in its best business interests. Sekiyu was interested in attracting a qualified person as its chief executive officer. Because of the unusual housing situation in Tokyo during the years in question, a person would have had to pay up to four times his U.S. housing costs to obtain comparable housing in Tokyo. Certainly, such a factor would have been a strong deterrent to any qualified person's interest in Sekiyu's presidency, absent a housing subsidy from Sekiyu. Furthermore, it was clearly in Mobil-Sekiyu's best business interests to maintain an equitable compensation relationship between its domestic employees and its American foreign-based ones. The housing subsidy was designed to accomplish that.

That the plaintiff also incurred a benefit from this residence and that it was, in part, a convenience to him, does not disturb the conclusion. As noted in William I. Olkjer, 32 T.C. 464, 469 (1959):

> No doubt the facilities furnished benefited the employee also. The test which the statute provides, however, is that of convenience to the employer. There is no provision to the effect that the employee is to be deprived of his right to exclude from gross income the value of food and lodging otherwise excludable because he, too, is convenienced.

See also United States Junior Chamber of Commerce v. United States, 334 F.2d 660, 167 Ct.Cl. 392 (1964); George I. Stone, 32 T.C. 1021, 1025 (1959).

The third and final test is whether the lodging was on the business premises of the employer. Observe first that "[t]he operative framework of [the clause 'on the business premises'] is at best elusive and admittedly incapable of generating any hard and fast line." Jack B. Lindeman, 60 T.C. 609, 617 (1973) (Tannenwald, J., concurring). This question is largely a factual one requiring a commonsense approach. The statute should not be read literally. As noted by the Tax Court in *Lindeman*, supra, 60 T.C. at 614:

> [T]he statutory language ordinarily would not permit any exclusion for lodging furnished a domestic servant, since a servant's lodging is rarely furnished on "the business premises of his employer"; yet the committee report * * * shows a clear intention to allow the exclusion where the servant's lodging is furnished in the employer's home.

In the original version of the [1986] Code, as enacted in the House, the term that was used in Section 119 was "place of employment." The Senate changed the wording to "business premises", which was accepted by the House. However, the change was without substance, for the House Conference Report stated that "[t]he term 'business premises of the employer' is intended, in general, to have the same effect as the term 'place of employment' in the House bill." H.Conf.Rep. No. 2543, 83d Cong., 2d Sess. 27, *reprinted in* [1954] U.S. Code Cong. & Admin. News, pp. 5280, 5286. The pertinent Treasury regulation similarly provides that "business premises" generally refers to the place of employment of the employee. Treas.Reg. Sec. 1.119–1(c)(1). The phrase, then, is not to be limited to the business compound or headquarters of the employer. Rather, the emphasis must be upon the place where the employee's duties are to be performed. See Comm'r. of Internal Revenue v. Anderson, 371 F.2d 59, 64 (6th Cir.1966), cert. denied 387 U.S. 906, 87 S.Ct. 1687, 18 L.Ed.2d 623 (1967). In United States Junior Chamber of Commerce v. United States, 334 F.2d at 664–65, 167 Ct.Cl. at 400, the court stated, "We think that the business premises of Section 119 means premises of the employer on which the duties of the employee are to be performed." The phrase has also been construed to mean either (1) living quarters that constitute an integral part of the business property, or (2) premises on which the company carries on some substantial segment of its business activities. Gordon S. Dole, 43 T.C. 697, 707 (1965), aff'd per curiam, 351 F.2d 308 (1st Cir. 1965).

In United States Junior Chamber of Commerce, supra, the taxpayer-president had an office in the employer-owned "White House" which he used at night for the conduct of business meetings. In addition, he used his residence for business entertainment purposes. The court held that, because of these two factors, the White House constituted a part of the business premises of the employer, though not physically contiguous to headquarters. In this case plaintiff, although he had an office at the employer's headquarters, worked in his residence in the evenings and on weekends, had business meetings and performed required business telephone calls from there which could not be made during normal business hours, and conducted regular business entertaining in the residence. In this sense plaintiff's residence was a part of the business premises of his employer, for it was a "premises on which the duties of the employee are to be performed", United States Junior Chamber of Commerce v. United States, 334 F.2d at 664-65, 167 Ct.Cl. at 400, and a "premises on which the company carries on some of its business activities." Gordon S. Dole, 43 T.C. at 707.

Interpretations of the phrase which are limited to the geographic contiguity of the premises or to questions of the quantum of business activities on the premises are too restrictive. But see Comm'r. of Internal Revenue v. Anderson, 371 F.2d 59 (6th Cir.1966). Rather, the statutory language "on the business premises of the employer" infers a functional rather than a spatial unity. In Rev.Rul. 75-540, 1975-2 Cum.Bull. 53, it was determined that the fair rental value of the official residence furnished a governor by the state is excludable from the governor's gross income under Section 119 of the Code. The Ruling noted that the business premises test was met because the residence provided by the state enabled the governor to carry out efficiently the administrative, ceremonial, and social duties required by his office. The governor's mansion, thus, served an important business function in that it was clearly identified with the business interests of the state. It was, in short, an inseparable adjunct. Similarly, in *United States Junior Chamber of Commerce*, supra, one of the main objectives of the employer was to promote and foster the growth of civic organizations in the United States. The White House, as official residence of the president of the organization, served a significant public relations function in furtherance of the organization's goals. In the present case, even apart from the strictly business activities which took place in plaintiff's residence, the house was a symbol to the Japanese business community of the status of Sekiyu's chief executive officer and a place where he officially entertained for business purposes. As such, it influenced plaintiff's effectiveness in the business community and directly served a business function for Sekiyu.

The situation, thus, is not the same as in James H. McDonald, 66 T.C. 223 (1976). In that case, the court found the quantum of business activities performed by the taxpayer in his home to be insignificant. There was no suggestion of prestige value to the employer or of its use for significant business entertainment. Also, the court held that the rental apartment supplied to the taxpayer was not closely identified with the business interests of his employer. Here, because plaintiff was the highest-ranking officer of his company, his status in the business community was extremely important to his employer. The residence supplied to him was closely identified with Sekiyu's business interests and was used to advance those interests.

We take cognizance of the admonition of Judge Raum to avoid "strained or eccentric" interpretations of the phrase "on the business premises." Gordon S. Dole, 43 T.C. at 708 (Raum, J., concurring), aff'd per curiam, 351 F.2d 308 (1st Cir.1965). However, we are persuaded that where, as here, (1) the residence was built and owned by the employer, (2) it was designed, in part, to accommodate the business activities of the employer, (3) the employee was required to live in the residence, (4) there were many business activities for the employee to perform after normal working hours in his home because of the extensive nature of the employer's business and the high-ranking status of the employee, (5) the employee did perform business activities in the residence,[17] and (6) the residence served an important business function of the employer, then the residence in question is a part of the business premises of the employer.

The three statutory requisites for exclusion are met. Accordingly, pursuant to Section 119 of the [1986] Code, the fair rental value of the residence is excludable from plaintiff's gross income. Plaintiffs are entitled to recover, and the amount will be determined under Rule 131(c).

Question

Do you agree with the court in Adams that a business premise for purposes of § 119 includes company-provided homes that are used only for entertainment and occasional office work? What impact did Japanese business customs have on the court's decision? Compare McDonald v. Commissioner, 66 T.C. 223 (1976) in which the vice-president and general manager of an American oil company's Japanese division was provided an apartment. Although the taxpayer conducted some business-related entertaining and made some overseas business telephone calls in the apartment, the Tax Court held the entertainment and the periodic use of the telephone did not constitute significant business activity and the apartment was not a business premise.

---

17. In addition to the consistent use of the den for work purposes, and the official phone calls, plaintiff used the house for gatherings of his staff with mixed business and social purposes and also for more extended business entertainment.

Courts have been reluctant to expand the definition "on the business premises" beyond the physical confines of the employee's primary place of business. With respect to the phrase "on the business premises of the employer" contained in § 119, the court in Commissioner v. Anderson, 371 F.2d 59, 67 (6th Cir.1966), cert. denied 387 U.S. 906, 87 S.Ct. 1687, 18 L.Ed.2d 623 (1967), stated that the phrase means that "in order for the value of meals or lodging to be excluded from gross income, the meals must be furnished or the lodging must be provided either at a place where the employee performs a significant portion of his duties or on the premises where the employer conducts a significant portion of his business." If lodging is furnished at a location at a distance (for example, two blocks) from the place where the employee works, the lodging is not furnished "on" the employer's business premises. The Code uses the phrase on the employer's business premises, not "in the vicinity of," "nearby," or "close to." However, a hotel manager's house across the street from the hotel and alongside the parking lots was held to be "on the business premises" in Lindeman v. Commissioner, 60 T.C. 609 (1973) (Acq. 1973–2 C.B. 2). The Tax Court considered the physical location of the house in relation to the hotel and the parking lots and the manager's obligations and significant amount of work he performed while he was at the house. Specifically, the manager was accessible by telephone; he could observe the hotel from the house; and he had an office in the home in which he conducted hotel business and entertained hotel guests in the house.

To be excluded from an employee's gross income, must meals (and lodging) be furnished in kind? Or may the employer reimburse an employee for the expenses of purchasing food? The next case considers this question.

COMMISSIONER v. KOWALSKI

Supreme Court of the United States, 1977.
434 U.S. 77, 98 S.Ct. 315, 54 L.Ed.2d 252.

MR. JUSTICE BRENNAN delivered the opinion of the Court.

This case presents the question whether cash payments to state police troopers, designated as meal allowances, are included in gross income under § 61(a) of the Internal Revenue Code of [1986], 26 U.S.C. § 61(a), and, if so, are otherwise excludable under § 119 of the Code, § 119.

I

The pertinent facts are not in dispute. Respondent is a state police trooper employed by the Division of State Police of the Department of Law and Public Safety of the State of New Jersey. During 1970, the tax year in question, he received a base salary of $8,739.38, and an additional $1,697.54 designated as an allowance for meals.

The State instituted the cash meal allowance for its state police officers in July 1949. Prior to that time, all troopers were provided with mid-shift[5] meals in kind at various meal stations located throughout the State. A trooper unable to eat at an official meal station could, however, eat at a restaurant and obtain reimbursement. The meal-station system proved unsatisfactory to the State because it required troopers to leave their assigned areas of patrol unguarded for extended periods of time. As a result, the State closed its meal stations and instituted a cash-allowance system. Under this system, troopers remain on call in their assigned patrol areas during their mid-shift break. Otherwise, troopers are not restricted in any way with respect to where they may eat in the patrol area and, indeed, may eat at home if it is located within that area. Troopers may also bring their mid-shift meal to the job and eat it in or near their patrol cars.

The meal allowance is paid biweekly in advance and is included, although separately stated, with the trooper's salary. The meal-allowance money is also separately accounted for in the State's accounting system. Funds are never commingled between the salary and meal-allowance accounts. Because of these characteristics of the meal-allowance system, the Tax Court concluded that the "meal allowance was not intended to represent additional compensation." 65 T.C. 44, 47.

Notwithstanding this conclusion, it is not disputed that the meal allowance has many features inconsistent with its characterization as a simple reimbursement for meals that would otherwise have been taken at a meal station. For example, troopers are not required to spend their meal allowances on their midshift meals, nor are they required to account for the manner in which the money is spent. With one limited exception not relevant here,[18] no reduction in the meal allowance is made for periods when a trooper is not on patrol because, for example, he is assigned to a headquarters building or is away from active duty on vacation, leave, or sick leave. In addition, the cash allowance for meals is described on a state police recruitment brochure as an item of salary to be received in addition to an officer's base salary and the amount of the meal allowance is a subject of negotiations between the State and the police troopers' union. Finally, the amount of an officer's cash meal allowance varies with his rank[19] and is included in his gross pay for purposes of calculating pension benefits.

On his 1970 income tax return, respondent reported $9,066 in wages. That amount included his salary plus $326.45 which represent-

5. While on active duty, New Jersey troopers are generally required to live in barracks. Meals furnished in kind at the barracks before or after a patrol shift are not involved in this case. Nor is the meal allowance intended to pay for meals eaten before or after a shift in those instances in which the trooper is not living in the barracks. However, because of the duration of some patrols, a trooper may be required to eat more than one meal per shift while on the road.

18. The amount of the allowance is adjusted only when an officer is on military leave.

19. Troopers, such as respondent, and other non-commissioned officers received $1,740 per year; lieutenants and captains received $1,776, majors $1,848, and the Superintendent $2,136.

ed cash meal allowances reported by the State on respondent's Wage and Tax Statement (Form W–2).[20] The remaining amount of meal allowance, $1,371.09, was not reported. On audit, the Commissioner determined that this amount should have been included in respondent's 1970 income and assessed a deficiency.

* * *

II

A

The starting point in the determination of the scope of "gross income" is the cardinal principle that Congress in creating the income tax intended "to use the full measure of its taxing power." In applying this principle to the construction of § 22(a) of the Internal Revenue Code of 1939 [21] this Court stated that "Congress applied no limitations as to the source of taxable receipts, nor restrictive labels as to their nature [, but intended] to tax all gains except those specifically exempted." Commissioner of Internal Revenue v. Glenshaw Glass Co., 348 U.S. 426, 429–430, 75 S.Ct. 473, 476, 99 L.Ed. 483 (1955). Although Congress simplified the definition of gross income in § 61 of the [1986] Code, it did not intend thereby to narrow the scope of that concept. See Commissioner of Internal Revenue v. Glenshaw Glass Co., supra, at 432, 75 S.Ct. at 477 and n. 11; H.R.Rep. No. 1337, 83d Cong., 2d Sess., A18 (1954); S.Rep. No. 1622, 83d Cong., 2d Sess., 168 (1954); U.S. Code Cong. & Admin.News 1954, p. 4025.[22] In the absence of a specific exemption, therefore, respondent's meal-allowance payments are income within the meaning of § 61 since, like the payments involved in *Glenshaw Glass Co.*, the payments are "undeniabl[y] accessions to wealth, clearly realized, and over which the [respondent has] complete dominion." Commissioner of Internal Revenue v. Glenshaw Glass Co., supra, at 431, 75 S.Ct. at 477. See also Commissioner of Internal Revenue v. LoBue, 351 U.S. 243, 247, 76 S.Ct. 800, 803, 100 L.Ed. 1142 (1956); Van Rosen v. Commissioner, 17 T.C. 834, 838 (1951).

Respondent contends, however, that § 119 can be construed to be a specific exemption covering the meal-allowance payments to New Jersey troopers. Alternatively, respondent argues that notwithstanding § 119 a specific exemption may be found in a line of lower-court cases and administrative rulings which recognize that benefits con-

---

20. On October 1, 1970, the Division of State Police began to withhold income tax from amounts paid as cash meal allowances. No claim has been made that the change in the division's withholding policy has any relevance for this case.

21. 53 Stat. 9, as amended, ch. 59, 53 Stat. 574. This section provided:

"(a) GENERAL DEFINITION.—'Gross income' includes gains, profits, and income derived from salaries, wages, or compensation for personal service, * * * or gains

or profits and *income derived from any source whatever.*" (Emphasis added.)

22. The House and Senate Reports state:

"[Section 61] corresponds to section 22(a) of the 1939 Code. While the language in existing section 22(a) has been simplified, the all-inclusive nature of statutory gross income has not been affected thereby. Section 61(a) is as broad in scope as section 22(a)." U.S.Code Cong. & Admin. News 1954, p. 4155.

ferred by an employer on an employee "for the convenience of the employer"—at least when such benefits are not "compensatory"—are not income within the meaning of the Internal Revenue Code. In responding to these contentions, we turn first to § 119. Since we hold that § 119 does not cover cash payments of any kind, we then trace the development over several decades of the convenience-of-the-employer doctrine as a determinant of the tax status of meals and lodging, turning finally to the question whether the doctrine as applied to meals and lodging survives the enactment of the Internal Revenue Code of [1986].

B

Section 119 provides that an employee may exclude from income "the value of any meals * * * furnished to him by his employer for the convenience of the employer, but only if * * * the meals are furnished on the business premises of the employer * * *." By its terms, § 119 covers *meals* furnished by the employer and not *cash* reimbursements for meals. This is not a mere oversight. As we shall explain at greater length below, the form of § 119 which Congress enacted originated in the Senate and the Report accompanying the Senate bill is very clear: "Section 119 applies only to meals or lodging furnished in kind." S.Rep. No. 1622, 83d Cong., 2d Sess., 190 (1954); U.S.Code Cong. & Admin.News 1954, p. 4825. See also Treas.Reg. § 1.119–1(c)(2), 26 CFR § 1.119–1 (1977). Accordingly, respondent's meal-allowance payments are not subject to exclusion under § 119.

C

The convenience-of-the-employer doctrine is not a tidy one. The phrase "convenience of the employer" first appeared in O.D. 265, 1 Cum.Bull. 71 (1919), in a ruling exempting from the income tax board and lodging furnished seamen aboard ship. The following year, T.D. 2992, 2 Cum.Bull. 76 (1920), was issued and added a convenience-of-the-employer section to Treas.Regs. 45, Art. 33, the income tax regulations then in effect. As modified, Art. 33 stated:

> "Art. 33. *Compensation paid other than in cash.* * * * When living quarters such as camps are furnished to employees for the convenience of the employer, the ratable value need not be added to the cash compensation of the employee, but where a person receives as compensation for services rendered a salary and in addition thereto living quarters, the value to such person of the quarters furnished constitutes income subject to tax. * * *"

While T.D. 2992 extended the convenience-of-the-employer test as a general rule solely to items received in kind, O.D. 514, 2 Cum.Bull. 90 (1920), extended the convenience-of-the-employer doctrine to cash payments for "supper money." [23]

---

23. " 'Supper money' paid by an employer to an employee, who voluntarily performs extra labor for his employer after regular business hours, *such payment not being considered additional compensation and not being charged to the salary account,* is considered as being paid for the

The rationale of both T.D. 2992 and O.D. 514 appears to have been that benefits conferred by an employer on an employee in the designated circumstances were not compensation for services and hence not income. Subsequent rulings equivocate on whether the noncompensatory character of a benefit could be inferred merely from its characterization by the employer or whether there must be additional evidence that employees are granted a benefit solely because the employer's business could not function properly unless an employee was furnished that benefit on the employer's premises. O.D. 514, for example, focuses only on the employer's characterization. Two rulings issued in 1921, however, dealing respectively with cannery workers [24] and hospital employees,[25] emphasize the necessity of the benefits to the functioning of the employer's business, and this emphasis was made the authoritative interpretation of the convenience-of-the-employer provisions of the regulations in Mim. 5023, 1940–1 Cum.Bull. 14.

Adding complexity, however, is Mim. 6472, 1950–1 Cum.Bull. 15, issued in 1950. This mimeograph states in relevant part:

> "The 'convenience of the employer' rule is simply an administrative test to be applied only in cases in which the compensatory character of * * * benefits is not otherwise determinable. It follows that the rule should not be applied in any case in which it is evident from the other circumstances involved that the receipt of quarters or meals by the employee represents compensation for services rendered." Ibid.

Mimeograph 6472 expressly modified all previous rulings which had suggested that meals and lodging could be excluded from income upon a simple finding that the furnishing of such benefits was necessary to allow an employee to perform his duties properly. However, the ruling apparently did not affect O.D. 514, which, as noted above, creates an exclusion from income based solely on an employer's characterization of a payment as noncompensatory.

Coexisting with the regulations and administrative determinations of the Treasury, but independent of them, is a body of case law also applying the convenience-of-the-employer test to exclude from an employee's statutory income benefits conferred by his employer.

---

convenience of the employer * * *." (Emphasis added.)

24. "Where, from the location and nature of the work, it is necessary that employees engaged in fishing and canning be furnished with lodging and sustenance by the employer, the value of such lodging and sustenance may be considered as being furnished for the convenience of the employer and need not, therefore, be included in computing net income * * *." O.D. 814, 4 Cum.Bull. 84, 84–85 (1921).

25. "Where the employees of a hospital are subject to immediate service on demand at any time during the twenty-four hours of the day and on that account are required to accept quarters and meals at the hospital, the value of such quarters and meals may be considered as being furnished for the convenience of the hospital and does not represent additional compensation to the employees. On the other hand, where the employees * * * could, if they so desired, obtain meals and lodging elsewhere than in the hospital and yet perform the duties required of them by such hospital, the ratable value of the board and lodging furnished is considered additional compensation." O.D. 915, 4 Cum.Bull. 85, 85–86 (1921).

An early case is Jones v. United States, 60 Ct.Cl. 552 (1925). There the Court of Claims ruled that neither the value of quarters provided an Army officer for nine months of a tax year nor payments in commutation of quarters paid the officer for the remainder of the year were includable in income. The decision appears to rest both on a conclusion that public quarters by tradition and law were not "compensation received as such" within the meaning of § 213 of the Revenue Act of 1921, 42 Stat. 237, and also on the proposition that "public quarters for the housing of * * * officers is as much a military necessity as the procurement of implements of warfare or the training of troops." 60 Ct.Cl., at 569; see id., at 565–568. The Court of Claims, in addition, rejected the argument that money paid in commutation of quarters was income on the ground that it was not "gain derived * * * from labor" within the meaning of Eisner v. Macomber, 252 U.S. 189, 40 S.Ct. 189, 64 L.Ed. 521 (1920), but apparently was at most a reimbursement to the officer for furnishing himself with a necessity of his job in those instances in which the Government found it convenient to leave the task of procuring quarters to an individual officer. 60 Ct. Cl., at 574–578.

Subsequent judicial development of the convenience-of-the-employer doctrine centered primarily in the Tax Court. In two reviewed cases decided more than a decade apart, Benaglia v. Commissioner, 36 B.T.A. 838 (1937), and Van Rosen v. Commissioner, 17 T.C. 834 (1951), that court settled on the business-necessity rationale for excluding food and lodging from an employee's income. *Van Rosen's* unanimous decision is of particular interest in interpreting the legislative history of the 1954 recodification of the Internal Revenue Code since it predates that recodification by only three years. There, the Tax Court expressly rejected any reading of *Jones,* supra, that would make tax consequences turn on the intent of the employer, even though the employer in *Van Rosen* as in *Jones* was the United States and, also as in *Jones,* the subsistence payments involved in the litigation were provided by military regulation.[26] In addition, *Van Rosen* refused to follow the *Jones* holding with respect to cash allowances, apparently on the theory that a civilian who receives cash allowances for expenses otherwise nondeductible has funds he can "take, appropriate, use and expend," 17 T.C. at 838, in substantially the same manner as "any other civilian employee whose employment is such as to permit him to live at home while performing the duties of his employment." Id., at 836; see id., at 839–840. It is not clear from the opinion whether the last conclusion is based on notions of equity among taxpayers or is simply an evidentiary conclusion that, since Van Rosen was allowed to live at home while performing his duties, there was no business purposes for the furnishing of food and lodging.

---

26. Van Rosen was a civilian ship captain employed by the United States Army Transportation Corps. Id., at 834. In this capacity, his pay and subsistence allowances were determined by the Marine Personnel Regulations of the Transportation Corps of the Army. Id., at 837. His principal argument in the Tax Court was the factual similarity of his case to Jones v. United States, 60 Ct.Cl. 552 (1925).

Two years later, the Tax Court in an unreviewed decision in Doran v. Commissioner, 21 T.C. 374 (1953), returned in part to the employer's-characterization rationale rejected by *Van Rosen*. In *Doran*, the taxpayer was furnished lodging in kind by a state school. State law required the value of the lodging to be included in the employee's compensation. Although the court concluded that the lodging was furnished to allow the taxpayer to be on 24-hour call, a reason normally sufficient to justify a convenience-of-the-employer exclusion, it required the value of the lodging to be included in income on the basis of the characterization of the lodging as compensation under state law. The approach taken in *Doran* is the same as that in Mim. 6472, supra. However, the Court of Appeals for the Second Circuit, in Diamond v. Sturr, 221 F.2d 264 (1955), on facts indistinguishable from *Doran,* reviewed the law prior to 1954 and held that the business-necessity view of the convenience-of-the-employer test, "having persisted through the interpretations of the Treasury and the Tax Court throughout years of re-enactment of the Internal Revenue Code," was the *sole* test to be applied. 221 F.2d at 268.

D

Even if we assume that respondent's meal-allowance payments could have been excluded from income under the 1939 Code pursuant to the doctrine we have just sketched, we must nonetheless inquire whether such an implied exclusion survives the 1954 recodification of the Internal Revenue Code. Cf. Helvering v. Winmill, 305 U.S. 79, 83, 59 S.Ct. 45, 46, 83 L.Ed. 52 (1938). Two provisions of the 1954 Code are relevant to this inquiry: § 119 and § 120,[27] now repealed,[28] which allowed police officers to exclude from income subsistence allowances of up to $5 per day.

In enacting § 119, the Congress was determined to "end the confusion as to the tax status of meals and lodging furnished an employee by his employer." H.R.Rep. No. 1337, 83d Cong., 2d Sess., 18 (1954); S.Rep. No. 1622, 83d Cong., 2d Sess., 19 (1954); U.S.Code Cong. & Admin.News 1954, p. 4042. However, the House and Senate initially differed on the significance that should be given the convenience-of-the-employer doctrine for the purposes of § 119. As explained in its Report, the House proposed to exclude meals from gross income "if they [were] furnished at the place of employment and the employee [was] required to accept them at the place of employment as a condition of

---

27. "Sec. 120. STATUTORY SUBSISTENCE ALLOWANCE RECEIVED BY POLICE.

"(a) *General Rule.—Gross income does not include any amount received as a statutory subsistence allowance by an individual who is employed as a police official* * * *.

"(b) *Limitations.—*

"(1) Amounts to which subsection (a) applies shall not exceed $5 per day.

"(2) If any individual receives a subsistence allowance to which subsection (a) applies, no deduction shall be allowed under any other provision of this chapter for expenses in respect of which he has received such allowance, except to the extent that such expenses exceed the amount excludable under subsection (a) and the excess is otherwise allowable as a deduction under this chapter." 68A Stat. 39.

28. See Technical Amendments Act of 1958, § 3, 72 Stat. 1607.

his employment." H.R.Rep. No. 1337, supra, at 18; see H.R. 8300, 83d Cong., 2d Sess., § 119 (1954); U.S.Code Cong. & Admin.News 1954, p. 4042. Since no reference whatsoever was made to the concept, the House view apparently was that a statute "designed to end the confusion as to the tax status of meals and lodging furnished an employee by his employer" required complete disregard of the convenience-of-the-employer doctrine; U.S.Code Cong. & Admin.News 1954, p. 4042.

The Senate, however, was of the view that the doctrine had at least a limited role to play. After noting the existence of the doctrine and the Tax Court's reliance on state law to refuse to apply it in *Doran v. Commissioner,* supra, the Senate Report states:

> "Your committee believes that the House provision is ambiguous in providing that meals or lodging furnished on the employer's premises, which the employee is required to accept as a condition of his employment, are excludable from income whether or not furnished as compensation. Your committee has provided that the basic test of exclusion is to be whether the meals or lodging are furnished primarily for the convenience of the employer (and thus excludable) or whether they were primarily for the convenience of the employee (and therefore taxable). However, in deciding whether they were furnished for the convenience of the employer, the fact that a State statute or an employment contract fixing the terms of the employment indicate the meals or lodging are intended as compensation is not to be determinative. This means that employees of State institutions who are required to live and eat on the premises will not be taxed on the value of the meals and lodging even though the State statute indicates the meals and lodging are part of the employee's compensation." S.Rep. No. 1622, supra, at 19; * * *.

In a technical appendix, the Senate Report further elaborated:

> "Section 119 applies only to meals or lodging furnished in kind. Therefore, any cash allowances for meals or lodging received by an employee will continue to be includible in gross income to the extent that such allowances constitute compensation." Id., at 190–191; * * *.

After conference, the House acquiesced in the Senate's version of § 119. Because of this, respondent urges that § 119 as passed did not discard the convenience-of-the-employer doctrine, but indeed endorsed the doctrine shorn of the confusion created by Mim. 6472 and cases like *Doran.* Respondent further argues that, by negative implication, the technical appendix to the Senate Report creates a class of noncompensatory cash meal payments that are to be excluded from income. We disagree.

The Senate unquestionably intended to overrule *Doran* and rulings like Mim. 6472. Equally clearly the Senate refused completely to abandon the convenience-of-the-employer doctrine as the House wished to do. On the other hand, the Senate did not propose to leave undisturbed the convenience-of-the-employer doctrine as it had evolved prior to the promulgation of Mim. 6472. The language of § 119 [29] quite plainly rejects the reasoning behind rulings like O.D. 514, see n. [23], supra, which rest on the employer's characterization of the nature of a payment.[30] This conclusion is buttressed by the Senate's choice of a term of art, "convenience of the employer," in describing one of the conditions for exclusion under § 119. In so choosing, the Senate obviously intended to adopt the meaning of that term as it had developed over time, except, of course, to the extent § 119 overrules decisions like *Doran.* As we have noted above, Van Rosen v. Commissioner, 17 T.C. 834 (1951), provided the controlling court definition at the time of the 1954 recodification and it expressly rejected the *Jones* theory of "convenience of the employer"—and by implication the theory of O.D. 514—and adopted as the exclusive rationale the business-necessity theory. See 17 T.C., at 838–840. The business-necessity theory was also the controlling administrative interpretation of "convenience of the employer" prior to Mim. 6472. See supra, at 320–321, and n. 19. Finally, although the Senate Report did not expressly define "convenience of the employer" it did describe those situations in which it wished to reverse the courts and create an exclusion as those where "[an] employee must accept * * * meals or lodging in order properly to perform his duties." S.Rep. No. 1622, supra, at 190; * * *.

As the last step in its restructuring of prior law, the Senate adopted an additional restriction created by the House and not theretofore a part of the law, which required that meals subject to exclusion had to be taken on the business premises of the employer. Thus § 119 comprehensively modified the prior law, both expanding and contracting the exclusion for meals and lodging previously provided, and it must therefore be construed as its draftsmen obviously intended it to be—as a replacement for the prior law, designed to "end [its] confusion."

Because § 119 replaces prior law, respondent's further argument—that the technical appendix in the Senate Report recognized the existence under § 61 of an exclusion for a class of noncompensatory cash payments—is without merit. If cash meal allowances could be excluded on the mere showing that such payments served the convenience of the employer, as respondent suggests, then cash would be more widely excluded from income than meals in kind, an extraordinary result given the presumptively compensatory nature of cash payments and the obvious intent of § 119 to narrow the circumstances in which meals could be excluded. Moreover, there is no reason to suppose that Congress would have wanted to recognize a class of excludable cash

29. "[T]he provisions of an employment contract * * * shall not be determinative of whether * * * meals * * * are intended as compensation."

30. We do not decide today whether, notwithstanding § 119, the "supper money" exclusion may be justified on other grounds. See, e.g., Treasury Department, Proposed Fringe Benefit Regulations, 40 Fed.Reg. 41118, 41121 (1975) (example 8). Nor do we decide whether sporadic meal reimbursements may be excluded from income. Cf. United States v. Correll, 389 U.S. 299, 88 S.Ct. 445, 19 L.Ed.2d 537 (1967).

meal payments. The two precedents for the exclusion of cash—O.D. 514 and Jones v. United States—both rest on the proposition that the convenience of the employer can be inferred from the characterization given the cash payments by the employer, and the heart of this proposition is undercut by both the language of § 119 and the Senate Report. *Jones* also rests on *Eisner v. Macomber,* 252 U.S. 189, 40 S.Ct. 189, 64 L.Ed. 521 (1920), but Congress had no reason to read *Eisner's* definition of income into § 61 and, indeed, any assumption that Congress did is squarely at odds with Commissioner of Internal Revenue v. Glenshaw Glass Co., 348 U.S. 426, 75 S.Ct. 473, 99 L.Ed.2d 483 (1955).[31] See id., at 430–431, 75 S.Ct. 475–476. Finally, as petitioner suggests, it is much more reasonable to assume that the cryptic statement in the technical appendix—"cash allowances ＊ ＊ ＊ will continue to be includable in gross income to the extent that such allowances constitute compensation"—was meant to indicate only that meal payments otherwise deductible under § 162(a)(2) of the [1986] Code were not affected by § 119.

Moreover, even if we were to assume with respondent that cash meal payments made for the convenience of the employer could qualify for an exclusion notwithstanding the express limitations upon the doctrine embodied in § 119, there would still be no reason to allow the meal allowance here to be excluded. Under the pre-1954 convenience-of-the-employer doctrine respondent's allowance is indistinguishable from that in *Van Rosen v. Commissioner,* supra, and hence it is income. Indeed, the form of the meal allowance involved here has drastically changed from that passed on in Saunders v. Commissioner of Internal Revenue, 215 F.2d 768 (CA3 1954), relied on by the Third Circuit below see supra, at 318, and in its present form the allowance is not excludable even under *Saunders'* analysis. In any case, to avoid the completely unwarranted result of creating a larger exclusion for cash than kind, the meal allowances here would have to be demonstrated to be necessary to allow respondent "properly to perform his duties." There is not even a suggestion on this record of any such necessity.

Finally, respondent argues that it is unfair that members of the military may exclude their subsistence allowances from income while respondent cannot. While this may be so, arguments of equity have little force in construing the boundaries of exclusions and deductions from income many of which, to be administrable, must be arbitrary. In any case, Congress has already considered respondent's equity argument and has rejected it in the repeal of § 120 of the 1954 Code. That

---

31. Moreover, it must be recognized that § 213 of the Revenue Act of 1921, 42 Stat. 237, which was involved in *Jones v. United States,* made a distinction by its terms between "gross income" which included "salaries, wages, or compensation for personal service" and the "compensation received as such" by an officer of the United States. See 60 Ct.Cl., at 563. The Court of Claims assumed that Congress by so distinguishing intended to tax United States officers more narrowly than other taxpayers by levying the income tax only on amounts expressly characterized by Congress as compensation. See ibid. For this reason, *Jones* is of limited value in construing § 61 which contains no language even remotely similar to § 213.

provision as enacted allowed state troopers like respondent to exclude from income up to $5 of subsistence allowance per day. Section 120 was repealed after only four years, however, because it was "inequitable since there are many other individual taxpayers whose duties also require them to incur subsistence expenditures regardless of the tax effect. Thus, it appears that certain police officials by reason of this exclusion are placed in a more favorable position tax-wise than the other individual income taxpayers who incur the same types of expense. * * *" H.R.Rep. No. 775, 85th Cong., 1st Sess., 7 (1957).

Reversed.

MR. JUSTICE BLACKMUN, with whom The Chief Justice joins, dissenting.

More than a decade ago the United States Court of Appeals for the Eighth Circuit, in United States v. Morelan, 356 F.2d 199 (1966), held that the $3-per-day subsistence allowance paid Minnesota state highway patrolmen was excludable from gross income under § 119 of the Internal Revenue Code of [1986], 26 U.S.C. § 119. It held, alternatively, that if the allowance were includable in gross income, it was deductible as an ordinary and necessary meal-cost trade or business expense under § 162(a)(2) of the Code, 26 U.S.C. § 162(a)(2). I sat as a Circuit Judge on that case. I was happy to join Chief Judge Vogel's opinion because I then felt, and still do, that it was correct on both grounds. Certainly, despite the usual persistent Government opposition in as many Courts of Appeals as were available, the ruling was in line with other authority at the appellate level at that time.

* * *

I have no particular quarrel with the conclusion that the payments received by the New Jersey troopers constituted income to them under § 61. I can accept that, but my stance in *Morelan* leads me to disagree with the Court's conclusion that the payments are not excludable under § 119. The Court draws an in-cash or in-kind distinction. This has no appeal or persuasion for me because the statute does not speak specifically in such terms. It does no more than refer to "meals * * * furnished on the business premises of the employer," and from those words the Court draws the in-kind consequence. I am not so sure. In any event, for me, as was the case in *Morelan,* the business premises of the State of New Jersey, the trooper's employer, are wherever the trooper is on duty in that State. The employer's premises are statewide.

The Court in its opinion makes only passing comment, with a general reference to fairness, on the ironical difference in tax treatment it now accords to the paramilitary New Jersey state trooper structure and the federal military. The distinction must be embarrassing to the Government in its position here, for the Internal Revenue Code draws no such distinction. The Commissioner is forced to find support for it—support which the Court in its opinion in this case does not stretch to find—only from a regulation. Treas.Reg. § 1.61–2(b), 26

CFR § 1.61–2(b) (1977), excluding subsistence allowances granted the military, and the general references in 37 U.S.C. § 101(25) (1970 ed., Supp. V), added by Pub.L. 93–419, § 1, 88 Stat. 1152, to "regular military compensation" and "Federal tax advantage accruing to the aforementioned allowances because they are not subject to Federal income tax." This, for me, is thin and weak support for recognizing a substantial benefit for the military and denying it for the New Jersey state trooper counterpart.

I fear that state troopers the country over, not handsomely paid to begin with, will never understand today's decision. And I doubt that their reading of the Court's opinion—if, indeed, a layman can be expected to understand its technical wording—will convince them that the situation is as clear as the Court purports to find it.

Questions

1. Could Kowalski have excluded the meal allowance under § 132 or another Code section? If Kowalski must include the meal allowance in gross income, can he take a deduction for meals actually purchased? Consider § 162(a). What result if the State of New Jersey paid the back taxes of its police? Reconsider the Old Colony case, p. 49.

2. In the Benaglia case, decided in 1937, the court applied the judicially developed convenience of employer doctrine. Section 119 was first enacted in 1954. Is the judicially developed doctrine still available with respect to meals and lodging?

Problems

1. John Doe is a physician with a wife and two small children. He is about to take a position as head of the medical department of the EZ Mine, operated by Colossal Metals Co., located seventy five miles west of Phoenix, Arizona. He will be "on call" outside business hours. His salary is to be $70,000 per year. The company wants Doe to live on the premises and will furnish living quarters, plus an expense account for money actually used for food costs for himself and his family. There is a clear indication that meals and lodging are to be taken into account in fixing the compensation. The value of these items is $27,000 annually.

(a) What would be the tax consequences of this proposal to Doe, under § 119 and the Regulations, if agreed to by the parties? Consider Reg. § 1.119–1(a)(1), –1(a)(2), –1(b), –1 (c)(1) and the Adams and Kowalski cases.

(b) What kind of clause would you draft for Doe's employment contract which will, so far as possible, protect Doe's income tax position? Would you change any part of the proposed arrangement? Should the meals and lodging be described in the contract as additional compensation? Could you give him an option to receive additional compensation in lieu of lodging?

(c) Consider the tax consequences to the Corporation under § 162(a).

2. Peterson owns a large poultry farm and performs various supervisory and managerial duties. He is considering the construction of a $100,000 house on the premises. Would you advise him to: (1) incorporate the business; (2) have the corporation construct and own the residence; (3) have the Board of Directors pass a resolution requiring Peterson, as President of the corporation, to live in the house as a condition of his employment; and (4) enter into a contract with corporation requiring Peterson, who will be on call 24 hours a day to supervise the poultry breeding process, to use the residence? Will the fair market rental value of the house be included in Peterson's gross income? As a dividend? Reconsider Problem 1(b)(i) at page 116.

3. Elton, a ski lift operator at a remote ski resort, is paid $6,000 for the season. His employer offers to provide him with a room for $150 a month. The employee can live elsewhere, but it would be more convenient if the employee lived at the resort. A comparable room in a nearby town would cost $200 a month. Assume Elton takes the room at the resort. What is his gross income? Consider §§ 119 and 132(a)(2) and (c).

4. Ted Player's law firm often requires him to work late at the office. At such times, Ted's dinner expenses and cab fare home are reimbursed from petty cash. Do such reimbursements constitute gross income? Are all the conditions of § 119 satisfied? Consider Reg. § 1.119–1(a)(2). See OD 514 cited in Kowalski at fns. 23 and 30. Did OD 514 survive the adoption of § 119 as part of the Code? How does § 132 treat the supper money and cab fare? Consider § 132(a)(3) and (4) and (d).

5. Should the exclusion for meals and lodging be based upon the "convenience of the employer"? Should § 119 be eliminated from the Code? Reconsider the advantages and disadvantages of taxing fringe benefits. Reread pp. 84–86. Consider the following excerpt from H. Simons, Personal Income Taxation 53 (1938):

> Let us consider here another of Kleinwachter's conundrums. We are asked to measure the relative incomes of an ordinary officer serving with his troops and a Flugeladjutant to the sovereign. Both receive the same nominal pay; but the latter receives quarters in the palace, food at the royal table, servants, and horses for sport. He accompanies the prince to theater and opera, and, in general, lives royally at no expense to himself and is able to save generously from his salary. But suppose, as one possible complication, that the Flugeladjutant detests opera and hunting.

> The problem is clearly hopeless. To neglect all compensation in kind is obviously inappropriate. On the other hand, to include the prerequisites as a major addition to the salary implies that all income should be measured with regard for the relative pleasurableness of different activities—which would be the negation of measurement. There is hardly more reason for imputing additional income to the Flugeladjutant on account of his luxurious wardrobe than for bringing into account the prestige and social distinction of a (German) university professor.

Reference: Kragen & Speer, IRC Section 119: Is Convenience of the Employer a Valid Concept? 29 Hastings L.J. 921 (1978).

3. EMPLOYEE DEATH BENEFITS

Introduction. Section 101(b) permits the beneficiaries of a deceased employee to exclude up to $5,000 paid by the employer by reason of the death of an employee. The exclusion is extremely broad and is available whether the benefits are paid in a single sum or installments, to the deceased employee's beneficiaries or his estate, outright or in trust. The exclusion is conditioned on the employee not having a "nonforfeitable right" to receive the amounts. § 101(b)(2)(B).

Is a Death Benefit in Excess of $5,000 a Gift or Compensation? Does the enactment of § 101(b), preclude the application of § 102 for payments in excess of $5,000? In Rev.Rul. 62–102, 1962–2 C.B. 37, the Service announced that it would continue to argue that widow's payments are generally not gifts, but it would no longer argue that § 101(b) automatically bars recourse to § 102. Therefore, under certain circumstances, payments in excess of $5,000 can be excluded if the trier of fact finds that a gift was intended. Section 102(c)(1) mandates the inclusion in gross income of all gifts by employers to employees. Is a death benefit received by a member of a deceased employee's family a gift to the decedent's estate or survivor, or is it a gift "to or for the benefit of the employee?" Consider why the death benefit was paid in the next case.

ESTATE OF CARTER v. COMMISSIONER
United States Court of Appeals, Second Circuit, 1971.
453 F.2d 61.

FRIENDLY, CHIEF JUDGE:

The taxpayers' appeal from a judgment of the Tax Court, 29 CCH Tax Ct.Mem. 1407 (1970), raises the frequently litigated question whether payments by an employer to the widow of a deceased employee constituted compensation to the latter, includible as gross income under I.R.C. § 61(a), or a gift to the survivor, excludible under § 102(a).

Sydney J. Carter had been employed by the New York City financial house of Salomon Bros. & Hutzler ("Salomon Bros.") for 38 years when he died on March 1, 1960. At that time he was working under a yearly employment contract entitling him to an annual salary of $15,000 and, if he was still in the firm's employ on September 30, 1960, the end of its fiscal year, to an additional amount equal to .55% of the firm's net profits. During his employment he had required hospitalization more than 20 times and had undergone seven major operations. On many of these occasions partners of Salomon Bros. called Mrs. Carter [32] to offer financial assistance; the Carters declined, preferring

32. Mrs. Carter was personally acquainted with many of the partners, in part because she had served as secretary to the manager of the firm's Cleveland office from November, 1929 to December, 1932, when she married Mr. Carter.

to manage on their own. Most of the Salomon Bros. partners attended Mr. Carter's funeral, two having flown in from Chicago despite a blizzard. Some of the partners later suggested that the Carters' son come to work for the firm, which he did for a while.

In 1960 Salomon Bros. was managed by an administrative committee, consisting of a number of the general partners. At a meeting of this committee held shortly after Mr. Carter's death, it was decided to pay Mrs. Carter what her husband would have earned under his contract if he had lived until the end of the firm's fiscal year. These payments amounted to $60,130.84, of which $8,653.80 (paid in 15 biweekly checks of $576.92) constituted what would have been Mr. Carter's salary and $51,477.04 was what would have been his .55% share in the firm's profits.

While no minutes were kept of the administrative committee meeting at which the payments to Mrs. Carter were authorized, two members of the committee testified before the Tax Court. They agreed that at the time of Mr. Carter's death, Salomon Bros. had no established plan or policy with respect to payments to the survivors of valued employees; indeed, Mr. Carter was the first "contract employee" to have died. Both attested to the affection and esteem in which Mr. Carter was held. One, Mr. William J. Salomon, now the managing partner, who was called by the Commissioner, testified that he felt sympathy for the widow, that this did not enter into the particular decision since "we would be sympathetic to any widow," but that, on the other hand, he doubted whether the payment would have been made if Mr. Carter had not been survived by a wife and son. He said further that, as was fairly obvious, Mr. Carter's past services were a factor in arriving at the decision. * * *

The joint return for 1960 filed by Mrs. Carter as executrix and for herself did not report as income the payments of $60,130.84, * * * The Commissioner assessed a deficiency for failure to include the former amount; Mrs. Carter petitioned the Tax Court to reconsider this; that court sustained the Commissioner; and this appeal followed. We reverse.

The Commissioner expectably relies on C.I.R. v. Duberstein, 363 U.S. 278, 80 S.Ct. 1190, 4 L.Ed.2d 1218 (1960), which included Stanton v. United States, and United States v. Kaiser, 363 U.S. 299, 80 S.Ct. 1204, 4 L.Ed.2d 1233 (1960). We believe he reads somewhat more into those decisions than they held. Apart from the fact that none of the three cases involved payments to a survivor of a deceased employee, we do not understand the Court's opinion to mean that every trier of the facts was to be free for all future time to disregard guidelines that other trial and appellate courts had developed concerning the weight to be given to recurring "relevant factual elements, with their various combinations," 363 U.S. at 289, see also p. 290, 80 S.Ct. at 1199. In refusing to adopt the Government's proposal that *any* business reason for a payment would prevent it from being considered a gift, see 363 U.S. at 284 n. 6

and 287, 80 S.Ct. at 1196 and 1197, and requiring inquiry in each case into "the dominant reason that explains his [the payor's] action in making the transfer," the Court scarcely intended to sanction disregard of the teaching of one of its greatest members:

> It will not do to decide the same question one way between one set of litigants and the opposite way between another.

Cardozo, The Nature of the Judicial Process 33 (1921). See also H.L.A. Hart, The Concept of Law 155–62 (1961).

When the Supreme Court decided *Duberstein, Stanton* and *Kaiser,* the Tax Court had already gone a considerable way toward structuring its position with respect to the taxable status of payments to the survivor of a deceased employee. In the often cited case of Estate of Hellstrom v. C.I.R., 24 T.C. 916 (1955), it held that payments to the widow of the president of a corporation of the amount the president would have received in salary if he had lived out the year constituted a gift. The court specifically gave no weight to the facts that the corporation took a deduction or that the gift was a function of the deceased's salary. It found the controlling facts to be that (1) the gift was made to the widow, rather than to the estate; (2) there was no obligation on the part of the corporation to make any further payments to the deceased; (3) the widow had never worked for the corporation; (4) the corporation received no economic benefit; and (5) the deceased had been fully compensated for his services. Applying a test of principal motive and thus anticipating *Duberstein,* the court found this to be a desire of the corporation to do an act of kindness for the widow. In Estate of Foote v. C.I.R., 28 T.C. 547 (1957), the Tax Court followed *Hellstrom* and found a gift in payments to the widow of the amount which her husband, a former officer of the corporation, would have received in salary if he had lived out the year. All the factors relied upon in *Hellstrom* were present, except that the gift was made to the estate of the deceased, rather than directly to the widow. There was an additional finding that the corporation had no policy of making such payments. In Estate of Luntz v. C.I.R., 29 T.C. 647 (1958), the Tax Court held that payments to the widow of a sum equivalent to two years salary of her husband, a former president were a gift, despite the fact that at the same time the corporation also provided for the wives of two living officers at the time of their death. In finding that the payments were a gift, the Tax Court repeated the five factors noted in *Hellstrom.*

Despite the fact that *Duberstein* had approved the substantive test applied in *Hellstrom* and *Luntz,* the Tax Court took an abrupt swerve in Estate of Pierpont v. C.I.R., 35 T.C. 65 (1960), decision of which had been postponed pending the Supreme Court's decision in *Duberstein* and which was reviewed by the full court. The majority, seeing in the Supreme Court's summarization of older cases an indication, not perceptible to us, that the Court was adopting a more restrictive notion of what constitutes a gift, found payments to a survivor to be income, despite the presence of the five factors held in *Hellstrom* and *Luntz* to point to a gift, because of the authorizing resolution's having used the phrases "in recognition of the services rendered," a factor obviously present in every such case—whether mentioned or not—and having described the payment as "a continuation" of decedent's salary, as the payments held to be gifts in *Hellstrom, Foote* and *Luntz* had also been, and of the absence of "solid evidence" that the payments "were motivated in any part by the widow's needs or by a sense of generosity or the like." 35 T.C. at 68.

The Tax Court's decision in *Pierpont* was reversed and remanded by the Fourth Circuit, Poyner v. C.I.R., 301 F.2d 287 (4 Cir.1962). Chief Judge Sobeloff, writing for a strong court, said, id. at 291–292 (footnote omitted):

> In every prior Tax Court case, essentially identical facts were held sufficient to support the conclusion that the dominant motive was sympathy for the taxpayer's widowed position. The only evidence on which the Tax Court specifically relies for its contrary finding is the wording of the authorizing corporate resolutions. While the language of the resolutions certainly merits consideration, never before has such language been deemed sufficient by itself, and in the face of the other above specified factors, to support a finding that the payments were compensation for services rendered. As the facts stipulated in this case do not differ from those deemed conclusive in past cases, a contrary finding seems to us without warrant.

> The Supreme Court in Duberstein did not destroy the authority of the earlier Tax Court cases and the guides enunciated in them for discovering motivation.

After summarizing *Duberstein,* the opinion continued, id. at 292 (footnotes omitted):

> On the other hand, Duberstein cannot be read as limiting inquiry by the trier of fact solely to the factors recognized by the earlier decisions. The objective is to discover which motive is dominant in a field of co-existing motives. In the task of sorting out the varying motives, the development of more reliable criteria by the triers of fact should not be curtailed. Indeed, the Tax Court since Duberstein has considered it necessary to inquire into the widow's stock holdings in the company and the knowledge or lack of it on the part of the Board of her financial status following the death of her husband. The Tax Court in the present case also seems to have thought that the directors' knowledge of "the widow's needs" was an important factor. These subjects are certainly relevant, and inquiry may properly be directed to them, and whatever other factors the trier of fact might think helpful.

As the record was silent with respect to these further factors, the court reversed in order to permit the parties to supplement it.

* * *

As previously noted, the Tax Court's finding of income has been upset in two cases since *Poyner.* The Sixth Circuit reversed in Kuntz' Estate v. C.I.R., 300 F.2d 849 (6 Cir.), cert. denied, 371 U.S. 903, 83 S.Ct.

208, 9 L.Ed.2d 165 (1962), in which the Tax Court had relied on its *Pierpont* opinion. The court of appeals did this although the corporation was a family company and the resolution referred to the payment of the former salary for an additional year "as additional compensation and in consideration of services heretofore rendered * * *," since two directors testified that the intention was to make a gift. The Eighth Circuit reversed in Olsen's Estate v. C.I.R., 302 F.2d 671 (8 Cir.), cert. denied, 371 U.S. 903, 83 S.Ct. 208, 9 L.Ed.2d 165 (1962), where, in a pre-*Duberstein* decision, the Tax Court had found a lump sum payment to be income, although the authorizing resolution did no more than acknowledge the decedent's valuable services, the president of the corporation testified the board had thought that a payment to the widow "was in order" and "she probably could use the money under those circumstances," and the company claimed the payment as a deduction, not for compensation, but under the heading "Other Deductions."

The course of decision in the district courts has been quite different from that in the Tax Court. Payments to a survivor, not specifically characterized as compensation, have been rather consistently held to be gifts except when the corporation was dominated by the decedent's immediate family or there was a plan, formal or informal, for making such payments. In United States v. Kasynski, 284 F.2d 143 (10 Cir. 1960), the court affirmed a decision of a district judge, rendered before *Duberstein,* holding the payment of an amount equivalent to two years salary, under circumstances remarkably parallel to those in the instant case, to be a gift. In United States v. Frankel, 302 F.2d 666 (8 Cir.), cert. denied, 371 U.S. 903, 83 S.Ct. 208, 9 L.Ed.2d 165 (1962), the court affirmed a district court's holding that payments to a widow of what the deceased would have received in salary and bonus for the rest of the year (February through December) was a gift, the court emphasizing that the company had no policy for payments of this type. In United States v. Pixton, 326 F.2d 626 (5 Cir.1964) (Wisdom, J.), the court affirmed a ruling that payments of one-half of the deceased's former salary were a gift, although the corporation, in an effort to protect its deduction, wrote the widow that the payments were not intended to be a gift but rather some form of salary continuation. Our own case of Fanning v. Conley, 357 F.2d 37 (2 Cir.1966), affirmed a finding of a gift where a corporation had paid the widow an amount equal to a half year's salary "as a salary continuation," the payments were charged to "miscellaneous expense" and a tax deduction was claimed under the heading "Other Deductions"—despite evidence that this was not the first payment to a survivor.[33] Where courts of appeals have affirmed district courts' findings of income or reversed their findings of gift, the facts have been far more favorable to the Government than here.

33. Another court of appeals decision affirming a district court finding of a gift, is Greentree v. United States, 338 F.2d 946 (4 Cir.1964)—a rather extreme case since the widow and her sons owned all the stock of the corporation.

* * * Quite obviously, the Tax Court and the district courts have been traveling different paths.

If Mrs. Carter had paid the tax here at issue and sued for a refund, the odds that a district court would have found the payments constituted a gift would thus have been overwhelming. If it had done so, Fanning v. Conley, supra, 357 F.2d 37, is proof positive that we would have affirmed. Not content with reliance on the "unless clearly erroneous" rule, F.R.Civ.P. 52(a), we went to pains to point out for the guidance of the district courts that the very factors here principally relied upon by the Commissioner to negate the inference of gift—the references to salary continuation, the deduction of the payment as a business expense, although not as compensation,[34] and the failure to investigate the widow's financial circumstances—"should not be the controlling or determinative factor," 357 F.2d at 41. Indeed, on the last item Mrs. Carter stands rather better than did Mrs. Fanning, in light of Salomon Bros.' knowledge of the heavy costs entailed by her husband's many hospitalizations.[35] We cannot believe the Supreme Court intended that, at least in an area where, in contrast to the entire field of controversy with respect to gifts versus compensation, similar fact patterns tend to recur so often, the result should depend on whether a widow could afford to pay the tax and sue for a refund rather than avail herself of the salutary remedy Congress intended to afford in establishing the Tax Court and permitting determination before payment.[36] The "mainsprings of human conduct," 363 U.S. at 289, 80 S.Ct. 1190, do not differ so radically according to who tries the facts.

Beyond all this, we join in Chief Judge Sobeloff's belief, expressed in Poyner v. C.I.R., supra, 301 F.2d at 291–292, that when the Supreme Court wrote as it did in *Duberstein*, it could reasonably have expected the Tax Court to continue to observe the sensible guidelines last enunciated in Luntz v. C.I.R., 29 T.C. 647, 650 (1958) supplemented by such others as experience should prove to be relevant, as aids to determining "the dominant reason that explains his [the payor's] action in making the transfer," 363 U.S. at 286, 80 S.Ct. at 1197. Each of the factors mentioned in *Luntz* as pointing to a gift is present here unless the one reading "the wife performed no services for the corporation" were to be read to include services that had ended 28 years before her

34. The Supreme Court instructed in *Duberstein* that courts should give little or no weight to "the peripheral deductibility of payments as business expenses," since such an inquiry "would summon one difficult and delicate problem of federal tax law as an aid to the solution of another." 363 U.S. at 288, 80 S.Ct. at 1198. Cf. 4A Mertens, Law of Federal Income Taxation, § 25.85 (1966 ed.).

35. Mrs. Carter's testimony that the family was almost totally dependent on her husband's salary is verified by the fact that the joint income tax return shows 1960 dividend and interest receipts of only $1,272.28.

36. For a further discussion of the inconsistent results between the tax court and the district courts in this area, and the resulting forum shopping for litigants who can afford it, see Note, Payments to Widows of Corporate Executives and Employees—Gifts or Income?, 49 Va.L.Rev. 74, 123 (1963); Note, Voluntary Payments to Widows of Corporate Executives: Gifts or Income?, 62 Mich.L.Rev. 1216, 1227–31 (1964).

husband's death, a construction that is patently unreasonable. If anything, Mrs. Carter's previous employment and her consequent acquaintance with Salomon Bros. partners tend in favor of the inference of a gift. The only factors mentioned in the judge's opinion as calling for a different result here than in *Luntz* are (1) the claim of a tax deduction by the payor, which the Supreme Court in *Duberstein,* see fn. 14, this court in *Fanning,* and the Tenth Circuit in *Kasynski,* have held to be without material probative significance; (2) the alleged failure to inquire into Mrs. Carter's financial condition, which was unnecessary in light of what the firm knew; (3) the reference to continuation of Carter's salary as a measure of the payment, a factor present in the great bulk of these cases and ruled by us not to be material in *Fanning,* supra, 357 F.2d at 41; and (4) the filing—by someone not identified * * *—of a form 1099 return with respect to the bonus portion of the payment. This last factor was outweighed by the inconsistent failure to file such a form with respect to the salary portion and the failure to denominate the payments as compensation in the partnership return.

* * *

We perceive no tenable distinction between the facts of this case and those that led the Eighth Circuit to reverse the Tax Court in Olsen's Estate v. C.I.R., supra, 302 F.2d 671. We think the facts here are more favorable to the taxpayer than those that led the Sixth Circuit to do the same in Kuntz Estate v. C.I.R., supra, 300 F.2d 849. On the other hand, we do not believe that reversal here would be inconsistent with any of the decisions by courts of appeals or the Court of Claims which we have discovered. Applying the criterion of United States v. United States Gypsum Co., 333 U.S. 364, 395, 68 S.Ct. 525, 92 L.Ed. 746 (1948), approved for use in this context by the Court in *Duberstein,* 363 U.S. at 290–291, 80 S.Ct. at 1199–1200, we are "left with the definite and firm conviction that a mistake has been committed."

The judgment is reversed, with instructions to enter judgment annulling the determination of a deficiency.

DAVIS, JUDGE (dissenting):

Chief Judge Friendly's comprehensive opinion demonstrates at least these two things: first, that since Commissioner of Internal Revenue v. Duberstein, 363 U.S. 278, 80 S.Ct. 1190, 4 L.Ed.2d 1218 (1960), there has been a perhaps unfortunate variety of judicial answers to the question whether payments to survivors were compensation or gifts, and, second, that in this case the trier of facts could have come to the other conclusion as many other judges probably would. Nevertheless, I depart from the court because the standards set by the Supreme Court, in delineating the roles of trier and reviewing tribunal, seem to me to call for affirmance of the Tax Court's result here, regardless of what we or some others would do as fact-finders.

* * *

The Tax Court below canvassed all the significant factors which have been mentioned as bearing on the issue but felt that the taxpayers had failed, on "conflicting evidence", to sustain their burden of showing that the employer had made a gift. Given *Duberstein's* accent on the trier's role and special function, I do not have the necessary "definite and firm conviction that a mistake has been committed" on this record. The testimony of William Salomon, managing partner of the employer, is especially damaging to the taxpayer. He said, in particular, that "the opinion of counsel was that we would be permitted to make these payments and it would be treated in the same manner as if he [Mr. Carter] were still alive, or as an employee would be considered exactly as far as the tax implications were concerned."

* * *

There remains to say only that, for me, the *Duberstein* teaching, insisting on the totality of the individual facts, reduces the impact of decisions by other courts on what are necessarily other factual patterns. In the only two rulings reversing outright a Tax Court holding of taxability (Kuntz v. Commissioner of Internal Revenue, 300 F.2d 849 (6th Cir.1962) and Olsen's Estate v. Commissioner of Internal Revenue, 302 F.2d 671 (8th Cir.1962)), there was no live and explicated testimony like that of William Salomon, but, at most, merely formal and summary indications in the authorizing resolutions that the payments were regarded as compensation. Affirmances of a trier's finding of a gift, like Fanning v. Conley, 357 F.2d 37 (2d Cir.1966), are, it goes without explanation, in quite a different class. As for the implied suggestion that the Tax Court should, in a case like this, bow to the assumed trend in the district courts, I see two obstacles: first, that nothing in the federal model of tax-determination sets one group of triers above another; and, second, that *Duberstein* contemplated lack of "symmetry" between "the variety of forums in which federal income tax cases can be tried" * * *.

Questions

1. Could the employer in Carter take a deduction for the payment to the widow? In Bank of Palm Beach & Trust Co. v. United States, 201 Ct.Cl. 325, 476 F.2d 1343 (Fed.Cir.1973), the employer of the taxpayer in the Carter decision, Salomon Bros., was allowed to deduct the full amount of the death benefit. The court found that "the dominant motivation prompting the payments was a business motivation. * * * The aspects of this dominant business motivation include the award of additional compensation as well as a general policy directed toward the increased morale of similarly situated employees." Judge Davis, who dissented in Carter, concurred in the result in Bank of Palm Beach & Trust Co., but supported the deduction on the ground that the payment was a business gift.

2. Is symmetry of treatment needed between the company's and widow's treatment of the payment given the nature of the question? (Note that the Carter case involved a taxable year prior to the enactment of § 274(b).)

3. What would be the effect of § 274(b) on the employer in Carter?

4. What would be the effect of § 102(c)(1) on the widow in Carter?

Problem

Ed, the vice-president of a local corporation, was killed in a plane crash while on company business. The board of directors wishes to make payments to his widow by continuing Ed's annual salary of $40,000 for the next two years. The widow also received a payment of $3,300, representing Ed's salary for the month the deceased worked before his death.

(a) How should the resolution by the directors be structured so that the payments to Ed's widow will be exempt from taxation? Consider § 102(c)(1) and Reg. § 1.274–3(b). Can the $3,300 of past due salary be treated as a death benefit? Consider § 101(b)(2)(B).

(b) Assume the trier of fact finds that the corporation intended to make a gift directly to Ed's widow. How will Ed's widow and the company treat the salary continuation payments? Consider §§ 101(b), 102, 162(a) and 274(b).

(c) Instead, assume the trier of fact finds that the company continued the deceased's salary to compensate for past services which had not been fully compensated for. How will Ed's widow and the company treat the payments?

(d) In each of the foregoing, assume Ed's widow owned a controlling interest in the company. How might this fact change the results? Reconsider Problem 1(b)(i) on page 116.

Question

Should the $5,000 exclusion for employer-provided death benefits be repealed? Consider the following excerpt:

OFFICE OF THE SECRETARY, DEPARTMENT OF THE TREASURY, TAX REFORM FOR FAIRNESS, SIMPLICITY, AND ECONOMIC GROWTH

Vol. 2 at 31–32 (1984).

REASON FOR CHANGE

The exclusion of certain death benefits from income creates an artificial preference for compensation to be paid in this form. The exclusion of such benefits from the tax base causes the tax rates on other compensation to increase. Moreover, the exclusion is unfair because it is not available to all taxpayers (such as self-employed individuals).

Finally, confusion exists under present law as to whether a payment by an employer to a deceased employee's family constitutes a death benefit subject to the $5,000 limitation or a fully excludable gift. Treatment of such a payment as a gift is contrary to economic reality and leads to different tax treatment on similar facts.

PROPOSAL

The proposal would repeal the $5,000 exclusion for employer-furnished death benefits. Any amount paid by or on behalf of an employer by reason of the death of an employee to the estate or a family member or other beneficiary of the decedent would be characterized as a taxable death benefit rather than as an excludable gift.

* * *

ANALYSIS

Approximately $400 million of employer-provided death benefits are excluded from income under current law. As with all exclusions, the tax benefit per dollar of the death benefit exclusion increases with the recipient's tax bracket. Thus, the exclusion provides the greatest assistance to high-income taxpayers, who are also more likely to receive such benefits than low-income taxpayers.

Moreover, the Treasury Department proposals would repeal the current exclusion from income of employer-provided group-term life insurance. Absent repeal of the death benefit exclusion, the taxation of employer-provided group-term life insurance would encourage employers to recharacterize life insurance as an excludable death benefit.

Finally, a specific provision that payments from an employer to a deceased employee's estate or family do not constitute gifts would simplify current law and also reduce the unfairness created by current law where similar facts may lead to different tax results.

4. INCOME IN RESPECT OF A DECEDENT

The term "income in respect of a decedent" (IRD) refers to income earned during a taxpayer's lifetime, which was not received by a cash method taxpayer before his death or did not accrue for an accrual method taxpayer before his death. Since the income was not included by decedent on his final income tax return, pursuant to § 691 the income will be included in the gross income of the decedent's estate or reported by the beneficiary who collects it. Under § 691, IRD is treated in a manner similar to what would occur had the decedent collected the payment during his lifetime. It is reported in gross income when received under § 691(a)(1) and retains same character it would have had if the decedent lived to collect it. § 691(a)(3). In order to effectuate the intent of § 691 and prevent payment from being treated as a return of basis, § 1014(c) denies IRD a stepped-up basis. The treatment of IRD, however, allows the assignment of income for personal services, an advantage if the assignee is in a lower tax bracket. Apparently, Congress is willing to allow this tax-saving assignment because an individual can use it only once during his lifetime. Generally, a taxpayer cannot assign (or split) personal service income to another. Personal service income is taxed to the individual who earns it. See Lucas v. Earl, page 707.

Although the term "income in respect of a decedent" is not defined in the Code (and the Regulations provide little guidance, Reg. § 1.691(a)–1(b)), many types of IRD are easily recognized. The most common type is salaries and wages unpaid at death. Accrued interest and unpaid dividends on stock (if decedent dies after the record date but before the payment date) are also IRD items. It is also clear that unrealized appreciation in an asset owned by decedent at the time of his death is not IRD and can receive a tax free stepped-up basis under § 1014(a).

ESTATE OF PETERSON v. COMMISSIONER
United States Court of Appeals, Eight Circuit, 1981.
667 F.2d 675.

MCMILLIAN, CIRCUIT JUDGE.

This is an appeal from the decision of the Tax Court holding that the sale proceeds received by the estate of Charley W. Peterson from the sale of 2,398 calves did not constitute "income in respect of a decedent" under § 691(a)(1) of the Internal Revenue Code * * *.

The facts are not disputed. The following statement of facts is based upon the Tax Court opinion. The decedent, Charley W. Peterson, was in the business of raising and selling cattle. On July 11, 1972, he entered into a "livestock sales contract" with the Max Rosenstock Co., through its agent R.E. Brickley. Under the terms of this contract, the decedent was to raise and sell to the Max Rosenstock Co. "approximately 3,300 calves" at $0.49 per pound, with the date of delivery to be designated by the decedent upon five days notice. One group of calves (the Brown County calves) was to be delivered no later than November 1, 1972; the other group (the Holt County calves) was to be delivered no later than December 15, 1972. The calves were to be from three to eleven months old and in "merchantable condition" when delivered. As provided in the contract, the Max Rosenstock Co. paid $46,500 in "earnest money" to the decedent on July 13, 1972. The risk of loss was on the decedent until delivery.

The decedent did not designate a delivery date or deliver any calves by the November 1 delivery date. The record contains no reason why the decedent did not designate a delivery date or deliver the Brown County calves on or before the November 1, 1972, delivery date specified in the contract. The decedent died on November 9, 1972. The estate (the taxpayer) assumed responsibility for the calves, designated several December delivery dates, and delivered a total of 2,929 calves, 2,398 owned by the estate and 531 owned by the decedent's sons, Willis Peterson and Charles R. Peterson. The calves were accepted by the Max Rosenstock Co. As found by the Tax Court, approximately two-thirds of the calves were in a "deliverable" condition as of the date of the decedent's death. The remaining calves were not "deliverable" on that date because they were too young.

The estate reported the sale of the calves on its fiduciary income tax return and computed the gain from the sale by subtracting the fair market value of the calves on the date of the decedent's death from the sale proceeds. The Commissioner, however, determined that the gain from the sale constituted "income in respect of a decedent" under § 691(a)(1) and recomputed the estate's gain on the sale by subtracting the decedent's adjusted basis in the calves from the sale proceeds. See §§ 691(a)(1), 1014(a) (basis of property acquired from decedent is the fair market value at date of decedent's death), 1014(c) (§ 1014(a) does not apply to property which constitutes a right to receive an item of income in respect of a decedent under § 691). The characterization of the sales transaction thus determines whether the estate uses the decedent's adjusted basis or a stepped-up basis (fair market value on date of death) in calculating the gain from the sale. * * *

The Tax Court decided that the sale proceeds did not constitute "income in respect of a decedent" under § 691(a)(1). 74 T.C. at 641. After noting that § 691 does not itself define "income in respect of a decedent," the Tax Court reviewed the history of the section,[37] referred to the applicable regulations, 26 C.F.R. § 1.691(a)(1)–(3) (1981), examined the case law, and distilled a four-factor test for determining whether sale proceeds constitute "income in respect of a decedent": (1) whether the decedent entered into a legally significant arrangement regarding the subject matter of the sale,[38] (2) whether the decedent performed the substantive (nonministerial) acts required as preconditions to the sale,[39] (3) whether there existed at the time of the dece-

---

37. As summarized in Keck v. Commissioner, 415 F.2d 531, 533 (6th Cir.1969):

Under the prior law, only the items which were accruable to a taxpayer at the time of his death were required to be included in the last return. This discriminated against accrual-basis taxpayers and allowed much income of cash-basis taxpayers to escape income tax. To correct this situation, Congress provided that in the case of both cash and accrual taxpayers, the last return must include all items accruable at death. The Supreme Court in Helvering v. Enright, 312 U.S. 636, 61 S.Ct. 777, 85 L.Ed. 1093 (1941), held that the term "accrual" in the statute was not to be construed narrowly in its accounting sense, but broadly to effectuate the purpose of the statute. However, such broad construction resulted in the bunching of income in the last return and its resultant taxation in higher surtax brackets.

It was to remedy this situation that Congress enacted the forerunner of Section 691, * * * which provides that such income as was formerly required to be included in the last return, because it was accrued though not actually re-

ceived, is taxable to the recipient and has the same character in his hands that it would have had in the hands of the decedent.

38. As noted by the Tax Court, "[t]his arrangement may take a variety of forms: an express executory contract of sale [as in Trust Co. v. Ross, supra, 392 F.2d 694]; an implied contract for sale [A delivers apples to Y, Y accepts the apples, A dies before Y can pay for them]; or a contractual arrangement with a cooperative marketing association [as in Commissioner v. Linde, supra, 213 F.2d 1 (no contract or sale, just delivery of grapes to marketing cooperative; proceeds held income in respect of a decedent when received)]." Estate of Peterson v. Commissioner, 74 T.C. 630, 639 (1980) (parentheticals substituted and expanded). See also Halliday v. United States, 655 F.2d 68, 72 (5th Cir.1981) (the right to income need not be legally enforceable).

39. "One indicium of whether a decedent has performed the applicable substantive acts is whether he has delivered, or somehow placed, the subject matter of the sale beyond his control prior to his death." Estate of Peterson v. Commissioner, supra,

dent's death any economically material contingencies which might have disrupted the sale,[40] and (4) whether the decedent would have eventually received the sale proceeds if he or she had lived. 74 T.C. at 639–41.

The Tax Court concluded that the decedent had entered into a legally significant agreement to sell the calves on the basis of the livestock sales contract. The Tax Court also found that there were no economically material contingencies which could potentially have disrupted the sale; the transaction was not contingent upon the actions or approval of third parties. Compare Keck v. Commissioner, 415 F.2d 531, 534 (6th Cir.1969). Further, the decedent, if he had lived, would have received the sale proceeds; the transaction was not effective only at death. * * * The Tax Court, however, concluded that the decedent had not performed the substantive acts required under the livestock sales contract. 74 T.C. at 644. At the date of the decedent's death one-third of the calves were not in "deliverable" condition; all the calves required care and feeding until actually delivered. The estate assumed responsibility for the care and feeding of all the calves until delivery (for approximately one month). The Tax Court concluded that the activities performed by the estate were not perfunctory or ministerial and that these activities were sufficient to remove the sale proceeds from the scope of § 691(a)(1). Id. at 644–45.

* * * However, in order to determine whether the Tax Court misapplied its four-factor test, we necessarily reach the Commissioner's apportionment or allocation argument. We think that the apportionment or allocation argument incorrectly emphasizes the condition or character of the subject matter of the sale instead of the status of the transaction itself at the time of the decedent's death. For the reasons discussed below, we affirm the decision of the Tax Court.

Stated in misleadingly simple terms, whether income is considered income in respect of a decedent under § 691 depends upon whether the decedent had a right to receive income at the time of his or her death. The focus is upon the decedent's *right or entitlement to income* at the time of death.

Although it is pertinent to inquire whether the income received after death was attributable to activities and economic efforts of the decedent in his lifetime, these activities and efforts must give rise to a right

74 T.C. at 640. Compare M. Ferguson, J. Freeland & R. Stephens, Federal Income Taxation of Estates and Beneficiaries, supra, 180–84 ("[E]ven where the property has been made the subject of a binding, executory contract of sale, if the benefits and hazards of ownership are still possessed by the decedent at his death, the property is entitled to a § 1014(a) basis in the hands of his estate, and his negotiated profit will not be taxed to his estate (or to anyone) under § 691 when the sale is completed after his death.") (footnote omitted), with Gordon, Income in Respect of a

Decedent and Sales Transactions, 1961 Wash.U.L.Q. 30, 37 (§ 691 should apply to sale proceeds from sales which at the time of the decedent's death are incomplete "only as to delivery of the res and receipt of the purchase price").

40. Cf. Keck v. Commissioner, supra, 415 F.2d at 534 (sale of stock was contingent upon Interstate Commerce Commission approval; proceeds held not income in respect of decedent where ICC approval not granted at time of the decedent's death).

to that income. And the right is to be distinguished from the activity which creates the right. Absent such a right, no matter how great the activities or efforts, there would be no taxable income under § 691.

Trust Co. v. Ross, 392 F.2d 694, 695 (5th Cir.1967) (per curiam), cert. denied, 393 U.S. 830, 89 S.Ct. 97, 21 L.Ed.2d 101 (1968) ∗ ∗ ∗.

The leading commentators have proposed the following as a "tentative working definition" of income in respect of a decedent:

> Items of income in respect of a decedent ∗ ∗ ∗ are payments received toward satisfaction of a right or expectancy created almost entirely through the efforts or status of the decedent and which, except for his death and without further action on his part, the decedent would have realized as gross income. Two observations should be made. First, the concept is manifestly broader than the mere accrued earnings of a cash basis decedent. Second, despite the breadth of this tentative definition, § 691 does not reach the income potential in a decedent's appreciated property, even if that appreciation is due to the decedent's own efforts. Further action on the decedent's part (e.g., a sale) would have been required for such appreciation to be realized as income. Within this definition farm produce inventories grown, harvested, and processed for market, but not delivered by the decedent before his death, even though they come very close to representing ordinary income actually realized, are "property" rather than a bare right to income until they are sold. Not being income in respect of a decedent, they qualify for a new basis at death under the fair market value provision of § 1014(a).

M. Ferguson, J. Freeland & R. Stephens, Federal Income Taxation of Estates and Beneficiaries 146 (1970) (footnote omitted).

"The impact of § 691 may vary according to the nature or origin of the income. Such variation extends to questions of timing and characterization and even to the question whether a particular receipt must be treated as income in respect of a decedent at all." Id. at 162. For example, items of income attributable to the decedent's services are generally income in respect of a decedent.[41] Characterization of items of income attributable to sales proceeds, as in the present case, however, is less clear, particularly because of the operation of the basis rules of § 1014. Id. at 177–78.

---

41. The decedent's personal services are the most common source of IRD [income in respect of a decedent], including payment for the decedent's final pay period, compensation paid in installments continuing after his death, billed but uncollected fees and commissions, and accrued vacation and leave pay. Items attributable to the decedent's services but dependent on future events can also constitute IRD, such as an insurance agent's right to receive renewal commissions on life insurance policies sold by him, a lawyer's right to share in contingent fees received by his firm in cases that are uncompleted at the time of his death, and a bonus paid after an employee's death by an employer under a plan that did not vest enforceable rights in the employees. More controversial are cases holding that allowances paid by employers to the surviving spouse or other dependents of a faithful employee, if not excludable from gross income as "gifts" or employee death benefits under IRC § 102 or § 101(b)(1), constitute IRD ∗ ∗ ∗.

3 B. Bittker, Federal Taxation of Income, Estates and Gifts, supra, ¶ 83.1.2, at 83–5 to –6 (footnotes omitted).

[I]t may be difficult to determine whether the decedent's steps prior to his death had proceeded sufficiently to treat sales proceeds received after death as income in respect of a decedent. The test here is not quite whether the decedent "closed" the sale or transferred title and possession of an asset before death. Rather, it is whether his successor acquired a right to receive proceeds from an asset's disposition on the one hand, or acquired the asset itself on the other. Depending upon the subject and the terms of a sale, death may interrupt the transaction at a number of stages which do not fall clearly on either side of this murky distinction.

Id. at 178–79.

As noted by Ferguson, Freeland and Stephens, "the definitional problem under § 691(a) is complicated by the general rule of § 1014(a) according a basis equal to estate tax value to the decedent's "property" other than such § 691(a) "rights." Id. at 180. As illustrated by the present case, the tax consequences of characterizing a particular item of income may be substantial. Ferguson, Freeland and Stephens apparently do not favor characterizing sales proceeds from sales transactions substantially "incomplete" [42] at the time of the decedent's death as income in respect of a decedent:

[W]here there is a contract of sale which would have been completed during the decedent's life but for his death, the proceeds received upon culmination of the sale by the decedent's transferee will be taxed as income in respect of a decedent if no substantial conditions remained to be performed by the decedent at his death. Thus, if the executor had only a passive or ministerial role to play in completing the sale, the proceeds should be taxed as income in respect of a decedent.

---

42. Tax commentators differentiate between "executory sales contracts" and "sales," even though such a distinction may not make much sense in contract law. See Note, Sales Transactions and Income in Respect of a Decedent, supra, 3 Ga.L. Rev. at 617 ("closed transaction"). As illustrated in the examples in the relevant regulations, [Reg. § 1.691(a)–1(b)], delivery or actual disposition of the subject of a sales contract before death is a "completed" sale and the sale proceeds received after death is income in respect of a decedent. Actual disposition of the subject matter, in the absence of any sales contract or agreement, was sufficient to make the post-death receipt of proceeds income in respect of a decedent in *Linde*, supra, 213 F.2d at 4–8 (decedent was a member of an agricultural marketing cooperative). If the decedent neither enters into a sales contract nor delivers the property before death, the post-death disposition of the property by the executor does not produce income in respect of a decedent.

The difficult question arises where the decedent has made arrangements to dispose of the property (such as entering into a sales contract) but dies before delivering or otherwise disposing of the property. In *Trust Co. v. Ross,* the subject matter of the sale was the controlling interest in a hotel chain. The negotiations were completed, the contract of sale was executed, and the stock was placed in escrow before the death of the decedent. After his death, the estate made some financial arrangements and formally closed the sale. The Fifth Circuit concluded that the execution of the contract created a right to the proceeds (and thus constituted income in respect of a decedent) because the tasks left to the executor were "minor." 392 F.2d at 697. Accord, Estate of Sidles, supra, 65 T.C. at 880–81 (on date of death decedent had performed enough substantive acts within his control to "perfect" his right to receive liquidating distribution of corporate assets, declaration of liquidating dividend and filing of articles of dissolution characterized as "mere formalities" and "ministerial acts").

* * * Whenever the decedent negotiates a contract enforceable by his executor after death, the profit may properly be attributed to the decedent's bargaining and other efforts, which would seem to suggest income treatment for a part of the post-death receipts. On the other hand, the basis rules of § 1014(a) suggest that, wherever the risks inherent in ownership remain with the decedent until death, adjustments to the property's basis (and hence variations in the amount of gain or loss under the contract) remain possible until actual disposition by the decedent's successor.

Id. at 183–84 (footnote omitted).

Here, the task remaining to be performed by the estate was performance of the contract. We agree with the conclusion of the Tax Court that performance of the contract, which, under the circumstances, involved care and feeding of livestock and delivery, cannot be characterized as a ministerial or minor act. However, we think that characterization of the tasks which remain after the death of the decedent should not necessarily depend upon the nature of the subject matter of the sales transaction. For example, the subject matter of the sales transaction in the present case was livestock, which obviously required care and feeding. What if the subject matter was not livestock but logs or refrigerators? It would still be the task of the decedent's transferee to deliver or otherwise dispose of the logs or refrigerators, even though that type of property does not require the care that livestock does.

We recognize that the analysis followed by the Tax Court emphasizes delivery or disposal of the subject matter of the sales transaction and, to a certain degree, discounts the significance of the sales contract. Compare Gordon, Income in Respect of a Decedent and Sales Transactions, 1961 Wash.U.L.Q. 30, 37–38 (proposing that § 691 should apply to sales proceeds if the contract of sale is incomplete at death "only as to delivery of the res and receipt of the purchase price"). Nonetheless, this analysis is not inconsistent with Trust Co. v. Ross, supra, 392 F.2d at 697, where the contract of sale was executed and the stock was placed in escrow before the death of the decedent and the tasks remaining for the estate were "minor," and Commissioner v. Linde, supra, 213 F.2d at 4–8, where the decedent had delivered the property before death to the marketing cooperative, thus "converting" the property into a right to receive income. Moreover, "while the death of a decedent can be a fortuitous event tax-wise, it is certainly hard to visualize death as a tax avoidance scheme." Note, Sales Transactions and Income in Respect of a Decedent, supra, 3 Ga.L.Rev. at 615. After all, the decedent in a sales case does not prearrange his death in order to shift the responsibility for delivering the subject matter of the sale transaction to his executor or to take advantage of the fair market value basis rule of § 1014(a) and thus avoid the reach of § 691.

Accordingly, the decision of the Tax Court is affirmed.

The Peterson case raises a problem where there has been a sale of appreciated property which was not completed prior to decedent's death. If the sale is complete but the purchase price is yet to be paid in full or in part, the gain on the sale is IRD. And if the sale consisted of a capital asset, the IRD will be reported as a capital gain when payment is received. If the sale has not been completed by the time of death, the gain is still in the form of unrealized appreciation and is eligible for the tax free stepped-up basis. Because the stakes are high, there has been considerable litigation over the issue of the completeness of the sale. The courts have used either an "economic activities" test which looks to whether the economic activities of the decedent produced the gain or a "right to income" test which uses a formalistic approach by looking at the time the sales contract became effective. See Commissioner v. Linde, 213 F.2d 1 (9th Cir.1954), cert. denied 348 U.S. 871, 75 S.Ct. 107, 99 L.Ed. 686 (1955) (sale proceeds of grapes delivered to co-ops prior to death and sold after death treated as IRD because the payments "had their source exclusively in decedent's contract and arrangement with the cooperative associations") and Trust Company of Georgia v. Ross, 392 F.2d 694 (5th Cir.1967), cert. denied 393 U.S. 830, 89 S.Ct. 97, 21 L.Ed.2d 10 (1968) (payments treated as IRD, notwithstanding amendments to the contract after decedent's death and existence of liquidated damage clause permitting the purchaser to terminate the contract by forfeiting the down payment).

Question

Is the formalistic approach found in the Regulations, § 1.691(a)–2(b) Example (5), preferable to looking at the decedent's economic activities?

An estate's claim for the unpaid wages of a deceased employee cannot receive a tax free stepped-up basis under § 1014(a). § 1014(c). Unpaid wages of a cash method employee cannot be included in income on the employee's final income tax return. And, if this claim takes a basis equal to its value at death, little or no income would be realized on the collection of the deceased employee's wages. Because an employee using the accrual method of accounting would have to report uncollected, but earned, wages on his final income tax return, an employee would be able to escape income taxation on wages based solely upon the choice of a method of accounting. One of the reasons Congress enacted §§ 691 and 1014(c) was to eliminate this disparate treatment between individuals using different accounting methods.

Problems

1. Dr. J. bills a patient $1,000 on June 30 for services rendered. Consider the tax consequences in each of the following if Dr. J. uses: (1) the cash method of accounting, or (2) the accrual method of accounting.

(a) Dr. J. dies on July 31. The receivable has a value of $1,000 at the time of his death. The estate collects the entire $1,000 outstanding balance on August 15. Consider § 1014(c) and Reg. § 1.446–1(c)(ii).

(b) Assume in "a" above that the estate receives a payment of only $950. Consider § 1014(c).

(c) Assume in "a" above that the estate sells the receivable to a collection company for $950 on August 1. The collection company collects the entire $1,000 on September 10. How does the collection company treat the $1,000 it receives?

2. Father, a cash method taxpayer, bills clients for services performed. Prior to the collection of his receivables, he gives them to his 15 year-old son. The father's basis in each receivable is zero.

(a) Who will realize the income, the father or the son?

(b) Assume the father gave the receivables, but died prior to their collection. Does § 1014(c) apply?

3. What is an advantage of gain in the form of unrealized appreciation in the value of property owned at death over gain earned by the performance of services?

5. OTHER EMPLOYEE BENEFITS EXCLUDED BY THE CODE FROM GROSS INCOME

Various types of insurance, including group life insurance and health benefit plans, and other plans, such as qualified group legal service plans, provide tax free income for employees. A primary danger of this type of device is that its benefits will not be generally available to all employees but will serve only as tax free rewards for top management. The Tax Reform Act of 1986 established comprehensive nondiscrimination rules for statutory employee benefit plans. § 89. The term "statutory employee benefit plan" includes: (1) a plan providing group term life insurance; and (2) an accident or health plan. § 89(i). Under the nondiscrimination tests, statutory employee benefit plans are subject to eligibility tests and a benefits test, applicable to each type of benefit. § 89(c), (d), (e) and (f). A highly compensated employee, as defined in § 414(g), who is a participant in any discriminatory statutory employee benefit plan is taxed only on the value of the discriminatory portion of the employer provided coverage under the plan. § 89(b) and (g)(3).

Group Life Insurance. Under § 79(a), premiums paid by an employer on group term life insurance represent gross income to each employee only to the extent that the coverage of such insurance exceeds $50,000. The premiums on group term life insurance with a face value below $50,000 are not taxed to an employee on the rationale: (1) that it is desirable to encourage employers to provide life insurance protection for their employees and (2) that a basic amount of insurance helps keep family units together when the principal breadwinner dies prematurely.

Question

Should the exclusion for employer-provided group term life insurance be repealed? Consider the following excerpt:

OFFICE OF THE SECRETARY, DEPARTMENT OF THE TREASURY, TAX REFORM FOR FAIRNESS, SIMPLICITY, AND ECONOMIC GROWTH
Vol. 2 at 29 (1984).

REASON FOR CHANGE

The exclusion of group-term life insurance from income causes significant inequities among taxpayers. Taxpayers receiving group-term life insurance through an employer-sponsored plan effectively purchase such insurance with pre-tax dollars, whereas taxpayers not covered by an employer plan must use after-tax dollars to acquire the same insurance. Thus, two taxpayers with identical real incomes may pay different amounts in income taxes. Moreover, even among taxpayers covered by employer plans, the exclusion of group-term life insurance favors high[er] bracket over low[er] bracket taxpayers. * * *

The group-term life insurance exclusion lowers the after-tax cost of term life insurance and thus encourages employees to request and employers to provide more insurance than the employees would be willing to pay for on their own. Because this subsidy for term life insurance is provided through the tax system, its actual cost to society is difficult to control or monitor. As with other fringe benefit exclusions, the group-term life insurance exclusion also narrows the tax base and thus causes higher than necessary marginal tax rates.

PROPOSAL

The exclusion of group-term life insurance from income would be repealed. Group-term life insurance provided by an employer would be taxable under the same general principles that apply to other employer-provided fringe benefits.

* * *

ANALYSIS

Almost one-half of all families receive some employer-provided group-term life insurance. Such insurance accounts for approximately 40 percent of the value of all life insurance in force. Given the lower rates available through group-term insurance, most employers are expected to continue to make such insurance available.

Accident and Health Plans. Section 106 excludes the premium costs of employer contributions to accident and health plans from an employee's gross income. Employer contributions to accident and health plans are deductible as ordinary and necessary business expense of the employer under § 162(a). Amounts received by an employee under employer provided health and accident plans to reimburse the employee for medical care expenses incurred for the employee, his spouse or dependents are excluded from the employee's gross income unless the expenses were deducted by the employee in a prior taxable year.   § 105(b).

Question

Should the exclusion for employer-provided health insurance be modified.   Consider the following excerpt:

OFFICE OF THE SECRETARY, DEPARTMENT OF THE TREASURY, TAX REFORM FOR FAIRNESS, SIMPLICITY, AND ECONOMIC GROWTH
Vol. 2 at 23–26 (1984).

REASONS FOR CHANGE

As with other tax-free fringe benefits, the exclusion of employer-provided health insurance from income subsidizes the cost of such insurance for eligible taxpayers.   Within limits, this tax-based incentive for employee health insurance is an appropriate part of the national policy to encourage essential health care services.   In its present unlimited form, however, the exclusion provides disproportionate benefits to certain taxpayers, encourages the overconsumption of health care services, and contributes to higher than necessary marginal tax rates.

The exclusion from income of employer-provided health insurance is unfair to individuals who are not covered by employer plans and who must therefore pay for their health care with after-tax dollars. * * *

Because many employer-provided plans are so generous that the employees pay very little, if anything, out-of-pocket for health services, the employees are more likely to overuse doctor and hospital services and medical tests.   The tax system subsidizes this overuse by reducing the effective cost of employer-provided insurance. * * * The rapid increase in the cost of health care services in recent years can be attributed at least in part to overconsumption of such services by employees for whom they are tax free and, in many cases, available without limit.

The unlimited exclusion for employer-provided health care has also contributed to the erosion of the tax base and to consequent high marginal tax rates.   Compensation paid in this nontaxable form has grown significantly in recent years.   Imposing reasonable limits on the amount of health care available tax-free is an important part of the effort to broaden the base of taxable income and reduce marginal tax rates.

* * *

PROPOSAL

Employer contributions to a health plan would be included in the employee's gross income to the extent they exceed $70 per month ($840 per year) for individual coverage of an employee, or $175 per month ($2,100 per year) for family coverage (i.e., coverage that includes the spouse or a dependent of the employee). These monthly dollar limits would be adjusted annually to reflect changes in the Consumer Price Index.

With respect to any employee, an employer's contribution to a health plan would be the annual cost of coverage of the employee under the plan reduced by the amount of the employee's contributions for such coverage. The annual cost of coverage with respect to an employee would be calculated by determining the aggregate annual cost of providing coverage for all employees with the same type of coverage (individual or family) as that of the employee, and dividing such amount by the number of such employees.

The annual cost of providing coverage under an insured plan (or any insured part of a plan) would be based on the net premium charged by the insurer for such coverage. The annual cost of providing coverage under a noninsured plan (or any noninsured part of a plan) would be based on the costs incurred with respect to the plan, including administrative costs. In lieu of using actual administrative costs, an employer could treat seven percent of the plan's incurred liability for benefit payments as the administrative costs of the plan. A plan would be a noninsured plan to the extent the risk under the plan is not shifted from the employer to an unrelated third party.

* * *

The proposal would require that the cost of coverage under the plan be determined in advance of the payroll period. The cost would be redetermined at least once every 12 months, and whenever there are significant changes in the plan's coverage or in the composition of the group of covered employees.

If the actual cost of coverage cannot be determined in advance, reasonable estimates of the cost of coverage would be used. If an estimated cost were determined not to be reasonable, the employer would be liable for the income taxes (at the maximum rate applicable to individuals) and the employment taxes (both the employer's and the employee's share) that would have been paid if the actual cost of coverage had been used. * * *

* * *

ANALYSIS

For 1987, the proposed cap on tax-free employee health care would increase the taxable income of only 30 percent of all civilian workers (or approximately one-half of civilian employees who receive some employer-provided insurance). Even for affected taxpayers, only the excess over the $175 family/$70 individual monthly ceilings would be included in gross income.

Most low-income employees would be unaffected by the proposed change because they generally receive employer-provided insurance (if at all) in amounts below the cap. Only about ten percent of those with incomes below the average for all taxpayers would have increased taxable income as a result of the proposal. In contrast, approximately 40 percent of the wealthiest one-fifth of all taxpayers would have additional taxable income as a result of the proposal, with 60 percent of the additional tax liability borne by that group. A small number of low-income workers now receive an extremely large proportion of their compensation in the form of health insurance; the impact on those workers, however, would be mitigated by the proposed increases in the personal exemptions and zero bracket amounts.

Group Legal Service Plan. Section 120 excludes from an employee's income, employer contributions to and the value of benefits received from qualified "group legal service plans" set up by an employer for the benefit of employees, their spouses and dependents. The plan must meet nondiscriminatory standards with respect to eligibility, contributions, and benefits. § 120(c). The plans can be funded by direct payments to law firms, through insurance companies, through certain tax-exempt organizations functioning solely to provide group legal services or through a combination of eligible organizations.

Question

Should the exclusion for employer-provided legal services be repealed? Consider the following excerpt:

OFFICE OF THE SECRETARY, DEPARTMENT OF THE TREASURY, TAX REFORM FOR FAIRNESS, SIMPLICITY, AND ECONOMIC GROWTH.
Vol. 2 at 33 (1984).

REASON FOR CHANGE

The exclusion from income of employer-provided group legal services encourages overconsumption of legal services by permitting employees to purchase them with pre-tax dollars. The exclusion is also unfair because it is not available to all taxpayers and, where available, is of greater benefit to high-income taxpayers. Finally, by encouraging employees to take more of their compensation in this untaxed form, the exclusion narrows the tax base and thus places upward pressure on marginal tax rates.

PROPOSAL

The group legal exclusion would be allowed to expire.

* * *

ANALYSIS

Expiration of the exclusion for group legal services will allow a market for such services to develop without tax-induced distortions.

———

Viewpoint of Organized Labor. In analyzing the treatment of these employee benefits currently excluded by statutory provision from gross income, the viewpoint of organized labor should be considered.

STATEMENT OF AFL–CIO PRESIDENT LANE KIRLAND ON FRINGE BENEFIT TAXATION
(January 11, 1985).

The AFL–CIO supports just and fair measures to reduce the deficit and make the nation's tax structure more efficient and productive, but merely to increase the taxes of working people and jeopardize benefits and protections that are essential to their welfare and that of their families would be unjust and unfair.

In the so-called fringe benefit group now being considered for taxation are widely used programs that fulfill major, demonstrable needs and social purposes that affect the great majority of working Americans.

Health insurance, pensions, day care, education programs, prepaid legal plans have evolved over many years to meet specific national social goals and have been subjected to the checks and balances of the legislative process, as well as the collective bargaining process.

These benefits are not frivolous "perks" or gimmicks to shelter income, generate phony losses or otherwise reduce the taxes of a privileged few. Most are longstanding economic buttresses of the tax code and are widely distributed among America's working population.

To qualify for tax exclusion, the plans must comply with stringent rules and contain limitations and constraints to prevent discrimination or favoritism.

That test distinguishes these provisions from many other so-called tax "preferences" which primarily benefit a privileged few and provide no assurance that their stated purpose will be served.

We strongly object, therefore, to these proposals on the grounds that:

- Any *revenue* attained by taxing fringes would be directly and exclusively taken out of the pockets of working people, and

- Any *changes* in relative tax burdens that might come about would be strictly the result of shifting and rearranging the tax liabilities of working people.

HEALTH CARE

Those who advocate eliminating the tax exclusion for employer *health insurance* contributions or placing a cap on tax-free employer contributions argue that an employee health tax would give consumers an incentive to reduce coverage which, in turn, would force a reduction in demand for health care; and doctors, hospitals and the health care "providers" would reduce prices.

But in health care, unlike other markets, consumers make almost no purchasing decisions. Physicians decide when patients need to go into the hospital, how long they stay, and what tests and medications they receive while they are there. To use a tax penalty to encourage patients to act in an area over which they have so little control makes no sense.

The most likely effect of scaling back benefits would be loss of coverage for preventive care, outpatient diagnostic services, dental care, eyeglasses and other benefits which, in fact, save money. What would be left intact is coverage for hospital and surgical benefits over which patients have very little control and which have been the major source of our health inflation problems.

*   *   *

We believe that current tax treatment of qualified *group legal service plans* helps to make such services available at minimal cost to many who would otherwise be denied such protection. There is no evidence that such plans have been abused, exploited as tax shelters, or led to inequities or discriminatory practices.

To heap more of the tax burden on working people—particularly in the areas of health, education, pensions, unemployment insurance and workers' compensation—would result in more injustice, not less. We urge Congress to concentrate on the long list of alternative means to increase revenue through improving not sacrificing equity.

C. INVESTMENT CONTEXT

1. MUNICIPAL BOND INTEREST

In general, Section 103(a) excludes from gross income interest received on state and local bonds.

Problems

1. Two taxpayers, one in the 33% marginal income tax bracket, the other in the 15% bracket, are considering whether to invest their savings in 10% taxable bonds or 8% tax-free bonds. What advice would you give each taxpayer?

2. Liz, an investor, purchases a $10,000 previously issued municipal bond paying interest of $500 per year from the bondholder for $7,000. Liz receives interest payments each year until the bond reaches maturity at which time she receives $10,000 from the municipality. Why must Liz

report $3,000 of income on the redemption of the bond at maturity? What is the reason for not excluding $3,000 of income? What is the character of the $3,000 of income? Consider §§ 1276(a)(1) and 1278(a)(1)(B)(ii).

Policy Aspects. The exclusion for municipal bond interest has been justified on the ground that it enables state and local governments to compete for funds in the financial markets at a lower cost. The exclusion has been criticized as an inefficient subsidy because it costs the Federal government more in lost tax revenues than the interest costs saved by state and local governments. It is also inequitable as it erodes the progressivity of the income tax. Despite its well-recognized problems, state and local governments have come to rely on this subsidy. Various proposals to remedy the problems have recognized that the subsidy must continue.

The Tax Reform Act of 1986 divides municipal bonds into three broad categories for Federal income tax purposes. The first category consists of "public purpose" bonds issued by state and local governments or their agencies to finance traditional governmental operations and functions, such as road building and public school construction. The interest on public purpose bonds generally continues to be excluded from gross income. § 103(a).

The second category consists of "private activity" bonds. § 141(a). Private activity bonds are issued for two broad purposes. The first type of private activity bond provides public financing for so-called public purposes such as financing private housing for persons below certain income levels (mortgage subsidy bonds) and providing student loans. In other words, the funds are used by nongovernmental persons. The second type of private activity bond provides public financing for properties used for private business use such as bonds used to finance an industrial park where the buildings are rented to private companies. The interest on any private activity bond is tax free only if the bond is also a "qualified" bond. §§ 141(d) and 142–145. For example, a private activity bond issued to finance a municipal airport, where space is rented to private airline companies, is a qualified bond. § 142(a)(1). If a private activity bond is not qualified, then the interest is taxable. For example, a private activity bond used to finance the building of a sport stadium is viewed as the providing of a public purpose that Congress does not feel is essential and is not a qualified bond.

Even though a private activity bond is also a qualified bond, the states are subject to volume caps on the amount of qualified private activity bonds that can be issued. § 146. In addition, taxpayers who buy qualified private activity bonds issued after August 7, 1986, generally must treat the interest on these bonds as a tax preference item which must be added to taxable income for purposes of calculating the alternative minimum tax. § 57(a)(5).

The third category consists of any state or local bonds where the proceeds of the public financing are invested (even if only for a short period) by the issuing governmental body in higher yielding, taxable obligations. Such bonds are used for arbitrage purposes. A government's arbitrage profits are perceived as being unrelated to the purpose of the borrowing. Under § 103(b)(2) the interest on any "arbitrage" bond, § 148(a), is taxable, even though the bond is otherwise tax exempt because it is a public purpose or qualified private activity bond. However, such bonds can retain their tax free status if the issuing governmental body rebates its arbitrage profits to the Federal government. § 148(f).

Any bond qualifying for tax free treatment, either because it is a public purpose or qualified private activity bond, will lose that tax exemption if it does not meet certain compliance requirements found in § 149, such as the requirement that the bond be in registered form. § 103(b)(3).

The following excerpt from the legislative history summarizes some of the concerns regarding an unrestricted ability of state and local governments to issue tax exempt bonds.

> The committee is concerned that the large volume of nongovernmental tax-exempt bonds and the accompanying ability of higher income taxpayers to avoid paying income tax erodes confidence in the equity of the tax system, increases the cost of financing traditional government activities, and results in an inefficient allocation of new capital. The committee desires to correct these problems without affecting the ability of State and local governments to issue tax-exempt bonds for general government operations or for the construction and operation of such governmental facilities as schools, highways, government buildings, and governmentally owned and operated sewage, solid waste, water, and electric facilities.

> The dollar volume of tax-exempt bonds issued for long-term nongovernmental purposes more than doubled in the three years between 1981 and 1984, from $30.9 billion to $71.7 billion. The committee believes that the volume of these bonds has reached unjustifiably high levels, despite recent Congressional attempts to control that volume. In 1984, these issues represented nearly two-thirds of the total tax-exempt bond market. In 1975, nongovernmental bond volume was less than one-third of the total tax-exempt bond market. Each dollar of nongovernmental bond volume represents an indirect subsidy by the Federal Government for the activities of nongovernmental persons. Absent further restrictions on nongovernmental bonds, the revenue cost of this tax subsidy is estimated to total $68.5 billion over the next five years.

> The large volume of tax-exempt bonds for nongovernmental persons affects the equity of the tax system in several ways. First, the equity of the tax system is harmed when high-income taxpayers and corporations have the ability to limit their tax liability by investing in tax-exempt securities. Due to the large volume of nongovernmental

tax-exempt obligations, tax-exempt yields are often only slightly less than taxable yields. Taxpayers with high marginal tax rates receive an after-tax yield on tax-exempt bonds much higher than the yield they would receive from investing in taxable bonds. A perception of inequity arises when these investors are able to reduce their tax liability and still receive a very high rate of return by investing in tax-exempt bonds. A smaller supply of bonds for activities of nongovernmental persons will reduce the benefit high marginal tax rate investors receive from investing in tax-exempt bonds.

Second, tax-exempt financing for certain activities of nongovernmental persons results in a misallocation of capital. The efficient allocation of capital requires that the social return from a marginal unit of investment be equal across activities. When there is no difference between the private return on capital and the social return, the output of capital will be maximized only if there is no preferential treatment for investment in certain activities. If the ability of nongovernmental activities to qualify for tax-exempt financing is restricted, capital may be more efficiently allocated.

Further, the large volume of nongovernmental tax-exempt bonds also increases the interest rates that State and local governments must pay to finance their activities. As the total volume of tax-exempt bonds increases, the interest rate on the bonds must increase to attract investment from competing sources. The additional bond volume caused by nongovernmental users in the tax-exempt market thus increases the cost of financing essential government services. Tax Reform Act of [1986], Report of the Committee on Ways and Means, House of Representatives, on H.R. 3838, 99th Cong., 1st Sess. 514–15 (1985).

Questions

1. Is § 103 necessary? How does the exclusion constitute a form of revenue sharing?

2. Why does Congress require that tax free municipal bonds be in registered form?

2. TRANSFER PAYMENTS

Despite the absence of any exclusionary provision in the Code, the Service, following a long-standing administrative position, did not tax governmental transfer payments, such as Social Security, unemployment insurance, veterans benefits, welfare and other assistance payments. The Service has excluded transfer payments by administrative pronouncement, citing no authority and giving no reasons for the exclusion. See I.T. 3447, 1941–1 C.B. 191, superceded by Rev.Rul. 70–217, 1970–1 C.B. 12.

There are two categories of transfer payments. The first category consists of those which are "income conditioned." These payments are designed to supplement income and bring the poor up to a subsistence income level. The second category consists of those which are "income replacements" or forms of deferred compensation. Income replacements are actually equivalent to a form of salary and have nothing to do with an individual's general well-being.

The question has frequently arisen as to whether governmental transfer payments should be subject to income taxation. It is generally agreed that the first category of payments, income conditioned, should not be taxed. Why? Even if they were taxed, the additional revenues would be relatively minor.

Commentators have frequently recommended that the second category, income replacements, be subject to taxation, especially because they are paid regardless of the need of the recipient. In an effort to raise tax revenues, Congress has decided to tax some transfer payments in the second category, but only as to individuals who do not rely on them for maintenance of a subsistence income level.

Pursuant to § 85, all unemployment compensation benefits are includible in gross income. The legislative history indicates: "The committee believes that unemployment compensation benefits, which essentially are wage replacement payments, should be treated for tax purposes in the same manner as wages or other wage-type payments. Also, when wage replacement payments are given more favorable tax treatment than wages, some individuals may be discouraged from returning to work." (Tax Reform Act of [1986], Report of the Committee on Ways and Means, House of Representatives on H.R. 3838, 99th Cong., 1st Sess. 98 (1985)).

Congress enacted the Social Security Amendments Act of 1983 in response to the imminent threat of insolvency of the Social Security system, not to raise tax revenues. It is estimated that the legislation will save the Social Security system approximately $165 billion from 1983 to 1989. As part of this legislation, under § 86, Social Security payments for taxpayers above a certain income level are partially included in gross income. In determining the amount of Social Security subject to taxation, the floor used includes tax-exempt interest income. § 86(b)(2)(8).

Question

Why would it be unconstitutional for an income tax to include the full amount of Social Security benefits in gross income? Consider Sullenger v. Commissioner, page 477.

Chapter 6

BUSINESS DEDUCTIONS

A. DEDUCTIONS: THE STATUTORY SCHEME

Deductions growing out of the taxpayer's trade or business or the taxpayer's transactions for profit are allowed under several Code sections. Section 162(a) permits deductions for the "ordinary and necessary" expenses of "carrying on" a "trade or business." For individuals engaged in profit-oriented transactions which do not constitute the carrying on of a "trade or business," deductions with respect to ordinary and necessary expenses for the "production or collection of income," and the "management, conservation, or maintenance of property held for the production of income," are available under § 212. Prior to the addition of the predecessor of § 212 in 1942, classification of an activity as an investment resulted in the disallowance of deductions for expenses incurred in an income producing activity. In Higgins v. Commissioner, 312 U.S. 212, 61 S.Ct. 475, 85 L.Ed. 783 (1941), the Supreme Court held that expenses incurred by an individual who managed his investment portfolio were not deductible under the predecessor of § 162 because his investment activity did not constitute a "trade or business." Why did the Supreme Court feel it was necessary to narrowly construe this deduction section? Congress quickly reacted to this rather harsh result by enacting the predecessor of § 212 which expressly allows an individual to deduct the ordinary and necessary expenses incurred in income-producing activities other than a trade or business. Why was it unnecessary to enact a deduction section similar to § 212 for corporations?

In analyzing the deductibility of expenses under §§ 162 and 212, you should distinguish the following:

(1) Was the cost incurred in a business venture or investment activity as opposed to a personal activity? Consider § 262.

(2) Even if the expenditure was made in a business or investment context, was the cost a current expense or a capital outlay? See § 263. This aspect of the deductibility of expenses will be analyzed in Chapter 7.

(3) Even if it was related to a business or investment activity and was a current expense, a deduction may be disallowed (See §§ 162(f) and 274(b)) or postponed (see §§ 163(d) and 469).

Under the Tax Reform Act of 1986 all of a taxpayer's income producing activities are divided into three broad categories: (i) activities generating regular income such as wages, salaries, professional fees and income from the active conduct of a trade or business; (ii) activities generating portfolio (investment) income such as dividends, interest from bonds and various forms of savings, and income from the sale of shares of stock; and (iii) passive activities used as tax shelters because they initially generate losses such as real estate investments. The category of an income producing activity is important because the classification will determine whether the deductions and losses generated by that activity may be taken currently or are subject to postponement. For example, there are limitations on the ability to currently deduct losses from an activity in the tax shelter category against income from the other two categories. Under § 469 losses generated by a tax shelter can offset income earned from tax shelter activities and can offset regular or portfolio income only upon a taxable disposition. The ability to deduct tax shelter losses is postponed until a taxpayer's tax shelter investments produce income or are sold at a gain. There are also limitations on the ability to currently deduct interest expenses incurred in an activity under the portfolio category. Under § 163(d) a taxpayer who borrows funds to make an investment in stocks and bonds will only be able to currently deduct the interest on that loan against an equal amount of income from his portfolio investments. Disallowed investment interest is carried forward indefinitely. Thus, regular income can be offset by business deductions, noninterest porfolio investment deductions and personal deductions such as charitable contributions, home mortgage interest (§ 163(h)(2)(D)) and property taxes.

Both §§ 162 and 212 embody the same ordinary and necessary requirement and are generally interpreted in a similar fashion. Thus, the standards for a deduction under both sections are the same. Despite a consistent application of the standards used in determining whether an item is deductible, a taxpayer may prefer to classify an activity as a business under § 162 rather than as an investment activity under § 212. For example, under § 172, net operating losses (as defined in § 172(c)) may be carried back and carried forward to other taxable years. Does a deduction under § 212 qualify as a net operating loss? Consider § 172(c) and (d)(4).

In addition to §§ 162 and 212, depreciation deductions are deductible under §§ 167 and 168, and losses sustained (realized and recognized) during the taxable year (and not compensated by insurance or otherwise) are deductible under § 165(a). For an individual, the deduction of losses is restricted by § 165(c) to three areas: (1) losses incurred in a trade or business; (2) losses incurred in a transaction entered into for profit; and (3) casualty and theft losses of personal property. However, casualty and theft losses are only deductible to a limited extent even though such losses are unconnected with a trade or business or a transaction entered into for profit. § 165(c)(3) and (h).

Sections 162, 212, 165(c)(1) and (2), 167 and 168 specify the deductions used in arriving at the "net" income of a business or investment activity. There are several business related expenses which are deductible under other specific Code provisions. Even though an item may be deductible under more than one provision, a taxpayer may take only one deduction. The premise common to all of the Internal Revenue Code provisions allowing business and investment deductions is that the taxpayer is engaged in a profit-seeking activity. Expenditures incurred in personal (non profit-seeking) activities are not deductible under the business and investment provisions in the Internal Revenue Code. The fundamental question in this chapter is how to draw the line between profit-seeking and personal expenditures.

Personal, living or family expenses are generally nondeductible under § 262. However, certain personal deductions, such as medical expenses, charitable contributions and alimony (which are considered in detail in Chapter 9) are permitted by statutory exceptions to the general rule of § 262. The taxpayer need not engage in a business or a profit-making transaction to qualify for these statutory personal deductions. However, the Tax Reform Act of 1986 severely limited the deductibility of personal interest. In brief, when phased-in, no deduction generally is allowed for personal interest (such as interest on car loans) paid or accured. § 163(h). Interest on debt secured by the principal residence or a second residence of the taxpayer is generally deductible subject to limitations. § 163(h)(2)(D) and (h)(3), (4) and (5) (A). The details of the limits on the interest deductions are considered in Chapter 9. If no deduction can be taken unless there is a specific statutory authorization for it, is it really necessary to have § 262 in the Code?

Even though an expenditure initially qualifies for a current deduction under a specific provision of the Internal Revenue Code, certain deductions are subject to an additional requirement before they can be taken on an individual's income tax return. Under § 67(a) a two percent floor is placed under any deduction classified as a "miscellaneous itemized deduction." § 67(b). For example, nonreimbursed employee business expenses, such as union dues, and investment expenses are subject to this limitation. These expenses are deductible only to the extent that they, in the aggregate, exceed two percent of the taxpayer's adjusted gross income. The legislative history, giving the reasons for this two percent floor, states:

> The committee believes that the [prior] law treatment of employee business expenses, investment expenses, and other miscellaneous itemized deductions [fostered] significant complexity. For taxpayers who [anticipated] claiming itemized deductions, [prior] law effectively [required] extensive recordkeeping with regard to what commonly [were]

small expenditures. Moreover, the fact that small amounts typically [were] involved [presented] significant administrative and enforcement problems for the Internal Revenue Service. These problems [were] exacerbated by the fact that taxpayers * * * frequently [made] errors of law regarding what types of expenditures [were] properly allowable as miscellaneous itemized deductions.

Since many taxpayers incur some expenses that are allowable as miscellaneous itemized deductions, but these expenses commonly are small in amount, the committee believes that the complexity created by [prior] law [was] undesirable. At the same time, the committee believes that taxpayers with unusually large employee business or investment expenses should be permitted an itemized deduction reflecting that fact. * * *

Accordingly, the committee believes that the imposition of a [two]-percent floor on miscellaneous itemized deductions constitutes a desirable simplification of the tax law. This floor will relieve taxpayers of the burden of recordkeeping unless they expect to incur expenditures in excess of the percentage floor. Also, the floor will relieve the Internal Revenue Service of the burden of auditing deductions for such expenditures when not significant in aggregate amount. (Tax Reform Act of [1986], Report of the Committee on Ways and Means, House of Representatives on H.R. 3838, 109–110 (1985)).

A detailed explanation as to what deductions are subject to the two percent limitation is found at p. 482.

B. BUSINESS OR PERSONAL CONSUMPTION?

The materials in this chapter deal with the problems of distinguishing between: (1) "personal, living or family expenses," which are nondeductible under § 262, and (2) business or investment expenses, which are deductible under §§ 162 or 212. The difficulty arises because certain business or investment activities benefit an individual by providing what may otherwise be an item of personal consumption. Also, certain personal activities may involve a business or investment element. The following materials consider the age-old question of whether individuals should be able to reap tax benefits in the form of business or investment deductions if they engage in activities that are not profit-motivated or engage in activities that have both a personal and a profit motive.

1. LACK OF A PROFIT MOTIVE

The "hobby loss" problem presented in the following case exemplifies the personal consumption vs. business expense dilemma.

SMITH v. COMMISSIONER

Tax Court of the United States, 1947.
9 T.C. 1130.

* * *

HILL, JUDGE: The question is whether petitioner operated the farm as a trade or business or for profit, on the one hand, or for recreational purposes or as a hobby, on the other. As is implicit or stated in the cases cited by both petitioner and respondent, the answer to this question lies in determining petitioner's intention from all of the evidence. We have concluded that the facts show that the petitioner's intent in operating the farm was primarily for the purpose of making a profit.

Respondent bases his argument that petitioner had no intent to operate the farm as a trade or business or for profit on the following points: (1) That the operation of the farm resulted in a series of uninterrupted losses,[1] (2) that petitioner's purchase of the farm was essentially motivated by his desire to have a country estate for his home, and (3) that petitioner operated the farm in order to supply his family with food for home consumption.

It is true that the petitioner has experienced continuous annual losses from the operation of his farm since its acquisition in 1933 and through the taxable years in question. Moreover, the record discloses that after the taxable years involved here there were further losses in 1944, 1945, and 1946. The fact that the operation of the farm has resulted in a series of losses, however, is not controlling if the other evidence shows there is a true intention of eventually making a profit. Respondent cites the case of Thacher v. Lowe, 282 Fed. 1944, to support his argument. The court in that case stated:

> * * * it is difficult to imagine how a farm which has been running the number of years which this had could be thought capable of turning a deficiency of 90 percent into a profit.

On the facts in the instant case, however, we can not say that there is no reasonable expectation of realizing a profit.

We do not agree with the respondent that petitioner purchased the farm primarily to satisfy his desire to live on a country estate. It may be true that petitioner experienced pleasure from residing in a country home, but this fact alone does not negative his intent to operate the farm for profit. Nor is such intent negatived by the fact assumed by respondent that petitioner, as a business executive, has received an annual salary sufficiently high to indicate no need to supplement his income by the farm operation.

We are convinced from the record that it has at all times been petitioner's intention to operate the farm for profit, and that he had

---

1. From 1940 to 1949, the net losses from the operation of the farm ranged from about $390 to $2800 per year. The taxpayer's compensation as a business executive was $65,000 in 1942 and $74,000 in 1943.—Eds.

reasonable expectations of accomplishing that result. His efforts to make a profit have included increasing the land in cultivation and in pasturage from 75 to 95 acres, renting the farm, employing an experienced farmer to operate it under his supervision, improving the land by reclamation practices and fertilization and soil conservation methods, and engaging at various times in a number of diversified types of farming. He spends most of his week ends working on the farm, performing such odd jobs as repairing buildings or equipment, feeding poultry, and spraying orchards. On week days he usually consults with his employee for 10 or 15 minutes each morning in connection with problems related to the operation of the farm. In addition he has expended a great deal of money in repairing farm buildings and buying farm equipment, all of which was for utilitarian rather than beautification purposes. He has always considered the farm separate from his home, he has segregated the capital and operating expenses of the residence from the farm expenses, and he has not used the farm for any social or recreational purposes, nor does it have any such facilities.

This leaves for our consideration respondent's argument that petitioner operated the farm primarily for the purpose of providing wholesome food for his family. It should be noted, first, that petitioner and his family consumed at the most only 10 per cent of the farm products on the average and that all of those used were included and reported in the farm income at regular prices. The other approximately 90 per cent of the farm produce was sold by the petitioner to local butchers and grocerymen, to purchasers stopping by the farm, and occasionally to the Delaware Packing Co. at Trenton. In addition to that, the types of products raised by petitioner included poultry, eggs, cattle, sheep, wheat, corn and hay, many of which are not readily adaptable to home consumption, and such of them as were so adaptable were produced in far greater quantities than his home consumption requirements. The petitioner's primary intention, therefore, was not to produce good food for home consumption. * * *

We hold that petitioner's farm operations during the taxable period here involved were a business regularly carried on by him for profit and that the losses in question resulted from ordinary and necessary expenses paid during such taxable period in carrying on such business and, therefore, are deductible for income tax purposes.

* * *

Section 183 reinforces § 262 by disallowing deductions attributable to "an activity * * * not engaged in for profit." Whether a taxpayer had a primary profit motive for an activity is a factual question. In determining a taxpayer's intent, § 183(d) creates a rebuttable presumption that, in general, an activity is engaged in for profit if the gross income from the activity exceeds the deductions attributable to it in three or more of the five consecutive tax years ending with the year in question, unless the Service establishes to the contrary. Failure to qualify for the presumption does not create a negative inference that the activity was not engaged in for profit. See Churchman v. Commissioner, 68 T.C. 696 (1977). Even if the taxpayer's activities are not profit-seeking, certain items for which a personal deduction is available, such as mortgage interest (§ 163(h)(2)(D)) and taxes (§ 164), are deductible without regard to whether the activity is engaged in for profit. § 183(b)(1). In addition, pursuant to § 183(b)(2), items which depend on the existence of a profit motive (e.g., depreciation, insurance and utility expenses), are deductible, but only to the extent that the gross income from the activity exceeds the personal deductions allowable under § 183(b)(1).

The term "activity not engaged in for profit" is defined in § 183(c) as any activity other than one with respect to which deductions are allowable under §§ 162 or 212(1) or (2). The Regulations require that the factual determination of whether an activity is engaged in for profit be based on objective standards, not the taxpayer's subjective intent. Reg. § 1.183–2(a). Reg. § 1.183–2(b) suggests nine relevant factors "which should normally be taken into account," in determining whether an activity is engaged in for profit. The Regulations further provide that no single fact or group of facts is controlling in each case and that "all facts and circumstances with respect to the activity are to be taken into account." Reg. § 1.183–2(b).

In interpreting § 183, the Tax Court in Jasionowski v. Commissioner, 66 T.C. 312, 321–322 (1976), stated:

The legislative history surrounding section 183 indicates that one of the prime motivating factors behind its passage was Congress' desire to create an objective standard to determine whether a taxpayer was carrying on a business for the purpose of realizing a profit or was instead merely attempting to create and utilize losses to offset other income. S.Rept. No. 91–552, to accompany H.R. 13270 (Pub.L. 91–172), 91st Cong., 1st Sess. 104 (1969).

* * *

Further, we note that the test under section 183 is not whether the taxpayer's intention and expectation of profit is reasonable but rather whether such intention and expectation is bona fide. S.Rept. No. 91–552, supra at 103; Sec. 1.–183–2(a), Income Tax Regs. * * *

Although section 183 has clearly placed a gloss on post-1969 judicial profit-motive inquiries, we think pre-1969 case law in this area remains relevant. We say this for two reasons. First, section 183(c) defines an "activity not engaged in for profit" as an activity with respect to which deductions would not be allowable under section 162 or section 212(1) or (2). Thus, prior cases dealing with profit motive under these sections retain their vitality. Second, the so-called "relevant factors" set forth in the regulations, [Reg. § 1.183–2(b)] are themselves derived from prior case law * * * and, therefore, we think such prior law has a role to play in their application.

Accordingly, determinations as to the existence or absence of a profit motive, whether directed toward years beginning prior or subsequent to December 31, 1969, will quite often be identical. * * *

In Dreicer v. Commissioner, 665 F.2d 1292 (D.C.Cir.1981), the taxpayer derived his income as the beneficiary of a trust fund. This allowed him to focus his attention on global travel and dining. In 1955 he published "The Diner's Companion," a commercial failure, compiling his opinions on dining throughout the world. He spent the next twenty years traveling around the world researching his next book, finally completing a draft entitled "My 27 Year Search for the Perfect Steak— Still Looking." This manuscript was rejected. Taxpayer, of course, claimed his travel as a business expense. At trial, the Tax Court applied a "bona fide expectation of profit" standard in finding there was not a profit motive. On appeal, the court said that this was not the proper test to use—the test is not dependent upon a profit "expectation" as one may embark upon an activity for the sincere purpose of eventually reaping a profit. Therefore, the court held that the proper test is the "objective" of making a profit, even if the probability of financial success is small or even remote. On remand, the Tax Court again denied the deduction finding that taxpayer had not convinced it that he had an honest and actual objective to make a profit. Dreicer v. Commissioner, 78 T.C. 642 (1982), affirmed without opinion 702 F.2d 1204 (D.C.Cir.1983).

If there is a finding that the farm is a profit seeking activity under either §§ 162 or 212, the ability to deduct the losses from that income producing activity may be restricted if § 469 applies. Section 469 applies to any income producing activity where the taxpayer does not "materially" participate. § 469(c)(1)(B) and (h). If there is a finding that the farm is operated primarily for personal pleasure, the expenditures deductible under § 183(b)(2) are miscellaneous itemized deductions subject to the two percent floor of § 67(a).

Question

Do the facts in the Smith case indicate that the taxpayer materially participated in the operation of his farm so as to avoid the application of § 469(a)?

Problems

1. After Ted Player became a partner in his law firm, he purchased a small farm outside of the city with the idea of continuing its operation as a working farm. Ted and Terri (and their two children) travel to the farm most weekends and stay in a small house on the farm. Ted hires a manager to operate the farm, but materially participates in the activity so that the passive loss limitations contained in § 469 are not applicable.

(a) During the first year after he purchased the farm, Ted sold most of the produce grown on the farm for $5,000. The remaining portion of the produce is consumed by the Player family or given away to friends.

Reconsider Problem 2 on page 69. The costs of maintaining the farm are as follows: $15,000 in operating expenses, $1,500 in real estate taxes and $1,000 in mortgage interest.

    i. Can Ted, engaged in a primary business, also have a separate business venture? Consider § 162(a).

    ii. What are the tax consequences if the trier of fact finds that Ted intended to operate the farm as a business? Consider §§ 162(a), 163, 164, 183, and Reg. §§ 1.183–2(a) and (b) and 1.162–12. Are the deductible expenses used in computing adjusted gross income? Consider § 62(1). What is the impact of § 67? How should he structure the venture so as to demonstrate an objective to make a profit?

    iii. What are the tax consequences if the trier of fact finds that Ted intended to operate the farm as a hobby? Consider §§ 62, 67, 183(c), (b), 163(a) and (h), 164(a), 162(a).

(b) Assume instead that the farm generated operating revenues the first year of $2,000, and Ted intended to operate it as a hobby. How would this change the tax consequences? Consider §§ 183(b), 163(a) and (h), 164 and 67.

2. You represent Franz who has advised you that he wishes to start an art collection as a hedge against inflation and with the expectation of selling it at a profit. How would you advise Franz to arrange his purchases and holdings so that:

(a) his expenses (for example, visits to galleries and museums and subscriptions to art journals) will be deductible under § 212. Consider §§ 67 and 183 and Reg. §§ 1.183–2(a) and (b) and 1.212–1(b) and (d).

(b) if he sells all or part of his collection at a loss, the loss would be deductible under § 165(c)(2). Consider the impact of §§ 67 and 62(3). What would be the character of the loss? Consider § 1221.

3. Dreamer decides to open an art gallery next to the local steel mill because that section of town has no galleries. All his friends and business associates tell him that this type of business will never succeed in that location. Dreamer realizes that it may take a long time for his business to catch on, but he is willing to sustain initial losses in anticipation of potentially large, but highly speculative, future profits. May Dreamer deduct his losses even though his "expectation" of producing a profit is unreasonable? Consider §§ 67 and 183 and Reg. § 1.183–2(a) and (b).

2. DUAL USE PROPERTY

A difficult determination arises where a taxpayer uses property for both personal and business (or investment) purposes. If a taxpayer uses the den in his personal residence to do work he brings home from the office, should he be allowed to take a business deduction for his home office? Section 280A does not bar a taxpayer from deducting those expenses attributable to office space in his home which are deductible in any event. § 280A(b). These non-profit-oriented deductions include mortgage interest (§ 163(a)) and real estate taxes (§ 164(a)). With respect to those expenses not otherwise deductible (e.g.

utilities, maintenance, insurance and depreciation), they are allowed as a deduction to the extent allocable to a portion of the taxpayer's home (§ 280A(f)(1)) which, according to § 280A(c)(1), is exclusively used on a regular basis: (1) as the principal place of any business of the taxpayer (a self-employed taxpayer who uses the home office as his principal place of business or an employee-taxpayer whose employer does not provide office space may deduct such expenses, but not a self-employed taxpayer or an employee-taxpayer whose principal office is located outside his home) or (2) as a place of business used by patients, clients or customers in meeting or dealing with the taxpayer in the normal course of his business although the office may not be the taxpayer's principal place of business (e.g. a physician or a salesman who meets with clients in a secondary office at home). If the taxpayer's business involves being an employee, he may take business deductions for his home office only if the use of the home office is for the convenience of the taxpayer's employer. § 280A(c)(1). Home office expenses are deductible (except for expenses that are deductible without regard to business use, such as home mortgage interest) only to the extent of net income from the business activity, i.e., the taxpayer's gross income less the deductions attributable to the business. § 280A(c)(5). Disallowed home office deductions may be carried forward to later years.

In Drucker v. Commissioner, 715 F.2d 67 (2d Cir.1983) the court held that three musicians who were employees of the New York Metropolitan Opera Association could deduct the expenses allocable to a room in their respective apartments devoted solely to the study and practice of music because such a room constituted the principal place of their business and it was maintained for the convenience of their employer. The court concluded that less than "half of each musician's working time was spent at Lincoln Center and the musicians' performances at Lincoln Center were made possible by their practice at home." The place of performance, according to the court, was immaterial so long as the musicians were prepared and most of their preparation occurred at home. Although each employee received no compensation from his employer for work performed at home, the musician's practice room constituted his principal place of business. After concluding that a practice room was the principal place of business for each musician, the court found that such workplace was a business necessity, not a matter of personal convenience, comfort or economy. Even though the Opera did not specifically require its musician-employees to practice individually outside of Lincoln Center, such practice was a tacit condition of employment. In other words, practice was determined to be the focal point of the business activity. Because the Opera did not provide facilities for such practice, the maintenance of a room at home for practice was done for the convenience of the employer even though the employer did not specifically request that such a place be maintained.

Can a law professor who grades his exams at home take a home office deduction? In Weissman v. Commissioner, 751 F.2d 512 (2d Cir.

1984) the court held that a college professor could deduct the cost of a home office. The professor spent about 20 percent of his worktime at the college campus, the remaining working hours he spent in his home office which he used exclusively for scholarly research and writing. The professor was provided an office on campus which he was required to share with other professors and it was not a safe place for him to leave teaching, writing or research materials and equipment. The determination of a taxpayer's principal place of business under § 280A, depends on the nature of the business activities, the attributes of the space in which such activities can be conducted, and the practical necessity of using a home office to carry out such activities. Because the professor spent a majority of his employment-related time researching and writing, he needed a place to think, read, and write without interruption. It was necessary for him to work at home because his shared campus office did not provide the privacy needed to undertake sustained scholarly research and writing. However, is the focal point of a professor the educational institution, or his research and writing? See also Meiers v. Commissioner, 782 F.2d 75 (7th Cir.1986), where the court held that in determining a taxpayer's principal place of business, a major consideration was the relative amounts of time spent at each location—laundromat and home office where the administrative work of the business was done. Other relevant factors were the importance of the functions performed at home and the business necessity of maintaining a home office. The court also pointed out that the taxpayer spent most of her time in the home office and probably performed most of her most important managerial functions there.

A back door way around the lack of success in deducting home office expenses was accepted by a divided court in Feldman v. Commissioner, 84 T.C. 1 (1985), affirmed 791 F.2d 781 (9th Cir.1986). Noting that the Tax Reform [Act] of 1986 would amend § 280A(c)(3) to disallow a taxpayer a deduction for the rental of his dwelling unit to his employer, the court in Feldman expressed a willingness to await the Congressional resolution of the issue. The taxpayer leased a room in his personal residence to his employer. Taxpayer then used this room as an office provided by his employer. Taxpayer reported the rental income and deducted the costs of maintaining the leased space. The court allowed the deductions, including depreciation, under § 280A(c) (3). The dissent argued that the doctrine of substance over firm mandates that the rental arrangement was merely a scheme designed to disguise compensation as rental income in order to avoid the strict requirements for deducting home office expenses under § 280A(c)(1). However, the Tax Reform Act of 1986 altered the result in the Feldman case. No home office deduction is allowable because of business use where the taxpayer leases a portion of his home to an employer. § 280A(c)(6). If a lease is subject to this rule, no home office deductions are allowed except to the extent they are allowable in the absence of any business use, for example, home mortgage interest and real estate taxes.

As an alternative test to deduct expenses of a home office, a taxpayer may use a home office on a regular basis to meet or deal with clients or customers. In Green v. Commissioner, 78 T.C. 428 (1982), reversed 707 F.2d 404 (9th Cir.1983), the taxpayer, an account executive for a real estate management firm, maintained a home office at which he received numerous telephone calls, on a regular basis, from his clients. Because the taxpayer was difficult to reach during the day, he received many calls from clients in the evening at a room at home used exclusively as his office. The Tax Court held that the telephone conversations with clients qualified as "meeting or dealing" with clients. However, on appeal, in Green v. Commissioner, 707 F.2d 404 (9th Cir.1983), the Ninth Circuit reversed, concluding that telephone calls are not "meeting or dealing." According to the appellate court, clients must actually visit the office to make it deductible. In Frankel v. Commissioner, 82 T.C. 318 (1984) the Tax Court bowed to the Ninth Circuit decision and rejected the taxpayer's deduction. The home office deduction available to an employee on his individual income tax return is a miscellaneous itemized deduction subject to the two percent floor in § 67(a). Read §§ 62(1) and (2) and 63(d).

3. PERSONAL AND BUSINESS MOTIVES COMBINED

Child Care. Generally, expenses which are common to everyone, whether they work or not, such as food, clothing, and shelter, are not deductible. § 262. Presumably, the wife in the next case would not have incurred babysitting fees if she had decided not to work. Can child care costs be deducted under § 162 because they relate only to employed persons? Do you agree with the result in the next case?

SMITH v. COMMISSIONER
40 B.T.A. 1038 (1939), affirmed per curiam
113 F.2d 114 (2d Cir.1940).

OPINION

OPPER: Respondent determined a deficiency of $23.62 in petitioner's 1937 income tax. This was due to the disallowance of a deduction claimed by petitioners, who are husband and wife, for sums spent by the wife in employing nursemaids to care for petitioners' young child, the wife, as well as the husband, being employed. The facts have all been stipulated and are hereby found accordingly.

Petitioners would have us apply the "but for" test. They propose that but for the nurses the wife could not leave her child; but for the freedom so secured she could not pursue her gainful labors; and but for them there would be no income and no tax. This thought evokes an array of interesting possibilities. The fee to the doctor, but for whose healing service the earner of the family income could not leave his sickbed; the cost of the laborer's raiment, for how can the world proceed about its business unclothed; the very home which gives us shelter and rest and the food which provides energy, might all by an extension of the same proposition be construed as necessary to the operation of business and to the creation of income. Yet these are the very essence of those "personal" expenses the deductibility of which is expressly denied. [§ 262].

We are told that the working wife is a new phenomenon. This is relied on to account for the apparent inconsistency that the expenses in issue are now a commonplace, yet have not been the subject of legislation, ruling, or adjudicated controversy. But if that is true it becomes all the more necessary to apply accepted principles to the novel facts. We are not prepared to say that the care of children, like similar aspects of family and household life, is other than a personal concern. The wife's services as custodian of the home and protector of its children are ordinarily rendered without monetary compensation. There results no taxable income from the performance of this service and the correlative expenditure is personal and not susceptible of deduction. Rosa E. Burkhart, 11 B.T.A. 275. Here the wife has chosen to employ others to discharge her domestic function and the services she performs are rendered outside the home. They are a source of actual income and taxable as such. But that does not deprive the same work performed by others of its personal character nor furnish a reason why its cost should be treated as an offset in the guise of a deductible item.

We are not unmindful that, as petitioners suggest, certain disbursements normally personal may become deductible by reason of their intimate connection with an occupation carried on for profit. In this category fall entertainment, Blackmer v. Commissioner, 70 Fed.(2d) 255 (C.C.A., 2d Cir.), and traveling expenses, Joseph W. Powell, 34 B.T.A. 655; affd., 94 Fed.(2d) 483 (C.C.A., 1st Cir.), and the cost of an actor's wardrobe, Charles Hutchison, 13 B.T.A. 1187. The line is not always an easy one to draw nor the test simple to apply. But we think its principle is clear. It may for practical purposes be said to constitute a distinction between those activities which, as a matter of common acceptance and universal experience, are "ordinary" or usual as the direct accompaniment of business pursuits, on the one hand; and those which, though they may in some indirect and tenuous degree relate to the circumstances of a profitable occupation, are nevertheless personal in their nature, of a character applicable to human beings generally, and which exist on that plane regardless of the occupation, though not necessarily of the station in life, of the individuals concerned. See Welch v. Helvering, 290 U.S. 111.

In the latter category, we think, fall payments made to servants or others occupied in looking to the personal wants of their employers. David Sonenblick, 4 B.T.A. 986. And we include in this group nurse-maids retained to care for infant children.

Questions

What test did the court in Smith apply to disallow the deduction for child care as an employee business expense? Are you satisfied with the court's rationale in the Smith case? What do you feel was the real justification for the disallowance of the deduction? Can the Smith case be justified on the ground that if Mrs. Smith had no children, she would not have been compelled to incur such costs if she worked? Is child care a result of the personal decision to have children?

Although Congress did not wish to overturn the Smith case, it clearly was not satisfied with the result. In 1954, Congress enacted § 214 which permitted taxpayers to deduct child care costs as a personal deduction. However, the child care deduction was not as generous as other personal deductions. The taxpayer could only deduct a specified maximum amount. The amount of the deduction was gradually phased out if taxpayers had income over a certain level and not all individuals were eligible for the deduction. In addition, the complexities of the deduction were criticized.

Could it be said that the child care deduction was a recognition of the failure to tax the imputed income supplied by a nonworking spouse who stays home to care for the children? Reconsider Problem 2 on page 69. Can the deduction be justified as a device to encourage housewives to seek employment outside of the home?

In 1976, Congress repealed the child care deduction and replaced it with the credit provided for in § 21. Congress sought to limit the complexities inherent in the deduction. Although a maximum limit exists on the amount of the credit, it is not completely phased out based on a taxpayer's (or a family's) income level. Congress subsequently expanded the credit to permit payments to relatives (e.g. grandparents) to qualify. In 1981, Congress increased the maximum amount of the child care expenses (more precisely defined as employment related expenses in § 21(b)(2)) qualifying for the credit from $2,000 to $2,400 if the taxpayer's household includes one dependent (more precisely defined as a qualifying individual in § 21(b)(1)) and from $4,000 to $4,800 for two or more dependents. Furthermore, child care expenses generally cannot exceed the earned income of the taxpayer, if single, or for a married couple, the earned income of the spouse with the lower earnings. For taxpayers below a certain income level, Congress raised the size of the credit to 30 percent of the child care expenses, with a graduated phase back of the credit to 20 percent of the child care expenses if the taxpayer's adjusted gross income exceeds $10,000. § 21(a)(2).

The conversion from a deduction to a credit permits families who do not itemize their deductions to obtain a tax benefit for child care costs. In making the tax benefit available to all working families with child care costs, Congress may have recognized that the costs of child care are part of earning a living rather than personal consumption. If viewed as a cost associated with producing income, should a maximum limit be placed on the size of the credit? If Congress believes that the child care credit provides a substantial work incentive for families with children, should low income families be entitled to a refund of the unused portion of their child care credit? Compare § 32, the earned income credit, which is refundable.

Questions

1. What is the impact of § 129?

2. Why did Congress change the personal deduction for child care to a credit under § 21? Reconsider the Problem on page 14. For those families who did not itemize their deductions (§ 63(b) and (c)), would it have been just as effective to place the child care deduction in § 62, the items of deductions used to compute adjusted gross income? Should the "write-off" for child care expenses take the form of a deduction or a credit? Consider the following excerpt:

OFFICE OF THE SECRETARY, DEPARTMENT OF THE TREASURY, TAX REFORM FOR FAIRNESS, SIM-PLICITY, AND ECONOMIC GROWTH
Vol. 2, 17–19 (1984).

REASONS FOR CHANGE

Child and dependent care expenses incurred in order to obtain or maintain employment affect a taxpayer's ability to pay tax in much the same manner as other ordinary business expenses. A family with $30,000 of income and $2,000 of employment-related child care expenses does not have greater ability to pay tax than one with $28,000 of income and no such expenses.

There is, of course, a personal element in dependent care expenses incurred for household services and the care of one or more qualifying individuals. No objective standards exist, however, for allocating child and dependent care expenses based upon the personal and business benefits derived. Moreover, the cost of dependent care is frequently substantially higher than other mixed business/personal expenses for which no deduction is allowed, such as the costs of commuting and most business clothing. Disallowance of all dependent care costs in the computation of taxable income thus could generate a significant work disincentive.

Allowance of a deduction is the appropriate treatment of costs incurred in producing income. The current credit for dependent care expenses is targeted for the benefit of low-income taxpayers, although these expenses reduce the ability to pay tax at all income levels. Tax relief for low-income taxpayers is provided best through adjustments in tax rates or in the threshold level of income for imposition of tax. Such changes benefit all similarly situated taxpayers.

Computation of the limits on the dependent care credit also adds to the complexity of the tax law.

PROPOSAL

A deduction from gross income would be provided for qualifying child and dependent care expenses up to a maximum of $2,400 per year for taxpayers with one dependent, and $4,800 per year for taxpayers with two or more dependents. Qualifying expenses would continue to be limited by the taxpayer's earned income, if single, or, in the case of married couples, by the earned income of the spouse with the lower earnings.

* * *

ANALYSIS

The proposal recognizes that child and dependent care expenses constitute legitimate costs of earning income. The extent to which such expenses also provide a personal benefit, however, varies in each situation. As with certain other expenditures that provide mixed business and personal benefits to taxpayers, such as business meal and entertainment expenses, the proposal sets an objective limitation on the amount allowed as a deduction. This limit to some extent serves to deny a deduction for the portion of dependent care expenses constituting personal rather than business benefit. An objective limit also simplifies the tax law.

Under the proposal, approximately five million families (65.5 percent of all families) would claim deductions for dependent care expenses totalling approximately $7 billion. Approximately 61 percent of these deductions would be claimed by families with incomes under $50,000. The deduction, however, is relatively less favorable to low-income families than is the current credit. The choice of the deduction reflects the view that progressivity should be provided directly through the rate structure.

Uniforms and Work Clothes. Because an individual is considered to be in a trade or business in his role as an employee, he may deduct employee business expenses under § 162(a). An employee may deduct the cost of items including union dues, memberships in professional associations, professional journals and unreimbursed business travel (such as attending a convention) if the requirements of § 162(a) are satisfied. Can an employee who does not itemize his deductions (§ 63(b) and (c)) receive a tax benefit from the above described employee business expenses? Consider § 62, especially § 62(2).

As in the case of other expenses deductible as miscellaneous itemized deductions, employee business expenses, such as uniforms and work clothes, are subject to a two percent floor. § 67(a). In view of this floor, why will employees push for their employers to reimburse them for these expenses? Read §§ 62(2)(A) and 63(d)(1).

The next case deals with the inability of the manager of a designer boutique to deduct the cost of purchasing and maintaining designer clothes as a business expense.

PEVSNER v. COMMISSIONER

United States Court of Appeals, Fifth Circuit, 1980.
628 F.2d 467.

SAM D. JOHNSON, CIRCUIT JUDGE:

This is an appeal by the Commissioner of Internal Revenue from a decision of the United States Tax Court. The tax court upheld taxpayer's business expense deduction for clothing expenditures in the amount of $1,621.91 for the taxable year 1975. We reverse.

Since June 1973 Sandra J. Pevsner, taxpayer, has been employed as the manager of the Sakowitz Yves St. Laurent Rive Gauche Boutique located in Dallas, Texas. The boutique sells only women's clothes and accessories designed by Yves St. Laurent (YSL), one of the leading designers of women's apparel. Although the clothing is ready to wear, it is highly fashionable and expensively priced. Some customers of the boutique purchase and wear the YSL apparel for their daily activities and spend as much as $20,000 per year for such apparel.

As manager of the boutique, the taxpayer is expected by her employer to wear YSL clothes while at work. In her appearance, she is expected to project the image of an exclusive lifestyle and to demonstrate to her customers that she is aware of the YSL current fashion trends as well as trends generally. Because the boutique sells YSL clothes exclusively, taxpayer must be able, when a customer compliments her on her clothes, to say that they are designed by YSL. In addition to wearing YSL apparel while at the boutique, she wears them while commuting to and from work, to fashion shows sponsored by the boutique, and to business luncheons at which she represents the boutique. During 1975, the taxpayer bought, at an employee's discount, the following items: four blouses, three skirts, one pair of slacks, one trench coat, two sweaters, one jacket, one tunic, five scarves, six belts, two pairs of shoes and four necklaces. The total cost of this apparel was $1,381.91. In addition, the sum of $240 was expended for maintenance of these items.

Although the clothing and accessories purchased by the taxpayer were the type used for general purposes by the regular customers of the boutique, the taxpayer is not a normal purchaser of these clothes. The taxpayer and her husband, who is partially disabled because of a severe heart attack suffered in 1971, lead a simple life and their social activities are very limited and informal. Although taxpayer's employer has no objection to her wearing the apparel away from work, taxpayer stated that she did not wear the clothes during off-work hours because she felt that they were too expensive for her simple everyday lifestyle. Another reason why she did not wear the YSL clothes apart from work was to make them last longer. Taxpayer did admit at trial, however, that a number of the articles were things she could have worn off the job and in which she would have looked "nice."

On her joint federal income tax return for 1975, taxpayer deducted $990 as an ordinary and necessary business expense with respect to her purchase of the YSL clothing and accessories. However, in the tax court, taxpayer claimed a deduction for the full $1381.91 cost of the apparel and for the $240 cost of maintaining the apparel. The tax court allowed the taxpayer to deduct both expenses in the total amount of $1621.91. The tax court reasoned that the apparel was not suitable to the private lifestyle maintained by the taxpayer. This appeal by the Commissioner followed.

The principal issue on appeal is whether the taxpayer is entitled to deduct as an ordinary and necessary business expense the cost of purchasing and maintaining the YSL clothes and accessories worn by the taxpayer in her employment as the manager of the boutique. This determination requires an examination of the relationship between Section 162(a) of the Internal Revenue Code of [1986], which allows a deduction for ordinary and necessary expenses incurred in the conduct of a trade or business, and Section 262 of the Code, which bars a deduction for all "personal, living, or family expenses." Although many expenses are helpful or essential to one's business activities— such as commuting expenses and the cost of meals while at work— these expenditures are considered inherently personal and are disallowed under Section 262. See, e.g. United States v. Correll, 389 U.S. 299, 88 S.Ct. 445, 19 L.Ed.2d 537 (1967); Commissioner v. Flowers, 326 U.S. 465, 66 S.Ct. 250, 90 L.Ed. 203 (1946).

The generally accepted rule governing the deductibility of clothing expenses is that the cost of clothing is deductible as a business expense only if: (1) the clothing is of a type specifically required as a condition of employment, (2) it is not adaptable to general usage as ordinary clothing, and (3) it is not so worn. Donnelly v. Commissioner, 262 F.2d 411, 412 (2d Cir.1959).[3]

In the present case, the Commissioner stipulated that the taxpayer was required by her employer to wear YSL clothing and that she did not wear such apparel apart from work. The Commissioner maintained, however, that a deduction should be denied because the YSL clothes and accessories purchased by the taxpayer were adaptable for general usage as ordinary clothing and she was not prohibited from using them as such. The tax court, in rejecting the Commissioner's argument for the application of an objective test, recognized that the test for deductibility was whether the clothing was "suitable for general or personal wear" but determined that the matter of suitability was to be judged subjectively, in light of the taxpayer's lifestyle. Although the court recognized that the YSL apparel "might be used by some members of society for general purposes," it felt that because the "wearing of YSL apparel outside work would be inconsistent with * * * [tax-

3. When the taxpayer is prohibited from wearing the clothing away from work a deduction is normally allowed. See Harsaghy v. Commissioner, 2 T.C. 484 (1943). However, in the present case no such restriction was placed upon the taxpayer's use of the clothing.

payer's] lifestyle," sufficient reason was shown for allowing a deduction for the clothing expenditures.

In reaching its decision, the tax court relied heavily upon Yeomans v. Commissioner, 30 T.C. 757 (1958). In *Yeomans,* the taxpayer was employed as fashion coordinator for a shoe manufacturing company. Her employment necessitated her attendance at meetings of fashion experts and at fashion shows sponsored by her employer. On these occasions, she was expected to wear clothing that was new, highly styled, and such as "might be sought after and worn for personal use by women who make it a practice to dress according to the most advanced or extreme fashions." 30 T.C. at 768. However, for her personal wear, Ms. Yeomans preferred a plainer and more conservative style of dress. As a consequence, some of the items she purchased were not suitable for her private and personal wear and were not so worn. The tax court allowed a deduction for the cost of the items that were not suitable for her personal wear. Although the basis for the decision in *Yeomans* is not clearly stated, the tax court in the case *sub judice* determined that

> [a] careful reading of *Yeomans* shows that, without a doubt, the Court based its decision on a determination of Ms. Yeomans' lifestyle and that the clothes were not suitable for her use in such lifestyle. Furthermore, the Court recognized that the clothes Ms. Yeomans purchased were suitable for wear by women who customarily wore such highly styled apparel, but such fact did not cause the court to decide the issue against her. Thus, *Yeomans* clearly decides the issue before us in favor of the petitioner.

T.C. Memo 1979–311 at 9–10.

Notwithstanding the tax court's decision in *Yeomans,* the Circuits that have addressed the issue have taken an objective, rather than subjective, approach. Stiner v. United States, 524 F.2d 640, 641 (10th Cir.1975); Donnelly v. Commissioner, 262 F.2d 411, 412 (2d Cir.1959). An objective approach was also taken by the tax court in Drill v. Commissioner, 8 T.C. 902 (1947). Under an objective test, no reference is made to the individual taxpayer's lifestyle or personal taste. Instead, adaptability for personal or general use depends upon what is generally accepted for ordinary street wear.

The principal argument in support of an objective test is, of course, administrative necessity. The Commissioner argues that, as a practical matter, it is virtually impossible to determine at what point either price or style makes clothing inconsistent with or inappropriate to a taxpayer's lifestyle. Moreover, the Commissioner argues that the price one pays and the styles one selects are inherently personal choices governed by taste, fashion, and other unmeasurable values. Indeed, the tax court has rejected the argument that a taxpayer's personal taste can dictate whether clothing is appropriate for general use. See Drill v. Commissioner, 8 T.C. 902 (1947). An objective test, although not perfect, provides a practical administrative approach that allows a taxpayer or revenue agent to look only to objective facts in determining whether clothing required as a condition of employment is adaptable to general use as ordinary streetwear. Conversely, the tax court's reliance on subjective factors provides no concrete guidelines in determining the deductibility of clothing purchased as a condition of employment.

In addition to achieving a practical administrative result, an objective test also tends to promote substantial fairness among the greatest number of taxpayers. As the Commissioner suggests, it apparently would be the tax court's position that two similarly situated YSL boutique managers with identical wardrobes would be subject to disparate tax consequences depending upon the particular manager's lifestyle and "socio-economic level." This result, however, is not consonant with a reasonable interpretation of Sections 162 and 262.

For the reasons stated above, the decision of the tax court upholding the deduction for taxpayer's purchase of YSL clothing is reversed. Consequently, the portion of the tax court's decision upholding the deduction for maintenance costs for the clothing is also

Reversed.

––––––––

The costs of employee uniforms are deductible if the tests mentioned in Pevsner are satisfied. Uniforms of nurses, athletes, police, firemen and others are deductible if the taxpayer objectively shows that the required uniforms are specifically required as a condition of employment and not suitable to ordinary wear. Rev.Rul. 70–474, 1970–2 C.B. 34. Reg. § 1.262–1(b)(8) takes the position that military uniforms of a regular officer are not deductible because they take the place of clothing that would be otherwise required as a civilian. However, a reserve officer can deduct the cost of his uniform because it is worn only occasionally. Can an enlisted man deduct the cost of military fatigues? Would the cost of an officer's ceremonial sword be deductible?

Questions

How did the court in Pevsner apply the test of whether the designer clothes were "adaptable to general usage as ordinary clothing?" Why did the court feel that it had to adopt such a restrictive interpretation?

Problems

1. (a) Can Ted Player, an attorney, deduct the cost of reading glasses because his job requires a great deal of reading?

(b) Can Ted deduct the cost of a three piece suit if he only wears it for court appearances?

2. Can Fernando, an entertainer, deduct the cost of his sequined, red velvet jumpsuit?

3. (a) Can Frank, a welder in a machine shop, deduct the cost of protective goggles for his job? Assume the cost of the goggles is not reimbursed by Frank's employer. What if Frank occasionally uses the goggles while chopping wood at his home.

(b) Assume the same facts as in (a) but the cost of the goggles is reimbursed by Frank's employer? Can Frank exclude the payment received for the goggles from gross income under the judicially developed convenience of the employer doctrine (reconsider the Benaglia case at p. 308) or as a working condition fringe benefit (§ 132(a)(3) and (d))?

4. In Problems 1 to 3 consider the impact of § 67. Also, in Problem 3, consider the tax consequences to the employee and to the employer if the employee is reimbursed for his employee business expenses. Examine §§ 62(2)(A) and 63(d).

Meals. What about the cost of business meals? Can an individual deduct the cost of a meal eaten at a business meeting? In Sutter v. Commissioner, 21 T.C. 170 (1953) (Acq. 1954–1 C.B. 6), a physician claimed a deduction for the entire cost of his lunches at the meetings of the local chamber of commerce and the local hospital council. The luncheon meetings were related to his business. The court agreed with the Commissioner's position that a taxpayer can only deduct the cost of his business meals to the extent it exceeds the amount he would have normally spent. The court disallowed any deduction because the taxpayer in Sutter failed to show that the meal costs were greater than those he would have incurred for his normal, personal meals. The court stated that the presumption of nondeductibility can be overcome "only by clear and detailed evidence as to each instance that the expenditure was different from or in excess of that which would have been made for the taxpayer's personal purposes." However, ascertaining excess cost is extremely difficult, if not impossible, to administer. Consequently, the Commissioner announced in Rev.Rul. 63–144, 1963–2 C.B. 129 (Question 31), that "[t]he Service practice has been to apply this rule largely to abuse cases where taxpayers claim deductions for substantial amounts of personal living expenses. The Service does not intend to depart from this practice." As a result of this ruling taxpayers were allowed to deduct the entire cost of valid business meals. In Letter Ruling 8006004 (CCH IRS Letter Rulings Reports No. 155 (1980)) a school systems administrator, whose duties required membership in several local organizations, the meetings of which generally included lunch or dinner, was able to demonstrate that (i) the meetings were directly business related and (ii) the cost of the meal consumed at each meeting was in excess of what he would have normally spent for personal purposes. A deduction was allowed for the excess amounts. Does this mean that a taxpayer who discusses business with a client over lunch is allowed to deduct the excess cost of his own lunch over what he normally would have spent? The problem caused by this approach is that taxpayers will be treated differently if they have different personal eating habits. The school administrator can obtain a business deduction because he normally eats in the school cafeteria or brown bags his lunch. While the doctor, who attends the same meeting as the school administrator, might receive no deduction because he normally eats an expensive lunch. The following case illustrates the business or personal quandary.

MOSS v. COMMISSIONER

United States Court of Appeals, Ninth Circuit, 1985.
758 F.2d 211.

POSNER, CIRCUIT JUDGE: The taxpayers, a lawyer named Moss and his wife, appeal from a decision of the Tax Court disallowing federal income tax deductions of a little more than $1,000 in each of two years, representing Moss's share of his law firm's lunch expense at the Cafe Angelo in Chicago. The Tax Court's decision in this case has attracted some attention in tax circles because of its implications for the general problem of the deductibility of business meals. See, e.g., McNally, Vulnerability of Entertainment and Meal Deductions Under the Sutter Rule, 62 Taxes 184 (1984).

Moss was a partner in a small trial firm specializing in defense work, mostly for one insurance company. Each of the firm's lawyers carried a tremendous litigation caseload, averaging more than 300 cases, and spent most of every working day in courts in Chicago and its suburbs. The members of the firm met for lunch daily at the Cafe Angelo near their office. At lunch the lawyers would discuss their cases with the head of the firm, whose approval was required for most settlements, and they would decide which lawyer would meet which court call that afternoon or the next morning. Lunchtime was chosen for the daily meeting because the courts were in recess then. The alternatives were to meet at 7:00 a.m. or 6:00 p.m., and these were less convenient times. There is no suggestion that the lawyers dawdled over lunch, or that the Cafe Angelo is luxurious.

The framework of statutes and regulations for deciding this case is simple, but not clear. Section 262 of the Internal Revenue Code (Title 26) disallows, "except as otherwise expressly provided in this chapter," the deduction of "personal, family, or living expenses." Section 119 excludes from income the value of meals provided by an employer to his employees for his convenience, but only if they are provided on the employer's premises; and section 162(a) allows the deduction of "all the ordinary and necessary expenses paid or incurred during the taxable year in carrying on any trade or business, including—* * *. (2) traveling expenses (including amounts expended for meals * * *) while away from home * * *." Since Moss was not an employee but a partner in a partnership not taxed as an entity, since the meals were not served on the employer's premises, and since he was not away from home (that is, on an overnight trip away from his place of work, see United States v. Correll, 389 U.S. 299, 88 S.Ct. 445, 19 L.Ed.2d 537

(1967)), neither section 119 nor section 162(a)(2) applies to this case. The Internal Revenue Service concedes, however, that meals are deductible under section 162(a) when they are ordinary and necessary business expenses (provided the expense is substantiated with adequate records, see section 274(d)) even if they are not within the express permission of any other provision and even though the expense of commuting to and from work, a traveling expense but not one incurred away from home, is not deductible. Treasury Regulations on Income Tax § 1.262–1(b)(5); Fausner v. Commissioner, 413 U.S. 838, 93 S.Ct. 2820, 37 L.Ed.2d 996 (1973) (per curiam).

The problem is that many expenses are simultaneously business expenses in the sense that they conduce to the production of business income and personal expenses in the sense that they raise personal welfare. This is plain enough with regard to lunch; most people would eat lunch even if they didn't work. Commuting may seem a pure business expense, but is not; it reflects the choice of where to live, as well as where to work. Read literally, section 262 would make irrelevant whether a business expense is also a personal expense; so long as it is ordinary and necessary in the taxpayer's business, thus bringing section 162(a) into play, an expense is (the statute seems to say) deductible from his income tax. But the statute has not been read literally. There is a natural reluctance, most clearly manifested in the regulation disallowing deduction of the expense of commuting, to lighten the tax burden of people who have the good fortune to interweave work with consumption. To allow a deduction for commuting would confer a windfall on people who live in the suburbs and commute to work in the cities; to allow a deduction for all business-related meals would confer a windfall on people who can arrange their work schedules so they do some of their work at lunch.

Although an argument can thus be made for disallowing *any* deduction for business meals, on the theory that people have to eat whether they work or not, the result would be excessive taxation of people who spend more money on business meals because they are business meals than they would spend on their meals if they were not working. Suppose a theatrical agent takes his clients out to lunch at the expensive restaurants that the clients demand. Of course he can deduct the expense of their meals, from which he derives no pleasure or sustenance, but can he also deduct the expense of his own? He can, because he cannot eat more cheaply; he cannot munch surreptitiously on a peanut butter and jelly sandwich brought from home while his client is wolfing down tournedos Rossini followed by souffié au grand marnier. No doubt our theatrical agent, unless concerned for his longevity, derives personal utility from his fancy meal, but probably less than the price of the meal. He would not pay for it if it were not for the business benefit; he would get more value from using the same money to buy something else; hence the meal confers on him less utility than the cash equivalent would. The law could require him to pay tax on the fair value of the meal to him; this would be (were it not for costs of administration) the economically correct solution. But the government does not attempt this difficult measurement; it once did, but gave up the attempt as not worth the cost, see United States v. Correll, supra, 389 U.S. at 301 n. 6, 88 S.Ct. at 446 n. 6. The taxpayer is permitted to deduct the whole price, provided the expense is "different from or in excess of that which would have been made for the taxpayer's personal purposes." Sutter v. Commissioner, 21 T.C. 170, 173 (1953).

Because the law allows this generous deduction, which tempts people to have more (and costlier) business meals than are necessary, the Internal Revenue Service has every right to insist that the meal be shown to be a real business necessity. This condition is most easily satisfied when a client or customer or supplier or other outsider to the business is a guest. Even if Sydney Smith was wrong that "soup and fish explain half the emotions of life," it is undeniable that eating together fosters camaraderie and makes business dealings friendlier and easier. It thus reduces the costs of transacting business, for these costs include the frictions and the failures of communication that are produced by suspicion and mutual misunderstanding, by differences in tastes and manners, and by lack of rapport. A meeting with a client or customer in an office is therefore not a perfect substitute for a lunch with him in a restaurant. But it is different when all the participants in the meal are coworkers, as essentially was the case here (clients occasionally were invited to the firm's daily luncheon, but Moss has made no attempt to identify the occasions). They know each other well already; they don't need the social lubrication that a meal with an outsider provides—at least don't need it daily. If a large firm had a monthly lunch to allow partners to get to know associates, the expense of the meal might well be necessary, and would be allowed by the Internal Revenue Service. See Wells v. Commissioner, 36 T.C.M. 1698, 1699 (1977), aff'd without opinion, 626 F.2d 868 (9th Cir.1980). But Moss's firm never had more than eight lawyers (partners and associates), and did not need a daily lunch to cement relationships among them.

It is all a matter of degree and circumstance (the expense of a testimonial dinner, for example, would be deductible on a morale-building rationale); and particularly of frequency. Daily—for a full year—is too often, perhaps even for entertainment of clients, as implied by Hankenson v. Commissioner, 47 T.C.M. 1567, 1569 (1984), where the Tax Court held nondeductible the cost of lunches consumed three or four days a week, 52 weeks a year, by a doctor who entertained other doctors who he hoped would refer patients to him, and other medical personnel.

We may assume it was necessary for Moss's firm to meet daily to coordinate the work of the firm, and also, as the Tax Court found, that lunch was the most convenient time. But it does not follow that the expense of the lunch was a necessary business expense. The members of the firm had to eat somewhere, and the Cafe Angelo was both convenient and not too expensive. They do not claim to have incurred a greater daily lunch expense than they would have incurred if there had been no lunch meetings. Although it saved time to combine lunch with work, the meal itself was not an organic part of the meeting, as in the examples we gave earlier where the business objective, to be fully achieved, required sharing a meal.

The case might be different if the location of the courts required the firm's members to eat each day either in a disagreeable restaurant, so that they derived less value from the meal than it cost them to buy it, cf. Sibla v. Commissioner, 611 F.2d 1260, 1262 (9th Cir.1980); or in a restaurant too expensive for their personal tastes, so that, again, they would have gotten less value than the cash equivalent. But so far as appears, they picked the restaurant they liked most. Although it must be pretty monotonous to eat lunch the same place every working day of the year, not all the lawyers attended all the lunch meetings and there was nothing to stop the firm from meeting occasionally at another restaurant proximate to their office in downtown Chicago; there are hundreds.

An argument can be made that the price of lunch at the Cafe Angelo included rental of the space that the lawyers used for what was a meeting as well as a meal. There was evidence that the firm's conference room was otherwise occupied throughout the working day, so as a matter of logic Moss might be able to claim a part of the price of lunch as an ordinary and necessary expense for work space. But this is cutting things awfully fine; in any event Moss made no effort to apportion his lunch expense in this way.

Affirmed.

In Wells v. Commissioner, 36 T.C.M. (CCH) 1698 (1977), affirmed 626 F.2d 868 (9th Cir.1980), the court, in dictum, indicated that in a law firm "an occasional luncheon meeting with the firm staff to discuss the operation of the firm would be regarded as an ordinary and necessary business expense." Compare the situation described in the Hankenson case, discussed in the Moss case, with an occasional business lunch between a law firm partner and a prospective client who the partner hoped to get business from or referrals. In Rev.Rul. 63–144, 1963–2 C.B. 129 (Question 20), the Service ruled that the cost of lunches is not deductible when a group of business executives regularly have lunch together for personal reasons and each pays the entire bill in rotation.

Effective for the 1987 tax year, the deduction for otherwise allowable business meals is limited to 80 percent of cost. § 274(n). Besides meals, expenses subject to the 80 percent limitation include taxes and tips related to the meal and other related expenses such as cover charges. However, transportation to and from the business meal is not subject to the 80 percent limitation.

Questions

1. Should an associate in Mr. Moss' law firm report the value of the meals at Cafe Angelo in gross income if they are provided at no cost? Consider § 132(d) and (e).

2. With the enactment of § 274(n) can a taxpayer, such as the school administrator in Letter Ruling 8006004, deduct 80 percent of his entire meal cost or only 80 percent of the excess?

Problem

Once a month Richard's law firm has a luncheon for the associates to promote good relations. Typically, one of the partners in the firm gives a short talk on what is happening in the firm. Can Richard deduct the cost of his meal? What if Richard does not normally eat lunch? Would it make a difference if attendance was required or expected?

C. THE GREAT AMERICAN GAME: DEDUCTION OF TRAVEL EXPENSES

The title of this section may be amusing, but there is a serious thought behind it. Our system of taxation is based on self-assessment. Governments can exist in a self-assessment context only where there is confidence in the system. The exaggeration and abuse of deductions for travel expenses, and those for entertainment, discussed in the next section, have been widespread and well known. The corrosive effect of these abuses on the tax structure cannot be overlooked: the search for these deductions has indeed become the great American game.

Unreimbursed employee travel and transportation expenses are deductible as itemized deductions and are used only if the aggregate of the taxpayer's miscellaneous itemized deduction is in excess of two percent of his adjusted gross income. § 67(a).

1. COMMUTING

General Principles. Commuting costs, that is, the expenses of transportation to and from work, are nondeductible. Reg. §§ 1.162–2(e), 1.212–1(f), and 1.262–1(b)(5). The rationale is that non-business, personal reasons entered into the taxpayer's choice of a place of residence. Once the taxpayer is at work, the commute has ended; business-related transportation costs then become deductible business expenses.

Even if the expenses of commuting are greater than "normal" because the taxpayer drives long distances, the deduction is disallowed. In Sanders v. Commissioner, 439 F.2d 296 (9th Cir.1971), a civilian employee on an Air Force base was not allowed to live on the base for security reasons and the nearest available residential area was 80 miles away. The court denied the deduction for the cost of driving to and from work on the ground that there was no way to distinguish this expense from those of suburban commuters who cannot find suitable housing near their place of employment.

The Exception for Tools. There are, however, some exceptions to the commuting rules, particularly if the transportation is necessary to transport tools or instruments. In Fausner v. Commissioner, 413 U.S. 838, 93 S.Ct. 2820, 37 L.Ed.2d 996 (1973), rehearing denied 414 U.S. 882, 94 S.Ct. 43, 38 L.Ed.2d 130 (1974) the taxpayer, a commercial airline pilot who regularly drove his automobile approximately 84 miles round trip from his home to his place of employment, claimed a deduction for commuting expenses because he carried a flight bag and an overnight bag in his automobile. The deduction was disallowed because the taxpayer did not incur additional expenses for transporting job-required tools to and from work. A commuter can deduct the cost of traveling with tools between the taxpayer's home and place of business only if the taxpayer incurs additional expenses in transporting the tools. In such a case, an allocation of cost between personal and business expenses may be feasible. For example, the expenses incurred by the taxpayer in renting a trailer in which to carry tools are deductible, but not the cost of driving to and from work in his car (to which the trailer is attached). Rev.Rul. 75–380, 1975–2 C.B. 59.

Taxpayers may encounter difficulty in showing that additional expenses were incurred when commuting with tools. The Service stated in Letter Ruling 8025167 (March 27, 1980) that the taxpayer must establish that it costs more to travel to and from work with the equipment than it does without the equipment.

Problems

1. (a) Ted Player drives his car to and from his office each workday and is not reimbursed for the cost of his parking. Can he deduct the cost of driving to and from work, his parking expenses, and his own lunches? Consider § 262 and Reg. §§ 1.162–2(e) and 1.262–1(b)(5). Reconsider Problem 2 on page 70.

(b) Assume Ted drives from his office to meet with a client and returns to his office after the meeting. Can he deduct these driving costs? What is the impact of § 67?

2. Fritz, a carpenter who works at construction projects located throughout the city, uses his van to commute to and from work each day. At some sites, there is no overnight storage for his radial arm saw. If there is no overnight storage, he puts the saw in his van. Public transportation is available to about half of his jobs, but it is impossible for him to carry his saw on public transportation. Can Fritz deduct all the costs of commuting? What key factor should he be prepared to establish?

2. OTHER TRAVEL EXPENSES PAID BY TAXPAYERS: IN GENERAL

Under § 162(a)(2) a deduction is available for traveling expenses, including transportation costs and expenditures for meals and lodging, other than those which are "lavish or extravagant under the circumstances," which are:

    a. "Ordinary and necessary,"

    b. Incurred while "away from home," and

    c. Incurred in the "pursuit of a trade or business." The third condition means that a direct connection must exist between the expenditures and the conduct of the taxpayer's business or the business of the taxpayer's employer.

Let us consider how these requirements have been interpreted.

a. The Overnight Rule

A simple example of travel expenses is seen where a lawyer tries a case in a nearby town or a salesman goes on the road to sell his wares. The taxpayer's transportation expenses are deductible if incurred within the exigencies of the taxpayer's trade or business. Section 162(a) does not contain a requirement that transportation expenses be incurred away from home. (But transportation costs may be nondeductible commuting expenses.) However, the expenses for meals and lodging are deductible under § 162(a)(2) only if the taxpayer is "away from home" on business. The following case develops the overnight rule to differentiate traveling expenses from everyday living costs. If the overnight test is met, all of the taxpayer's expenses for meals and lodging on a business trip are deductible, not just the extra costs incurred by the taxpayer over what he would have expended if at home.

UNITED STATES v. CORRELL

Supreme Court of the United States, 1967.
389 U.S. 299, 88 S.Ct. 445, 19 L.Ed.2d 537.

MR. JUSTICE STEWART delivered the opinion of the Court.

The Commissioner of Internal Revenue has long maintained that a taxpayer traveling on business may deduct the cost of his meals only if his trip requires him to stop for sleep or rest. The question presented here is the validity of that rule.

The respondent in this case was a traveling salesman for a wholesale grocery company in Tennessee. He customarily left home early in the morning, ate breakfast and lunch on the road, and returned home in time for dinner. In his income tax returns for 1960 and 1961, he deducted the cost of his morning and noon meals as "traveling expenses" incurred in the pursuit of his business "while away from home" under § 162(a)(2) of the Internal Revenue Code of 1954. Because the respondent's daily trips required neither sleep nor rest, the Commissioner disallowed the deductions, ruling that the cost of the respondent's meals was a "personal, living" expense under § 262 rather than a travel expense under § 162(a)(2). The respondent paid the tax, sued for a refund in the District Court, and there received a favorable jury verdict. The Court of Appeals for the Sixth Circuit affirmed, holding that the Commissioner's sleep or rest rule is not "a valid regulation under the present statute." 369 F.2d 87, 90. In order to resolve a conflict among the circuits on this recurring question of federal income tax administration, we granted certiorari. 388 U.S. 905, 87 S.Ct. 2115, 18 L.Ed.2d 1346.

Under § 162(a)(2), taxpayers "traveling * * * away from home in the pursuit of a trade or business" may deduct the total amount "expended for meals and lodging." [4] As a result, even the taxpayer who incurs substantial hotel and restaurant expenses because of the special demands of business travel receives something of a windfall, for at least part of what he spends on meals represents a personal living expense that other taxpayers must bear without receiving any deduction at all.[5] Not surprisingly, therefore, Congress did not extend the special benefits of § 162(a)(2) to every conceivable situation involving business travel. It made the total cost of meals and lodging deductible only if incurred in the course of travel that takes the taxpayer "away from home." The problem before us involves the meaning of that limiting phrase.

In resolving that problem, the Commissioner has avoided the wasteful litigation and continuing uncertainty that would inevitably accompany any purely case-by-case approach to the question of whether a particular taxpayer was "away from home" on a particular day. Rather than requiring "every meal-purchasing taxpayer to take pot luck in the courts," [6] the Commissioner has consistently construed travel "away from home" to exclude all trips requiring neither sleep nor rest,[7] regardless of how many cities a given trip may have touched,[8]

---

4. Prior to the enactment in 1921 of what is now § 162(a)(2), the Commissioner had promulgated a regulation allowing a deduction for the cost of meals and lodging away from home, but only to the extent that this cost exceeded "any expenditures ordinarily required for such purposes when at home." Treas.Reg. 45 (1920 ed.), Art. 292, 4 Cum.Bull. 209 (1921). Despite its logical appeal, the regulation proved so difficult to administer that the Treasury Department asked Congress to grant a deduction for the "entire amount" of such meal and lodging expenditures. See Statement of Dr. T.S. Adams, Tax Adviser, Treasury Department, in Hearings on H.R. 8245 before the Senate Committee on Finance, 67th Cong., 1st Sess., at 50, 234–235 (1921). Accordingly, § 214(a)(1) of the Revenue Act of 1921, c. 136, 42 Stat. 239, for the first time included the language that later became § 162(a)(2).

5. Because § 262 makes "personal, living, or family expenses" nondeductible, * * * the taxpayer whose business requires no travel cannot ordinarily deduct the cost of the lunch he eats away from home. But the taxpayer who can bring himself within the reach of § 162(a)(2) may deduct what he spends on his noontime meal although it costs him no more, and relates no more closely to his business, than does the lunch consumed by his less mobile counterpart.

6. Commissioner v. Bagley, 1 Cir., 374 F.2d 204, 207.

7. The Commissioner's interpretation, first expressed in a 1940 ruling, I.T. 3395, 1940–2 Cum.Bull. 64, was originally known as the overnight rule. See Commissioner v. Bagley, supra, at 205.

8. The respondent lived in Fountain City, Tennessee, some 45 miles from his

how many miles it may have covered,[9] or how many hours it may have consumed.[10] By so interpreting the statutory phrase, the Commissioner has achieved not only ease and certainty of application but also substantial fairness, for the sleep or rest rule places all one-day travelers on a similar tax footing, rather than discriminating against intracity travelers and commuters, who of course cannot deduct the cost of the meals they eat on the road. See Commissioner Internal Revenue v. Flowers, 326 U.S. 465, 66 S.Ct. 250, 90 L.Ed. 203.

Any rule in this area must make some rather arbitrary distinctions,[11] but at least the sleep or rest rule avoids the obvious inequity of permitting the New York who makes a quick trip to Washington and back, missing neither his breakfast nor his dinner at home, to deduct the cost of his lunch merely because he covers more miles than the salesman who travels locally and must finance all his meals without the help of the Federal Treasury. And the Commissioner's rule surely makes more sense than one which would allow the respondent in this case to deduct the cost of his breakfast and lunch simply because he spends a greater percentage of his time at the wheel than the commuter who eats breakfast on his way to work and lunch a block from his office.

The Court of Appeals nonetheless found in the "plain language of the statute" an insuperable obstacle to the Commissioner's construction. 369 F.2d 87, 89. We disagree. The language of the statute— "meals and lodging * * * away from home"—is obviously not self-defining.[12] And to the extent that the words chosen by Congress cut in either direction, they tend to support rather than defeat the Commis-

employer's place of business in Morristown. His territory included restaurants in the cities of Madisonville, Engelwood, Etowah, Athens, Sweetwater, Lake City, Caryville, Jacksboro, La Follette, and Jellico, all in eastern Tennessee.

9. The respondent seldom traveled farther than 55 miles from his home, but he ordinarily drove a total of 150 to 175 miles daily.

10. The respondent's employer required him to be in his sales territory at the start of the business day. To do so, he had to leave Fountain City at about 5 a.m. He usually finished his daily schedule by 4 p.m., transmitted his orders to Morristown, and returned home by 5:30 p.m.

11. The rules proposed by the respondent and by the two *amici curiae* filing briefs on his behalf are not exceptional in this regard. Thus, for example, the respondent suggests that § 162(a)(2) be construed to cover those taxpayers who travel outside their "own home town," or outside "the greater * * * metropolitan area" where they reside. One *amicus* stresses the number of "hours spent and miles traveled away from the taxpayer's principal post of duty," suggesting that some emphasis should also be placed upon the number of meals consumed by the taxpayer "outside the general area of his home."

12. The statute applies to the meal and lodging expenses of taxpayers "traveling * * * away from home." The very concept of "traveling" obviously requires a physical separation from one's house. To read the phrase "away from home" as broadly as a completely literal approach might permit would thus render the phrase completely redundant. But of course the words of the statute have never been so woodenly construed. The commuter, for example, has never been regarded as "away from home" within the meaning of § 162(a)(2) simply because he has traveled from his residence to his place of business. See Commissioner v. Flowers, 326 U.S. 465, 473, 66 S.Ct. 250, 254, 90 L.Ed. 203. More than a dictionary is thus required to understand the provision here involved, and no appeal to the "plain language" of the section can obviate the need for further statutory construction.

sioner's position, for the statute speaks of "meals and lodging" as a unit, suggesting—at least arguably—that Congress contemplated a deduction for the cost of meals only where the travel in question involves lodging as well. Ordinarily, at least, only the taxpayer who finds it necessary to stop for sleep or rest incurs significantly higher living expenses as a direct result of his business travel,[13] and Congress might well have thought that only taxpayers in that category should be permitted to deduct their living expenses while on the road.[14] In any event, Congress certainly recognized, when it promulgated § 162(a)(2), that the Commissioner had so understood its statutory predecessor.[15] This case thus comes within the settled principle that "Treasury regulations and interpretations long continued without substantial change, applying to unamended or substantially reenacted statutes, are deemed to have received congressional approval and have the effect of law."

13. The taxpayer must ordinarily "maintain a home for his family at his own expense even when he is absent on business." Barnhill v. Commissioner Internal Revenue, 4 Cir., 148 F.2d 913, 917, and if he is required to stop for sleep or rest, "continuing costs incurred at a permanent place of abode are duplicated." James v. United States, 9 Cir., 308 F.2d 204, 206. The same taxpayer, however, is unlikely to incur substantially increased living expenses as a result of business travel, however far he may go, so long as he does not find it necessary to stop for lodging. One *amicus curiae* brief filed in this case asserts that "those who travel considerable distances such as [on] a one-day jet trip between New York and Chicago" spend more for "comparable meals [than] those who remain at their home base" and urges that all who travel "substantial distances" should therefore be permitted to deduct the entire cost of their meals. It may be that eating at a restaurant costs more than eating at home, but it cannot seriously be suggested that a taxpayer's bill at a restaurant mysteriously reflects the distance he has traveled to get there.

14. The court below thought that "[i]n an era of supersonic travel, the time factor is hardly relevant to the question of whether or not ∗ ∗ ∗ meal expenses are related to the taxpayer's business ∗ ∗ ∗." 369 F.2d 87, 89–90. But that completely misses the point. The benefits of § 162(a)(2) are limited to business travel "away from home," and *all* meal expenses incurred in the course of such travel are deductible, however unrelated they may be to the taxpayer's income-producing activity. To ask that the definition of "away from home" be

responsive to the business necessity of the taxpayer's meals is to demand the impossible.

15. In considering the proposed 1954 Code, Congress heard a taxpayer plea for a change in the rule disallowing deductions for meal expenses on one-day trips. Hearings on General Revision of the Internal Revenue Code before the House Committee on Ways and Means, 83d Cong., 1st Sess., pt. 1, at 216–219 (1953); Hearings on H.R. 8300 before the Senate Committee on Finance, 83d Cong., 2d Sess., pt. 4, at 2396 (1954). No such change resulted.

In recommending § 62(2)(C) of the 1954 Code, permitting employees to deduct certain transportation expenses in computing adjusted gross income, the Senate Finance Committee stated:

"At present, business transportation expenses can be deducted by an employee in arriving at adjusted gross income only if they are reimbursed by the employer or if they are incurred while he was *away from home overnight.* ∗ ∗ ∗

"Because these expenses, when incurred, usually are substantial, it appears desirable to treat employees in this respect like self-employed persons. For this reason both the House and your committee's bill permit employees to deduct business transportation expenses in arriving at adjusted gross income even though the expenses are not incurred in travel *away from home* or not reimbursed by the employer. ∗ ∗ ∗" S.Rep. No. 1622, 83d Cong., 2d Sess., 9 (1954) (emphasis added).

∗ ∗ ∗

Alternatives to the Commissioner's sleep or rest rule are of course available. Improvements might be imagined. But we do not sit as a committee of revision to perfect the administration of the tax laws. Congress has delegated to the Commissioner, not to the courts, the task of prescribing "all needful rules and regulations for the enforcement" of the Internal Revenue Code. 26 U.S.C. § 7805(a). In this area of limitless factual variations "it is the province of Congress and the Commissioner, not the courts, to make the appropriate adjustments." Commissioner v. Stidger, 386 U.S. 287, 296, 87 S.Ct. 1065, 1071, 18 L.Ed. 2d 53. The rule of the judiciary in cases of this sort begins and ends with assuring that the Commissioner's regulations fall within his authority to implement the congressional mandate in some reasonable manner. Because the rule challenged here has not been shown deficient on that score, the Court of Appeals should have sustained its validity. The judgment is therefore reversed.

Reversed.

Mr. Justice Marshall took no part in the consideration or decision of this case.

Mr. Justice Douglas, with whom Mr. Justice Black and Mr. Justice Fortas concur, dissenting.

The statutory words "while away from home," 26 U.S.C. § 162(a) (2), may not in my view be shrunken to "overnight" by administrative construction or regulations. "Overnight" injects a time element in testing deductibility, while the statute speaks only in terms of geography. As stated by the Court of Appeals:

"In an era of supersonic travel, the time factor is hardly relevant to the question of whether or not travel and meal expenses are related to the taxpayer's business and cannot be the basis of a valid regulation under the present statute." Correll v. United States, 369 F.2d 87, 89–90.

I would affirm the judgment below.

---

b. *Away From Home*

HANTZIS v. COMMISSIONER

United States Court of Appeals, First Circuit, 1981.
638 F.2d 248.
Cert. denied 452 U.S. 962, 101 S.Ct. 3112, 69 L.Ed. 973 (1981).

Levin H. Campbell, Circuit Judge.

The Commissioner of Internal Revenue (Commissioner) appeals a decision of the United States Tax Court that allowed a deduction under 26 U.S.C. § 162(a)(2) (1976) for expenses incurred by a law student in the course of her summer employment. The facts in the case are straightforward and undisputed.

In the fall of 1973 Catharine Hantzis (taxpayer), formerly a candidate for an advanced degree in philosophy at the University of California at Berkeley, entered Harvard Law School in Cambridge, Massachusetts, as a full-time student. During her second year of law school she sought unsuccessfully to obtain employment for the summer of 1975 with a Boston law firm. She did, however, find a job as a legal assistant with a law firm in New York City, where she worked for ten weeks beginning in June 1975. Her husband, then a member of the faculty of Northeastern University with a teaching schedule for that summer, remained in Boston and lived at the couple's home there. At the time of the Tax Court's decision in this case, Mr. and Mrs. Hantzis still resided in Boston.

On their joint income tax return for 1975, Mr. and Mrs. Hantzis reported the earnings from taxpayer's summer employment ($3,750) and deducted the cost of transportation between Boston and New York, the cost of a small apartment rented by Mrs. Hantzis in New York and the cost of her meals in New York ($3,204). The deductions were taken under 26 U.S.C. § 162(a)(2) (1976) * * *.

The Commissioner disallowed the deduction on the ground that taxpayer's home for purposes of section 162(a)(2) was her place of employment and the cost of traveling to and living in New York was therefore not "incurred * * * while away from home." The Commissioner also argued that the expenses were not incurred "in the pursuit of a trade or business." Both positions were rejected by the Tax Court, which found that Boston was Mrs. Hantzis' home because her employment in New York was only temporary and that her expenses in New York were "necessitated" by her employment there. The court thus held the expenses to be deductible under section 162(a)(2).

In asking this court to reverse the Tax Court's allowance of the deduction, the Commissioner has contended that the expenses were not incurred "in the pursuit of a trade or business." We do not accept this argument; nonetheless, we sustain the Commissioner and deny the deduction, on the basis that the expenses were not incurred "while away from home."

I.

Section 262 of the Code, 26 U.S.C. § 262 (1976), declares that "except as otherwise provided in this chapter, no deductions shall be allowed for personal, living, or family expenses." Section 162 provides less of an exception to this rule than it creates a separate category of deductible business expenses. This category manifests a fundamental principle of taxation: that a person's taxable income should not include the cost of producing that income. See Note, The Additional Expense Test: A Proposal to Help Solve the Dilemma of Mixed Business and Personal Expenses, 1974 Duke L.J. 636, 636. "[O]ne of the specific examples given by Congress" of a deductible cost of producing income is travel expenses in section 162(a)(2). Commissioner v. Flowers, 326 U.S. 465, 469, 66 S.Ct. 250, 252, 90 L.Ed. 203 (1946). See Rev.Rul. 60–16, 1960–1 C.B. 58, 60.

The test by which "personal" travel expenses subject to tax under section 262 are distinguished from those costs of travel necessarily incurred to generate income is embodied in the requirement that, to be deductible under section 162(a)(2), an expense must be "incurred * * * in the pursuit of a trade or business." In *Flowers* the Supreme Court read this phrase to mean that "[t]he exigencies of business rather than the personal conveniences and necessities of the traveler must be the motivating factors." 326 U.S. at 474, 66 S.Ct. at 254.[16] Of course, not every travel expense resulting from business exigencies rather than personal choice is deductible; an expense must also be "ordinary and necessary" and incurred "while away from home." 26 U.S.C. § 162(a) (2) (1976); Flowers, 326 U.S. at 470, 66 S.Ct. at 252. But the latter limitations draw also upon the basic concept that only expenses necessitated by business, as opposed to personal, demands may be excluded from the calculation of taxable income.

With these fundamentals in mind, we proceed to ask whether the cost of taxpayer's transportation to and from New York, and of her meals and lodging while in New York, was incurred "while away from home in the pursuit of a trade or business."

II.

The Commissioner has directed his argument at the meaning of "in pursuit of a trade or business." He interprets this phrase as requiring that a deductible traveling expense be incurred under the demands of a trade or business which predates the expense, i.e., an "already existing" trade or business. Under this theory, section 162(a)(2) would invalidate the deduction taken by the taxpayer because she was a full-time student before commencing her summer work at a New York law firm in 1975 and so was not continuing in a trade or business when she incurred the expenses of traveling to New York and living there while her job lasted. The Commissioner's proposed interpretation erects at the threshold of deductibility under section 162(a)(2) the requirement that a taxpayer be engaged in a trade or business before incurring a travel expense. Only if that requirement is satisfied would an inquiry into the deductibility of an expense proceed to ask whether the expense was a result of business exigencies, incurred while away from home, and reasonable and necessary.

Such a reading of the statute is semantically possible and would perhaps expedite the disposition of certain cases.[17] Nevertheless, we

16. *Flowers* denied a deduction claimed by the taxpayer as not involving expenses required by the taxpayer's *employer's* business. It is now established, however, that a taxpayer may be in the trade or business of being an employee. See, e.g., Primuth v. Commissioner, 54 T.C. 374, 377–78 (1970) (citing cases); Rev.Rul. 77–16, 1977–1 C.B. 37; Rev.Rul. 60–16, 1960–1 C.B. 58. Thus, expenses necessitated by the exigencies of an employee's occupation, without regard to the demands of the employer's business, are also deductible.

17. We do not see, however, how it would affect the treatment of this case. The Commissioner apparently concedes that upon starting work in New York the taxpayer engaged in a trade or business. If we held—as we do not—that an expense is deductible only when incurred in connection with an already existing trade or business, our ruling would seem to invalidate

reject it as unsupported by case law and inappropriate to the policies behind section 162(a)(2).

The two cases relied on by the Commissioner do not appear to us to establish that traveling expenses are deductible only if incurred in connection with a preexisting trade or business. The seminal interpretation of section 162(a)(2), Flowers v. Commissioner, supra, 326 U.S. 465, 66 S.Ct. 250, 90 L.Ed. 203, is as equivocal upon that point as the statutory language it construes. Commissioner v. Janss, 260 F.2d 99 (8th Cir.1958), a case with facts somewhat akin to the present, did not articulate any such theory. In *Janss,* a college student from Des Moines, Iowa, worked in Alaska during the summer between his freshman and sophomore years of school and sought to deduct from his taxable income the cost of transportation to and from Alaska as well as the cost of meals and lodging while there. Despite testimony from the personnel manager of the construction company for which Janss worked indicating that workers were available in Alaska and that Janss had been employed there largely as a personal favor, the Tax Court allowed the deduction. The Eighth Circuit reversed. It held, under *Flowers,* that Janss' travel to Alaska was not motivated by the exigencies of the employer's business. 260 F.2d at 104. The Eighth Circuit placed no emphasis on the fact that Janss had no previously existing trade or business.

Nor would the Commissioner's theory mesh with the policy behind section 162(a)(2). As discussed, the travel expense deduction is intended to exclude from taxable income a necessary cost of producing that income. Yet the recency of entry into a trade or business does not indicate that travel expenses are not a cost of producing income. To be sure, the costs incurred by a taxpayer who leaves his usual residence to begin a trade or business at another location may not be truly *travel* expenses, i. e., expenses incurred while "away from home," see infra, but practically, they are as much incurred "in the pursuit of a trade or business" when the occupation is new as when it is old.

An example drawn from the Commissioner's argument illustrates the point. The Commissioner notes that "if a construction worker, who normally works in Boston for Corp. A, travels to New York to work for Corp. B for six months, he is traveling * * * in the pursuit of his own trade as a construction worker." Accordingly, the requirement that travel expenses be a result of business exigencies is satisfied. Had a construction worker just entering the labor market followed the same course his expenses under the Commissioner's reasoning would not satisfy the business exigencies requirement.[18] Yet in each case, the

merely the deduction of the cost of taxpayer's trip from Boston to New York to begin work (about $64). We would still need to determine, as in any other case under section 162(a)(2), whether the expenses that arose *subsequent* to the taxpayer's entry into her trade or business were reasonable and necessary, required by business exigencies and incurred while away from home.

18. It could be argued that people enter the trade or business of "being employees," * * * upon becoming available for employment rather than upon actually starting work. If correct, the two hypothetical taxpayer's travel expenses would be costs of earning an income and not merely incidents of personal lifestyle. Requiring that the finding of business exigency necessary to deductibility under section 162(a)(2) be predicated upon the prior existence of a trade or business would thus captiously restrict the meaning of "in pursuit of a trade or business."

Insofar as any cases bear on the issue, they seem to support this conclusion. In United States v. LeBlanc, 278 F.2d 571 (5th Cir.1960), a justice of the Louisiana supreme court who resided in Napoleanville sought to deduct as a travel expense the cost of an apartment in New Orleans, where the court sat. Because Louisiana law required justices both to maintain a residence in their home districts and be present at court functions, the cost of the apartment was found to have been necessitated by business exigencies. Such a result is inconsistent with the rule proposed by the Commissioner. The taxpayer in *LeBlanc* was not previously engaged in the trade or business which he began upon arriving in New Orleans. At least for the period of his first term on the court, therefore, the taxpayer's expenses in New Orleans were not incurred in connection with an already existing occupation and so, by the Commissioner's reasoning, should have been disallowed.[19] In another case, Kroll v. Commissioner, 49 T.C. 557 (1968), the court expressly found that the taxpayer, an eight-year-old actor, was not engaged in an already existing trade or business. Indeed, before coming to New York to begin acting, he "had never engaged in a trade or business." 49 T.C. at 558. That this fact might have been dispositive was never mentioned by the court, which noted that the expenses in question were incurred in connection with an ongoing trade or business, id., at 561, and so went on to address the requirement that they have arisen while away from home.

In other contexts the phrase "in the pursuit of a trade or business" may permit the interpretation urged upon us by the Commissioner,[20]

situations would not necessarily produce different results. So interpreted, however, the Commissioner's argument would create an administrative nightmare. In every case in which the issue arose, the Commissioner and the courts would be presented with the task of determining at just what point a person could be said to have actually entered his trade or business. Further, such a position might well imply that Mrs. Hantzis actually entered her trade or occupation while still in Boston, and not upon arriving at the offices of the New York firm.

19. The tax years at issue in *LeBlanc* were 1950 and 1951. The taxpayer began his tenure on the court in December 1949. 278 F.2d at 572. Thus, it could be argued that as of January 1, 1950 the taxpayer was engaged in a previously existing trade or business. This rationalization of the case exposes the weaknesses of the Commissioner's position. It is not clear to us why a month's prior employment would provide prima facie evidence of the business purpose behind the taxpayer's expenses. And if it did, the question would further arise how much previous work would constitute an already existing trade or business. A week? A day? A few hours on the train between Napoleanville and New Orleans? The difficulty in administering such a rule is obvious.

20. Under the general provision of section 162(a), no deduction is allowed for expenses incurred in preparing to enter a new business and the phrase "in the pursuit of a trade or business" has in cases concerned with such expenses been read to "presuppose [ ] an existing business with which [the taxpayer] is connected." Frank v. Commissioner, 20 T.C. 511, 513–14 (1953).

but to require under section 162(a)(2) that a travel expense be incurred in connection with a preexisting trade or business is neither necessary nor appropriate to effectuating the purpose behind the use of that phrase in the provision. Accordingly, we turn to the question whether, in the absence of the Commissioner's proposed threshold limit on deductibility, the expenses at issue here satisfy the requirements of section 162(a)(2) as interpreted in *Flowers v. Commissioner.*

III.

As already noted, *Flowers* construed section 162(a)(2) to mean that a traveling expense is deductible only if it is (1) reasonable and necessary, (2) incurred while away from home, and (3) necessitated by the exigencies of business. Because the Commissioner does not suggest that Mrs. Hantzis' expenses were unreasonable or unnecessary, we may pass directly to the remaining requirements. Of these, we find dispositive the requirement that an expense be incurred while away from home. As we think Mrs. Hantzis' expenses were not so incurred, we hold the deduction to be improper.

The meaning of the term "home" in the travel expense provision is far from clear. When Congress enacted the travel expense deduction now codified as section 162(a)(2), it apparently was unsure whether, to be deductible, an expense must be incurred away from a person's residence or away from his principal place of business. See Note, A House is not a Tax Home, 49 Va.L.Rev. 125, 127–28 (1963). This ambiguity persists and courts, sometimes within a single circuit, have divided over the issue. Compare Six v. United States, 450 F.2d 66 (2d Cir.1971) (home held to be residence) and Rosenspan v. United States, 438 F.2d 905 (2d Cir.), cert. denied, 404 U.S. 864, 92 S.Ct. 54, 30 L.Ed.2d 281 (1971) and Burns v. Gray, 287 F.2d 698 (6th Cir.1961) and Wallace v. Commissioner, 144 F.2d 407 (9th Cir.1944) with Markey v. Commissioner, 490 F.2d 1249 (6th Cir.1974) (home held to be principal place of business) and Curtis v. Commissioner, 449 F.2d 225 (5th Cir.1971) and Wills v. Commissioner, 411 F.2d 537 (9th Cir.1969).[21] It has been suggested that these conflicting definitions are due to the enormous factual variety in the cases. See Bell v. United States, 591 F.2d 647, 649 (Ct.Cl.1979) ("We believe that much of the problem in differing definitions is the result of attempting to conceptualize the reasons for decisions which are based on widely varying factual situations."); Brandl v. Commissioner, 513 F.2d 697, 699 (6th Cir.1975) ("Because of the almost infinite variety of the factual situations involved, the courts have not formulated a concrete definition of the term 'home' capable of universal application.") We find this observation instructive, for if the cases that discuss the meaning of the term "home" in section 162(a)(2) are interpreted on the basis of their unique facts as well as the

---

21. The Tax Court has, with a notable exception, consistently held that a taxpayer's home is his place of business. See Daly v. Commissioner, 72 T.C. 190 (1979); Foote v. Commissioner, 67 T.C. 1 (1976); Montgomery v. Commissioner, 64 T.C. 175 (1975), aff'd, 532 F.2d 1088 (6th Cir.1976); Blatnick v. Commissioner, 56 T.C. 1344 (1971). The exception, of course, is the present case.

fundamental purposes of the travel expense provision, and not simply pinioned to one of two competing definitions of home, much of the seeming confusion and contradiction on this issue disappears and a functional definition of the term emerges.

We begin by recognizing that the location of a person's home for purposes of section 162(a)(2) becomes problematic only when the person lives one place and works another. Where a taxpayer resides and works at a single location, he is always home, however defined; and where a taxpayer is constantly on the move due to his work, he is never "away" from home. (In the latter situation, it may be said either that he has no residence to be away from, or else that his residence is always at his place of employment. See Rev.Rul. 60–16, 1960–1 C.B. 58, 62.) However, in the present case, the need to determine "home" is plainly before us, since the taxpayer resided in Boston and worked, albeit briefly, in New York.

We think the critical step in defining "home" in these situations is to recognize that the "while away from home" requirement has to be construed in light of the further requirement that the expense be the result of business exigencies. The traveling expense deduction obviously is not intended to exclude from taxation every expense incurred by a taxpayer who, in the course of business, maintains two homes. Section 162(a)(2) seeks rather "to mitigate the burden of the taxpayer who, *because of the exigencies of his trade or business, must* maintain two places of abode and thereby incur additional and duplicate living expenses." Kroll, supra, 49 T.C. at 562 (emphasis added). See Brandl, supra, 513 F.2d at 699; Daly, supra, 72 T.C. at 195. Consciously or unconsciously, courts have effectuated this policy in part through their interpretation of the term "home" in section 162(a)(2). Whether it is held in a particular decision that a taxpayer's home is his residence or his principal place of business, the ultimate allowance or disallowance of a deduction is a function of the court's assessment of the reason for a taxpayer's maintenance of two homes. If the reason is perceived to be personal, the taxpayer's home will generally be held to be his place of employment rather than his residence and the deduction will be denied. See, e.g., Markey, supra, 490 F.2d at 1252–55; Wills, supra, 411 F.2d at 540–41; Daly, supra, 72 T.C. at 195–98; Lindsay v. Commissioner, supra, 34 B.T.A. at 843–44. If the reason is felt to be business exigencies, the person's home will usually be held to be his residence and the deduction will be allowed. See, e.g., Frederick v. United States, 603 F.2d 1292 (8th Cir.1979); Wright v. Hartsell, 305 F.2d 221 (9th Cir. 1962); Harvey v. Commissioner, 283 F.2d 491 (9th Cir.1960); LeBlanc, supra, 278 F.2d 571. We understand the concern of the concurrence that such an operational interpretation of the term "home" is somewhat technical and perhaps untidy, in that it will not always afford bright line answers, but we doubt the ability of either the Commissioner or the courts to invent an unyielding formula that will make sense in all cases. The line between personal and business expenses winds through infinite factual permutations; effectuation of the travel expense provision requires that any principle of decision be flexible and sensitive to statutory policy.

Construing in the manner just described the requirement that an expense be incurred "while away from home," we do not believe this requirement was satisfied in this case. Mrs. Hantzis' *trade or business* did not require that she maintain a home in Boston as well as one in New York. Though she returned to Boston at various times during the period of her employment in New York, her visits were all for personal reasons. It is not contended that she had a business connection in Boston that necessitated her keeping a home there; no professional interest was served by maintenance of the Boston home—as would have been the case, for example, if Mrs. Hantzis had been a lawyer based in Boston with a New York client whom she was temporarily serving. The home in Boston was kept up for reasons involving Mr. Hantzis, but those reasons cannot substitute for a showing by *Mrs.* Hantzis that the exigencies of *her* trade or business required *her* to maintain two homes.[22] Mrs. Hantzis' decision to keep two homes must be seen as a choice dictated by personal, albeit wholly reasonable, considerations and not a business or occupational necessity. We therefore hold that her home for purposes of section 162(a)(2) was New York and that the expenses at issue in this case were not incurred "while away from home." [23]

We are not dissuaded from this conclusion by the temporary nature of Mrs. Hantzis' employment in New York. Mrs. Hantzis argues that the brevity of her stay in New York excepts her from the business exigencies requirement of section 162(a)(2) under a doctrine supposedly enunciated by the Supreme Court in Peurifoy v. Commissioner, 358 U.S. 59, 79 S.Ct. 104, 3 L.Ed.2d 30 (1958) (per curiam).[24] The Tax Court

22. In this respect, Mr. and Mrs. Hantzis' situation is analogous to cases involving spouses with careers in different locations. Each must independently satisfy the requirement that deductions taken for travel expenses incurred in the pursuit of a trade or business arise while he or she is away from home. See Chwalow v. Commissioner, 470 F.2d 475, 477–78 (3d Cir. 1972) ("Where additional expenses are incurred because, for personal reasons, husband and wife maintain separate domiciles, no deduction is allowed."); Hammond v. Commissioner, 213 F.2d 43, 44 (5th Cir. 1954); Foote v. Commissioner, 67 T.C. 1 (1976); Coerver v. Commissioner, 36 T.C. 252 (1961). This is true even though the spouses file a joint return. Chwalow, supra, 470 F.2d at 478.

23. The concurrence reaches the same result on essentially the same reasoning, but under what we take to be an interpretation of the "in pursuit of business" requirement. We differ from our colleague,

it would seem, only on the question of which precondition to deductibility best accommodates the statutory concern for "'the taxpayer who, because of the exigencies of his trade or business, must maintain two places of abode and thereby incur additional and duplicate living expenses.'" * * * Neither the phrase "away from home" nor "in pursuit of business" effectuates this concern without interpretation that to some degree removes it from "the ordinary meaning of the term." (Keeton, J., concurring). However, of the two approaches, we find that of the concurrence more problematic than that adopted here.

24. In *Peurifoy,* the Court stated that the Tax Court had "engrafted an exception" onto the requirement that travel expenses be dictated by business exigencies, allowing "a deduction for expenditures * * * when the taxpayer's employment is 'temporary' as contrasted with 'indefinite' or 'indeterminate.'" 358 U.S. at 59, 79 S.Ct. at 104. Because the Commissioner here held that Boston was the taxpayer's home because it would have been unreasonable for her to move her residence to New York for only ten weeks. At first glance these contentions may seem to find support in the court decisions holding that, when a taxpayer works for a limited time away from his usual home, section 162(a)(2) allows a deduction for the expense of maintaining a second home so long as the employment is "temporary" and not "indefinite" or "permanent." See, e.g., Frederick, supra, 603 F.2d at 1294; Six, supra, 450 F.2d at 69; Wright, supra, 304 F.2d at 224–25; Coburn v. Commissioner, 138 F.2d 763, 764–65 (2d Cir. 1943). This test is an elaboration of the requirements under section 162(a)(2) that an expense be incurred due to business exigencies and while away from home. See note 12, supra. Thus it has been said,

> "Where a taxpayer reasonably expects to be employed in a location for a substantial or indefinite period of time, the reasonable inference is that his choice of a residence is a personal decision, unrelated to any business necessity. Thus, it is irrelevant how far he travels to work. The normal expectation, however, is that the taxpayer will choose to live near his place of employment. Consequently, when a taxpayer reasonable [sic] expects to be employed in a location for only a short or temporary period of time and travels a considerable distance to the location from his residence, it is unreasonable to assume that his choice of a residence is dictated by personal convenience. The reasonable inference is that he is temporarily making these travels because of a business necessity."

Frederick, supra, 603 F.2d at 1294–95 (citations omitted).

The temporary employment doctrine does not, however, purport to eliminate any requirement that continued maintenance of a first home have a business justification. We think the rule has no application where the taxpayer has no business connection with his usual place of residence. If no business exigency dictates the location of the taxpayer's usual residence, then the mere fact of his taking temporary employment elsewhere cannot supply a compelling business reason for continuing to maintain that residence. Only a taxpayer who lives one place, works another and has business ties to *both* is in the ambiguous situation that the temporary employment doctrine is designed to resolve. In such circumstances, unless his employment away from his

did not challenge this exception, the Court did not rule on its validity. It instead upheld the circuit court's reversal of the Tax Court and disallowance of the deduction on the basis of the adequacy of the appellate court's review. The Supreme Court agreed that the Tax Court's finding as to the temporary nature of taxpayer's employment was clearly erroneous. Id. at 60–61, 79 S.Ct. at 105.

Despite its inauspicious beginning, the exception has come to be generally accepted. Some uncertainty lingers, however, over whether the exception properly ap-

plies to the "business exigencies" or the "away from home" requirement. Compare Brandl, supra, 513 F.2d at 699 and Blatnick v. Commissioner, 56 T.C. 1344, 1348 (1971) with Frederick, supra, 603 F.2d at 1294. In fact, it is probably relevant to both. See Six, supra, 450 F.2d at 69 n. 1; Note, supra, 49 Va.L.Rev. at 136–45.

Because we treat these requirements as inextricably intertwined, see supra, we find it unnecessary to address this question: applied to either requirement, the temporary employment doctrine affects the meaning of both.

usual home is temporary, a court can reasonably assume that the taxpayer has abandoned his business ties to that location and is left with only personal reasons for maintaining a residence there. Where only personal needs require that a travel expense be incurred, however, a taxpayer's home is defined so as to leave the expense subject to taxation. See supra. Thus, a taxpayer who pursues temporary employment away from the location of his usual residence, but has no business connection with that location, is not "away from home" for purposes of section 162(a)(2). See Cockrell v. Commissioner, 321 F.2d 504, 507 (8th Cir.1963); Tucker v. Commissioner, 55 T.C. 783, 786–88 (1971).

On this reasoning, the temporary nature of Mrs. Hantzis' employment in New York does not affect the outcome of her case. She had no business ties to Boston that would bring her within the temporary employment doctrine. By this holding, we do not adopt a rule that "home" in section 162(a)(2) is the equivalent of a taxpayer's place of business. Nor do we mean to imply that a taxpayer has a "home" for tax purposes only if he is already engaged in a trade or business at a particular location. Though both rules are alluringly determinate, we have already discussed why they offer inadequate expressions of the purposes behind the travel expense deduction. We hold merely that for a taxpayer in Mrs. Hantzis' circumstances to be "away from home in the pursuit of a trade or business," she must establish the existence of some sort of business relation both to the location she claims as "home" and to the location of her temporary employment sufficient to support a finding that her duplicative expenses are necessitated by business exigencies. This, we believe, is the meaning of the statement in *Flowers* that "[b]usiness trips are to be identified *in relation to* business demands and the traveler's business headquarters." 326 U.S. at 474, 66 S.Ct. at 254 (emphasis added). On the uncontested facts before us, Mrs. Hantzis had no business relation to Boston; we therefore leave to cases in which the issue is squarely presented the task of elaborating what relation to a place is required under section 162(a)(2) for duplicative living expenses to be deductible.

Reversed.

KEETON, DISTRICT JUDGE, concurring in the result.

Although I agree with the result reached in the court's opinion, and with much of its underlying analysis, I write separately because I cannot join in the court's determination that New York was the taxpayer's home for purposes of 26 U.S.C. § 162(a)(2). In so holding, the court adopts a definition of "home" that differs from the ordinary meaning of the term and therefore unduly risks causing confusion and misinterpretation of the important principle articulated in this case.

In adopting section 162(a)(2), Congress sought "to mitigate the burden of the taxpayer who, because of the exigencies of his trade or business, must maintain two places of abode and thereby incur additional and duplicate living expenses." Kroll v. Commissioner, 49 T.C.

557, 562 (1962). See Rosenspan v. United States, 438 F.2d 905, 912 (2d Cir.), cert. denied, 404 U.S. 864, 92 S.Ct. 54, 30 L.Ed.2d 108 (1971); James v. United States, 308 F.2d 204, 206–07 (9th Cir.1962). In the present case, the taxpayer does not contend that she maintained her residence in Boston for business reasons. Before working in New York, she had attended school near her home in Boston, and she continued to do so after she finished her summer job. In addition, her husband lived and worked in Boston. Thus, on the facts in this case, I am in agreement with the court that the taxpayer's deductions must be disallowed because she was not required by her trade or business to maintain both places of residence. However rather than resting its conclusion on an interpretation of the language of section 162(a)(2) taken as a whole, which allows a deduction for ordinary and necessary expenses incurred "while away from home in the pursuit of trade or business," the court reaches the same result by incorporating the concept of business-related residence into the definition of "home," thereby producing sometimes, but not always, a meaning of "home" quite different from ordinary usage.

The Supreme Court has noted that "[t]he meaning of the word 'home' in [the predecessor of § 162(a)(2)] with reference to a taxpayer residing in one city and working in another has engendered much difficulty and litigation." Commissioner v. Flowers, 326 U.S. 465, 471, 66 S.Ct. 250, 253, 90 L.Ed. 203 (1946). The Court has twice rejected opportunities to adopt definitive constructions of the term. Flowers, supra, 326 U.S. at 472, 66 S.Ct. at 253. Commissioner v. Stidger, 386 U.S. 287, 292, 87 S.Ct. 1065, 1068, 17 L.Ed.2d 51 (1967). See also Peurifoy v. Commissioner, 358 U.S. 59, 79 S.Ct. 104, 3 L.Ed.2d 30 (1958). Moreover, as the court's opinion in the present case points out, the courts of appeals have split on whether a taxpayer's "home" is her (or his) principal residence or principal place of business.

The court enters this conflict among circuits with a "functional" definition of home not yet adopted by any other circuit. I read the opinion as indicating that in a dual residence case, the Commissioner must determine whether the exigencies of the taxpayer's trade or business require her to maintain both residences. If so, the Commissioner must decide that the taxpayer's *principal residence* is her "home" and must conclude that expenses associated with the secondary residence were incurred "while away from home," and are deductible. If not, as in the instant case, the Commissioner must find that the taxpayer's *principal place of business* is her "home" and must conclude that the expenses in question were not incurred "while away from home." The conclusory nature of these determinations as to which residence is her "home" reveals the potentially confusing effect of adopting an extra-ordinary definition of "home."

A word used in a statute can mean, among the cognoscenti, whatever authoritative sources define it to mean. Nevertheless, it is a distinct disadvantage of a body of law that it can be understood only by those who are expert in its terminology. Moreover, needless risks of misunderstanding and confusion arise, not only among members of the public but also among professionals who must interpret and apply a statute in their day-to-day work, when a word is given an extraordinary meaning that is contrary to its everyday usage.

The result reached by the court can easily be expressed while also giving "home" its ordinary meaning, and neither Congress nor the Supreme Court has directed that "home" be given an extraordinary meaning in the present context. See Flowers, supra, Stidger, supra, and Peurifoy, supra. In Rosenspan v. United States, supra, Judge Friendly, writing for the court, rejected the Commissioner's proposed definition of home as the taxpayer's business headquarters, concluding that in section 162(a)(2) " 'home' means 'home.' " Id. at 912.

> When Congress uses a non-technical word in a tax statute, presumably it wants administrators and courts to read it in the way that ordinary people would understand, and not "to draw on some unexpressed spirit outside the bounds of the normal meaning of words." Addison v. Holly Hill Fruit Prods., Inc., 322 U.S. 607, 617, 64 S.Ct. 1215, 1221, 88 L.Ed. 1488 (1944).

Id. at 911. Cf. United States v. New England Coal and Coke Co., 318 F.2d 138, 142 (1st Cir.1963) ("Unless the contrary appears, it is presumed that statutory words were used in their ordinary sense").

In analyzing dual residence cases, the court's opinion advances compelling reasons that the first step must be to determine whether the taxpayer has business as opposed to purely personal reasons for maintaining both residences. This must be done in order to determine whether the expenses of maintaining a second residence were, "necessitated by business, as opposed to personal, demands," and were in this sense incurred by the taxpayer "while away from home in pursuit of trade or business." Necessarily implicit in this proposition is a more limited corollary that is sufficient to decide the present case: When the taxpayer has a business relationship to only one location, no traveling expenses the taxpayer incurs are "necessitated by business, as opposed to personal demands," regardless of how many residences the taxpayer has, where they are located, or which one is "home."

In the present case, although the taxpayer argues that her employment required her to reside in New York, that contention is insufficient to compel a determination that it was the nature of her trade or business that required her to incur the additional expense of maintaining a second residence, the burden that section 162(a)(2) was intended to mitigate. Her expenses associated with maintaining her New York residence arose from personal interests that led her to maintain two residences rather than a single residence close to her work. While traveling from her principal residence to a second place of residence closer to her business, even though "away from home," she was not "away from home in pursuit of business." Thus, the expenses at issue in this case were not incurred by the taxpayer "while away from home in pursuit of trade or business."

In the contrasting case in which a taxpayer has established that both residences were maintained for business reasons, section 162(a)(2) allows the deduction of expenses associated with travel to, and maintenance of, one of the residences if they are incurred for business reasons *and that abode is not the taxpayer's home.* A common sense meaning of "home" works well to achieve the purpose of this provision.

In summary, the court announces a sound principle that, in dual residence cases, deductibility of traveling expenses depends upon a showing that both residences were maintained for business reasons. If that principle is understood to be derived from the language of section 162(a)(2) taken as a whole, "home" retains operative significance for determining *which* of the business-related residences is the one the expense of which can be treated as deductible. In this context, "home" should be given its ordinary meaning to allow a deduction only for expenses relating to an abode that is not the taxpayer's principal place of residence. On the undisputed facts in this case, the Tax Court found that Boston was the taxpayer's "home" in the everyday sense, i.e., her principal place of residence. Were the issue relevant to disposition of the case, I would uphold the Tax Court's quite reasonable determination on the evidence before it. However, because the taxpayer had no business reason for maintaining both residences, her deduction for expenses associated with maintaining a second residence closer than her principal residence to her place of employment must be disallowed without regard to which of her two residences was her "home" under section 162(a)(2).

Question

Do you support the "tax home" theory rejected by the majority in Hantzis? Why was the temporary job exception unavailable?

In Daly v. Commissioner, 662 F.2d 253 (4th Cir.1981), a salesman, who maintained a personal residence in Virginia regularly traveled to other states for selling purposes. The court found his tax home to be the area he served as a traveling salesman, even though he prepared sales and other business reports at his Virginia residence. The salesman chose not to relocate his family because his wife would be forced to abandon her job and the move itself would be inconvenient. Finding the taxpayer's reasons personal, the court concluded that the travel expenses from his residence to his sales territory were not incurred for business reasons. A concurring judge was not satisfied with the result, stressing the need for Congressional action to change the outcome in cases where both spouses work and have legitimate reasons for maintaining their own tax homes. See also Comment, Daly v. Commissioner: Effect of the Tax Home Rule Under Section 162 on Two Earner

Families, 34 Tax Lawyer 829 (1981), and Note, Section 162(a)(2): Resolving the Tax Home Dispute, 2 Virginia Tax Rev. 153 (1982).

Two factual variations, the temporary job and the taxpayer working at two business locations, must be developed. The deductibility of travel expenses under § 162(a)(2) usually turns on the necessities of business. If the taxpayer travels to a temporary job and stays overnight, the taxpayer's cost of transportation to and from the temporary job location may be deductible under § 162(a)(2). Food and lodging at the temporary job location are also deductible if the taxpayer remains at least one night at the temporary post. Temporary employment, as opposed to indefinite employment, generally requires a stay whose termination is foreseeable within a fixed and reasonably short period, usually less than twelve months. The rationale of the temporary exception is premised on the unreasonableness of forcing a taxpayer to move his family to a new location for a job of a short duration. The taxpayer's additional costs are treated as business expenses. The nondeductibility of the expenses for an indefinite assignment is based on the rationale that factors of personal convenience, not business necessity, enter into the taxpayer's failure to move his home. Tucker v. Commissioner, 55 T.C. 783, 786 (1971).

Although the one-year rule is only a guideline, the Service's view is rather strict. According to Rev.Rul. 83–82, 1983–1 C.B. 45, where a taxpayer anticipates that the employment will last for less than one year, whether the employment is temporary is determined on all the facts and circumstances. Employment anticipated to last for more than one year but less than two years is presumed to be indefinite. The presumption can be rebutted if the taxpayer realistically expected the job to last less than two years and intended to return to his claimed tax home after the job terminated. The taxpayer must show that his claimed tax home is his "regular place of abode in a real and substantial sense". Three factors may be used to determine the bona fides of the latter assertion: (1) incurring duplicate living expenses because work requires him to be away from the claimed abode; (2) using the original residence while performing work in the vicinity immediately prior to the current job and continuing to maintain work contracts (e.g., job seeking) in that area during the temporary job; and (3) showing that family members currently reside at the original residence or that taxpayer continues to use the original residence as his lodging. If all these factors are satisfied, the taxpayer will be considered temporarily away from home. If only two factors are satisfied, all the facts and circumstances of the case will be closely scrutinized to make the determination. If only one factor is satisfied, the taxpayer will be considered as employed at the new location indefinitely. A stay of two years or more will be considered indefinite regardless of whether the three factors are satisfied.

Judicial application of the temporary—indefinite dichotomy is uncertain. In Holter v. Commissioner, 37 T.C.M. (CCH) 1707 (1978), the court found a job lasting nearly 19 months to be temporary. The taxpayer accepted a job in a remote location 300 miles from his home. Local employment was unavailable near his residence and the taxpayer continually looked for employment closer to his residence. Family circumstances made it unreasonable for him to uproot his family from their accustomed home to relocate at a job where the project could be expected, on the average, to last for six months and had never previously lasted more than a year. The continuing intent to find employment near the taxpayer's home if it became available strongly indicated the unreasonableness of moving. However, in Babeaux v. Commissioner, 601 F.2d 730 (4th Cir.1979), deductions were denied in three employment situations lasting from 19 to 32 months. The court characterized the positions as indefinite. In each case, the employee voluntarily terminated his employment for personal reasons when work was still available for people in his trade. The construction projects, which involved nuclear power plants, were of a long-term duration.

In Frederick v. United States, 603 F.2d 1292 (8th Cir.1979), a taxpayer, who was a carpenter, was allowed to deduct, under § 162(a), mileage incurred over a three-year period while working at a missile site. He drove back and forth daily between his residence and the work site, a distance of about 80 miles each way. According to the court, the "prospects for continued employment" determine if a job is temporary or not. The outlook for the taxpayer's continued employment at the site was not good. Most carpenters at the site were laid off each winter. The taxpayer was laid off when the project was completed. In Rev.Rul. 80–333, 1980–2 C.B. 60, the Service announced it will not follow Frederick. Is the Frederick decision consistent with the long commute in the Sanders decision at p. 385? Does it conflict with the Babeaux case at p. 405? With the Flowers case cited in the Hantzis decision?

Another factual variation concerns the taxpayer involved in two occupations or a single occupation at two posts of duty which require him to spend a substantial amount of time at each location. According to the Commissioner, an individual's tax home is his principal place of business. See e.g. Rev.Rul. 75–432, 1975–2 C.B. 60. The determination of a taxpayer's principal place of business depends on where the taxpayer: (1) spends more time; (2) engages in a greater degree of business activity; and (3) derives a greater portion of his income. Markey v. Commissioner, 490 F.2d 1249 (6th Cir.1974). Where the taxpayer maintains a permanent residence at or near the minor post of duty and another residence at or near the principal post of duty, Rev. Rul. 63–82, 1963–1 C.B. 33, 34 provides: "A taxpayer can deduct his expenses for meals and lodging while his duties require him to be at his minor place of business and away from his principal post of duty at least overnight. A taxpayer may also deduct the cost of transportation on all trips made between such locations for business reasons, whether or not they are overnight trips." Rev.Rul. 75–432, 1975–2 C.B. 60, 61 adds, "Of course, the deduction is limited to that portion of the family expenses for meals and lodging that is properly attributable to the employee's presence there in the actual performance of business duties." Rev.Rul. 63–145, 1963–2 C.B. 86 allows the taxpayer who resides at either a temporary or a minor post to deduct the cost of commuting from his lodging to his place of business at the temporary or minor post. The commuting costs must, however, be incurred while the taxpayer is away from home in pursuit of his business and must be reasonable. Reference: Rose, The Deductibility of Daily Transportation Expenses To and From Distant Temporary Work Sites, 36 Vanderbilt L.Rev. 541 (1983).

c. Requirements Pertaining to the Deductibility of Meals

Before the enactment of the predecessor of § 162(a)(2) in 1921, a taxpayer could deduct the costs of business meals and lodging while away from home only to the extent the amount exceeded "any expenditures ordinarily required for such purposes when at home." T.D. 3101, 3 C.B. 191 (1920). This regulation proved difficult to administer. Congress then allowed a deduction for the full amount spent on meals and lodging while away from home except "amounts which are lavish or extravagant under the circumstances." §§ 162(a)(2) and 274(k)(1)(A). See footnote 4 in the Correll case.

In addition to the requirements contained in § 162(a)(2), a business meal expense generally is not deductible under § 274(a)(1)(A) unless there is a "substantial and bona fide business discussion during, directly preceding, or directly following the meal. However, in the case of an individual who is away from home in pursuit of a trade or business and who eats alone, the absence of a business discussion does not preclude satisfying the 'directly related' or 'associated with' requirement." (Tax Reform Act of [1986], Report of the Committee on Ways and Means, House of Representatives on H.R. 3838, 125–26 (1985)). In other words, being on travel status automatically qualifies the meal as being related to his business.

The amount of an otherwise allowable deduction for a meal is reduced by 20 percent. § 274(n)(1)(A). Thus, if a taxpayer spends $100 for food or beverage costs incurred in the course of travel away from home which, but for this rule, would be fully deductible, the amount of the allowable deduction equals $80. The 20 percent reduction rule "reflects the fact that meals * * * inherently involve an element of personal living expenses, but still allows an 80 percent deduction where such expenses also have an identifiable business purpose." (Tax Reform Act of [1986], Report of the Committee on Ways and Means, House of Representatives on H.R. 3838, 121 (1985)).

Problems

1. Assume that Ted Player flies out-of-town to visit a client and returns that night. Can he deduct the cost of his airfare, cabs, airport parking and his meals? Consider §§ 67(a) and 162(a)(2).

2. If Ted decides to fly in the night before so that he can be fresh for his meeting the next morning, can he deduct the cost of his transportation, meals and lodging? He has incurred an additional meal by flying in the night before. Consider the Correll case and §§ 67(a), 162(a)(2) and 274(k) and (n).

3. Travel As A Form Of Education

No deduction is allowed for travel as a form of education. § 274(m) (2). The legislative history indicates:

> The committee is concerned about deductions claimed for travel as a form of "education." The committee believes that any business purpose served by traveling for general educational purposes, in the absence of a specific need such as engaging in research which can be performed only at a particular facility, is at most indirect and insubstantial. By contrast, travel as a form of education may provide substantial personal benefits by permitting some individuals in particular professions to deduct the cost of a vacation out of after-tax dollars, no matter how educationally stimulating the travel may be. Accordingly, the * * * [Act] disallows deductions for travel that can be claimed only on the ground that the travel itself is "educational," but permits deductions for travel that is a necessary adjunct to engaging in an activity that gives rise to business deductions relating to education. (Tax Reform [Act] of [1986], Report of the Committee on Ways and Means, House of Representatives on H.R. 3838, 99th Cong., 1st Sess. 122 (1985)).

Question

Can a tax lawyer who attends a continuing education program on The Tax Reform Act of 1986 deduct the costs of his travel (e.g., transportation, meals and lodging) and the program registration fee? Would it make any difference if this program was held in the middle of the winter in Miami instead of Chicago?

* * *

3. BUSINESS TRAVEL WITH A SPOUSE

Reg. § 1.162–2(c) denies a deduction for travel expenses of the taxpayer's spouse, unless the spouse's presence had a "bona fide business purpose." This means that the spouse must perform more than "some incidental service." In United States v. Disney, 413 F.2d 783 (9th Cir.1969) the employer "virtually insisted" on the presence of spouses to enhance the corporation's reputation for producing family entertainment. The court concluded that the deductibility of a spouse's expenses turned on whether: (1) the dominant purpose of the trip was to serve the taxpayer's business purpose; and (2) the spouse spent a substantial amount of time assisting the taxpayer-spouse fulfill that purpose. Reconsider problem 2 at p. 69.

4. ALLOCATION OF TRAVEL EXPENSES: COMBINED BUSI-NESS-PLEASURE TRAVEL

Primary Purpose Test. Throughout the Code the exigencies of administration often require Congress to attempt the impossible. Nowhere is this more manifest than in the provisions which authorize deductions for travel of employees. For in many cases travel expenses are undertaken by employees for a twofold purpose: (1) to pursue, in some measure, the commercial objectives of the employer, and (2) to receive a reward for being a diligent and hardworking employee. The industrialist who travels to seek new markets or new sources of raw material may also have a dual objective. The problem is that in many cases travel has business and personal overtones which are inextricably mixed. The Regulations state that if a trip is taken during which the taxpayer engages in both business and personal activities, the transportation expenses are deductible only if the trip was "primarily" for business purposes; however, meals and lodging are always deductible for those portions of the trip during which business activities are carried on. Reg. § 1.162–2(b). Of course, circumstances differ from case to case. Each taxpayer and revenue agent is likely to have a different abstract concept of the meaning of "primarily".

There are some limits. If a taxpayer spends five weeks on a vacation and one week on business during a six week trip, it seems probable that the trip will be considered primarily personal in nature (Reg. § 1.162–2(b)(2)), though time alone certainly cannot be considered determinative. In Holswade v. Commissioner, 82 T.C. 686 (1984) the court identified five factors to be considered in determining the primary purpose of a vacation cruise which combined on-board seminars and stopping at various ports of call for shopping and sightseeing: (1) the comparison between the length of the seminar lectures and the length of the cruise; (2) the features of the ship; (3) the nature of the ports of call and the sightseeing activities while ashore; (4) the availability of similar course work at lower cost and in surroundings more conducive to learning; and (5) the amount of study or preparation required for each seminar. Furthermore, deductions for conventions or seminars held on cruise ships are subject to additional limitations. No deduction is allowed unless the cruise ship is registered in the United States and only docks at ports of call in the United States. § 274(h)(2). And, a taxpayer may not deduct more than $2,000 annually for such business travel.

Where sums are expended for the travel expenses of several people, the expenses may, if the taxpayer is unable to establish the portion of such amount attributable to each person, be allocated pro rata to each member of the group. Reg. § 1.274–5T(c)(6)(ii).

Foreign Travel. Travel outside the United States must not only meet the tests of § 162(a) (or § 212), but also the standards imposed by § 274(c). Section 274(c)(1) disallows the deduction for expenses not allocable to business or profit activities, including an appropriate part of the taxpayer's expenses travelling to and from the foreign business location. If an individual engages in both business and personal activities while outside the United States, the deduction is computed by multiplying the otherwise allowable amount by the ratio of business days to the total number of days overseas. If the travel outside the United States away from home is less than one week or if less than 25% of the total time of such travel is devoted to personal activity, then pursuant to § 274(c)(2), § 274(c)(1) is inapplicable. Despite the restrictions imposed by § 274(c)(1), the deduction is, however, available under an advance reimbursement arrangement. Reg. § 1.274–4(a).

REV.RUL. 84–55
1984–1 C.B. 29.

ISSUE

Are expenses for overseas travel in attending a "continuing education program" deductible under section 162 of the Internal Revenue Code under the factual situation set forth below?

FACTS

A taxpayer, a salesperson in a large corporation, is a member of a local university's alumni association. The university, through a travel agency, arranges trips by airline to more than 22 foreign countries for members of its alumni association. The university represents that the trips are part of a continuing education program and that the academic exercises and conferences it sets up are designed to acquaint individuals in most occupations with selected facilities in several regions of the world. However, none of the conferences are directed toward specific occupations or professions, and it is up to the initiative of each participant to seek out specialists and organizational settings appropriate to their occupational interests. The stated aim of the program is to improve and enhance the human relations and professional skills required of individuals in their work settings. The objectives of the program include increased self-understanding, understanding of others, and increased awareness of the factors which promote or inhibit interpersonal effectiveness in business, professional, educational and organizational settings. The participants may attend by themselves, or with friends or families.

Three-hour sessions are held each day over a five-day period at each of the selected overseas facilities where participants can meet with individual practitioners. These sessions are composed of a variety of activities, including workshops, mini-lectures, role playing, skill development, and exercises. Professional conference directors schedule and conduct the sessions. Participants are free to choose those sessions they wish to attend.

The taxpayer's spouse and two minor children accompanied the taxpayer. The taxpayer spent approximately two hours at each of the planned sessions, and the remainder of the time touring and participating in recreational and sight-seeing activities with the family. The trip lasted less than one week.

LAW AND ANALYSIS

Section 162(a) of the Code allows as a deduction ordinary and necessary expenses paid or incurred during the taxable year in carrying on any trade or business.

Section 262 of the Code provides, with exceptions not here material, that no deduction is allowed for personal, living, or family expenses.

Section 1.162–2(a) of the Income Tax Regulations provides that only such traveling expenses as are reasonable and necessary in the conduct of the taxpayer's business and directly attributable to it may be deducted. If the trip is undertaken for other than business purposes, the travel fares and expenses incident to travel are personal expenses and the meals and lodging are living expenses. If the trip is solely on business, the reasonable and necessary traveling expenses, including travel fares, meals and lodging, and expenses incident to travel, are business expenses.

Under section 1.162–2(b)(1) of the regulations, if a taxpayer travels to a destination and while at such destination engages in both business and personal activities, traveling expenses to and from such destination are deductible only if the trip is related primarily to the taxpayer's trade or business. If the trip is primarily personal in nature, the traveling expenses to and from the destination are not deductible even though the taxpayer engages in business activities while at such destination. However, expenses while at the destination that are properly allocable to the taxpayer's trade or business are deductible even though the traveling expenses to and from the destination are not deductible.

Section 1.162–2(b)(2) of the regulations provides that whether a trip is related primarily to the taxpayer's trade or business or is primarily personal in nature depends upon the facts and circumstances in each case. The amount of time during the period of the trip that is spent on personal activities compared to the amount of time spent on activities directly relating to the taxpayer's trade or business is an important factor in determining whether the trip is primarily personal.

Section 1.162–2(d) of the regulations provides that expenses paid or incurred by a taxpayer in attending a convention or other meeting may constitute an ordinary and necessary business expense depending upon the facts and circumstances of each case. No distinction will be made between self-employed persons and employees. The allowance of deductions depends upon whether there is a sufficient relationship between the taxpayer's trade or business and attendance at the convention so that the taxpayer is benefiting or advancing the interests of the trade or business by such attendance.

Section 1.162–5(e)(1) of the regulations provides that if an individual travels away from home primarily to obtain education, the expenses of which are deductible under this section, the taxpayer's expenditures for travel, meals and lodging while away from home are deductible. However, if as an incident of such a trip the individual engages in some personal activity such as sightseeing, social visiting or entertaining, or other recreation, the portion of the expenses attributable to such personal activity constitutes nondeductible personal or living expenses and is not allowable as a deduction. If the individual's travel away from home is primarily personal, the individual's expenditures for travel, meals and lodging (other than meals and lodging during the time spent in participating in deductible education pursuits) are not deductible. Whether a particular trip is primarily personal or primarily to obtain education the expenses of which are deductible under this section depends upon all the facts and circumstances of each case. An important factor to be taken into consideration in making the determination is the relative amount of time devoted to personal activity as compared with the time devoted to educational pursuits. The rules set forth in this paragraph are subject to the provisions of section 162(a)(2), relating to deductibility of certain traveling expenses, and sections 274(c) and (d), relating to allocation of certain foreign travel expenses and substantiation required, respectively, and the regulations thereunder.

Section 274(h) of the Code provides for the disallowance of travel expenses incurred to attend a convention, seminar, or similar meeting outside the North American area unless the taxpayer establishes that the meeting is directly related to the active conduct of the taxpayer's trade or business and that, after taking into account certain specified factors, it is as reasonable for the meeting to be held outside the North American area as within the North American area.

In determining allowable deductions with respect to attendance at a foreign convention, the business purpose test of section 162 of the Code is a threshold test. If the convention trip is related primarily to the taxpayer's trade or business, then travel, transportation and subsistence expenses are deductible, provided it was as reasonable to hold the convention outside the North American area as within the North American area. If the nature of the trip is primarily personal, no deduction is allowable under section 162 for travel and transportation costs; however, those subsistence expenses that are properly allocable to the taxpayer's trade or business are deductible, subject to the provisions of section 274(h).

In this case, applying the principles described above, the fact that the taxpayer attended a continuing education program did not convert what was in all other respects a vacation into a business trip. The expenses incurred are not materially different from those reasonably incurred by any other tourist on a sight-seeing trip abroad. See Kadivar v. Commissioner, 32 T.C.M. 427 (1973), and Gino v. Commissioner, 60 T.C. 304 (1973) rev'd on another issue [76–2 USTC ¶ 9528], 538 F.2d 833 (9th Cir.1976), cert. denied 429 U.S. 979 (1976). The arrangements for the trip did not differ from those of any vacation or recreational trip. The taxpayer was accompanied by the taxpayer's spouse and children, and the major portion of the taxpayer's time was spent on personal, recreational, and sight-seeing activities. See Rev. Rul. 79–425, 1979–2 C.B. 81, which reaches a similar nondeductible conclusion regarding a taxpayer attending six brief sessions of a ten-day annual convention of a local professional association held in a foreign country; and Rev.Rul. 74–292, 1974–1 C.B. 43, which reaches a similar nondeductible conclusion regarding a taxpayer attending six brief professional seminars held abroad during the 14-day trip.

HOLDING

The taxpayer's expenses for the trip are not deductible under section 162 of the Code, except to the extent they are for registration fees and any other expenses incurred by the taxpayer that are directly attributable and properly allocable to the taxpayer's trade or business, subject, where applicable, to the provisions of section 274(h) and section 274(d).

Luxury Water Travel. Limits are placed on the allowable deductions for travel by luxury water transportation, for example, ocean liner or cruise ship. § 274(m)(1). In brief, the deduction allowable for luxury water travel cannot exceed twice the highest amount generally allowable with respect to a day of travel to employees of the executive branch of the Federal government while away from home but serving in the United States, multiplied by the number of days the taxpayer was engaged in luxury water travel.

5. POLICY ASPECTS

Question

Should the rules relating to the deductibility of travel expenses be modified? Consider the following excerpt:

OFFICE OF THE SECRETARY, DEPARTMENT OF THE TREASURY, TAX REFORM FOR FAIRNESS, SIMPLICITY, AND ECONOMIC GROWTH

Vol. 2, 87–90 (1984).

REASONS FOR CHANGE

The present limitations on deductions for business travel fail to establish reasonable distinctions between costs incurred for business purposes and costs reflecting personal consumption. The deduction for expenses for meals and lodging incurred "away from home" is premised on the assumption that the business traveler incurs additional costs while away from home. Restaurant meals are likely to be more expensive than the cost to the taxpayer of eating at home, and hotel accommodations are a duplicative expense for the taxpayer who maintains regular living quarters elsewhere. These excess costs incurred by a taxpayer away from home are, at least in part, legitimate business expenses.

[Prior] law, however, [did] not limit the deduction for away from home meals and lodging to the portion of the cost that represents an extra or duplicate expense. The * * * deductibility of such travel expenses permits a taxpayer who is away from home to deduct some costs that would be incurred even if he had stayed at home. * * * Moreover, the * * * deductibility of business travel expenses encourages excessive spending. * * *

The liberality of current law is greatest for taxpayers who remain away from home in a single city for an extended period of time. Extended travel status permits the taxpayer to take advantage of certain economies not available on shorter trips. For example, a professor visiting another university for a year probably will spend the same amount for lunch or dinner as he or she would have spent at home. Similarly, a taxpayer on extended travel at a single location ordinarily will be able to reduce the incidental costs of travel, such as laundry or transportation to the office.

In addition, the current tax treatment of trips that combine business travel with a vacation create opportunities for abuse. Many travel and business publications feature articles and promotional material that explain how taxpayers can pay for vacations with tax deductible dollars. These abuses distort business decisions and reduce the efficiency of the economy. For example, a taxpayer may alter the place and timing of business meetings for no reason other than to coincide with vacation plans. The current rules are also unfair. Some individuals are able to take deductions for personal expenses simply because they are better informed about the law. The presence of such obvious abuses undercut taxpayer trust in the integrity of the tax system.

* * *

PROPOSALS

1. Deductions for meals, lodging, and incidental travel expenses incurred by a taxpayer while located in one city away from home for 30 days or less would be limited to 200 percent of the maximum Federal reimbursement rate per day for that city, as published in the Federal Property Management Regulations, 101–7, G.S.A. Bulletin F.P.M.R. A–40. For example, the current applicable limit for a taxpayer located in Baltimore, Maryland for 30 days or less would be $150 per day. Deductions for expenses for meals and lodging incurred by a taxpayer while located in one city away from home for more than 30 days would be limited to 150 percent of the Federal per diem rate for that city. No deduction would be allowed for incidental travel expenses (e.g., laundry, taxi fares) incurred by a taxpayer while located in one city away from home for more than 30 days. For purposes of determining whether a taxpayer is away from home, travel assignments which extend for more

than one year in one city would be considered indefinite, and travel deductions be allowed.

2. A deduction for the daily transportation expenses of taxpayers (such as construction workers) who have no regular place of work and must travel·at least 35 miles (one way) to job assignments that last less than one year would be allowed for the commuting expenses incurred for mileage in excess of 35 miles (one way).

3. For purposes of determining whether a taxpayer is away from home, travel assignments which extend for more than one year in one city would be considered indefinite, and no travel deductions would be allowed.

* * *

ANALYSIS

The proposed limitations on travel expense deductions are designed to provide reasonable boundaries and eliminate the most extreme cases of abuse without unduly restricting deductions for legitimate business expenses. The dollar limitations are intentionally quite generous and are intended to deny deductions for that portion of travel expenses that is most likely to constitute personal satisfaction rather than business convenience. Expenditures in excess of the applicable limitation are deemed to represent luxury accommodations and meal costs incurred for personal rather than business reasons. The lower limits for trips lasting longer than 30 days reflect the economies that are available during extended periods of travel; the disallowance of incidental expenses after 30 days in one city recognizes the significant personal component of such expenses.

The proposed treatment for taxpayers, such as construction workers, who have no regular place of work addresses an area of the law that is a continuing source of litigation and confusion. Although commuting expenses to and from a regular place of work are nondeductible without regard to the length of the commute, it is reasonable to permit a deduction for transportation expenses to a nonregular place of work, such as a construction site, where the taxpayer is employed for a temporary period. Commuting expenses generally are disallowed on the theory that where a taxpayer chooses to reside—whether near or far from the workplace—is a matter of personal choice. That rationale is inappropriate when a taxpayer's workplace is constantly shifting, the jobs are temporary in nature, and the taxpayer must travel long distances to reach the job site.

The special commuting deduction would be allowed only for transportation expenses in excess of 35 miles (one way), would not extend to meal costs, and would be available only for job assignments that last less than one year. By using an objective mileage standard rather than requiring that travel be outside the "metropolitan area," the proposal would eliminate uncertainty and create uniformity among taxpayers located in different parts of the country.

The one-year rule for defining temporary employment would eliminate a significant source of dispute between taxpayers and the Internal Revenue Service, and would provide a reasonable division between temporary and indefinite assignments. One year is sufficient time for regular living patterns to be established at the new location and, thus, food and lodging expenses would no longer need to be duplicative or more expensive than comparable costs at the original job site.

6. MOVING EXPENSES

Section 217 provides for the deduction for certain moving expenses incurred by an individual. Amounts allowed under § 217 as moving expenses are itemized deductions, but are not subject to the two percent floor on miscellaneous itemized deductions. § 67(b)(6). The moving expenses (as defined in § 217(b)) must be incurred by the taxpayer in connection with his "commencement of work" as an employee or self-employed individual at a new principal place of work. § 217(a) and Reg. § 1.217-2(a)(3). The deduction is allowed for a taxpayer's first job, for a new job with a different employer, or for a job with the same employer at a new location. However, the taxpayer's employment at the new location must be permanent, not temporary. In Goldman v. Commissioner, 32 T.C.M. (CCH) 574 (1973), affirmed 497 F.2d 382 (6th Cir.1974), cert. denied 419 U.S. 1021, 95 S.Ct. 496, 42 L.Ed.2d 295 (1974) moving expenses from Washington back to Kentucky were disallowed because the taxpayer deducted travel expenses and rent for the temporary one year job. To assure that the moving expenses are tied to a business nexus, § 217(c) contains a geographical (minimum distance) test and a time (duration of employment) test. Not all moving expenses, even if reasonable, may be deducted in full. § 217(b)(3). Under § 82, an employee must include in his gross income the reimbursement of moving expenses by an employer. Although generally the reimbursement and the deduction constitute a wash, the realization and recognition of gross income under § 82 and the deduction of moving expenses under § 217 may occur in different tax years.

Problems

1. Ned is a member of a work crew responsible for the construction and maintenance of certain public utility facilities in a 12-state region. Ned owns a house in Kansas City where he lives when not away on work assignments and where his family resides at all times. Ned receives his assignments to various work locations from the regional office of his employer, which is in the vicinity of his permanent residence. His work locations change frequently. Almost all of his work locations require the taxpayer to be at the job sites overnight. Can Ned deduct: (1) the cost of transportation to his work locations; (2) his meals and lodging while away from Kansas City; and (3) his daily commuting expenses? Why? Consider §§ 67 and 274(k) and (n).

2. Sharpeyes, an accountant, is employed by an accounting firm with offices all over the country. He lives and works in Chicago.

(a) His firm sends him to Boca Raton, Florida to set up the firm's new office. He expects to be there for only a year, after which time he will return to the Chicago office. His family stays in Chicago. Can he deduct the cost of (1) his transportation to and from Florida; (2) his meals and lodging while in Florida; and (3) his daily commuting costs in Florida? Why?

(b) Assume his family moves with him to Florida and he rents his Chicago home for the year they are away. What expenses can be deducted? Why? Is there a duplication of living expenses? How should he treat the rental of his Chicago home?

(c) Assume Sharpeyes is asked to stay in Florida for as long as it takes to establish the practice. When he asked how long that might be, he was told that might take from one to three years.

    i. What expenses can he deduct?

    ii. In the alternative, can he deduct his moving expenses under § 217? Consider § 67(b)(6) and Reg. § 1.217–2(a)(1), –2(a)(3), and –2(c)(3).

3. Joan and her husband, Jim, live in New York City and her husband works there. Joan works in Washington, D.C. and travels to New York City to see Jim on weekends. Joan rents an efficiency apartment in Washington. Advise them on the deductibility of her transportation to and from Washington, her meals and lodging in Washington and New York, and commuting expenses while in Washington.

4. Eric works as a ski patrolman during the winter months in Vermont. During the summer, he is a lifeguard in Rehobeth Beach, Delaware. He spends about six months in each location. Can Eric deduct any of his transportation expenses, meals and lodging?

5. Dave lives and works in Minnesota. He purchased a condominium in Miami as an investment and rents it on a yearly lease. Every February, he travels to Miami to inspect his property and work with a local accountant on the books. This takes two afternoons. He usually spends the entire week in Miami as a mini vacation.

(a) Can Dave deduct the cost of: (1) his transportation to and from Miami; (2) his meals and lodging for the week; and (3) his daily commuting expenses? Would it make any difference if he made his yearly trip in August? Assume that the standards of § 162(a)(2) are read into § 212. Consider Regs. § 1.162–2(a) and (b), and §§ 62(4), 67 and 274(n).

(b) Assume Dave's wife accompanies him on his yearly inspection trip. Are any of her travel expenses deductible? Consider Regs. § 1.162–2(c).

D. THE GREAT AMERICAN GAME CONTINUED: DEDUCTION OF ENTERTAINMENT EXPENSES

1. INTRODUCTION

The ingenuity expended to obtain deductions for travel expenses which satisfy a personal urge for change, recreation and status is multiplied where the search is undertaken for entertainment deductions.

In 1961 President Kennedy called for the disallowance of business entertainment expenses. Because entertainment is essentially personal, it was felt that no deductions should be allowed for personal consumption even though it served a valuable business purpose. Despite the fact that a taxpayer may obtain some personal benefit from a legitimate business activity, a more important reason for this proposal was that the area had gotten out of hand. Too many taxpayers had devised means of disguising personal living expenses as business entertainment and travel deductions. President Carter made a similar pitch in his 1978 tax message to Congress, condemning the three-martini lunch and other situations where taxpayers were deducting expenditures that provided personal enjoyment with little or no business benefit.

The problems reached unmanageable proportions due to two factors, the first the degree of proof courts accepted to sustain a deduction under § 162, and the second, the ease with which taxpayers could substantiate the amount of the deduction. The case of Sanitary Farms Dairy, Inc. v. Commissioner, 25 T.C. 463 (1955), illustrates the minimal business connection needed to satisfy the business purpose requirement under § 162. In that case, the principal shareholder and president of a local dairy went on an African safari with his wife. He was a life-long hunting enthusiast. He claimed that by showing films of the safari to local groups, displaying the trophies he brought back at a museum located in the dairy, and inviting customers to dinner (where the main course often consisted of the game he shot), he obtained valuable advertising and goodwill for his business. The court allowed the corporation to deduct all the expenses of the safari. The court noted that "enjoyment of one's work does not make that work a personal hobby." The court concluded that the taxpayer undertook the trip for the purpose of benefiting the dairy and the trip provided the dairy with extremely good advertising. Although you would think that the business purpose should be the primary reason for incurring the expense, this case clearly illustrates that the showing of only a casual business purpose suffices to meet the requirements of § 162.

Although rejecting President Kennedy's proposal for a complete disallowance of entertainment expenses, Congress recognized the need to tighten up these deductions. In the Revenue Act of 1962 Congress laid down addition requirements before entertainment deductions would be allowed. Congress enacted § 274(a) which requires stricter standards for the deduction of business entertainment than would be required under the "ordinary and necessary" test of § 162(a). In addition, § 274(d) established new rules for the substantiation of travel and entertainment expenses. The Tax Reform Act of 1986 imposes a separate statutory rule (§ 274(k)) for business meals, additional limits on entertainment tickets (§ 274(l)), and generally reduces the amount of an otherwise allowable deduction for an entertainment expense by 20 percent. § 274(n)(1)(B). According to the legislative history, "This reduction rule reflects the fact that * * * entertainment inherently [involves] an element of personal living expenses, but still allows an 80 percent deduction where such expenses also have an identifiable business relationship." Senate Finance Committee Report on H.R. 3838, 99th Cong., 2d Sess. 68 (1986). Certain exceptions, spelled out in § 274(n)(2), exist to the 20 percent reduction rule. Thus, entertainment expenses must meet the tests of § 162 (or § 212), run the gauntlet of disallowance under § 274(a), (k) and (l) and be substantiated under § 274(d). Then, only 80 percent is allowed as a deduction under § 274(n). Furthermore, entertainment expenses, if unreimbursed, are subject to the two percent floor set forth in § 67(a).

2. ENTERTAINMENT ACTIVITY EXPENSES

Introduction. Entertainment activity expenses must run the hurdles set up by § 274(a)(1)(A) and the accompanying regulations. Section 274(a) disallows deductions with respect to activities which are of a type generally considered to constitute entertainment, amusement, or recreation, including meal expenses, unless the taxpayer establishes that the activity: (1) was "directly related" to the active conduct of the taxpayer's business; or (2) was "associated with" the active conduct of the taxpayer's business, if the item directly precedes or follows a substantial and bona fide business discussion. Pursuant to § 274(a)(2) (B), profit-oriented activities are treated as a trade or business.

The time and travail you expend in pursuit of interpreting these principles are not wasted: all must learn the semantics of the game. It must, however, be realized by all that as Justice Holmes said, "general propositions do not decide concrete cases." What then, does the attorney do in fact with issues involving entertainment expenses? Obviously, the attorney must obey the law. But is there in fact any law in this area? How are the words "directly related to" and "associated with" to be interpreted? If we cannot find out how the rules are interpreted by the Service, the lawyer cannot measure the facts in a client's case against day to day national application of the generalities in the statute and Regulations and against the innumerable cases that arise. Is there any way counsel can find out how, nationwide, these abstractions are applied to facts? It would seem not, for the facts are so kaleidoscopic and decisions so subjective that it would be impossible to weigh in each case the last gram of equity between taxpayers similarly situated. Beyond this, there is no current way of assembling information from the various revenue districts to make a composite national picture: this arises again from the multiplicity of facts and the subjective nature of the judgment to be made.

In most instances, the patterns developed in this area through judicial decisions cannot be expected to be reliable. The way of the tax attorney will be hard. Hence, in these cases, there may be an increasing tendency to grab everything in sight, throw the return in the hopper and hold one's ears. Although this is not very high-minded advice to given to students, it may be realistic.

WALLISER v. COMMISSIONER
Tax Court of the United States, 1979.
72 T.C. 433.

[The taxpayer, James Walliser, was vice president and branch manager of a local bank (First Federal). His primary responsibility was the marketing of permanent and interim loans. During 1973 and 1974 taxpayer and his wife traveled abroad in tour groups organized primarily for people involved in the building industry. Although the bank expected taxpayer to be active in cultivating new customers, it did not reimburse him for the cost of these trips. However, the bank did give taxpayer leave with pay to participate in the tours.]

TANNENWALD, JUDGE: * * *

* * * Petitioners, however, went on the tours because James found that they provided an unusual opportunity to associate with many potential and actual customers and believed that the tours would generate business, thereby helping him to meet his loan production quotas and obtain salary raises. He spent as much time as possible talking with builders whom he already knew and getting acquainted with builders he had not previously met to make them aware of First Federal's services and of his own skills. His conversations frequently centered on conditions in the building industry and the availability of loans for builders, but he did not negotiate specific business transactions on the tours or conduct formal business meetings. Social relationships formed or renewed on the tours between petitioners and builders and their spouses resulted in a substantial amount of loan business for First Federal.

Because James spent so much time with actual or potential customers, petitioners found the tours to be strenuous, and Carol, in particular, did not enjoy them. Petitioners took vacations with their family in the vicinity of Austin, Tex., in 1973 and in Puerto Vallarta, Mexico, in 1974.

* * *

On their 1973 and 1974 tax returns, petitioners deducted, as employee business expenses, one-half of the price of each of the tours (the portion attributable to James' travel) * * *.

OPINION

[The portion of the Tax Court's opinion dealing with the question whether James' expenses were deductible under § 162(a)(2) is omitted. The court held that the expenses were "ordinary and necessary" business expenses under that section.]

* * *

We now turn our attention to the applicability of section 274, the issue on which respondent has concentrated most of his fire. That section disallows a deduction in certain instances for expenses which would otherwise be deductible under section 162. Respondent argues that the requirements of section 274 are applicable here and have not been satisfied in that petitioners have failed: (1) To show that James' trips were "directly related" to the active conduct of his business (sec. 274(a)); (2) to substantiate the business purpose of his expenditures (sec. 274(d)); and (3) to allocate his time spent in foreign travel between personal and business activities (sec. 274(c)).

* * *

Petitioners urge that the "directly related" test of section 274(a) is not applicable because the expenditures at issue were incurred for travel, not entertainment. We disagree.

Section 274(a) relates to activities of a type generally considered to constitute "entertainment, amusement, or recreation." Section 1.274–2(b), Income Tax Regs., defines "entertainment, amusement, or recreation" as follows:

(b) *Definitions*—(1) *Entertainment defined* —(i) *In general.* For purposes of this section, the term *"entertainment" means any activity which is of a type generally considered to constitute entertainment, amusement, or recreation, such as* entertaining at night clubs, cocktail lounges, theaters, country clubs, golf and athletic clubs, sporting events, and on hunting, fishing, *vacation and similar trips, including such activity relating solely to the taxpayer* or the taxpayer's family.

* * *

(ii) *Objective test. An objective test shall be used to determine whether an activity is of a type generally considered to constitute entertainment.* Thus, if an activity is generally considered to be entertainment, it will constitute entertainment for purposes of this section and section 274(a) regardless of whether the expenditure can also be described otherwise, and even though the expenditure relates to the taxpayer alone. This objective test precludes arguments such as that "entertainment" means only entertainment of others or that an expenditure for entertainment should be characterized as an expenditure for advertising or public relations.

[Emphasis added.]

This regulation is squarely based on the language of the legislative history of section 274 and we find it to be valid as it relates to the issue herein.

* * *

Although the participants in the tours that petitioners took were drawn, for the most part, from the building industry, their activities—sightseeing, shopping, dining—were the same as those of other tourists. Fedders presented some awards to persons considered outstanding in its sales or promotional programs on the tours but did not conduct any business meetings. Nor is there any evidence that any business meetings were conducted on the 1973 General Electric tour; on the itinerary for the 1974 tour, for which petitioners canceled their reservation, only 1 hour out of 10 days of guided tours, dinners, and cocktail parties, was set aside for a business meeting. Under the objective test set forth in the regulations, it is irrelevant that petitioners did not regard the trips as vacations or did not find them relaxing. Clearly, the tours were of a type generally considered vacation trips and, thus, under the objective test, constituted entertainment for the purposes of section 274(a). Therefore, the requirements of that section must be satisfied.

For a deduction to be allowed for any item under section 274(a)(1) (A), the taxpayer must establish that the item was directly related to the active conduct of the taxpayer's trade or business or, in the case of an item directly preceding or following a substantial and bona fide business discussion, that such item was associated with the active conduct of the taxpayer's trade or business.

The "directly related" test requires that a taxpayer show a greater degree of proximate relationship between an expenditure and the taxpayer's trade or business than that required by section 162. H.Rept. 1447, supra, 1962–3 C.B. at 424; Conf.Rept. 2508, 87th Cong., 2d Sess. (1962), 1962–3 C.B. 1129, 1143–1144. Section 1.274–2(c)(3), Income Tax Regs., provides that, for an expenditure to be directly related to the active conduct of the taxpayer's trade or business, it must be shown that the taxpayer had more than a general expectation of deriving some income or business benefit from the expenditure, *other than the goodwill* of the person or persons entertained. While the language of this regulation is awkward and not completely apt in a situation where the entertainment expenditure relates to the taxpayer alone, it is clear, nevertheless, that more than a general expectation of deriving some income at some indefinite future time is necessary for an expenditure to be deductible under section 274(a). H.Rept. 1447, supra, 1962–3 C.B. at 424; Conf.Rept. 2508, supra.

The record shows that petitioners participated in the builders' tours because they provided an opportunity for James to meet new people who might be interested in the services he, and First Federal, had to offer and to maintain good personal relations with people already using those services. While James discussed business continually during the tours, his wife testified that this was typical of his behavior during all social activities. He engaged in general discussions about business conditions and the services he could provide to a builder but did not engage in business meetings or negotiations on the tours. James could not directly connect particular business transactions with specific discussions which occurred during the trips. In short, petitioners' purpose in taking the trips was to create or maintain goodwill for James and First Federal, his employer, in order to generate some future business. Although the evidence tends to indicate that the trips did, in fact, enhance goodwill and contribute to James' success in loan production and otherwise constituted ordinary and necessary business expenses deductible under section 162, we hold, nevertheless, that Congress intended, by means of the more stringent standard of the "directly related" test in section 274(a), to disallow deductions for this type of activity, which involves merely the promotion of goodwill in a social setting. See St. Petersburg Bank & Trust Co. v. United States, 362 F.Supp. 674, 680 (M.D.Fla.1973), affd. in an unpublished order 503 F.2d 1402 (5th Cir.1974).

We also hold that the petitioners' trips do not qualify as entertainment "associated with" the active conduct of a trade or business. To be deductible, entertainment "associated with" the active conduct of a trade or business must directly precede or follow a substantial business discussion. In St. Petersburg Bank & Trust Co. v. United States, supra, a decision affirmed by the Fifth Circuit, the District Court concluded that the phrase "directly preceding or following" in section 274(a)(1)(A) should be read restrictively in cases in which entertainment expenditures are related to the taxpayer's trade or business only in that they promote goodwill. In view of the legislative history, which reveals that the "associated with" test is an exception to the general rule intended to limit deductions for entertainment which has as its sole business purpose the promotion of goodwill, we agree with the District Court's conclusion. Accordingly, we do not consider the costs of the vacation trips to be deductible under section 274(a)(1)(A) as entertainment directly preceded or followed by a substantial and bona fide business discussion merely because James had general discussions of a business nature intended to promote goodwill during the course of the trips. See St. Petersburg Bank & Trust Co. v. United States, supra at 681.

We conclude that section 274(a) bars a deduction for the costs of James' trips. Because of this conclusion, we do not consider whether those costs were substantiated in accordance with the requirements of section 274(d) or properly allocated between personal and business activities under section 274(c).

Decision will be entered for the respondent.

Questions

1. Why did the entertainment in Walliser fail to meet both the directly related to and the associated with tests?

2. Compare the situation described in the Hankenson case, discussed in Moss at p. 383, with an occasional business lunch between a law firm partner and a prospective client whom the partner hopes to get business

from. For example, suppose the lawyer wants the prospective client to use his firm to handle a securities registration statement because the prospective client's company is going public? When does general goodwill entertainment cease and a specific business deal begin?

———

Business Meals. For purposes of deducting meal expenses as entertainment, the business discussion requirement of § 274(a)(1)(A), which applies to any business meal (except one consumed by an individual travelling away from home on business who has a meal alone or with persons, such as family members, who are not business-connected, but a deduction is claimed only for the meal of the individual), is not generally met if neither the taxpayer nor any employee of the taxpayer is present at the meal. § 274(k)(1)(B). For example, if one party to a contract negotiation buys lunch for other parties involved in the negotiation but does not attend the lunch, the deduction is denied even if the other parties engage in a business discussion. A business meal expense also cannot be "lavish or extravagant." § 274(k)(1)(A).

Taxpayer's (and Spouse's) Own Business Meals. A question not entirely resolved, despite the enactment of § 274(a) and (k), is the deductibility of a taxpayer's own meals (and those of his spouse) while entertaining a business client. In Sutter v. Commissioner, 21 T.C. 170 (1953) (Acq. 1954–1 C.B. 6), discussed at p. 380, the court agreed with the Commissioner's position that a taxpayer can only deduct the cost of his own meal to the extent it exceeds the amount he would have normally spent. As to the taxpayer's spouse see Reg. §§ 1.162–2(c) and 1.274–2(d)(4) and United States v. Disney, 413 F.2d 783 (9th Cir.1969), which are discussed at page 407. Consider the impact of § 274(n) on a spouse's meals.

Tickets. The deduction for entertainment tickets is generally limted, prior to the application of the 20 percent reduction rule, to the face value of the ticket. § 274(*l*)(1)(A). The payment to a "scalper" for a ticket is not deductible (even if not disallowed as an illegal payment under § 162(c) as discussed later in this chapter) to the extent that the amount paid exceeds the face value of the ticket.

Policy Aspects. The participants generally enjoy some personal benefit from business-related entertainment. How should the dual aspects of the entertainment expenses be handled? What if the taxpayer would have eaten a less expensive lunch, if he dined alone, or purchased a less expensive ticket, if he went to the theatre alone? Does the present system encourage taxpayers to favor entertainment expenses over other forms of consumption expenditures? Should all (or only certain) business-related entertainment be nondeductible, or should the deduction be limited to a fixed percentage or specific dollar amount? Should the client being entertained include its value in gross income?

The Tax Reform Act of 1986 deals with the problem that deductible travel and entertainment expenses convey substantial personal benefits to the recipient. Section 274(n) reduces the amount of an otherwise allowable deduction for a meal or entertainment expense by 20 percent. The 20 percent reduction rule reflects the element of personal living expenses inherent in meals and entertainment expenditures. The legislative history provides:

> The committee believes that [prior] law, by not focusing sufficiently on the personal-consumption element of deductible meal and entertainment expenses, unfairly [permitted] taxpayers who can arrange business settings for personal consumption to receive, in effect, a Federal tax subsidy for such consumption that is not available to other taxpayers. The taxpayers who [benefitted] from deductibility under [prior] law tend to have relatively high incomes, and in some cases the consumption may bear only a loose relationship to business necessity. For example, when executives have dinner at an expensive restaurant following business discussions and then deduct the cost of the meal, the fact that there may be some bona fide business connection does not alter the imbalance between the treatment of those persons, who have effectively transferred a portion of the cost of their meal to the Federal Government, and other individuals, who cannot deduct the cost of their meals.

> The significance of this imbalance is heightened by the fact that business travel and entertainment often may be more lavish than comparable activities in a nonbusiness setting. For example, meals at expensive restaurants and season tickets for luxury boxes at sporting events are purchased to a significant degree by taxpayers who claim business deductions for these expenses. This disparity is highly visible, and contributes to public perceptions that the tax system is unfair. Polls indicate that the public identifies the deductibility of normal personal expenses such as meals to be one of the most significant elements of disrespect for and dissatisfaction with the present tax system.

(Tax Reform Act of [1986], Report of the Committee on Ways and Means, House of Representatives on H.R. 3838, 120–121 (1985)).

Consider also the following excerpt.

OFFICE OF THE SECRETARY, DEPARTMENT OF THE TREASURY, TAX REFORM FOR FAIRNESS, SIMPLICITY, AND ECONOMIC GROWTH
Vol. 2, 82–85 (1984).

REASONS FOR CHANGE

In General. The special requirements for deductibility of business entertainment expenses have been the subject of repeated Congressional concern since their enactment in 1962. The existing requirements are an attempt to provide taxpayers and the Internal Revenue Service with standards for deductibility. Current standards, however, are predominantly subjective, leaving application of the law uncertain and creating significant opportunities for abuse. Under present law, the costs of country club memberships, football and theater tickets, parties, and lunches and dinners at expensive restaurants are all deductible, if a plausible business connection can be demonstrated. The existing tests for whether a business connection exists are premised upon the taxpayer's expectations and intentions, and thus may result in a deduction being allowed in cases where less time was devoted to business than to entertainment, no business was discussed, or the taxpayer was not even present at the entertainment activity.

The liberality of the law in this area is in sharp contrast to the treatment of other kinds of expenses that provide both business and personal benefits. In some cases, such as work-related clothing, the presence of any personal benefit is deemed sufficient reason to disallow any deduction. In other cases, taxpayers are allowed to deduct only the proportion of expenses allocated to business. In contrast, present law often allows [80%] deductibility of certain entertainment expenses even though the connection between the entertainment expense and business activity is extremely tenuous.

Efficiency. The treatment of "business related" entertainment under current law encourages excessive spending on entertainment. * * * The taxpayer's choice of meals is much more likely to be based on personal rather than business considerations, but the deductibility of the expense makes selection of the expensive meal more likely than in a nonbusiness context. * * *

Present law [subject to the 20% reduction under § 274(n)] has no effective response to these practices because it attempts to separate personal from business entertainment expenses on the basis of the taxpayer's intentions and purposes. It is frequently possible to demonstrate an actual business purpose or connection for an entertainment expense that nevertheless has a strong, if not predominant, element of personal consumption. The problem is exacerbated by the fact that no objective standards exist for determining whether an expense is based upon the personal or business benefits derived. The use of the subjective terms "directly related" and "associated with" leads to liberal interpretations by taxpayers, who cannot reasonably be expected to deny themselves the benefit of any doubt. Moreover, as an administrative matter, entertainment expense deductions are often difficult to audit. The cost of giving a party for friends who are also business associates is often allowed even if the primary motive for the party was personal enjoyment, not business benefit.

Fairness. The current treatment of business entertainment expenses encourages taxpayers to indulge personal entertainment desires while at work or in the company of business associates. The majority of taxpayers, however, do not benefit from this incentive. Most hold jobs that do not permit business entertainment, and many others are scrupulous in claiming business deductions for personal entertainment.

Current law thus creates a preference for the limited class of taxpayers willing and able to satisfy personal entertainment desires in a setting with at least some business trappings. Lunches are [80%] deductible for a business person who eats with clients at an elegant restaurant, but not for a plumber who eats with other workers at the construction site. A party for friends of a business person is deductible if they are business associates, but a party for friends of a secretary, sales clerk, or nurse is not deductible.

Extreme abuses of these deductions are frequently cited by those who assail the tax system as unfair. Abuses, even if rare, seriously undermine the integrity of the tax system and undercut the public trust that is essential to it. Some limitation on the deductibility of entertainment expenses is necessary if such perceptions of unfairness are to be eliminated.

PROPOSAL

No deduction would be allowed for entertainment expenses, except for certain business meals. A deduction would be allowed for ordinary and necessary business meals furnished in a clear business setting (as defined in Treasury regulations). For each person participating in each business meal, this deduction would be limited to $10 for breakfast, $15 for lunch, and $25 for dinner. The meal cost limitations would include gratuities and tax with respect to the meal.

ANALYSIS

Business Meal Limitations. Business meals provide a mixture of business and personal benefits. The extent to which a meal provides a personal benefit will vary, and it is not possible to develop rules that would specify the precise percentage of personal benefit in specific cases. The proposal, therefore, provides objective limitations that are intentionally quite generous, yet are intended to deny deductions for that portion of meal costs which is most likely to constitute personal rather than business benefit. Expenses in excess of the limitation are deemed to be incurred for personal rather than business reasons. The deduction will be disallowed only for the amount above the stated limit.

Representatives of the restaurant industry in testimony before Congress have provided several estimates of the average cost of restaurant meals. If adjusted for inflation, those estimates would range between $6.50 and $10.00 for 1983. In addition, Census data shows that only about 2.5 percent of all restaurant meals in 1977 were in restaurants where the average bill exceeded $10.00. Adjusted for inflation, this suggests that only about 2.5 percent of all meals were in restaurants with average bills over $17.00 in 1983.

While the proposal will reduce the number of expensive business meals, it is expected that the limitations will not have a significant impact on more than five percent of restaurants. Moreover, since some high-cost meals will be replaced by moderate-cost meals, the effect on total employment in the restaurant industry is expected to be modest.

Businesses are currently required to keep detailed records for all deductible meals. Therefore, the additional recordkeeping costs should be minimal.

Placing ceilings on the deductibility of business meals would eliminate the extreme cases of abuse—those that affect the average taxpayer the most. Despite its small revenue effect, the proposal would be of significant assistance in restoring trust in the tax system.

The Elimination of Other Entertainment Deductions. The proposal would completely eliminate deductions for entertainment expenses such as tickets to professional sporting events, tickets to the theater, the costs of fishing trips, and country club dues. Because all such entertainment has a large personal component, the proper tax treatment, on both efficiency and equity grounds, is to disallow a deduction.

Approximately one-third of all baseball tickets and over one-half of all hockey tickets are purchased by businesses. The net effect is often to raise the cost of tickets for those who are not subsidized through the tax system for their purchases. Some performing arts organizations also sell large proportions of their tickets to businesses. Some tickets bought by businesses would remain deductible as gifts to their employees, but only if individual gifts are valued at less than $25.

If a public subsidy of such entertainment is desirable, a direct expenditure program could better target the aid. Further, current law raises serious equity questions by increasing the demand for tickets thereby causing the price of tickets to rise for the general public.

Reference: Halperin, Business Deduction for Personal Living Expenses: A Uniform Approach to an Unsolved Problem, 122 U.Pa.L.Rev. 859 (1974).

3. SUBSTANTIATION OF TRAVEL, MEAL AND ENTERTAINMENT EXPENSES

Proof and Deductions. One taxpayer claims a deduction of $300 for travel, meals, or entertainment expenses; another claims $1,000. Do both win?

The minimal requirements needed to substantiate entertainment deductions were laid down in Cohan v. Commissioner, 39 F.2d 540 (2d Cir.1930), where the taxpayer spent substantial sums on travel and entertainment, but kept no records as to any of these expenditures. The court held that absolute certainty was not needed and ordered the trial court to "make as close an approximation as it can, bearing heavily if it chooses upon the taxpayer whose inexactitude is of his own making." 39 F.2d at 544. As a result of the Cohan [25] rule deductions were frequently allowed for estimates of the amount spent on business

---

25. The Cohan rule is: if the evidence indicates that a taxpayer incurred a deductible expense but the exact amount cannot be determined, the court should make an approximation and not disallow the deduction entirely.

entertainment in the absence of anything more than self-serving testimony that business entertainment took place. Many taxpayers deliberately overstated unsubstantiated entertainment expenses knowing that on audit or at trial a portion of the claimed deduction would be disallowed. Because most taxpayers are never audited, those who deliberately overstated these deductions received an unjustified windfall. Also by not requiring documentation, taxpayers could fairly easily show that the entertainment served a business purpose.

A partial answer to these problems is found in the quantum of proof now necessary to support a deduction for travel, meals, and entertainment expenses. With the adoption of § 274(d) by the Revenue Act of 1962 Congress added special substantiation requirements to satisfy before a taxpayer is allowed a deduction. In effect, Congress rejected the use of the Cohan rule for all deductions required to meet the substantiation requirements of § 274(d). No deduction is allowed for travel or meal expenses or an entertainment activity or facility "unless the taxpayer substantiates by adequate records or by sufficient evidence corroborating the taxpayer's own statement (A) the amount of such expense * * *, (B) the time and place of the travel, entertainment * * *, (C) the business purpose of the expense * * *, and (D) the business relationship to the taxpayer of persons entertained * * *." Both local and out-of-town travel are subject to the § 274(d) substantiation standards. In addition, the business use of property described in § 280F (such as most passenger vehicles and computers) and business gifts must satisfy these same substantiation standards. All business expenditures not subject to § 274(d) need only satisfy the more lenient substantiation requirements applicable under § 162, which have been interpreted to permit in certain circumstances uncorroborated statements by taxpayers.

The documentation taxpayers are required to maintain or prepare is found in Reg. §§ 1.274–5T and –6T. Regulations § 1.274–5T(c) reiterate the Congressional intent that no deduction is to be allowed on the basis of approximations. A taxpayer must substantiate each element of an expenditure or use so as to establish the four elements found in § 274(d)(A)–(D) by means of (1) adequate records or (2) the taxpayer's own statement corroborated by other sufficient evidence. Reg. § 1.274–5T(c)(1). Written evidence has considerably more probative value than oral evidence alone, and the value of written evidence is greater the closer in time it relates to the expenditure or use. Reg. § 1.274–5T(c)(1).

Adequate records include an account book, diary, statement of expense or similar records kept by the taxpayer and documentation that, in combination, are sufficient to establish each of the four elements. Reg. § 1.274–5T(c)(1)(i). Contemporaneous records, or at least records made at or near the time of the expenditure or use, are preferred. Reg. § 1.274–5T(c)(1). The requisite information is to be recorded at or near the time of the expenditure or use when the taxpayer has "full present knowledge of each element of the expenditure or use." Reg. § 1.274–5T(c)(2)(ii)(A). Documentary evidence, such as receipts, are required for away from home lodging expenditures and other expenses in excess of $25, except transportation charges. Reg. § 1.274–5T(c)(2)(ii)(D). The account book and the receipt should "complement each other in an orderly manner." Reg. § 1.274–5T(c)(2)(i).

Moreover, the taxpayer can substantiate his claim by other available evidence if "exceptional circumstances" are present. Reg. § 1.274–5T(c)(4). If a taxpayer establishes that the failure to produce adequate records is due to the loss of such records through circumstances beyond the taxpayer's control, such as destruction by fire or other casualty, then the taxpayer may substantiate a deduction by a reasonable reconstruction of the records. Reg. § 1.274–5T(c)(5).

However, the Treasury, having marched the Service's forces up the hill, thereafter marches them down: it is suggested that the proof required may be dispensed with if there is substantiation by other evidence, including the taxpayer's own statement (be it oral or written) and other corroborative evidence sufficient to establish each element. This corroborating evidence can be oral, such as testimony from a disinterested, unrelated party describing the taxpayer's business activities. Reg. § 1.274–5T(c)(3)(i). The Temporary Regulations further indicate, "[T]he corroborative evidence required to support a statement not made at or near the time of the expenditure or use must have a high degree of probative value to evaluate such statement and evidence to the level of credibility reflected by a record made at or near the time of the expenditure or use supported by sufficient documentary evidence." Reg. § 1.274–5T(c)(1). However, an uncorroborated statement by the taxpayer will not be sufficient to justify a business deduction under § 274(d). The Conference Report to Accompany H.R. 3838, Tax Reform Act of 1986, 99th Cong., 2d Sess. II–27 (1987), concludes: "It is reemphasized that under the conference agreement * * *, the Internal Revenue Service and the courts are not to apply the *Cohan* approximation rule to allow deductibility of any food or beverage expense, other entertainment expense, or other expenditure subject to substantiation pursuant to section 274(d) if the expenditure is not substantiated in accordance with section 274(d) and the regulations thereunder."

The Tax Reform Act of 1984 was an attempt to tighten up the travel and entertainment area by first eliminating the less rigorous method whereby a taxpayer could submit his own corroborated statement and secondly, imposed a "contemporaneous" requirement for the maintenance of adequate records. As a practical matter a taxpayer was required to keep a daily written record in a log or diary. If contemporaneous records were not maintained on a daily basis, no deduction was allowed. In 1985 Congress repealed the "contemporaneous" requirement for adequate records and reinstated the rules in existence prior to the 1984 legislation, including the use of taxpayer's own corroborated statement. This was done in response to complaints that the contemporaneous rules and the Regulations adopted to implement them required costly, complex and unreasonable recordkeeping. Do you agree? Were there any advantages to the 1984 changes?

To relieve taxpayers of the burden of keeping records to substantiate the cost of meals consumed while traveling away from home on business, Rev.Proc. 83–71, 1983–2 C.B. 590, provides for an optional meal deduction. A taxpayer may deduct $14 per day as a business deduction for the cost of meals for each day he is away from home on business, provided that he stays in the area for less than 30 days. If he stays in the area for 30 days or more, only $9 per day is allowed.

Reimbursement. If an employee is on an expense account, he need not report the reimbursement as income nor account on his tax return for amounts expended solely for the benefit of the employer where the taxpayer makes an "adequate accounting" to the employer and does not claim expenses in excess of the amounts reimbursed. Reg. §§ 1.162–17(b)(1) and 1.274–5T(f)(2)(i). And, the employee is not subject to the 80 percent limitation. § 274(n)(2)(A). A proper accounting by the employee shifts the obligation to comply with § 274(d) to the employer. And, § 274(n) applies to the employer's deductions for meals and entertainment.

If an employee claims expenses in excess of the amount reimbursed, he must maintain additional evidence and substantiate that the expenses were paid in carrying out the employee's trade or business, not the employer's trade or business. Reg. §§ 1.274–5T(f)(2)(iii) and 1.162–17(b)(3). The employee must show that part of his job involves the entertainment, at his expense, of the employer's customers. If the reimbursement exceeds the employee's expenses, the employee must include such excess in income. Reg. §§ 1.162–17(b)(2) and 1.274–5T(f)(2)(ii).

Where a taxpayer is not fully reimbursed for the costs of his business travel, business meals and business entertainment, the amount of the reimbursement is reported as income and any of these employee business expenses, up to the amount of the reimbursement, are taken as above-the-line deductions. § 62(a)(2)(A). Any deduction claimed as an above-the-line deduction is not an itemized deduction and is, therefore, not subject to the 80 percent limitation nor the two percent floor. §§ 63(d), 67(a) and 274(e)(3) and (n)(2)(A). Instead, the 80 percent limitation applies to the employer who is entitled to a business deduction for the reimbursement of an employee's business meals and entertainment. § 274(n). Any employee business expenses for travel, meals and entertainment in excess of the reimbursement becomes a below-the-line "miscellaneous itemized deduction." An employee's business deduction for the excess costs of transportation and lodging are subject to the two percent floor. The business deduction for the excess costs of meals and entertainment is first subject to the 80 percent limitation of § 274(n), and then the reduced amount is subject to the two percent floor of § 67(a).

Example 1. During the year Ted Player, an associate in a large law firm, incurs and pays $1,000 of business entertainment expenses and $1,200 of business travel expenses (consisting of $600 for transportation, $400 for lodging and $200 for meals while away from home). Ted is not reimbursed for any of these employee business expenses. His gross income and adjusted gross income is $20,000. Ted's allowable, below-the-line itemized deduction for these costs is computed as follows:

Entertainment	$1,000
Meals	200
	$1,200
less: 20% disallowed	240
	$ 960
plus: transportation	600
lodging	400
	$1,960
less: 2% of AGI	400
Amount allowed	$1,560

Example 2. Assume that Ted is reimbursed by his employer for $700 of his entertainment costs and $900 of his travel costs (consisting of $800 for transportation and lodging and $100 for meals). Ted's adjusted gross income is:

Gross income	$20,000
plus: reimbursement	1,600
less: costs up to amount of reimbursement	1,600
Adjusted gross income	$20,000

Ted's allowable, below-the-line deductions are:

Excess cost of entertainment	$300
Excess cost of meals	100
	$400
less: 20% disallowed	80
	$320
plus: excess cost of transportation and lodging	200
	$520
less: 2% of AGI	400
Amount allowed	$120

Problem

Ned is an employee of the Trendy Corp., a clothing manufacturer having its principal offices in New York City. A buyer from a Midwest department store came to New York with his wife to purchase a line of women's dresses. The buyer has been a steady customer of the Trendy Corp. for a number of years.

The buyer and his wife arrived in town on Monday. That evening Ned and his wife took the buyer and his wife to a night club for dinner, drinks and a floor show. The total bill for the evening was $400. Between acts at the night club, Ned and the buyer discussed Ned's line of women's apparel for about 15 minutes. The two couples were in the night club for about four hours.

On Tuesday morning, the buyer visited Ned's employer's office and ordered $26,000 worth of merchandise. After completing their business, Ned took the buyer to lunch at a nearby restaurant. Ned paid the bill for the luncheon (at which no business was discussed) which amounted to $100. Taxpayer also purchased two theater tickets to a matinee for Ned's wife and the buyer's wife, paying $46 for the two tickets. The buyer and his wife flew home the next day.

(a) Assume Ned's employer does not reimburse him for any of the above expenses.

i. What expenses, if any, may Ned deduct as ordinary and necessary business expenses under § 162? Consider §§ 274(a)(1)(A), (k) and (n), and 102(c). As to the "directly related to" standard consider Reg. § 1.274–2(c)(3) and (7). As to the "associated with" test consider Reg. § 1.274–2(d)(1), (2), and (3). What is the impact of the "lavish or extravagant" standard contained in Reg. § 1.274–1? § 274(k). As to the expenses of the spouses (including the taxpayer's) consider § 274(b) and Reg. § 1.274–2(e)(2) and (3) and –2(d)(4). Reconsider § 274(d). What is the impact of § 67?

ii. Would the deductions be disallowed because they were paid by Ned in carrying on the business of his employer, not his own business? Can the employee overcome this obstacle by showing that part of the obligation of his job is the entertainment of customers?

(b) Assume the company reimburses Ned for all of the entertainment expenses. What are the tax consequences to both Ned and the company? Consider §§ 274(e)(2) and (3) and (n), 62(a)(2)(A) and 67. What effect will reimbursement have on the adequacy of the employee's records? Consider Reg. §§ 1.162–17(b) and 1.274–5T(f)(2).

4. EXPENSES OF ENTERTAINMENT FACILITIES

Section 274(a)(1)(B) disallows any deduction for facilities used in conjunction with an activity constituting entertainment, amusement, or recreation, even though such expenses would be deductible under § 162(a). Examples of entertainment facilities include yachts, hunting lodges, swimming pools, airplanes, apartments, and vacation homes. The disallowance of expenses of entertainment facilities applies, pursuant to § 274(a)(2)(A), to dues or fees paid to social, athletic or sporting clubs. However, if the taxpayer establishes, under § 274(a)(2)(C), that the facility was used primarily for the furtherance of his business and the amount paid was directly related to the active conduct of his business then, in the case of a club, the disallowance rule of § 274(a)(1)

(B) will not apply. A taxpayer meets the definition of using a facility primarily for the furtherance of his business, according to Reg. § 1.274–2(e)(4)(iii), if more than 50 percent of the total calendar days of use of the facility by the taxpayer were days of "business use". Use of a facility during one calendar day constitutes a day of business use if the "primary use of the facility on such day was ordinary and necessary within the meaning of section 162 or 212 and the regulations thereunder." Reg. § 1.274–2(e)(4)(iii).

The legislative history explains the interrelationship of deductions for an entertainment activity and an entertainment facility as follows:

> Moreover, the deductions for otherwise allowable business entertainment activities and business meals are not affected by this legislation. For example, if a salesman took a customer hunting for a day at a commercial shooting preserve, the expenses of the hunt (such as hunting rights, dogs, a guide, etc.) would be deductible provided that the current law requirements of substantiation, adequate records, ordinary and necessary, directly related, etc. are met. However, if the hunters stayed overnight at a hunting lodge on the shooting preserve, the cost attributable to the lodging would be non-deductible but expenses for any meals would be deductible if they satisfied the requirements of current law. The shooting preserve should provide the taxpayer with an allocation of charges attributable to the overnight lodging for the taxpayer and guests. Conference Report, Revenue [Act] of 1978, 95th Cong. 2d Sess. 691 (1978).

Problems

1. George entertains a client of Service Corporation at the company's yacht docked in San Francisco. Both George and the client stay on the yacht. All expenses for the weekend are paid by George who is reimbursed by the corporation. What expenses can the corporation deduct? What about the cost of maintaining the yacht? Is the cost of business entertainment (food, drinks) on board deductible? Is interest on a loan to finance the yacht deductible? Consider §§ 67 and 274(a)(1)(A) and (B), (f), (h)(2)(A), (k) and (n).

2. (a) The Widget Corporation paid the dues at a country club for Susan, an executive of the corporation. Widget reimburses Susan for meals at the club which she takes with business clients. Advise the Corporation as to the deductibility of these items. Consider §§ 67(a) and 274(a)(1)(A) and (a)(2)(C), (k) and (n) and Reg. § 1.274–2(e)(2), (e)(3)(ii), and (e)(4)(i) and (iii).

(b) As to Susan, will the reimbursement of these items represent gross income? Can an employee deduct the amount of reimbursed expenses? Consider § 274(e)(2) and (3). Consider also Reg. §§ 1.274–5(T)(f)(2) and 1.162–17(b). What is the impact of §§ 67(a)(2)(A), 67(a) and 274(n)?

5. CONVENTION EXPENSES

Expenses paid or incurred by the taxpayer in going to a convention may be deducted, even though attendance is voluntary. Expenses related to attending a convention, seminar, or similar meeting are only deductible under § 162 as ordinary and necessary expenses of carrying on a trade or business. Thus, expenses of attending a convention which relate to financial or tax planning, which would be deductible under § 212 rather than § 162, are disallowed. § 274(h)(7). The legislative history indicates:

> The committee is concerned about deductions claimed for travel and other costs of attending conventions or other meetings that relate to financial or tax planning, rather than to a trade or business of the taxpayer. * * * In many cases, these seminars are held in locations (including some that are overseas) that are attractive for vacation purposes, and are structured so as to permit extensive leisure activities on the part of attendees. Since investment purposes do not relate to the taxpayer's means of earning a livelihood (i.e., a trade or business), the committee believes that these abuses, along with respect to any deduction for personal living expenses, justify denial of any deduction for the costs of attending a nonbusiness seminar or similar meeting that does not relate to a trade or business of the taxpayer. (Tax Reform Act of [1986], Report of the Committee on Ways and Means House of Representatives on H.R. 3838, 123 (1985)).

With respect to business convention expenses, the principal issue is "whether there is a sufficient relationship between the taxpayer's trade or business and his attendance at the convention or other meeting so that he is benefiting or advancing the interests of his trade or business by such attendance." Reg. § 1.162–2(d). Traveling expenses for family members are not deductible unless the family member's presence on the trip has a "bona fide business purpose" and they perform more than "some incidental service" for the head of the family. Reg. § 1.162–2(c). Section 274(h) contains additional restrictions on the deductibility of foreign convention expenses.

RUDOLPH v. UNITED STATES

Supreme Court of the United States, 1962.
370 U.S. 269, 82 S.Ct. 1277, 8 L.Ed.2d 484.

Per Curiam.

The petition for certiorari in this case was granted because it was thought to present important questions involving the definition of "income" and "ordinary and necessary" business expenses under the Internal Revenue Code. 368 U.S. 913, 82 S.Ct. 195, 7 L.Ed.2d 130. An insurance company provided a trip from its home office in Dallas, Texas, to New York City for a group of its agents and their wives. Rudolph and his wife were among the beneficiaries of this trip, and the Commissioner assessed its value to them as taxable income. It appears to be agreed between the parties that the tax consequences of the trip turn upon the Rudolphs' "dominant motive and purpose" in taking the trip and the company's in offering it. In this regard the District Court, on a suit for a refund, found that the trip was provided by the company for "the primary purpose of affording a pleasure trip * * * in the nature of a bonus, reward, and compensation for a job well done" and that from the point of view of the Rudolphs it "was primarily a pleasure trip in the nature of a vacation * * *." D.C., 189 F.Supp. 2, 4–5. The Court of Appeals approved these findings. 5 Cir., 291 F.2d 841. * * *

Writ of certiorari dismissed.

Separate opinion of MR. JUSTICE HARLAN.

Although the reasons given by the Court for dismissing the writ as improvidently granted should have been persuasive against granting certiorari, now that the case is here I think it better to decide it, two members of the Court having dissented on the merits.

The courts below concluded (1) that the value of this "all expense" trip to the company-sponsored insurance convention constituted "gross income" to the petitioners within the meaning of § 61 of the Internal Revenue Code of [1986] and (2) that the amount reflected was not deductible as an "ordinary and necessary" business expense under § 162 of the Code. * * *.

The basic facts, found by the District Court, are as follows. Petitioners, husband and wife, reside in Dallas, Texas, where the home office of the husband's employer, the Southland Life Insurance Company, is located. By having sold a predetermined amount of insurance, the husband qualified to attend the company's convention in New York City in 1956 and, in line with company policy, to bring his wife with him. The petitioners, together with 150 other employees and officers of the insurance company and 141 wives, traveled to and from New York City on special trains, and were housed in a single hotel during their two-and-one-half-day visit. One morning was devoted to a "business meeting" and group luncheon, the rest of the time in New York City to "travel, sight-seeing, entertainment, fellowship or free time." The entire trip lasted one week.

The company paid all the expenses of the convention-trip which amounted to $80,000; petitioners' allocable share being $560. When petitioners did not include the latter amount in their joint income tax return, the Commissioner assessed a deficiency which was sustained by the District Court, 189 F.Supp. 2, and also by the Court of Appeals, one judge dissenting, in a per curiam opinion, 291 F.2d 841, * * *.

I.

Under § 61 of the [1986] Code was the value of the trip to the taxpayer-husband properly includible in gross income? * * *

Petitioners do not claim that the value of the trip is within one of the statutory exclusions from "gross income" * * * as did the taxpayer in Patterson v. Thomas, 289 F.2d 108, 111–112; rather they characterize the amount as a "fringe benefit" not specifically excluded from § 61 by other sections of the statute, yet not intended to be encompassed by its reach. Conceding that the statutory exclusions from "gross income" are not exhaustive, as the Government seems to recognize is so under Glenshaw, it is not now necessary to explore the extent of any such nonstatutory exclusions. For it was surely within the Commissioner's competence to consider as "gross income" a "reward, or a bonus given to * * * employees for excellence in service," which the District Court found was the employer's primary purpose in arranging this trip. I cannot say that this finding, confirmed as it has been by the Court of Appeals, is inadequately supported by this record.

II.

There remains the question whether, though income, this outlay for transportation, meals, and lodging was deductible by petitioners as an "ordinary and necessary" business expense under § 162.[26] * * *

Where, as here, it may be arguable that the trip was both for business and personal reasons, the crucial question is whether, under all the facts and circumstances of the case, the purpose of the trip was "related primarily to business" or was, rather, "primarily personal in nature." That other trips to other conventions or meetings by other taxpayers were held to be primarily related to business is of no relevance here; that certain doctors, lawyers, clergymen, insurance agents or others have or have not been permitted similar deductions only shows that in the circumstances of those cases, the courts thought that the expenses were or were not deductible as "related primarily to business."

The husband places great emphasis on the fact that he is an entrapped "organization man," required to attend such conventions, and that his future promotions depend on his presence. Suffice it to say that the District Court did not find any element of compulsion; to the contrary, it found that the petitioners regarded the convention in New York City as a pleasure trip in the nature of a vacation. Again, I cannot say that these findings are without adequate evidentiary support.

The trip not having been primarily a business trip, the wife's expenses are not deductible. It is not necessary, therefore, to examine whether they would or would not be deductible if, to the contrary, the husband's trip was related primarily to business.

Where, as here, two courts below have resolved the determinative factual issues against the taxpayers, according to the rules of law set

---

26. No question is raised in this case as to whether the $80,000 paid by the company for the total convention expense is deductible by the corporation.

There is no need to explore the lack of symmetry in certain "income" and "deductibility" areas in the 1954 Code permitting employers to provide certain "fringe benefits" to employees—such as parking facilities, swimming pools, medical services—which have not generally been considered income to the employee, but which, if paid for by the employee with his own funds, would not be a deductible expense. The practicalities of a tax system do not demand hypothetical or theoretical perfection, and these workaday problems are properly the concern of the Commissioner, not of the Courts.

forth in the statute and regulations, it is not for this Court to re-examine the evidence, and disturb their findings, unless "clearly erroneous." That is not the situation here.

I would affirm.

MR. JUSTICE DOUGLAS, with whom MR. JUSTICE BLACK joins, dissenting.

I.

It could not, I think, be seriously contended that a professional man, say a Senator or a Congressman, who attends a convention to read a paper or conduct a seminar *with all expenses paid* has received "income" within the meaning of the Internal Revenue Code. Nor would it matter, I assume, that he took his wife and that her expenses were also paid. Income has the connotation of something other than the mere payment of expenses. The statute, 26 U.S.C. § 61, 26 U.S. C.A. § 61, speaks in terms of financial gain, of compensation for services, "including fees, commissions, and similar items." The form of payment for services covers a wide range. Treasury Regulations § 1.61–1 provide:

> "Gross income includes income realized in any form, whether in money, property, or services. Income may be realized, therefore, in the form of services, meals, accommodations, stock, or other property, as well as in cash."

The formula "all expenses paid" might be the disguise whereby compensation "for services" is paid. Yet it would be a rare case indeed where one could conclude that a person who gets only his expenses for attendance at one convention gets "income" in the statutory sense. If this arrangement were regular and frequent or if it had the earmarks of a sham device as a cloak for remuneration, there would be room for fact-finders to conclude that it was evasive. But isolated engagements of the kind here in question have no rational connection with compensation "for services" rendered.

It is true that petitioner was an employee and that the expenses for attending the convention were paid by his employer. He qualified to attend the convention by selling an amount of insurance that met a quota set by the company. Other salesmen also qualified, some attending and some not attending. They went from Dallas, Texas, to New York City, where they stayed two and a half days. One day was given to a business session and a luncheon; the rest of the time was left for social events.

On this record there is no room for a finding of fact that the "expenses paid" were "for services" rendered. They were apparently a proper income tax deduction for the employer. The record is replete with evidence that from management's point of view it was good business to spend money on a convention for its leading agents—a convention that not only kept the group together in New York City, but in transit as well, giving ample time for group discussions, exchanges of experience, and educational training. It was the exigencies of the employment that gave rise to the convention. There was nothing dishonest, illegitimate, or unethical about this transaction. No services were rendered. New York City may or may not have been attractive to the agents and their wives. Whether a person enjoys or dislikes the trip that he makes "with all expenses paid" has no more to do with whether the expenses paid were compensation "for services" rendered than does his attitude toward his job.

In popular understanding a trip to a convention "with all expenses paid" may be an award. Yet the tax laws are filled with exemptions for "awards" which are not considered to be income. The exemption of gifts is one example. Others are the exemptions of the proceeds of life insurance payable at death, disability benefits, the rental values of parsonages, scholarship and fellowship grants, allowances of U.S. employees abroad, mustering-out payments to members of the Armed Forces, etc. Employees may receive from their employers many fringe benefits that are not income. * * *

II.

The expenses, if "income," are plainly deductible. The Government, however, says that our problem is to determine "whether it is consistent with the ends of an equitable and workable tax system" to make them such. The problem of designing an "equitable" tax system is, however, for Congress, not for the Court.

* * *

I see no reason to take this case out of the main stream of precedents and establish a special rule for insurance conventions. Judge Brown, dissenting in the Court of Appeals, shows how discriminatory this decision is:

"Deductions have been allowed as 'ordinary and necessary' to clergymen attending a church convention; to expenses of an employee attending conventions of a related business group; to a lawyer attending a meeting of the American Bar Association; to a legal secretary attending the national convention of the National Association; to physicians attending medical conventions; to certified public accountants attending conventions; to university teachers in attending conventions or scientific meetings; to professional cartoonists attending political conventions; to persons attending the Red Cross Convention; to school teachers attending summer school; to attorneys attending an institute on Federal taxation; to employees sent to refresher courses to become more acquainted with new processes in the industry; to a furniture store sending its buyers to the annual furniture mart; to representatives to annual conventions of trade associations; and to an insurance agent away from home on business." 291 F.2d 841, 844–845.

Insurance conventions go back at least to 1924 (Report No. 15, Life Insurance Sales Research Bureau, Nov. 1924) and are premised on the idea that agents and companies benefit from the knowledge and increase in morale which result from them. Why they should be treated differently from other conventions is a mystery. It cannot be, as the district judge thought and as the Government seems to argue, because going to New York City is, as a matter of law, a "pleasure trip." If we are in the field of judicial notice, I would think that some might conclude that the weekend in New York City was a chore and that those who went sacrificed valuable time that might better have been spent on the farm, in the woods, or along the seashore.

Moreover, federal revenue agents attending their convention are given a deduction for the expenses they incur. We are advised that

" * * * the Commissioner has recently withdrawn his objections in two Tax Court cases to the deduction of convention expenses incurred by two IRS employees in attending conventions of the National Association of Internal Revenue Employees.

"No explanation has been given publicly for the Tax Court action of the Commissioner, it being generally presumed that the IRS employees met the tests of Reg. § 1.162–2(d) by showing a sufficient relationship between the trade or business of being an IRS employee and attendance at conventions of the NAIRE. The National Association of Internal Revenue Employees has hailed the Commissioner's actions as setting a precedent which can be cited by IRS employees when taking deductions for expenses incurred in attending NAIRE conventions." CCH Standard Federal Tax Reports No. 23, April 19, 1961, pt. 1, p. 2.

It is odd, indeed, that revenue agents need make no accounting of the movies they saw or the nightclubs they attended, in order to get the deduction, while insurance agents must.

III.

The wife's expenses are, on this record, also deductible. The Treasury Regulations state in § 1.162–2(c):

"Where a taxpayer's wife accompanies him on a business trip, expenses attributable to her travel are not deductible unless it can be adequately shown that the wife's presence on the trip has a bona fide business purpose. The wife's performance of some incidental service does not cause her expenses to qualify as deductible business expenses. The same rules apply to any other members of the taxpayer's family who accompany him on such a trip."

The civil law philosophy, expressed in the community property concept, attributes half of the husband's earnings to the wife—an equitable idea that at long last was reflected in the idea of income splitting under the federal income tax law. The wife's contribution to the business productivity of the husband in at least some activities is well known. It was specially recognized in the insurance field long before the issue of deductibility of her expenses arose under the federal income tax. Business reasons motivated the inclusion of wives in this particular insurance convention. An insurance executive testified at this trial:

"Q. I hand you Plaintiff's Exhibit 15, and you will notice it is a letter addressed to 'John Doe'; also a bulletin entitled 'A New Partner Has Been Formed.'

"Will you tell us what that consists of?

"A. This is a letter addressed to the wife of an agent, a new agent, as we make the contract with him. This letter is sent to his wife within a few days after the contract, enclosing this booklet explaining to her how she can help her husband in the life insurance business.

* * *

"Q. Please tell us, as briefly as you can and yet in detail, how you as agency director for Southland attempt to integrate the wives' performance with the performance of agents in the life insurance business.

"A. One of the important functions we have in mind is the attendance at these conventions. In addition to that communication, occasionally there are letters that will be written to the wife concerning any special sales effort that might be desired or promoted. The company has a monthly publication for the agents and employees that is mailed to their homes so the wife will have a convenient opportunity to see the magazine and read it.

"At most of our convention program[s], we have some specific reference to the wife's work, and in quite a few of the convention programs we have had wives appear on the program.

"Q. Suppose you didn't have the wives and didn't seek to require their attendance at a convention, would there be some danger that your meetings and conventions would kind of degenerate into stag affairs, where the whole purpose of the meeting would be lost?

"A. I think that would definitely be a tendency."

I would reverse the judgments below and leave insurance conventions in the same category as conventions of revenue agents, lawyers, doctors, business men, accountants, nurses, clergymen and all others, until and unless Congress decides otherwise.

Problem

Sales Corporation proposes to have a convention annually in the United States at which all its sales representatives who have sold a minimum number of units are to be invited at the expense of the company. The convention will last four days and will always be held at a noted resort within the United States. Each morning, from 9:00 to 10:30 a.m., a lecture on company sales policies and techniques will be given, at which attendance is to be required. During the remainder of the day and evening the employer will make golfing, fishing, tennis, horseback riding and other activities available to its employees, their spouses and children. The cost of the convention will be about $2,500 per family. Representatives of Sales Corporation ask you whether:

(a) Under this proposal the Corporation could deduct the expenses of the convention? Consider § 274(a)(1)(A). If this convention is "entertainment, amusement, or recreation," how will the requirement of a substantial and bona fide business discussion associated with the active conduct of the taxpayer's business be met? Consider Reg. § 1.274–2(d)(2) to (4) (is this a convention?) and –2(f)(2)(v) and (vi). What about the expenses for families of the employees? Consider Reg. § 1.162–2(c) and (d) and § 274(e)(2) and (3). What is the impact of § 274(e)(1), (2) and (4), (k) and (n)?

(b) Would the employees realize gross income if the plan were adopted? Consider the Rudolph case and § 132. Could the employees deduct their expenses (and those of their families) under §§ 162 and 274(a)? Consider Reg. § 1.162–2(b), (c), and (d). What is the impact of §§ 67 and 274(n)?

E. CONVERSION OF PERSONAL ASSETS

An individual is not allowed to deduct losses on the sale of personal assets, such as a personal residence; however, losses on the sale of trade or business property and investments are allowed. § 165(a) and (c)(1) and (2). Additionally, the costs of maintaining personal property (with the exception of taxes and interest) are not deductible. §§ 162, 212, and 262. To deduct the costs of maintaining property and any loss on sale, an individual will argue that he converted the property from personal to business or investment use. This controversy often arises where a taxpayer moves out of his personal residence and wishes to deduct the costs of maintaining the property after he ceases to occupy it and any loss on its subsequent sale. Although the courts tend to be skeptical of taxpayer's claims that a personal residence has been converted to business or investment use, certain taxpayers have been successful in convincing the trier-of-fact that an actual conversion took place after they moved out.

In Gevirtz v. Commissioner, 123 F.2d 707 (2d Cir.1941), a taxpayer originally purchased land for an apartment building but constructed a personal residence instead after deciding that the location was not then appropriate for additional rental units. After living in the home for several years she moved out and was unsuccessful in either renting it or selling it. She finally abandoned the property, allowing the mortgage holder to take it. She attempted to deduct her loss based upon her contention that she never converted the property from her original investment motive. She claimed that the house was designed to allow its conversion into several rental units. The court found that her motive in holding the property became personal when she occupied it as a residence. It concluded that the investment motive was abandoned. Why do you feel the court in Gevirtz was reluctant to accept taxpayer's contention of a continuation of her original profit motive?

In Weir v. Commissioner, 109 F.2d 996 (3d Cir.1940), an individual purchased stock in a realty company which owned the apartment building he lived in as a tenant. He purchased the stock to make sure that as a stockholder he had a say in the management of the building. After he moved out, he sold the stock at a loss. Even though the origin for his purchase was personal, the court allowed the taxpayer to deduct the loss under § 165(c)(2). The court stated that because the stock paid dividends, it was property "used to produce taxable income" so no need existed to look at his motive for the purchase. Why was the court in Weir inclined to hold for the taxpayer while in a case like Gevirtz courts are generally reluctant to find for the taxpayer? Sometimes, as the following case indicates, the taxpayer is successful in proving a conversion took place.

LOWRY v. UNITED STATES

United States District Court, Central District of New Hampshire, 1974.
384 F.Supp. 257.

OPINION

BOWNES, DISTRICT JUDGE.

Plaintiffs bring this action to recover federal income taxes and interest, in the amount of $1,072, which they allege were erroneously or illegally assessed and collected. Jurisdiction is based on 28 U.S.C. § 1346(a)(1).

The issue is whether plaintiffs, who ceased to use their summer house as residential property in 1967 and immediately offered it for sale without attempting to rent the property, converted it into "income producing property," thereby entitling them to deduct the maintenance expenses incurred after it was put on the market and prior to its sale in 1973. The Internal Revenue Service allowed plaintiffs to take maintenance deductions in the tax years 1968 and 1969. They disallowed similar maintenance deductions in the tax year 1970. The only year in issue is 1970.[27]

Plaintiffs are husband and wife domiciled in Peterborough, New Hampshire. (Since Edward G. Lowry, Jr., is the principal party in this case, he alone will hereinafter be referred to as plaintiff.) Plaintiff filed a joint federal income tax return for 1970 with the District Director of Internal Revenue in Portsmouth, New Hampshire. On his 1970 income tax return, plaintiff deducted expenditures made for the care and maintenance of his former summer residence. He based these deductions upon the premise that the summer residence was no longer personal property, but was property "held for the production of income." Int.Rev.Code of [1986] § 212. The Internal Revenue Service disagreed with plaintiff and disallowed the deduction basing its decision on Internal Revenue Code of [1986] § 262 which provides:

> Except as otherwise expressly provided in this chapter, no deductions shall be allowed for personal, living, or family expenses.

---

27. Plaintiff, due to his own mistake, failed to take the allowable depreciation deductions and that matter is not before this court.

On November 27, 1971, plaintiff paid the disputed $1,072 under written protest.

The property in question is plaintiff's former summer residence on Martha's Vineyard (hereinafter referred to as Vineyard property). The Vineyard property is part of a cooperative community known as Seven Gates Farm Corporation.

Seven Gates was formed in 1921 by five persons, one of whom was plaintiff's father. Upon forming the corporation, plaintiff's father acquired the Vineyard property. In 1942, plaintiff acquired "title" to the property by gift from his father.

Legal title to the Vineyard property is held by Seven Gates. In 1970, plaintiff had a lease for the Vineyard property and was a 3% stockholder in the corporation. The leasing arrangement treated plaintiff as the de facto owner of the property. It ran for the life of the corporation with the proviso that, upon dissolution of the corporation, it would automatically be converted into a fee title. No stockholder-lessee, however, could sell his stock and lease without the prior consent of 75% of the stockholder-lessees. Each lease further provided that a rental for a year or less required the prior consent of the Committee on Admissions and that a lease for more than a year required the prior consent of 75% of the other stockholder-lessees.

In 1966, plaintiff owned three residential properties: he maintained his legal residence in Maryland; he had a winter residence in Florida; and the Vineyard property. During 1966, plaintiff sold his Maryland home and purchased a house in Peterborough, New Hampshire. Because the Peterborough house did "all the things that the house in Martha's Vineyard did," plaintiff decided, in 1967, to sell the Vineyard property and put a sales price on it of $150,000. From 1921 through 1967, plaintiff had spent nearly all of his summers at the Vineyard property.

After it was put on the market, the house was never again used as residential property. Each spring plaintiff went to Martha's Vineyard, opened the house, put up curtains, pruned the shrubbery, generally cleaned and spruced up the property, and then left. This took two or three days and plaintiff occupied the house during this period. Each fall plaintiff returned and closed the house for the winter. The closing also took two to three days and plaintiff stayed in the house. The only other time that plaintiff occupied the property was once a year, when the corporation had its annual meeting of stockholders. As evidence of his intent to treat the Vineyard property as a business asset, plaintiff testified that in 1971 his daughter, after returning from abroad, requested the use of the property. Plaintiff refused, stating that the property was a business proposition. As a fatherly gesture, however, he rented a summer home in Maine for her use.

Plaintiff made no attempt to rent the house for the following reasons: He believed that it would be easier to sell a clean empty house than one occupied by tenants; the house being suitable for summer occupancy only, would have had to have been rented completely equipped, which would have required the plaintiff to purchase linen, silver, blankets, and recreational equipment at a cost which would not have been justified by any possible rental; rental prices bore no reasonable relation to the value of the property and the expected sales price; and rental was complicated by the restrictive provisions of the corporation's bylaws.

In 1968, a prospective purchaser offered to buy the property for $150,000. Plaintiff, however, could not obtain the necessary 75% approval of the stockholders of Seven Gates and the sale was not completed. In 1973, plaintiff received a cash offer of $150,000 for the property and the sale was closed in September of 1973. Plaintiff's 1973 tax return showed a net long-term capital gain of $100,536.50, as a result of the sale.

RULINGS OF LAW

The tax issue in this case is: When and how does residential property become converted into income producing property?

The Tax Court, in attempting to establish a clear guideline in a murky area, created a simple test: The taxpayer had to make a bona fide offer to rent in order to convert residential property into "income producing property." The Tax Court's *sine qua non* was a product of administrative reality. There are three basic reasons why the Government established a rental prerequisite. First, it stemmed from a fear that taxpayers would countermand the listing for sale after taking a series of deductions and reoccupy the house on a personal basis. Mary Laughlin Robinson, 2 T.C. 305, 309 (1943). Second, the rental requisite provided a clear and convenient administrative test. Warren Leslie, Sr., 6 T.C. 488, 494 (1946). Third, the rental requirement found some implied support in Treas.Reg. § 1.212–1(h), which provides:

> Ordinary and necessary expenses paid or incurred in connection with the management, conservation, or maintenance of property held for use as a residence by the taxpayer are not deductible. However, ordinary and necessary expenses paid or incurred in connection with the management, conservation, or maintenance of property held by the taxpayer as rental property are deductible even though such property was formerly held by the taxpayer for use as a home.

In Hulet P. Smith, 26 T.C.M. 149 (1967), aff'd 397 F.2d 804 (9th Cir. 1968), the Tax Court abandoned the rental test and held that an offer for sale plus an abandonment transformed the property into an investment asset. The Court of Appeals, in affirming, circumspectly stated:

> The Government makes a strong case for reversal. See Recent Development, Hulet P. Smith, 66 Mich.L.Rev. 562 (1968). Unusual circumstances are present, however, and we are not persuaded that the Tax

Court's factual finding and its consequent conclusions are clearly wrong.[28] *Smith,* supra, 397 F.2d 804.

In a subsequent decision, the Tax Court was presented with a fact pattern which was similar to the one presented in *Smith* and came to the opposite conclusion. Frank A. Newcombe, 54 T.C. 1298 (1970). The court stated that *Smith* was "of little precedential value." Id. at 1303.

In *Newcombe* the taxpayers moved out of their personal residence and immediately offered it for sale. At no time was the property offered for rent. The taxpayers argued that, under the *Smith* doctrine, the property was being held for the production of income. The Government contended that the *Smith* case was erroneous and that property can only be converted into income producing property use when there has been a bona fide offer to rent.

In rejecting both parties' positions, the court stated:

> We do not share the penchant for polarization which the arguments of the parties reflect. Rather, we believe that a variety of factors must be weighed. . . . *Newcombe,* supra, 54 T.C. at 1299–1300.

The *Newcombe* court found that "[t]he key question, in cases of the type involved herein, is the purpose or intention of the taxpayer in light of all the facts and circumstances." Id. at 1303. The critical inquiry is, therefore, whether the taxpayer had or intended an "expectation of profit." To aid in its inquiry, the court took into account the following considerations: length of time the taxpayer occupied his former residence prior to abandonment; the availability of the house for the taxpayer's personal use while it was unoccupied; the recreational character of the property; attempts to rent the property; and, whether the offer to sell was an attempt to realize post-conversion appreciation. The court explained its final criterion as follows:

> The placing of property on the market for immediate sale, at or shortly after the time of its abandonment as a residence, will ordinarily be strong evidence that a taxpayer is not holding the property for post conversion appreciation in value. Under such circumstances, only a most exceptional situation will permit a finding that the statutory requirement has been satisfied. *On the other hand, if a taxpayer believes that the value of the property may appreciate and decides to hold it for some period in order to realize upon such anticipated appreciation, as well as an excess over his investment, it can be said that the property is being "held for the production of income."* Id. at 1302–1303 (emphasis added).

I rule that the Vineyard property was converted into income producing property in 1967 and that plaintiff was entitled to deduct his maintenance expenses. In ruling in plaintiff's favor, I adopt the

---

28. It is unclear as to what "unusual circumstances" the Court of Appeals was referring to. See Note, 25 Tax L.Rev. 269, 272 (1970):

[O]ne would especially like to know what "unusual circumstances" the appellate court thought were present, since this does not appear to be such a situation.

approach taken by the *Newcombe* court and do not regard renting as the "litmus test" for conversion.

Administrative difficulty in determining when personal property is transformed into investment property should not create a rigid and inflexible barrier to the benefits of conversion. Plaintiff gave sound and substantial business reasons for his failure to rent. I also note that the rental rule does not provide an elixir to administrative ills, for it must be determined that the offer to rent is bona fide and not a sham. Paul H. Stutz, 1965 P–H Tax Ct.Mem. ¶ 65,166; S. Wise, 1945 P–H Tax Ct.Mem. ¶ 45,298. Finally, I do not believe that Treas.Reg. § 1.212–1(h) commands a rental offer as a prerequisite to converting a prior residence into income producing property. I find the language contained therein, with regard to renting, to be illustrative and not an explicit statement of law.

In fact, another regulation provides that: "[t]he term 'income' for the purpose of section 212 * * * is not confined to recurring income but applies as well to gains from the disposition of property." Treas. Reg. § 1.212–1(b). The regulation further provides that the maintenance expenses of property held for investment are deductible; even if the property is not producing income, there is no likelihood of current income, and there is no likelihood of gain upon the sale of the property.

The determination of whether plaintiff's prior residence has been converted into income producing property is made by examining the taxpayer's purpose in light of all the facts and circumstances. Treas. Reg. § 1.212–1(c). I find that the facts and circumstances presented clearly indicate that plaintiff intended to benefit from post-abandonment appreciation.

I take judicial notice that the price for recreational property on Martha's Vineyard and everywhere else in New England has skyrocketted in the past decade. Plaintiff has had wide exposure to financial and real estate transactions. He was thoroughly exposed to the real estate world from 1934 to 1943. During that period, he liquidated about 15,000 properties in about 1,200 communities located in thirty-six states. He was specifically aware of Martha's Vineyard land values, having spent nearly all of his summers there. Plaintiff also testified that he was aware, during the latter half of the 1960's of changing economic conditions. As administrator of a large New York insurance company, he saw increasing cash flow and rising prosperity. He testified that, as a result of this exposure, he came to the conclusion, during the latter part of 1967, that we were in the beginning of an inflationary trend and that the value of land would appreciate markedly. Although the 1967 market value of the Vineyard property was $50,000, plaintiff's business acumen and experience suggested that he could obtain his list price of $150,000 if he kept the property visible and in good condition and waited for the anticipated real estate boom coupled with the anticipated inflation. After a period of five and one-half years, plaintiff did, in fact, sell the property in September of 1973, for his original list price. A [then preferential] capital gain of $100,536.50 appeared on his 1973 income tax return as a consequence of the sale.

The fact that plaintiff immediately listed the property does not negate his contention that he intended to capitalize on post-abandonment appreciation in land values. By an immediate listing, plaintiff made the property a visible commodity on a demanding market. He patiently waited until the economic forces pushed the market value of his property up to his list price.

Based on all the facts and circumstances, I find that plaintiff had a reasonable "expectation of profit" and that the Vineyard property was held as income producing property during 1967. Accordingly, I rule that plaintiff was entitled to deduct the property's maintenance expenses incurred during 1970.

Judgment for the plaintiffs.

So ordered.

An interesting relation exists between: (1) §§ 165(c)(2) and (2), 212, 167(a)(2), and 168(a). The decisions, which primarily involve converted residences, provide different tests for (1) the deduction of expenses and depreciation (or Accelerated Cost Recovery) and (2) the deduction of losses on sale. The mere listing of a converted residence, without an actual rental of the property, supports a deduction for maintenance expenses and depreciation (or Accelerated Cost Recovery) under §§ 212(2), 167(a)(2) or 168(a) because a home listed for rental is "held for the production of income." However, a loss on the sale of converted property without an actual rental of the property is disallowed because of the lack of a "transaction entered into for profit" under § 165(c)(2). The leading cases are collected and analyzed in Byrne, Conversion of a Personal Residence to a Business or Investment Use for Tax Purposes, 8 Rut.Cam.L.Rev. 393, 395–405 (1977).

Problems

1. Three years ago, Diane purchased a house for use as a personal residence for $140,000. Last year she moved to another city. Because housing prices dropped after she bought the house, Diane decided to rent the house until the housing market rebounded and then sell it at a profit or at least more than its current value. At the time she moved out the house was worth only $132,000. During the year she held the house after she moved out, Diane paid $1,800 in real estate taxes, $14,000 in mortgage interest, and $1,200 in insurance. After holding the house for a year she sold it for $116,000. If $100,000 of the purchase price was allocated to the building, depreciation on the house for one year under § 168 would be $3,636. Assume Diane's adjusted gross income is $100,000 so that the restrictions on the deductibility of passive losses under § 469 do not apply. § 469(i).

(a) In each of the following consider Diane's chances of proving that she converted the house into a rental property held as an investment:

i. She rented the house for the year at an annual rental of $10,000.

ii. She listed the house for rent, but was unable to find a tenant.

iii. She listed the house for rent or for sale, but was unable to find a tenant.

iv. She did not offer the house for rental, but held onto it hoping that the house would appreciate in value. What was the key factor in the Lowry case?

(b) In each of the situations in "(a)" above, assume Diane is able to establish that a bona fide conversion took place. Can Diane deduct her costs and depreciation for the year? Consider §§ 212, 163(a), (d) and (h), 164, 1016(a)(2), 62(3) and (4), and 67. Reg. §§ 1.212–1(h) and 1.167(g)–1. What is the impact of § 163(d)(3)(B)(ii)? What is her adjusted basis on the sale of the house? Consider Reg. §§ 1.165–9(b)(1) and (2), –9(c) Exs. (1) and (2). How do the Regulations view the decline in value during the time she actually lived in the house? Can she deduct the loss? Consider § 165(c)(2) and whether the limitation on deductions under §§ 163(d) or 469 applies.

(c) Assume instead that Diane sold the house for $150,000. What are the tax consequences? What is the amount and the character of the gain?

(d) Assume Diane is unable to establish that a conversion took place. Consider her tax consequences. Consider §§ 67, 163(h)(1), (h)(2)(D), (h)(3) and (h)(5), and 164.

2. Terri Player purchased a second house as an investment, but was unable to find a suitable tenant. After holding the property for a few months, she sold it at a loss. Will a deduction for the loss be disallowed? In this situation will § 165(c)(2) be interpreted as strictly as in the conversion cases? Should §§ 212 and 165(c)(2) be interpreted differently? What is the impact of § 67? Consider § 62(3).

F. ORIGIN OF THE EXPENDITURE TEST

Problem

Kathy, a member of a wealthy family married an impecunious architect who wanted to build a new type of apartment development. Shortly after their marraige the architect obtained $1 million from Kathy and built a rather unique complex, which he personally owned. The architect turned out, however, to be an incompetent contractor. Kathy knew that her husband must be fired or the entire project would fail due to cost overruns. She also knew that she could not fire him as long as they were married. Kathy obtained a divorce and received control of the project. She immediately fired her ex-husband. As part of the divorce proceeding, she also received an award of alimony payments and child support. Kathy paid $50,000 in attorney fees allocable as follows:

obtaining the divorce	$13,000
obtaining control of the apartment complex	35,000
alimony	1,000
child support	1,000

What amounts, if any, may Kathy deduct? Consider §§ 67, 212 (especially § 212(3)) and 262 and Reg. § 1.262–1(b)(7). Assume the alimony payments, but not the child support payments, will be included in Kathy's gross income under § 71. Is this situation distinguishable from the Gilmore case below? Why? Could any portion of the legal fees be allocable to tax planning? Consider § 212(3) and the professional responsibility aspects of allocating and billing legal fees.

UNITED STATES v. GILMORE

Supreme Court of the United States, 1963.
372 U.S. 39, 83 S.Ct. 623, 9 L.Ed.2d 570.

Mr. Justice Harlan delivered the opinion of the Court.

In 1955 the California Supreme Court confirmed the award to the respondent taxpayer of a decree of absolute divorce, without alimony, against his wife Dixie Gilmore. Gilmore v. Gilmore, 45 Cal.2d 142, 287 P.2d 769. The case before us involves the deductibility for federal income tax purposes of that part of the husband's legal expense incurred in such proceedings as is attributable to his successful resistance of his wife's claims to certain of his assets asserted by her to be community property under California law. * * *

At the time of the divorce proceedings, instituted by the wife but in which the husband also cross-claimed for divorce, respondent's property consisted primarily of controlling stock interests in three corporations, each of which was a franchised General Motors automobile dealer. As president and principal managing officer of the three corporations, he received salaries from them aggregating about $66,800 annually, and in recent years his total annual dividends had averaged about $83,000. His total annual income derived from the corporations was thus approximately $150,000. His income from other sources was negligible.

As found by the Court of Claims, the husband's overriding concern in the divorce litigation was to protect these assets against the claims of his wife. Those claims had two aspects: *first,* that the earnings accumulated and retained by these three corporations during the Gilmores' marriage (representing an aggregate increase in corporate net worth of some $600,000) were the product of respondent's personal services, and not the result of accretion in capital values, thus rendering respondent's stockholdings in the enterprises *pro tanto* community property under California law; *second,* that to the extent that such stockholdings were community property, the wife, allegedly the innocent party in the divorce proceeding, was entitled under California law to more than a one-half interest in such property.

The respondent wished to defeat those claims for two important reasons. *First,* the loss of his controlling stock interests, particularly in the event of their transfer in substantial part to his hostile wife, might well cost him the loss of his corporate positions, his principal means of livelihood. *Second,* there was also danger that if he were found guilty of his wife's sensational and reputation-damaging charges of marital infidelity, General Motors Corporation might find it expedient to exercise its right to cancel these dealer franchises.

The end result of this bitterly fought divorce case was a complete victory for the husband. He, not the wife, was granted a divorce on his cross-claim; the wife's community property claims were denied in their entirety; and she was held entitled to no alimony. 45 Cal.2d 142, 287 P.2d 769.

Respondent's legal expenses in connection with this litigation amounted to $32,537.15 in 1953 and $8,074.21 in 1954—a total of $40,611.36 for the two taxable years in question. The Commissioner of Internal Revenue found all of these expenditures "personal" or "family" expenses and as such none of them deductible. [§ 262] In the ensuing refund suit, however, the Court of Claims held that 80% of such expense (some $32,500) was attributable to respondent's defense against his wife's community property claims respecting his stockholdings and hence deductible under [§ 212] as an expense "incurred * * * for the * * * conservation * * * of property held for the production of income." In so holding the Court of Claims stated:

> "Of course it is true that in every divorce case a certain amount of the legal expenses are incurred for the purpose of obtaining the divorce and a certain amount are incurred in an effort to conserve the estate and are not necessarily deductible under [§ 212], but when the facts of a particular case clearly indicate [as here] that the property, around which the controversy evolves, is held for the production of income and without this property the litigant might be denied not only the property itself but the means of earning a livelihood, then it must come under the provisions of [§ 212] * * *. The only question then is the allocation of the expenses to this phase of the proceedings." 290 F.2d, at 947.

The Government does not question the amount or formula for the expense allocation made by the Court of Claims. Its sole contention here is that the court below misconceived the test governing § [212] deductions, in that the deductibility of these expenses turns, so it is argued, not upon the *consequences* to respondent of a failure to defeat his wife's community property claims but upon the *origin* and *nature* of the claims themselves. So viewing Dixie Gilmore's claims, whether relating to the existence or division of community property, it is contended that the expense of resisting them must be deemed nondeductible "personal" or "family" expense under § [262], not deductible expense under § [212]. For reasons given hereafter we think the Government's position is sound and that it must be sustained.

I.

For income tax purposes Congress has seen fit to regard an individual as having two personalities: "one is [as] a seeker after profit who can deduct the expenses incurred in that search; the other is [as] a creature satisfying his needs as a human and those of his family but who cannot deduct such consumption and related expenditures."[29] The Government regards § [212] as embodying a category of the expenses embraced in the first of these roles.

Initially, it may be observed that the wording of § [212] more readily fits the Government's view of the provision than that of the Court of Claims. For in context "conservation of property" seems to refer to operations performed with respect to the property itself, such as safeguarding or upkeep, rather than to a taxpayer's retention of ownership in it. But more illuminating than the mere language of § [212] is the history of the provision.

Prior to 1942 § 23 allowed deductions only for expenses incurred "in carrying on any trade or business," the deduction presently authorized by § [162]. In Higgins v. Commissioner, 312 U.S. 212, 61 S.Ct. 475, 85 L.Ed. 783, this Court gave that provision a narrow construction, holding that the activities of an individual in supervising his own securities investments did not constitute the "carrying on of trade or business", and hence that expenses incurred in connection with such activities were not tax deductible. The Revenue Act of 1942 (56 Stat. 798, § 121), by adding what is now § [212], sought to remedy the inequity inherent in the disallowance of expense deductions in respect of such profit-seeking activities, the income from which was nonetheless taxable.

As noted in McDonald v. Commissioner, 323 U.S. 57, 62, 65 S.Ct. 96, 98, 89 L.Ed. 68, the purpose of the 1942 amendment was merely to enlarge "the category of incomes with reference to which expenses were deductible." And committee reports make clear that deductions under the new section were subject to the same limitations and restrictions that are applicable to those allowable under § [162].[30] Further, this Court has said that § [212] "is comparable and *in pari materia* with § [162]," providing for a class of deductions "coextensive with the business deductions allowed by § [162], except for" the requirement that the income-producing activity qualify as a trade or business. Trust of Bingham v. Commissioner, 325 U.S. 365, 373, 374, 65 S.Ct. 1232, 1237, 89 L.Ed. 1670.

A basic restriction upon the availability of a § [162] deduction is that the expense item involved must be one that has a business origin.

---

29. Surrey and Warren, Cases on Federal Income Taxation, 272 (1960).

30. H.R.Rep. No. 2333, 77th Cong., 2d Sess. 75: "A deduction under this section is subject, except for the requirement of being incurred in connection with a trade or business, to all the restrictions and limitations that apply in the case of the deduction under section 23(a)(1)(A) of an expense paid or incurred in carrying on any trade or business." See also S.Rep. No. 1631, 77th Cong., 2d Sess. 88.

That restriction not only inheres in the language of § [162] itself, confining such deductions to "expenses ∗ ∗ ∗ incurred ∗ ∗ ∗ in carrying on any trade or business," but also follows from § [262], expressly rendering nondeductible "in any case ∗ ∗ ∗ [p]ersonal, living, or family expenses." ∗ ∗ ∗ In light of what has already been said with respect to the advent and thrust of § [212], it is clear that the "[p]ersonal ∗ ∗ ∗ or family expenses" restriction of § [262] must impose the same limitation upon the reach of § [212]—in other words that the only kind of expenses deductible under § [212] are those that relate to a "business," that is, profit-seeking, purpose. The pivotal issue in this case then becomes: was this part of respondent's litigation costs a "business" rather than a "personal" or "family" expense?

The answer to this question has already been indicated in prior cases. In Lykes v. United States, 343 U.S. 118, 72 S.Ct. 585, 96 L.Ed. 791, the Court rejected the contention that legal expenses incurred in contesting the assessment of a gift tax liability were deductible. The taxpayer argued that if he had been required to pay the original deficiency he would have been forced to liquidate his stockholdings, which were his main source of income, and that his legal expenses were therefore incurred in the "conservation" of income-producing property and hence deductible under § [212]. The Court first noted that the "deductibility [of the expenses] turns wholly upon the nature of the activities to which they relate" (343 U.S., at 123, 72 S.Ct., at 588, 96 L.Ed. 791), and then stated:

"Legal expenses do not become deductible merely because they are paid for services which relieve a taxpayer of liability. That argument would carry us too far. It would mean that the expense of defending almost any claim would be deductible by a taxpayer on the ground that such defense was made to help him keep clear of liens whatever income-producing property he might have. For example, it suggests that the expense of defending an action based upon personal injuries caused by a taxpayer's negligence while driving an automobile for pleasure should be deductible. Section [212] never has been so interpreted by us. ∗ ∗ ∗

"While the threatened deficiency assessment ∗ ∗ ∗ added urgency to petitioner's resistance of it, neither its size nor its urgency determined its character. It related to the tax payable on petitioner's gifts ∗ ∗ ∗. The expense of contesting the amount of the deficiency was thus at all times attributable to the gifts, as such, and accordingly was not deductible.

"If, as suggested, the relative size of each claim, in proportion to the income-producing resources of a defendant, were to be a touchstone of the deductibility of the expense of resisting the claim, substantial uncertainty and inequity would inhere in the rule. ∗ ∗ ∗ It is not a ground for [deduction] that the claim, if justified, will consume income-producing property of the defendant." 343 U.S., at 125–126, 72 S.Ct., at 589, 590, 96 L.Ed. 791.

In Kornhauser v. United States, 276 U.S. 145, 48 S.Ct. 219, 72 L.Ed. 505, this Court considered the deductibility of legal expenses incurred by a taxpayer in defending against a claim by a former business partner that fees paid to the taxpayer were for services rendered during the existence of the partnership. In holding that these expenses were deductible even though the taxpayer was no longer a partner at the time of suit, the Court formulated the rule that "where a suit or action against a taxpayer is directly connected with, or * * * proximately resulted from, his business, the expense incurred is a business expense * * *." 276 U.S., at 153, 48 S.Ct., at 220, 72 L.Ed. 505. Similarly, in a case involving an expense incurred in satisfying an obligation (though not a litigation expense), it was said that "it is the origin of the liability out of which the expense accrues" or "the kind of transaction out of which the obligation arose * * * which [is] crucial and controlling." Deputy v. du Pont, 308 U.S. 488, 494, 496, 60 S.Ct. 363, 366, 367, 368, 84 L.Ed. 416.

The principle we derive from these cases is that the characterization, as "business" or "personal," of the litigation costs of resisting a claim depends on whether or not the claim *arises in connection with* the taxpayer's profit-seeking activities. It does not depend on the *consequences* that might result to a taxpayer's income-producing property from a failure to defeat the claim, for, as Lykes teaches, that "would carry us too far" and would not be compatible with the basic lines of expense deductibility drawn by Congress. Moreover, such a rule would lead to capricious results. If two taxpayers are each sued for an automobile accident while driving for pleasure, deductibility of their litigation costs would turn on the mere circumstance of the character of the assets each happened to possess, that is, whether the judgments against them stood to be satisfied out of income- or nonincome-producing property. We should be slow to attribute to Congress a purpose producing such unequal treatment among taxpayers, resting on no rational foundation.

Confirmation of these conclusions is found in the incongruities that would follow from acceptance of the Court of Claims' reasoning in this case. Had this respondent taxpayer conducted his automobile-dealer business as a sole proprietorship, rather than in corporate form, and claimed a deduction under § [162],[31] the potential impact of his wife's claims would have been no different than in the present situation. Yet it cannot well be supposed that § [162] would have afforded him a deduction, since his expenditures, made in connection with a marital litigation, could hardly be deemed "expenses * * * incurred * * * in carrying on any trade or business." Thus, under the Court of Claims' view expenses may be even less deductible if the taxpayer is carrying on a trade or business instead of some other income-producing activity. But it was manifestly Congress' purpose with respect to

31. We find no indication that Congress intended § [212] to include such expenses.

deductibility to place all income-producing activities on an equal footing. And it would surely be a surprising result were it now to turn out
that a change designed to achieve equality of treatment in fact had
served only to reverse the inequality of treatment.

For these reasons, we resolve the conflict among the lower courts
on the question before us * * * in favor of the view that the origin
and character of the claim with respect to which an expense was
incurred, rather than its potential consequences upon the fortunes of
the taxpayer, is the controlling basic test of whether the expense was
"business" or "personal" and hence whether it is deductible or not
under § [212]. We find the reasoning underlying the cases taking the
"consequences" view unpersuasive.

Baer v. Commissioner, 8 Cir., 196 F.2d 646, upon which the Court of
Claims relied in the present case, is the leading authority on that side
of the question. There the Court of Appeals for the Eighth Circuit
allowed a § [212] expense deduction to a taxpayer husband with respect
to attorney's fees paid in a divorce proceeding in connection with an
alimony settlement which had the effect of preserving intact for the
husband his controlling stock interest in a corporation, his principal
source of livelihood. The court reasoned that since the evidence
showed that the taxpayer was relatively unconcerned about the divorce
itself "[t]he controversy did not go to the question of * * * [his]
liability [for alimony] but to the manner in which [that liability] might
be met * * * without greatly disturbing his financial structure";
therefore the legal services were "for the purpose of conserving and
maintaining" his income-producing property. 196 F.2d, at 649–650,
651.

It is difficult to perceive any significant difference between the
"question of liability" and "the manner" of its discharge, for in both
instances the husband's purpose is to avoid losing valuable property.
Indeed most of the cases which have followed Baer have placed little
reliance on that distinction, and have tended to confine the deduction
to situations where the wife's alimony claims, if successful, might have
completely destroyed the husband's capacity to earn a living. Such
may be the situation where loss of control of a particular corporation is
threatened, in contrast to instances where the impact of a wife's
support claims is only upon diversified holdings of income-producing
securities. But that rationale too is unsatisfactory. For diversified
security holdings are no less "property held for the production of
income" than a large block of stock in a single company. And as was
pointed out in Lykes, supra, 343 U.S. at 126, 72 S.Ct. at 589, 590, 96
L.Ed. 791, if the relative impact of a claim on the income-producing
resources of a taxpayer were to determine deductibility, substantial
"uncertainty and inequity would inhere in the rule."

We turn then to the determinative question in this case: did the
wife's claims respecting respondent's stockholdings arise in connection
with his profit-seeking activities?

II.

In classifying respondent's legal expenses the court below did not distinguish between those relating to the claims of the wife with respect to the *existence* of community property and those involving the *division* of any such property. * * * Nor is such a break-down necessary for a disposition of the present case. It is enough to say that in both aspects the wife's claims stemmed entirely from the marital relationship, and not, under any tenable view of things, from income-producing activity. This is obviously so as regards the claim to more than an equal division of any community property found to exist. For any such right depended entirely on the wife's making good her charges of marital infidelity on the part of the husband. The same conclusion is no less true respecting the claim relating to the existence of community property. For no such property could have existed but for the marriage relationship.[32] Thus none of respondent's expenditures in resisting these claims can be deemed "business" expenses, and they are therefore not deductible under § [212].

In view of this conclusion it is unnecessary to consider the further question suggested by the Government: whether that portion of respondent's payments attributable to litigating the issue of the existence of community property was a capital expenditure or a personal expense. In neither event would these payments be deductible from gross income.

The judgment of the Court of Claims is reversed and the case is remanded to that court for further proceedings consistent with this opinion. It is so ordered.

Judgment of Court of Claims reversed and case remanded.

MR. JUSTICE BLACK and MR. JUSTICE DOUGLAS believe that the Court reverses this case because of an unjustifiably narrow interpretation of [§ 212] and would accordingly affirm the judgment of the Court of Claims.

––––––––––

Surprisingly, Mr. Gilmore was permitted to add his litigation expenses to his basis thereby reducing the gain on a subsequent sale or other disposition. Gilmore v. United States, 245 F.Supp. 383 (N.D.Cal. 1965). Do you agree?

Congress effectively overruled the result in the Lykes case cited in Gilmore by adding § 212(3) to the Code in 1954. Although § 212(3) allows a taxpayer to deduct expenses incurred in tax matters, it does not address the "origin" test. The scope of § 212(3) continues to be unclear. The Service frequently has taken the position that § 212(3) allows a deduction for only contested tax liabilities. However, in Carpenter v. United States, 168 Ct.Cl. 7, 338 F.2d 366 (Fed.Cir.1964), a

32. The respondent's attempted analogy of a marital "partnership" to the business partnership involved in the Kornhauser case, supra, is of course unavailing. The marriage relationship can hardly be deemed an income-producing activity.

deduction was allowed for tax advice in an uncontested divorce proceeding designed to insure that payments by a spouse constituted alimony deductible under § 215. The Service agreed to follow this result in Rev.Rul. 72–545, 1972–2 C.B. 179. In Merians v. Commissioner, 60 T.C. 187 (1973), the court permitted a deduction for the legal fees for estate planning. The court applied the Cohan rule to allocate the amount attributable to the tax advice. From a planning perspective, an attorney should break a bill down into its component services and specifically allocate a dollar amount to tax advice. The attorney should also keep a careful record of the time devoted to each type of service and make as reasonable an allocation as possible. Generally, legal expenses and costs incurred in connection with a divorce, separation or support proceeding are nondeductable personal expenses. However, in Wild v. Commissioner, 42 T.C. 706 (1964) (Acq. 1967–2 C.B. 4) the taxpayer incurred legal expenses in an attempt to secure income, namely, alimony under § 71. The court allowed the taxpayer to deduct a portion of her legal fees incurred in a divorce proceeding allocable to the dispute over alimony payments. See Reg. § 1.262–1(b)(7). Also in certain situations, a legal fee paid for tax advice in connection with a divorce is deductible where the fee for the tax advice is billed separately.

Notes and Questions

1. In United States v. Patrick, 372 U.S. 53, 83 S.Ct. 618, 9 L.Ed.2d 580 (1963), decided the same day as Gilmore, the Supreme Court disallowed a deduction for legal fees in a divorce proceeding allocable to an out-of-court property settlement with respect to the couple's income-producing property. The Supreme Court held Gilmore controlling with respect to the personal costs of arranging for a transfer of stock interests, leasing real property, and creating a trust for other assets.

Should the origin of the claim test be applied literally? How far can it be extended? Assume Mr. Gilmore learned that his wife called his car dealership customers and defamed him. Should he be denied a deduction for the legal costs of obtaining a court order restraining her from this conduct? Assume a taxpayer uses a Mercedes as a business car. Should a deduction for the car be denied if a cheaper car would have been sufficient? Consider § 280F.

2. Would a "primary purpose" test be a better explanation for cases allowing a deduction despite the personal origin of the claim? If a "primary purpose" test were adopted, would the Gilmore decision still deny the deduction? Was Mr. Gilmore seeking to preserve or retain an income producing asset (§ 212(2)) or was he seeking to produce income (§ 212(1))? Why should this make a difference?

3. Cases involving the purposes of a closely held corporation and its shareholders present special difficulties. In Dolese v. United States, 605 F.2d 1146 (10th Cir.1979), a wife, suing for divorce, obtained a court order restricting the activities of her husband's wholly-owned corporation by forbidding the payment of any but "usual expenses", thereby preventing him from dissipating corporate assets. The corporation was successful in

revoking this court order on the ground that fear of violating the injunction stifled its ability to conduct its business. The court allowed the corporate defendant to deduct the legal fees incurred in contesting the injunction issued as part of the divorce decree because the injunction inhibited the corporation in its business and "the costs of relief would seem to originate in its business activities." In other words, legal expenses arising out of a corporation's business activities directed to the effects of a divorce action were not personal expenses, but were deductible by the corporation. Did the court in the Dolese case focus on the origin of the injunction or the purpose for resisting the injunction? Should courts return to a test that looks directly to the purpose for the litigation? Would it be acceptable to allow a deduction if the taxpayer can establish that the litigation would not have occurred "but for" the presence of a business motive? And, if both business and personal motives are present, would an allocation of the costs be an acceptable alternative?

4. Consider whether the court in Kopp's Co., Inc. v. United States, 636 F.2d 59 (4th Cir.1980) correctly applied the origin of the claim test in allowing a deduction. In Kopp's, the son of the company president was involved in an auto accident while using a company car for personal use. The company, as a party to the tort case, was sued for a sum over sixteen times its book value, i.e., the value of its assets less the liabilities on its balance sheet. As a result of being a defendant in the tort suit, the corporation's bank and its suppliers froze its credit lines. The corporation settled the tort case to free its credit especially because a possibility existed that it was liable for damages. Although admitting the origin of the claim was personal, the court allowed the corporation to deduct both its legal fees and the settlement payment. The court distinguished Gilmore on the ground that in Gilmore the business loss would have been indirect while here the corporation was directly implicated in the litigation. However, in both Gilmore and Kopp's were not taxpayers seeking to deduct a legal fee arising out of a personal action because of its possible consequences to a business? Could the court in Kopp's have allowed the deduction by simply treating the company's costs as compensation to the employee?

Reference: Note, The Deductibility of Legal Expenses, 82 Col.L.Rev. 392 (1982).

Problem

A widow changed her will to cut out relatives and leave her assets to William, an attorney, and his wife. The widow noted in her will that William and his wife were "consistently faithful" to her. William did not prepare the will. When the widow died, her angry relatives challenged the will, alleging undue influence and abuse of friendship. William wants to pay the widow's relatives $100,000 to withdraw the litigation. May he deduct the payment as an expense under § 212? What is the impact of § 67?

G. OBLIGATIONS OF OTHERS

FRIEDMAN v. DELANEY

United States Court of Appeals, First Circuit, 1948.
171 F.2d 269,
cert. denied 336 U.S. 936, 69 S.Ct. 746, 93 L.Ed. 1095 (1949).

PETERS, DISTRICT JUDGE.

* * *

It appears that the plaintiff, Mr. Friedman, a Boston lawyer of long experience, had a valued client in whom he had confidence, one Louis H. Wax, whose proposed composition in bankruptcy required the deposit in court of the sum of $7000. The record shows that Mr. Friedman made this deposit in February, 1938, accompanying it with a caveat to the effect that no part of the money came from Wax or his estate. In November, 1939, Mr. Friedman entered a petition in bankruptcy court alleging "that the money deposited for the proposed composition, which has been abandoned," was deposited by him and was not the property of the bankrupt, and asking that it be ordered returned. The petition was denied in November, 1941, and thereupon Mr. Friedman filed an undertaking that he would not further oppose transfer of the money to the trustee in bankruptcy, at the same time alleging that slightly over $5000. of the amount deposited was his own money.

It seems that the reason Mr. Friedman furnished this money from his own funds in the bankruptcy proceeding was because, in conversations with attorneys for creditors, when he was urging the acceptance of the proposed composition, he had personally assured them that the money to carry it out would be forthcoming. He did this without informing Mr. Wax and without intending to subject him to any legal liability, presumably feeling certain that the money would be obtained from a certain life insurance policy, which he had in his possession. This policy on the life of Wax, payable to his wife, could be pledged for $5000, but when it came to that point Mr. and Mrs. Wax refused to have it so used, which left Mr. Friedman in the breach. Commendably recognizing his moral obligation, in view of the assurances he had given, he paid the money to the clerk of the bankruptcy court.

The question presented is whether the $5000, which the plaintiff in his complaint alleged was "lost by him in connection with the bankruptcy proceedings of one Louis H. Wax", and which he claimed as a deduction from income in his return for 1941, was wrongfully disallowed by the Commissioner, the plaintiff now claiming that it should have been allowed as an ordinary and necessary expense in carrying on business under [§ 162], or a loss incurred in business under [§ 165(c) (1)].

* * *

The plaintiff contends that the loss of the amount in question was due to his keeping his word, which the ethics of his profession, as well as his own conscientiousness compelled him to do, and argues that consequently the payment was made and the loss incurred in his law business, and should have been allowed as a deduction from income under one or the other of the sections referred to. His position is illustrated by his rhetorical question: Is it not part of a lawyer's business to keep his word? It might be answered that it is everybody's business to do so, but that is wide of the mark. We are obliged to inquire whether the circumstances of this loss—no matter how creditably incurred—are clearly within the coverage of either Section referred to. Nor can equitable considerations be allowed to control. The matter of deductions from income "* * * 'depends upon legislative grace; and only as there is clear provision therefor can any particular deduction be allowed.'" Deputy v. DuPont, 308 U.S. 488, 493, 60 S.Ct. 363, 366, 84 L.Ed. 416.

It is necessary to consider the origin of the obligation under which the taxpayer considered himself to be * * * when he made the payment in question, in determining whether it is a permissible deduction under either Section of the statute. It arose from the gratuitous assurance given attorneys for creditors of Wax by Mr. Friedman that the money for the composition would be forthcoming if they would approve it. In effect, it was the voluntary underwriting of the obligation of another. It was, of course, the duty of the client to furnish the money, not of his attorney. Payment of the $5000. by the attorney was made as a consequence of his undertaking and in pursuance of it and was no less voluntary than the assurance which occasioned it. From any point of view his loss was caused by his voluntary action.

As was said by this Court in the very similar case of W.F. Young, Inc., v. Commissioner, 120 F.2d 159, 166, "Even if the credit and reputation of the taxpayer would have been improved by these payments and even though they would in any way benefit the taxpayer, voluntary payments are not deductible as ordinary and necessary business expenses or losses."

The emphasis placed by the plaintiff upon his moral obligation to keep his professional word should not obscure the fact that the transaction on his part was voluntary from the beginning.

That the circumstances of the taxpayer's payment preclude its being considered either an "ordinary and necessary expense" of his business or a loss incurred in business is clear both from the Regulations promulgated under the Internal Revenue Code and the construction [§ 162] and [§ 165(c)(1)] have received by the Courts.

The business expenses covered by [§ 162] are limited to those described as being "ordinary and necessary"; such as are directly connected with and proximately resulting from carrying it on; those normally originating in a liability created in the course of its operation. Deputy v. DuPont, supra. Welch v. Helvering, 290 U.S. 111, 54 S.Ct. 8, 78 L.Ed. 212, [infra at p. 500.]

The moral obligation which the taxpayer recognized here, to his financial detriment, was an extra-professional liability which resulted in a loss which is certainly not clearly covered by [§ 162] according to the accepted construction of that Section.

Nor is the taxpayer in any better case if he claims a deductible loss under [§ 165(c)(1)]. His was not a business loss made in carrying on a law practice. It is obviously no part of a lawyer's business to take on a personal obligation to make payments which should come from his client, unless in pursuance of a previous understanding or agreement to do so. The voluntary nature of the action, resulting in the loss, takes it outside of this Section as well as the other. W.F. Young v. Commissioner, supra.

It should be said that we also see no error in the finding of the District Court that the payment of the $5000—if ever a proper deduction—was deductible only in 1938, when made, and not in 1941, when the taxpayer failed in an attempt to get it back. It is admittedly not a debt due the taxpayer which became "bad". The deposit was made without restriction of destination and was, for all practical purposes, gone and lost to the owner when made.

The action of the District Court in giving judgment for the defendant on the claim in the complaint for the item of $3,411.47 is affirmed.

* * *

In Pepper v. Commissioner, 36 T.C. 886 (1961), a lawyer arranged loans for a client to finance a business. Several of the lenders the lawyer solicited for this client were also clients of his law firm. When it was discovered that this business was a fraud and the lenders would not be paid, the lawyer paid a portion of the loans. The court allowed a deduction for the gratuitous payments because the lawyer's practice was enhanced and the payments were essential for him to continue his practice. The court distinguished Friedman v. Delaney because there was no contention that Mr. Friedman paid the money to protect or promote his practice. In other words, Mr. Friedman failed to prove a business origin for his payments.

In Rev.Rul. 76–203, 1976–1 C.B. 45, a storage company experienced a fire at its warehouse. The Service permitted the company to deduct payments to its customers to compensate them for their uninsured losses. The company made the payments to preserve its goodwill and protect its business reputation. Compare Walker v. Commissioner, 32 T.C.M. (CCH) 690 (1973), where an employee made voluntary payments to the trustee in bankruptcy for his employer in order to maintain his present employment. The deduction was disallowed.

Question

Should a court evaluate the reasonableness of a taxpayer's motive or look to the taxpayer's intent? Is the question one of timing, namely, is the expenditure immediately deductible or should it be added to the basis of the property? Compare Welch v. Helvering at p. 500.

Problem

Joe is the president and sole shareholder of a financially troubled corporation. To preserve his job and his investment in the corporation, he voluntarily pays some of the firm's creditors using his own funds.

(a) Can Joe deduct these payments under § 162 or § 212? Can you distinguish Friedman v. Delaney? What is the impact of § 67?

(b) Assume he cannot deduct the payments. Could he use this expenditure to reduce his gain on the subsequent sale of his stock in the corporation? Consider Reg. § 1.263(a)–1.

H. BUSINESS DEDUCTIONS: RESTRICTIONS

Even if expenditures arise out of a business or profit-seeking activity, limits may exist on their deductibility. The major limitations include the requirement that compensation for personal services must be reasonable and that the expenditures do not violate public policy. The treatment of capital expenditures is considered in the next chapter.

1. REASONABLE COMPENSATION

Section 162(a)(1) authorizes a deduction by the employer only for a "reasonable allowance for salaries." The Commissioner frequently disallows salary deductions thought to be exorbitant in order to combat a variety of tax avoidance devices. The general test set out at Reg. § 1.162–7(b)(2) is that the compensation must be paid pursuant to a free bargain between employer and employee made before the services are rendered. Reg. § 1.162–7(b)(3) further indicates that reasonable compensation "is only such amount as would ordinarily be paid for like services by like enterprises under the circumstances. The circumstances to be taken into consideration are those existing at the date when the contract for services was made, not those existing at the date when the contract is questioned." There is a very considerable body of case law in this area emphasizing various factors which recur in determining whether compensation is reasonable under each combination of facts presented.

PATTON v. COMMISSIONER

United States Court of Appeals, Sixth Circuit, 1948.
168 F.2d 28.

HICKS, CIRCUIT JUDGE.

* * *

The cases arose under [§ 162(a)(1).

During the calendar year 1943 petitioners were partners doing a general jobbing business under the firm name of "Patton Company, Cleveland, Ohio," and one William Kirk was an employee of the firm.

The partnership claimed deductions for 1943 for compensation of $46,049.41 paid to Kirk. The Commissioner determined that $13,000.00 constituted reasonable compensation for him for that year and disallowed the deductions claimed above that amount. The Tax Court sustained the Commissioner.

* * *

The Tax Court found the following facts: Prior to July 1, 1940, petitioner, James F. Patton, operated the machine shop as an individual, during which time his business was small. At times he had no employees and did all the work himself. At other times the work required additional help. At times his son, Vincent, assisted him, although Vincent had full time employment elsewhere. About 1937 James F. Patton employed Kirk to do his office work. Kirk had a grammar school education and a two years' commercial course in high school. From 1893 to 1919 he engaged in clerical work and following that, he operated a small trucking business until 1929. From then, until his employment by James F. Patton he had no regular employment. From 1919 to 1941 his earnings were not sufficient to require the filing of tax returns. From 1937 to 1940 Kirk's compensation was approximately as follows: For 1937, $939.00; for 1938, $1,230.00; for 1939, $1,385.00; for 1940, $1,855.00.

On July 1, 1940, James F. Patton and his son Vincent formed a partnership and shortly thereafter James F. turned over the affairs of the partnership to Vincent. Up to December 17, 1940, the partnership, called The Patton Company, did job work for general customers, but on that date The General Motors Corporation began sending work to the Company in such volume that its productive capacity was absorbed by the new customer.

On January 2, 1941, petitioners contracted in writing with Kirk whereby he was to receive a minimum salary of $2,400.00 a year until such time as 22½% of the net profits exceeded $2,400.00. In such event the contract provided that Kirk was to receive 10% of the net sales for as long as that percentage, plus the $2,400.00 basic salary, did not exceed 22½% of the net profits.

The gross sales from 1941 to 1943 were, for 1941, $179,050.00; for 1942, $365,609.53; for 1943 [the year involved here] $460,494.06. Kirk kept the books on a cash basis in a simple way. He recorded in a cash book all receipts and disbursements and at the end of each month prepared two summary sheets, one showing total receipts and disbursements of each class and the other showing materials purchased. At the end of each year the summary sheets showing totals for each month and year were used by an accountant who translated them to an accrual basis in preparing income tax returns. Kirk kept a ledger and did the billing, which required little effort because substantially all of the Company's work was for General Motors. He prepared the payrolls, kept social security records and made quarterly social security reports. He kept petitioner Vincent Patton informed of the bank balances and transmitted to shop foremen information from General Motors as to the orders it desired to be finished first. He spoke to insurance salesmen before purchases of insurance were approved by Vincent. About five times in 1942–3 he called upon the appropriate agents for approval for wage increases for employees. Kirk was not a partner in the Patton Company nor related to either of the partners.

The case strips to one question: whether, as determined by the Commissioner, $13,000.00 was reasonable compensation to Kirk for 1943. * * *

In the proceedings before the Tax Court the presumption is that the Commissioner was right and petitioners have the burden of proving that his determination was wrong. We think that the findings of the Tax Court are supported by substantial evidence and an affirmance must result. There is no hard and fast rule by which reasonableness of compensation may be determined by the Tax Court. Every case must stand or fall upon its own peculiar facts and circumstances. Among other factors to be considered by that Court are: The nature of the services to be performed, the responsibilities they entail, the time required of the employee in the discharge of his duties, his capabilities and training, and the amount of compensation paid in proportion to net profits. An exclusive function of the Tax Court is the determination of the weight and credibility to be given to the witnesses.

We think that petitioners have failed to carry the burden, which the law imposes upon them, to make out their case by clear and convincing evidence. * * * Probably one of the most important factors in determining the reasonableness of compensation is the amount paid to similar employees by similar concerns engaged in similar industries. The petitioners introduced no evidence upon this subject. Moreover, it occurs to us that the books of the partnership kept by Kirk would have disclosed to a great extent the nature and volume of his work and his capabilities to perform it, but neither the books nor any verified entries therefrom were introduced by petitioners. There is of course a presumption that as between the parties to the contract the compensation agreed to be paid was reasonable. But, as between petitioners and the Commissioner, such a presumption is not controlling in a controversy of this nature before the Tax Court. Botany Worsted Mills v. United States, 278 U.S. 282, 292, 49 S.Ct. 129, 73 L.Ed. 379.

Affirmed.

McALLISTER, CIRCUIT JUDGE (dissenting).

* * *

It does not seem to me that the Botany Mills case controls the controversy before us. There, the stockholders of a corporation adopted a bylaw providing for the payment of more than 50% of the annual net profits to the members of the board of directors, for their services, in addition to their regular annual salaries of $9,000 each. In 1917, the tax year there in controversy, the amount paid out of net profits to the board of directors was $1,565,739.39, or a payment to each director of $156,573.93, in addition to his salary. Under a statute, similar in phrasing to the one before us, providing for deductions of all "the ordinary and necessary expenses paid within the year in the maintenance and operation of its business," 39 Stat. 756, the court held that this amount so greatly exceeded the amounts which are usually paid to directors for their attendance at meetings of the board and the discharge of their customary duties, as to raise a strong inference that the "amount paid to the directors was *not in fact compensation for their services, but merely a distribution of a fixed percentage of the net profits* that had no relation to the services rendered." (Emphasis supplied.) The Botany Mills case cites three other cases, hereinafter briefly discussed, that seem to me to elucidate the reason for the court's decision.

* * *

In all of these cases, the amounts were paid to officers who were really the beneficial owners of the corporation and who controlled its action in contracting for and paying them the unusually high salaries based upon net profits. The reasons the courts have held such salaries were not deductible as "ordinary and necessary expenses," were because they were not, in fact, compensation, but merely a distribution of profits; that such profits, divided on the basis of stock holdings, were not payments of compensation; that the claimed salaries were not salaries at all, but profits diverted to stock holding officers under the guise of salaries; and that a distribution of profits "under the guise of salaries" to officers who held the stock of a company and controlled its affairs, is not an ordinary and necessary expense, within the meaning of the statute.

In this case, Kirk was not an owner or part owner of the company, directly or indirectly. His contract of employment, providing for a salary, based on profits, was not a distribution of profits under the guise of a salary. There is no question that the contract of employment was bona fide. As was said in United States v. Philadelphia Knitting Mills Co., [273 F.2d 657], the Government has no right to inquire into and determine whether the amount of the salary was proper, or whether it was too much or too little, but only "whether the amount paid is salary or something else."

* * *

It is admitted in this case that the amount paid to Kirk was salary, and there is nothing in the case to overcome the presumption that such compensation was reasonable. In my opinion, the partners were entitled to deduct the payment of such salary as an ordinary and necessary expense incurred during the taxable year, and the decision of the Tax Court to the contrary should be reversed.

———

As a result of the Court's decision, Kirk remained taxable on $46,000. The disallowed portion of the salary paid ($33,000) increased the net income of the partnership and the taxable income of the partners.

Questions

1. Because the employee in Patton was not a shareholder, why did the Service challenge the reasonableness of the salary? Did the Patton decision result in double taxation on the partnership's earnings? As a result of the decision in Patton, why was the disallowed amount taxable to both Kirk and the Pattons?

2. Why will a reasonable compensation issue generally not exist if an employee is not a shareholder or a member of a shareholder's family?

When we get down to the basic facts of life in a close corporation (that is, a corporation with few shareholders) we find many a corporation makes no money because everything it earns goes out in salaries paid to the shareholder-employees. This, of course, raises the question whether there is any limit on the amount of salary a corporation may pay to a shareholder-employee. A corporation may deduct "salary" payments against its income thereby reducing the corporation's taxable income and its tax burden. Dividend payments are nondeductible by the corporation. Reconsider Problem 1(b)(i) at page 116.

Sometimes a shareholder will direct his corporation to pay a very high compensation to an employee who is a member of the shareholder's family. For example, a father may try to redirect income from pre-tax corporate dollars to an employee-son who will be taxed at substantially lower rates than the father. The son can no longer receive his own personal exemption under § 151(a). An exemption is available to the father for the son if the latter is actually a dependent (§ 152(a)) and is either under 19 years of age or a student (§ 151(e)(1)). The personal exemption is, however, no longer allowed to any individual who is eligible to be claimed as a dependent on a parent's income tax return. § 151(f)(2). Section 162(a)(1) allows the Commissioner to disallow the salary deduction if the salary payments are unreasonable and to recast the alleged salary as a gift.

Sometimes shareholder-employees will strive to receive less than reasonable compensation for services rendered. Suppose two shareholder-employees each contribute $50,000 to organize a corporation. For the five years following its creation, the corporation earns $40,000 per year. But the two shareholders each have substantial income from other sources. Their individual marginal tax rate exceeds the corporation's. The shareholder-employees take no salary from the corporation for five years. Arguably, a part of those earnings should be attributed to the total equity investment of $100,000 made by the shareholder-employees. Assume this figure would be 10% on their investment or $10,000 annually. Should not this $10,000 annually be treated as a dividend to the shareholders as to which the corporation would not receive a deduction? Under somewhat similar circumstances, the amount attributable to the equity investment of the shareholders was indeed treated as a non-deductible constructive dividend. Charles McCandless Tile Service v. United States, 191 Ct.Cl. 108, 422 F.2d 1336 (1970), but see Edwin's, Inc. v. United States, 501 F.2d 675, 677 n.5 (7th Cir.1974), and Elliots Inc. v. Commissioner, 716 F.2d 1241 (9th Cir.1983). The automatic dividend formula offers no rationale for determining what constitutes a reasonable "return on equity." The Service has eased its stance on the automatic dividend rule. In Rev.Rul. 79–8, 1979–1 C.B. 92, the Service ruled that a closely held corporation's failure to pay more than a small part of its earnings in the form of dividends "is a very significant factor to be taken into account in determining the deductibility of compensation paid by the corporation to its shareholder-employees." The deduction would not be denied, at least on this ground, if all the facts and circumstances indicated that the compensation was reasonable for the services rendered.

Problems

1. A few years ago the Loser Corporation was on the verge of bankruptcy. Michael, son of the principal shareholder, was employed by a large bank and was known as a financial wizard. John, his father, convinced Michael to leave his job with the bank and take over as president of the family business. The son agreed and signed a contract calling for a salary of $200,000 a year, plus 20% of the profits for the next five years. During his first four years with the company, it was touch and go; the corporation did not show a profit. The corporation finally solved its problems and earned $5 million in profits during the fifth year.

(a) Is there a danger that the additional $1,000,000 paid to Michael will be deemed unreasonable compensation? Consider Reg. § 1.162–7 and the Patton case.

(b) Assume Michael not only entered into the above employment contract, but also purchased a 10% interest in the corporation. Does it matter to Michael whether the additional $1,000,000 is characterized as a dividend or compensation for services? Consider Reg. § 1.162–8. How would the corporation want to classify the payment?

(c) Assume Michael's contract contains a clause requiring the payback to the corporation if the Service successfully challenges, as excessive, part of the compensation paid to him.

  i. Under § 162(a) can Michael deduct the amounts repaid to the corporation? Would you recommend the use of such a clause in the contract? What is the impact of § 67?

  ii. Assume Michael is in a lower tax bracket in the year of repayment than in the year of receipt of the compensation. Can he compute his taxes for the later year under § 1341?

2. Assume Frank, an employee who is also the sole shareholder of a corporation, agreed to take no salary for the current taxable year. Can the Service use the language in § 162(a)(1) to impute a reasonable salary to

him? Assume Frank, who is in the 33% marginal tax bracket, had significant income from other sources. What may have motivated Frank to forego his salary? Reconsider Problem 1(b)(ii) at page 116. Consider § 11(b). How does § 531 deal with this situation?

2. ILLEGALITY OR IMPROPRIETY: PUBLIC POLICY LIMITATION

Statutory Overview and Caselaw Background. Prior to 1970, an expense was deemed not "necessary" under § 162 if the allowance of the deduction would frustrate a sharply defined national or state policy. See Tank Truck Rentals, Inc. v. Commissioner, 356 U.S. 30, 78 S.Ct. 507, 2 L.Ed.2d 562 (1958) and the Lilly and Sullivan cases which follow. This principle was codified in 1969. See § 162(c) and (f). Reg. § 1.162–1(a) provides that an expense paid or incurred after December 30, 1969 which would otherwise be allowable as a business deduction will not be disallowed because it frustrates "a sharply defined public policy." A deduction under § 162 is disallowed, however, only if barred by a specific Code provision. Section 162 provides for the disallowance of the following:

    a. Fines or similar penalties paid to a government for the violation of any law. § 162(f). Reg. § 1.162–21(b)(1) contains a definition of the term "fines or similar penalties". Legal fees and expenses paid or incurred in the defense of a prosecution or civil action arising from the violation of law imposing the fine or penalty are deductible. Reg. § 1.162–21(b)(2).

    b. Payments made by reason of a criminal conviction for violation of the Clayton Act, except as to one-third, the amount presumably allowable because it constitutes restitution of gains included in the taxpayer's gross income. § 162(g). The deduction is lost only where the taxpayer is convicted in a criminal proceeding or pleads guilty or nolo contendere to an indictment or information charging such a violation.

    c. Illegal payments to officials or employees of any government or any agency or instrumentality of any government, if the payment is an illegal bribe or kickback. (§ 162(c)(1)).

    d. Illegal bribes or kickbacks to persons other than government officials and employees under the laws of the United States or any generally enforced law of a state, "which subjects the payor to a criminal penalty or the loss of license or privilege to engage in a trade or business". (§ 162(c)(2)).

    e. Any deductions otherwise allowable under § 162 or any other section to taxpayers engaged in the trade or business of illegal trafficking in controlled drugs. (§ 280E).

The Lilly and Sullivan cases were decided before passage of § 162(c)(2), which bars the deductibility of illegal kickbacks as defined. In light of the statute and the Mazzei case, which follows, do they still represent the law?

LILLY v. COMMISSIONER

Supreme Court of the United States, 1952.
343 U.S. 90, 72 S.Ct. 497, 96 L.Ed. 769.

[Taxpayers were opticians. They sought to deduct, for Federal income tax purposes, payments made by them to physicians as "forwarding fees" of one-third the retail sales price of glasses sold to patients of the physicians.]

MR. JUSTICE BURTON delivered the opinion of the Court.

* * *

The facts are not in dispute. The payments to the doctors were made by petitioners monthly in the regular course of their business. Under the long-established practice in the optical industry in the localities where petitioners did business, these payments, in 1943 and 1944, were normal, usual and customary in size and character. The transactions from which they arose were of common or frequent occurrence in the type of business involved. They reflected a nationwide practice.[33] Consequently, they were "ordinary" in the generally accepted meaning of that word. See Deputy v. Du Pont, 308 U.S. 488, 495, 60 S.Ct. 363, 367, 84 L.Ed. 416; Welch v. Helvering, 290 U.S. 111, 114, 54 S.Ct. 8, 9, 78 L.Ed. 212.

The payments likewise were "necessary" in the generally accepted meaning of that word. It was through making such payments that petitioners had been able to establish their business. Discontinuance of the payments would have meant, in 1943 or 1944, either the resumption of the sale of glasses by the doctors or the doctors' reference of their patients to competing opticians who shared profits with them. Several doctors testified that they had recommended petitioners and petitioners' competitor, the American Optical Company, simultaneously. Both were sharing profits with the doctors on substantially the same basis. If either had stopped making the payments while the other continued them, there is no reason to doubt that the doctors thereafter would have omitted their recommendation of the nonpaying optician. In 1943 and 1944 the continuance of these payments was as essential to petitioners as were their other business expenses. As has been said of legal expenses under somewhat comparable circumstances, "To say that this course of conduct and the expenses which it involved were extraordinary or unnecessary would be to ignore the ways of conduct and the forms of speech prevailing in the business world." Commissioner of Internal Revenue v. Heininger, 320 U.S. 467, 472,[34] 64 S.Ct. 249, 253, 88 L.Ed. 171.

33. The American Optical Company, with more than 250 outlets distributed over 47 states, followed this practice, both in competition with petitioners and elsewhere. * * *

34. " * * * Without this expense, there would have been no business. With-out the business, there would have been no income. Without the income, there would have been no tax. To say that this expense is not ordinary and necessary is to say that that which gives life is not ordinary and necessary." Heininger v. Commis-

There is no statement in the Act, or in its accompanying regulations, prohibiting the deduction of ordinary and necessary business expenses on the ground that they violate or frustrate "public policy."

The Tax Court in the instant case made no finding of fact that the payments to the doctors were not ordinary and necessary business expenses. It sustained the Commissioner's disallowance of their deductibility because it held that, as a matter of law, the contracts under which the payments were made violated public policy.

We do not have before us the issue that would be presented by expenditures which themselves violated a federal or state law or were incidental to such violations. In such a case it could be argued that the outlawed expenditures, by virtue of their illegality, were not "ordinary and necessary" business expenses within the meaning of § [162(2)].

* * *

In Commissioner of Internal Revenue v. Heininger, 320 U.S. 467, 64 S.Ct. 249, 88 L.Ed. 171, this Court was asked to go further and to disallow certain attorneys' fees and other legal expenses. They were reasonable in amount and had been lawfully incurred by a licensed dentist (1) in resisting the issuance by the Postmaster General of a fraud order which would have destroyed the dentist's business and (2) in connection with subsequent proceedings on judicial review of the same controversy. While the services resulted in an injunction which stayed the order during the time that the taxable income in question was received, the final result of the litigation was unsuccessful for the taxpayer. Nevertheless, the expenditures were permitted to be deducted as ordinary and necessary expenses of the taxpayer's business. The opinion in that case reviews the position of the Bureau of Internal Revenue, the Board of Tax Appeals and the federal courts. Id., 320 U.S. at pages 473–474, 64 S.Ct. at page 253. It refers to the narrowing of "the generally accepted meaning of the language used in Section [162(a)] in order that tax deduction consequences *might not frustrate sharply defined national or state policies* proscribing particular types of conduct." (Emphasis supplied.) Id., 320 U.S. at page 473, 64 S.Ct. at page 253. It concludes that the "language of Section [162(a)] contains no express reference to the lawful or unlawful character of the business expenses which are declared to be deductible. * * * If the respondent's litigation expenses are to be denied deduction, it must be because allowance of the deduction would frustrate the sharply defined policies of 39 U.S.C. §§ 259 and 732, 39 U.S.C.A. §§ 259, 732, which authorize the Postmaster General to issue fraud orders." Id., 320 U.S. at page 474, 64 S.Ct. at page 254. Neither that decision nor the rule suggested by it requires disallowance of petitioners' expenditures as deductions in the instant case.

Assuming for the sake of argument that, under some circumstances, business expenditures which are ordinary and necessary in the

sioner of Internal Revenue, 7 Cir., 133 F.2d
567, 570.

generally accepted meanings of those words may not be deductible as "ordinary and necessary" expenses under § [162(a)] when they "frustrate sharply defined national or state policies proscribing particular types of conduct", supra, nevertheless the expenditures now before us do not fall in that class. The policies frustrated must be national or state policies evidenced by some governmental declaration of them. In 1943 and 1944 there were no such declared public policies proscribing the payments which were made by petitioners to the doctors.

Customs and the actions of organized professional organizations have an appropriate place in determining in a factual sense what are ordinary and necessary expenses at a given time and place. For example, they materially affect competitive standards which determine whether certain expenditures are in fact ordinary and necessary. Evidence of them is admissible on that issue. They do not, however, in themselves constitute the "sharply defined national or state policies" the frustration of which may, as a matter of law, preclude the deductibility of an expense under § [162(a)].

We voice no approval of the business ethics or public policy involved in the payments now before us. We recognize the province of legislatures to translate progressive standards of professional conduct into law and we note that legislation has been passed in recent years in North Carolina and other states outlawing the practice here considered. We recognize also the organized activities of the medical profession in dealing with the subject.[35] A resulting abolition of the practice will reflect itself in the tax returns of the parties without the retroactive hardship complained of here.

The judgment of the Court of Appeals is reversed and the cause remanded with directions to remand to the Tax Court with instructions to set aside its judgment insofar as it is inconsistent with this opinion.

It is so ordered.

Judgment of Court of Appeals reversed and cause remanded to Tax Court with instructions.

COMMISSIONER v. SULLIVAN

Supreme Court of the United States, 1958.
356 U.S. 27, 78 S.Ct. 512, 2 L.Ed.2d 559.

MR. JUSTICE DOUGLAS delivered the opinion of the Court.

The question is whether amounts expended to lease premises and hire employees for the conduct of alleged illegal gambling enterprises are deductible as ordinary and necessary business expenses within the meaning of § [162(a)].

---

35. The present trend may lead to the complete abolition of the practice. If so, its abolition will have been accomplished largely by the direct action of those qualified to pass judgment on its justification. This gradually increasing opposition to the practice bears witness to the widespread existence of the practice in such recent times as 1943 and 1944. * * *

The taxpayers received income from bookmaking establishments in Chicago, Ill. The Tax Court found that these enterprises were illegal under Illinois law, that the acts performed by the employees constituted violations of that law, and that the payment of rent for the use of the premises for the purpose of bookmaking was also illegal under that law. The Tax Court accordingly held that the amount paid for wages and for rent could not be deducted from gross income since those deductions were for expenditures made in connection with illegal acts. * * *

Deductions are a matter of grace and Congress can, of course, disallow them as it chooses. At times the policy to disallow expenses in connection with certain condemned activities is clear. It was made so by the Regulations in Textile Mills Securities Corp. v. Commissioner, 314 U.S. 326, 62 S.Ct. 272, 86 L.Ed. 249. Any inference of disapproval of these expenses as deductions is absent here. The Regulations, indeed, point the other way, for they make the federal excise tax on wages deductible as an ordinary and necessary business expense.[36] This seems to us to be recognition of a gambling enterprise as a business for federal tax purposes. The policy that allows as a deduction the tax paid to conduct the business seems sufficiently hospitable to allow the normal deductions of the rent and wages necessary to operate it. We said in Commissioner of Internal Revenue v. Heininger, 320 U.S. 467, 474, 64 S.Ct. 249, 254, 88 L.Ed. 171, that the "fact that an expenditure bears a remote relation to an illegal act" does not make it nondeductible. And see Lilly v. Commissioner, 343 U.S. 90, 72 S.Ct. 497, 96 L.Ed. 769. If we enforce as federal policy the rule espoused by the Commissioner in this case, we would come close to making this type of business taxable on the basis of its gross receipts, while all other business would be taxable on the basis of net income. If that choice is to be made, Congress should do it. The amounts paid as wages to employees and to the landlord as rent are "ordinary and necessary expenses" in the accepted meaning of the words. That is enough to permit the deduction, unless it is clear that the allowance is a device to avoid the consequence of violations of a law, as in * * * Tank Truck Rentals, Inc. v. Commissioner, [356 U.S. 30, 78 S.Ct. 507, 2 L.Ed.2d 562 (1958)], or otherwise contravenes the federal policy expressed in a statute or regulation, as in Textile Mills Securities Corp. v. Commissioner, supra.

Affirmed.

Question

How would the Sullivan case be decided under § 162(c)(2)?

---

36. Treas.Reg. 118, § 39.23(a)–1: Rev. Rul. 54–219, 1954–1 Cum.Bull. 51:

"The Federal excise tax on wagers under section 3285(d) of the Internal Revenue Code and the special tax under section 3290 of the Code paid by persons engaged in receiving wagers are deductible, for Federal income tax purposes, as ordinary and necessary business expenses under section 23(a) of the Internal Revenue Code, provided the taxpayer is engaged in the business of accepting wagers or conducting wagering pools or lotteries, or is engaged in receiving wagers for or on behalf of any person liable for the tax under section 3285(d) of the Code."

MAZZEI v. COMMISSIONER

Tax Court of the United States, 1972.
61 T.C. 497.

[The taxpayer entered into a conspiracy to produce counterfeit U.S. currency. However, the real intent of his coconspirators was to defraud the taxpayer. He gave them $20,000 in $100 bills for reproduction. They took the money, left taxpayer with a black box used for the reproduction of currency and were never heard from again.]

QUEALY, JUDGE: * * *

OPINION

Petitioner contends that the fact that he incurred a loss is substantiated by the evidence and that such loss is deductible under section 165(c)(2) or section 165(c)(3). Respondent contends initially that petitioner has failed to prove that a loss was in fact suffered, and, further, that even if a loss were proven in fact, a deduction for such loss would not be allowed under section 165(c)(2) or section 165(c)(3) on the grounds that allowance of such a deduction would be contrary to public policy. As our findings of fact indicate, the Court is convinced that petitioner, in fact, incurred a loss in the sum of $20,000, as the result of being defrauded. However, the deductibility of such loss is precluded by our decision in Luther M. Richey, Jr., 33 T.C. 272 (1959).

In the *Richey* case, the taxpayer became involved with two other men in a scheme to counterfeit United States currency. The taxpayer observed a reproduction process involving the bleaching out of $1 bills and the transferring of the excess ink from $100 bills onto the bleached-out bills. Upon observing this demonstration, the taxpayer became convinced that the process could reproduce money. When the taxpayer later met with the other men in a hotel room to carry out the scheme, the taxpayer turned over to one of the other men $15,000 which was to be used in the duplication process. Before the process was completed, one of the other men to whom the taxpayer had given the $15,000 left the room under the pretext of going to get something and never returned. The taxpayer later discovered that his money was gone and was not able to recover it. We disallowed the taxpayer's claimed loss deduction under section 165(c)(2) and section 165(c)(3), on the grounds that to allow the loss deduction would constitute an immediate and severe frustration of the clearly defined policy against counterfeiting obligations of the United States as enunciated by title 18, U.S.C., sec. 471.[37] This Court said:

> The record establishes that petitioner's conduct constituted an attempt to counterfeit, an actual start in the counterfeiting activity,

---

[37]. 18 U.S.C., sec. 471:

Whoever, with intent to defraud, falsely makes, forges, counterfeits, or alters any obligation or other security of the United States, shall be fined not more than $5,000 or imprisoned not more than fifteen years, or both.

and overt acts looking to consummation of the counterfeiting scheme. Petitioner actively participated in the venture. He withdrew money from the bank and changed it into high denomination bills with the full knowledge and intention that the money would be used to duplicate other bills. He was physically present at the place of alteration, and assisted in the process by washing the bills and otherwise aiding Randall and Johnson in their chores. He was part and parcel of the attempt to duplicate the money. Petitioner's actions are no less a violation of public policy because there was another scheme involved, namely, that of swindling the petitioner. From the facts, we hold that to allow the loss deduction in the instant case would constitute a severe and immediate frustration of the clearly defined policy against counterfeiting obligations of the United States. [33 T.C. at 276–277.]

Petitioner would distinguish the *Richey* case on the grounds that there the taxpayer was involved in an actual scheme to duplicate money where the process was actually begun, only to have the taxpayer swindled when his cohorts made off with his money, whereas in the instant case there never was any real plan to counterfeit money, it being impossible to duplicate currency with the black box. Petitioner contends that, from the inception, the only actual illegal scheme was the scheme to relieve petitioner of his money, and petitioner was a victim and not a perpetrator of the scheme.

In our opinion, the fact that the petitioner was victimized in what he thought was a plan or conspiracy to produce counterfeit currency does not make his participation in what he considered to be a criminal act any less violative of a clearly declared public policy. Not only was the result sought by the petitioner contrary to such policy, but the conspiracy itself constituted a violation of law.[38] The petitioner conspired with his covictim to commit a criminal act, namely, the counterfeiting of United States currency and his theft loss was directly related to that act. If there was a transaction entered into for profit, as petitioner argues, it was a conspiracy to counterfeit.

While it is also recognized that the Supreme Court in Commissioner v. Tellier, 383 U.S. 687 (1966), may have redefined the criteria for the disallowance on grounds of public policy of an otherwise deductible business expense under section 162(a), we do not have that type of case. The loss claimed by the petitioner here had a direct relationship to the purported illegal act which the petitioner conspired to commit. Compare Commissioner v. Heininger, 320 U.S. 467 (1943).

We also do not feel constrained to follow Edwards v. Bromberg, 232 F.2d 107 (C.A. 5, 1956), wherein the court allowed a deduction for a loss

38. 18 U.S.C., sec. 371:

If two or more persons conspire either to commit any offense against the United States, or to defraud the United States, or any agency thereof in any manner or for any purpose, and one or more of such persons do any act to effect the object of the conspiracy, each shall be fined not more than $10,000 or imprisoned not more than five years, or both.

If, however, the offense, the commission of which is the object of the conspiracy, is a misdemeanor only, the punishment for such conspiracy shall not exceed the maximum punishment provided for such misdemeanor.

incurred by the taxpayer when money, which he thought was being bet on a "fixed" race, was stolen from him. The taxpayer never intended to participate in "fixing" the race.

The ultimate question for decision in this case is whether considerations of public policy should enter into the allowance of a theft loss under section 165(c)(3) where there is a "theft"—and the loss by the petitioner of his money would certainly qualify as such—the statute imposes no limitation on the deductibility of the loss. Nevertheless, in Luther M. Richey, Jr., supra, this Court held that the deduction of an admitted theft was properly disallowed on grounds of public policy in a factual situation which we find indistinguishable. We would follow that case.

Reviewed by the Court.

Decision will be entered for the respondent.

STERRETT, J., I respectfully dissent from the majority opinion for the following reasons:

In Tank Truck Rentals v. Commissioner, 356 U.S. 30, 33, 35 (1958), the Supreme Court laid down the test for denying a deduction on the grounds of public policy. An otherwise allowable deduction may be denied if allowance would "severely and immediately" frustrate "sharply defined national or State policies proscribing particular types of conduct, evidenced by some governmental declaration thereof." Frustration of a particular State policy "is most complete and direct when the expenditure for which deduction is sought is itself prohibited by statute." Tank Truck Rentals v. Commissioner, supra at 35. If the expenditure is payment of a penalty imposed by the State because of an illegal act, allowance of a deduction would clearly frustrate State policy by reducing the "sting" of the penalty imposed. Accordingly, the Supreme Court disallowed the deduction of fines the taxpayer had paid during the course of its trucking operations. The Court said, "To allow the deduction sought here would but encourage continued violations of State law by increasing the odds in favor of noncompliance." Tank Truck Rentals v. Commissioner, supra at 35.

In Commissioner v. Sullivan, 356 U.S. 27 (1958), decided the same day as Tank Truck Rentals, the Court refused to disallow the deduction of rent and wage expenses in operating an illegal bookmaking establishment. The Court stated, "The fact that an expenditure bears a remote relation to an illegal act does not make it nondeductible." Commissioner v. Sullivan, supra at 29. See also Commissioner v. Heininger, 320 U.S. 467 (1943); Lilly v. Commissioner, 343 U.S. 90 (1952). Once again in Commissioner v. Tellier, 383 U.S. 687, 694 (1966), the Supreme Court reiterated and emphasized its position that an otherwise allowable deduction should only be disallowed when in violation of a public policy that is sharply limited and carefully defined.

Against this background, Congress as part of the Tax Reform Acts of 1969 and 1971 attempted to set forth categories of expenditures within the purview of section 162 which were to be denied on the grounds of public policy. The Senate Finance Committee report for the 1969 Tax Reform Act states "The provision for the denial of the deduction for payments in these situations [39] which are deemed to violate public policy is intended to be *all inclusive.* Public policy, in other circumstances, generally is not sufficiently clearly defined to justify the disallowance of deductions." (Emphasis added.) S.Rept. No. 91–552, 91st Cong., 1st Sess. (1969), 1969–3 C.B. 597. In expanding the category of nondeductible expenditures, the legislative history of the 1971 Tax Reform Act states, "The committee continues to believe that the determination of when a *deduction* should be *denied* should remain under the *control* of *Congress.*" (Emphasis added.) S.Rept. No. 92–437, 92d Cong., 1st Sess. (1971), 1972–1 C.B. 599.

While the above statements have direct effect under section 162, where most of the public policy decisions have arisen, it does seem to call for judicial restraint in other areas where Congress has not specifically limited deductions. Moreover, such statements may have been a reaction to widely varied decisions such as those in Edwards v. Bromberg, 232 F.2d 107 (C.A.5, 1956), and Luther M. Richey, Jr., 33 T.C. 272 (1959), which we think are not fairly distinguishable, and have led to the disparate results so inimical to the uniform administration of the tax laws.[40]

Despite the above, the majority seeks to invoke public policy as the tool to deny the petitioner an otherwise allowable theft loss. While congressional intent could logically be read to remove public policy considerations from the Internal Revenue Code where not specifically included, at a minimum the strict test laid down by the Supreme Court must be met.

In the majority opinion, as in *Richey,* we apparently pay lip service to the Supreme Court by stating "that to allow the loss deduction would constitute an immediate and severe frustration of the clearly defined policy against counterfeiting obligations of the United States." Unfortunately in both cases we fail to discuss precisely how that frustration will occur. In the case of illegal payments such as bribes and kickbacks and the payment of fines, we are able to see a direct relationship between the allowance of the deduction and encouragement of continued violations of the law. In essence, the Government underwrites a portion of the expenses. However in the instant case we cannot see how counterfeiting will be encouraged in any manner by allowing the petitioner a theft loss deduction arising out of a distinctly different act. At best, the relationship is more remote than that in *Sullivan,* for the

39. Fines, a portion of treble damages under antitrust laws, bribes to public officials, and other unlawful bribes and kickbacks.

40. We note that our decision in *Richey* did not mention or discuss Edwards v. Bromberg, 232 F.2d 107 (C.A.5, 1956), decided 3½ years earlier.

term "theft" presupposes that the victim has not voluntarily parted with his property.[41]

The majority seems to indicate that a deduction can be denied where there is *any* relationship between the loss or expense and the illegal activity, a position specifically rejected by *Sullivan*. Such reasoning does not readily lend itself to being "sharply limited" or "carefully defined." Had petitioner contracted pneumonia on his New York excursion, would the majority also deny him a medical expense deduction?

Or assume that customers on the premises of the bookmaking establishment involved in *Sullivan* were robbed by an outside intruder. Would the majority deny them a theft loss because they were engaged in an illegal activity? Or would the majority have this Court of special jurisdiction add to its assigned duties of interpreting the Internal Revenue Code the task of grading criminal activity, a task for which we obviously have no particular expertise. The authority for undertaking such additional duties remains obscure to me and would also be, I suspect, obscure to Congress.

Congress has authorized the imposition of severe punishment upon those found guilty of counterfeiting United States currency. It is designed to repress such criminal conduct. In the interest of uniform application of the Internal Revenue Code, where the frustration of State or national policy is neither severe nor immediate, we must not be tempted to impose a "clean hands doctrine" as a prerequisite to deductibility. To hold otherwise, especially in light of the broad brushstroke of public policy applied by the majority opinion, makes the taxing statute an unwarranted instrument of further punishment.

FORRESTER, FEATHERSTON, HALL, and WILES, JJ., agree with this dissent.

In Rev.Rul. 81–24, 1981–1 C.B. 79, the Service ruled that the frustration of public policy doctrine continues to be applicable to deny a claim for a deduction, at least for a loss under § 165.

Questions

1. What is the basic issue with respect to the public policy limitation on deductions? Should the issue be approached in terms of a tax on net income (regardless of the nature of the expense) or disallowance of a deduction which would frustrate public policy?

41. This should be contrasted with the situation where a counterfeiter has money and equipment confiscated during a legal search by police. Allowance of a casualty loss would frustrate public policy by lessening the adverse effect of proper governmental action directly related to the counterfeiting. Cf. Hopka v. United States, 195 F.Supp. 474 (N.D.Iowa 1961).

2. Did Congress change prior case law in this area by enacting § 162(c), (f) and (g)?

---

3. ILLEGAL BUSINESS PAYMENTS AND SECTION 162

The Federal income tax is premised only on gross income, not on every type of receipt. Computing the cost of goods (or services) sold is an essential element of figuring gross income, which is, in turn, the starting point in determining taxable income. Thus, the business taxpayer must subtract from gross receipts the usual items included in the cost of goods (or services) sold, such as labor, materials and overhead expenses, to arrive at gross income. Read Reg. § 1.61–3(a) and reconsider the excerpt from Doyle v. Mitchell Brothers Co. set out on page 142. From gross income, the business taxpayer subtracts allowable deductions to determine taxable income. Reconsider §§ 62 and 63.

SULLENGER v. COMMISSIONER
Tax Court of the United States, 1948.
11 T.C. 1076.

OPINION

MURDOCK, JUDGE: * * * The parties have entered into a stipulation which leaves for decision only the question of whether the Commissioner erred in failing to subtract from gross receipts, as cost of goods sold, the excess over the O.P.A. price paid by J.H. Sullenger for meat which he then sold through his business conducted under the name of Select Meat Co. The stipulation of facts is adopted as the findings of fact.

* * *

The petitioner purchased a business known as Select Meat Co. in 1942. He has since operated it as a sole proprietorship. He keeps his accounts upon an accrual basis, using a fiscal year ending June 30.

The petitioner paid to wholesale meat packing firms during the taxable years, for meats purchased from them, amounts in excess of the O.P.A. prices in effect at the time of the purchases. The petitioner then sold the meat and the income from those sales is being taxed. The Commissioner, in determining the deficiencies, failed to recognize the excess over O.P.A. prices as cost of goods sold.

The respondent argues that the amounts paid in excess of the O.P.A. prices were "not truly a part of cost of goods sold" but were "in reality nothing but a 'bribe' to the various packing firms or amounts paid to them illegally to induce them to sell the goods to petitioner at the ceiling price." He then argues that the amounts must be considered from the standpoint of deductions, deductions are a matter of grace and not of right, to allow these amounts as deductions would be contrary to public policy, and, therefore, the determination of the Commissioner must be affirmed.

The trouble with his argument is that its major premise is unsound. The amounts in question were actually, as the stipulation shows, a part of the cost of goods sold and are not being claimed by this petitioner as a deduction under section 23. Section 23 makes no provision for the cost of goods sold, but the Commissioner has always recognized, as indeed he must to stay within the Constitution, that the cost of goods sold must be deducted from gross receipts in order to arrive at gross income. No more than gross income can be subjected to income tax upon any theory. The income from a business which is wholly illegal was held subject to income tax in United States v. Sullivan, 274 U.S. 259. Nevertheless, it was necessary to determine what that income was, and the cost of an illegal purchase of liquor was subtracted from proceeds of the illegal sale of the liquor in order to arrive at the gain from the illegal transactions which were subjected to income tax in that case. This is not a case of penalties provided for violation of the O.P.A. regulations. See the Emergency Price Control Act of 1942 (Title 50, App.U.S.C.A., sec. 901 et seq.). No authority has been cited for denying to this taxpayer the cost of goods sold in computing his profit, which profit alone is gross income for income tax purposes. It is unnecessary to discuss cases involving deductions, since this case does not involve any deduction. The point in controversy is decided for the petitioners.

Reviewed by the Court.

Decisions will be entered under Rule 50.

————

The Service initially acquiesced in the Sullenger decision (1952–2 C.B. 3), but subsequently substituted a nonacquiescence (1976–1 C.B. 1). Other cases have rejected the constitutional theory advanced in Sullenger. See e.g., Commissioner v. Weisman, 197 F.2d 221 (1st Cir.1952), where the court held deductible the unlawful portion paid for inventory in excess of the OPA price ceiling.

Illegal business bribes, kickbacks, or payments, although nondeductible under § 162(c)(2), can be part of the cost of goods or services sold if the payments come directly from the seller of goods or services and are directly related to the cost of his sales. Section 162(c)(2) precludes a taxpayer from deducting certain illegal payments as business expense. However, when a seller makes an "adjustment" to the sales price, he establishes, in effect, the maximum net price at which he can make a sale. The "adjustment" may take the form of a trade discount or an otherwise illegal rebate. Nevertheless, instead of being an expense of doing business, the adjustment is, in economic reality, a reduction in gross receipts sustained as part of the cost of completing the sale. In short, it is a cost of the goods or services sold.

For instance, in Max Sobel Wholesale Liquors v. Commissioner, 69 T.C. 477 (1977), affirmed 630 F.2d 670 (9th Cir.1980), a wholesale liquor dealer rebated additional merchandise to selected customers in violation of state law; while in Haas Brothers Inc. v. Commissioner, 73 T.C. 1217 (1980), another liquor dealer paid a similar rebate in cash. Although, as a matter of tax policy, taxpayers generally should not benefit from illegal payments, courts recognize that § 162(c) does not extend to the determination of the cost of goods (or services) sold. Section 162(c) is solely concerned with deductions from gross income and provides no authority to adjust exclusions required to compute gross income. The Service has also acceded to this conclusion. In Rev. Rul. 82–149, 1982–2 C.B. 56, the Service ruled that a taxpayer may subtract illegal payments from gross sales to determine gross income. The Service reasoned that "illegal rebates made by a seller directly to a purchaser are allowable adjustments to the sales price of the merchandise (or cost of goods sold as in Max Sobel) for purposes of calculating gross income."

One limitation exists on the rationale of the Sobel type cases, as explained in Alex v. Commissioner, 628 F.2d 1222 (9th Cir.1980). In the Alex case, a life insurance agent sold insurance in violation of state law by reimbursing some insureds' premium payments and by paying other insureds' premiums himself. The court distinguished between discounts or rebates to which customers became entitled at the time of sale and costs incurred in the form of illegal payments, or payments to third parties, which were not made pursuant to an agreement between the buyer and the seller. In the latter instance, the seller is not adjusting the price. The insurance agent in the Alex case merely generated additional commission and bonus income for himself through a fraudulent scheme. He had no product to adjust in price because his "product" belonged to the insurance company. Furthermore, as an accounting matter, any expenses incurred which are indirectly related to a transaction do not qualify as a cost of goods sold. Such indirect expenses can only be classified as potential business expense deductions. Then, of course, when such discounts or rebates are made illegally, § 162(c)(2) disallows any deduction based on them.

This treatment of cost of goods sold has continued to be respected. Section 280E was added to the Code to prohibit deductions for expenditures for items such as telephone, auto and rentals if incurred in the illegal trafficking in drugs. The legislative history provides: "To preclude possible challenges on constitutional grounds, the adjustment to gross receipts with respect to costs of goods sold is not affected by this provision of the Act". Staff of the Joint Committee, General Explanation of the Revenue Provisions of the Tax Equity and Fiscal Responsibility Act of 1982 at 264 (1982).

Problems

1. (a) Beleagured, the owner of an appliance store, must pay regular sums to hoodlums as "protection" money to conduct his business in peace.

i. Will the payments be deductible under § 162(c)(2)? Consider the Lilly and Mazzei cases and Reg. § 1.162–1(a).

ii. Assume the payments are deductible under § 162(c)(2), will the payments be "ordinary and necessary" expenses deductible under § 162(a)? Reconsider Friedman v. Delaney, page 458, and the impact of § 67.

iii. Assume the payments are not deductible under § 162(c). Will they constitute a cost of goods sold? Consider the Sullenger case and Reg. § 1.61–3(a).

(b) What if he must make protection payments to the police? Consider § 162(c)(1) and Reg. § 1.61–3(a).

2. After finishing law school, Terri Player became a tax lawyer. Terri pays a referring lawyer 20 percent of the fees received from any client referred to her by another lawyer. May Terri deduct the payments? Consider § 162(c) and (a), Reg. § 1.61–3(a) and the Lilly case. Rule 1.5 of the American Bar Association, Model Rules of Professional Conduct (1983) provides:

(e) A division of fee between lawyers who are not in the same firm may be made only if:

(1) the division is in proportion to the services performed by each lawyer or, by written agreement with the client, each lawyer assumes joint responsibility for the representation;

(2) the client is advised of and does not object to the participation of all the lawyers involved; and

(3) the total fee is reasonable.

Comment

* * *

Division of Fee

A division of fee is a single billing to a client covering the fee of two or more lawyers who are not in the same firm. A division of fee facilitates association of more than one lawyer in a matter in which neither alone could serve the client as well, and most often is used when the fee is contingent and the division is between a referring lawyer and a trial specialist. Paragraph (e) permits the lawyers to divide a fee on either the basis of the proportion of services they render or by agreement between the participating lawyers if all assume responsibility for the representation as a whole and the client is advised and does not object. It does not require disclosure to the client of the share that each lawyer is to receive. * * *

3. Enterprising sells slot machines, an activity prohibited by State law. State law also makes illegal the purchase of slot machines from

outside jurisdictions. Assume this year Enterprising purchased slot machines from manufacturers in Nevada at a cost of $100,000. He conducted his operations in leased premises, paying rent in the amount of $5,000 and reasonable salaries in the amount of $30,000. He sold the slot machines to his customers for a total amount of $400,000. In order to avoid trouble with local authorities, he paid $80,000 to various officials as bribes. Despite these payments, taxpayer was prosecuted for the illegal sale of one slot machine. He incurred legal expenses of $5,000 in connection with this litigation. He was found guilty and paid a fine of $5,000. Assume Enterprising had no other income or itemized deductions. What was his adjusted gross income? Consider §§ 62(1), 67, 162(a), (c), (f), and 1001(a), Reg. §§ 1.61–3(a), and 1.162–21(b)(2) and the Sullivan and Sullenger cases.

4. DEDUCTIBILITY OF LOBBYING EXPENSES

Activities of lobbyists are not generally considered to represent the highest social good for which expenses may be deducted by taxpayers. Thus, judicial and administrative enthusiasm respecting claims for Federal income tax deductions arising from lobbying expenses have been notable for their restraint. As a general rule, the Service and the courts have been inclined to assert that expenses for the promotion and defeat of legislation are not "ordinary and necessary" expenses which may be deducted. In Cammarano v. United States, 358 U.S. 498, 79 S.Ct. 524, 3 L.Ed.2d 462 (1959), amounts expended to persuade the public to reject an initiative measure were held not deductible. As the Supreme Court stated in the Cammarano case, the denial of deductions for business-related political activity "express[ed] a determination by Congress that since purchased publicity can influence the fate of legislation which will affect, directly or indirectly, all in the community, everyone in the community should stand on the same footing as regards its purchase so far as the Treasury of the United States is concerned." (358 U.S. at 513), 79 S.Ct. at 533, 3 L.Ed.2d at 472.)

The Code allows a deduction for lobbying expenses in connection with legislation or proposed legislation "of direct interest to the taxpayer." § 162(e). The taxpayer's "direct interest" pertains to legislation or proposed legislation which will, or may reasonably be expected, to affect the taxpayer's trade or business. Reg. § 1.162–20(c)(2)(ii)(b). Explicitly excluded is legislation that will merely affect business or economic conditions in general.

Expenses incurred for the purpose of influencing the public with respect to legislative matters are expressly excluded. § 162(e)(2)(B). Thus, a taxpayer cannot deduct any expenses incurred in grass roots campaigns to present and develop a public position even if it relates to a matter of direct interest to the taxpayer.

Problems

1. Mark owns a beer distributorship in Oregon and is a member of the Oregon Beer Distributors Institute. A movement is being undertaken by Oregon citizens to forbid the sale of beer except through state owned stores.

Taxpayer is asked to contribute funds to the Institute to be used to persuade the legislature and the public not to support the proposed legislation. You are asked by Mark to inform him respecting the best way to block the legislation while getting a deduction for his expenses in doing so. Consider §§ 62(1), 67, 162(e) and Reg. § 1.162–20(a)(2), (c)(2), and (d)(1).

2. Terri Player, a public spirited tax attorney, wishes to deliver testimony before a Congressional committee on a tax reform matter, not connected with her practice. May she deduct her expenses? Consider § 162(e) and Reg. § 1.162–20(d)(1). Reconsider Problem 3 at page 35.

I. MISCELLANEOUS ITEMIZED DEDUCTIONS

There are two tiers of itemized deductions for individuals. Those deductions placed in the first tier are not subject to the two percent floor of § 67. Examine § 67(b). Any itemized deductions not specifically exempted from the impact of § 67(a) by § 67(b) are treated as tier two deductions and are deductible only to the extent they cumulatively exceed wto percent of adjusted gross income. No tier one itemized deductions nor the aggregate of tier two itemized deductions in excess of two percent of adjusted gross income are deducted on an individual's income tax return if that taxpayer does not itemize deductions because the standard deduction is used to compute taxable income under § 63(b). Examine § 63. Any above-the-line deduction used in computing adjusted gross income under § 62 and the personal exemptions provided by § 151 are not itemized deductions so that they are not subject to the § 67(a) two percent floor. § 63(d). In addition, above-the-line deductions and the personal exemptions remain deductible on an individual's income tax return if that taxpayer uses the standard deduction.

The following list is illustrative of those expenses initially qualifying for a deduction but subject to the two percent floor:

Employee Business Expenses

1. 80% of unreimbursed employee entertainment and meal expenses, including meals away from home.

2. Unreimbursed employee travel expenses for transportation and lodging.

3. Dues to unions and professional associations.

4. Home office expenses.

5. Professional journals.

6. Uniforms and work clothes.

7. Costs of seeking employment.

8. Education related to a taxpayer's employment or profession.

9. Malpractice insurance.

Expenses for the Production of Income

1. Cost of safe deposit box to store stocks and non-tax exempt bonds.
2. Fees for investment advice.
3. Legal and accounting fees.
4. Costs of collecting investment income.
5. Travel costs for investments.

Other Expenses

1. Tax return preparation costs.
2. Fees for tax planning and advice.

Chapter 7

BUSINESS DEDUCTIONS: CURRENT DEDUCTION OR CAPITAL EXPENDITURE

A. INTRODUCTION

Deductions and Tax Accounting: General Principles. It should first be noted that the timing of a taxpayer's deductions will generally be controlled by whether he is on the cash or accrual method. This may be illustrated by the following example:

Assume that the taxpayer purchased office supplies on December 15 and paid for them by a check issued on January 15. He reported income on the calendar year. If he were on the cash method he would have a deduction for the cost of his office supplies in January. More specifically, a cash method taxpayer's check constitutes payment when issued to the payee provided it is honored on presentation. If he were on the accrual method he would have a deduction in December. § 461(a); Reg. § 1.461–1(a)(1) and (2). The item is said to have accrued when all events have occurred which fix the fact of liability, if the amount thereof can be ascertained with reasonable accuracy. In addition, under § 461(h), the all events test is deemed not to be met any earlier than when "economic performance" occurs with respect to the item. Under § 461(h)(2)(A)(ii) economic performance occurred when the taxpayer was provided with the office supplies. Reread pp. 226 to 231. An exception to the economic performance test exists, under § 461(h)(3) for certain recurring items. This exception is designed to avoid upsetting normal accounting and business practices and imposing undue burdens on taxpayers.

Having disposed of this fairly elementary aspect of tax accounting with respect to deductions, we proceed to issues of considerably greater sophistication.

Expenses Which Must Be Spread Over Years. The Code generally prohibits deductions for capital expenses. Let us first engage in a review by reference to an example:

Assume that T, a cash method taxpayer, projects taxable income of $100,000 for his current tax year. This amount is abnormally high compared to his usual earnings. He owns raw land. Foreseeing the high tax liability, he builds a structure for the sum of $100,000 on the land and seeks to deduct the entire amount in the current tax year.

This device will not work. Neither the cash method nor the accrual method taxpayer may currently deduct an expenditure which results in the creation of an asset with a useful life which extends substantially beyond the close of the taxable year. Reg. § 1.461–1(a)(1) and (2).

Section 263(a)(1) provides that no deduction is allowed for amounts paid for new buildings or permanent improvements made to increase the value of property. Section 263(a)(2) also provides that no amount is deductible in restoring property or making good any exhaustion thereof for which an allowance is or has been made. However, if the useful life of an addition or improvement is twelve months or less, the taxpayer may currently deduct the entire cost of the item even if the taxpayer will use the item over two taxable years. Rev.Rul. 73–357, 1973–2 C.B. 40 and Colorado Springs Nat'l Bank v. United States, 505 F.2d 1185 (10th Cir.1974).

An amount which is capitalized becomes part of the taxpayer's basis in the asset with respect to which the expenditure is incurred. The cost of a capital improvement may sometimes be recovered on a year-to-year basis by depreciation deductions under § 167, for eligible property placed in service after December 31, 1980, by deductions under the Accelerated Cost Recovery System (§ 168) or by amortization deductions under other Code sections.

The rationale for the treatment of capital expenditures turns on the basic accounting concept requiring the matching of expenditures with the revenues the expenditures generate. Where a taxpayer produced or acquired an asset which will generate income over a period of years the expenses entailed in producing or acquiring that asset should be deducted over a similar period or, as the Supreme Court stated in Commissioner v. Idaho Power Co., 418 U.S. 1, 16, 94 S.Ct. 2757, 2766, 41 L.Ed.2d 535, 546–547 (1974):

> The purpose of § 263 is to reflect the basic principal that a capital expenditure may not be deducted from current income. It serves to prevent a taxpayer from utilizing currently a deduction properly attributable, through amortization, to later tax years when the capital [expenditure] becomes income producing.

If a depreciation, an accelerated cost recovery, or an amortization deduction is not available (for example, on an asset with an indefinite useful life, such as land), the capital expenditure will increase the taxpayer's basis thereby reducing the gain (or increasing the loss) realized and recognized when the asset is eventually sold. Where many installations of equipment and improvements are made, evidence must be adduced to show which items the taxpayer may treat as capital expenditures and which may be currently deducted.

In certain cases, Congress has thought it desirable to relax the strictures of § 263, even for assets with indefinite useful lives, presumably in order to encourage investments in particular areas. Thus, the rule is relaxed as to certain expenses including, among others, pollution control facilities (§ 169), research and experimental expenditures (§ 174), items related to soil and water conservation (§ 175), and those for mineral development (§ 616). The capitalization rule is also relaxed for relatively small amounts (§ 179).

Question

Why does a taxpayer usually prefer to deduct the full cost of an expenditure in the year of payment?

B. CAPITAL EXPENDITURE VERSUS DEDUCTIBLE EXPENSE

1. REPAIRS VERSUS IMPROVEMENTS

The distinction between: (a) a repair on business property or property held for investment which is deductible as an expense and (b) an expense of such a major proportion requiring capitalization, has always been difficult to draw. Generally stated, a capital expenditure adds to the value of property, prolongs the life of the property or expands the property to a new or different use. A repair keeps property in an ordinary efficient operating condition, but does not materially add to the value of the property or appreciably prolong its life. See Reg. §§ 1.162–4 and 1.263(a)–1(b). "Repairs in the nature of replacements" are (in contrast with "incidental repairs") classified as capital expenditures, according to Reg. § 1.162–4, if they arrest deterioration and appreciably prolong the life of the property. Consider the criteria used by the Tax Court to distinguish repairs from improvements and replacements in the following cases.

MIDLAND EMPIRE PACKING CO. v. COMMISSIONER

Tax Court of the United States, 1950.
14 T.C. 635.

* * *

OPINION

ARUNDELL, JUDGE: The issue in this case is whether an expenditure for a concrete lining in petitioner's basement to oilproof it against an oil nuisance created by a neighboring refinery is deductible as an ordinary and necessary expense under [§ 162(a)] of the Internal Revenue Code, on the theory it was an expenditure for a repair, or, in the alternative, whether the expenditure may be treated as the measure of the loss sustained during the taxable year and not compensated for by insurance or otherwise within the meaning of [§ 165(a)] of the Internal Revenue Code.

The respondent has contended, in part, that the expenditure is for a capital improvement and should be recovered through depreciation charges and is, therefore, not deductible as an ordinary and necessary business expense or as a loss.

It is none too easy to determine on which side of the line certain expenditures fall so that they may be accorded their proper treatment for tax purposes. Treasury Regulations [§ 1.162–4], from which we quote in the margin, is helpful in distinguishing between an expenditure to be classed as a repair and one to be treated as a capital outlay. In Illinois Merchants Trust Co., Executor, 4 B.T.A. 103, at page 106, we discussed this subject in some detail and in our opinion said:

> It will be noted that the first sentence of the article [now with minor changes, Reg. § 1.162–4] relates to repairs, while the second sentence deals in effect with replacements. In determining whether an expenditure is a capital one or is chargeable against operating income, it is necessary to bear in mind the purpose for which the expenditure was made. To repair is to restore to a sound state or to mend, while a replacement connotes a substitution. A repair is an expenditure for the purpose of keeping the property in an ordinarily efficient operating condition. It does not add to the value of the property, nor does it appreciably prolong its life. It merely keeps the property in an operating condition over its probable useful life for the uses for which it was acquired. Expenditures for that purpose are distinguishable from those for replacements, alterations, improvements, or additions which prolong the life of the property, increase its value, or make it adaptable to a different use. The one is a maintenance charge, while the others are additions to capital investment which should not be applied against current earnings.

It will be seen from our findings of fact that for some 25 years prior to the taxable year petitioner had used the basement rooms of its plant as a place for the curing of hams and bacon and for the storage of meat and hides. The basement had been entirely satisfactory for this purpose over the entire period in spite of the fact that there was some seepage of water into the rooms from time to time. In the taxable year it was found that not only water, but oil, was seeping through the concrete walls of the basement of the packing plant and, while the water would soon drain out, the oil would not, and there was left on the basement floor a thick scum of oil which gave off a strong odor that permeated the air of the entire plant, and the fumes from the oil created a fire hazard. It appears that the oil which came from a nearby refinery had also gotten into the water wells which served to furnish water for petitioner's plant, and as a result of this whole condition the Federal meat inspectors advised petitioner that it must discontinue the use of the water from the wells and oil-proof the basement, or else shut down its plant.

To meet this situation, petitioner during the taxable year undertook steps to oilproof the basement by adding a concrete lining to the walls from the floor to a height of about four feet and also added concrete to the floor of the basement. It is the cost of this work which it seeks to deduct as a repair. The basement was not enlarged by this work, nor did the oilproofing serve to make it more desirable for the purpose for which it had been used through the years prior to the time that the oil nuisance had occurred. The evidence is that the expenditure did not add to the value or prolong the expected life of the property over what they were before the event occurred which made the repairs necessary. It is true that after the work was done the seepage of water, as well as oil, was stopped, but, as already stated, the presence of the water had never been found objectionable. The repairs merely served to keep the property in an operating condition over its probable useful life for the purpose for which it was used.

While it is conceded on brief that the expenditure was "necessary," respondent contends that the encroachment of the oil nuisance on petitioner's property was not an "ordinary" expense in petitioner's particular business. But the fact that petitioner had not theretofore been called upon to make a similar expenditure to prevent damage and disaster to its property does not remove that expense from the classification of "ordinary" for, as stated in Welch v. Helvering, 290 U.S. 111, "ordinary in this context does not mean that the payments must be habitual or normal in the sense that the same taxpayer will have to make them often. * * * the expense is an ordinary one because we know from experience that payments for such a purpose, whether the amount is large or small, are the common and accepted means of defense against attack. Cf. Kornhauser v. United States, 276 U.S. 145. The situation is unique in the life of the individual affected, but not in the life of the group, the community, of which he is a part." Steps to protect a business building from the seepage of oil from a nearby refinery, which had been erected long subsequent to the time petitioner started to operate its plant, would seem to us to be a normal thing to do, and in certain sections of the country it must be a common experience to protect one's property from the seepage of oil. Expenditures to accomplish this result are likewise normal.

In American Bemberg Corporation, 10 T.C. 361, we allowed as deductions, on the ground that they were ordinary and necessary expenses, extensive expenditures made to prevent disaster, although the repairs were of a type which had never been needed before and were unlikely to recur. In that case the taxpayer, to stop cave-ins of soil which were threatening destruction of its manufacturing plant, hired an engineering firm which drilled to the bedrock and injected grout to fill the cavities where practicable, and made incidental replacements and repairs, including tightening of the fluid carriers. In two successive years the taxpayer expended $734,316.76 and $199,154.33, respectively, for such drilling and grouting and $153,474.20 and

$79,687.29, respectively, for capital replacements. We found that the cost (other than replacement) of this program did not make good the depreciation previously allowed, and stated in our opinion:

> In connection with the purpose of the work, the * * * program was intended to avert a plant-wide disaster and avoid forced abandonment of the plant. The purpose was not to improve, better, extend, or increase the original plant, nor to prolong its original useful life. Its continued operation was endangered; the purpose of the expenditures was to enable petitioner to continue the plant in operation not on any new or better scale, but on the same scale and, so far as possible, as efficiently as it had operated before. The purpose was not to rebuild or replace the plant in whole or in part, but to keep the same plant as it was and where it was.

The petitioner here made the repairs in question in order that it might continue to operate its plant. Not only was there danger of fire from the oil and fumes, but the presence of the oil led the Federal meat inspectors to declare the basement an unsuitable place for the purpose for which it had been used for a quarter of a century. After the expenditures were made, the plant did not operate on a changed or larger scale, nor was it thereafter suitable for new or additional uses. The expenditure served only to permit petitioner to continue the use of the plant, and particularly the basement for its normal operations.

In our opinion, the expenditure of $4,868.81 for lining the basement walls and floor was essentially a repair and, as such, it is deductible as an ordinary and necessary business expense. This holding makes unnecessary a consideration of petitioner's alternative contention that the expenditure is deductible as a business loss * * *.

Decision will be entered under Rule 50.

———

In Mt. Morris Drive-In Theater Co. v. Commissioner, 25 T.C. 272 (1955), affirmed 238 F.2d 85 (6th Cir.1956), the taxpayer cleared a tract of land for use as a drive-in theater. The clearing and grading resulted in a substantial increase in the drainage of surface water onto the adjacent property. Three years later, after the adjacent landowner threatened to sue, the taxpayer installed a drainage system at a cost of $8,224. The Tax Court required the expenditure to be capitalized as a cost of preparing the property for use as a drive-in theater. It found that since there was a foreseeable need for this drainage system, the site was not completed until the drainage system was added. The concurring opinion would have required the cost be capitalized even though the need for it could not be foreseen. Furthermore, the time the cost was incurred, according to the concurring opinion, has no bearing on whether the cost should be capitalized. The dissent argued that the cost was a current deduction as the drainage system "did not improve, better, extend, increase or prolong the useful life of the property."

Question

Can you reconcile the results in the Midland Empire Packing and Mt. Morris Drive-In Theatre cases? How do these cases impact on the accounting principle requiring the matching of revenues and expenditures?

———

In Evans v. Commissioner, 33 T.C.M. (CCH) 1192 (1974), reversed on this point 557 F.2d 1095 (5th Cir.1977), a farmer paid for repairs to a dam and reservoir on his farm. The Tax Court concluded that the repairs increased the capacity of the dam and reservoir and prolonged their useful life. One-third of the dam was replaced by the substitution of a clay seam for gravel composition dirt that had run the length of the dam. In holding the expenditure a repair, the Fifth Circuit looked at the purpose for which the repairs were undertaken, namely, to return the repaired items to the condition they were in prior to the occurrence of water seepage. The expenditure did not constitute a "material increase in value". Is the appellate decision consistent with Reg. § 1.162–4?

Contrast, however, the following excerpt from Hotel Sulgrave, Inc. v. Commissioner, 21 T.C. 619, 621 (1954):

> We do not agree that the installation of the sprinkler system [in a hotel] constituted a repair made "for the purpose of keeping the property in an ordinarily efficient operating condition." Cf. Illinois Merchants Trust Co., 4 B.T.A. 103, 106, cited by petitioner. It was a permanent addition to the property ordered by the city of New York to give the property additional protection from the hazard of fire. It was an improvement or betterment having a life extending beyond the year in which it was made and which depreciates over a period of years. While it may not have increased the value of the hotel property or prolonged its useful life, the property became more valuable for use in the petitioner's business by reason of compliance with the city's order. The respondent did not err in determining that the cost of this improvement or betterment should be added to petitioner's capital investment in the building, and recovered through depreciation deductions in the years of its useful life.

The uniform capitalization rules to be promulgated by the Treasury under § 263A "are not intended to apply to expenditures properly treated as repair costs * * * that do not relate to the manufacture, remanufacture, or production of property." Senate Finance Committee Report on H.R. 3838, 99th Cong., 2d Sess. 143 (1986).

2. PREPAYMENT OF EXPENSES

A cash method taxpayer may, among other techniques, control the amount of net income for the current year by paying or forebearing to pay deductible items. Reg. § 1.461–1(a)(1) recites that if a taxpayer expends funds to create an asset having a useful life which extends substantially beyond the tax year, it may not be deductible at all, or it may only be deductible, in part, for the taxable year in which it is made. Consider the treatment of fire insurance premiums in the next case.

COMMISSIONER v. BOYLSTON MARKET ASSN.

United States Court of Appeals, First Circuit, 1942.
131 F.2d 966.

MAHONEY, CIRCUIT JUDGE.

* * *

The taxpayer in the course of its business, which is the management of real estate owned by it, purchased from time to time fire and other insurance policies covering periods of three or more years. It keeps its books and makes its returns on a cash receipts and disbursements basis. The taxpayer has since 1915 deducted each year as insurance expenses the amount of insurance premiums applicable to carrying insurance for that year regardless of the year in which the premium was actually paid. This method was required by the Treasury Department prior to 1938 by G.C.M. 13148, XIII–1 Cum.Bull. 67 (1934). Prior to January 1, 1936, the taxpayer had prepaid insurance premiums in the amount of $6,690.75 and during that year it paid premiums in an amount of $1082.77. The amount of insurance premiums prorated by the taxpayer in 1936 was $4421.76. Prior to January 1, 1938, it had prepaid insurance premiums in the amount of $6148.42 and during that year paid premiums in the amount of $890.47. The taxpayer took a deduction of $3284.25, which was the amount prorated for the year 1938. The Commissioner in his notice of deficiency for the year 1936 allowed only $1082.77 and for the year 1938 only $890.47, being the amounts actually paid in those years, on the basis that deductions for insurance expense of a taxpayer on the cash receipts and disbursements basis is limited to premiums paid during the taxable year.

We are asked to determine whether a taxpayer who keeps his books and files his returns on a cash basis is limited to the deduction of the insurance premiums actually paid in any year or whether he should deduct for each tax year the pro rata portion of the prepaid insurance applicable to that year. The pertinent provisions of the statute are [§§ 162 and 461].

This court in Welch v. DeBlois, 1 Cir., 1938, 94 F.2d 842, held that a taxpayer on the cash receipts and disbursements basis who made prepayments of insurance premiums was entitled to take a full deduction for these payments as ordinary and necessary business expenses in the year in which payment was made despite the fact that the insurance covered a three-year period. The government on the basis of that decision changed its earlier G.C.M. rule, supra, which had required the taxpayer to prorate prepaid insurance premiums. The Board of Tax Appeals has refused to follow that case in George S. Jephson v. Com'r, 37 B.T.A. 1117; Frank Real Estate & Investment Co., 40 B.T.A. 1382, unreported memorandum decision Nov. 15, 1939, and in the instant case. The arguments in that case in favor of treating prepaid insurance as an ordinary and necessary business expense are persuasive. We are, nevertheless, unable to find a real basis for distinguishing between prepayment of rentals, Baton Coal Co. v. Commissioner, 3 Cir., 1931, 51 F.2d 469, certiorari denied 284 U.S. 674, 52 S.Ct. 129, 76 L.Ed. 570; Galatoire Bros. v. Lines, 5 Cir., 1928, 23 F.2d 676; See Main & McKinney Building Co. v. Commissioner, 5 Cir., 1940, 113 F.2d 81, 82, certiorari denied 311 U.S. 688, 61 S.Ct. 66, 85 L.Ed. 444; bonuses for the acquisition of leases, Home Trust Co. v. Commissioner, 8 Cir., 1933, 65 F.2d 532; J. Alland & Bro., Inc. v. United States, D.C.Mass.1928, 28 F.2d 792; bonuses for the cancellation of leases, Steele-Wedeles Co. v. Commissioner, 30 B.T.A. 841, 842; Borland v. Commissioner, 27 B.T.A. 538, 542; commissions for negotiating leases, see Bonwit Teller & Co. v. Commissioner, 2 Cir., 1931, 53 F.2d 381, 384, 82 A.L.R. 325, and prepaid insurance. Some distinctions may be drawn in the cases cited on the basis of the facts contained therein, but we are of the opinion that there is no justification for treating them differently insofar as deductions are concerned. All of the cases cited are readily distinguishable from such a clear cut case as a permanent improvement to a building. This latter is clearly a capital expenditure. See Parkersburg Iron & Steel Co. v. Burnet, 4 Cir., 1931, 48 F.2d 163, 165. In such a case there is the creation of a capital asset which has a life extending beyond the taxable year and which depreciates over a period of years. The taxpayer regardless of his method of accounting can only take deductions for depreciation over the life of the asset. Advance rentals, payments of bonuses for acquisition and cancellation of leases, and commissions for negotiating leases are all matters which the taxpayer amortizes over the life of the lease. Whether we consider these payments to be the cost of the exhaustible asset, as in the case of advance rentals, or the cost of acquiring the asset, as in the case of bonuses, the payments are prorated primarily because the life of the asset extends beyond the taxable year. To permit the taxpayer to take a full deduction in the year of payment would distort his income. Prepaid insurance presents the same problem and should be solved in the same way. Prepaid insurance for a period of three years may be easily allocated. It is protection for the entire period and the taxpayer may, if he desires, at any time surrender the insurance policy. It thus is clearly an asset having a longer life than a single taxable year. The line to be drawn between capital expenditures and ordinary and necessary business expenses is not always an easy one, but we are satisfied that in treating prepaid insurance as a capital expense we are obtaining some degree of consistency in these matters. We are, therefore, of the opinion that Welch v. DeBlois, supra, is incorrect and should be overruled.

The decision of Board of Tax Appeals is affirmed.

———

A result contrary to the Boylston case was reached in Waldheim Realty and Investment Co. v. Commissioner, 245 F.2d 823 (8th Cir.

1957), where the court allowed a cash method taxpayer to deduct prepaid insurance in accordance with past practice which did not substantially distort income because the deduction produced results comparable to a pro rata capitalization. The Commissioner has reiterated the position that the Boylston case represents the law. Rev.Rul. 70–413, 1970–2 C.B. 104.

In general, prepayments of rentals must be capitalized over the term of a lease. These prepayments must be amortized because the life of the asset extends beyond the taxable year. A full deduction for several years' rentals in the year of payment would materially distort income in that year.

However, in Zaninovich v. Commissioner, 616 F.2d 429 (9th Cir. 1980), the court allowed the taxpayer to deduct a prepayment of rent for a twelve-month period even though eleven of those months were in the taxable year following the year in which the taxpayer made the prepayment. The Ninth Circuit decided that the "one year" rule, which treats a payment as a capital expenditure if it creates an asset or provides an advantage to a capital asset which has a useful life in excess of one year, applied to distinguish currently deductible expenses and capital expenditures. The court noted: "The one-year rule is useful because it serves to segregate from all business costs those which cannot possibly be considered capital in nature because of their transitory utility to the taxpayer." 616 F.2d at 432. In short, the court concluded that if the prepayment relates to a period of one year or less, the prepayment was currently deductible in the year in which it was made as no evidence existed that this constituted a material distortion of income. The overriding advantage of this rule is the ease of application. The court pointed out that requiring the taxpayers to capitalize their rental payments sacrifices the simplicity of the cash payment for an inconsequential change in the timing of deductions. Note that § 461(i), added in 1984, may result in a postponement of the deduction if taxpayer is a cash method tax shelter as defined in § 461(i) (3). Deduction for payment by a cash method tax shelter is allowed only when the activity to which the expenditure relates has been economically performed as contemplated by § 461(h).

In other situations, a cash method taxpayer may currently deduct an expenditure if a good business reason exists for the prepayment. For example, a person in the business of feeding cattle for market may purchase feed in Year 1 which will be consumed by cattle in Year 2. The cash method taxpayer may seek to deduct the expense in Year 1, the year in which the feed was purchased, but not used. Whether the cash method farmer will be successful in deducting the prepayment depends, according to the Service in Rev.Rul. 79–229, 1979–2 C.B. 210, on meeting three tests: 1) the expenditure must be a payment for feed (a purchase) and not a deposit; 2) the payment must serve a valid business purpose; and 3) the deduction must not result in a material distortion of income. See Rev.Rul. 75–152, 1975–1 C.B. 144. In Commissioner v. VanRaden, 650 F.2d 1046 (9th Cir.1981) the court allowed a deduction for prepaid feed, which was substantially consumed within one year of purchase. The court relied on the Zaninovich case that an expense may be deducted in the year of payment where the expenditure creates an asset having a useful life of one year or less. In VanRaden the cattle feeding operation was not taxpayer's principal business; rather it was designed to produce losses that could be used to offset income from other sources. For a long time cash basis farmers have been permitted to deduct as current operating costs a wide variety of expenses other taxpayers would have to capitalize.

The high tax bracket individual not actively engaged in the business of farming, may seek to prepay the cost of feeding cattle. A deduction in the year of the prepayment would reduce the individual's current income from other sources. If the cattle are sold in the following year, any gain will be realized and recognized at that time. By deducting the cost of feed in the current year and thereby reducing taxable income, the individual achieves a one-year deferral of the taxes on his earnings.

A taxpayer who invests in a farming syndicate, as defined in § 464(c), as a passive investor for the purpose of sheltering income from other sources is subject to the limitations of § 464. In brief, the rules of § 464 apply to limit the deductions of a farming syndicate regardless of its method of accounting. See §§ 448(a), (b)(1), (d)(1), and 263A(e)(4). The cost of feed, among other items of farm supplies, may only be deducted in the tax year when "actually used or consumed." § 464(a). Then the economic performance rules are applied to limit the timing of deductions. § 464(i)(4). In addition, the limitation on the deductibility of passive activity losses under § 469 may also postpone the deductions generated from a passive investment in a farming activity.

The above limitations on deductions arising from a farming activity only apply to the passive investor. Can an individual, using the cash method, who materially participates in the active conduct of a farming activity, currently use the deductions generated by prepayments against income from other sources? The answer is generally yes if the three requirements of Rev.Rul. 79–229, discussed at p. 493, are satisfied. However, even if the taxpayer is a real farmer, if the prepayments exceed more than 50 percent of the taxpayer's total deductible farming expenses for the year, excluding prepaid supplies, then § 464(f) places limitations on the deductibility of the prepaid items. If § 464(f) applies, then such expenses may be deducted only in the year in which the supplies are actually used or consumed. For purposes of the 50 percent test, deductible farming expenses include the normal operating expenses, including taxes, interest and depreciation. § 464(f)(4)(C).

Section 461(g) requires cash method taxpayers to capitalize prepaid interest and deduct such interest ratably over the period of the loan. Read page 644. Accrual method taxpayers generally amortize the prepayment of interest over the period of a loan.

Uniform capitalization rules exist for determining what costs, that may otherwise appear to be deductible as current operating expenses, must be capitalized by a taxpayer. § 263A. These capitalization rules only apply to a taxpayer who manufactures or produces real or personal property for resale, to a taxpayer who acquires inventory for resale, and to taxpayers who manufacture or construct assets for self use. § 263A(b). For example, certain expenditures and other deductions normally deductible as current operating expenses must generally be capitalized and added to the basis of property being constructed if they are related to the asset under construction and are incurred during its construction period. See Commissioner v. Idaho Power Company, 418 U.S. 1 (1974), at p. 586. There are special rules for the treatment of interest on a loan used to finance the construction of an asset. See § 263A(f).

Problems

1. (a) Gerri, a doctor on the cash method, passed the State Board examination in January and began to establish her practice. Which of the following items are currently deductible and which must be capitalized?

i. She rents office space in a highly desirable professional building, paying an under the table $10,000 cash "bonus" to the landlord for a long-term lease. Her monthly rental is $1,000. Consider Reg. § 1.461–1(a)(1).

ii. She buys $15,000 worth of goods for her office, including office furniture, medical equipment, medical books, and a computer, and also purchases $5,000 worth of supplies (paper, pencils, etc.). She wants to deduct the entire $20,000 in the year of the purchase. Consider Reg. §§ 1.162–3, and 1.162–6. What purpose is served by § 179? Read page 574. Should questionable items be claimed as an expense deduction on a tax return on the premise that buried in a list of deductions they may slip by on audit or be available to concede on audit? Reconsider pp. 19–35. Consider § 6661. Why may Gerri want to capitalize these items? Is she able to do so?

iii. She pays an interior decorator $4,000 to fix up her waiting room; the decorating includes a paint job which costs her an additional $2,000. Consider Reg. §§ 1.162–4 and 1.263(a)–1.

iv. She pays an electrician to fix a broken air conditioner in the office. Assume the electrician replaces the compressor unit. Consider Reg. § 1.162–4.

v. She pays for a three years' advance subscription to a medical journal. Consider the Boylston case and Reg. §§ 1.162–6 and 1.461–1(a).

vi. She pays the utility bills for her office.

(b) Would your answers be different if Gerri were an accrual method taxpayer? Consider Reg. § 1.461–1(a) and § 461(h). Reread pp. 226–232.

(c) Consider the tax consequences to Gunther, Gerri's landlord of the following:

i. What is the effect of the bonus payment as to Gunther, a cash method taxpayer? Consider Reg. § 1.61–8(b).

ii. $100 for newspaper advertisements offering the space Gerri rented on a long-term lease. Consider Reg. § 1.162–3.

iii. $18 for adding a mailbox for Gerri. Consider § 179 and Reg. § 1.162–3.

iv. $200 for constructing a sign to replace one destroyed by vandals. The old sign had an adjusted basis of $175. Consider §§ 165(a) and (c)(1), 179 and Reg. 1.162–3.

v. $10,000 for patching the entire asphalt parking lot. Consider the Midland Empire case.

vi. $100 for a plumber to unclog a drain.

vii. An OSHA inspector requires the installation of a wheelchair ramp in the building at a cost of $5000.

2. Gary, a cash method taxpayer, is in the 33 percent tax bracket and expects to remain in this tax bracket for the next five years. He purchased an old hotel in an area of town where tourists congregate. For the past several years he has been operating it on a marginal basis. Gary has now decided to undertake an extensive rehabilitation program. This involves replacement of the following: floors on the ground level, all hardware and plumbing fixtures, and painting and decorating throughout. Gary is undecided whether to have the work done in one year or to spread it over a five-year period. Your partner is working on the contracts and asks whether, for tax purposes, you have any suggestions respecting the manner and timing of the rehabilitation program. Advise her. Consider Reg. §§ 1.162–4 and 1.263(a)–1 and –2, and § 168(c) and (i)(6).

3. COSTS OF ACQUIRING AND DISPOSING OF PROPERTY

Expenses incurred in the acquisition or disposition of capital assets are capital expenditures. The cost of the acquisition of property "having a useful life substantially beyond the taxable year" is also a capital expenditure. Reg. § 1.263(a)–2(a).

Ancillary expenses for the acquisition or disposition of an asset (e.g. commissions paid on purchasing shares of stock) also comprise a part of the cost of an asset. Reg. § 1.263(a)–2(e). Likewise, on the disposition of property, selling commissions (except by dealers) are not deductible but must be offset against the amount realized in figuring the taxpayer's gain (or loss). Reg. § 1.263(a)–2(e).

Expenses to perfect or defend title to property (as opposed to amounts expended for the production of income, such as the cost of investment advice, which are deductible under § 212) generally must be capitalized and added to the basis of the property. Section 263(a) requires that the expenses of improvements to property must be capitalized if they increase the value of any property or estate. If the taxpayer buys property and thereafter expends sums to perfect title, for example, by removing a cloud on title, he is obviously increasing the value of the property. Consonant with this statutory requirement are

Reg. §§ 1.212–1(k) and 1.263(a)–2(c). It does not follow as a matter of logic from the foregoing that where an individual has continued in undisturbed possession of property over a considerable period of time and suddenly finds he must repel an attack on his title, the act of repelling increases the value of the property or estate which he previously owned. The statutory requirement respecting capitalization concerns expenses which actually increase the value of the property or estate. Nevertheless, it has been held that the expenses incurred to defend an existing title must be capitalized. Lewis v. Commissioner, 253 F.2d 821, 827–828 (2d Cir.1958) and Cruttenden v. Commissioner, 644 F.2d 1368 (9th Cir.1981). However, an expense for defending both present title and past receipt of rentals is to be allocated between a capital expense and a current deduction. Morgan's Estate v. Commissioner, 332 F.2d 144 (5th Cir.1964).

Whatever the theoretical weakness of the Regulations, the consistent support given to the Regulations by the courts makes it dubious whether the taxpayer should plan any transaction in reliance on deducting the full expense of an unwarranted attack upon title, even where the taxpayer has held undisturbed possession of the property in question over a long period of time. In other contexts, however, the drawing of a line between a capital expenditure, and a deductible expense may prove difficult.

WOODWARD v. COMMISSIONER

Supreme Court of the United States, 1970.
397 U.S. 572, 90 S.Ct. 1302, 25 L.Ed.2d 577.

[T]he taxpayers, the majority shareholders of the corporation, voted to renew the corporation's charter. Under state law, shareholders voting for such an extension were required to purchase the shares of any dissenters. The taxpayers incurred substantial litigation expenses in connection with a state court proceeding to determine the value of the dissenters' shares.

MR. JUSTICE MARSHALL delivered the opinion of the Court.

* * *

More difficult questions arise with respect to another class of capital expenditures, those incurred in "defending or perfecting title to property." Treas.Reg. on Income Tax § 1.263(a)–2(c). In one sense, any lawsuit brought against a taxpayer may affect his title to property—money or other assets subject to lien.[1] The courts, not believing that Congress meant all litigation expenses to be capitalized, have created the rule that such expenses are capital in nature only where the taxpayer's "primary purpose" in incurring them is to defend or perfect title. See, e.g., Rassenfoss v. Commissioner of Internal Revenue, 158 F.2d 764 (C.A. 7th Cir.1946); Industrial Aggregate Co. v.

1. See Hochschild v. Commissioner of Internal Revenue, 161 F.2d 817, 820 (C.A. 2d Cir.1947) (Frank, J., dissenting).

United States, 284 F.2d 639, 645 (C.A. 8th Cir.1960). This test hardly draws a bright line, and has produced a melange of decisions, which, as the Tax Court has noted, "[i]t would be idle to suggest *   *   * can be reconciled." Ruoff v. Commissioner, 30 T.C. 204, 208 (1958).

Taxpayers urge that this "primary purpose" test, developed in the context of cases involving the costs of defending property, should be applied to costs incurred in acquiring or disposing of property as well. And if it is so applied, they argue, the costs here in question were properly deducted, since the legal proceedings in which they were incurred did not directly involve the question of title to the minority stock, which all agreed was to pass to taxpayers, but rather was concerned solely with the value of that stock.

We agree with the Tax Court and the Court of Appeals that the "primary purpose" test has no application here. That uncertain and difficult test may be the best that can be devised to determine the tax treatment of costs incurred in litigation that may affect a taxpayer's title to property more or less indirectly, and that thus calls for a judgment whether the taxpayer can fairly be said to be "defending or perfecting title." Such uncertainty is not called for in applying the regulation that makes the "cost of acquisition" of a capital asset a capital expense. In our view application of the latter regulation to litigation expenses involves the simpler inquiry whether the origin of the claim litigated is in the process of acquisition itself.

A test based upon the taxpayer's "purpose" in undertaking or defending a particular piece of litigation would encourage resort to formalisms and artificial distinctions. For instance, in this case there can be no doubt that legal, accounting, and appraisal costs incurred by taxpayers in *negotiating* a purchase of the minority stock would have been capital expenditures. See Atzingen-Whitehouse Dairy, Inc. v. Commissioner, 36 T.C. 173 (1961). Under whatever test might be applied, such expenses would have clearly been "part of the acquisition cost" of the stock. Helvering v. Winmill, 305 U.S. 79, 59 S.Ct. 45, 83 L.Ed. 52 (1938). Yet the appraisal proceeding was no more than the substitute that state law provided for the process of negotiation as a means of fixing the price at which the stock was to be purchased. Allowing deduction of expenses incurred in such a proceeding, merely on the ground that title was not directly put in question in the particular litigation, would be anomalous.

Further, a standard based on the origin of the claim litigated comports with this Court's recent ruling on the characterization of litigation expenses for tax purposes in United States v. Gilmore, 372 U.S. 39, 83 S.Ct. 623, 9 L.Ed.2d 570 (1963). This Court there held that the expense of defending a divorce suit was a nondeductible personal expense, even though the outcome of the divorce case would affect the taxpayer's property holdings, and might affect his business reputation. The Court rejected a test that looked to the consequences of the litigation, and did not even consider the taxpayer's motives or purposes in undertaking defense of the litigation, but rather examined the origin and character of the claim against the taxpayer, and found that the claim arose out of the personal relationship of marriage.

The standard here pronounced may, like any standard, present borderline cases, in which it is difficult to determine whether the origin of particular litigation lies in the process of acquisition. This is not such a borderline case. Here state law required taxpayers to "purchase" the stock owned by the dissenter. In the absence of agreement on the price at which the purchase was to be made, litigation was required to fix the price. Where property is acquired by purchase, nothing is more clearly part of the process of acquisition than the establishment of a purchase price.[2] Thus the expenses incurred in that litigation were properly treated as part of the cost of the stock that the taxpayers acquired.

Affirmed.

Disposition expenses present the issue whether they are deductible against ordinary income or are used as an offset against amount realized in computing the taxpayer's capital gain (or loss). After the Woodward case, courts have required taxpayers to offset expenses incurred in the disposition of property, such as legal and accounting fees, against the amount realized. See e.g. Third Nat'l Bank in Nashville v. United States, 427 F.2d 343 (6th Cir.1970), and Von Hafften v. Commissioner, 76 T.C. 831 (1981).

Problem

Ron purchases 100 shares of stock at $50 per share and pays his broker a $100 commission. During the time he held the stock, he purchased a subscription to the Wall Street Journal to follow his investment. He also paid $20 annually for the rental of a safe deposit box to hold the stock certificate. The stock paid dividends of $850 during the two years he held it. At the end of the two years he sold the stock for $60 per share, paying his broker another $100 commission.

   a. Can Ron deduct the $5,000 he paid for the stock under § 212(1)?

2. Taxpayers argue that "purchase" analysis cannot properly be applied to the appraisal situation, because the transaction is an involuntary one from their point of view—an argument relied upon by the District Court in the Smith Hotel Enterprises case, supra, n. 1. In the first place, the transaction is in a sense voluntary, since the majority holders know that under state law they will have to buy out any dissenters. More fundamentally, however, wherever a capital asset is transferred to a new owner in exchange for value either agreed upon or determined by law to be a fair *quid pro quo*, the payment itself is a capital expenditure, and there is no reason why the costs of determining the amount of that payment should be considered capital in the case of the negotiated price and yet considered deductible in the case of the price fixed by law. See Isaac G. Johnson & Co. v. United States, 149 F.2d 851 (C.A. 2d Cir.1945) (expenses of litigating amount of fair compensation in condemnation proceeding held capital expenditures).

b. Can Ron deduct the purchase commission, the subscription and the safe deposit rental under § 212(2)?

c. What is the amount of Ron's gain upon the sale? Consider Reg. § 1.263(a)–2(e) and the impact of § 67.

4. CURRENT DEDUCTION—CAPITALIZATION QUANDARY CONTINUED

The next case illustrates that sometimes capitalization is the rationale for denying a current deduction without the court recognizing that principle.

WELCH v. HELVERING
Supreme Court of the United States, 1933.
290 U.S. 111, 54 S.Ct. 8, 78 L.Ed. 212.

MR. JUSTICE CARDOZO delivered the opinion of the Court.

The question to be determined is whether payments by a taxpayer, who is in business as a commission agent, are allowable deductions in the computation of his income if made to the creditors of a bankrupt corporation in an endeavor to strengthen his own standing and credit.

In 1922 petitioner was the secretary of the E.L. Welch Company, a Minnesota corporation, engaged in the grain business. The company was adjudged an involuntary bankrupt, and had a discharge from its debts. Thereafter the petitioner made a contract with the Kellogg Company to purchase grain for it on a commission. In order to re-establish his relations with customers whom he had known when acting for the Welch Company and to solidify his credit and standing, he decided to pay the debts of the Welch business so far as he was able. In fulfillment of that resolve, he made payments of substantial amounts during five successive years. In 1924, the commissions were $18,028.20, the payments $3,975.97; in 1925, the commissions $31,377.07, the payments $11,968.20; in 1926, the commissions $20,925.25, the payments $12,815.72; in 1927, the commissions $22,119.61, the payments $7,379.72; and in 1928, the commissions $26,177.56, the payments $11,068.25. The Commissioner ruled that these payments were not deductible from income as ordinary and necessary expenses, but were rather in the nature of capital expenditures, an outlay for the development of reputation and good will. The Board of Tax Appeals sustained the action of the Commissioner (25 B.T.A. 117), and the Court of Appeals for the Eighth Circuit affirmed. 63 F.(2d) 976. The case is here on certiorari.

> "In computing net income there shall be allowed as deductions * * * all the ordinary and necessary expenses paid or incurred during the taxable year in carrying on any trade or business." [§ 162].

We may assume that the payments to creditors of the Welch Company were necessary for the development of the petitioner's business, at least in the sense that they were appropriate and helpful.

McCulloch v. Maryland, 4 Wheat. 316, 4 L.Ed. 579. He certainly thought they were, and we should be slow to override his judgment. But the problem is not solved when the payments are characterized as necessary. Many necessary payments are charges upon capital. There is need to determine whether they are both necessary and ordinary. Now, what is ordinary, though there must always be a strain of constancy within it, is none the less a variable affected by time and place and circumstance. Ordinary in this context does not mean that the payments must be habitual or normal in the sense that the same taxpayer will have to make them often. A lawsuit affecting the safety of a business may happen once in a lifetime. The counsel fees may be so heavy that repetition is unlikely. None the less, the expense is an ordinary one because we know from experience that payments for such a purpose, whether the amount is large or small, are the common and accepted means of defense against attack. Cf. Kornhauser v. United States, 276 U.S. 145, 48 S.Ct. 219, 72 L.Ed. 505. The situation is unique in the life of the individual affected, but not in the life of the group, the community, of which he is a part. At such times there are norms of conduct that help to stabilize our judgment, and make it certain and objective. The instance is not erratic, but is brought within a known type.

The line of demarcation is now visible between the case that is here and the one supposed for illustration. We try to classify this act as ordinary or the opposite, and the norms of conduct fail us. No longer can we have recourse to any fund of business experience, to any known business practice. Men do at times pay the debts of others without legal obligation or the lighter obligation imposed by the usages of trade or by neighborly amenities, but they do not do so ordinarily, not even though the result might be to heighten their reputation for generosity and opulence. Indeed, if language is to be read in its natural and common meaning (Old Colony R. Co. v. Commissioner, 284 U.S. 552, 560, 52 S.Ct. 211, 76 L.Ed. 484; Woolford Realty Co. v. Rose, 286 U.S. 319, 327, 52 S.Ct. 568, 76 L.Ed. 1128), we should have to say that payment in such circumstances, instead of being ordinary is in a high degree extraordinary. There is nothing ordinary in the stimulus evoking it, and none in the response. Here, indeed, as so often in other branches of the law, the decisive distinctions are those of degree and not of kind. One struggles in vain for any verbal formula that will supply a ready touchstone. The standard set up by the statute is not a rule of law; it is rather a way of life. Life in all its fullness must supply the answer to the riddle.

The Commissioner of Internal Revenue resorted to that standard in assessing the petitioner's income, and found that the payments in controversy came closer to capital outlays than to ordinary and necessary expenses in the operation of a business. His ruling has the support of a presumption of correctness, and the petitioner has the burden of proving it to be wrong. Wickwire v. Reinecke, 275 U.S. 101,

48 S.Ct. 43, 72 L.Ed. 184; Jones v. Commissioner (C.C.A.) 38 F.(2d) 550, 552. Unless we can say from facts within our knowledge that these are ordinary and necessary expenses according to the ways of conduct and the forms of speech prevailing in the business world, the tax must be confirmed. But nothing told us by this record or within the sphere of our judicial notice permits us to give that extension to what is ordinary and necessary. Indeed, to do so would open the door to many bizarre analogies. One man has a family name that is clouded by thefts committed by an ancestor. To add to this own standing he repays the stolen money, wiping off, it may be, his income for the year. The payments figure in his tax return as ordinary expenses. Another man conceives the notion that he will be able to practice his vocation with greater ease and profit if he has an opportunity to enrich his culture. Forthwith the price of his education becomes an expense of the business, reducing the income subject to taxation. There is little difference between these expenses and those in controversy here. Reputation and learning are akin to capital assets, like the good will of an old partnership. Cf. Colony Coal & Coke Corp. v. Commissioner (C.C.A.) 52 F.(2d) 923. For many, they are the only tools with which to hew a pathway to success. The money spent in acquiring them is well and wisely spent. It is not an ordinary expense of the operation of a business.

Many cases in the federal courts deal with phases of the problem presented in the case at bar. To attempt to harmonize them would be a futile task. They involve the appreciation of particular situations, at times with border-line conclusions. Typical illustrations are cited in the margin.[3]

The decree should be

Affirmed.

---

3. Ordinary expenses: Commissioner v. People's Pittsburgh Trust Co. (C.C.A.) 60 F.(2d) 187, expenses incurred in the defense of a criminal charge growing out of the business of the taxpayer; American Rolling Mill Co. v. Commissioner (C.C.A.) 41 F.(2d) 314, contributions to a civic improvement fund by a corporation employing half of the wage earning population of the city, the payments being made, not for charity, but to add to the skill and productivity of the workmen (cf. the decisions collated in 30 Columbia Law Review 1211, 1212, and the distinctions there drawn); Corning Glass Works v. Lucas, 59 App.D.C. 168, 37 F.(2d) 798, 68 A.L.R. 736, donations to a hospital by a corporation whose employees with their dependents made up two-thirds of the population of the city; Harris & Co. v. Lucas (C.C.A.) 48 F.(2d) 187, payments of debts discharged in bankruptcy, but subject to be revived by force of a new promise. Cf. Lucas v. Ox Fibre Brush Co., 281 U.S. 115, 50 S.Ct. 273, 74 L.Ed.

733, where additional compensation, reasonable in amount, was allowed to the officers of a corporation for services previously rendered.

Not ordinary expenses: Hubinger v. Commissioner (C.C.A.) 36 F.(2d) 724, payments by the taxpayer for the repair of fire damage, such payments being distinguished from those for wear and tear; Lloyd v. Commissioner (C.C.A.) 55 F.(2d) 842, counsel fees incurred by the taxpayer, the president of a corporation, in prosecuting a slander suit to protect his reputation and that of his business; One Hundred Five West Fifty-Fifth Street v. Commissioner (C.C.A.) 42 F.(2d) 849, and Blackwell Oil & Gas Co. v. Commissioner (C.C.A.) 60 F.(2d) 257, gratuitous payments to stockholders in settlement of disputes between them, or to assume the expense of a lawsuit in which they had been made defendants; White v. Commissioner (C.C.A.) 61 F.(2d) 726, payments in settlement of a

In Commissioner v. Tellier, 383 U.S. 687, 689–690, 86 S.Ct. 1118, 1120, 16 L.Ed.2d 185, 188 (1966), the Supreme Court stated:

> The principal function of the term "ordinary" in § 162(a) is to clarify the distinction, often difficult, between those expenses that are currently deductible and those that are in the nature of capital expenditures, which, if deductible at all, must be amortized over the useful life of the asset.

See also Bertolini Trucking Co. v. Commissioner, 736 F.2d 1120 (6th Cir.1984). Note also that § 263(a) takes precedence over § 162.

Question

Is Welch v. Helvering distinguishable from Friedman v. Delaney, at p. 458? Should a deduction be denied merely because it is unusual? What was the tacit justification for not allowing Mr. Welch a current deduction? Did the Supreme Court view Mr. Welch's expenditure as the purchase of an asset? What would you call this asset? In light of the Supreme Court's decision, could Mr. Welch ever recover the cost of this asset? Consider Reg. § 1.167(a)–3.

Problems

1. Stan is an insurance broker. What are the tax consequences if he reimburses customers for losses they suffered when an insurer he represented went bankrupt?

2. A fire destroyed the warehouse owned by Security Storage Co. What are the tax consequences if the firm voluntarily pays customers whose uninsured goods were destroyed by the fire? Consider Welch v. Helvering and Friedman v. Delaney (p. 458).

5. COSTS OF STARTING-UP OR EXPANDING A BUSINESS

Start-Up Expenditures. For start-up expenses incurred prior to the enactment of § 195, the Service and the courts literally interpreted § 162(a). Until the regular activities for which the business was formed were engaged in, the taxpayer was not "carrying on" a trade or business. For example, in construing the phrase "carrying on any trade or business" under § 162(a) the court in Richmond Television Corp. v. United States, 345 F.2d 901, 907 (4th Cir.1965), reversed and remanded on another issue, 382 U.S. 68, 86 S.Ct. 233, 15 L.Ed.2d 143 (1965) (per curiam), reversed on another issue, 354 F.2d 410 (4th Cir. 1965), overruled on other issues, N.C.N.B. Corp. v. United States, 684 F.2d 285, 289 (4th Cir.1982), stated:

> The uniform teaching of these several cases is that, even though a taxpayer has made a firm decision to enter into business and over a considerable period of time spent money in preparation for entering that business, he still has not "engaged in carrying on any trade or business" with the intendment of section 162(a) until such time as the

lawsuit against a member of a partnership, the effect being to enable him to devote his undivided efforts to the partnership business and also to protect its credit.

business has begun to function as a going concern and performed those activities for which it was organized.

Thus, expenses incurred prior to the establishment of a business (so-called preopening expenses) were nondeductible. Those nondeductible start-up or preopening expenses, incurred subsequent to a decision to acquire or establish a specific business, but prior to its actual operation, could be capitalized as intangible assets. Expenditures relating to specific physical assets could be added to the basis of the assets. A corporation or a partnership could (and continues to be able) elect to amortize start-up costs which qualify as "organizational expenditures." §§ 248 and 709(b). Other start-up costs, for example, which relate to assets with an unlimited or indeterminate useful life or which do not qualify as "organizational expenditures," could only be recovered on the sale or termination of a business.

In addition to the issue of deductibility under § 162, consider how the Tax Court in the next case handled the possibility of a deduction under § 212 or § 165(c)(2). Were the business investigatory expenses in question deductible, or must such expenses be capitalized, or were they viewed as personal?

FRANK v. COMMISSIONER

Tax Court of the United States, 1953.
20 T.C. 511.

[Prior to World War II the taxpayer had been employed as a newspaperman. After his discharge from military service in November, 1945, the taxpayer and his wife (who had been employed by several government agencies during World War II), travelled in search of a radio station or newspaper to purchase and operate. Taxpayer and his wife were employed by a newspaper in Phoenix, Arizona for about six months in 1946. They continued to examine other newspapers that were for sale. They purchased a newspaper in Canton, Ohio in November, 1946 and immediately began publication.]

* * *

OPINION

VAN FOSSAN, JUDGE: The only question presented is whether the petitioners may deduct $5,965 in the determination of their net income for the year 1946 as ordinary and necessary business expenses or as losses. The petitioners base their claim for deductions upon [§§ 162(a), 212, and 165(c)(2)]. The evidence reasonably establishes that the petitioners expended the amount of expenses stated in our Findings of Fact during the taxable year in traveling, telephone, telegraph, and legal expenses in the search for and investigation of newspaper and radio properties. This total amount was spent by the petitioners in their travels through various states in an endeavor to find a business which they could purchase and operate. These expenses do not include amounts spent while living in Phoenix, Arizona.

The travel expenses and legal fees spent in searching for a newspaper business with a view to purchasing the same cannot be deducted under the provisions of [§ 162(a)]. The petitioners were not engaged in any trade or business at the time the expenses were incurred. The trips made by the taxpayers from Phoenix, Arizona, were not related to the conduct of the business that they were then engaged in but were preparatory to locating a business venture of their own. The expenses of investigating and looking for a new business and trips preparatory to entering a business are not deductible as an ordinary and necessary business expense incurred in carrying on a trade or business. George C. Westervelt, 8 T.C. 1248. The word "pursuit" in the statutory phrase "in pursuit of a trade or business" is not used in the sense of "searching for" or "following after," but in the sense of "in connection with" or "in the course of" a trade or business. It presupposes an existing business with which petitioner is connected. The fact that petitioners had no established home during the period of their travels further complicates the question and alone may be fatal to petitioners' case. If they had no home, how could they have expenses "away from home"? The issue whether all or part of the expenses so incurred were capital expenditures is not raised or argued and we do not pass judgment on such question.

Neither are the travel and legal expenses incurred by the petitioners in their attempt to find and purchase a business deductible under [§ 212], which allows the deduction of expenses incurred in the production or collection of income or in the management, conservation, or maintenance of property held for the production of income. There is a basic distinction between allowing deductions for the expense of producing or collecting income, in which one has an existent interest or right, and expenses incurred in an attempt to obtain income by the creation of some new interest. Marion A. Burt Beck, 15 T.C. 642, affd. 194 F.2d 537. The expenses here involved are of the latter classification. The traveling costs were incurred in an endeavor to acquire a business which might, in the future, prove productive of income. It might reasonably be said that petitioners were engaged in the active search of employment as newspaper owners, but that cannot be regarded as a business. It is much like the situation obtaining in Mort L. Bixler, 5 B.T.A. 1181, or like that found in McDonald v. Commissioner, 323 U.S. 57, where it was held that a Pennsylvania court of common pleas judge seeking reelection could not deduct under [§ 212] expenses of such campaign. The Supreme Court said " * * * his campaign contributions were not expenses incurred in being a judge but in trying to be a judge for the next ten years."

The petitioners contend finally that the expenses in question must be allowed as deductions as nonbusiness losses under [§ 165(c)(2)]. This subsection of the Code provides a deduction for losses incurred in transactions entered into for profit. The only transaction entered into for profit by the petitioners, as disclosed by the facts, was the purchase of a newspaper in Canton, Ohio. Other possible transactions were investigated and rejected or otherwise not entered into. It cannot be said that the petitioners entered into a transaction every time they visited a new city and examined a new business property. Nor can we hold that petitioners entered into such transactions and then abandoned them, as they here contend. Rather, they refused to enter into such transactions after the preliminary investigation. If the general search for a suitable business property itself be considered as a transaction entered into for profit, no abandonment of such project occurred in the taxable year so as to enable deduction of these expenses as losses. Travel and legal expenses, such as were incurred here by petitioners, are not deductible as losses. Robert Lyons Hague, 24 B.T.A. 288; cf. Charles T. Parker, 1 T.C. 709. The cases cited by the petitioners concern instances where transactions were actually entered into and losses were then sustained upon abandonment. We cannot find this situation here.

We conclude that the petitioners may not deduct the expenses claimed for 1946 under the applicable provisions of the Internal Revenue Code.

Decision will be entered for the respondent.

———

To encourage the formation of new business and reduce litigation, investigatory and start-up expenses paid or incurred after July 29, 1980 may be amortized, under § 195, over a period of not less than 60 months. "Start-up expenditures" are defined in § 195(c)(1) as expenses paid or incurred in investigating the creation or acquisition of an active trade or business, creating an active trade or business, or "any activity engaged in for profit and for the production of income before the day on which the active trade or business begins, in anticipation of such activity becoming an active trade or business * * *." The Treasury is authorized to promulgate Regulations determining when an active trade or business begins. § 195(c)(2)(A). Start-up expenditures allowable as deductions under §§ 164 and 163(a) (taxes and certain interest expenditures, which are allowable without regard to whether they were incurred in a business context) are not treated as start-up expenditures for purposes of § 195 amortization. § 195(c)(1).

The expenditures must relate to investigating or creating an active trade or business, not an investment. Examples of an active trade or business include the operation of an apartment complex, an office building or a shopping center. Moreover, "* * * in the case of investigatory expenditures incurred by a taxpayer with respect to the acquisition of an existing trade or business, the taxpayer will be considered to have entered into a trade or business only if the taxpayer has an equity interest in, and actively participates in the management of, the trade or business." Senate Finance Committee, Report No. 96–

1036, Miscellaneous Revenue Act of 1980, 96th Cong.2d Sess. 12–13 (1980).

Examples of investigatory costs include expenses incurred in analyzing potential markets, products, labor and transportation facilities. Start-up costs consist, among other items, of advertising, employee training expenses, and professional consultant fees.

Despite the legislative attempt in 1980 it remained unclear whether certain costs were start-up expenditures. For example, in Hoopengarner v. Commissioner, 80 T.C. 538 (1983) the taxpayer acquired, in April, 1976, a 52½ year leasehold interest in an undeveloped parcel of land. In 1976 the taxpayer paid rent as lessee of the land. In February, 1977, the taxpayer commenced construction of an office building on the parcel. The building was completed in September, 1977 and occupied by tenants in late 1977. Although barring the taxpayer from deducting his 1976 rent expenses under § 162(a), a majority of the Tax Court concluded that the taxpayer could deduct his 1976 rent payment under § 212(2). The majority indicated that the taxpayer's leasehold interest qualified as "property" under § 212(2). Although the taxpayer realized no income from his leasehold interest during 1976, the leasehold constituted property held for the production of income because the taxpayer held the leasehold for the production of future rental income and future appreciation. Section 263 was deemed inapplicable because the rent did not result in the acquisition of an asset with a useful life in excess of one year. The taxpayer's possessory right to the land arising from the rent payment, according to the majority, was completely consummed within one year of payment.

The purpose for renting the land in Hoopengarner was to obtain a site for the building. Because taxpayer's motive was to operate a building to produce a profit, the taxpayer's rental payments incurred prior to the completion of the building are really allocable to future revenues from the building. Congress amended § 195 in 1984 to ensure the capitalization of expenditures made in anticipation of entering into a trade or business. Note the broadened definition of start-up expenses contained in § 195(c)(1)(A)(iii). This definition would require the capitalization of the rent expenses allowed as a current deduction in Hoopengarner.

What if an individual, who is not engaged in the particular trade or business, incurs expenses in investigating the prospects for creating or acquiring a trade or business, but does not in fact commence or acquire the business? Senate Finance Committee, Report No. 96–1036, Miscellaneous Revenue Act of 1980, 96th Cong., 2d Sess. 13 (1980) states: "[n]o deduction is allowed under [§ 195] with respect to items incurred incident to a trade or business which actually is not commenced or acquired by the taxpayer." Thus, investigatory expenses incurred in the course of a general search for or preliminary investigation of a business are not deductible under § 162(a) because no business exists. Likewise, under § 212 until a transaction is complete and the business is commenced or acquired there is no production of income from the taxpayer's business. Investigatory expenses incurred in an unsuccessful attempt to acquire a specific business are, however, deductible as a loss under § 165(c)(2). The expenses may be deductible under § 165(c)(2) as a loss incurred in a transaction entered into for profit only if the taxpayer has gone beyond a general investigatory search to focus on the acquisition of a specific business or investment. Rev.Rul. 77–254, 1977–2 C.B. 63, 64. See also Seed v. Commissioner, 52 T.C. 880 (1969) (Acq. 1970–2 C.B. xxi). Investigatory expenses incurred by a taxpayer who is engaged in the same type of business, but does not consummate the acquisition of the specific business, are also deductible as a loss under § 165(c)(2). Rev.Rul. 74–104, 1974–1 C.B. 70. Finally, § 195(a) now states that except as provided under § 195, no deduction is allowed for start-up expenditures, including investigatory expenses.

Start-up expenses must be distinguished from the ordinary and necessary expenses of expanding an existing business which are currently deductible. Senate Finance Committee, Report No. 96–1036, Miscellaneous Revenue Act of 1980, 96th Cong., 2d Sess. 12 (1980) states: "In the case of an existing business, eligible start-up expenditures do not include deductible ordinary and necessary expenses paid or incurred in connection with an expansion of the business. As under present law, these expenses will continue to be currently deductible. The determination of whether there is an expansion of an existing trade or business or a creation or acquisition of a new trade or business is to be based on the facts and circumstances of each case under present law."

Expanding a Business. The line between expenditures by a going business for the purpose of expanding the current business (which probably are currently deductible) and those for the purpose of entering a new business (which must be capitalized) raises a difficult factual issue.

In Briarcliff Candy Corporation v. Commissioner, 475 F.2d 775 (2d Cir.1973), the taxpayer was engaged in the manufacture and sale of candy products. It instituted a program for soliciting independently operated retail outlets, primarily drug stores, to sell its candies. Taxpayer set up a new franchise division to pursue this expansion. The Commissioner argued that the costs incurred in establishing a division for obtaining a new marketing outlet for its products should be capitalized as taxpayer's efforts amounted to the creation of an asset, a new distribution system for its products. The court allowed a current deduction as it found that this was nothing more than the expansion of an existing business, not the creation of "separate and distinct assets." Courts following Briarcliff Candy have held that an expenditure that merely provides a benefit in future years is not to be capitalized if that cost does not serve to create or enhance what is essentially a separate and distinct asset. For example, courts have held that the commencement of a credit card division by a bank constituted the extension of the banking business, not a new business, even though the bank had not previously engaged in the consumer credit card business. Colorado Springs National Bank v. United States, 505 F.2d 1185 (10th Cir.1974); First Security Bank of Idaho, N.A. v. Commissioner, 592 F.2d 1050 (9th Cir.1979); Iowa Des Moines National Bank v. Commissioner, 592 F.2d 433 (8th Cir.1979).

An excellent analysis of § 195 is contained in Mundstock, Taxation of Business Intangible Capital, Pennsylvania Law Review, June, 1987.

Problems

1. Martin is a stockbroker who has inherited several million dollars from a wealthy uncle. Martin's lifelong ambition has been to go into the magazine publishing business. Martin wants to invest part of his fortune in acquiring a magazine.

(a) Assume he investigates and then consummates the purchase of one magazine. Consider § 195. He incurs various expenses including appraisals, legal fees, travel costs, and telephone. What expenses are deductible? When are they deductible?

(b) Assume he investigates several magazines, but purchases one magazine. Consider the Frank case and §§ 195, 162, 212, and 165(c)(2). Assume Martin incurred $80,000 of expenses in his search and $60,000 are allocable to the magazines he did not buy. Reconsider the materials on the legal expenses incident to divorce and separation at pp. 448–457.

(c) Assume he undertakes a preliminary investigation in connection with the purchase of a specific magazine, which is then abandoned. How may he treat these costs? Consider §§ 195, 162, 212, and 165(c).

(d) Assume he conducts a general investigation of several magazines, but does not focus on a specific magazine. He never acquires any magazine. Consider the Frank case and §§ 195, 162, 212, and 165(c)(2).

2. You represent The Last National Bank located in Metroville. Because of population shifts, the bank wants to open new branches in the suburbs. Consider the tax consequences of the bank engaging consultants to prepare general marketing studies of the suburbs and feasibility studies focusing on potential locations for future bank branches. The bank wants to devote staff time to planning and implementing the projects and applying for permission of Federal regulatory authorities to open branches. The bank also desires to expend funds for attorney's fees and permit fees for licensing the new branches. Determine the tax treatment of these expenditures. Consider §§ 162(a), 263 and 195.

6. EXPENSES OF EDUCATION

Problems

1. Scientific Research Corporation has a policy of hiring only candidates for a Ph.D. degree in Geophysics for the position of project research

director. The Corporation hired Jane Doe, who had a master's degree in Geophysics, as a member of the research staff with an eye to grooming her for advancement to the project research director position. After being hired, she enrolled as a part-time candidate for a Ph.D. degree in Geophysics at State Institute of Technology. Her tuition, fees, books and supplies cost $15,000 per year.

(a) Consider the tax consequences to Jane if she is not reimbursed for her expenses and wishes to itemize her deductions. Consider § 67 and Reg. § 1.162–5(a), (b) and (c). How should the Corporation structure the employment and educational requirements to assure that the expenses are deductible by Jane?

(b) How many of the above expenses can the Corporation deduct if it pays them? Consider § 162.

(c) Would Jane realize gross income if Scientific reimburses Jane for the above expenses (or Scientific paid for these items)? Consider the question apart from § 127 by examining §§ 61(a), 62(a)(2)(A), 67 and 132, and Reg. §§ 1.162–5(a), (b) and (c) and 1.162–17(b)(1) and then under § 127. What if Jane cannot deduct these expenses?

2. Can a taxpayer, who is a doctor, deduct the travel expenses and registration fee of attending an investment seminar in another city on "How to make money in the stock market"? Consider § 274(h)(7). Would the result be different if taxpayer is a stock broker?

Employee's Viewpoint. Two groups of education expenses (so-called job-related education expenses) are deductible. The first group is composed of courses that maintain or improve skills needed in an individual's present job or employment. Reg. § 1.162–5(a) and (c)(1). For example, short refresher courses taken by a physician to improve his skills are deductible. A teacher may deduct the expenses of courses in broad subject areas. See e.g. Ford v. Commissioner, 56 T.C. 1300 (1971), affirmed per curiam 487 F.2d 1025 (9th Cir.1973). Even if the courses qualify an individual for substantial advancement, they are deductible if taken primarily to maintain or improve skills needed in his present employment. The second group of courses are those which are required by an individual's employer, or applicable law or regulations, as a condition to an individual's retention of a present job or rate of pay. Reg. § 1.162–5(a) and (c)(2). This standard is satisfied only by employer educational requirements which are imposed for a bona fide business purpose of the employer. The employer mandated standard only applies to the cost of the minimum required education.

However, the education expenses: (1) to meet the minimum entry educational requirements of the taxpayer's chosen employment or trade or business (Reg. § 1.162–5(b)(2)) or (2) to qualify an individual for a new trade or business (Reg. § 1.162–5(b)(3)) (as opposed to new duties involving the same type of work as the individual's present employment) are nondeductible personal expenses. For example, law school expenses of a practicing accountant are nondeductible. The expenses which qualify the accountant for a new trade or business are nondeductible whether or not he intends to enter the legal profession. Reg. § 1.162–5(b)(3) (especially Example 1). The Regulations state that nondeductible educational expenses which meet minimum educational requirements or qualify an individual for a new trade or business are "personal expenditures or constitute an inseparable aggregate of personal and capital expenditures." Reg. § 1.162–5(b)(1). Furthermore, expenses falling under Reg. § 1.162–5(b)(2) or (3) may not be deducted even if the education maintains or improves the skills required by the individual in the individual's job or meets the express requirements of the individual's employer or applicable law or regulations. Reg. § 1.162–5(c)(2).

In sum, educational expenses are deductible, subject to the two percent floor imposed in § 67(a), if the taxpayer expends funds to maintain skills or because of an employer or legal mandate but not to meet minimum educational requirements in the taxpayer's trade or business or qualify him for a new trade or business. A deductible education expense can be viewed as an intellectual repair.

SHARON v. COMMISSIONER

Tax Court of the United States, 1976.
66 T.C. 515, affirmed 591 F.2d 1273 (9th Cir.1978).

SIMPSON, JUDGE: * * *

FINDINGS OF FACT

Some of the facts have been stipulated, and those facts are so found.

* * *

Bar Admission Expenses

The petitioner attended Brandeis University from September 1957 to June 1961 and received a bachelor of arts degree upon his graduation. * * *

After graduation from Brandeis University, the petitioner entered Columbia University School of Law, receiving a bachelor of laws degree in June 1964. * * *

* * * The petitioner expended a total of $210.20 in gaining admission to practice law in the State of New York. This amount included $175.20 for bar review courses and materials related thereto and a New York State bar examination fee of $25.

The petitioner was admitted to practice law in the State of New York on December 22, 1964. Thereafter, he was employed as an attorney by a law firm in New York City until 1967, when he accepted a position in the Office of Regional Counsel, Internal Revenue Service, and moved to California.

Although not required by his employer to be a member of the California bar, the petitioner decided to become a member of that

State's bar after moving there. However, he found that the study of California law, which he undertook in preparation for the California bar examination, was helpful in his practice of law as an attorney in the Regional Counsel's office. The petitioner spent the following amounts in order to gain membership in the California bar:

Registration as law student in California	$ 20
California bar review course	230
General bar examination fee	150
Attorney's bar examination fee	375
Admittance fee	26
Total	801

In 1969, the petitioner also spent a total of $11 in order to be admitted to practice before the U.S. District Court for the Northern District of California and the U.S. Court of Appeals for the Ninth Circuit. The petitioner's employer required only that he be admitted to practice before the U.S. Tax Court.

In 1970, the petitioner incurred the following expenses in connection with his admission to the U.S. Supreme Court:

Round trip air fare, San Francisco to New York	$238.35
Round trip rail fare, New York to Washington, and miscellaneous expenses	75.00
Total	313.35

The petitioner's employer did not require that he be admitted to practice before the U.S. Supreme Court but did assist him in this matter. The Chief Counsel of the IRS personally moved the admission of a group of IRS attorneys, including the petitioner. Furthermore, two of his supervisors signed his application as personal references.

During 1970, the U.S. Supreme Court rules required a personal appearance before it in Washington, D.C., to be admitted to practice.

On their return for 1969, the petitioners claimed a deduction for "Dues and Professional Expenses" of $492. The Commissioner disallowed $385 of such deduction on the grounds that the disallowed portion was not a deductible business expense, but was a nondeductible capital expenditure. On their return for 1970, the petitioners claimed a deduction of $313.35 for the cost of petitioner Joel A. Sharon's admission to practice before the U.S. Supreme Court. The Commissioner also disallowed such deduction. In addition to challenging the disallowed deductions, the petitioners alleged in their petition that they were entitled to amortize or depreciate the cost of petitioner Joel A. Sharon's education. The Commissioner denied this allegation in his answer.

* * *

OPINION

* * *

2. Amortization of License to Practice Law in New York

The next issue to be decided is whether the petitioner may amortize the cost of obtaining his license to practice law in New York. The petitioner contends that he is entitled under section 167 to amortize the cost of such license over the period from the date of his admission to the bar to the date on which he reaches age 65, when he expects to retire. In his cost basis of this "intangible asset," he included the costs of obtaining his college degree ($11,125), obtaining his law degree ($6,910), a bar review course and related materials ($175.20), and the New York State bar examination fee ($25). As justification for including these education expenses in the cost of his license, he points out that, in order to take the New York bar examination, he was required to have graduated from college and an accredited law school.

The petitioners rely upon section 1.167(a)–3 of the Income Tax Regulations, which provides in part:

> If an intangible asset is known from experience or other factors to be of use in the business or in the production of income for only a limited period, the length of which can be estimated with reasonable accuracy, such an intangible asset may be the subject of a depreciation allowance. * * *

There is no merit in the petitioner's claim to an amortization deduction for the cost of his education and related expenses in qualifying himself for the legal profession. His college and law school expenses provided him with a general education which will be beneficial to him in a wide variety of ways. See James A. Carroll, 51 T.C. 213, 216 (1968). The costs and responsibility for obtaining such education are personal. Section 1.262–1(b)(9) of the Income Tax Regulations provides that expenditures for education are deductible only if they qualify under section 162 and section 1.162–5 of the regulations. In the words of section 1.162–5(b), all costs of "minimum educational requirements for qualification in * * * employment" are "personal expenditures or constitute an inseparable aggregate of personal and capital expenditures." There is no "rational" or workable basis for any allocation of this inseparable aggregate between the nondeductible personal component and a deductible component of the total expense. Fausner v. Commissioner, 413 U.S. 838, 839 (1973). Such expenses are not made any less personal or any more separable from the aggregate by attempting to capitalize them for amortization purposes. Since the inseparable aggregate includes personal expenditures, the preeminence of section 262 over section 167 precludes any amortization deduction. Cf. Commissioner v. Idaho Power Co., 418 U.S. at 17; Bodzin v. Commissioner, 509 F.2d at 681. The same reasoning applies to the costs of review courses and related expenses taken to qualify for the practice of a profession. William D. Glenn, 62 T.C. 270, 274–276 (1974).

In his brief, the petitioner attempts to distinguish our opinion in *Denman* by asserting that he is not attempting to capitalize his educational costs, but rather, the cost of his license to practice law. Despite the label which the petitioner would apply to such costs, they nonetheless constitute the costs of his education, which are personal and nondeductible. Moreover, in his petition, he alleged that the capital asset he was seeking to amortize was his education.

There remains the $25 fee paid for the petitioner's license to practice in New York. This was not an educational expense but was a fee paid for the privilege of practicing law in New York, a nontransferable license which has value beyond the taxable years, and such fee is a capital expenditure. * * * The Commissioner has limited his argument to the educational expenses and apparently concedes that the fee may be amortized. Since the amount of the fee is small, the petitioner might, ordinarily, be allowed to elect to deduct the full amount of the fee in the year of payment, despite its capital nature. Cf. sec. 1.162–12(a), Income Tax Regs., with respect to the treatment of inexpensive tools. However, since the fee was paid prior to the years in issue, we cannot allow a current deduction in this case. Therefore, in view of the Commissioner's concession and our conclusion with respect to the third and fourth issues, a proportionate part of such fee may be added to the amounts to be amortized in accordance with our resolution of the third issue.

3. License to Practice Law in California

The next issue to be decided is whether the petitioner may deduct or amortize the expenses he incurred in gaining admission to practice before the State and Federal courts of California. The Commissioner disallowed the amounts paid in 1969 to take the attorney's bar examination in California and the amounts paid for admission to the bar of the U.S. District Court for the Northern District of California and for admission to the U.S. Court of Appeals for the Ninth Circuit. He determined that such expenses were capital expenditures. In his brief, the petitioner argues for a current deduction only if the costs of his license to practice in California are not amortizable.

It is clear that the petitioner may not deduct under section 162(a) the fees paid to take the California attorney's bar examination and to gain admission to practice before two Federal courts in California. In *Arthur E. Ryman, Jr.,* supra, an associate professor of law sought to deduct as an ordinary business expense the cost of his admission to the bar of the State in which he resided. We held that since the taxpayer could reasonably expect the useful life of his license to extend beyond 1 year, the cost of such license was a capital expenditure and not a currently deductible business expense. Unlike the small fee paid to New York, the aggregate amount of such payments in 1969 is too large to disregard their capital nature and allow the petitioners to deduct them currently.

In connection with his alternative claim that he be allowed to amortize the costs of acquiring his license to practice law in California, the petitioner asserts that such costs total $801. Such amount includes the cost of a California bar review course, registration fees, and other items specified in our Findings of Fact. However, the petitioner is in error in including the cost of his bar review course, $230, in the capital cost of his license to practice in California.

* * * Although the petitioner was authorized to practice law in some jurisdictions when he took the California bar review course, such course was nevertheless educational in the same sense as the first bar review course. * * *

Nor may the petitioner treat the payment for the California bar review course as a part of the costs of acquiring his license to practice in California. Educational expenses which are incurred to meet the minimum educational requirements for qualification in a taxpayer's trade or business or which qualify him for a new trade or business are "personal expenditures or constitute an inseparable aggregate of personal and capital expenditures." Sec. 1.162–5(b), Income Tax Regs. We find that the bar review course helped to qualify the petitioner for a new trade or business so that its costs are personal expenses.

* * *

Before taking the bar review course and passing the attorney's bar examination, the petitioner was an attorney licensed to practice law in New York. As an attorney for the Regional Counsel, he could represent the Commissioner in this Court. However, he could not appear in either the State courts of California, the Federal District Courts located there, nor otherwise act as an attorney outside the scope of his employment with the IRS. See Cal.Bus. & Prof.Code sec. 6125 (West 1974); 20 Op.Cal.Atty.Gen. 291 (1952). If he had done so, he would have been guilty of a misdemeanor. Cal.Bus. & Prof.Code sec. 6126 (West 1974). Yet, after receiving his license to practice law in California, he became a member of the State bar with all its accompanying privileges and obligations. He could appear and represent clients in all the courts of California. By comparing the tasks and activities that the petitioner was qualified to perform prior to receiving his license to practice in California with the tasks and activities he was able to perform after receiving such license, it is clear that he has qualified for a new trade or business. Consequently, the expenses of his bar review course were personal and are not includable in the cost of his license to practice law in California.

It is true that even before he became a member of the bar of California, the petitioner was engaged in the business of practicing law. Cf. David J. Primuth, 54 T.C. 374 (1970). However, in applying the provisions of section 1.162–5 of the regulations to determine whether educational expenses are personal or business in nature, it is not enough to find that the petitioner was already engaged in some business—we must ascertain the particular business in which he was previously engaged and whether the education qualified him to engage in a different business. Before taking the bar review course and becoming a member of the bar of California, the petitioner could not generally engage in the practice of law in that State, but the bar review course helped to qualify him to engage in such business.

The Commissioner does not argue that the capital expenditures incurred in obtaining his license to practice law in California may not be amortized. In a series of cases, the courts have held that the fees paid by physicians to acquire hospital privileges are not current business expenses but are capital expenditures amortizable over the doctor's life expectancy. Walters v. Commissioner, 383 F.2d 922, 924 (6th Cir.1967). * * * We hold that the petitioner may treat the costs of acquiring his license to practice in California in a similar manner. * * * Although the petitioner testified that he would retire at age 65 if he were financially able to do so, such testimony is not sufficient to establish the shorter useful life for which he argues.

We are aware that the petitioner's business as an employee of the Office of Regional Counsel did not require him to become a member of the California bar, and it may be argued that, within the meaning of section 167(a)(1), this intangible asset was not "used" in the petitioner's business during 1969 and 1970. However, the record does demonstrate that membership in the California bar was of some assistance to the petitioner in those years. Furthermore, when an attorney commences the practice of law, it is impossible to anticipate where his work will take him. He cannot with certainty establish what work he will receive and what bar memberships will be useful to him. Once he launches into the practice of law, he must decide what bars to join, and so long as there is some rational connection between his present or prospective work and those that he joins, we think that the expenses of joining them should be accepted as an appropriate cost of acquiring the necessary licenses to practice his profession. Since in 1969 and 1970, the petitioner was working in California, he had reason to anticipate that he might eventually leave the Government and enter into the private practice of law in that State; thus, when that possibility is considered together with the immediate benefit to be derived from membership in the California bar, there was ample reason for him to join such bar at that time. For these reasons, we are satisfied that in 1969 and 1970, the petitioner did make use of the tangible asset constituting the privilege of practicing law in California.

4. Supreme Court Admission

The fourth issue to be decided is whether the petitioner may either deduct or amortize the cost of gaining admission to practice before the U.S. Supreme Court. The petitioner deducted the travel costs he incurred in 1970 in traveling to Washington, D.C., to be personally present for the Supreme Court admission, as required by that Court's rules. The Commissioner disallowed the deduction and argued in his brief that such expenditures were capital in nature since the petitioner acquired an asset with a useful life beyond 1 year.

In his brief, the petitioner concedes that he may not deduct the costs he incurred if we find that his license to practice before the Supreme Court is an intangible asset with a useful life of more than 1 year. For the same reasons that we have concluded that the petitioner's New York and California licenses were intangible assets with a useful life of more than 1 year, we also hold that his Supreme Court license is an intangible asset with a useful life exceeding 1 year. Thus, the petitioner may not deduct under section 162 the cost of obtaining such license.

In order for such license to be amortizable pursuant to section 167, the petitioner must show that it was property used in his trade or business. There is little evidence concerning the petitioner's "use" in 1970 of his license to practice before the Supreme Court. However, he did testify that the admission to various bars was a factor used in evaluating attorneys for promotion by his employer, and the Commissioner never disputed such testimony. Furthermore, it is altogether appropriate for any attorney-at-law to become a member of the bar of the Supreme Court whenever it is convenient for him to do so. No one can know when the membership in such bar may be useful to him in the practice of law—it may bring tangible benefits today, tomorrow, or never; yet, if one holds himself out to practice law, there is ample reason for him to acquire membership in the bar of the Supreme Court. Under these circumstances, we find that the intangible asset acquired by becoming a member of such bar was used by the petitioner in 1970 and hold that he may amortize the costs of acquiring such asset over his life expectancy.

* * *

To reflect the foregoing,

Decisions will be entered under Rule 155.

Reviewed by the Court.

RAUM and HALL, JJ., did not participate in the consideration and disposition of this case.

* * *

IRWIN, J., dissenting: I disagree with that portion of the majority opinion which holds that petitioner may not treat the payment for the California bar review course as a part of the cost of acquiring his license to practice law in California. In the past, we have indeed adopted a "commonsense approach" in determining whether an educational expenditure qualifies a taxpayer for a new trade or business. Kenneth C. Davis, 65 T.C. 1014, 1019 (1976); William D. Glenn, 62 T.C. 270, 275 (1974); Ronald F. Weiszmann, 52 T.C. 1106, 1110 (1969), affd. 443 F.2d 29 (9th Cir.1971). However, I think we depart from that approach when we hold that an attorney, licensed to practice law in New York, qualifies for a new trade or business when he obtains a license to practice law in California. In William D. Glenn, supra at 275, we stated:

We have not found a substantial case law suggesting criteria for determining when the acquisition of new titles or abilities constitutes the entry into a new trade or business for purposes of section 1.162–5(c) (1), Income Tax Regs. What has been suggested, and we uphold such suggestion as the only commonsense approach to a classification, is that a comparison be made between the *types of tasks and activities which the taxpayer was qualified to perform before the acquisition of a particular title or degree, and those which he is qualified to perform afterwards.* Ronald F. Weiszmann, 52 T.C. 1106, 1110 (1969), affd. 443 F.2d 29 (C.A.9, 1971). Where we have found such activities and abilities to be significantly different, we have disallowed an educational expense deduction, based on our finding that there had been qualification for a new trade or business. *Ronald F. Weiszmann,* supra. [Emphasis supplied.]

In my view there is no difference in the *types* of tasks and activities which petitioner was qualified to perform before and after he acquired his California license. By virtue of being licensed to practice in California, petitioner could perform the same types of tasks and activities in that state as he was already qualified to perform in New York. In this regard, respondent takes the position that once an individual is qualified to teach in State A, a college course taken in order to qualify for a teaching position in State B is neither a minimum educational requirement of his trade or business nor education qualifying him for a new trade or business. Rev.Rul. 71–58, 1971–1 C.B. 55. I would similarly conclude that once an individual is qualified to practice law in one State, a bar review course taken in preparation for the bar exam of another State is not education leading to qualification for a new trade or business.

———

On appeal, the Ninth Circuit, in affirming the denial of the expenses for the taxpayer's college and law school education and the bar review course, stated that the "allocation of those expenses between the nondeductible personal component and any deductible capital component would not be feasible." Sharon v. Commissioner, 591 F.2d 1273 (9th Cir.1978), cert. denied 442 U.S. 941, 99 S.Ct. 2883, 61 L.Ed.2d 311 (1979).

Question

In the Sharon case why was taxpayer allowed to capitalize certain costs and amortize them over their useful lives? How did the court determine useful life?

———

The educational expenses of an individual who is unemployed or inactive in his business or profession generally are nondeductible. In Wassenaar v. Commissioner, 72 T.C. 1195 (1979), a law student who completed law school and immediately enrolled in a master's program in taxation could not deduct the cost of his graduate tax study because he did not establish his trade or business as a tax lawyer prior to beginning graduate study. The moral is clear: a professional who hopes to deduct the expenses of graduate studies should first be certified to practice his profession and then practice it even for a brief period to give effect to the actual certification to practice represented by his license. Could a practicing lawyer who quit his job and took a full year off to study for an LL.M. degree deduct these educational costs? In Rev.Rul. 68–591, 1968–2 C.B. 73, the Service concluded that a suspension of employment or business activities for one year or less, followed by the resumption of the same employment or business, constitutes a temporary interruption and does not prevent the deduction of otherwise qualified education expenses. The cases draw the line between a temporary and an indefinite suspension on all the facts and circumstances. See e.g., Sherman v. Commissioner, 36 T.C.M. (CCH) 1191 (1977).

Employer's Viewpoint. What if an employer furnishes educational assistance to an employee? Such assistance may take the form of:

(1) the employer reimbursing the employee for educational expenses;

(2) the employer directly paying the employee's educational expenses;

(3) the employer directly furnishing the educational services to the employee.

Unless the educational expenses are deductible to the individual under Reg. § 1.162–5, an employee will generally have income with respect to employer-provided educational assistance which is not offset by any deduction. The employer receives a deduction for the amounts paid to provide educational assistance because such amounts constitute compensation to the employee.

Section 127 excludes up to $5,250 annually from an employee's gross income of employer-provided educational assistance under a qualified program. § 127(a)(1) and (b). A qualified program, among other items, must be nondiscriminatory with respect to eligibility and participation. § 127(b)(2) and (3). The employer may elect to treat an educational assistance program as a statutory employee benefit plan, § 89(i)(2)(B), and thus be subject to the nondiscrimination rules imposed by § 89. Educational assistance excludable from gross income is defined in § 127(c)(1).

Question

Should the exclusion for employer-provided educational assistance be repealed? Are the benefits of the exclusion fairly distributed? Is this exclusion more valuable to certain taxpayers? If so, high-income or low-income taxpayers? Does this exclusion avoid the regular oversight and administrative controls which apply to direct budgetary expenditures? As a result, is this exclusion "unsound"?

References: Mylan, Current Tax Treatment of Educational Costs, 32 Univ.Fla.L.Rev. 387 (1980); Schoenfeld, The Educational Expense Deduction: The Need for a Rational Approach, 27 Villanova L.Rev. 237 (1982).

Question

Should educational costs generally be capitalized, like an investment in a physical asset, and be recoverable through annual depreciation (amortization) deductions? What should be included in educational costs—what expenses and for which educational institutions (college, graduate, professional, vocational, technical or other schools)? Does an individual's life or career expectancy supply an ascertainable useful life? Should the depreciation (amortization) deductions be available to a student or to his parents? Consider the Sharon case and the following commentary.

R. GOODE, THE INDIVIDUAL INCOME TAX
80, 83–87 (Rev. ed. 1976).

* * *

Educational Expenditures

Expenditures for education that increases earning capacity or is intended to do so are a strategically important cost of earning income but are deductible to only a limited extent. Those who invest in themselves are discriminated against compared with persons who have spent little in preparation for their occupations. The tax provisions are paradoxical at a time when the country has become more aware of the need for highly trained persons and of the contribution of education to economic progress.

* * *

A person who holds a job on a provisional or temporary basis, subject to the completion of certain educational requirements, may not deduct the cost of meeting these requirements, since this is a minimum condition of the employment. If, however, the requirements for the position are changed after the person has once fully qualified, the cost of meeting the new standard is deductible. For an employee, a change of duties does not involve a new trade or business if the employee continues in the same general type of work. The regulations state (sec. 1.162–5[b][i]) that for this purpose "all teaching and related duties shall be considered to involve the same general type of work."

Illustrating the application of the rules, the authors of the regulations mention the case of A, the holder of a bachelor's degree who is employed as a high school teacher in a state where a condition of continued employment is the completion of a fifth year of college within ten years after being hired. A completes the additional year of study and obtains a standard certificate. The cost is deductible inasmuch as the fifth year of training is not a minimum requirement of employment. B, who also holds a bachelor's degree, is temporarily employed as an instructor at a university while studying for an advanced degree. He may become a regular faculty member only if he obtains the graduate degree and may continue as an instructor only so long as he makes satisfactory progress toward obtaining the degree. The cost of the graduate studies is not deductible because they are part of the minimum requirements for qualification in B's trade or business. C, a self-employed accountant, attends law school at night and earns a law degree. The expenditures are not deductible because the course of study qualifies C for a new trade or business. D, a practicing psychiatrist, pursues a program of study and training at an accredited psychoanalytic institute which will lead to qualifying him to practice psychoanalysis. Expenditures for the program are deductible because it maintains or improves skills required by D in his trade or business and does not qualify him for a new trade or business.

* * * [s]ome of the distinctions that are drawn in the regulations appear to be formalistic or arbitrary.

By denying deductions for the cost of education intended to meet the minimum requirements of obtaining employment or of qualifying for different work, the Treasury regulations exclude deductions for outlays that contribute to future earning capacity and that have great economic significance for the individual and the community. If a similar attitude were taken toward physical capital, deductions from taxable income presumably would be allowed for maintenance expenses and capital replacement costs, but would be denied for depreciation of capital used to establish new firms, to enlarge existing enterprises, or to introduce new products. The regulations concerning educational expenditures are less favorable to the young and the ambitious than to the established and the timeserver.

* * *

Possible Revisions

By analogy with the treatment of investment in physical capital, persons who make expenditures for education that increases their earning power, or is intended to do so, should be permitted to capitalize those outlays and write them off against taxable income through depreciation or amortization allowances. Income-producing educational expenditures are investments with a limited life and, if it is feasible, they should be given the same tax treatment as other investments. Failure to allow tax-free recovery of educational outlays means that the income tax falls in part on the return of capital rather than on net income.

To bring out significant issues, I shall attempt to give the broad outlines of a suitable plan. The suggestions are intended to serve as a basis for discussion rather than as recommendations for immediate legislation. The plan, in brief, is that part of the personal costs of college education and professional, technical, and vocational education should be capitalized and written off against the student's future earned income over a period of ten to twenty years or more. Minor costs of part-time study would be currently deducted. Provisions limiting deductions to expenses relating to the taxpayer's current position would be dropped.

If the amortization of educational expenditures is justified as a refinement in the definition of income, the deductions should be taken against the income attributable to the education. The deduction should be taken by the student rather than the parents, even when the latter pay the educational expenses. Expenditures by parents, relatives, or friends may be considered gifts. The student would be allowed to recover free of income tax the value of these gifts just as the cost of a depreciable asset acquired as a gift can be written off against the income of the recipient. The privilege of writing off the value of gifts in the form of education should not extend to scholarships and other aid received from educational institutions, governments, corporations, or other organized bodies.

The personal costs of education are far less than total costs because of heavy expenditures by governments and nonprofit institutions. Personal costs are those met by students, parents, and other private individuals. They include (1) money outlays for tuition and fees, books and supplies, and travel; (2) any additional living expenses of the student; and (3) earnings forgone while studying. Forgone earnings are by far the largest component of the costs of college and graduate education, and they constitute an important part of high school costs. This part of costs is already excluded from the tax base, and no special deduction is necessary or appropriate.[4] Although living expenses above those that would be incurred by a person who was not a student should be deductible, it would be difficult to distinguish these additional expenses from ordinary living costs; therefore, as a practical matter, no allowance is suggested for additional living expenses. The costs to be capitalized and amortized would be those listed under item 1 above.

In principle, expenditures for education should be classified as costs of earning income when incurred for that purpose, regardless of whether they could be shown to result in additional income. The taxpayer's intention is the dominant factor governing the distinction between other "ordinary and necessary" business and professional expenses and personal expenses. Mixed motives are especially common, however, with respect to education, and there are no accounting and administrative rules to distinguish one kind of educational outlay from another.

As a practical possibility, the current deduction or amortization of educational expenditures might be allowed for: (1) any course creditable toward a degree at an accredited college or university, regardless of whether a degree is earned; (2) vocational training at a recognized trade school, business college, or similar institution; and (3) a supple-

---

4. The freedom of forgone earnings from income tax is in some respects similar to rapid amortization of this part of students' investment. See Gary S. Becker, Human Capital: A Theoretical and Empirical Analysis, with Special Reference to Education (National Bureau of Economic Research, 1964), pp. 14–15, 149; * * *.

mentary, continuation, or refresher course of a predominantly professional or vocational nature taken at a recognized or accredited institution. Part-time studies and correspondence courses as well as full-time resident study should be eligible. Expenditures for ordinary high school studies and elementary school would be classified as personal expenses rather than costs of earning income.

For college and university studies, this plan would err on the side of liberality, because it would cover some educational expenditures that are predominantly consumption, as judged by presumed motivation or apparent influence on income. Most college and university education, however, seems to add to earning capacity, and it is difficult to rule out the possibility of economic motivation in connection with any part of it. With all private costs, including forgone earnings, treated as investment, the rate of private return has been estimated at about 15 percent a year for both college education and graduate instruction and research. If a large fraction of the costs were classified as consumption expenditures, the calculated rate of return on the remaining outlays would be high indeed. The imperfections resulting from a liberal allowance for college costs seem less objectionable than the present practice of permitting virtually none of these expenditures to be charged against taxable income.

The diversity of trade schools, business colleges, and similar institutions and the absence of a comprehensive accrediting system for them would complicate the application of administrative checks to ensure that the expenses of study at these institutions were legitimate educational expenditures. A difficulty in connection with supplementary training and continuation or refresher courses would be to identify vocational courses. Many extension courses, evening classes, and correspondence courses are almost entirely consumption, dealing with subjects such as hobbies, arts and crafts, current events, and music appreciation. Courses cannot always be distinguished on the basis of their content. A music course, for example, may be vocational training for one person but avocational for another. It seems that the best rule would be to allow current deductions or amortization charges only for expenses relating to education which the taxpayer represents as being primarily vocational or professional and which the authorities consider reasonably related to his occupation or occupational plans. This standard would be harder to apply than the present rule on education but little if any more difficult than the rules on a number of other deductions. The amounts involved may be smaller and many may feel that it is sound public policy to be more liberal about educational expenses than about some of the items now deductible.

The suggestion that no income tax allowance be made for ordinary high school education is debatable. There is considerable overlap between high school courses and the training offered by trade schools and business colleges, on the one hand, and by liberal arts colleges, on the other. For pupils in public high schools, however, the amount that could be written off would be small. Since most young people now go to high school, the principal effect of an income tax allowance for the personal costs of secondary education would be to encourage attendance at private schools.

It would seem reasonable to limit the deductions or amortization charges to taxable earned income, without insisting that a direct link be shown between the education and the taxpayer's occupation. Although education may make one a better investor, the relation between property income and education is tenuous. If educational expenditures could be written off against property income, persons with inherited wealth might gain an undue advantage. * * *

The requirement that deductions or amortization charges be taken only against taxable earned income would disqualify housewives when they were not working outside the home.[5] This would not be as unfair as it may seem. Although a housewife's services have economic value and her contribution to the family's economic welfare is enhanced by her education, the value of her services does not enter into taxable income. Hence denial of a writeoff for educational costs that qualify the housewife to perform her services at home more effectively cannot be regarded as discriminatory in the same way as failure to take account of costs of earning a taxable income.

By analogy with physical assets, educational expenditures should be capitalized and written off against taxable income over the period in which they contribute to earnings—ordinarily the whole working life of the person. This approach, however, might be cumbersome for major expenditures and ridiculous for small items. A practical procedure would be to allow persons incurring large educational expenses to capitalize them and amortize them over a fixed period of, say, ten or twenty years, or the period ending at the age of sixty-five if that is shorter. Students could be permitted to begin amortization immediately or to postpone it until they are established in their occupations. Taxpayers incurring minor educational expenses might be given the option of capitalizing their outlays or deducting them currently.

Persons who become totally and permanently disabled and the estates of those who die before completing the amortization of their educational expenses might appropriately be allowed to deduct the unamortized balance in the last taxable year and be granted a carryback of net loss and refund of prior-year taxes if the deduction reduced the last year's income below zero. Similar treatment might be urged for women who withdraw from the labor force after marriage, but this would be questionable since many of these women later resume outside employment.

* * *

5. The attribution to a wife of part of the earnings of her husband under a state community property law should be disregarded in determining qualification for the deduction.

C. ACCRUAL METHOD TAXPAYERS: ADVANCE RECEIPTS AND RESERVES FOR ESTIMATED EXPENSES

1. ADVANCE UNEARNED RECEIPTS

A corollary to the capitalization of expenditures is the capitalization of current receipts. Accrual method taxpayers have sought to defer the reporting of prepaid income for services to be performed in the future. The Service and the courts have usually rejected the attempts of accrual method taxpayers to delay the reporting of income until the services are performed and thereby match revenue and expenses.

Given that a purpose of the accrual method of accounting is to match income with the deductions that will be incurred in generating that income, it would seem logical that accounting principles would allow the taxpayer to report income in the year it is earned, specifically the year the taxpayer actually performs the services. For example, in Beacon Publishing Co. v. Commissioner, 218 F.2d 697 (10th Cir.1955) a newspaper publishing company, an accrual method taxpayer, was allowed to postpone reporting prepaid subscribers as income until the years it subsequently delivered the newspapers. The court allowed this postponement because treating prepayments as income in the year payment was received would fail to match income with its related expenses thereby producing a distortion of the taxpayer's true income for the current year. Despite the court in Beacon Publishing adopting the matching concept of generally accepted accounting principles (GAAP), the Commissioner has been successful in requiring accrual method taxpayers to report prepaid income in the year of receipt on the ground that the taxpayers have, at that point in time, the unrestricted use of the cash and therefore, have the ability to pay the tax on such income. How can the claim of right doctrine discussed in the North American Oil Consolidated case at page 175 be distinguished from the prepaid services cases? Consider when the income was earned in both situations.

In Automobile Club of Michigan v. Commissioner, 353 U.S. 180, 77 S.Ct. 707, 1 L.Ed.2d 746 (1957), an accrual method taxpayer received annual fees for repair services it was contractually obligated to perform over the next twelve months. Taxpayer allocated the fees uniformly over the twelve month period. The Supreme Court required the taxpayer to report the entire fee when received on the ground that taxpayer's ratable method did not clearly reflect income because there was no fixed obligation to perform these services at specified times in the future. In American Automobile Association v. United States, 367 U.S. 687, 81 S.Ct. 1727, 6 L.Ed.2d 1109 (1961), the taxpayer tried to meet the Court's objections in the Automobile Club of Michigan decision by arguing that its ratable method of allocating the fees was in accordance with GAAP, that it had consistently been using this method for reporting purposes over the past twenty years, and that this method was the customary practice in its line of business. The Court concluded that taxpayer's attempt to prove that its method of allocating the prepaid fees clearly reflected income was artificial, and stated that:

> When their receipt as earned income is recognized ratably over two calendar years, without regard to correspondingly fixed individual expense or performance justifications, but consistently with overall experience, their accounting doubtless presents a rather accurate image of the total financial structure, but fails to respect the criteria of annual tax accounting and may be rejected by the Commissioner. (367 U.S. at 692, 81 S.Ct. at 1730, 6 L.Ed.2d at 1113).

In Schlude v. Commissioner, 372 U.S. 128, 83 S.Ct. 601, 9 L.Ed.2d 633 (1963), an accrual method taxpayer who operated a dance studio received prepayments for future dancing lessons. The Supreme Court disregarded GAAP and required the taxpayer to treat the prepayments as income in the year received, again expressing its concern that the taxpayer could not predict when, if at all, it would be required to give the dance lessons. Does Schlude distort income by requiring unearned receipts to be treated as income? Are the results in these cases consistent with § 446(a) and Reg. § 1.446–1(a)(2)? Why did the Commissioner cite the Schlude case as authority for his position in Rev.Rul. 83–163 at p. 212.

In Artnell Co. v. Commissioner, 400 F.2d 981 (7th Cir.1968), the court considered the timing of payments received by a professional baseball team, an accrual method taxpayer, for advance ticket sales, advance radio and television revenues, and sales of season parking passes. Each of these items related to baseball games to be played after the end of the taxable year in question. The Commissioner maintained that an accrual method taxpayer must include in gross income in the year of receipt prepaid items for which services will be performed in a later year. The Seventh Circuit noted that the Supreme Court cases dealing with the prepaid income of accrual method taxpayers involved situations where the time and the extent of the performance of future services were uncertain. The court stated, "[T]he deferred income was allocable to games which were to be played on a fixed schedule. Except for rain dates, there was certainty. We would have no difficulty in distinguishing the instant case in this respect." 400 F.2d at 984. The court remanded the case to determine whether the taxpayer's method of accounting clearly reflected income. On remand, the Tax Court allowed the taxpayer to continue to defer its income. 29 T.C.M. (CCH) 403 (1970).

The Tax Court followed Artnell in Collegiate Cap & Gown Co. v. Commissioner, 37 T.C.M. (CCH) 960 (1978), where an accrual method taxpayer received advance rental payments for the use of caps and gowns. The Tax Court held that the advance payments were not taxable until the apparel was actually used. The key factor was the certainty as to the time of future performance, i.e. the graduation date.

BOISE CASCADE CORP. v. UNITED STATES

United States Court of Claims, 1976.
208 Ct.Cl. 619, 530 F.2d 1367.

OPINION

PER CURIAM:

These are consolidated cases, in which plaintiffs seek the recovery of nearly $2,400,000 in income taxes plus interest thereon, paid for the years 1955 through 1961. They now come before the court on exceptions by the parties to the recommended decision filed by Trial Judge Lloyd Fletcher, on September 20, 1974, pursuant to Rule 134(h), having been submitted to the court on the briefs and oral argument of counsel. He held for the plaintiffs on all the significant issues. After briefing and oral argument, the court agrees with the trial judge in part, and disagrees in part. * * *

We agree substantially with the portions of the recommended opinion that hold the Commissioner of Internal Revenue to have abused his discretion under IRC § 446(b), in determining that Ebasco's method of accounting failed to reflect income clearly for Federal Income Tax purposes and in requiring a change in such method as set forth below. * * *

Trial Judge Fletcher's opinion, as modified by the court, follows:

The plaintiffs are Boise Cascade Corporation and several of its subsidiary companies. The original petition was filed by Ebasco Industries Inc. and its subsidiary companies which had filed consolidated tax returns for the taxable years 1955 through 1958. Later, Ebasco Industries was merged with Boise Cascade in a non-taxable transaction, and the necessary steps were taken thereafter to consolidate the actions now before the court.

Ebasco Industries was engaged in holding various investments during the years 1955 through August 31, 1969, the date of its merger into Boise Cascade. These investments included marketable securities, short-term investments, and ownership interests in various operating subsidiaries which were (and continue to be) engaged primarily in rendering engineering, construction, architectural, and consulting services. Two of such subsidiaries were Ebasco Services, Inc. (Ebasco) and Chemical Construction Corporation (Chemical Construction). Ebasco Industries owned stock possessing at least 80 percent of the voting power of all classes of stock of those subsidiary corporations.

The plaintiffs' annual shareholder reports included a certification by independent accountants that the financial statements were prepared in conformity with generally accepted accounting principles applied on a basis consistent with that of the preceding year.

In its business, Ebasco Services enters into contracts to perform engineering and similar services. Under the various terms of these contracts, Ebasco is entitled to bill fixed sums either in monthly, quarterly, or other periodic installments, plus such additional amounts as may be provided for in a particular contract. Depending on the terms of the different contracts, payments may in some cases be due prior to the annual period in which such services are to be performed, and in some cases subsequent thereto.

For a number of years prior to 1959 and continuing to the time of trial, Ebasco included in its income for both book and tax purposes amounts attributable to services which it performed during the taxable year, a procedure accepted by the Internal Revenue Service on prior audits. * * *

Where Ebasco billed for services prior to the tax year in which they were performed, it credited such amounts to a balance sheet account called "Unearned Income". Where the services were performed in a subsequent period, the "Unearned Income" account was debited, and such amounts were included in an income account called "Service Revenues." The amount recorded in the latter account was included in income for both book and tax purposes. In determining the amount which was to be included in the "Unearned Income" account, the costs of obtaining the contract were not taken into account;[6] and, with the exception of prepaid insurance and similar items, all such amounts were expensed in the tax year during which they were incurred. The amounts in the "Unearned Income" account were treated as liabilities and were excluded from gross income for each tax year consistently in Ebasco's books, records, and shareholder reports, as well as in its tax returns. All of the amounts included in the account during one tax year were earned through the performance of services during the following year and were included in income for such following tax year. When the amounts credited to the "Unearned Income" account were collected, Ebasco had an unrestricted right to the use of such funds.

During the three tax years in issue, an average of over 94 percent of the amounts included in the "Unearned Income" account was received by Ebasco under contracts which obligated it to perform engineering services in connection with the design and construction of electric generating plants. These contracts either required that services be performed by a specified date or required that Ebasco should perform those services "with all reasonable dispatch and diligence," as "expeditiously as possible," or some comparable requirement. The small remaining amounts in the account were received either under contracts which required Ebasco to perform specific services in connection with a specific project of a client, or required Ebasco to provide consultation and advice on an annual basis for an annual fee.

6. These amounts included the cost of preparing bids, proposals, and estimates, overhead, advertising, and selling expenses.

In addition to its "Unearned" account, Ebasco maintained an "Unbilled Charges" account computed in the same manner as the "Unearned Income" account. The balance in such account represented amounts earned through the rendering of services, or on partially completed contracts, or earned prior to contracting under all of which payment was not then due by the terms of a contract or was not billable and due prior to execution of a future contract. Stated another way, the amounts included in this account were those which Ebasco was not entitled to bill or receive until a year subsequent to the year in which the services were actually rendered. Such amounts were recorded in "Service Revenues" and included in income for tax as well as book purposes in the taxable year in which the services were rendered. Likewise, the costs attributable to the rendering of services which produced the year-end balance in the "Unbilled Charges" account were deducted from gross income in the year such services were rendered. In 1959, 1960, and 1961 there were approximately $405,000, ($56,000), and $179,000 of such net amounts, respectively, carried in the "Unbilled Charges" account.

Plaintiffs' consolidated income tax returns for 1959 through 1961 were audited by the Government, and the amounts in the "Unearned Income" account were included in taxable income for Federal tax purposes. These adjustments were made pursuant to section 446(b) of the [1986] Code under which the Commissioner determined that plaintiffs' deferral method of accounting did not clearly reflect income. During the same examination for the same tax years, no adjustments were made to the "Unbilled Charges" or the "Service Revenues" accounts.

At trial Ebasco presented expert testimony related solely to the accounting practices described above. The sole witness was a qualified certified public accountant * * *

He testified that the method of accounting used by Ebasco which employs both an "Unearned Income" account and an "Unbilled Charges" account and is based on accruing amounts as income at the time the related services are performed is in accordance with recognized and generally accepted accounting principles and clearly reflects Ebasco's income. He indicated that this method properly matched revenues with costs of producing such revenues and is particularly appropriate in this case because almost all of Ebasco's income is derived from the performance of services by its own personnel. He further testified that this method of accounting was widely used by companies engaged in rendering engineering and similar services, and that such method clearly reflected the income of Ebasco.

With respect to costs incurred in obtaining contracts, such as bid preparation, overhead, advertising, and other selling expenses, the witness considered them to be properly deducted in the year incurred as continuing costs of doing and developing business.[7] He explained that these costs should not properly be amortizable over the life of any particular contract since they were costs connected with new business development and were unrelated to performance of the contract.

The accounting method proposed by the Commissioner requires Ebasco to accrue as income the amounts included in the "Unearned Income" account and also requires the accrual, consistent with plaintiffs' accounting method, of amounts in the "Unbilled Charges" account. In the opinion of plaintiffs' expert, this method of accounting was not in accordance with generally accepted accounting principles and did not clearly reflect Ebasco's income. To him, the Commissioner's method was erroneous in that it required the inclusion in income of amounts billed but not yet earned on contracts in one accounting period without at the same time acknowledging the obligations and costs to be incurred by Ebasco in the future performance of such contractual commitments. He termed such method as "hybrid" in that while it recognized the accrual method with respect to unbilled charges which were earned but not yet billable, it had the effect of imposing a cash basis method as to the billed but unearned charges in the "Unearned Income" account.

Finally, the witness testified that if Ebasco were to use a method of accounting under which amounts in the "Unearned Income" account would be accrued as income and amounts in the "Unbilled Charges" account would *not* be accrued as income, such method would more clearly reflect the income of Ebasco than the method of accounting proposed by the Commissioner. He stated that, while such method was not technically in accordance with generally accepted accounting principles, it was a more logical and consistent approach to use in determining the income of Ebasco than the Commissioner's method.

* * *

These issues present but another facet in the continuing controversy over the proper timing for Federal income tax purposes of various income and expense items incurred by an accrual basis taxpayer. Based on expert accounting testimony presented by Ebasco at trial, it can hardly be disputed that Ebasco's system for deferral of unearned income is in full accord with generally accepted accounting principles as that phrase is used in financial or commercial accounting. But such a showing alone is not determinative for income tax purposes. The taxpayer must also show that its method clearly reflects income for the purposes of the Internal Revenue Code. Thus, while generally accepted methods of accounting are of probative value and are treated with respect by Treas.Reg. § 1.446–1(a)(2), they are not necessarily synonymous with the proper tax accounting to be afforded an accrual item in a given situation.

7. The witness distinguished such costs from commissions which in some instances may properly be amortized where they re-

late directly to the contract involved and thus reduce the amount realizable under such contract.

This variance is especially noticeable in cases where the taxpayer's accounting method results in the deferment of income. The taxpayer in such a situation is generally relying on well-known accounting principles which essentially focus on a conservative matching of income and expenses to the end that an item of income will be related to its correlative expenditure. Tax accounting, on the other hand, starts from the premise of a need for certainty in the collection of revenues and focuses on the concept of ability to pay. Thus, under this theory, where an item of income has been received even though as yet unearned, it should be subject to taxation because the taxpayer has in hand (or otherwise available) the funds necessary to pay the tax due.

Putting such theoretical considerations aside for the moment, it may be helpful briefly to resummarize Ebasco's long-consistent method of accounting under which receipts are accrued and reported as income only at the time the engineering and similar services which generate such receipts are rendered. In many cases, Ebasco's right to bill or receive payment arose prior to the annual accounting period in which the related services were to be performed. In other cases, the right to bill or receive payment arose subsequent to the annual accounting period in which the services were performed.

When under the terms of a contract Ebasco billed a client prior to the accounting period in which the related services were rendered, Ebasco debited the amount billed to accounts receivable and credited it to a balance sheet liability account called "Unearned Income." Subsequently, when the services were rendered, the income earned was debited to the "Unearned Income" account and credited to the income account "Service Revenues." The amounts recorded in the "Service Revenues" account were reported as income for both book and tax purposes. All of the amounts which were included in the "Unearned Income" account at the end of a taxable year were earned through the performance of services in the next succeeding year and were accrued and reported as income in such next succeeding taxable year for both book and tax purposes.

When services were performed in an annual accounting period and Ebasco was not entitled to bill a client for such services until a subsequent annual accounting period under the terms of a contract, Ebasco debited the amount attributable to such services to the balance sheet account "Unbilled Charges" and credited a like amount to "Service Revenues." The amount recorded in the "Service Revenues" account was reported as income for both book and tax purposes. Ebasco's cost of rendering the services which produced the amounts recorded in the "Unbilled Charges" account were deducted from gross income for that year for both book and tax purposes.

Thus, it can readily be seen that, under Ebasco's system, all amounts reported as income were determined with reference to the related services performed within the annual accounting period. The record clearly establishes that such system is a generally accepted accounting method for a business such as Ebasco's. Does it clearly reflect income as required by section 446 of the Code?

Defendant stoutly responds to that question in the negative. It relies heavily on the decisions of the Supreme Court in American Automobile Ass'n v. United States, 367 U.S. 687, 81 S.Ct. 1727, 6 L.Ed. 2d 1109 (1961) and Schlude v. Commissioner of Internal Revenue, 372 U.S. 128, 83 S.Ct. 601, 9 L.Ed.2d 633 (1963), which cases defendant contends have firmly established the rule that, in the absence of a specific statutory exception, a taxpayer has no right to defer recognition of income received or accrued under a contract for the performance of services.

Counsel for Ebasco respond with equal vigor that Ebasco's accounting system does, in fact, clearly reflect income. To them, the Supreme Court in the above-cited decisions only held that the Commissioner of Internal Revenue did not abuse his discretion under section 446 by rejecting what the Court referred to as a "purely artificial" accounting method. Ebasco's counsel are astonished that defendant could in this case interpret *American Automobile* and *Schlude* as preventing any income deferral when, as recently as 1971, the Commissioner, in Rev. Proc. 71–21, 1971–2 C.B. 549 has held that taxpayers may defer the inclusion in income of payments received in one taxable year for services to be performed in the next succeeding year.

Although one can hardly speak with complete confidence in this troublesome and confusing area of tax law as affected by modern accounting methods, I think it fair to conclude that, on balance, Ebasco's position in this litigation is the reasonable one of the conflicting viewpoints.

The starting point, of course, must involve a close look at the trilogy of Supreme Court decisions dealing with the problem of income deferral. Those cases are Automobile Club of Michigan v. Commissioner of Internal Revenue, 353 U.S. 180, 77 S.Ct. 707, 1 L.Ed.2d 746 (1957); American Automobile Ass'n v. United States, supra, and Schlude v. Commissioner, supra.

In *Michigan,* the Court sustained the action of the Commissioner of Internal Revenue in rejecting the taxpayer's method of deferral accounting pursuant to the authority of section 41 of the 1939 Code, the predecessor of [1986] Code section 446(b), supra. The taxpayer was engaged in performing various services to the automotive industry including the rendition of services to members of the club but only upon their specific request. Under its method of accounting, the club deferred taking into income the full amount of annual membership dues which the club required to be paid in advance, irrespective of whether the dues-paying member might call upon the club for any services during the 12-month period. Upon collection, these prepaid amounts were deposited in the club's regular bank account and used for general corporate purposes. In its books, the club entered these prepaid amounts into a liability account titled "Unearned Membership Dues," and thereafter for each of the 12 months of membership, one-twelfth of the amounts so paid was credited to an account called "Membership Income." In sustaining the Commissioner's rejection of this accounting method as not clearly reflecting income, the Court held:

> The pro rata allocation of the membership dues in monthly amounts is *purely artificial and bears no relation to the services which petitioner may in fact be called upon to render for the member.* Section 41 vests the Commissioner with discretion to determine whether the petitioner's method of accounting clearly reflects income. We cannot say, in the circumstances here, that the discretionary action of the Commissioner, sustained by both the Tax Court and the Court of Appeals, exceeded permissible limits * * * 353 U.S. 189, 77 S.Ct. 712. [Emphasis supplied.]

Four years later, the issue returned to the Court in the *American Automobile case.* While the facts were essentially similar to those in *Michigan,* it was contended in *American Automobile* that the earlier case did not control because the Court had before it at last a full record containing expert accounting testimony that the system used was in accord with generally accepted accounting principles, that proof of membership service cost was detailed, and that the correlation between such cost and the period of time over which the dues were credited as income was shown and justified by proof of experience.

The Court, however, was unimpressed. Unable to perceive any significant difference between the methods of operation and accounting employed by the two automobile clubs, the Court held that, just as in *Michigan,* the American Automobile Association's system of accounting was "purely artificial" because "substantially all services are performed only upon a member's demand and the taxpayer's performance was not related to fixed dates after the tax year." 367 U.S. 691, 81 S.Ct. 1729. The Court explained at 692, 81 S.Ct. at 1729:

> It may be true that to the accountant the actual incidence of cost in serving an individual member in exchange for his individual dues is inconsequential, or, from the viewpoint of commercial accounting, unessential to determination and disclosure of the overall financial condition of the Association. That "irregularity," however, is highly relevant to the clarity of an accounting system which defers receipt, as earned income, of dues to a taxable period *in which no, some, or all of the services paid for by those dues may or may not be rendered.* The Code exacts its revenue from the individual member's dues which, no one disputes, constitute income. When their receipt as earned income is recognized ratably over two calendar years, *without regard to corre-spondingly fixed individual expense or performance justification,* but consistently with overall experience, their accounting doubtless presents a rather accurate image of the total financial structure, but

fails to respect the criteria of annual tax accounting and may be rejected by the Commissioner. [Emphasis supplied.] [8]

The third of this trilogy of cases is *Schlude v. Commissioner,* supra, where the Court again rejected an attempt by an accrual basis taxpayer to defer prepaid amounts for future services. The taxpayers there operated a dance studio and offered dancing lessons under contracts which required the students to pay their tuition in advance with no right to refund, i.e., the studio was entitled to receive the advance payments under the contracts irrespective of whether the studio was ever called upon to render any teaching services.[9] At the end of each fiscal period, the total number of actually taught hours were multiplied by the applicable hourly rate. The resulting sum was then deducted from the deferred income account and reported as earned income on taxpayers' financial statements and income tax returns.

The Court held that the case was "squarely controlled by American Automobile Association," (372 U.S. 134, 83 S.Ct. 604) and sustained the Commissioner's rejection of Schlude's accounting method. Said the Court at 135–136, 83 S.Ct. at 605:

> The *American Automobile Association* case rested upon an additional ground which is also controlling here. Relying upon Automobile Club of Michigan v. Commissioner, 353 U.S. 180, 77 S.Ct. 707, 1 L.Ed.2d 746, the Court rejected the taxpayer's system as *artificial since the advance payments related to services which were to be performed only upon customers' demands without relation to fixed dates in the future. The system employed here suffers from that very same vice,* for the studio sought to defer its cash receipts on the basis of contracts which did not provide for lessons on fixed dates after the taxable year, but left such dates to be arranged from time to time by the instructor and his student. Under the contracts, the student could arrange for some or all of the additional lessons or could simply allow their rights under the contracts to lapse. But even though the student did not demand the remaining lessons, the contracts permitted the studio to insist upon payment in accordance with the obligations undertaken and to retain whatever prepayments were made without restriction as to use and without obligation of refund. At the end of each period, while the number of lessons taught had been meticulously reflected, the studio was uncertain whether none, some or all of the remaining lessons would be rendered. *Clearly, services were rendered solely on demand in the fashion of the American Automobile Association and Automobile Club of Michigan cases.* [Emphasis supplied.]

It seems clear to me that, despite defendant's vigorous contention to the contrary, this trilogy of Supreme Court decisions cannot be said to have established an unvarying rule of law that, absent a specific

8. Discussion of the Court's treatment of "other considerations" bearing upon its decision appears below.

9. No dates for dancing lessons were fixed but simply left to a mutually agreeable arrangement between student and teacher. Significant amounts of income flowed from cancellations resulting in no performance of services.

statutory exception, a taxpayer may never defer recognition of income received or accrued under a contract for the performance of future services, no matter whether such deferral clearly reflects income.

Defendant persuasively argues, however, that its interpretation of the cases is justified by the Court's additional ground for decision in both *American Automobile* and *Schlude*. In both cases, it is true, the Court's majority and minority opinions gave close consideration to the legislative history of sections 452 and 462 of the 1954 Code. These sections contained the first explicit legislative sanctions of deferral of income (§ 452) and deduction of future estimated expenses (§ 462). In the next year, however, both sections were retroactively repealed. Ch. 143, 69 Stat. 134. To the majority in *American Automobile*, this repealer action constituted "clearly a mandate from the Congress that petitioner's system was not acceptable for tax purposes." 367 U.S. 695, 81 S.Ct. 1731. The dissent, of course, viewed the legislative history in different perspective.[10]

To me, the dilemma and its likely solution, have been gracefully and accurately stated by the able and comprehensive opinion of the Fifth Circuit Court of Appeals in Mooney Aircraft, Inc. v. United States, 420 F.2d 400, 408–409 (5th Cir., 1969) where the court observed:

> This alternative ground, based on legislative intent, would seem to dispose of the entire question: *all* deferrals and accruals are bad unless specifically authorized by Congress. But the Court was careful to discuss the legislative history as dictum and restricted its holding to a finding that the Commissioner did not abuse his discretion in rejecting the *AAA's* accounting system. It specifically refrained from overruling *Beacon* [Beacon Publishing Co. v. Commissioner of Internal Revenue, 218 F.2d 697 (10th Cir.1955) (deferral of prepaid subscriptions)] and *Schuessler* [Schuessler v. Commissioner of Internal Revenue, 230 F.2d 722 (5th Cir.1956) (accrual of expenses of 5-year service period)], distinguishing them on the ground that future performance was certain. *AAA*, supra, 367 U.S. at 692, n. 4, 81 S.Ct. 1727. It seems, then, that the Court is for the present taking a middle ground pending Congressional reform and clarification in this extremely confused area of the law: While the repeal of §§ 452 and 462 does not absolutely preclude deferrals and accruals, it indicates that the Commissioner should have very broad discretion to disallow such accounting techniques when there is any reasonable basis for his action.

10. For example, in his *Schlude* dissent, Mr. Justice Stewart observed at 372 U.S. 139–140, 83 S.Ct. 607:

"For the reasons I have elsewhere stated at some length, to rely on the repeal of §§ 452 and 462 as indicating congressional disapproval of accrual accounting principles is conspicuously to disregard clear evidence of legislative intent. The Secretary of the Treasury, who proposed the repeal of these sections, made explicitly clear that no inference of disapproval of accrual accounting principles was to be drawn from the repeal of the sections. So did the Senate Report. The repeal of these sections was occasioned solely by the fear of temporary revenue losses which would result from the taking of "double deductions" during the year of transition by taxpayers who had not previously maintained their books on an accrual basis." [Footnotes omitted.]

The *Mooney Aircraft* approach was foreshadowed by the Seventh Circuit's decision in Artnell Company v. Commissioner of Internal Revenue, 400 F.2d 981 (7th Cir., 1968). There, Chicago White Sox, Inc. had received and accrued in a deferred unearned income account amounts attributable to advance ticket sales and revenues for other services related to baseball games to be played thereafter during the 1962 season. Prior to such performance, however, Artnell acquired Chicago White Sox, Inc., liquidated it, and continued operation of the team. In the final short-year return filed as transferee by Artnell in behalf of White Sox, Inc., Artnell excluded the deferred unearned income previously received by White Sox. The Commissioner required such amounts to be accrued as income to White Sox on receipt, and the Tax Court sustained him. In reversing and remanding, the Seventh Circuit analyzed the Supreme Court's trilogy, supra, and said at 400 F.2d 984–985:

> Has the Supreme Court left an opening for a decision that under the facts of a particular case, the extent and time of future performance are so certain, and related items properly accounted for with such clarity, that a system of accounting involving deferral of prepaid income is found clearly to reflect income, and the commissioner's rejection deemed an abuse of discretion? Or has it decided that the commissioner has complete and unreviewable discretion to reject deferral of prepaid income where Congress has made no provision? The tax court apparently adopted the latter view, for it concluded "that the Supreme Court would reach the same decision regardless of the method used by the taxpayer for deferring prepaid income."

> It is our best judgment that, although the policy of deferring, where possible, to congressional procedures in the tax field will cause the Supreme Court to accord the widest possible latitude to the commissioner's discretion, there must be situations where the deferral technique will so clearly reflect income that the Court will find an abuse of discretion if the commissioner rejects it.

> Prior to 1955 the commissioner permitted accrual basis publishers to defer unearned income from magazine subscriptions if they had consistently done so in the past. He refused to allow others to adopt the method. In 1955 his refusal was held, by the tenth circuit, in *Beacon,* to be an abuse of discretion. In *Automobile Club of Michigan,* the Supreme Court distinguished *Beacon,* on its facts, because "performance of the subscription, in most instances, was, in part, necessarily deferred until the publication dates after the tax year." The Court, however, expressed no opinion upon the correctness of *Beacon.* In 1958, Congress dealt specifically with the *Beacon,* problem. It is at least arguable that the deferral as income of prepaid admissions to events which will take place on a fixed schedule in a different taxable year is so similar to deferral of prepaid subscriptions that it would be an abuse of discretion to reject similar accounting treatment.

> In any event the prepaid admission situation approaches much closer to certainty than the situations considered in *Automobile Club of*

Michigan, American Automobile Association, or *Schlude.* [Footnotes omitted.]

Judicial reaction to *Artnell* has been mixed. Compare, for example, Hagen Advertising Displays, Inc. v. Commissioner of Internal Revenue, 407 F.2d 1105 (6th Cir., 1969) and Angelus Funeral Home v. Commissioner of Internal Revenue, 407 F.2d 210 (9th Cir., 1969), cert. denied, 396 U.S. 824, 90 S.Ct. 65, 24 L.Ed.2d 74; with New Eng. Tank Indus. of N.H., Inc. v. Commissioner of Internal Revenue, 413 F.2d 1038 (1st Cir., 1969). See, also, Petroleum Heat and Power Co. v. United States, 405 F.2d 1300, 1302–1304, 186 Ct.Cl. 486, 492–495 (1969). Defendant's reaction, of course, is simply that *"Artnell* was wrongly decided." Df's Br. p. 33.

Out of this mélange, one must choose a path. To use one of Justice Holmes' favorite expressions, I "can't help" but conclude that what Ebasco is pleased to call its "balanced and symmetrical" method of accounting does in fact clearly reflect its income. It achieves the desideratum of accurately matching costs and revenues by reason of the fact that the costs of earning such revenues are incurred at the time the services are performed. See, *Mooney Aircraft,* supra, 420 F.2d at 403. Entirely unlike the factual situations before the Supreme Court in the automobile club and dance studio cases, Ebasco's contractual obligations were fixed and definite. In no sense was Ebasco's performance of services dependent solely upon the demand or request of its clientele.[11]

Based upon the foregoing considerations, it is necessary to conclude that Ebasco's method of accounting under which income is accrued as the related services are performed clearly reflects its income, and, accordingly, the Commissioner is not authorized by § 446(b) to impose another method of accounting. That this is true becomes particularly obvious when it is realized that the accounting method imposed upon Ebasco by the Commissioner is a classic example of a hybrid system combining elements of the accrual system with a cash system, a mixture generally viewed with disfavor. See, Hackensack Water Co. v. United States, 173 Ct.Cl. 606, 611, 352 F.2d 807, 809 (1965). Thus, where Ebasco's billing precedes the rendition of its contracted-for services, the Commissioner proposes to tax as income amounts billed even though such amounts have not then been earned by performance. On the other hand, where the performance of services precedes billing,

---

11. By way of illustrating the point, the overwhelming majority of the amounts carried in the "Unearned Income" account were paid to Ebasco pursuant to contracts for the performance of engineering services in the design and construction of electric generating plants. The construction of such a plant is, of course, a vast and complicated project involving many contractors and suppliers whose activities must be closely coordinated under rigid schedules. Therefore, as pointed out by Ebasco, there was never any question but that Ebasco had to perform its engineering services all of which were absolutely necessary to completion of the project. Many contracts contained fixed and specific dates for Ebasco's performance; others simply required Ebasco to proceed as "expeditiously as possible" or similar language. Thus, unlike the taxpayers in the Supreme Court decisions, Ebasco had a fixed obligation to perform its services without the uncertainty as to performance so prominent in those cases.

the Commissioner would tax amounts as income at the time the services are rendered even though, under such contracts, Ebasco has no present right to bill, or receive payment of such amounts. The inconsistency within the Commissioner's method is strident.

His method would appear to the ordinary mind to distort income instead of clearly reflecting it. Judging both by what he has rejected and what he would impose he has abused his discretion within the meaning of the authority cited, *Mooney Aircraft* and *Artnell*. Ebasco has demonstrated not only that its method of accounting is in accordance with generally accepted accounting principles but, in addition, clearly reflects its income, treating these issues to be discrete, as we must. Therefore, the amounts accrued in Ebasco's "Unearned Income" account are not taxable until the year in which Ebasco performs the services which earn that income.

* * *

Conclusion of Law

Upon the findings of fact and opinion, which are adopted by the court and made a part of the judgment herein, the court concludes as a matter of law that plaintiff is entitled to recover on the accounting issue and judgment is entered to that effect, with the determination of the amount of recovery to be reserved for further proceedings under Rule 131(c) in accordance with this opinion. Judgment is entered for defendant * * *.

Questions

1. Why are generally accepted accounting principles (GAAP) not followed for tax purposes where a taxpayer receives prepayments?

2. If the prepayments are not refundable, can the claim of right doctrine be used to justify the reporting of income as payments are received? Is the claim of right doctrine consistent with GAAP? What result if the prepayments are refundable if the future services are not performed?

2. DOES FINANCIAL ACCOUNTING OR TAX ACCOUNTING CONTROL?

In *Commission v. Idaho Power Co.*, p. 586, the Supreme Court relied on financial accounting (GAAP) to require the taxpayer to capitalize the depreciation on construction equipment used in building property as part of the cost of that property. Yet, we have seen the Court reject the use of financial accounting principles in the prepaid services line of cases, although it failed to give any reason in these cases for rejecting the use of financial accounting. Does this mean that financial accounting is at least presumptively correct? The Supreme Court faced the question of whether "generally accepted accounting principles" are presumptively correct in the tax field in the following case. Consider whether the reasoning of Boise Cascade is still valid after reading this case.

THOR POWER TOOL CO. v. COMMISSIONER

Supreme Court of the United States, 1979.
439 U.S. 522, 99 S.Ct. 773,
58 L.Ed.2d 785.

[Taxpayer had carried certain inventory on its books at cost and wanted to write it down to its scrap value because the inventory had become worthless. Although financial accounting principles permitted the writedown, the Supreme Court rejected taxpayer's treatment, relying upon Reg. § 1.446–1(a)(2) which provides that an accounting method is not acceptable unless approved by the Commissioner. The Court read the Schlude line of cases as support for its interpretation of this regulation. The Court went on to discuss the impact of financial accounting principles as follows]:

MR. JUSTICE BLACKMUN delivered the opinion of the Court.

* * *

I

THE INVENTORY ISSUE

A

* * *

* * * On audit, the Commissioner disallowed the write-down in its entirety, asserting that it did not serve clearly to reflect Thor's 1964 income for tax purposes.

The Tax Court, in upholding the Commissioner's determination, found as a fact that Thor's write-down of excess inventory did conform to "generally accepted accounting principles"; indeed, the court was "thoroughly convinced * * * that such was the case." 64 T.C., at 165. The court found that if Thor had failed to write down its inventory on some reasonable basis, its accountants would have been unable to give its financial statements the desired certification. Id., at 161–162. The court held, however, that conformance with "generally accepted accounting principles" is not enough; § 446(b), and § 471 as well, of the [1986] Code, 26 U.S.C. §§ 446(b) and 471, prescribe, as an independent requirement, that inventory accounting methods must "clearly reflect income." The Tax Court rejected Thor's argument that its write-down of "excess" inventory was authorized by Treasury Regulations, 64 T.C., at 167–171, and held that the Commissioner had not abused his discretion in determining that the write-down failed to reflect 1964 income clearly.

B

Inventory accounting is governed by §§ 446 and 471 of the Code, 26 U.S.C. §§ 446 and 471. Section 446(a) states the general rule for methods of accounting: "Taxable income shall be computed under the method of accounting on the basis of which the taxpayer regularly computes his income in keeping his books." Section 446(b) provides, however, that if the method used by the taxpayer "does not clearly reflect income, the computation of taxable income shall be made under such method as, in the opinion of the [Commissioner], does clearly reflect income." Regulations promulgated under § 446 and in effect for the taxable year 1964, state that "no method of accounting is acceptable unless, in the opinion of the Commissioner, it clearly reflects income." Treas.Reg. § 1.446–1(a)(2), 26 CFR § 1.446–1(a)(2).[12]

Section 471 prescribes the general rule for inventories. It states:

> "Whenever in the opinion of the [Commissioner] the use of inventories is necessary in order clearly to determine the income of any taxpayer, inventories shall be taken by such taxpayer on such basis as the [Commissioner] may prescribe as conforming as nearly as may be to the best accounting practice in the trade or business and as most clearly reflecting the income."

As the Regulations point out, § 471 obviously establishes two distinct tests to which an inventory must conform. First, it must conform "as nearly as may be" to the "best accounting practice," a phrase that is synonymous with "generally accepted accounting principles." Second, it "must clearly reflect the income." Treas.Reg. § 1.471–2(a)(2), 26 CFR § 1.471–2(a)(2).

It is obvious that on their face, §§ 446 and 471, with their accompanying Regulations, vest the Commissioner with wide discretion in determining whether a particular method of inventory accounting should be disallowed as not clearly reflective of income. This Court's cases confirm the breadth of this discretion. In construing § 446 and its predecessors, the Court has held that "[t]he Commissioner has broad powers in determining whether accounting methods used by a taxpayer clearly reflect income." Commissioner of Internal Revenue v. Hansen, 360 U.S. 446, 467, 79 S.Ct. 1270, 1282, 3 L.Ed.2d 1360 (1959). Since the Commissioner has "[m]uch latitude for discretion," his interpretation of the statute's clear-reflection standard "should not be interfered with unless clearly unlawful." Lucas v. American Code Co., 280 U.S. 445, 449, 50 S.Ct. 202, 203, 74 L.Ed. 538 (1930). To the same effect are United States v. Catto, 384 U.S. 102, 114, 86 S.Ct. 1311, 1317, 16 L.Ed. 2d 398 (1966); Schlude v. Commissioner of Internal Revenue, 372 U.S. 128, 133–134, 83 S.Ct. 601, 604, 9 L.Ed.2d 633 (1963); American Automobile Assn. v. United States, 367 U.S. 687, 697–698, 81 S.Ct. 1727, 1732, 6 L.Ed.2d 1109 (1961); Automobile Club of Michigan v. Commissioner of Internal Revenue, 353 U.S. 180, 189–190, 77 S.Ct. 707, 712–713, 1 L.Ed.2d 746 (1957); Brown v. Helvering, 291 U.S. 193, 203, 54 S.Ct. 356, 360, 78 L.Ed. 725 (1934). In construing § 203 of the Revenue Act of 1918, 40 Stat. 1060, a predecessor of § 471, the Court held that the taxpayer bears a "heavy burden of [proof]," and that the Commissioner's disallowance of an inventory accounting method is not to be set

---

12. The Regulations define "method of accounting" to include "not only the overall method of accounting of the taxpayer but also the accounting treatment of any item." Treas.Reg. § 1.446–(a)(1), 26 CFR § 1.446–1(a)(1).

aside unless shown to be "plainly arbitrary." Lucas v. Structural Steel Co., 281 U.S. 264, 271, 50 S.Ct. 263, 266, 74 L.Ed. 848 (1930).

As has been noted, the Tax Court found as a fact in this case that Thor's write-down of "excess" inventory conformed to "generally accepted accounting principles" and was "within the term, 'best accounting practice,' as that term is used in section 471 of the Code and the regulations promulgated under that section." 64 T.C., at 161, 165. Since the Commissioner has not challenged this finding, there is no dispute that Thor satisfied the first part of § 471's two-pronged test. The only question, then, is whether the Commissioner abused his discretion in determining that the write-down did not satisfy the test's second prong in that it failed to reflect Thor's 1964 income clearly. Although the Commissioner's discretion is not unbridled and may not be arbitrary we sustain his exercise of discretion here, for in this case the write-down was plainly inconsistent with the governing Regulations which the taxpayer, on its part, has not challenged.

* * *

* * * [W]e agree with the Tax Court and with the Seventh Circuit that the Commissioner acted within his discretion in deciding that Thor's write-down of "excess" inventory failed to reflect income clearly. In the light of the well-known potential for tax avoidance that is inherent in inventory accounting, the Commissioner in his discretion may insist on a high evidentiary standard before allowing write-downs of inventory to "market." Because Thor provided no objective evidence of the reduced market value of its "excess" inventory, its write-down was plainly inconsistent with the Regulations, and the Commissioner properly disallowed it.

C

The taxpayer's major argument against this conclusion is based on the Tax Court's clear finding that the write-down conformed to "generally accepted accounting principles." Thor points to language in Treas. Reg. § 1.446–1(a)(2), 26 CFR § 1.446–1(a)(2), to the effect that "[a] method of accounting which reflects the consistent application of generally accepted accounting principles * * * *will ordinarily be regarded as clearly reflecting income*" (emphasis added). Section 1.471–2(b), 26 CFR § 1.471–2(b), of the Regulations likewise stated that an inventory taken in conformity with best accounting practice "can, *as a general rule,* be regarded as clearly reflecting * * * income" (emphasis added). These provisions, Thor contends, created a *presumption* that an inventory practice conformable to "generally accepted accounting principles" is valid for income tax purposes. Once a taxpayer has established this conformity, the argument runs, the burden shifts to the Commissioner affirmatively to demonstrate that the taxpayer's method does *not* reflect income clearly. Unless the Commissioner can show that a generally accepted method "demonstrably distorts income," Brief for Chamber of Commerce of the United States as *Amicus Curiae* 3, or that the taxpayer's adoption of such method was "motivated by tax avoidance," Brief for Petitioner 25, the presumption in the taxpayer's favor will carry the day. The Commissioner, Thor concludes, failed to rebut that presumption here.

If the Code and Regulations did embody the presumption petitioner postulates, it would be of little use to the taxpayer in this case. As we have noted, Thor's write-down of "excess" inventory was inconsistent with the Regulations; any general presumption obviously must yield in the face of such particular inconsistency. We believe, however, that no such presumption is present. Its existence is insupportable in light of the statute, the Court's past decisions, and the differing objectives of tax and financial accounting.

First, as has been stated above, the Code and Regulations establish two distinct tests to which an inventory must conform. The Code and Regulations, moreover, leave little doubt as to which test is paramount. While § 471 of the Code requires only that an accounting practice conform "as nearly as may be" to best accounting practice, § 1.446–1(a)(2) of the Regulations states categorically that "*no* method of accounting is acceptable unless, in the opinion of the Commissioner, it clearly reflects income" (emphasis added). Most importantly, the Code and Regulations give the Commissioner broad discretion to set aside the taxpayer's method if, "in [his] opinion," it does not reflect income clearly. This language is completely at odds with the notion of a "presumption" in the taxpayer's favor. The Regulations embody no presumption; they say merely that, in most cases, generally accepted accounting practices will pass muster for tax purposes. And in most cases they will. But if the Commissioner, in the exercise of his discretion, determines that they do not, he may prescribe a different practice without having to rebut any presumption running against the Treasury.

Second, the presumption petitioner postulates finds no support in this Court's prior decisions. It was early noted that the general rule specifying use of the taxpayer's method of accounting "is expressly limited to cases where the Commissioner believes that the accounts clearly reflect the net income." Lucas v. American Code Co., 280 U.S., at 449, 50 S.Ct., at 203. More recently, it was held in *American Automobile Assn. v. United States,* that a taxpayer must recognize prepaid income when received, even though this would mismatch expenses and revenues in contravention of "generally accepted commercial accounting principles." 367 U.S., at 690, 81 S.Ct., at 1730. "[T]o say that in performing the function of business accounting the method employed by the Association is in accord with generally accepted commercial accounting principles and practices," the Court concluded, "is not to hold that for income tax purposes it so clearly reflects income as to be binding on the Treasury." Id., at 693, 81 S.Ct., at 1730. "[W]e are mindful that the characterization of a transaction for financial accounting purposes, on the one hand, and for tax purposes, on the other, need not necessarily be the same." Frank Lyon Co. v. United

States, 435 U.S. 561, 577, 98 S.Ct. 1291, 1300, 55 L.Ed.2d 550 (1978). See Commissioner of Internal Revenue v. Idaho Power Co., 418 U.S. 1, 15, 94 S.Ct. 2757, 2765, 41 L.Ed.2d 535 (1974). Indeed, the Court's cases demonstrate that divergence between tax and financial accounting is especially common when a taxpayer seeks a current deduction for estimated future expenses or losses. E.g., Commissioner of Internal Revenue v. Hansen, 360 U.S. 446, 79 S.Ct. 1270, 3 L.Ed.2d 1360 (1959) (reserve to cover contingent liability in event of nonperformance of guarantee); Brown v. Helvering, 291 U.S. 193, 54 S.Ct. 356, 78 L.Ed. 725 (1934) (reserve to cover expected liability for unearned commissions on anticipated insurance policy cancellations); *Lucas v. American Code Co.*, supra (reserve to cover expected liability on contested lawsuit). The rationale of these cases amply encompasses Thor's aim. By its president's concession, the company's write-down of "excess" inventory was founded on the belief that many of the articles inevitably would become useless due to breakage, technological change, fluctuations in market demand, and the like. Thor, in other words, sought a current "deduction" for an estimated future loss. Under the decided cases, a taxpayer so circumstanced finds no shelter beneath an accountancy presumption.

Third, the presumption petitioner postulates is insupportable in light of the vastly different objectives that financial and tax accounting have. The primary goal of financial accounting is to provide useful information to management, shareholders, creditors, and others properly interested; the major responsibility of the accountant is to protect these parties from being misled. The primary goal of the income tax system, in contrast, is the equitable collection of revenue; the major responsibility of the Internal Revenue Service is to protect the public fisc. Consistently with its goals and responsibilities, financial accounting has as its foundation the principle of conservatism, with its corollary that "possible errors in measurement [should] be in the direction of understatement rather than overstatement of net income and net assets." In view of the Treasury's markedly different goals and responsibilities understatement of income is not destined to be its guiding light. Given this diversity, even contrariety, of objectives, any presumptive equivalency between tax and financial accounting would be unacceptable.

This difference in objectives is mirrored in numerous differences of treatment. Where the tax law requires that a deduction be deferred until "all the events" have occurred that will make it fixed and certain, United States v. Anderson, 269 U.S. 422, 441, 46 S.Ct. 131, 134, 70 L.Ed. 347 (1926), accounting principles typically require that a liability be accrued as soon as it can reasonably be estimated. Conversely, where the tax law requires that income be recognized currently under "claim of right," "ability to pay," and "control" rationales, accounting principles may defer accrual until a later year so that revenues and expenses may be better matched. Financial accounting, in short, is hospitable to estimates, probabilities, and reasonable certainties; the tax law, with its mandate to preserve the revenue, can give no quarter to uncertainty. This is as it should be. Reasonable estimates may be useful, even essential, in giving shareholders and creditors an accurate picture of a firm's overall financial health; but the accountant's conservatism cannot bind the Commissioner in his efforts to collect taxes. "Only a few reserves voluntarily established as a matter of conservative accounting," Mr. Justice Brandeis wrote for the Court, "are authorized by the Revenue Acts." Brown v. Helvering, 291 U.S., at 201–202, 54 S.Ct., at 360.

Finally, a presumptive equivalency between tax and financial accounting would create insurmountable difficulties of tax administration. Accountants long have recognized that "generally accepted accounting principles" are far from being a canonical set of rules that will ensure identical accounting treatment of identical transactions. "Generally accepted accounting principles," rather, tolerate a range of "reasonable" treatments, leaving the choice among alternatives to management. Such, indeed, is precisely the case here. Variances of this sort may be tolerable in financial reporting, but they are questionable in a tax system designed to ensure as far as possible that similarly situated taxpayers pay the same tax. If management's election among "acceptable" options were dispositive for tax purposes, a firm, indeed, could decide unilaterally—within limits dictated only by its accountants—the tax it wished to pay. Such unilateral decisions would not just make the Code inequitable; they would make it unenforceable.

* * *

The judgment of the Court of Appeals is affirmed.

It is so ordered.

3. LIMITED LEGISLATIVE AND ADMINISTRATIVE DEFERRALS

The differences between financial accounting and tax accounting have been narrowed in response to the Supreme Court's refusal to do so. See § 455 permitting the deferral of certain prepaid subscription income and § 456, changing the result in the AAA case, by providing for the deferral of prepaid dues received by certain membership organizations. Reg. § 1.451–5, added in 1971, allows certain accrual method taxpayers, receiving prepayments for goods to be delivered in the future, a limited deferral. Consider how the following administrative pronouncement permits a limited deferral for that portion of a prepayment received for services to be performed in the following year. Is it consistent with § 446? However, a prepayment of income that does not fall under any of the administrative or statutory concessions is presumably governed by the case law which requires reporting a prepayment as income when received.

REV.PROC. 71-21

1971-2 C.B. 549.

SECTION 1. PURPOSE

The purpose of this Revenue Procedure is to implement an administrative decision, made by the Commissioner in the exercise of his discretion under section 446 of the Internal Revenue Code of 1954, to allow accrual method taxpayers in certain specified and limited circumstances to defer the inclusion in gross income for Federal income tax purposes of payments received (or amounts due and payable) in one taxable year for services to be performed by the end of the next succeeding taxable year. Amounts due and payable are, for purposes of this Revenue Procedure, treated as payments received.

SEC. 2. BACKGROUND

In general, tax accounting requires that payments received for services to be performed in the future must be included in gross income in the taxable year of receipt. However, this treatment varies from financial accounting conventions consistently used by many accrual method taxpayers in the treatment of payments received in one taxable year for services to be performed by them in the next succeeding taxable year. The purpose of this Revenue Procedure is to reconcile the tax and financial accounting treatment of such payments in a large proportion of these cases without permitting extended deferral in the time of including such payments in gross income for Federal income tax purposes. Such reconciliation will facilitate reporting and verification of such items from the standpoint of both the taxpayers affected and the Internal Revenue Service.

SEC. 3. PERMISSIBLE METHODS

.01 An accrual method taxpayer who receives a payment for services to be performed by him in the future and who includes such payment in gross income in the year of receipt is using a proper method of accounting.

.02 An accrual method taxpayer who, pursuant to an agreement (written or otherwise), receives a payment in one taxable year for services, where all of the services under such agreement are required by the agreement as it exists at the end of the taxable year of receipt to be performed by him before the end of the next succeeding taxable year, may include such payment in gross income as earned through the performance of the services, subject to the limitations provided in [section] 3.08. However, if the inclusion in gross income of payments received is properly deferred under the preceding sentence and for any reason a portion of such services is not performed by the end of the next succeeding taxable year, the amount allocable to the services not so performed must be included in gross income in such next succeeding year, regardless of when (if ever) such services are performed.

.03 Except as provided in sections 3.04 and 3.05 [these sections are omitted], a payment received by an accrual method taxpayer pursuant to an agreement for the performance by him of services must be included in his gross income in the taxable year of receipt if under the terms of the agreement as it exists at the end of such year:

(a) Any portion of the services is to be performed by him after the end of the taxable year immediately succeeding the year of receipt; or

(b) Any portion of the services is to be performed by him at an unspecified future date which may be after the end of the taxable year immediately succeeding the year of receipt.

*   *   *

.08 This Revenue Procedure has no application to amounts received under guaranty or warranty contracts or to prepaid rent or prepaid interest. However, for purposes of this Revenue Procedure and section 1.61–8(b) of the Income Tax Regulations (requiring "advance rentals" to be included in income in the year of receipt), the term "rent" does not include payments for the use or occupancy of rooms or other space where significant services are also rendered to the occupant, such as for the use or occupancy of rooms or other quarters in hotels, boarding houses, or apartment houses furnishing hotel services, or in tourist homes, motor courts, or motels. See section 1.1372–4(b)(5) (vi) of the regulations.

*   *   *

.12 The above rules may be illustrated in part as follows:

(1) On November 1, 1970, A, a calendar year accrual method taxpayer in the business of giving dancing lessons, receives a payment for a one-year contract commencing on that date which provides for 48 individual, one-hour lessons. Eight lessons are provided in 1970. Under the method prescribed in section 3.02, A must include 1/6 of the payment in income for 1970, and 5/6 of such payment in 1971, regardless of whether A is for any reason unable to give all the lessons under the contract by the end of 1971.

(2) Assume the same facts as in Example 1 except that the payment is received for a two-year contract commencing on November 1, 1970, under which 96 lessons are provided. The taxpayer must include the entire payment in his gross income in 1970 since a portion of the services may be performed in 1972.

(3) On June 1, 1970, B, a calendar year accrual method taxpayer who is a landscape architect, receives a payment for services which, under the terms of the agreement, must be completed by December, 1971. On December 31, 1970, B estimates that 3/4 of the work under the agreement has been completed. Under the method prescribed in section 3.02, B must include 3/4 of the payment in 1970. The remaining 1/4 of such payment must be included in 1971, regardless of whether B is for any reason unable to complete the job in 1971.

*   *   *

4. RESERVE FOR ESTIMATED EXPENSES

The general rule for accrual method taxpayers that prepaid income is taxable when received (even though the services paid for have not been performed and later expenses must be incurred to earn the income) obviously creates unnatural peaks and valleys of income for taxpayers. It is natural that accrual method taxpayers would try to alleviate this by taking, in the year they are charged with income, deductions for the estimated expenses of producing the income which will be incurred in later years. But for accrual method taxpayers, expenses are deductible in the year in which "all events have occurred which determine the fact of the liability and the amount thereof can be determined with reasonable accuracy." Reg. § 1.461–1(a)(2). According to Rev.Rul. 76–345, 1976–2 C.B. 134, the Service permits an accrual only "when the fact of the liability to a specified individual * * * has been clearly established and the amount of the liability to each individual can be determined with reasonable accuracy."

In addition, under § 461(h), no deduction is permitted until both the "all events test" is satisfied and "economic performance" has occurred. Reread pp. 226–232. The taxpayer may seek to transfer much of the income into a reserve for future estimated expenses and deduct the amounts allocated to the reserve. Generally this may not be done.

Although the matching principle under GAAP requires that the expenses of earning income be reported in the year the income is reported (the year of "realization") in order to prevent a "material distortion" of the net income of the business, tax accounting (with some limited exceptions such as § 166(c)) generally disallows a current deduction for estimated future expenses even though the income has been reported currently. Consider how the following case dealt with a current deduction for future expenses related to income reported currently. Also, consider whether the future expenses satisfied the "all events" test for accrual method taxpayers, and when "economic performance" occurred.

MOONEY AIRCRAFT, INC. v. UNITED STATES

United States Court of Appeals, Fifth Circuit, 1969.
420 F.2d 400.

* * *

This is yet another case in the continuing conflict between commercial accounting practice and the federal income tax. The facts, as accepted by the parties for the purpose of the motion for summary judgment, may be summarized as follows:

During the years 1961 through 1965 taxpayer was in the business of manufacturing and selling single-engine, executive aircraft. The taxpayer's practice was to sell exclusively to regional distributors throughout the United States and Canada. These distributors sold to more localized dealers who in turn sold to the ultimate consumers.

During the fiscal years ending October 31, 1961, 1963, 1964 and 1965 taxpayer issued, with each aircraft which it manufactured and sold, a document captioned "Mooney Bond" setting out an unconditional promise that taxpayer would pay to the bearer of the document the sum of $1,000 when the corresponding aircraft should be permanently retired from service. By far the great majority of the "Mooney Bonds" issued by the taxpayer were retained by the distributors to whom they were originally issued, or by persons related to such distributors as the result of reorganizations, liquidations, etc. By October 31, 1965 many distributors had accumulated quite large holdings in the certificates; one distributor, for example, held no less than 122.

Taxpayer seeks to exclude or deduct from gross income the face value of either all Mooney Bonds, or those Mooney Bonds which it is estimated will ultimately be redeemed,[3] in the year the instruments were issued. It is the Government's position that the Mooney Bonds may be deducted only in the year the aircraft to which it relates is in fact permanently retired from service. The Government has alleged, and the taxpayer has not denied, that perhaps 20 or more years may elapse between issuance of the Bonds and retirement of the aircraft. The district court sustained the Government's position and, for the reasons to be discussed, we affirm the judgment of the district court.

The issue in this case is whether the taxpayer's "accrual" system of accounting is acceptable for tax purposes. In order to better understand this issue it may be helpful to first discuss the purpose and techniques of accrual accounting as they relate to the federal income tax.

"Income" has been defined as "a net or resultant determined by matching revenues with related expenses." Since the Internal Revenue Code allows the deduction of substantially all business expenses it seems reasonably clear that Congress intended to tax only net business income. This objective, however, is complicated by the fact that the tax is exacted on an annual basis whereas business transactions are often spread over two or more years. A business may receive payment for goods or services in one tax year but incur the related expenses in subsequent tax years. The result is that the expenses cannot be used to offset the receipts, and the full amount of the receipts is taxed as though it were all net "profit." [7]

---

3. Taxpayer attempted to introduce an expert study estimating what number of the bonds would actually be presented for redemption.

Taxpayer also raises a separate issue, namely, claimed net operating losses sustained in the fiscal years 1961 and 1963, which result from the deduction from income of the face amount of the bonds. These he wishes to carry-back to fiscal years 1959 and 1962.

7. The expenses incurred in a subsequent year can, of course, be used to offset receipts for that year; but there may be no receipts for that year, or the receipts may be less than the expenses. In other words, the relationship between expenses incurred in producing the revenues of an earlier year, and the revenues received in the year the expenses are incurred, may well be random and thus produce a distortion of "income" for that year.

The purpose of "accrual" accounting in the taxation context is to try to alleviate this problem by matching, in the same taxable year, revenues with the expenses incurred in producing those revenues. Accurate matching of expenses against revenues in the same taxable year may occur either by "deferring" receipts until such time as the related expenses are incurred or by "accruing" estimated future expenses so as to offset revenue. Under the deferral concept present receipts are not recognized as "income" until they are "earned" by performing the related services or delivering goods. It is thus not the actual receipt but the right to receive which is controlling; and, from an accounting (if not from a tax) point of view, that "right" does not arise until the money is "earned." [10] A corresponding principle states that expenses are to be reported in the year the related income is "earned" whether or not actually paid in that year.

Another accounting technique for matching expenses and revenues is the "accrual" of estimated future expenses which has been described as follows:

> "The professional accountant recognizes estimated future expenses when the current performance of a contract to deliver goods or render services creates an incidental obligation in the seller which may require him to incur additional expenses at some future time. Instead of deferring the recognition of a portion of the revenue from the sale transaction until such time as the future expenses are incurred, accepted accounting procedures require inclusion of the total revenue in the current determination of income when the contract has been substantially performed, and the simultaneous deduction of all the related expenses, including a reasonable estimate for future expenses." [12]

* * *

* * * The Commissioner has consistently opposed deferment of prepaid income, or accrual of estimated future expenses, on the ground that for tax purposes such methods do not clearly reflect income. In the "deferral" cases he has argued that when the taxpayer receives payment under "claim of right,"—i.e., without restriction as to disposition—deferring such payments to a future year violates the annual accounting concept, and they must therefore be reported in the year received. * * * The principle question in the present case is whether, in the light of the statutory policies these doctrines are intended to implement, the Commissioner was justified in disallowing a present deduction of the Mooney Bonds as "not clearly reflecting income."

Although the Government admits that the retirement of the aircraft in this case is inevitable, it contends, nevertheless, that taxpayer cannot deduct the bonds in the year of issuance because the obligation they represent is contingent upon the happening of a future event—

---

10. See, e.g., American Automobile Association v. United States, 367 U.S. 687, 699, 81 S.Ct. 1727, 6 L.Ed.2d 1109 (1961) (Justice Stewart, dissenting opinion).

12. See Comment, 61 Mich.L.Rev. 148, 151 (1962).

retirement of the related aircraft. Therefore, "all the events" creating the liability have not occurred in the taxable year. We cannot agree. In all the cases cited by the Government there was uncertainty as to whether the future event would actually happen;[25] here there is none. There is no contingency in this case as to the fact of liability itself; the only contingency relates to when the liability will arise.[26] To be sure, technically, the liability is "created" by the event of the retirement of a particular plane; if a plane lasted forever there would be no liability. But taxation has been called a "practical field," and we do not see how the technical position the Government takes is designed to further the purpose of the statute. One commentator has argued, and we think justly, that the all events test is designed to protect tax revenues by "[insuring] that the taxpayer will not take deductions for expenditures that might never occur. . . ."[27] If there is any doubt whether the liability will occur courts have been loathe to interfere with the Commissioner's discretion in disallowing a deduction. * * * But here, there is no doubt at all that the liability will occur since airplanes, like human beings, regrettably must cease to function.[28]

The "all events test," however, is not the only basis upon which the Commissioner can disallow a deduction. Under § 4[4]6(b) he has discretion to disallow any accounting method which does not clearly reflect income. As previously stated, the Commissioner has often relied on the "claim of right test," to disallow a deduction or a deferral of income in cases where the taxpayer's receipt of the funds was unrestricted. He

---

25. In Brown v. Helvering, 291 U.S. 193 (1934) taxpayer attempted to deduct from commissions for the sale of insurance the estimated amounts that would have to be refunded because of future cancellations. The Supreme Court disallowed the deduction because there was no assurance that any single policy would be cancelled and the expense incurred: "In respect to no particular policy written within the year could it be known that it would be cancelled in a future year. . . . ." Id. at 201.

In Simplified Tax Records, Inc. v. Commissioner, 41 T.C. 75 (1963) the taxpayer contracted to prepare income tax reports for its subscribers, receiving payment in advance. Since, however, this service was available only upon a subscriber's demand there was no assurance that taxpayer would render services to any individual subscriber in the future, and a deduction for the estimated expense of such future services was disallowed. Cf. Schlude v. Commissioner, 372 U.S. 128 (1963); American Automobile Assn. v. United States, 367 U.S. 687 (1961). In these cases then, although there is a great probability that the expense will occur, it is not certain; and in cases of doubt the courts have usually deferred to the Commissioner: "Experience

taught that there is a strong probability that many of the policies written during the taxable year will be . . . cancelled. But experience taught also that we are not dealing here with certainties. Brown v. Helvering, 291 U.S. 193." (Brandeis, J.)

26. See, e.g., Revenue Ruling 57–105, 1957–1 Cum.Bull. 193: ". . . an obligation is considered contingent when the existence of any liability at all is uncertain or when its existence depends upon the happening of a future *contingent* event. (Emphasis added)

Although, strictly speaking, liability in the present case depends upon a future event, it does not depend upon a future *contingent* event, since retirement of the planes is certain.

27. Comment, Notre Dame Lwyr. 511, 520 (1967).

28. Even if the fact of the liability seems certain or highly probable some decisions have disallowed a deduction if the *amount* is uncertain or at least cannot be reasonably estimated. See, e.g., Brown v. Helvering, 291 U.S. 193 (1934). Since there is no finding by the trial judge on this issue, and since, as appears below, its resolution is not necessary for the decision of this case, we do not reach it.

appears to be doing so here, for the Government says in its brief, "Taxpayer received the full economic benefit of these proceeds, without any restriction as to use or enjoyment, and without any duty to return or transfer any part of these proceeds." The claim of right doctrine, however, has not enjoyed universal acceptance in the courts, see e.g., Schuessler v. Commissioner, 230 F.2d 722 (5th Cir. 1956); Beacon Publishing Co. v. Commissioner, 218 F.2d 697 (10th Cir. 1955), and in two recent major decisions in this area, American Automobile Assn. v. United States * * * (hereafter AAA) and Schlude v. Commissioner * * * (hereafter Schlude), the Supreme Court seems to have placed little if any reliance on the doctrine.

Both AAA and Schlude involved an attempt to defer prepaid receipts to the future years when they allegedly would be "earned." * * *

Insofar as AAA and Schlude concerned inaccurate matching of revenues and expenses, both seem distinguishable from the present case. For one thing, this case involves an attempt to deduct future expenses rather than to defer present receipts. Cf. Schuessler v. Commissioner, 230 F.2d 722 (5th Cir. 1966) with Beacon Publishing Co. v. Commissioner, 218 F.2d 697 (10th Cir. 1955); * * * Although the net effect of deferral of income and deduction of future expenses is often identical, deferral creates a greater risk of loss of tax revenues, since at least in the accrual of expenses situation income is reported and taxed when received. See, e.g., Comment, 42 Notre Dame Lwyr. 511, 520 (1967). But even if "deferral" and "accrual" are identical for tax purposes, there is no doubt in this case that taxpayer will incur the "costs" necessary to pay the bonds on dates after the tax year.[30] The Government argues that Schlude and AAA require that these costs must arise on fixed dates. But we think that the relevance of the "fixed dates" criteria in Schlude and AAA was that since there were no fixed dates on which services had to be performed, there was no assurance that services would be performed after the tax year. If it is certain that there will be services (or costs) after the tax year, why should it make any difference that the date of those services (or costs) is uncertain? All that Schlude and AAA would seem to require is that the deferred income is reported as the related costs do in fact occur. If this were a deferral case, the taxpayer would report the "income" represented by the bonds in the years they were redeemed and paid.

---

30. Cf. Simplified Tax Records, Inc. v. Commissioner, 41 T.C. 75 (1963), note 25, supra. In this case the Tax Court relied on Schlude and AAA to reject an accrual of future expenses. Taxpayer had contracted to provide tax returns for subscribers for a period of two years and had been paid in advance. There was no obligation to make the returns, however, unless a subscriber made a specific request. Held, since the service was available only on demand of the members, there was, as in Schlude and AAA, no assurance that the services would be performed and thus deduction of the future expenses involved could be disallowed. This is not dissimilar from the holding in Brown v. Helvering, * * *. In a sense, then, Schlude and AAA only represent the application of the "all events" test to deferral cases. In the present case we think the all events test has been met since it is certain that the bonds will be redeemed in future years. * * *

Schlude and AAA, however, have significance far beyond their particular facts. For in both these cases the Court announced an additional reason for its decision which indicated that even if the taxpayer's system did truly reflect income it still might be rejected. * * * [T]he Court restricted its holding to a finding that the Commissioner did not abuse his discretion in rejecting the AAA's accounting system It specifically refrained from overruling Beacon and Schuessler, distinguishing them on the ground that future performance was certain. * * * [T]he Commissioner should have very broad discretion to disallow such accounting techniques when there is any reasonable basis for his action. This is the construction given these two Supreme Court cases by the United States Tax Court:

> "We suspect, because of its repeated emphasis on the Commissioner's discretion * * * Sec. 446 * * * that the majority of the Supreme Court stand for the principle that, absent statutory sanction for it, unless the taxpayer can show that the Commissioner clearly abused his discretion in disallowing deferral of prepaid income or accrual of estimated future expenses, this exercise of the Commissioner's discretion will not be disturbed by the Court even though the taxpayer's method of accounting is in accord with generally accepted principles of commercial accounting. * * *

The question remains: Was there reasonable basis for the Commissioner's action in this case? It appears to us there was ample basis.

The most salient feature in this case is the fact that many or possibly most of the expenses which taxpayer wishes to presently deduct will not actually be paid for 15, 20 or even 30 years (the taxpayer has not attempted to deny this). In no other case coming to our attention have we found anything even comparable to the time span involved in this case. In virtually all these other cases, even though a taxpayer may have received money under "claim or right" and had unrestricted use of the funds, there was still some relationship between those funds and related expenses which, more or less proximately, had to be borne. If there were no actual strings there were at least invisible strings attached to the money. Taxpayers could not use the money without at least an eye to the upcoming expenses or services to be performed. In this case, however, the related expenditure is so distant from the time the money is received as to completely attenuate if not break any relationship between the two. For all practical purposes the revenue taxpayer received from the sale of the planes is his to use as he pleases. Rather than being set up as a reserve to pay an impending expense it is far more probable that the money will be used as capital to expand the business. In what sense, then, is it an accurate reflection of income to regard it as an expense of doing business in the current year? To so regard it is to let an accounting fiction obscure the business and fiscal realities that are the heart of this case. In exercising his discretion the Commissioner need not close his eyes to these realities and to the actual facts. We feel that from both a business and tax standpoint the accounting systems rejected by the

Supreme Court in Schlude and AAA were much more reasonable than the one involved here, and that to allow a present deduction in this case would distort rather than reflect income. We therefore find no difficulty in concluding that the Commissioner had a reasonable basis for disallowing the deduction as not clearly reflecting income.

There is yet another reason why the time span is too long. The longer the time the less probable it becomes that the liability, though incurred, will ever in fact be paid. Some courts have held that the improbability of payment is not a ground for disallowing the accrual of a future expense.[38] Yet under 452 of the Internal Revenue Code of 1954 * * * the first express legislative sanction of deferral of income (repealed in 1955, * * *), Congress specifically limited the length of time income could be deferred to five years. * * * It seems to us that these time limits are founded on the need to protect tax revenues, since the longer the interval between receipt of the funds and imposition of the tax the greater the risk the funds will be dissipated or that the taxpayer will die or that a business will be dissolved. A similar risk of loss of revenues exists in the case of accruals. Indeed, the very purpose of the "all events test" is to make sure that the taxpayer will not deduct expenses that might never occur. Just as in the deferral situation, the longer the time interval between receipt of money and payment of the related expense the greater the chance that the money will be dissipated and never paid. If it is never paid, it is not an expense and should have been taxed. In the present case the taxpayer could in all good faith use all the monies it has received as capital to expand its business; if one day it became insolvent the expense might never be paid, yet the money would have been used as tax-free income. We repeat that because of the inordinate length of time involved in this case the Commissioner was clearly within his discretion in disallowing deduction of the "Mooney Bonds" as a current expense.

* * *

We affirm the judgment of the District Court.

Affirmed.

Questions

Are you satisfied with the reasoning of the court in the Mooney Aircraft case? Consider whether the case would have been decided differently if § 461(h) had been in effect. Would a more realistic approach have been to allow a deduction for the discounted present value of the future obligation? Did the taxpayer actually sell two separate items, an airplane and an original issue discount bond? As an alternative could it be argued that the "bond" represented a rebate of the purchase price?

38. The Zimmerman Steel Co. v. Commissioner, 130 F.2d 1011 (8th Cir.1942), originated this rather dubious rule of tax accounting (all the more dubious now in light of Schlude and AAA).

Consider how the next case dealt with the "all events" test and the taking of a current deduction for an estimate of future expenses related to income currently reported.

BROWN v. HELVERING

Supreme Court of the United States, 1934.
291 U.S. 193, 54 S.Ct. 356, 78 L.Ed. 725.

[The taxpayer, a general insurance agent on the accrual method, was entitled to receive "overriding commissions" on fire insurance policies written through local agents. The taxpayer was obligated to refund, to the insurance company, a part of commission payments received in the event a policyholder cancelled a policy in the future and became entitled to the return of a portion of the premiums paid. The taxpayer reported as gross income the "overriding commissions" in the year the policies were written. The taxpayer set up a liability account called "Return Commission" and sought to charge off payments, estimated on the basis of past experience, of the future liability to refund commissions with respect to policies written during the taxable year.]

MR. JUSTICE BRANDEIS delivered the opinion of the Court.

* * *

First. The Commissioner properly disallowed the deductions on account of the credits to the "Return Commission" account. Under the Revenue Acts, taxable income is computed for annual periods. If the accounts are kept on the accrual basis, the income is to be accounted for in the year in which it is realized, even if not then actually received; and the deductions are to be taken in the year in which the deductible items are incurred. * * *

The overriding commissions were gross income of the year in which they were receivable. As to each such commission there arose the obligation—a contingent liability—to return a proportionate part in case of cancellation. But the mere fact that some portion of it might have to be refunded in some future year in the event of cancellation or reinsurance did not affect its quality as income. Compare American National Co. v. United States, 274 U.S. 99, 47 S.Ct. 520, 71 L.Ed. 946. When received, the general agent's right to it was absolute. It was under no restriction, contractual or otherwise, as to its disposition, use, or enjoyment. Compare North American Oil Consolidated v. Burnet, 286 U.S. 417, 424, 52 S.Ct. 613, 76 L.Ed. 1197. The refunds during the tax year of those portions of the overriding commissions which represented cancellations during the tax year had, prior to the tax return for [the earliest tax year in question] always been claimed as deductions; and they were apparently allowed as "necessary expenses paid or incurred during the taxable year." The right to such deductions is not now questioned. Those which the taxpayer claims now are of a very different character. They are obviously not "expenses paid during the taxable year." They are bookkeeping charges representing credits to a reserve account.

These charges on account of credits to the "Return Commission" reserve account are claimed as deductions on the ground that they are expenses "incurred," "during the taxable year." It is true that, where a liability has "accrued during the taxable year," it may be treated as an expense incurred; and hence as the basis for a deduction, although payment is not presently due, United States v. Anderson, 269 U.S. 422, 440, 441, 46 S.Ct. 131, 70 L.Ed. 347, and although the amount of the liability has not been definitely ascertained. United States v. Anderson, supra. Compare Continental Tie & Lumber Co. v. United States, 286 U.S. 290, 296, 52 S.Ct. 529, 76 L.Ed. 1111. But no liability accrues during the taxable year on account of cancellations which it is expected may occur in future years, since the events necessary to create the liability do not occur during the taxable year. Except as otherwise specifically provided by statute, a liability does not accrue as long as it remains contingent.

The liability of [the taxpayer] arising from expected future cancellations was not deductible from gross income because it was not fixed and absolute. In respect to no particular policy written within the year could it be known that it would be canceled in a future year. Nor could it be known that a definite percentage of all the policies will be canceled in the future years. Experience taught that there is a strong probability that many of the policies written during the taxable year will be so canceled. But experience taught also that we are not dealing here with certainties. This is shown by the variations in the percentages in the several five-year periods of the aggregate of refunds to the aggregate of overriding commissions.

* * *

[The taxpayer] argues also that the Revenue Acts required him to make his return "in accordance with the method of accounting regularly employed in keeping the books;" and that in making the deductions based on the credits to "Return Commission" account he complied with this requirement. * * *

The accrual method of accounting had been regularly employed by [the taxpayer] before 1923, but no "Return Commission" account had been set up. Moreover, the method employed by the taxpayer is never conclusive. If in the opinion of the Commissioner it does not clearly reflect the income, "the computation shall be made upon such basis and in such manner" as will, in his opinion, do so. United States v. Anderson, 269 U.S. 422, 439, 46 S.Ct. 131, 70 L.Ed. 347. In assessing the deficiencies, the Commissioner required in effect that the taxpayer continue to follow the method of accounting which had been in use prior to the change made in 1923. To so require was within his administrative discretion. Compare Bent v. Com'r Int. Rev. (C.C.A.) 56 F.(2d) 99.

* * *

Affirmed.

Question

What barred the Court from adopting a more lenient approach in this area?

———

Rev.Proc. 71–21, set out above, alleviates some of the pressure for establishing and deducting a reserve for estimated future liabilities. And, the courts have sometimes allowed taxpayers to establish reserves for estimated expenses. For example, in Schuessler v. Commissioner, 230 F.2d 722 (5th Cir.1956), taxpayer sold furnaces which included a contract that he would turn them on and off during each heating season for the next five years. The court allowed a current deduction for the estimated cost of this service. Taxpayer had shown that he charged more for his furnaces to cover the cost of the future services he was obligated to perform. Would the taxpayer in Schuessler be allowed a current deduction under the exception for recurring items in the economic performance test contained in § 461(h)? Consider § 461(h)(3).

Problem

Security Storage Co. is a public warehouse company using the accrual method. When a customer puts goods in storage, he is required to pay a "handling out" fee in advance; when the goods are in fact "handled out" at the end of storage the customer is not required to pay for loading and other services included in the charge. The fee is credited against such a charge.

The accountant for the firm seeks to minimize the receipt of taxable income until the latest possible date and asks you to give her your best judgment concerning the following methods of attack:

(a) She will claim that the "handling out" fee is not includible in gross income when received. Consider the trilogy of Supreme Court cases (Automobile Club of Michigan, American Automobile Association, and Schlude) (are these cases distinguishable?), Boise Cascade, and Rev.Proc. 71–21.

(b) She will, in the alternative, seek to offset income by establishing on the books a "Reserve for Handling Out" based on the liability of the firm to its customers for this item. The liability will be fixed by an annual inventory of stored property on hand at the end of each year, for which a handling charge had been collected; the handling charge would be allocated 40% for handling in and 60% for handling out. This division represents the experience in the industry and bookkeeping similar to this represents a past practice of the taxpayer. The taxpayer will deduct, for Federal income tax purposes, the amounts charged to the reserve. The accountant is very concerned about taking the deduction for the reserve. Can you reassure the accountant? Do you get any help from § 162, Reg. § 1.461–1(a)(2), § 461(h), or the Brown case? See Pacific Grape Products Co. v. Commissioner, 219 F.2d 862 (9th Cir.1955).

Chapter 8

RECOVERY OF CAPITAL COSTS: DEPRECIATION—A COST ALLOCATION SYSTEM

A. INTRODUCTION

In Chapter 7, we discussed § 263 which requires the capitalization of certain expenditures that create assets with a useful life extending substantially beyond the close of the taxable year. Reread Reg. § 1.461–1(a)(1) and (2). Although capital [1] expenditures may not be deducted currently, in most cases capital expenditures may be the subject of a deduction in future taxable years. The capitalization requirement of § 263 simply precludes the taxpayer from taking a current deduction under §§ 162 or 212 for the full amount of the expenditure in the year the asset is acquired.

This chapter considers cost allocation methods known as depreciation and its current embodiment under the Accelerated Cost Recovery System. Depreciation provides methods for the taxpayer to deduct the cost of certain property over a period of time. The cost is recovered by deductions over the asset's useful life (for assets subject to traditional depreciation) or over a statutory recovery period (for assets subject to the Accelerated Cost Recovery System). In the alternative, if the cost of an asset which must be capitalized is not depreciable, the cost is recovered as an offset against the amount realized in computing gain (or loss) on the sale or other disposition (or as a loss on the abandonment) of the asset.

---

1. The term "capital asset" used in connection with § 263 must be distinguished from the same term used in connection with § 1221. Section 263 requires the capitalization of all expenditures that create assets with a useful life extending substantially beyond the close of the taxable year in which the expenditure is made. The expenditures which are capitalized under § 263 create "assets" for § 263 purposes. Nevertheless, these same expenditures and the capitalization requirement of § 263 do not automatically render an "asset" a "capital asset" for the capital gain purposes of § 1221. Section 1221 excludes assets created by capitalizing expenditures that are property used in a trade or business from the definitions of capital assets. Nevertheless, these business assets may qualify as quasi-capital assets by application of § 1231. For a discussion of the mechanics of § 1231 see pp. 975–977.

B. TRADITIONAL DEPRECIATION

1. INTRODUCTION

Depreciation of a capitalized expenditure involves the allocation of the cost of using certain property to its period of use in a trade or business or for the production of income. A deduction is allowed for the exhaustion, wear and tear, and obsolescence of qualified property, based on the asset's cost or other basis. In effect, the depreciation deduction permits the taxpayer to recover his capital tax free, and the deduction is allocated over the property's estimated useful life.

Where a taxpayer buys a business or investment related asset which wears out, fairness requires that a deduction be given as a part of the cost of doing business or producing income in subsequent years to the extent that the asset has been consumed. Consider the following illustration:

> X pays $5,000 for a machine which he expects to use in his business for five years. X cannot deduct the entire $5,000 expenditure in the year of payment. However, as X uses the machine in his business, he is consuming the machine to produce income. Consequently, he should be allowed to deduct a portion of the $5,000 cost each year. The depreciation deduction accomplishes that result. In effect, the $5,000 cost of the machine is matched to the years in which the machine generates revenue. Deducting the entire cost in the year the machine is paid for would be a material distortion of the financial picture of that business. Instead, a more accurate result would be to deduct $1,000 each year over a five year period.

Until the enactment of § 168 in 1981, depreciation allocated the cost of an asset, which had a limited life and contributed to income for more than one taxable year, over the appropriate accounting periods to determine taxable income during each of these periods. In theory, the depreciation deduction equalled the amount of the asset "used up" during each annual period. The depreciation deduction under § 167 permitted the taxpayer to recoup annually a portion of the basis (not the current value) of a wasting asset through deductions from ordinary income.

Historically, the accounting profession developed the term "depreciation" to describe the process that occurs over time and eventually renders an asset incapable of servicing the production or service needs of its owner. Depreciation is composed of two factors that contribute to the decline in an asset's usefulness, namely, physical depreciation and functional depreciation. Physical depreciation involves the wear and tear attributable to the asset's use and deterioration from the action of the elements. Functional depreciation, on the other hand, involves the recognition that an asset will become inadequate and obsolete as changes in production or technology occur. An asset becomes physically inadequate when it cannot be used to satisfy increased production needs. Conversely, an asset is rendered functionally obsolete if the goods it produces are no longer in demand or if technology changes so that a new, more cost efficient asset, which can produce goods of equal or higher quality, may be purchased. Because depreciation is a book-keeping entry, not a bank deposit, it is not a replacement fund with which new assets may be purchased. The depreciation deduction bars the overstatement of profits during the years the asset is used.

The last decade has witnessed a high degree of technical innovation in numerous fields. Perhaps the greatest rate of technological change has taken place in the computer and electronics industries. Consequently, the rate at which the technological innovations have rendered computers obsolete is a classic example of functional depreciation. IBM, a computer manufacturer and the leader in the business information industry, has continually introduced new lines of computers that render each predecessor line as obsolete as the abacus. The rate of obsolescence in the computer industry affected the manner in which taxpayers depreciated their computers, assuming they decided to buy rather than lease. As a general rule, taxpayers selected a very short useful life and deducted the bulk of the cost in the early years of the useful life, even though the asset can be used for a longer period.

If an asset is eligible for depreciation, the next question is how much of the asset depreciates (or is "used up") in a given tax year? Prior to the adoption of the Accelerated Recovery Cost System under § 168 (beginning January 1, 1981), § 167 governed the amount and calculation of depreciation deductions. The concept of depreciation as embodied in § 167 parallels the accounting concept of depreciation. The depreciation deduction under § 167 strives to match the revenues generated by the asset over its useful life with a portion of its cost. Consequently, a number of factors affect the determination of the annual depreciation deduction. These factors are:

1. the taxpayer's adjusted basis in the asset as determined by reference to §§ 1011, 1012, and 1016,

2. the asset's expected useful life,

3. the method of depreciation chosen,

4. the amount which the taxpayer expects to realize on the sale or other disposition of the asset at the end of its useful life (salvage value).

The two key factors in the traditional approach are: (1) the asset's useful life and (2) the method of depreciation (the rate at which the asset is depreciated). Depreciation allocates the cost of the asset over its useful life, which is defined as an estimate of the future time period over which the asset will be economically productive.

Consider the taxpayer who buys a new machine costing $100,000 for her factory. Under § 263, none of the $100,000 would be deductible currently. Section 263 provides that no deduction is available, with certain exceptions, for amounts paid out for new buildings or permanent improvements. Such expenditures are capital expenditures and contribute to income producing activities for periods beyond the current tax year. Deductions for the cost of the machine were traditionally obtained through depreciation deductions as the machine wears out. Under § 167(a) a depreciation deduction is available to the extent of " * * * a reasonable allowance for the exhaustion, wear and tear * * * (1) of property used in the trade or business, or (2) of property held for the production of income." Pursuant to § 167, depreciation might be taken under the straight line method under which the basis (cost) of the asset was deducted in equal annual installments over the asset's useful life. If the machine costs $100,000 and has a useful life of 25 years, the depreciation deduction is $4,000 per year (for the purposes of this example we do not consider salvage value). Each depreciation deduction also reduces the asset's adjusted basis. § 1016(a)(2). At the end of 25 years, the taxpayer's adjusted basis would be zero. If, at the end of 25 years, the taxpayer then sold the machine for $20,000, the taxpayer would have a gain of $20,000.

Although the taxpayer does not have a current deduction of $100,000, she has a depreciation deduction against current income of $4,000 in each tax year. In short, depreciation allocates the cost of an asset, which has a limited life and contributes to income for more than one tax year, over appropriate periods to determine taxable income during each of these future periods. This matching process prevents a material distortion of the taxpayer's net income for the years in question.

2. LIMITATIONS ON THE DEPRECIATION DEDUCTION

A number of limitations exist with respect to depreciation deductions. Most of these limitations on the depreciation deduction involve the class of property to which the deduction applies. As a general rule only property used in a trade or business or used for the production of income may be the subject of the depreciation deduction. § 167(a). In the case of tangible property placed in service after December 31, 1980, § 168 governs the deduction of the cost of business or investment property. For property placed in service prior to 1981, § 167 governs the determination of a taxpayer's annual depreciation deduction, even for years after 1980. A taxpayer's inventory or stock in trade, which is held for sale, did not (and does not) qualify for depreciation. Section 167 continues to apply to intangible property acquired after December 31, 1980, as deductions under the Accelerated Cost Recovery System (§ 168) are only available for tangible property. § 168(a).

In order to be depreciable, the subject property must have an ascertainable useful life and be consumed, deteriorate, become obsolete, or be rendered useless through the passage of time. An example of an asset which must be capitalized pursuant to § 263, but which, because of an unascertainable useful life, may not be depreciated is goodwill. See Reg. § 1.167(a)–3. The capitalized cost of unimproved land or stock in a corporation may not be depreciated because land and stock last forever.

Even though the fair market value of property may be greater, the taxpayer may not take depreciation deductions in excess of his basis in the subject property. Generally, a taxpayer's basis in depreciable property is the historical cost of such property under § 1012, adjusted as provided in § 1016. Moreover, the taxpayer's basis for depreciation includes not only the monies expended for the property, but also the amount of any indebtedness he assumed, entered into, or took the property subject to. See Chapter 11 dealing with determination of basis and determination of amount realized, and the landmark case of Crane v. Commissioner, 331 U.S. 1, 67 S.Ct. 1047, 91 L.Ed. 1301 (1947), p. 766. Take a typical example of the inclusion of indebtedness in basis. Assume a taxpayer purchases a building to be used as a warehouse for his business, and he pays 20% of the purchase price in cash and obtains a mortgage for the balance. If he purchases the warehouse for $100,000 and he mortgages $80,000 of the purchase price, what is his basis? The purchase price of $100,000 or the $20,000 cash down payment? Is not the term "cost" under § 1012 synonymous with "purchase price" if interpreted as commonly understood? Assuming he makes the payments on the mortgage, will his equity investment, and consequently, his basis, in the property increase as he pays off the principal balance of the mortgage? Is it proper to carry this logic one step further and create a presumption that the taxpayer will eventually satisfy the mortgage obligation in order to retain ownership to the property? In most legitimate situations the mortgage indebtedness is included in the taxpayer's basis to determine depreciation deductions because it is reasonable to presume that the taxpayer will satisfy the indebtedness in order to retain ownership in the property or be able to realize his equity investment therein on a subsequent sale or exchange of the property. However, would this same conclusion apply if the property's fair market value as of the date of acquisition is less than the outstanding principal balance of the mortgage? See Estate of Franklin v. Commissioner, 544 F.2d 1045 (9th Cir.1976), p. 798.

When the taxpayer depreciates property and receives an annual depreciation deduction, the taxpayer's basis must be adjusted (reduced) each year by the amount of the depreciation deduction. § 1016(a)(2)(A). The basis reduction increases the taxpayer's gain (or reduces his loss) on the sale or other subsequent disposition of the property. The interrelation between depreciation deductions and adjusted basis is considered on page 762.

3. PERIOD OF TIME OVER WHICH DEPRECIATION MAY BE TAKEN: THE CONCEPT OF USEFUL LIVES

As mentioned earlier in this chapter, depreciation involves a cost allocation process. The cost of a depreciable asset, which has been capitalized pursuant to § 263, is allocated to the income generated by the asset via the depreciation deductions contained in § 167. The practice of matching the costs of producing income to the years the income is reported was developed by the accounting profession and is known as the "matching principle". Of course, the discussion, for the present moment, assumes that § 168 does not control. Section 168 is a mandatory section applicable to all depreciable tangible property used in a trade or business or for the production of income placed in service after December 31, 1980. Section 168 disregards the "matching principle" and applies a cost recovery system that generally allows a taxpayer to recover his cost in the subject property well before it ceases to be useful in the income-producing activity.

A number of depreciation methods were developed prior to or after the adoption of § 167. These depreciation methods are based on the "matching principle" which strives to match all revenues generated by a depreciable asset with a portion of its cost. For instance, assume a depreciable asset generates $100,000 of revenues throughout its useful life and the asset costs $10,000. An ideal application of the matching principle would be to match every $1 of revenue with $.10 of cost. In other words, the depreciation expense for each dollar of revenue equals:

$$\frac{\$\ 10,000\ (\text{cost})}{\$100,000\ (\text{revenue})} = \$.10$$

Nevertheless, an accurate application of the matching principle is not a reality that can easily, if ever, be attained because the revenues expected from a depreciable asset must be estimated. Experience with forecasting methods indicates that it is not possible, without divine inspiration, to predict revenue flows with exactitude. Consequently, we are relegated to making estimates based on our best judgment and experience, which we hope will not be far off target. The depreciation methods discussed below illustrate an attempt to arrive at a better matching of revenues with costs of producing those revenues and, particularly, the costs of utilizing depreciable assets to produce revenues.

Before discussing depreciation methods, it is important to examine the practical administrative difficulties encountered by a massive organization which utilizes a large group of depreciable assets to generate revenues, and the legislative and administrative responses to these problems. It is easy to imagine the bookkeeping difficulties associated with keeping track of a large pool of depreciable assets and recording the depreciation deductions. Because a taxpayer may not deduct an aggregate amount for depreciation which exceeds his basis in the subject property, the taxpayer must maintain an accurate record of his past depreciation deductions associated with his depreciable assets. The accounting profession has established a rule that requires that all amounts taken as depreciation be credited to an account termed "Accumulated Depreciation" (also labelled "Reserve for Depreciation") and, of course, debited to an account termed "Depreciation Expense". The "Accumulated Depreciation" account is reported on the balance sheet as a contra-asset account offsetting the amount reported as the historical cost or other basis of depreciable assets as adjusted for capital improvements and abandonments, sales, exchanges, or other dispositions. If an asset originally cost $42,000 and had been depreciated $12,000 in prior years, its adjusted basis would be $30,000. That information would appear on the taxpayer's financial statement as:

Asset	$42,000
Less: Accumulated Depreciation	12,000
	$30,000

A taxpayer with a large pool of depreciable assets must find a way to minimize the transaction costs of accounting for depreciation. Absent a short-cut method, the taxpayer would have to conduct a particularized analysis of each asset. The asset-by-asset approach epitomizes the classical analysis which a taxpayer, at one time, had to conduct. Typically, the taxpayer would have to estimate the asset's salvage value (its estimated resale or scrap value at the end of its estimated useful life) as well as its useful life, which is defined as an estimate of the future time period over which an asset would be economically productive based on the individual taxpayer's judgment and prior experience (or industry wide experience). Taxpayers generally chose the shortest possible useful life for an asset to accelerate deductions against ordinary income. For instance, assume a taxpayer purchases an asset for $10,000 which has an expected useful life of 10 years and no salvage value. If the taxpayer used a method of depreciation known as straight line, which is based on the assumption that an asset depreciates evenly throughout its useful life, then the yearly depreciation deduction is $1,000 computed as:

$$\frac{\text{Cost Less Salvage Value}}{\text{Useful Life}} = \frac{\$10,000}{10 \text{ years}} = \$1,000$$

Assume that the taxpayer succeeds in convincing the Service that the asset's correct useful life is 5 years, not 10 years. This ploy enables the taxpayer to increase the annual depreciation deduction from $1,000 to $2,000 $\left(\frac{\$10,000}{5} = \$2,000\right)$ for the first five years. After the fifth year no further deductions are permitted as the taxpayer has recovered his entire basis in the property.

Reducing the estimated useful life increased the deferral effect of the depreciation deduction. In other words, the taxpayer may shelter $10,000 worth of ordinary income from income taxation more quickly over a 5-year period rather than a 10-year period. In addition to paying less taxes during the first five years, the deferral also gives the taxpayer the use of the amount of taxes otherwise payable on which he may earn interest. Reread page 17. Therefore, given the obvious advantages to the taxpayer of using a shorter useful life to depreciate assets and, conversely, the obvious disadvantages to the Service from such action by the taxpayer, it is easy to understand the cause of substantial litigation between the Service and taxpayers over the assignment of useful lives to depreciable assets. The test used for estimating an asset's useful life was based on the particular "facts and circumstances" of the taxpayer's situation. Needless, considerable litigation occurred over this question. Under the "facts and circumstances" test, a taxpayer claiming depreciation was required to estimate the useful life for each item of depreciable property.

As a consequence of the volume of litigation and the administrative difficulties associated with the "facts and circumstances" standard, the Service issued tables of estimated or "guideline" useful lives for tangible depreciable assets in 1942 and again in 1962. (Bulletin F and Rev. Proc. 62–21, 1962–2 C.B. 418). Bulletin F contained thousands of standardized asset lives which approximated actual physical life. The guideline lives of Rev.Proc. 62–21 were approximately 30 percent to 40 percent shorter than the Bulletin F lives, and assets were grouped by broad industrial classifications and by certain broad general asset classifications, with a "guideline life" established for each of these classes. The "guideline lives" tables were subsequently replaced in 1971 by the Asset Depreciation Range system (ADR) under § 167(m). "The Guideline system [of Rev.Proc. 62–21] * * * recognized the impossibility of the administering the depreciation provisions on an individualized basis. The ADR system is realistic and forthright in recognizing this same impossibility. ADR gears the annual depreciation allowance * * * to industry average lives and experience." Announcement 71–76, 1971–2 C.B. 503, 514. ADR assets were similarly grouped by industrial and asset classification.

A taxpayer electing to use ADR could rely on the lives for the classes of assets without regard to the particular facts and circumstances of each asset. Under ADR the taxpayer was granted an election to use a useful life which ranged from 80 percent to 120 percent of the prescribed guideline life. For property not covered by ADR (or all of the taxpayer's property if the taxpayer did not elect to use ADR), the determination of useful life continued to be based on actual facts and circumstances of each asset.

For property acquired after 1980 the facts and circumstances standard is applicable only to intangibles. All tangible property placed in service after 1980, with a few exceptions, is subject to § 168, a mandatory provision known as the Accelerated Cost Recovery System. Under § 168, the taxpayer is required to recover the cost of a tangible asset placed in service after 1980 under one of several recovery periods assigned by the Code. Under the Accelerated Cost Recovery System the determination of the recovery period for an asset is based on the class life assigned to that asset under ADR. § 168(c), (e) and (i)(1).

4. DEPRECIATION METHODS: THE TRADITIONAL APPROACH

Traditional depreciation methods are grouped into two categories: straight line and accelerated. Under the straight line method, the taxpayer's depreciation deductions are spaced evenly throughout an asset's useful life. Thus, an equal amount of depreciation is taken and allowed for each year of the asset's useful life. Consider the following example of the straight line method of depreciation:

> A taxpayer purchases a machine to be used in her business at a cost of $110,000. She estimates that the asset will have a useful life of 10 years and a salvage value of $10,000. If the straight line method is used the taxpayer's annual depreciation deduction ($10,000) is based upon the following formula:

$$\text{annual depreciation deduction} = \frac{\text{Cost less salvage value}}{\text{estimated useful life}}$$

$$\$10,000 = \frac{\$110,000 - \$10,000}{10 \text{ years}}$$

The accelerated methods of depreciation (§ 167(b)) permit taxpayers to allocate larger depreciation deductions to the earlier years of an asset's useful life and smaller deductions in the later years. The accelerated methods permit a quicker recovery of a larger part of the taxpayer's cost. Some of the accelerated depreciation methods include: the double declining balance method, the 150% declining balance method, the sum-of-the-years-digits method, the income forecast method, and the units of production method.

The declining balance methods apply a fixed percentage each year to the property's adjusted basis at the beginning of the tax year to determine the annual depreciation deduction. The 150% declining balance method and the double declining balance method are similar in all but one major aspect (obviously, certain other technical differences exist which have been omitted from this discussion). The double declining method applies a rate of two times the straight line rate to the taxpayer's adjusted basis in the property, as reduced for prior years' depreciation, to arrive at the current year's depreciation deduction. The 150% declining balance method utilizes a rate that is 1.5 times the straight line rate.

Under the declining balance methods no provision is made for salvage value in computing the depreciation deduction. However, these methods always leave a remaining balance, or adjusted basis, at the end of the asset's estimated useful life which is treated as salvage value. Thus, a salvage value is automatically built into the declining balance methods.

The sum-of-the-years-digits method of computing depreciation provides the greatest deferral and time value of money advantages for taxpayers. The basic underlying premise of the sum-of-the-years-digits method is that more of the cost of the asset will be used up or dissipated by obsolescence in the early years of its life. The method is appropriate, for example, when dealing with the high rate of functional depreciation which plagues the business information industry in the area of computer technology.

Consider the following example of sum-of-the-years-digits depreciation.

Assume that an asset which costs $110,000 has a salvage value of $10,000, and has an estimated useful life of ten years.

The first step is to determine the depreciable base:

Cost of asset $110,000
Less salvage value   10,000
Depreciable base $100,000

To find the sum-of-the-years-digits, the digit of each year is progressively numbered and then added up. The sum-of-the-years-digits for ten years is 55 (10 + 9 + 8 + 7 + 6 + 5 + 4 + 3 + 2 + 1). The first year's depreciation is 10/55, the second year's 9/55, the third year's 8/55, and so on.

The following table compares the depreciation deductions using the straight line method and two different accelerated methods:

Assume the same facts as in the previous example. (Cost = $110,000; salvage value = $10,000; expected useful life of 10 years).

Annual depreciation deductions

Year	Straight Line	Double Declining Balance	Sum-of-the-Years-Digits
1	$ 10,000	$22,000	$ 18,182
2	10,000	17,600	16,364
3	10,000	14,080	14,545
4	10,000	11,264	12,727
5	10,000	9,011	10,909
6	10,000	7,209	9,091
7	10,000	5,767	7,273
8	10,000	4,614	5,455
9	10,000	3,691	3,636
10	10,000	2,953	1,818
Total depreciation:	$100,000	$98,189	$100,000

Because the straight line rate is 10%, the annual straight line depreciation deduction is $10,000. Assuming that the double declining balance method of depreciation is used, the rate of depreciation is 20%, or twice the straight line rate of 10%. Under the double declining balance method of depreciation each year's depreciation deduction is 20 percent of the property's adjusted basis as of the beginning of the year. The depreciation deduction for the first year is 20 percent of $110,000, and the adjusted basis at the beginning of the next year is $88,000. The depreciation deduction for the second year is 20 percent of $88,000, leaving an adjusted basis of $70,400. For the third year the depreciation deduction is 20 percent of $70,400. And so on for each succeeding year. If we used the 150% declining balance method, the rate would have been 15% and the depreciation deduction for the first year would have been $16,500 (15% × $110,000). It is important to note when using an accelerated declining balance method that the taxpayer's adjusted basis in the property at the end of its useful life will approximate the expected salvage value of $10,000.

The income forecast method of depreciation was developed primarily to deal with the special matching problems encountered in fields like the movie industry. Section 263, you will recall, requires the capitalization of expenditures which create an asset with a useful life extending substantially beyond the tax year in which the expenditures are made. Most of the costs associated with the production of movies are capital in nature. Consequently, such costs must be capitalized. A problem arises when the taxpayer attempts to match the costs of the movie with the revenues it generates. Most movies generate the greatest portion of revenues in their first year of release. Thereafter, the revenue flows generally slow down to a trickle as compared to the initial revenue flows. Consider the following example:

> A taxpayer produces a movie titled "Marsha Goes to Law School" at a cost of $1,000,000 with a salvage value of zero. He expects the film to generate $10 million of revenues. The actual revenue flows are: year one—$7 million, year two—$2 million, year three—$2 million, year four—$1 million and thereafter—$0. His depreciation deductions under the income forecast method compares the actual revenues in each year to the total estimated revenues. Since he expects to gross $10 million and receives $7 million the first year, he is allowed to deduct 70% of the movie's basis that first year. § 167(b)(4). Once his basis is fully recovered, no further deductions are allowed even though the film continues to generate revenues.

Year	Cost	% of Total Estimated Income	Depreciation Deductions
1	$1,000,000	70%	$ 700,000
2	1,000,000	20%	200,000
3	1,000,000	10%	100,000
4 & thereafter		0%	–0–
		100%	$1,000,000

The units of production method relates depreciation to the estimated production flows of the asset and is denominated in a rate per unit or rate per hour. The formula for calculating depreciation under the units of production method is based upon a comparison of actual production each year to total estimated production.

rate per unit =   Cost less salvage value
or per hour   estimated units or hours during its useful life.

Consider the following illustration:

> A taxpayer purchases a machine to be used in the production of consumer goods. The machine cost $110,000 and has a salvage value of $10,000. Its estimated useful life, in hours, is 100,000 hours.

The depreciation rate per hour is:

$$\frac{\$100,000 \ (Cost) - \$10,000 \ (Salvage \ value)}{100,000 \ hours \ (estimated \ useful \ life \ in \ hours)} = \begin{array}{l} \$1.00 \ of \ depreciation \\ per \ hour \end{array}$$

The depreciation deduction for a given tax year is computed as follows:

Year	§ 1016 Adjusted Basis less Salvage Value	Actual Production Hours	Rate	Depreciation Deduction
0	$100,000	–	–	–
1	80,000	20,000	$1.00	$ 20,000
2	40,000	40,000	1.00	40,000
3	20,000	20,000	1.00	20,000
4	10,000	10,000	1.00	10,000
5	–0–	20,000	1.00	10,000
		110,000 hours		$100,000

The machine's § 1016 adjusted basis at the end of year five will equal its expected salvage value of $10,000. Since a taxpayer may not take deductions greater than his basis in an asset, the depreciation deduction for year five may not exceed $10,000. Under the units of production method, the taxpayer's adjusted basis in the machine at the end of year five must equal its expected salvage value. If a depreciation deduction of $20,000 (20,000 hours at $1.00 per hour or $20,000) rather than $10,000 is taken for year five, the taxpayer's adjusted basis in the property at the end of year five, computed pursuant to § 1016, would be $0 and not $10,000, its expected salvage value.

In sum, the accelerated methods of computing depreciation share one basic characteristic, they permit taxpayers to allocate larger depreciation deductions to the early years of an asset's useful life and lesser deductions in the later years. Taxpayers receive a benefit from using accelerated depreciation methods. They are able to reduce the current year's tax liability and defer the payment of taxes on ordinary income to which the depreciation deductions are applied and, consequently, receive what amounts to an interest free loan from the United States Government. The value of the deferral hinges on the taxpayer's ability to invest the money required to pay the ultimate tax liability. The value of a tax deferral is function of: (1) the rate of return the taxpayer can earn on the amount of taxes deferred and (2) timing, i.e., how long the tax liability can be deferred. Reread page 17.

Question

Section 167(b)(4) provides for the use of other methods of writing off the cost of an asset not mentioned in the Code. How do the income forecast method and the units of production method more accurately reflect the matching of income to expenses than a method expressed in a term of years? Why would a taxpayer adopt any of these other methods? Note also that the income forecast method and the units of production method may be used for property placed in service after 1980.   § 168(f)(1)(B).

C. ACCELERATED COST RECOVERY SYSTEM

1. INTRODUCTION

During 1981 Congress, in an attempt to provide the investment stimulus for economic expansion, enacted § 168, which contains the Accelerated Cost Recovery System (ACRS).   Section 168 represents a substantial restructuring of the concept of depreciation deductions.   It provides more rapid cost recovery deductions than permitted under § 167. The new cost recovery system, ACRS, abandons the concept of economic useful life.   The cost of an asset is recovered, under ACRS, over a statutorily prescribed recovery period.   § 168(c). Because salvage value is ignored for ACRS, the taxpayer may deduct over the appropriate recovery period the full cost of a tangible asset placed in service after December 31, 1980.   § 168(b)(4). Moreover, ACRS does not distinguish between new and used real property. See § 167(j).

The Senate Finance Committee set forth the basic policy rationale underlying § 168 in its report to Congress. S. Report No. 97–144, Economic Recovery Tax Act of 1981, 97th Cong., 1st Sess. 47 (1981). The Committee stated:

> The committee believes that present rules for determining depreciation allowances * * * need to be replaced because they do not provide the investment stimulus that is essential for economic expansion.   The committee also believes that present rules are unnecessarily complicated.

> The real value of depreciation deductions allowed under present rules has declined for several years due to successively higher rates of inflation.   Reductions in the real value of depreciation deductions diminish the profitability of investment and discourage businesses from replacing old equipment and structures with more modern assets that reflect recent technology.   The committee agrees with numerous witnesses who testified that a substantial restructuring of depreciation deductions * * * will be an effective way of stimulating capital formation, increasing productivity and improving the nation's competitiveness in international trade.   The committee therefore believes that a new capital cost recovery system is required which provides for the more rapid acceleration of cost recovery deductions * * *.

> The committee heard copious testimony that the present rules are too complex.   These rules require determinations on matters, such as useful life and salvage value, which are inherently uncertain and, thus, too frequently result in unproductive disagreements between taxpayers and the Internal Revenue Service.   Current regulations provide numerous elections and exceptions which taxpayers—especially small businesses—find difficult to master and expensive to apply.   The committee believes that a new capital cost recovery system should be structured which de-emphasizes the concept of useful life, minimize the

number of elections and exceptions, and so is easier to comply with and to administer.

An examination of the wording of §§ 167(a) and 168(a) indicates that depreciation is only available for property used in a trade or business or held for the production of income (§§ 162 or 212 activities). However, the Accelerated Cost Recovery System cannot be used for those assets described in § 168(f)(2)–(5). A taxpayer may also elect not to use ACRS for any property he wishes to depreciate using a method not expressed in a term of years. § 168(f)(1). It is important to note at this juncture that § 168 does not have any retroactive effect. In other words, § 168 applies only to recovery property which is placed in service after December 31, 1980. Consequently, the depreciation of tangible property placed in service before January 1, 1981, with some exceptions, is still governed by § 167 pursuant to which taxpayers use the facts and circumstances test or the Asset Depreciation Range System to arrive at a proper allowance for depreciation. Intangibles, regardless of when placed in service, are not eligible for § 168, and are still governed by § 167.

2. COMPUTING THE ACRS DEPRECIATION DEDUCTIONS

Generally, for tangible property placed in service after 1980, the depreciation deduction provided by § 167(a) is determined under the Accelerated Cost Recovery System. § 168(a). Under ACRS the annual depreciation deductions are determined by using:

(1) the applicable recovery period, § 168(c);

(2) the applicable depreciation method, § 168(b); and

(3) the applicable convention, § 168(d).

Recovery periods. The taxpayer begins by determining the appropriate recovery period to which the subject property belongs. For each asset this determination is based on either the class life assigned to that asset under the Asset Depreciation Range system (ADR), (more specifically, its ADR midpoint life as announced in Rev.Proc. 83–35, 1983–1 C.B. 745), § 168(e)(1) and (i)(1)(A), or as otherwise provided in § 168(e)(2) and (3). Once the property is classified under § 168(e), § 168(c) assigns each classification to one of eight recovery periods, 3-year, 5-year, 7-year, 10-year, 15-year, 20-year, 27½-year, or 31½-year.* The 5-year recovery period includes autos and light trucks. § 168(e)(3)(B)(i). Office furniture and equipment is in the 7-year recovery period. However, computers and their peripheral

* From 1981 to 1986 there were basically only five recovery periods under ACRS, 3-year, 5-year, 10-year, 15-year and 19-year. Autos and light trucks were in the 3-year recovery period, and almost all machinery and equipment was in the 5-year recovery period. Many taxpayers will now have to contend with three separate sets of depreciation rules: (i) the "useful life" system under § 167 is still used for property placed in service prior to 1981; (ii) the original ACRS continues to apply to eligible assets placed in service between 1981 and 1986; and (iii) the revised ACRS applies to all assets placed in service after 1986. The reason for this treatment is because all of an asset's depreciation deductions are determined by the depreciation rules in effect for the year an asset was placed in service. Therefore, a building placed in service prior to 1981, where a 40-year useful life was adopted, continues to be depreciated using that 40-year useful life, even though newly-acquired buildings can use the shorter recovery periods available under ACRS. The anti-churning rules contained in § 168(f)(5) prevent a taxpayer from obtaining shorter recovery periods by engaging in churning transactions for property already owned by the taxpayer or related parties.

equipment are in the 5-year recovery period. Most types of machinery and equipment used in manufacturing belong to the 7-year recovery period although some is either in the 5-year or 10-year recovery period. For example, machinery and equipment used in the manufacture of motor vehicles has an ADR midpoint life of 12 years and is therefore 7-year property under § 168(e)(1) and has a 7-year recovery period under § 168(c). Machinery used for petroleum refining has an ADR midpoint life of 16 years and is therefore assigned to the 10-year recovery period. See Rev.Proc. 83–35, 1983–1 C.B. 745. The applicable recovery period for buildings is not determined by reference to an ADR class life. Instead, § 168(e)(2) assigns a mandatory 27.5-year recovery period to residential rental property and a 31.5-year recovery period to nonresidential real property. Residential rental property is a building or structure with respect to which 80 percent or more of the gross rental income is derived from dwelling units, i.e. a house of apartment used to provide living accommodations. §§ 168(e)(2)(A) or 167(j)(2)(B). Nonresidential real property is defined in § 168(e)(2)(B) and includes office buildings, retail stores, warehouses and manufacturing plants.

The recovery periods under ACRS frequently ignore the concept of "useful life" because the recovery periods assigned to most assets are shorter than actual or estimated useful lives. Examine § 168(e)(1). For example, new buildings placed in service prior to 1981 were depreciable over a useful life that ranged between 35 to 40 years.** The Treasury Department is authorized to adjust the "class life" under ADR of all assets (except residential rental property and nonresidential real property) based on actual experience. § 168(i)(1)(B). Any class life prescribed or modified under the Secretary's authority must "reasonably reflect the anticipated decline in value over time, of the property to the industry or other group." § 168(i)(1).

Depreciation methods. Next, the method of depreciation to be used for each of the eight recovery periods must be determined. ACRS generally utilizes an accelerated method of depreciation to generate larger deductions in the earlier years that eligible personal property is being depreciated over. The double declining balance method is applicable to property included in the 3-year, 5-year, 7-year and 10-year recovery periods. § 168(b)(1). Property placed in the 15-year and 20-year recovery periods uses the 150 percent declining balance method. § 168(b)(2). Both of the available declining balance methods switch to the straight line method to recover an asset's remaining adjusted basis. § 168(b)(1)(B). The switch occurs at the point where the straight line write-off of the remaining adjusted basis is greater than the deduction available if that declining balance method were continued. The cost of property in the 27.5-year and 31.5-year recovery periods is depreciated using the straight line method. § 168(b)(3). The entire cost of property in any of the recovery periods is depreciated because ACRS treats an asset's salvage value as zero. § 168(b)(4). A taxpayer may elect, on a year-by-year basis, to recover the cost of ACRS property over its assigned

** Under ACRS the recovery period for buildings dropped all the way to 15 years if placed in service after 1980, edged up to 18 years if placed in service after March 15, 1984, and went to 19 years if placed in service after May 8, 1985. Currently, for buildings placed in service after 1986, the recovery periods are either 27.5 or 31.5 years.

recovery period using the straight line method. § 168(b)(5). If a taxpayer makes this election for any one asset, that election is also binding on all other assets in that same recovery period that are placed in service in that year. § 168(b)(5). A taxpayer may also elect to use the alternative depreciation system set forth in § 168(g)(2). § 168(g)(7). The alternative depreciation system uses the straight line method over longer recovery periods than those assigned under § 168(c). For example, a taxpayer may elect to depreciate a machine with a 12-year ADR class life over 12 years rather than its 7-year recovery period under § 168(c). Finally, it should be mentioned that for a limited category of assets the longer recovery periods under the alternative depreciation system are mandatory. § 168(g)(1).

Depreciation conventions. The taxpayer must be aware that the recovery period begins on the date the property is deemed to be placed in service under the applicable convention, either the half-year convention or the mid-month convention. The half-year convention applies to all depreciable personal property. § 168(d)(1) and (2). Under the half-year convention an asset is deemed to have been placed in service in the middle of the year regardless of when it was actually placed in service by the taxpayer. § 168(d)(4)(A). For example, whether an asset is actually placed in service on January 1 or December 31 of the year, the taxpayer is entitled to treat it as if it were used for half a year and is entitled to a half year's depreciation for that first year of use. A half year of depreciation is also allowed for the year in which the property is disposed of, or is otherwise retired from service, regardless of when during that year the disposition actually occurs. § 168(d)(4)(A). For example, if a taxpayer purchases 5-year recovery property and sells it during the fourth year of use, he is entitled to a half year's depreciation for the first and fourth years and a full year's depreciation for the second and third years. If a taxpayer continues to use depreciable property after the end of its recovery period, no further depreciation deductions are allowed because he has deducted his entire basis in the property. In other words, the aggregate of a taxpayer's depreciation deductions are limited to his basis in the property, not its value. Since the half-year convention treats property as placed in service in the middle of the first year, the statutory recovery period begins in the middle of the year and continues for the number of years assigned to that recovery period. For example, because an auto (5-year recovery property), placed in service any time during 1987, is treated as placed in service on July 1, 1987, its entire basis will be recovered over a five-year period, commencing from July 1, 1987. In effect, the cost of that auto will be depreciated over six taxable years. This means that the actual write-off periods for all assets subject to the half-year convention are 4, 6, 8, 11, 16, and 21 years.

In the case of residential rental property and nonresidential real property there is no half-year convention. Instead, a mid-month convention applies. § 168(d)(4)(B). Under the mid-month convention the depreciation deduction for the first year a building is placed in service is based on the number of months the property was actually in use. Property placed in service at any time during a month is treated as having been placed in service in the middle of the month. And, if the property has not been fully depreciated by the time it is disposed of, it is treated as having been disposed of in the middle of the month that disposition occurs. For example, if a building is purchased on November 30 and is sold the following March 1, the taxpayer is entitled to 1½ months of depreciation for the year of acquisition and 2½ months of depreciation for the year of sale.

A mid-quarter convention may apply to property otherwise eligible for the half-year convention. § 168(d)(3)(A). For purposes of determining whether the mid-quarter convention will apply, residential rental property and nonresidential real property are not taken into account. § 168(d)(3)(B). The mid-quarter convention treats all property placed in service during any quarter of a taxable year as placed in service at the midpoint of that quarter. The use of the mid-quarter convention is required if more than 40 percent of all depreciable property (other than real property) is placed in service during the last three months of the taxable year. § 168(d)(3)(A).

Other considerations. The recovery period for any improvement or addition (a capitalized cost instead of a currently deductible repair) to real or personal property by a taxpayer who owns that property is also eligible for depreciation under ACRS. However, each addition or improvement has its own separate recovery period. And, the recovery period begins on the later of: (i) the date on which the addition or improvement is placed in service, or (ii) the date on which the property with respect to which such addition or improvement was made is placed in service. § 168(i)(6)(B). The depreciation deduction for the addition or improvement to recovery property is computed in the same manner that the depreciation deduction for the underlying recovery property would be computed if such property were placed in service at the same time as the addition or improvement. § 168(i)(6)(A). For example, suppose an office building (31.5-year recovery property) is placed in service during 1987, and an addition is added to the building during 1992. The cost of the addition is treated as the acquisition of a separate 31.5-year recovery asset in 1992 and is depreciated over its own 31.5-year recovery period, beginning in 1992.

The cost of leasehold improvements made by a tenant to or on the leased property can be depreciated by the tenant. If the leasehold improvement creates an asset having an ACRS recovery period longer than the remaining term of the lease and the tenant will surrender the leasehold improvement at the end of the lease, then the leasehold improvement has a "useful life" to the tenant of this shorter period. However, under § 168(i)(8), the cost of any leasehold improvement must be depreciated over its assigned ACRS recovery period despite the fact that the remaining lease term is a shorter period. When the lease is terminated the tenant may take a loss for his remaining unrecovered adjusted basis in the leasehold improvement. See problem 2 at page 122.

D. ITEMS WHICH CANNOT BE DEPRECIATED

The availability of a depreciation deduction on an asset also turns on whether or not it:

(1) is used in a trade or business or held for the production of income and

(2) has a limited useful life which can be estimated with reasonable accuracy (it is a wasting asset).

Both criteria must be met before a depreciation deduction is permitted.

Not all assets constitute property for purposes of the Accelerated Cost Recovery System. For purposes of the Accelerated Cost Recovery System, intangible property and property subject to amortization are not eligible for § 168. But § 167 is available.

Not all assets can be depreciated. Neither inventories (or stock in trade) nor raw land may be depreciated because depreciation is limited to items subject to "wear and tear, to decay or decline from natural causes, to exhaustion, and to obsolescence." Reg. § 1.167(a)–2 and –9. The purchaser of real estate must, therefore, allocate his cost between the land and the building in proportion to their fair market values on the date of acquisition.

E. EXPENSING CERTAIN BUSINESS ASSETS

Section 179 allows the taxpayer an election to deduct up to $10,000 of the cost of certain expenditures that would otherwise be capitalized. § 179(a) and (b). Only certain properties qualify for this election. § 179(d)(1). "Section 179 property" is limited to depreciable property used by a taxpayer in the active conduct of a trade or business. Therefore, any taxpayer who does not take an active role in the business is not eligible for this election. § 179(b)(3)(A). In addition, the § 179 election is not available for property used in an activity held for the production of income (a § 212 investment activity). If he qualifies for the election, a taxpayer may deduct up to $10,000 each year of any capital expenditure within the meaning of § 263 as long as the asset is depreciable. Also, the election does not apply to buildings. There exists a limit on the election to expense qualifying property if the aggregate cost of qualifying property placed in service during the taxable year exceeds $200,000. § 179(b)(2). For every dollar of investment in excess of $200,000, the maximum dollar ceiling is reduced by one dollar. Furthermore, the amount eligible to be expensed is limited to the taxable income derived from the trade or business in which the related property is used. § 179(b)(3). A subsequent conversion of the expensed property to personal use any time before the end of that property's ACRS recovery period results in the taxpayer having to report as income the excess of the expensed amount over the ACRS depreciation deduction that would have been allowed for the expensed amount. § 179(d)(10).

F. BUSINESS–PERSONAL USE OF AUTOMOBILES: DEPRECIATION DEDUCTIONS

Taxpayers who own automobiles, among other types of "listed property" defined in § 280F(d)(4), and claim business-related tax benefits of ACRS often deployed this tax benefit to subsidize an element of personal consumption associated with the use of expensive passenger cars. To meet this concern, as well as the perception of widespread abuse and the overstatement of the business-use portion of passenger cars, Congress, in 1984, imposed limitations on the depreciation deductions for passenger cars. If a taxpayer uses an automobile 100% for business purposes, the maximum depreciation deduction is $2,560 in the year the car is placed in service, $4,100 for the second year in the recovery period, $2,450 for the third year in the recovery period, and $1,475 for each succeeding year in the recovery period. § 280F(a)(2). The caps under § 280F only come into play if the cost of the car exceeds $12,800. The entire cost of the car can be depreciated. All that § 280F does is limit the depreciation deductions during the recovery period to $12,800. Any costs in excess of $12,800 can be depreciated in the years following the end of the ACRS recovery period. However, the depreciation deduction for any year following the end of the recovery period cannot exceed $1,475 annually. § 280F(a)(2)(B). The $2,560 deduction limitation for the first year may not be increased by making an election under § 179. § 280F(d)(1). These amounts will be indexed for inflation beginning in 1989. § 280F(d)(7). Where the business use is less than 100%, the depreciation limits are reduced proportionately, subject to a 50% test which requires that an automobile be used more than 50% in a "qualified business use" (i.e. the taxpayer's trade or business). § 280F(b)(4). For automobiles not meeting the 50% test, depreciation is calculated on the straight line method over five years on that portion allocable to business use. § 280F(b)(2). If the 50% test is met, depreciation deductions may be claimed based on the applicable percentage of business use. Taxpayers are required to substantiate automobile business-use deductions by keeping "adequate records." § 274(d), and Temp.Reg. § 1.274–6T.

Problems

1. (a) Harriet purchases a personal residence for $140,000 in the current tax year, paying $40,000 in cash as a down payment and obtaining a mortgage of $100,000 from a local bank. Can she take a recovery deduction under § 168 or a depreciation deduction under § 167 for her home? What is her basis for the residence?

(b) Assume, in the next tax year, Harriet expends $13,000 to add a swimming pool to her home and pays $1,400 in maintenance and other repairs on the home. She sells the house at the end of the tax year for $173,000. May she take a deduction for depreciation after she lists the house for sale? May she deduct the maintenance and repair expenses? Reconsider Lowry v. United States, page 442 and Problem 1 on pp. 447–448. What is her adjusted basis for the house? Consider § 1016. What is the amount of her gain? Consider § 1016(a)(1). What is the character of her gain?

(c)(i) Assume the same facts as in (b). In the current tax year Harriet decided not to live in the house or sell it, but, instead listed the property for rent. May she take a recovery deduction under § 168 or depreciation deduction under § 167? What is her adjusted basis for the house? May she deduct maintenance and repair expenses? Reconsider Problem 1 on pp. 447–448. What is the impact of § 67(a)? Assume that Harriet's adjusted gross income is less than $100,000 so that the restrictions on the use of passive losses under § 469 are inapplicable.

(ii) What if she subsequently moves back into the house after the termination of the lease? May she continue to take a depreciation deduction under § 167? May she deduct maintenance and repair expenses?

2. (a) On January 1, 1980, Henry purchased a machine for use in his business at a cost of $110,000. The machine had an ADR guideline life of 10 years and a salvage value of $10,000. Compute (under § 167) annual depreciation deductions for each year using the:

(a) straight line method

(b) double declining balance method

(c) sum-of-the-years-digits method

Compare the tax savings for each of these methods. Consider Reg. § 1.167(b)–(0), –1, –2.

(b) Assume Henry purchased an identical machine on January 1 of the current tax year for $110,000. How does the Accelerated Cost Recovery System impact on the cost allocation process? What type of recovery property is the machine? Consider § 168(c) and (e). What is the recovery period? What is the applicable deduction percentage? Consider 168(b). What accelerated depreciation method does ACRS use for this machine?

(c) Will the aggregate recovery deductions under ACRS exceed the total depreciation deductions under § 167?

(d) A year after placing the machine in service Henry spends $6,000 to modify the machine for a new use. How does he treat this $6,000 expenditure? § 168(i)(6).

3. Ted Player has recently become a partner in his law firm. He is in the 33% marginal income tax bracket because of the rate surcharge. On January 1 of the current year he buys an apartment building as an investment for $500,000 with $450,000 of the purchase price allocated to the building and the remaining $50,000 to the land. Reg. § 1.167(a)–5. Why does Ted favor allocating as much as possible to the building? He invests $100,000 of his own money and finances the balance by giving a mortgage note in the sum of $400,000 for the balance. The mortgage is payable over a term of twenty-five years. He receives gross rentals of $52,500 yearly and has operating expenses and real estate taxes of $10,000 yearly. His yearly mortgage payments are $42,500, broken down as follows:

Year	Principal	Interest
1	$4,000	$38,500
2	$5,000	$37,500
3	$6,000	$36,500

(a) What is his basis in the building when he purchased the property and at the end of each of the first three years? Consider §§ 1011, 1012, and 1016(a)(2).

(b) What is his tax picture in the year of purchase and for the next two years? Specifically, determine his income, his deductions, and his tax loss? Consider §§ 162(a), 163(a), (d)(3)(B)(ii) and (h), 164, and 168(a), (b), (c), (d) and (e). Why is this investment considered a tax shelter? Assume that Ted actively participates in the management of this investment and that his adjusted gross income is less than $100,000 so that § 469 does not apply.

(c) What will his situation be if he is able to increase the rentals by $5,000 in the third year? Does this investment have a positive cash flow?

(d) Now consider what would happen if he had put the $100,000 into common stock paying dividends of $6,000 per year. Consider the impact of the tax structure on whether investors prefer real estate or common stock.

(e) What was the impact on real estate as a tax shelter after the Tax Reform Act of 1986 increased the recovery period for buildings from 19 years to the present 27.5 or 31.5 years?

Question

Do you favor or oppose the Accelerated Cost Recovery System as a means of cost allocation? In analyzing the following proposal for the Capital Cost Recovery System (CRRS), reconsider the criteria for the policy set forth on pp. 40–43.

THE PRESIDENT'S TAX PROPOSALS TO THE CONGRESS FOR FAIRNESS, GROWTH AND SIMPLICITY
134–151, 160–163 (1985).

REASONS FOR CHANGE

Disregard of Economic Depreciation. Depreciation allowances should reflect the economic fact that, on average, the values of assets decline over time due to a variety of factors, including declining productivity, wear and tear, and obsolescence. If depreciation allowances understate real economic depreciation of a particular asset, income from the investment is overtaxed and a tax disincentive is created which impairs capital formation and retards the economy's productive capacity. Similarly, if depreciation allowances exceed real economic depreciation, incentives are created for investment in depreciable property.

The pre-ACRS depreciation system required capital costs to be recovered over the useful economic life of particular property. Generally, useful lives for particular types of property were significantly longer than the recovery periods introduced with ACRS. The rate of recovery over the useful life was often determined by election of the taxpayer. The pre-ACRS depreciation system did not take account of inflation. Thus, pre-ACRS depreciation deductions for many assets understated real economic depreciation and thus resulted in overtaxation of the income from such assets.

The cost recovery system introduced with ACRS addressed the prior overtaxation of capital investment by providing for more rapid acceleration of depreciation deductions. However, at low inflation rates, ARCS reverses the general overtaxation of capital investment. * * * In addition, ACRS continues to base depreciation allowances on historic costs rather than current replacement costs; thus, the present value of fixed depreciation deductions varies with the rate of inflation.

* * *

Non-neutrality of ACRS Investment Incentives. * * *

Investment distortions created by ACRS, * * * and other capital cost recovery provisions hamper economic efficiency. The tax code guides the allocation of capital, overriding private market forces and the individually expressed consumer preferences they represent. Paradoxically, these distortions do not reflect stated government policy to favor particular assets or industries. As a result, ACRS operates as an undeclared government industrial policy which largely escapes public scrutiny and systematic review.

ACRS also fails to provide a systematic level of investment incentives. Since ACRS does not take inflation or real replacement costs into account, the benefits of accelerated depreciation diminish as inflation increases. The variability of inflation over time precludes certainty as to the incentive actually provided for an investment in depreciable property. Such uncertainty acts as a depressant on economic activity. Increasing the certainty of obtaining inflation-proof cost recovery would stimulate risk taking and lead to more efficient allocation of investment funds.

* * *

PROPOSAL

New capital cost recovery rules would be established that preserve investment incentives while explicitly accounting for inflation and different rates of economic depreciation. The new Capital Cost Recovery System ("CCRS") would modify ACRS in several important respects. First, CCRS would allow cost recovery of the real or inflation-adjusted cost of depreciable assets, rather than only the original, nominal cost. Second, CCRS would assign property among new recovery classes based upon economic depreciation rates. Third, CCRS would prescribe depreciation schedules and recovery periods which produce systematic investment incentives that are neutral across recovery classes.

Under CCRS, all depreciable tangible assets would be assigned to one of six classes, which would replace the present * * * ACRS recovery classes. Each CCRS class would be assigned a declining-balance depreciation rate, ranging from 55 percent to four percent. The depreciation rate would be applied to an asset's inflation-adjusted basis in a manner described below. Applying a fixed declining-balance depreciation rate of less than 100 percent to the adjusted basis of an asset would never fully recover such basis. To ensure that depreciation accounts close out in a reasonable number of years, each CCRS class would be assigned a recovery period of between four and 28 years. The recovery period is not an estimate of the economic useful life of an asset and hence, is not comparable to recovery periods under pre-ACRS depreciation rules based on economic useful lives.

To avoid bunching of the depreciation allowance in the last year of the recovery period, CCRS depreciation schedules for each class would switch from the declining-balance rate to the straight-line depreciation method in the year in which, assuming a half-year convention, the straight-line method yields a higher allowance than the declining-balance rate. The half-year convention means that, for the CCRS class with a four year recovery period, the straight-line method is applied assuming placement in service on July 1 of the first year and retirement on July 1 of the fifth year. Since a half-year convention is assumed for purposes of determining the year in which the depreciation schedule switches from the declining-balance rate to the straight-line method, depreciation schedules cover one year more than the assigned recovery period.

Under CCRS, the first-year depreciation rate would be prorated based upon the number of months an asset was placed in service. A mid-month convention would be assumed for the month an asset is placed in service. For example, an asset placed in service by a calendar year taxpayer during any part of April would obtain a depreciation rate equal to the full first-year rate multiplied by a percentage equal to $(12-3.5)/12$.

Table 2 lists the CCRS depreciation schedules for each of the six recovery classes. The schedules for each class prescribe the depreciation rate which would be applied to the adjusted basis of an asset in each year. Table 2 identifies the year in which the depreciation schedule switches from the declining-balance rate to the straight-line method. The apparent increase in depreciation rates after the switchover to the straight-line method does not mean that CCRS would be a back-loaded depreciation system. Relative to inflation-adjusted original cost, the straight-line method produces constant depreciation rates. It is only with respect to adjusted basis that straight-line method depreciation rates increase over time. Thus, under the straight-line method, in the close-out year, the applicable depreciation rate is always 100 percent and the remaining adjusted basis of an asset is fully recovered.

* * *

CCRS would adjust depreciation allowances for inflation by means of a basis adjustment. Under ACRS, only the unadjusted original cost basis of an asset is recovered over the class recovery period. Under CCRS, after adjustment for allowable depreciation in the prior year, an asset's unrecovered basis would be adjusted for inflation during the current year using an appropriate government price index. The applicable depreciation rate would be applied to the resulting adjusted basis. There would be no inflation adjustment in the year in which an asset is placed in service; inflation adjustments would begin with the second year in which the asset is in service. Thus, the scheduled depreciation rate in Table 2 would be applied as of the end of a taxable year to an asset's basis which had been adjusted first for the prior year's depreciation and then for the current year's inflation. An asset's unrecovered basis would continue to be indexed for inflation after the switch-over to the straight-line method. The year in which the switch-over occurs would be dependent only on the class depreciation rate and recovery period, and not on the inflation rate.

Table 7.01–2

Capital Cost Recovery System Depreciation Schedule (as a Percent of Inflation-Adjusted Basis) [1]

Year	Class					
	1	2	3	4	5	6
1 [2]	27.5	22	16.5	11	8.5	2.00
2	55	44	33	22	17	4.00
3	55	44	33	22	17	4.00
4	67	44	33	22	17	4.00
5	100	67	40	29	17	4.08
6		100	67	40	18	4.26
7			100	67	22	4.44
8				100	29	4.65
9					40	4.88
10					67	5.13
11					100	5.41
12						5.71
13						6.06
14						6.45
15						6.90
16						7.41
17						8.00
18						8.70
19						9.53
20						10.53
21						11.76
22						13.33
23						15.38
24						18.18
25						22.22
26						28.57

Year	Class					
	1	2	3	4	5	6
27						40.00
28						66.67
29						100.00

1. A half-year convention is assumed for purposes of determining the year in which the depreciation schedule switches from the declining-balance rate to the straight-line method. Consequently, the depreciation schedules cover one year more than the recovery period for each class.

2. First-year allowance shown assumes an asset is placed in service by a calendar year taxpayer on July 1, without regard to the mid-month convention. Actual allowance in first year would vary depending on when asset is placed in service.

Although there would be no inflation adjustment to basis for purposes of determining depreciation in the year in which an asset is placed in service, there would be a full year's inflation adjustment in the close-out year if property is retained in service to the end of the close-out year. Retirement of an asset prior to the end of the close-out year would be treated as a disposition, upon which a taxpayer would obtain full recovery of an asset's remaining adjusted basis and recognize gain or loss. For retirements and other taxable dispositions, such as sales, there would be a pro-rata inflation adjustment to basis in the year of disposition for purposes of computing gain or loss. Such pro-rata adjustment would be based on the number of full months the asset was held during the year of disposition.

An asset's adjusted basis for depreciation purposes would be used for purposes of computing gain or loss upon disposition of a depreciable asset. * * * Losses from sales or dispositions of depreciable property would not offset capital gains but would be fully deductible against ordinary income. * * *

Intangible assets would not be subject to CCRS and would be amortized generally under current law rules. For example, assets that are depreciable under the income forecast method or other method not measured in terms of years, such as motion pictures, would continue to be depreciable under rules similar to current law. The basis of depreciable property not subject to CCRS would be indexed for inflation beginning with the second year of amortization. Similarly, gains from sales or dispositions of amortized property which is indexed for inflation would be taxed at ordinary income rates.

Assets that are eligible for cost depletion, such as timber, oil and coal, would not be subject to CCRS. Depletable assets would be indexed for inflation, by means of an inflation adjustment to an asset's cost depletion basis used for purposes of determining ordinary income realized upon sale of the asset.

* * *

* * * CCRS would retain the current law distinction between deductible repairs and expenditures that appreciably prolong an asset's useful life or materially add to its value, and thus, must be capitalized. Capitalized costs would generally be added to the adjusted basis of the underlying asset or, in some cases, depreciated separately. Each CCRS class would be assigned a safe-harbor repair allowance factor. The safe-harbor would permit expenses incurred after the asset is placed in service to be deducted without challenge, if such expenses are allocable to the asset and do not exceed the product of the asset's remaining inflation-adjusted basis and the repair allowance factor.

* * *

Table 4 summarizes the classification of ACRS assets among the six CCRS classes.

* * *

The principle underlying CCRS classification of assets among the six CCRS recovery classes is that assets should be grouped on the basis of equivalent economic depreciation rates. Treasury Department empirical studies show that a geometric pattern of constant-dollar depreciation is generally an appropriate method to apply to all classes of business assets, even though the geometric pattern may not accurately characterize economic depreciation for all items within a class. Each of the six CCRS classes that resulted from the Treasury Department studies is comprised of a group of asset-types that, on average, have approximately the same present value of economic depreciation. The six CCRS classes are organized so as to minimize the variance in observed economic depreciation rates for assets within a class. (For a published account of Treasury Department commissioned studies, see "The Measurement of Economic Depreciation," by Charles R. Hulten and Frank C. Wykoff in *Depreciation, Inflation, and the Taxation of Income from Capital* (ed. C. Hulten, 1981.)

Table 7.01–4

CCRS Asset Classes

CCRS Class	Classification of ACRS Property [1]	Depreciation Rate [2]	Recovery Period [3]
Class 1	3-year property	55%	4
Class 2	Trucks, Buses, and Trailers, Office, Computing, and Accounting Equipment	44%	5

CCRS Class	Classification of ACRS Property [1]	Depreciation Rate [2]	Recovery Period [3]
Class 3	Construction Machinery, Tractors, Aircraft, Mining and Oil Field Machinery, Service Industry Machinery, and Instruments	33%	6
Class 4	5-year, 10-year, and 15-year public utility property not assigned to Class 2, 3, or 5—E.g., Metal Working Machinery, Furniture and Fixtures, General Industrial Machinery, Other Electrical Equipment, Communications Equipment, Fabricated Metal Products, and Railroad Track and Equipment	22%	7
Class 5	Railroad Structures, Ships and Boats, Engines and Turbines, Plant and Equipment for Generation, Transmission and Distribution of Electricity, Gas and Other Power, and Distribution Plant for Communications Services	17%	10
Class 6	18-year property; 15-year low-income housing [under prior law]	4%	28

1. Items of property are assigned to CCRS classes under rules described in the text of the General Explanation.

2. The depreciation method switches from a constant declining-balance rate to the straight-line method in the year of service in which the straight-line method produces greater depreciation allowances than the declining-balance rate would, assuming a half-year convention for computation of the straight-line method.

3. The recovery period is the number of years over which cost recovery is computed under the straight-line method. A consequence of assuming a half-year convention for purposes of computing depreciation rates under the straight-line method is that depreciation schedules cover one year more than the recovery periods.

* * *

The proposed CCRS system contemplates that the Treasury Department would establish permanent facilities to conduct empirical studies of economic depreciation. Such studies would gather evidence for all types of assets of changing economic depreciation rates due to such factors as technological obsolescence, changing market conditions or changing utilization rates. In addition, the Treasury Department would develop data that would enable economic depreciation rates to be measured more precisely for specific asset-types within each CCRS class. The Treasury Department would review data on economic depreciation and would promulgate regulations to reclassify asset-types upon evidence that economic depreciation for an asset-type deviates significantly from its class norm. Pending development of an institutionalized process for reviewing economic depreciation rates, ACRS property would be classified among CCRS classes in the manner described above.

* * *

ANALYSIS

Improvements in Capital Cost Recovery System. The proposed CCRS depreciation system * * * makes possible a substantial lowering of statutory tax rates for individuals and corporations. This reduction in statutory tax rates is accomplished without sacrificing investment incentives necessary to stimulate continued economic growth for the economy as a whole. The CCRS depreciation rates and recovery periods produce effective tax rates which would stimulate new investment in depreciable assets. The indexing of depreciation allowances for inflation and the classification of assets on the basis of economic depreciation would ensure that the CCRS system provides neutral investment incentives. Thus, CCRS, * * * would correct three principal defects of the capital cost recovery system of current law—the variance in effective tax rates among different assets and industries; the volatility of effective tax rates in response to fluctuating inflation * * *

CCRS would be less distortive of economic choices among new investments in equipment and structures in different industries. Since CCRS incentive depreciation rates are derived separately for each CCRS class based upon economic depreciation rates, the variance of effective tax rates across different industries and assets would be minor compared to the unsystematic distortions created under current law. Some differences would remain, however, in the effective tax rates on income from depreciable and non-depreciable assets.

CCRS would contribute further to economic neutrality by accounting for the effects of inflation. For each recovery class, CCRS would produce the same real present value of depreciation deductions regardless of inflation rates, while ACRS and unindexed straight-line methods, which recover original cost only, yield real present value deductions which decrease as inflation increases. Moreover, for all six CCRS classes, at an assumed inflation rate of five percent and an assumed real discount rate of four percent, the incentive depreciation rates under CCRS produce greater present value depreciation benefits than does ACRS without the investment tax credit [which, prior to 1987, enabled a taxpayer to take as a credit, dollar-for-dollar, against his tax liability an amount equal to 10 percent of the cost of certain property]. At higher assumed inflation rates, the CCRS incentives are even greater relative to ACRS. The CCRS incentives are provided without the front-loaded acceleration of depreciation deductions available under ACRS.

Investment Incentives. CCRS would provide depreciation rates in excess of estimated economic depreciation rates. CCRS recovery periods would be shorter than the recovery periods under a system of real economic depreciation. CCRS depreciation rates and recovery periods would combine to produce approximately equivalent effective tax rates of 18 percent on all types of equipment and machinery, regardless of the inflation rate. The effective tax rate on structures would be higher, although the recovery period would be significantly shorter than under a system with real economic depreciation rates. Moreover, the disparity under [prior] law in effective tax rates for machinery and equipment compared to structures would be substantially narrowed under CCRS. When the effects of debt finance are taken into account, the difference in effective tax rates would likely be reduced further.

* * *

Neutrality of CCRS Asset Classification. CCRS is designed to provide neutral investment incentives while at the same time preserving the simplicity of a depreciation system based on relatively few classes of property, each of which would have a single depreciation rate to be applied to inflation-adjusted basis. In modifying the ACRS class-based system, CCRS does not revert to prior flawed methods of depreciation which depended upon determining each asset's useful life, without regard to the pattern of economic depreciation over such life. Rather, CCRS is premised on the theory that a neutral depreciation system is one which produces the same effective tax rate for all depreciable assets. The equivalence of effective tax rates can be accomplished by classifying property on the basis of economic depreciation. Even though CCRS depreciation rates contain incentives in excess of economic depreciation rates, classification of assets on the basis of economic depreciation permits the investment incentives to be of approximately equal effect for all depreciable assets, regardless of inflation.

* * *

Simplification of Other Tax Provisions. CCRS and other proposed reforms of the capital cost recovery system of current law would permit a further simplification of the tax system. Even where existing complex rules are retained, their significance to taxpayers and the Internal Revenue Service would be lessened with a more neutral measure of taxable income. * * *

CCRS would apply to mixed-use property which is partially used for personal use and partially for business purposes. For taxpayers whose portion of business use varies over time, indexing of depreciable basis may require more complicated recordkeeping than is customary under current law.

References: Auerbach, The New Economics of Accelerated Depreciation, 23 B.C.L.Rev. 1327 (1982); R. McIntyre, and D. Tipps, Inequity and Decline 37–45 (1983); Solomon and Grossman, Tax and Non-Tax Policies to Promote Capital Formation: Stimulating High Technology in the 1980's, 1 Amer.J. Tax Policy, 63, 89–95 (1982).

G. DEPRECIATION (OR ACCELERATED COST RECOVERY) AS A CAPITAL EXPENDITURE

The following materials consider the tax treatment of a taxpayer who uses depreciable equipment (or recovery property) to construct a long-lived asset.

COMMISSIONER v. IDAHO POWER CO.

Supreme Court of the United States, 1974.
418 U.S. 1, 94 S.Ct. 2757, 41 L.Ed.2d 535.

MR. JUSTICE BLACKMUN delivered the opinion of the Court.

This case presents the sole issue whether, for federal income tax purposes, a taxpayer is entitled to a deduction from gross income, under § 167(a) of the Internal Revenue Code of [1986], 26 U.S.C. § 167(a), for depreciation on equipment the taxpayer owns and uses in the construction of its own capital facilities, or whether the capitalization provision of § 263(a)(1) of the Code, 26 U.S.C. § 263(a)(1), bars the deduction.

* * *

I

Nearly all the relevant facts are stipulated. The taxpayer-respondent, Idaho Power Company, is a Maine corporation organized in 1915, with its principal place of business at Boise, Idaho. It is a public utility engaged in the production, transmission, distribution, and sale of electric energy. * * *

For many years, the taxpayer has used its own equipment and employees in the construction of improvements and additions to its capital facilities. The major work has consisted of transmission lines, transmission switching stations, distribution lines, distribution stations, and connecting facilities.

During 1962 and 1963, the tax years in question, taxpayer owned and used in its business a wide variety of automotive transportation equipment, including passenger cars, trucks of all descriptions, power-operated equipment, and trailers. Radio communication devices were affixed to the equipment and were used in its daily operations. The transportation equipment was used in part for operation and maintenance and in part for the construction of capital facilities having a useful life of more than one year.

On its books, the taxpayer used various methods of charging costs incurred in connection with its transportation equipment either to current expense or to capital accounts. To the extent the equipment was used in construction, the taxpayer charged depreciation of the equipment, as well as all operating and maintenance costs (other than pension contributions and social security and motor vehicle taxes) to the capital assets so constructed. This was done either directly or through clearing accounts in accordance with procedures prescribed by the Federal Power Commission and adopted by the Idaho Public Utilities Commission.

For federal income tax purposes, however, the taxpayer treated the depreciation on transportation equipment differently. It claimed as a deduction from gross income *all* the year's depreciation on such equipment, including that portion attributable to its use in constructing capital facilities. The depreciation was computed on a composite life of 10 years and under straight-line and declining-balance methods. The other operating and maintenance costs the taxpayer had charged on its books to capital were not claimed as current expenses and were not deducted.

* * *

Upon audit, the Commissioner of Internal Revenue disallowed the deduction for the construction-related depreciation. He ruled that that depreciation was a nondeductible capital expenditure to which § 263(a)(1) had application. He added the amount of the depreciation so disallowed to the taxpayer's adjusted basis in its capital facilities, and then allowed a deduction for an appropriate amount of depreciation on the addition, computed over the useful life (30 years or more) of the property constructed. A deduction for depreciation of the transportation equipment to the extent of its use in day-to-day operation and maintenance was also allowed. * * *

* * *

It is worth noting the various items that are not at issue here. * * * The taxpayer has capitalized, as part of its cost of acquisition of capital assets, the operating and maintenance costs (other than depreciation, pension contributions, and social security and motor vehicle taxes) of the transportation equipment attributable to construction. This is not contested. The Commissioner does not dispute that the portion of the transportation equipment's depreciation allocable to operation and maintenance of facilities, in contrast with construction thereof, qualifies as a deduction from gross income. There is no disagreement as to the allocation of depreciation between construction and maintenance. The issue, thus comes down primarily to a question of timing, as the Court of Appeals recognized, 477 F.2d, at 692, that is, whether the construction-related depreciation is to be amortized and deducted over the *shorter* life of the equipment or, instead, is to be amortized and deducted over the *longer* life of the capital facilities constructed.

II

Our primary concern is with the necessity to treat construction-related depreciation in a manner that comports with accounting and taxation realities. Over a period of time a capital asset is consumed and, correspondingly over that period, its theoretical value and utility are thereby reduced. Depreciation is an accounting device which recognizes that the physical consumption of a capital asset is a true cost, since the asset is being depleted.[3] As the process of consumption continues, and depreciation is claimed and allowed, the asset's adjusted income tax basis is reduced to reflect the distribution of its cost over the accounting periods affected. The Court stated in Hertz Corp. v. United States, 364 U.S. 122, 126, 80 S.Ct. 1420, 1422, 4 L.Ed.2d 1603 (1960): "[T]he purpose of depreciation accounting is to allocate the expense of using an asset to the various periods which are benefited by that asset." * * * When the asset is used to further the taxpayer's day-to-day business operations, the periods of benefit usually correlate with the production of income. Thus, to the extent that equipment is used in such operations, a current depreciation deduction is an appropriate offset to gross income currently produced. It is clear, however, that different principles are implicated when the consumption of the asset takes place in the construction of other assets that, in the future, will produce income themselves. In this latter situation, the cost represented by depreciation does not correlate with production of current income. Rather, the cost, although certainly presently incurred, is related to the future and is appropriately allocated as part of the cost of acquiring an income-producing capital asset.

The Court of Appeals opined that the purpose of the depreciation allowance under the Code was to provide a means of cost recovery, * * * and that this Court's decisions, * * * endorse a theory of replacement through "a fund to restore the property." Although tax-free replacement of a depreciating investment is one purpose of depreciation accounting, it alone does not require the result claimed by the taxpayer here. Only last Term, in United States v. Chicago, B. & Q.R. Co., 412 U.S. 401, 93 S.Ct. 2169, 37 L.Ed.2d 30 (1973), we rejected replacement as the strict and sole purpose of depreciation:

> "Whatever may be the desirability of creating a depreciation reserve under these circumstances, as a matter of good business and accounting practice, the answer is * * * '[d]epreciation reflects the cost of an existing capital asset, not the cost of a potential replacement.' " Id., at 415, 93 S.Ct., at 2177.

Even were we to look to replacement, it is the replacement of the constructed facilities, not the equipment used to build them, with which we would be concerned. If the taxpayer now were to decide not to construct any more capital facilities with its own equipment and

---

3. The Committee on Terminology of the American Institute of Certified Public Accountants has discussed various definitions of depreciation and concluded that:

"These definitions view depreciation, broadly speaking, as describing not downward changes of value regardless of their causes but a money cost incident to exhaustion of usefulness. The term is sometimes applied to the exhaustion itself, but

the committee considers it desirable to emphasize the cost concept as the primary if not the sole accounting meaning of the term: thus, *depreciation* means the cost of such exhaustion, as *wages* means the cost of labor." 2 APB Accounting Principles, Accounting Terminology Bulletin No. 1— Review and Resume ¶ 48, p. 9512 (1973) (emphasis in original).

employees, it, in theory, would have no occasion to replace its equipment to the extent that it was consumed in prior construction.

Accepted accounting practice and established tax principles require the capitalization of the cost of acquiring a capital asset. In Woodward v. Commissioner of Internal Revenue, 397 U.S. 572, 575, 90 S.Ct. 1302, 1305, 25 L.Ed.2d 577 (1970), the Court observed: "It has long been recognized, as a general matter, that costs incurred in the acquisition * * * of a capital asset are to be treated as capital expenditures." This principle has obvious application to the acquisition of a capital asset by purchase, but it has been applied, as well, to the costs incurred in a taxpayer's construction of capital facilities. * * *

There can be little question that other construction-related expense items, such as tools, materials, and wages paid construction workers, are to be treated as part of the cost of acquisition of a capital asset. The taxpayer does not dispute this. Of course, reasonable wages paid in the carrying on of a trade or business qualify as a deduction from gross income. § 162(a)(1) of the [1986] Code, 26 U.S.C. § 162(a)(1). But when wages are paid in connection with the construction or acquisition of a capital asset, they must be capitalized and are then entitled to be amortized over the life of the capital asset so acquired. Briarcliff Candy Corp. v. Commissioner of Internal Revenue, 475 F.2d 775, 781 (CA2 1973).

Construction-related depreciation is not unlike expenditures for wages for construction workers. The significant fact is that the exhaustion of construction equipment does not represent the final disposition of the taxpayer's investment in that equipment; rather, the investment in the equipment is assimilated into the cost of the capital asset constructed. Construction-related depreciation on the equipment is not an expense to the taxpayer of its day-to-day business. It is, however, appropriately recognized as a part of the taxpayer's cost or investment in the capital asset. The taxpayer's own accounting procedure reflects this treatment, for on its books the construction-related depreciation was capitalized by a credit to the equipment account and a debit to the capital facility account. By the same token, this capitalization prevents the distortion of income that would otherwise occur if depreciation properly allocable to asset acquisition were deducted from gross income currently realized. * * *

An additional pertinent factor is that capitalization of construction-related depreciation by the taxpayer who does its own construction work maintains tax parity with the taxpayer who has its construction work done by an independent contractor. The depreciation on the contractor's equipment incurred during the performance of the job will be an element of cost charged by the contractor for his construction services, and the entire cost; of course, must be capitalized by the taxpayer having the construction work performed. The Court of Appeals' holding would lead to disparate treatment among taxpayers because it would allow the firm with sufficient resources to construct its own facilities and to obtain a current deduction, whereas another firm without such resources would be required to capitalize its entire cost including depreciation charged to it by the contractor.

Some, although not controlling, weight must be given to the fact that the Federal Power Commission and the Idaho Public Utilities Commission required the taxpayer to use accounting procedures that capitalized construction-related depreciation. * * * The opinions in American Automobile Ass'n v. United States, 367 U.S. 687, 81 S.Ct. 1727, 6 L.Ed.2d 1109 (1961), and Schlude v. Commissioner of Internal Revenue, 372 U.S. 128, 83 S.Ct. 601, 9 L.Ed.2d 633 (1963), urged upon us by the taxpayer here, are not to the contrary. In the former case it was observed that merely because the method of accounting a taxpayer employs is in accordance with generally accepted accounting procedures, this "is not to hold that for income tax purposes it so clearly reflects income as to be binding on the Treasury." 367 U.S., at 693, 81 S.Ct., at 1730. Nonetheless, where a taxpayer's generally accepted method of accounting is made compulsory by the regulatory agency *and* that method clearly reflects income, it is almost presumptively controlling of federal income tax consequences.

The presence of § 263(a)(1) in the Code is of significance. Its literal language denies a deduction for "[a]ny amount paid out" for construction or permanent improvement of facilities. The taxpayer contends, and the Court of Appeals held, that depreciation of construction equipment represents merely a decrease in value and is not an amount "paid out," within the meaning of § 263(a)(1). We disagree.

The purpose of § 263 is to reflect the basic principle that a capital expenditure may not be deducted from current income. It serves to prevent a taxpayer from utilizing currently a deduction properly attributable, through amortization, to later tax years when the capital asset becomes income producing. The regulations state that the capital expenditures to which § 263(a) extends include the "cost of acquisition, construction, or erection of buildings." Treas.Reg. § 1.263(a)–2(a). This manifests an administrative understanding that for purposes of § 263(a)(1), "amount paid out" equates with "cost incurred." The Internal Revenue Service for some time has taken the position that construction-related depreciation is to be capitalized. Rev.Rul. 59–380, 1959–2 C.B. 87; Rev.Rul. 55–252, 1955–1 Cum.Bull. 319.

There is no question that the cost of the transportation equipment was "paid out" in the same manner as the cost of supplies, materials, and other equipment, and the wages of construction workers.[4] The

---

4. The taxpayer contends that depreciation has been held not to be an expenditure or payment for purposes of a charitable contribution under § 170 of the Code, 26 U.S.C. § 170, e.g., Orr v. United States, 343 F.2d 553 (CA5 1965); Mitchell v. Commissioner, 42 T.C. 953, 973–974 (1964), or for purposes of a medical-expense deduction under § 213, 26 U.S.C. § 213, e.g., Gordon v. Commissioner, 37 T.C. 986 (1962). Section 263 is concerned, however, with the capital nature of an expenditure and not with its timing, as are the phrases "payment * * * within the taxable year" or "paid during the taxable year," respectively used in §§ 170 and 213. The treatment of depreciation under those sections has no relevance to the issue of capitalization

taxpayer does not question the capitalization of these other items as elements of the cost of acquiring a capital asset. We see no reason to treat construction-related depreciation differently. In acquiring the transportation equipment, taxpayer "paid out" the equipment's purchase price; depreciation is simply the means of allocating the payment over the various accounting periods affected. As the Tax Court stated in Brooks v. Commissioner, 50 T.C., at 935, "depreciation—inasmuch as it represents a using up of capital—is as much an 'expenditure' as the using up of labor or other items of direct cost."

Finally, the priority-ordering directive of § 161—or, for that matter, § 261 of the Code, 26 U.S.C. § 261—requires that the capitalization provision of § 263(a) take precedence, on the facts here, over § 167(a).

* * *

The Court of Appeals concluded, without reference to § 161, that § 263 did not apply to a deduction, such as that for depreciation of property used in a trade or business, allowed by the Code even though incurred in the construction of capital assets.[5] We think that the court erred in espousing so absolute a rule, and it obviously overlooked the contrary direction of § 161. * * *

We hold that the equipment depreciation allocable to taxpayer's construction of capital facilities is to be capitalized.

The judgment of the Court of Appeals is reversed.

It is so ordered.

Judgment of Court of Appeals reversed.

Mr. Justice Douglas, dissenting.

* * *

Now that we are on our own I disagree with the Court in disallowing the present claim for depreciation. A company truck has, let us say, a life of 10 years. If it cost $10,000, one would expect that "a

here. See, e.g., Producers Chemical Co. v. Commissioner, 50 T.C. 940, 959 (1968).

5. The Court of Appeals relied on All-Steel Equipment, Inc. v. Commissioner, 54 T.C. 1749 (1970), rev'd in part, 467 F.2d 1184 (CA7 1972), in holding that § 263 was inapplicable to deductions specifically allowed by the Code. 477 F.2d, at 693. In *All-Steel*, the Tax Court faced the question whether taxes, losses, and research and experimental expenses incurred in manufacturing inventory items were currently deductible and did not have to be capitalized. The Tax Court held that these items were deductible, and that the taxpayer's method of accounting did not clearly reflect income. The Court of Appeals, in contrast, held that certain repair expenses incurred in producing inventory could be deducted "only in the taxable year in which the manufactured goods to which the repairs relate are sold." 467 F.2d, at

1186. We need not decide this issue, but we note that § 263(a)(1)(B) excepts research and experimental expenditures from capitalization treatment, see Snow v. Commissioner of Internal Revenue, 416 U.S. 500, 94 S.Ct. 1876, 40 L.Ed.2d 336 (1974), and that § 266 of the Code, 26 U.S.C. § 266, creates a further exception by providing taxpayers with an election between capitalization and deduction of certain taxes and carrying charges. The Tax Court, in discussing deductions for taxes, losses, and research and experimental expenditures, observed that "deductions expressly granted by statute are not to be deferred even though they relate to inventory or capital items." 54 T.C., at 1759. This statement, when out of context, is subject to overbroad interpretation and, as is evident from our holding in the present case, has decided limitations in application.

reasonable allowance for the exhaustion, wear and tear" of the truck would be $1,000 a year within the meaning of 26 U.S.C. § 167(a). That was the provision in the House Report of the 1954 Code when it said that it provided for "a liberalization of depreciation with respect to both the estimate of useful life of property and the method of allocating the depreciable cost over the years of service." H.R.Rep. No. 1337, 83d Cong., 2d Sess., 22.

Not so, says the Government. Since the truck was used to build a plant for the taxpayer and the plant has a useful life of 40 years, a lower rate of depreciation must be used—a rate that would spread out the life of the truck for 40 years even though it would not last more than 10. Section 167 provides for a depreciation deduction with respect to property "used in the (taxpayer's) trade or business" or "held for the production of income" by the taxpayer. There is no intimation that § 167(a) is not satisfied. The argument is rested upon § 161 which allows the deductions specified in § 167(a) "subject to the exceptions" in § 263(a) * * *.

I agree with the Court of Appeals that depreciation claimed on a truck whose useful life is 10 years is not an amount "paid out" within the meaning of § 263(a)(1). If "payment" in the setting of § 263(a)(1) is to be read as including depreciation, Congress—not the courts—should make the decision.

I suspect that if the life of the vehicle were 40 years and the life of the building were 10 years the Internal Revenue Service would be here arguing persuasively that depreciation of the vehicle should be taken over a 40-year period. That is not to impugn the integrity of the IRS. It is only an illustration of the capricious character of how law is construed to get from the taxpayer the greatest possible return that is permissible under the Code.

* * *

Depreciation on an automobile is not allowed as a charitable deduction, Orr v. United States, 343 F.2d 553; Mitchell v. Commissioner, 42 T.C. 953, 973–974, since it is not a "payment" within the meaning of § 170(a)(1). Likewise depreciation on an automobile used to transport the taxpayer's son to a doctor is not deductible as a medical expense under § 213 because it is not an expense "paid" within the meaning of the section. Gordon v. Commissioner, 37 T.C. 986; Calafut v. Commissioner, 23 T.C.M. 1431.

* * *

If the test under § 263(a)(1) were the cost of capital improvements, the result would be different. But, as noted, the test is "any amount paid out," which certainly does not describe depreciation deductions unless words are to acquire esoteric meanings merely to accommodate the IRS. Congress is the lawmaker; and taking the law from it, we should affirm the Court of Appeals.

Question

Can Idaho Power be reconciled with Thor Power Tool, at p. 539?

Section 263A, enacted as part of the Tax Reform Act of 1986, mandates the capitalization of all costs incurred in producing real or tangible personal property or in acquiring real or personal property for resale. § 263A(b). In the case of personal property acquired by a taxpayer for resale, the uniform capitalization rules do not apply if the taxpayer's annual gross receipts for the three preceding taxable years were 10 million or less. § 263A(b)(2)(B). Furthermore, these rules do not apply to personal use property. § 263A(c)(1). Taxpayers subject to these uniform capitalization rules are required to capitalize not only the direct costs of such property but also an allocable portion of indirect costs that benefit the assets produced or acquired for resale, including taxes and general and administrative overhead costs. § 263A(b)(2).

Special rules apply to the allocation of interest to property constructed by the taxpayer. § 263A(f). The allocation rules, set forth in § 263A(f)(2), apply to: (1) interest paid or incurred during the production (i.e., construction) period (as defined in § 263A(f)(4)(B)) allocable to real or tangible property constructed by the taxpayer which has a long useful life, as defined in § 263A(f)(4)(A), or a specified production period, as defined in § 263A(f)(4)(B).

Problem

Herb uses one of his business machines to construct a fixture. He places this fixture in use in one of his stores. The fixture has a useful life of 10 years. The materials for the fixture cost $1,500. Taxpayer paid $2,500 in wages to an employee to construct the fixture. The recovery deduction on the machine for the time Herb used it to construct the fixture equalled $800. What is Herb's basis in this self-constructed asset? Are any other indirect costs included in his basis? Consider § 263A(b)(2) and its impact on the Idaho Power case.

H. AMORTIZATION OF INTANGIBLES

Intangibles are excluded from the definition of property eligible for the Accelerated Cost Recovery System. § 168(a). Under the traditional allowance for depreciation, some intangibles, such as goodwill (business reputation, location, and established clientele) are not depreciable. Goodwill, which supposedly lasts as long as the taxpayer remains in a business, generally lacks an ascertainable useful life—an indispensable element of depreciation. If goodwill is sold or worthless when the business is terminated or destroyed (recall the Ratheyon Production Corp. at pp. 143–146), the cost of goodwill will be deductible at that time or recovered as a tax free return of capital.

On the other hand, intangibles may be amortized under § 167 if they have limited useful lives. This can be provided by contract (e.g. covenant not to compete) or by statute (e.g. patents or copyrights). Reg. § 1.167(a)–3. Following the straight line method, amortization deductions generally must be spread evenly over the useful life of the intangible asset. For some intangibles with an indefinite life, specific Code provisions permit certain expenditures, e.g., the expense of organizing a corporation (§ 248) or a partnership (§ 709), to be amortized over a stated period. In these instances, the Code provides a limited life for expenditures of indefinite duration and permits amortization over a statutorily prescribed period. Why in the following case was the taxpayer prohibited from amortizing the entire cost of acquiring a liquor license?

NACHMAN v. COMMISSIONER

United States Court of Appeals, Fifth Circuit, 1951.
191 F.2d 934.

STRUM, CIRCUIT JUDGE.

* * *

Desiring to enter the retail liquor business as partners in Jacksonville, Florida, petitioners on April 25, 1944, purchased from one Baker Bryan for $8,000 an existing liquor license, good until September 30, 1944, issued to Bryan by the City of Jacksonville for $750, the fee fixed by ordinance therefor. The difference between the official fee of $750 and the purchase price of $8,000 was a premium which Bryan was enabled to exact from petitioners because these licenses were restricted by law to approximately 76 for the entire City of Jacksonville, all of which were then issued. Many more persons desired them than could obtain them directly from the city, so they were in great demand, even at a premium. These licenses were assignable, and carried with them valuable renewal privileges, as it was the established practice in issuing renewal licenses from year to year to prefer the holders of existing licenses over other applicants. Because of this known practice, and the limited number of licenses available, persons wishing to enter the liquor business in Jacksonville were willing to pay a substantial premium in order to acquire a license from an existing licensee.

In making their income tax returns for the tax year involved, petitioners deducted as an ordinary and necessary business expense, the entire $8,000 paid for the license. The Commissioner disallowed all except 5/12th of the $750 annual fee, representing the unexpired portion of the license extending from April 25, 1944, the date of purchase, to September 30, 1944, when it expired. The Commissioner entered a deficiency assessment accordingly. On appeal, the Tax Court held that petitioners were entitled to deduct as ordinary business expense the entire $750 official fee, but no more, and reduced the deficiency accordingly. It is the latter determination by the Tax Court that petitioners bring here for review.

* * * The license carried with it by established custom, if not by law, a valuable renewal privilege indispensable to petitioners' continuance in business in subsequent years. In purchasing the license, petitioners bought not only the operating right for the current year but also renewal privileges for future years. This privilege, entitling petitioners to preference over non-license holders in the issuance of renewal licenses, was of substantial value, of which the seller and the purchasers of this license were well aware. No one would pay $8,000 for a $750, license having only five months to run, unless the purchaser was reasonably sure it carried with it appurtenant privileges of substantial future value to the purchaser. It was these considerations that prompted petitioners to pay $8,000 for a $750 license, of which only $5/12$ths remained.

Of the $8,000 paid for the license in question, the official cost of issuance, $750, was an ordinary and necessary business expense. The remaining $7,250 was the expenditure of capital in the acquisition of a capital asset reasonably expected to serve petitioners through future years, the cost of which is not deductible as an ordinary expense. * * *

Petitioners further contend that if the $7,250 in question be regarded as the purchase price of a capital asset and therefore not deductible as ordinary business expense, they are entitled to an amortized depreciation allowance on such capital asset under [§ 167], and [Reg. § 1.167(a)–3], relating to depreciation of intangible property. Depreciation allowance on intangibles, however, is confined to those definitely limited in duration, such as patents, franchises, copyrights, licenses for fixed periods, and the like, the partial exhaustion of which may be computed with reasonable certainty.

It is clear that the renewal privilege appurtenant to this license extends beyond, and was actually exercised beyond, the taxable year in question. Presumably the petitioners may continue to exercise their renewal privileges as long as they desire, as there is no indication that the City will depart from its custom of renewing existing licenses. How long petitioners may wish to continue exercising their renewal privileges is indeterminable. It might be for one year, or many. It was exercised by them at least as late as 1949. The basis for depreciation of an intangible capital asset is partial exhaustion due to lapse of time. This renewal privilege being of indefinite duration, dependent upon petitioners' wishes as well as upon the City's future course of action, there is no rational basis for prediction as to duration.

Moreover, if petitioners elect to discontinue the exercise of their renewal rights, it is reasonable to assume that they will sell them, just as did their predecessor Bryan, either recouping their investment or sustaining a deductible loss. We conclude therefore, as did the Tax Court, that the renewal privilege incident to the license is a nondepreciable capital asset. * * *

Fed'l Inc. Tax (S. & H.) ACB—22   * * *

Problem

Can a taxpayer amortize the cost of an easement which lasts forever, such as the right-of-way for a gas transmission pipeline? According to industry practice, when a pipeline wears out, pipeline companies typically abandon the pipeline and the accompanying easement. May the taxpayer use an accelerated recovery method? Consider § 167(c).

WESTINGHOUSE BROADCASTING CO.
v. COMMISSIONER

United States Court of Appeals, Third Circuit, 1962.
309 F.2d 279, cert. denied 372 U.S. 935.
83 S.Ct. 881, 9 L.Ed.2d 766 (1963).

KALODNER, CIRCUIT JUDGE.

Is a television network affiliation contract for a two-year term, automatically renewable in the absence of termination notice for successive two-year terms, a depreciable asset?

That is the question presented by this petition for review of the Decision of the Tax Court which answered it in the negative premised on its determination that the contract had "an indeterminate useful life" as of the close of the tax years here involved.

The facts critical to our disposition may be summarized as follows:

On June 1, 1953, Westinghouse Broadcasting Company, Inc. ("taxpayer") purchased from Philco Corporation ("Philco") for $8,534,000 all of the assets of television station WPTZ in Philadelphia, Pennsylvania, including its network affiliation contract with National Broadcasting Company (NBC) which was to expire on January 1, 1954.[6]

The network affiliation contract was renewable automatically for successive two-year terms unless, at least 90 days prior to the expiration of any two-year term, either party sent the other written notice of its intention not to renew.[7]

---

6. The network affiliation contract set forth the terms of WPTZ's affiliation with NBC. By the terms of the affiliation contract, NBC agreed to supply to WPTZ a variety of network television programs, sponsored or unsponsored and to give WPTZ the right of first refusal to broadcast such programs in the Philadelphia area. WPTZ agreed, with certain exceptions, to broadcast sponsored programs of the NBC network during hours designated in the contract as "network option time". The financial arrangement set forth in the contract called for a division between WPTZ and NBC of gross billings to network advertisers for WPTZ's station time, WPTZ receiving a one-third share and NBC receiving a two-thirds share, except that for the first 24 hours of network programs broadcast by WPTZ each month billings were to be paid entirely to NBC. Billing rates were specified in the contract and were subject to change by NBC under conditions therein specified.

7. The renewal provision reads as follows:

"23. This agreement * * * shall remain in effect for a period of two years. It shall then be renewed on the same terms and conditions for a further period of two years, and so on for successive further periods of two years each unless and until either party shall, at least three months prior to the expiration of the then current term, give the other party written notice that it does not desire to have the contract renewed for a further period."

The agreement between Philco and taxpayer allocated $5,000,000 of the $8,500,000 purchase price of WPTZ to the network affiliation contract, $1,500,000 to good will and the balance to tangible assets and receivables.

The network affiliation contract was automatically renewed on January 1, 1954 for a two-year term expiring January 1, 1956. On September 28, 1954 NBC informed taxpayer that it desired to acquire a television station in Philadelphia and sometime prior to November 15, 1954 taxpayer was further advised by NBC that it would not renew the network affiliation contract beyond January 1, 1956.[8] On October 1, 1955 pursuant to the 90-day notice provision of the affiliation contract NBC gave formal notice to taxpayer of termination of the network affiliation contract on January 1, 1956.

The network affiliation contract had been entered into between NBC and Philco Television Broadcasting Corporation on November 23, 1949 for a two-year term commencing January 1, 1950 and automatically renewed on January 1, 1952 for a further two-year term expiring January 1, 1954. It had been assigned to Philco by Philco Television Broadcasting Corporation on May 14, 1952 during the renewed term.

Federal Communications Commission (FCC) regulations in effect during 1953 and 1954 prohibited any contract providing for network affiliation for a term longer than two years.

The average earnings *before taxes* of WPTZ for 1951 and 1952 were $1,704,459. The net broadcast income of WPTZ for 1951 and 1952 exceeded the broadcast income of WFIL–TV, the ABC affiliate in Philadelphia, by $748,000 and $1,250,000 respectively, and such excess was attributed by taxpayer's expert, Howard E. Stark, to WPTZ's affiliation with NBC.

Between January 1, 1953, and April 1, 1960, a total of 87 NBC affiliation agreements expired in circumstances other than a station going off the air or the acquisition of the affiliate by the network.

Taxpayer, on its books, and federal income tax returns for 1953 and 1954, depreciated its cost of the $5,000,000 network affiliation contract over a 55-month period ending January 1, 1958, i.e., the 7-month term in existence on June 1, 1953, plus two renewal terms of two years each (January 1, 1954 to January 1, 1956 and January 1, 1956 to January 1, 1958) based on taxpayer's assumption that network affiliation contracts may normally be expected to be renewed for two terms. Subsequently, in the course of the proceedings below, taxpayer contended that the network affiliation contract was depreciable over a 31-month period— the 7-month term ending January 1, 1954 and the 24-month period ending January 1, 1956 when the contract was actually terminated.

8. On May 16, 1955 taxpayer entered into an agreement with NBC whereby it agreed to exchange the assets of WPTZ and its Philadelphia radio station for the assets of NBC's Cleveland, Ohio television and radio station plus $3,000,000. The actual exchange of stations took place on January 21, 1956.

Taxpayer here contends that the Tax Court erred in its finding that the network affiliation contract did not have a "determinable useful life" as of the close of 1953 and 1954, the tax years under review. It urges that "as a matter of law, a business contract with a specific term and provision for renewal is definitely limited in duration to that term and such renewal terms as are reasonably certain to occur", and, that "as a matter of fact, there was no reasonable certainty of renewal indefinitely with respect to the affiliation agreement" and that "the maximum period of renewal was to January 1, 1958."

The record, taken as a whole, says taxpayer, "establishes that at the time of acquisition of the affiliation agreement on June 1, 1953, two renewals, i.e. renewals to January 1, 1958, might be reasonably certain, but that a renewal beyond January 1, 1959 was not reasonably certain", and that "Thus the contract, under the reasonable certainty rule, had a maximum useful life of 55 months at the end of 1953 and 1954." In support, taxpayer cites the testimony of its expert, Stark: "If you could not assume two renewals, I don't think I would advise anyone to enter into a contract, but beyond that you can't foresee anything in this business." [9]

The sum of the Commissioner's position is that Section 23(*l*) of the Internal Revenue Code of 1939 (applicable here to the year 1953) and Section 167(a) of the Internal Revenue Code of [1986] (applicable here to 1954) provide for a depreciation deduction in circumstances where such deduction represents "a reasonable allowance for the exhaustion * * * of property used in the trade or business"; that Treasury Regulations 118 (1939) Code, Sec. 39.23(1)–3 and Treasury Regulations on Income Tax ([1986] Code), Section 1.167(a)–3, provide that if an intangible asset is known from experience to be of use in the business or in the production of income for only a limited period, the length of which can be estimated with "reasonable" certainty, such intangible asset may be the subject of a depreciation allowance; that both the 1939 and [1986] Treasury Regulations impose upon the taxpayer the burden of establishing the reasonableness of the deduction for depreciation allowance,[10] and finally, that the record discloses that taxpayer had failed to establish with "reasonable" certainty that the maximum period of renewal of the network affiliation contract was to January 1, 1958.

The Tax Court held that "Insufficient evidence was introduced from which could be calculated either the average useful life of network affiliation contracts or their useful life span", and further stated its conclusion "that petitioner [taxpayer] has not only failed to persuade us that the contract had a 55-month useful life but also that it has failed

9. Stark, a broker specializing in the purchase and sale of radio and television stations, played no part in the transaction in which taxpayer acquired station WPTZ from Philco.

10. * * * Treas.Reg. on Income Tax Sec. 1.167(b)–O.

to persuade us respondent [Commissioner] erred in his determination that the contract had an indeterminable useful life".

On review of the record we agree with the Tax Court's holding that taxpayer failed to prove that at the close of the taxable years 1953 and 1954 it was "reasonably certain" that the network affiliation contract had a maximum useful life of but 55 months from the date of its acquisition by taxpayer on June 1, 1953.

The burden of proof to do so was on taxpayer not only under the applicable revenue statutes and the Treasury Regulations pertaining to them, earlier cited, but by reason of the well-settled principle that the Commissioner's determination of a deficiency in tax bears a presumption of correctness. Hoffman v. Commissioner, 298 F.2d 784, 788 (3 Cir. 1962).

Taxpayer did not adduce any testimony to the effect that based on "experience" in the television industry the number of renewals of the network affiliation contract could be "estimated" with "reasonable certainty" or "reasonable accuracy" as required by the Treasury Regulations earlier cited.

While taxpayer's expert, Stark, in substantiating the $5,000,000 consideration paid for the network affiliation contract, testified that he had assumed a useful life for the contract which contemplated two renewals after acquisition, or 55 months in this case, he did not say that his assumed premise of such two renewals was based on "experience" with such contracts. All that Stark said was that it was the "practice" of experts in evaluating network affiliation contracts "to anticipate the likelihood of two separate renewals * * * following the expiration of the unexpired term of the contract", to which he added that in his post-evaluation of the contract here involved he had in mind that anticipation and "the hope that it would be continued beyond that date [two separate renewals]".

It must be stressed that nowhere in his testimony did Stark say that the "practice" of experts in anticipating two renewals of network affiliation contracts was based on "experience" with respect to contract renewals.

Under the circumstances we agree with the Tax Court that the "practice" of the experts in figuring on two renewals of a network affiliation contract was not "a sufficient indication of that contract's probable useful life."

Nor can any probative value with respect to the "probable useful life" of the network affiliation contract here be attributed to the stipulated fact that "between January 1, 1953 and April 1, 1960, a total of 87 NBC affiliation agreements expired in circumstances other than a station going off the air or the acquisition of the affiliate by the network" since there was no evidence as to the actual life span of those agreements or as to the number of their renewals.

This too must be said. Taxpayer based its 55-month useful life estimate of the network affiliation contract on its premise that there was reasonable certainty of only 48 months plus the 7 months of its unexpired term. The premise was in turn sub-based, so to say, on the theory that network affiliation contracts have a life span of 72 months, their original two-year term and two renewals. Taxpayer disregards the fact that the network affiliation contract here had actually run for 24 months (January 1, 1950 to January 1, 1952) prior to the renewed term (January 1, 1952 to January 1, 1954) during which it was acquired by taxpayer on June 1, 1953.

It would serve no useful purpose to discuss the cases cited by taxpayer and the Commissioner since the facts in those cases vary significantly from those existing here.

For the reasons stated the decision of the Tax Court will be affirmed.

HOUSTON CHRONICAL PUBLISHING CO. v. UNITED STATES

United States Court of Appeals, Fifth Circuit, 1973.
481 F.2d 1240, cert. denied 414 U.S. 1129,
94 S.Ct. 867, 38 L.Ed.2d 754 (1974).

GOLDBERG, CIRCUIT JUDGE:

This is a tax case raising three complex and unrelated issues, none of which admits of facile solution. Taxpayer, the Houston Chronicle Publishing Company, is a Texas corporation that publishes *The Houston Chronicle,* a major daily newspaper. From 1963 to 1966 taxpayer engaged in the series of actions to expand its facilities and operations that gave rise to the tax questions now before us. Simply stated, those issues are:

> (1) Under the Internal Revenue Code of [1986], may a newspaper publisher ever amortize costs incurred in acquiring subscription lists, and if so, has this taxpayer shown itself to be entitled to claim such amortization?

* * *

I. AMORTIZATION OF NEWSPAPER SUBSCRIPTION LISTS

* * *

A. *The Operative Facts*

Prior to 1964, taxpayer was in competition with a second afternoon newspaper, *The Houston Press,* which was published by the Houston Press Company [hereinafter The Press]. In late 1963 or early 1964, taxpayer resumed previously discontinued negotiations with The Press, aimed at acquiring the assets of *The Houston Press.* The negotiations were successful, and on March 20, 1964, taxpayer entered into a contract with The Press under which taxpayer acquired the land, improvements, fixtures, inventory, equipment, library, and subscription lists owned by The Press.[11]   In addition to these assets, taxpayer received a noncompetition agreement from The Press and E.W. Scripps Company restricting the latter from engaging in the publication of any weekly, daily, or Sunday newspaper in the Houston area for a period of ten years. Taxpayer paid The Press a total consideration of $4,500,000, none of which was allocated among the various items prior to the time of sale.

Under the purchase agreement, taxpayer was entitled to receive all subscription lists of *The Houston Press,* and it eventually did receive the lists. The Press had distributed its newspapers by means of district managers. Each manager supervised a specific area and was responsible for distributing newspapers to the paperboys and street vending boxes in his area. The district managers were employees of The Press and maintained the lists of subscribers to *The Houston Press* within their respective areas. The Press maintained a list of the aggregate number of subscribers, but only the district managers maintained lists showing the names and addresses of the subscribers.

Sometime after the sale, taxpayer engaged the services of the firm of Marshall & Stevens, Inc., Valuation Engineers, to evaluate the various assets acquired from The Press. *The Houston Press* had a circulation of approximately 89,000, and the valuation engineers estimated that about 40% of these would become subscribers to *The Houston Chronicle.* The anticipated number of new subscribers, approximately 35,600, was multiplied by the average cost of obtaining a new subscriber, $2.00, to arrive at a total value of the subscription lists of $71,200. That figure is not in dispute.

On the date that the purchase arrangement was announced to the public, March 20, 1964 (which was also the last day *The Houston Press* was published), taxpayer's president directed his staff to attempt to obtain employment contracts from the district managers previously employed by The Press. In compliance with this directive, taxpayer's city manager went to the offices of The Press on March 20, 1964. Through his efforts, at least 24 of the 28 to 30 district managers of The Press signed contracts to become independent contractors with taxpayer. In essence, then, taxpayer ultimately acquired virtually all of the distribution structure that The Press had utilized.

Taxpayer had agreed to complete all subscriptions to *The Houston Press,* and in addition, taxpayer furnished former subscribers to *The Houston Press* with one month's free delivery of *The Houston Chronicle* in order to acquaint them with that newspaper. As a result of these various efforts, approximately 36,000 Press subscribers ultimately began subscribing to *The Houston Chronicle.*

Because taxpayer had no intention of continuing publication of *The Houston Press,* it did not consider the subscription lists to be self-

---

11. The right to use the Scripps-Howard "lighthouse" design, a trademark registered with the United States Patent Office, and the Scripps-Howard slogan was expressly excluded from the conveyance.

regenerating assets and considered them valuable only to the extent they furnished names and addresses of prospective subscribers to *The Houston Chronicle.* Concluding that the expected useful life of the lists was five years, taxpayer claimed as an amortization deduction for the taxable years here in question, 1964 and 1965, one-fifth of the assigned value per year.

In connection with an audit of taxpayer's income tax returns, the Commissioner disallowed the amortization expense deductions claimed for the subscription lists. Taxpayer paid the resulting deficiencies and filed claims for a refund, which were ultimately unsuccessful. Taxpayer thereafter filed the instant suit for a refund.

B. Action Below

Taxpayer's position is that it may claim an amortization deduction under § 167(a) of the Internal Revenue Code of [1986] for the subscription lists, an intangible capital asset, if the asset has (1) a limited useful life that is (2) of ascertainable duration. The government admits that those two qualities generally do allow an intangible capital asset to qualify for such a deduction but insists that subscription lists must be treated as being akin to the "goodwill" of a business, which is non-amortizable as a matter of law. The court below agreed with taxpayer and heard evidence on the question of whether these lists had ascertainable limited lives.

In addition to arguing that these subscription lists were non-amortizable as a matter of law, however, the government argued at the close of the evidence that taxpayer had failed to produce that quantum of evidence that would entitle it to go to the jury under Boeing Co. v. Shipman, 5 Cir.1969, 411 F.2d 365. The trial court again agreed with taxpayer and ruled that the evidence adduced was sufficient to prevent a directed verdict for the government and submitted the case to the jury on special issues.

The jury was first asked to allocate a portion of the purchase price to various assets and items. Their verdict on this issue was as follows:

(a)	Goodwill	$775,400
(b)	Covenant not to Compete	$1,809,400
(c)	Library or Morgue	$350,000
(d)	Subscription List	$71,200

In addition, the jury specifically found that "on March 20, 1964, the subscription list had a reasonably ascertainable useful life * * * [of] 5 years."

The government filed a motion for judgment notwithstanding the verdict and renewed in support thereof its arguments that subscription lists are non-amortizable as a matter of law and that even if such lists sometimes are amortizable, taxpayer had not satisfied its burden of producing sufficient evidence to support the jury's verdict. This motion was denied and judgment was entered for taxpayer. The government brings this appeal and again presents its dual argument that the subscription lists in question do not entitle taxpayer to claim an amortization expense deduction.

C. Whether Newspaper Subscription Lists Are Non-Amortizable as a Matter of Law

The government does not contend that these newspaper subscription lists are non-amortizable because they are *intangible* capital assets. Indeed, it could not, for we have previously said:

> "Under the present law, a reasonable amortization deduction is allowed for the exhaustion, wear and tear of property used in the taxpayer's business, or of property held for the production of income, I.R.C. § 167(a) [1986]. The property, to be depreciable, must be an inherently wasting asset, but this allowance is not limited to tangible assets."

Griswold v. Commissioner, 5 Cir.1968, 400 F.2d 427, 433. Also, the Treasury Regulations specifically provide for amortization or depreciation of intangible capital assets:

> "If an intangible asset is known from experience or other factors to be of use in the business or in the production of income for only a limited period, the length of which can be estimated with reasonable accuracy, such an intangible asset may be the subject of a depreciation allowance. Examples are patents and copyrights. An intangible asset, the useful life of which is not limited, is not subject to the allowance for depreciation. No allowance will be permitted merely because, in the unsupported opinion of the taxpayer, the intangible asset has a limited useful life. No deduction for depreciation is allowable with respect to goodwill * * *."

Treas.Reg. § 1.167(a)–3. On the other hand, not every intangible capital asset is depreciable:

> "Thus the statute does not include all property. There are even some kinds of property used in business on which depreciation is not allowable because none is sustained, and other property on which it is not allowable because any exhaustion which may occur is not susceptible of accurate measurement. Accordingly, in order to establish the right to depreciation, it is necessary to show that the property, whether tangible or intangible, will become exhausted within a definite period, which is known as its useful life, and which can be ascertained from specific terms, such as a contract, or can be determined from available facts."

Pohlen v. Commissioner, 5 Cir.1948, 165 F.2d 258, 259.

Taxpayer admits that it bears all burdens in regard to establishing its right to claim a § 167(a) deduction. *See* Bennett v. Commissioner, 8 Cir.1944, 139 F.2d 961 * * *. This being so, taxpayers frequently are prevented from taking § 167(a) deductions because they are unable to prove affirmatively that the particular asset involved satisfies all of the prerequisites for amortizability. Many of the reported cases turn on this factual question and thus stand not so much for the proposition that the type of asset is never amortizable as they do for the conclusion that the very asset involved failed to qualify for one or more particular reasons.

* * *

The most frequently reported cases—those involving denials of § 167(a) amortization deductions for intangible capital assets where the taxpayer failed to carry his burden of convincing the trier of fact that the asset has a limited useful life of ascertainable duration—are similarly distinguishable. In denying a § 167(a) deduction in Griswold v. Commissioner, supra, for example, we emphasized that taxpayers had "offered no evidence to accurately establish the duration of the assets." 400 F.2d at 434. Similarly, in a case involving "insurance renewals," we denied amortization deductions where taxpayers had "adduced no controverting evidence of a limited useful life" of the asset. Salome v. United States, 5 Cir.1968, 395 F.2d 990.

Indeed, most of the cases denying § 167(a) deductions to intangibles clearly rest on a failure of the taxpayer to carry his burden of proof. In International Textbook Co. v. United States, 1930, 44 F.2d 254, 71 Ct.Cl. 132, taxpayer had incurred substantial expenses in obtaining the right to market certain educational programs. In denying a depreciation deduction in connection with this asset, the court found that the rights were of indefinite duration and noted that taxpayer had failed to provide any "basis for the computation of exhaustion" of the asset. 44 F.2d at 257. In Dunn v. United States, 10 Cir.1969, 400 F.2d 679, the court held that various payments made in connection with a "Dairy Queen" franchise were non-amortizable where no certain life of the franchise agreement had been shown. The court in Gant v. Commissioner, 6 Cir.1959, 263 F.2d 558, pinioned its refusal to allow the purchaser of a distributorship to amortize monthly payments to the seller on the fact finding that the future period of the arrangement was "entirely unascertainable." 263 F.2d at 559. A claimed depreciation deduction was disallowed for a somewhat different reason in Klein v. Commissioner, 2 Cir.1966, 372 F.2d 261. Taxpayer furnished exterminating and pest-control services, and he expanded his business by buying the accounts of other exterminators. His attempt to depreciate the cost of those purchases was thwarted when he failed to satisfy § 167(a)'s requirement that he establish the cost basis of the asset. Each of these cases represents the failure of a given taxpayer to carry his burden of bringing his claim within the *factual* borders that would support an amortization deduction—none rules that the asset involved is *per se* non-amortizable.

Some intangible capital assets are, of course, non-amortizable as a matter of law, with the most frequently litigated example being the "goodwill" of an ongoing business. Treasury Regulation § 1.167(a)–3 specifically provides, "No deduction for depreciation is allowable with respect to goodwill," and the cases are consistent in applying that regulation strictly. E.g., Winn-Dixie Montgomery, Inc. v. United States, 5 Cir.1971, 444 F.2d 677; United States v. Cornish, 9 Cir.1965,

348 F.2d 175; Dodge Brothers, Inc. v. United States, 4 Cir.1941, 118 F.2d 95. Indeed, this proposition is so well settled that the only question litigated in recent years regarding this area of the law is whether a particular asset is "goodwill."

We have previously spoken at length to the question of what constitutes goodwill:

"[T]he nature of goodwill * * * is the expectancy that 'the old customers will resort to the old place.' Commissioner of Internal Revenue v. Killian, 314 F.2d 852, 855 (C.A.5, 1963); Nelson Weaver Realty Co. v. Commissioner of Internal Revenue, 307 F.2d 897, 901 (C.A.5, 1962); Karan v. Commissioner of Internal Revenue, 319 F.2d 303, 306 (C.A.7, 1963). '[T]he essence of goodwill is the expectancy of continued patronage, for whatever reason.' Boe v. Commissioner of Internal Revenue, 307 F.2d 339, 343 (C.A.9, 1962) * * *. [T]o the extent [a given item or asset] contributes to the expectancy that the old customers will resort to the old place it is an element of goodwill. Commissioner of Internal Revenue v. Seaboard Finance Co., 367 F.2d 646, 651 n. 6 (C.A.9, 1966); Boe v. Commissioner of Internal Revenue, supra, 307 F.2d at 343.

"* * *

"This Court has held that * * * goodwill is acquired by the purchaser of a going concern where the 'transfer enables the purchaser to step into the shoes of the seller.' Balthrope v. Commissioner of Internal Revenue, 356 F.2d 28, 32 n. 1 ([C.A.5] 1966); Masquelette's Estate v. Commissioner of Internal Revenue, 239 F.2d 322, 325 ([C.A.5] 1956). We have also said that goodwill is transferred where, as here, the buyer continues the seller's business uninterrupted, using primarily the seller's employees, and utilizing the seller's name. Barran v. Commissioner of Internal Revenue, supra, 334 F.2d 58, 61 ([C.A.5] 1964). It is immaterial that the agreement did not use the term 'goodwill,' for '[t]he use of these words is, of course, not necessary if in fact what is transferred does give to the purchaser everything that can effectively aid him to step into the shoes of the seller.' Masquelette's Estate v. Commissioner of Internal Revenue, supra, at 325; see also Barron v. Commissioner of Internal Revenue, supra, at 61 * * *."

Winn-Dixie Montgomery, Inc. v. United States, supra, 444 F.2d at 681–682. Thus, the precise issue is often whether or not the asset involved is either ordinary goodwill or so much like goodwill that the reasons for denying amortization deductions for goodwill are fully applicable. Foremost among those reasons is the conclusive presumption that goodwill is a non-depreciating capital asset. See, e.g., Id.; Golden State Towel & Linen Service, Ltd. v. United States, 1967, 373 F.2d 938, 179 Ct.Cl. 300. Viewed in a business context, the economic value of a taxpayer's continuing goodwill within his field of operations is seen as an ongoing asset that fluctuates but does not necessarily diminish.[12]

12. The government's brief summarizes this position as follows:

"Since the nature of goodwill is the expectancy that old customers will resort to

The crucial question becomes one of asking whether the intangible capital asset involved necessarily possesses similar characteristics.

Many reported cases apply this analytical approach. Clark Thread Co. v. Commissioner, 3 Cir.1939, 100 F.2d 257, is an early example. Taxpayer had incurred expenses in securing a competitor's agreement to discontinue using the trade name "Clark." When taxpayer attempted to treat this cost as a business expense deduction, the court looked to the substance of the transaction and concluded that taxpayer had acquired the right to use the trade name free of competition. The deduction was disallowed because trade names are like goodwill in their economic characteristics and effect. Both may vary in value through the years, but both will be of ongoing usefulness indefinitely, presumptively for as long as the business continues to operate. In J.C. Cornillie Co. v. United States, E.D.Mich.1968, 298 F.Supp. 887, a contract under which fuel oil customers would be referred to taxpayer by a former supplier was held to constitute the purchase of goodwill, and the claimed deduction was accordingly disallowed. What taxpayer had obtained was the ongoing expectation that customers would utilize its services in the future, the archetypical element of goodwill. In Falstaff Beer, Inc. v. Commissioner, 5 Cir.1963, 322 F.2d 744, taxpayer attempted to treat the cost of purchasing an existing marketing structure as an ordinary business expense deduction under § 162 of the Internal Revenue Code. Recognizing that what was actually transferred was the seller's goodwill, we found the purchase price to be a capital investment that "unquestionably added value, permanently or at least for many years" to the purchaser's business, 322 F.2d at 748, and we therefore denied the § 162 deduction. In Sammons v. Commissioner, 7 Cir.1949, 177 F.2d 837, the cost of obtaining existing "Who's Who" biographical sketches was found to be allocable, as a factual matter, to goodwill and other non-deductible intangibles.

None of the foregoing cases supports the government's argument that subscription lists are non-amortizable as a matter of law. Nor does the case most closely in point to the one before us support the government's position. In Blaine v. United States, 5 Cir.1971, 441 F.2d 917, taxpayer attempted to depreciate the cost of obtaining "insurance expiration" lists and a covenant not to compete from the seller.

"The Commissioner disallowed the depreciation deductions for the stated reason that [lists of] insurance expirations do not have a reasonably ascertainable useful life, and are in the nature of goodwill. The taxpayers paid the resulting deficiencies, and filed a claim for a refund. The refund claims were disallowed. Suit for refunds was brought in the district court. The jury returned a special verdict finding that the

the old places and the expectancy of continued patronage * * * the term goodwill, for tax purposes, encompasses a wide spectrum of intangibles which are associated with favorable customer patronage * * *. Thus, goodwill is the sum total of all the imponderable qualities which attract customers and bring patronage to the business. By its very nature, goodwill is not a depreciable asset since it is self-regenerating and its benefits extend over a substantial period of time which cannot be estimated with reasonable accuracy."

expirations involved had a useful life of six years. Judgment was entered for tax refunds reflecting the allowance of * * * depreciation deductions over a six year period. Motion for judgment notwithstanding the verdict was made and overruled. The United States brings this appeal contending that insurance expirations are goodwill * * * and not depreciable as a matter of law, and even if they are depreciable the finding of a useful life of six years is clearly erroneous. * * *"

441 F.2d at 918. Although we reversed the case, we did so only on the ground that taxpayer had failed to produce that quantum of evidence that would withstand a motion for judgment notwithstanding the verdict under Boeing Co. v. Shipman, supra. In other words, we refused to find that the lists there involved were non-amortizable as a matter of law; to the contrary, we treated the issue [as] a factual question, i.e., *whether* the limited and ascertainable lives of the intangibles had been proven by sufficient competent evidence.

The government's posture in the instant case is on all fours with the position it took in Blaine v. United States, supra. That case alone would control our disposition of the question of whether such lists are non-amortizable as a matter of law were it not for the fact that the government here raises an argument not discussed in *Blaine.* As a refinement of its argument that lists such as those before us are to be treated as goodwill for tax purposes, the government argues that the so-called "mass asset" or "indivisible asset" rule requires that amortization be denied.

The "mass asset" rule has been applied where arguably distinct assets are "inextricably" linked to goodwill, see Golden State Towel & Linen Service, Ltd. v. United States, supra, and where the seemingly separate assets possess the same qualities as goodwill, possessing no determinable useful life and having self-regenerating capability, see Winn-Dixie Montgomery, Inc. v. United States, supra. The government here invokes that "rule" to insist that the instant taxpayer cannot amortize the cost of obtaining these lists. We cannot agree, and we do not read the "mass asset" cases as controlling this case.

Most of the cases purporting to apply the "mass asset" rule involve evidentiary failures on the part of the taxpayer. In Thrifticheck Service Corp. v. Commissioner, 2 Cir.1961, 287 F.2d 1, the amount paid for customer contracts was not entitled to be deducted as a depreciable expense and was instead lumped together into one non-depreciable asset that included the expectation of future business coming to taxpayer. The holding rested squarely on the failure of taxpayer to prove a reasonable period over which the amounts should have been amortized, and the case stands for little more. Similarly, in Marsh & McLennan, Inc. v. Commissioner, 3 Cir.1969, 420 F.2d 667, the cost of acquiring "insurance expiration" lists was not allowed to be depreciated. The court rested its holding on two findings: "first, the expirations were inextricably linked with elements of goodwill such that they had no determinable value in themselves; and second, the taxpayer had not proved that the expirations had a limited useful life, determinable with 'reasonable accuracy.'" 420 F.2d at 667. The dissenting opinion of Judge Van Dusen characterized these fact findings as being "clearly erroneous" and emphasized that the "mass asset" rule turns on factual questions. Without compiling the myriad cases that discuss the "mass asset" rule, we are satisfied that the rule does not establish a *per se* rule of non-amortizability in every case involving both goodwill and other intangible assets. In the light of § 167(a) of the Code and Regulation § 1.167(a)–3, we are convinced that the "mass asset" rule does not prevent taking an amortization deduction if the taxpayer properly carries his dual burden of proving that the intangible asset involved (1) has an ascertainable value separate and distinct from goodwill, and (2) has a limited useful life, the duration of which can be ascertained with reasonable accuracy.

Where the taxpayer has been able to satisfy this perhaps extremely difficult burden, depreciation expense deductions have been allowed. In Western Mortgage Co. v. United States, C.D.Cal.1969, 308 F.Supp. 333, the taxpayer established that loan service contracts carried with them no expectancy of continued patronage or repeat business, and in addition, proved that as a result of the contracts it would

> "receive a determinable amount of income over a 'limited period, the length of which can be estimated with reasonable accuracy.' Treasury Regulations, Section 1.167(a)–3 (1954). The parties stipulated that the * * * loans had an average life of 7 years. This average life complies with Treasury Regulations, Section 1.167(a)–3 (1954). * * * Accordingly, plaintiff is entitled to amortize over a 7-year period that portion of the purchase price properly allocable to the right to service the * * * loans."

308 F.Supp. at 340–341. In Commissioner v. Seaboard Finance Co., 9 Cir.1966, 367 F.2d 646, affirming T.C.Memo. 1904–253, the "premium" paid for acquiring outstanding loans and other assets was found to be amortizable. The Commissioner had argued that the entire premium was allocable to goodwill and other non-depreciable assets, but the taxpayer was able to obtain a fact finding that only 30% of the premium was allocable to those items. Accordingly, when taxpayer established the value and reasonably ascertainable useful life of the remaining 70% attributable to the loan accounts, the claimed deduction was allowed.

Two Sixth Circuit cases relied upon by the government also demonstrate that the amortizability of a given intangible capital asset turns on its *factual* characteristics. Both Skilken v. Commissioner, 6 Cir. 1969, 420 F.2d 266 (terminable-at-will vending machine locations), and Toledo Blade Co. v. Commissioner, 6 Cir.1950, 180 F.2d 357, affirming 11 T.C. 1079 (transfer of newspaper's intangible assets, including covenant not to compete), denied amortization expense deductions. In both cases, however, the taxpayer had failed to establish one or more of the factual prerequisites to amortizability—no ascertainable useful life was shown in *Skilken* and no definite value was shown in *Toledo Blade*.

Only in the Eighth Circuit has the position here urged by the government been approached. Willcuts v. Minnesota Tribune Co., 8 Cir.1939, 103 F.2d 947, denied ordinary expense deductions to the cost of purchasing another newspaper's circulation, but the court made clear that taxpayer's failure to carry the evidentiary burdens compelled that result:

> "The record is entirely silent on [the actual costs and values involved]. The assessment of the Commissioner of Internal Revenue is, however, presumptively correct. The burden of proof was on the taxpayer to overcome this burden. * * *"

103 F.2d at 951. See also National Weeklies v. Commissioner, 8 Cir. 1943, 137 F.2d 39, 42 (no depreciation deduction for newspaper subscription lists where "the evidence in any event failed to establish the depreciation basis necessary"). Meredith Publishing Co. v. Commissioner, 8 Cir.1933, 64 F.2d 890, denied ordinary expense deductions to the cost of building up a magazine's circulation, but the case involved a situation where taxpayer was claiming and receiving annual deductions for the cost of replacing each subscription that expired. More recently, however, the Eighth Circuit has allowed expenses incurred in obtaining intangible capital assets used in the trade or business to be depreciated where the proper supportive facts are present. See Northern Natural Gas Co. v. O'Malley, 8 Cir.1960, 277 F.2d 128. As the concurring opinion of then-Circuit Judge Blackmun makes clear, if the asset is shown to be a wasting one used in taxpayer's trade or business, a reasonable deduction must be allowed. 277 F.2d at 139–141.

Finally, we note that even the Tax Court, which in several early cases denied depreciation deductions for customer lists involved in particular situations, see, e.g., Anchor Cleaning Service, Inc. v. Commissioner, 1954, 22 T.C. 1029; Danville Press, Inc. v. Commissioner, 1925, 1 B.T.A. 1171; Herald-Despatch Co. v. Commissioner, 1926, 4 B.T.A. 1096, has recently allowed the cost of customer lists to be depreciated in Manhattan Co. of Virginia, Inc. v. Commissioner, 1968, 50 T.C. 78. In that case, the court allocated the purchase price to various specific intangible assets. Finding that "75 percent of the cost * * * of the customer lists is allocable to the depreciable part of the intangible asset consisting of the information acquired by [taxpayers] from the customer lists which enabled them to contact customers * * * and in many instances to obtain their business," 50 T.C. at 93, the court concluded:

> "The record here shows that of the typical customers acquired by [taxpayers] from the * * * lists, they could expect to lose approximately 20 percent a year. From this and the other evidence in this record, we conclude that from the experience of [taxpayers] the information on the customer lists which had a limited useful life had such a useful life of approximately 5 years. We therefore conclude that the 75 percent of the cost of the customer lists which we have allocated to

an intangible asset of a wasting nature should be depreciated on a 5-year basis."

Id. See also First Pennsylvania Banking & Trust Co. v. Commissioner, 1971, 56 T.C. 677.

Finding that the instant lists met the requirements of § 167(a) of the Code and the Regulations promulgated thereunder, we explicitly hold that which we left unsaid in Blaine v. United States, 5 Cir.1971, 441 F.2d 917—newspaper subscription lists such as those before us are intangible capital assets that may be depreciated for tax purposes if taxpayer sustains his burden of proving that the lists (1) have an ascertainable value separate and distinct from goodwill, and (2) have a limited useful life, the duration of which can be ascertained with reasonable accuracy. Cf. Commissioner v. Killian, 5 Cir.1963, 314 F.2d 852. Therefore, as we did in *Blaine*, we must now turn to a consideration of whether the instant findings supporting amortizability, i.e., the jury's verdict, can withstand appellate review.

D. Whether the Jury's Verdict Is Sufficiently Supported by the Evidence

The dispositive findings made by the jury in its special verdict were (1) that the lists here involved had a separate value of $71,200, and (2) that the lists "had a reasonably ascertainable useful life * * * [of] 5 years." The government does not challenge the first finding but insists that insufficient evidence was before the jury from which the second finding could have been made. If the evidence was insufficient, the government's motions for a directed verdict and for judgment notwithstanding the verdict should have been granted. We hold that the trial judge correctly determined that the evidence was sufficient to entitle taxpayer to submit the case to the jury.

Because so few taxpayers have obtained favorable findings in cases such as the one before us, there is a paucity of reported cases discussing the level of evidence that must be surpassed if a favorable finding is to withstand appellate review. * * * [T]wo tax cases involving this very issue are particularly instructive. First, in Blaine v. United States, 5 Cir.1971, 441 F.2d 917, we found that the evidence adduced was insufficient to support the jury's verdict in favor of taxpayer. Finding much of the evidence regarding the useful life of the disputed asset to be without legal bearing, we characterized the remaining evidence as "opinions unsupported by facts of substance and materiality * * *." 441 F.2d at 919. Thus, * * * we reversed with directions that judgment be entered for the government.

On the other hand, in Manhattan Co. of Virginia, Inc. v. Commissioner, 1968, 50 T.C. 78, the Tax Court found that the following evidence was competent on the depreciability issue:

—testimony that the lists could be assigned a value separate from the other assets acquired;

—testimony that the cost of the lists correlated with anticipated revenues, computed on a per customer average;

—testimony regarding taxpayer's normal attrition rate, which averaged 20% per year; and

—evidence that 25% of the value of the lists would continue indefinitely and that the remaining 75% would become valueless at the normal attrition rate.

Finding this evidence properly relevant to the inquiry at hand—i.e., whether this particular asset was factually a wasting asset to which a value could be assigned and whether the limited useful life of the asset could be ascertained with reasonable certainty—the Tax Court allowed taxpayer to depreciate 75% of the costs of the list over a five-year period. 50 T.C. at 92–94.

We have parsed and thoroughly scrutinized the record produced in the instant case, and we find in it sufficient evidence to defeat the government's motions and to sustain the jury's verdict. Of particular importance, we find, *inter alia:*

—testimony from taxpayer's officers and employees, based upon their experience as publishers of an afternoon newspaper in the Houston area, regarding the cost of obtaining new subscriptions;

—corroborative testimony from the valuation engineers, based upon their study, discussed *supra;*

—testimony from taxpayer's officers and employees, again based on their experience, regarding the anticipated useful life of a subscription list used in connection with the publication of an afternoon newspaper in the Houston area;

—corroborative testimony from the valuation engineers, again based upon their study; and

—the results of a survey of *The Houston Chronicle's* current subscribers regarding the useful life of an average subscription, and testimony connecting the survey with *The Houston Press* subscription lists, i.e., testimony that conditions in the afternoon newspaper market in the Houston area had not been materially altered during the years in question.

We think that this direct testimony rises above the level of "unsupported opinion of the taxpayer" * * * and we conclude that the very able trial judge correctly submitted the case to the jury. The government's remaining objections on this issue pertain to the weight that should have been given to this testimony, but as we have said before:

"It is not our function to comment upon the weight of [the] evidence, nor are we in a position to say how we would decide the case were we the jurors. It is for the jury, once competent evidence has been introduced from which the necessary facts can be found, 'to weigh conflicting evidence and inferences and determine the credibility of witnesses.' Boeing Co. v. Shipman, 411 F.2d at 375.

" * * * In a case such as we have here, where shades of evidence have been produced on opposite sides of [the] issue, jury exile should be almost as rare as a museum piece * * *."

Jones v. Concrete Ready-Mix, Inc., 5 Cir.1972, 464 F.2d 1323, 1326. This issue having been properly submitted to the jury, and the jury having found the controlling facts from competent evidence, this issue will be affirmed.

E. Conclusion

Judicial tolerance compels us to say that many jurists and scholars could diagnose tax non-depreciability in the muscles and tendons of list transactions. We reject, however, the establishment of a *per se* rule and a monolithic "mass asset" theory that would amalgamate all subscriptions lists with goodwill.

Our view—that amortizability for tax purposes must turn on factual bases—is more in accord with the realities of modern business technology in a day when lists are bartered and sold as discrete vendible assets. Extreme exactitude in ascertaining the duration of an asset is a paradigm that the law does not demand. All that the law and regulations require is reasonable accuracy in forecasting the asset's useful life.

The burden to prove that an asset qualifies for tax amortizability is cast upon the taxpayer, and this taxpayer has manfully carried that heavy load as weighed by the jury. After studying the Code, Regulations, cases, testimony, and the jury's verdict, all in the light of the trial judge's meticulously thorough instructions, we can find no Achilles heel to the amortizability of these subscription lists.

* * *

See also Los Angeles Cent. Animal Hospital, Inc. v. Commissioner, 68 T.C. 269 (1977) (Acq. 1978–2 C.B. 2) where the court distinguished medical records of a veterinary hospital from goodwill; the taxpayer could amortize the amount allocable to the records over a seven-year period. However, in General Television, Inc. v. United States, 449 F.Supp. 609 (D.Minn.1978), affirmed 598 F.2d 1148 (8th Cir.1979), subscriber contracts of purchased cable television companies were deemed indistinguishable from goodwill and, therefore, could not be amortized.

Problems

1. Television Station, Inc. is a corporation operating a television station. It sold all of its assets to KFOX Corporation on the first day of the latter's tax year. Included among the assets of Television was a transferable contract with "Wolfman" Bonner, a sports announcer of national renown, running for a period of five years from the date of sale. This contract was automatically renewable for another period of five years

unless one of the parties exercises an option to terminate within a stated period of time.

During the tax year, KFOX claimed a deduction for the amortization of Bonner's contract. KFOX placed a five year estimated useful life on the contract and allocated the sum of $2,000,000 to the employment contract out of a total of $8,000,000 paid for the business. A specific sum was also allocated to goodwill. Representatives of the Internal Revenue Service objected, vaguely referring to the mass asset rule and the Westinghouse case.

(a) KFOX asks for your advice with reference to:

(1) Its prospects for establishing the deduction in the contract. Consider the Westinghouse Broadcasting Company, Nachman, and Houston Chronicle cases and Reg. § 1.167(a)–3.

(2) What information it should gather?

(b) How should Bonner's contract have been structured to eliminate any tax problems? What other difficulties would then be presented?

(c) Assume also that when KFOX was organized it expended $500,000 in various fees in order to obtain a broadcasting license which runs for three years. Taxpayer wanted to deduct the $500,000 over a three year period. The Service refused to permit any deduction. Taxpayer asks you to explain the probable reason for the refusal and the likely result. Assume also that when the seller was organized it expended $500,000 in various fees to obtain a broadcasting license which runs for three years. Is this expenditure deductible? If so, over how long a period? Consider § 195.

2. (a) Reconsider the Big Mac Food Services Corporation, the purchaser of the Papa Schultz grocery store in Problem 1 on page 151. How can the purchaser recover the cost of the various assets it acquired, including the amount paid for goodwill? See Reg. § 1.167(a)–3 and reconsider the Raytheon case on page 143.

(b) Assume the sales contract contained a covenant not to compete by Papa Schultz, which runs for five years. The contract allocates $50,000 of the purchase price to this promise not to compete.

(i) How will the purchaser treat the $50,000 it paid for the covenant?

(ii) How must the seller treat the $50,000 received for his promise not to compete? Is it includible in gross income? If so, when, and what is the character of that income?

(iii) Why will the Service usually accept the contract's labelling of the $50,000 as an amount paid for goodwill or for a covenant not to compete?

3. Tex purchased a professional football team for $50,000,000. Among the rights he acquired were a franchise in the NFL, a stadium lease with five years left to run, the right to participate in the annual NFL draft of college football players, the right to proceeds from the league's television contracts, and the right to royalties earned by NFL Films and NFL Properties. He also acquired the 50 players presently under contract to

the team. What assets may be written off under § 168? Under § 167? What useful lives would you have for those assets? Consider Reg. § 1.167(a)–3. How would you allocate the purchase price among the acquired assets? Compare Selig v. United States, 740 F.2d 572 (7th Cir. 1984), with Laird v. United States, 556 F.2d 1224 (5th Cir.1977), cert. denied 434 U.S. 1014, 98 S.Ct. 729, 54 L.Ed.2d 758 (1978).

Chapter 9

PERSONAL DEDUCTIONS

A. INTRODUCTION

Although personal expenses are generally nondeductible under § 262, the Code permits a variety of deductions for expenses clearly personal in nature. This chapter considers medical expenses (§ 213), charitable contributions (§ 170), alimony (§ 215), interest (§ 163), taxes (§ 164) and casualty and theft losses (§ 165(c)(3)). Note that all of these deductions, with the exception of alimony, are specifically exempted from the two percent floor on itemized deductions. § 67(b). Alimony is deductible from gross income in computing adjusted gross income and is therefore, not an itemized deduction subject to § 67(a). § 62(a)(10).

Allowance for personal deductions is usually perceived to represent significant departures from the economic concept of net income as the relevant tax base. However, is this always true? Personal deductions are generally allowed to achieve some Congressional purpose. As you examine each personal deduction provision covered in this chapter you should attempt to determine and analyze the policy rationale for that deduction and whether that Code provision effectively achieves the desired purpose.

References: Andrews, Personal Deductions in an Ideal Income Tax, 86 Harv.L.Rev. 309 (1972); Bittker, Income Tax Deductions, Credits, and Subsidies for Personal Expenditures, 16 J. of Law and Econ. 193 (1973); Turnier, Evaluating Personal Deductions in an Income Tax— The Ideal, 66 Cornell L.Rev. 262 (1981).

B. MEDICAL EXPENSES

Introduction. Under § 213, medical and dental care expenses incurred by a taxpayer, the taxpayer's spouse, and the taxpayer's dependents and paid by the taxpayer during the year, if not compensated by insurance, may be deducted by the taxpayer within specified limits. The annual deduction is limited to medical expenses in excess of 7.5 percent of the taxpayer's adjusted gross income. § 213(a). Drug expenses which qualify for the deduction are limited to two categories: prescription drugs (defined in § 213(d)(3)) and insulin. Remember that § 106 excludes medical insurance premiums paid by an employer from an employee's gross income. Reread pp. 350–353.

The legislative history reproduced here indicates the Congressional rationale for the medical expense deduction and provides several reasons why Congress revamped the medical expense deduction in 1982. Consider the following excerpt from the Joint Committee on Taxation, General Explanation of the Revenue Provisions of the Tax Equity and Fiscal Responsibility Act of 1982, 24–25 (1982):

> The primary rationale for allowing an itemized deduction for medical expenses is that "extraordinary" medical costs—those in excess of a floor designed to exclude predictable, recurring expenses—reflect an economic hardship, beyond the individual's control, which reduces the ability to pay Federal income tax. In recent years, however, because medical costs have risen faster than incomes and because of the broad coverage of expenses (such as capital expenses and transportation expenses), an increasing number of individuals have claimed deductions for expenses in excess of the [then] floor of 3 percent of adjusted gross income. As a result, a larger number of individuals have, in effect, received partial reimbursement for their medical expenses, thereby creating an incentive for further health care spending and exacerbating the problem of rising medical care expenditures. Further, many of the expenses which are small relative to income do not significantly reduce ability to pay taxes, especially since they could have been avoided by the purchase of insurance. Finally, the medical expense deduction is complex, since detailed records must be kept and difficult distinctions must be made between expenses for medical treatment (deductible) and expenses for ordinary consumption (nondeductible). For these reasons, Congress decided to limit the use of the medical expense deduction by raising the floor from 3 to 5 percent of adjusted gross income.

> Further, the separate deduction for health insurance premiums and the separate 1-percent floor for drugs complicated the computation of the deduction, and Congress decided to eliminate them. Finally, Congress eliminated the deduction for non-prescription drugs other than insulin to simplify the deduction, to conform its coverage more closely to the coverage of private health insurance policies, and because expenses for non-prescription drugs are more likely to represent expenses for ordinary consumption than "extraordinary" medical costs that should be deductible.

The Tax Reform Act of 1986 increased the percentage floor from 5 to 7.5 percent of adjusted gross income. The legislative history states:

> By utilizing a deduction floor of [7.5] percent of the taxpayer's adjusted gross income, the [Act] continues the benefit of deductibility where an individual incurs extraordinary medical expenses—for example, as a result of uninsured surgery, severe chronic disease, or catastrophic illness. Thus, the [Act] retains deductibility where the ex-

penses are so great that they absorb a substantial portion of the taxpayer's income and hence substantially affect the taxpayer's ability to pay taxes. The committee also believes that the higher floor, by reducing the number of returns claiming the deduction, will alleviate complexity associated with the deduction, including substantiation and audit verification problems and numerous definitional issues. (Senate Finance Committee Report on H.R. 3838, 99th Cong., 2d Sess. 59 (1986)).

Questions

1. Why will most, if not all of, the increased tax receipts from the 1982 and 1986 changes come from middle income taxpayers rather than the wealthy? Could Congress have solved its concerns without the burden falling on the middle class?

2. (a) In considering the rationale for the medical expense deduction, do medical care expenses reduce the taxpayer's net worth or ability to pay taxes? Does the medical expense deduction serve "to measure the taxpayer's income in assessing his taxpaying capacity"[1] and, therefore, should it be more valuable to higher bracket taxpayers? Contrast expenditures for food and clothing.

(b) Why is a 7.5% floor imposed? Does the 7.5% floor serve the Congressional purpose of only allowing a deduction for medical expenses which impose a large and unexpected burden on a taxpayer's resources? Should the 7.5% floor be raised or lowered?

(c) What about individuals with little or no income against which to apply the deduction? Should the deduction be replaced with a (refundable) credit? Would a credit measure taxpaying capacity?

Reference: Newman, The Medical Expense Deduction: A Preliminary Postmortem, 53 So.Calif.L.Rev. 787 (1980).

Definition of Medical Care. Problems arise concerning what items may be considered "medical care." Under § 213(d), the term "medical care" includes payments for prevention, diagnosis, treatment and cure of disease, as well as for transportation primarily for and essential to medical care, and insurance covering medical care. A gloss on the definition is found in Reg. § 1.213–1(e)(1)(ii) and in the legislative history of the statute:

SENATE REPORT NO. 1622
83rd Cong. 2d Sess. 219–220 (1954).

Subsection (e) defines medical care to mean amounts paid for the diagnosis, cure, mitigation, treatment, or prevention of diseases or for the purpose of affecting any structure or function of the body (including

1. Bittker, Income Tax Deductions, Credits and Subsidies for Personal Expend- itures, 16 J. of Law and Econ. 193, 208 (1973).

amounts paid for accident or health insurance), or for transportation primarily for and essential to medical care. The deduction permitted for "transportation primarily for and essential to medical care" clarifies existing law in that it specifically excludes deduction of any meals and lodging while away from home receiving medical treatment. For example, if a doctor prescribes that a patient must go to Florida in order to alleviate specific chronic ailments and to escape unfavorable climatic conditions which have proven injurious to the health of the taxpayer, and the travel is prescribed for reasons other than the general improvement of a patient's health, the cost of the patient's transportation to Florida would be deductible * * *. However, if a doctor prescribed an appendectomy and the taxpayer chose to go to Florida for the operation not even his transportation costs would be deductible. The subsection is not intended otherwise to change the existing definitions of medical care, to deny the cost of ordinary ambulance transportation nor to deny the cost of food or lodging provided as part of a hospital bill.

A taxpayer who uses his own car for transportation for medical care purposes cannot claim a medical expense deduction for depreciation (or Accelerated Cost Recovery), but he can deduct the mileage at a specified rate per mile. In Rev. Proc. 64–15, 1964–1 C.B. (Part I) 676, the Service concluded that depreciation (Accelerated Cost Recovery) is not an amount paid for purposes of § 213(d). See also, Weary v. United States, 510 F.2d 435 (10th Cir.1975).

A review of the scope of medical costs which are deductible provides the taxpayer with a useful guide for determining how expenditures should be structured in order to better insure deductibility. It is not assumed that the taxpayer will incur medical costs merely because they are deductible from his adjusted gross income. Medical expenses are likely to be nondiscretionary. The problem in this area is that certain expenses of the ill resemble expenses healthy individuals make for their comfort and enjoyment. The following materials provide examples of the nature of this problem.

Unfortunately, the line between nondeductible personal expenses (§ 262) and deductible medical expenses (§ 213) cannot be drawn with precision. For example, the Service ruled that expenses for marriage counseling were not deductible in Rev.Rul. 75–319, 1975–2 C.B. 88, noting that the expenditure was not incurred for the prevention or alleviation of a medical condition but to improve the marriage. Yet, in Rev.Rul. 75–187, 1975–1 C.B. 92, the cost of psychiatric treatment for a couple's sexual inadequacy and incompatibility was deductible. More surprising was Rev.Rul. 76–332, 1976–2 C.B. 81, allowing a deduction for cosmetic plastic surgery for a face lift. Even though its purpose was solely to improve taxpayer's personal appearance, it constituted medical care since the operation affected the body.

However, virtue may also be its own reward. Rev.Rul. 79–162, 1979–1 C.B. 116 concerned a taxpayer who, at his physician's suggestion, took part in a nine-week course on how to quit smoking by changing his personal habits. The taxpayer took the course not to cure a specific ailment, but to improve his general health and well-being. Notwithstanding the doctor's recommendation, the fee paid for the smoke-quitter course was deemed a nondeductible medical expense. No deduction, the Service reiterated, is allowable for something merely beneficial to one's health or for personal, living or family expenses. Rev.Rul. 79–151, 1979–1 C.B. 116, described a taxpayer, whose physician advised him to lose weight, and who enrolled in a course to learn how to draw up a diet and stick with it. Again, the fee for the diet course was nondeductible. The objective of improving one's appearance, health and sense of well-being was viewed as insufficient to qualify as medical care. However, in Letter Ruling 8004111 (October 31, 1979), a taxpayer was allowed a deduction for the cost incurred in a weight reduction program because two physicians recommended such a program for the treatment of specific diseases, namely, hypertension and obesity.

A particularly difficult problem arises with swimming pools. When can the cost of a swimming pool be a deductible medical cost? In Rev.Rul. 83–33, 1983–1 C.B. 70, an individual was suffering from a degenerative disease that resulted in a progressive weakness and decreased use of the knees and legs. To slow the effects of the disease, his doctor prescribed a treatment of swimming several times a day. The taxpayer constructed an indoor lap pool in order to follow the prescribed exercise program. A deduction for medical care was allowed but only to the extent the cost of the pool exceeded the resulting increase in the value of his home. A key factor in allowing the medical expense deduction was the finding that the primary purpose for the installation of the pool was directly related to taxpayer's medical care.

In Ferris v. Commissioner, 582 F.2d 1112 (7th Cir.1978), the taxpayer expended $195,000 to construct a pool which was architecturally and aesthetically compatible with his luxury residence. The court remanded to determine the difference between the amount expended and the minimum reasonable cost of a functionally adequate swimming pool. Although the excessive costs would not be a deductible medical care expense, such costs may be capitalized and added to the basis of the house. Read Reg. § 1.213–1(e)(1)(iii).

The more difficult situations involve expenditures which would never be incurred but for a medical problem. In Levine v. Commissioner, 695 F.2d 57 (2d Cir.1982), cert. denied 462 U.S. 1132, 103 S.Ct. 3113, 77 L.Ed.2d 1367 (1983), the taxpayers provided an apartment and an automobile for their mentally ill son to permit him to continue medically necessary treatment at a nearby clinic on an outpatient basis. No deduction was permitted for these costs because they were not necessary to the legitimate medical treatment received. The court went on and stated:

> We are not unsympathetic to the argument presented by Mrs. Levine and to the efforts she and her husband are making to provide their son Guy with the best medical care available. However, a court's personal view of what is wise, enlightened or compassionate should not substitute for legislative judgment. We are constrained by the statutes and regulations as written, and by the expressed purposes of those who wrote them (695 F.2d at 58).

Congress responded to the harshness of denying deductions for the costs of lodging incurred while away from home to obtain medical care by adding § 213(d)(2) in 1984. Does this Code provision mean that a parent accompanying a child to an out-of-town hospital can deduct his lodging costs while his child is receiving the specialized care? Note that the parent must qualify for the transportation deduction under § 213(d)(1)(B). How did Congress deal with the concern that a taxpayer may seek to deduct lodging while on a vacation?

Despite this most recent attempt to do equity, there still exist situations where expenditures incurred only because of a bona fide medical condition are not allowed as a medical deduction. Compare the following situation with the Smith case on child care at p. 371.

REV. RUL. 78–266
1978–2 C.B. 123.

Advice has been requested whether, under the circumstances described below, a medical expense deduction is allowable to a taxpayer for amounts paid for care of the taxpayer's children to enable the taxpayer to visit a physician for medical treatment.

The taxpayer, *B*, has an ailment that requires treatment in a physician's office twice weekly on a regular basis. *B* is the parent of three normal, healthy children under six years of age. *B* hires a baby sitter to care for the children each time *B* goes to the physician's office and receives medical treatment.

* * *

Section 213(e) of the Code defines the term "medical care" as amounts paid for the diagnosis, cure, mitigation, treatment or prevention of disease, or for the purpose of affecting any structure or function of the body; for insurance covering such medical care; or for transportation primarily for and essential to medical care.

Section 1.213–1(e)(1)(ii) of the Income Tax Regulations provides that deductions for expenditures for medical care allowable under section 213 will be confined strictly to expenses incurred primarily for the prevention or alleviation of a physical or mental defect or illness.

The courts have denied a medical expense deduction for expenses that are not directly for medical care, even though the expense may have some relation to medical care. For example, in Ochs v. Commissioner, 195 F.2d 692 (2d Cir.1952), cert. denied, 344 U.S. 827 (1952), a deduction was denied for expenditures incurred to send the taxpayer's children to a boarding school on a physician's advice to alleviate the taxpayer's spouse's suffering from throat cancer that required her to rest her voice. In McVicker v. United States, 194 F.Supp. 607 (S.D.Cal. 1961), a deduction was denied for the taxpayers' payments to a domestic servant hired on a physician's advice that housework would cause a relapse of the taxpayer-wife's illness. In Wendell v. Commissioner, 12 T.C. 161 (1949), a medical expense deduction was denied for salaries paid to practical nurses employed to care for a child whose mother died at childbirth, the child being normal and having no unusual illness.

In Gerstacker v. Commissioner, 414 F.2d 448 (6th Cir.1969), the court permitted a medical expense deduction for legal expenses necessary to establish guardianship for the taxpayer's wife, a mental patient, in order to keep her in a mental institution for care. Rev.Rul. 71–281, 1971–2 C.B. 165, announces that the Internal Revenue Service will follow *Gerstacker*. The facts in the instant care are distinguishable from *Gerstacker* and Rev.Rul. 71–281 because in *Gerstacker* the expense was essential to the medical treatment of the person for whom the expense was incurred in that the payment for legal services for the taxpayer's wife was made to obtain the medical treatment.

In the instant case, as in *Ochs, McVicker,* and *Wendell*, the expenditures for the care of *B*'s children are not expenses for medical care, even though the expenditures have some relation to medical care. Accordingly, a medical expense deduction is not allowable to *B* for amounts paid for the care of *B*'s children to enable *B* to visit a physician for medical treatment. Such expenditures are personal expenses within the meaning of section 262 of the Code and, therefore, are nondeductible.

Rev.Rul. 73–597, 1973–2 C.B. 69, similarly denies a charitable contributions deduction under section 170 of the Code for amounts paid for a baby sitter to care for the taxpayers' children to enable the taxpayer to perform gratuitous services for a charitable organization to which contributions are deductible.

Rev.Rul. 71–281 is distinguished.

Reference: Feld, Abortion to Aging: Problems of Definition in the Medical Expense Tax Deduction, 58 B.U. L.Rev. 165 (1978).

Timing the Payment of Medical Expenses. Section 213(a) permits a deduction for medical expenses paid during the taxable year, regardless of whether the taxpayer uses the cash or accrual method. Reg. § 1.213–1(a). The widespread use of credit cards to purchase goods and services raises the question of when an otherwise deductible expenditure may be deducted when the taxpayer "charges" a purchase. Section 213(a) requires deductible medical care expenses to be "paid" during the taxable year. Read Reg. § 1.213–1(a)(1). See also § 170(a)(1) and Reg. § 1.170A–1(a)(1). In Rev.Rul. 78–39, 1978–1 C.B. 73, the Service allowed a taxpayer to deduct a medical expense when the taxpayer charged the item on his credit card. The credit card holder immediately incurs a debt to a third party when the card is used. When a deductible payment is made with borrowed money, the taxpayer receives the deduction in the year the expense is paid, not when the loan is repaid provided the taxpayer does not borrow the funds from the person to whom payment is made. Granan v. Commissioner, 55 T.C. 753 (1971). The use of a credit card is deemed the equivalent to the payment of the medical expense with borrowed funds.

Problems

1. Sally is a resident of New York. She was ordered by her doctor to spend the winter in Florida to alleviate a heart condition that would be aggrevated by remaining in cold weather at home. Assume it is not disputed that the trip is a medical necessity (often taxpayers have not established a direct relationship between the treatment of a disease and a trip to a warmer climate, see Reg. § 1.213–1(e)(1)(iv)). Sally went to Florida and incurred the following expenses:

(a) fees for a doctor in Florida;

(b) transportation expenses to Florida and back;

(c) meals and lodging in Florida and en route. If taxpayer is a diabetic, may she deduct the cost of specially prepared food?

(d) expense of hospitalization in Florida due to a sudden respiratory illness;

(e) expense of a weight reduction program pursuant to a physician's recommendation;

(f) the purchase of eye glasses;

(g) transportation, meals and lodging expenses of her husband to and from Florida and while in Florida;

(h) on her return to New York, taxpayer installed a central home air conditioning system at a cost of $5,000. Her doctor advised her such installation was required to care for her respiratory condition. After the installation, the value of the taxpayer's house increased $3,000.

What expenses constitute medical care? Consider § 213(d) and Reg. § 1.213–1(e)(1)(iii)–(v).

2. Henry, a single taxpayer, incurred and paid $2,300 in qualified medical care expenses during Year 1. His adjusted gross income for Year 1 equaled $20,000. Henry's itemized deductions for Year 1 equaled $6,700 (including $800 in medical deductions). Why can he only deduct $800 in medical care expenses, when his qualified medical care expenses were $2,300? Consider §§ 67(b)(5) and 213(a). During Year 2 Henry is reimbursed $1,900 by his health insurance company. What are the income tax

consequences for both years? Consider §§ 213(a), 63, 105(b), 111, and Reg. § 1.213–1(g).

C. CHARITABLE CONTRIBUTIONS

1. CHARITY CONSTRUED: MAXIMUM ANNUAL DEDUCTIONS FOR INDIVIDUALS

Individuals may annually deduct up to 20 percent of their adjusted gross income (more precisely, their charitable contribution base [2]) for gifts to certain charitable organizations. § 170(b)(1)(B). The requirements for these organizations are listed at § 170(c) and include those organized and operated exclusively for religious, charitable, scientific, literary, or educational purposes, or to foster national or international amateur sports competition, or for the prevention of cruelty to children or animals. No part of the net earnings of such organization may inure to the benefit of any private person. The organization may not attempt to influence legislation or participate or intervene in political campaigns on behalf of candidates to public office.

Deduction of an additional 30 percent, making a total of 50 percent annually, is authorized by § 170(b)(1)(A) for gifts by individuals to (but not for the use of) certain types of organizations (so-called public charities), including churches, educational organizations, hospitals or medical research organizations, and publicly supported organizations.

If a taxpayer makes contributions to 50 percent charities and 20 percent charities in the same year, the taxpayer first takes a deduction against the limit of contributions to the 50 percent charities. If the taxpayer's contribution to the 50 percent charities do not exhaust the limit on 50 percent charities, the taxpayer may contribute the lesser of: (1) contributions to the 20 percent charities up to 20 percent of his charitable contribution base or (2) the remaining amount on the 50 percent limit. § 170(b)(1)(B).

A carry forward is available to the taxpayer who exceeds the 50 percent limit on contributions to 50 percent charities. § 170(d)(1). A taxpayer may not carry forward contributions to 20 percent charities in excess of the limit for a taxable year. § 170(d)(1). In determining the availability of a carry forward, a taxpayer takes contributions to 50 percent charities in a taxable year against the 50 percent limit and then considers contributions to 20 percent charities. § 170(d)(1).

Reference: Wittenbach, Charting the Current Rules on Charitable Contributions, 63 Taxes 541 (1985).

2. SOME LIMITATIONS ON CHARITABLE CONTRIBUTIONS

No deduction is allowable for a contribution of services to a charity and no income is imputed to the taxpayer for the value of such services. Reg. § 1.170A–1(g). Section 170(a)(1) requires the payment of a contri-

---

2. A taxpayer's charitable contribution base equals his adjusted gross income without regard to any net operating loss carryback authorized by § 172. § 170(b)(1)(F).

bution, presumably in money or other property. Unreimbursed expenses (for example, travel expenses, but not the prorated depreciation on a personal automobile) in connection with services donated to a charity are, however, deductible. Reg. § 1.170A–1(g) and Orr v. United States, 343 F.2d 553 (5th Cir.1965). Other deductible unreimbursed out-of-pocket expenses incurred while performing charitable services include telephone calls, cost and maintenance of uniforms, and special equipment and materials required to perform duties. However, the parents of an Olympic figure skater could not deduct the cost of skating lessons and travel expenses of the skater and her mother as unreimbursed expenses made incident to rendering services to the U.S. Olympic Committee. In Babilonia v. Commissioner, 681 F.2d 678 (9th Cir.1982), the court reasoned that the taxpayer's daughter skated for her own benefit, not to render services to the Olympic Committee; also all of the expenditures conferred a substantial, direct benefit on the taxpayer and her daughter.

Child care expenses which free the taxpayer to perform gratuitous services for the charity are nondeductible. Rev.Rul. 73–597, 1973–2 C.B. 69. Reconsider Rev.Rul. 78–266 discussed earlier in this chapter.

Pursuant to § 170(k), no charitable deduction is allowed for traveling expenses (including costs for meals and lodging) incurred in performing services away from home for a charitable organization unless "there is no significant element of personal pleasure, recreation, or vacation in such travel." The legislative history of the Tax Reform Act of 1986 (Tax Reform Act of [1986], Report of the Committee on Ways and Means, House of Representatives on H.R. 3838, 99th Cong. 1st Sess. 129 (1985)) indicates that this rule applies to expenses relating to travel by the taxpayer or a person associated with the taxpayer (for example, a family member). However, the rule "does not apply to the extent that the taxpayer pays for travel by third parties who are participants in the charitable activity (for example, expenses for travel by children unrelated to the taxpayer, personally incurred by the troop leader for a tax-exempt youth group who takes children belonging to the group on a camping trip)". A key interpretative issue is whether the travel away from home involves a significant element of personal pleasure, recreation or vacation. The legislative history notes, "[T]he fact that a taxpayer enjoys providing services to the charitable organization will not lead to denial of the deduction. For example, a troop leader for a tax-exempt youth group who takes children belonging to the group on a camping trip may qualify for a charitable deduction with respect to his or her own travel expenses if he or she is on duty in a genuine and substantial sense throughout the trip, even if he or she enjoys the trip or enjoys supervising the children." (Tax Reform Act of [1986], Report of the Committee on Ways and Means, House of Representatives on H.R. 3838, 99th Cong. 1st Sess. 129 (1985).)

Section 170(f)(3) generally disallows the deduction for the gift to a charity of the use of property, except if such interest is transferred in trust. Section 162(b) prevents a deduction under § 162(a) if the deduction would have been available under § 170 but for the percentage limitations of § 170.

To be deductible in a particular year, the taxpayer must pay the charitable contribution within that year. § 170(a)(1). A taxpayer makes a contribution by effectuating delivery. Reg. § 1.170A–1(b). A contribution charged to a donor's credit card is paid when the taxpayer makes the charge, not when the taxpayer pays the bank. Rev.Rul. 78–38, 1978–1 C.B. 67.

The limitations imposed on the contribution of assets which have appreciated in value are considered at pp. 1020–1023.

Reference: Newman, The Inequitable Tax Treatment of Expenses Incident to Charitable Service, 47 Ford.L.Rev. 139 (1978).

Problems

1. Can Giver receive a charitable contribution deduction if he

(a) gives cash to an individual on welfare? Consider § 170(a)(1), (b)(1)(A), and (c). What if he gave cash to a charitable organization which solicits funds for designated needy beneficiaries?

(b) attends a fund raising dinner for a local charity, paying $150 per plate? The value of the meal is $35. Consider § 170(c). Would it make a difference if Giver wrote a check for $150 payable to the charity? What if Giver does not attend the dinner?

(c) teaches Sunday school at his church each week? Is the value of his services deductible? Consider Reg. § 1.170A–1(g). Is this correct? Why? Is the cost of his travel deductible? Can he deduct the depreciation, insurance, maintenance, and repairs on his car used for travel to his church? Consider § 170(k).

(d) allows his church to use an empty retail store in his building for a rummage sale. The space normally rents for $850 per month? Can he deduct the rental value of the store? Will the rental value of the store be included in his gross income?

2. What problem would you foresee if the trustees of a private school determine not to raise tuition but rather to put on a high-pressure fund-raising effort among parents, pointing out to them how contributions will cost the parents less than an equal number of dollars of increased tuition?

3. What is the rationale for the charitable contribution deduction? Consider: (1) the benefits of a pluralistic system in terms of spending and decision-making, the encouragement of experimental programs and ideas, and the dispersion of power; (2) the relief given to the public, particularly governmental units, from certain burdens; (3) the incentive to private giving, a. socially desirable activity. Is the tax deduction "fair" with respect to taxpayers in different tax brackets? Do the deductions benefit upper income taxpayers? Do wealthy individuals exercise "excessive" control over charities? Do the financial needs of charities and their reliance on gifts of appreciated property outweigh any inequities?

Consider also the following alternatives:

(a) limiting the charitable contribution deduction to the amount by which contributions exceed a stated percentage (for example, 2%) of the taxpayer's adjusted gross income. Consider the administrative difficulties in monitoring small donations to eligible charities and the income tax deduction as an incentive for the contribution of small amounts to charitable organizations (what is the efficiency of the deduction mechanism?) As giving reaches what percentage of income, are taxes likely to affect the actual level of donations?

(b) allowing a deduction equal to 100% of adjusted gross income or removing the percentage limitation on gifts to or for the use of 50 percent charities.

(c) replacing the deduction with a credit;

References: Bittker, Charitable Contributions: Tax Deductions or Matching Grants? 28 Tax L.Rev. 37 (1972); McDaniel, Federal Matching Grants for Charitable Contributions: A Substitute for the Income Tax Deduction, 27 Tax L.Rev. 377 (1972); Andrews, Personal Deductions in an Ideal Income Tax, 86 Harv.L.Rev. 309, 347–48, 354–70 (1972).

D. MARITAL DISSOLUTIONS: SEPARATION AND DIVORCE

From a tax-planning point of view, separation and divorce raise issues concerning the income tax treatment of alimony or support payments, property settlements, child support and legal expenses incurred in marital dissolutions. In addition, gift and estate tax considerations must be addressed. The tax consequences of separation and divorce raise complex questions not often perceived or understood by couples in the process of dissolving their marital relationship.

1. ALIMONY PAYMENTS

Section 71 provides that certain payments for alimony or support designated as alimony are included in the recipient's gross income. Section 215 then gives a deduction to the payor spouse for alimony payments taxable to the recipient spouse under § 71. The purpose of this symmetrical system for inclusion and deduction was to relieve the tax burden otherwise placed on the payor spouse. Prior to 1942, the payor received no deduction for the payment of alimony and the recipient did not have to include the payments in gross income. Gould v. Gould, 245 U.S. 151, 38 S.Ct. 53, 62 L.Ed. 211 (1917). During the early years of the income tax law this was not a harsh result as income tax rates were relatively low. However, this situation became an intolerable burden on the payor spouse when income tax rates increased to high levels to raise the revenues necessary to finance the war effort. The legislative history allowing the current tax treatment for alimony payments expressed the concern that a spouse's alimony and income tax payments could exhaust his entire income:

> The existing law does not tax alimony payments to the wife who receives them, nor does it allow the husband to take any deduction on account of his entire net income even though a large portion of his income goes to his wife as alimony * * *. The increased tax rates would intensify this hardship and in many cases the husband would not have sufficient income left after paying alimony to meet his income tax obligation. H.R.Rep. No. 2333, 77th Cong. 2d Sess. 46 (1942).

Treating alimony payments as income to the recipient and giving the payor a deduction shifts the tax burden of that income to the spouse who actually has the economic use of these funds. However, this symmetrical objective was not always achieved because the alimony deduction was originally an itemized deduction. If the payor did not itemize his personal deductions (i.e., if he had no excess itemized deductions using current terminology), he would not be able to use the alimony deduction; while the recipient still included the alimony in gross income. Congress remedied this problem in 1976 by allowing the payor spouse to deduct alimony in computing his adjusted gross income under § 62(13).

Although the Tax Reform Act of 1984 maintained the income/deduction symmetry for alimony payments, it significantly altered the complex and sometimes rigid statutory rules for determining what constituted alimony payments. According to the legislative history, Congress sought to eliminate the confusion as to what constitutes alimony for income tax purposes.

> The committee believes that the present law definition of alimony is not sufficiently objective. Differences in State laws create differences in Federal tax consequences and administrative difficulties for the IRS. The committee believes that a uniform Federal standard should be set forth to determine what constitutes alimony for Federal tax purposes. This will make it easier for the Internal Revenue Service, the parties to a divorce, and the courts to apply the rules to the facts in any particular case and should lead to less litigation. The committee bill attempts to define alimony in a way that would conform to general notions of what type of payments constitute alimony as distinguished from property settlements and to prevent the deduction of large, one-time lump-sum property settlements. H.R.Rep. No. 432, 98th Cong.2d Sess. 1495 (1984).

An alimony payment for purposes of the deduction provided in § 215(a) and the inclusion in gross income under § 71(a) must satisfy all of the requirements of § 71(b) and not be for child support within the meaning of § 71(c). These requirements are as follows:

> (1) The payments can only be in cash. § 71(b)(1). Under prior law alimony could be in property which raised problems as to the value of that property. A payment can also qualify where a cash payment is made to a third party for the benefit of the payee spouse.

Fed'l Inc. Tax (S. & H.) ACB—23

(2) The payments can only be made under a divorce or separation instrument. § 71(b)(1)(A). Qualifying divorce or separation instruments are defined in § 71(b)(2). An oral separation agreement is not sufficient even though it may be valid under state law.

(3) The divorce or separation instrument does not designate the payment as not includible in gross income under § 71 and not deductible under § 215. § 71(b)(1)(B). This provision allows spouses flexibility in determining the income tax consequences of payments made as part of the dissolution of their marriage. The planner should be aware that the parties are given the option by written agreement that payments otherwise qualifying as alimony need not be so treated for income tax purposes. Seemingly, such a designation could be changed by a later amendment to the agreement.

(4) The liability for the payments must cease on the death of the recipient. § 71(b)(1)(D). This requirement is intended to prevent the deduction for payments which are in effect part of a property settlement unrelated to the support needs of the recipient. Furthermore, payments will not qualify to the extent there is any liability to make any payment in cash or property as a substitute for such payments after the death of the recipient.

(5) The payments cannot be fixed as child support for a child of the payor spouse. § 71(c)(1).

(6) The spouses, if legally separated under a decree of divorce or separate maintenance, may not be members of the same household at the time the payments are made. § 71(b)(1)(C). If a spouse is immediately preparing to depart from the household of the other spouse, the payments will qualify.

(7) The payments must not be front-loaded. § 71(f). Special rules are provided to ensure that payments for property settlements are not disguised as alimony payments. In brief, the Tax Reform Act of 1986 provides that excess alimony payments for the first and second post-separation years are includible in the payor spouse's gross income (and are deductible by the payee spouse) beginning in the third post-separation year. The excess payments for the first and second post-separation years are defined, respectively, in § 71(f)(3) and (f)(4). The term "post-separation years" is defined in § 71(f)(6). As a result, any payment initially qualifying as deductible alimony under § 71(b) may later lose that status if it runs afoul of § 71(f). § 71(f)(1).

The legislative history states:

* * * [I]f the alimony payments in the first year exceed the average payments in the second and third year by more than $15,000, the excess amounts are recaptured in the third year by requiring the payor to include the excess in income and allowing the payee who previously included the alimony in income a deduction for that amount in computing adjusted gross income. A similar rule applies to the extent the payments in the second year exceed the payments in the third year by more then $15,000. This rule is intended to prevent persons whose divorce occurs near the end of the year from making a deductible

property settlement at the beginning of the next year. Recapture is not required if either party dies or if the payee spouse remarries by the end of the calendar year which is two years after the payments began and payments cease by reason of that event. Also the rule does not apply to temporary support payments (described in sec. 71(b)(2)(C)) or to payments which fluctuate as a result of a continuing liability to pay, for at least three years, a fixed portion or portions of income from the earnings of a business, property or services.

Thus, for example, if the payor makes alimony payments of $50,000 in the first year and no payments in the second or third year, $35,000 will be recaptured (assuming none of the exceptions apply). If instead the payments are $50,000 in the first year, $20,000 in the second year and nothing in the third year, the recapture amount will consist of $5,000 from the second year (the excess over $15,000) plus $27,500 for the first year (the excess of $50,000 over the sum of $15,000 plus $7,500). (The $7,500 is the average payments for years two and three after reducing the payments by the $5,000 recaptured from year two.)

(Tax Reform Act of 1986, Conference Report to Accompany H.R. 3838, House of Representatives, 99th Cong. 2d Sess. II–849 (1986)).

If these statutory conditions are met, then the payments are alimony. It is immaterial that the payments may be specifically designated as consideration for property.

If the payments do not satisfy the statutory conditions, then under § 71(b) they do not constitute alimony (or separate maintenance) payments. Accordingly, the recipient does not realize any income and the payor receives no deduction. Instead, the payments are treated as either for child support or as a payment for property, as considered below. In brief, a payment which is part of a property settlement is not treated as alimony because the payor essentially purchases the recipient's property. For example, if a married couple owns their home jointly and the husband desires to continue to reside in it, the payments to the wife for her share of the house should not give rise to a deduction for alimony payments.

Reference: Hjorth, Divorce, Taxes, And The 1984 Tax Reform Act: An Inadequate Response To An Old Problem, 61 Wash.L.Rev. 151 (1986).

2. CHILD SUPPORT PAYMENTS

Since amounts payable for the support of minor children are not income to the recipient or deductible by the payor under §§ 71(c) and 215(b), it is important to determine whether cash payments are alimony or child support. A key issue is whether or not the amounts payable for child support are specifically designated as such in the operative decree, instrument or agreement as required by § 71(c)(1). Without the ability to determine the exact portion of a cash payment allocable to child support the payment will be fully taxable as alimony to the recipient and deductible by the payor. However, a reference to a specific amount is no longer necessary. Under § 71(c)(2) a payment is "fixed" as child support if it is reduced or eliminated on the happening of a contingency or event involving a child (e.g. attaining a specified age). The same rule applies if the reduction is to occur at a time that can be "clearly associated" with such a contingency or event relating to the child.

For tax planning purposes, it may be advantageous to treat undesignated child support payments as taxable alimony if the recipient spouse is in a lower marginal income tax bracket than the payor spouse. Part of the tax savings to the payor could be passed on to the recipient in the form of larger alimony payments.

Generally, a parent's obligation to support a child terminates when the child reaches the age of majority. However, payments which must be used for the support of children even after they reach adulthood are not alimony for income tax purposes. See Emmons v. Commissioner, 36 T.C. 728 (1961), affirmed 311 F.2d 223 (6th Cir.1962); Mandel v. United States, 229 F.2d 382 (7th Cir.1956). This result is justified as the recipient spouse must use the payments for the support of the adult children. It would be unfair to require the recipient to treat the payments as income where the recipient is only a conduit for the payments.

Problems

1. H is required to pay W $3,000 per month under the terms of their divorce decree. The payments are reduced by $1,000 per month when their only child, who is living with W, reaches age 21 or graduates from college, whichever is later. In the event W dies, the payments terminate. If she remarries the payments are reduced by $2,000 per month. Determine the income tax consequences to H and W of these payments. Consider § 71(a), (b), (c) and (f).

2. Assume the same facts as in Problem 1. H also agrees to pay for all of W's medical expenses. The obligation for these payments will also terminate upon W's remarriage. During the first year W has no medical expenses. The second year H pays $680 directly to W's doctor. What are the income tax consequences to H and W of these payments? Consider § 71(b).

3. H agrees to pay W $1,000 a month for the next 10 years under the terms of their separation agreement, but payments will terminate if she dies. Determine the income tax consequences. Consider § 71(b).

4. As part of their divorce decree H agrees to pay W's law school tuition for the next three years. Assume that W's tuition payments are $9,000 for the first year, $10,000 the second year and $11,000 the third year. He will also pay her $1,000 a month until she takes a bar exam, after which time she will receive $400 a month for the next three years. All the payments will terminate in the event H or W dies. Determine the income tax consequences to H and W. Consider § 71(a), (b), and (f).

5. (a) H agrees to pay W alimony for the next 10 years according to a fixed payment schedule. H makes payments to W of $45,000 in Year 1, $30,000 in Year 2, $15,000 in Year 3, and $6,000 annually for Years 4 through 10. Pursuant to the divorce decree, H's obligation to make these payments was to terminate in the event of W's death. Determine the income tax consequences for each of the 10 years as the payments are made. Consider the impact of § 71(f). (b) What result if W dies in the middle of the third year so that H made no payments after her death? Consider § 71(f)(5).

6. H agrees to pay W $1,000 a month for the rest of her life. Normally, H sends W a check every month. However, this month H is short on cash and W agrees to accept in satisfaction of the $1,000 alimony obligation for this month stock owned by H with a value of $1,000. H's basis in the stock is $850. Does the satisfaction of the obligation to pay $1,000 in cash with appreciated property satisfy the "in cash" requirement of § 71(b)(1)?

3. PROPERTY SETTLEMENTS

Frequently, separation or divorce involves a transfer of property between spouses. When payment is made in the form of cash the key question is whether the transaction represents an alimony payment or a payment for property. Recall that a payment for property neither results in a current deduction for the payor nor gross income under § 71(a) to the recipient. The label applied to the payments (alimony, support or property settlement) is not determinative. Instead, the intent of the parties and the facts surrounding the decree, instrument or agreement are controlling. In the past lawyers, accountants, the Service and the courts struggled to distinguish alimony from property settlements. An objective of the 1984 legislation was tax simplification. The newly-formulated standards found in § 71(b) are intended to make the distinction between alimony and property settlements clearer.

A transfer of property other than cash can never be treated as alimony because of the requirement contained in § 71(b)(1) that alimony payments can only be made in cash. If a cash payment otherwise meets the operative requirements of § 71(b), it is alimony deductible by the payor and includible in the income of the recipient, unless the parties have agreed otherwise in accordance with § 71(b)(1)(B). If a cash payment is not alimony or child support, the payment is now governed by § 1041 which treats property settlements as gifts. In effect, a payment to a spouse or an ex-spouse incident to a divorce is now either alimony, child support, or a gift. (Under some limited circumstances the payment may also be classified as compensation for services.)

Once it is determined that the transfer of property (including cash) between spouses is part of a property settlement, the recipient's basis in the property received must be determined. Another question is whether gain or loss is realized on the exchange of property. The next case illustrates the tax consequences of the transfer of appreciated property in exchange for marital rights under prior law.

UNITED STATES v. DAVIS
Supreme Court of the United States, 1962.
370 U.S. 65, 82 S.Ct. 1190, 8 L.Ed.2d 335.

MR. JUSTICE CLARK delivered the opinion of the Court.

These cases involve the tax consequences of a transfer of appreciated property by Thomas Crawley Davis to his former wife pursuant to a property settlement agreement executed prior to divorce, as well as the deductibility of his payment of her legal expenses in connection therewith. * * *

In 1954 the taxpayer and his then wife made a voluntary property settlement and separation agreement calling for support payments to the wife and minor child in addition to the transfer of certain personal property to the wife. Under Delaware law all the property transferred was that of the taxpayer, subject to certain statutory marital rights of the wife including a right of intestate succession and a right upon divorce to a share of the husband's property. Specifically as a "division in settlement of their property" the taxpayer agreed to transfer to his wife, *inter alia,* 1,000 shares of stock in the E.I. du Pont de Nemours & Co. The then Mrs. Davis agreed to accept this division "in full settlement and satisfaction of any and all claims and rights against the husband whatsoever (including but not by way of limitation, dower and all rights under the laws of testacy and intestacy) * * *." Pursuant to the above agreement which had been incorporated into the divorce decree, one-half of this stock was delivered in the tax year involved, 1955, and the balance thereafter. Davis' cost basis for the 1955 transfer was $74,775.37, and the fair market value of the 500 shares there transferred was $82,250. * * *

I.

The determination of the income tax consequences of the stock transfer described above is basically a two-step analysis: (1) Was the transaction a taxable event? (2) If so, how much taxable gain resulted therefrom? Originally the Tax Court (at that time the Board of Tax Appeals) held that the accretion to property transferred pursuant to a divorce settlement could not be taxed as capital gain to the transferor because the amount realized by the satisfaction of the husband's marital obligations was indeterminable and because, even if such benefit were ascertainable, the transaction was a nontaxable division of property. Mesta v. Commissioner, 42 B.T.A. 933 (1940); Halliwell v. Commissioner, 44 B.T.A. 740 (1941). However, upon being reversed in quick succession by the Courts of Appeals of the Third and Second Circuits, Commissioner of Internal Revenue v. Mesta, 123 F.2d 986 (C.A.3d Cir. 1941); Commissioner of Internal Revenue v. Halliwell, 131 F.2d 642 (C.A.2d Cir.1942), the Tax Court accepted the position of these courts and has continued to apply these views in appropriate cases since that time, * * * In Mesta and Halliwell the Courts of Appeals reasoned that the accretion to the property was "realized" by the transfer and that this gain could be measured on the assumption that the relinquished marital rights were equal in value to the property transferred. The matter was considered settled until the Court of Appeals for the Sixth Circuit, in reversing the Tax Court, ruled that, although such a transfer might be a taxable event, the gain realized thereby could not be determined because of the impossibility of evaluating the fair market value of the wife's marital rights. Commissioner of Internal Revenue v. Marshman, 279 F.2d 27 (1960). In so holding that court specifically rejected the argument that these rights could be presumed to be equal in value to the property transferred for their release. This is essentially the position taken by the Court of Claims in the instant case.

II.

We now turn to the threshold question of whether the transfer in issue was an appropriate occasion for taxing the accretion to the stock. There can be no doubt that Congress, as evidenced by its inclusive definition of income subject to taxation, i.e., "all income from whatever source derived, including * * * [g]ains derived from dealings in property,"[3] intended that the economic growth of this stock be taxed. The problem confronting us is simply *when* is such accretion to be taxed. Should the economic gain be presently assessed against taxpayer, or should this assessment await a subsequent transfer of the property by the wife? The controlling statutory language, which provides that gains from dealings in property are to be taxed upon "sale or other disposition,"[4] is too general to include or exclude conclusively the transaction presently in issue. Recognizing this, the Government and the taxpayer argue by analogy with transactions more easily classified as within or without the ambient of taxable events. The taxpayer asserts that the present disposition is comparable to a nontaxable division of property between two co-owners,[5] while the Government contends it more resembles a taxable transfer of property in exchange for the release of an independent legal obligation. Neither disputes the validity of the other's starting point.

In support of his analogy the taxpayer argues that to draw a distinction between a wife's interest in the property of her husband in a common-law jurisdiction such as Delaware and the property interest of a wife in a typical community property jurisdiction would commit a double sin; for such differentiation would depend upon "elusive and

---

3. § 61(a).

4. § 1001.

5. Any suggestion that the transaction in question was a gift is completely unrealistic. Property transferred pursuant to a negotiated settlement in return for the release of admittedly valuable rights is not a gift in any sense of the term. To intimate that there was a gift to the extent the value of the property exceeded that of the rights released * * * invokes the erroneous premise that every exchange not precisely equal involves a gift * * *.

subtle casuistries which * * * possess no relevance for tax purposes,"
Helvering v. Hallock, 309 U.S. 106, 118, 60 S.Ct. 444, 450, 84 L.Ed. 604
(1940), and would create disparities between common-law and community property jurisdictions in contradiction to Congress' general policy
of equality between the two. The taxpayer's analogy, however, stum-
bles on its own premise, for the inchoate rights granted a wife in her
husband's property by the Delaware law do not even remotely reach
the dignity of co-ownership. The wife has no interest—passive or
active—over the management or disposition of her husband's personal
property. Her rights are not descendable, and she must survive him to
share in his intestate estate. Upon dissolution of the marriage she
shares in the property only to such extent as the court deems "reasonable." 13 Del.Code Ann. § 1531(a). What is "reasonable" might be
ascertained independently of the extent of the husband's property by
such criteria as the wife's financial condition, her needs in relation to
her accustomed station in life, her age and health, the number of
children and their ages, and the earning capacity of the husband. See,
e.g., Beres v. Beres, 2 Storey 133, 52 Del. 133, 154 A.2d 384 (1959).

This is not to say it would be completely illogical to consider the
shearing off of the wife's rights in her husband's property as a division
of that property, but we believe the contrary to be the more reasonable
construction. Regardless of the tags, Delaware seems only to place a
burden on the husband's property rather than to make the wife a part
owner thereof. In the present context the rights of succession and
reasonable share do not differ significantly from the husband's obligations of support and alimony. They all partake more of a personal
liability of the husband than a property interest of the wife. The
effectuation of these marital rights may ultimately result in the ownership of some of the husband's property as it did here, but certainly this
happenstance does not equate the transaction with a division of property by co-owners. Although admittedly such a view may permit different tax treatment among the several States, this Court in the past has
not ignored the differing effects on the federal taxing scheme of
substantive differences between community property and common-law
systems. E.g., Poe v. Seaborn, 282 U.S. 101, 51 S.Ct. 58, 75 L.Ed. 239
(1930). To be sure Congress has seen fit to alleviate this disparity in
many areas, e.g., Revenue Act of 1948, 62 Stat. 110, but in other areas
the facts of life are still with us.

Our interpretation of the general statutory language is fortified by
the long-standing administrative practice as sounded and formalized by
the settled state of law in the lower courts. The Commissioner's
position was adopted in the early 40's by the Second and Third Circuits
and by 1947 the Tax Court had acquiesced in this view. This settled
rule was not disturbed by the Court of Appeals for the Sixth Circuit in
1960 or the Court of Claims in the instant case, for these latter courts
in holding the gain indeterminable assumed that the transaction was
otherwise a taxable event. Such unanimity of views in support of a

position representing a reasonable construction of an ambiguous statute will not lightly be put aside. It is quite possible that this notorious construction was relied upon by numerous taxpayers as well as the Congress itself, which not only refrained from making any changes in the statutory language during more than a score of years but re-enacted this same language in 1954.

III.

Having determined that the transaction was a taxable event, we now turn to the point on which the Court of Claims balked, viz., the measurement of the taxable gain realized by the taxpayer. The Code defines the taxable gain from the sale or disposition of property as being the "excess of the amount realized therefrom over the adjusted basis * * *." I.R.C. [1986] § 1001(a). The "amount realized" is further defined as "the sum of any money received plus the fair market value of the property (other than money) received." I.R.C. [1986] § 1001(b). In the instant case the "property received" was the release of the wife's inchoate marital rights. The Court of Claims, following the Court of Appeals for the Sixth Circuit, found that there was no way to compute the fair market value of these marital rights and that it was thus impossible to determine the taxable gain realized by the taxpayer. We believe this conclusion was erroneous.

It must be assumed, we think, that the parties acted at arm's length and that they judged the marital rights to be equal in value to the property for which they were exchanged. There was no evidence to the contrary here. Absent a readily ascertainable value it is accepted practice where property is exchanged to hold, as did the Court of Claims in Philadelphia Park Amusement Co. v. United States, 126 F.Supp. 184, 189, 130 Ct.Cl. 166, 172 (1954), that the values "of the two properties exchanged in an arms-length transaction are either equal in fact or are presumed to be equal." * * * To be sure there is much to be said of the argument that such an assumption is weakened by the emotion, tension and practical necessities involved in divorce negotiations and the property settlements arising therefrom. However, once it is recognized that the transfer was a taxable event, it is more consistent with the general purpose and scheme of the taxing statutes to make a rough approximation of the gain realized thereby than to ignore altogether its tax consequences. * * *.

Moreover, if the transaction is to be considered a taxable event as to the husband, the Court of Claims' position leaves up in the air the wife's basis for the property received. In the context of a taxable transfer by the husband,[6] all indicia point to a "cost" basis for this property in the hands of the wife. Yet under the Court of Claims' position her cost for this property, i.e., the value of the marital rights relinquished therefor, would be indeterminable, and on subsequent

---

6. Under the present administrative practice, the release of marital rights in exchange from property or other considera- tion is not considered a taxable event as to the wife. * * * See Rev.Rul. 67-221— Eds.

disposition of the property she might suffer inordinately over the Commissioner's assessment which she would have the burden of proving erroneous, Commissioner of Internal Revenue v. Hansen, 360 U.S. 446, 468, 79 S.Ct. 1270, 3 L.Ed.2d 1360 (1959). Our present holding that the value of these rights is ascertainable eliminates this problem; for the same calculation that determines the amount received by the husband fixes the amount given up by the wife, and this figure, i.e., the market value of the property transferred by the husband, will be taken by her as her tax basis for the property received.

Finally, it must be noted that here, as well as in relation to the question of whether the event is taxable, we draw support from the prior administrative practice and judicial approval of that practice. * * * We therefore conclude that the Commissioner's assessment of a taxable gain based upon the value of the stock at the date of its transfer has not been shown erroneous.

* * *

Reversed in part and affirmed in part.

MR. JUSTICE FRANKFURTER took no part in the decision of these cases.

MR. JUSTICE WHITE took no part in the consideration or decision of these cases.

———

The Davis case illustrates some of the confusion as to the treatment of transfers of property incident to a separation or divorce. Typically, the parties to marital property settlements view the transfer of property between them as a division of their assets, not as a taxable event giving rise to the realization of gain. The Tax Reform Act of 1984 overruled the result in the Davis case to achieve tax simplification and uniform treatment among all taxpayers regardless of the differences in the property laws of their states or in the nature of the ownership of the transferred property. The legislative history indicates:

> The committee believes that, in general, it is inappropriate to tax transfers between spouses. This policy is already reflected in the Code rule that exempts marital gifts from the gift tax, and reflects the fact that a husband and wife are single economic unit.

> The current rules governing transfers of property between spouses or former spouses incident to divorce have not worked well and have led to much controversy and litigation. Often the rules have proved a trap for the unwary as, for example, where the parties view property acquired during marriage (even though held in one spouse's name) as jointly owned, only to find that the equal division of the property upon divorce triggers recognition of gain.

> Furthermore, in divorce cases, the government often gets whipsawed. The transferor will not report any gain on the transfer, while the recipient spouse, when he or she sells, is entitled under the Davis

rule to compute his or her gain or loss by reference to a basis equal to the fair market value of the property at the time received.

The committee believes that to correct these problems, and make the tax laws as unintrusive as possible with respect to relations between spouses, the tax laws governing transfers between spouses and former spouses should be changed. H.R.Rep. No. 432, 98 Cong. 2d Sess. 1491 (1984).

Under § 1041(a), a transfer of property between spouses while married or incident to a divorce (as defined in § 1041(c)) is no longer treated as a taxable event giving rise to a realization of gain or loss. Instead, the transfer is treated as a gift with the transferee taking the transferor's basis and holding period. The only difference from a normal transfer by gift is that §§ 1041(b)(2) and 1015(e) allow unrealized losses to be assigned to the transferee spouse or former spouse. Why does this special rule exist? This nonrecognition treatment applies whether the transfer is for the release of marital rights, cash or other property, the assumption of liabilities in excess of the adjusted basis of the property, or for other consideration (but not services).

The tax planner must still be careful as gift treatment is available only if the requirements of § 1041 are satisfied. A transfer occurring as part of an ante-nuptial agreement, for example, the Farid-Es-Sultaneh case at pp. 282–287, still results in a realization of gain by the transferor. Reconsider Problems 1 and 2 at page 288. The Service has issued a series of questions and answers illustrating the treatment of transfers between spouses or transfers incident to a divorce. Temp. Reg. § 1.1041–1T.

Problems

1. H owns stock with a basis of $100 and a fair market value of $180, which he acquired several years ago. H sells this property to his wife, W, for $180 in cash. Does H realize any gain? Consider § 1041(a). What is W's basis in the stock she purchased? Consider § 1041(b).

2. H owns stock, acquired several years ago, with a basis of $90,000 and a fair market value of $80,000. What are the tax consequences to H (is there a realization of gain (or loss)?) and to W (what is her basis and holding period?) if:

(a) While married, W pays H $80,000 in cash for the stock. Consider § 1041(a) and (b). Can H report a loss on the sale? Are § 267(a) and (d) necessary?

(b) While married W receives the stock as a gift from H. Does § 1041(b) or § 1015(a) control? Examine § 1015(e).

(c) W receives the stock pursuant to the terms of their divorce decree by agreeing to release all of her marital rights in his estate. Consider §§ 1041(a) and (b), and 1015(e).

(d) What result in each of the above situations if W subsequently sells the stock for $80,000 three months after acquiring it? Consider § 1223(2).

3. H and W purchased 200 shares of stock many years ago for $8,600, taking title as joint tenants with the right of survivorship. Pursuant to the terms of their divorce decree new stock certificates were issued whereby H and W each owned 100 shares individually. The stock was worth $12,000 at the time of the divorce. Prior to § 1041 this was a division of property which did not result in a realization of gain. Did § 1041 change the tax result?

4. H and W purchased a personal residence many years ago for $30,000 as joint tenants with the right of survivorship. They were divorced this year. The home is currently valued at $160,000. Assume the mortgage has been paid in full. H gives W $80,000 for her half interest in the house.

   (a) What were the tax consequences of this transaction prior to the effective date of § 1041? Consider the Davis case. Determine the consequences to the W and the basis and holding period H would have in the house.

   (b) Determine the tax consequences to both parties if the transfer occurred today. Consider §§ 1041 and 1223(2).

   (c) Assume instead, H gave W stock purchased two years ago for $60,000, and having a current fair market value of $80,000, for her half interest in the house. Determine whether any gain is realized and the bases and holding periods for the house and the stock. Consider §§ 1041 and 1223(2).

   (d) Assume the unpaid balance of mortgage equals $30,000. H gave W $65,000 for her half interest agreeing to assume the liability for the entire mortgage. What result?

4. DEPENDENCY EXEMPTION

A problem often overlooked in connection with a divorce or legal separation relates to which spouse will receive the dependency exemptions for the children. An individual taxpayer is allowed a deduction (indexed for inflation starting in 1990 under § 151(f)), as the dependency exemption (§ 151) for each qualified dependent. Under prior law it was confusing and often difficult to determine which parent, after a separation or divorce, should receive the dependency exemption. As the legislative history illustrates, the 1984 Act sought simplification, flexibility and administrative convenience in this area:

> The present rules governing the allocations of the dependency exemption are often subjective and present difficult problems of proof and substantiation. The Internal Revenue Service becomes involved in many disputes between parents who both claim the dependency exemption based on providing support over the applicable thresholds. The cost to the parties and the Government to resolve these disputes is relatively high and the Government generally has little tax revenue at stake in the outcome. The committee wishes to provide more certainty by allowing the custodial spouse the exemption unless that spouse

waives his or her right to claim the exemption. Thus, dependency disputes between parents will be resolved without the involvement of the Internal Revenue Service. H.R.Rep. No. 432, 98th Cong.2d Sess. 1498 (1984).

As provided in § 152(e)(1), the parent having custody of a child for the greater part of the year is entitled to the dependency exemption for the child even though the noncustodial parent provides more support payments than the custodial parent.

There are two major exceptions to the general rule allowing the custodial parent to take the dependency exemption. The first provides negotiating flexibility by allowing the noncustodial parent to take the dependency exemption if the custodial parent signs a written declaration releasing the claim to the dependency exemption for one or more specified years or permanently. § 152(e)(2)(A). This declaration must then be attached to the noncustodial parent's tax returns. § 152(e)(2) (B). From a planning standpoint, the custodial spouse should consider releasing the right to the dependency exemption annually in order to better insure the receipt of child support payments. Since the dependency exemption is worth more to the parent in the higher marginal tax bracket, a lower bracket custodial parent may be willing to surrender the exemption in exchange for larger child support or other payments. Secondly, the general rule will not apply if a multiple support agreement exists. § 152(e)(3). The general rule also does not apply to a qualified decree or agreement executed prior to January 1, 1985, if the custodial parent agrees to release his claim to the dependency exemption to the noncustodial parent, and the noncustodial parent provides at least $600 for the support of the child during the year. § 152(e)(4). Of course, a pre-1985 instrument may be modified so that the new rules will apply.

Although a taxpayer is allowed a deduction under § 213(a) for the costs of medical care for a dependent, § 213(d)(5) provides that a child of separated or divorced parents will be treated as a dependent of both parents. Thus, a parent paying medical expenses for a child can claim a deduction for medical care expenditures even if the other parent is allowed the dependency exemption for the child, provided that the parent's payments exceed the 7.5% floor.

5. FILING STATUS

A key factor often overlooked is the filing status under § 1 after the spouses are divorced or separated. The 1984 legislation provided that any custodial parent releasing a claim to a dependency exemption will be treated as entitled to the dependency exemption for the purpose of qualifying for the more favorable head of household filing status under § 1(b) as defined in § 2(b). § 2(b)(1)(A)(i). Can a custodial parent who is not entitled to the dependency exemption for the child claim the child care credit under § 21? Examine § 21(e)(5).

Problems

1. Will a spouse with a dependent child be compelled to file under § 1(d) as a married individual filing separately if she is abandoned by her husband? Consider § 7703(b).

2. H and W live in a state where the only ground for a no-fault divorce is to be separated and living apart under a voluntary separation agreement for a period of one year. (A voluntary separation agreement is not a decree of separate maintenance under state law.) During the year they are separated, they maintain separate residences and conduct their personal affairs as if they were single. Can they file a joint return while they are separated? Consider §§ 6013 and 7703(a). Can they file as unmarried individuals under § 1(c) or must they use the higher rates under § 1(d) for married individuals filing separately?

6. LEGAL EXPENSES INCIDENT TO DIVORCE AND SEPARATION

Taxpayers may not deduct all of the legal expenses incident to a divorce or separation. General legal advice in connection with obtaining a divorce is nondeductible under § 262. Expenses incurred in a divorce suit or negotiated arrangement are deductible under § 212(2) only if the origin of the claim arose in connection with the spouse's profit-seeking activities (i.e., the production of income or the management or conservation of income-producing property) and then only to that extent. Reconsider the problem at page 448, and reread the Gilmore case at page 449. However, a spouse can deduct the legal costs attributable to the production and collection of taxable income, such as legal fees to negotiate alimony payments and to recover alimony arrearages. Reg. § 1.262–1(b)(7).

Legal expenses for obtaining tax advice incident to a divorce or separation, including the tax effects of agreements concerning alimony, child support and property settlements are deductible under § 212(3). See the Carpenter case and Rev.Rul. 72–545 at page 456. Yet, in United States v. Patrick, 372 U.S. 53, 83 S.Ct. 618, 9 L.Ed.2d 580 (1963), a husband's payments to his attorney and his wife's attorney for tax advice regarding an out of court property settlement were held nondeductible under the rationale of Gilmore decision. Remember that expenses deductible under § 212 are subject to the two percent floor of § 67(a).

An attorney should make a "reasonable allocation" of the legal expenses incurred in connection with a divorce or separation, distinguishing between nondeductible advice with respect to obtaining a divorce and deductible advice with respect to the tax consequences of alimony payments and property settlements. Evidence of a "reasonable allocation" may consist of: (1) the attorney's opinion; (2) reliable records of services rendered; or (3) a history of tax and investment advice given before marital difficulties arose.

E.   INTEREST

After the Tax Reform Act of 1986 the interest deduction cannot be discussed by a simple recital that a taxpayer gets a deduction for interest paid or accrued by him, whether it is paid with respect to:

a. a business

b. an investment

c. a personal expense, such as interest on the mortgage on a home.

Because this is a work devoted to tax planning—a study which necessarily emphasizes the shortcomings and inconsistencies of the tax structure—it is appropriate to examine the use of and complexities of the interest deduction.

1. HOW THE INTEREST DEDUCTION OPERATES

Interest is Deductible Though Unrelated to Production of Income. The Code has long contained a provision that interest payments by the taxpayer are deductible from his gross income. Deductibility is not limited to such payments as are related to a trade or business or the production of income. Section 163(a) provides: "There shall be allowed as a deduction all interest paid or accrued within the taxable year on indebtedness."

How "Interest" is Defined. Interest may generally be defined as "compensation for the use or forbearance of money." Deputy v. du-Pont, 308 U.S. 488, 498, 60 S.Ct. 363, 368, 84 L.Ed. 416, 424 (1940). There is no interest unless there is a valid and subsisting, legally enforceable indebtedness which may, however, originally have been incurred without consideration. For example, interest may be paid a creditor for forbearing to demand the payment of money legally due. A payment will not be deductible as interest if it is gratuitous. Of course, the interest paid must be bona fide to be deductible.

Interest Paid for Another. Interest paid on behalf of another generally is not deductible as interest by the person who makes the payment. For example, if the taxpayer, the president of a corporation, in his individual capacity, agrees to pay interest on a corporate note as part of an agreement between the corporation and the note holder to reduce the interest rate and extend the maturity, a deduction for the interest the taxpayer paid would be disallowed. The indebtedness must be an obligation of the taxpayer. Sheppard v. Commissioner, 37 B.T.A. 279 (1938). If a father pays the mortgage on his son's home, the father is treated as having made a gift to the son, and the son is entitled to the interest deduction.

Exceptions exist to the general rule. A deduction may be allowed under § 162(a) for the taxpayer who makes interest payments on behalf of a corporation where the taxpayer does so to protect his business reputation. Reconsider the note on page 460. Interest paid on a real estate mortgage where the payor is the legal or equitable owner of the real estate is deductible even though the taxpayer is not directly liable on the obligation. Reg. § 1.163–1(b). Interest paid on the mortgage of a cooperative housing corporation by tenant-stockholders is deductible to the extent of their proportionate share of the total interest due on the mortgage. § 216(a)(2). Where parties are jointly and severally liable with respect to a note, all of the interest paid by one of the parties is deductible by such individual. Mason v. United States, 453 F.Supp. 845 (N.D.Cal.1978).

2. LIMITATIONS ON THE DEDUCTIBILITY OF INTEREST

Three major limitations exist with respect to the deductibility of interest, namely restrictions on the deductibility of:

    (1) personal interest;

    (2) prepaid interest; and

    (3) investment interest.

Even though one of the above limitations do not apply, for interest incurred in a business or investment activity there is another factor that may prohibit the current deduction of a taxpayer's interest costs. Under § 263A a taxpayer may be required to capitalize his interest costs as part of the basis of a self-constructed asset.

Personal Interest. Generally, no deduction is permitted for personal interest. § 163(h)(1). Personal interest includes all interest except: (i) qualified residence interest, § 163(h)(2)(D); (ii) interest incurred or continued in connection with the conduct of a trade or business (except the performance of services as an employee), § 163(h)(2)(A); (iii) any investment interest as defined in § 163(d), § 163(h)(2)(B); and (iv) interest taken into account in computing income or loss from a passive activity, § 163(h)(2)(C). Therefore, taxpayers are precluded from deducting interest on consumer purchases such as an auto loan.

Qualified residence interest is deductible. § 163(h)(2)(D). Qualified residence interest consists of interest paid or accrued on indebtedness secured by the taxpayer's principal residence (as defined in § 1034) and a second residence. § 163(h)(3) and (h)(5)(A)(i). Qualified residence interest equals the interest on debt secured by such a residence not in excess of the taxpayer's basis for such residence (including the cost of improvements as opposed to repairs but excluding other adjustments to basis such as depreciation) plus the amount incurred after August 16, 1986, for qualified medical and educational expenses. § 163(h)(4)(A). If a residence is worth less than its basis, qualified residence interest does not include interest on any portion of such debt in excess of the fair market value of the residence at the time the taxpayer incurs the indebtedness. § 163(h)(3)(B). If the principal amount of any indebtedness incurred on or before August 16, 1986, and secured by the residence on August 16, 1986, exceeds the taxpayer's basis for the residence, such amount is substituted for the taxpayer's basis in computing the limitation on the amount of qualified residence interest. § 163(h)(3)(C).

In short, interest on indebtedness secured by the taxpayer's principal (or second residence), at least up to the amount of the taxpayer's basis, constitutes qualified residence interest. For example, if a taxpayer's basis in his principal residence equals $100,000 (and this amount does not exceed the fair market value of the residence) and the indebtedness secured by the residence equals $60,000, interest on a refinancing of $100,000 (the original $60,000 indebtedness plus an additional $40,000) is treated as qualified residence interest. If the debt exceeds the taxpayer's basis, the interest on the excess is deductible only to the extent the borrowed amounts are used for qualified educational or medical purposes. The terms "qualified medical expenses" and "qualified educational expenses" are defined, respectively, in § 163(h)(4)(B) and (C). Tuition expenses for primary, secondary, college, and graduate level education generally are included in the term "qualified educational expenses." Interest on indebtedness used to pay qualified medical or educational expenses must be secured by the taxpayer's principal or second residence and such expenses must be paid or incurred within a "reasonable period of time before or after such indebtedness is incurred." § 163(h)(4)(A).

If a taxpayer borrows against the equity in his home to make an investment, the interest that is not deductible as qualified residence interest may be deducted as investment interest under the limitations contained in § 163(d).

In limiting, but not eliminating the deductibility of personal interest, the legislative history states:

> [The Code] excludes or mismeasures income arising from the ownership of housing and other consumer durables. [Reread pages 64 to 68]. Investment in such goods allows consumers to avoid the tax that would apply if funds were invested in assets producing taxable income and to avoid the cost of renting these items, a cost which would not be deductible in computing tax liability. Thus, the tax system provides an incentive to consume rather than save.

> Although the committee believes that it would not be advisable to subject to income tax imputed rental income with respect to consumer durables owned by the taxpayer, it does believe that it is appropriate and practical to address situations where consumer expenditures are financed by borrowing. By phasing out the [former] deductibility of [personal] interest, the committee believes that it has eliminated from the [Code] a significant disincentive to saving.

> While the committee recognizes that the imputed rental value of owner-occupied housing may be a significant source of untaxed income, the committee nevertheless, believes that encouraging home ownership is an important policy goal achieved in part by providing a deduction for residential mortgage interest. (Senate Finance Committee Report on H.R. 3838, 99th Cong. 2d Sess. 804 (1986)).

The limitation on the deduction of personal interest is phased in over a five-year period. § 163(h)(6) and (d)(6)(B). The applicable percentage is 35 percent in 1987, 60 percent in 1988, 80 percent in 1989, 90 percent in 1990 and 100 percent in 1991.

Prepaid Interest. Consider the case of the taxpayer who has very high income in a tax year, so that he urgently needs a deduction. Consequently he buys a parcel of raw land for $100,000, making a cash down payment of 10% of the purchase price and prepaying interest for five years on the $90,000 mortgage which will mature in five years. It is his hope that the value of the land will appreciate. He feels reasonably sure that he will be able to sell his equity in the property some time before the expiration of the five years for at least as much as he has invested in the property. The hoped for tax consequence is that he will get a deduction in the tax year for the full amount of prepaid interest. If he ultimately sells the property for the amount of his investment, his basis on the sale will be $100,000 (the amount representing the interest payments was taken as a deduction and will not be added to the property's basis). If the interest payments were $30,000 and he sold the property for $120,000, he would have a capital gain of $20,000. Thus, he would have taken an interest deduction of $30,000, dollar-for-dollar, against other sources of ordinary income in the year of purchase. The taxpayer would achieve the deferral of the amount of taxes otherwise due on the other sources of income at the cost of paying taxes on the $20,000 gain.

Under § 461(g), all cash method taxpayers must capitalize prepayments of interest for the use of money for a period of time after the close of the taxable year in which paid, and deduct such payments in the period to which the interest is allocable. This rule applies to interest prepayments for business, investment and personal purposes and is designed to allocate interest payments to reflect the cost of using money.

Thus the taxpayer, who bought the parcel of raw land for $100,000 with a 10% down payment, could not deduct the prepayment of interest allocable to any period falling after the year of the purchase. In the year subsequent to the year of the purchase, only the interest allocable to that period could be deducted and so forth. A cash method taxpayer can therefore deduct prepaid interest no earlier than in the taxable year the interest represents a charge for the use of borrowed money during that period.

An accrual method taxpayer deducts interest on a daily basis over the life of the loan, irrespective of when the interest on the loan is due or payable. Rev.Rul. 68–643, 1968–2 C.B. 76.

Under § 461(g)(2) "points" (an additional interest charge imposed by the lender, usually on the closing of a loan) are currently deductible by a cash method taxpayer if "incurred in connection with the purchase or improvement of, and secured by, the principal residence of the taxpayer to the extent that * * * such payment of points is an established business practice in the area in which such indebtedness is incurred, and the amount of such payment does not exceed the amount generally charged in such area." However, points paid to refinance a home mortgage must be amortized over the term of the new loan. I.R. 86–88. According to the Service, points paid to refinance a mortgage are not paid in connection with the purchase or improvement of a home; rather, they are paid to retire an existing indebtedness.

Investment Interest. Assume again the taxpayer who, as the saying goes, is shopping for a deduction. As in the example discussed with respect to prepaid interest, he wants to do so by creating a large interest deduction. This he does, again, by a small investment on a large purchase. Thus he gets substantial leverage. As in the case of prepaid interest, he seeks a tax advantage because the interest cost is deductible dollar-for-dollar against the taxpayer's other sources of ordinary income. He also hopes to realize investment income (for example, interest on bonds purchased with the borrowed funds) in subsequent years.

Although an interest expense may initially qualify for an interest deduction, substantial limitations on the deduction are imposed by § 163(d) which is concerned with the mismatching caused if a current deduction is allowed for investment interest expenses while the related investment income is realized and reported in later years. Section 163(d) is designed to prevent "taxpayers from sheltering or reducing tax on other, non-investment income by means of the unrelated interest deduction." Senate Finance Committee Report on H.R. 3838, 99th Cong., 2d Sess. 803 (1986). The effect of § 163(d) is to adopt the matching concept by requiring that the deductions for interest expenses incurred with respect to a taxpayers investments be reported in the same taxable year as the income from a taxpayer's investments. If an individual is able to postpone the reporting of his investment income, then § 163(d) postpones the deduction for his investment interest expenses. Accordingly, an individual's expenditures for "investment interest" are currently deductible only to the extent of his "net investment income" for that year. § 163(d)(1). Interest deductions disallowed under § 163(d)(1) are carried forward and treated as investment interest expenses in the succeeding taxable year. § 163(d)(2). However, the interest deduction disallowed and carried forward is allowed as a deduction in a subsequent year only to the extent the taxpayer has net investment income in such year. Although § 163(d)(2) provides only for a carryover of disallowed investment interest to the next taxable year, Congress intended that the unused interest deduction be carried over until any year where there is sufficient investment income against which to offset it. Staff of the Joint Committee on Taxation, General Explanation of the Tax Reform Act of 1976, 94th Cong., 2d Sess. 103 (1976).

The limitations imposed by § 163(d) only apply to "investment interest" as defined in § 163(d)(3). Although interest expenses incurred by a taxpayer engaged in the active conduct of a trade or business are not investment interest, other limitations, such as the capitalization rules under § 263A, may prevent a current deduction. Interest qualifying for the personal deduction available for "qualified residence interest", as defined in § 163(h)(3), is not investment interest and is, therefore, not subject to the § 163(d) limitations. § 163(d)(3)(B)(i). Any interest expense which is taken into account under § 469 in computing gain or loss from a passive activity is subject to the limitations on the deduction of passive losses and is not investment interest for purposes of § 163(d). The passive loss rules under § 469 are discussed in Chapter 11. Interest allocable to a rental real estate activity in which the taxpayer "actively" participates is not treated as investment interest as the deductibility of losses from these activities are also subject to the passive loss rules under § 469. § 163(d)(3)(B)(ii). Since § 469 already limits a taxpayer's ability to deduct losses from passive activities, there is no need for § 163(d) to also limit such interest deductions.

"Investment interest" subject to the § 163(d)(1) limitation is defined as "any interest paid or accrued on indebtedness incurred or continued to purchase or carry property held for investment." § 163(d)(3)(A). The term "property held for investment" is defined in § 163(d)(5) and includes property that produces interest or dividends. § 163(d)(5)(A)(i). Investment interest may include interest on loans used to purchase or carry investments in a limited partnership or S corporation. Also, investment interest includes any interest expenses incurred in an activity involving the conduct of a trade or business in which the taxpayer does not "materially" participate if that activity is not a passive activity subject to the passive loss rules under § 469. § 163(d)(5)(A)(ii).

A taxpayer's "net investment income" equals the excess of his "investment income" (as defined in § 163(d)(4)(B)) over his "investment expenses" (as defined in § 163(d)(4)(C)). § 163(d)(4)(A). Investment income includes: (i) gross income from property held as an investment, such as dividends, interest, rents and royalties; (ii) gain attributable to the disposition of property held for investment; (iii) amounts treated as gross portfolio income under the passive loss rules; and (iv) income from interest in activities involving a trade or business in which the taxpayer does not materially participate, if that activity is not treated as a passive activity under the passive loss rules (§ 163(d)(5)(A)(ii)). Investment expenses are deductible expenses (other than interest) directly connected with the production of investment income, including depreciation. § 163(d)(4)(C). In determining deductible investment expenses, only those expenses allowed after the application of the two percent floor on miscellaneous itemized deductions are considered. "In computing the amount of expenses that exceed the two percent floor, expenses that are not investment expenses are intended to be disallowed before any investment expenses are disallowed." Conference Report to Accompany H.R. 3838, Tax Reform Act of 1986, 99th Cong., 2d Sess. II–154 (1986). Finally, it should be noted that investment income and investment expenses do not include any income or expenses from passive activities taken into account under the passive loss rules of § 469. § 163(d)(4)(D).

The limits on the deduction of investment interest under § 163(d) are to be phased in over a five-year period. § 163(d)(6).

Capitalization of Certain Interest. Interest on debt must be capitalized if such debt is paid or incurred during the production period (as defined in § 263A(f)(4)(B) and (g)(1)) and is allocable to real or tangible personal property constructed by the taxpayer. Furthermore, such property must have either: (i) a long useful life (i.e. a class life of 20 years or more) or (ii) a specified production period. § 263A(f)(1).

3. INTEREST TO PURCHASE OR CARRY TAX-EXEMPT SECURITIES

A taxpayer must avoid the trap of § 265(2). Section 265(2) disallows the deduction for interest "incurred or continued to purchase or carry [tax-exempt] obligations." Section 265(2) is intended to restrain efforts by higher bracket taxpayers to borrow funds and invest in tax free bonds thereby using the interest deduction on the borrowed funds to reduce the taxpayer's income from other sources. With respect to § 163(d) the legislative history notes, "The investment interest limitation is not intended to disallow a deduction for interest expense which in the same year is * * * disallowed under Sec. 265 * * *." Tax Reform Act of 1986, Conference Report To Accompany H.R. 3838, House of Representatives, 99th Cong., 2d Sess. II–154 (1986). Seemingly, if a taxpayer surmounts the hurdle posed by § 265(2), he must then run the gauntlet of § 163(d).

Reference: Asimow, The Interest Deduction, 24 UCLA L.Rev. 749 (1977); Mundstock, Accelerated Depreciation and the Interest Deduction: Can Two Rights Really Make a Wrong?, 29 Tax Notes 1253 (1985).

Questions

1. Three individuals are all interested in purchasing 100 shares of stock in Arbitrage Corporation. The stock is currently selling at $80 a share and does not pay any dividends. The first taxpayer borrows $8,000 at 10 percent interest and uses the loan proceeds to purchase 100 shares at a cost of $8,000. The second taxpayer owns a bond valued at $8,000, paying $800 of interest each year. He sells the bond and uses the $8,000 of sales proceeds to purchase the stock. The third taxpayer also owns a bond worth $8,000, paying $800 annual interest. He decides to keep his bond. Instead, he borrows $8,000 at 10 percent interest and uses the loan proceeds to purchase the stock. What income and deductions can each taxpayer report? From a practical point of view have not all three taxpayers incurred the same costs? Why are their income tax consequences different? Assume they have no other investment income or investment expenses.

2. Sam and Carl each have $50,000 of gross income. Sam's $50,000 is earned income received as a salary. Carl's $50,000 is all income from his

investments. Both taxpayers borrow money to use for investment in a growth stock that pays no dividends. Does Carl receive more favorable income tax treatment than Sam? Is this disparity justified?

3. Although the matching principle is the stated Congressional reason for § 163(d), is it sound as a matter of tax policy? Consider the tracing and arbitrage assumptions made by § 163(d).

Problems

1. Enid, a 33 percent bracket taxpayer, borrows $10,000 at 9 percent interest from her local bank. She uses the loan proceeds to purchase a municipal bond paying 6 percent interest. What purpose does § 265(2) serve? Is § 265(2) consistent with the Haverly case at page 208?

Suppose Enid already owns the $10,000 municipal bond and pledges that bond as collateral for the $10,000 loan from her local bank. Does § 265(2) apply?

2. A taxpayer has been making the mortgage payments on his son's mortgage loan. Is the interest deductible by the father? Consider the Old Colony case at page 49.

3. Assume the quality of living quarters suitable for Robert would cost $1,200 in monthly rent. Assume his monthly salary equals $3,500. If he purchases a home comparable to the house he would rent, his interest payments in the early years of the mortgage would approximate $14,000 per year. His real estate taxes would be $3,000 per year and his homeowner's insurance would be $600 annually.

   a) Assume Robert is in the 28 percent marginal income tax bracket. The house he is considering may be purchased for $160,000. He would borrow $120,000 from a bank. He has $40,000 in cash presently earning 10 percent interest in a money market fund to use as his down payment. Should he buy or rent? How does the rate of inflation affect this decision?

   b) Do the tax laws favor the homeowner? How are renters discriminated against? What changes would you recommend in order to treat those who rent on an equal footing with those who own their houses? Are such changes practical? Reconsider problem 3 at page 69.

4. Diane purchased a home several years ago for $100,000 and no improvements have been made. As of January 1, 1987, the balance on her original mortgage was $60,000 and the house was worth $200,000. On January 1, 1987, Diane refinanced her home with her original mortgage holder and obtained a new mortgage for $150,000, thereby netting $90,000 in cash from the refinancing. Her mortgage interest for the 1987 year totalled $18,000, and she paid the bank $3,000 in points for the refinancing of her mortgage. She invests the $90,000 in corporate bonds, paying $5,500 in interest for 1987. Assume that she has no other investment income or investment expenses for the year. How much of the $18,000 in mortgage interest can she deduct for 1987? Can any of the disallowed interest deduction be carried forward?

5. (a) Should a dollar limitation be placed on the amount of deductible home mortgage interest instead of the present treatment?

(b) Should the deduction for home mortgage interest be allowed only for interest on a taxpayer's principal residence?

(c) Should the deduction for home mortgage interest be changed to a credit? Reconsider the problem at page 43.

Consider the following report:

CONGRESSIONAL BUDGET OFFICE, THE TAX TREATMENT OF HOMEOWNERSHIP: ISSUES AND OPTIONS 21–22, 27–40
(September, 1981).

The current tax treatment of homeownership reduces the after-tax cost of owning a home, enabling more families to buy homes and allowing homes to be of better quality. But the same tax provisions that make homeowning more affordable also increase the rate of return on homeownership as an investment. They divert personal savings from business investment into home building, reduce the demand for and production of rental housing, and raise house prices (thereby offsetting some of the effects of tax savings on homeownership costs). The tax benefits provided to homeowners also increase with taxable income and cause homeowners and renters to be taxed differently. These effects became especially pronounced during the inflationary period of the 1970s, in part because taxpayers were pushed into higher marginal tax brackets—thereby increasing the rate of subsidy provided by the tax provisions.

* * *

EFFECTS ON THE COST AND EXTENT OF HOMEOWNERSHIP

Effects on Homeownership Costs

Tax subsidies reduce the apparent cost of owning a home. They also increase the rate of return on homeownership as an investment.

The actual decrease in homeownership costs is hard to estimate, for two reasons. First, the reduction in tax liabilities, together with other tax provisions, has increased the demand for owner-occupied housing, thereby raising house prices and interest rates. Second, the provisions have enabled people to afford larger homes, giving a further boost to the price of the average house. On the basis of present housing prices and mortgage interest rates, however, the pre-tax cost of homeownership has been reduced by 35 percent or more in some cases—the amount depending on house prices, interest rates, and the taxpayer's marginal tax rate. * * *

Effects on the Extent of Homeownership

The current tax provisions also appear to increase the extent of homeownership. Most of the studies analyzing this issue have found that the provisions raise the incidence of homeownership by about 3 to

5 percentage points—meaning a 5 to 8 percent rise in the fraction of households owning a house or apartment, or about one-fourth of the total increase in homeownership observed since World War II. For example, Harvey Rosen estimates in a study based on a cross-section of households surveyed during 1970 that the proportion owning their own homes would have been 2.5 to 5.5 percentage points lower (depending on income level) if deductions for mortgage interest and property taxes had been disallowed and net imputed rental income had been taxed. In addition, those owning homes would have held units costing an average of 10 to 20 percent less than the homes they actually held. * * * A third study, by Patric Hendershott and James Shilling, which uses data through 1978, found a slightly larger effect on homeownership. Their results suggest that the homeownership rate would have been about 4 to 5 percentage points lower than observed in 1978 if property taxes and mortgage interest payments had not been deductible. This larger impact may reflect the particular circumstances that developed during the last half of the 1970s, when inflation made homeownership particularly attractive by greatly increasing the magnitude of tax savings from these deductions.

OTHER CONSEQUENCES

Besides their effect on the extent and after-tax cost of homeownership, the tax subsidies also have other economic consequences. First, they decrease business investment by increasing the attractiveness of homeownership as a use of personal savings. Second, they weaken the market for rental housing by enhancing the attractiveness of homeowning as an investment and by lowering its cost. Third, the tax subsidies help to raise the price of housing, particularly during periods of inflation when the interaction of inflation with the income tax increases the tax benefits for homeownership and decreases those for other types of assets (particularly depreciable business plant and equipment). Fourth, the tax subsidies alter the structure of the individual income tax and require significantly higher marginal tax rates to obtain any specified level of federal revenues. None of these consequences, though they flow naturally from the effects of the current tax code on the demand for homeownership as against renting and other types of investments, was a matter of much concern when the various tax provisions were adopted. Each one, though, has attracted growing attention during the last several years as declining productivity growth, a dwindling supply of rental housing, and rapidly escalating house prices have become major concerns.

Effects on Business Capital Formation and Productivity

Tax subsidies for homeownership tend to reduce business investment because they raise the rate of return on homeownership as an investment, thereby attracting more personal savings. This effect can be measured by examining the impact of homeownership subsidies on the after-tax cost of capital for homeownership and other types of investment projects, since projects with lower after-tax costs of capital tend to obtain more funds than do those with higher costs.

A recent study by Patric Hendershott and Sheng-Cheng Hu suggests that the average, risk-adjusted net cost of capital for owner-occupied housing in 1964–1965 was 5.3 percent, compared with 9.5 to 10 percent for investments in corporate plant and equipment and 7 to 7.4 percent for investments in noncorporate structures and equipment, and in rental housing. For the years 1976–1977, the figures were 5.3 percent for owner-occupied housing, 11.5 percent for corporate equipment, 12.8 percent for corporate structures, and 8 to 8.8 percent for noncorporate investment and rental housing.[8] These large differences in the cost of funds imply a substantial diversion of funds from other investment assets, particularly from corporate plant and equipment into owner-occupied housing. They also imply a corresponding loss in economic output, because the lower costs of funds for homeownership allow funds to be bid away from higher-cost projects whose true (before-tax) rate of return is higher. Hendershott and Hu's figures suggest that as much as 23 percent of the owner-occupied housing in 1964–1965 and 33 percent of that in 1976–1977 represented construction that was induced by the effects of the tax provisions in lowering the cost of capital for homeownership as against business investment. At 1976–1977 levels, these investment shifts implied an annual economic loss of about $6 billion in 1972 dollars, or 0.4 percent of GNP, if based on the standard assumption that the marginal rate of return from investments equals the marginal cost, meaning that these induced increases in the stock of owner-occupied housing represented less productive uses of funds than the business investments from which they were diverted.

During the last decade of persistent inflation and sluggish economic growth, the effects of homeownership tax provisions on business investment have received particular attention because of the relationship between business investment and productivity growth. Recent studies suggest that the virtual halving in the growth rate of nonresidential investment between the years 1965–1973 and 1974–1979 may have contributed to the simultaneous dramatic decline in productivity growth during the late 1970s.[9]

Although many factors other than the homeownership tax provisions were responsible for the slowdown in net business investment, including a stagnant economy and large federal deficits that absorbed much of the expanding credit in the economy, shifts of personal saving into homeownership may also have played a role. Between 1970 and 1979, for example, the percentage of personal savings devoted to net

8. See Patric H. Hendershott and Sheng-Cheng Hu, "Government-Induced Biases in the Allocation of the Stock of Fixed Capital in the United States," in George M. Von Furstenberg, ed., *Capital, Efficiency, and Growth* (Ballinger, 1980), Table 4–5, p. 343.

9. See Congressional Budget Office, *The Productivity Problem: Alternatives for Action* (January 1981), Tables 11 and 13, pp. 30 and 34.

investments in owner-occupied housing more than doubled, from 13.6 to 28.0 percent.[10] Perhaps more striking, between 1975–1976 and 1977–1979 the fraction of disposable income used for net purchases of owner-occupied housing rose by more than half, from 2.4 percent to 3.8 percent, while the share devoted to net financial investments fell from 4.3 percent to 1.0 percent.[11] These figures do not necessarily "prove" that homeownership was attracting funds from business investment, because shifts in this direction could have resulted from the rapid growth in the number of younger households, which traditionally devote more of their resources to acquiring homes and other consumer durables than do the older households that were more prevalent at the end of the 1960s. Nevertheless, they are consistent with research indicating that, between 1972 and 1979, homeowners earned rates of return on their homes averaging 10 percentage points higher (7.6 percentage points in real terms) than were available from other financial assets.[12]

Whether these extraordinary returns on homeownership, and the corresponding effects on the allocation of savings, will continue over the next decade is uncertain. The development in the last several years of new mortgage instruments whose interest rates fluctuate with market conditions will probably decrease the attractiveness of homeownership as an investment, as will the continuation of high interest rates, which raise the cost of capital for owner-occupied housing. Similarly, the growth of money market funds and the gradual lifting of interest ceilings on savings accounts are providing alternative ways for homeowners to earn a high return on their savings. Passage of the Economic Recovery Tax Act of 1981, with its faster depreciation writeoffs for business investment, may also stem the flow of savings out of financial assets by offsetting the decline in depreciation allowances caused by inflation, thus increasing the returns from nonresidential investment. On the other hand, the number of households with a head aged 25–34—the demographic group that includes most first-time homebuyers—will outnumber those with heads of age 55 to 64 by at least 50 percent through the year 2000. This rough index of housing demand pressure suggests that the underlying demand for homeownership will remain strong over the next two decades so long as income levels, interest rates, and mortgage instruments make homeownership accessible to a large share of these households.

If the demand for homeownership remains strong, savings could continue to be diverted into housing at a time when capital markets will already be under heavy pressure to finance the increased business

10. Ibid., Table 9, p. 14.

11. See Carol Corrado and Charles Steindel, "Perspectives on Personal Saving," *Federal Reserve Bulletin*, vol. 66 (August 1980), Table 2, p. 615.

12. Patric H. Hendershott and Sheng-Cheng Hu, "Inflation and Extraordinary Returns on Owner-Occupied Housing: Some Implications for Capital Allocation and Productivity Growth," *Journal of Macroeconomics*, vol. 3 (Spring 1981), Tables 1 and 2, pp. 188 and 191.

investment resulting from the 1981 tax law changes. This, in turn, could generate strong upward pressure on interest rates. In addition, continuation of the present tax incentives for homeownership during the coming period of high demographic pressures for homeownership could exacerbate what is likely to be an excess of single-family homes by the time the current members of the postwar "baby boom" generation enter retirement. Census Bureau data project a sharp rise in the percentage of the population aged 65 and older beginning about the year 2015. From then through at least the year 2030 these persons will represent between 14 and 18 percent of the population, as against 11.2 percent in 1980 and 11.7 percent in 1985. The percentage of the population aged 25 to 34, by comparison, will fall by 2025 to about 13 percent, compared with about 17 percent in 1985. Because younger families traditionally favor larger homes while the elderly prefer smaller, less expensive units, these trends suggest there would already be an excess of single-family homes and a shortage of smaller units by that time. Current tax law, by creating incentives to purchase homes, could well increase that imbalance of housing units.

Effects on Rental Housing

Tax subsidies reduce the demand for rental housing by decreasing the relative cost of homeownership as a consumption good and increasing its attractiveness as an investment. This lower demand, in turn, leads to the construction of less rental housing. * * *

Over the last several years, the role of tax subsidies for rental housing has gained particular attention because of the shrinking rental housing market in the United States. Rental housing construction since the 1974–1975 recession has averaged about 10 percent less than that during the last economically stable period, the late 1960s, based on figures for multifamily housing construction. * * * Moreover, during the last five years, an important new trend—the conversion of rental units into owner-occupied condominiums and cooperatives—has developed. * * *

The decline in rental housing construction and the conversion of rental units to ownership status can be traced to many causes. Rising costs of housing maintenance and construction, for example, are a factor in both developments, as is the spread of rent control, which has made it hard for landlords to keep rents in line with costs and with the rate of return available on other investments. Another factor that has encouraged both condominium conversion and the shifting of multiunit construction toward condominiums has been the rise in the number of small, higher-income families that prefer smaller homes in urban centers—a change attributable largely to the maturation of the postwar "baby boom" generation and, to some extent, the rise in divorce rates.

A major impetus both for conversions and for decreased rental construction, however, has been a further drop in the demand for rental housing among middle- and high-income households, thus leaving landlords to meet higher expenses with an increasingly poorer clientele. Between 1970 and 1977, for example, the median income of renter households fell by 10 percent in real terms. In 1979, the median rental household income was only $10,000. The declining economic position of renter households, together with rent control, helps to explain why rent levels increased only 67 percent between 1970 and 1979 as against a 200 percent rise in operating costs for rental housing.

Much of the "disappearance" of higher-income households from the rental market can be traced to the combined effects of tax subsidies for homeownership and inflation-induced "bracket creep," although the prospect of investment gains from house price inflation has also played a role. Inflation, which pushed middle- and upper-income households into steadily higher tax brackets, greatly increased the value of the various tax benefits for homeownership, thereby increasing the appeal of homeowning. The tax benefits also enabled these households to pay substantially more for housing if they owned rather than rented. Thus, it became attractive for some landlords to convert rental units and for builders to shift some rental construction to condominiums and cooperatives.

*Effect on House Prices, the Inflation Rate, and
Inflation-Indexed Benefits*

Tax benefits for homeownership, by increasing the demand for homeowning, tend to raise the price of homes. In the long run, house prices can be expected to reach a point where, on average, the rate of return to homeownership as an investment should equal that for other investments. During periods of economic stability, when the age structure of the population and the magnitudes of tax benefits are relatively constant, house prices should also be stable. House prices can increase rapidly, however, during periods of inflation or when changing demographics increase the rate of household formation and, thus, the demand for housing units.

In the past decade, and particularly the past five years, the price of homes has increased dramatically in the United States. Between 1969 and 1979, the median sales prices for new and existing homes and the "average" price of a new, constant-quality house all rose by 140 to 160 percent—roughly one and one-half times as fast as the Consumer Price Index (CPI) or GNP deflator, two general measures of inflation. These price increases have given existing homeowners substantial investment gains but made it far harder for nonhomeowners to enter the market, since incomes over this period increased only about as fast as the general inflation rate.[14] Housing price increases have also increased benefit levels and expenditures for many federal programs and raised

14. Between 1969 and 1979, median household income in the United States rose by 97.3 percent, as against 98.0 percent for the Consumer Price Index. Median household income for households with heads of age 25–34, the most common age group for first-time homebuyers, rose by 95.6 percent over this period. * * *

wage levels for many private employees, because house prices enter directly into the Consumer Price Index, and the CPI is used to adjust benefit levels for Social Security and Food Stamp payments, in addition to setting wage rates under many private labor contracts.

The increase in the relative price of homes during this period can be traced to many factors. The rapid rate of household formation during this period, discussed earlier, was clearly one influence, since new households have a heavy demand for consumer durables and for housing in particular. Another factor was the highly cyclical nature of the homebuilding industry, which experienced unusually rapid cost increases because of more stringent government regulations and the need to recruit workers and reassemble capital after the housing downturn of 1969–1970 and the much greater recession of 1974–1975. But the interaction of inflation with the existing tax provisions for homeownership, coupled with, until recently, fairly low real rates of interest, also had an important influence. The rise in the value of tax subsidies attributable to inflation greatly increased the investment returns for homeownership, thereby encouraging households to pay steadily higher prices for new and existing homes. This trend was encouraged by tax policies that limited business earnings by requiring firms to use historical rather than current values for equipment in claiming depreciation allowances. The sharp rise in mortgage interest rates since 1979 has reduced the rate of house price appreciation, but a return on interest rates return to more normal levels could accelerate it again because of the strong, underlying demand for housing. On the other hand, future appreciation rates could be lower than during the 1970s if greater use of variable-rate mortgages makes homebuying a riskier financial proposition, thereby decreasing the investment demand for housing.

Effect on the Federal Tax System

The present tax treatment for homeownership has three major effects on the federal income tax. First, by narrowing the tax base, it requires higher marginal tax rates to collect any desired amount of revenue. These higher tax rates, in turn, can create disincentives for savings, investment, and labor supply if they are at all sizable. Second, the provision of tax benefits for homeowners causes homeowners and renters in otherwise equal circumstances to be taxed differently. Third, these benefits reduce the progressivity of the income tax, partly because higher-income households own, on average, more expensive homes that have greater tax-subsidized expenses and partly because the form in which the benefits are provided gives taxpayers a higher rate of subsidy the higher is their taxable income. Thus, the current tax provisions benefits most those least likely to need help in buying a home. * * * This "upward tilt" of the tax benefits is especially great for the home mortgage interest and property tax deductions, since these are limited to taxpayers who itemize—a group consisting disproportionately of taxpayers with expanded incomes of $30,000 or more.[15]

* * *

The indirect rate-increasing effects of the current tax provisions for homeownership have become quite substantial with the recent increases in house prices and interest rates. Using the arithmetic sum of the five key tax expenditures for homeownership[16] CBO estimates that, eliminating these provisions would allow marginal tax rates to be more than 10 percent lower with no change in aggregate tax revenues. The actual erosion of the tax base because of these five provisions and the exclusion of imputed net rental income may be less than estimated, since if they were not available taxpayers might shift some of their income and savings into other tax-favored forms. Nevertheless, these figures suggest that the current tax provisions for homeownership have had a substantial impact on the tax base.

4. JUDICIAL TECHNIQUES IN COMBATING TAX AVOIDANCE [17]

Problem

Mrs. Moneybags, a wealthy widow, has been advised by Mr. Sharpeyes, her accountant, to purchase U.S. Treasury bonds (paying 8 percent on the face value of $400,000), selling at discount, for $300,000. The bonds, commonly known, as "flower bonds", may, prior to maturity be applied at face value in the payment of the holder's Federal estate taxes. Sharpeyes recommends that, because Mrs. Moneybags lacks sufficient liquid assets to buy the bonds, she should borrow $300,000 from a bank at a cost of 12 percent interest. Consider the income tax consequences of this transaction to Mrs. Moneybags. Assume she has no income or losses from passive activities. Consider the Goldstein case, §§ 163(d), 183, 461(g) and 1276–1278. What other information should you ascertain?

——————

Introduction. From time to time tax counsel will shape transactions in an artificial fashion, but in reliance on formal compliance with a statute, hoping to create favorable tax consequences for clients. They are able to find such opportunities because the tax structure is necessarily general. This in turn arises from at least two factors: even the most imaginative drafter of statutes cannot forecast in advance how imaginative taxpayers may arrange transactions for tax benefits and a

15. Estimates using the Treasury Department's Tax Calculator indicate that less than half of all taxpayers with incomes below $30,000 now [prior to the Tax Reform Act of 1986] itemize deductions, compared with more than 75 percent of those with incomes above that level.

16. The major tax expenditures for homeownership are: deductibility of mortgage interest on owner-occupied homes; deductibility of property taxes on owner-occupied homes; deferral of capital gains on sales of owner-occupied homes; exclusion of capital gain on sales of owner-occupied homes for persons aged 55 and older; exclusion of interest on state and local bonds for owner-occupied housing.—Eds.

17. Adapted from Rice, Judicial Techniques in Combating Tax Avoidance, 51 Mich.L.Rev. 1021 (1952).

structure in which such particularity was sought would be so complex as to be incomprehensible.

One fundamental problem in federal tax law is the rationale (or lack of it) that underlies the conduct of the courts in striking down tax avoidance devices and refusing to recognize business arrangements which meet statutory requirements for tax saving but fail to meet judicial standards of tax morality.

The cases in the area are, of course, legion. Some arrangement of transactions so as to achieve maximum tax advantages has always been approved; these are the cases involving so-called tax "avoidance" as a legal means to minimize taxes, rather than "evasion", a fraudulent conduct. As Mr. Justice Holmes stated: "The only purpose of the [taxpayer] was to escape taxation. * * * The fact that it desired to evade the law, as it is called, is immaterial, because the very meaning of a line in the law is that you intentionally may go as close to it as you can if you do not pass it." (Superior Oil Co. v. Mississippi, 280 U.S. 390, 395–96, 50 S.Ct. 169, 170, 74 L.Ed. 504, 508 (1930)). Reread pages 26–35.

It likewise is inevitable that taxpayers will sometimes avoid taxes by tendering purely formal compliance with statutory requirements as a justification for nontaxability. The basis for their success is reasonably apparent: there are obvious reasons why a statute should be considered to mean no more and no less than it says. To abandon the moorings established through the statutory structure might "create difficulties and uncertainties more objectionable in their results than any seeming inequities which would be eliminated or prevented." Eaton v. White, 70 F.2d 449, 452 (1st Cir.1934). Tax consequences may determine not only how but whether many business transactions of a nature vital to national economic well being will be consummated. Such transactions may be impeded or altogether foregone where tax consequences are governed by a statute which is continually extended to mean something other than what it says. While the effects of such uncertainty can be, and indeed have been overstated the argument is not without force. Even beyond the economic need for certainty, it is at least doubtful how far judicial legislation should go as a matter of self-imposed judicial restraint. For if the courts enacted the plain provisions of the code, relying on the vague contours of statutory "policy" requirements which exist only in the hearts and minds of the jurists, we may well be coming uncomfortably close to judicial absolutism. Certainly prediction of the outcome of cases will become more difficult.

The alternative is no less distressful. When one taxpayer effects a transaction with only literal conformance to the statute and thereby contrives to avoid tax, the damage is not measured solely in terms of the dollar loss of revenue under his own return. Success in one transaction emboldens attempts by others, and the taxpayer, as with all successful individuals, will have his imitators. Thus there is always the danger that the good fortune of the taxpayer in a single case will be the fountainhead from which will spring multiple transactions in which tax avoidance is the sole, primary, or contributing purpose.

Reaction of the courts to this problem has been indecisive. One approach familiar to all has been to recite that a tax avoidance device is unsuccessful where it is a "sham", "unreal", or a "mere formalism," or that "substance must be regarded rather than form." Another invokes such terms as "good faith" and "bona fide". Other courts refer to "common sense" and still others to whether the transaction was binding.

Judicial Principles Restricting Tax Avoidance: The View that The Revenue Must Come First. The foregoing approaches, used in approval of tax saving doctrines, are confused and self-contradictory.

Other courts support their decisions by reliance on the conclusion that the revenue must come first. Other decisions speak specifically of frustrating evasions of tax liability [18] defeating the payment of taxes, and conduct intended "solely to reduce tax liability." [19]

No court has said, however, and none is expected to say, that a person who would incur tax liability if he handled a transaction in a certain manner should always be said to have incurred that liability even though he in fact concluded the transaction so as to avoid the tax. Hence, these comments do not really aid in drawing the line between the success and failure of tax avoidance devices.

The Business Purpose Rule. A leading principle in this area is expressed in the view that a transaction which formally complies with statutory requirements will be unavailing to reduce taxes unless undertaken with a business purpose. There is a deficiency in the doctrine: only the most unimaginative of tax counsel will find it difficult to project innumerable business reasons supporting any device to save taxes.

Another problem of theory may be noted. The courts have repeated to the point of boredom that an intention to save taxes is immaterial in measuring the tax consequences of any transaction. However, (to restate the business purpose rule) it is equally well established that an intention to consummate a transaction for purposes other than business does govern tax liability. Actually there are only two purposes which are pertinent in these cases: If the courts find that no business purpose exists, the clear corollary is that the sole purpose of the taxpayer was to save taxes. Then the intention of the taxpayer to save taxes clearly becomes material, for it is abundantly clear that a tax saving purpose alone is not a business purpose. On the other hand, where a transaction is consummated partly with a view to saving taxes, and partly for business reasons, there is not necessarily conflict between the business purpose rule and the view that a tax saving purpose is immaterial; as

18. Morgan Mfg. Co. v. Commissioner, 124 F.2d 602, 605 (4th Cir.1941).

19. Higgens v. Smith, 308 U.S. 473, 476, 60 S.Ct. 355, 357, 84 L.Ed. 406, 410 (1940).

has been noted some courts have reconciled the views by holding that where both purposes are present the existence of a tax saving intention does not contaminate.

Leaving the question of theory to one side, grave problems of consistency in applying the doctrine appear. It is clearly a doctrine of last resort, invoked only where no more concrete and measurable principle is available to lend respectability to the decision of the court. Like other rules, it is invoked when it suits the pleasure of the court to decide for the Commissioner, and is ignored in cases when recognition would be embarrassing. In this area, no less than others in the law, courts occasionally find it more convenient to ignore than to distinguish precedents.

Differences in result frequently arise to the extent that various courts emphasize or ignore either the business or tax avoidance purposes respectively advanced by the taxpayer and the Commissioner. The effect of the doctrine where both business and tax saving motives are present has not been definitively stated. Finally and most importantly, the application of the doctrine is whimsical; it is invoked when thought desirable and ignored when it is inconvenient.

The Search for Legislative Intention. Sometimes when courts are faced with a new and wondrous mechanism by which the ever hopeful taxpayer seeks to insure tax savings, they prudently retire behind the statement that the statute was not intended to authorize the result sought by the taxpayer. In the entire cabinet of bromides for use on such occasions, there is none to cause the analytical taxpayer more anguish. These references go beyond recourse to traditional legislative materials; in many cases the congressional debates and committee reports are silent on the subject. Rather what is here involved is that Congress did not intend a purely formal compliance with statutory requirements to be effective in avoiding a tax. We are not accorded an explanation of how the court arrived at the conclusion that Congress intended the statute to be read in a manner other than it was written, and no extrinsic evidence on that subject is available. Accordingly, it may not be unkind to entertain the thought that when the Supreme Court says Congress did not intend to permit tax avoidance, it really means only that the Court refuses to permit it. This brings us once again to the most baffling of all questions: upon what basis does the Supreme Court distinguish the cases in which a wholly literal compliance with statutory terms will be effective to save taxes, from those in which such tax savings is frustrated?

Summary. The nature of the taxation process requires that statutes be drafted so as to establish only the broad outlines of revenue responsibility. Frequently, this impels taxpayers to engage in commercially astonishing transactions which would result in tax savings under a literal interpretation of the statute. In measuring the tax consequences of such conduct, courts must weigh the dangers of successful tax avoidance against the perils of imposing tax responsibility by judicial fiat in cases where no such responsibility is imposed by statute. The issue explored is both where and how the line is to be drawn.

In terms of this objective, the comments of the courts and the doctrines they have enunciated are discouraging. It is all very well to call a transaction a sham, but one undertaking to predict the outcome of litigation might find it comforting to be informed of the difference between "sham" and "non-sham". And while all may agree that form must not be exalted over substance, one may properly be concerned at the failure of the courts to establish the point at which form ends and substance begins. Similarly, it is hardly open to doubt that transactions which are not "realistic," or "bona fide," should be ignored; but that does not inform us how or where the line between purity and unrighteousness should be traced. Finally, when a court rejects a tax saving device by looking to the intention of Congress in enacting the statute, that case has no value of any kind in predicting the treatment of a different tax saving device in the future. Standards of "policy" and "congressional intention" may be altogether intuitive.

This raises the question of whether we have not been barking up the wrong tree in trying to formulate general principles respecting tax avoidance devices. The major premises under which tax avoidance is frustrated in some cases and allowed in others are simply too ephemeral to be articulated. And if articulation were possible, it would only serve to challenge further the ingenuity of the taxpayer.

To approach the problem sanely we must do two things. We must first remember that the justification for preventing tax avoidance is rational and legitimate: the need for protection of the federal revenues by preservation of public confidence in our system of taxation. To measure the length to which a court will go, we must stop reaching for the easy, general rule expressed in terms of business purpose and devote our energies to charting what the courts have done in fact.

Areas are frequent in which successions of cases have occurred in sufficient volume to establish patterns which furnish a basis for reasonable predictions of the outcome of similar cases which may arise in the future. As tax saving devices recur in the same general form, legal principles will emerge. In this sense, "law" is being made, and prediction becomes increasingly accurate under the judicial processes of inclusion and exclusion. The prospect does not entirely please, but we may console ourselves that our blindnesses and uncertainties are only those which fall to all of us seeking the "solid land of fixed and settled rules."

The foregoing necessarily suffers from the perils of generality. Let us analyze how courts go about rationalizing tax avoidance doctrines.

GOLDSTEIN v. COMMISSIONER

United States Court of Appeals, Second Circuit, 1966.
364 F.2d 734, cert. denied 385 U.S. 1005.
87 S.Ct. 708, 17 L.Ed.2d 543 (1967).

WATERMAN, CIRCUIT JUDGE.

Tillie Goldstein and her husband petition to review a decision of the Tax Court disallowing as deductions for federal income tax purposes payments totaling $81,396.61 made by petitioner to certain banks, which payments petitioner claimed were payments of interest on indebtedness within Section 163(a) of the 1954 Internal Revenue Code. * * * A majority of the Tax Court held for several reasons to be considered in the body of this opinion that these payments were not deductible. Goldstein v. Commissioner, 44 T.C. 284 (1965). We affirm on one of the grounds mentioned by the Tax Court.

During the latter part of 1958 petitioner received the good news that she held a winning Irish Sweepstakes ticket and would shortly receive $140,218.75. This windfall significantly improved petitioner's financial situation, for she was a housewife approximately 70 years old and her husband was a retired garment worker who received a $780 pension each year. In 1958 the couple's only income, aside from this pension and the unexpected Sweepstakes proceeds, was $124.75, which represented interest on several small savings bank accounts. The petitioner received the Sweepstakes proceeds in December 1958 and she deposited the money in a New York bank. She included this amount as gross income in the joint return she and her husband filed for 1958 on the cash receipts and disbursements basis.

Petitioner's son, Bernard Goldstein, was a certified public accountant, practicing in New York in 1958. In November of that year Bernard either volunteered or was enlisted to assist petitioner in investing the Sweepstakes proceeds, and in minimizing the 1958 tax consequences to petitioner of the sudden increase in her income for that year. A series of consultations between Bernard and an attorney resulted in the adoption of a plan, which, as implemented, can be summarized as follows: During the latter part of December 1958 petitioner contacted several brokerage houses that bought and sold securities for clients and also arranged collateral loans. With the assistance of one of these brokerage houses, Garvin, Bantel & Co., petitioner borrowed $465,000 from the First National Bank of Jersey City. With the money thus acquired, and the active assistance of Garvin, Bantel, petitioner purchased $500,000 face amount of United States Treasury ½% notes, due to mature on October 1, 1962. Petitioner promptly pledged the Treasury notes so purchased as collateral to secure the loan with the Jersey City Bank. At approximately the same time in 1958 Bernard secured for petitioner a $480,000 loan from the Royal State Bank of New York. With the assistance of the Royal State Bank petitioner purchased a second block of $500,000 face amount of

United States Treasury 1½% notes, due to mature on October 1, 1961. Again the notes were pledged as collateral with this bank to secure the loan. Bernard testified that the petitioner purchased the Treasury notes because he believed "the time was ripe" to invest in this kind of government obligation. Also, pursuant to the prearranged plan, petitioner prepaid to the First National Bank of Jersey City and to the Royal State Bank the interest that would be due on the loans she had received if they remained outstanding for 1½ to 2½ years. These interest prepayments, made in late December of 1958, totaled $81,396.61.[20] Petitioner then claimed this sum as a Section 163(a) deduction on the 1958 income tax return she filed jointly with her husband.

After reviewing these transactions in detail the Tax Court held the $81,396.61 was not deductible as "interest paid or accrued" on "indebtedness" under Section 163(a). In large part this holding rested on the court's conclusion that both loan transactions were "shams" that created "no genuine indebtedness." To support this conclusion the court stressed that, even though petitioner was borrowing approximately one half million dollars from each bank, the banks had agreed to the loans without any of their officers or employees having met petitioner or having investigated her financial position. The court noted that in each of the loan transactions petitioner was not required to commit any of her funds toward the purchase of the Treasury notes in their principal amount. And at several points the court appears to have attached great weight to the fact that most of the relevant transactions were apparently conducted by Garvin, Bantel and the Jersey City Bank, or by Bernard and the Royal State Bank, without petitioner's close supervision. Taking all these factors together, the Tax Court decided that, in fact, each transaction was " * * * an investment *by the bank* in Treasury obligations; wherein the bank, in consideration for prepayment to it of 'interest' by a customer * * * would carry such Treasury notes in the customer's name as purported collateral for the 'loan.' " 44 T.C. at 299 (italics in original). The court went on to say that " * * * if it is necessary to characterize the customer's payment, we would say that it was a fee to the bank for providing the 'facade' of a loan transaction." Ibid.

There is a certain force to the foregoing analysis. Quite clearly the First National Bank of Jersey City and the Royal State Bank of New York preferred to engage in the transactions they engaged in here rather than invest funds directly in Treasury notes because petitioner's loans bore interest at an appreciably higher rate than that yielded by the government obligations. This fact, combined with the impeccable property pledged as security for the loans, may have induced these banks to enter into these transactions without all the panoply that the court indicates usually accompanies loan transactions of such size.

---

20. The prepaid interest on the Jersey City Bank loan totaled $52,596.61 and covered a future period of two years and 9½ months; the prepaid interest on the Royal State Bank loan totaled $28,800 and covered a future period of 1½ years.

Indeed, while on its face purporting to be a debtor-creditor transaction between a taxpayer and a bank, in fact there can be a situation where the bank itself is, in effect, directly investing in the securities purportedly pledged by taxpayer as collateral to taxpayer's obligation; in such a transaction the taxpayer truly can be said to have paid a certain sum to the bank in return for the "facade" of a loan transaction. For Section 163(a) purposes such transactions are properly described as "shams" creating no "genuine indebtedness" and no deduction for the payment of "interest" to the bank should be allowed. * * * Cf. Knetsch v. United States, 364 U.S. 361, 81 S.Ct. 132, 5 L.Ed.2d 128 (1960).

In our view, however, the facts of the two loan arrangements now before us fail in several significant respects to establish that these transactions were clearly shams. We agree with the dissent below that the record indicates these loan arrangements were " * * * regular and, moreover, indistinguishable from any other legitimate loan transaction contracted for the purchase of Government securities." 44 T.C. at 301 (Fay, J., dissenting). In the first place, the Jersey City Bank and the Royal State Bank were independent financial institutions; it cannot be said that their sole function was to finance transactions such as those before us. Compare Lynch v. Commissioner of Internal Revenue, 273 F.2d 867 (2 Cir.1959); Goodstein v. Commissioner of Internal Revenue, 267 F.2d 127 (1 Cir.1959). Second, the two loan transactions here did not within a few days return all the parties to the position from which they had started. Ibid. Here the Royal State Bank loan remained outstanding, and, significantly, that Bank retained the Treasury obligations pledged as security until June 10, 1960, at which time petitioner instructed the bank to sell the notes, apply the proceeds to the loan, and credit any remaining balance to her account. The facts relating to the Jersey City Bank loan are slightly different: this loan was closed in June 1959 when the brokerage house of Gruntal & Co. was substituted for the Jersey City Bank as creditor. Gruntal received and retained the 1962 Treasury 1½%'s originally pledged as security for the loan until December 1, 1959 when, pursuant to instructions from petitioner and her advisors, these notes were sold, and $500,000 face amount of United States Treasury 2½% bonds were purchased to replace them as security. Petitioner's account with Gruntal was not finally closed until June 13, 1960 when the last of these substituted bonds were sold, the petitioner's note was marked fully paid, and the balance was credited to petitioner. Third, the independent financial institutions from which petitioner borrowed the funds she needed to acquire the Treasury obligations possessed significant control over the future of their respective loan arrangements: for example, the petitioner's promissory note to the Jersey City Bank explicitly gave either party the right to accelerate the maturity of the note after 30 days, and it was the Jersey City Bank's utilization of this clause that necessitated recourse to Gruntal; the Royal State Bank had the right at any time to demand that petitioner increase her collateral or liquidate the loan, and on several occasions it made such a demand. Fourth, the notes signed by petitioner in favor of both banks were signed with recourse. If either of the independent lending institutions here involved had lost money on these transactions because of the depreciation of the collateral pledged to secure the loans we are certain that, upon petitioner's default of payment, they would have without hesitation proceeded against petitioner to recover their losses. Compare Lynch v. Commissioner of Internal Revenue, supra (nonrecourse notes). * * * Moreover, all things being equal, the banks' chances of judgments in their favor would have been excellent. In view of this combination of facts we think it was error for the Tax Court to conclude that these two transactions were "shams" which created no genuine indebtedness. Were this the only ground on which the decision reached below could be supported we would be compelled to reverse.

In reaching this conclusion we recognize that at least one other United States Court of Appeals has disallowed a deduction for interest in a closely analogous case on the ground the transactions there were "sham." Bridges v. Commissioner of Internal Revenue, 325 F.2d 180 (4 Cir.1963). We think the interest of candor is better served if the "sham" and "absence of indebtedness" rationales are reserved for cases like Lynch v. Commissioner of Internal Revenue, supra, and Goodstein v. Commissioner of Internal Revenue, supra. Different considerations govern decisions as to whether interest payments are deductible by a taxpayer who borrows money from an independent lending institution, executes a promissory note with recourse, and purchases Treasury obligations that are then in fact pledged with the lender as security for the loan for a significant period of time, unless it can be concluded from other facts (not present in this case) that the transaction is simply a sham.

One ground advanced by the Tax Court seems capable of reasoned development to support the result reached in this case by that court. The Tax Court found as an ultimate fact that petitioner's purpose in entering into the Jersey City Bank and Royal State Bank transactions "was not to derive any economic gain or to improve here [sic] beneficial interest; but was *solely* an attempt to obtain an interest deduction as an offset to her sweepstake winnings." 44 T.C. at 295 (emphasis added). This finding of ultimate fact was based in part on a set of computations made by Bernard Goldstein shortly after the Jersey City Bank and Royal State Bank loan transactions had been concluded. These computations were introduced by the Commissioner below and they indicated that petitioner and her financial advisors then estimated that the transactions would produce an economic loss in excess of $18,500 inasmuch as petitioner was out of pocket the 4% interest she had prepaid and could expect to receive 1½% interest on the Treasury obligations she had just purchased plus a modest capital gain when the obligations were sold. This computation also reflected Bernard's realization that if the plan was successful this economic loss would be more than offset by the substantial reduction in petitioner's 1958 income tax liability due to the large deduction for interest "paid or accrued" taken in that year. The memorandum drawn up by Bernard is set out in full in the opinion of the Tax Court. 44 T.C. 292–293. In fact, petitioner sustained a $25,091.01 economic loss on these transactions for some of the Treasury obligations were ultimately sold for less than the price that had been originally anticipated by petitioner's advisors.

Before the Tax Court, and before us, petitioner has argued that she realistically anticipated an economic gain on the loan transactions due to anticipated appreciation in the value of the Treasury obligations, and that this gain would more than offset the loss that was bound to result because of the unfavorable interest rate differential. In support of this position, Bernard testified, and documentary evidence was introduced, to the effect that in December 1958 the market for Treasury obligations was unreasonably depressed, and that many investors at that time were favorably disposed toward their purchase. In short, petitioner argued that she intended a sophisticated, speculative, sortie into the market for government securities.

In holding that petitioner's "sole" purpose in entering into the Jersey City Bank and Royal State Bank transactions was to obtain an interest deduction, the Tax Court rejected this explanation of her purpose in entering into these transactions. For several reasons we hold that this rejection was proper. First, petitioner's evidence tending to establish that she anticipated an economic profit on these transactions due to a rising market for Treasury obligations is flatly contradicted by the computations made by Bernard contemporaneously with the commencement of these transactions and introduced by the Commissioner at trial. These computations almost conclusively establish that petitioner and her advisors from the outset anticipated an economic loss. Petitioner's answer to this damaging evidence is that the set of Bernard's computations introduced by the Commissioner was only one of several arithmetic projections made at the same time by Bernard, and that Bernard intended the computations introduced by the Commissioner to represent the worst that could befall the plan if prices for government obligations continued to decline. The petitioner introduced several exhibits that purported to be reconstructions of the other arithmetic projections made by Bernard contemporaneously with the computations introduced by the Commissioner. Exhibit 83, introduced by petitioner, purported to be an arithmetic projection of petitioner's expected profit on the assumption that the market for Treasury obligations remained at the level it had reached at the close of 1958; this exhibit showed an economic profit on both transactions over a two-year period totaling a meager $2,075.00. Exhibit 84, also introduced by petitioner, purported to be an arithmetic projection of petitioner's expected profit on the assumption that the market for Treasury obligations reverted to previous highs; this exhibit projected an economic profit on both transactions over a two year period totaling $22,875.00.

The Tax Court's ground (or grounds) for refusing to credit these exhibits and related evidence does not clearly appear in its opinion, but sufficient grounds are not hard to find. First, unlike the computations made by Bernard that the Commissioner introduced, Exhibits 83 and 84 purported only to be reconstructions of calculations made by Bernard in late December 1958. The originals of Exhibits 83 and 84 were not produced; no explanation of petitioner's failure to do so was given. On this ground the Tax Court might have decided that Exhibits 83 and 84 were especially prepared for this litigation and had not entered into Tillie's calculations at the outset. Second, even if we assume Exhibits 83 and 84 represent computations made contemporaneously with petitioner's entrance into these transactions, they far from establish that the transactions were undertaken with a realistic expectation of economic profit. For example, Exhibit 83 purports to establish that, assuming the market for Treasury obligations remained constant, petitioner and her advisors anticipated an economic profit of $2,075.00 over a two year period on these transactions. But Exhibit 83 fails to reflect the $6,500 fee paid to Bernard and tax counsel for their work in planning these transactions. Once this fee is included in these computations all economic profit disappears. Inclusion of this $6,500 item similarly reduces the total economic profit as computed in Exhibit 84. Furthermore, although petitioner made an outlay of "prepaid interest" on the Royal State Bank loan for a period of 1½ years, Exhibits 83 and 84 compute the outlay on this loan as if there had been an interest payment for only one year. The payment of interest on the Jersey City Bank loan similarly is computed on a two-year basis instead of the basis of the actual outlay, which extended for two years, nine and one half months. Such computations presuppose petitioner could, at her option, terminate the loans prior to their due dates, sell the securities, and be reimbursed for the portions of the prepaid interest not yet earned by the banks. However, neither loan agreement contains a provision entitling petitioner to be reimbursed for any unearned portion of the prepaid interest if the loan is terminated *by the petitioner* prior to the due date. And, in the case of the Royal State Bank transaction, it is not even clear that petitioner had the power to prepay the principal of the loan prior to its maturity date. This uncertainty in the consequences of a sale by petitioner of the Treasury obligations prior to their due date might have led the Tax Court to conclude that petitioner and her advisors could not have entertained a realistic hope of economic profit when these loan transactions were commenced. Finally, Exhibit 84 is predicated on the remote possibility that the Treasury obligations could be sold considerably in excess of par, thereby yielding an effective rate of interest well below 1½%, even though it would be unlikely that investors would purchase them for such a small return when they were to mature at par in the near future.

For all of the above reasons the Tax Court was justified in concluding that petitioner entered into the Jersey City Bank and Royal State Bank transactions without any realistic expectation of economic profit and "solely" in order to secure a large interest deduction in 1958 which could be deducted from her sweepstakes winnings in that year. This conclusion points the way to affirmance in the present case.

We hold, for reasons set forth hereinafter, that Section 163(a) of the [1986] Internal Revenue Code does not permit a deduction for interest paid or accrued in loan arrangements, like those now before us, that can not with reason be said to have purpose, substance, or utility apart from their anticipated tax consequences. See Knetsch v. United States, 364 U.S. 361, 366, 81 S.Ct. 132, 5 L.Ed.2d 128 (1960) * * *. Although it is by no means certain that Congress constitutionally could tax gross income, see Surrey & Warren, Federal Income Taxation 228–29 (1960 ed.), it is frequently stated that deductions from "gross income" are a matter of "legislative grace." E.g., Deputy v. DuPont, 308 U.S. 488, 493, 60 S.Ct. 363, 84 L.Ed. 416 (1940). There is at least this much truth in this oft-repeated maxim: a close question whether a particular Code provision authorizes the deduction of a certain item is best resolved by reference to the underlying Congressional purpose of the deduction provision in question.[21]

Admittedly, the underlying purpose of Section 163(a) permitting the deduction of "all interest paid or accrued within the taxable year on indebtedness" is difficult to articulate because this provision is extremely broad: there is no requirement that deductible interest serve a business purpose, that it be ordinary and necessary, or even that it be reasonable. 4 Mertens, Law of Federal Income Taxation § 26.01 (1960 ed.). Nevertheless, it is fair to say that Section 163(a) is not entirely unlimited in its application and that such limits as there are stem from the Section's underlying notion that if an individual or corporation desires to engage in purposive activity, there is no reason why a taxpayer who borrows for that purpose should fare worse from an income tax standpoint than one who finances the venture with capital that otherwise would have been yielding income.

In order fully to implement this Congressional policy of encouraging purposive activity to be financed through borrowing, Section 163(a) should be construed to permit the deductibility of interest when a taxpayer has borrowed funds and incurred an obligation to pay interest in order to engage in what with reason can be termed purposive activity, even though he decided to borrow in order to gain an interest deduction rather than to finance the activity in some other way. In other words, the interest deduction should be permitted whenever it can be said that the taxpayer's desire to secure an interest deduction is only one of mixed motives that prompts the taxpayer to borrow funds; or, put a third way, the deduction is proper if there is some substance to the loan arrangement beyond the taxpayer's desire to secure the deduction. After all, we are frequently told that a taxpayer has the

---

21. The proposition that because deductions are a matter of "legislative grace" they should be strictly construed is much more doubtful as an interpretive guide. See Note, An Argument Against the Doctrine That Deductions Should be Narrowly Construed as a Matter of Legislative Grace, 56 Harv.L.Rev. 1142 (1943).

right to decrease the amount of what otherwise would be his taxes, or altogether avoid them, by any means the law permits. E.g., Gregory v. Helvering, 293 U.S. 465, 55 S.Ct. 266, 79 L.Ed. 596 (1935). On the other hand, and notwithstanding Section 163(a)'s broad scope this provision should not be construed to permit an interest deduction when it objectively appears that a taxpayer has borrowed funds in order to engage in a transaction that has no substance or purpose aside from the taxpayer's desire to obtain the tax benefit of an interest deduction: and a good example of such purposeless activity is the borrowing of funds at 4% in order to purchase property that returns less than 2% and holds out no prospect of appreciation sufficient to counter the unfavorable interest rate differential. Certainly the statutory provision's underlying purpose, as we understand it, does not require that a deduction be allowed in such a case. Indeed, to allow a deduction for interest paid on funds borrowed for no purposive reason, other than the securing of a deduction from income, would frustrate Section 163(a)'s purpose; allowing it would encourage transactions that have no economic utility and that would not be engaged in but for the system of taxes imposed by Congress. When it enacted Section 163(a) Congress could not have intended to permit a taxpayer to reduce his taxes by means of an interest deduction that arose from a transaction that had no substance, utility, or purpose beyond the tax deduction. See Knetsch v. United States, supra, [364] U.S. at 367, 81 S.Ct. 132.

In many instances transactions that lack all substance, utility, and purpose, and which can only be explained on the ground the taxpayer sought an interest deduction in order to reduce his taxes, will also be so transparently arranged that they can candidly be labeled "shams." In those instances both the rationale of the decision we announce today, and that of Goodstein v. Commissioner of Internal Revenue, supra, and its progeny, are available as grounds for disallowing the deduction. The present case makes plain, however, that these rationales are distinct from each other, and that a court need not always first label a loan transaction a "sham" in order to deny a deduction for interest paid in connection with the loan.

In Knetsch v. United States, supra, [364] U.S. at 365, 81 S.Ct. 132, the Supreme Court cautions us, by reiteration there of what the Court had said in Gregory v. Helvering, supra, 55 S.Ct. at page 267 at 469, that in cases like the present "the question for determination is whether what was done, apart from the tax motive, was the thing which the statute intended." We here decide that Section 163(a) does not "intend" that taxpayers should be permitted deductions for interest paid on debts that were entered into solely in order to obtain a deduction. It follows therefore from the foregoing, and from the Tax Court's finding as a matter of "ultimate" fact that petitioner entered into the Jersey City Bank and Royal State Bank transactions without any expectation of profit and without any other purpose except to obtain an interest deduction, and that the Tax Court's disallowance of the deductions in this case must be affirmed.

Question

Does the limitation of the deductibility of interest paid on loans incurred in connection with an investment (§ 163(d)), cast doubt on the validity of the Goldstein case?

F. TAXES

Section 164 outlines the deductibility of taxes whether or not they were paid in connection with business or profit-seeking transactions. State and local property taxes, both real and personal, are deductible even though they arise from non-business transactions, such as property used as the taxpayer's residence. State and local income taxes, but not state and local sales taxes, are also deductible.

Any state, local, or foreign tax not described in the first sentence of § 164(a), for example, nondeductible sales taxes, incurred by a taxpayer in connection with the acquisition or disposition of property is treated as a part of the cost of the acquired property, or as a reduction in the amount realized on the disposition of property. § 164(a). Thus, a sales tax is included in the basis of the acquired property under such circumstances.

Federal income taxes, social security taxes paid by an employee and estate, gift, and inheritance taxes whether federal or state, are nondeductible. § 275. Special assessments for improvements which increase the value of the assessed property are nondeductible. § 164(c) (1). Instead, they can be capitalized as part of the cost of the related property.

Problem

Bonny agrees to purchase a parcel of land, valued at $10,150, from Stephanie for $10,000 in cash. In addition, Bonny agrees to pay the real estate taxes on the property for the year in the amount of $300. The real estate taxes are due on the last day of the year. The sale takes place on July 1. Bonny pays the $300 in real estate taxes on December 31. Can she take a deduction for the entire amount under § 164? Consider § 164(d). What basis does Bonny take in the land?

Notes and Questions

Should the deduction for state and local taxes be repealed? Or do state and local taxes reduce a taxpayer's ability to pay his Federal tax liabilities? Because of the diversities in state and local tax systems, if the deduction for state and local income taxes were not allowed, taxpayers in the same levels of gross income would differ in their abilities to meet their Federal income tax liabilities. Thus, the deduction for state and local income taxes serves as "an important means of accommodation where both the state and local government on one hand and the Federal Government on the other hand tap this same revenue source * * *." (H.R.Rep. No. 749, 88th Cong., 1st Sess. 48 (1963)). Deductibility favors the objective of fiscal coordination among various governmental levels (Federal, state, and local) by preventing the confiscation of income, giving state and local governments more freedom to tax, and lessening the impact of the Federal tax system on a jurisdiction's population by reducing income tax differentials between jurisdictions, and enabling states and localities to finance more adequately public services. The deductibility of sales and property taxes enable states and localities to structure freely their tax systems in a neutral environment (H.R.Rep. No. 749, 88th Cong., 1st Sess. 48–50 (1963)). The denial of the deduction for sales taxes would discourage state and local governments from using this revenue source to meet their financial needs. However, the sales and property taxes represent a cost of consumption and the tax deduction thereby subsidizes personal consumption. Is this inequitable? Sales and property taxes finance public, not private, uses of resources. Consider the impact of the real estate tax deduction on the Federal tax burden borne by homeowners and renters.

Recently, the deduction for state and local taxes has come under attack. Consider the following proposal.

THE PRESIDENT'S TAX PROPOSALS TO THE CONGRESS FOR FAIRNESS, GROWTH AND SIMPLICITY
62–66 (1985).

* * *

REPEAL DEDUCTION OF STATE AND LOCAL TAXES

General Explanation

* * *

Reasons for Change

Fairness. The current deduction for State and local taxes disproportionately benefits high-income taxpayers residing in high-tax States. The two-thirds of taxpayers who do not itemize deductions are not entitled to deduct State and local taxes, and even itemizing taxpayers receive relatively little benefit from the deduction unless they reside in high-tax States. Although the deduction for State and local taxes thus benefits a small minority of U.S. taxpayers, the cost of the deduction is borne by all taxpayers in the form of significantly higher marginal tax rates.

* * *

Erosion of the Tax Base. The deduction for State and local taxes is one of the most serious omissions from the Federal income tax base. Repeal of the deduction is projected to generate $33.8 billion in revenues for 1988. Recovery of those revenues will permit a substantial reduction in marginal tax rates. Indeed, unless those revenues are recovered, tax rates will almost certainly remain at the current unnecessarily high levels.

The Fallacy of the "Tax on a Tax" Argument. Some argue that the deductibility of State and local taxes is appropriate because individuals should not be "taxed on a tax." The argument is deficient for a number of reasons. First, it ignores the effect of State and local tax deductibility on the Federal income tax base. Deductibility not only reduces aggregate Federal income tax revenues, it shifts the burden of collecting those revenues from high-tax to low-tax States. High-tax States effectively shield a disproportionate share of their income from Federal taxation, leaving a relatively greater share of revenues to be collected from low-tax States. Absent the ability to impose Federal income tax on amounts paid in State and local taxes, the Federal government loses the ability to control its own tax base and to insist that the burden of Federal income taxes be distributed evenly among the States.

Second, the "tax on a tax" argument suggests that amounts paid in State or local taxes should be exempt from Federal taxation because they are involuntary and State or local taxpayers receive nothing in return for their payments. Neither suggestion is correct. State and local taxpayers have ultimate control over the taxes they pay through the electoral process and through their ability to locate in jurisdictions with amenable tax and fiscal policies. Moreover, State and local taxpayers receive important personal benefits in return for their taxes, such as public education, water and sewer services and municipal garbage removal. In this respect, the determination by State and local taxpayers of their levels of taxation and public service benefits is analogous to their individual decisions over how much to spend for the purchase of private goods.

It is, of course, true that not all benefits provided by State and local governments are directly analogous to privately purchased goods or services. Examples include police and fire protection, judicial and administrative services and public welfare. These services nevertheless provide substantial personal benefits to State and local taxpayers, whether directly or by enhancing the general quality of life in State and local communities.

Finally, the "tax on a tax" argument is contradicted by the practice of most States with respect to their own tax systems, including many of those with high tax rates. Federal income taxes are allowable as a deduction from State individual income taxes in only 16 States and from State corporate income taxes in only seven States. New York and California, States with very high tax rates, are among the States that deny a deduction for Federal income taxes.

Inefficient Subsidy. The deduction for State and local taxes may also be regarded as providing a subsidy to State and local governments, which are likely to find it somewhat easier to raise revenue because of the deduction. A general subsidy for spending by State and local governments can be justified only if the services which State and local governments provide have important spillover benefits to individuals in other communities. The existence of such benefits has not been documented.

Even if a subsidy for State and local government spending were desired, provision of the subsidy through a deduction for State and local taxes is neither cost effective nor fair. On average, State and local governments gain less than fifty cents for every dollar of Federal revenue lost because of the deduction. Moreover, a deduction for State and local taxes provides a greater level of subsidy to high-income States and communities than to low-income States and communities. In addition, a deduction for taxes does not distinguish between categories of State and local spending on the basis of their spillover effects, but is as much a subsidy for spending on recreational facilities as for public welfare spending. Finally, the deduction distorts the revenue mix of State and local governments by creating a bias against the imposition of user charges in favor of more general taxes.

Proposal

The itemized deduction for State and local income taxes and for other State and local taxes that are not incurred in carrying on a trade or business or income-producing activity would be repealed. State and local taxes (other than income taxes) which currently are deductible only by itemizers, but which are incurred in carrying on an income-producing activity, would be aggregated with employee business expenses and other miscellaneous deductions and would be deductible subject to a threshold.

* * *

Analysis

While only one-third of all families itemized deductions in 1983, this group included most high-income families (more than 95 percent of families with income over $100,000 itemized tax deductions) and very few low-income families (2 percent of families with income of $10,000 or less itemized tax deductions). * * * Two-thirds of the total deductions for State and local tax payments were claimed by families with economic income of $50,000 or more. The benefits are even further skewed toward high-income families because deductions are worth more to families which face higher marginal tax rates.

The tax savings from deductibility vary widely among the States and, * * *, provide the greatest benefits to individuals in high-income States. Because this tax expenditure requires tax rates for all individuals to be higher than they otherwise would be, those in the 15 States with above-average tax savings per capita currently gain at the expense of taxpayers in the other 35 States. Even within the high-tax States, less than one-half of all taxpayers itemize deductions.

Recent estimates indicate that the effect of tax deductibility on the level of State and local government spending is not large. A National League of Cities study found that total State and local spending is about 2% higher because of the existence of tax deductibility. This estimated effect is low in part because less than one-third of total State and local spending is financed by taxes potentially deductible from the Federal individual income tax. Because State and local spending has been growing by about 7% per year since 1980, the elimination of tax deductibility would not reduce the absolute level of State and local spending, but only reduce its rate of growth. However, because the proportion of taxpayers who itemize varies a great deal among the States as well as among local governments within a State, the effect on spending for a particular State or local government would be larger than 2 percent for a high-income community and may not affect spending at all in low-income communities where few residents itemize deductions.

The three most important sources of State and local tax revenue in the U.S. are general sales, personal income and property taxes. Some argue that itemized deductions should be eliminated for some of these taxes, but retained for others. * * * [However], elimination of any one tax deduction would have an uneven effect on taxpayers among the States. In addition, since State and local governments would be likely to increase reliance on the remaining deductible taxes, disallowing deductions for particular taxes is likely to lead to sizeable distortions in State and local revenue mixes. For example, disallowing only the sales tax deduction might force a State, like Washington, that relies heavily on a general sales tax but does not have an individual income tax, to adopt one.

BILLMAN AND CUNNINGHAM, NONBUSINESS STATE AND LOCAL TAXES: THE CASE FOR DEDUCTIBILITY

28 Tax Notes 1107, 1107–1120 (1985).

A. INTRODUCTION

In the ongoing debate about fundamental tax reform, the deduction for nonbusiness state and local taxes has come under repeated fire. No major tax reform proposal has left it untouched, and the Department of the Treasury has twice proposed that the deduction be completely repealed.[22] This article evaluates the merits of the various arguments that have been made for the elimination of the deduction. In addition, the article examines other arguments that have been given little attention in the debate over its future.

History of the Deduction for State and Local Taxes

Since 1861, amounts paid as state and local taxes have been deductible for purposes of the federal income tax. Over the years, two quite different rationales have been offered in support of the deduction. First, the deduction has been justified as being necessary to properly

---

22. See U.S. Dept. of Treasury, Tax Reform for Fairness, Simplicity, and Economic Growth 77–81 (1984) (hereinafter cited as "Treasury I, Vol. 1"); U.S. Dept. of Treasury, Tax Reform for Fairness, Simplicity, and Economic Growth—General Explanation of the Treasury Department Proposals 66–71 (1984) (hereinafter cited as "Treasury I, Vol. 2"); The President's Tax Proposals to the Congress for Fairness, Growth, and Simplicity 62–69 (1985) (hereinafter cited as "Treasury II").

measure an individual's taxable income. Under this view, an amount paid in state and local taxes reduces an individual's ability to pay federal taxes. From a tax policy perspective, an appropriate remedy in such a situation is to grant a deduction for the payment, thereby removing the amount of the payment from the federal income tax base. Implicit in this rationale is the conclusion that the deduction is not a tax expenditure; rather, it is a necessary adjustment to properly define the tax base.

The second rationale is that the deduction, to the extent that it is not necessary to define the proper federal income tax base, facilitates fiscal coordination in our federal system. Under this rationale, the deduction is a tax expenditure and must be analyzed and justified as such. As viewed by some, this tax expenditure is a subsidy to state and local governments; as viewed by others, it is a crucial component of the overall financing scheme of our federal system of government.

Summary of Treasury Position

In Treasury II and in congressional testimony, the Treasury has offered several arguments in support of the repeal of the nonbusiness state and local tax deduction for itemizing taxpayers. First is "Fairness." Treasury II states that the deduction is unfair because it disproportionately benefits high-income individuals residing in high-tax states. As further explained, this creates two types of inequities. As between itemizing and nonitemizing taxpayers (regardless of location), the deduction benefits only those who itemize their deductions. Treasury II finds this to be unfair because only about one-third of all taxpayers itemize their deductions, with the clear implication that the predominant number of itemizers are higher-income taxpayers. In addition, as between itemizing taxpayers, the deduction benefits taxpayers residing in high-tax jurisdictions more than those in lower-tax states.

Second, the deduction creates an "Erosion of the Tax Base." Viewing the deduction as a tax expenditure and as revenue that the federal government could, but does not, collect, Treasury II states that marginal tax rates could be lowered significantly if the taxable income represented by this deduction were included in the tax base.

Third is the "Fallacy of the 'Tax on a Tax' Argument." One component of the tax on a tax argument is the question as to whether the deduction for state and local taxes is necessary for the proper definition of the federal tax base. Treasury II answers this question in the negative, arguing that state and local taxes are "voluntary" payments made by residents of a particular jurisdiction in exchange for public goods and services that represent items of "personal consumption." As such, they should not be allowed as reductions in the federal tax base.

Treasury II also criticizes the deduction on this level because it shifts the burden of the federal income tax from high-tax to low-tax states. It inhibits the ability of the federal government to insist that the federal income tax burden be distributed evenly among the states. In addition, Treasury II maintains that the repeal of the deduction is critical, because the federal government must be able to control its own tax base. With the deduction, state and local jurisdictions effectively control the federal tax base by being able to increase their taxes and diminish federal revenue.

Fourth, Treasury II argues that the deduction for state and local taxes is an "Inefficient Subsidy" to state and local governments. The basic point of this argument is that the federal government should only be spending money (either directly or indirectly through the tax system) on projects that are national in character—i.e., that have benefits that cross or "spill over" individual state and local boundaries. Treasury II finds support for its position in favor of repeal in the absence of strong evidence that these spillover items make up a significant portion of all state and local expenditures. Moreover, even though Treasury II does acknowledge that certain spillover expenditures do exist in almost every state and local jurisdiction, the deduction does not properly identify what expenditures are local and national in character.

Evaluating the Deduction for State and Local Taxes

Treasury II's position arguing for repeal of the deduction for nonbusiness state and local taxes is based upon two fundamental premises that reject the historical justifications for the deduction: First, the deduction is not necessary to define the federal income tax base properly. As such, the deduction represents a tax expenditure. Second, Treasury II has concluded that, viewed as a tax expenditure, the deduction cannot be justified on the basis of economic considerations. This article examines both of these premises.

With regard to whether the deduction for state and local taxes is necessary for the proper definition of the federal income tax base, the first section of this article draws upon two theoretical models—a time-honored economic model of the ideal federal system of government (sometimes referred to as "fiscal federalism") and a model of the comprehensive income tax base—and explores the role of the deduction for state and local taxes in a world with both of these models in place. Once these models have been developed, the article then compares these theoretical constructs with the real world, seeking to determine whether Treasury II's proposed repeal of the deduction for state and local taxes produces a federal income tax system that, in fact, better measures the income of all taxpayers.

The second part of this article examines the deduction for state and local taxes as a tax expenditure, both in its own right and in comparison with other significant tax expenditures, such as the deductions for home mortgage interest and charitable contributions. Each of Treasury II's arguments regarding the deduction is explored in detail in this section of the article.

The article concludes that Treasury II has not made the case for repeal of the deduction. Treasury II does not explicitly address the question of whether the deduction is necessary to properly define taxable income. As developed below, a deduction for state and local taxes would not be necessary in the ideal economic world of fiscal federalism. Presumably, Treasury II's position is based upon this ideal model. In fact, the real world diverges from the ideal in so many significant ways that it is highly questionable whether repeal of the deduction will result in a better formulation of the federal tax base. Indeed, its repeal may actually increase inter-taxpayer unfairness by overstating the taxable income of many taxpayers.

At the tax expenditure level, the article concludes that Treasury II overstates the arguments against the deduction for state and local taxes, especially when compared to the proposed retention of both the home mortgage interest and charitable contribution deductions under Treasury II. From a tax policy perspective, it is difficult to rationalize the repeal of the deduction for state and local taxes alongside the retention of many other similar expenditure items, especially the deduction for charitable contributions. Both of these deductions in many ways seek to accomplish similar goals and purposes and, as tax expenditures, both have very similar effects upon the fairness, efficiency, and neutrality of the tax base. The repeal/retention dichotomy in this particular comparison is quite stark, and clearly calls into question the merits of Treasury II's position. The article now turns to a detailed development of these arguments.

B. STATE AND LOCAL TAX DEDUCTION AS PART OF IDEAL TAX BASE

A Theoretical Model for a Multiunit Taxing System

The deduction for nonbusiness state and local taxes is somewhat unique because, at least in the past, it has been viewed as an element of a much larger picture, namely, the manner in which our complicated federal system, with a multitude of federal, state, and local jurisdictions, is financed.* * * *

Fiscal Functions of Government. In the theoretical model of one noted economist, Professor Richard A. Musgrave, governments perform at least three major fiscal functions—allocation, distribution, and stabilization. Under the allocation function, governments make decisions as to what portion of total resources are to be dedicated to so-called public or social goods—goods that will not be provided at all, or at socially desirable levels, if left to the private marketplace. Examples of public goods include national defense, education, and police and fire protection. In addition, governments also determine what the resource allocation mix among the various public goods should be. Under the

* A recent text put the number of state and local jurisdictions at approximately 80,000. See R. Musgrave and P. Musgrave, Public Finance in Theory and Practice 501 (4th ed. 1984) (hereinafter cited as "Musgrave & Musgrave").

distribution function, governments determine through fiscal policies what the fair distribution of income and wealth in society should be. Through the stabilization function, governments seek through economic policy to maintain high employment, a reasonable level of price stability, and an appropriate rate of economic growth for society.

The Ideal Multiunit System. The Musgrave model posits that it is not only appropriate, but economically efficient, to divide these basic governmental functions among various levels of government, with each level performing those functions for which it is best (i.e., most efficiently) suited. Hence, a federal system comprised of both a central or national government, and state and local governments, not only makes sense from a political perspective, but it may be economically efficient and desirable as well. The most important division of labor among the various levels of government in a multiunit or federal system arises with respect to the allocation function.

A central premise of the Musgrave optimal allocation function is "the spatial limitation of benefit incidence." This maxim of allocation theory assumes that different public goods and services benefit different regions within a country ("benefit regions"). In the context of multiunit governmental structure, there are thus essentially two types of public goods—those goods whose benefits are "federation-wide" (national goods) and those goods whose benefits are less than federation-wide (regional or local goods).

Under allocation theory generally, the optimum level of goods and services is determined by the preferences of the consumers of those goods and services in society. Consumers reveal their preferences for types and amounts of private goods and services via their purchases in the marketplace. For social or public goods, the basic manner in which consumer preferences are revealed is through the political process (i.e., voting and other mechanisms of representative government). Given the manner in which consumer preferences for public goods are determined through the political process, the model assumes that the ideal multiunit governmental system should seek to correlate benefit regions with the political constituency that both votes and pays for the benefits.

For example, national goods, such as national defense, whose benefits are "federation-wide," should be provided by the central or national government, because all consumers in the country benefit from these national goods and their preferences should be ascertained to determine the optimum levels for the various potential national benefits. Local goods, those with less than federation-wide benefits, should be provided by the local governments whose citizens benefit therefrom and whose citizens' preferences should determine the proper level of benefit provision. These local goods will not be provided at optimum levels of efficiency if consumer preferences beyond the proper benefit region are taken into account (through the political process) in establishing the allocation level.

Under the Musgrave model, the distribution function, unlike the allocation function, must be provided only at the national or central government level. To do otherwise would create disparities among various jurisdictions with different redistributional policies, thereby causing high-income individuals to move to low-tax jurisdictions and vice versa. Because this would result in all low-income individuals residing in the high redistribution jurisdictions, the local redistribution scheme would fall apart unless restrictions on mobility were put in place. Finally, the model assumes that the stabilization function must be within the province of the national government, because local jurisdictions do not have the capacity to affect the entire nation's economy in a uniform manner.

Thus, under this ideal model of fiscal federalism, national governments would generally provide goods that had benefits that were "national" in nature, and local governments would provide those goods that were "local" in nature. In this ideal world, to the extent that a particular public good was somewhere in between purely local and clearly national, i.e., a good that had benefits that "spilled over" local boundaries, but did not necessarily rise to a truly national level, the national government would aid in the provision of such goods through a series of grants to local or regional governments. On the other hand, the national government would engage in income redistribution among the national citizenry, with the regional and local governments only seeking to raise revenue to provide the social goods within the purview of the regional and local governments.

How the Model Translates Into a Tax System. This ideal model of multiunit government fiscal coordination translates directly into a general taxation scheme. The guiding principle is that the residents of each benefit region or jurisdiction establish a desired level of benefits (expressing their preferences through the political process), and then they pay for the services provided by that jurisdiction through taxes. This implies that all taxes at the local level *should* be based upon benefits received—so-called "benefits received" taxation. In an ideal world in which individuals have ready mobility, if the level of benefits (and thus the level of taxes) did not correspond to an individual's level and mix of preferences for public goods, such individual would be able to relocate to a benefit region that allocated its resources more in line with that individual's preferences.[23]

The national government would impose broad-based taxes, independent of the location or residence of any particular taxpayer. Since this level of government is solely responsible for the distribution function, it

---

23. In a world in which individuals have ready mobility and in which local jurisdictions only provide local goods, the taxes imposed by the local jurisdiction can be imposed on a number of different bases, e.g., property, income, or consumption. Although these are not explicitly tied to actual benefits, by choosing to live in a particular locale, an individual has revealed his or her preference for the mix and the level of services he or she desires, with overall taxes thereby being equated with overall benefits received.

would not be restricted to benefits received taxation. If it chose to engage in income redistribution, it could adopt a tax based solely upon each individual's ability to pay taxes, regardless of the benefits that the individual receives—so-called "ability-to-pay" taxes. Ability-to-pay taxes are not assessed on the basis of the level of services or goods a taxpayer receives in exchange therefor. Rather, these taxes primarily carry out the income redistribution goals of society. Under the ideal federal model, since only the national government would be charged with any income redistribution responsibility, it would be the only government imposing ability-to-pay taxes. Conversely, since the local jurisdictions would not be engaged in income distribution, but only resource allocation, such jurisdictions would impose only benefits received taxes upon their taxpayers.

Fundamentals of Tax Policy

Under the ideal model of fiscal federalism, the central or national government would be charged with income redistribution. Assuming that the nation as a whole had determined that income redistribution should be accomplished, what would the national tax system look like? There are several potential models for a redistributive tax system, but this article will concentrate upon the comprehensive income tax, since that has been the basic model used in the United States to date, and since it seems likely that an income-based tax will remain the goal of our federal taxing scheme. The most important aspect of the design of an appropriate income tax is the determination of the proper tax base. Once the tax base is established, the tax rates can be set to raise any level of revenue necessary to support the desired level of national goods and services. Hence, the goal would be to define "income" in a fair, efficient, and neutral manner for all taxpayers.

Defining a Comprehensive Income Tax Base. Although no single ideal definition of "income" has been adopted as part of the ongoing debate regarding broad-based tax reform, the Haig-Simons definition is the starting point for most discussions: Income is the sum of a taxpayer's consumption and his change in wealth over a period of time, usually a year.[24] This definition is very broad, and it brings within its reach certain items that cannot reasonably or practically be included within an administrable tax base. For example, the Haig-Simons definition of income would include unrealized appreciation on non-marketable assets and the imputed income that arises from owner-occupied homes. Nonetheless, this definition provides a useful frame of reference by setting the outer limits of a model comprehensive income tax base, and by allowing each potential exclusion from the tax base to be judged against a uniform standard.

The Haig-Simons definition of income is somewhat different from what most taxpayers normally think of as income (e.g., wages, divi-

24. See *H. Simons, Personal Income Taxation: The Definition of Income as a Problem of Fiscal Policy 50* (1938).

dends, interest, etc.). Under present law, the starting point for measuring taxable income is a taxpayer's sources or receipts for the appropriate year. Yet under the Haig-Simons definition, income is measured by its uses, not by its sources. Under this scheme, a basic equality is assumed: If a taxpayer purchases or consumes a good or service in the market, the value received is equal to the price paid for the good or service. Hence, the uses of income should be equal to the sources of income, and either side of this equation may be used as the measure of income in a given period. Moreover, under the Haig-Simons definition, there are only two categories of potential uses of income—current consumption and savings. If a person does not currently use income, it is saved. Hence, the notion of the increase in a taxpayer's net worth in a given period of time is synonymous with savings. Whatever a taxpayer does not consume, of necessity, adds to the taxpayer's net worth. Thus, a taxpayer's income in a given period can be measured by looking at the sum of his or her consumption and additions to savings during that period.

State and Local Taxes Under a Comprehensive Definition of Income. Keeping in mind the basic equality between the amount paid for goods and services and the value of those goods and services, it is possible to analyze how state and local tax payment transactions should be treated under a comprehensive income tax base. In any state and local tax transaction, two basic events take place: (1) A taxpayer makes tax payments to the government, and (2) the same taxpayer receives certain goods and services for those payments. Since step (1), the payment of taxes, is neither consumption nor savings, the payment of taxes would not be included in the tax base. Under the Haig-Simons definition of income, however, the value of the benefits received by the taxpayer in step (2) does constitute income and should be included in the base. Similarly, under the Musgrave model, state and local taxes would all be based on benefits received; therefore, the amount paid in taxes would be deemed to be equal to the value of the benefits received. One could effectively include the value of these benefits simply by denying a deduction for the state and local taxes.

To illustrate, if a person earns $200 in a year, this amount would be the person's Haig-Simons income for that year if nothing else happened, because it would represent savings of $200. If the same person also paid $50 of state and local taxes, and received $50 in goods and services in return, although the tax payments would be, in effect, deductible in computing taxable income (because they represent neither consumption nor savings), the $50 in goods and services received would represent consumption (and thus income) creating a wash. The person would still have $200 of taxable income—$150 of savings and $50 of consumption. In other words, in cases in which the amount of taxes paid equals goods and services received, the comprehensive income tax would allow no net deduction for state and local taxes.

In an income-based, ability-to-pay federal income tax scheme, denying a deduction for state and local taxes only produces the proper result if the state and local taxes are imposed on a benefits received basis. If, for example, the above taxpayer paid $50 in state and local taxes, but received only $25 in goods and services in return (as would be the case, for example, in a state or local jurisdiction engaged in income redistribution), his or her Haig-Simons income would be $175 ($150 savings plus $25 of consumption). Completely denying a deduction for state and local taxes in this case would result in the person being overtaxed. In this example, a state and local tax deduction should be eliminated only to the extent of the benefits received from the state and local governments. The ability-to-pay portion of the state and local levies must be deductible to measure income properly.

Fiscal Federalism, the Income Tax, and the Real World

Since, under the ideal model of federalism, no state or local jurisdiction would impose anything other than benefits received tax levies, there would never be a case in this ideal world in which state and local taxes reduced a taxpayer's taxable income. The taxes paid would always be washed out by benefits received, creating the net effect of no deduction for state and local taxes. The real world, however, differs from the Musgrave ideal in several important respects.

First, state and local governments do not only provide local goods that benefit only their residents. Rather, they frequently must provide at least two different types of public goods, whose benefits flow beyond the benefit region of the government in question. One such type of good—public welfare transfer payments—actually puts state and local governments in the role of providing goods that are national in character. In other words, the Musgrave model of ideal fiscal federalism is not borne out by reality, because the national government does not always perform all of the allocation functions that it ideally should under that model. In the recent past, the national government has increased the number of these national resource allocation priorities that have been "turned back" to the state and local jurisdictions.

Another example of this type of public good is the spillover good. Even though its benefits are not national in nature (and thus it would not be the responsibility of the national government directly), such benefits extend beyond the governmental region that is providing the good. To illustrate, certain expenditures for environmental protection may create benefits for neighboring jurisdictions as well as the jurisdiction making the expenditure. Under the Musgrave model, national grants or subsidies are intended to deal with this type of spillover situation. In reality, many state and local jurisdictions must provide these spillover goods without the help of a federal grant.

Perhaps the most important aspect of this first divergence of reality from the ideal model is that the situation is not one that has been voluntarily created by the citizens of the state and local government. Especially in the case of public welfare transfer payments, state and local governments have established these programs at least partially in response to national goals. The same is true for many of the spillover situations. To say that a state or local jurisdiction can easily move toward the ideal model of fiscal federalism ignores the reality of the situation. Until the federal government plays its proper role under the model of fiscal federalism, i.e., by providing all significant national goods and aiding states with spillover situations, it is unrealistic and inappropriate to assume that state and local governments will do the same.

A second, related way in which state and local government policies do not reflect the Musgrave model is that states and, to a lesser extent local governments, impose taxes on the basis of their residents' ability to pay, not upon the benefits they receive. In other words, state and local governments do engage in income redistribution, in violation of the ideal model of fiscal federalism. Once again, however, the impetus for this conduct seems to be closely related to the real world distortions in the model allocation function. If the state and local jurisdictions are forced to provide resources of a national character, such as welfare, it is almost inevitable that these jurisdictions will have to engage in income redistribution through the tax system. Welfare payments are the means by which income redistribution is accomplished. They are not most effectively provided through benefits received taxation. Hence, the reality is that state and local governments do engage in both benefits received and ability-to-pay taxation to provide the public goods within their benefit regions.

A third way in which the real world diverges from the ideal model is that individuals do not have ready mobility. The model assumes that all individuals may express their preferences for public goods initially through the political process. If, under traditional majority rule procedures, a particular individual ends up living in a benefit region that provides public goods differently from that individual's preferences, the model assumes that the individual is free to relocate in a jurisdiction that allocates goods more in line with the individual's preferences. In fact, no such absolute mobility exists. In the real world, many individuals live in jurisdictions that may overprovide public goods from their perspective, but those individuals may not be perfectly free to "vote with their feet" and leave that benefit region.

This lack of mobility is especially important when examining the nature of the state and local taxation system. If an individual is not free to move out of a high-tax jurisdiction, then the taxes of that jurisdiction become all the more involuntary to that individual. He or she is locked in, by both majority rule and the lack of perfect mobility, to paying taxes for public goods and services from which he or she receives no benefits.[25] This involuntary aspect of the present state and local taxing scheme is quite important to the overall question of whether those taxes should be deductible for federal income tax purposes.

25. As Musgrave and Musgrave have characterized the situation, "Taxpayers must pay the tax, and while they have a vote, they do not have a veto."

The significance of these differences between the ideal fiscal federalism model and reality is that they directly contradict the theoretical equality between state and local taxes paid and benefits received. Since this equality does not exist in the real world, denying the deduction of state and local taxes is not equivalent, in terms of the tax base, to including the government benefits received in the base. Thus, under the Haig-Simons definition of income, the only accurate measure of income will be the value of the government benefits received by each individual.

It is also very difficult, if not impossible, however, to measure the value of the consumption-type benefits received by any individual from state and local government goods and services. Thus, the comprehensive income tax model is left in a quandary. The posited equality between tax payments and benefits received is not present, and the precise portion of those tax payments corresponding to benefits received cannot be ascertained. Hence, only two basic solutions are available: (1) Allow the deduction for state and local taxes, except in cases in which there is an ascertainable relationship between the tax payment and the benefit received; or (2) Disallow the deduction completely on the assumption that the predominant portion of state and local taxes involves a direct correlation between benefits and tax payments.*

Neither of these two solutions is perfect. Under the first solution, the value of most public goods and services consumed by taxpayers will be excluded from the tax base. As with other exclusions, this solution will create a bias in favor of local public goods over individual private expenditures. Under the second solution, the federal government will be arbitrarily overtaxing a considerable portion of its citizenry, while at the same time undertaxing another segment of society.[26]

Denying the deduction completely is particularly troublesome, given the reasons why reality diverges from the ideal. In fact, state and local tax levies go beyond benefits received taxation in large part to allow the state and local jurisdictions to carry out national resource allocation goals. When combined with the lack of perfect mobility, a solution that eliminates the deduction for state and local taxes completely ignores the significant portion of state and local taxes that is both involuntary in nature and redistributive in purpose.

---

* An intermediate approach would be artificially to establish a percentage of state and local taxes that, on average, represents consumption. Only state and local taxes in excess of this amount would be deductible. * * *

26. As described in more detail in the text * * * disallowance of the deduction, in effect, correctly taxes government benefits received only for those individuals whose state and local taxes paid exactly equal government benefits received. If the state and local jurisdictions engage in income redistribution, there will be a substantial number of taxpayers for whom this equality does not exist. If taxes paid are greater than government benefits received, disallowance of the deduction overtaxes, because only the benefits received should be included in the tax base. If benefits received exceed taxes paid, disallowance of the deduction does nothing to remedy the undertaxation that arises because benefits received are not presently included in the base.

Treasury II, Fiscal Federalism and
Comprehensive Income Taxes

* * * Treasury I quite clearly took the position that most state and local tax levies do represent so-called "benefits received" taxation—i.e., that most state and local taxes are levies to pay for specific goods and services received by taxpayers of that jurisdiction. Another way of looking at this type of state and local tax levy is that it is essentially a "user charge" for the services received. User charges are currently excluded from the category of deductible nonbusiness taxes. Treasury II also seems to place state and local taxes under the consumption category when it refers to such taxes as "voluntary" payments by taxpayers. In general, voluntary payments would be indicative of consumption-type expenditures and of a benefits received situation.[27]

It seems clear that Treasury II, in large measure, assumes the existence of a pure system of federalism as set out in the Musgrave model. Under that view, all state and local taxes would be of the benefits received variety, and a deduction for those taxes would not be required in measuring income under a comprehensive income tax. Much of the language and rationale of the report can be understood in light of this theoretical construct. Treasury II simply refuses to acknowledge that state and local taxes are actually based upon something other than the benefits received by the taxpayers in those jurisdictions. Moreover, Treasury II seems to assume a very high degree of taxpayer mobility among state and local jurisdictions, a fact that arguably is not borne out by reality. Treasury II's position would be wholly defensible if the real world actually reflected the state of affairs postulated in the ideal model of fiscal federalism.

The real nature of state and local taxes is far less clear than Treasury II would suggest. To the extent that state and local taxes are based upon an ability to pay, and not upon a benefits received, policy, there are two strong arguments that full deductibility is preferable to nondeductibility. The first argument is premised upon the fact that there is not adequate correspondence between the amount of taxes paid by a particular individual and the value of government benefits received. Although allowing a full deduction has the effect of excluding from the federal tax base the value of most services provided by state and local governments, arguably this result is preferable to denying the deduction completely and, thereby, overtaxing many individuals, while undertaxing many others. * * *

The second argument is that once it is recognized that multiple levels of government share in the distribution function by imposing

---

27. Under the ideal model, all state and local tax payments would be "voluntary" also in the sense that, with perfect mobility, an individual who paid those taxes had acquiesced in the level of public goods and services being provided by the jurisdiction in question. Mobility allows an individual only to pay that level of taxes that coincides with the individual's preferences for public goods.

ability-to-pay taxes, it becomes essential for at least one level of government to provide for deductibility of these taxes in order to integrate an overall measure of ability to pay. Allowing a deduction at the federal level is most consistent with Musgrave's ideal model and allows the federal government to act as "the primary and the final arbiter of the national distribution of income and wealth." This is also the practical choice because the federal government has greater ability to effect national income redistribution than does any one state, as well as a greater ability to adjust for the deduction. * * *

The basic question is whether state and local taxes are benefits received or ability-to-pay taxes. This determines how any particular state and local tax should be treated under a comprehensive income tax model. If any substantial portion of state and local taxes is assessed on an ability-to-pay basis, Treasury II is significantly flawed in its definition of the income tax base. Ability-to-pay state and local taxes, however inconsistent with the ideal model of federalism, are not properly part of a comprehensive federal income tax base. The failure of Treasury II to acknowledge this fact represents the most serious fundamental weakness in the position of the report.

The clearest example of an ability-to-pay levy is a state and local income tax. It is reasonably clear that most of these taxes are not established on a benefits received or user charge basis, and thus should be deducted when measuring income under a comprehensive base. A broad-based sales tax is a little less clear but, unless one believes that the distribution of governmental benefits is similar to the distribution of expenditures subject to the sales tax, it too should be considered an ability-to-pay tax.

The property tax is probably more in the nature of a benefits received tax than either the income tax or sales tax. While state governments generally use a sales tax and/or an income tax, the property tax is almost exclusively within the province of local governments. There may be some basis for the assertion that local governments spend a higher percentage of their revenue on public goods that only benefit their particular region than do state governments. If this is true, there probably would be a higher degree of correlation between taxes paid and benefits received for the property tax than with the other two general levies. On the other hand, even in the case of property taxes, it is quite possible that the relationship between taxes paid and benefits received may be sufficiently attenuated to warrant classifying the property tax as an ability-to-pay tax.

Many commentators argue that the federal government should be neutral with respect to how state and local governments choose to raise revenue. For this reason, if state and local income taxes are deductible, these commentators favor retaining the deduction for both property [28] and sales taxes. If a deduction were permitted only for income

---

28. The property tax is the most questionable of these three levies. Many economists believe that property taxes are passed on by landlords to tenants in the

taxes, undue pressure would be placed on state and local governments to use this type of levy, even though it might not otherwise be appropriate.

Should the Federal Income Tax Base Be Evenly Distributed Among the States? One further point deserves comment under the discussion of the model comprehensive income tax. A stated goal of Treasury II is to produce a more even distribution of the burden of federal income taxes among the states. This report concludes that the present deductibility of state and local taxes skews the distribution of federal income taxes in favor of high-tax jurisdictions, with low-tax jurisdictions bearing an unfair share of the total federal income tax burden. There are problems with this approach.

First, this argument is interesting in that it explicitly focuses on inter-regional, rather than inter-individual, equities. Since the federal income tax is imposed upon individuals and not upon regions, the argument must be implying that the state and local tax deduction is not necessary to properly measure federal taxable income. Absent the deduction, the federal income tax base will be defined without regard to the taxing policies of the various state and local jurisdictions, thereby treating two individuals in different jurisdictions alike, irrespective of the amount of state and local taxes that each has to pay. In terms of Treasury II, both individuals would bear an equal share of the federal tax burden.

The important question, however, is the one that Treasury II has ignored—whether it is fair to define the federal income tax base without regard to state and local taxes. To the extent that such taxes do affect an individual's ability to pay, the federal tax base should be reduced for such taxes. Treasury II again skips over this crucial point, assuming that those taxes are properly part of the tax base.

Moreover, under both the Musgrave theoretical model of fiscal federalism and under most comprehensive income tax models, it is clear that the individual is the proper level for income measurement. It is the individual's ability to pay with which the federal income tax should be concerned. Therefore, if a state and local tax levy is truly an ability-to-pay tax, it is properly excluded from the tax base, because it does not represent amounts that are available for either consumption or savings of that individual. The distribution of the effect of that deduction among the various states has little to do with the proper measurement

form of higher rents; tenants, however, are not given a deduction. Since the property tax deduction is only available to homeowners, it "gravely discriminates against renters." R. Goode, The Individual Income Tax 171 (1976). This is the position taken in Blueprints for Basic Tax Reform. See U.S. Dept. of the Treasury, Blueprints for Basic Tax Reform 86–88, 93 (1977). On the other hand, certain economists, viewing the problem from a national perspective, believe that landlords, not tenants, bear the burden of the property tax. Under this latter view, the discrimination against renters is entirely a product of the exclusion from income of the gross imputed fair rental value of owner-occupied homes. See, e.g., Comments by Charles E. McClure, Jr., in Comprehensive Income Taxation 69, 71–72 (J. Pechman ed. 1977). The authors take no position with respect to this particular issue.

of income under a comprehensive federal income tax that measures only an individual's ability to pay.

Conclusion

Under a comprehensive federal income tax, state and local taxes that represent ability-to-pay tax levies should be deductible in determining income. In the absence of the ability to ascertain precisely what portion of state and local taxes represents ability-to-pay levies, at least some deduction for those taxes must be maintained in the federal income tax system in order to avoid the unfairness of forcing taxpayers to pay federal income tax upon amounts that are not properly part of a comprehensive tax base. If partial deductibility is not possible, then full deductibility is a very defensible solution, given the lack of any significant degree of correlation between government benefits received and taxes paid in many jurisdictions. To keep the federal income tax neutral with respect to the use of different types of taxes by state and local governments, the deduction should not distinguish among various types of state and local tax levies.

C. STATE AND LOCAL TAXES AS A TAX EXPENDITURE

The deduction for state and local taxes can properly be viewed as a tax expenditure only if the deduction is not necessary to properly define the income tax base. As a tax expenditure, however, it is still possible to justify the deduction. Historically, the basic rationale for the deduction as a tax expenditure has been that it facilitates fiscal coordination in our federal system.

The primary focus of this rationale is that serious equity problems may arise if several independent taxing jurisdictions use the same tax base (e.g., a tax based upon income) to raise revenue. For example, under our federal system of government, it is not unusual for an individual to be both a resident and a taxpayer in three or more jurisdictions simultaneously. These various levels of government often use the same tax base to raise revenue and, if they operated independently, certain groups of taxpayers might be burdened by excessively high rates of tax. At present, the federal government, 45 states, the District of Columbia, and numerous local jurisdictions all impose a tax on income. In the absence of a deduction for state and local income taxes at the federal level, the combined marginal tax rate on a taxpayer's income might approach, or even exceed, 100 percent. Although confiscatory rates are currently unlikely,[29] the possibility of confiscation does illustrate the potential inequities that could result from a lack of fiscal coordination. * * *

Since the deduction reduces the impact of state and local taxes on residents, it can also be viewed as a form of financial aid from the federal government to facilitate the financing of local public services. Some observers also believe that the existence of the deduction reduces

---

29. Although the maximum marginal rate for individuals at the federal level is currently only [33] percent, it has been as high as 94 percent.

local opposition to ability-to-pay taxes, thereby promoting a more equitable overall tax system. Finally, the deduction reduces the tax differential among states and other communities, thereby reducing the economic inefficiencies created by large geographic differentials.

Treasury II

The Treasury has apparently rejected the notion that the deduction is necessary to properly define the income tax base. Moreover, Treasury II has also rejected as unnecessary the role that the deduction plays in fiscal coordination. Rather, the report has taken the position that the state and local tax deduction should be repealed in its entirety. There are a number of problems with the arguments used in Treasury II to defend the repeal of the deduction for nonbusiness state and local taxes. To address some of these problems, it is helpful to examine three similar itemized deductions under current law—nonbusiness interest deductions, especially for owner-occupied homes; charitable contributions; and state and local taxes. Under Treasury II, there is some cutback in the interest deduction,[30] there is very little direct change in the charitable contribution deduction, and there is a total repeal of the state and local tax deduction. Can the obvious discrepancy between the actions proposed by Treasury II for interest and charitable contributions on the one hand, and state and local taxes on the other, be rationalized in an appropriate way?

Fairness. Treasury II takes the position that the state and local tax deduction disproportionately benefits high-income taxpayers residing in high-income states. Under this view, the deduction has the effect of requiring taxpayers in low-tax states to subsidize taxpayers in other communities. Furthermore, Treasury II argues that since only one-third of all taxpayers itemize, the federal level deduction effectively skews the burden of the state and local taxes within a particular community, because the deduction makes those taxes less costly to those higher income taxpayers who, in effect, have part of their state and local tax burden paid by the federal government through the itemized deduction.

The issue of fairness is directly tied to the appropriate definition of taxable income. Treasury II's position with respect to fairness is tenable only in the Musgrave model of the ideal fiscal world. As discussed above, our federal system deviates from this world in significant ways. Because of these deviations, there is, in fact, no equality between the amount paid in state and local taxes and the governmental benefits received by individual taxpayers. This is particularly true with respect to residents of high-tax states that actively engage in income redistribution. In these jurisdictions, there is little doubt that

---

30. In general terms, Treasury II proposes to disallow deductions for nonbusiness interest (i.e., interest on nonprincipal residences, consumer interest, and most other interest not incurred in the conduct of a trade or business) to the extent that those deductions exceed the sum of $5,000 plus the taxpayer's net investment income. See *Treasury II* at 323.

as the amount paid in taxes increases, the value of benefits received as a percentage of these taxes decreases.

If one returns to the Haig-Simons definition of income, it is clear that the present law benefits *both* lower- and higher-income taxpayers. As the previous discussion developed, under that general definition of income, consumption-type items (including the benefits received from state and local governments in the form of public goods and services) are properly part of a comprehensive income tax base. At present, however, because of the difficulty of measuring the value of those public goods and services received, the tax base generally does not include the value of those consumption items.

This imperfection in the tax base does benefit those individuals who receive a deduction for state and local taxes, to the extent that those taxpayers actually receive benefits from state and local governments in the form of public goods and services. Equally as important in this context, however, is the benefit received by lower-income taxpayers who are not taxed upon the benefits they receive in the form of public goods and services from state and local governments. In a world in which state and local governments engage in any significant degree of income redistribution through ability-to-pay state and local taxes, it is difficult to say precisely where the greater benefit of the present system lies. It is quite clear, however, that the benefits of the present system do not run solely to higher-income taxpayers at the expense of lower-income taxpayers.

Denying the deduction for state and local taxes is an expedient, but not a fair, mechanism to insure that the value of public goods and services provided by state and local governments will be included in the tax base. Under the Haig-Simons definition of income, the repeal of the deduction for state and local taxes would have the effect of including the value of the government benefits received in the income tax base. Only where a pure benefits received taxation scheme is in place, however, is such a structure fair among all taxpayers. If, in the real world, state and local governments engage in a significant degree of ability-to-pay taxation, repeal of the deduction overtaxes individuals whose taxes exceed government benefits received, while undertaxing those lower-income taxpayers whose government benefits received exceed taxes paid. It is difficult to agree with Treasury II that such a state of affairs is "fair" in any overall sense, and it may well be seen as adding a significant degree of unfairness to the system.

Treasury II makes a further argument that the deduction for state and local taxes discriminates among citizens of the same jurisdiction depending on whether they itemize their deductions. At present, for those taxpayers who do not itemize, a portion of their standard deduction or "zero bracket amount" is deemed to represent state and local taxes paid. Simplicity and administrability have dictated the standard deduction approach. Treasury II, however, seems to lose sight of the relationship between the amount of the standard deduction and personal deductions, such as state and local taxes. Contrary to Treasury II, it is an appropriate view of the present tax system that all taxpayers receive a deduction for state and local taxes—in the form, first, of the standard deduction and, second, of itemized deductions, if itemized deductions exceed the standard deduction.

Finally, from the perspective of low-income taxpayer/high-income taxpayer equity, it is difficult to justify the conclusion of unfairness with respect to the state and local tax deduction in light of the proposed treatment of home mortgage interest and charitable contributions in Treasury II. Both of the latter deductions are also itemized deductions and have the same general distribution among the income brackets. Both of the latter are utilized disproportionately by higher-income taxpayers. If fairness and equity are truly at the heart of a fundamental tax reform proposal, it is difficult to reconcile the liberal treatment of home mortgage interest and charitable contributions with the repeal of the state and local tax deduction.

Erosion of the Tax Base. Treasury II describes the state and local tax deduction as "one of the most serious omissions from the federal income tax base." Under recent estimates by the Joint Committee on Taxation, repeal of the deduction would generate $44.4 billion in 1988 at present tax rates. Treasury II implies that without the repeal of this deduction, tax rates, which are at "unnecessarily high levels," cannot be reduced.

Although the repeal of this deduction would generate a great deal of federal revenue, that fact, by itself, does not justify its demise. Rather, as a tax expenditure, the deduction should be analyzed as a spending program and its merits judged alongside other comparable spending programs. As articulated above, this deduction has long been justified as playing a significant fiscal coordination role in the federal system. Moreover, the state and local tax deduction is not often thought of as a "loophole," or a "tax shelter," and has never been the principal target of tax reform. Although some observers advocate the repeal of this section, this is invariably in the context of an overall reform of the tax base, in which such preferences as depletion, capital gains, fringe benefits, charitable contributions, nonbusiness interest, and qualified deferred compensation are also being carefully scrutinized. What appears to be lacking in Treasury II is the balanced scrutiny of all tax expenditures that traditional tax expenditure analysis requires.

Treasury II takes the position that the repeal of the deduction for state and local taxes is necessary in the overall effort to reduce unnecessarily high tax rates. This argument may be facially accurate, but it has little to do with the overall process of fundamental tax reform. Initially, it is not necessary to reduce tax rates as part of the process of fundamental tax reform, so long as the tax base is broadened in a fair and efficient manner. For example, it would not be irrational for Congress to broaden the tax base without reduction in rates to deal with the federal government deficit. Furthermore, if Congress decides to lower rates as part of a revenue neutral tax reform package, there are numerous possible sources of revenue that are worth considering.

* * *

The Fallacy of the "Tax on a Tax" Argument

Treasury II states that some argue that state and local taxes should be deductible to avoid imposing a "tax on a tax." Treasury II finds this argument deficient for three reasons: First, the argument ignores the effect of the deduction for state and local taxes on the federal income tax base. The report states that this provision effectively permits state and local governments to define the federal tax base. Second, the argument suggests that the state and local taxes are involuntary and citizens of the jurisdiction receive nothing for their taxes. Treasury II disagrees with both suggestions. Finally, Treasury II concludes that the argument is contradicted by the practice of denying a deduction at the state and local level for federal taxes. Whether taken alone or cumulatively, none of Treasury II's reasons is convincing.

Who Should Define the Federal Tax Base? Treasury II argues that, through the deduction for state and local taxes, state and local jurisdictions are inappropriately but effectively in a position to define the federal income tax base. By enacting additional deductible taxes, a state or local government can reduce the federal tax base and shift the burden of the federal income tax to other jurisdictions.

Several points deserve attention here. First, as previously noted, the federal income tax is imposed on individuals, not jurisdictions. Second, it can be argued that the basic definition of income, not state and local taxing policies, define the federal income tax base. If ability-to-pay state and local taxes are not part of a proper federal income tax base, that is the result of the theoretical underpinnings of a comprehensive income tax, not the policies of state and local governments. Third, to the extent that fiscal coordination is a desired objective, there is little doubt that the federal government, given its greater resources and financial strength, is in a better position than most state and local governments to coordinate overlapping demands on the same tax base.

Finally, if the question is whether a particular deduction or credit involves a loss of federal power over its own tax base, every tax expenditure violates this standard. The home mortgage interest and the charitable contribution deductions are but two of many examples of cases in which the federal government has effectively ceded the power to define its tax base in a manner at least as great as that claimed by Treasury II with respect to state and local taxes. The home mortgage interest deduction allows every individual to redefine the federal tax base by excluding his or her mortgage interest payments from that base. Under the same rationale, when an individual makes a charitable contribution, that individual is redefining the federal tax base. At least in the case of state and local tax deductions, there is a degree of public control over the definition of the federal tax base that is not present when an individual deducts home mortgage interest or charitable contributions. Hence, it is difficult to justify the repeal of the state and local tax deduction on the basis that it represents a loss of control over the federal tax base, given the even greater loss of control over that base represented by other tax expenditures. A tax reform program aimed at fairness and simplicity would seem to require a more consistent treatment of essentially the same types of expenditure.

The Voluntariness of the Payment. Treasury II maintains that state and local taxes are essentially voluntary payments made in exchange for items of personal consumption. On that basis, it would repeal the deduction for state and local taxes. Apart from the theoretical discussion of the proper elements of the tax base above, if voluntariness of the payment is to be a proper measure of the deductibility of a personal expenditure, it is difficult to justify the proposed retention of the home mortgage interest and charitable contribution deductions alongside of the repeal of the state and local tax deduction. Both a payment of mortgage interest and a charitable contribution involve transactions at least as voluntary as the payment of state and local taxes. At best, taxpayers have only indirect control over state and local tax burdens through their ability to elect the legislative body. In addition, although Treasury II asserts that taxpayers can move from high-tax to low-tax jurisdictions if they do not approve of the former's taxing policies, such a move is a very complicated matter in a world in which taxpayers clearly do not enjoy perfect mobility. The payment of state and local taxes, therefore, involves only a limited degree of voluntariness. On the other hand, the making of a charitable contribution is completely voluntary. So is choosing to place a roof over one's head with a debt-financed purchase of property.

If the voluntariness of a payment is the appropriate criterion for measuring deductibility, the treatment of these three important itemized deductions in Treasury II is inconsistent and indefensible.

Payment for Personal Consumption. Under current law, payments to charities and state and local governments are generally treated consistently. In each case, not every payment to such an entity is deductible. In both cases, if a taxpayer receives, in exchange for that payment, a direct benefit, no deduction is allowed. For example, a taxpayer is not entitled to any deduction for tuition payments made to a private, tax-exempt school, despite its charitable status, because of the direct benefit received in the form of educational services. Similarly, a payment to a state or local government for a sewer assessment is not deductible, despite the fact that it is levied by a taxing jurisdiction, because it is in exchange for sewer services.

On the other hand, if a payment to a charity or a state and local government can only be said to be indirectly in exchange for any specific service or benefit, the payment is usually deductible. For example, the Internal Revenue Service has ruled that undifferentiated payments made by a member of a church as an annual contribution to support all church activities will be deductible in full, even though the member's children may benefit from one of the church's activities—free secular and religious education. This is essentially the same analysis that is applied to allow a full deduction for state and local taxes under a comprehensive income tax, even though there may be some indirect benefits passing to a given taxpayer. As long as the payments (whether charitable contributions or taxes) are not directly linked to benefits received, they should be deductible.

There is yet another similarity between the function of charities and state and local governments that makes any differentiation in the tax treatment of charitable contributions and state and local taxes difficult to defend. In many cases, governments and charities provide similar services to the public at large. For example, the Internal Revenue Service has ruled that payments to a charitable organization performing volunteer fire department services in the locality of the taxpayer's home are deductible. Apparently, despite the clear benefits received by the taxpayer from this form of fire protection, the payment was not directly in exchange for fire protection and thus still deductible. It would certainly be anomalous under Treasury II for such a payment to remain deductible if made as a charitable contribution but not deductible if made in the form of taxes to a state and local government. Such a distinction would create inequities and inefficiencies and would violate a basic principle of neutrality upon which fundamental tax reform is based.

Both the theory and the practice behind the taxation of payments to charities and state and local governments reflect the strong similarities between the purposes of, and the functions performed by, both types of entities. On the level of personal consumption, it is difficult to repeal the deduction for state and local taxes in full, without questioning the basis upon which the charitable contribution deduction remains intact. To be consistent, both types of payments should be treated similarly for federal income tax purposes.

Must State and Local Governments Allow a Deduction for Federal Taxes? Treasury II takes the position that the fact that only 16 states allow a deduction for federal income taxes at the state level contradicts the "tax on a tax" argument. It is not clear which underlying rationale for the deductibility of state and local taxes this aspect of Treasury II's argument is intended to address.

If this point is intended to address the rationale of fiscal coordination (i.e., alleviation of the burden of overlapping taxes), the deduction is only necessary at one level in order to prevent overburdening of the tax base. Assuming a deduction at the federal level, a similar deduction for federal taxes at the state and local level would not be required.

Treasury II may also be suggesting that because most states do not have such a deduction, state and local taxes are not actually based on ability to pay. The implication is that if a state desired to impose an income tax based on the ability to pay of its residents, the base would be determined on an amount *net* of federal tax liability. This argument is not persuasive. Given the lack of true taxpayer mobility and the fact that most states currently engage in income redistribution among their citizenry, it is beyond peradventure to suggest that state income taxes are not based, at least in part, on ability to pay. In addition, although deductibility at both the federal, and state and local, levels may be preferable in terms of pureness in measuring a taxpayer's ability to pay, it has been shown that federal deductibility alone may be sufficient for overall equity in a federal tax system.

Inefficient Subsidy. Treasury II states that the deduction for state and local taxes could be regarded as a subsidy to state and local governments. Viewed in this way, Treasury II argues that the subsidy is both inefficient and unfair. The existence of the deduction also encourages state and local governments to impose general taxes rather than user charges.

It must be conceded that if the deduction for state and local taxes were solely a subsidy, it would be hard to defend. Although those who favor the deduction on other grounds might consider the subsidy aspects an added plus, no one defends the deduction on this ground alone.

Summary

This article has evaluated the itemized deduction for nonbusiness state and local taxes from two perspectives: Whether such deduction is required in the process of defining the appropriate federal income tax base, and whether, even if the answer to the first question is assumed to be in the negative, the deduction can be justified as a proper exercise of fiscal policy by the federal government. On both counts, this article concludes that the treatment of the deduction in Treasury II is less than adequate. It virtually ignores the role of the deduction in properly defining a comprehensive income tax base. In addition, if the deduction is to be examined as a tax expenditure, Treasury II is questionable. Especially when Treasury II's treatment of home mortgage interest and charitable contributions is lined up against the proposed repeal of the state and local tax deduction, the report cannot be said to be either fair or neutral.

G. CASUALTY AND THEFT LOSSES

1. INTRODUCTION

Under § 165(c), individual taxpayers may deduct the following: (1) trade or business losses, (2) losses incurred in transactions entered into for profit, and (3) personal casualty losses. The losses covered by § 165(c)(3) are described as those arising from "fire, storm, shipwreck, or other casualty, or from theft." However, no deduction is allowed for a loss to the extent compensated for by insurance. An individual taxpayer is not permitted to deduct a casualty loss under § 165(c)(3) for damages to personal assets unless the taxpayer, if he has casualty insurance, files a timely insurance claim with respect to the damage to that property. § 165(h)(4).

According to the legislative history (S.Reg. No. 830, 88th Cong., 2d Sess., reprinted in 1964–1 (Part 2) C.B. 505, 561), the casualty loss deduction is confined to "extraordinary, non-recurring losses [that] go beyond the average or usual losses incurred by most taxpayers in day-to-day living." The distinction between extraordinary and ordinary losses is achieved through two means. First, a casualty or theft loss is taken into account only to the extent that the loss exceeds $100 for any occurrence. § 165(h)(1). Second, casualty and theft losses are deductible only to the extent that the total amount of all such losses, after subtracting the $100 floor per casualty, sustained during a tax year exceeds 10 percent of the taxpayer's adjusted gross income. § 165(h)(2). The legislative history (Joint Committee on Taxation, General Explanation of the Tax Equity and Fiscal Responsibility Act of 1982, 26–27 (1982)) indicates the rationale for adding the 10% floor:

> In order to reduce the number of users of this complex deduction and the partial reimbursement of losses provided by the tax system, while maintaining the deduction for losses which significantly affect an individual's ability to pay taxes, Congress decided to put a percentage-of-adjusted-gross-income floor under the casualty loss deduction similar to the floor under the medical expense deduction. A floor of this type is fair to taxpayers of all income levels because the size of a loss that significantly reduces an individual's ability to pay tax varies with his income.

Questions

1. Why did Congress allow a personal deduction for casualty losses? Is a casualty loss a part of the risk of living and thus nondeductible, or does a casualty loss for personal use property reduce a taxpayer's wealth and disposable income without any personal satisfaction or utility? In other words, does a casualty loss deduction correctly measure the taxpayer's taxable income and his ability to pay income taxes?

2. How does the casualty loss deduction benefit those taxpayers who cannot bear the economic impact of such a loss more than those who can?

2. DEFINITION OF THEFT OR OTHER CASUALTY

Section 165(c)(3) allows a taxpayer to deduct unreimbursed theft or casualty losses even if the property stolen or damaged is used for personal purposes as opposed to property of a business or investment character.

Section 165(c)(3) contemplates some sort of physical damage, not merely a decline in market value due to extraneous events. An "other casualty" loss must be a sudden, unexpected and unusual event similar to a fire, storm, or shipwreck mentioned in § 165(c)(3). Rev.Rul. 72–

592, 1972–2 C.B. 101. Thus, normal wear and tear, or damage to property that occurs over time is not a casualty loss. See e.g. Rev.Rul. 63–232, 1963–2 C.B. 97, (losses from termites are not casualty losses because the damage occurs gradually). See generally the Appendix in Maher v. Commissioner, 680 F.2d 91 (11th Cir.1982).

CARPENTER v. COMMISSIONER
25 T.C.M. (CCH) 1186 (1966).

MEMORANDUM FINDINGS OF FACT AND OPINION

WITHEY, JUDGE: * * *.

FINDINGS OF FACT

* * *

During 1962 petitioner Nancy Carpenter owned a diamond engagement ring. At an undisclosed time in 1962 she placed the ring in a waterglass of ammonia for the purpose of cleaning it. The glass containing the ring was left "next" to the kitchen sink. While petitioner William Carpenter was washing dishes, he inadvertently "picked up the glass and emptied its contents down the" sink drain, not realizing the ring was part of such contents. He then activated the garbage disposal unit in the sink damaging the ring. The damaged ring was recovered and taken to a jeweler for appraisal. His appraisal was that the ring was a total loss.

* * *

Nancy had a loss as a result of the above facts in the amount of the difference between the fair market value of her original ring immediately before it was damaged and its fair market value immediately after in the resulting amount of $980.

OPINION

Respondent's position here is that Nancy did not suffer a casualty loss within the meaning of section 165(a) and (c)(3) of the Internal Revenue Code of 1954 in that, by applying the principle of *ejusdem generis,* it cannot be said that the events which gave rise to the ring damage were like or similar to a "fire, storm, [or] shipwreck" and therefore do not amount to "other casualty" under that section. He also takes the position that, should we hold to the contrary on this point, * * * the salvage value of the damaged ring must be offset against the gross loss suffered by Nancy.

Because William's testimony and his demeanor on the witness stand satisfies us that he is not the type of person who would deliberately and knowingly do so, we have concluded that his placing of the original ring in the disposal unit was inadvertent and accidental. We in turn conclude from this that the damage to the ring resulted from the destructive force of the disposal coupled with the accident or mischance of placing it therein; that, because this is so, the damage must be said to have arisen from fortuitous events over which petitioners had no control.

While the application of the principle of *ejusdem generis* has been consistent in reported cases under this section of the Code and its predecessors, from at least Shearer v. Anderson, 16 F.2d 995 (C.A. 2), the application has been clearly and consistently broadened. Automobile accidental damage has been likened to shipwreck, Shearer v. Anderson, supra; earthslide damage to a building, to fire, storm, and shipwreck, Harry Heyn 46 T.C. 302; and drought damage to buildings, to storm damage, Maurer v. United States, 178 F.Supp. 223, reversed on other grounds 284 F.2d 122. Respondent has gone so far as to allow deduction for damage caused by the sonic boom of a speeding airplane as an "other casualty." See Rev.Rul. 59–344, 1959–2 C.B. (Part 2) 74, superseded by Rev.Rul. 60–329, 1960–2 C.B. (Part 2) 67, only to clarify the former. This Court has held that "other casualty" includes damage caused by an infestation by termites, E.G. Kilroe, 32 T.C. 1304, in noway departing from the principle in doing so.

We think the principle of *ejusdem generis* as now applied fulfills congressional intent in the use of the phrase "other casualty" in that it is being generally held that wherever force is applied to property which the owner-taxpayer is either unaware of because of the hidden nature of such application or is powerless to act to prevent the same because of the suddenness thereof or some other disability and damage results, he has suffered a loss which is, in that sense, like or similar to losses arising from the enumerated causes. Of course, we do not mean to say that one may willfully and knowingly sit by and allow himself to be damaged in his property and still come within the statutory ambit of "other casualty."

Nancy sustained a loss here under circumstances which it is true may be due to her or her husband's negligence, but this has no bearing upon the question whether an "other casualty" has occurred absent any willfulness attributable thereto. Harry Heyn, supra.

* * *

Decision will be entered under Rule 50.

In Keenan v. Bowers, 91 F.Supp. 771 (E.D.S.C.1950), a wife wrapped a ring in tissue paper and left it on a night stand. Her husband mistakenly flushed the tissue paper down a toilet. The court disallowed deduction. In White v. Commissioner, 48 T.C. 430 (1967) (Acq. C.B. 1969–1, 21), a car door slammed on a taxpayer's hand, dislodging the diamond out of her ring; the diamond, worth $1,200, was not found even though a diligent search was made. The court allowed the deduction.

Questions

1. Is it possible to reconcile the White case with Keenan v. Bowers?

2. Does the taxpayer's negligence enter into the determination of whether an "other casualty" exists? Consider Reg. § 1.165–7(a)(3). What if the casualty was caused by the taxpayer's wilful act or wilful negligence?

In order to take a deduction for a loss by theft, the taxpayer must establish that a criminal taking of money or property in fact occurred (Rev.Rul. 72–112, 1972–1 C.B. 60), although the thief need not be identified or apprehended. See, e.g., Jacobson v. Commissioner, 73 T.C. 610 (1979) (the taxpayer proved that valuable items disappeared from her house; the court concluded that it was very unlikely that a large number of valuable personal items would disappear without being stolen). See also Jones v. Commissioner, 24 T.C. 525 (1955) (Acq.1955–2 C.B. 7). A mere loss or disappearance of property will not suffice. A criminal appropriation of property must occur which benefits the taker.

A theft loss is deductible in the year when discovered. § 165(e). A casualty loss is deductible in the year when sustained. § 165(a).

Problem

1. Terri Player left her engagement ring, pearl necklace and earings in the hotel room after she checked out. She returned the next day and found the jewelry missing. Is this a theft? Consider Reg. § 1.165–8(d).

2. Taxpayer incurs a loss in the conduct of an illegal business. Can Taxpayer deduct the loss under 1) § 165 or 2) § 162(a)? Consider whether § 162(c) and (f) apply to § 165(c)(3)? Reconsider pp. 467–478.

3. Rochelle, an accomplished author, is on the cash method of accounting. Her literary agent collects $75,000 of her royalties in Year 1 and embezzles such funds. Rochelle never knew of the embezzled royalties until Year 3. She recovers only $25,000 from the embezzler.

(a) What are the tax consequences of the above transactions to Rochelle? Did she constructively receive the royalties in Year 1? Consider Reg. § 1.451–2(a). Did Rochelle sustain a loss under § 165(c)(3) in Year 1 or in Year 3 or no loss at all? Consider § 165(b).

(b) What are the tax consequences of the above transactions to the embezzler? Reconsider Problem 2 on page 181. Consider also the applicability of §§ 67 and 1341.

3. AMOUNT OF CASUALTY OR THEFT LOSS

The amount of the deduction for a casualty loss under § 165(c)(3) involving personal use property which is completely destroyed equals the lesser of: (1) the taxpayer's adjusted basis for the property or (2) the decline in the fair market value of the property as a result of the casualty. Reg. § 1.165–7(b)(1).

If the casualty involves business or investment property which is totally destroyed, the deductible loss equals the adjusted basis of the property. Reg. § 1.165–7(b)(1). If the property was converted from personal to business or investment use prior to the casualty, the taxpayer's basis for computing the casualty loss equals the lesser of: (1) the property's adjusted basis, or (2) the fair market value of the property at the date of conversion. Reg. § 1.165–7(a)(5).

If the casualty does not totally destroy the property, the amount of the casualty loss equals the lesser of: (1) the property's adjusted basis or (2) the decline in the fair market value of the property. Reg. § 1.165–7(b). This rule applies to personal use property as well as business or investment property. The amount of the deductible casualty loss taken on property which is not completely destroyed reduces, of course, the adjusted basis of the property. § 1016(a)(1).

The amount of the theft loss is determined in the same manner as a casualty loss, but the value of the property after the theft is zero. Reg. § 1.165–8(c). The diminution in fair market value generally must be ascertained by competent appraisal. Reg. § 1.165–7(a)(2)(i). Taxpayers often establish the fair market value before the casualty by the replacement cost of the item which is then reduced to reflect the time the taxpayer held the item. See e.g. Pfalzgraf v. Commissioner, 67 T.C. 784 (1977) (Acq. 1977–2 C.B. 2). See also Reg. § 1.165–7(a)(2)(ii).

A casualty or theft loss is not deductible if the taxpayer is compensated by insurance (or otherwise) for his loss. § 165(a). See § 165(h)(4). However, a business taxpayer, fearing the cancellation of his insurance policy, who does not file a claim for an insured loss, is allowed to deduct the loss under § 165(a) without filing an insurance claim. Hills v. Commissioner, 76 T.C. 484 (1981), affirmed 691 F.2d 997 (11th Cir.1982); Miller v. Commissioner, 733 F.2d 399 (6th Cir.1984) (en banc).

Finally, losses incurred in investment activities are subject to the two percent floor imposed by § 67(a) on miscellaneous itemized deductions. Trade or business losses are above-the-line deductions, § 62(a)(1), and are therefore not itemized deductions. See also § 67(b)(3). Recall that casualty or theft losses involving personal use property are subject to a $100 nondeductible floor per casualty or theft. After the $100 floor is applied, the taxpayer's personal casualty and theft losses are aggregated and are deductible only if the total amount for the year exceeds 10 percent of the taxpayer's adjusted gross income. § 165(h).

Problems

1. Rebecca purchased a car for personal use at a cost of $8,000. When the value of the car equalled $5,800, it was stolen. The theft was not covered by insurance.

(a) What is the amount of the taxpayer's loss deduction? Assume the taxpayer's adjusted gross income in the year of the theft equals $10,000. Consider § 165(h) and Reg. §§ 1.165–8 and –7(b). What is the character of the deduction? Consider § 1222(2) and (4). Consider the impact of § 67.

(b) What result if there is an insurance recovery of $5,000? Of $8,000?

2. Richard purchased a car for use in his business at a cost of $10,000. He has taken $4,500 of Accelerated Cost Recovery Deductions on the car. The car was stolen. The theft was not covered by insurance. When the car was taken, it was worth $7,500. What is the amount of the taxpayer's loss deduction? Consider §§ 165(c), (b), 1011, 1012, 1016(a)(2) and Reg. § 1.165–8 and –7(b).

Chapter 10

FAMILY TRANSACTIONS—
REDIRECTING INCOME

A. SPLITTING OF INCOME BETWEEN SPOUSES UNDER THE CODE

In 1948 the Internal Revenue Code equalized the status of married couples living in common law and in community property states by authorizing all married couples to file a joint income tax return. §§ 1(a) and 6013(a). For the entire nation, Congress adopted the result in Poe v. Seaborn, 282 U.S. 101, 51 S.Ct. 58, 75 L.Ed. 239 (1930), where the Supreme Court held that the earnings of each spouse in a community property state were taxable one half to each. A joint tax return enables a husband and wife to aggregate their income and deductions, even if one spouse has no income or deductions. Under the rate structure enacted in 1948, a married couple filing a joint return paid a tax equal to twice the tax a single person would have paid on half their aggregate taxable income.

The revision to the rate structure enacted in 1969 gave rise to a "marriage penalty" when persons with relatively equal incomes married each other. These married couples paid a tax significantly higher than the aggregate taxes they would have paid if each taxpayer were single.

Former § 221 provided a special deduction for married couples in which both spouses earn personal service income. Such couples filing a joint return receive a "two earner" deduction in computing their adjusted gross income equal to 10 percent of the lower spouse's qualified earned income for the taxable year, as defined, up to $30,000. Consider the following excerpt from the Joint Committee on Taxation, General Explanation of the Economic Recovery Act of 1981, 33 (1981):

REASONS FOR CHANGE

The Congress was concerned about the marriage tax penalty and decided that a suitable response to this problem was to allow married couples a new deduction equal to a percentage of the earnings of the spouse with lower earnings.

Any attempt to alleviate the marriage penalty involves the reconciliation of several competing objectives of tax policy. For many years, one accepted goal has been the equal taxation of married couples with equal incomes. This has been viewed as appropriate because married couples frequently pool their income and consume as a unit, and thus it has been thought that married couples should pay the same amount of tax regardless of how the income is divided between spouses. This result generally was achieved under prior law.

The Congress believed that alleviation of the marriage penalty was necessary because large tax penalties on marriage undermined respect for the family by affected individuals and for the tax system itself. To do this, the Congress was obliged to make a distinction between one-earner and two-earner married couples. The simplest way to alleviate the marriage penalty was to allow a percentage of the earned income of the spouse with the lower earnings to be, in effect, free from income tax.

This provision also alleviates another effect of the prior system on all married couples—high effective marginal tax rates on the second earner's income. Recent studies have shown that these high marginal rates had a significant adverse effect on second earners' decisions to seek paying jobs. The ten-percent reduction in marginal tax rates for second earners provided by the new deduction will reduce this work disincentive. In addition, some contend that two-earner couples are less able to pay income tax than one-earner couples with the same amount of income because the former have more expenses resulting from earning income, as well as less free time. Under this concept, the new deduction will improve equity by reducing the tax burdens of two-earner couples compared to one-earner couples.

The second-earner deduction reduces the marriage penalty and improves work incentives for second earners without abandoning the basic principle of encouraging joint returns. Allowing married couples to file separate returns as single taxpayers would have been very complex because of the necessity for rules to allocate income and deductions between the spouses. If separate filing were optional, many couples would have been burdened by having to compute tax liability under both options (separately and jointly) in order to determine which method minimized their liability. Further, separate filing would have provided tax reductions with respect to all types of income received by married couples, while the Congress believed that relief was essential for wages and salaries received by second earners. Also, separate filing would have reduced taxes only for couples affected by the marriage penalty, but the Congress believed that there should be a tax reduction for all two-earner married couples.

In repealing the two-earner deduction, the legislative history of the Tax Reform Act of 1986 indicates:

The adjustment of the standard deduction and the rate schedule in the [Tax Reform Act of 1986] also makes it possible to minimize the marriage penalty while repealing the complicated two-earner deduction. As a result, single individuals who marry will retain more of the total standard deduction for two single individuals than under [prior] law.

* * * In spite of the repeal of the two-earner deduction, marriage penalties generally are either smaller than [prior] law or only a nominal amount under the [Tax Reform Act of 1986]. The only exceptions to this result occur for certain relatively high income couples, e.g., where the two spouses have incomes of $100,000 and $30,000. (Tax Reform Act of [1986], Report of the Committee on Ways and Means, House of Representatives on H.R. 3838, 99th Cong., 1st Sess. 88 (1985)).

For critical assessment of § 221, see Gann, Abandoning Marital Status as a Factor in Allocating Income Tax Burdens, 59 Texas L.Rev. 1 (1980). See generally Bittker, Federal Income Taxation and the Family, 27 Stan.L.Rev. 1389 (1975).

B. SPLITTING OF INCOME BY PRIVATE ARRANGEMENT: INTRODUCTION

Three points must be noted at the outset in order for the student to understand the phenomenon of income splitting by private arrangement. First, each member of the family is a separate individual for Federal income tax purposes, and every individual is entitled to file his own separate income tax return. § 6012(a). Although parents and their minor children are members of the same household, income generated from property owned by a child is taxable to that child, not to the parents, even though the income-producing property may have been received as a gift from the parents.

The Tax Reform Act of 1986 contains a mechanism designed to discourage parents, whose income from property would otherwise be taxed at the parent's high marginal tax rate, from transferring income-producing property to a child in the hope of having the income subject to taxation at a child's lower marginal rates. As stated in the legislative history:

The committee believes that the present law rules governing the taxation of minor children provide inappropriate tax incentives to shift income-producing assets among family members. In particular, the committee is aware that the treatment of a child as a separate taxpayer encourages parents whose income would otherwise be taxed at a high marginal rate bracket to transfer income-producing property to a child to ensure that the income is taxed at the child's lower marginal rates. In order to reduce the opportunities for tax avoidance through intra-family transfers of income-producing property, the committee concluded that it is generally appropriate to tax the income on property transferred * * * to a minor child at the parent's marginal rates. Senate Finance Committee Report on H.R. 3838, Tax Reform [Act] of 1986, 99th Cong., 2d Sess. 862 (1986).

An assignment of income from property is still permitted if the child becomes the owner of the income-producing property. All that § 1(i) does is compute the tax on a child's taxable income in excess of $500.00, (if it is attributable to unearned income) at the parent's marginal tax rate. The child's earned income continues to be taxed to the child at the child's marginal tax rate. A child's unearned income is subject to taxation at the parent's marginal tax rate regardless of when the child received the income-producing property or its source. It is irrelevant that the property was given to the child prior to 1987 (§ 1(i) is effective after December 31, 1986), or that the property was obtained as a gift from someone other than the parents, such as the grandparents. There still remains an income tax savings if $1,000 of unearned income can be taxable to a child under age 14. A child is entitled to a $500 standard deduction, § 63(c)(5)(A), which can be deducted against $500 of unearned income. In addition, the next $500 of unearned income, which is taxable, is taxed to the child at the child's marginal tax rate. § 1(i)(4)(A)(ii). In effect, a child's first $1,000 of unearned income is not subject to taxation at the parent's rate. Therefore, a child will pay only $75 in taxes on the first $1,000 of unearned income (15% times $500 of taxable income) for an effective rate of only 7.5 percent. If the parents are in the 28 percent marginal tax bracket, the ability to shift $1,000 of income to a child represents an annual tax savings of $255. Once a child reaches age 14, § 1(i) no longer applies, and the bracket shifting advantage is then available for taxable income up to $17,850 for each child. § 1(c). The ability to shift $18,350 of income to a child over age 13 results in an annual tax savings of $2,460.50 ($17,850 of taxable income plus a $500 standard deduction that will escape tax at the parents' 28 percent rate). If the parents are subject to the 5 percent rate surcharge, so that their marginal rate is 33 percent, then it may be advantageous to shift even more than $18,350 of income to a child.

The special rules for calculating the income tax liability of a child who has unearned income are contained in § 1(i). These rules only apply to a child who has not attained age 14 before the close of the taxable year and who has at least one living parent. § 1(i)(2). Apparently, age 14 was selected because this is the age at which children may work in certain employment under the Fair Labor Standards Act. Pursuant to § 1(i)(1), the tax imposed equals the greater of:

(1) the tax imposed on the child's income without regard to the special rules for the taxation of certain unearned income or

(2) the sum of

    a. the tax that would be imposed if the taxable income of the child for the taxable year were reduced by the child's "net unearned income" and

    b. the child's share of the "allocable parental tax."

"Net unearned income" means that portion of the child's gross income that is not earned income (as defined in § 911(d)(2)) regardless of the source of the assets creating the child's net unearned income, reduced by the sum of: (1) $500 plus (2) the greater of (a) $500 or (b) the amount of the allowable deductions directly connected with the production of unearned income. § 1(i)(4)(A). The $500 figures are adjusted for inflation beginning in 1988. § 63(c)(5).

The term "allocable parental tax" is the excess of:

(1) the tax that would be imposed on the parent's taxable income if that income included the net unearned income of each child of the parent under age 14, over;

(2) the tax actually imposed on the parent's taxable income. § 1(i)(3)(A).

If there is more than one child with unearned income subject to taxation at the parents' rates, each child's share of any allocable parental tax equals an amount that bears the same ratio to the total allocable parental tax as the net unearned income of each child bears to the aggregate net unearned income of all children of such parent under age 14. § 1(i)(3)(B). In the case of divorced parents, the parent whose income is taken into account for purposes of computing the tax on the child's income is the custodial parent of the child. § 1(i)(5)(A).

The following examples from the legislative history (Tax Reform Act of 1986, Conference Report to Accompany H.R. 3838, House of Representatives 99th Cong. 2d Sess. II 768–69 (1986)) illustrate the tax consequences of § 1(i) with respect to unearned income of a dependent child under age 14 in 1988:

Example 1. If the child has $400 of unearned income and no earned income, the child's standard deduction is $400 which is allocated against the child's unearned income, so that the child has no Federal income tax liability.

Example 2. If the child has $900 of unearned income and no earned income, the child's standard deduction is $500 which is allocated against the first $500 of unearned income. The child's net unearned income is $400. Because the child's net unearned income is less than $500, the net [un]earned income is taxed at the child's rates.

Example 3. If the child has $1,300 of unearned income and no earned income, the child's standard deduction is $500 which is allocated against unearned income. The child has net unearned income equal to $800 of which the first $500 is taxed at the child's rates, and the remaining $300 of unearned income is taxed at the top rate of the parents.

Second, each individual filing a tax return generally has a personal exemption (§ 151) and a standard deduction (§ 63(c)). However, the personal exemption is disallowed for an individual who is eligible to be claimed as a dependent on another taxpayer's return (for example, a child eligible to be claimed on his parents' return). § 151(f)(2). Furthermore, as previously noted, a dependent may use up to $500 of his standard deduction to offset unearned income. § 63(c)(5). Thus, § 1(i), which taxes all of the unearned income of a child under age 14 in excess of $500 to the child at the top marginal tax rate of his parents, generally applies only to unearned income of such child in excess of $1,000.

Third, the two bracket rate structure (together with the 5 percent rate surcharge) still affords incentives for parents to attempt to shift income to children who have attained age 14 before the close of a taxable year and who presumably are and will be in a lower marginal tax bracket. A family unit composed of a couple with two children who have attained age 14 will pay less overall taxes if the income can be divided by the parents and the two children than if all the income were taxable to the parents. Thus, the race is on to redirect income to children who have attained age 14 through gifts of income from both personal services and property. The materials in this chapter consider whether these techniques will (and should) be successful.

Problems

1. (a) On January 1 of the current year Nicole's parents, who are in the 33 percent bracket because of the 5 percent surcharge, transfer a substantial amount into a custodial bank account for their daughter. During the year the savings account earns $10,000 of interest. Assume that Nicole is 13 at the end of the tax year and that she has no other unearned income and no itemized deductions directly connected with the production of income. What are the income tax consequences to Nicole for the $10,000 of income she must report? Consider §§ 1(i), 63(c)(5) and 151(f)(2). What amount in taxes was saved by this assignment of income from the parents to their child?

     (b) Determine the tax savings for the following year, when Nicole turned 14, if her unearned income was $10,600 for that year.

2. When Dana was eight years old she appeared in a movie and earned a $50,000 fee. How much income tax must Dana pay on this earned income? Assume Dana has no expenses and that her parents are in the 33 percent marginal tax bracket. After paying the income taxes on Dana's income her parents deposited the remaining amount in a savings account in Dana's name. How is the interest income on Dana's savings taxed? Consider §§ 1(c), (g) and (i) and 63(c)(2) and (5).

The materials in this chapter examine various attempts to assign income to family members. Some have been successful, others have not. As you examine the various income-shifting devices, consider the underlying principles allowing successful assignments of income. Also, consider why the alimony rules under §§ 71 and 215 sanction a valid assignment of income and the tax savings divorcing spouses can achieve when they take this into consideration.

C. GIFTS OF PERSONAL SERVICE INCOME

The following case bars a husband's attempt to give his wife (as assignee) a portion of his future earnings and thus reduce his gross income. Personal service income, therefore, is taxed to the individual who earns it. Although the allowance of joint returns has eliminated the need to assign income to a spouse in a lower tax bracket,[1] there remains an advantage in shifting income from parents to their children over the age of 13.

LUCAS v. EARL

Supreme Court of the United States, 1930.
281 U.S. 111, 50 S.Ct. 241, 74 L.Ed. 731.

MR. JUSTICE HOLMES delivered the opinion of the Court.

This case presents the question whether the respondent, Earl, could be taxed for the whole of the salary and attorney's fees earned by him in the years 1920 and 1921, or should be taxed for only a half of them in view of a contract with his wife which we shall mention. The Commissioner of Internal Revenue and the Board of Tax Appeals imposed a tax upon the whole, but their decision was reversed by the Circuit Court of Appeals, 30 F.(2d) 898. A writ of certiorari was granted by this court.

By the contract, made in 1901, Earl and his wife agreed "that any property either of us now has or may hereafter acquire * * * in any way, either by earnings (including salaries, fees, etc.), or any rights by contract or otherwise, during the existence of our marriage, or which we or either of us may receive by gift, bequest, devise, or inheritance, and all the proceeds, issues, and profits of any and all such property shall be treated and considered, and hereby is declared to be received, held, taken, and owned by us as joint tenants, and not otherwise, with the right of survivorship." The validity of the contract is not questioned, and we assume it to be unquestionable under the law of the State of California, in which the parties lived. Nevertheless we are of opinion that the Commissioner and Board of Tax Appeals were right.

The Revenue Act of 1918 approved February 24, 1919, c. 18, §§ 210, 211, 212(a), 213(a), 40 Stat. 1057, 1062, 1064, 1065, imposes a tax upon the net income of every individual including "income derived from salaries, wages, or compensation for personal service * * * of whatever kind and in whatever form paid," § 213(a). [§ 61(a)] * * * A very forcible argument is presented to the effect that the statute seeks to tax only income beneficially received, and that taking the question more technically the salary and fees became the joint property of Earl and his wife on the very first instant on which they were received. We well might hesitate upon the latter proposition, because however the matter

---

1. In states that do not allow joint returns for state income tax returns, the ability to shift income to a spouse can reduce state income taxes.

might stand between husband and wife he was the only party to the contracts by which the salary and fees were earned, and it is somewhat hard to say that the last step in the performance of those contracts could be taken by anyone but himself alone. But this case is not to be decided by attenuated subtleties. It turns on the import and reasonable construction of the taxing act. There is no doubt that the statute could tax salaries to those who earned them and provide that the tax could not be escaped by anticipatory arrangements and contracts however skilfully devised to prevent the salary when paid from vesting even for a second in the man who earned it. That seems to us the import of the statute before us and we think that no distinction can be taken according to the motives leading to the arrangement by which the fruits are attributed to a different tree from that on which they grew.

Judgment reversed.

THE CHIEF JUSTICE took no part in this case.

Notes

Should Lucas v. Earl be limited to income to be earned by the performance of future services? One interpretation of the decision was that the person providing the future services retained control over the assignee's ability to receive it as he could always refuse to perform the services. What if the taxpayer attempts to assign, by contract, to his spouse income to be derived from services which have been completed? In Helvering v. Eubank, 311 U.S. 122, 61 S.Ct. 149, 85 L.Ed. 81 (1940), rehearing denied 312 U.S. 713, 61 S.Ct. 609, 85 L.Ed. 1144 (1941), the taxpayer, a general life insurance agent, after the termination of his insurance agency contracts and services as an agent, assigned (in advance of payment) the right to receive future renewal commissions which had been earned for services rendered in the prior sale of insurance policies. As a cash method taxpayer, the taxpayer would have been taxable on the renewal commissions when received. Despite the assignment, the renewal commissions, when paid to the assignee, were held taxable to the taxpayer-assignor, not to the assignee. The income derived from past services could not be transformed by a contractual assignment into property which could be gratuitously assigned to another. The assignee has a mere power to collect. Thus, under the Earl and Eubank cases the assignment of past and future salary and retirement benefits will be taxed to the employee-assignor. The assignments in these situations, whether the right to receive income is assigned before or after the income is earned, will fail to deflect income from an assignor to an assignee.

In Commissioner v. Giannini, 129 F.2d 638 (9th Cir.1942), the taxpayer was president and a director of a large banking corporation. On June 22, 1927, the board of directors of the corporation fixed his compensation, in lieu of salary, at 5% of the corporation's net profits per year, with a guaranteed minimum of $100,000 per year, commencing January 1, 1927. On July 22, 1927, the taxpayer informed the board of directors that he would not accept any more compensation for that year and "suggested that the corporation do something worthwhile with the money." On January 20, 1928, the board adopted a resolution stating that the taxpayer was entitled to $1,500,000 for his services computed from July 23, 1927 to January 20, 1928 and that he refused to accept it. The board directed that the sum of $1,500,000 be donated to the University of California to establish a Foundation of Agricultural Economics named after the taxpayer. In holding that the money was not includible in the taxpayer's income, the court indicated that the taxpayer did not beneficially receive the money and did not direct its disposition. The court stated that "we cannot say as a matter of law that the money was beneficially received by the taxpayer." (129 F.2d at 641). The corporation made all arrangements with the University of California regarding the corporate donation to the Foundation; the taxpayer only participated as an officer of the corporation.

Consider a situation involving the assignment of income required by factors beyond the assigner's control. In Commission v. First Security Bank of Utah, 405 U.S. 394, 92 S.Ct. 1085, 31 L.Ed.2d 318 (1972), the Supreme Court refused to require the taxpayer to report "income that he did not receive and that he was prohibited from receiving." The Court refused to extend the assignment of income principles developed in Lucas v. Earl beyond situations where "income would have been received by the taxpayer had he not arranged for it to be paid another", 405 U.S. at 403–404, 92 S.Ct. at 1091, 31 L.Ed.2d at 326, stressing the fact that the taxpayer was legally prohibited from receiving such income. Taxpayer was a bank owned by a holding company. Taxpayer's parent also owned an affiliated insurance company. Since taxpayer was prohibited by law from acting as an insurance agent, it could not write insurance policies for its borrowers who needed life insurance to cover their loans with the taxpayer. Instead, the taxpayer referred its borrowers to an independent insurance company who, in turn, reinsured the policies with the affiliated insurance company owned by taxpayer's parent holding company. This affiliated insurance company received the commissions for these policies. The Commissioner argued that taxpayer should be taxable on these insurance commissions because it was the taxpayer who originated the insurance policies, and by not charging for its referrals, taxpayer had effectively diverted income to its affiliate.

After the First Security Bank of Utah decision, it was feared that taxpayers would achieve an assignment of income by structuring contractual arrangements which required the person who earned the income to transfer it to another. However, these fears were soon laid to rest in United States v. Basye, 410 U.S. 441, 93 S.Ct. 1080, 35 L.Ed.2d 412 (1973). The Supreme Court held that the First Security Bank of Utah case is to be confined to situations where the transfer of the right to payment is compelled by law. The Court refused to permit as assignment of income resulting from the consensual agreement of two parties acting at arm's length. A partnership providing services was required to report the income from those services even though payment was received by another under a bona fide and enforceable contractual arrangement entered into by the partnership.

Yet, in Teschner v. Commissioner, 38 T.C. 1003 (1962), an assignment of income was permitted in an abberational situation. A father won a contest sponsored by an unrelated party. The contest rules provided that only persons under 17 were eligible to receive any prize and that any entrant over 17 must designate a younger person to receive the winnings. Taxpayer designated his daughter when he submitted his entry. Since taxpayer's inability to receive the prize was attributable entirely to the contest rules, over which taxpayer had no influence, a mere power to direct payment to another was not sufficient to require the contest winner to report the income.

Problems

1. An executive of the Production Corporation, a calendar year taxpayer who earns $100,000 per year, directs on January 1 that:

(a) $10,000 of his salary be paid to his 14 year old daughter. Consider the rationale for the Lucas v. Earl decision.

(b) $10,000 of his salary be paid to a tax-exempt organization selected by Production's board of directors (the executive is not a member of the Corporation's board of directors). Consider the Giannini case and the economic benefit and constructive receipt doctrines.

Who is taxed when the assignee collects the income? Examine Reg. § 1.102–1(e). When is the income taxed?

2. Lucky enters an essay writing contest sponsored by an unrelated corporation. The prize consists of an annuity of $1,000 per year for 20 years payable to some person under age 17 on entering the contest. Lucky designates his 15 year old son as the annuity recipient. Lucky wins the contest. What are the tax consequences to Lucky and his son? Consider the Basye and Tescher cases.

3. (a) Rod, a talented high school baseball player, entered into a contract in Year 1 with his father, a former semiprofessional baseball player, to compensate his father for services as coach, agent, and business manager. In Year 2, Rod signed a professional baseball contract and received a $100,000 signing bonus pursuant to the contract. He paid $50,000 from his bonus to his father. What are the tax consequences to Rod and his father? Consider § 162.

(b) What result if Rod's father rendered these services gratuitously, there being no contract with his father? Consider the imputed income materials at pp. 64–69.

4. An entertainer would like to make a contribution to a charity. What is the difference between:

(a) the entertainer agreeing to perform services in consideration of the third party sponsor of the performance contributing the entertainer's fee to a charity designated by the entertainer. What is the applicability of § 170(b)(1)(A), which mandates that an individual's charitable contributions to certain charities cannot exceed 50 percent of the donor's adjusted gross income?

(b) the entertainer arranging with the charity to provide his services without charge to a charity which sponsors an entertainment event. What if the entertainer fits the charity into a prearranged series of performances?

In analyzing whether the entertainer would have taxable income, consider Reg. § 1.61–2(c), Problem 1 at page 68, the Basye decision, and the following Revenue Rulings:

REV. RUL. 71
1953–1 C.B. 18.

Advice has been requested relative to circumstances in which the second sentence of [Reg. § 1.61–2(c)] will apply. * * *.

The typical case in which the second sentence of [Reg. § 1.61–2(c)] is applicable is one in which a radio sponsor or motion picture producer engages the services of an artist and by agreement with the artist turns over the payment for those services to a charitable organization designated by the artist.

Instances also arise in which an artist enters into an agreement with a charitable organization to render services to it, and the charitable organization in turn agrees with a sponsor or producer to make those services available to such sponsor or producer in consideration of a sum to be paid to the charitable organization. Such an arrangement often constitutes an attempt, by act of the parties, to channel to an exempt organization income which would normally be that of the individual artist and thereby to avoid the percentage limitation on the deduction of charitable contributions provided in section [170(b)] of the Code. In such situation the tax consequences will be the same as those attending the type of transaction described in the preceding paragraph. The rule that income is taxable to the one who earns it cannot be avoided by such an anticipatory arrangement.

Thus, for example, if an actor, whose contract with the studio regularly employing him permits, enters into a contract with a university, under which the actor may or may not have nominal duties at the university but in fact renders services principally to a third party, such as a radio sponsor or motion picture producer, payment for his services to be made to the university, such an arrangement constitutes an attempt to do indirectly the same thing that is done in the typical case hereinabove described. Accordingly, it is held that in such circumstances the sums paid to the charitable organization are includible in gross income of the individual rendering the services.

There are instances, however, in which an individual is under contract of employment or other obligation entered into in good faith for purposes other than avoidance of the percentage limitation imposed on the deduction of contributions by section [170(b)] of the Code, and, as an incident of his normal duties and obligations, his employer or other superior makes his services available to a third party, payment being made to the employer or other superior. In such a case, if the individual does not participate directly or indirectly in the contract pursuant to which his services are made available to the third party and if he has no right to receive, or direct the use or disposition of, the amounts so paid, such amounts are not includible in his gross income. This conclusion would be the same whether the employer or other superior having control of the services is a commercial organization or an organization described in section [170(b)] of the Code. However, it must be clearly shown that the relationship was entered into in good faith for purposes other than avoidance of the percentage limitation imposed by section [170(b)] on deduction of contributions, and that the organization is entitled, in substance as well as form, to the services which it makes available to the third party. The execution of a legally sufficient contract of employment or other document purporting to establish the obligation contemplated is a fact with evidentiary value, but is not necessarily dispositive of any case. Good faith and reality are not ascertained by any mechanical or formalistic test. The effect for tax purposes of the contract of employment or other obligation will be determined by a consideration of all the circumstances.

REV. RUL. 68–503

1968–2 C.B. 44.

At the request of a political fund-raising organization, an individual taxpayer gratuitously rendered professional services as a featured performer in entertainment programs planned, organized, promoted, and scheduled by the fund-raising organization. He was not entitled to, and received no payment for these services. Admissions were charged for the programs, and the net proceeds inured solely to the fund-raising organization.

Held, under these facts, no amount is includible in the individual's gross income as a result of the gratuitous services rendered. In the present case, the fund-raising organization is the promoter of the entertainment programs, and the fact that services are contributed in connection therewith does not, of itself, result in gross income to the contributor. See section 1.61–2(c) of the Income Tax Regulations, * * *.

D. GIFTS OF INCOME FROM PROPERTY

1. INTRODUCTION

It is clear that if a father gives a gift to his adult son of income-producing property, the son would report the income because the son now owns that property. The tax laws do allow an assignment of income, but it is restricted to income from property and does not extend to income from services. For example, if a father gives his adult son stock, the subsequently collected dividends are reported by the son. The price the father must pay for obtaining an assignment of income is giving up all control over the property. However, where a gift is made and the donor retains certain elements of control over the income-producing property, the courts may look at the practical realities and treat the donor as the real owner of the property. For example, in Commissioner v. Sunnen, 333 U.S. 591, 68 S.Ct. 715, 92 L.Ed. 898 (1948), an inventor transferred all of his rights under certain royalty contracts with a corporation to his wife. Taxpayer retained no direct control over these royalty contracts. However, taxpayer was the controlling shareholder of the corporation obligated to make the payments under these royalty contracts. The Supreme Court noted that as controlling shareholder he could control the corporation's performance under its royalty contracts and, therefore, indirectly control the royalties paid to his wife. This led the Court to tax him on the royalties received by his wife.

It should also be noted that a gift of income producing property can only shift that income earned after the date of the gift. The donor must report any income earned prior to the time of the gift, even if it is collected by the donee.

Assume a father owns a $1,000 bond with 10 percent interest coupons. Interest is payable annually on December 31. The father is in the 33 percent tax bracket. In order to redirect income to his 15 year old son (who has no taxable income), on December 1, the father detaches and gives to his son a coupon which entitles the son to collect the $100 interest payment due on December 31. The father retains the bond and the remaining coupons. Depending on the discount rate applied, the value of the coupon on the date of the gift is less than $100. In the rural vernacular, the father gives the eggs but keeps the hen. Should this transfer of an income item be effective to redirect income from the father to the son for tax purposes? This was the issue considered in the next case.

HELVERING v. HORST

Supreme Court of the United States, 1940.
311 U.S. 112, 61 S.Ct. 144, 85 L.Ed. 75.

[A father owned negotiable bonds with interest coupons in bearer form. He detached and gave to his son coupons representing $25,000 in future interest payments shortly before their due date, retaining the other interest coupons and the right to receive the redemption proceeds upon maturity of the bonds. The Supreme Court held that the interest income was taxable to the father and not the son.]

MR. JUSTICE STONE delivered the opinion of the Court.

* * *

The holder of a coupon bond is the owner of two independent and separable kinds of right. One is the right to demand and receive at maturity the principal amount of the bond representing capital investment. The other is the right to demand and receive interim payments of interest on the investment in the amounts and on the dates specified by the coupons. Together they are an obligation to pay principal and interest given in exchange for money or property which was presumably the consideration for the obligation of the bond. Here respondent, as owner of the bonds, had acquired the legal right to demand payment at maturity of the interest specified by the coupons and the power to command its payment to others which constituted an economic gain to him.

Admittedly not all economic gain of the taxpayer is taxable income. From the beginning the revenue laws have been interpreted as defining "realization" of income as the taxable event rather than the acquisition of the right to receive it. And "realization" is not deemed to occur until the income is paid. But the decisions and regulations have consistently recognized that receipt in cash or property is not the only characteristic of realization of income to a taxpayer on the cash receipts basis. Where the taxpayer does not receive payment of income in money or property realization may occur when the last step is taken by which he obtains the fruition of the economic gain which has already accrued to him. Old Colony Trust Co. v. Commissioner, 279 U.S. 716, 49 S.Ct. 499, 73 L.Ed. 918; Corliss v. Bowers, 281 U.S. 376, 378, 50 S.Ct. 336, 74 L.Ed. 916. Cf. Burnet v. Wells, 289 U.S. 670, 53 S.Ct. 761, 77 L.Ed. 1439.

In the ordinary case the taxpayer who acquires the right to receive income is taxed when he receives it, regardless of the time when his right to receive payment accrued. But the rule that income is not taxable until realized has never been taken to mean that the taxpayer, even on the cash receipts basis, who has fully enjoyed the benefit of the economic gain represented by his right to receive income, can escape taxation because he has not himself received payment of it from his obligor. The rule, founded on administrative convenience, is only one of postponement of the tax to the final event of enjoyment of the income, usually the receipt of it by the taxpayer, and not one of exemption from taxation where the enjoyment is consummated by some event other than the taxpayer's personal receipt of money or property. Cf. Aluminum Castings Co. v. Routzahn, 282 U.S. 92, 98, 51 S.Ct. 11, 13, 75 L.Ed. 234. This may occur when he has made such use or disposition of his power to receive or control the income as to procure in its place other satisfactions which are of economic worth. The question here is, whether because one who in fact receives payment for services or interest payments is taxable only on his receipt of the payments, he can escape all tax by giving away his right to income in advance of payment. If the taxpayer procures payment directly to his creditors of the items of interest or earnings due him, see Old Colony Trust Co. v. Commissioner, supra; Bowers v. Kerbaugh-Empire Co., 271 U.S. 170, 46 S.Ct. 449, 70 L.Ed. 886; United States v. Kirby Lumber Co., 284 U.S. 1, 52 S.Ct. 4, 76 L.Ed. 131, or if he sets up a revocable trust with income payable to the objects of his bounty, * * * Corliss v. Bowers, supra; cf. Dickey v. Burnet, 8 Cir., 56 F.2d 917, 921, he does not escape taxation because he did not actually receive the money. Cf. Douglas v.

Willcuts, 296 U.S. 1, 56 S.Ct. 59, 80 L.Ed. 3, Helvering v. Clifford, 309 U.S. 331, 60 S.Ct. 554, 84 L.Ed. 788.

Underlying the reasoning in these cases is the thought that income is "realized" by the assignor because he, who owns or controls the source of the income, also controls the disposition of that which he could have received himself and diverts the payment from himself to others as the means of procuring the satisfaction of his wants. The taxpayer has equally enjoyed the fruits of his labor or investment and obtained the satisfaction of his desires whether he collects and uses the income to procure those satisfactions, or whether he disposes of his right to collect it as the means of procuring them. Cf. Burnet v. Wells, supra.

Although the donor here, by the transfer of the coupons, has precluded any possibility of his collecting them himself he has nevertheless, by his act, procured payment of the interest, as a valuable gift to a member of his family. Such a use of his economic gain, the right to receive income, to procure a satisfaction which can be obtained only by the expenditure of money or property, would seem to be the enjoyment of the income whether the satisfaction is the purchase of goods at the corner grocery, the payment of his debt there, or such non-material satisfactions as may result from the payment of a campaign or community chest contribution, or a gift to his favorite son. Even though he never receives the money he derives money's worth from the disposition of the coupons which he has used as money or money's worth in the procuring of a satisfaction which is procurable only by the expenditure of money or money's worth. The enjoyment of the economic benefit accruing to him by virtue of his acquisition of the coupons is realized as completely as it would have been if he had collected the interest in dollars and expended them for any of the purposes named. Burnet v. Wells, supra.

In a real sense he has enjoyed compensation for money loaned or services rendered and not any the less so because it is his only reward for them. To say that one who has made a gift thus derived from interest or earnings paid to his donee has never enjoyed or realized the fruits of his investment or labor because he has assigned them instead of collecting them himself and then paying them over to the donee, is to affront common understanding and to deny the facts of common experience. Common understanding and experience are the touchstones for the interpretation of the revenue laws.

The power to dispose of income is the equivalent of ownership of it. The exercise of that power to procure the payment of income to another is the enjoyment and hence the realization of the income by him who exercises it. We have had no difficulty in applying that proposition where the assignment preceded the rendition of the services, Lucas v. Earl, 281 U.S. 111, 50 S.Ct. 241, 74 L.Ed. 731; Burnet v. Leininger, 285 U.S. 136, 52 S.Ct. 345, 76 L.Ed. 665, for it was recognized in the Leininger case that in such a case the rendition of the service by the assignor was the means by which the income was controlled by the donor and of making his assignment effective. But it is the assignment by which the disposition of income is controlled when the service precedes the assignment and in both cases it is the exercise of the power of disposition of the interest or compensation with the resulting payment to the donee which is the enjoyment by the donor of income derived from them.

This was emphasized in Blair v. Commissioner, 300 U.S. 5, 57 S.Ct. 330, 81 L.Ed. 465, on which respondent relies, where the distinction was taken between a gift of income derived from an obligation to pay compensation and a gift of income-producing property. In the circumstances of that case the right to income from the trust property was thought to be so identified with the equitable ownership of the property from which alone the beneficiary derived his right to receive the income and his power to command disposition of it that a gift of the income by the beneficiary became effective only as a gift of his ownership of the property producing it. Since the gift was deemed to be a gift of the property the income from it was held to be the income of the owner of the property, who was the donee, not the donor, a refinement which was unnecessary if respondent's contention here is right, but one clearly inapplicable to gifts of interest or wages. Unlike income thus derived from an obligation to pay interest or compensation, the income of the trust was regarded as no more the income of the donor than would be the rent from a lease or a crop raised on a farm after the leasehold or the farm had been given away. Blair v. Commissioner, supra, 300 U.S. 12, 13, 57 S.Ct. 333, 81 L.Ed. 465 and cases cited.
* * *

The dominant purpose of the revenue laws is the taxation of income to those who earn or otherwise create the right to receive it and enjoy the benefit of it when paid. See, Corliss v. Bowers, supra, 281 U.S. 378, 50 S.Ct. 336, 74 L.Ed. 916; Burnet v. Guggenheim, 288 U.S. 280, 283, 53 S.Ct. 369, 370, 77 L.Ed. 748. The tax laid by the 1934 Revenue Act upon income "derived from * * * wages, or compensation for personal service, of whatever kind and in whatever form paid * * *; also from interest * * *" therefore cannot fairly be interpreted as not applying to income derived from interest or compensation when he who is entitled to receive it makes use of his power to dispose of it in procuring satisfactions which he would otherwise procure only by the use of the money when received.

It is the statute which taxes the income to the donor although paid to his donee. Lucas v. Earl, supra; Burnet v. Leininger, supra. True, in those cases the service which created the right to income followed the assignment and it was arguable that in point of legal theory the right to the compensation vested instantaneously in the assignor when paid although he never received it; while here the right of the assignor to receive the income antedated the assignment which transferred the right and thus precluded such an instantaneous vesting. But the statute affords no basis for such "attenuated subtleties." The distinction was explicitly rejected as the basis of decision in Lucas v. Earl. It should be rejected here, for no more than in the Earl case can the purpose of the statute to tax the income to him who earns, or creates and enjoys it be escaped by "anticipatory arrangements * * * however skilfully devised" to prevent the income from vesting even for a second in the donor.

Nor is it perceived that there is any adequate basis for distinguishing between the gift of interest coupons here and a gift of salary or commissions. The owner of a negotiable bond and of the investment which it represents, if not the lender, stands in the place of the lender. When, by the gift of the coupons, he has separated his right to interest payments from his investment and procured the payment of the interest to his donee, he has enjoyed the economic benefits of the income in the same manner and to the same extent as though the transfer were of earnings and in both cases the import of the statute is that the fruit is not to be attributed to a different tree from that on which it grew. See Lucas v. Earl, supra, 281 U.S. 115, 50 S.Ct. 241, 74 L.Ed. 731.

Reversed.

* * *

Question

Could the Supreme Court have viewed the son as obtaining the coupon for its present discounted value? Thus, the son would be taxed on the difference between the amount collected and the discounted value of the coupon on the date of purchase. Reconsider the allocation of basis for the bond in light of Irwin v. Gavitt, at p. 264.

The father's retention of the bond, in our example, appears to be the key element. The father retains ownership and control over the payment of the income or over the management and use of the bond which generates the income stream. He possesses the ability to allocate periodically the income from the bond to different individuals. Various donees may be selected in different years. The retention of control over the income flow (the right to demand payment of interest represented by the coupons) is deemed to be the equivalent of the receipt of the income represented by the coupon. Under these circumstances, the assignor realizes income in the year in which the income is paid to the assignee.

Consider the next case where the assignor only has a right to collect the income from property but no right to the income-producing property itself. Recall, that in Irwin v. Gavitt, at p. 264, the income beneficiary of a trust must report the entire amount of each income payment received from the trust. Can the life tenant of a trust give his beneficial interest in the trust to his children and successfully redirect the taxability of that income?

BLAIR v. COMMISSIONER
Supreme Court of the United States, 1937.
300 U.S. 5, 57 S.Ct. 330, 81 L.Ed. 465.

MR. CHIEF JUSTICE HUGHES delivered the opinion of the Court.

This case presents the question of the liability of a beneficiary of a testamentary trust for a tax upon the income which he had assigned to his children prior to the tax years and which the trustees had paid to them accordingly.

The trust was created by the will of William Blair, a resident of Illinois who died in 1899, and was of property located in that State. One-half of the net income was to be paid to the donor's widow during her life. His son, the petitioner Edward Tyler Blair, was to receive the other one-half and, after the death of the widow, the whole of the net income during his life. In 1923, after the widow's death, petitioner assigned to his daughter, Lucy Blair Linn, an interest amounting to $6,000 for the remainder of that calendar year, and to $9,000 in each calendar year thereafter, in the net income which the petitioner was then or might thereafter be entitled to receive during his life. At about the same time, he made like assignments of interests, amounting to $9,000 in each calendar year, in the net income of the trust to his daughter Edith Blair and to his son, Edward Seymour Blair, respectively. In later years, by similar instruments, he assigned to these children additional interests, and to his son William McCormick Blair other specified interests, in the net income. The trustees accepted the assignments and distributed the income directly to the assignees.

* * *

Third. The question remains whether, treating the assignments as valid, the assignor was still taxable upon the income under the federal income tax act. That is a federal question.

Our decisions in Lucas v. Earl, 281 U.S. 111, 50 S.Ct. 241, 74 L.Ed. 731, and Burnet v. Leininger, 285 U.S. 136, 52 S.Ct. 345, 76 L.Ed. 665, are cited. In the Lucas Case the question was whether an attorney was taxable for the whole of his salary and fees earned by him in the tax years or only upon one-half by reason of an agreement with his wife by which his earnings were to be received and owned by them jointly. We were of the opinion that the case turned upon the construction of the taxing act. We said that "the statute could tax salaries to those who earned them and provide that the tax could not be escaped by anticipatory arrangements and contracts however skilfully devised to prevent the salary when paid from vesting even for a second in the man who earned it." That was deemed to be the meaning of the statute as to compensation for personal service and the one who earned the income was held to be subject to the tax. In Burnet v. Leininger, supra, a husband, a member of a firm, assigned future partnership income to his wife. We found that the revenue act dealt explicitly with the liability of partners as such. The wife did not become a member of the firm;

the act specifically taxed the distributive share of each partner in the net income of the firm; and the husband by the fair import of the act remained taxable upon his distributive share. These cases are not in point. The tax here is not upon earnings which are taxed to the one who earns them. Nor is it a case of income attributable to a taxpayer by reason of the application of the income to the discharge of his obligation. Old Colony Trust Company v. Commissioner, 279 U.S. 716, 49 S.Ct. 499, 73 L.Ed. 918. There is here no question of evasion or of giving effect to statutory provisions designed to forestall evasion; or of the taxpayer's retention of control. Corliss v. Bowers, 281 U.S. 376, 50 S.Ct. 336, 74 L.Ed. 916; Burnet v. Guggenheim, 288 U.S. 280, 53 S.Ct. 369, 77 L.Ed. 748.

In the instant case, the tax is upon income as to which, in the general application of the revenue acts, the tax liability attaches to ownership. See Poe v. Seaborn, 282 U.S. 101, 51 S.Ct. 58, 75 L.Ed. 239; Hoeper v. Tax Commission, 284 U.S. 206, 52 S.Ct. 120, 76 L.Ed. 248.

The Government points to the provisions of the revenue acts imposing upon the beneficiary of a trust the liability for the tax upon the income distributable to the beneficiary. But the term is merely descriptive of the one entitled to the beneficial interest. * * * The one who is to receive the income as the owner of the beneficial interest is to pay the tax. If under the law governing the trust the beneficial interest is assignable, and if it has been assigned without reservation, the assignee thus becomes the beneficiary and is entitled to rights and remedies accordingly. We find nothing in the revenue acts which denies him that status.

The decision of the Circuit Court of Appeals turned upon the effect to be ascribed to the assignments. The court held that the petitioner had no interest in the corpus of the estate and could not dispose of the income until he received it. Hence it was said that "the income was *his*" and his assignment was merely a direction to pay over to others what was due to himself. The question was considered to involve "the date when the income became transferable." 83 F.(2d) 655, at page 662. The Government refers to the terms of the assignment—that it was of the interest in the income "which the said party of the first part now is, or may hereafter be, entitled to receive during his life from the trustees." From this it is urged that the assignments "dealt only with a right to receive the income" and that "no attempt was made to assign any equitable right, title or interest in the trust itself." This construction seems to us to be a strained one. We think it apparent that the conveyancer was not seeking to limit the assignment so as to make it anything less than a complete transfer of the specified interest of the petitioner as the life beneficiary of the trust, but that with ample caution he was using words to effect such a transfer. That the state court so construed the assignments appears from the final decree which described them as voluntary assignments of interests of the petitioner "in said trust estate," and it was in that aspect that petitioner's right to make the assignments was sustained.

The will creating the trust entitled the petitioner during his life to the net income of the property held in trust. He thus became the owner of an equitable interest in the corpus of the property. By virtue of that interest he was entitled to enforce the trust, to have a breach of trust enjoined and to obtain redress in case of breach. The interest was present property alienable like any other, in the absence of a valid restraint upon alienation. The beneficiary may thus transfer a part of his interest as well as the whole. See Restatement of the Law of Trusts, §§ 130, 132 et seq. The assignment of the beneficial interest is not the assignment of a chose in action but of the "right, title, and estate in and to property." See Bogert, Trusts and Trustees, vol. 1, § 183, pp. 516, 517; 17 Columbia Law Review, 269, 273, 289, 290.

We conclude that the assignments were valid, that the assignees thereby became the owners of the specified beneficial interests in the income, and that as to these interests they and not the petitioner were taxable for the tax years in question. The judgment of the Circuit Court of Appeals is reversed and the cause is remanded with direction to affirm the decision of the Board of Tax Appeals.

It is so ordered.

However, if in the Blair situation, the taxpayer, a life beneficiary under a trust, assigned a portion of his income interest for only one year, the attempted redirection of income would be unsuccessful and the income would be taxed to the assignor. Harrison v. Schaffner, 312 U.S. 579, 61 S.Ct. 759, 85 L.Ed. 1055 (1941). The taxpayer-donor continues to be free to allocate subsequent payments as he chooses. The Horst decision denies the effectiveness of a temporary income allocation. More generally, where the donor retains substantial controls over a source of recurrent receipts, the income from the source will be attributed to the donor.

2. GRATUITOUS ASSIGNMENTS OF COPYRIGHTS AND PATENTS

An author may give away his interest in an effort to redirect income. The gift of an entire interest in a copyright or separate rights in a copyright (for example, the right to publish or the right to use for motion pictures) transfers an item of property. The income from the entire interest or separate rights in a copyright is generally taxable to the donee as ordinary income. The donor has parted with all or a portion of the underlying property; each right in a copyright is a separate item of property. Furthermore, the donee's ownership of the entire interest or separate rights in a copyright includes the ability to license the use of or to sell the property and to negotiate the terms and conditions of the license or sale. The donee, therefore, has control over the property assigned and contributes to the production of income from the copyright or an interest in a copyright. However, if the donor gives a copyright or an interest in a copyright, but retains extensive controls over such interest, an assignment of the copyright or an interest in the copyright will not generally redirect income to the donee.

An interesting dichotomy involves the famous author, P.G. Wodehouse, who assigned a half interest in three unpublished stories to his wife. The Tax Court found that, although the transfers of the three stories were separately made, all three transfers were essentially the same and held that taxpayer, not his spouse, was taxable on royalty payments received in 1938, 1940 and 1941. Wodehouse v. Commissioner, 8 T.C. 637 (1947). In Wodehouse v. Commissioner, 178 F.2d 987 (4th Cir.1949), involving the royalties for two of the stories received in 1938 and 1941, the court held that the assignment lacked economic reality and required the taxpayer to report the income received by his wife. Yet, in Wodehouse v. Commissioner, 177 F.2d 881 (2d Cir.1949), involving royalties for the third story received in 1940, the assignment of income was allowed because the royalties arose from a contract negotiated by her agent on her behalf.

If an inventor licenses a manufacturer to use a patent under a royalty agreement, the gratuitous assignment of the royalty agreement is generally sufficient to redirect income to the assignee. In Heim v. Fitzpatrick, 262 F.2d 887 (2d Cir.1959), the assignment of patent rights (like the assignment of a copyright) was successful to redirect income to the assignee. It seems that the gift of the royalty agreement would also be viewed as a gratuitous transfer of property. Yet, in Strauss v. Commissioner, 168 F.2d 441 (2d Cir.1948), a transferor of royalty rights was taxable on the royalty payments received by the transferee. Are Heim and Strauss consistent? Reconsider Helvering v. Eubank at page 708. The gratuitous transfer route should not be used to attempt to redirect income to the assignee where the assignor retains substantial controls over the patent or over the receipt of income. A gift was held ineffective to redirect income where the donor, as president, director and owner of 89% of the shares of a corporation had licensed a patent from the inventor-donor, on a non-exclusive basis, pursuant to a license agreement with no specified minimum royalties and terminable, without liability, by either party on notice to the other party. The donor "retained very substantial interests in the contracts themselves, as well as power to control the payments of royalties to his wife [the donee] * * *." Commissioner v. Sunnen, 333 U.S. 591, 608, 68 S.Ct. 715, 724, 92 L.Ed. 898 (1948).

Problem

1. Ted Player buys a $1,000 face amount corporate coupon bond on January 1 for $1,000. The bond will mature on January 1 in 10 years. The bond has 10 interest coupons, each paying $100 interest annually on December 31. What are the tax consequences, in terms of who is taxed, when, and in what amounts, if:

(a) on July 1 of the year of purchase, Ted gives to his 16 year old son, Tim, one interest coupon due on December 31 of that year.

(b) on July 1 of the year of purchase, Ted gives Tim all the interest coupons.

(c) on December 31 of the year of purchase, Ted gives Tim the bond with all the interest coupons attached (except for the interest coupon payable on that date).

(d) on July 1 of the year of purchase, Ted gives Tim a 25% interest in the bond and all the interest coupons.

(e) on December 15 of the year of purchase, Ted sells the bond for $1,050 and directs that the sale proceeds be paid directly to Tim.

Ted and Tim are cash method, calendar year taxpayers. The impact of § 1286(b) is discussed at 1001–1003.

2. (a) Mother owns a building which she leases to a tenant for eleven years. Mother assigns to her daughter all of her right, title and interest in the leasehold. When the daughter collects the rents is Mother or her daughter taxable on the rent paid by the tenant?

(b) What result if the lease runs for 99 years?

3. (a) Terri Player writes an income tax treatise. After completion of the manuscript, but prior to the publication of the book, she assigns all of her right, title, and interest in the copyright to her children ages 10 and 15. Who is taxable on the income? What if, instead, Terri had assigned the anticipated royalties to her children? Consider the impact of § 1(i).

(b) Assume Terri in her will names her children as beneficiaries of the copyright and royalties? After her death her children collect the royalties. Who is taxed on the income? Consider §§ 691(a) and 1014(c).

4. Ted Player buys a lottery ticket and before the drawing gives it as a gift to his 15 and 17 year old children. Who is taxed on the income if, after the gift, the children, who hold the winning ticket, collect the prize?

E. SPLITTING OF INCOME THROUGH TRANSFERS IN TRUST

1. INTRODUCTION

A person may transfer property to a trust to save income taxes by shifting income to family members in lower tax brackets. An outright gift of property may be satisfactory if: (1) the gifts are small in amount; (2) the donee is an adult; and (3) the donor will retain substantial property after the gift. Absolute gifts should not be made without consideration of the advantages of making a transfer in trust.

Under a trust arrangement, the property owner (the grantor) transfers property to a trustee, an individual or entity with investment skills, who manages the property for the benefit of a beneficiary. The trustee can be authorized to make distributions of trust income or principal to one or more beneficiaries in varying proportions at a time and under circumstances which may produce the greatest tax benefit for the recipients. There may also be substantial tax advantages in authorizing the trustee to accumulate income rather than distributing it to the beneficiary as earned. The grantor may wish to reserve the right to receive all or a portion of the income, to recover the principal of the trust on the termination of the beneficiary's income interest, or to revoke the trust. The grantor may allocate the beneficial ownership of the property over several generations by using life estates with remainders. The grantor may seek to insulate the beneficiaries against claims by their creditors. But the grantor's most basic desire, at least from an income tax standpoint, is to redirect income to family members in lower tax brackets without giving up effective control over the property. Income tax problems arise when the grantor retains an interest in or a power over the trust so that the grantor continues in substance to be regarded as the owner of the trust property.

2. IRREVOCABLE TRUSTS: GRANTORS RESERVE LITTLE OR NO CONTROL

We begin, however, with the situation in which the grantor establishes an irrevocable trust and retains little or no control over the trust or trustee. Where the grantor is willing to cut the strings to the trust property, the income from the trust will be taxed to the beneficiary, to the trust, or in part to each, but not to the grantor.

A trust generally computes its taxable income and determines its tax liability in the same manner as an individual. A trust usually serves as a conduit to pass income to the beneficiary. Two aspects of the conduit treatment must be noted. First, trust income is taxed only once on its way to the beneficiary. The beneficiary is taxed on income either distributed or to which the beneficiary is entitled, whether or not actually distributed. If the trust is not required to disburse the income annually and does not do so, the trust is taxed. Elaborate rules (so-called throwback rules) surround the taxation of accumulated income which the trust ultimately pays out to the beneficiary. Second, the trust income received by the beneficiary retains the same character in the hands of the beneficiary as it had when received by the trust.

3. GRANTOR TRUSTS: GRANTORS RETAIN CONTROL

The grantor may retain one or more controls (or strings) over the trust or the trustee, including reserving: (1) the power of revocation (§ 676); (2) the income for the grantor's (or grantor spouse's) benefit (§ 677); (3) a reversion in the trust principal (§ 673); or (4) the power to control beneficial enjoyment of trust income or principal (§ 674). The reservation of these powers may make the income from the trust taxable to the grantor, not to the trust or the beneficiary (§ 671). Although the grantor has placed the property in trust, the grantor may be regarded as the owner of the property because of his control over the trust property. But in such situations the grantor faces a severe pinch problem; the grantor must bear the tax liability without actually receiving the trust income. The retention of certain controls by grantors is, therefore, effectively discouraged for taxpayers of modest wealth.

The Tax Reform Act of 1986 also blocks planning techniques designed to avoid the application of the grantor trust provisions by having prohibited powers or interests become effective in the grantor's spouse. Senate Finance Committee Report on H.R. 3838, 99th Cong., 2d Sess. 871 (1986). Section 672(e) provides that for purposes of the grantor trust rules, the grantor is treated as holding any power or interest held by the grantor's spouse if that spouse is living with the grantor at the time of the creation of any power or interest held by such spouse.

Power of Revocation. In Corliss v. Bowers, 281 U.S. 376, 50 S.Ct. 336, 74 L.Ed. 916 (1930), the grantor-taxpayer created a trust to pay income to his wife for life, with remainder to their children. In the trust instrument, the taxpayer reserved the power "to modify or alter in any manner, or revoke in whole or in part, this indenture and the trusts then existing, and the estates and interests in property hereby created." The grantor's power to revoke the trust, recapture the property transferred in trust, and stop the payment of income to the beneficiary before it took place was the equivalent to ownership of the trust property. Everything the beneficiary had could be taken back by the grantor. In taxing the income from the revocable trust to the grantor, although the income was actually paid to the beneficiary, the Supreme Court stated:

> * * * if a man disposes of a fund in such a way that another is allowed to enjoy the income which it is in the power of the first to appropriate, it does not matter whether the permission is given by assent or by failure to express dissent. The income that is subject to a man's unfettered command and that he is free to enjoy at his own option may be taxed to him as his income, whether he sees fit to enjoy it or not. (281 U.S. at 378, 50 S.Ct. at 337, 74 L.Ed. at 917–918).

Section 676(a) taxes the income of a trust to the grantor if a power to revoke the trust and receive all or any part of the trust principal is exercisable by the grantor alone, by a nonadverse party (as defined in § 672(b) and (a)) alone, or by the grantor and a nonadverse party acting together. If such a power to revoke exists, even if the power is not exercised, the grantor remains in substance the owner of the trust property. But if, for example, the grantor makes an adverse party (as defined in § 672(a)) the co-trustee, then § 676(a) will not apply.

Income for Grantor's (or Grantor's Spouse's) Benefit. The grantor is deemed to be the owner of the trust and the income from the trust is taxed under § 677(a) to the grantor if the income from all or a portion of the trust may be distributed, or held or accumulated for later distribution, to the grantor or the grantor's spouse without the consent of an adverse party. The mere existence of a power to make such a distribution, and not its exercise, makes the income taxable to the grantor. The grantor will, however, not be taxed on the income from the trust if such power can be exercised only with the consent or approval of an adverse party. The grantor is also taxed if the income may be applied to discharge the grantor's (or his spouse's) legal obligations.

When the income from a trust is distributed or applied to support or maintain a beneficiary whom the grantor is "legally obligated to support," the grantor is taxed on the income so used as opposed to the mere power to do so. § 677(b) and Reg. § 1.677(b)–1(a). Except to the extent the trust income is so applied or distributed, the grantor will not be taxed on trust income, which, in the trustee's discretion, may be distributed to maintain or support a trust beneficiary (except the grantor's spouse) whom the grantor is obligated to support or maintain. Section 677(b) does not apply to income that may be used to discharge the grantor's legal obligation to support his spouse or is available to discharge legal obligations of the grantor or the grantor's spouse, except the duty to support or maintain a trust beneficiary.

Right of Reversion. The taxpayer may be willing to give up all income rights in the property, if after a certain time period, or on the occurrence of certain conditions, the property will come back to him.

HELVERING v. CLIFFORD

Supreme Court of the United States, 1940.
309 U.S. 331, 60 S.Ct. 554, 84 L.Ed. 788.

MR. JUSTICE DOUGLAS delivered the opinion of the Court.

In 1934 respondent declared himself trustee of certain securities which he owned. All net income from the trust was to be held for the "exclusive benefit" of respondent's wife. The trust was for a term of five years, except that it would terminate earlier on the death of either respondent or his wife. On termination of the trust the entire corpus was to go to respondent, while all "accrued or undistributed net income" and "any proceeds from the investment of such net income" was to be treated as property owned absolutely by the wife. During the continuance of the trust respondent was to pay over to his wife the whole or such part of the net income as he in his "absolute discretion" might determine. And during that period he had full power (a) to exercise all voting powers incident to the trusteed shares of stock; (b) to "sell, exchange, mortgage, or pledge" any of the securities under the declaration of trust "whether as part of the corpus or principal thereof or as investments or proceeds and any income therefrom, upon such terms and for such consideration" as respondent in his "absolute discretion may deem fitting"; (c) to invest "any cash or money in the trust estate or any income therefrom" by loans, secured or unsecured, by deposits in banks, or by purchase of securities or other personal property "without restriction" because of their "speculative character" or "rate of return" or any "laws pertaining to the investment of trust funds"; (d) to collect all income; (e) to compromise, etc., any claims held by him as trustee; (f) to hold any property in the trust estate in the names of "other persons or in my own name as an individual" except as otherwise provided. Extraordinary cash dividends, stock dividends, proceeds from the sale of unexercised subscription rights, or any enhancement, realized or not, in the value of the securities were to be treated as principal, not income. An exculpatory clause purported to protect him from all losses except those occasioned by his "own wilful and deliberate" breach of duties as trustee. And finally it was provided that neither the principal nor any future or accrued income should be liable for the debts of the wife; and that the wife could not transfer, encumber, or anticipate any interest in the trust or any income therefrom prior to actual payment thereof to her.

It was stipulated that while the "tax effects" of this trust were considered by respondent they were not the "sole consideration" involved in his decision to set it up, as by this and other gifts he intended to give "security and economic independence" to his wife and children. It was also stipulated that respondent's wife had substantial income of her own from other sources; that there was no restriction on her use of the trust income, all of which income was placed in her personal checking account, intermingled with her other funds, and expended by her on herself, her children and relatives; that the trust was not designed to relieve respondent from liability for family or household expenses and that after execution of the trust he paid large sums from his personal funds for such purposes.

Respondent paid a federal gift tax on this transfer. During the year 1934 all income from the trust was distributed to the wife who included it in her individual return for that year. The Commissioner, however, determined a deficiency in respondent's return for that year on the theory that income from the trust was taxable to him. The Board of Tax Appeals sustained that redetermination. 38 B.T.A. 1532. The Circuit Court of Appeals reversed. 8 Cir., 105 F.2d 586. We granted certiorari because of the importance to the revenue of the use of such short term trusts in the reduction of surtaxes.   *   *   *

  *   *   * The broad sweep of [the] language [in § 61(a)] indicates the purpose of Congress to use the full measure of its taxing power within those definable categories. Hence our construction of the statute should be consonant with that purpose. Technical considerations, niceties of the law of trusts or conveyances, or the legal paraphernalia which inventive genius may construct as a refuge from surtaxes should not obscure the basic issue. That issue is whether the grantor after the trust has been established may still be treated, under this statutory scheme as the owner of the corpus. See Blair v. Commissioner, 300 U.S. 5, 12, 57 S.Ct. 330, 333, 81 L.Ed. 465. In absence of more precise standards or guides supplied by statute or appropriate regulations, the answer to that question must depend on an analysis of the terms of the trust and all the circumstances attendant on its creation and operation. And where the grantor is the trustee and the beneficiaries are members of his family group, special scrutiny of the arrangement is necessary

lest what is in reality but one economic unit be multiplied into two or more by devices which, though valid under state law, are not conclusive so far as [§ 61(a)] is concerned.

In this case we cannot conclude as a matter of law that respondent ceased to be the owner of the corpus after the trust was created. Rather, the short duration of the trust, the fact that the wife was the beneficiary, and the retention of control over the corpus by respondent all lead irresistibly to the conclusion that respondent continued to be the owner for purposes of [§ 61(a)].

So far as his dominion and control were concerned it seems clear that the trust did not effect any substantial change. In substance his control over the corpus was in all essential respects the same after the trust was created, as before. The wide powers which he retained included for all practical purposes most of the control which he as an individual would have. There were, we may assume, exceptions, such as his disability to make a gift of the corpus to others during the term of the trust and to make loans to himself. But this dilution in his control would seem to be insignificant and immaterial, since control over investment remained. If it be said that such control is the type of dominion exercised by any trustee, the answer is simple. We have at best a temporary reallocation of income within an intimate family group. Since the income remains in the family and since the husband retains control over the investment, he has rather complete assurance that the trust will not effect any substantial change in his economic position. It is hard to imagine that respondent felt himself the poorer after this trust had been executed or, if he did, that it had any rational foundation in fact. For as a result of the terms of the trust and the intimacy of the familial relationship respondent retained the substance of full enjoyment of all the rights which previously he had in the property. That might not be true if only strictly legal rights were considered. But when the benefits flowing to him indirectly through the wife are added to the legal rights he retained, the aggregate may be said to be a fair equivalent of what he previously had. To exclude from the aggregate those indirect benefits would be to deprive [§ 61(a)] of considerable vitality and to treat as immaterial what may be highly relevant considerations in the creation of such family trusts. For where the head of the household has income in excess of normal needs, it may well make but little difference to him (except income-tax-wise) where portions of that income are routed—so long as it stays in the family group. In those circumstances the all-important factor might be retention by him of control over the principal. With that control in his hands he would keep direct command over all that he needed to remain in substantially the same financial situation as before. Our point here is that no one fact is normally decisive but that all considerations and circumstances of the kind we have mentioned are relevant to the question of ownership and are appropriate foundations for findings on that issue. Thus, where, as in this case, the benefits directly or indirectly retained blend so imperceptibly with the normal concepts of full ownership, we cannot say that the triers of fact committed reversible error when they found that the husband was the owner of the corpus for the purposes of [§ 61(a)]. To hold otherwise would be to treat the wife as a complete stranger; to let mere formalism obscure the normal consequences of family solidarity; and to force concepts of ownership to be fashioned out of legal niceties which may have little or no significance in such household arrangements.

The bundle of rights which he retained was so substantial that respondent cannot be heard to complain that he is the "victim of despotic power when for the purpose of taxation he is treated as owner altogether." See Du Pont v. Commissioner, 289 U.S. 685, 689, 53 S.Ct. 766, 767, 77 L.Ed. 1447.

* * *

The judgment of the Circuit Court of Appeals is reversed and that of the Board of Tax Appeals is affirmed.

It is so ordered.

Reversed.

Prior to the Tax Reform Act of 1986, former § 673(a) treated the grantor as the owner of a trust if he had a reversionary interest in the principal or income of a trust that "will or may reasonably be expected to take effect in possession or enjoyment within ten years, commencing with the date of the transfer of that portion of the trust." Under former § 673(a) this meant that the income of a trust could be reported by the income beneficiary of a trust if the income interest lasted for at least ten years and one day, with a reversion at the end of the trust term in the settlor.

The Tax Reform of 1986 repealed the so-called 10-year rule for transfers in trust made after March 1, 1986 "so that a trust would be treated as a grantor trust in all cases where there is any significant possibility that interests and powers in the trust may become effective in the grantor after the creation of the trust." Senate Finance Committee Report on H.R. 3838, 99th Cong., 2d Sess. 871 (1986). Section 673(a) now treats a trust as a grantor trust, with the income taxed to the grantor, if he (or his spouse) has a reversionary interest in trust principal or income provided that "as of the inception of that portion of the trust, the value of such interest exceeds 5 percent of the value of such portion." For example, if a father transfers income-producing property to a trust, giving an income interest to his children for the next 32 years, at which time the trust is to terminate and the property is to be returned to the father, an assignment of income will be permitted because the present value of the reversion retained by the father is worth less than 5 percent.

To facilitate ease of administration, an exception exists under which the grantor is deemed not to be the owner of a portion of a trust because of a reversionary interest if such portion passes to the grantor (or his spouse) only after the death of a trust beneficiary before such beneficiary attains age 21 provided the beneficiary is a lineal descendant of the grantor who holds all of the present interests in any portion of the trust. § 673(b).

In sum, § 673(a) imposes a severe penalty on the grantor who retains a reversionary interest. From a planning standpoint, the grantor should not retain a reversionary interest in a trust created to serve as an income splitting vehicle.

Power to Control Beneficial Enjoyment. If the grantor reserves the power to control the beneficial enjoyment of trust income or principal, the grantor, with certain exceptions, is viewed as the owner of the trust property for income tax purposes and the income from the trust is required to be included in the grantor's taxable income. Section 674(a) treats the grantor as the owner of any portion of a trust if the "beneficial enjoyment of the corpus or income" is subject to a "power of disposition," exercisable by the grantor, a nonadverse party (§ 672(b) and (a)) or the grantor and nonadverse party acting together, without the approval or consent of any adverse party. Power to control the beneficial enjoyment includes the retention of the power to add beneficiaries to those named in the trust instrument, to vary the proportions in which the principal or income is to be paid to the specified beneficiaries, to select the ultimate beneficiary or beneficiaries, and to accelerate or postpone the time when distributions are to be made. According to Reg. § 1.674(a)–1(a), § 674(c) reaches "every case in which [the grantor] or a nonadverse party can affect the beneficial enjoyment of a portion of a trust," unless the power is subject to the certain limitations.

Section 674 is subject to a number of exceptions contained in § 674(b), (c), and (d). The scope of the exceptions depends on whether the grantor (1) serves as trustee or appoints a related or subordinate party (§ 672(c)) or (2) appoints an "independent" trustee. If the grantor wishes the trustee's powers with respect to the control of beneficial enjoyment to be limited by § 674(b), the grantor can name anyone as trustee, including himself. If the grantor wants to give the trustee greater flexibility in determining who will enjoy the benefits of the trust, the grantor may confer broader discretionary powers on a narrower group of trustees in accordance with § 674(c) and (d).

Section 674(b) permits limited discretionary powers to be vested in anyone as trustee without causing trust income to be attributed to the grantor. The power to invade the trust principal and distribute the principal will cause the grantor to be taxed on the trust income, unless the principal can be distributed to or for:

(1) a beneficiary, beneficiaries, or a class of beneficiaries, if the power is limited by a "reasonably definite standard" established in the

trust instrument. § 674(b)(5)(A). A reasonably definite standard "＊ ＊ ＊ is a clearly measurable standard under which the holder of a power is legally accountable ＊ ＊ ＊. For instance, a power to distribute corpus for the education, support, maintenance, or health of a beneficiary; for his reasonable support and comfort; or to enable him to maintain his accustomed standard of living; or to meet an emergency ＊ ＊ ＊." Reg. § 1.674(b)–1(b)(5)(i). The grantor, acting as trustee, is viewed as implementing the terms of the trust instrument; or

(2) any current income beneficiary, if the distribution is charged against the proportionate share of the income to such beneficiary. § 674(b)(5)(B). The income beneficiary need not be a remainderman.

In addition to the power to distribute principal, the grantor may desire the power to withhold income temporarily. The power to withhold and accumulate income for a current income beneficiary will not result in the grantor being taxed on the trust's income if the accumulated income is ultimately payable: (1) on the termination of the trust or on the distribution of principal plus accumulated income "to the current income beneficiaries in shares which have been irrevocably specified in the trust instrument" or (2) to the beneficiary, his estate, or, with limitations, his appointees. § 674(b)(6).

The provisions discussed above apply to the power to allocate principal or income among named beneficiaries. This restriction prevents persons holding these powers from introducing strangers into the group of beneficiaries or class of beneficiaries after the trust is set up. The restriction does not apply to the inclusion of after-born or after-adopted children.

Section 674(c) permits broader discretionary powers to be vested in the trustee, but the grantor has less freedom in choosing the trustee or trustees. The grantor cannot serve as the sole trustee or one of the trustees. At least one-half of the trustees must be independent trustees who are not a related or subordinate party to the grantor and who are not subservient to the grantor's wishes. A related or subordinate party is defined in § 672(c). The powers specified pertain to payments of income or principal to be made from the trust. Under § 674(c), the trustee may not only accumulate income or distribute trust principal, but also decide which individual or individuals from among a group or class of beneficiaries will receive the income or principal, in what proportions, and when.

Under § 674(d), the grantor's close relatives (but not the grantor or the grantor's spouse who is living with the grantor) or employees can serve as trustee and be given discretionary power to distribute, apportion, allocate, or accumulate income (but not principal) to or for a beneficiary, beneficiaries or within a class of beneficiaries, if the power is limited by a reasonably definite standard set forth in a trust instrument. As to a reasonably definite standard, see Reg. § 1.674(b)–1(b)(5).

Problem

An insurance agent establishes a trust, providing that all of the income from the trust is to be paid to his children, with any property remaining in the trust after the death of the last surviving child to be paid over to the grandchildren. He transfers into the trust his right to future renewal commissions arising from life insurance policies he has sold. Will this irrevocable transfer in trust be effective to shift the reporting of the income to the trust beneficiaries? Consider § 671, Reg. § 1.671–1(c), and Lucas v. Earl at page 707.

F. GIFT–LEASEBACK ARRANGEMENTS

We next examine the problem of the grantor who places property in trust and then leases it back from the trust. The taxpayer hopes to redirect income to a lower tax bracket family member by placing the property in a trust. The taxpayer also hopes to deduct the rental payments made to the trust.

Problem

Gino owns and operates a restaurant in a building he owns. He proposes to transfer the building in trust for the benefit of his 15 year old son. Gino's income from the restaurant business is $100,000. Gino wants to lease the building back from the trust at a fair rental value of $20,000 per year. Thus Gino's income will be reduced (the exact figure depends on a comparison of the rental payments with deductions for depreciation (Accelerated Cost Recovery), maintenance, taxes, interest, and insurance and the son's gross income will be $20,000 per year (assuming no income from other sources).

(a) Will the rental payment be deductible by Gino under § 162(a)(3) and taxable to the son?

(b) How would you structure this transaction to achieve the result sought by Gino? Who should obtain the trust corpus on the termination of the trust? Consider §§ 673(a) and 672(e). What other controls could Gino retain? Consider § 674(b).

ROSENFELD v. COMMISSIONER

United States Court of Appeals, Second Circuit, 1983.
706 F.2d 1277.

IRVING R. KAUFMAN, CIRCUIT JUDGE:

For as long as governments have taxed their citizens, individuals have sought to minimize their tax burdens. On occasion, members of the public have employed elaborate devices to defer taxes or shift income to their associates and relatives in lower tax brackets. When such schemes completely lack legitimate purposes and affect no real economic or beneficial interests, courts have not hesitated to pierce the formal arrangements and examine the substance of the underlying transaction. At the same time, judges have recognized that taxpayers are generally free to order their investment and business decisions to reduce their tax liability. As Judge Learned Hand eloquently noted, "one may so arrange his affairs that his taxes shall be as low as possible; he is not bound to choose that pattern which will best pay the Treasury; there is not even a patriotic duty to increase one's taxes." Helvering v. Gregory, 69 F.2d 809, 810 (2d Cir.1934), *aff'd*, 293 U.S. 465, 55 S.Ct. 266, 79 L.Ed. 596 (1935).

This case calls upon us to draw, once again, the fine line between valid business transactions and illegitimate tax avoidance ploys. We are required to determine, as a matter of first impression within this Circuit, whether a taxpayer who gives property to his children in trust may lease back that property for use as a professional office, and deduct the rent payments from his income pursuant to I.R.C. § 162(a)(3). Because we believe these transactions involved real transfers of economic interests, and for other reasons set forth below, we affirm the Tax Court's order allowing the rent deductions.

I

Since the underlying facts are important to the resolution of this dispute, we set them forth in some detail.

In 1963 George B. Rosenfeld, a doctor practicing in Cheektowaga, New York, purchased a parcel of land in that town. Shortly thereafter, Rosenfeld arranged for a building to be constructed on the property, intended for use as a medical office. Since the completion of the building in 1964, Rosenfeld has been its sole occupant.

In 1969 Rosenfeld decided to establish a trust for the benefit of his three daughters, and to transfer the land and medical office to the trust. Prior to executing this transaction, he arranged for an independent firm, Grant Appraisal & Research Corporation, to value the property. After the appraiser concluded that the fair rental of the property was $14,000 per year, Rosenfeld created an irrevocable trust, and arranged for Samuel Goldman, his accountant, and Ira Powsner, his attorney, to act as trustees. Pursuant to the terms of the agreement, the trustees were responsible for collecting income produced by the property and investing it, until the termination of the trust, at which time the accumulated proceeds would be distributed to the beneficiaries.

The trust was to have a term of 10½ years, and Rosenfeld retained a reversionary interest in the corpus.* During the period of the trust, he remained liable for the mortgage payments and general upkeep of the property. The trustees were responsible for the payment of real estate taxes. Rosenfeld had no right to alter the terms of the trust, and was legally obligated to fulfill its requirements.

* The Tax Reform Act of 1986 repealed the income splitting benefits of the 10-year reversionary trust.—Eds.

The trust agreement was executed on July 1, 1969, and on that same date, Rosenfeld entered into a lease with the trustees. Rosenfeld agreed to rent the medical property for the entire term of the trust for annual payments of $14,000, the amount fixed by the appraisers as fair and reasonable. The lease also required Rosenfeld to pay utility and other incidental expenses, and granted him the right to construct additions to the building at his expense.

In 1973, Rosenfeld decided to transfer his reversionary interest in the trust property to his wife.** Two years later, appellee and the trustees agreed upon further changes and amended the trust to extend its termination date for 5 years, from 1980 to 1985. Also in 1975 the lease agreement was modified to increase the annual rent to $15,000, and alter the rental term to one year, renewable for an additional year at Rosenfeld's option.

We now approach the core of this dispute. In his tax returns for 1974 and 1975, Rosenfeld claimed a deduction for his rent payments to the trust pursuant to I.R.C. § 162(a)(3), which allows a taxpayer to deduct from his income "ordinary and necessary" rent expenses incurred as a condition of the taxpayer's trade or business. The trust filed fiduciary returns, and reported the amounts paid by appellee as income. The trust also claimed deductions for real estate taxes and depreciation on the property. After auditing Rosenfeld's returns, the Commissioner disallowed the deductions for the rent expenses in 1974 and 1975. In October 1977, appellee received a statutory notice of deficiency, and, as one would anticipate under these circumstances, he challenged the Commissioner's assessment.

Eventually the case was heard by Judge Simpson, who concluded the rent payments were properly deducted by the taxpayer pursuant to § 162(a)(3). Accordingly, the judge recalculated the deficiencies, and for the years 1974 and 1975 found Rosenfeld liable for items other than the rent deductions. Rosenfeld does not challenge these assessments. The Commissioner, however, filed a notice of appeal, questioning the Tax Court's rejection of the deficiencies relating to the rent deductions.

II

While, as we have noted, this appeal raises a question of first impression in this Circuit, we are not writing on a *tabula rasa*. The issue on this appeal has not suffered from lack of consideration by various tribunals. The Tax Court has been confronted with this problem on numerous occasions, and several other Circuits have also expressed their views. These authorities, however, have been divided on the proper tax treatment of a claimed deduction in a gift-leaseback situation. Generally the Tax Court's recent decisions have allowed deductions in similar situations. But we find the Courts of Appeals

** Section 672(e) now provides that for purposes of the grantor trust rules (§§ 671–677), the grantor is treated as holding any power or interest held by the grantor's spouse if that spouse is living with the grantor at the time of the creation of any power or interest held by such spouse.—Eds.

have split on this issue. The Third, Seventh, Eighth and Ninth Circuits have held in favor of the taxpayer,[9] while the Fourth and Fifth Circuits have adopted the Commissioner's view.[10] It is against this background of divergent views that we are called upon to exercise our Solomonic powers and resolve the instant dispute, by determining which of the conclusions reached among the Circuits accords with the law, and, indeed, is the fairer course to follow.

We commence our consideration by looking to the language of the statute. On its face it appears to grant a taxpayer the right to deduct his rent expenses, even where he previously owned the leased property. In relevant part, I.R.C. § 162(a) provides:

> There shall be allowed as a deduction all the ordinary and necessary expenses paid or incurred during the taxable year in carrying on any trade or business, including—
>
> * * *
>
> (3) rentals and other payments required to be made as a condition to the continued use or possession, for purposes of the trade or business, of property to which the taxpayer has not taken or is not taking title or in which he has no equity.

But the Commissioner claims Rosenfeld has no right to a deduction pursuant to this provision, because he voluntarily entered into the arrangement which created the need to pay rent. Appellant urges us to adopt the view that the gift-leaseback arrangement is a sham and the taxpayer should be prevented from taking advantage of his self-created rent liability to reduce his taxes.

In considering the validity of a claimed deduction in a gift-lease-back situation, we have been given some guidance by the Tax Court which has devised a four-prong test. To receive the deduction, "1) [t]he grantor must not retain substantially the same control over the property that he had before he made the gift, 2) [t]he leaseback should normally be in writing and must require the payment of a reasonable rent, 3) [t]he leaseback (as distinguished from the gift) must have a bona fide business purpose, [and] 4) [t]he grantor must not possess a disqualifying 'equity' in the property within the meaning of section 162(a)(3)." May v. Commissioner, 76 T.C. 7, 13 (1981), appeal pending (9th Cir. No. 82–7658); see Mathews v. Commissioner, 61 T.C. 12 (1973), rev'd, 520 F.2d 323 (5th Cir.1975), cert. denied, 424 U.S. 967, 96 S.Ct. 1463, 47 L.Ed.2d 734 (1976); see also Quinlivan v. Commissioner, 599 F.2d 269, 272 (8th Cir.), cert. denied, 444 U.S. 996, 100 S.Ct. 531, 62 L.Ed.2d 426 (1979).

9. See, e.g., Brown v. Commissioner, 180 F.2d 926 (3d Cir.), cert. denied, 340 U.S. 814, 71 S.Ct. 42, 95 L.Ed. 598 (1950); Skemp v. Commissioner, 168 F.2d 598 (7th Cir.1948); Quinlivan v. Commissioner, 599 F.2d 269 (8th Cir.), cert. denied, 444 U.S. 996, 100 S.Ct. 531, 62 L.Ed.2d 426 (1979); Brooke v. United States, 468 F.2d 1155 (9th Cir.1972).

10. See, e.g., Perry v. United States, 520 F.2d 235 (4th Cir.1975), cert. denied, 423 U.S. 1052, 96 S.Ct. 782, 46 L.Ed.2d 641 (1976); Van Zandt v. Commissioner, 341 F.2d 440 (5th Cir.), cert. denied, 382 U.S. 814, 86 S.Ct. 32, 15 L.Ed.2d 62 (1965).

For reasons stated below, we believe this test is an appropriate measure of the legitimacy of a deduction in a gift-leaseback situation. The Commissioner has conceded that the lease was properly executed and does not challenge the reasonableness of the rent. Appellant, however, asserts that Rosenfeld did not satisfy the first element of the May test because, in fact, he retained control of the property. The Commissioner also challenges the third prong of this test, contending that the gift and leaseback considered together must have a demonstrable bona fide business purpose. See Perry v. United States, 520 F.2d 235 (4th Cir.1975), cert. denied, 423 U.S. 1052, 96 S.Ct. 782, 46 L.Ed.2d 641 (1976); Van Zandt v. Commissioner, 341 F.2d 440 (5th Cir.), cert. denied, 382 U.S. 814, 86 S.Ct. 32, 15 L.Ed.2d 62 (1965).

Judge Simpson's opinion is enlightening. He found the first part of the May test was met, because Rosenfeld surrendered control over the property he deeded to the trust. Pursuant to the terms of the trust agreement, the trustees were authorized to mortgage or sell the property, grant easements, and exercise other powers traditionally associated with ownership. Moreover, Rosenfeld was obligated to pay rent, and although the initial lease granted a right of occupancy for the entire term of the trust, the amended lease was only for a single year, renewable for one additional year. Rosenfeld was also prohibited from subletting the property or assigning his rights under the lease.

In addition, the Tax Court found the trustees were independent, and appellant has presented nothing which would persuade us to reject this finding. In some cases in which a taxpayer has been prevented from taking a rent deduction, the trustees were not truly independent, and the decisions in those cases are clearly distinguishable on that basis. See, e.g., Van Zandt v. Commissioner, supra (grantor is also trustee); see also White v. Fitzpatrick, 193 F.2d 398, 402 n. 2 (2d Cir. 1951) ("the factor of independent trusteeship is crucial"), cert. denied, 343 U.S. 928, 72 S.Ct. 762, 96 L.Ed. 1338 (1952); Quinlivan v. Commissioner, supra, 599 F.2d at 273 n. 4 (distinguishing Van Zandt and Perry v. United States, supra, because of the lack of independence of the trustees in those cases). We are of the view that in this case the broad grants of power to the trustees, the concomitant diminution of Rosenfeld's rights, and the actual independence of the trustees, adequately satisfies the first element of the Tax Court's test.

The Commissioner also claims, as we have indicated, that the entire transaction, and not merely the leaseback, must be imbued with a valid business purpose. But we are of the view that such a requirement is too harsh for it would lead inevitably to a denial of the rent deduction, despite its clear business purpose, because the gift of the land was not *ipso facto* a business transaction. The Commissioner's argument calls for a test which is overly stringent, particularly in the circumstances here. Many financial decisions are motivated by the prospect of legitimate tax savings, rather than business concerns, and we have already expressed our agreement with Judge Learned Hand's view that a transaction which is otherwise legitimate, is not unlawful merely because an individual seeks to minimize the tax consequences of his activities. See Helvering v. Gregory, supra; Gilbert v. Commissioner, 248 F.2d 399, 411 (2d Cir.1957) (L. Hand dissenting).

We have frequently noted in our decisions that the propriety of conduct should be determined by examining all that occurred. *White v. Fitzpatrick,* supra. This does not, of course, imply that we should blindly apply the business purpose standard (or some other test) without consideration of other factors which bear on the case. To illustrate, Congress has explicitly considered the gift aspect of this transaction which the Commissioner finds objectionable. The so-called Clifford trust provisions of the Internal Revenue Code, 26 U.S.C. §§ 671–678, specifically [addressed] the creation of short-term trusts, and impose minimum requirements which must be satisfied before the trust income can be taxed to the beneficial owner. While these provisions are not dispositive of the issue whether payments to the trust may be deducted, see S.Rep. No. 1622, 83d Cong., 2d Sess., reprinted in, 1954 U.S.Code Cong. & Ad.News 4621, 5006; 26 C.F.R. § 1.671–1(c) (1982), we cannot blind ourselves to the interplay between these provisions and § 162(a) (3). Quinlivan v. Commissioner, supra, 599 F.2d at 273–74; Lerner v. Commissioner, 71 T.C. 290, 301–02 (1978).

The Commissioner's position that both the trust and the leaseback must have a legitimate business purpose, ignores the Congressional policy inherent in the Clifford sections. It is difficult to imagine a case in which the establishment of such a trust could be viewed as furthering a taxpayer's business objectives. Quite simply, Clifford trusts [previously were] income-shifting devices designed to shelter income, and we cannot lightly overlook the legislative determination that trusts which comply with §§ 671–678 are legitimate.[11] Accepting the Commissioner's view, as noted in Quinlivan v. Commissioner, supra, 599 F.2d at 274, "would produce a benefit only in cases where investment property—not used in the grantor's trade or business—is placed in trust. Persons whose assets consist largely of business property would be excluded from a tax benefit clearly provided by Congress."

Accordingly, we decline appellant's invitation to adopt a business purpose standard of review. Rather, we believe our inquiry should focus on whether there has been a change in the economic interests of

---

11. Indeed, we note many commentators have criticized those decisions which adopt the Commissioner's position. Our dissenting brother's reasoning essentially follows the views of those Circuits with which we disagree. The authorities forcefully argue that compliance with the Clifford sections of the Tax Code should be sufficient to ensure the deductibility of rent payments in a gift-leaseback situation. See, e.g., Froehlich, Clifford Trusts: Use of Partnership Interests as Corpus; Leaseback Arrangements, 52 Calif.L.Rev. 956, 973–74 (1964); Note, Clifford Trusts: A New View Towards Leaseback Deductions, 43 Alb.L.Rev. 585, 594–95 (1979); Note, Gifts and Leasebacks: Is Judicial Consensus Impossible?, 49 U.Cin.L.Rev. 379, 393–94 (1980); Comment, Gift Leaseback Transactions: An Unpredictable Tax-Savings Tool, 53 Temple L.Q. 569 (1980). En passant, we note that our views have prevailed in the greater number of Circuits which have already considered the issue now before us.

the relevant parties. If their legal rights and beneficial interests have changed, there is no basis for labeling a transaction a "sham" and ignoring it for tax purposes. Indeed, our prior decisions have indicated that this is the relevant inquiry. Gilbert v. Commissioner, supra, 248 F.2d at 411–12 (L. Hand, dissenting); United States v. Ingredient Technology Corp., slip op. at 1027, 1040 (2d Cir. Jan. 5, 1983); see also Frank Lyon Co. v. United States, 435 U.S. 561, 98 S.Ct. 1291, 55 L.Ed.2d 550 (1978); Brooke v. United States, 468 F.2d 1155, 1158 (9th Cir.1972).

It is readily apparent here that there has been a real change in the legal rights and interests of the parties. As we noted, the trustees were granted broad powers over the corpus of the trust, which necessarily reduced Rosenfeld's authority. Moreover, during the years in issue, Rosenfeld had no present or future interest in the property. When he deeded his reversion in 1973, he retained no legal or equitable right to the trust property. See White v. Fitzpatrick, supra, 193 F.2d at 401 (court distinguishes Skemp v. Commissioner, supra, and Brown v. Commissioner, 180 F.2d 926 (3d Cir.), cert. denied, 340 U.S. 814, 71 S.Ct. 42, 95 L.Ed. 598 (1950), on the ground that grantor did not retain a reversion in those cases). In addition, Rosenfeld was legally obligated to pay rent. The trustees were required to collect a fixed rent which the Commissioner concedes is fair, and also to discharge their fiduciary duties to the trust beneficiaries. Although the lease was initially coterminous with the trust, the lease amendments required renegotiation on an annual basis if Rosenfeld was to continue to occupy the building, and there is nothing presented to us to cause us to believe that this bargaining would not be carried out at arm's length.

In addition to these substantial changes in the economic positions of the parties, there were legitimate non-tax motives for the creation of the trust and the leaseback. Rosenfeld understandably wanted to guarantee his children's financial well-being, and the trust helped assure realization of this objective. See Brooke v. United States, supra, 468 F.2d at 1158; cf. Parshelsky's Estate v. Commissioner, 303 F.2d 14, 18–19 (2d Cir.1962) (court considering tax consequences of corporate reorganization examines non-tax-avoidance motives of both corporation and shareholders). The leaseback was also clearly motivated by concerns other than tax savings and was a business necessity. Rosenfeld required an office to practice medicine, and the rental payments were a condition of continued occupancy.

While recognizing these factors, the Commissioner asserts, nonetheless, that nothing changed because Rosenfeld was occupying the same premises as a lessee which he previously used as the owner. This argument is disingenuous. Rosenfeld could have given the property to his children in trust and leased property from a third party for an amount equally fair and reasonable for his medical office. It is clear, and indeed, counsel conceded at oral argument, that a rent deduction would have been entirely proper in such a case. See Frank Lyon Co. v. United States, supra. In real terms, there is little difference between this hypothetical case and the events the Commissioner challenges. In both cases Rosenfeld would have voluntarily relinquished his right to occupy his offices rent-free, and created the need to lease other premises. It can hardly be a matter of concern for the Commissioner whether Rosenfeld rents from the trust rather than from some third party. In either situation he would be required to pay rent, and the trust could receive rental income from the property it owned.

III

In sum, we believe the gift-leaseback transaction substantially altered Rosenfeld's economic and beneficial rights, and accordingly, the arrangement, which was otherwise proper under both the Clifford sections of the Internal Revenue Code and § 162(a)(3), was not rendered objectionable merely because Rosenfeld's rent payments were made to a trust which he established for the benefit of his children. The Tax Court properly concluded that Rosenfeld had a right to deduct his rent expenses pursuant to I.R.C. § 162(a)(3).

The order is affirmed.

MacMAHON, DISTRICT JUDGE, dissenting:

I respectfully dissent. It is fundamental that in determining liability for income taxes courts consider the economic reality, not the form, of financial transactions. In the words of Judge Learned Hand:

> The Income Tax Act imposes liabilities upon taxpayers based upon their financial transactions, and it is of course true that the payment of the tax is itself a financial transaction. *If, however, the taxpayer enters into a transaction that does not appreciably affect his beneficial interest except to reduce his tax, the law will disregard it;* for we cannot suppose that it was part of the purpose of the act to provide an escape from the liabilities that it sought to impose.

Gilbert v. Commissioner, 248 F.2d 399, 411 (2d Cir.1957) (L. Hand, J., dissenting) (emphasis added). Since I find that the transaction here does not appreciably affect the beneficial interest of the taxpayer, except to reduce his tax, I cannot agree with the majority. Nor can I find either a business purpose in the transaction or a significant transfer of control over the property.

I. Business Purpose

Those courts that have permitted deduction of rental payments after a gift and leaseback have taken a "bifurcated" approach, viewing the gift and the leaseback as separate transactions, while those that have denied deductions have looked at the contemporaneous gift and leaseback as one transaction. See Perry v. United States, 520 F.2d 235, 238 (4th Cir.1975), cert. denied, 423 U.S. 1052, 96 S.Ct. 782, 46 L.Ed.2d 641 (1976); Brooke v. United States, 468 F.2d 1155, 1160 (9th Cir.1972) (Ely, J., dissenting). The government argues that we should consider the contemporaneous gift and leaseback as a single transaction and apply the business purpose rule to the taxpayer's claimed deduction for rental payments. The majority characterizes this argument as requiring a business purpose for the gift and a business purpose for the leaseback. It is illogical to require a business purpose for a gift, and this is not the government's argument. The government argues that the contemporaneous gift and leaseback be viewed as one transaction and that the business purpose rule be applied to the taxpayer's claimed deduction for the "business expense" of the resulting rental payments.

Both the facts of the instant case and the relevant legal standards compel the conclusion that the gift and leaseback must be viewed as a single transaction. The uncontroverted evidence is that Dr. Rosenfeld approached his lawyer and his accountant because he wanted to make lifetime gifts to his children. The trust, deed and lease were executed the same day, July 1, 1969, and the lease was coterminous with the trust. It also is undisputed that the terms of the trust and of the lease were fixed before that day.

The total payments made by Dr. Rosenfeld were far in excess of the reasonable rental value of the office. This court previously has recognized, in a gift-leaseback, the significance of the fact that the transaction is disadvantageous to the business. White v. Fitzpatrick, 193 F.2d 398, 400 (2d Cir.1951), cert. denied, 343 U.S. 928, 72 S.Ct. 762, 96 L.Ed. 1338 (1952). In the instant case, Dr. Rosenfeld initially paid $14,000 per year, which was the gross rental, as determined by an independent appraiser, necessary to carry the building's fair market value. However, the appraiser determined that the highest and best use of the building was as a professional office, with the unfinished one-third of the building "finished and occupied." But Dr. Rosenfeld paid the full appraised rent while using the one-third unfinished space not for an office but for storage. In addition, Dr. Rosenfeld remained liable on the mortgage and continued to make the monthly payments. The standard in this court for determining whether a business expense is "ordinary and necessary," 26 U.S.C. § 162(a), and therefore deductible, is whether a hard-headed businessman, under the circumstances, would have incurred the expense. Cole v. Commissioner, 481 F.2d 872, 876 (2d Cir. 1973). These terms, I submit, are not the terms on which a hard-headed businessman would sign a lease for an office he already owned and occupied. Dr. Rosenfeld remained liable on the mortgage so that the gift of the building to the trust would be of greater value to his daughters and, presumably, because the interest deductions were of more value to him than to the trust. He was willing to pay a high rent because the greater the rent, the greater the gift to his daughters and the lower the family's taxes. As in Mathews v. Commissioner, 520 F.2d 323, 325 (5th Cir.1975), cert. denied, 424 U.S. 967, 96 S.Ct. 1463, 47 L.Ed.2d 734 (1976), "the fact rent negotiations produced 'reasonable' results is totally irrelevant. Any bargaining is simply not at arm's length, because any rent exceeding expenses stays in the * * * family."

Dr. Rosenfeld's scheme amounts in substance to an assignment of $14,000 of his yearly income to the trust. Such an assignment would not be recognized by the tax law. In *White v. Fitzpatrick,* supra, the taxpayer owned and operated a company which owned a certain patent essential to its business. The taxpayer transferred the patent to his wife for ten dollars, and the following day the wife licensed the exclusive manufacturing rights to the taxpayer for the term of the patent. This court described the transaction thus: "The sole practical effect of these transactions * * * was to create a right to income in the wife, while leaving untouched in all practical reality the husband-donor's effective dominion and control over the properties in question." 193 F.2d at 400. The court denied the taxpayer a business deduction for the resulting royalties, stating that the taxpayer's scheme "in effect * * * is not different from claiming that the gift itself made the original income [his wife's] in the first place." Id. at 401. In the instant case, Dr. Rosenfeld in effect diverted $14,000 of his income to the trust by taking a business deduction for rent. The only conclusion that can be drawn from these facts is that the trust, deed and lease were conceived and executed at the same time and for the same purpose and that the purpose was to make gifts to Dr. Rosenfeld's children.

It is beyond question that courts will look to the substance of transactions in determining their tax consequences. See Diedrich v. Commissioner, 457 U.S. 191, 194–96, 102 S.Ct. 2414, 2417–18, 72 L.Ed.2d 777 (1982); Knetsch v. United States, 364 U.S. 361, 81 S.Ct. 132, 5 L.Ed. 2d 128 (1960) * * *. This court has repeatedly recognized this salutary principle. See Hoffman Motors Corp. v. United States, 473 F.2d 254, 257 (2d Cir.1973) ("[C]ourts will look through the 'form' of a business transaction and rule on the basis of its 'substance.' "); Philipp Bros. Chemicals, Inc. (N.Y.) v. Commissioner, 435 F.2d 53, 57 (2d Cir. 1970) ("[I]t is economic reality, rather than legal formality, which determines who earns income."); Lubin v. Commissioner, 335 F.2d 209, 213 (2d Cir.1964) ("[O]ur taxing statutes are intended to take cognizance of realities and not mere appearances or facades.").[12] Furthermore, this court has answered the question of whether a deduction is permissible for rental payments arising from a gift-leaseback in *White v. Fitzpatrick,* supra. The court denied the deduction,[13] stating:

> Gift and retained control must be regarded as inseparable parts of a single transaction, especially since it was only in their sum total that they had any reality in regard to the conduct of [taxpayer's] business. To isolate them * * * is to hide business reality behind paper pretense.

12. See Mathews v. Comm'r, 520 F.2d 323, 325 (5th Cir.1975), cert. denied, 424 U.S. 967, 96 S.Ct. 1463, 47 L.Ed.2d 734 (1976):

In deciding the federal questions of income tax law, we must examine transactions with substance rather than form in mind. If we stood at the top of the world and looked down on this transaction— ignoring the flyspeck of legal title under state law—we would see the same state of affairs the day after the trust was created that we saw the day before.

13. See also Hall v. United States, 208 F.Supp. 584 (N.D.N.Y.1962) (denying deduction for rental payments made by grantor-doctor after gift-leaseback of medical office property).

White v. Fitzpatrick, supra, 193 F.2d at 400. White was cited in Perry v. United States, supra, in which the Fourth Circuit Court of Appeals denied a deduction for rental payments arising from a gift-leaseback. See 520 F.2d at 238 n. 3.

Nonetheless, the majority struggles to avoid application of the business purpose rule by arguing that, although it is proper to determine tax consequences by "examining all that occurred," this "does not, of course, imply that we should blindly apply the business purpose standard * * * without consideration of other factors which bear on the case." Here, the majority points, "[t]o illustrate," to the validity of the trust as one of these "other factors," but the majority does not point to any other transaction for which a deduction under Section 162(a) is allowed without a business purpose. It is clear that, rather than using the trust as an "illustration," the majority relies on the validity of the trust in allowing the deduction. The majority offers the validity of the trust as the sole "other factor" to be considered. In addition, the majority concludes that the test to be applied to the gift is whether the gift was a "sham." In other words, if the gift is valid, the deduction is allowed; if the gift is a sham, the deduction is denied. The majority, and the other courts which have reached the same result,[14] have been unfaithful to the cases cited above because they have been seduced by the Clifford trust. However, the majority's reliance on the validity of the trust does not withstand analysis.

First, the legislative history plainly states that the Clifford trust sections are irrelevant in determining the deductibility of Dr. Rosenfeld's rental payments. The Senate Finance Committee Report states:

> The effect of this provision is to insure that taxability of Clifford type trusts shall be governed solely by this subpart [rather than by 26 U.S.C. § 61]. However, this provision does not affect the principles governing the taxability of income to a grantor or assignor other than by reason of his dominion and control over the trust * * *. *This subpart also has no application in determining the right of a grantor to deductions for payments to a trust under a transfer and leaseback arrangement.*

S.Rep. No. 1622, 83d Cong., 2d Sess., *reprinted in* [1954] U.S.Code Cong. & Ad.News 4621, 5006 (emphasis added). See also Perry v. United States, supra, 520 F.2d at 237 n. 2. This language could hardly be clearer.

Second, the majority relies on the argument, advanced by the Eighth Circuit Court of Appeals in Quinlivan v. Commissioner, 599 F.2d 269 (8th Cir.), cert. denied, 444 U.S. 996, 100 S.Ct. 531, 62 L.Ed.2d 426

---

14. Brown v. Comm'r, 180 F.2d 926 (3d Cir.), cert. denied, 340 U.S. 814, 71 S.Ct. 42, 95 L.Ed. 598 (1950) (2–1 decision) (trust of up to 21 years duration); Skemp v. Comm'r, 168 F.2d 598 (7th Cir.1948) (trust to terminate after 20 years or upon deaths of grantor and wife, whichever first oc-curs); Quinlivan v. Comm'r, 599 F.2d 269 (8th Cir.), cert. denied, 444 U.S. 996, 100 S.Ct. 531, 62 L.Ed.2d 426 (1979) (Clifford trust); Brooke v. United States, 468 F.2d 1155 (9th Cir.1972) (2–1 decision) (guardianship which constituted a Clifford trust).

(1979), that to deny a deduction here "would produce a benefit only in cases where investment property—not used in the grantor's trade or business—is placed in trust. Persons whose assets consist largely of business property would be excluded from a tax benefit clearly provided by Congress." Id. at 274. The infirmities of this argument are many. First, it is an argument about legislative intent, but is of course unaccompanied by citation to the legislative history. Second, it ignores the fact that this "benefit clearly provided" is not "provided" to the majority of taxpayers who do not have assets lying around that they can give away for ten years at a time. Third, there would be no such "unfairness" if the taxpayer had assets other than business property which could form the corpus of a Clifford trust. The record does not indicate, nor does the opinion in *Quinlivan,* whether the respective taxpayers had other assets substantial enough to form the corpus of a Clifford trust.

Most importantly, however, the *Quinlivan* argument ignores the fact that the "tax benefit" is not the deduction of rental payments but the diversion of income from the grantor to the trust. The argument is that it is somehow unfair, or contrary to Congress' intent, that persons whose *only* asset substantial enough to form the corpus of a Clifford trust is business property are excluded from taking advantage of the Clifford trust provisions. The remedy, the argument runs, is for the courts to ignore the business purpose rule and the substance of the transaction and grant the taxpayer a business expense deduction. But owners of other types of assets which produce no income, such as commodities or residences, also are unable to take advantage of the Clifford trust provisions. If Dr. Rosenfeld placed his residence in a Clifford trust, no court would permit him to deduct the resulting rent in order to effectuate the Clifford trust provisions. In the instant case, Dr. Rosenfeld, instead of purchasing the land and building in question, could have purchased some other asset and placed that asset in a Clifford trust. But he did not because he wanted not only a tenant's but also a landlord's control over his office. See infra Part II.

The majority also argues, later in its opinion, that there is no difference "in real terms" between this case and the hypothetical case where Dr. Rosenfeld leases office space somewhere else and the trust property is leased to a third party. But there is a difference, as shown in Part II of this dissent. Dr. Rosenfeld exerted substantial control over the property by remaining in a building he previously owned and that he, and later his wife, would own in the future, and by dealing with trustee-lessors who were his personal advisors, and later his daughter. Although his legal interest in the property was a leasehold, he acted as both tenant and landlord and claimed the tax deductions available to both a tenant (rent) and an owner (interest on the mortgage). In short, Dr. Rosenfeld wants to have his cake, or more accurately the Treasury's, and eat it too.

In sum, Dr. Rosenfeld began paying rent on July 1, 1969, not in order to have an office in which to practice medicine, because he already had such an office. He began paying rent so that the trust would have income and his purpose of making a lifetime gift to his children would be fulfilled. There was simply no business purpose in this transaction. Moreover, the majority's adoption of the Tax Court's four-part test is unnecessary because the business purpose rule has no infirmity in this context. This exception to the business purpose rule increases the complexity of the law in an area where I had thought the complexity already sufficient. Adoption of the four-part test, involving a factual inquiry into the particular circumstances of the taxpayer's scheme years after the scheme is implemented, will make it even more difficult for taxpayers to plan their affairs. A holding that rental payments arising from a gift-leaseback are not deductible simply would require taxpayers to find other, less hypocritical means of avoiding their taxes.

II. Retention of Control

The government argues that, even if the bifurcated approach to the gift and leaseback is adopted, Dr. Rosenfeld should not be granted a deduction for his rental payments. The government bases this argument on the principles that transactions lacking in economic substance cannot form the basis for tax deductions, see Knetsch v. United States, supra, 364 U.S. at 366, 81 S.Ct. at 135; Goldstein v. Commissioner, 364 F.2d 734, 741 (2d Cir.1966), cert. denied, 385 U.S. 1005, 87 S.Ct. 708, 17 L.Ed.2d 543 (1967); Gilbert v. Commissioner, supra, 248 F.2d at 411 (L. Hand, dissenting), and that transactions entered into among family members for the purpose of splitting income must be examined with strict scrutiny, see Commissioner v. Tower, 327 U.S. 280, 291, 66 S.Ct. 532, 537, 90 L.Ed. 670 (1946); Helvering v. Clifford, 309 U.S. 331, 335, 60 S.Ct. 554, 556, 84 L.Ed. 788 (1940); White v. Fitzpatrick, supra, 193 F.2d at 402. The majority ignores these principles, applying instead the first prong of the Tax Court's special four-part test. This prong requires that the grantor, in order to receive a deduction, must not retain "substantially the same control over the property that he had before he made the gift." Because I believe that even this requirement has not been met, I must dissent on this ground also.

The original trustees, Mr. Powsner and Mr. Goldman, were Dr. Rosenfeld's advisors. They were the individuals who concocted the gift-leaseback scheme, and it is to be expected that they would want Dr. Rosenfeld to be satisfied with the arrangement. Nor surprisingly, the trustees never spoke with another potential tenant in 1969, and there is no evidence that they did so in 1975 when the new lease was signed. The trustees' purpose obviously was to satisfy both their fiduciary duties and Dr. Rosenfeld, and, indeed, Mr. Goldman testified that he saw no reason for contacting other potential tenants and "disturbing the doctor's practice." Moreover, it is fair to say that the original trustees, if not bosom buddies, certainly were located less than an arm's length from Dr. Rosenfeld. The trustees, for example, never attempted to improve or lease the unfinished one-third of the building because, in

Mr. Goldman's words on redirect examination, "I was informed by *Dr. Rosenfeld, who inquired about it on our behalf,* that the cost of making it into finished office space was very prohibitive, and would not be worth the rent that would be collectible, and this would be an enormous cost to the—to the parties involved" (emphasis added). The fact that "the tenant" is able to instruct "the landlord" whether to improve the building surely amounts at least to " 'passive acquiescence to the will of the donor.' " White v. Fitzpatrick, supra, 193 F.2d at 402 (quoting Commissioner v. Culbertson, 337 U.S. 733, 747, 69 S.Ct. 1210, 1216, 93 L.Ed. 1659 (1949).

The lease also granted Dr. Rosenfeld the right to build onto the building, an indicia of ownership one would not expect to find in a tenant's hands. Moreover, as explained in Part I, supra, the total payments made by Dr. Rosenfeld were excessive. Dr. Rosenfeld was willing to pay a premium because he was more than a tenant.

In 1973 Dr. Rosenfeld deeded his reversion in the trust corpus to his wife. The possibility, urged by Dr. Rosenfeld's counsel, that the Rosenfelds might obtain a divorce in the future is mere speculation, while the question before us is one of fact. The reversion in Dr. Rosenfeld's wife is of little relevance because the question is one of control, not one of equity. Moreover, once the property is in the hands of his wife, pursuant to his gift, deductions for his rental payments will not be allowed. *White v. Fitzpatrick,* supra. In short, that Dr. Rosenfeld became wise enough in 1973 to deed the reversion to his wife does nothing to weaken the substantial control he retained.

In 1975 Dr. Rosenfeld amended the trust, extending its term five and one-half years. He was able to extend the trust even though, having already deeded his reversion to his wife, he had no beneficial interest in the corpus. By extending the trust, Dr. Rosenfeld shifted from his wife to his daughters the income of the property for the period covered by the extension. And there is little chance that Dr. Rosenfeld would be opposed in another attempt to extend the trust: his daughters would not object, and his wife is not likely to object because her income from the property would be taxed to him. *White v. Fitzpatrick,* supra. Dr. Rosenfeld, for all practical purposes, has the power to determine who receives the income from the property.

Moreover, when Dr. Rosenfeld amended the trust, he appointed his daughter Barbara and Robert Swados, an attorney, as trustees.[15] The amendment provided that the trustees could act by majority vote, but only if Barbara Rosenfeld was among the majority. In other words, the trustees could take no action opposed by Barbara Rosenfeld, who was, of course, the grantor's daughter, a beneficiary of the trust and a recipient of her father's largesse.

In sum, the question before us is not what amount of control Dr. Rosenfeld gave to the trustees, but whether the control he retained was

---

15. Mr. Powsner had died before this.

"substantially the same [as] he had before he made the gift." Dr. Rosenfeld determined whether to improve the unfinished space in the building, and he had the right to build onto the building. He paid all expenses of the land and building except real estate taxes and structural repairs, the deduction which he shifted to his family. He faced no competitors either time he signed a lease with the trustees. The trustees were his advisors and, later, his daughter Barbara, one of the recipients of his largesse. Dr. Rosenfeld extended the trust once, installing his daughter as a trustee with an essential vote, and might do so again. This, I think, is enough control over the building to be "substantially the same * * * [as] he had before he made the gift," and to make Dr. Rosenfeld, like the taxpayer in *White v. Fitzpatrick*, supra, the "actual enjoyer and owner of the property." 193 F.2d at 402. As this court recently stated, " '*for tax purposes*, there was not a sufficient severance of the [taxpayer's] ownership over the assets for the transaction to create the tax consequence' intended for her." Blake v. Commissioner, 697 F.2d 473, 480 (2d Cir.1982) (quoting United States v. General Geophysical Co., 296 F.2d 86, 90 (5th Cir.1961), cert. denied, 369 U.S. 849, 82 S.Ct. 932, 8 L.Ed.2d 8 (1962) (on petition for rehearing)).

Reference: Peroni, Untangling The Web of Gift-Leaseback Jurisprudence, 68 Minn.L.R. 735 (1984).

G. EXPENSES AND LOSSES ARISING FROM TRANSACTIONS BETWEEN FAMILY MEMBERS

Assume Father owns stock in Production Corporation which has decreased in value. He sells the stock to his son and wants to take a deduction for the loss. Section 267(a)(1) disallows deductions for losses from sales or exchanges of property, directly or indirectly, between certain related persons. The relationships to which the prohibitions apply include: (1) the taxpayer and certain family members as set forth in § 267(c)(4); and (2) an individual and a corporation more than 50% owned, directly or indirectly, by or for the individual as set forth in § 267(b)(2). The loss on Father's sale of shares to his son would be nondeductible. § 267(a)(1), (b)(1), and (c)(4).

Although § 267(a)(1) disallows the seller a loss on a sale to a related party, the buyer may subsequently be able to take advantage of the disallowed loss. If the property increases in value after its acquisition by the buyer, he is taxable only to the extent his gain exceeds the disallowed loss. § 267(d). If the buyer sells the property at a loss, he is only able to deduct his actual loss. § 267(d). In this situation, the disallowed loss has no effect.

Section 267(a)(1) applies if a taxpayer sells marketable securities at a loss on a stock exchange and concurrently instructs his broker to buy for his wife's account the same number of shares of the same stock at, if possible, the same price. In McWilliams v. Commissioner, 331 U.S. 694, 67 S.Ct. 1477, 91 L.Ed. 1750 (1947), the Supreme Court held that this type of transaction is a sale, directly or indirectly, at a loss to a related party for purposes of § 267(a)(1) even though the shares were not identical and the purchaser from the husband and the seller to the wife were unknown strangers. Consider how the enactment of § 1041 eliminated the need for § 267(a) to apply to sales between spouses. See § 267(g).

Problems

1. Mother runs a business using the accrual method. Mother hires her son, who uses the cash method. The son performs services during the current year. Although Mother does not actually pay her son, she claims she is entitled to a deduction for the expense because she is entitled to accrue the salary as an expense. This would normally not constitute income for the son because he is on the cash method and never received any money. Examine §§ 267(a)(2) as to the availability of the deduction for Mother. What result if Mother subsequently pays her son the following year?

2. Mother owned property with a basis of $20,000. She sold the property to her daughter for $10,000, its fair market value.

(a) Can Mother deduct the loss? Consider §§ 267(a)(1), (b)(1), (c)(4), and 1041.

(b) The daughter thereafter sold the property for (1) $30,000 or (2) for $16,000. How much gain does the daughter realize and recognize? Consider § 267(d) and Reg. § 1.267(d)–1(a)(2) and (4) Example (1). When does the daughter's holding period begin?

(c) What if the daughter sold the property for $5,000? Consider § 267(d) and Reg. § 1.267(d)–1(a)(4) Example (2).

(d) What if the daughter subsequently gives the property as a gift to a third party who sells the property for $40,000. How much gain does the third party realize and recognize? Consider Reg. § 1.267(d)– 1(a)(4) Example (3) and § 1015. When does the third party's holding period begin? Consider § 1223(1).

3. (a) John Doe owns a patent. He also owns 95% of the stock of the Doe Manufacturing Corp. He is on the cash method; the corporation is on the accrual method. Both use a calendar year for tax purposes. He leases the patent to the Corporation on January 1 of the tax year, at a stated royalty, payable at annual intervals on December 31. By December 31, royalties in the sum of $10,000 had accrued in the tax year. The royalties were paid to him by the Corporation on April 1 of the following year. What are the tax consequences of this transaction to the Corporation? Consider § 267(a)(2) and (b)(2), and Reg. §§ 1.451–2(a), and 1.446–1(c)(1)(ii).

(b) Could Doe have avoided the impact of § 267(a)(2)? Would you advise payment by a negotiable promissory note? What if Doe timely receives payment and concurrently returns the amount paid by the Corporation as a loan?

H. INTEREST–FREE LOANS

Given the income tax savings available if a taxpayer in a high marginal tax bracket is able to assign income to a taxpayer in a low marginal tax bracket, we have seen various attempts to accomplish assignments of income. For example, in Helvering v. Horst, discussed at page 713 of this chapter, where a father detached the interest coupons from a bond and gave the coupons to his son as a gift, the interest was taxed to the father when the son cashed the coupons. We have also seen at pp. 70–84 that the value of the right of an employee to use his employer's property free of charge is treated as compensation income to the employee. Logically, one would surmise that if any employee was allowed to use his employer's money free of any interest charges, or if a father gave his son an interest-free loan, that similar results would follow. However, the courts consistently refused to extend these principles to interest-free loans. The leading case, Dean v. Commissioner, 35 T.C. 1083 (1961), (non-acq. 1973–2 C.B. 4), involved a non-interest bearing loan of over two million dollars by a closely-held corporation to its two shareholders. The court distinguished the rent-free use of property from the interest-free use of money in that in the former situation a benefit is conferred upon the employee which would not give rise to a deduction by the employee, whereas, in the later situation, the value of the benefit received by the borrower would give rise to an offsetting deduction. That is, if the employee's income was increased by the amount of interest he should have been charged, the employee would also receive an interest deduction under § 163 of the same amount. Other courts consistently used the analysis formulated in the Dean case to hold that an interest-free loan did not result in any income to the borrower.

It is apparent that an interest-free loan is the economic equivalent of a loan bearing a market rate of interest and an accompanying payment by the lender to the borrower to fund the payment of interest by the borrower. The failure by the courts to treat interest-free loans in accordance with their economic substance provided taxpayers with opportunities to circumvent well-established principles of taxation.

Interest-free loans were used by families to avoid the prohibition against an assignment of income without giving up the underlying property producing that income. For example, assume a father lent his son $100,000, charging 12% interest. If the son invested the loan proceeds in a one-year certificate of deposit paying 12%, the son reported $12,000 of interest income and had an offsetting $12,000 deduction for the interest paid to his father. The father reported $12,000 of interest income while the net result to the son was zero. Assume instead that the loan to the son was interest-free. The failure of the courts to treat interest-free loans in accordance with the above-described substance resulted in no income reported by the father, and no deduction reported by the son. The net result was that the son was taxed on $12,000 of income earned by investing the loan proceeds, thereby achieving an assignment of $12,000 of income to the lower bracket son. The Supreme Court in Dickman v. Commissioner, 465 U.S. 330, 104 S.Ct. 1086, 79 L.Ed.2d 343 (1984), treated the father, in our example, as making a gift subject to Federal gift tax. If market interest rates equalled 12%, the amount of the gross gift would most likely be $12,000, the amount of interest the father could have charged the son.

Section 7872 simply imputes the result that should have occurred had a market rate of interest, of say 12%, been charged. For example, if a father gives his son a $100,000 interest-free loan, § 7872 would impute $12,000 of interest income to the father and a $12,000 interest deduction for the son. § 7872(a)(1). The legislative history provides:

> The Act adds to the Code new section 7872 (relating to the tax treatment of loans that, in substance, result in a gift, payment of compensation, dividend, capital contribution, or other similar payment from the lender to the borrower). Loans that are subject to the provision and that do not require payment of interest, or require payment at a rate below the statutory rate (referred to as the "applicable Federal rate"), are recharacterized as an arm's-length transaction in which the lender made a loan to the borrower in exchange for a note requiring the payment of interest at the applicable Federal rate. This rule results in the parties being treated as if:
>
> (1) The borrower paid interest to the lender that may be deductible to the borrower and is included in income by the lender; and
>
> (2) The lender (a) made a gift subject to the gift tax (in the case of a gratuitous transaction) * * *. Joint Committee on Taxation, General Explanation of the Revenue Provisions of the Deficit Reduction Act of 1984, 528–529 (1984).

Question

Examine § 7872 and how it handles interest-free loans between individuals. Note that § 7872 also applies to loans with below market rates of interest. § 7872(a)(1) and (e)(1). Consider how the appropriate rate of interest is determined as authorized by § 7872(e)(2) and (f)(2). Although de minimis exceptions are available, the legislation goes on to provide situations where these de minimis exceptions cannot be used. § 7872(c)(2). Consider also how § 7872 provides for the timing of the income and the deductions it imputes. § 7872(a)(2). Finally, what difference would it make if the loan were a term loan instead of a demand loan?

Another area of concern involved the making of interest-free loans from corporations to their shareholders to circumvent the fact that a corporation receives no deduction for the payment of dividends. An interest-free loan in this context is the economic equivalent of a loan to a shareholder requiring the shareholder to pay interest to the corporation and a distribution by the corporation of an identical amount as a dividend. Prior to the enactment of § 7872 the corporation did not have to report any interest income that would have otherwise been paid by the shareholder-borrower. The effect was to give the corporation a deduction for dividends. Examine § 7872(c)(1)(C).

Finally, interest-free loans to employees were being used to avoid the rules requiring the payment of employment taxes and the rules of §§ 163(d) and 265(2) limiting an individual's otherwise allowable interest deductions. An interest-free loan to an employee is the economic equivalent of a loan requiring the payment of interest to the employer and a payment to the employee of compensation in an equal amount. Without imputing the interest income and the interest deduction the employee could then invest the loan proceeds and avoid the limitations imposed by §§ 163(d) and 265(2) as he did not pay any interest on the borrowed funds. Examine § 7872(c)(1)(B). The Regulations provide for the exemption of certain interest-free or below-market loans, such as employee relocation loans, from the application of § 7872 under the delegation to the Commissioner of rule-making authority granted in § 7872(g)(1)(C). Reg. § 1.7872–5T(b).

There are situations outside the scope of § 7872 which involve interest-free loans and where the interest element should be imputed. For example, consider a taxpayer who sells an asset on credit without charging any interest but charges a higher price than the property is worth. These problems are addressed in §§ 483 and 1274 discussed in Chapter 11.

Chapter 11

INTRODUCTION TO PROPERTY TRANSACTIONS

A. OVERVIEW

Subsection 61(a)(3) includes in gross income "gains" derived from dealings in property." It is significant that the reference is to "gains" from the dealing in property rather than a broader term like "receipts" from dealings in property. The concept of gain carries with it an implicit notion that, when we are dealing with property, some portion of the receipts is not included in gross income despite the general comprehensiveness of the concept of gross income in § 61.

This notion is further developed by § 1001(a), which provides that "the gain from the sale or other disposition of property shall be the excess of the amount realized therefrom over the adjusted basis." These words directly bring in two important concepts and indirectly a third. It is obvious, on the face of this language, that a determination must be made of the "amount realized" and of the "basis of the property;" what is not explicit, but is equally important, is the concept that the gains from the property are only those that are realized. Inherent in this concept is that changes in value are not a realization.

To some degree the requirement of a realization is the analogue of the requirement for accrual of income. In general, the keystone of accrual accounting for the recognition of income is an actual or constructive receipt of cash or cash equivalent or an event that generates the unconditional right to receive the income.

The requirement of a realization and the determination of the amount realized are closely related questions but not completely the same. Some cases seem to indicate that if the amount realized cannot be valued there has not been a realization. On the other hand, the ability to determine a value for the amount realized may be used by the courts to strengthen a conclusion that a realization event has occurred. These issues are addressed particularly in the well-known case of Burnet v. Logan that we will consider in this chapter.

The remaining issue in the statutory equation contained in § 1001(a) is the determination of basis. Basis is a specific tax term, which stands for the same concept as the accountant's concept of cost. It is usually not difficult to determine the cost of property when the property is acquired for cash, but there may be greater difficulty when property is acquired in an exchange. Is cost to be measured by the value of the property acquired, the value of the property given up, or some other measure?

Although, as indicated, there are some problems in determining realization, basis, and the amount realized in dealing with unencumbered tangible property, the problems in this area are reasonably well resolved and are not too difficult. When attention turns to the liability side of the balance sheet, however, there has been considerably more difficulty in dealing with these questions. In a real sense, liabilities are just the flip side or the analogue of assets. Nevertheless, neither the Code nor the "common law" of taxation has developed the analogue concepts to amount realized and basis for liabilities. There has been more difficulty, for example, in determining when a debtor is permitted to discharge a liability for an amount different than the amount incurred. In this situation a realization event occurs that is the analogue of disposing of a property for an amount different from the original basis. The cases, however, concluded that income from such cancellation of indebtedness is indeed income. This concept is now codified in § 61(a)(13).

Similarly, there have been considerable difficulties in determining the consequences of the debt financed acquisition and disposition of property. When property is purchased with funds borrowed from a third party, little difficulty exists in determining that the basis should include the amount paid with borrowed funds. Is the same result to apply when the funds are in effect supplied by the seller of the property in the form of purchase money financing? Does it make any difference if the liability is a nonrecourse liability, i.e. one in which the property stands as the sole source of payment, with the buyer having no obligation to pay the obligation and having the opportunity to simply surrender the property to satisfy the liability? Similar questions arise in connection with the disposition of property subject to a liability. If the property is used to pay off a liability, does the value of the property matter in determining the amount realized? What is the effect of amount of the debt? Is there any difference if the property is subject to a recourse or a nonrecourse liability? In this connection there is some interplay between the concept of cancellation of indebtedness income and the concept of amount realized. To the degree that a purchase money obligation is cancelled is it proper to characterize the resulting gain as an income from the cancellation of indebtedness or as an adjustment of purchase price? After some years of controversy and litigation, the Code now makes the question partially irrelevant by providing in § 108 that in certain circumstances the income from cancellation of indebtedness can be in effect deferred by adjusting the basis of property, including both property acquired by the indebtedness and property not so acquired. What is the effect of this issue in determining the questions of the amount realized and the cancellation of indebtedness?

The final issue in connection with property transactions, which is primarily related to the determination of capital gains, (which will be considered in the next chapter) is the determination of the holding period. Special capital gains treatment is only given for property held for more than a requisite holding period. How is the beginning and end of the holding period to be measured? Is it to be measured from the time the taxpayer acquires title to the property or by using some other method?

B. IS THERE A REALIZATION? WHAT IS THE AMOUNT REALIZED?

By this time, it should be apparent that taxpayers do not report fluctuations in value as gains or losses. Both §§ 61(a)(3) and 1001(a) demonstrate that the Code requires something more, some type of transaction, before a taxable event exists. What is needed is referred to as a "realization." Although the Code contains no specific definition of the term, it does offer some insight as to what events constitute a realization. Section 1001(a) provides that a sale or other disposition of property results in a realization. And, § 61(a)(3) refers to gains from dealings in property as giving rise to gross income but fails to define the term "dealings." Does this mean that dealings are broader in scope than sales or other dispositions? A realization does not automatically follow every time there is a transaction. What characteristics must exist for a transaction to be treated as a taxable realization? Reconsider the following: Eisner v. Macomber (page 106); the treatment of gifts and bequests (pp. 257–261); the treatment of marital property settlements (pp. 631–637); and the Oates case (page 251).

Study Problem

Mrs. Logan owned all the shares in a mining company with a basis of $173,000. In 1916, she sold her shares for $137,500 in cash and future payments based upon the production from the mine. The production payments called for the purchaser to pay 60 cents for each ton of ore extracted. Mrs. Logan received production payments of $20,000 in 1917, $15,500 in 1918, $19,000 in 1919 and $10,000 in 1920. In 1916, an appraiser estimated that the present discounted value of the production payments was approximately $105,000 with an expected payout period of 45 years. Why was there a realization in the Burnet v. Logan case while there was no realization in the Eisner v. Macomber case? Can there be a realization where the amount realized cannot be determined?

BURNET v. LOGAN

Supreme Court of the United States, 1931.
283 U.S. 404, 51 S.Ct. 550, 75 L.Ed. 1143.

MR. JUSTICE McREYNOLDS delivered the opinion of the Court.

* * *

Prior to March, 1913, and until March 11, 1916, respondent, Mrs. Logan, owned 250 of the 4,000 capital shares issued by the Andrews & Hitchcock Iron Company. It held 12 per cent. of the stock of the Mahoning Ore & Steel Company, an operating concern. In 1895 the latter corporation procured a lease for 97 years upon the "Mahoning" mine and since then has regularly taken therefrom large, but varying, quantities of iron ore—in 1913, 1,515,428 tons; in 1914, 1,212,287 tons; in 1915, 2,311,940 tons; in 1919, 1,217,167 tons; in 1921, 303,020 tons; in 1923, 3,029,865 tons. The lease contract did not require production of either maximum or minimum tonnage or any definite payments. Through an agreement of stockholders (steel manufacturers), the Mahoning Company is obligated to apportion extracted ore among them according to their holdings.

On March 11, 1916, the owners of all the shares in Andrews & Hitchcock Company sold them to Youngstown Sheet & Tube Company, which thus acquired, among other things, 12 per cent. of the Mahoning Company's stock and the right to receive the same percentage of ore thereafter taken from the leased mine.

For the shares so acquired, the Youngstown Company paid the holders $2,200,000 in money, and agreed to pay annually thereafter for distribution among them 60 cents for each ton of ore apportioned to it. Of this cash Mrs. Logan received 250/4000—$137,500; and she became entitled to the same fraction of any annual payment thereafter made by the purchaser under the terms of sale.

Mrs. Logan's mother had long owned 1,100 shares of the Andrews & Hitchcock Company. She died in 1917, leaving to the daughter one-half of her interest in payments thereafter made by the Youngstown Company. This bequest was appraised for federal estate tax purposes at $277,164.50.

During 1917, 1918, 1919, and 1920 the Youngstown Company paid large sums under the agreement. Out of these respondent received on account of her 250 shares $9,900 in 1917; $11,250 in 1918; $8,995.50 in 1919; $5,444.30 in 1920—$35,589.80. By reason of the interest from her mother's estate, she received $19,790.10 in 1919, and $11,977.49 in 1920.

Reports of income for 1918, 1919, and 1920 were made by Mrs. Logan upon the basis of cash receipts and disbursements. They included no part of what she had obtained from annual payments by the Youngstown Company. She maintains that until the total amount actually received by her from the sale of her shares equals their value on March 1, 1913, no taxable income will arise from the transaction. Also that, until she actually receives by reason of the right bequeathed to her a sum equal to its appraised value, there will be no taxable income therefrom.

On March 1, 1913, the value of the 250 shares then held by Mrs. Logan exceeded $173,089.80—the total of all sums actually received by her prior to 1921 from their sale ($137,500 cash in 1916, plus four annual payments amounting to $35,589.80). That value also exceeded original cost of the shares. The amount received on the interest devised by her mother was less than its valuation for estate taxation; also less than the value when acquired by Mrs. Logan.

The Commissioner ruled that the obligation of the Youngstown Company to pay 60 cents per ton had a fair market value of $1,942,111.46 on March 11, 1916; that this value should be treated as so much cash, and the sale of the stock regarded as a closed transaction with no profit in 1916. He also used this valuation as the basis for apportioning subsequent annual receipts between income and return of capital. His calculations, based upon estimates and assumptions, are too intricate for brief statement.[1] He made deficiency assessments according to the view just stated, and the Board of Tax Appeals approved the result.

The Circuit Court of Appeals held that, in the circumstances, it was impossible to determine with fair certainty the market value of the agreement by the Youngstown Company to pay 60 cents per ton. Also that respondent was entitled to the return of her capital—the value of 250 shares on March 1, 1913, and the assessed value of the interest derived from her mother—before she could be charged with any taxable income. As this had not in fact been returned, there was no taxable income.

1. In the brief for petitioner the following appears:

The fair market value of the Youngstown contract on March 11, 1916, was found by the Commissioner to be $1,942,111.46. This was based upon an estimate that the ore reserves at the Mahoning mine amounted to 82,858,535 tons; that all such ore would be mined; that 12 per cent. (or 9,942,564.2 tons) would be delivered to the Youngstown Company. The total amount to be received by all the vendors of stock would then be $5,965,814.52 at the rate of 60 cents per ton. The Commissioner's figure for the fair market value on March 11, 1916, was the then worth of $5,965,814.52, upon the assumption that the amount was to be received in equal annual installments during 45 years, discounted at 6 per cent., with a provision for a sinking fund at 4 per cent. For lack of evidence to the contrary,

this value was approved by the Board. The value of the 550/4000 interest which each acquired by bequest was fixed at $277,164.50 for purposes of federal estate tax at the time of the mother's death.

During the years here involved, the Youngstown Company made payments in accordance with the terms of the contract, and respondents respectively received sums proportionate to the interests in the contract which they acquired by exchange of property and by bequest.

The Board held that respondents' receipts from the contract, during the years in question, represented "gross income"; that respondents should be allowed to deduct from said gross income a reasonable allowance for exhaustion of their contract interests; and that the balance of the receipts should be regarded as taxable income.

We agree with the result reached by the Circuit Court of Appeals.

The 1916 transaction was a sale of stock—not an exchange of property. We are not dealing with royalties or deductions from gross income because of depletion of mining property. Nor does the situation demand that an effort be made to place according to the best available data some approximate value upon the contract for future payments. This probably was necessary in order to assess the mother's estate. As annual payments on account of extracted ore come in, they can be readily apportioned first as return of capital and later as profit. The liability for income tax ultimately can be fairly determined without resort to mere estimates, assumptions, and speculation. When the profit, if any, is actually realized, the taxpayer will be required to respond. The consideration for the sale was $2,200,000 in cash and the promise of future money payments wholly contingent upon facts and circumstances not possible to foretell with anything like fair certainty. The promise was in no proper sense equivalent to cash. It had no ascertainable fair market value. The transaction was not a closed one. Respondent might never recoup her capital investment from payments only conditionally promised. Prior to 1921, all receipts from the sale of her shares amounted to less than their value on March 1, 1913. She properly demanded the return of her capital investment before assessment of any taxable profit based on conjecture.

"In order to determine whether there has been gain or loss, and the amount of the gain if any, we must withdraw from the gross proceeds an amount sufficient to restore the capital value that existed at the commencement of the period under consideration." Doyle v. Mitchell Bros. Co., 247 U.S. 179, 184, 185, 38 S.Ct. 467, 469, 62 L.Ed. 1054. Revenue Act 1916, § 2, 39 Stat. 757, 758; Revenue Act 1918, c. 18, 40 Stat. 1057. Ordinarily, at least, a taxpayer may not deduct from gross receipts a supposed loss which in fact is represented by his outstanding note. Eckert v. Burnet, 283 U.S. 140, 51 S.Ct. 373, 75 L.Ed. 911 (1931). And, conversely, a promise to pay indeterminate sums of money is not necessarily taxable income. "Generally speaking, the income tax law is concerned only with realized losses, as with realized gains." Lucas v. American Code Co., 280 U.S. 445, 449, 50 S.Ct. 202, 203, 74 L.Ed. 538.

From her mother's estate, Mrs. Logan obtained the right to share in possible proceeds of a contract thereafter to pay indefinite sums. The value of this was assumed to be $277,164.50, and its transfer was so taxed. Some valuation—speculative or otherwise—was necessary in order to close the estate. It may never yield as much, it may yield more. If a sum equal to the value thus ascertained had been invested in an annuity contract, payments thereunder would have been free from income tax until the owner had recouped his capital investment. We think a like rule should be applied here. The statute definitely excepts bequests from receipts which go to make up taxable income.

See Burnet, Commissioner, v. Whitehouse, 283 U.S. 148, 51 S.Ct. 374, 75 L.Ed. 916 (1931).

The judgments below are affirmed.

———

The satisfaction of an obligation with property is a taxable event giving rise to a gain or loss. The result would be the same if the taxpayer sold his property for cash and used the proceeds of the sale to pay the obligation. This principle applies to the satisfaction of almost any obligation. For example, a company uses a capital asset with a basis of $100 and a fair market value of $150 to pay an employee for a wage obligation of $150. The employee reports $150 in income as wages. The company has a $50 gain. Consider also the character of the gain and why the company has a $150 business deduction under § 162.

Where a decedent's estate distributes appreciated property in satisfaction of a pecuniary bequest, the estate will realize a gain equal to the extent the amount of the pecuniary bequest exceeds the fair market value of the property at the date of death. § 1001(a). This result is justified since a cash bequest creates an obligation of the estate to pay a specific sum to that beneficiary. However, a distribution of an asset (which has appreciated in value after the date of death) to a beneficiary who was entitled to that asset as a specific bequest in decedent's will is not a realization to the estate. Under state law, the beneficiary becomes the owner of property received as a specific bequest at the moment of death. The reason for this difference can best be justified by focusing upon who bears the burden of any post-death decreases in value and who benefits from any post-death increases in value.

Problems

1. Janet owns a building valued at $220,000 with an adjusted basis of $150,000 which she has owned for three years.

(a) Assume the building is completely destroyed by fire, and Janet collects insurance proceeds in the sum of $220,000.

  i. Does Janet realize gain? What is the amount of the gain? What additional facts are necessary to determine the character of the gain?

  ii. Consider the impact of § 1033 if she uses the insurance proceeds to buy a replacement building. Read pages 846–847 in this chapter.

(b) Assume Janet contributes the building to a corporation in exchange for stock in that corporation worth $220,000.

  i. Does Janet realize gain? If so, what is the amount realized.

  ii. Will the realized gain be recognized? Consider § 351.

(c) Assume Janet gratuitously transfers the building to her son, Michael.

    i. Is a gift an "other disposition" for purposes of § 1001(a)? Reconsider page 204 and Problem 1 on p. 263 in Chapter 5.

    ii. What is Michael's basis in the building? Consider § 1015(a). Can Michael add on (tack) Janet's holding period to his holding period? Consider § 1223(2).

(d) What result if Janet sells the building to her husband for $220,000? Consider § 1041. Reconsider Problems 1 through 4 on pages 637–638 of Chapter 9.

2. Karen owns a restored 1955 Thunderbird with a basis of $5,000 and a fair market value of $15,000. Karen bought the car ten years ago.

(a) Karen gives the car to Raoul in return for painting Karen's portrait.

    i. Does Karen realize gain? If so, what is the amount and the character of the gain? Consider § 1001(a); Regs. §§ 1.1001–1(e) and 1.1015–4, and the Philadelphia Park Amusement Co. case on page 760 of this Chapter.

    ii. What is Karen's basis in the painting? Consider § 1012.

    iii. What is Raoul's basis in the car? Consider § 1012. When does Raoul's holding period in the car begin?

(b) Karen transfers the car to John in satisfaction of a $15,000 tort judgment against her.

    i. Does Karen realize gain? If so, what is the amount and the character of the gain?

    ii. Does John realize income? Consider § 104(a)(2). What is John's basis in the car? When does John's holding period in the car begin? Reconsider Problem 1(d) on page 141.

(c) Assume Karen transfers the car to Kristen in exchange for a contract right (the right to service vending machines) held by her.

    i. Does Karen realize gain? Consider the Philadelphia Park Amusement case on page 760 of this chapter. If so, what is the amount and the character of the gain? What is Karen's basis in the contract right?

    ii. What is Kristen's basis for the car?

3. Lori, a cash method taxpayer, borrows $5,000 from Sam, an accrual method taxpayer, in Year 1 when she purchased a $5,000 stereo system at Sam's store on credit. Lori satisfies this obligation in full in Year 2 by transferring to Sam appreciated stock worth $4,000 (having a basis to Lori of $3,500) and $1,000 in cash. The stereo system cost Sam $3,500.

(a) Does Lori realize gain? If so, what is the character of that gain, and when does she recognize the gain?

(b) Does Sam realize a gain? If so, what is the character of the gain and when does he recognize the gain? Consider § 1221(1).

(c) What is Lori's basis in the stereo? What is Sam's basis in the stock?

(d) Can Lori and Sam start their holding periods in Year 1? Consider § 1223(1) and (2).

4. Decedent, who died on January 1 of the current tax year, owned land with a basis of $6,000 and a fair market value of $10,000 at the time of death. Consider whether a realization occurs in each of the following, as well as the transferee's basis and holding period for the land:

(a) Decedent leaves his son a general (pecuniary) devise of $11,000 in his will. The land increases in value to $11,000 after the date of death. The estate satisfies this devise by transfering the property to the son. What is the estate's basis in the land? Consider § 1014(a). If a realization occurs, what is the amount and character of the estate's gain? Consider § 1223(11). What is the son's basis in the land?

(b) Decedent leaves the land to his son by a specific bequest in his will. The estate distributes the land to the son when it is worth $9,000. With respect to the son's holding period consider § 1223(11).

5. Gene, an agent with the Impermanent Life Insurance Co., entered into an agreement with the company whereby he gave up the right to receive future renewal commissions which are contingent on customers' renewals of existing life insurance policies, in return for a contract providing for fixed monthly payments over a specified number of years. Consider Gene's tax consequences. Is the transaction a realization or merely a substitution of one contract for another with a different manner of payment? Consider § 1001(a), the Oates case at page 251 and the Drescher case at page 160 in Chapter 3.

6. Reconsider Problem 2 on page 103 dealing with stock options. Assume the employee realizes $11 in income per share (or a total of $1,100) when he exercises the option.

(a) What is his basis in the stock?

(b) When does his holding period for the stock begin? Consider §§ 1223 and 83(f).

7. Bob paid $500 for an option from Tom to purchase land for $25,000 anytime within the next three years. Tom had a basis of $20,000 in the property. Bob exercised the option at a time when the land was worth $29,000.

(a) Did Tom realize gain on the grant or the exercise of the option? What amount of gain did Tom realize? What if the option were not exercised; when would Tom realize and recognize income?

(b) What is Bob's basis in the land? Consider § 1012.

(c) Why was the stock option in Problem 6 above treated differently?

(d) When does Bob's holding period for the land begin? Consider § 1223.

8. (a) Vera buys shares of stock in X Corp. How would Vera treat commissions paid to a broker for the purchase of stock? Consider Reg.

§ 1.1012–1(a). How does she treat commissions paid on the sale of the stock? Consider Reg. § 1.263(a)–2(e). Reconsider the Problem on page 499.

(b) Assume Vera purchased 10 shares in X Corp. for $65 a share. Later, she purchased 20 shares in X Corp. for $52 a share. Finally, she purchased 15 shares in X Corp. for $58 a share. Vera now sells 5 shares of X Corp. What is her basis in the stock sold? Consider Reg. § 1.1012–1(c) (1). How may Vera avoid the general rule provided for by Reg. § 1.1012–1(c)(1)? Consider Reg. § 1.1012–1(c)(2) and (3).

C. DETERMINATION OF BASIS

When a taxpayer acquires property by purchase, § 1012 provides that the basis in property generally equals its cost. Although cost connotes the amount paid for property, for purposes of § 1012 it is more than the cash purchase price of property. Purchases can be made indirectly. For example, if an employee receives an asset worth $100 as compensation for services, her basis in that asset is $100. This is the same as if the employer gave an employee $100 in cash and the employee used that cash to purchase the asset. The employee is allowed to take the $100 basis in the asset because she included that amount in her gross income. Read Reg. § 1.61–2(d)(2) and reconsider the problem at pp. 95–96.

However, not all compensatory transfers are treated in this manner. If an employee receives a retirement annuity under a qualified plan, he does not include the value of that annuity in gross income. When the funds are placed in the qualified plan his basis in the annuity will be zero. Accordingly, when the employee retires and starts receiving payments under his retirement annuity, the entire amount of the payments is taxable, since he received no basis for this compensatory transfer. See § 72(c)(1) and reconsider Problem 1(a) at page 155.

An employee who receives a bottle of liquor worth $20 at the company Christmas party may exclude the value of this payment in kind from gross income under the de minimis provisions of § 132(a)(4). If he later sells the bottle for $25, his gain will only be $5. He takes a tax-free $20 basis; the exclusion is, therefore, permanent with respect to the receipt of the liquor.

Property acquired by gift generally takes a carryover basis (unless it has decreased in value) in the hands of the donee. § 1015(a). Reconsider page 257. Sometimes, a transfer is partially gratuitious. Suppose a father who owns shares of stock with basis and a fair market value of $10,000, sells the shares to his son for only $6,000. The son has acquired 6/10ths of the stock by purchase and 4/10ths by gift. The son's basis is $10,000, $6,000 by purchase and $4,000 by gift. Reg. §§ 1.1001–1(e) and 1.1015–4 detail the treatment of part-sale/part-gift transactions.

The next case considers the basis of property acquired in an exchange transaction.

PHILADELPHIA PARK AMUSEMENT CO. v. UNITED STATES

130 Ct.Cl. 166, 126 F.Supp. 184 (1954).

[In 1889, the taxpayer received a 50-year franchise to operate a passenger railway in Fairmount Park, Philadelphia. At a cost of $381,000, it built the Strawberry Bridge which was used by its street-cars. In 1934, it deeded the bridge to the city in exchange for a ten year extension of its franchise. In 1946 when the extended franchise still had several years to run, it was abandoned, and the taxpayer arranged bus transportation for visitors to its amusement park. The taxpayer's basis for the ten year extension of its franchise became important when the taxpayer asserted depreciation deductions based on the cost of the extension and a loss on abandonment of the franchise.]

LARAMORE, JUDGE.

* * *

This brings us to the question of what is the cost basis of the 10-year extension of taxpayer's franchise. Although defendant contends that Strawberry Bridge was either worthless or not "exchanged" for the 10-year extension of the franchise, we believe that the bridge had some value, and that the contract under which the bridge was transferred to the City clearly indicates that the one was given in consideration of the other. * * *

The gain or loss, whichever the case may have been, should have been recognized, and the cost basis under section [1012] of the Code, of the 10-year extension of the franchise was the cost to the taxpayer. The succinct statement in [§ 1012] that "the basis of property shall be the cost of such property" although clear in principle, is frequently difficult in application. One view is that the cost basis of property received in a taxable exchange is the fair market value of the property *given* in the exchange. The other view is that the cost basis of property received in a taxable exchange is the fair market value of the property *received* in the exchange. As will be seen from the cases and some of the Commissioner's rulings [2] the Commissioner's position has not been altogether consistent on this question. The view that "cost" is the fair market value of the property given is predicated on the theory that the cost to the taxpayer is the economic value relinquished. The view that "cost" is the fair market value of the property received is based upon the theory that the term "cost" is a tax concept and must be considered in the light of the * * * prime role that the basis of property plays in determining tax liability. We believe that when the question is considered in the latter context that the cost basis of the property received in a taxable exchange is the fair market value of the property *received* in the exchange.

---

2. Compare I.T. 2212, IV–2 C.B. 118 with I.T. 3523, 1941–2 C.B. 124 and the Commissioner's equivocal acquiescence in Estate of Isadore L. Myers case, [I.T.C. 100] 1943–1 C.B. 17.

When property is exchanged for property in a taxable exchange the taxpayer is taxed on the difference between the adjusted basis of the property given in exchange and the fair market value of the property received in exchange. For purposes of determining gain or loss the fair market value of the property received is treated as cash and taxed accordingly. To maintain harmony with the fundamental purpose of these sections, it is necessary to consider the fair market value of the property received as the cost basis to the taxpayer. The failure to do so would result in allowing the taxpayer a stepped-up basis, without paying a tax therefor, if the fair market value of the property received is less than the fair market value of the property given, and the taxpayer would be subjected to a double tax if the fair market value of the property received is more than the fair market value of the property given. By holding that the fair market value of the property received in a taxable exchange is the cost basis, the above discrepancy is avoided and the basis of the property received will equal the adjusted basis of the property given plus any gain recognized, or that should have been recognized, or minus any loss recognized, or that should have been recognized.

Therefore, the cost basis of the 10-year extension of the franchise was its fair market value on August 3, 1934, the date of the exchange. The determination of whether the cost basis of the property received is its fair market value or the fair market value of the property given in exchange therefor, although necessary to the decision of the case, is generally not of great practical significance because the value of the two properties exchanged in an arms-length transaction are either equal in fact, or are presumed to be equal. The record in this case indicates that the 1934 exchange was an arms-length transaction and, therefore, if the value of the extended franchise cannot be determined with reasonable accuracy, it would be reasonable and fair to assume that the value of Strawberry Bridge was equal to the 10-year extension of the franchise. The fair market value of the 10-year extension of the franchise should be established but, if that value cannot be determined with reasonable certainty, the fair market value of Strawberry Bridge should be established and that will be presumed to be the value of the extended franchise. This value cannot be determined from the facts now before us since the case was prosecuted on a different theory.

The taxpayer contends that the market value of the extended franchise or Strawberry Bridge could not be ascertained and, therefore, it should be entitled to carry over the undepreciated cost basis of the bridge as the cost of the extended franchise under [§ 7701(a)(42)]. If the value of the extended franchise or bridge cannot be ascertained with a reasonable degree of accuracy, the taxpayer is entitled to carry over the undepreciated cost of the bridge as the cost basis of the extended franchise. Helvering v. Tex-Pen Oil Co., 300 U.S. 481, 499, 57 S.Ct. 569, 81 L.Ed. 755; Gould Securities Co. v. United States, 2 Cir., 96 F.2d 780. However, it is only in rare and extraordinary cases that the value of the property exchanged cannot be ascertained with reasonable accuracy. We are presently of the opinion that either the value of the extended franchise or the bridge can be determined with a reasonable degree of accuracy. Although the value of the extended franchise may be difficult or impossible to ascertain because of the nebulous and intangible characteristics inherent in such property, the value of the bridge is subject to more exact measurement. Consideration may be given to expert testimony on the value of comparable bridges, Strawberry Bridge's reproduction cost and its undepreciated cost, as well as other relevant factors.

Therefore, because we deem it equitable, judgment should be suspended and the question of the value of the extended franchise on August 3, 1934, should be remanded to the Commissioner of this court for the taking of evidence and the filing of a report thereon.

The failure of taxpayer to properly record the transaction in 1934 and thereafter does not prevent the correction of the error, especially under the circumstances of this case. Countway v. Commissioner, 1 Cir., 127 F.2d 69. * * *

* * *

We, therefore, conclude that the 1934 exchange was a taxable exchange and that the taxpayer is entitled to use as the cost basis of the 10-year extension of its franchise its fair market value on August 3, 1934, for purposes of determining depreciation and loss due to abandonment, as indicated in this opinion.

Accordingly, judgment will be suspended and the question of the value of the extended franchise on August 3, 1934, is remanded to the Commissioner of this court for the taking of evidence and the filing of a report thereon.

JONES, CHIEF JUDGE, and MADDEN, WHITAKER, and LITTLETON, JUDGES, concur.

D. ADJUSTMENTS TO BASIS

Sections 1011 and 1016 deal with adjustments to basis. A taxpayer's original basis in an asset is subject to upward or downward adjustment to reflect subsequent events having tax consequences. Additional capital outlays with respect to an asset increase a taxpayer's adjusted basis for the asset. Why is it important to differentiate between capital improvements as opposed to repairs? Read § 1016(a) (1). Conversely, certain deductions decrease a taxpayer's adjusted basis with respect to an asset.

Pursuant to § 1016(a)(2), depreciation (Accelerated Cost Recovery) deductions reduce a taxpayer's adjusted basis because the taxpayer is writing off his investment. Note that under § 167(a), cost recovery deductions under § 168 constitute allowances for exhaustion, wear and tear, and obsolescence, and thus are covered by § 1016(a)(2). Does it make a difference if the taxpayer fails to take depreciation (Accelerated

Cost Recovery) deductions on business or investment property? Read § 1016(a)(2)(A).

What happens to the basis of an asset subject to a casualty loss? Read § 1016(a)(1). For example, a taxpayer owns a personal use auto, with an original cost of $8,000, and a current fair market value of $5,000. The car is damaged, reducing its value by $1,000. The taxpayer receives $1,000 from the other driver's insurance company to cover his damages. Instead of repairing his car, the taxpayer pockets the damage payment. Does the taxpayer realize $1,000 of gross income? What is his basis in his car?

The next case considers the problems of allocating the basis of an asset to the portion sold.

INAJA LAND CO. v. COMMISSIONER

Tax Court of the United States, 1947.
9 T.C. 727 (Acq. 1948–1 C.B. 2).

[In 1928 the taxpayer paid $61,000 for 1236 acres of land on the banks of the Owens River, Mono County, California, together with certain water rights, for use as a private fishing club. The City of Los Angeles constructed a tunnel nearby in 1934 and commenced to divert polluted waters into the Owens River, and this action had a deleterious effect on the fishing on the taxpayer's preserve. In 1939 the City paid taxpayer $50,000 for a release of any liability for this diversion of foreign waters, and for an easement to continue to divert such waters, into the Owens River. In settling its claim against the City, the taxpayer incurred attorneys' fees and costs of $1,000.]

OPINION

LEECH, JUDGE:

The question presented is whether the net amount of [$49,000] received by petitioner in the taxable year 1939 * * * constitutes taxable income under [§ 61(a)] or is chargeable to capital account. The respondent contends: (a) That the $50,000, less [$1000] expenses incurred, which petitioner received from the city of Los Angeles * * * represented compensation for loss of present and future income and consideration for release of many meritorious causes of action against the city, constituting ordinary income; and, (b) since petitioner has failed to allocate such sum between taxable and nontaxable income, it has not sustained its burden of showing error. Petitioner maintains that the language of the [agreement] and the circumstances leading up to its execution demonstrate that the consideration was paid for the easement granted to the city of Los Angeles and the consequent damage to its property rights; that the loss of past or future profits was not considered or involved; that the character of the easement rendered it impracticable to attempt to apportion a basis to the property affected; and, since the sum received is less than the basis of the entire property, taxation should be postponed until the final disposition of the property.

* * *

Upon this record we have concluded that no part of the recovery was paid for loss of profits, but was paid for the conveyance of a right of way and easements, and for damages to petitioner's land and its property rights as riparian owner. Hence, the respondent's contention has no merit. Capital recoveries in excess of cost do constitute taxable income. Petitioner has made no attempt to allocate a basis to that part of the property covered by the easements. It is conceded that all of petitioner's lands were not affected by the easements conveyed. Petitioner does not contest the rule that, where property is acquired for a lump sum and subsequently disposed of a portion at a time, there must be an allocation of the cost or other basis over the several units and gain or loss computed on the disposition of each part, except where apportionment would be wholly impracticable or impossible. Nathan Blum, 5 T.C. 702, 709. Petitioner argues that it would be impracticable and impossible to apportion a definite basis to the easements here involved, since they could not be described by metes and bounds; that the flow of the water has changed and will change the course of the river; that the extent of the flood was and is not predictable; and that to date the city has not released the full measure of water to which it is entitled. In Strother v. Commissioner, 55 Fed.(2d) 626, the court says:

> * * * A taxpayer * * * should not be charged with gain on pure conjecture unsupported by any foundation of ascertainable fact. See Burnet v. Logan, 283 U.S. 404; 51 S.Ct. 550, 75 L.Ed. 1143.

This rule is approved in the recent case of *Raytheon Production Corporation v. Commissioner,* [pages 143–146]. Apportionment with reasonable accuracy of the amount received not being possible [because what was sold cannot be determined and, therefore, there is no way to allocate the taxpayer total cost against the amount received], and this amount being less than petitioner's cost basis for the property, it can not be determined that petitioner has, in fact, realized gain in any amount. Applying the rule as above set out, no portion of the payment in question should be considered as income, but the full amount must be treated as a return of capital and applied in reduction of petitioner's cost basis. Burnet v. Logan, 283 U.S. 404.

Reviewed by the Court.

Decision will be entered for the petitioner.

Questions

1. Why is the result in Inaja Land very favorable to the taxpayer? What is the taxpayer's remaining basis for property as a result of the decision?

2. Under what circumstances can the taxpayer use the cost recovery principle set forth in Inaja Land?

Problems

1. Farmer Brown purchased his 100 acre farm many years ago for $15,000. All 100 acres are used to grow his Indian hemp crop.

(a) The state decides to build a new highway through Brown's land. The state uses its power of eminent domain and takes two acres of his land. Brown receives $3,000 as a condemnation award. Does Brown realize gain? What is the amount of Brown's gain? Consider Reg. § 1.61–6(a). What basis does he have in the property he did not sell?

(b) A public utility decides to string a power line over Brown's land. He receives $3,000 in return for granting the utility company the necessary air rights easement. The farmer still has the use of all of his land.

    i. What are the tax consequences to Brown? Consider Reg. § 1.61–6(a) and the Inaja Land case.

    ii. Assume Brown sells his farm, including the land subject to the easement, at a later date for $40,000. What are the tax consequences for Brown?

(c) i. Assume in (b) above Brown receives $61,000 for granting the easement. What are his tax consequences?

    ii. Assume, after receiving $61,000 for granting the easement, Brown subsequently sells his farm for $40,000. What are his tax consequences?

2. Leisure purchased 100 acres for $15,000. An appraisal report, made at the time Leisure purchased the land, stated that the value of the two acres fronting on a lake were worth $2,000 and that the remaining 98 acres were worth $13,000. Several years later, Leisure decides to sell the two acre lakefront tract for $8,000.

(a) How would you allocate the basis for this sale? Would an allocation based on some physical measure be the most advantageous method for Leisure? Consider the Inaja Land case.

(b) Can you devise an alternative allocation method? Consider Reg. § 1.61–6(a) Ex. (2).

E. TREATMENT OF LIABILITIES

1. IMPACT OF LIABILITIES ON BASIS AND AMOUNT REALIZED

Question

Examine Reg. § 1.1001–2(c) Ex. (8) and Problem 3 on page 757. Why is it important to distinguish between the satisfaction of a liability and the cancellation of a liability?

Section 1001(b) defines the "amount realized" as the sum of any money received plus the fair market value of property (other than money) received. Other property received includes services (performed or to be performed) and goodwill. Relief from personal liability, for example, an employer's payment of an employee's income taxes, constitutes an amount realized. Reread Old Colony Trust Co. v. Commissioner, page 49. Amounts received for reasons other than the sale or disposition of property are excluded from the computation of gain or loss. § 1001(a).

The Crane case considers two important questions. First, what is a taxpayer's basis for property acquired subject to a nonrecourse liability? As we have seen, basis is important for depreciation (Accelerated Cost Recovery) purposes. Second, what is the amount realized on the disposition of property subject to a nonrecourse liability? The concept of a mortgage and the difference between recourse and nonrecourse financing is considered at page 886.

CRANE v. COMMISSIONER

Supreme Court of the United States, 1947.
331 U.S. 1, 67 S.Ct. 1047, 91 L.Ed. 1301.

[This case involved a taxpayer who obtained by bequest an apartment building subject to a mortgage with a principal amount of $255,000 and $7,000 of unpaid interest, the property having been appraised at a fair market value equal to the amount of the unpaid amount of the debt. The taxpayer took depreciation on this basis for a number of years, and then sold the property to a third party for $2,500 net cash, subject to the mortgage of $255,000. The Court held that the taxpayer's basis under the former section corresponding to § 1014(a) (providing that in the case of property acquired by bequest the basis shall be "the fair market value of such property" at the date of death) equaled the fair market value of the property apart from the mortgage, here $262,000, and not merely the value of the equity, here zero.]

MR. CHIEF JUSTICE VINSON delivered the opinion of the Court.

The question here is how a taxpayer who acquires depreciable property subject to an unassumed mortgage, holds it for a period, and finally sells it still so encumbered, must compute her taxable gain.

Petitioner was the sole beneficiary and the executrix of the will of her husband, who died January 11, 1932. He then owned an apartment building and lot subject to a mortgage,[3] which secured a principal debt of $255,000.00 and interest in default of $7,042.50. As of that date, the property was appraised for federal estate tax purposes at a value exactly equal to the total amount of this encumbrance. Shortly after her husband's death, petitioner entered into an agreement with the mortgagee whereby she was to continue to operate the property—

3. The record does not show whether he was personally liable for the debt.

collecting the rents, paying for necessary repairs, labor, and other operating expenses, and reserving $200.00 monthly for taxes—and was to remit the net rentals to the mortgagee. This plan was followed for nearly seven years, during which period petitioner reported the gross rentals as income, and claimed and was allowed deductions for taxes and operating expenses paid on the property, for interest paid on the mortgage, and for the physical exhaustion of the building. Meanwhile, the arrearage of interest increased to $15,857.71. On November 29, 1938, with the mortgagee threatening foreclosure, petitioner sold to a third party for $3,000.00 cash, subject to the mortgage, and paid $500.00 expenses of sale.

Petitioner reported a taxable gain of $1,250.00. Her theory was that the "property" which she had acquired in 1932 and sold in 1938 was only the equity, or the excess in the value of the apartment building and lot over the amount of the mortgage. This equity was of zero value when she acquired it. No depreciation could be taken on a zero value.[4] Neither she nor her vendee ever assumed the mortgage, so, when she sold the equity, the amount she realized on the sale was the net cash received, or $2,500.00. This sum less the zero basis constituted her gain, of which she reported half as taxable on the assumption that the entire property was a "capital asset".

The Commissioner, however, determined that petitioner realized a net taxable gain of $23,767.03. His theory was that the "property" acquired and sold was not the equity, as petitioner claimed, but rather the physical property itself, or the owner's rights to possess, use, and dispose of it, undiminished by the mortgage. The original basis thereof was $262,042.50, its appraised value in 1932. Of this value $55,000.00 was allocable to land and $207,042.50 to building.[5] During the period that petitioner held the property, there was an allowable depreciation of $28,045.10 on the building,[6] so that the adjusted basis of the building at the time of sale was $178,997.40. The amount realized on the sale was said to include not only the $2,500.00 net cash receipts, but also the principal amount [7] of the mortgage subject to which the property was sold, both totaling $257,500.00. The selling price was allocable in the proportion, $54,471.15 to the land and $203,028.85 to the building. The Commissioner agreed that the land was a "capital asset", but thought that the building was not. Thus, he determined that petitioner sustained a capital loss of $528.85 on the land, of which 50% or $264.42

4. This position is, of course, inconsistent with her practice in claiming such deductions in each of the years the property was held. The deductions so claimed and allowed by the Commissioner were in the total amount of $25,500.00.

5. The parties stipulated as to the relative parts of the 1932 appraised value and of the 1938 sales price which were allocable to land and building.

6. The parties stipulated that the rate of depreciation applicable to the building was 2% per annum.

7. The Commissioner explains that only the principal amount, rather than the total present debt secured by the mortgage, was deemed to be a measure of the amount realized, because the difference was attributable to interest due, a deductible item.

was taken into account, and an ordinary gain of $24,031.45 on the building, or a net taxable gain as indicated.

The Tax Court agreed with the Commissioner that the building was not a "capital asset." In all other respects it adopted petitioner's contentions, and expunged the deficiency.[8] Petitioner did not appeal from the part of the ruling adverse to her, and these questions are no longer at issue. On the Commissioner's appeal, the Circuit Court of Appeals reversed, one judge dissenting.[9] We granted certiorari because of the importance of the questions raised as to the proper construction of the gain and loss provisions of the Internal Revenue Code.

[§ 1001(a)] defines the gain from "the sale or other disposition of property" as "the excess of the amount realized therefrom over the adjusted basis provided in [§ 1011] * * *." It proceeds, [§ 1001(b)], to define "the amount realized from the sale or other disposition of property" as "the sum of any money received plus the fair market value of the property (other than money) received." Further, in [§ 1011], the "adjusted basis for determining the gain or loss from the sale or other disposition of property" is declared to be "the basis determined under [§ 1012], adjusted * * * for exhaustion, wear and tear, obsolescence, amortization * * * [§ 1016(a)(2)]. The basis [of property acquired from a decedent] [§ 1014(a)] is "the fair market value of [the property at the date of the decedent's death * * *"]

Logically, the first step under this scheme is to determine the unadjusted basis of the property, under [§ 1014(a)], and the dispute in this case is as to the construction to be given the term "property". If "property", as used in that provision, means the same thing as "equity", it would necessarily follow that the basis of petitioner's property was zero, as she contends. If, on the contrary, it means the land and building themselves, or the owner's legal rights in them, undiminished by the mortgage, the basis was $262,042.50.

We think that the reasons for favoring one of the latter constructions are of overwhelming weight. In the first place, the words of statutes—including revenue acts—should be interpreted where possible in their ordinary, everyday senses.[10] The only relevant definitions of "property" to be found in the principal standard dictionaries [11] are the two favored by the Commissioner, i.e., either that "property" is the

---

8. 3 T.C. 585. The Court held that the building was not a "capital asset" within the meaning of [§ 1221] and that the entire gain on the building had to be taken into account * * * because it found that the building was of a character subject to physical exhaustion and that petitioner had used it in her trade or business.

But because the Court accepted petitioner's theory that the entire property had a zero basis, it held that she was not entitled to the 1938 depreciation deduction on the building which she had inconsistently claimed.

For these reasons, it did not expunge the deficiency in its entirety.

9. 2 Cir., 153 F.2d 504.

10. Old Colony R. Co. v. Commissioner, 284 U.S. 552, 560, 52 S.Ct. 211, 213, 76 L.Ed. 484.

11. See Webster's New International Dictionary, Unabridged, 2d Ed.; Funk & Wagnalls' New Standard Dictionary; Oxford English Dictionary.

physical thing which is a subject of ownership, or that it is the aggregate of the owner's rights to control and dispose of that thing. "Equity" is not given as a synonym, nor do either of the foregoing definitions suggest that it could be correctly so used. Indeed, "equity" is defined as "the value of a property * * * above the total of the liens. * * *"[12] The contradistinction could hardly be more pointed. Strong countervailing considerations would be required to support a contention that Congress, in using the word "property", meant "equity", or that we should impute to it the intent to convey that meaning.

In the second place, the Commissioner's position has the approval of the administrative construction of [§ 1014(a)]. With respect to the valuation of property under that section [Reg. § 1.1014–1(a)] provides that ["the basis of property acquired from a decedent is the fair market value of such property at the date of the decedent's death * * *.] The land and building here involved were so appraised in 1932, and their appraised value—$262,042.50—was reported by petitioner as part of the gross estate. This was in accordance with the estate tax law and regulations, which had always required that the value of decedent's property, undiminished by liens, be so appraised and returned, and that mortgages be separately deducted in computing the net estate.[13] As the quoted provision of the Regulations has been in effect since 1918, and as the relevant statutory provision has been repeatedly reenacted since then in substantially the same form, the former may itself now be considered to have the force of law.[14]

Moreover, in the many instances in other parts of the Act in which Congress has used the word "property", or expressed the idea of "property" or "equity", we find no instances of a misuse of either word or of a confusion of the ideas.[15] In some parts of the Act other than the gain and loss sections, we find "property" where it is unmistakably used in its ordinary sense.[16] On the other hand, where either Congress or the Treasury intended to convey the meaning of "equity," it did so by the use of appropriate language.[17]

A further reason why the word "property" in [§ 1012] should not be construed to mean "equity" is the bearing such construction would

12. See Webster's New International Dictionary, supra.

13. See City Bank Farmers' Trust Co. v. Bowers, 2 Cir., 68 F.2d 909, certiorari denied, 292 U.S. 644, 54 S.Ct. 778, 78 L.Ed. 1495; Rodiek v. Helvering, 2 Cir., 87 F.2d 328; Adriance v. Higgins, 2 Cir., 113 F.2d 1013.

14. Helvering v. R.J. Reynolds Co., 306 U.S. 110, 114, 59 S.Ct. 423, 425, 83 L.Ed. 536.

15. Cf. Helvering v. Stockholms Enskilda Bank, 293 U.S. 84, 87, 55 S.Ct. 50, 51, 79 L.Ed. 211.

16. [§ 162(a)(3)] permits the deduction from gross income of "rentals * * * required to be made as a condition to the continued use * * * for purposes of the trade or business, of *property* * * * in which he [the taxpayer] has no *equity*."

[Section 167(a)] permits the deduction from gross income of "a reasonable allowance for the exhaustion, wear and tear of *property* used in the trade or business * * *."

* * *

17. See [§ 162(a)(3)] * * *.

have on the allowance of deductions for depreciation and on the collateral adjustments of basis.

Section [167(a)] permits deduction from gross income of "a reasonable allowance for the exhaustion, wear and tear of property * * *." [The basis for depreciation is defined in § 167(g).]

Under these provisions, if the mortgagor's equity were the [§ 1012] basis, it would also be the original basis from which depreciation allowances are deducted. If it is, and if the amount of the annual allowances were to be computed on that value, as would then seem to be required,[18] they will represent only a fraction of the cost of the corresponding physical exhaustion, and any recoupment by the mortgagor of the remainder of that cost can be effected only by the reduction of his taxable gain in the year of sale. If, however, the amount of the annual allowances were to be computed on the value of the property, and then deducted from an equity basis, we would in some instances have to accept deductions from a minus basis or deny deductions altogether.[19] The Commissioner also argues that taking the mortgagor's equity as the [§ 1012] basis would require the basis to be changed with each payment on the mortgage,[20] and that the attendant problem of repeatedly recomputing basis and annual allowances would be a tremendous accounting burden on both the Commissioner and the taxpayer. Moreover, the mortgagor would acquire control over the timing of his depreciation allowances.

Thus it appears that the applicable provisions of the Act expressly preclude an equity basis, and the use of it is contrary to certain implicit principles of income tax depreciation, and entails very great administrative difficulties.[21] It may be added that the Treasury has never furnished a guide through the maze of problems that arise in connection with depreciating an equity basis, but, on the contrary, has consistently permitted the amount of depreciation allowances to be computed on the full value of the property, and subtracted from it as a basis. Surely, Congress' long-continued acceptance of this situation gives it full legislative endorsement.[22]

We conclude that the proper basis under [§ 1014(a)] is the value of the property, undiminished by mortgages thereon, and that the correct

---

18. [§ 167(g)], in defining the "basis upon which" depreciation is "to be allowed", [does] not distinguish between basis as the minuend from which the allowances are to be deducted, and as the dividend from which the amount of the allowance is to be computed. * * *

19. So long as the mortgagor remains in possession, the mortgagee can not take depreciation deductions, even if he is the one who actually sustains the capital loss, as [§ 167(a)] allows them only on property "used in the trade or business."

20. Sec. [1016(a)(1)] requires adjustment of basis "for expenditures * * *

properly chargeable to capital account * * *."

21. Obviously we are not considering a situation in which a taxpayer has acquired and sold an equity of redemption only, i.e., a right to redeem the property without a right to present possession. In that situation, the right to redeem would itself be the aggregate of the taxpayer's rights and would undoubtedly constitute 'property' within the meaning of [§ 1012]. No depreciation problems would arise. See note 28.

22. See note [14].

basis here was $262,042.50. The next step is to ascertain what adjustments are required under [§ 1011(a)]. As the depreciation rate was stipulated, the only question at this point is whether the Commissioner was warranted in making any depreciation adjustments whatsoever.

Section [1016(a)(2)] provides that "proper adjustment in respect of the property *shall in all cases be made* * * * for exhaustion, wear and tear * * * to the extent of the amount [A] allowed * * * but not less than the amount allowable * * *." The Tax Court found on adequate evidence that the apartment house was property of a kind subject to physical exhaustion, that it was used in taxpayer's trade or business, and consequently that the taxpayer would have been entitled to a depreciation allowance under [§ 167(a)], except that, in the opinion of that Court, the basis of the property was zero, and it was thought that depreciation could not be taken on a zero basis. As we have just decided that the correct basis of the property was not zero, but $262,042.50, we avoid this difficulty, and conclude that an adjustment should be made as the Commissioner determined.

Petitioner urges to the contrary that she was not entitled to depreciation deductions, whatever the basis of the property, because the law allows them only to one who actually bears the capital loss,[23] and here the loss was not hers but the mortgagee's. We do not see, however, that she has established her factual premise. There was no finding of the Tax Court to that effect, nor to the effect that the value of the property was ever less than the amount of the lien. Nor was there evidence in the record, or any indication that petitioner could produce evidence, that this was so. The facts that the value of the property was only equal to the lien in 1932 and that during the next six and one-half years the physical condition of the building deteriorated and the amount of the lien increased, are entirely inconclusive, particularly in the light of the buyer's willingness in 1938 to take subject to the increased lien and pay a substantial amount of cash to boot. Whatever may be the rule as to allowing depreciation to a mortgagor on property in his possession which is subject to an unassumed mortgage and clearly worth less than the lien, we are not faced with that problem and see no reason to decide it now.

At last we come to the problem of determining the "amount realized" on the 1938 sale. [Section 1001(b)], it will be recalled, defines the "amount realized" from "the sale * * * of property" as "the sum of any money received plus the fair market value of the property (other than money) received," and [§ 1001(a)] defines the gain on "the sale * * * of property" as the excess of the amount realized over the basis. Quite obviously, the word "property", used here with reference to a sale, must mean "property" in the same ordinary sense intended by the use of the word with reference to acquisition and depreciation in [§§ 1011, 1012 and 1016], both for certain of the reasons stated hereto-

23. See Helvering v. F. & R. Lazarus & Co., 308 U.S. 252, 60 S.Ct. 209, 84 L.Ed. 226; Duffy v. Central R. Co., 268 U.S. 55, 64, 45 S.Ct. 429, 431, 69 L.Ed. 846.

fore in discussing its meaning in [§§ 1011, 1012 and 1016], and also because the functional relation of the two sections requires that the word mean the same in one section that it does in the other. If the "property" to be valued on the date of acquisition is the property free of liens, the "property" to be priced on a subsequent sale must be the same thing.[24]

Starting from this point, we could not accept petitioner's contention that the $2,500.00 net cash was all she realized on the sale except on the absurdity that she sold a quarter-of-a-million dollar property for roughly one per cent of its value, and took a 99 per cent loss. Actually, petitioner does not urge this. She argues, conversely, that because only $2,500.00 was realized on the sale, the "property" sold must have been the equity only, and that consequently we are forced to accept her contention as to the meaning of "property" in [§§ 1011, 1012, and 1016]. We adhere, however, to what we have already said on the meaning of "property", and we find that the absurdity is avoided by our conclusion that the amount of the mortgage is properly included in the "amount realized" on the sale.

Petitioner concedes that if she had been personally liable on the mortgage and the purchaser had either paid or assumed it, the amount so paid or assumed would be considered a part of the "amount realized" within the meaning of [§ 1001(b)].[25] The cases so deciding have already repudiated the notion that there must be an actual receipt by the seller himself of "money" or "other property", in their narrowest senses. It was thought to be decisive that one section of the Act must be construed so as not to defeat the intention of another or to frustrate the Act as a whole,[26] and that the taxpayer was the "beneficiary" of the payment in "as real and substantial [a sense] as if the money had been paid it and then paid over by it to its creditors." [27]

Both these points apply to this case. The first has been mentioned already. As for the second, we think that a mortgagor, not personally liable on the debt, who sells the property subject to the mortgage and for additional consideration, realizes a benefit in the amount of the mortgage as well as the boot.[28] If a purchaser pays boot, it is immateri-

24. See Maguire v. Commissioner, 313 U.S. 1, 8, 61 S.Ct. 789, 794, 85 L.Ed. 1149.

We are not troubled by petitioner's argument that her contract of sale expressly provided for the conveyance of the equity only. She actually conveyed title to the property, and the buyer took the same property that petitioner had acquired in 1932 and used in her trade or business until its sale.

25. United States v. Hendler, 303 U.S. 564, 58 S.Ct. 655, 82 L.Ed. 1018; Brons Hotels, Inc., 34 B.T.A. 376; Walter F. Haass, 37 B.T.A. 948. See Douglas v. Willcutts, 296 U.S. 1, 8, 56 S.Ct. 59, 62, 80 L.Ed. 3, 101 A.L.R. 391.

26. See Brons Hotels, Inc., supra, 34 B.T.A. at page 381.

27. See United States v. Hendler, supra, 303 U.S. at page 566, 58 S.Ct. at page 656, 82 L.Ed. 1018.

28. Obviously, if the value of the property is less than the amount of the mortgage, a mortgagor who is not personally liable cannot realize a benefit equal to the mortgage. Consequently, a different problem might be encountered where a mortgagor abandoned the property or transferred it subject to the mortgage without receiving boot. That is not this case. [In the original case this footnote was number 37.—Eds.]

al as to our problem whether the mortgagor is also to receive money from the purchaser to discharge the mortgage prior to sale, or whether he is merely to transfer subject to the mortgage—it may make a difference to the purchaser and to the mortgagee, but not to the mortgagor. Or put in another way, we are no more concerned with whether the mortgagor is, strictly speaking, a debtor on the mortgage, than we are with whether the benefit to him is, strictly speaking, a receipt of money or property. We are rather concerned with the reality that an owner of property, mortgaged at a figure less than that at which the property will sell, must and will treat the conditions of the mortgage exactly as if they were his personal obligations.[29] If he transfers subject to the mortgage, the benefit to him is as real and substantial as if the mortgage were discharged, or as if a personal debt in an equal amount had been assumed by another.

Therefore we conclude that the Commissioner was right in determining that petitioner realized $257,500.00 on the sale of this property.

The Tax Court's contrary determinations, that "property", as used in [§ 1012] and related sections, means "equity", and that the amount of a mortgage subject to which property is sold is not the measure of a benefit realized, within the meaning of [§ 1001(b)], announced rules of general applicability on clear-cut questions of law.[30] The Circuit Court of Appeals therefore had jurisdiction to review them.[31]

Petitioner contends that the result we have reached taxes her on what is not income within the meaning of the Sixteenth Amendment. If this is because only the direct receipt of cash is thought to be income in the constitutional sense, her contention is wholly without merit.[32] If it is because the entire transaction is thought to have been "by all dictates of common-sense * * * a ruinous disaster", as it was termed in her brief, we disagree with her premise. She was entitled to depreciation deductions for a period of nearly seven years, and she actually took them in almost the allowable amount. The crux of this case, really, is whether the law permits her to exclude allowable deductions from consideration in computing gain.[33] We have already

29. For instance, this petitioner returned the gross rentals as her own income, and out of them paid interest on the mortgage, on which she claimed and was allowed deductions. * * *

30. See Commissioner v. Wilcox, 327 U.S. 404, 410, 66 S.Ct. 546, 550; Bingham's Trust v. Commissioner, 325 U.S. 365, 369–372, 65 S.Ct. 1232, 1234–1236, 89 L.Ed. 1670. Cf. John Kelley Co. v. Commissioner, 326 U.S. 521, 527, 698, 66 S.Ct. 299, 302; Dobson v. Commissioner, 320 U.S. 489, 64 S.Ct. 239, 88 L.Ed. 248.

31. Ibid; * * *.

32. Douglas v. Willcutts, supra, 296 U.S. at page 9, 56 S.Ct. at page 62, 80 L.Ed. 3, 101 A.L.R. 391; Burnet v. Wells, 289 U.S. 670, 677, 53 S.Ct. 761, 763, 77 L.Ed. 1439.

33. In the course of the argument some reference was made, as by analogy, to a situation in which a taxpayer acquired by devise property subject to a mortgage in an amount greater than the then value of the property, and later transferred it to a third person, still subject to the mortgage, and for a cash boot. Whether or not the difference between the value of the property on acquisition and the amount of the mortgage would in that situation constitute either statutory or constitutional income is a question which is different from the one before us, and which we need not presently answer.

showed that, if it does, the taxpayer can enjoy a double deduction, in effect, on the same loss of assets. The Sixteenth Amendment does not require that result any more than does the Act itself.

Affirmed.

MR. JUSTICE JACKSON, dissenting.

The Tax Court concluded that this taxpayer acquired only an equity worth nothing. The mortgage was in default, the mortgage debt was equal to the value of the property, any possession by the taxpayer was forfeited and terminable immediately by foreclosure, and perhaps by a receiver pendente lite. Arguments can be advanced to support the theory that the taxpayer received the whole property and thereupon came to owe the whole debt. Likewise it is argued that when she sold she transferred the entire value of the property and received release from the whole debt. But we think these arguments are not so conclusive that it was not within the province of the Tax Court to find that she received an equity which at that time had a zero value. Dobson v. Commissioner, 320 U.S. 489, 64 S.Ct. 239, 88 L.Ed. 248; Commissioner v. Scottish American Investment Co., Ltd., 323 U.S. 119, 65 S.Ct. 169, 89 L.Ed. 113. The taxpayer never became personally liable for the debt, and hence when she sold she was released from no debt. The mortgage debt was simply a subtraction from the value of what she did receive, and from what she sold. The subtraction left her nothing when she acquired it and a small margin when she sold it. She acquired a property right equivalent to an equity of redemption and sold the same thing. It was the "property" bought and sold as the Tax Court considered it to be under the Revenue Laws. We are not required in this case to decide whether depreciation was properly taken, for there is no issue about it here.

We would reverse the Court of Appeals and sustain the decision of the Tax Court.

MR. JUSTICE FRANKFURTER and MR. JUSTICE DOUGLAS join in this opinion.

PARKER v. DELANEY

United States Court of Appeals, First Circuit, 1950.
186 F.2d 455, cert. denied 341 U.S. 926, 71 S.Ct. 797, 95 L.Ed. 1357 (1951).

[In 1933, 1934, and 1936 Parker acquired four apartment houses from banks, which owned the properties as a result of foreclosure proceedings. He paid no money for the properties, and took them subject to mortgage liens totaling $273,000. He did not become personally liable for the mortgage debt. While holding the properties Parker deducted $45,280.48 as depreciation. He paid off $13,989.38 of principal on the mortgages. In 1945 the mortgages were in default, and Parker conveyed the properties to the banks.

On his 1945 return, Parker reported a $31,291.10 long-term capital gain from the sale of the apartment properties to the banks. After thinking the matter over he sued for a refund, claiming that his "amount realized" under the predecessor of § 1001 was zero, since he "realized nothing when the properties were reconveyed to the banks in 1945 and so there was legally nothing to tax as a gain * * *."]

FAHY, CIRCUIT JUDGE.

* * *

That there was a disposition of the properties by appellant in 1945 seems clear. Appellant had regularly reported for tax purposes all income and had taken all deductions, including those for depreciation, to which he would be entitled as owner. The serious question is not whether there was a disposition within the meaning of [§ 1001], as to which we are clear, but whether a gain was realized from such disposition. * * * [T]he question is whether taxpayer received from his disposition of the apartment houses money or other property of a value in excess of the amount of their adjusted basis, that is, in excess of the cost of the properties less depreciation.

In applying the foregoing formula to the facts we may conveniently consider first the question of the cost of the properties to appellant. During the years of his operation of them he took deductions for depreciation on a cost basis equal to the amount of the first mortgage liens. In this court he expressly disclaims any contention that their value for depreciation purposes was less than those liens. These mortgages represented the prices paid, or the consideration, for the properties. The properties became subject to these liens and appellant considered them as the cost in deducting depreciation. Nothing appears to the contrary and we must, as did the court below, accept these figures of cost used by appellant. Indeed we do not understand him to dispute this treatment of the cost question.

The depreciation deductions, taken on the basis discussed above, amounted to $45,280.48. We come to the time of disposition, therefore, with that amount having been set aside from gross income and put in capital account for replacement purposes, the justification for permitting depreciation deductions in computing taxable income. Detroit Edison Co. v. Commissioner, 319 U.S. 98, 63 S.Ct. 902, 87 L.Ed. 1286 * * *. The adjusted basis in 1945 accordingly was $273,000 less $45,280.48, or $227,719.52. The question is whether more than this was realized from disposition of the properties in that year. If so it was taxable gain * * *. It is here the real controversy arises. Appellant contends that he realized nothing or in any event nothing in excess of the adjusted basis of $227,719.52, though the amount of the mortgages then was $31,291.10 in excess of said adjusted basis. * * *

The burden of deciding whether or not the last named figure was gain we think has been assumed by Crane v. Commissioner, 331 U.S. 1, 67 S.Ct. 1047, 91 L.Ed. 1301. In that case there was a sale of improved real estate to a third party subject to the amount of the mortgage, plus $3,000 boot paid to the seller. The latter, like appellant here, was not personally liable on the mortgage. In the instant case the disposition was to the mortgagees instead of to a third party purchaser and no boot was paid.

In the Crane case the taxpayer contended that all she received was the boot, and that its amount, less expenses of the sale, was the amount of gain realized. But the Supreme Court held that the taxpayer received benefit in the amount of the mortgage as well as the boot. We see no logical or practical distinction which takes the present case out of the rationale of that decision. If the amount of the unassumed mortgage in the Crane case was properly included in the amount realized on the sale, the amounts of the unassumed mortgages should be held to have been realized on the disposition in this case. In both, such amounts had been considered in determining the unadjusted basis. Since in the Crane case taxpayer obtained the property by devise, the basis was the fair market value at the time of acquisition. [§ 1014]. In the case at bar the basis was cost. [§ 1012]. Depreciation had been computed and deducted on such amounts; and their relationship under [§ 1016] to the question of gain realized under [§ 1001] requires that account be taken of such value or cost in determining the realization on disposition. Furthermore, the property in the hands of appellant was relieved at the time of disposition of the mortgage liens and obligations. So far as appellant was concerned as owner these were paid even though he was not personally liable for them. The matter was so treated in the Crane case, 331 U.S. at page 13, 67 S.Ct. at page 1054. The added factor there, not present here, that boot was paid over and above the mortgage, is not material so long as the value of the properties was not less than the liens. Boot served to show this in the Crane case, but the payment of boot is of course not the only means of showing whether or not value is equal to or more than the liens on the property disposed of.

This brings us to appellant's contention that in fact the value was less and the Crane doctrine accordingly does not apply. He points out that the Supreme Court, in such a situation, reserved decision: "Obviously, if the value of the property is less than the amount of the mortgage, a mortgagor who is not personally liable cannot realize a benefit equal to the mortgage. Consequently, a different problem might be encountered where a mortgagor abandoned the property or transferred it subject to the mortgage without receiving boot. That is not this case." Footnote 37, 331 U.S. at page 14, 67 S.Ct. at page 1054 [footnote 28 on page 772].

This statement is predicated upon a situation where the value of the property when disposed of is less than the mortgage. There is no evidence to that effect in this case. The District Court treated the value as equal to the mortgages and we have no basis for doing otherwise. The critical point is that the value equaled the mortgages, not that it exceeded them, and on this factual matter we must on the record support the conclusion of the District Court.

Appellant also contends that the property was abandoned to the banks and accordingly that there could be no capital gain * * *. We are not concerned with the computation of the amount to be taxed, that is, whether it was properly computed as a gain on the sale or exchange of a capital asset or should have been computed as an ordinary gain. The appellee Collector concedes that it is too late to make an additional assessment on the theory of ordinary gain. Accordingly it does not help appellant to term the transaction an abandonment if it was nevertheless a disposition within the meaning of [§ 1001] upon which a gain was realized and if, as we hold, it was then of a value equal to the first mortgage liens. In these circumstances the unpaid amount of the liens is carried forward, as it were, from the time of acquisition to the time of disposition. They are treated as cost at the earlier time and so must be treated as value at the later time. The result in the end is that the taxpayer accounts to the taxing authorities for the gain realized by his deductions for depreciation in excess of his own investment.

The judgment of the District Court is affirmed.

MAGRUDER, CHIEF JUDGE (concurring).

I concur. The logic of the court's opinion is inescapable, with Crane v. Commissioner, 331 U.S. 1, 67 S.Ct. 1047, 91 L.Ed. 1301, as the starting point.

As an original matter, I would have had some difficulty in understanding how the taxpayer in the Crane case realized more than $3,000 from her sale of the mortgaged property there involved, in view of the definition of "amount realized" in [§ 1001(b)] of the Internal Revenue Code. By the same token in the case at bar, under the more natural and obvious reading of [§ 1001(b)] it would seem that the amount realized by the taxpayer herein was zero, when he caused his straw man to quitclaim to the banks, for no cash consideration, properties then subject to mortgages up to their full value, the taxpayer not being liable on the mortgage debt. To reach the conclusion that the taxpayer thereby "realized" the amount of the outstanding mortgage debt would seem to require a somewhat esoteric interpretation of the statutory language. Also, I do not clearly understand why the Treasury allowed the taxpayer deductions for depreciation, under [§ 167], in the total amount of $45,280.48, taking the taxpayer's original "cost" basis as the amount of the mortgages, though he made no cash investment in the properties upon acquisition, nor did he obligate himself on the mortgage debt. But that matter need not concern us here, because depreciation in the amount of $45,280.48 was in fact "allowed"; and under [§ 1016(a)(2)], the adjusted basis for determining gain or loss from the sale or other disposition of the property takes account of depreciation "to the extent [of the amount (A) allowed * * * but not less than the amount allowable * * *"] under the income tax laws.

Perhaps the net result reached by the court here might be arrived at by another mode of computation with less strain upon the statutory language. Thus, the adjusted basis for determining gain or loss under [§ 1016(a)(2)] might be computed as follows: Original cost, zero, plus $13,989.38, the total amount which taxpayer paid in reduction of the mortgage debt while he held the properties, minus $45,280.48, the amount of depreciation "allowed", which comes out to an adjusted basis of minus $31,291.10. Now, apply that adjusted basis of minus $31,291.10 to the computation of gain or loss under the formula in [§ 1001(a)]: The "amount realized" upon taxpayer's disposition of the properties, zero (as suggested above), minus the adjusted basis as computed under [§ 1016], or in other words, minus $31,291.10 subtracted from zero, comes out to a plus figure of $31,291.10, representing the amount of the taxpayer's gain, upon which the tax would be computed.

———

The suggestion in Parker v. Delaney by Judge Magruder that the basis of property should not include the amount of the mortgage has never been adopted by the courts or the Commissioner. The concept of a negative basis has been rejected because of the administrative problems it would cause when the mortgagor-owner makes principal payments on the loan.

Questions

1. Would it have been simpler to apply the negative basis approach suggested by Judge Magruder in Parker v. Delaney? For example, what would have been the result under this approach if Mrs. Crane did not depreciate the property, i.e. took no depreciation deductions on her tax return?

2. Does the tax benefit rule require the inclusion of the balance of the mortgage in the amount realized by Mrs. Crane? What benefit did she derive from the property?

3. Would it have made a difference whether Mrs. Crane's purchaser paid off the mortgage rather than taking the property subject to the mortgage?

2. LIABILITIES IN CONNECTION WITH APPRECIATED PROPERTY

WOODSAM ASSOCIATES, INC. v. COMMISSIONER

United States Court of Appeals, Second Circuit, 1952.
198 F.2d 357.

CHASE, CIRCUIT JUDGE.

The petitioner paid its income and declared value excess profits taxes for 1943 as computed upon returns it filed which included as part of its gross income $146,058.10 as gain realized upon the mortgage foreclosure sale in that year of improved real estate which it owned and which was bid in by the mortgagee for a nominal sum. It filed a timely claim for refund on the ground that its adjusted basis for the property had been understated and its taxable gain, therefore, was less than that reported. The refund claim was denied and a deficiency in both its income taxes and declared value excess profits taxes was determined which was affirmed, without dissent, in a decision reviewed by the entire Tax Court. The decisive issue now presented is whether the basis for determining gain or loss upon the sale or other disposition of property is increased when, subsequent to the acquisition of the property, the owner receives a loan in an amount greater than his adjusted basis which is secured by a mortgage on the property upon which he is not personally liable. If so, it is agreed that part of the income taxes and all of the declared value excess profits taxes paid for 1943 should be refunded.

A comparatively brief statement of the admitted facts and their obvious, and conceded, tax consequences will suffice by way of introduction.

On December 29, 1934, Samuel J. Wood and his wife organized the petitioner and each transferred to it certain property in return for one-half of its capital stock. One piece of property so transferred by Mrs. Wood was the above mentioned parcel of improved real estate consisting of land in the City of New York and a brick building thereon divided into units suitable for use, and used, in retail business. The property was subject to a $400,000 mortgage on which Mrs. Wood was not personally liable and on which the petitioner never became personally liable. Having, thus, acquired the property in a tax free exchange, [§ 351], the petitioner took the basis of Mrs. Wood for tax purposes. [§ 362(a)]. Upon the final disposition of the property at the foreclosure sale there was still due upon the mortgage the principal amount of $381,000 and, as the petitioner concedes,[34] the extent to which the amount of the mortgage exceeds its adjusted basis was income taxable to it even though it was not personally liable upon the mortgage. Crane v. C.I.R., 331 U.S. 1, 67 S.Ct. 1047, 91 L.Ed. 1301.

Turning now to the one item whose effect upon the calculation of the petitioner's adjusted basis is disputed, the following admitted facts need to be stated. Mrs. Wood bought the property on January 20, 1922 at a total cost of $296,400. She paid $101,400 in cash, took the title subject to an existing mortgage for $120,000 and gave a purchase money bond and second mortgage for $75,000. She had made payments on the first mortgage reducing it to $112,500, when, on December 30, 1925, both of the mortgages were assigned to the Title Guarantee and Trust Company. On January 4, 1926 Mrs. Wood borrowed $137,500

34. The petitioner requested a finding that the value of the property was less than the principal amount due on the mortgage which, it was apparently urged, prevented it from realizing the full amount due thereon. The authority cited was footnote 37 in Crane v. Commissioner, 331 U.S. 1, 67 S.Ct. 1047, 1054, 91 L.Ed. 1301, where the Court said, "Obviously, if the value of the property is less than the amount of the mortgage, a mortgagor who is not personally liable cannot realize a benefit equal to the mortgage. Consequently, a different problem might be encountered where a mortgagor abandoned the property or transferred it subject to the mortgage without receiving boot. * * *" However, the petitioner has disclaimed reliance upon that and, we think, advisedly so. Cf. Parker v. Delaney, 1 Cir., 186 F.2d 455.

from the Title Guarantee & Trust Company and gave it a bond and mortgage for $325,000 on which she was personally liable, that being the amount of the two existing mortgages, which were consolidated into the new one, plus the amount of the cash borrowed. On June 9, 1931 this consolidated mortgage was assigned to the East River Savings Bank and, shortly thereafter, Mrs. Wood borrowed an additional $75,000 from that bank which she received upon the execution of a second consolidated mortgage for $400,000 comprising the principal amount due on the first consolidated mortgage plus the additional loan. However, this transaction was carried out through the use of a "dummy" so that, under New York law, Mrs. Wood was not personally liable on this bond and mortgage. See In re Childs Co., 2 Cir., 163 F.2d 379. This was the mortgage, reduced as above stated, which was foreclosed.

The contention of the petitioner may now be stated quite simply. It is that, when the borrowings of Mrs. Wood subsequent to her acquisition of the property became charges solely upon the property itself, the cash she received for the repayment of which she was not personally liable was a gain then taxable to her as income to the extent that the mortgage indebtedness exceeded her adjusted basis in the property. That being so, it is argued that her tax basis was, under familiar principles of tax law, increased by the amount of such taxable gain and that this stepped up basis carried over to the petitioner in the tax free exchange by which it acquired the property.

While this conclusion would be sound if the premise on which it is based were correct, we cannot accept the premise. It is that the petitioner's transferor made a taxable disposition of the property, within the meaning of [§ 1001], when the second consolidated mortgage was executed, because she had, by then, dealt with it in such a way that she had received cash, in excess of her basis, which, at that time, she was freed from any personal obligation to repay. Nevertheless, whether or not personally liable on the mortgage, "The mortgagee is a creditor, and in effect nothing more than a preferred creditor, even though the mortgagor is not liable for the debt. He is not the less a creditor because he has recourse only to the land, unless we are to deny the term to one who may levy upon only a part of his debtor's assets." C.I.R. v. Crane, 2 Cir., 153 F.2d 504, 506. Mrs. Wood merely augmented the existing mortgage indebtedness when she borrowed each time and, far from closing the venture, remained in a position to borrow more if and when circumstances permitted and she so desired. And so, she never "disposed" of the property to create a taxable event which [§ 1001] makes a condition precedent to the taxation of gain. "Disposition," within the meaning of [§ 1001], is the " 'getting rid, or making over, of anything; relinquishment' ". Herber's Estate v. Commissioner, 3 Cir., 139 F.2d 756, 758, certiorari denied 322 U.S. 752, 64 S.Ct. 1263, 88 L.Ed. 1582. Nothing of that nature was done here by the mere execution of the second consolidated mortgage; Mrs. Wood was the owner of this property in the same sense after the execution of this mortgage that she was before. As was pointed out in our decision in the Crane case, supra, 153 F.2d at 505–506, " * * * the lien of a mortgage does not make the mortgagee a cotenant; the mortgagor is the owner for all purposes; indeed that is why the 'gage' is 'mort,' as distinguished from a '*vivum vadium.*' Kortright v. Cady, 21 N.Y. 343, 344, 78 Am.Dec. 145. He has all the income from the property; he manages it; he may sell it; any increase in its value goes to him; any decrease falls on him, until the value goes below the amount of the lien." Realization of gain was, therefore, postponed for taxation until there was a final disposition of the property at the time of the foreclosure sale. See Lutz & Schramm Co., 1 T.C. 682; Mendham Corp., 9 T.C. 320. Therefore, Mrs. Wood's borrowings did not change the basis for the computation of gain or loss.

Affirmed.

From a financial perspective when property is used as collateral for a nonrecourse loan, the loan proceeds generate the same amount of cash as if the property were actually sold for an equivalent amount. For example, if a taxpayer who owns $80,000 worth of land free and clear of any liabilities (with a basis of $25,000) uses it as collateral for an $80,000 nonrecourse loan, he has obtained $80,000 in cash from the property. Since the taxpayer can keep the loan proceeds even though the land become worthless, he has received $55,000 of cash in excess of his basis in the land. Financially, this has the appearance of a gain. One could conceivably view the nonrecourse borrowing as a sale with option to repurchase the land for $80,000.

Was the court in Woodsam correct in holding that § 1001(a) requires a disposition of the property before there can be a realization? Since Mrs. Wood was able to convert a portion of her unrealized appreciation into cash, should it matter that she still owned the property? If the borrowing had been found by the court to be a taxable event, there would be no financial hardship in reporting the gain at that time as the transaction did generate cash with which to pay any tax on the gain.

Given that borrowing against property a taxpayer already owns is not a realization, we will consider later in this chapter the tax consequences if the newly pledged property is subsequently sold, the purchaser taking the property subject to the nonrecourse liability. Since the receipt of the loan proceeds is not treated as a sale when the loan is made, think about how the disposition of the property should be treated when the taxpayer keeps the loan proceeds and surrenders the property to another. As will be discussed later in this chapter, a disposition of property subject to a liability, whether by sale or by gift, gives rise to a realization with the transferor having to account for the liability at that time.

3. IMPACT OF LIABILITIES IN EXCESS OF THE FAIR MAR-KET VALUE OF PROPERTY

COMMISSIONER v. TUFTS

Supreme Court of the United States, 1983.
461 U.S. 300, 103 S.Ct. 1826, 75 L.Ed.2d 863.

JUSTICE BLACKMUN delivered the opinion of the Court.

Over 35 years ago, in Crane v. Commissioner, 331 U.S. 1, 67 S.Ct. 1047, 91 L.Ed. 1301 (1947), this Court ruled that a taxpayer, who sold property encumbered by a nonrecourse mortgage (the amount of the mortgage being less than the property's value), must include the unpaid balance of the mortgage in the computation of the amount the taxpayer realized on the sale. The case now before us presents the question whether the same rule applies when the unpaid amount of the nonrecourse mortgage exceeds the fair market value of the property sold.

I

On August 1, 1970, respondent Clark Pelt, a builder, and his wholly owned corporation, respondent Clark, Inc., formed a general partnership. The purpose of the partnership was to construct a 120-unit apartment complex in Duncanville, Tex., a Dallas suburb. Neither Pelt nor Clark, Inc., made any capital contribution to the partnership. Six days later, the partnership entered into a mortgage loan agreement with the Farm & Home Savings Association (F & H). Under the agreement, F & H was committed for a $1,851,500 loan for the complex. In return, the partnership executed a note and a deed of trust in favor of F & H. The partnership obtained the loan on a nonrecourse basis: neither the partnership nor its partners assumed any personal liability for repayment of the loan. Pelt later admitted four friends and relatives, respondents Tufts, Steger, Stephens, and Austin, as general partners. None of them contributed capital upon entering the partnership.

The construction of the complex was completed in August 1971. During 1971, each partner made small capital contributions to the partnership; in 1972, however, only Pelt made a contribution. The total of the partners' capital contributions was $44,212. In each tax year, all partners claimed as income tax deductions their allocable shares of ordinary losses and depreciation. The deductions taken by the partners in 1971 and 1972 totalled $439,972. Due to these contributions and deductions, the partnership's adjusted basis in the property in August 1972 was $1,455,740.

In 1971 and 1972, major employers in the Duncanville area laid off significant numbers of workers. As a result, the partnership's rental income was less than expected, and it was unable to make the payments due on the mortgage. Each partner, on August 28, 1972, sold his partnership interest to an unrelated third party, Fred Bayles. As consideration, Bayles agreed to reimburse each partner's sale expenses up to $250; he also assumed the nonrecourse mortgage.

On the date of transfer, the fair market value of the property did not exceed $1,400,000. Each partner reported the sale on his federal income tax return and indicated that a partnership loss of $55,740 had been sustained.[35] The Commissioner of Internal Revenue, on audit, determined that the sale resulted in a partnership capital gain of approximately $400,000. His theory was that the partnership had realized the full amount of the nonrecourse obligation.[36]

Relying on Millar v. Commissioner, 577 F.2d 212, 215 (CA3), cert. denied, 439 U.S. 1046, 99 S.Ct. 721, 58 L.Ed.2d 704 (1978), the United States Tax Court, in an unreviewed decision, upheld the asserted deficiencies. 70 T.C. 756 (1978). The United States Court of Appeals for the Fifth Circuit reversed. 651 F.2d 1058 (1981). That court expressly disagreed with the *Millar* analysis, and, in limiting *Crane v. Commissioner,* supra, to its facts, questioned the theoretical underpinnings of the *Crane* decision. We granted certiorari to resolve the conflict. 456 U.S. 960, 102 S.Ct. 2034, 72 L.Ed.2d 483 (1982).

II

Section 752(d) of the Internal Revenue Code of [1986] 26 U.S.C. § 752(d), specifically provides that liabilities incurred in the sale or exchange of a partnership interest are to "be treated in the same manner as liabilities in connection with the sale or exchange of property not associated with partnerships." Section 1001 governs the determination of gains and losses on the disposition of property. Under § 1001(a), the gain or loss from a sale or other disposition of property is defined as the difference between "the amount realized" on the disposition and the property's adjusted basis. Subsection (b) of § 1001 defines "amount realized": "The amount realized from the sale or other disposition of property shall be the sum of any money received plus the fair market value of the property (other than money) received." At issue is the application of the latter provision to the disposition of property encumbered by a nonrecourse mortgage of an amount in excess of the property's fair market value.

A

In *Crane v. Commissioner,* supra, this Court took the first and controlling step toward the resolution of this issue. Beulah B. Crane

---

35. The loss was the difference between the adjusted basis, $1,455,740, and the fair market value of the property, $1,400,000. On their individual tax returns, the partners did not claim deductions for their respective shares of this loss. In their petitions to the Tax Court, however, the partners did claim the loss.

36. The Commissioner determined the partnership's gain on the sale by subtracting the adjusted basis, $1,455,740, from the liability assumed by Bayles, $1,851,500. Of the resulting figure, $395,760, the Commissioner treated $348,661 as capital gain, pursuant to § 741 of the Internal Revenue Code, 26 U.S.C. § 741, and $47,099 as ordinary gain under the recapture provisions of § 1250 of the Code. The application of § 1250 in determining the character of the gain is not at issue here.

was the sole beneficiary under the will of her deceased husband. At his death in January 1932, he owned an apartment building that was then mortgaged for an amount which proved to be equal to its fair market value, as determined for federal estate tax purposes. The widow, of course, was not personally liable on the mortgage. She operated the building for nearly seven years, hoping to turn it into a profitable venture; during that period, she claimed income tax deductions for depreciation, property taxes, interest, and operating expenses, but did not make payments upon the mortgage principal. In computing her basis for the depreciation deductions, she included the full amount of the mortgage debt. In November 1938, with her hopes unfulfilled and the mortgagee threatening foreclosure, Mrs. Crane sold the building. The purchaser took the property subject to the mortgage and paid Crane $3,000; of that amount, $500 went for the expenses of the sale.

Crane reported a gain of $2,500 on the transaction. She reasoned that her basis in the property was zero (despite her earlier depreciation deductions based on including the amount of the mortgage) and that the amount she realized from the sale was simply the cash she received. The Commissioner disputed this claim. He asserted that Crane's basis in the property, under * * * (the current version is § 1014 of the Code, as amended, 26 U.S.C. § 1014) was the property's fair market value at the time of her husband's death, adjusted for depreciation in the interim, and that the amount realized was the net cash received plus the amount of the outstanding mortgage assumed by the purchaser.

In upholding the Commissioner's interpretation of [§ 1014], the Court observed that to regard merely the taxpayer's equity in the property as her basis would lead to depreciation deductions less than the actual physical deterioration of the property, and would require the basis to be recomputed with each payment on the mortgage. 331 U.S., at 9–10, 67 S.Ct., at 1052. The Court rejected Crane's claim that any loss due to depreciation belonged to the mortgagee. The effect of the Court's ruling was that the taxpayer's basis was the value of the property undiminished by the mortgage. Id., at 11, 67 S.Ct., at 1053.

The Court next proceeded to determine the amount realized under * * * § 1001(b) of the 1954 Code, 26 U.S.C. § 1001(b). In order to avoid the "absurdity," see 331 U.S., at 13, 67 S.Ct., at 1054, of Crane's realizing only $2,500 on the sale of property worth over a quarter of a million dollars, the Court treated the amount realized as it had treated basis, that is, by including the outstanding value of the mortgage. To do otherwise would have permitted Crane to recognize a tax loss unconnected with any actual economic loss. The Court refused to construe one section of the Revenue Act so as "to frustrate the Act as a whole." Ibid.

Crane, however, insisted that the nonrecourse nature of the mortgage required different treatment. The Court, for two reasons, disagreed. First, excluding the nonrecourse debt from the amount realized would result in the same absurdity and frustration of the Code. Id., at 13–14, 67 S.Ct., at 1054. Second, the Court concluded that Crane obtained an economic benefit from the purchaser's assumption of the mortgage identical to the benefit conferred by the cancellation of personal debt. Because the value of the property in that case exceeded the amount of the mortgage, it was in Crane's economic interest to treat the mortgage as a personal obligation; only by so doing could she realize upon sale the appreciation in her equity represented by the $2,500 boot. The purchaser's assumption of the liability thus resulted in a taxable economic benefit to her, just as if she had been given, in addition to the boot, a sum of cash sufficient to satisfy the mortgage.[37]

In a footnote, pertinent to the present case, the Court observed:

"Obviously, if the value of the property is less than the amount of the mortgage, a mortgagor who is not personally liable cannot realize a benefit equal to the mortgage. Consequently, a different problem might be encountered where a mortgagor abandoned the property or transferred it subject to the mortgage without receiving boot. That is not this case." Id., at 14, n. 37, 67 S.Ct., at 1054–55, n. 37 [footnote 28 on page 772].

B

This case presents that unresolved issue. We are disinclined to overrule *Crane,* and we conclude that the same rule applies when the unpaid amount of the nonrecourse mortgage exceeds the value of the property transferred. *Crane* ultimately does not rest on its limited theory of economic benefit; instead, we read *Crane* to have approved the Commissioner's decision to treat a nonrecourse mortgage in this context as a true loan. This approval underlies *Crane's* holdings that the amount of the nonrecourse liability is to be included in calculating both the basis and the amount realized on disposition. That the amount of the loan exceeds the fair market value of the property thus becomes irrelevant.

When a taxpayer receives a loan, he incurs an obligation to repay that loan at some future date. Because of this obligation, the loan proceeds do not qualify as income to the taxpayer. When he fulfills the obligation, the repayment of the loan likewise has no effect on his tax liability.

Another consequence to the taxpayer from this obligation occurs when the taxpayer applies the loan proceeds to the purchase price of

---

37. Crane also argued that even if the statute required the inclusion of the amount of the nonrecourse debt, that amount was not Sixteenth Amendment income because the overall transaction had been "by all dictates of common sense * * * a ruinous disaster." Brief for Petitioner in Crane v. Commissioner, O.T.1946, No. 68, p. 51. The Court noted, however, that Crane had been entitled to and actual-ly took depreciation deductions for nearly seven years. To allow her to exclude sums on which those deductions were based from the calculation of her taxable gain would permit her "a double deduction * * * on the same loss of assets." The Sixteenth Amendment, it was said, did not require that result. 331 U.S., at 15–16, 67 S.Ct., at 1055.

property used to secure the loan. Because of the obligation to repay, the taxpayer is entitled to include the amount of the loan in computing his basis in the property; the loan, under § 1012, is part of the taxpayer's cost of the property. Although a different approach might have been taken with respect to a nonrecourse mortgage loan,[38] the Commissioner has chosen to accord it the same treatment he gives to a recourse mortgage loan. The Court approved that choice in *Crane,* and the respondents do not challenge it here. The choice and its resultant benefits to the taxpayer are predicated on the assumption that the mortgage will be repaid in full.

When encumbered property is sold or otherwise disposed of and the purchaser assumes the mortgage, the associated extinguishment of the mortgagor's obligation to repay is accounted for in the computation of the amount realized.[39] See United States v. Hendler, 303 U.S. 564, 566–567, 58 S.Ct. 655, 656, 82 L.Ed. 1018 (1938). Because no difference between recourse and nonrecourse obligations is recognized in calculating basis,[40] *Crane* teaches that the Commissioner may ignore the nonrecourse nature of the obligation in determining the amount real-

38. The Commissioner might have adopted the theory, implicit in Crane's contentions, that a nonrecourse mortgage is not true debt, but, instead, is a form of joint investment by the mortgagor and the mortgagee. On this approach, nonrecourse debt would be considered a contingent liability, under which the mortgagor's payments on the debt gradually increase his interest in the property while decreasing that of the mortgagee. Note, Federal Income Tax Treatment of Nonrecourse Debt, 82 Colum.L.Rev. 1498, 1514 (1982); Lurie, Mortgagor's Gain on Mortgaging Property for More than Cost Without Personal Liability, 6 Tax.L.Rev. 319, 323 (1951); cf. Brief for Respondents 16 (nonrecourse debt resembles preferred stock). Because the taxpayer's investment in the property would not include the nonrecourse debt, the taxpayer would not be permitted to include that debt in basis. Note, 82 Colum.L.Rev., at 1515; cf. Gibson Products Co. v. United States, 637 F.2d 1041, 1047–1048 (CA5 1981) (contingent nature of obligation prevents inclusion in basis of oil and gas leases of nonrecourse debt secured by leases, drilling equipment, and percentage of future production).

We express no view as to whether such an approach would be consistent with the statutory structure and, if so, and *Crane* were not on the books, whether that approach would be preferred over *Crane's* analysis. We note only that the *Crane* Court's resolution of the basis issue presumed that when property is purchased with proceeds from a nonrecourse mortgage, the purchaser becomes the sole own-

er of the property. 331 U.S., at 6, 67 S.Ct., at 1050. Under the *Crane* approach, the mortgagee is entitled to no portion of the basis. * * * The nonrecourse mortgage is part of the mortgagor's investment in the property, and does not constitute a coinvestment by the mortgagee. But see Note, 82 Colum.L.Rev., at 1513 (treating nonrecourse mortgage as coinvestment by mortgagee and critically concluding that *Crane* departed from traditional analysis that basis is taxpayer's investment in property).

39. In this case, respondents received the face value of their note as loan proceeds. If respondents initially had given their note at a discount, the amount realized on the sale of the securing property might be limited to the funds actually received. See Commissioner v. Rail Joint Co., 61 F.2d 751, 752 (CA2 1932) (cancellation of indebtedness); Fashion Park, Inc. v. Commissioner, 21 T.C. 600, 606 (1954) (same). See generally J. Sneed, The Configurations of Gross Income 319 (1967) ("[I]t appears settled that the reacquisition of bonds at a discount by the obligor results in gain only to the extent the issue price, where this is less than par, exceeds the cost of reacquisition").

40. The Commissioner's choice in *Crane* "laid the foundation stone of most tax shelters," Bittker, Tax Shelters, Nonrecourse Debt, and the *Crane* Case, 33 Tax.L.Rev. 277, 283 (1978), by permitting taxpayers who bear no risk to take deductions on depreciable property. * * *

ized upon disposition of the encumbered property. He thus may include in the amount realized the amount of the nonrecourse mortgage assumed by the purchaser. The rationale for this treatment is that the original inclusion of the amount of the mortgage in basis rested on the assumption that the mortgagor incurred an obligation to repay. Moreover, this treatment balances the fact that the mortgagor originally received the proceeds of the nonrecourse loan tax-free on the same assumption. Unless the outstanding amount of the mortgage is deemed to be realized, the mortgagor effectively will have received untaxed income at the time the loan was extended and will have received an unwarranted increase in the basis of his property.[41] The Commissioner's interpretation of § 1001(b) in this fashion cannot be said to be unreasonable.

C

The Commissioner in fact has applied this rule even when the fair market value of the property falls below the amount of the nonrecourse obligation. Treas.Reg. § 1.1001–2(b), 26 CFR § 1.1001–2(b) (1982);[42] Rev.Rul. 76–111, 1976–1 Cum.Bull. 214. Because the theory on which the rule is based applies equally in this situation, see Millar v. Commissioner, 67 T.C. 656, 660 (1977), aff'd on this issue, 577 F.2d 212, 215–216 (CA3), cert. denied, 439 U.S. 1046, 99 S.Ct. 721, 58 L.Ed.2d 704 (1978);[43] Mendham Corp. v. Commissioner, 9 T.C. 320, 323–324 (1947); Lutz & Schramm Co. v. Commissioner, 1 T.C. 682, 688–689 (1943), we have no reason, after *Crane,* to question this treatment.[44]

41. Although the *Crane* rule has some affinity with the tax benefit rule, see Bittker, supra, at 282; Del Cotto, Sales and Other Dispositions of Property Under Section 1001: The Taxable Event, Amount Realized and Related Problems of Basis, 26 Buffalo L.Rev. 219, 323–324 (1977), the analysis we adopt is different. Our analysis applies even in the situation in which no deductions are taken. It focuses on the obligation to repay and its subsequent extinguishment, not on the taking and recovery of deductions. See generally Note, 82 Colum.L.Rev., at 1526–1529.

42. The regulation was promulgated while this case was pending before the Court of Appeals for the Fifth Circuit. T.D. 7741, 45 Fed.Reg. 81743, 1981–1 Cum. Bull. 430 (1980). It merely formalized the Commissioner's prior interpretation, however.

43. The Court of Appeals for the Third Circuit in *Millar* affirmed the Tax Court on the theory that inclusion of nonrecourse liability in the amount realized was necessary to prevent the taxpayer from enjoying a double deduction. 577 F.2d, at 215; cf. n. 4, supra. Because we resolve the question on another ground, we do not address the validity of the double deduction rationale.

44. Professor Wayne G. Barnett, as amicus in the present case, argues that the liability and property portions of the transaction should be accounted for separately. Under his view, there was a transfer of the property for $1.4 million, and there was a cancellation of the $1.85 million obligation for a payment of $1.4 million. The former resulted in a capital loss of $50,000, and the latter in the realization of $450,000 of ordinary income. Taxation of the ordinary income might be deferred under § 108 by a reduction of respondents' bases in their partnership interests.

Although this indeed could be a justifiable mode of analysis, it has not been adopted by the Commissioner. Nor is there anything to indicate that the Code requires the Commissioner to adopt it. We note that Professor Barnett's approach does assume that recourse and nonrecourse debt may be treated identically.

The Commissioner also has chosen not to characterize the transaction as cancellation of indebtedness. We are not presented with and do not decide the contours of the cancellation-of-indebtedness doctrine. We note only that our approach does not fall within certain prior interpretations of that doctrine. In one view, the doctrine

Respondents received a mortgage loan with the concomitant obligation to repay by the year 2012. The only difference between that mortgage and one on which the borrower is personally liable is that the mortgagee's remedy is limited to foreclosing on the securing property. This difference does not alter the nature of the obligation; its only effect is to shift from the borrower to the lender any potential loss caused by devaluation of the property.[45] If the fair market value of the property falls below the amount of the outstanding obligation, the mortgagee's ability to protect its interests is impaired, for the mortgagor is free to abandon the property to the mortgagee and be relieved of his obligation.

This, however, does not erase the fact that the mortgagor received the loan proceeds tax-free and included them in his basis on the understanding that he had an obligation to repay the full amount. See Woodsam Associates, Inc. v. Commissioner, 198 F.2d 357, 359 (CA2 1952); Bittker, 33 Tax.L.Rev., at 284. When the obligation is canceled, the mortgagor is relieved of his responsibility to repay the sum he originally received and thus realizes value to that extent within the meaning of § 1001(b). From the mortgagor's point of view, when his obligation is assumed by a third party who purchases the encumbered property, it is as if the mortgagor first had been paid with cash borrowed by the third party from the mortgagee on a nonrecourse basis, and then had used the cash to satisfy his obligation to the mortgagee.

rests on the same initial premise as our analysis here—an obligation to repay—but the doctrine relies on a freeing-of-assets theory to attribute ordinary income to the debtor upon cancellation. See Commissioner v. Jacobson, 336 U.S. 28, 38–40, 69 S.Ct. 358, 363–64, 93 L.Ed. 477 (1949); United States v. Kirby Lumber Co., 284 U.S. 1, 3, 52 S.Ct. 4, 76 L.Ed. 131 (1931). According to that view, when nonrecourse debt is forgiven, the debtor's basis in the securing property is reduced by the amount of debt canceled, and realization of income is deferred until the sale of the property. See Fulton Gold Corp. v. Commissioner, 31 B.T.A. 519, 520 (1934). Because that interpretation attributes income only when assets are freed, however, an insolvent debtor realizes income just to the extent his assets exceed his liabilities after the cancellation. Lakeland Grocery Co. v. Commissioner, 36 B.T.A. 289, 292 (1937). Similarly, if the nonrecourse indebtedness exceeds the value of the securing property, the taxpayer never realizes the full amount of the obligation canceled because the tax law has not recognized negative basis.

Although the economic benefit prong of *Crane* also relies on a freeing-of-assets theory, that theory is irrelevant to our broader approach. In the context of a sale or disposition of property under § 1001, the extinguishment of the obligation to repay is not ordinary income; instead, the amount of the canceled debt is included in the amount realized, and enters into the computation of gain or loss on the disposition of property. According to *Crane*, this treatment is no different when the obligation is nonrecourse: the basis is not reduced as in the cancellation-of-indebtedness context, and the full value of the outstanding liability is included in the amount realized. Thus, the problem of negative basis is avoided.

45. In his opinion for the Court of Appeals in *Crane*, Judge Learned Hand observed:

"[The mortgagor] has all the income from the property; he manages it; he may sell it; any increase in its value goes to him; any decrease falls on him, until the value goes below the amount of the lien * * *. When therefore upon a sale the mortgagor makes an allowance to the vendee of the amount of the lien, he secures a release from a charge upon his property quite as though the vendee had paid him the full price on condition that before he took title the lien should be cleared * * *." 153 F.2d 504, 506 (CA2 1945).

Moreover, this approach avoids the absurdity the Court recognized in *Crane*. Because of the remedy accompanying the mortgage in the nonrecourse situation, the depreciation in the fair market value of the property is relevant economically only to the mortgagee, who by lending on a nonrecourse basis remains at risk. To permit the taxpayer to limit his realization to the fair market value of the property would be to recognize a tax loss for which he has suffered no corresponding economic loss.[46] Such a result would be to construe "one section of the Act * * * so as * * * to defeat the intention of another or to frustrate the Act as a whole." 331 U.S., at 13, 67 S.Ct., at 1054.

In the specific circumstances of *Crane*, the economic benefit theory did support the Commissioner's treatment of the nonrecourse mortgage as a personal obligation. The footnote in *Crane* acknowledged the limitations of that theory when applied to a different set of facts. *Crane* also stands for the broader proposition, however, that a nonrecourse loan should be treated as a true loan. We therefore hold that a taxpayer must account for the proceeds of obligations he has received tax-free and included in basis. Nothing in either § 1001(b) or in the Court's prior decisions requires the Commissioner to permit a taxpayer to treat a sale of encumbered property asymmetrically, by including the proceeds of the nonrecourse obligation in basis but not accounting for the proceeds upon transfer of the encumbered property. See Estate of Levine v. Commissioner, 634 F.2d 12, 15 (CA2 1980).

* * *

IV

When a taxpayer sells or disposes of property encumbered by a nonrecourse obligation, the Commissioner properly requires him to include among the assets realized the outstanding amount of the obligation. The fair market value of the property is irrelevant to this calculation. We find this interpretation to be consistent with Crane v. Commissioner, 331 U.S. 1, 67 S.Ct. 1047, 91 L.Ed. 1301 (1947), and to implement the statutory mandate in a reasonable manner. National Muffler Dealers Assn. v. United States, 440 U.S. 472, 476, 99 S.Ct. 1304, 1306, 59 L.Ed.2d 519 (1979).

The judgment of the Court of Appeals is therefore reversed.

It is so ordered.

JUSTICE O'CONNOR, concurring.

46. In the present case, the Government bore the ultimate loss. The nonrecourse mortgage was extended to respondents only after the planned complex was endorsed for mortgage insurance under §§ 221(b) and (d)(4) of the National Housing Act, 12 U.S.C. § 1715*l* (b) and (d)(4) (1976 ed. and Supp. V). After acquiring the complex from respondents, Bayles operated it for a few years, but was unable to make it profitable. In 1974, F & H foreclosed, and the Department of Housing and Urban Development paid off the lender to obtain title. In 1976, the Department sold the complex to another developer for $1,502,000. The sale was financed by the Department's taking back a note for $1,314,800 and a nonrecourse mortgage. To fail to recognize the value of the nonrecourse loan in the amount realized, therefore, would permit respondents to compound the Government's loss by claiming the tax benefits of that loss for themselves.

I concur in the opinion of the Court, accepting the view of the Commissioner. I do not, however, endorse the Commissioner's view. Indeed, were we writing on a slate clean except for the *Crane* decision, I would take quite a different approach—that urged upon us by Professor Barnett as *amicus*.

Crane established that a taxpayer could treat property as entirely his own, in spite of the "coinvestment" provided by his mortgagee in the form of a nonrecourse loan. That is, the full basis of the property, with all its tax consequences, belongs to the mortgagor. That rule alone, though, does not in any way tie nonrecourse debt to the cost of property or to the proceeds upon disposition. I see no reason to treat the purchase, ownership, and eventual disposition of property differently because the taxpayer also takes out a mortgage, an independent transaction. In this case, the taxpayer purchased property, using nonrecourse financing, and sold it after it declined in value to a buyer who assumed the mortgage. There is no economic difference between the events in this case and a case in which the taxpayer buys property with cash; later obtains a nonrecourse loan by pledging the property as security; still later, using cash on hand, buys off the mortgage for the market value of the devalued property; and finally sells the property to a third party for its market value.

The logical way to treat both this case and the hypothesized case is to separate the two aspects of these events and to consider, first, the ownership and sale of the property, and, second, the arrangement and retirement of the loan. Under *Crane*, the fair market value of the property on the date of acquisition—the purchase price—represents the taxpayer's basis in the property, and the fair market value on the date of disposition represents the proceeds on sale. The benefit received by the taxpayer in return for the property is the cancellation of a mortgage that is worth no more than the fair market value of the property, for that is all the mortgagee can expect to collect on the mortgage. His gain or loss on the disposition of the property equals the difference between the proceeds and the cost of acquisition. Thus, the taxation of the transaction *in property* reflects the economic fate of the *property*. If the property has declined in value, as was the case here, the taxpayer recognizes a loss on the disposition of the property. The new purchaser then takes as his basis the fair market value as of the date of the sale. See, e.g., United States v. Davis, 370 U.S. 65, 72, 82 S.Ct. 1190, 1194, 8 L.Ed.2d 335 (1962); Gibson Products Co. v. United States, 637 F.2d 1041, 1045, n. 8 (CA5 1981) (dictum); see generally Treas.Reg. § 1.1001–2(a)(3), 26 CFR § 1.1001–2(a)(3) (1982); B. Bittker, 2 Federal Income Taxation of Income, Estates and Gifts, ¶ 41.2.2., at 41–10–41–11 (1981).

In the separate borrowing transaction, the taxpayer acquires cash from the mortgagee. He need not recognize income at that time, of course, because he also incurs an obligation to repay the money. Later, though, when he is able to satisfy the debt by surrendering property that is worth less than the face amount of the debt, we have a classic situation of cancellation of indebtedness, requiring the taxpayer to recognize income in the amount of the difference between the proceeds of the loan and the amount for which he is able to satisfy his creditor. 26 U.S.C. § 61(a)(12). The taxation of the financing transaction then reflects the economic fate of the loan.

The reason that separation of the two aspects of the events in this case is important is, of course, that the Code treats different sorts of income differently.   *   *   * Not only does Professor Barnett's theory permit us to accord appropriate treatment to each of the two types of income or loss present in these sorts of transactions, it also restores continuity to the system by making the taxpayer-seller's proceeds on the disposition of property equal to the purchaser's basis in the property. Further, and most important, it allows us to tax the events in this case in the same way that we tax the economically identical hypothesized transaction.

Persuaded though I am by the logical coherence and internal consistency of this approach, I agree with the Court's decision not to adopt it judicially. We do not write on a slate marked only by *Crane*. The Commissioner's longstanding position, Rev.Rul. 76–111, 1976–1 C.B. 214, is now reflected in the regulations. Treas.Reg. § 1.1001–2, 26 CFR § 1.1001–2 (1982). In the light of the numerous cases in the lower courts including the amount of the unrepaid proceeds of the mortgage in the proceeds on sale or disposition, see, e.g., Estate of Levine v. Commissioner, 634 F.2d 12, 15 (CA2 1980); Millar v. Commissioner, 577 F.2d 212 (CA3), cert. denied, 439 U.S. 1046, 99 S.Ct. 721, 58 L.Ed.2d 704 (1978); Estate of Delman v. Commissioner, 73 T.C. 15, 28–30 (1979); Peninsula Properties Co., Ltd. v. Commissioner, 47 B.T.A. 84, 92 (1942), it is difficult to conclude that the Commissioner's interpretation of the statute exceeds the bounds of his discretion. As the Court's opinion demonstrates, his interpretation is defensible. One can reasonably read § 1001(b)'s reference to "the amount realized *from* the sale or other disposition of property" (emphasis added) to permit the Commissioner to collapse the two aspects of the transaction. As long as his view is a reasonable reading of § 1001(b), we should defer to the regulations promulgated by the agency charged with interpretation of the statute. National Muffler Dealers Association v. United States, 440 U.S. 472, 488–489, 99 S.Ct. 1304, 1312–13, 59 L.Ed.2d 519 (1979); United States v. Correll, 389 U.S. 299, 307, 88 S.Ct. 445, 449, 19 L.Ed.2d 537 (1967); see also Fulman v. United States, 434 U.S. 528, 534, 98 S.Ct. 841, 845, 55 L.Ed.2d 1 (1978). Accordingly, I concur.

Questions

1. What basis did the purchaser in the Tufts case take, $1.8 million, $1.4 million or 0? Consider the Estate of Franklin case (page 798 of this chapter), §§ 1274(b)(3) and 7701(g).

2. Assume the purchaser in the Tufts case used a $1.4 million basis for the property and took depreciation deductions of $200,000, paid

$200,000 to reduce the principal of the loan, and then abandoned the property. What are the tax consequences to the purchaser? Consider Reg. § 1.1001–2(a)(3).

————

In Allan v. Commissioner, 86 T.C. 655 (1986), the court applied the Tufts rationale (that an obligation be included in the amount realized), holding that an obligation that was not included in the basis of any asset, but was deducted instead, must be included as part of the amount realized. The taxpayer had taken deductions for mortgage interest and real estate taxes because it used the accrual method of accounting. The taxpayer never paid its obligations for taxes and interest and later transferred the property to the mortgage holder in lieu of foreclosure. What would have been the result in this situation had the taxpayer in Allan used the cash method of accounting and never taken a deduction for the liability for real estate taxes and mortgage interest? Examine § 108(e)(2) and problem 5 at p. 241.

4. FURTHER IMPLICATIONS OF LIABILITIES ON BASIS

It is universally accepted that a liability (including nonrecourse loans) incurred as part of the acquisition of property is included in the basis of that property. The Mayerson case considers this bedrock principal of tax law. The Estate of Franklin case illustrates a well-established, but draconian, exception to this proposition.

MAYERSON v. COMMISSIONER
Tax Court of the United States, 1966.
47 T.C. 340.

[Taxpayer wished to purchase a building from the seller. Conventional bank financing was unavailable because of the building's age and bad condition. Taxpayer bought the building for $332,500 by paying $5,000 immediately and $5,000 within the first month of the next tax year. The remainder of the purchase price was paid by taxpayer giving the seller a nonrecourse purchase money mortgage (that is, the seller of the property financed the purchase) calling for annual interest payments on the mortgage. No principal payments were required for 99 years, when the entire principal would become due. The taxpayer had the option of finding conventional mortgage financing and paying off the entire purchase money obligation within the first two years. Five years after the "sale," the taxpayer obtained a conventional mortgage loan from a financial institution. The taxpayer and the seller agreed to discharge the note and the purchase-money mortgage for $200,000. The issue was whether the taxpayer's basis was $10,000 or $332,500 (the cash down payment plus the nonrecourse mortgage).]

HOYT, JUDGE: * * *

ULTIMATE FINDINGS OF FACTS

The petitioner acquired the 8th and Walnut Building in an arm's-length transaction which constituted a bona fide purchase and created a valid debt obligation. Petitioner's gross investment in this property for computing depreciation for the years 1960 and 1961 was $332,500.

OPINION

* * *

Respondent determined that petitioner's claimed deduction for depreciation of the 8th and Walnut Building was excessive and not allowable under section 167 during the years in question. A depreciation deduction is allowed for property used in a trade or business or held for the production of income. Section 167(g) of the Code provides that the basis for the depreciation deduction is the adjusted basis provided in section 1011 for the purpose of determining the gain on the sale or other disposition of such property. Generally, the adjusted basis for determining gain or loss from the sale of property is the amount paid for such property in cash or other property. Sec. 1.1012–1, Income Tax Regs. Thus, in a situation of outright purchase, the amount paid for the property constitutes the depreciable basis. Moreover, it is well accepted that a purchase-money debt obligation for part of the price will be included in basis. This is necessary in order to equate a purchase-money mortgage situation with the situation in which the buyer borrows the full amount of the purchase price from a third party and pays the seller in cash. It is clear that the depreciable basis should be the same in both instances.

Respondent's position is essentially that the purchase-money mortgage involved in this case was a nullity and that a capital investment in the subject property had not occurred. The $10,000 cash downpayment was treated [by the respondent] as the cost of obtaining a 99-year lease, thus qualifying for amortization deductions over the term of the lease. This treatment gives rise to the inference that respondent determined that the transaction actually resulted in the creation of a long-term lease. On brief, respondent adds the additional contention that in effect all petitioner acquired was an option to purchase at any time during the alleged lease.

Respondent's position apparently results from his objections to certain features of the purchase-money mortgage. Petitioner was not personally liable on the mortgage, and the only recourse available to the mortgagee in case of default was foreclosure against the property; the property was the only security under the mortgage agreement. Respondent argues that when there is no enforceable and binding personal obligation with respect to the purchase price, no debt is created.

The absence of a debt is also indicated by the indefinite amount of the alleged obligation, according to respondent. This is evidently a reference to the fact that petitioner could pay off the mortgage in the first or 2 succeeding years with an amount stipulated in the purchase-money mortgage which was less than the face amount due after the expiration of 3 years. Thus, the amount due on the mortgage could fluctuate between three different sums depending upon whether payment occurred within the first year, the second, or third year, or years thereafter.

Respondent also emphasizes the fact that after two initial payments of $5,000 each, no portion of the principal of the purchase-money mortgage was due on or before 99 years from the date of the obligation. Petitioner did have the option, however, to make payments of principal at any time during the term of the mortgage. Petitioner was obligated to pay a fixed sum of $18,000 per year, designated as interest, in monthly installments. If the principal due on the mortgage was reduced below $300,000, then interest was payable at the rate of 6 percent per year on the unpaid balance.

It is undisputed that petitioner became the owner of legal title to the 8th and Walnut Building. There is no hint of a sham transaction in the transfer of title to the building and respondent makes no contention that the transaction was a sham or rigged to appear to be a sale and mortgage back when it was in fact something else. We are concerned with an arm's-length transaction entered into between knowledgeable strangers for business motives. It is well accepted, however, that depreciation is not predicated upon ownership of property but rather upon an investment in property. Gladding Dry Goods Co., 2 B.T.A. 336 (1925). It therefore follows that the benefit of the depreciation deduction should inure to those who would suffer an economic loss caused by wear and exhaustion of the business property. See Thomas W. Blake, Jr., 20 T.C. 721 (1953).

Respondent relies upon the preceding cases and general statements in Weiss v. Wiener, 279 U.S. 333 (1929), to the effect that only a capital investment is depreciable, to support his view that the petitioner did not have a depreciable interest in the 8th and Walnut Building.

We must first decide whether the absence of personal liability with respect to the purchase-money mortgage precludes the inclusion of any amount attributable to the mortgage in the depreciable basis of the property. If this is true, depreciation based on the purchase-money mortgage should be denied regardless of the existence of a bona fide debt obligation for the mortgage. An analysis of this question must begin with the Supreme Court's landmark decision in Crane v. Commissioner, 331 U.S. 1 (1947). The *Crane* case involved the question of what the proper basis of inherited property was for the purpose of computing the taxable gain on the sale of the property. The property was received subject to an unassumed mortgage and was sold still so encumbered. The Court held that the basis of the property was the value at the date of death undiminished by the mortgage. The inclusion of the indebtedness in basis was balanced by a similar inclusion of the indebtedness in amount realized upon the ultimate sale of the property to a nonassuming grantee.

The relevance of the *Crane* case to the issue of depreciable basis arises due to section 167(g) which states that the basis for depreciation shall be the same as the basis for gain or loss on a sale or exchange under section 1011. Thus, the *Crane* case constitutes strong authority for the proposition that the basis used for depreciation as well as the computation of gain or loss would include the amount of an unassumed mortgage on the property.

This position was expressly adopted by this Court in Blackstone Theatre Co., 12 T.C. 801, 804 (1949), acq. 1949-2 C.B. 1, with the following language:

> From *Crane* we can deduce the following applicable principles: (a) the basis for given property includes liens thereon, even though not personally assumed by the taxpayer; and (b) the depreciation allowance should be computed on the full amount of this basis. * * *

The respondent argues that the *Crane* case should not apply in a purchase situation since the basis in that case started with fair market value and not cost, as in the case of a purchase. The reasoning of the *Crane* case, however, seems equally applicable to a purchase situation and indeed was so applied in the Blackstone Theatre Co. case and Parker v. Delaney, 186 F.2d 455 (C.A.1, 1950). It should also be applied here.

The element of the lack of personal liability has little real significance due to common business practices. As we have indicated in our findings it is not at all unusual in current mortgage financing of income-producing properties to limit liability to the property involved. Taxpayers who are not personally liable for encumbrances on property should be allowed depreciation deductions affording competitive equality with taxpayers who are personally liable for encumbrances or taxpayers who own unencumbered property. The effect of such a policy is to give the taxpayer an advance credit for the amount of the mortgage. This appears to be reasonable since it can be assumed that a capital investment in the amount of the mortgage will eventually occur despite the absence of personal liability. The respondent has not suggested any rationale that would reasonably require a contrary conclusion. The lien created by the purchase-money mortgage, like the tax liens in the *Blackstone Theatre* case, should be included in basis for the purpose of computing depreciation.

Having determined that the absence of personal liability with respect to a purchase-money mortgage does not preclude the inclusion of the mortgage in the depreciable basis of the property, we must decide whether the purchase-money mortgage involved in this case should be considered a bona fide debt obligation. Respondent argues that even if the usual purchase-money mortgage should be included in depreciable basis, this doctrine would be inapplicable in a situation where the alleged debt instrument does not create any obligation to pay the purchase price.

The bases for respondent's contention that no debt obligation was created are the absence of personal liability on the mortgage and the fact that the principal of the mortgage was not due for 99 years. We have already discussed the relative unimportance of personal liability in modern business transactions. We hold that this does not affect the validity of the mortgage debt. Therefore, if we are to conclude that there was no debt it must be because of the 99-year term for maturity. Although this term does seem unusually long, after viewing the totality of the circumstances and all the evidence of record we have found and hold that a valid debt obligation was created by the purchase-money mortgage in question.

Contrary to respondent's asserted position, we do not believe that this transaction was in reality or substance a lease with an option to purchase. The uncontroverted testimony of petitioner and a representative of the [seller] was that a sale was intended with an understanding that there would be a conversion to institutional mortgage financing as soon as possible. These witnesses were forthright, impressive, and entirely believable. It is clear that the 99-year term was never expected to run its course, but even absent this factor, it should be realized that a definite contractual obligation was created which would have had to be fulfilled by or before a definite date in the future. The sales transaction was normal in every other way, and the actions of the parties to the transaction certainly support our conclusions that a bona fide sale occurred and a valid debt obligation for most of the purchase price was created. Petitioner invested in improvements for the building and undertook the usual duties of a property owner. He worked diligently to find the highest and best use for the property so that he could obtain conventional financing. Within a few years he succeeded and retired the mortgage as the parties understood and hoped.

As we view the evidence before us, we do not have a substance versus form situation here because substance and form coincide. Although it can be argued that the economic realities of the transaction would be the same whether the transaction was characterized as a sale with a purchase-money mortgage or a long-term lease with an option to purchase at any time, the evidence is convincing that the parties to the transaction intended a sale and mortgage and the form was consistent with this intent. We therefore hold that the transaction was in substance as well as form an effective sale and purchase-money mortgage for income tax purposes.

Respondent's final argument for denial of the depreciation deductions on the 8th and Walnut Building is based on the proposition that even though the purchase-money mortgage imposed an obligation on petitioner, the obligation cannot be considered as part of the depreciable basis since the cost of property for the purpose of determining basis for depreciation does not include any amount with respect to obligations which are contingent and indefinite in nature. Columbus & Greenville Railway Co., 42 T.C. 834 (1964); Albany Car Wheel Co., 40 T.C. 831 (1963), affirmed per curiam 333 F.2d 653 (C.A.2, 1964); Lloyd H. Redford, 28 T.C. 773 (1957). An example of the type of contingency referred to in the preceding proposition was present in the Albany Car Wheel Co. case. In that case we found that the purchaser-taxpayer's obligation under the purchase agreement to procure a release of the predecessor's liability under a union contract for severance pay was of such a contingent nature that it could not be considered a part of the cost of the assets acquired. Whether it would ever be necessary to satisfy any severance pay obligations was unknown at the time of the sale.

Similarly, in the *Lloyd H. Redford* case the amount of a note was held not to be includable in basis since the note was only payable from profits and it was uncertain whether there would ever be profits.

It was held in the *Columbus & Greenville Railway Co.* case that basis did not include any amount of a mortgage where there was no primary responsibility and no fixed indebtedness for which the taxpayer or its property was liable.

We hold that the doctrine supported by the foregoing cases is inapplicable to the subject purchase-money mortgage. Respondent contends that the amount of the obligation was indefinite because of the varying amounts due under the terms of the instrument and the fact that the purchase-money mortgage was eventually settled for the negotiated price of $200,000, a substantial reduction from the amount due under the instrument.

There were only two variables in the overall purchase price of the property, and they were specified in dollar amounts. The price depended then upon whether the purchase-money mortgage was paid within the first year, the second year, or years thereafter. We would classify such a price reduction for early payment as a bonus discount. The presence of such optional discounts does not make the purchase price indefinite. It merely provided an incentive for very early retirement of the mortgage which did not occur. The cost basis at the time of purchase should be the nondiscount price; the entire principal of the note and mortgage was due unless the discounted sums were paid in the first 2 years. It was not prepaid so as to provide for the application of the discount provisions and hence no adjustment in basis is required during the years before us. It is evident from the record that if the lien on the property provided by the mortgage were to be discharged at any time prior to its due date, the then fixed amount would necessarily have to be paid. There was nothing contingent or indefinite about the obligation here.

The subsequent settlement of the purchase-money mortgage for less than the amount due under the terms of the instrument should not affect the allowable depreciation in taxable years prior to the settlement. In the *Blackstone Theatre Co.* case, the taxpayer acquired real estate with outstanding tax liens exceeding $120,000. Although there was no personal liability as to these liens and although the liens were settled 5 years after the acquisition for $50,000, the depreciable basis for the intervening years was held to include the full $120,000. Here we are concerned with an arm's-length business transaction and there is no logical basis for disregarding the purchase price provided for in the purchase-money mortgage.

* * *

Decision will be entered under Rule 50.

Although the Internal Revenue Service acquiesced in the Mayerson decision, 1969–1 C.B. 21, the Service emphasized "that its acquiescence in Mayerson is based on the particular facts in the case and will not be relied upon in the disposition of other cases except in situations where it is clear that the property has been acquired at its fair market value in an arm's length transaction creating a bona fide purchase and a bona fide debt obligation." Rev.Rul. 69–77, 1969–1 C.B. 59.

Question

Why do purchasers of real estate feel so strongly about including nonrecourse loans as part of the property's basis?

ESTATE OF FRANKLIN v. COMMISSIONER
United States Court of Appeals, Ninth Circuit, 1967.
544 F.2d 1045.

SNEED, CIRCUIT JUDGE:

This case involves another effort on the part of the Commissioner to curb the use of real estate tax shelters.[47] In this instance he seeks to disallow deductions for the taxpayers' distributive share of losses reported by a limited partnership with respect to its acquisition of a motel and related property. These "losses" have their origin in deductions for depreciation and interest claimed with respect to the motel and related property. These deductions were disallowed by the Commissioner on the ground either that the acquisition was a sham or that the entire acquisition transaction was in substance the purchase by the

---

47. An early skirmish in this particular effort appears in Manuel D. Mayerson, 47 T.C. 340 (1966), which the Commissioner lost. The Commissioner attacked the substance of a nonrecourse sale, but based his attack on the nonrecourse and long-term nature of the purchase money note, without focusing on whether the sale was made at an unrealistically high price. In his acquiescence to Mayerson, 1969–2 Cum. Bull. xxiv, the Commissioner recognized that the fundamental issue in these cases generally will be whether the property has been "acquired" at an artificially high price, having little relation to its fair market value. "The Service emphasizes that its acquiescence in Mayerson is based on the particular facts in the case and will not be relied upon in the disposition of other cases except where it is clear that the property has been acquired at its fair market value in an arm's length transaction creating a bona fide purchase and a bona fide debt obligation." Rev.Rul. 69–77, 1969–1 Cum.Bull. 59.

partnership of an option to acquire the motel and related property on January 15, 1979. The Tax Court held that the transaction constituted an option exercisable in 1979 and disallowed the taxpayers' deductions. Estate of Charles T. Franklin, 64 T.C. 752 (1975). We affirm this disallowance although our approach differs somewhat from that of the Tax Court.

The interest and depreciation deductions were taken by Twenty-Fourth Property Associates (hereinafter referred to as Associates), a California limited partnership of which Charles T. Franklin and seven other doctors were the limited partners. The deductions flowed from the purported "purchase" by Associates of the Thunderbird Inn, an Arizona motel, from Wayne L. Romney and Joan E. Romney (hereinafter referred to as the Romneys) on November 15, 1968.

Under a document entitled "Sales Agreement," the Romneys agreed to "sell" the Thunderbird Inn to Associates for $1,224,000. The property would be paid for over a period of ten years, with interest on any unpaid balance of seven and one-half percent per annum. "Prepaid interest" in the amount of $75,000 was payable immediately; monthly principal and interest installments of $9,045.36 would be paid for approximately the first ten years, with Associates required to make a balloon payment at the end of the ten years of the difference between the remaining purchase price, forecast as $975,000, and any mortgages then outstanding against the property.

The purchase obligation of Associates to the Romneys was nonrecourse; the Romneys' only remedy in the event of default would be forfeiture of the partnership's interest. The sales agreement was recorded in the local county. A warranty deed was placed in an escrow account, along with a quitclaim deed from Associates to the Romneys, both documents to be delivered either to Associates upon full payment of the purchase price, or to the Romneys upon default.

The sale was combined with a leaseback of the property by Associates to the Romneys; Associates therefore never took physical possession. The lease payments were designed to approximate closely the principal and interest payments with the consequence that with the exception of the $75,000 prepaid interest payment no cash would cross between Associates and Romneys until the balloon payment. The lease was on a net basis; thus, the Romneys were responsible for all of the typical expenses of owning the motel property including all utility costs, taxes, assessments, rents, charges, and levies of "every name, nature and kind whatsoever." The Romneys also were to continue to be responsible for the first and second mortgages until the final purchase installment was made; the Romneys could, and indeed did, place additional mortgages on the property without the permission of Associates. Finally, the Romneys were allowed to propose new capital improvements which Associates would be required to either build themselves or allow the Romneys to construct with compensating modifications in rent or purchase price.

In holding that the transaction between Associates and the Romneys more nearly resembled an option than a sale, the Tax Court emphasized that Associates had the power at the end of ten years to walk away from the transaction and merely lose its $75,000 "prepaid interest payment." It also pointed out that a *deed* was never recorded and that the "benefits and burdens of ownership" appeared to remain with the Romneys. Thus, the sale was combined with a leaseback in which no cash would pass; the Romneys remained responsible under the mortgages, which they could increase; and the Romneys could make capital improvements.[48] The Tax Court further justified its "option" characterization by reference to the nonrecourse nature of the purchase money debt and the nice balance between the rental and purchase money payments.

Our emphasis is different from that of the Tax Court. We believe the characteristics set out above can exist in a situation in which the sale imposes upon the purchaser a genuine indebtedness within the meaning of section 167(a), Internal Revenue Code of [1986], which will support both interest and depreciation deductions. They substantially so existed in Hudspeth v. Commissioner, 509 F.2d 1224 (9th Cir.1975) in which parents entered into sale-leaseback transactions with their children. The children paid for the property by executing nonnegotiable notes and mortgages equal to the fair market value of the property; state law proscribed deficiency judgments in case of default, limiting the parents' remedy to foreclosure of the property. The children had no funds with which to make mortgage payments; instead, the payments were offset in part by the rental payments, with the difference met by gifts from the parents to their children. Despite these characteristics this court held that there was a bona fide indebtedness on which the children, to the extent of the rental payments, could base interest deductions. See also American Realty Trust v. United States, 498 F.2d 1194 (4th Cir.1974); Manuel D. Mayerson, 47 T.C. 340 (1966).

In none of these cases, however, did the taxpayer fail to demonstrate that the purchase price was at least approximately equivalent to the fair market value of the property. Just such a failure occurred here. The Tax Court explicitly found that on the basis of the facts before it the value of the property could not be estimated. 64 T.C. at 767–768.[49] In our view this defect in the taxpayers' proof is fatal.

48. There was evidence that not all of the benefits and burdens of ownership remained with the Romneys. Thus, for example, the leaseback agreement appears to provide that any condemnation award will go to Associates. Exhibit 6–F, at p. 5.

49. The Tax Court found that appellants had "not shown that the purported sales price of $1,224,000 (or any other price) had any relationship to the actual market value of the motel property * * *." 64 T.C. at 767.

Petitioners spent a substantial amount of time at trial attempting to establish that, whatever the actual market value of the property, Associates acted in the good faith *belief* that the market value of the property approximated the selling price. However, this evidence only goes to the issue of sham and does not supply substance to this transaction. "Save in those instances where the statute itself turns on intent, a matter so real as taxation must depend on objective realities, not on the varying subjective beliefs of individual tax-

Reason supports our perception. An acquisition such as that of Associates if at a price approximately equal to the fair market value of the property under ordinary circumstances would rather quickly yield an equity in the property which the purchaser could not prudently abandon. This is the stuff of substance. It meshes with the form of the transaction and constitutes a sale.

No such meshing occurs when the purchase price exceeds a demonstrably reasonable estimate of the fair market value. Payments on the principal of the purchase price yield no equity so long as the unpaid balance of the purchase price exceeds the then existing fair market value. Under these circumstances the purchaser by abandoning the transaction can lose no more than a mere chance to acquire an equity in the future should the value of the acquired property increase. While this chance undoubtedly influenced the Tax Court's determination that the transaction before us constitutes an option, we need only point out that its existence fails to supply the substance necessary to justify treating the transaction as a sale *ab initio*. It is not necessary to the disposition of this case to decide the tax consequences of a transaction such as that before us if in a subsequent year the fair market value of the property increases to an extent that permits the purchaser to acquire an equity.[50]

Authority also supports our perception. It is fundamental that "depreciation is not predicated upon ownership of property *but rather upon an investment in property*. Gladding Dry Goods Co., 2 BTA 336 (1925)." *Mayerson*, supra at 350 (italics added). No such investment exists when payments of the purchase price in accordance with the

payers." Lynch v. Commissioner, 273 F.2d 867, 872 (2d Cir.1959). See also Bornstein v. Commissioner, 334 F.2d 779 (1st Cir. 1964); MacRae v. Commissioner, 294 F.2d 56 (9th Cir.1961).

In oral argument it was suggested by the appellants that neither the Tax Court nor they recognized the importance of fair market value during the presentation of evidence and that this hampered the full and open development of this issue. However, upon an examination of the record, we are satisfied that the taxpayers recognized the importance of presenting objective evidence of the fair market value and were awarded ample opportunity to present their proof; appellants merely failed to present clear and admissible evidence that fair market value did indeed approximate the purchase price. Such evidence of fair market value as was relied upon by the appellants, *viz.* two appraisals, one completed in 1968 and a second in 1971, even if fully admissible as evidence of the truth of the estimates of value appearing therein, does not require us to set aside the Tax Court's finding. As the Tax Court found, the 1968 appraisal was "error-filled,

sketchy" and "obviously suspect." 64 T.C. at 767 n. 13. The 1971 appraisal had little relevancy as to 1968 values. On the other side, there existed cogent evidence indicating that the fair market value was substantially less than the purchase price. This evidence included (i) the Romneys' purchase of the stock of two corporations, one of which wholly-owned the motel, for approximately $800,000 in the year preceding the "sale" to Associates ($660,000 of which was allocable to the sale property, according to Mr. Romney's estimate), and (ii) insurance policies on the property from 1967 through 1974 of only $583,200, $700,000, and $614,000. 64 T.C. at 767–768.

Given that it was the appellants' burden to present evidence showing that the purchase price did not exceed the fair market value and that he had a fair opportunity to do so, we see no reason to remand this case for further proceedings.

50. These consequences would include a determination of the proper basis of the acquired property at the date the increments to the purchaser's equity commenced.

design of the parties yield no equity to the purchaser. Cf. Decon Corp., 65 T.C. 829 (1976); David F. Bolger, 59 T.C. 760 (1973); Edna Morris, 59 T.C. 21 (1972). In the transaction before us and during the taxable years in question the purchase price payments by Associates have not been shown to constitute an *investment in the property*. Depreciation was properly disallowed. Only the Romneys had an investment in the property.

Authority also supports disallowance of the interest deductions. This is said even though it has long been recognized that the absence of personal liability for the purchase money debt secured by a mortgage on the acquired property does not deprive the debt of its character as a bona fide debt obligation able to support an interest deduction. *Mayerson*, supra at 352. However, this is no longer true when it appears that the debt has economic significance only if the property substantially appreciates in value prior to the date at which a very large portion of the purchase price is to be discharged. Under these circumstances the purchaser has not secured "the use or forbearance of money." See Norton v. Commissioner, 474 F.2d 608, 610 (9th Cir.1973). Nor has the seller advanced money or forborne its use. See Bornstein v. Commissioner, 334 F.2d 779, 780 (1st Cir.1964); Lynch v. Commissioner, 273 F.2d 867, 871–872 (2d Cir.1959). Prior to the date at which the balloon payment on the purchase price is required, and assuming no substantial increase in the fair market value of the property, the absence of personal liability on the debt reduces the transaction in economic terms to a mere chance that a genuine debt obligation may arise. This is not enough to justify an interest deduction. To justify the deduction the debt must exist; potential existence will not do. For debt to exist, the purchaser, in the absence of personal liability, must confront a situation in which it is presently reasonable from an economic point of view for him to make a capital investment in the amount of the unpaid purchase price. See *Mayerson*, supra at 352.[51] Associates, during the taxable years in question, confronted no such situation. Compare Crane v. Commissioner, 331 U.S. 1, 11–12, 67 S.Ct. 1047, 91 L.Ed. 1301 (1947).

Our focus on the relationship of the fair market value of the property to the unpaid purchase price should not be read as premised upon the belief that a sale is not a sale if the purchaser pays too much. Bad bargains from the buyer's point of view—as well as sensible bargains from buyer's, but exceptionally good from the seller's point of view—do not thereby cease to be sales. See Commissioner v. Brown, 380 U.S. 563, 67 S.Ct. 1047, 91 L.Ed. 1301 (1965); Union Bank v. United States, 285 F.2d 126, 128, 152 Ct.Cl. 126 (1961). We intend our holding

---

51. Emphasis on the fair market value of the property in relation to the apparent purchase price animates the spirit, if not the letter, of Rev.Rul. 69–77, 1969–1 Cum. Bull. 59.

and explanation thereof to be understood as limited to transactions substantially similar to that now before us.

Affirmed.

Section 6659 provides for a penalty if the value or the adjusted basis of property reported on any income tax return exceeds 150 percent of the correct value or adjusted basis. The penalty equals a percentage of the underpayment of tax resulting from the overstatement of value or adjusted basis. The percentage depends on the size of the overstatement of value or adjusted basis.

Questions

1. Why was the purchaser in Estate of Franklin willing to pay more for the property than the property was worth?

2. As a result of the Estate of Franklin case, what was the buyer's basis in the property? Was the mortgage includible in the property's basis?

5. CONTINGENT LIABILITIES

Liabilities which are contingent and indefinite are not included in the purchaser's basis. In the following case analyze how the court concluded that severance pay dependent on the number of employees remaining on a firm's payroll in the event of a future plant closing was deemed a contingent liability.

ALBANY CAR WHEEL CO. v. COMMISSIONER

Tax Court of the United States, 1963.
40 T.C. 8321, affirmed per curiam 333 F.2d 653 (2d Cir.1964).

Respondent determined a deficiency in income tax of petitioner in the amount of $16,959.40 for the year 1955.

The sole question is whether petitioner overstated its cost basis in computing depreciation and gain on sale with respect to certain assets which it purchased in 1955.

* * *

The starting point in this case is section 1012 of the [1986] Code which provides that "The basis of property shall be the cost of such property * * * [except in certain situations not applicable here]." Accordingly, the decisive question before us is: What did petitioner pay for the assets that it acquired from the Old Co.?

According to the stipulation of facts and the evidence before us, petitioner paid $15,000 in cash on a note to the Old Co., and assumed certain specified liabilities of the Old Co. in the net amount of $74,360.35. The Commissioner insists that the sum of these two figures, namely, $89,360.35, represents the "cost" of the assets purchased. Petitioner, on the other hand, claimed a cost of $137,543.95, which was the book value of the assets in the hands of the Old Co. Petitioner undertook to support its higher cost basis by contending that, in addition to the foregoing $89,360.35 which it paid for the assets in the manner described, it also assumed an obligation of the Old Co. for severance pay to its employees under a union contract, that such obligation was equal to at least the difference between the $89,360.35 and the book value of the assets in the hands of the Old Co., and that it therefore represented an additional item of cost for the assets which it thus acquired. We disagree. We hold that although petitioner did in fact procure the cancellation of the Old Co.'s contingent liability in respect of severance pay by executing a new and different type of contract with the union, petitioner's obligation under the new contract was of such contingent character that it could not be considered part of the cost of the assets which it acquired, and that any such obligation which might actually result in a fixed liability in a later year may properly be taken into account in petitioner's behalf as a deduction in such later year.

The Old Co.'s contract with the union provided that, upon permanent closing of the plant, employees with from 1 to 5 years of service were to be allowed 4 weeks' severance pay and employees with 5 or more years of service were to be allowed 8 weeks' severance pay. It had 111 employees in 1955, and when Cooley was negotiating for the purchase of the assets, he was naturally concerned about any liability that might result in respect of severance pay, particularly since the chilled iron wheel industry was moribund. Indeed the evidence shows that he had calculations made showing that if the plant were to close at that time, the liability for severance pay would be approximately $48,000 in respect of the employees then working for the Old Co. Had the petitioner assumed fixed obligations in any such amount we would agree that such assumption would constitute a part of its cost of the assets acquired. But that is not what occurred.

In the first place, and perhaps of lesser importance, the Old Co.'s contract in respect of severance pay spelled out a liability to employees *as of the time of closing.* There was no liability for severance pay in respect of those employees who had died or who had voluntarily terminated their employment.[52] In the second place, and of greater significance here, petitioner did not assume the Old Co.'s liabilities in respect of severance pay. While it is true that section XXII of petitioner's new agreement with the union recites that "The Union recognizes

52. Thus, of the 111 employees in 1955, only 58 remained in 1960 when the plant was actually closed, and if petitioner had in fact assumed the Old Co.'s obligations under the contract in force in 1955, its contingent liability in respect of the 111 employees would have become fixed only as to 58 of them. And of course, any liability to employees hired after petitioner began business could not properly be regarded as part of the cost of the assets acquired from the Old Co.

that by entering into this Agreement the present Company has in effect assumed substantially the same obligations to the Union and to the employees as those which had been undertaken by the predecessor Company," the fact is that petitioner did not assume the Old Co.'s obligations and that its own obligations under the new contract were radically different from those of the Old Co.

Petitioner's obligations, set forth in section XIV of the new contract, revolved primarily around *notice*. Under these provisions petitioner's liability to its employees at the time of permanent closing of the plant could be met by giving 6 weeks' written notice to employees with from 1 to 5 years of service and 12 weeks' written notice to employees with 5 or more years of service.[53] Petitioner was liable for severance pay under the new contract only where it failed to give the specified notice. And the record shows that when petitioner in fact determined to close its plant in 1960 it gave the required notice to its employees. As a consequence, it paid their wages for work performed during the 6- or 12-week periods prior to closing, but they received no severance pay whatever. Those wages were deducted in petitioner's 1960 income tax return, in determining cost of goods sold in that year. Petitioner recognizes that it cannot have it both ways—i.e., it concedes that if it is entitled to have severance pay included as part of the cost of assets acquired in 1955, the deduction for wages paid in 1960 must be reduced by a like amount. However, we think that petitioner's method of reporting for 1960 was correct, that the wages paid in that year during the notice period prior to closing were properly deductible in 1960, and that they were not in any part a component of the "cost" of the assets acquired in 1955.

Of course, there was always the possibility that petitioner might become liable for severance pay, if, for example, the plant should burn down and the employees were thrown out of work without having received the required notice. But petitioner protected itself against this contingency by insurance, and the premiums paid therefor were plainly deductible as a business expense. We think that petitioner's liability for severance pay, in view of the notice provisions, was so speculative that its obligations under the union contract cannot fairly be regarded as part of the "cost" of the assets acquired from the Old Co. To the extent that any liability might accrue in a later year as a result of that contract, payments thereunder may properly be taken into account at such later time; they may not be used to increase the cost of

---

53. The union construed the contract under the seniority provisions as applying also to employees who had been laid off within 2 years, and, under this interpretation, petitioner was compelled to rehire 14 employees for periods of 6 weeks each at the time of closing in 1960. However, the evidence discloses that every one of these 14 employees was originally hired by petitioner several years after it commenced business in 1955, and petitioner had incurred no obligation as to them, contingent or otherwise, when it acquired the assets of the Old Co.

goods sold in an earlier year or to increase the amount of the depreciation allowance for such earlier year.

Both parties have cited a number of cases, which we have examined and considered. However, we find that none of them is sufficiently close to the present case to warrant discussion.

Decision will be entered for the respondent.

Questions

1. After reading the Meyerson, Estate of Franklin, and Albany Car Wheel cases, when is (and should) a liability be included in basis?

2. Compare the approach used in Estate of Franklin to deny the taxpayer a basis to that used in Albany Car Wheel. How do they differ?

3. Reconsider Question 1, page 791 of this chapter.

In Commercial Security Bank v. Commissioner, 77 T.C. 145 (1981) the Tax Court held that the diminution in the sales price received by the seller on account of the buyer agreeing to pay the seller's "accrued business liabilities" was the equivalent of the seller paying off these liabilities. Therefore, the seller could deduct the accrued liabilities as paid. The buyer, according to the court in David R. Webb Co. v. Commissioner, 708 F.2d 1254 (7th Cir.1983), affirming 77 T.C. 1134 (1981), does not receive a deduction for paying off the seller's liability. Instead, the amount of the payment becomes part of the purchase price and thus comprises part of the basis of the acquired property.

In Zappo v. Commissioner, 81 T.C. 77 (1983), the Tax Court held that the taxpayers could not reduce the amount of their debt cancellation income by the future possibility of having to make additional payments. A contingent liability did not constitute a sufficient liability to prevent debt cancellation income.

The Taxpayers in Zappo borrowed money in connection with a real estate venture from New Investors. Subsequently, after a dispute with the lender, they entered into a settlement agreement in which they transferred their shares in the real estate venture company to New Investors in exchange for a release from the prior loan obligations. On the same day, the taxpayers sold the incompleted properties for cash and a contingent agreement to pay up to $78,500 of the profit on the properties. Taxpayers guaranteed that the former lender would receive at least $53,500 under the contingent agreement. The taxpayers contended that their obligations under the guarantee agreement offset their discharge of indebtedness income. After holding that the existence of separate agreements did not overcome the fact that the two agreements were inseparably linked, the Tax Court rejected the argument that the taxpayers were entitled to offset the two obligations. The court reasoned as follows (81 T.C. at 89):

When an obligation is highly contingent and has no presently ascertainable value, it cannot refinance or substitute for the discharge of a true debt. The very uncertainty of the highly contingent replacement obligation prevents it from reencumbering assets freed by discharge of the true debt until some indeterminable date when the contingencies are removed. In a word, there is no real continuation of indebtedness when a highly contingent obligation is substituted for a true debt. Consequently, the rule in *Kirby Lumber* applies, and gain is realized to the extent the taxpayer is discharged from the initial indebtedness.

This approach, which merely affects the timing of tax consequences, was summarized concisely by the First Circuit as follows:

> it is simpler, when faced with obligations to pay that are highly uncertain, to wait and see if the contingency occurs. If it does not occur, the obligations need never enter basis, for they do not represent any obligation to pay. If it does occur, the extent of the monetary obligation will be reasonably capable of calculation, and * * * can then be determined. [*Brountas v. Commissioner*]

We find this approach applicable to the case before us.

Problems

1. Sheila owns property encumbered by a $260,000 mortgage. She is personally liable on the mortgage. Bob buys the property from Sheila. He pays $40,000 cash for the property and assumes the mortgage liability. What is the amount realized on the sale? Would it make any difference for basis purposes if the mortgage was nonrecourse? Consider Reg. § 1.1001–2(a) and (b) (read carefully) and the Crane and Tufts cases (respectively, pp. 766 and 782 of this chapter).

2. Terri Player purchased an apartment house for $200,000 in Year 1, paying $50,000 in cash and borrowing $150,000 from a bank, secured by a first mortgage with recourse on the property. She held the building for investment purposes. By the end of Year 4, the property increased in value to $400,000 and Terri had taken depreciation deductions of $25,000. In Year 4, she borrowed an additional $200,000 from a bank, secured by a nonrecourse second mortgage on the property. In Year 7, after taking an additional $15,000 in depreciation deductions (for an aggregate of $40,000), Terri sells the property. Burt gives Terri $250,000 in cash and takes the property subject to both the first and second mortgages. Assume that the principal amount of the mortgages remain, respectively, at $150,000 and $200,000.

(a) What is the amount of Terri's gain? What is the character of her gain? Consider the Woodsam Associates, Inc. case (page 778 of this chapter).

(b) Assume the principal amount of the mortgages when Terri sells the property equal, respectively, $140,000 and $190,000. Terri receives $270,000 in cash for the property. What are the tax consequences to her?

3. Gogetter purchased an existing business. The sales contract called for him to pay $25,000 in cash and to assume the following: (1) a current mortgage for $100,000 on the business's real estate; (2) outstanding notes for $75,000 owed to unsecured creditors; and (3) any liability for severance pay that might become due to the existing employees. If all of the employees entitled to severance pay are laid off, the maximum payments would total $18,000. Gogetter also agrees to pay all of the property taxes on the existing business for the entire year. The sale took place on June 30. The $12,000 in property taxes for the year are due on December 31.

(a) What is Gogetter's basis in the business? Consider the Albany Car Wheel case (page 803 in this chapter).

(b) What is the seller's amount realized?

(c) How are the property taxes paid by Gogetter handled? Are they a deduction? If so, by whom? Are they added to Gogetter's basis in the business?

4. (a) Scott purchased an apartment house for $100,000, paying $10,000 in cash and taking the property subject to a $90,000 nonrecourse mortgage. At the time of the purchase the building was worth $80,000 and the land, $20,000. Over the next ten years, Scott took $40,000 in depreciation deductions on the building. He also paid $15,000 of principal on the loan so that the unpaid mortgage equaled $75,000. Scott then sells the real estate to Barbara for $25,000 cash with Barbara taking the property subject to the mortgage. What is the amount of Scott's realized gain?

(b) Assume the property in part (a) is only worth $75,000 at the end of ten years and Scott is unable to dispose of it.

i. What are the tax consequences to Scott and the mortgagee if he deeds the property over to the mortgagee? Is this a cancellation of indebtedness or the satisfaction of a liability?

ii. Assume, instead, Scott abandons the property. What are the tax consequences to him? Consider § 165(a) and (c).

(c) Assume the property in (a) above is only worth $65,000 at the end of ten years and Scott is unable to dispose of it. Assume Scott surrenders the property to the mortgagee. Do footnote 37 in the Crane case (footnote 28 on page 772 of this chapter) and the Tufts decision limit his gain to $5,000? Can the other $10,000 be treated as cancellation of indebtedness income? Consider Reg. § 1.1001–2(c) Ex. 8.

5. Margo purchased an apartment building on leased land for $100,000, paying no cash, and obtaining a $100,000 nonrecourse mortgage from a bank. The mortgage provides for annual interest payments with the entire principal amount payable (ballooning) at the end of 27½ years. Margo writes off the entire cost of the building over the next 27½ years under § 168. At the end of 27½ years Margo discovers that the building was constructed on a former chemical dump site. This news immediately made the building worthless. Margo abandons the building rather than paying off the loan. Why must Margo recognize a realized gain of $100,000? Consider the applicability of the tax benefit concept as applied in the Tufts case.

6. Dave purchased an unimproved parcel of land for $100,000, paying no cash, and obtaining a nonrecourse loan for the entire purchase price from a bank. After paying $2,000 of the principal on the loan, Dave discovers that the land is not suitable for development because it is in a flood area. Dave abandons the land. May Dave claim a $100,000 loss for his unrecovered basis in the land? Read footnote 8 in the Tufts case (footnote 41 on page 787 of this chapter). Do you agree with the Court's view? What is the character of the loss?

F. PART SALE/PART GIFT TRANSACTIONS

A taxpayer may engage in a part gift/part sale transaction by selling property for less than its fair market value. Assume a father transfers property (which is free and clear of liability), with a basis of $50 and a fair market value of $875, to his son as a gift on the condition that his son pay any gift taxes on the property. The amount of the gift for purposes of the gift tax is the fair market value of the property less the gift tax. This is commonly referred to as a "net gift." Assume that the gift tax is $75. The Supreme Court in Diedrich v. Commissioner, 457 U.S. 191, 102 S.Ct. 2414, 72 L.Ed.2d 777 (1982), which we next consider, held that this type of transaction should be viewed as a part sale/part gift. The Court treated the son as paying the father $75 for the property so that the father realized a gain of $25, the amount by which the liability exceeded the father's basis in the donated property. Reg. §§ 1.1001–1(e) and 1.1015–4. In other words, where the amount paid exceeds the father's basis in the transferred property, the father realizes a gain equal to the amount of the excess. Unless the part sale/part gift transfer is made to a charity, the taxpayer allocates his entire basis to the amount realized to determine his gain. If the taxpayer makes a part sale/part gift to a qualified charity, the taxpayer allocates his basis between the part of the property he sold to the charity and the part he gave away. § 1011(b).

DIEDRICH v. COMMISSIONER
Supreme Court of the United States, 1982.
457 U.S. 191, 102 S.Ct. 2414, 72 L.Ed.2d 777.

CHIEF JUSTICE BURGER delivered the opinion of the Court.

We granted certiorari to resolve a circuit conflict as to whether a donor who makes a gift of property on condition that the donee pay the resulting gift tax receives taxable income to the extent that the gift tax paid by the donee exceeds the donor's adjusted basis in the property transferred. ____ U.S. ____, 102 S.Ct. 89, 70 L.Ed.2d 82 (1981). The United States Court of Appeals for the Eighth Circuit held that the donor realized income. 643 F.2d 499 (1981). We affirm.

I

A

Diedrich v. Com'r Internal Revenue

In 1972 petitioners Victor and Frances Diedrich made gifts of approximately 85,000 shares of stock to their three children, using both a direct transfer and a trust arrangement. The gifts were subject to a condition that the donees pay the resulting federal and state gift taxes. There is no dispute concerning the amount of the gift tax paid by the donees. The donors' basis in the transferred stock was $51,073; the gift tax paid in 1972 by the donees was $62,992. Petitioners did not include as income on their 1971 federal income tax returns any portion of the gift tax paid by the donees. After an audit the Commissioner of Internal Revenue determined that petitioners had realized income to the extent that the gift tax owed by petitioners but paid by the donees exceeded the donors' basis in the property. Accordingly, petitioners' taxable income for 1972 was increased by $5,959.[54] Petitioners filed a petition in the United States Tax Court for redetermination of the deficiencies. The Tax Court held for the taxpayers, concluding that no income had been realized [39 TCM 433 (1979)].

* * *

C

The United States Court of Appeals for the Eighth Circuit consolidated the two appeals [Diedrich and another case presenting the same issue] and reversed, concluding that "to the extent the gift taxes paid by donees" exceeded the donors' adjusted bases in the property transferred, "the donors realized taxable income." 643 F.2d 499, 504 (1981). The Court of Appeals rejected the Tax Court's conclusion that the taxpayers merely had made a "net gift" of the difference between the fair market value of the transferred property and the gift taxes paid by the donees. The court reasoned that a donor receives a benefit when a donee discharges a donor's legal obligation to pay gift taxes. The Court of Appeals agreed with the Commissioner in rejecting the holding in Turner v. Commissioner, 49 T.C. 356 (1968), aff'd per curiam, 410 F.2d 752 (CA6 1969), and its progeny, and adopted the approach of Johnson v. Commissioner, 59 T.C. 791 (1973), aff'd, 495 F.2d 1079 (CA6), cert. denied, 419 U.S. 1040, 95 S.Ct. 527, 42 L.Ed.2d 317 (1974), and Estate of Levine v. Commissioner, 72 T.C. 780 (1979), aff'd, 634 F.2d 12 (CA2 1980). We granted certiorari to resolve this conflict, ___ U.S. ___, 102 S.Ct. 89, 70 L.Ed.2d 82 (1981), and we affirm.

54. Subtracting the stock basis of $51,073 from the gift tax paid by the donees of $62,992, the Commissioner found that petitioners had realized a long term capital gain of $11,919. After a 50% reduction in long term capital gain, [former] 26 U.S.C. § 1202 (1976), the Diedrichs' taxable income increased by $5,959.

II

A

Pursuant to its Constitutional authority, Congress has defined "gross income" as income "from whatever source derived," including "[i]ncome from discharge of indebtedness." 26 U.S.C. § 61 (1976).[55] This Court has recognized that "income" may be realized by a variety of indirect means. In Old Colony Tr. Co. v. Commissioner, 279 U.S. 716, 49 S.Ct. 499, 73 L.Ed. 918 (1929), the Court held that payment of an employee's income taxes by an employer constituted income to the employee. Speaking for the Court, Chief Justice Taft concluded that "[t]he payment of the tax by the employer[ ] was in consideration of the services rendered by the employee and was a gain derived by the employee from his labor." Id., at 729, 49 S.Ct. at 504. The Court made clear that the substance, not the form, of the agreed transaction controls. "The discharge by a third person of an obligation to him is equivalent to receipt by the person taxed." Ibid. The employee, in other words, was placed in a better position as a result of the employer's discharge of the employee's legal obligation to pay the income taxes; the employee thus received a gain subject to income tax.

The holding in Old Colony was reaffirmed in Crane v. Commissioner, 331 U.S. 1, 67 S.Ct. 1047, 91 L.Ed. 1301 (1947). In Crane the Court concluded that relief from the obligation of a nonrecourse mortgage in which the value of the property exceeded the value of the mortgage constituted income to the taxpayer. The taxpayer in *Crane* acquired depreciable property, an apartment building, subject to an unassumed mortgage. The taxpayer later sold the apartment building, which was still subject to the nonrecourse mortgage, for cash plus the buyer's assumption of the mortgage. This Court held that the amount of mortgage was properly included in the amount realized on the sale, noting that if the taxpayer transfers subject to the mortgage,

> "the benefit to him is as real and substantial as if the mortgage were discharged, or as if a personal debt in an equal amount had been assumed by another." Id., at 14, 67 S.Ct. at 1054.

Again, it was the "reality," not the form, of the transaction that governed. Ibid. The Court found it immaterial whether the seller received money prior to the sale in order to discharge the mortgage, or whether the seller merely transferred the property subject to the mortgage. In either case the taxpayer realized an economic benefit.

---

55. The United States Constitution provides that Congress shall have the power to lay and collect taxes on income "from whatever source derived." Art. I, § 8, cl. 1; Amendment XVI.

In Helvering v. Bruun, 309 U.S. 461, 469, 60 S.Ct. 631, 634, 84 L.Ed. 864 (1940), the Court noted:

"While it is true that economic gain is not always taxable as income, it is set-

tled that the realization of gain need not be in cash derived from the sale of an asset. Gain may occur as a result of exchange of property, payment of the taxpayer's indebtedness, relief from a liability, or other profit realized from the completion of a transaction." (Emphasis supplied.)

B

The principles of *Old Colony* and *Crane* control.[56] A common method of structuring gift transactions is for the donor to make the gift subject to the condition that the donee pay the resulting gift tax, as was done in each of the cases now before us. When a gift is made, the gift tax liability falls on the donor under 26 U.S.C. § 2502(d).[57] When a donor makes a gift to a donee, a "debt" to the United States for the amount of the gift tax is incurred by the donor. Those taxes are as much the legal obligation of the donor as the donor's income taxes; for these purposes they are the same kind of debt obligation as the income taxes of the employee in *Old Colony,* supra. Similarly, when a donee agrees to discharge an indebtedness in consideration of the gift, the person relieved of the tax liability realizes an economic benefit. In short, the donor realizes an immediate economic benefit by the donee's assumption of the donor's legal obligation to pay the gift tax.

An examination of the donor's intent does not change the character of this benefit. Although intent is relevant in determining whether a gift has been made, subjective intent has not characteristically been a factor in determining whether an individual has realized income.[58] Even if intent were a factor, the donor's intent with respect to the condition shifting the gift tax obligation from the donor to the donee was plainly to relieve the donor of a debt owed to the United States;

---

56. Although the Commissioner has argued consistently that payment of gift taxes by the donee results in income to the donor, several courts have rejected this interpretation. See, e.g., Turner v. Commissioner, 49 T.C. 356 (1968), aff'd per curiam, 410 F.2d 752 (CA6 1969); Hirst v. Commissioner, 572 F.2d 427 (CA4 1978) (en banc). Cf. Johnson v. Commissioner, 495 F.2d 1079 (CA6), cert. denied, 419 U.S. 1040, 95 S.Ct. 527, 42 L.Ed.2d 317 (1974).

It should be noted that the *gift* tax consequences of a conditional gift will be unaffected by the holding in this case. When a conditional "net" gift is given, the gift tax attributable to the transfer is to be deducted from the value of the property in determining the value of the gift at the time of transfer. See Rev.Rul. 75–72, 1975–1 C.B. 310 (general formula for computation of gift tax on conditional gift); Rev.Rul. 71–232, 1971–1 C.B. 275.

57. "The tax imposed by section 2501 shall be paid by the donor."

Section 6321 imposes a lien on the personal property of the donor when a tax is not paid when due. The donee is secondarily responsible for payment of the gift tax should the donor fail to pay the tax.

26 U.S.C. § 6324(b). The donee's liability, however, is limited to the value of the gift. Ibid. This responsibility of the donee is analogous to a lien or security. Ibid. See also S.Rep. No. 665, 72d Cong., 1st Sess. 42 (1932); H.R.Rep.No. 708, 72d Cong., 1st Sess. 30 (1932).

58. Several courts have found it highly significant that the donor intended to make a gift. *Turner v. Commissioner,* supra; *Hirst v. Commissioner, supra.* It is not enough, however, to state that the donor intended simply to make a gift of the amount which will remain after the donee pays the gift tax. As noted above, subjective intent has not characteristically been a factor in determining whether an individual has realized income. In Commissioner v. Duberstein, 363 U.S. 278, 286, 80 S.Ct. 1190, 1197, 4 L.Ed.2d 1218 (1960), the Court noted that " * * * the donor's characterization of his action is not determinative * * *." See also Minnesota Tea Co. v. Helvering, 302 U.S. 609, 613, 58 S.Ct. 393, 394, 82 L.Ed. 474 (1938) ("[a] given result at the end of a straight path is not made a different result because reached by following a devious path").

the choice was made because the donor would receive a benefit in relief from the obligation to pay the gift tax.[59]

Finally, the benefit realized by the taxpayer is not diminished by the fact that the liability attaches during the course of a donative transfer. It cannot be doubted that the donors were aware that the gift tax obligation would arise immediately upon the transfer of the property; the economic benefit to the donors in the discharge of the gift tax liability is indistinguishable from the benefit arising from discharge of a preexisting obligation. Nor is there any doubt that had the donors sold a portion of the stock immediately before the gift transfer in order to raise funds to pay the expected gift tax, a taxable gain would have been realized. § 1001. The fact that the gift tax obligation was discharged by way of a conditional gift rather than from funds derived from a pregift sale does not alter the underlying benefit to the donors.

Consistent with the economic reality, the Commissioner has treated these conditional gifts as a discharge of indebtedness through a part gift and part sale of the gift property transferred. The transfer is treated as if the donor sells the property to the donee for less than the fair market value. The "sale" price is the amount necessary to discharge the gift tax indebtedness; the balance of the value of the transferred property is treated as a gift. The gain thus derived by the donor is the amount of the gift tax liability less the donor's adjusted basis in the entire property. Accordingly, income is realized to the extent that the gift tax exceeds the donor's adjusted basis in the property. This treatment is consistent with § 1001 of the Internal Revenue Code, which provides that the gain from the disposition of property is the excess of the amount realized over the transferor's adjusted basis in the property.

III

We recognize that Congress has structured gift transactions to encourage transfer of property by limiting the tax consequences of a transfer. See, e.g., 26 U.S.C. § 102 (gifts excluded from donee's gross income). Congress may obviously provide a similar exclusion for the conditional gift. Should Congress wish to encourage "net gifts," changes in the income tax consequences of such gifts lie within the legislative responsibility. Until such time, we are bound by Congress' mandate that gross income includes income "from whatever source derived." We therefore hold that a donor who makes a gift of property on condition that the donee pay the resulting gift taxes realizes taxable

---

59. The existence of the "condition" that the gift will be made only if the donee assumes the gift tax consequences precludes any characterization that the payment of the taxes was simply a gift from the donee back to the donor.

A conditional gift not only relieves the donor of the gift tax liability, but also may enable the donor to transfer a larger sum of money to the donee than would otherwise be possible due to such factors as differing income tax brackets of the donor and donee.

income to the extent that the gift taxes paid by the donee exceed the donor's adjusted basis in the property.

The judgment of the United States Court of Appeals for the Eighth Circuit is

Affirmed.

JUSTICE REHNQUIST, dissenting.

It is a well-settled principle today that a taxpayer realizes income when another person relieves the taxpayer of a legal obligation in connection with an otherwise taxable transaction. See Crane v. Commissioner, 331 U.S. 1, 67 S.Ct. 1047, 91 L.Ed. 1301 (1947) (sale of real property); Old Colony Tr. Co. v. Commissioner, 279 U.S. 716, 49 S.Ct. 499, 73 L.Ed. 918 (1929) (employment compensation). In neither *Old Colony* nor *Crane* was there any question as to the existence of a taxable transaction; the only question concerned the amount of income realized by the taxpayer as a result of the taxable transaction. The Court in this case, however, begs the question of whether a taxable transaction has taken place at all when it concludes that "[t]he principles of *Old Colony* and *Crane* control" this case. Ante, at 2418.

In *Old Colony*, the employer agreed to pay the employee's federal tax liability as part of his compensation. The employee provided his services to the employer in exchange for compensation. The exchange of compensation for services was undeniably a taxable transaction. The only question was whether the employee's taxable income included the employer's assumption of the employee's income tax liability.

In *Crane*, the taxpayer sold real property for cash plus the buyer's assumption of a mortgage. Clearly a sale had occurred, and the only question was whether the amount of the mortgage assumed by the buyer should be included in the amount realized by the taxpayer. The Court rejected the taxpayer's contention that what she sold was not the property itself, but her equity in that property.

Unlike *Old Colony* or *Crane*, the question in this case is not the amount of income the taxpayer has realized as a result of a concededly taxable transaction, but whether a taxable transaction has taken place at all. Only *after* one concludes that a partial sale occurs when the donee agrees to pay the gift tax do *Old Colony* and *Crane* become relevant in ascertaining the amount of income realized by the donor as a result of the transaction. Nowhere does the Court explain why a gift becomes a partial sale merely because the donor and donee structure the gift so that the gift tax imposed by Congress on the transaction is paid by the donee rather than the donor.

In my view, the resolution of this case turns upon congressional intent: whether Congress intended to characterize a gift as a partial sale whenever the donee agrees to pay the gift tax. Congress has determined that a gift should not be considered income to the donee. 26 U.S.C. § 102. Instead, gift transactions are to be subject to a tax system wholly separate and distinct from the income tax. See id.

§ 2501 et seq. Both the donor and the donee may be held liable for the gift tax. Id. §§ 2502(d), 6324(b). Although the primary liability for the gift tax is on the donor, the donee is liable to the extent of the value of the gift should the donor fail to pay the tax. I see no evidence in the tax statutes that Congress forbade the parties to agree among themselves as to who would pay the gift tax upon pain of such an agreement being considered a taxable event for the purposes of the income tax. Although Congress could certainly determine that the payment of the gift tax by the donee constitutes income to the donor, the relevant statutes do not affirmatively indicate that Congress has made such a determination.

I dissent.

The following revenue ruling considers the bargain sale of encumbered real property to a charitable organization.

REV.RUL. 81–163
1981–1 C.B. 433.

Issue

What is the amount of gain recognized by an individual on the bargain sale of real property to a charitable organization under the circumstances described below?

Facts

During the taxable year, an individual taxpayer transferred unimproved real property subject to an outstanding mortgage of 10x dollars to an organization described in section 170(c) of the Internal Revenue Code. On the date of transfer the fair market value of the property was 25x dollars, and the taxpayer's adjusted basis in the property was 15x dollars. The taxpayer had held the property for more than one year and made no other charitable contributions during the taxable year. The property was a capital asset in the taxpayer's hands. Thus, under the provisions of section 170 the taxpayer made a charitable contribution to the organization of 15x dollars (25x dollars fair market value less 10x dollars mortgage).

Law and Analysis

Section 1011(b) of the Code and § 1.1011–2(b) of the Income Tax Regulations provide that, if a deduction is allowable under § 170 (relating to charitable contributions) by reason of a sale, the adjusted basis for determining the gain from the sale is the portion of the adjusted basis of the entire property that bears the same ratio to the adjusted basis as the amount realized bears to the fair market value of the entire property.

Section 1.1011–2(a)(3) of the regulations provides that, if property is transferred subject to an indebtedness, the amount of the indebtedness must be treated as an amount realized for purposes of determining whether there is a sale or exchange to which § 1011(b) of the Code and § 1.1011–2 apply, even though the transferee does not agree to assume or pay the indebtedness.

Because the outstanding mortgage of 10x dollars is treated as an amount realized, the taxpayer's adjusted basis for determining gain on the bargain sale is 6x dollars (15x dollars adjusted basis of the entire property X 10x dollars amount realized divided by 25x dollars fair market value of the entire property).

HOLDING

The taxpayer recognizes long-term capital gain of 4x dollars (10x dollars amount realized less 6x dollars adjusted basis) on the bargain sale of the property to the charitable organization.

In Ebben v. Commissioner, 783 F.2d 906 (9th Cir.1986), the court held that a donation to charity of property encumbered by a mortgage resulted in a bargain sale and the basis must be computed under the allocation rule of § 1011(b). According to the court, the donation of encumbered property was included within the meaning of the word "sale" in § 1011(b). Because the donation of encumbered property relieves the transferor of his primary obligation to repay the loan, it is as though the transferor received cash.

Problems

1.   (a) Martin owns land with a fair market value of $15,000 and a basis of $6,000. Martin sells the property to his son for $10,000.

i.   Does Martin realize gain? What is the amount of the gain? Consider Reg. §§ 1.1001–1(e) and 1.1015–4(a).

ii.   What is the son's basis in the property? Consider Reg. § 1.1015–4(a).

iii.   What is the son's holding period for the property? Consider § 1223.

(b) What result in "a" above if Martin's basis in the land was $11,000?

(c) Martin owns a second parcel of land with a value of $15,000 and a basis of $6,000. Martin sells the property to a charity for $10,000. Does Martin realize gain? What is the amount of Martin's gain on the sale? Consider § 1011(b).

2.   (a) Susan purchased a building for $60,000, paying $10,000 in cash and obtaining a $50,000 nonrecourse mortgage. Susan took $36,000 in depreciation deductions on the building resulting in an adjusted basis for the building of $24,000. Assume that Susan did not repay any of the mortgage principal. Susan gives the building, subject to the mortgage, to a charity at a time when it has a fair market value of $75,000. What is the amount of Susan's charitable deduction under § 170 and her gain, if any? Consider § 1011(b). Will the allocation of basis required by § 1011(b) cause

the realization of gain by Susan? Can a taxable realization arise in a donative setting? Consider the Crane case. Is the finding of a realization an application of the tax benefit doctrine?

(b) Assume Susan gives the building to her son who takes the property subject to the mortgage. What are the tax consequences to Susan? Will the transfer of property, subject to a nonrecourse liability, result in the debt being an amount realized by Susan? What is her son's basis in and holding period for the building? Consider § 1223(2).

(c) Assume Susan gives the property to her son as a bequest in her will. What are the tax consequences to the son? What is his basis in and holding period for the property? Consider §§ 1014 and 1223(11) and Reg. § 1.1001–2(c) Ex. (8). Reconsider Problem 4 on page 10 of this Chapter.

3. H owns a parcel of land with a basis of $25,000 and a value of $100,000. The land is subject to a $65,000 nonrecourse mortgage as H had pledged the land as collateral for a loan last year. H gives this land, subject to the mortgage, to his wife as a gift. Does H realize a gain on the disposition of this property? What basis does W take in the property? Consider the implications to be drawn from § 1041(e). Does § 1041(a) negate the realization of gain attributable to the liability? Consider Reg. § 1.1041–1T(b) Q & A 12.

G. DEFERRAL OF REALIZED GAIN

1. INSTALLMENT SALES

We next consider a method of deferring income common to investors and entrepreneurs under which gain arising from the sale of property is allocated to the years in which payments are received by the seller.

Introduction. One of the earlier devices used by taxpayers to avoid pyramiding income in a single year was the installment sale. This device was soon recognized as fulfilling a valid purpose from which legitimate tax savings might follow. The method and measure by which tax savings from installment sales become available is currently set out at §§ 453, 453A and 453B which represent a refinement of many earlier statutes on the subject. Section 453 provides the rules for sales of real property and casual sales of personal property. Section 453A contains rules covering dealer transactions in personal property, while § 453B contains rules covering the dispositions of installment obligations. The installment sale method permits both cash and accrual taxpayers to spread income resulting from current sales of realty and personalty (other than inventory), over later taxable years. However, a taxpayer who sells stock or securities traded on an established securities market cannot use the installment sale method. § 453(j). Section 453C also limits the use of the installment sale method for certain transactions based on the amount of the taxpayer's outstanding indebtedness.

The manner in which installment sales may save taxes is illustrated by the following example:

Taxpayer, on the cash method, owns raw land (a capital asset) with a basis of $1,000. He sells it in Year 1 for a total price of $2,500. Of course, he has gain to the extent by which the amount realized from the sale exceeds his basis; this is $1,500. However, he will receive payment in five future equal annual installments of $500 each, plus interest on the outstanding balance. In the absence of a statutory provision, the entire $1,500 gain from the sale of the land would be attributable to Taxpayer in Year 1, notwithstanding that he actually will receive the sales proceeds over a period of five years. Section 453 allows Taxpayer to postpone the recognition of income and spread the $1,500 gain from the sale over five years.

The installment sale method of reporting is mandatory with respect to qualifying sales of real estate and casual sales of eligible personalty unless the taxpayer elects to the contrary and thereby recognizes his gain, in full, in the year of the sale. § 453(d). When the taxpayer can use the installment method, there are very substantial advantages. Payment of taxes is postponed until the years in which the taxpayer receives the gain in cash or its equivalent thereby avoiding the pinch problem. The recognition of gain is matched with the realization of cash. Because the gain is not bunched into one year, the impact of progressive tax rates may be lessened. The seller's aggregate cost is also reduced as the deferral of the payment of tax confers a substantial benefit on the taxpayer.

Question

Should the Code provide for an interest charge for the use of the installment method, specifically, interest on the amount of the delayed tax payment? Examine § 453C(e)(4)(B).

In analyzing the installment sale method three questions must be considered: the amount of gain, the timing of gain, and the character of gain. The balance of this section ignores the treatment of dealers in personal property and the disposition of personal property of a kind which is required to be included in the taxpayer's inventory. It must be remembered that the installment method only defers the reporting of the gain on the sale of the property and does not determine the timing of the interest inherent in any deferred payment situation.

Amount and Timing of Gain. Under prior law, a sale of realty or nondealer disposition of personalty qualified for installment sale treatment only if seller received 30 percent or less of the selling price in the year of the sale. This provision has been repealed. Senate Finance Committee Report No. 96–1000, Installment Sales Revision Act of 1980, 96th Cong.2d Sess. 8–9 (1980) states:

A number of problems have arisen in connection with the 30-percent initial payment requirement which was designed to limit installment sale reporting to transactions where hardships might result from current imposition of tax on uncollected amounts. Some have argued that it is an arbitrary limitation which has unduly complicated and interfered with normal business transactions. In addition, it has been argued that the limitation has operated as a trap for the unwary. If a taxpayer fails to secure competent advice and inadvertently exceeds the 30-percent limitation, however slightly, the entire gain must be recognized in the year of sale. The limitation has produced an inordinate amount of litigation and confusion.

No longer must payments for the sale of realty or a casual sale of personal property be made in two or more installments payable in two or more taxable years to qualify such sale for installment treatment. Under § 453(b)(1), to qualify as an installment sale there must be a "disposition of property where at least one payment is to be received after the close of the taxable year in which the disposition occurs." Installment reporting is now available to a taxpayer who receives a lump sum payment in a taxable year subsequent to the year of sale. § 453(b)(1).

The installment sale method is defined in § 453(c) as "a method under which the income recognized for any taxable year from a disposition is that proportion of the payments received in that year which the gross profit (realized or to be realized when payment is completed) bears to the total contract price." Generally excluded are evidence of the purchaser's indebtedness, but the buyer's notes payable on demand are included in the "payment" concept. § 453(f)(3) and (4).

The allocation of gain to the years over which the payments are made is described in Temp.Reg. § 15A.453–1(b)(2). In effect, the gain is spread proportionately over the payment period. Under the installment sale method, the gross profit ratio (Temp.Reg. § 15A.453–1(b)(2) (i)), i.e., the proportion of gross profit as defined in Temp.Reg. § 15A.453–1(b)(2)(v) to the contract price as defined in Temp.Reg. 15A.453–1(b)(2)(iii), is computed. The gross profit ratio is applied to each installment payment when received and that part of each payment representing the element of gain is included in the seller's gross income.

Read carefully Temp.Reg. § 15A.453–1(b)(5) Ex. (1) and (2) which illustrate the installment method of reporting income. Note that if the property is subject to a mortgage which the purchaser assumes or takes subject thereto, the contract price only includes the amount of the mortgage in excess of the seller's basis in the property. Reg. § 1.453–4(c) and Temp.Reg. § 15A.453–1(b)(3).

Question

How does the gross profit ratio (Temp.Reg. § 15A.453–1(b)(2)(i)) compare with the exclusion ratio for an annuity (Reg. § 1.72–4(a))? Reconsider pp. 152–153.

Character of Gain. Under the installment sale method, gain is characterized by the original transaction and depends on the nature of the asset and the period for which the asset was held. In effect, the installment method is only a timing device for the gain realized on the sale of the property.

Losses. A loss sustained on an installment sale of qualified assets is deductible only in the taxable year in which the sale is made. The loss cannot be spread over the years during which the payments of the selling price are received. Rev.Rul. 70–430, 1970–2 C.B. 51. The spreading of losses may be accomplished by the capital loss carryover provided by § 1212(b).

Practical Problems Arising From the Installment Method: Dispositions of Installment Obligations. In the course of his business or investment operations, the taxpayer using the installment method of accounting may need cash. One way of getting the cash is to sell the remaining installment obligations to a bank or other purchaser at a discount; this is, of course, a well established commercial practice, but it may raise serious tax questions.

Under § 453B, tax consequences may arise when an installment obligation is "satisfied at other than its face value or distributed, transmitted, sold, or otherwise disposed of * * *." A disposition includes transfers which are not generally realization transactions, such as gifts and transfers in trust, but not the transmission of installment obligations at death (except as provided in § 691). The amount of gain or loss recognized upon a disposition is the difference between the basis of the obligation (defined in § 453B(b) as the face amount of the obligation less the amount which would be realized as income were the obligation satisfied in full) and either: (1) the amount realized on the sale or exchange of the obligation or a satisfaction for less than face value; or (2) the fair market value of the obligation at the time of the disposition other than a sale or exchange. § 453B(a). In general, the reporting of the remaining unreported gain with respect to the entire transaction is accelerated to the time of the disposition; this result is, of course, reasonable because the taxpayer, at this point, has realized the entire gain, in both fact and theory.

The gain (or loss) on the disposition of an installment obligation is treated as arising from a sale or exchange of the property in respect of which the property was received. § 453B(a). The character of the original transaction giving rise to the installment obligation controls. Therefore, the sale of an installment obligation, prior to 1988, held for a short-term holding period which was received on the sale of a capital asset held for a long-term holding period still receives long-term capital gain (or loss) treatment.

Impact of Borrowing on Installment Sales. The rationale for allowing a taxpayer to use the installment method to postpone the reporting of gain until the payments under the sales contract are actually received is premised on the hardship current recognition would cause. It would be unfair, and may create a pinch on a taxpayer's other resources, to require a taxpayer to currently report a gain when the receipt of the cash from the sale generating that gain is to be paid in subsequent taxable years. However, if a taxpayer is able to obtain the necessary cash, either directly by pledging his installment receivables as collateral for a loan, or indirectly through unrelated borrowings, he has a much better cash flow position and requiring the taxpayer to report the gain in the year of sale would not impose the same hardships. In fact, where a taxpayer pledges his installment receivables as collateral for a loan, there is no hardship at all in currently reporting the gain. Where the taxpayer has borrowed money in any manner, the use of the installment sale method to defer the reporting of gain on the sale of an asset is limited by § 453C. The legislative history explains the reasons for adopting the so-called proportionate disallowance rule as follows:

> In general, the underlying reason for allowing the reporting of gain on the installment method for Federal income tax purposes is that the seller may be unable to pay tax currently because no cash may be available until payments under the obligation are received. The committee believes that the ability to defer taxation under the installment sales method is inappropriate in the case of * * * gains realized on certain business or rental property, to the extent that the taxpayer has been able to receive cash from borrowings related to its installment obligations.

> The committee believes that the borrowings of a taxpayer generally are related to its installment obligations in one of two ways. In general, either the taxpayer would not undertake all or a portion of the borrowings but for its extending credit in connection with the sale of its property or the taxpayer's borrowing ability is enhanced by the presence of the installment obligations among the taxpayer's assets. The committee recognizes, however, that it is extremely difficult to determine with any precision the extent of the nexus between the taxpayer's borrowings and its installment obligations. Hence, the committee believes it appropriate to adopt a rule which assumes that the borrowings of the taxpayer may be allocated among the taxpayer's assets on a pro rata basis. Nevertheless, the committee believes that farm property and personal use property, as well as indebtedness relating to such property, should not be taken into account.

> The committee recognizes that arguments may be made that, in certain circumstances, a taxpayer's borrowings may appear to have no nexus whatsoever to its installment obligations, and that in other circumstances, a taxpayer's borrowings may appear to be so closely related to its installment obligations that the installment obligations could appropriately be treated as having been disposed of. Nevertheless, rather than making necessary the difficult and subjective inquiry regarding the nexus between the borrowings of a taxpayer and its installment obligations, the committee believes that imposing a limitation based on a pro rata allocation of the taxpayer's borrowings is an

appropriate accommodation of competing concerns. (Senate Finance Committee Report on H.R. 3838, 99th Cong., 2d Sess. 123–24 (1986)).

The proportionate disallowance rule of § 453C places a limit on the deferral available under the installment method by creating the fiction that a payment is received in the year of sale. § 453C(a)(2). The deemed payment is called "allocable installment indebtedness" and is computed by reference to a taxpayer's outstanding liabilities ("applicable installment obligations").

A taxpayer's "allocable installment indebtedness" (AII) is generally determined by:

(1) dividing the face amount of the taxpayer's "applicable installment obligations" outstanding at the end of the year by the sum of:

(a) the face amount of all installment obligations (i.e. applicable installment obligations and other installment obligations) and

(b) the adjusted basis of all of the taxpayer's other assets (except installment obligations);

(2) multiplying the resultant quotient by the taxpayer's average quarterly indebtedness for the taxable year (or, for casual sales the taxpayer's indebtedness at the close of the taxable year), § 453C(b)(4);

(3) subtracting any AII that is attributable to applicable installment obligations arising in previous years, § 453C(b)(1) and (2).

In computing the AII for the year, a taxpayer does not take into account assets that comprise personal property, as defined in § 1275(b)(3), or indebtedness arising from the sale of such property. § 453C(b)(3). "Applicable installment obligations" are installment obligations arising from a sale after February 28, 1986, of, among other items:

(1) real property (except personal use property of an individual or certain farm property) held by the taxpayer for sale to customers in the ordinary course of the taxpayer's trade or business (as considered in Chapter 12), or

(2) real property (except personal use property of an individual or certain farm property) used in the taxpayer's trade or business or held for the production of rental income, provided that the selling price of the property exceeds $150,000. § 453C(e)(1)(A) and (B).

In each subsequent taxable year, the taxpayer is not required to recognize gain attributable to the "applicable installment obligations" arising in any prior year to the extent that the payments do not exceed the amount of AII attributable to such obligations. § 453C(c)(1). On the receipt of such payments, the AII attributable to the obligation on which the payment is received is reduced by the amount of such payments. § 453C(c)(2).

Example. In Year 1 a taxpayer sells land held for the production of rental income for $90,000, taking back the purchaser's note in the amount of $90,000, due one year from the date of sale, with interest. During Year 1 the taxpayer borrows $180,000 to finance the purchase of another parcel of land costing $180,000. The taxpayer's basis in the property sold is $60,000. Assume that the taxpayer has no other assets or liabilities. Applying the 33⅓ percent gross profit ratio to the $60,000 of "allocable installment indebtedness" for Year 1 results in $20,000 of gain on the sale being reported in Year 1. The $60,000 amount for the AII for the year is computed by multiplying:

(1) the taxpayer's indebtedness at the end of Year 1 ($180,000), by

(2) the quotient of

(a) the total face amount of the taxpayer's outstanding applicable installment receivables ($90,000), over

(b) the sum of

(i) the total face amount of the taxpayer's outstanding installment receivables ($90,000), and

(ii) the adjusted basis of its other assets at the end of Year 1 ($180,000).

The taxpayer is treated as having received a $60,000 payment as of the close of Year 1. When the taxpayer receives the actual $90,000 payment in Year 2, the prior year's AII reduces the amount subject to installment reporting. Therefore, only $30,000 of the $90,000 payment for Year 2 is subject to the gross profit ratio, so that only $10,000 of gain is reported in Year 2. In effect, any actual payment is first deemed to be a tax-free return of the amounts previously reported as AII. Had there been a second installment sale in Year 2, the amount treated as AII in Year 1 reduces the AII amount for the second year. § 453C(c)(1).

A taxpayer's indebtedness is defined very broadly and includes all accounts payable and accrued expenses, as well as the usual forms of indebtedness. Evidently, cash basis taxpayers will have to include these liabilities as well. A taxpayer with indebtedness in excess of the aggregate basis of his assets cannot get any benefit from installment sale reporting. A taxpayer's liabilities are involved in the computation of AII even though the debt may have been incurred in a year prior to the sale. Apparently, there need be no connection between a taxpayer's liabilities and the installment receivables.

QUESTION

The proportionate disallowance rule was adopted ostensibly as an attempt to bring more equity into the tax laws. Typically, more equity means more complexity. Is § 453C consistent with the tax simplification theme of the Tax Reform Act of 1986?

For those who wish to study this topic in more detail the following examples from the legislative history should suffice:

The application of the rules of the bill may be illustrated by the following example. The example assumes that the taxpayer is a dealer in real property, uses the calendar year as its taxable year, and that its operations began in 1987.

Calendar year 1987.—During 1987, the taxpayer sells one property [7] for $90,000, taking back the purchaser's note for the entire purchase price.[8] The property was sold at a profit. No payments are received on the obligation before the end of the year.

The aggregate adjusted basis of the taxpayer's assets, other than the installment obligation,[9] is $310,000 as of the end of 1987. The taxpayer's average quarterly indebtedness for 1987 is $200,000.

The taxpayer's AII for 1987 would be $45,000. This amount is computed by multiplying (1) the taxpayer's average quarterly indebtedness for 1987 ($200,000) by (2) the quotient of (a) the total face amount of taxpayer's outstanding applicable installment obligations ($90,000) and (b) the sum of (i) the total face amount of the taxpayer's installment obligations ($90,000) and (ii) the adjusted basis of its other assets as of the end of 1987 ($310,000). The taxpayer would be treated as receiving a payment of $45,000 on the outstanding installment obligation as of the close of 1987.[10]

Calendar year 1988.—During 1988, the taxpayer sells another property for $110,000, taking back the purchaser's note for the entire purchase price. The property was sold at a profit. No payments were received in 1988 on either the 1987 or 1988 installment obligations held by the taxpayer.

The aggregate adjusted basis of the taxpayer's assets, other than the installment obligations, is $400,000 as of the end of 1988. The taxpayer's average quarterly indebtedness for 1988 is $300,000.

The taxpayer's AII for 1988 would be $55,000. This amount is computed by multiplying (1) the taxpayer's average quarterly indebtedness for 1988 ($300,000) by (2) the quotient of (a) the total face amount of the taxpayer's outstanding applicable installment obligations ($200,000) and (b) the sum of (i) the total face amount of the taxpayer's installment obligations ($200,000) and (ii) the adjusted basis of its other assets as of the end of 1988 ($400,000), and (3) subtracting the amount of AII allocated to applicable installment obligations that arose prior to 1988 ($45,000). The taxpayer would be treated as having received a payment of $55,000 on the installment obligation that arose in 1988, as of the close of 1988.

---

7. All sales referred to in the example are assumed to be of property that is held for sale to customers in the ordinary course of the taxpayer's trade or business.

8. All installment obligations received in this example are assumed not to be payable on demand or readily tradable (within the meaning of sec. 453(f)). In addition, such installment obligations are assumed to have stated interest sufficient to avoid the recharacterization of any portion of the principal amount as interest under section 483 or section 1274. Payments referred to in the example are payments of principal on the obligations.

9. It is assumed that none of the taxpayer's assets in the example other than its applicable installment obligations are installment obligations. If so, these assets would be taken into account at their face amount rather than their adjusted basis.

10. Where the taxpayer has more than one applicable installment obligation outstanding as of the close of the taxable year, the amount of AII for the year would be allocated pro rata (by outstanding face amount) to the obligations, and the proportionately allocated amount would be treated as a payment on each respective outstanding obligation.

Calendar year 1989.—In 1989, the taxpayer sells a third property for $130,000. The property was sold at a profit. Also in 1989, the installment obligation that the taxpayer received in 1987 is paid in full. No payments are received on either the obligation that was received in 1988 or the one received in 1989.

The aggregate adjusted basis of the taxpayer's assets, other than its installment obligations, is $360,000 as of the end of 1989. The taxpayer's average quarterly indebtedness for 1989 is $500,000.

With respect to the $90,000 payment that was received on the installment obligation that arose in 1987, the first $45,000 of the payment would not result in the recognition of any additional gain with respect to the obligation, and would reduce the amount of AII that is treated as allocated to that obligation. The next $45,000 would be treated as an additional payment on the obligation that results in the recognition of additional gain under the installment method.

Taking into account the payment on the 1987 installment obligation, the AII allocated to taxable years before 1989, for purposes of computing AII for 1989, would be $55,000 ($45,000 of AII from 1987 plus $55,000 of AII from 1988 minus $45,000 of AII from 1987 returned in 1989).

The taxpayer's AII for 1989 would be $145,000. This amount is computed by multiplying (1) the taxpayer's average quarterly indebtedness for 1989 ($500,000) by (2) the quotient of (a) the total face amount of the taxpayer's outstanding applicable installment obligations as of the end of 1989 ($110,000 plus $130,000, or $240,000) and (b) the sum of (i) the total face amount of the taxpayer's installment obligations ($240,000) and (ii) the adjusted basis of its other assets as of the end of 1989 ($360,000), and (3) subtracting the amount of AII allocated to applicable installment obligations that arose prior to 1989 $55,000).

Since taxpayer's AII for 1989 ($145,000) exceeds the amount of applicable installment obligations arising in 1989 and outstanding at the end of the year ($130,000), the taxpayer is treated as having received a payment, as of the close of 1989, of $130,000 on the installment obligation that arose in 1989, and a payment of $15,000 (i.e., the excess of $145,000 over $130,000) on the installment obligation that arose in 1988. (Senate Finance Committee Report on H.R. 3838, 99th Cong., 2nd Sess. 127–129 (1986)).

Problems

1. Siegmund, a cash method taxpayer, owns an apartment building free and clear. His adjusted basis in the building is $20,000 and the fair market value is $100,000. He sells the building to Bart for $100,000, receiving $10,000 in cash as a down payment and Bart's promissory note for $90,000. The note calls for Bart to make equal annual installments of $10,000 each for the next nine years, the first installment due in one year. Bart also agrees to pay 10% interest each year on the unpaid balance at the end of each year. Assume this interest rate meets the imputed interest requirements. Because the claim to future payments is a valuable proper-

ty right under state law with a fair market value equal to its face amount, Siegmund has an amount realized of $100,000 at the time of the sale. He further realizes a gain of $80,000. Siegmund is in the 28% income tax bracket.

(a) What problems may Siegmund face if he has to pay the entire tax liability in the year of sale?

(b) Is the transaction an installment sale? Consider § 453(b).

(c) If so, how much gain is recognized and when? Consider § 453(c) and Temp.Reg. § 15A.453–1(b)(2). What is the gross profit? Consider Temp.Reg. § 15A.453–1(b)(2)(v). What is the contract price? Consider Temp.Reg. § 15A.453–1(b)(2)(iii) and (ii). What is the gross profit ratio? Consider Temp.Reg. § 15.453–1(b)(2)(i). How are the annual interest payments treated? Assume that Siegmund has no outstanding liabilities so that § 453C does not apply.

(d) Would it make any difference if Siegmund were on the accrual method of accounting? Consider 453(a).

(e) What if the note given by Bart were due on demand? Consider § 453(c), (f)(3) and (4).

(f) What if Siegmund, after receiving the $10,000 down payment, but before collecting any payments on the nondemand promissory note, sells the note for $85,000. Is this a disposition? If so, what are the tax consequences to Siegmund; specifically, what is the amount of his gain, when is the gain recognized, and what is the character of the gain? Or, is there a loss on selling the note? Consider § 453B(a) and (b) and Reg. § 1.453–9(b)(3) Ex. (1).

2. (a) Stan owns a parcel of land held for investment purposes with a basis of $30,000 and a fair market value of $100,000. The land is subject to a $30,000 nonrecourse mortgage. Stan sells the land for $20,000 in cash and a $50,000 note, payable at the rate of $10,000 per year, plus 10% annual interest on the unpaid balance of the note. The first annual payment on the note is due one year from the date of sale. In addition, Pat, the purchaser, agrees to take the land subject to the mortgage. When does Stan report the $70,000 gain realized on this sale? Consider § 453(c) and Temp.Reg. § 15A.453–1(b)(2), –(b)(3), and –1(b)(5) Ex. (2) and Ex. (3) and Reg. § 1.453–4(c).

(b) Assume the same facts as in (a), except the mortgage is with recourse. Does this affect when Stan will report the gain? Consider Temp. Reg. § 15A.453–1(b)(2), –1(b)(3) and Reg. § 1.453–4(c).

(c) Assume the same facts as in (a), except that the outstanding mortgage on the land is in the amount of $40,000 and Stan receives only $10,000 in cash in the year of sale. When will Stan report the $70,000 realized gain in this sale? What is the gross profit ratio? How does Temp. Reg. § 15A.453–1(b)(2)(iii) accommodate the Crane and Tufts cases?

2. OPEN TRANSACTIONS

If the purchaser's deferred payment obligations received by the vendor do not have an ascertainable fair market value, such obligations may not be deemed an amount realized (or the equivalent of cash) and the transaction is said to be open. In an open transaction, which is also called the cost recovery method, where the obligations received by the vendor lack a fair market value or are not the equivalent of cash, the payments received by the seller in the form of cash and other property having an ascertainable fair market value are applied against and reduce the basis of the property sold. When the amount applied against the basis of the property sold exceeds the basis, then the excess is treated as gain realized. Reg. § 1.453–6(a)(2). Thus, following the cost recovery concept, the initial cash received and subsequent payments of the obligations are applied first against the basis of the property. Once the basis of the property has been recovered, subsequent payments, when received, are realized and recognized as gain. The character of all gain (including an unexpected gain) realized and recognized on an open transaction, even after the recovery of basis, is determined by reference to the character of the property sold.

Study Problem Continued

Mrs. Logan owned all the shares in a mining company with a basis in the stock of $173,000. In 1916 she sold her shares for $137,500 in cash and future payments based on the production from the mine. The production payments called for the purchaser to pay 60 cents for each ton of ore extracted. Mrs. Logan received production payments of $20,000 in 1917, $15,500 in 1918, $19,000 in 1919 and $10,000 in 1920. An appraiser estimated that the present discounted value of the production payments in 1916 was approximately $105,000 with an expected payout period of 45 years.

(a) What were the tax consequences for Mrs. Logan? Consider Burnet v. Logan (page 753 of this chapter) and Reg. § 1.453–6(a)(2).

(b) How did the Commissioner wish to treat the transaction?

(c) From Mrs. Logan's viewpoint which is the better outcome: (1) a finding of a closed transaction and using the installment sales method or (2) a finding that the amount realized lacks an ascertainable fair market value? Does § 453(j)(2) overrule Burnet v. Logan? Note: In 1916 the installment sale method had not yet been enacted and there was no special treatment for capital gains.

(d) What was the purchaser's basis in the shares he acquired from Mrs. Logan? Consider the Albany Car Wheel case at page 803.

The expansion of installment reporting to sales subject to a contingency will reduce substantially the justification for treating a transaction as open and using the cost recovery method sanctioned by Burnet v. Logan, page 753 of this chapter. Section 453(j) permits installment method reporting for sales with a contingent selling price. This provision will significantly expand the availability of installment reporting. See Temp.Reg. § 15A.453–1(c)(1). Consider also Reg. § 1.1001–1(a).

Senate Finance Committee, Report No. 96–1000, Installment Sales Revision Act of 1980, 96th Cong.2d Sess. 23, 24 (1980) provides:

However, it is intended that, for sales under which there is a stated maximum selling price, the regulations will permit basis recovery on the basis of a gross profit ratio determined by reference to the stated maximum selling price. For purposes of this provision, incidental or remote contingencies are not to be taken into account in determining if there is a stated maximum selling price. In general, the maximum selling price would be determined from the "four corners" of the contract agreement as the largest price which could be paid to the taxpayer assuming all contingencies, formulas, etc., operate in the taxpayer's favor.

Income from the sale would be reported on a pro rata basis with respect to each installment payment using the maximum selling price to determine the total contract price and gross profit ratio. If, pursuant to standards prescribed by regulations, it is subsequently determined that the contingency will not be satisfied in whole or in part, thus reducing the maximum selling price, the taxpayer's income from the sale would be recomputed. The taxpayer would then report reduced income as adjusted, with respect to each installment payment received in the taxable year of adjustment and subsequent taxable years. If the maximum price is reduced in more than one taxable year, e.g., because of successive changes in the status of the contingency, each such year of reduction would constitute an adjustment year.

* * *

In cases where the sales price is indefinite and no maximum selling price can be determined but the obligation is payable over a fixed period of time, it is generally intended that basis of the property sold would be recovered ratably over that fixed period. In a case where the selling price and period are both indefinite but a sale has in fact occurred, it is intended that the regulations would permit ratable basis recovery over some reasonable period of time.

[I]t is the Committee's intent that the cost-recovery method not be available in the case of sales for a fixed price (whether the seller's obligation is evidenced by a note, contractual promise, or otherwise), and that its use be limited to those rare and extraordinary cases involving sales for a contingent price where the fair market value of the purchaser's obligation cannot reasonably be ascertained.

Problem

Mark owns all of the rights to a new electronic device for the computer-assisted study for law school examinations. His basis in the rights is $36,000. He sells the rights to this device to S & K Outlines, Inc. for $24,000 cash, plus 25% of the earnings generated by the device over the next 12 years. What are the tax consequences to Mark? Consider Burnet v. Logan, § 453(j)(2), and Temp.Reg. § 15A.453–1(c)(1) and (3).

Questions and Notes

For a cash method taxpayer, is a purchaser's unsecured nonnegotiable promissory note the equivalent of cash? Consider § 1001(b) and Reg. §§ 1.61–2(d)(4) and 1.451–2(a). What if the taxpayer were on the accrual method?

In Warren Jones Co. v. Commissioner, 524 F.2d 788 (9th Cir.1975), reversing 60 T.C. 663 (1973), the taxpayer, using the cash method of accounting, sold a building by using a land sale contract for $153,000, receiving $20,000 in cash and a contract calling for payment of the balance, $133,000, over fifteen years. In the year of sale, the taxpayer received $24,000, and because the taxpayer had a basis of $61,913.34 in the building, the taxpayer postponed reporting the gain until it recovered its basis. Evidence was presented that the $133,000 contract could have been sold in the marketplace at a discounted price of only $76,980.[60] The Tax Court held that the taxpayer properly deferred reporting gain, that the contract was not "property (other than money)" under § 1001(b), and that the contract was not the equivalent of cash since, with a fair market value of $76,980, it could not be sold for anywhere near its $133,000 face amount. The Ninth Circuit reversed, interpreting the legislative history of § 1001(b) to mean that Congress intended to establish a definite rule that if the fair market value of the property received in an exchange can be ascertained, the fair market value must be reported as the amount realized, rejecting the argument that cash equivalency close to face amount of an obligation was an element to be considered in determining whether fair market value could be ascertained. The Ninth Circuit reasoned that § 453, providing for installment reporting, served as Congress's way of providing relief from the hardships of § 1001(b).

In Rev.Rul. 79–292, 1979–2 C.B. 287, the Service ruled that the amount realized under § 1001(b) on the sale by an accrual method taxpayer who received long-term obligations from the buyer was the face amount of the obligations. According to the Service, valuing the obligation at fair market value would be "inconsistent with the well-established principle that an accrual method taxpayer includes in income amounts which it has a right to receive." Accordingly, the accrual method taxpayer who elects out of the installment method under § 453(d) must report the entire gain (except the interest) in the year of sale. Reg. § 15A.453–1(d)(2)(ii).

The cash method taxpayer who elects out under § 453(d) must treat the fair market value of the debt as part of his amount realized in the year of sale, regardless of whether it is a cash equivalent. Compare the Warren Jones Co. case, at p. 829, to Reg. § 15A.453–1(d)(2)(ii). If the fair market value of the debt is less than the face amount of the debt, the excess of the face amount of the note over its value is also income and the timing of this

---

60. In accordance with prevailing business practices any potential buyer for the contract would likely have required the taxpayer to deposit $41,000 of the proceeds from the sale of the contract in an escrow account securing the first $41,000 of payments. Although the court found that the taxpayer could have sold the contract for $117,980, it determined its fair market value to be only $76,980.

excess must be determined. For example, a seller receives a $50.00 note paying an adequate rate of interest, with installments of $10.00 a year for five years. The fair market value of the note is $25.00. If he elects to opt out of installment reporting under § 453(d), this $25.00 value is part of his amount realized in the year of sale and he takes a $25.00 basis in the note. Does he allocate $5.00 of basis to each $10.00 annual payment, thereby reporting $5.00 of income each year? Or can he recover his entire $25.00 basis before reporting any income? In Shafpa Realty Corp. v. Commissioner, 8 B.T.A. 283 (1927), a pro rata allocation of basis to each payment was permitted for an obligation fixed in amount. The court in Underhill v. Commissioner, 45 T.C. 489 (1966), reached the same result. However, in Dorsey v. Commissioner, 49 T.C. 606 (1968), involving the payment of an indefinite amount over a stated number of years, full recovery of basis was allowed before any income was reported.

A separate question concerns the character of this income. Can the $25.00 excess qualify as a capital gain if the underlying property was a capital asset? In Waring v. Commissioner, 412 F.2d 800 (3d Cir.1969), the court treated this excess as ordinary income. The court noted that since the sale took place in the year the capital asset was sold and was treated as a closed transaction in that year, the receipt of the excess did not arise out of that prior sale. Capital gain treatment is not available since § 1223 requires a sale or exchange in order for taxpayer to report a capital gain.

3. DEFERRED PAYMENT TRANSACTIONS AND IMPUTED INTEREST: THE TIME VALUE OF MONEY

Introduction. The tax treatment of debt instruments given in consideration for the sale of property or for cash has been addressed at various times for over three decades, culminating in the massive and complex changes enacted in 1984. Congress gradually realized that if the tax reporting of a transaction is not in conformity with the economic or financial realities of that transaction, substantial distortions, particularly with respect to the treatment of interest, may result. Taxpayers structured their transactions so as to obtain the maximum tax savings these distortions offer. A high level of inflation with its accompanying high interest rates only served to exacerbate these distortions. Numerous tax shelter devices were feasible only because of their ability to exploit the general failure of the tax laws to take into account such distortions. As previously discussed at pp. 231–232, dealing with structured settlements, the ability to deduct currently an amount to be paid in the future constitutes a distortion. The failure of the tax accounting rules dealing with timing to take into account the time value of money allowed taxpayers to obtain substantial tax savings without any financial or economic justification for these windfalls.

Before studying the rules currently in force, it is extremely helpful to examine some of the distortions caused by the fact that, in the past, tax accounting concepts sometimes conflicted with financial accounting principles in areas such as the manner in which interest was determined and when interest was reported. At the same time, we will examine some of the prior legislative responses to these distortions.

The first financial concept a student must master is the nature of, and difference between, simple and compound interest. This can best be understood by reference to Table 1. If an individual deposits $100,000 in a bank account paying 10% annual interest and leaves all the monies on deposit for a term of eight years, how much will be in that bank account at the end of eight years? Using simple interest, only the original deposit of $100,000 would earn interest each year. Therefore, at 10% annual simple interest, he would earn $10,000 of interest each year and have a total of $180,000 on deposit at the end of eight years. If the interest is compounded, the interest earned each year is added to the balance earning interest during each succeeding year. The amount of interest earned each year increases (or compounds) because the amount on deposit correspondingly increases. Therefore, at 10% annual compound interest, a total of $214,358.88 would be on deposit at the end of eight years.

Table 1

	10% Annual Compound Interest		10% Annual Simple Interest	
Year	Money on deposit at the end of year	Interest earned during each year	Money on deposit at the end of year	Interest earned during each year
1	$110,000	$10,000	$110,000	$10,000
2	121,000	11,000	120,000	10,000
3	133,100	12,100	130,000	10,000
4	146,410	13,310	140,000	10,000
5	161,051	14,641	150,000	10,000
6	177,156.10	16,105.10	160,000	10,000
7	194,871.71	17,715.61	170,000	10,000
8	214,358.88	19,487.17	180,000	10,000
Total interest earned		$114,358.88		$80,000

Debt Instruments Issued for Cash Prior to 1984. Prior to 1954 the Internal Revenue Code contained no provision recognizing that interest may be disguised (or understated). This omission encouraged purchasers of corporate bonds to treat the interest earned on their bonds as capital gains then eligible for preferential treatment. For example, if a corporation needed to borrow $100,000 and pay 10% interest annually, it could issue a non-interest bearing bond with a face amount of $214,358.88, the face amount payable at the end of eight years. (This is commonly referred to as a zero-coupon bond.) The issuing corporation would receive $100,000 in cash for its bond. As can be seen from Table 1, the amount of the discount, the difference between the issue price, $100,000, and the redemption price, $214,358.88, represents $114,358.88 of compound interest earned over eight years. The bondholder contended that the entire amount of this interest income was capital gain. See United States v. Midland-Ross Corp. at p. 996. And, if the bondholder used the cash method of accounting, he realized and recognized this gain in the year the corporation retired the bond and paid him the face amount of the obligation. Congress added legislation in 1954 requiring that this gain be treated as ordinary income (referred to as "original issue discount" (OID)) since it is measured by the difference between the issue price and the redemption amount, a difference which is, in effect, compound interest on the issue price for the term of the obligation. Congress was only concerned with the potential for reporting interest income as preferential capital gain when it enacted its first OID rule in 1954. It did not focus on the timing of the interest element. As a result, there was a lack of symmetry between the bondholder and the corporation. The accrual method corporation deducted as its interest expense a portion of the total unstated interest each year, and the bondholder, usually using the cash method of accounting, reported the entire amount of interest income in the year he received it (i.e., the year the bond was redeemed or sold). Additionally, the corporation and the bondholder treated as their annual interest income and interest expense, $14,294.86 ($\frac{1}{8} \times$ $114,358.88), a level, ratable amount. This allowed an artificial acceleration of the interest to the early years of the loan, since, as Table 1 shows, annual compound interest is less than this level amount for the first four years. Finally, this early OID legislation was limited in its application to corporate and government bonds treated by the bondholders as capital assets. And, it was not clear whether bonds issued for property were covered by this legislation.

Congress became concerned about this lack of symmetry between the cash method bondholder and the accrual method corporation with respect to timing of the interest. In 1969 Congress amended the OID provisions to provide for mandatory annual inclusion of the original issue discount interest so that the bondholder reported the same amount of interest income the corporation deducted as an interest expense each year. In effect, cash method bondholders were put on a type of accrual reporting for OID bonds. Although matching was achieved, a significant distortion remained as the amount of interest reported was still the ratable, level amount which failed to reflect the compounding effect of unpaid interest. And, although the cash basis bondholder was required to report interest income before he received payment, this matching only applied to bonds issued for cash. Taxpayers still successfully contended that debt instruments issued for property were not subject to these OID rules.

Congress allowed ratable, level reporting of interest on the assumption that both parties to a loan transaction would have conflicting interests and the bondholder would object to front-loading his interest income. This broke down with the advent of high market interest rates and the fact that many bondholders were pension funds or other tax-exempt institutions indifferent to the front-loading of their interest income. For example, assume a corporation issued a $10,000,000 zero coupon bond due in 30 years for $120,000 in cash so as to yield 15% a year. The corporation could deduct $329,333 a year as interest ($1/30 \times$ $9,880,000) when in reality its interest expense for the first year was only $18,000 (15% $\times$ $120,000). If the bondholder did not pay taxes on its income, it did not care that its income for the early years was overstated. Once Congress realized that certain bondholders had no conflicting interest with respect to an overstatement of their initial interest income, Congress, in 1982, added §§ 163(e) and 1232A (equivalent to what is now § 1272(a)) requiring the financial accrual of interest based upon the compounding of unpaid interest for debt instruments issued for cash. This legislation required the accrual of the "daily portion" of original issue discount in determining both interest income and deductions. Accordingly, both parties, in our example, would have accrued only $18,000 as interest in the first year.

JOINT COMMITTEE ON TAXATION, GENERAL EXPLANATION OF THE REVENUE PROVISIONS OF THE TAX EQUITY AND FISCAL RESPONSIBILITY ACT OF 1982

158–163 (1983).

PRIOR LAW

Tax treatment of corporate original issue discount bonds

Normally, a bond is issued at a price approximately equal to the amount for which the bond will be redeemed at maturity, and the return to the holder of the bond is entirely in the form of periodic interest payments. However, in the case of original issue discount (OID) bonds, the issue price is below the redemption price, and the holder receives some or all of his return in the form of price appreciation. The spread between the issue price and redemption price is the original issue discount. The extreme case of an OID bond is a zero coupon bond, on which there are no periodic interest payments, and the holder's entire return comes from price appreciation.

Under prior law, for bonds issued by a corporation and for which the period between the issue date and the stated maturity date exceeded one year, the original issue discount was treated as accruing in equal monthly installments over the life of the bond. Thus, an issuer of an OID bond deducted, as interest, both any periodic interest payments and a ratable portion of the original issue discount each year, and the holder of the bond included this same amount in income. For example, if a corporation issued a $1,000, 25-year bond paying a $70 annual coupon for an issue price of $500, it would deduct $90 for each full year over the life of the bond ($70 annual coupon plus $1/25$th of the $500 original issue discount). The original holder of the bond would also report $90 of income for each full year he held the bond. The basis of the bond in the hands of the holder was adjusted for the discount required to be included in income. Amounts included in income as original issue discount for each purchaser after the original holder were reduced by spreading any purchase premium (the excess of the purchase price over the issue price plus previous OID income inclusions) over the remaining life of the bond and deducting it on a ratable monthly basis from OID included in income.

* * *

Prior statutory rules explicitly prescribed the treatment of OID only with respect to holders of corporate and taxable government obligations that were capital assets in the hands of the holder (sec. 1232). The rule for holders of short-term corporate bonds was in section 1.1232–3A(b)(2) of the income tax regulations. For corporate issuers, the analogous rules governing the deduction of OID were prescribed by section 1.163–4 of the income tax regulations. The treatment of issuers prescribed by the regulations applied to both cash and accrual basis issuers. This regulatory treatment of corporate issuers achieved substantial parity of treatment between issuers and the holders of corporate bonds, who were required by section 1232 to include OID in taxable income ratably over the life of the bond.

Tax treatment of noncorporate original issue discount bonds

The statutory rules applicable to holders of OID bonds (sec. 1232) did not require OID on noncorporate bonds to be included in income ratably over the life of the bond. For government bonds, such rules required ordinary income treatment of the portion of any gain from the sale or redemption consisting of accrued OID. A cash basis holder of noncorporate bonds deferred the inclusion of OID in income until the bond was sold or redeemed.

Example comparing corporate OID and ordinary bonds

Assume a 15-percent interest rate. Suppose a business wants to borrow $1 and then borrow at the end of the year to pay all interest charges for the year, and repeat this sequence each year for 30 years. Its interest payments would be 15 cents in the first year, 17.3 cents the second year (15 percent interest on the outstanding balance of $1.15), and so on, and would grow exponentially, eventually equaling $8.64 in the 30th year. At the end of 30 years, the overall debt would mount up to $66.21. A total of $65.21 in interest would be paid, and deducted, over the period, but the deductions would start small and grow.

The taxpayer could achieve the same substantive result by issuing a zero-coupon bond at a price of $1 redeemable for $66.21 in 30 years. However, by using the OID bond, the taxpayer could obtain a deduction of $2.17 each year ($65.21 divided by 30). Thus, the OID bond allowed larger interest deductions in early years than borrowing the same amount with ordinary loans. In this example, the taxpayer deducted in the first year more than twice the amount borrowed and more than 14 times the real interest. Conversely, the purchaser of the OID bond included more interest in his income in early years than the purchaser of an ordinary bond.

Table 1 shows the different patterns of deductions for the issuer and income inclusion for the holder between a zero-coupon bond and borrowing with ordinary loans under prior law.

Table 1. Comparison of Interest Deductions and Income Inclusion Between Borrowing $1 With Zero-Coupon Bonds and With Ordinary Loans Under Prior Law

[Dollars]

Year	Ordinary loans	Zero-coupon bond	Difference
1982	0.150	2.174	2.024
1983	.173	2.174	2.001
1984	.198	2.174	1.976
1985	.228	2.174	1.946
1986	.262	2.174	1.912
1987	.302	2.174	1.872
1988	.347	2.174	1.827
1989	.399	2.174	1.775
1990	.459	2.174	1.715
1991	.528	2.174	1.646
1992	.607	2.174	1.567
1993	.698	2.174	1.476
1994	.803	2.174	1.371
1995	.923	2.174	1.251
1996	1.061	2.174	1.113
1997	1.221	2.174	.953
1998	1.404	2.174	.770
1999	1.614	2.174	.560
2000	1.856	2.174	.318
2001	2.135	2.174	.039
2002	2.455	2.174	− .281
2003	2.823	2.174	− .649
2004	3.247	2.174	−1.073
2005	3.734	2.174	−1.560
2006	4.294	2.174	−2.120
2007	4.938	2.174	−2.764
2008	5.679	2.174	−3.505
2009	6.530	2.174	−4.356
2010	7.510	2.174	−5.336
2011	8.636	2.174	−6.462
Total	65.212	65.212	0
Present value (computed at 8.1 percent after-tax rate)	11.738	24.245	12.505

Assumptions for Table 1—

Ordinary bond: Taxpayer borrows $1 in 1981 and borrows every year to pay the interest on the outstanding indebtedness. Interest rates remain at 15 percent. All debt repaid in 2011.

Zero-coupon bond: Taxpayer issues bond for price of $1 with no coupon, maturing in 30 years at a price of $66.21 (15-percent yield to maturity).

REASONS FOR CHANGE

The larger deductions allowed to issuers of OID bonds in the early years of a bond's term relative to deductions allowed issuers of interest-bearing bonds not issued at a discount were a substantial tax advantage to the former, an advantage that increased with the term of the bonds. The ratable OID amortization formula was adopted at a time when interest rates were considerably lower than at present and when the formula involved a much smaller distortion. The formula was significantly different from the formula which issuers use to compute interest deductions on financial statements and did not represent a proper measurement of interest costs to the issuer. There was no justification for providing what was, in effect, a tax incentive for issuing long-term OID bonds.

Moreover, the larger income inclusion for OID bond purchasers in early years, relative to purchasers of nondiscount bonds, unjustifiably penalized those who wished to take advantage of the opportunity the OID bond provides to guarantee the reinvestment of the interest payments at the bond's initial yield to maturity. Under prior law, only tax-exempt borrowers, such as pension funds, could avoid this penalty.

Congress also believed that the treatment of holders of OID bonds should be comparable, whether the bonds are corporate or noncorporate obligations, and that the treatment of taxable, noncorporate issuers of OID bonds should be comparable to the treatment of corporate issuers.

EXPLANATION OF PROVISION

The Act provides new rules for computing the method of amortizing original issue discount, using a method that parallels the manner in which interest would accrue through borrowing with interest-paying, nondiscount bonds.

Under the formula prescribed in the Act, the OID is allocated over the life of the bond through a series of adjustments to the issue price for each "bond period." The adjustment to the issue price for any bond period is determined by multiplying the adjusted issue price (i.e., the issue price as increased by adjustments prior to the beginning of the bond period) by the bond's yield to maturity and then by subtracting the interest payable during the bond period. The adjustment to the issue price for any bond period is the amount of the OID allocated to that bond period.

Except as regulations may provide otherwise, a bond period for any given bond is each one-year period beginning on the date of issue of the bond and each anniversary thereof, or the shorter period to maturity for the last bond period. The increase in the adjusted issue price for any bond period is allocated ratably to each day in the bond period.

Each bondholder must include in income the sum of the daily portions of OID so determined for each day during the taxable year the bond is held. When the taxable year of a holder overlaps more than one bond period (which will generally be the case unless the bond period happens to coincide with the holder's taxable year), the holder must include the appropriate daily portions for each of the relevant bond periods. The daily portions of OID includible in income or deductible will be reflected in the current earnings and profits of corporate bondholders and issuers.

* * *

* * * As under prior law, the basis of a bond will be increased for OID included in income, * * *

The aggregate daily portions of OID determined under the new rules that accrue during the taxable year of the issuer are the amount that the issuer may deduct. * * *

Although the 1982 legislation finally provided for the realistic financial reporting of the interest element by both the bondholder and the corporation, this approach applied to only those debt instruments governed by the OID rules. Many common transactions were not governed by these rules. Debt instruments excluded from the OID rules included: debt instruments issued by individuals, debt instruments issued in reorganizations (although this was changed by the Technical Corrections Act of 1982), and debt instruments issued for property (other than traded securities). Section 483 previously governed debt instruments issued for property.

Debt Instruments Issued for Property Prior to 1984. The ability to convert interest income into capital gain, which received preferential tax treatment prior to 1988, existed in deferred payment sales of property by understating the amount of interest to be paid on the debt used to finance the purchase price. Congress added § 483 in 1964 to deal with the problem of inadequate interest in deferred payment sales transactions including those under § 453. Suppose a taxpayer has a basis of $20,000 for raw land held as a capital asset. The taxpayer could sell it for $30,000, taking back a note carrying 10% interest due in one year, or the taxpayer could sell it for $33,000, taking back an interest-free note due one year in the future. Could the taxpayer avoid the ordinary income which would be attributed to him if he received the $3,000 as part of the sales price? Section 483 is designed "to prohibit a seller from avoiding ordinary income liability by merely labeling receipts as selling price rather than interest * * *." Robinson v. Commissioner, 439 F.2d 767, 768 (8th Cir.1971). On the buyer's side, § 483 is designed to prevent a buyer from overstating his basis in the acquired property.

Prior to its amendment by the Tax Reform Act of 1984, § 483 provided that where no interest was stated in a contract (or where the stated interest was below the minimum "safe harbor" rate specified in the Regulations) for the sale or exchange of property, the seller was deemed to have received and the buyer was deemed to have paid interest at a specified rate (Reg. § 1.483–1(c)(2)(ii)(B)) on payments due more than six months after the date of sale under a contract that provided for one or more payments due more than one year after the date of the sale. § 483(c)(1). Part of each payment, as received, was imputed as interest income (payment for the use of money) to the seller and the buyer treated a like amount as an interest deduction when paid. Reg. § 1.483–2(a)(1)(ii). Therefore, both buyers and sellers were required to report their interest deductions and income when payments were made, regardless of their methods of accounting. Reg. § 1.483–2(a)(1)(iii). The Regulations provided tables for calculating the interest element applied to each payment. Reg. § 1.483–1(g)(2). If interest were imputed under § 483, the imputed interest was excluded from the selling price for installment sale purposes. Temp.Reg. § 15A.453–1(b)(2)(ii).

However, the imputed interest rules under § 483 did not adequately deal with the economic reality of deferred payment sales of property for three important reasons. First, was the failure to use adequate, market rates of interest. Interest was imputed only if the interest rate stated in the sales contract failed to meet a "simple" interest test rate, most recently, 9% simple interest. A below market, safe-harbor test rate using simple, rather than compound interest, still allowed some conversion of ordinary income into capital gains. For example, a 25-year mortgage, paying 6% interest on the unpaid principal each year, met the 9% simple interest safe harbor. And, the same test rate was used regardless of the maturity of the obligation. This failed to take into account the fact that the rate of interest increases with the length of a loan. Finally, if the simple interest safe harbor was not satisfied, § 483 determined the amount of the hidden interest using an interest rate one point above the test rate, most recently 10%, compounded semi-annually. The rate used to impute interest was frequently below actual market interest rates. This failure permitted some conversion of ordinary income into capital gains which received preferential treatment prior to 1988, and allowed purchasers to overstate the basis of purchased property. Secondly, once the amount of unstated interest was determined, the Regulations under § 483 did not allocate the interest to each taxable year in a financially realistic manner. Instead, the total unstated interest was allocated ratably in equal amounts to each installment payment over the entire term of the sales contract. Third, the year in which the buyer and seller reported the interest was determined when payments were made rather than when the interest actually accrued.

The following example illustrates some of these distortions which existed prior to the 1984 legislation. Suppose a taxpayer owned a valuable asset with a $20,000 basis. Assume that the item was a capital asset in his hands as he purchased it for use in his personal residence. Another taxpayer wished to purchase this asset for use in his restaurant business as 5-year ACRS property. The taxpayer could sell it for its $100,000 fair market value, taking back a $100,000 note, paying 10% annual compound interest on the unpaid balance, with all payments (totalling $214,358.88) due at the end of eight years. If the parties used this arrangement, the seller would report $80,000 of capital gain, which received preferential treatment prior to 1988, and $114,358.88 of ordinary income. Suppose instead, that the taxpayer sold the asset for $124,627.25, with 9% simple interest, all payments due at the end of eight years. Again, the total to be paid will be $214,358.88 (the interest portion being $11,216.45 per year (9% × $124,627.25) for eight years, or $89,731.63). Since the 9% simple interest safe-harbor had been satisfied, § 483 did not impute any additional interest; the seller had a capital gain of $104,627.25 and ordinary income of $89,731.63. If market interest rates are 10%, $24,627.25 of interest income was converted into capital gain which received preferential tax treatment prior to 1988. The advantages to the buyer were even more pronounced. The buyer received a 10% investment tax credit on the purchase price. Inflating the purchase price by $24,627.25 gave the buyer a windfall by allowing him a larger investment tax credit, prior to 1987, than he would otherwise receive. If the $24,627.25 were treated as an interest expense, the buyer would normally deduct it over the eight-year term. Since this extra amount is part of the basis in the asset, he could deduct it over five years. Although the buyer lost an interest deduction, he received a depreciation deduction in the same amount.

The legislative history of the 1984 Tax Reform Act illustrated an extreme distortion that could be caused by allocating the interest ratably between the payments made.

A further problem with section 483 under prior law was its method of allocating unstated interest among deferred payments. Some tax shelters were exploiting this method of allocation to accelerate several years' interest charges into the year of the sale.

To illustrate, assume property with an established fair market value of $100,000 is sold for $2,500 in cash and two negotiable $100,000 notes, one maturing six months and one day after the sale (payments on an obligation are within the scope of section 483 only if they are due more than six months after the sale), the other thirty years after the sale. The present value of the cash and notes, assuming a 12 percent interest rate, would approximately equal the $100,000 value of the property. Since the notes have no stated interest, section 483 of prior law imputed interest at a rate of 10 percent, compounded semiannually. Applying this rate, the total unstated interest in the deferred purchase contract would be $99,408 (the $200,000 aggregate face value of the notes less $100,592, the sum of their present values).

Since deferred payments in this example are to be made in two equal installments, the total unstated interest of $99,408 would be allocated (under prior section 483) one-half ($49,704) to the first note and one-half to the second. Thus, the purchaser arguably would be entitled to deduct as interest almost one-half the cost of the property in the year of purchase when, economically, virtually all of the imputed interest actually would be paid in the second payment. Joint Committee on Taxation, General Explanation of the Revenue Provisions of the Deficit Reduction Act of 1984, 113 (1984).

Current Legislative Approach. The 1984 Tax Reform Act extended the coverage of true financial accounting for interest. The key elements of this legislation include: (1) expanding the use of market interest rates to determine whether a debt instrument issued for property understates the interest and using market rates to impute any unstated interest; (2) the recognition that interest accrues each year based upon the compounding effect of unpaid interest, and (3) the requirement that interest be reported in the year it accrues regardless of when payment is made, effectively putting both the buyer and the seller on the accrual method of accounting. However, there remain situations where some or all of these elements do not apply.

Debt Instruments Issued for Cash (§§ 1272 and 1273). The character and timing rules for bonds remain essentially unchanged. The entire amount of the original issue discount continues to be characterized as interest income. And, both parties are required to report the interest each year, with the amount of the annual interest being computed using the compounding effect of unpaid interest. The rules under §§ 1272 and 1273 do not impute any additional interest as the parties have already determined the amount of the interest by issuing the bond for cash. Section 1272(a)(2) contains a list of debt instruments issued for cash which are exempt from this treatment. For example, the interest on U.S. savings bonds and on loans for $10,000 or less between individuals, may continue to be reported by cash method taxpayers when paid.

Debt Instruments Issued for Property (§ 1274). Since the true issue price of a debt instrument given for property is the value of property and since that value is not automatically determined by the parties, Congress has provided for an indirect determination by use of prescribed interest rates. The prescribed rate is called the "applicable Federal rate" (AFR) and the AFR varies with the maturity of the debt instrument. § 1274(d)(1)(A). The Service issues new rates every month. § 1274(d)(1)(B). If it is found that sufficient interest is not provided for, then the same AFR is used to impute the amount of unstated interest.

The basic approach of § 1274 is to use the compounding of interest, applying market rates of interest, to determine: (a) whether sufficient interest is stated, (b) if not, the amount of unstated interest, and (c) the amount of each year's interest. And, the OID approach requires both interest income and interest deductions to be reported as they accrue each year, regardless of whether the interest is paid.

An example is helpful in explaining the application of the OID approach under § 1274 for a debt issued for property. Assume a seller receives no cash and takes back a debt instrument to finance the sale of property. The debt instrument is issued in the face amount of $10,000,000, maturing in five years, and has 5% simple interest, payable annually. Therefore, $500,000 of interest will be paid each year for five years, and the $10,000,000 principal amount will be paid at the end of the fifth year. Assume that the AFR is 10%, compounded semiannually.

The first step is to determine whether the debt instrument provides for "adequate stated interest." That is, have the parties provided for the payment of sufficient interest on the debt? This will automatically be the case if the stated interest rate is at least equal to the AFR and is payable at least semiannually. In all other cases the Code provides a complex process for determining the "true" sales price. There is "adequate stated interest" if the "stated principal amount" for the debt is less than or equal to the the "imputed principal amount." § 1274(c)(2). The "imputed principal amount" is the sum of the present values, using the AFR as the discount rate, of all payments due under the debt instrument whether labelled by the parties as principal or interest. § 1274(b)(1). In effect, the "imputed principal amount" represents the Code's determination of the fair market value or sales price of the property sold. The following table illustrates the computation of the amount that § 1274(a) treats as the true debt principal in our example.

Table 2

Year	Present Value at 10% Compounded Semiannually		Annual Payment		Present Value of Annual Payments
1	.907029	×	$500,000	=	$ 453,514.50
2	.822702	×	500,000	=	411,351.00
3	.746215	×	500,000	=	373,107.50
4	.676839	×	500,000	=	338,419.50
5	.613913	×	10,500,000	=	6,446,086.50
Imputed principal amount:					$8,022,479.00

Since the $10,000,000 "stated principal amount" exceeds the "imputed principal amount" (or true sales price), this debt instrument does not provide "adequate stated interest." The "imputed principal amount" is treated exactly as if it was the cash issue price under the OID rules.

The parties will report as interest each year the interest on the "imputed principal amount," using the AFR compounded semiannually, with the difference between this amount and the interest actually paid each year being imputed. The next table illustrates how the amount and timing of the imputed interest is determined.

Table 3

Year	Adjusted Issue Price *	Annual Interest on Adjusted Issue Price at 10% Compounded Semiannually	Annual Interest Paid	Annual Interest Imputed
1	$ 8,022,479.00	$ 822,304.00	$ 500,000	$ 322,304.00
2	8,344,783.00	855,340.00	500,000	355,340.20
3	8,700,123.00	891,762.60	500,000	391,762.60
4	9,091,885.80	931,919.00	500,000	431,919.00
5	9,523,804.00	976,190.00	500,000	476,190.00
		$4,477,515.80	$2,500,000	$1,997,515.80

* The issue price is the imputed principal amount. § 1274(a)(2). The issue price is increased each year by the amount of the prior year's imputed interest. As a result the amount of the unpaid debt principal increases each year.

The $1,977,515.80 of imputed interest is treated as "original issue discount" under § 1273(a). This OID amount is taken into income by the seller under § 1272(a) and is deducted by the buyer under § 163(e). Accordingly, the buyer and seller will report a total of $4,477,515.80 of interest, allocable to each year as indicated in Table 3 even though the parties only provided for interest payments totalling $2,500,000.

Continued Availability of § 483. Although the scope of § 483 has been reduced, it is still available and will apply to any deferred payment transaction involving the sale of property exempted from the OID rules under § 1274, such as the sale of a principal residence, sales involving total payments of $250,000 or less, and sales of farmland for $1,000,000 or less. Examine §§ 1274(c)(3) and 483(d)(1). The key difference between a § 483 transaction from an OID transaction under § 1274 is one of timing for the taxpayers. Under § 483 both cash method buyers and cash method sellers continue to report the interest income and expense when payment is made instead of when the interest accrues. Accrual method sellers and accrual method buyers also are required to report the interest when payment is made (or due) as § 483 requires that the imputed interest be allocated to "payments." § 483(a). Examine Reg. § 1.483–2(a)(1)(ii) and (iii). See Rev.Rul. 82–124, 1982–1 C.B. 89, and Rev.Rul. 77–421, 1977–2 C.B. 188.

Section 483(e) provides for a 6% semiannual compound rate to impute the amount of unstated interest for sales between family members of land for $500,000 or less. However, interest will still be accrued using the compounding effect.

Sections 483(d)(2) to (d)(4) provide for situations where no interest will be imputed. For example, under § 483(d)(2) only transactions with a sales price exceeding $3,000 are covered by § 483. In addition, § 1275(b)(1) provides that for "personal use property" no interest is imputed under §§ 483 or 1274. Certain annuities governed by § 72 are also exempted from both §§ 483 and 1274. § 1275(a)(1)(B).

Availability of § 1274A. In 1985, under the guise of simplification of the imputed interest rules, Congress added another exception to §§ 483 and 1274 allowing lower imputed interest rates for certain smaller transactions. Examine § 1274A(a). Under this provision, if the amount of seller financing does not exceed $2,800,000, the amount of interest to be imputed may not exceed 9%. Indexing of this $2,800,000 threshold begins after 1989. § 1274A(d)(2). For purposes of qualifying for the 9% imputation rate, sales which are related are treated as one sale under § 1274A(d)(1), thereby aggregating the underlying debt instruments.

Section 1274A also provides that in situations providing financing not exceeding $2,000,000, the timing of the interest income and deductions can be reported on the cash method of accounting. § 1274A(c). To qualify for this treatment the lender cannot be a dealer in the type of property financed and must already be using the cash method. § 1274(c)(2)(B). Both the lender and the borrower must jointly elect such treatment. § 1274A(c)(2)(D). A debt instrument meeting these requirements is known as a "cash-method debt instrument."

References: Halperin, Interest in Disguise: Taxing the Time Value of Money, 95 Yale L.J. 506 (1986); Kiefer, The Tax Treatment of a Reverse Investment, 26 Tax Notes 925 (1985); Halperin, The Time Value of Money–1984, 23 Tax Notes 751 (1984); Sunley, Observations on the Appropriate Tax Treatment of Future Costs, 23 Tax Notes 719 (1984); Stier, Original Issue Discount Rules and the Time Value of Money, 23 Tax Notes 1101 (1984); Cannellos and Kleinbrand, The Miracle of Compound Interest: Interest Deferral and Discount After 1982, 38 Tax.L.Rev. 565 (1983).

An article contends that, even with imputed interest, the deduction of accrued liabilities can yield "cost-free" liabilities. That is, the tax savings from including the liability in basis can be worth more to a taxpayer than paying the liability hurts a taxpayer. The article feels that the 1984 legislative remedies did not entirely cure the problem and suggests that cash accounting may be required, even at the sacrifice of the matching concept. See Johnson, Silk Purses from a Sow's Ear: Cost Free Liabilities under the Income Tax, 3 Am.J. of Tax Policy 231 (1984).

Problems

1. Seller owns a capital asset with a basis of $6,000,000 and agrees to sell it to Buyer for $13,400,964. The entire purchase price is payable three years from the date of the sales contract and no interest is payable. The Applicable Federal Rate (AFR) at the time the sale takes place is 10%,

compounded semiannually. Both parties use the cash method. Assume § 453C does not apply.

(a) Determine the amount and character of Seller's income and when the income is reported. Consider §§ 453 and 1274 and Reg. § 15A.453–1(b)(2). What is Seller's imputed principal amount, § 1274(b), interest income, gross profit ratio and amount realized?

(b) Determine Buyer's basis in the property he purchased, the amount of his interest deductions and the timing of the interest deductions. Assume Buyer uses the property in his business.

2. Sam owns a capital asset with a basis of $5,721,735 and agrees to sell it to Ben for ten payments of $1,000,000 each, payable every six months over the next five years. No interest is stated in the sales contract. How will the parties treat the $10,000,000 in payments? The AFR is 10%, compounded semiannually. Both parties use the cash method.

(a) What is the amount and character of Sam's income and when does he report the income? Consider §§ 453 and 1274.

(b) What is the amount and timing of Ben's interest deductions?

3. On January 1, of Year 1, S agrees to sell land held as an investment to B for $2,500,000. B agrees to pay the contract price in five annual payments of $500,000, the first payment due on January 1, of Year 2. S has a $1,000,000 basis in the land. Both S and B use the cash method. The AFR is 12%.

(a) Determine the character and timing of S's income. Consider §§ 453, 1274, 1274A(a) and (b).

(b) Determine B's basis in the acquired property and the amount and timing of his interest deductions.

4. S agrees to sell land held as an investment to B for $500,000. The sale took place on January 1, of Year 1. B agreed to pay the contract price in five annual payments of $100,000, the first payment due on January 1, of Year 2. S has a $100,000 basis in the land. Both S and B use the cash method. Both S and B jointly make the election permitted by § 1274A(c). The AFR is 12%.

(a) Determine the character and timing of S's income. What is the significance of an election under § 1274A(c)?

(b) Determine B's basis in the land and the amount and timing of his interest deductions.

5. S is a dealer who agrees to sell a machine to B for use in B's business. The sales contract, entered into on January 1, of Year 1, requires B to pay for the machine in four annual installments of $50,000, the first payment due on January 1, of Year 2. Both S and B use the accrual method. S's basis in the machine is $100,000. The AFR is 12%.

(a) Determine the character and timing of S's income. Consider §§ 453, 483(a), (b) and (c), 1274(c)(3)(C), 1274A(a) and (c), and Regs. §§ 15A.453–1(b)(2); 1.483–1(a)(2) Ex. 1; 1.483–1(c)(2)(ii)(C); 1.483–2(a)(1)(ii) and (iii).

(b) Determine B's basis in the machine and the amount and timing of his interest deductions.

The following tables should be used in answering the above problems:

Semiannual Compound Interest and Annuity 10.00%

	Amount of 1	Present Worth of 1	Present Worth of 1 Per Period	
	What a single $1 deposit grows to in the future. The deposit is made at the beginning of the first period.	What $1 to be paid in the future is worth today. Value today of a single payment tomorrow.	What $1 to be paid at the end of each period is worth today. Value today of a series of payments tomorrow.	
Year				**Period**
	1.050 000	0.952 381	0.952 381	1
	1.102 500	0.907 029	1.859 410	2
1	1.102 500	0.907 029	1.859 410	2
2	1.215 506	0.822 702	3.545 951	4
3	1.340 096	0.746 215	5.075 692	6
4	1.477 455	0.676 839	6.463 213	8
5	1.628 895	0.613 913	7.721 735	10

Semiannual Compound Interest and Annuity 9.00%

	Amount of 1	Present Worth of 1	
Year			**Period**
	1.045 000	0.956 938	1
	1.092 025	0.915 730	2
1	1.092 025	0.915 730	2
2	1.192 519	0.838 561	4
3	1.302 260	0.767 896	6
4	1.422 101	0.703 185	8
5	1.552 969	0.643 928	10

Deferred Payments for the Use of Property or for Services. As discussed in connection with the all-events test at pp. 231–232, the accrual method of accounting distorted the matching of income and deductions by allowing a current deduction for the entire amount of a future obligation. When the accrual of the deduction was coupled with the absence of any requirement limiting the amount of the current deduction to its present discounted value, accrual method taxpayers obtained unwarranted tax savings. This resulted because the timing of the income and deduction from a transaction, such as the rental of property, depended upon each party's method of accounting. Assume a landlord, who used the cash method, leased property to a tenant, who used the accrual method, for a period of three years. The entire rental of $300,000 was payable at the end of the third year. The cash method landlord reported rental income only when he collected the rental at the end of the lease, and then he treated the entire $300,000 as rental income. The accrual method tenant deducted, in each year, a ratable portion of the $300,000 rental obligation, or $100,000 a year, on the theory that this portion of his liability was fixed annually.

Congress believed that the lack of symmetry between the tenant and landlord should be eliminated. Moreover, Congress believed that where the payment of rentals is deferred, an interest element is present, and that the interest element should be realized and recognized by cash and accrual taxpayers. Assuming a 10% market interest rate, $23,255 of interest is present in the above 3-year deferral.

The 1984 legislation added new § 467 to cover the potential abuses found in deferred rental transactions. Generally, the landlord and tenant must report their rental income and deductions using the accrual method of accounting. § 467(a)(1). The amount of rent accrued for each year is determined by § 467(b)(1) which allocates the rents in accordance with the rental agreement. In addition, the parties must annually accrue any interest on the accrued but unpaid rents (§ 467(a)(2)); the unstated interest being determined under § 467(e)(4). However, this approach is not applied to any rental agreement involving total payments of $250,000 or less. § 467(d)(2). The § 467 approach also applies to the deferred payments for services if so provided in the Regulations. § 467(g).

Problem

Starstruck, an actor, enters into an arrangement with Motion Pictures, Inc., under which he will render services in a motion picture during Year 1. The services are completed by December 31 of Year 1. In return, Motion Pictures, Inc. will pay Starstruck $1,331,000, but payment will be deferred until January 1 of Year 5. (Assume an interest rate of 10%, compounded annually.) Starstruck uses the cash method of accounting; Motion Pictures, Inc. uses the accrual method of accounting.

    (a) What is the amount of income Starstruck must report? When is it included in gross income? Consider § 467(g), (a)(1), (a)(2), and (e)(4).

    (b) What are the amounts of Motion Picture's deductions? When can the corporation take its deductions? When does the corporation satisfy the "all events" and "economic performance" tests. Consider § 461(h). Reconsider Problem 1 on page 254. Consider § 467(g).

H. NONRECOGNITION OF REALIZED GAINS AND LOSSES

1. NONRECOGNITION TRANSACTIONS: AN OVERVIEW

The term recognition connotes that a taxpayer's gain or loss will be taken into account for tax purposes. Generally, realized gains or losses are recognized unless a statutory provision provides for nonrecognition.

Nonrecognition provisions permit the taxpayer to realize gains on certain dispositions without payment of tax. Nonrecognition of a realized gain defers the payment of taxes until the taxpayer makes a disposition of the property that does not qualify for nonrecognition treatment. Installment sale treatment is another form of nonrecognition for a realized gain. As previously discussed, the deferral of tax on a realized gain can be very valuable.

Losses may also not be recognized. Since an unrecognized loss cannot be used to offset income from other sources, nonrecognition of a realized loss accelerates the payment of taxes.

Nonrecognition of gains and losses is founded on several premises. Nonrecognition may flow from the continuity of a taxpayer's investment (or economic position) which exists despite a change in the form or identity of the taxpayer's property. Certain hardship situations may also result in nonrecognition.

We have already considered several nonrecognition provisions. Section 1033 (page 147 and Problem 1(a)(ii) at page 756) provides for the nonrecognition of gain (but not loss) on involuntary conversions of property. An involuntary conversion encompasses the destruction of property (in whole or in part), theft, seizure, requisition, or condemnation. Section 1033 is premised on hardship. It is unlikely that the taxpayer intended to cash in his investment and realize and recognize a gain at the time of the involuntary conversion. For example, if a taxpayer's truck, with an adjusted basis of $12,000, is destroyed by fire, and he receives insurance proceeds of $14,500 for the truck, he realizes a gain of $2,500. If the taxpayer reinvests the insurance proceeds in property "similar or related in service and use" within two years, he need not recognize the realized gain, provided the qualified replacement property he purchased has a cost at least equal to the amount realized. § 1033(a)(2)(A). Where the truck is destroyed and thus involuntarily converted to cash, the taxpayer may elect whether or not to recognize the realized gain. His adjusted basis in the new truck equals its cost as adjusted downward to insure that the taxpayer's realized gain of $2,500 will eventually be recognized on the subsequent sale or other disposition of the vehicle. § 1033(b).

Also reconsider §§ 108 and 1017 (pp. 237–243) and §§ 109 and 1019 (pp. 121–122).

2. NONRECOGNITION ON THE SALE OF TAXPAYER'S PRINCIPAL RESIDENCE

Section 1034 constitutes, along with the exclusion from gross income of the imputed rental value of a residence and deductions for interest paid on a qualified residence and real estate taxes, another tax benefit for home owners in comparison with renters. Under § 1034, the realized gain on the sale of the taxpayer's principal residence is not recognized if the taxpayer purchases and uses a new principal residence within two years before or after the sale of the old residence, provided the cost of the new residence is at least as much as the adjusted sales price, as defined, of the old residence. Individuals who relocate for employment purposes may generally use the rollover provision more than once in a two year period. § 1034(d)(2). The unrecognized gain on the sale of the old residence is deducted from the adjusted basis of the new residence thereby deferring the taxation of the gain. § 1034(e). If the new residence is less costly, the taxpayer's realized gain is recognized, but only to the extent the adjusted sales price of the old residence exceeds the cost of the new residence. The taxpayer tacks on the holding period of the old residence to the holding period of the new residence. § 1223(7).

Section 1034 is designed "to eliminate a hardship under existing law * * * [which is] accentuated when the transactions are necessitated by such facts as an increase in the size of the family or a change in the place of the taxpayer's employment. In these situations the transaction partakes of the nature of an involuntary conversion." H.R. Rep. No. 586, 82d Cong. 1st Sess. (1951) reprinted in 1951–2 C.B. 357, 377. But do taxpayers generally sustain a hardship in selling their principal residence? Don't individuals decide to move after balancing the advantages and disadvantages?

Section 121 provides that an individual who attains age 55 may exclude from gross income, on a one-time, elective basis, up to $125,000 of gain from the sale of residence which the seller occupied for at least three out of the preceding five years. How does § 121 account for inflation? There is only one lifetime election with respect to married taxpayers. Taxpayers age 55 and above may use both the nonrecognition provision of § 1034 and the $125,000 exclusion provision of § 121.

Problem

Senior purchased a home for $42,000 fifteen years ago. This year he retired at age 65 and moved to Florida. Senior sold his home up north for $187,000 and used $52,000 of the proceeds to buy a condominium as his new home.

    (a) Does he have to recognize any of his gain? Consider §§ 1034 and 121 (especially § 121(d)(7)) and Reg. § 1.121–5(g).

    (b) What is his basis and holding period in the condominium? Consider § 1223(7).

3. LIKE-KIND EXCHANGES: NONRECOGNITION BECAUSE OF CONTINUITY OF INVESTMENT

Section 1031 provides for the mandatory nonrecognition of the gain or loss on the exchange, but not the sale, of "like kind" productive property (but not inventory or property held primarily for sale) or investment property (but not stocks and bonds). Productive property may be swapped for investment property in a like-kind exchange and vice versa. Reg. § 1.1031(a)–1(a). See also Reg. § 1.1031(a)–1(b).

As an example of a "like-kind" exchange, Al and Bob, the owners of two apartment buildings, may swap their properties. Under § 1031, the gain or loss realized by each owner is not recognized because each owner maintains a continuity of investment in property of the same type as originally held. As to each owner, the new building received is not substantially different from the old building. Each owner is still an owner of rental real estate and the exchange transaction is not deemed the appropriate time to recognize the gain or loss. Nonrecognition of gain or loss is accomplished by the taxpayer's adjusted basis for his old building becoming the taxpayer's adjusted basis for his new building. This is the so-called "substituted basis". § 1031(d). Recognition of gain or loss is postponed until the taxpayer sells the new building or exchanges it for dissimilar property.

Section 1223(1) provides that the holding period of property acquired in a "like-kind" exchange under § 1031 includes the taxpayer's holding period for the property given up in the exchange.

Reference: Jensen, The Uneasy Justification for Special Treatment of Like-Kind Exchanges, 4 Am.J.Tax Policy 193 (1985).

Question

What is the rationale for § 1031? If a realized gain is not recognized, does this mean that the gain is excluded and never subject to taxation? If not, is the recognition merely postponed? How is this deferral accomplished? What kind of basis rules are involved in a like-kind exchange? Examine § 1031(d).

It is a rare situation where there is an exchange of like-kind assets with identical values. One party usually exchanges property that has a value less than the value of the property received. As part of the exchange that party also transfers cash or other property not qualifying for nonrecognition treatment (commonly referred to as "boot") thereby equalizing the exchange. If boot is part of a like-kind exchange, is nonrecognition still available? Assume the fair market value of Al's building is $100,000 (and the adjusted basis is $60,000) and the fair market value of Bob's building is $90,000 (and the adjusted basis is $50,000). To consummate the exchange, Bob transfers his building to Al plus $10,000 in cash. Al realizes a gain of $40,000, that is, the building received with a fair market value of $90,000 plus $10,000 cash, less the adjusted basis ($60,000) of Al's building. But Al recognizes a gain of only $10,000, the amount of the cash (the "boot") received. This is because under § 1031(b) the gain recognized cannot exceed the value of the boot received. Bob realizes a gain of $40,000, that is, the building received, with a fair market value of $100,000, less the adjusted basis ($50,000) of the building given up and the basis ($10,000) in the cash. Because Bob did not receive any cash or nonqualifying property, Bob does not recognize any gain. § 1031(a) and (b).

What is the basis of the properties exchanged?   Under § 1031(d), Al's basis for the new building equals $60,000, that is, Al's old basis ($60,000) plus the gain recognized ($10,000) less the cash received ($10,000) on the exchange.   Reg. § 1.1031(d)–1(e).   The unrecognized portion of the realized gain ($30,000), will eventually be taxed when the newly-acquired building is sold or exchanged for dissimilar property. Bob's basis for the new building is $60,000, that is, the adjusted basis ($50,000) of the property given up plus $10,000 in cash transferred less the money received (zero), plus the gain recognized (zero).

If property exchanged is subject to a mortgage, under § 1031(b), the amount realized by the transferor includes the amount of the mortgage, which is viewed as cash, whether the transferee assumes the mortgage or takes the property subject to the mortgage.   The amount of the mortgage is treated as boot received by the transferor for purposes of determining the gain recognized (Reg. § 1.1031(b)–1(c)), and accordingly reduces the taxpayer's basis in the acquired property.   The taxpayer's basis in the acquired property is increased by the amount of any mortgage to which such property is subject.   The intricacies with respect to the treatment of liabilities in like-kind exchange transactions are detailed in Reg. § 1.1031(d)–2.

Section 1031(c) does not permit a realized loss to be recognized, despite the receipt of boot.   Taxpayers normally do not desire the nonrecognition of losses on properties which have declined in value. Taxpayers would rather sell loss property for cash, recognize the loss (the deductibility of the loss turns on meeting the requirements of § 165; the character of the loss must also be considered) and invest the proceeds in the new property.   The sale of property for cash would bar the application of the nonrecognition provisions of § 1031.   Section 1031 appears to be a mandatory provision, but with planning, it becomes an elective provision.

Problems

1.   Ernie exchanges his old pickup truck, used in his business, which has an adjusted basis of $2,800 and fair market value of $4,800, for a new truck which sells for $5,800.   Ernie gives up his old truck and $1,000 in cash.   The new truck will be put to the same use in his business.

(a) Is Ernie's exchange of a used truck for a new truck a like kind exchange?   Consider § 1031(a) and Reg. § 1.1031(a)–1(b).

(b) What is the amount of Ernie's realized gain and recognized gain?   Consider § 1031(b).

(c) What is Ernie's basis in the new truck?   Consider § 1031(d).

(d) What is Ernie's holding period in the new truck?   Consider § 1223(1).

2.   Assume Ernie exchanges his old pickup truck, used in his business, which has an adjusted basis of $2,800 and a fair market value of $4,800, for another pickup truck with a fair market value of $4,600 and $200 in cash.

Does Ernie recognize any gain? Consider § 1031(b). What is Ernie's basis in the acquired truck? Consider § 1031(d) and Reg. § 1.1031(d)–1(b) Ex.

3. Al exchanges an apartment building, with an adjusted basis of $170,000 and a fair market value of $200,000, for an apartment building owned by Bob, with an adjusted basis of $135,000 and a fair market value of $180,000. Bob also transfers $20,000 in cash to Al.

(a) Is the application of § 1031 elective in this situation? Consider § 1031(a).

(b) What is Al's realized gain, recognized gain, and basis in the property received? Consider § 1031(b) and (d).

(c) What is Bob's realized gain, recognized gain, and basis in the property received? Consider § 1031(b) and (d).

(d) What are Al and Bob's holding periods in the respective properties acquired. Consider § 1223(1).

4. Carl owns land with a basis of $10,000 and a fair market value of $12,500. Carl exchanges the land with Don for parcel of land worth $9,000, an auto worth $2,000, and $1,500 in cash. What is Carl's realized gain, recognized gain, and basis in the acquired assets? Consider § 1031(b), (d), and Reg. § 1.1031(d)–1(c) Ex.

5. Ellen purchased an apartment building several years ago for $80,000, paying $20,000 in cash and taking the building subject to an existing $80,000 nonrecourse mortgage. Currently, Ellen's adjusted basis in the building is $60,000 and the outstanding mortgage is $40,000. Ellen's building has a fair market value of $140,000.

Frank owns a building, free and clear, with a fair market value of $90,000. Frank's adjusted basis in his building is $35,000. Frank gives the building and $10,000 in cash to Ellen, in exchange for Ellen's building subject to the existing mortgage.

(a) What is the amount of Ellen's realized gain and recognized gain? Consider Reg. 1.1031(d)–2 which treats a mortgage assumed as money received if the property given up in the exchange is subject to a mortgage. What is the reason for this rule and is this consistent with the Tufts decision.

(b) What is Ellen's basis in the newly acquired building? Consider § 1031(d).

(c) What is the amount of Frank's realized gain and recognized gain? Consider § 1031(b).

(d) What is Frank's basis in the newly acquired building? Consider § 1031(d).

(e) What are Ellen and Frank's holding periods in the respective properties acquired? Consider § 1223(1).

(f) What is the amount and character of Ellen's gain on the subsequent sale of the newly acquired building for $90,000 two months later.

Fed'l Inc. Tax (S. & H.) ACB—30

I. SALE OR LEASE

1. SALE-LEASEBACK TRANSACTIONS

A sale and leaseback transaction involves the taxpayer, who already owns an asset, selling that asset and leasing it back from the purchaser. The sale and leaseback transaction enables the taxpayer to raise cash and realize and recognize a loss on the property without surrendering possession of the property over the term of the lease. Typically, the lease will be a net lease with the seller-lessee paying a monthly rental which is roughly equal to the amortized repayment of the principal and interest on the buyer's financing plus a return on the buyer's investment. The rental payments made by the seller-lessee are deductible. This is helpful if the value of the property consists mostly of land or if the building has been fully depreciated by the seller. At the expiration of the lease, the buyer-lessor will take possession of the property. The arrangements may contain options to cancel or extend the lease and options for the lessee to buy back the property at an amount generally equivalent to the unpaid principal on the purchaser-lessor's financing plus a return on the purchaser's investment.

JORDAN MARSH CO. v. COMMISSIONER

United States Court of Appeals, Second Circuit, 1959.
269 F.2d 453.

HINCKS, CIRCUIT JUDGE.

* * *

The transactions giving rise to the dispute were conveyances by the petitioner in 1944 of the fee of two parcels of property in the city of Boston where the petitioner, then as now, operated a department store. In return for its conveyances the petitioner received $2,300,000 in cash which, concededly, represented the fair market value of the properties. The conveyances were unconditional, without provision of any option to repurchase. At the same time, the petitioner received back from the vendees leases of the same properties for terms of 30 years and 3 days, with options to renew for another 30 years if the petitioner-lessee should erect new buildings thereon. The vendees were in no way connected with the petitioner. The rentals to be paid under the leases concededly were full and normal rentals so that the leasehold interests which devolved upon the petitioner were of no capital value.

In its return for 1944, the petitioner, claiming the transaction was a sale under [§ 1001(c)], sought to deduct from income the difference [$2,500,000] between the adjusted basis of the property [$4,800,000] and the cash received [$2,300,000]. The Commissioner disallowed the deduction, taking the position that the transaction represented an exchange of property for other property of like kind. Under [§ 1031(a)] such exchanges are not occasions for the recognition of gain or loss; and even the receipt of cash or other property in the exchange of the properties of like kind is not enough to permit the taxpayer to recognize loss. [§ 1031(c)] Thus the Commissioner viewed the transaction, in substance, as an exchange of a fee interest for a long term lease, justifying his position by [Reg. § 1.1031(a)–1(c)] which provides that a leasehold of more than 30 years is the equivalent of a fee interest.

* * *

Upon this appeal, we must decide whether the transaction in question here was a sale or an exchange of property for other property of like kind within the meaning of [§ 1031(a) and (c)]. If we should find that it is an exchange, we would then have to decide whether the Commissioner's regulation, declaring that a leasehold of property of 30 years or more is property "of like kind" to the fee in the same property, is a reasonable gloss to put upon the words of the statute. The judge in the Tax Court felt that Century Electric Co. v. Commissioner of Internal Rev., 8 Cir., 192 F.2d 155, certiorari denied 342 U.S. 954, 72 S.Ct. 625, 96 L.Ed. 708, affirming 15 T.C. 581, was dispositive of both questions. In the view which we take of the first question, we do not have to pass upon the second question. For we hold that the transaction here was a sale and not an exchange.

The controversy centers around the purposes of Congress in enacting [§ 1031(a)], dealing with non-taxable exchanges. The section represents an exception to the general rule, stated in [§ 1002] that upon the sale or exchange of property the entire amount of gain or loss is to be recognized by the taxpayer. The first Congressional attempt to make certain exchanges of this kind non-taxable occurred in Section 202(c), Revenue Act of 1921, c. 135, 42 Stat. 227. Under this section, no gain or loss was recognized from an exchange of property unless the property received in exchange had a "readily realizable market value." In 1924, this section was amended to the form in which it is applicable here. Discussing the old section the House Committee observed:

> "The provision is so indefinite that it cannot be applied with accuracy or with consistency. It appears best to provide generally that gain or loss is recognized from all exchanges, and then except specifically and in definite terms those cases of exchanges in which it is not desired to tax the gain or allow the loss. This results in definiteness and accuracy and enables a taxpayer to determine prior to the consummation of a given transaction the tax liability that will result." (Committee Reports on Rev.Act of 1924, reprinted in Int.Rev.Cum.Bull. 1939–1 (Part 2), p. 250.)

Thus the "readily realizable market value" test disappeared from the statute. A later report, reviewing the section, expressed its purpose as follows:

> "The law has provided for 12 years that gain or loss is recognized on exchanges of property having a fair market value, such as stocks, bonds, and negotiable instruments; on exchanges of property held primarily for sale; or on exchanges of one kind of property for another kind of property; but not on other exchanges of property solely for property of like kind. In other words, profit or loss is recognized in the case of exchanges of notes or securities, which are essentially like

money; or in the case of stock in trade; or in case the taxpayer exchanges the property comprising his original investment for a different kind of property; but *if the taxpayer's money is still tied up in the same kind of property* as that in which it was originally invested, he is not allowed to compute and deduct his theoretical loss on the exchange, nor is he charged with a tax upon his theoretical profit. The calculation of the profit or loss is deferred until it is realized in cash, marketable securities, or other property not of the same kind having a fair market value." (House Ways and Means Committee Report, reprinted in Int.Rev.Cum.Bull.1939–1 (Part 2), p. 564.) [61]

These passages lead us to accept as correct the petitioner's position with respect to the purposes of the section. Congress was primarily concerned with the inequity, in the case of an exchange, of forcing a taxpayer to recognize a paper gain which was still tied up in a continuing investment of the same sort. If such gains were not to be recognized, however, upon the ground that they were theoretical, neither should equally theoretical losses. And as to both gains and losses the taxpayer should not have it within his power to avoid the operation of the section by stipulating for the addition of cash, or boot, to the property received in exchange. These considerations, rather than concern for the difficulty of the administrative task of making the valuations necessary to compute gains and losses, were at the root of the Congressional purpose in enacting [§ 1031(a) and (c)]. Indeed, if these sections had been intended to obviate the necessity of making difficult valuations, one would have expected them to provide for nonrecognition of gains and losses in all exchanges, whether the property received in exchanges were "of a like kind" or *not* of a like kind. And if such had been the legislative objective, [§ 1031(b)], providing for the recognition of gain from exchanges not wholly in kind, would never have been enacted.

That such indeed was the legislative objective is supported by Portland Oil Co. v. Commissioner of Internal Revenue, 1 Cir., 109 F.2d 479. There Judge Magruder, in speaking of a cognate provision contained in [§ 351(a)], said at page 488:

> "It is the purpose of [§ 351(a)] to save the taxpayer from an immediate recognition of a gain, or to intermit the claim of a loss, in certain transactions where gain or loss may have accrued in a constitutional sense, but where in a popular and economic sense there has been a mere change in the form of ownership and the taxpayer has not really 'cashed in' on the theoretical gain, or closed out a losing venture."

In conformity with this reading of the statute, we think the petitioner here, by its unconditional conveyances to a stranger, had done more than make a change in the *form of ownership:* it was a change as to the *quantum* of ownership whereby, in the words just quoted, it had "closed out a losing venture." By the transaction its

---

61. Emphasis supplied.

capital invested in the real estate involved had been completely liquidated for cash to an amount fully equal to the value of the fee. This, we hold, was a sale—not an exchange within the purview of [§ 1031].

The Tax Court apparently thought it of controlling importance that the transaction in question involved no change in the petitioner's possession of the premises: it felt that the decision in Century Electric Co. v. Commissioner of Internal Rev., supra, controlled the situation here. We think, however, that that case was distinguishable on the facts. For notwithstanding the lengthy findings made with meticulous care by the Tax Court in that case, 15 T.C. 581, there was no finding that the cash received by the taxpayer was the full equivalent of the value of the fee which the taxpayer had conveyed to the vendee-lessor, and no finding that the lease back called for a rent which was fully equal to the rental value of the premises. Indeed, in its opinion the Court of Appeals pointed to evidence that the fee which the taxpayer had "exchanged" may have had a value substantially in excess of the cash received. And in the Century Electric case, the findings showed, at page 585, that the taxpayer-lessee, unlike the taxpayer here, was not required to pay "general state, city and school taxes" because its lessor was an educational institution which under its charter was exempt from such taxes. Thus the leasehold interest in Century Electric on this account may well have had a premium value. In the absence of findings as to the values of the properties allegedly "exchanged," necessarily there could be no finding of a loss. And without proof of a loss, of course, the taxpayer could not prevail. Indeed, in the Tax Court six of the judges expressly based their concurrences on that limited ground. 15 T.C. 596.

* * *

* * * Here plainly the petitioner by the transfer finally closed out a losing venture. And it cannot justly be said that the economic situation of the petitioner was unchanged by a transaction which substituted $2,300,000 in cash for its investment in real estate and left it under a liability to make annual payments of rent for upwards of thirty years. Many *bona fide* business purposes may be served by such a transaction. Cary, Corporate Financing through the Sale and Lease-Back of Property: Business, Tax, and Policy Considerations, 62 Harv.L. Rev. 1.

In ordinary usage, an "exchange" means the giving of one piece of property in return for another—not, as the Commissioner urges here, the return of a lesser interest in a property received from another. It seems unlikely that Congress intended that an "exchange" should have the strained meaning for which the Commissioner contends. For the legislative history states expressly an intent to correct the indefiniteness of prior versions of the Act by excepting from the general rule "specifically and in definite terms those cases of exchanges in which it is not desired to tax the gain or allow the loss."

But even if under certain circumstances the return of a part of the property conveyed may constitute an exchange for purposes of [§ 1031], we think that in this case, in which cash was received for the full value of the property conveyed, the transaction must be classified as a sale. Standard Envelope Manufacturing Co. v. C.I.R., 15 T.C. 41; May Department Stores Co. v. C.I.R., 16 T.C. 547.

Reversed.

A carved out right held by the seller (for example, the retention of a lease) may be deemed a retained interest or an amount realized by him. For example, the seller, in consideration of the payment of $750,000 by the buyer, transferred to the buyer title to a warehouse worth $1,000,000. The buyer assumed control of the premises and bore the risks and benefits of ownership. However, the seller retained the right to use the warehouse, without payment of rent, for the next $2\frac{1}{2}$ years. The $1,000,000 sales price equalled the value of the cash received and the present value of the leasehold interest retained by seller. The seller realized $1,000,000 on the sale and had a deduction for prepaid rent in the sum of $250,000 (the present value of the leasehold interest), which must be amortized over the next $2\frac{1}{2}$ years. Steinway and Sons v. Commissioner, 46 T.C. 375 (1966) (Acq. 1967–2 C.B. 3). The buyer realized $250,000 in rental income over the $2\frac{1}{2}$ year period and took a $1,000,000 basis in the warehouse. In Alstores Realty Co. v. Commissioner, 46 T.C. 363 (1966) (Acq. 1967–2 C.B. 1), the Tax Court held that the buyer received the value of the leasehold which was used to pay for the property. The Tax Court reasoned as follows (46 T.C. at 370–374):

> Petitioner contends that even if the space-occupancy agreement should be regarded as a lease, there was, nonetheless, no income produced to the "lessor" since the "lease" was rent free. While it may be true that no rent was due or to be paid after Steinway's [the seller's] occupancy was to begin as petitioner's tenant, the agreement of the parties recognizes that it was because prepayment had been made by Steinway. As disclosed by our findings the contract itself speaks in terms of "further payment," an obvious recognition by the parties at that time that payment had already been made. The answer to petitioner's contention here is that although there were no cash payments to petitioner designated as rent after the property was deeded to it, Steinway's right of occupancy thereafter was a valuable one for which petitioner must have received consideration in some form, and that consideration was in the form of Steinway's conveyance to petitioner of fee title to the entire building—to the extent that the purchase price of the building exceeded the $750,000 cash paid therefor, or $253,090.75, as determined by respondent. This approach to a similar transaction was taken in Famous Foods, Inc. v. United States, 215 F.Supp. 206 (W.D.Pa.1963).

> The alternative analysis of the situation looks to the substance of the transaction. Petitioner here argues that, although in form there

may have been a sale and leaseback, in substance there was a conveyance of a *future interest* with Steinway reserving to itself, or carving
out, a term of 2½ years in a portion of the property. Hence, Steinway
in substance retained its right to occupancy not as a lessee of petitioner, but as a legal owner of a reserved term for years. This approach is
supported by *Kruesel v. United States,* an unreported case (D.Minn.
1963, 12 A.F.T.R.2d 5701, 63–2 U.S.T.C. par. 9714).

Although at first blush petitioner's argument is an appealing one,
we conclude that it must be rejected and we must hold for respondent.
Steinway did not in form or substance reserve an estate for years.

An analogous situation was presented in McCulley Ashlock, 18
T.C. 405 (1952). There the building in question was subject to a lease
to a third party at the time it was purchased by the taxpayer. The
contract of sale provided that the buyer would pay $40,000 cash but the
seller was to retain "possession" of the premises and all the rights to
the rental income from the lessee until the expiration of the primary
term of the existing lease (about 28 months from date of the sale
contract). The Commissioner determined that the rent received by the
seller subsequent to conveyance of title to the taxpayer purchaser was
really taxable income to the taxpayer purchaser. We rejected the
Commissioner's approach in that case, holding that the seller had
reserved an ownership interest in the property (an estate for years) and
that the rents received were income to the seller for occupancy of what
was still his property—not income to the purchaser, who did not then
have a present legal ownership interest but only a future interest. The
essence of our reasoning in the *Ashlock* case was as follows (pp. 411–
412).

> Here, the trustees [the sellers of the property] not only re-
> tained the rents legally but they also retained control and benefits
> of ownership. Under the contract of sale on April 18, 1945, the
> trustees specifically agreed to pay property taxes, insurance premi-
> ums, and "all normal maintenance items and expenses," so that
> the property would be delivered to * * * [the buyer] in the
> present condition except for normal wear and tear. Furthermore,
> the June 11, 1945, agreement stated that in the event that the
> property was damaged or destroyed, and loss of income during the
> period of repair or reconstruction would be the trustees' loss. It
> further provided that insurance proceeds would be devoted to
> restore and repair the property, except in the event of total
> destruction petitioner would have the option of rebuilding the
> premises or compensating the trustees for unpaid rent. Thus the
> trustee bore the risks of ownership of the rents and managed the
> property. Larger expenses or a cessation of rents were risks
> incurred by the trustees. * * *

A directly analogous problem, solved by the same type of reasoning
may be found in the "oil payment" line of cases in which the question
is whether or not the vendor of an oil lease retains an economic
interest in the oil in place. See Thomas v. Perkins, 301 U.S. 655
(1937).

The same factors which we looked to in *Ashlock* in deciding in favor of the purchaser, analyzed in the factual posture of the instant case, dictate the opposite result here. Petitioner, the buyer, assumed control of the premises and the benefits of ownership. Petitioner, the buyer, specifically agreed to pay for and supply to Steinway, the seller, heat, electricity, and water. The space-occupancy agreement stated that in the event the property was damaged or destroyed and Steinway's occupancy was thereby destroyed or impaired the burden of loss would be upon *petitioner* (with petitioner agreeing to pay Steinway 6¼ cents per square foot per month for space so affected). It is clear in the instant case that the buyer bore the risks and burdens of ownership during the term of the space-occupancy agreement. Such was not the case in *McCulley Ashlock*, supra, nor apparently in *Kruesel v. United States*, supra, relied upon by petitioner.

Furthermore, the rights of Steinway, the seller, as occupant were not those of a holder of a legal estate for years but were specifically limited to those of a lessee. The standard terms and conditions of a New York Real Estate Board form lease were imposed. For example, Steinway could not alter or improve the building nor sublet or assign its interest without the consent of petitioner.

Of key significance in this case is the fact that petitioner was required to pay to Steinway 6¼ cents per square foot per month for space which Steinway was entitled to occupy but which it may have been unable to occupy by reason of an act of God or the fault of petitioner, or which it may have elected to vacate during the last one-half year of the space occupancy agreement. This arrangement is entirely inconsistent with the theory that Steinway had a reserved estate for years; why would petitioner, the alleged remainderman, be required to make payments to Steinway, the alleged owner of an estate for years, as a result of nonoccupancy by the latter? What we really have here is a provision for reimbursement of prepaid rent in the event the tenant is denied (or, during the last one-half year of the term, elects abandonment of) its right of unfettered occupancy, the prepaid rent being in the form of the value of the property received by petitioner in excess of the $750,000 cash paid therefor.

Petitioner emphasizes the fact that it received no cash rental payments at any time; it merely purchased real estate for cash. This is partly true, but one need not receive cash to have received income. In Pembroke v. Helvering, 70 F.2d 850 (C.A.D.C.1934), affirming 23 B.T.A. 1176 (1931), the taxpayer was held to have received rent income in the amount of the value of the equity in certain property received in partial consideration for granting a long-term leasehold on other property owned by the taxpayer. In the instant case petitioner received, in exchange for the lease interest granted to Steinway, rent income in the amount of the excess of the value of the property that petitioner received over the cash which it paid.

Rather than to rely on its argument that it received no cash payments labeled as rent, petitioner might have attempted to show that it did not receive on the purchase any value in excess of the cash consideration paid so that it received nothing which could be considered rent, even constructively. However, such a showing has not been made and we have found as an ultimate fact that the property had a fair market value of [$1,000,000] at the time of transfer.

* * *

Possibly the result in the instant case would be different if the parties had in fact *intended* to carve out a reserved term for years in Steinway and had structured their transaction in that form. See *Kruesel v. United States*, supra. We do not agree with petitioner, however, that to hold that there was a sale of the fee and a simultaneous leaseback here is to exalt form over substance. The so-called space-occupancy agreement placed the two parties' rights, obligations, and risks as they would be allocated in a typical lease arrangement. Hence, the arrangement was a lease in substance as well as in form.

* * *

In Wagner v. Commissioner, 518 F.2d 655 (10th Cir.1975), a landlord owned real estate subject to an existing lease which expired on August 31, 1970. The taxpayer executed a contract to purchase the property from the landlord on June 26, 1969, for $610,000. The property was listed for $675,000. Other pertinent provisions of the contract were:

1. The landlord would retain all rents under the existing lease until its expiration on August 31, 1970. These rents would total $48,000;

2. The landlord would pay all real estate taxes on the property until August 31, 1970. This would total $24,000;

3. The taxpayer would obtain possession of the property on termination of the lease;

4. The taxpayer did not have to pay interest on the unpaid purchase price until termination of the lease. Interest would otherwise have been $54,000.

A warranty deed was executed on November 24, 1969. The taxpayer claimed he became the owner on June 26, 1969, the date of the contract, and began taking depreciation deductions as of that date. The Commissioner argued that the taxpayer did not become the owner until termination of the lease. The court held for the taxpayer noting that the fact that property is sold subject to an existing lease will not postpone the time of sale. The court noted that the total purchase price was agreed on and the tradeouts on taxes and rents were negotiated as part of the purchase price.

Question

Consider the Alstore Realty and Wagner cases. Specifically:

(a) In each situation, what was sold? Was it the sale of a present right to property or a future right to the property?

(b) Depending on the nature of the transaction, what were the tax consequences?

2. REALITY OF A "SALE" (SALE v. LEASE)

A number of significant tax consequences turn on who is the owner of property. One issue that may arise is whether a taxpayer has purchased property or has merely leased property from the owner. A sale may create gain for the seller which he hopes to characterize as capital gains eligible for preferential tax treatment prior to 1988, with the depreciation (cost recovery) on the property thereafter going to the buyer. A lease creates "rents", a deductible item to the lessee and taxable as ordinary income to the lessor who may seek to retain the benefits of depreciation (cost recovery) and to avoid the recapture of depreciation and the investment tax credit (§§ 47, 1245, 1250). The user of the property may, however, desire a lease if the rental deduction is greater than the depreciation and other deductions, such as taxes. This is also advantageous if the property is land which is not depreciable. But if the lessee has no taxable income and is, therefore, unable to use the depreciation and other deductions, then having the lessor retain the deductions and the investment tax credit may result in lower rental for the lessee. The Commissioner seeks to impose criteria to differentiate leases from sales thereby limiting the freedom of the parties to structure a transaction for their own benefit. If there is a difference in the tax rates between the parties or if only one party has taxable income, the concern of the Internal Revenue Service will be stimulated.

In some cases, it is hard to determine whether a sale or lease took place. Answering this question is not an easy one since the ownership of property involves a number of rights which may be placed in different persons. Similarly a transfer of rights can involve a transfer of all or part of those rights and can be made absolute or contingent.

In the classic case of Clay Brown, which follows, the taxpayer transferred the stock of his corporation to a charity for nonrecourse consideration which was based completely on a percentage of the income of the business over a number of years. The Internal Revenue Service contended that this transaction could not be considered a sale, but the Supreme Court held that the fact that the buyer had no risk in connection with the reacquisition did not prevent a sale from occurring.

COMMISSIONER v. BROWN

Supreme Court of the United States, 1965.
380 U.S. 563, 85 S.Ct. 1162, 14 L.Ed.2d 75.

MR. JUSTICE WHITE delivered the opinion of the Court.

In 1950, when Congress addressed itself to the problem of the direct or indirect acquisition and operation of going businesses by charities or other tax-exempt entities, it was recognized that in many of the typical sale and lease-back transactions, the exempt organization was trading on and perhaps selling part of its exemption. H.R.Rep. No. 2319, 81st Cong., 2d Sess., pp. 38–39; S.Rep. No. 2375, 81st Cong., 2d Sess., pp. 31–32, U.S.Code Congressional Service 1950, p. 3053. For this and other reasons the Internal Revenue Code was accordingly amended in several respects, of principal importance for our purposes by taxing as "unrelated business income" the profits earned by a charity in the operation of a business, as well as the income from long-term leases of the business.[62] The short-term lease, however, of five years or less, was not affected and this fact has moulded many of the transactions in this field since that time, including the one involved in this case.

The Commissioner, however, in 1954, announced that when an exempt organization purchased a business and leased it for five years to another corporation, not investing its own funds but paying off the purchase price with rental income, the purchasing organization was in danger of losing its exemption; that in any event the rental income would be taxable income; that the charity might be unreasonably accumulating income; and finally, and most important for this case, that the payments received by the seller would not be entitled to capital gains treatment. Rev.Rul. 54–420, 1954–2 Cum.Bull. 128.

This case is one of the many in the course of which the Commissioner has questioned the sale of a business concern to an exempt organization. The basic facts are undisputed. Clay Brown, members of his family and three other persons owned substantially all of the stock in Clay Brown & Company, with sawmills and lumber interests near Fortuna, California. Clay Brown, the president of the company and spokesman for the group, was approached by a representative of California Institute for Cancer Research in 1952, and after considerable negotiation the stockholders agreed to sell their stock to the Institute for $1,300,000, payable $5,000 down from the assets of the company and the balance within 10 years from the earnings of the company's assets. It was provided that simultaneously with the transfer of the stock, the Institute would liquidate the company and lease its assets for five years to a new corporation, Fortuna Sawmills, Inc., formed and wholly owned by the attorneys for the sellers.[63] Fortuna would pay to the Institute

---

62. The Revenue Act of 1950, * * * [added what] are now §§ 501 through 504 and 511 through 515 of the Internal Revenue Code of [1986]. [The Tax Reform Act of 1969 further amended these sections.— Eds.]

63. The net current assets subject to liabilities were sold by the Institute to For-

80% of its operating profit without allowance for depreciation or taxes, and 90% of such payments would be paid over by the Institute to the selling stockholders to apply on the $1,300,000 note. This note was noninterest bearing, the Institute had no obligation to pay it except from the rental income and it was secured by mortgages and assignments of the assets transferred or leased to Fortuna. If the payments on the note failed to total $250,000 over any two consecutive years, the sellers could declare the entire balance of the note due and payable. The sellers were neither stockholders nor directors of Fortuna but it was provided that Clay Brown was to have a management contract with Fortuna at an annual salary and the right to name any successor manager if he himself resigned.[64]

The transaction was closed on February 4, 1953. Fortuna immediately took over operations of the business under its lease, on the same premises and with practically the same personnel which had been employed by Clay Brown & Company. Effective October 31, 1954, Clay Brown resigned as general manager of Fortuna and waived his right to name his successor. In 1957, because of a rapidly declining lumber market, Fortuna suffered severe reverses and its operations were terminated. Respondent sellers did not repossess the properties under their mortgages but agreed they should be sold by the Institute with the latter retaining 10% of the proceeds. Accordingly, the property was sold by the Institute for $300,000. The payments on the note from rentals and from the sale of the properties totaled $936,131.85. Respondents returned the payments received from rentals as the gain from the sale of capital assets. The Commissioner, however, asserted the payments were taxable as ordinary income and were not capital gain within the meaning of § 1222(3). * * *

In the Tax Court, the Commissioner asserted that the transaction was a sham and that in any event respondents retained such an economic interest in and control over the property sold that the transaction could not be treated as a sale resulting in a long-term capital gain. A divided Tax Court, 37 T.C. 461, found that there had been considerable good-faith bargaining at arm's length between the Brown family and the Institute, that the price agreed upon was within a reasonable range in the light of the earnings history of the corporation and the adjusted net worth of its assets, that the primary motivation for the Institute was the prospect of ending up with the assets of the business free and clear after the purchase price had been fully paid, which would then permit the Institute to convert the property and the money for use in cancer research, and that there had been a real

tuna for a promissory note which was assigned to sellers. The lease covered the remaining assets of Clay Brown & Company. Fortuna was capitalized at $25,000, its capital being paid in by its stockholders from their own funds.

64. Clay Brown's personal liability for some of the indebtedness of Clay Brown & Company, assumed by Fortuna, was continued. He also personally guaranteed some additional indebtedness incurred by Fortuna.

change of economic benefit in the transaction.[65] Its conclusion was that the transfer of respondents' stock in Clay Brown & Company to the Institute was a bona fide sale arrived at in an arm's-length transaction and that the amounts received by respondents were proceeds from the sale of stock and entitled to long-term capital gains treatment under [former provisions of] the Internal Revenue Code. The Court of Appeals affirmed, 9 Cir., 325 F.2d 313, and we granted certiorari, 377 U.S. 962, 84 S.Ct. 1647, 12 L.Ed.2d 734.

Having abandoned in the Court of Appeals the argument that this transaction was a sham, the Commissioner now admits that there was real substance in what occurred between the Institute and the Brown family. The transaction was a sale under local law. The Institute acquired title to the stock of Clay Brown & Company and, by liquidation, to all of the assets of that company, in return for its promise to pay over money from the operating profits of the company. If the stipulated price was paid, the Brown family would forever lose all rights to the income and properties of the company. Prior to the transfer, these respondents had access to all of the income of the company; after the transfer, 28% of the income remained with Fortuna and the Institute. Respondents had no interest in the Institute nor were they stockholders or directors of the operating company. Any rights to control the management were limited to the management contract between Clay Brown and Fortuna, which was relinquished in 1954.

Whatever substance the transaction might have had, however, the Commissioner claims that it did not have the substance of a sale within the meaning of § 1222(3). His argument is that since the Institute invested nothing, assumed no independent liability for the purchase price and promised only to pay over a percentage of the earnings of the company, the entire risk of the transaction remained on the sellers. Apparently, to qualify as a sale, a transfer of property for money or the promise of money must be to a financially responsible buyer who undertakes to pay the purchase price other than from the earnings or the assets themselves or there must be a substantial down payment which shifts at least part of the risk to the buyer and furnishes some cushion against loss to the seller.

To say that there is no sale because there is no risk-shifting and that there is no risk-shifting because the price to be paid is payable only from the income produced by the business sold, is very little different from saying that because business earnings are usually taxable as ordinary income, they are subject to the same tax when paid over as the purchase price of property. This argument has rationality but it places an unwarranted construction on the term "sale," is contrary to

65. The Tax Court found nothing to indicate that the arrangement between the stockholders and the Institute contemplated the Brown family's being free at any time to take back and operate the business.

the policy of the [former] capital gains provisions of the Internal Revenue Code, and has no support in the cases. We reject it.

"Capital gain" and "capital asset" are creatures of the tax law and the Court has been inclined to give these terms a narrow, rather than a broad, construction. Corn Products Co. v. Commissioner, 350 U.S. 46, 52, 76 S.Ct. 20, 24, 100 L.Ed. 29. A "sale," however, is a common event in the non-tax world; and since it is used in the Code without limiting definition and without legislative history indicating a contrary result, its common and ordinary meaning should at least be persuasive of its meaning as used in the Internal Revenue Code. "Generally speaking, the language in the Revenue Act, just as in any statute, is to be given its ordinary meaning, and the words 'sale' and 'exchange' are not to be read any differently." Helvering v. William Flaccus Oak Leather Co., 313 U.S. 247, 249, 61 S.Ct. 878, 880, 85 L.Ed. 1310; Crane v. Commissioner, 331 U.S. 1, 6, 67 S.Ct. 1047, 1050, 91 L.Ed. 1301; Old Colony R. Co. v. Commissioner, 284 U.S. 552, 560, 52 S.Ct. 211, 213, 76 L.Ed. 484.

> "A sale, in the ordinary sense of the word, is a transfer of property for a fixed price in money or its equivalent," State of Iowa v. McFarland, 110 U.S. 471, 478, 4 S.Ct. 210, 214, 28 L.Ed. 198; it is a contract "to pass rights of property for money,—which the buyer pays or promises to pay to the seller * * *," Williamson v. Berry, 8 How. 495, 544, 12 L.Ed. 1170. Compare the definition of "sale" in § 1(2) of the Uniform Sales Act and in § 2–106(1) of the Uniform Commercial Code. The transaction which occurred in this case was obviously a transfer of property for a fixed price payable in money.

* * *

As of January 31, 1953, the adjusted net worth of Clay Brown & Company as revealed by its books was $619,457.63. This figure included accumulated earnings of $448,471.63, paid in surplus, capital stock and notes payable to the Brown family. The appraised value as of that date, however, relied upon by the Institute and the sellers, was $1,064,877, without figuring interest on deferred balances. Under a deferred payment plan with a 6% interest figure, the sale value was placed at $1,301,989. The Tax Court found the sale price agreed upon was arrived at in an arm's-length transaction, was the result of real negotiating and was "within a reasonable range in light of the earnings history of the corporation and the adjusted net worth of the corporate assets." 37 T.C. 461, 486.

Obviously, on these facts, there had been an appreciation in value accruing over a period of years, Commissioner v. Gillette Motor Transport, Inc., 364 U.S. 130, 80 S.Ct. 1497, 4 L.Ed.2d 1617, and an "increase in the value of the income-producing property." Commissioner v. P.G. Lake, Inc., 356 U.S. 260, 266, 78 S.Ct. 691, 695. This increase taxpayers were entitled to realize at [the former preferential] capital gains rates on a cash sale of their stock; and likewise if they sold on a deferred payment plan taking an installment note and a mortgage as security. Further, if * * * the transaction otherwise satisfied [§ 453], the gain itself could be reported on the installment basis.

In the actual transaction, the stock was transferred for a price payable on the installment basis but payable from the earnings of the company. Eventually $936,131.85 was realized by respondents. This transaction, we think, is a sale, and so treating it is wholly consistent with the purposes of the Code to allow capital gains treatment for realization upon the enhanced value of a capital asset.

The Commissioner, however, embellishes his risk-shifting argument. Purporting to probe the economic realities of the transaction, he reasons that if the seller continues to bear all the risk and the buyer none, the seller must be collecting a price for his risk-bearing in the form of an interest in future earnings over and above what would be a fair market value of the property. Since the seller bears the risk, the so-called purchase price *must* be excessive and *must* be simply a device to collect future earnings at [the former preferential] capital gains rates.

We would hesitate to discount unduly the power of pure reason and the argument is not without force. But it does present difficulties. In the first place, it denies what the tax court expressly found—that the price paid was within reasonable limits based on the earnings and net worth of the company; and there is evidence in the record to support this finding. We do not have, therefore, a case where the price has been found excessive.

Secondly, if an excessive price is such an inevitable result of the lack of risk-shifting, it would seem that it would not be an impossible task for the Commissioner to demonstrate the fact. However, in this case he offered no evidence whatsoever to this effect; and in a good many other cases involving similar transactions, in some of which the reasonableness of the price paid by a charity was actually contested, the Tax Court has found the sale price to be within reasonable limits, as it did in this case.

Thirdly, the Commissioner ignores as well the fact that if the rents payable by Fortuna were deductible by it and not taxable to the Institute, the Institute could pay off the purchase price at a considerably faster rate than the ordinary corporate buyer subject to income taxes, a matter of considerable importance to a seller who wants the balance of his purchase price paid as rapidly as he can get it. The fact is that by April 30, 1955, a little over two years after closing this transaction, $412,595.77 had been paid on the note and within another year the sellers had collected another $238,498.80, for a total of $651,094.57.

Furthermore, risk-shifting of the kind insisted on by the Commissioner has not heretofore been considered an essential ingredient of a sale for tax purposes. In LeTulle v. Scofield, 308 U.S. 415, 60 S.Ct. 313, 84 L.Ed. 355, one corporation transferred properties to another for cash and bonds secured by the properties transferred. The Court held that there was "a sale or exchange upon which gain or loss must be reckoned in accordance with the provisions of the revenue act dealing with the recognition of gain or loss upon a sale or exchange," id., at 421, 60 S.Ct. at 316, since the seller retained only a creditor's interest rather than a proprietary one. "[T]hat the bonds were secured solely by the assets transferred and that upon default, the bondholder would retake only the property sold, [did not change] his status from that of a creditor to one having a proprietary stake." Ibid. Compare Marr v. United States, 268 U.S. 536, 45 S.Ct. 575, 69 L.Ed. 1079. To require a sale for tax purposes to be to a financially responsible buyer who undertakes to pay the purchase price from sources other than the earnings of the assets sold or to make a substantial down payment seems to us at odds with commercial practice and common understanding of what constitutes a sale. The term "sale" is used a great many times in the Internal Revenue Code and a wide variety of tax results hinge on the occurrence of a "sale." To accept the Commissioner's definition of sale would have wide ramifications which we are not prepared to visit upon taxpayers, absent congressional guidance in this direction.

The Commissioner relies heavily upon the cases involving a transfer of mineral interests, the transferor receiving a bonus and retaining a royalty or other interest in the mineral production. Thomas v. Perkins, 301 U.S. 655, 57 S.Ct. 911, 81 L.Ed. 1324. Thomas v. Perkins is deemed particularly pertinent. There a leasehold interest was transferred for a sum certain payable in oil as produced and it was held that the amounts paid to the transferor were not includable in the income of the transferee but were income of the transferor. We do not, however, deem either Thomas v. Perkins or the other cases controlling.

First, "Congress * * * has recognized the peculiar character of the business of extracting natural resources," Burton-Sutton Oil Co. v. Commissioner, 328 U.S. 25, 33, 66 S.Ct. 861, 866 * * *.

Second, Thomas v. Perkins does not have unlimited sweep. The Court in Anderson v. Helvering, [310 U.S. 404, 60 S.Ct. 952, 84 L.Ed. 1277], pointed out that it was still possible for the owner of a working interest to divest himself finally and completely of his mineral interest by effecting a sale. In that case the owner of royalty interest, fee interest and deferred oil payments contracted to convey them for $160,000 payable $50,000 down and the balance from one-half the proceeds which might be derived from the oil and gas produced and from the sale of the fee title to any of the lands conveyed. The Court refused to extend Thomas v. Perkins beyond the oil payment transaction involved in that case. Since the transferor in Anderson had provided for payment of the purchase price from the sale of fee interest as well as from the production of oil and gas, "the reservation of this additional type of security for the deferred payments serve[d] to distinguish this case from Thomas v. Perkins. It is similar to the reservation in a lease of oil payment rights together with a personal guarantee by the lessee that such payments shall at all events equal the specified sum." Anderson v. Helvering, supra, 310 U.S. at 412–413, 60 S.Ct. at

956. Hence, there was held to be an outright sale of the properties, all of the oil income therefrom being taxable to the transferee notwithstanding the fact of payment of part of it to the seller. The respondents in this case, of course, not only had rights against income, but if the income failed to amount to $250,000 in any two consecutive years, the entire amount could be declared due, which was secured by a lien on the real and personal properties of the company.[66]

There is another reason for us not to disturb the ruling of the Tax Court and the Court of Appeals. In 1963, the Treasury Department, in the course of hearings before the Congress, noted the availability of [the former preferential] capital gains treatment on the sale of capital assets even though the seller retained an interest in the income produced by the assets. The Department proposed a change in the law which would have taxed as ordinary income the payments on the sale of a capital asset which were deferred over more than five years and were contingent on future income. Payments, though contingent on income, required to be made within five years would not have lost capital gains status nor would payments not contingent on income even though accompanied by payments which were. Hearings before the House Committee on Ways and Means, 88th Cong., 1st Sess., Feb. 6, 7, 8 and 18, 1963, Pt. I (rev.), on the President's 1963 Tax Message, pp. 154–156.

Congress did not adopt the suggested change[67] but it is significant for our purposes that the proposed amendment did not deny the fact or

66. Respondents place considerable reliance on the rule applicable where patents are sold or assigned, the seller or assignor reserving an income interest. In Rev.Rul. 58–353, 1958–2 Cum.Bull. 408, the Service announced its acquiescence in various Tax Court cases holding that the consideration received by the owner of a patent for the assignment of a patent or the granting of an exclusive license to such patent may be treated as the proceeds of a sale of property for income tax purposes, even though the consideration received by the transferor is measured by production, use, or sale of the patented article. The Government now says that the Revenue Ruling amounts only to a decision to cease litigating the question, at least temporarily, and that the cases on which the rule is based are wrong in principle and inconsistent with the cases dealing with the taxation of mineral interests. We note, however, that in Rev.Rul. 60–226, 1960–1 Cum.Bull. 26, the Service extended the same treatment to the copyright field. Furthermore, the Secretary of the Treasury in 1963 recognized the present law to be that "the sale of a patent by the inventor may be treated as the sale of a capital asset," Hearings before the House Committee on Ways and Means, 88th Cong., 1st Sess., Feb. 6, 7, 8 and 18, 1963, Pt. I (rev.), on the President's

1963 Tax Message, p. 150, and the Congress failed to enact the changes in the law which the Department recommended.

These developments in the patent field obviously do not help the position of the Commissioner. Nor does I.R.C. § 1235, which expressly permits specified patent sales to be treated as sales of capital assets entitled to [the former preferential] capital gains treatment. We need not, however, decide here whether the extraction and patent cases are irreconcilable or whether, instead, each situation has its own peculiar characteristics justifying discrete treatment under the sale and exchange language of § 1222. Whether the patent cases are correct or not, absent § 1235, the fact remains that this case involves the transfer of corporate stock which has substantially appreciated in value and a purchase price payable from income which has been held to reflect the fair market value of the assets which the stock represents.

67. It did, however, accept and enact another suggestion made by the Treasury Department. Section 483, which was added to the Code, provided for treating a part of the purchase price as interest in installment sales transactions where no interest was specified. The provision was to apply as well when the payments provided for

occurrence of a sale but would have taxed as ordinary income those income-contingent payments deferred for more than five years. If a purchaser could pay the purchase price out of earnings within five years the seller would have capital gain rather than ordinary income. The approach was consistent with allowing appreciated values to be treated as capital gain but with appropriate safeguards against reserving additional rights to future income. In comparison, the Commissioner's position here is a clear case of "overkill" if aimed at preventing the involvement of tax-exempt entities in the purchase and operation of business enterprises. There are more precise approaches to this problem as well as to the question of the possibly excessive price paid by the charity or foundation. And if the Commissioner's approach is intended as a limitation upon the tax treatment of sales generally, it represents a considerable invasion of [the former] capital gains policy, a matter which we think is the business of Congress, not ours.

The problems involved in the purchase of a going business by a tax-exempt organization have been considered and dealt with by the Congress. Likewise, it has given its attention to various kinds of transactions involving the payment of the agreed purchase price for property from the future earnings of the property itself. In both situations it has responded, if at all, with precise provisions of narrow application. We consequently deem it wise to "leave to the Congress the fashioning of a rule which, in any event, must have wide ramifications." American Automobile Ass'n v. United States, 367 U.S. 687, 697, 81 S.Ct. 1727, 1732, 6 L.Ed.2d 1109.

Affirmed.

MR. JUSTICE HARLAN, concurring.

Were it not for the tax laws, the respondents' transaction with the Institute would make no sense, except as one arising from a charitable impulse. However the tax laws exist as an economic reality in the businessman's world, much like the existence of a competitor. Businessmen plan their affairs around both, and a tax dollar is just as real as one derived from any other source. The Code gives the Institute a tax exemption which makes it capable of taking a greater after-tax return from a business than could a non-tax-exempt individual or corporation. Respondents traded a residual interest in their business for a faster payout apparently made possible by the Institute's exemption. The respondents gave something up; they received something substantially different in return. If words are to have meaning, there was a "sale or exchange."

Obviously the Institute traded on its tax exemption. The Government would deny that there was an exchange, essentially on the theory that the Institute did not put anything at risk; since its exemption is

were indefinite as to their size, as for example "where the payments are in part at least dependent upon future income derived from the property." S.Rep. No. 830, 88th Cong., 2d Sess., p. 103, U.S.Code Congressional and Administrative News 1964, p. 1776. This section would apparently now apply to a transaction such as occurred in this case.

unlimited, like the magic purse that always contains another penny, the Institute gave up nothing by trading on it.

One may observe preliminarily that the Government's remedy for the so-called "bootstrap" sale—defining sale or exchange so as to require the shifting of some business risks—would accomplish little by way of closing off such sales in the future. It would be neither difficult nor burdensome for future users of the bootstrap technique to arrange for some shift of risks. If such sales are considered a serious abuse, ineffective judicial correctives will only postpone the day when Congress is moved to deal with the problem comprehensively. Furthermore, one may ask why, if the Government does not like the tax consequences of such sales, the proper course is not to attack the exemption rather than to deny the existence of a "real" sale or exchange.

The force underlying the Government's position is that the respondents did clearly retain some risk-bearing interest in the business. Instead of leaping from this premise to the conclusion that there was no sale or exchange, the Government might more profitably have broken the transaction into components and attempted to distinguish between the interest which respondents retained and the interest which they exchanged. The worth of a business depends upon its ability to produce income over time. What respondents gave up was not the entire business, but only their interest in the business' ability to produce income in excess of that which was necessary to pay them off under the terms of the transaction. The value of such a residual interest is a function of the risk element of the business and the amount of income it is capable of producing per year, and will necessarily be substantially less than the value of the total business. Had the Government argued that it was that interest which respondents exchanged, and only to that extent should they have received capital gains treatment, we would perhaps have had a different case.

* * *

MR. JUSTICE GOLDBERG, with whom THE CHIEF JUSTICE and MR. JUSTICE BLACK join, dissenting.

The essential facts of this case which are undisputed illuminate the basic nature of the transaction at issue. Respondents conveyed their stock in Clay Brown & Co., a corporation owned almost entirely by Clay Brown and the members of his immediate family, to the California Institute for Cancer Research, a tax-exempt foundation. The Institute liquidated the corporation and transferred its assets under a five-year lease to a new corporation, Fortuna, which was managed by respondent Clay Brown, and the shares of which were in the name of Clay Brown's attorneys, who also served as Fortuna's directors. The business thus continued under a new name with no essential change in control of its operations. Fortuna agreed to pay 80% of its pretax profits to the Institute as rent under the lease, and the Institute agreed to pay 90% of this amount to respondents in payment for their shares until the respondents received $1,300,000, at which time their interest would terminate and the Institute would own the complete beneficial interest as well as all legal interest in the business. If remittances to respondents were less than $250,000 in any two consecutive years or any other provision in the agreements was violated, they could recover the property. The Institute had no personal liability. In essence respondents conveyed their interest in the business to the Institute in return for 72% of the profits of the business and the right to recover the business assets if payments fell behind schedule.

At first glance it might appear odd that the sellers would enter into this transaction, for prior to the sale they had a right to 100% of the corporation's income, but after the sale they had a right to only 72% of that income and would lose the business after 10 years to boot. This transaction, however, afforded the sellers several advantages. The principal advantage sought by the sellers was [the former preferential treatment of] capital gain, rather than ordinary income, treatment for that share of the business profits which they received. Further, because of the Tax Code's charitable exemption [68] and the lease arrangement with Fortuna,[69] the Institute believed that neither it nor Fortuna would have to pay income tax on the earnings of the business. Thus the sellers would receive free of corporate taxation, and subject only to personal taxation at [the former preferential] capital gains rates, 72% of the business earnings until they were paid $1,300,000. Without the sale they would receive only 48% of the business earnings, the rest going to the Government in corporate taxes, and this 48% would be subject to personal taxation at ordinary rates. In effect the Institute sold the respondents the use of its tax exemption, enabling the respondents to collect $1,300,000 from the business more quickly than they otherwise could and to pay taxes on this amount at [the former preferential] capital gains rates. In return, the Institute received a nominal amount of the profits while the $1,300,000 was being paid, and it was to receive the whole business after this debt had been paid off. In any realistic sense the Government's grant of a tax exemption was used by the Institute as part of an arrangement that allowed it to buy a business that in fact cost it nothing. I cannot believe that Congress intended such a result.

* * *

The purpose of the [former] capital gains provisions of the Internal Revenue Code, § 1201 et seq., is to prevent gains which accrue over a

68. See I.R.C. § 501(c)(3).

69. This lease arrangement was designed to permit the Institute to take advantage of its charitable exemption to avoid taxes on payment of Fortuna's profits to it, with Fortuna receiving a deduction for the rental payments as an ordinary and necessary business expense, thus avoiding taxes to both. Though unrelated business income is usually taxable when received by charities, an exception is made for income received from the lease of real and personal property of less than five years. See I.R.C. § 514; Lanning, Tax Erosion and the "Bootstrap Sale" of a Business—I, 108 Pa.L.Rev. 623, 684–689. Though denial of the charity's tax exemption on rent received from Fortuna would also remove the economic incentive underlying this bootstrap transaction, there is no indication in the Court's opinion that such income is not tax exempt. See the Court's opinion, ante, at 1163–1164.

long period of time from being taxed in the year of their realization through a sale at high rates resulting from their inclusion in the higher tax brackets. Burnet v. Harmel, 287 U.S. 103, 106, 53 S.Ct. 74, 75, 77 L.Ed. 199. These provisions are not designed, however, to allow [the former preferential] capital gains treatment for the recurrent receipt of commercial or business income. In light of these purposes this Court has held that a "sale" for capital gains purposes is not produced by the mere transfer of legal title. Burnet v. Harmel, supra; Palmer v. Bender, 287 U.S. 551, 53 S.Ct. 225, 77 L.Ed. 489. Rather, at the very least, there must be a meaningful economic transfer in addition to a change in legal title. See Corliss v. Bowers, 281 U.S. 376, 50 S.Ct. 336, 74 L.Ed. 916. Thus the question posed here is not whether this transaction constitutes a sale within the terms of the Uniform Commercial Code or the Uniform Sales Act—we may assume it does—but, rather, the question is whether, at the time legal title was transferred, there was also an economic transfer sufficient to convert ordinary income into [the former preferential] capital gain by treating this transaction as a "sale" within the terms of I.R.C. § 1222(3).

In dealing with what constitutes a sale for capital gains purposes, this Court has been careful to look through formal legal arrangements to the underlying economic realities. Income produced in the mineral extraction business, which "resemble[s] a manufacturing business carried on by the use of the soil," Burnet v. Harmel, supra, 287 U.S. at 107, 53 S.Ct. at 76, is taxed to the person who retains an economic interest in the oil. Thus, while an outright sale of mineral interests qualifies for capital gains treatment, a purported sale of mineral interests in exchange for a royalty from the minerals produced is treated only as a transfer with a retained economic interest, and the royalty payments are fully taxable as ordinary income. Burnet v. Harmel, supra. See Palmer v. Bender, supra.

In Thomas v. Perkins, 301 U.S. 655, 57 S.Ct. 911, 81 L.Ed. 1324, an owner of oil interests transferred them in return for an "oil production payment," an amount which is payable only out of the proceeds of later commercial sales of the oil transferred. The Court held that this transfer, which constituted a sale under state law, did not constitute a sale for tax purposes because there was not a sufficient shift of economic risk. The transferor would be paid only if oil was later produced and sold; if it was not produced, he would not be paid. The risks run by the transferor of making or losing money from the oil were shifted so slightly by the transfer that no § 1222(3) sale existed, notwithstanding the fact that the transaction conveyed title as a matter of state law, and once the payout was complete, full ownership of the minerals was to vest in the purchaser.

I believe that the sellers here retained an economic interest in the business fully as great as that retained by the seller of oil interests in Thomas v. Perkins. The sellers were to be paid only out of the proceeds of the business. If the business made money they would be paid; if it did not, they would not be paid. In the latter event, of course, they could recover the business, but a secured interest in a business which was losing money would be of dubious value. There was no other security. The Institute was not bound to pay any sum whatsoever. The Institute, in fact, promised only to channel to the sellers a portion of the income it received from Fortuna.

Moreover, in numerous cases this Court has refused to transfer the incidents of taxation along with a transfer of legal title when the transferor retains considerable control over the income-producing asset transferred. See, e.g., Commissioner v. Sunnen, 333 U.S. 591, 68 S.Ct. 715, 92 L.Ed. 898; Helvering v. Clifford, 309 U.S. 331, 60 S.Ct. 554, 84 L.Ed. 788; Corliss v. Bowers, supra. Control of the business did not, in fact, shift in the transaction here considered. Clay Brown, by the terms of the purchase agreement and the lease was to manage Fortuna. Clay Brown was given power to hire and arrange for the terms of employment of all other employees of the corporation. The lease provided that "if for any reason Clay Brown is unable or unwilling to so act, the person or persons holding a majority interest in the principal note described in the Purchase Agreement shall have the right to approve his successor to act as general manager of Lessee company." Thus the shareholders of Clay Brown & Co. assured themselves of effective control over the management of Fortuna. Furthermore, Brown's attorneys were the named shareholders of Fortuna and its Board of Directors. The Institute had no control over the business.

I would conclude that on these facts there was not a sufficient shift of economic risk or control of the business to warrant treating this transaction as a "sale" for tax purposes. Brown retained full control over the operations of the business; the risk of loss and the opportunity to profit from gain during the normal operation of the business shifted but slightly. If the operation lost money, Brown stood to lose; if it gained money Brown stood to gain, for he would be paid off faster. Moreover, the entire purchase price was to be paid out of the ordinary income of the corporation, which was to be received by Brown on a recurrent basis as he had received it during the period he owned the corporation. I do not believe that Congress intended this recurrent receipt of ordinary business income to be taxed at [the former preferential] capital gains rates merely because the business was to be transferred to a tax-exempt entity at some future date. For this reason I would apply here the established rule that, despite formal legal arrangements, a sale does not take place until there has been a significant economic change such as a shift in risk or in control of the business.[70]

To hold as the Court does that this transaction constitutes a "sale" within the terms of I.R.C. § 1222(3), thereby giving rise to [the former

---

70. The fact that respondents were to lose complete control of the business after the payments were complete was taken into account by the Commissioner, for he treated the business in respondents' hands as a wasting asset, see I.R.C. § 167, and allowed them to offset their basis in the stock against the payments received.

preferential] capital gain for the income received, legitimates considerable tax evasion. Even if the Court restricts its holding, allowing only those transactions to be § 1222(3) sales in which the price is not excessive, its decision allows considerable latitude for the unwarranted conversion of ordinary income into capital gain. Valuation of a closed corporation is notoriously difficult. The Tax Court in the present case did not determine that the price for which the corporation was sold represented its true value; it simply stated that the price "was the result of real negotiating" and "within a reasonable range in light of the earnings history of the corporation and the adjusted net worth of the corporate assets." 37 T.C., at 486. The Tax Court, however, also said that "[i]t may be * * * that petitioner [Clay Brown] would have been unable to sell the stock at as favorable a price to anyone other than a tax-exempt organization." 37 T.C., at 485. Indeed, this latter supposition is highly likely, for the Institute was selling its tax exemption, and this is not the sort of asset which is limited in quantity. Though the Institute might have negotiated in order to receive beneficial ownership of the corporation as soon as possible, the Institute, at no cost to itself, could increase the price to produce an offer too attractive for the seller to decline. * * *

Although the Court implies that it will hold to be "sales" only those transactions in which the price is reasonable, I do not believe that the logic of the Court's opinion will justify so restricting its holding. If this transaction is a sale under the Internal Revenue Code, entitling its proceeds to [the former preferential] capital gains treatment because it was arrived at after hard negotiating, title in a conveyancing sense passed, and the beneficial ownership was expected to pass at a later date, then the question recurs, which the Court does not answer, why a similar transaction would cease to be a sale if hard negotiating produced a purchase price much greater than actual value. * * *

Further, a bootstrap tax avoidance scheme can easily be structured under which the holder of any income-earning asset "sells" his asset to a tax-exempt buyer for a promise to pay him the income produced for a period of years. The buyer in such a transaction would do nothing whatsoever; the seller would be delighted to lose his asset at the end of, say, 30 years in return for [the former preferential] capital gains treatment of all income earned during that period. It is difficult to see, on the Court's rationale, why such a scheme is not a sale. And, if I am wrong in my reading of the Court's opinion, and if the Court would strike down such a scheme on the ground that there is no economic shifting of risk or control, it is difficult to see why the Court upholds the sale presently before it in which control does not change and any shifting of risk is nominal.

I believe that the Court's overly conceptual approach has led to a holding which will produce serious erosion of our progressive taxing system, resulting in greater tax burdens upon all taxpayers. The tax avoidance routes opened by the Court's opinion will surely be used to advantage by the owners of closed corporations and other income-producing assets in order to evade ordinary income taxes and pay at [the former preferential] capital gains rates, with a resultant large-scale ownership of private businesses by tax-exempt organizations. While the Court justifies its result in the name of conceptual purity,[71] it simultaneously violates long-standing congressional tax policies that [the former preferential] capital gains treatment is to be given to significant economic transfers of investment-type assets but not to ordinary commercial or business income and that transactions are to be judged on their entire substance rather than their naked form. Though turning tax consequences on form alone might produce greater certainty of the tax results of any transaction, this stability exacts as its price the certainty that tax evasion will be produced. In Commissioner v. P.G. Lake, Inc., 356 U.S. 260, 265, 78 S.Ct. 691, 694, 2 L.Ed.2d 743, this Court recognized that the purpose of the [former] capital gains provisions of the Internal Revenue Code is " 'to relieve the taxpayer from * * * excessive tax burdens on gains resulting from a conversion of capital investments, and to remove the deterrent effect of those burdens on such conversions.' * * * And this exception has always been narrowly construed so as to protect the revenue against artful devices." I would hold in keeping with this purpose and in order to prevent serious erosion of the ordinary income tax provisions of the Code, that the bootstrap transaction revealed by the facts here considered is not a "sale" within the meaning of the capital gains provisions of the Code, but that it obviously is an "artful device," which this Court ought not to legitimate. The Court justifies the untoward result of this case as permitted tax avoidance; I believe it to be a plain and simple case of unwarranted tax evasion.

Question

What factors led the Supreme Court to conclude that a sale occurred in Clay Brown?

———

Another round in the battle over whether a transaction is characterized as a purchase or sale was won by the taxpayer in Frank Lyon Company v. United States, 435 U.S. 561, 98 S.Ct. 1291, 55 L.Ed.2d 550 (1978), reversing 536 F.2d 746 (8th Cir.1976).

In the Frank Lyon case, a bank planned to construct a multi-story bank and office building in order to remain competitive with other banks. However, the bank could not finance the building itself because of various Federal and state regulations. Consequently, an arrangement was worked out whereby the taxpayer was to buy the building as

---

71. It should be noted, however, that the Court's holding produces some rather unusual conceptual results. For example, after the payout is complete the Institute presumably would have a basis of $1,300,000 in a business that in reality cost it nothing. If anyone deserves such a basis, it is the Government, whose grant of tax exemption is being used by the Institute to acquire the business.

it was constructed. The building was then leased back to the bank for a primary term of 25 years with options to extend the lease to a maximum of 65 years. The total rent for the building over the 25-year primary term equalled the principal and interest payments on the mortgage. Under the lease, the bank was responsible for all maintenance expenses. The bank had the option to repurchase the building at various times for prices that equalled the outstanding balance of the mortgage plus the taxpayer's investment. Under the mortgage agreement, the taxpayer warranted that it would lease the building to the bank under the terms mentioned. The taxpayer agreed to make payments on the mortgage equal to the rentals received.

In contrast to the usual two-party arrangement, the Frank Lyon case involved three independent parties, the taxpayer, Frank Lyon Company (Lyon), the bank, Worthen Bank & Trust Company (Worthen), and the mortgage lender (New York Life).

In holding for the taxpayer, the Supreme Court stated (435 U.S. at 572–585, 98 S.Ct. at 1298–1304, 55 L.Ed.2d at 560–567):

II

This Court, almost 50 years ago, observed that "taxation is not so much concerned with the refinements of title as it is with actual command over the property taxed—the actual benefit for which the tax is paid." Corliss v. Bowers, 281 U.S. 376, 378, 50 S.Ct. 336, 74 L.Ed. 916 (1930). In a number of cases, the Court has refused to permit the transfer of formal legal title to shift the incidence of taxation attributable to ownership of property where the transferor continues to retain significant control over the property transferred. E.g., Commissioner of Internal Revenue v. Sunnen, 333 U.S. 591, 68 S.Ct. 715, 92 L.Ed. 898 (1948); Helvering v. Clifford, 309 U.S. 331, 60 S.Ct. 554, 84 L.Ed. 788 (1940). In applying this doctrine of substance over form, the Court has looked to the objective economic realities of a transaction rather than to the particular form the parties employed. The Court has never regarded "the simple expedient of drawing up papers," Commissioner of Internal Revenue v. Tower, 327 U.S. 280, 291, 66 S.Ct. 532, 538, 90 L.Ed. 670 (1946), as controlling for tax purposes when the objective economic realities are to the contrary. "In the field of taxation, administrators of the laws and the courts are concerned with substance and realities, and formal written documents are not rigidly binding." Helvering v. Lazarus & Co., 308 U.S., at 255, 60 S.Ct., at 210. Nor is the parties' desire to achieve a particular tax result necessarily relevant. Commissioner of Internal Revenue v. Duberstein, 363 U.S. 278, 286, 80 S.Ct. 1190, 4 L.Ed.2d 1218 (1960).

In the light of these general and established principles, the Government takes the position that the Worthen-Lyon transaction in its entirety should be regarded as a sham. The agreement as a whole, it is said, was only an elaborate financing scheme designed to provide economic benefits to Worthen and a guaranteed return to Lyon. The latter was but a conduit used to forward the mortgage payments, made under the guise of rent paid by Worthen to Lyon, on to New York Life as mortgagee. This, the Government claims, is the true substance of the transaction as viewed under the microscope of the tax laws. Although the arrangement was cast in sale-and-leaseback form, in substance it was only a financing transaction, and the terms of the repurchase options and lease renewals so indicate. It is said that Worthen could reacquire the building simply by satisfying the mortgage debt and paying Lyon its $500,000 advance plus interest, regardless of the fair market value of the building at the time; similarly, when the mortgage was paid off, Worthen could extend the lease at drastically reduced bargain rentals that likewise bore no relation to fair rental value but were simply calculated to pay Lyon its $500,000 plus interest over the extended term. Lyon's return on the arrangement in no event could exceed 6% compound interest (although the Government conceded it might well be less, Tr. of Oral Arg. 32). Furthermore, the favorable option and lease renewal terms made it highly unlikely that Worthen would abandon the building after it in effect had "paid off" the mortgage. The Government implies that the arrangement was one of convenience which, if accepted on its face, would enable Worthen to deduct its payments to Lyon as rent and would allow Lyon to claim a deduction for depreciation, based on the cost of construction ultimately borne by Worthen, which Lyon could offset against other income, and to deduct mortgage interest that roughly would offset the inclusion of Worthen's rental payments in Lyon's income. If, however, the Government argues, the arrangement was only a financing transaction under which Worthen was the owner of the building, Worthen's payments would be deductible only to the extent that they represented mortgage interest, and Worthen would be entitled to claim depreciation; Lyon would not be entitled to deductions for either mortgage interest or depreciation and it would not have to include Worthen's "rent" payments in its income because its function with respect to those payments was that of a conduit between Worthen and New York Life.

The Government places great reliance on *Helvering v. Lazarus & Co.*, supra, and claims it to be precedent that controls this case. The taxpayer there was a department store. The legal title of its three buildings was in a bank as trustee for land-trust certificate holders. When the transfer to the trustee was made, the trustee at the same time leased the buildings back to the taxpayer for 99 years, with option to renew and purchase. The Commissioner, in stark contrast to his posture in the present case, took the position that the statutory right to depreciation followed legal title. The Board of Tax Appeals, however, concluded that the transaction between the taxpayer and the bank in reality was a mortgage loan and allowed the taxpayer depreciation on the buildings. This Court, as had the Court of Appeals, agreed with that conclusion and affirmed. It regarded the "rent" stipulated in the leaseback as a promise to pay interest on the loan, and a "depreciation fund" required by the lease as an amortization fund designed to pay off the loan in the stated period. Thus, said the Court, the Board justifiably concluded that the transaction, although in written form a transfer of ownership with a leaseback, was actually a loan secured by the property involved.

The *Lazarus* case, we feel, is to be distinguished from the present one and is not controlling here. Its transaction was one involving only two (and not multiple) parties, the taxpayer-department store and the trustee-bank. The Court looked closely at the substance of the agreement between those two parties and rightly concluded that depreciation was deductible by the taxpayer despite the nomenclature of the instrument of conveyance and the leaseback.

The present case, in contrast, involves three parties, Worthen, Lyon, and the finance agency. The usual simple two-party arrangement was legally unavailable to Worthen. Independent investors were interested in participating in the alternative available to Worthen, and Lyon itself (also independent from Worthen) won the privilege. Despite Frank Lyon's presence on Worthen's board of directors, the transaction, as it ultimately developed, was not a familial one arranged by Worthen, but one compelled by the realities of the restrictions imposed upon the bank. Had Lyon not appeared, another interested investor would have been selected. The ultimate solution would have been essentially the same. Thus, the presence of the third party, in our view, significantly distinguishes this case from *Lazarus* and removes the latter as controlling authority.

III

It is true, of course, that the transaction took shape according to Worthen's needs. As the Government points out, Worthen throughout the negotiations regarded the respective proposals of the independent investors in terms of its own cost of funds. It is also true that both Worthen and the prospective investors compared the various proposals in terms of the return anticipated on the investor's equity. But all this is natural for parties contemplating entering into a transaction of this kind. Worthen needed a building for its banking operations and other purposes and necessarily had to know what its cost would be. The investors were in business to employ their funds in the most remunerative way possible. And, as the Court has said in the past, a transaction must be given its effect in accord with what actually occurred and not in accord with what might have occurred.

There is no simple device available to peel away the form of this transaction and to reveal its substance. The effects of the transaction on all the parties were obviously different from those that would have resulted had Worthen been able simply to make a mortgage agreement with New York Life and to receive a $500,000 loan from Lyon. Then *Lazarus* would apply. Here, however, and most significantly, it was Lyon alone, and not Worthen, who was liable on the notes, first to City Bank, and then to New York Life. Despite the facts that Worthen had agreed to pay rent and that this rent equaled the amounts due from Lyon to New York Life, should anything go awry in the later years of the lease, Lyon was primarily liable. No matter how the transaction could have been devised otherwise, it remains a fact that as the agreements were placed in final form, the obligation on the notes fell squarely on Lyon. Lyon, an ongoing enterprise, exposed its very business well-being to this real and substantial risk.

The effect of this liability on Lyon is not just the abstract possibility that something will go wrong and that Worthen will not be able to make its payments. Lyon has disclosed this liability on its balance sheet for all the world to see. Its financial position was affected substantially by the presence of this long-term debt, despite the offsetting presence of the building as an asset. To the extent that Lyon has used its capital in this transaction, it is less able to obtain financing for other business needs.

In concluding that there is this distinct element of economic reality in Lyon's assumption of liability, we are mindful that the characterization of a transaction for financial accounting purposes, on the one hand, and for tax purposes, on the other, need not necessarily be the same. Commissioner of Internal Revenue v. Lincoln Savings & Loan Assn., 403 U.S. 345, 355, 91 S.Ct. 1893, 29 L.Ed.2d 519 (1971); Old Colony R. Co. v. Commissioner of Internal Revenue, 284 U.S. 552, 562, 52 S.Ct. 211, 76 L.Ed. 484 (1932). Accounting methods or descriptions, without more, do not lend substance to that which has no substance. But in this case accepted accounting methods, as understood by the several parties to the respective agreements and as applied to the transaction by others, gave the transaction a meaningful character consonant with the form it was given.[72] Worthen was not allowed to enter into the type of transaction which the Government now urges to be the true substance of the arrangement. Lyon and Worthen cannot be said to have entered into the transaction intending that the interests involved were allocated in a way other than that associated with a sale-and-leaseback.

Other factors also reveal that the transaction cannot be viewed as anything more than a mortgage agreement between Worthen and New York Life and a loan from Lyon to Worthen. There is no legal obligation between Lyon and Worthen representing the $500,000 "loan" extended under the Government's theory. And the assumed 6% return on this putative loan—required by the audit to be recognized in the taxable year in question—will be realized only when and if Worthen exercises its options.

The Court of Appeals acknowledged that the rents alone, due after the primary term of the lease and after the mortgage has been paid, do not provide the simple 6% return which, the Government urges, Lyon is guaranteed, 536 F.2d, at 752. Thus, if Worthen chooses not to

---

72. We are aware that accounting standards have changed significantly since 1968 and that the propriety of Worthen's and Lyon's methods of disclosing the transaction in question may be a matter for debate under these new standards. * * *

exercise its options, Lyon is gambling that the rental value of the building during the last 10 years of the ground lease, during which the ground rent is minimal, will be sufficient to recoup its investment before it must negotiate again with Worthen regarding the ground lease. There are simply too many contingencies, including variations in the value of real estate, in the cost of money, and in the capital structure of Worthen, to permit the conclusion that the parties intended to enter into the transaction as structured in the audit and according to which the Government now urges they be taxed.

It is not inappropriate to note that the Government is likely to lose little revenue, if any, as a result of the shape given the transaction by the parties. No deduction was created that is not either matched by an item of income or that would not have been available to one of the parties if the transaction had been arranged differently. While it is true that Worthen paid Lyon less to induce it to enter into the transaction because Lyon anticipated the benefit of the depreciation deductions it would have as the owner of the building, those deductions would have been equally available to Worthen had it retained title to the building. The Government so concedes. * * * The fact that favorable tax consequences were taken into account by Lyon on entering into the transaction is no reason for disallowing those consequences. We cannot ignore the reality that the tax laws affect the shape of nearly every business transaction. See Commissioner of Internal Revenue v. Brown, 380 U.S. 563, 579–580, 85 S.Ct. 1162, 14 L.Ed.2d 75 (1965) (Harlan, J., concurring). Lyon is not a corporation with no purpose other than to hold title to the bank building. It was not created by Worthen or even financed to any degree by Worthen.

The conclusion that the transaction is not a simple sham to be ignored does not, of course, automatically compel the further conclusion that Lyon is entitled to the items claimed as deductions. Nevertheless, on the facts, this readily follows. As has been noted, the obligations on which Lyon paid interest were its obligations alone, and it is entitled to claim deductions therefor under § 163(a) of the 1954 Code, 26 U.S.C. § 163(a).

As is clear from the facts, none of the parties to this sale-and-leaseback was the owner of the building in any simple sense. But it is equally clear that the facts focus upon Lyon as the one whose capital was committed to the building and as the party, therefore, that was entitled to claim depreciation for the consumption of that capital. The Government has based its contention that Worthen should be treated as the owner on the assumption that throughout the term of the lease Worthen was acquiring an equity in the property. In order to establish the presence of that growing equity, however, the Government is forced to speculate that one of the options will be exercised and that, if it is not, this is only because the rentals for the extended term are a bargain. We cannot indulge in such speculation in view of the District Court's clear finding to the contrary. We therefore conclude that it is

Lyon's capital that is invested in the building according to the agreement of the parties, and it is Lyon that is entitled to depreciation deductions, under § 167.

IV

* * *

In short, we hold that where, as here, there is a genuine multiple-party transaction with economic substance which is compelled or encouraged by business or regulatory realities, is imbued with tax-independent considerations, and is not shaped solely by tax-avoidance features that have meaningless labels attached, the Government should honor the allocation of rights and duties effectuated by the parties. Expressed another way, so long as the lessor retains significant and genuine attributes of the traditional lessor status, the form of the transaction adopted by the parties governs for tax purposes. What those attributes are in any particular case will necessarily depend upon its facts. It suffices to say that, as here, a sale-and-leaseback, in and of itself, does not necessarily operate to deny a taxpayer's claim for deductions.

* * *

Questions

1. What factors were critical in the Supreme Court's determination that the form of the transaction was controlling in Frank Lyon?

2. Who had the risk of loss in Frank Lyon, the taxpayer or the bank?

———

Subsequent decisions have applied the Lyon test of whether there is a business purpose for a sale-leaseback arrangement apart from tax advantages and whether there is economic substance to the arrangement. Courts may disregard the form of a transaction which is devoid of economic substance. Hilton v. Commissioner, 74 T.C. 305 (1980), affirmed per curiam 671 F.2d 316 (9th Cir.1982), involved a newly constructed building which was sold to a finance company and leased back under a long-term net lease. The Tax Court denied sale-leaseback treatment after evaluating the economic substance of the transaction. The value of the interest acquired by the purchaser was less than the amount paid for the building, apart from the tax benefits from the transaction. The court regarded the purported lease as nothing more than a disguised financing arrangement.

In Rice's Toyota World, Inc. v. Commissioner, 81 T.C. 184 (1983), affirmed 752 F.2d 89 (4th Cir.1985), a retail car dealership entered into a sale-leaseback arrangement with a computer equipment leasing corporation. The taxpayer was not entitled to depreciation deductions on its purported investment in the property. The Tax Court viewed the transaction as a sham, the sole purpose of which was to provide the taxpayer with deductions to offset income from other sources. There was no business purpose for entering into the transaction. An objective analysis of the transaction indicated that the dealership did not have a reasonable possibility of profit from the transaction apart from the tax benefit. Also, the purchase was illusory because the taxpayer was building no equity in the asset.

In Swift Dodge v. Commissioner, 692 F.2d 651 (9th Cir.1982), reversing 76 T.C. 547 (1981), the court grappled with the question of whether an auto dealer sold or leased cars to the users. More specifically, could the auto dealer or the users claim the investment tax credit and depreciation? The purported leases were open-ended in that they contained a clause whereby the user had to make up for any difference between the projected value of the cars at the end of the lease term and the actual value. If a car was worth less than projected, the user assumed the risk of depreciable loss. If the car was worth more, the user would receive the gain. The users paid for all maintenance and insurance. The dealer retained legal title in the cars. A user could have the car on the termination of the lease by paying the dealer, in cash, the car's full depreciated value.

The Tax Court concluded that each transaction was a lease. It perceived the need for the lessor to retain significant and genuine attributes of the traditional lease form. The Tax Court stated that a transaction is a lease if the lessor assumes burdens other than those of a lendor and is subject to significant risks not ordinarily incident to a secured loan.

The Ninth Circuit reversed, finding that the transactions were nothing more than conditional sales with a final lump-sum payment due at the end of the payment period. The appellate court noted that the only risk the dealer had was the risk of default by the purchaser, the same risk borne by the holder of a security interest.

The Swift Dodge case was distinguished in Estate of Thomas v. Commissioner, 84 T.C. 412 (1985) where the Tax Court found that a computer sale-leaseback transaction satisfied the economic substance test, even though nonrecourse financing was used to finance the purchase of computers. There was a reasonable expectation of profit. On the termination of the leases it was projected that the computers would have a residual value of approximately 14 to 30% of their original purchase price. The lessor retained significant and genuine attributes of a traditional lessor. In short, the lease arrangement had economic substance; it was entered into for business reasons and not solely for tax avoidance purposes.

Some planning guideposts were provided in Rev.Rul. 55–540, 1955–2 C.B. 39, and Rev.Proc. 75–21, 1975–1 C.B. 715, modified by Rev.Proc. 76–30, 1976–2 C.B. 647. The Service suggested that to preserve lease status, among other items, the rental payments should not exceed the fair rental value of the property, and no portion of the payments should be designated as "interest" or be applicable to an equity interest to be acquired by the lessee.

In 1981 Congress, somewhat dissatisfied with the Service's rules and in part to encourage the transfer of tax benefits from a taxpayer who could not use them to a taxpayer who could, provided for so-called safe-harbor leasing. Under these provisions, a transaction that would not meet the standards of a bona fide lease was nevertheless treated as such for tax purposes. The safe-harbor leasing rules proved to be overly generous and were substantially cut back in 1982. The safe-harbor rules were followed by rules providing for a special category of finance leasing which were, in turn, repealed by the Tax Reform Act of 1986.

In summary, the sale versus lease issues have proven to be intractable largely because the conflict in a very real sense is not between the parties to the transaction but between the user's own tax and economic desires. In any leasing transaction of the type we are considering here, the user of the property is perfectly happy to give the lessor the tax benefits. A major purpose of the transaction is to pass on those tax benefits from one who cannot use them to one who can with the understanding that the lessor will pass some of those benefits back to the lessee in form of reduced rents. On the other hand, the lessee wants to be absolutely certain that it has complete control over the use of the property, including as a practical matter, any residual benefits. The lessor, on the other hand, usually has no interest in using the property or obtaining those benefits as long as the lease rentals during any primary term provide it with an adequate return on its money. Accordingly, the lessee is happy to take the risks on the lease residual, and the lessor is happy to get rid of such risks, but as indicated above the tax law wants the lessor, not the lessee, to bear the risks. It is far from clear that these conflicts have been adequately resolved.

————

Reference: Simonson, Determining Tax Ownership of Leased Property, 38 Tax Lawyer 1 (1984); Solomon and Fones, Sale-Leaseback and the Shelter-Oriented Investor; An Analysis of Frank Lyon Co. and Estate of Franklin, 56 Taxes 618 (1978).

Problems

1. Suppose Doe, who is not a builder or a dealer, owns and proposes to lease raw land with a basis of $50,000 to Roe for use as a parking lot under an agreement providing for rent of a stated sum per month. Roe will have an option to purchase the land for $100,000 within three years; Roe may apply the amounts paid as rent against the purchase price of the property if he exercises the option at any time during the three-year period.

(a) Roe consults you regarding the tax consequences of the arrangement and asks whether you could work out a more advantageous arrangement from a tax viewpoint. If a lease with an option to purchase is desired, how should the arrangement be structured? Consider § 162(a)(3), and the Rosenfeld case at page 731.

(b) You represent Doe. What are the tax consequences if the arrangement is recast as a sale? When will Doe realize and recognize the gain? Why? What is the character of the gain?

2. The Production Corporation owns, free-and-clear of any mortgage, the land and building in which it manufactures widgets. The Corporation is strapped for cash. Evaluate the tax considerations to the Corporation in recommending that it:

(a) mortgage the land and building. Reconsider the Woodsam Associates case, page 32 of this chapter;

(b) sell the land and building to a purchaser for $2,000,000 in cash, its fair market value, with the purchaser entering into a long-term lease for the property with the Corporation. Under the lease, the Corporation will pay not only rent but also taxes, utilities, insurance and maintenance expenses on the property. The Corporation's adjusted basis in the land and building equals $3,000,000. The rentals under the lease would be at fair market value. How long should the term of the lease run? Consider Reg. § 1.1031(a)–1(c). Note that Reg. § 1.1002–1(d) provides: "Ordinarily, to constitute an exchange, the transaction must be a reciprocal transfer of property, as distinguished from a transfer of property for money consideration only." What is the significance of the Jordan Marsh case? Why might the Corporation want to structure the transaction as an exchange rather than a sale and leaseback? Consider § 1031(c). Consider also the impact of § 469 discussed at pp. 884 to 898 of this chapter.

(c) the same facts as in (b) above, but the purchaser will buy the land and building for $1,000,000 in cash and allow the Corporation to occupy the premises at a lower rent for thirty years (or more). What if the term of the lease exceeds the useful life of the building? How may the Service recast the transaction? What tax consequences will result to the Corporation and the purchaser if the transaction is recast? What is the significance of a bargain (less than market) rental for the premises? Is this a loan by the "purchaser" to the Corporation, secured by the property? Consider the Helvering v. Lazarus & Co. case discussed in the Frank Lyon decision. Consider also the Alstors Realty Co. case.

(d) the same facts as in (b) above, but the Corporation will also have an option to repurchase the property for an "inadequate" price. How may the Service recast the transaction? What tax consequences will result to the Corporation and the purchaser if the transaction is recast?

J. TAX SHELTERS

1. INTRODUCTION

Prior to the Tax Reform Act of 1986, tax shelters took a wide variety of forms and covered many activities. The common characteristic of tax shelters was the generation of tax losses (many times in excess of a taxpayer's actual investment) which served as deductions, not only against the taxpayer's share of the income from his tax shelter investment, but also against his income from other sources, such as a lucrative medical practice or interest and dividends from his investments in stocks and bonds. A taxpayer with substantial income that would otherwise be subject to taxation at his high marginal rates could use a tax shelter to reduce his overall tax liability on this real income.

At the outset, the student should note that a real estate investment, to use a typical tax shelter vehicle, offered the following major deductions: (i) depreciation; (ii) interest on borrowed funds (divided between interest expenses incurred during the construction period and interest incurred after the building was placed in operation); (iii) real estate taxes (again divided between taxes incurred during the construction period and after completion of construction); and (iv) the costs to operate and maintain the property, such as management fees, insurance and repairs. The skillful attorney would combine these deductions with discrete tax provisions to build a tax shelter.

The deductions generated by a tax shelter investment generally provided two important benefits: (i) the deferral of taxation on the income offset by its deductions, and (ii) the conversion of ordinary income into capital gains. And, these two benefits could be increased by the use of borrowed funds (financial leverage).

Deferral. The typical tax shelter investment generated a substantial portion of its deductions, and consequently tax losses used to reduce his tax liability on income from other sources, during the early years of the investment. The typical tax shelter generated taxable income, if any, only in later years. When a tax shelter investment ceased to generate tax losses and began to report taxable income, the tax shelter aspect of the investment was over. In effect, the government provided the taxpayer with an interest-free loan (unsecured by any collateral) equal to the amount of taxes which would be paid on his income from other sources but for the tax losses. Repayment of this "loan" occurred when the tax shelter investment reached either the "cross over" point, by starting to generate taxable income in excess of the cash flow from the investment, or when the taxpayer sold or exchanged his tax shelter investment in a recognition transaction, thereby giving rise to a gain on the disposition. The advantage of this deferral depended primarily on the length of the deferral, but a taxpayer's marginal income tax bracket and market rates of interest were also factors to consider in determining the advantages to be obtained from the deferral.

In a real estate investment, for example, several factors contributed to the ability to take a substantial amount of the deductions generated by the investment during the early years of that investment. Most notably, the Accelerated Cost Recovery System under § 168 (prior to the Tax Reform Act of 1986) provided accelerated depreciation deductions by adopting a 19-year recovery period and using the 175 percent declining balance method of depreciation. However, real estate is now depreciated over a longer recovery period (either 27.5 or 31.5 years) using the straight line method.

Another aspect of accelerating deductions occurred when certain expenditures were deducted as incurred rather than spreading the deductions over the useful life of the investment. Prior to the Tax Reform Act of 1976, taxpayers could deduct, when paid or accrued, loan interest and real estate taxes incurred during the construction period of an asset. In 1976, as a result of the concern about real estate tax shelters, Congress enacted provisions requiring that interest and real estate taxes paid or accrued during the construction of an asset be capitalized, thereby prohibiting the deduction, and allowing the deduction of these costs over a five-year period. (See § 189, repealed by the Tax Reform Act of 1986). The current embodiment of this approach is found in § 263A(f). Furthermore, under the uniform capitalization rules found in § 263A, all other costs incurred in the construction of real property held for profit must be capitalized. Under § 263A all costs added to the basis of the property under construction are to be recovered over the useful life (ACRS recovery period) of the asset.

Conversion. Many tax shelters allowed a taxpayer to convert ordinary income into capital gains, which received preferential treatment prior to 1988. This conversion took place on either the sale or other disposition of the property used by the tax shelter investment or the sale or other disposition of the taxpayer's interest in the tax shelter investment vehicle. The conversion arose because the depreciation deductions (which reduce an asset's basis, § 1016(a)(2)) are ordinary deductions and offset ordinary income. The conversion occurs on the taxable sale or other taxable disposition of the property because all or a portion of the gain attributable to prior depreciation deductions (the difference between original cost and adjusted basis) was characterized as a capital gain. The depreciation recapture provisions (§§ 1245 and 1250), which are examined in Chapter 12, were designed to prevent this conversion. After the Tax Reform Act of 1986, which ended preferential tax rates for capital gains, the conversion aspect of a tax shelter is no longer an advantage of tax shelter investments.

Financial leverage. If a taxpayer borrowed funds as part of his tax shelter investment, he could make a larger investment, thereby increasing his deductions and making the tax shelter more attractive. As discussed earlier in this chapter, both the funds an individual invests and any liabilities incurred as part of the acquisition of property are used in determining the basis of the property acquired. For example, if an investor purchased a building by providing a $20,000 down payment in cash and obtaining $80,000 of mortgage financing, his basis would be $100,000. As we have seen, the general rule is that the depreciation deductions are taken on a taxpayer's basis in the property, not the amount of cash the individual has invested. By the use of borrowed funds a taxpayer can significantly increase the benefits of deferral by increasing his deductions, particularly depreciation deductions. Frequently, the deductions generated by a tax shelter exceed a taxpayer's equity investment in the tax shelter vehicle. Consider how much income tax could be deferred by a taxpayer in the 50 percent marginal income tax bracket if he could depreciate the entire $100,000 basis in the above building, and compare the amount of income taxes not paid because of $100,000 in deductions to his $20,000 investment in the building. During the early years of a typical real estate venture the depreciation deductions exceeded the principal payments on the mortgage loan, so that it was not uncommon during the early years for the aggregate tax losses to exceed the taxpayer's original investment.

In analyzing the benefits of leverage, two concepts must be understood: (1) what a mortgage is and (2) what the difference between recourse and nonrecourse financing is. Real property acquisitions are usually financed by secured loans. A mortgage is not a loan made on real property. A mortgage represents a security interest in property given by a borrower to a creditor to secure a loan. In the event of a default in the payment of interest or principal on a loan, a mortgage enables a lender-mortgagee to foreclose on the property, sell it at auction, and apply the proceeds to satisfy the loan obligation. The loan is evidenced by a borrower's (mortgagor's) note or bond and is usually repayable in equal installments (covering both interest and principal) over a specified time period.

Real estate, and other assets as well, may be financed by means of recourse or nonrecourse loans. If an individual borrows through a recourse loan, he is personally liable for the satisfaction of the debt in the event of default. Thus, if a mortgagee forecloses on property given as security and the proceeds of a sale are inadequate to satisfy the loan obligation, the mortgagee can go against the borrower's other assets to recover the shortfall. Funds also may be borrowed through a nonrecourse loan. The borrower does not assume personal liability for the repayment of the debt. The creditor is limited to the proceeds obtained on the foreclosure of the mortgage and the sale of the property. The race is on for real estate investors to utilize nonrecourse financing which allows the investors to increase their deductions without risking their own capital.

Occasionally, investors may fail to report the gross income which arises on the disposition of property subject to nonrecourse indebtedness, usually inadvertently, but sometimes intentionally. By failing to report this income, the tax deferral resulting from shelters is made permanent.

To attack the benefits of leverage which permits taxpayers who bore no risk to take deductions on depreciable property, Congress enacted the "at risk" rules in 1976. See § 465. Section 465(a) limits tax losses (defined as the deductions for one taxable year from any activity in excess of the income for that year from the same activity (§ 465(d)) which can be offset against a taxpayer's other sources of income, including salaries and dividends, to the amount he has "at risk" in the activity at the end of the taxable year. In other words, taxpayers cannot deduct losses in excess of their actual financial investment in the activity. A taxpayer is "at risk" only with respect to: (1) cash or other property (to the extent of its basis) he invested in the activity; (2) amounts borrowed with recourse for use in or contributed to the activity; and (3) net income from the activity. Stated differently, a taxpayer is not "at risk" with respect to nonrecourse loans. The amount at risk is decreased by cash withdrawn from the activity and net losses from the activity used against other income. § 465(b). A taxpayer may only deduct net losses from an activity up to the amount of his at risk investment. Stated differently, losses are deductible under the at risk rules only up to the amount a taxpayer can actually lose by engaging in the activity.

The Tax Reform Act of 1986 extended the application of the "at risk" rules to real estate activities that used seller financing or obtained mortgage loans from related parties. Prior to 1987 all investments in real estate were exempt from the at risk limitations on deductions. The legislative history of the Tax Reform Act of 1986 provides that Congress extended the coverage of the at risk rules to certain real estate investments "so as to limit the opportunity for overvaluation of property (resulting in inflated deductions)." Tax Reform [Act] of [1986], Report of the Committee on Ways and Means, House of Representatives on H.R. 3838, 99th Cong., 1st Sess. 293 (1985).

The at risk limitations will not apply in the case of an activity involving the holding of real property (as defined in § 465(b)(6)(E)) if a taxpayer uses "qualified nonrecourse financing." In other words, a taxpayer is treated at risk with respect to certain types of nonrecourse financing. Essentially, qualified nonrecourse financing is financing that is not provided by the seller as long as the lender is not related to the purchaser. § 465(b)(6)(B). Nonrecourse financing provided by or guaranteed by a governmental body or loaned by a "qualified person," as defined in §§ 465(b)(6)(D) and 46(c)(8)(D)(iv), is not subject to the at risk limitations. Basically, Congress was suspicious of seller-provided financing as exhibited in the legislative history, which provides:

> Nonrecourse financing by the seller of real property * * * is not treated as an amount at risk * * * because there may be little or no incentive to limit the amount of such financing to the value of the property. In the case of * * * third party commercial financing secured by the real property, however, the lender is much less likely to make loans which exceed the property's value or cannot be serviced by the property; it is more likely that such financing will be repaid and

that the purchaser has or will have real equity in the activity. Tax Reform [Act] of [1986], Report of the Committee on Ways and Means, House of Representatives on H.R. 3838, 99th Cong., 1st Sess. 293 (1985).

Question

Consider the impact of the extension of the at risk rules to real estate investments using seller-provided nonrecourse financing on the need to challenge the validity of the financing arrangement in Estate of Franklin at page 798.

———

The at risk rules determine the maximum amount that can be deducted by a taxpayer engaged in an activity subject to its limitations. § 465(c)(1) and (3). Because losses generated by an activity using bona fide third party financing are not subject to the at risk rules, a taxpayer could still use these losses to shelter other sources of income. Congress perceived that the at risk rule is "not a sufficient basis for determining whether or when net losses from an activity should be deductible against other sources of income, or for determining whether an ultimate economic loss has been realized." Senate Finance Committee Report on H.R. 3838, 99th Cong., 2d Sess. 717 (1986). In order to achieve these goals Congress enacted limitations on the ability to deduct so-called passive losses not restricted by the at risk rules. This new weapon, added by the Tax Reform Act of 1986, is discussed next in this chapter.

2. PASSIVE LOSS LIMITATIONS

Having gone as far as it felt was possible with the at risk rule, Congress further attacked tax shelter investments by eliminating the ability in most instances of using losses generated by tax shelter investments to offset income from other sources. In enacting the limitations on the ability to use passive losses described in § 469(d), the legislative history stressed a concern with the inequities caused in the tax system by the use of tax shelters. These inequities were analyzed as follows:

In recent years, it has become increasingly clear that taxpayers are losing faith in the Federal income tax system. This loss of confidence has resulted in large part from the interaction of two of the system's principal features: its high marginal rates (in 1986, 50 percent for a single individual with taxable income in excess of $88,270), and the opportunities it provides for taxpayers to offset income from one source with tax shelter deductions and credits from another.

The prevalence of tax shelters in recent years—even after the highest marginal rate for individuals was reduced in 1981 from 70 percent to 50 percent—has been well documented. For example, a recent Treasury study[2] revealed that in 1983, out of 260,000 tax

2. Treasury Department, "Taxes Paid by High-Income Taxpayers and the Growth of Partnerships," reprinted in IRS Statistics of Income Bulletin (Fall 1985), beginning at page 55.

returns reporting "total positive income"[3] in excess of $250,000, 11 percent paid taxes equaling 5 percent or less of total positive income, and 21 percent paid taxes equaling 10 percent or less of total positive income. Similarly, in the case of tax returns reporting total positive income in excess of $1 million, 11 percent paid tax equaling less than 5 percent of total positive income, and 19 percent paid tax equaling less than 10 percent of total positive income.[4]

Such patterns give rise to a number of undesirable consequences, even aside from their effect in reducing Federal tax revenues. Extensive shelter activity contributes to public concerns that the tax system is unfair, and to the belief that tax is paid only by the naive and the unsophisticated. This, in turn, not only undermines compliance, but encourages further expansion of the tax shelter market, in many cases diverting investment capital from productive activities to those principally or exclusively serving tax avoidance goals.

The committee believes that the most important sources of support for the Federal income tax system are the average citizens who simply report their income (typically consisting predominantly of items such as salaries, wages, pensions, interest, and dividends) and pay tax under the general rules. To the extent that these citizens feel that they are bearing a disproportionate burden with regard to the costs of government because of their unwillingness or inability to engage in tax-oriented investment activity, the tax system itself is threatened.

Under these circumstances, the committee believes that decisive action is needed to curb the expansion of tax sheltering and to restore to the tax system the degree of equity that is a necessary precondition to a beneficial and widely desired reduction in rates. So long as tax shelters are permitted to erode the Federal tax base, a low-rate system can provide neither sufficient revenues, nor sufficient progressivity, to satisfy the general public that tax liability bears a fair relationship to the ability to pay. In particular, a provision significantly limiting the use of tax shelter losses is unavoidable if substantial rate reductions are to be provided to high-income taxpayers without disproportionately reducing the share of total liability under the individual income tax that is borne by high-income taxpayers as a group.

The question of how to prevent harmful and excessive tax sheltering is not a simple one. One way to address the problem would be to eliminate substantially all tax preferences in the Internal Revenue Code. For two reasons, however, the committee believes that this course is inappropriate.

3. Total positive income was defined as the sum of salary, interest, dividends, and income from profitable businesses and investments, as reported on tax returns.

4. Other studies have similarly reached the conclusion that tax shelters, by flowing through tax benefits to individuals with positive sources of income, have permitted some taxpayers with sizeable economic incomes substantially to reduce their tax liabilities. *See* Joint Committee on Taxation, *Tax Reform Proposals: Tax Shelters and Minimum Tax* (JCS-34-85), August 7, 1985.

First, while the [Act] reduces or eliminates some tax preference items that the committee believes do not provide social or economic benefits commensurate with their cost, there are many preferences that the committee believes are socially or economically beneficial. This is especially true when such preferences are used primarily to advance the purposes upon which Congress relied in enacting them, rather than to avoid taxation of income from sources unrelated to the preferred activity.

Second, it would be extremely difficult, perhaps impossible, to design a tax system that measures income perfectly. For example, the statutory allowance for depreciation, * * * reflects broad industry averages, as opposed to providing precise item-by-item measurements. * * *

Even to the extent that rules for the accurate measurement of income can theoretically be devised, such rules may involve undue complexity from the perspective of many taxpayers. For example, a system that required all taxpayers to use a theoretically pure accrual method of accounting (e.g., including unrealized appreciation, and allowing only the amount of depreciation actually incurred for each specific asset in each taxable year) would create serious difficulties in both compliance and administration.

However, when the tax system, in order to avoid such complexity, permits simpler rules to be applied (e.g., generally not taxing unrealized gain, and allowing depreciation based on broad industry averages), opportunities for manipulation are created. Taxpayers may structure transactions specifically to take advantage of the situations in which the simpler rules lead to undermeasurement or deferral of income.

The question of what constitutes a tax shelter that should be subject to limitations is closely related to the question of who Congress intends to benefit when it enacts tax preferences. For example, in providing preferential depreciation for real estate or favorable accounting rules for farming, it was not Congress's primary intent to permit outside investors to avoid tax liability with respect to their salaries by investing in limited partnership syndications. Rather, Congress intends to benefit and provide incentives to taxpayers active in the businesses to which the preferences were directed.

In some cases, the availability of tax preferences to nonparticipating investors has even harmed the industries that the preferences were intended to benefit. For example, in the case of farming, credits and favorable deductions have often encouraged investments by wealthy individuals whose principal or only interest in farming is to receive an investment return, largely in the form of tax benefits to offset tax on positive sources of income. Since such investors may not need a positive cash return from farming in order to profit from their investments, they have a substantial competitive advantage in relation to active farmers, who commonly are not in a position to use excess tax benefits to shelter unrelated income. This has significantly contributed to the serious economic difficulties presently being experienced by many active farmers.

The availability of tax benefits to shelter positive sources of income also has harmed the economy generally, by providing a non-economic return on capital for certain investments. This has encouraged a flow of capital away from activities that may provide a higher pre-tax economic return, thus retarding the growth of the sectors of the economy with the greatest potential for expansion. Tax Reform Act of 1986, Senate Finance Committee Report on H.R. 3838, 99th Cong., 2d Sess. 713–716 (1986).

General rules. As discussed previously at page 361, all of a taxpayer's income-producing activities are divided into three broad categories: (i) activities generating income from the active conduct of a trade or business in which the taxpayer materially participates; (ii) income from portfolio investments; and (iii) "passive activities" in which the taxpayer does not materially participate. Losses from a passive activity generally may only be deducted against the income from that particular passive activity or another passive activity and generally may not be deducted against income from the other two categories. § 469(a) and (d). Similarly, tax credits from passive activities can only offset the income taxes attributable to income from passive activities. § 469(a) and (d). In effect, there is a general prohibition against using losses and credits from passive activities to shelter income from one's business or portfolio investments. However, there are a few limited exceptions allowing passive activity losses to be used against income in the other two categories. § 469(c)(3), (g) and (i). Any passive losses not allowed as deductions in the year incurred are not disallowed forever. Instead, they may be carried forward (but not back) indefinitely and can be used to offset income from a passive activity in a subsequent taxable year. § 469(b). Even without income from a passive activity, suspended passive activity losses are deductible in full in the year a taxpayer disposes of his entire interest in the passive activity that generated the suspended losses if the disposition is a taxable transaction. § 469(g). The suspended passive activity loss must first be applied against any gain realized and recognized from the disposition of that passive activity, § 469(g)(1)(A)(i), and then against income from other passive activities. § 469(g)(1)(A)(ii). Any excess remaining after offsetting gains and other income from passive activities can then be deducted in the year of disposition against income from the other two categories. § 469(g)(1)(A)(iii).

Losses from the active conduct of a trade or business in which the taxpayer materially participates are not subject to the passive loss restrictions under § 469(a) and may immediately be used to offset income from all three categories.

Before the limitations on the deduction of passive losses under § 469(a) are applied, a taxpayer must first ascertain whether a current deduction is allowed under the at risk rule of § 465. If the at risk rule does not suspend the deduction, then the taxpayer must overcome the hurdles under the passive loss rule before a current deduction is allowed.

Since many taxpayers do not actively participate in the management of their portfolio investments, portfolio income, which includes interest, dividends and royalties, as well as gain from the sale of stocks and bonds, could just as easily have been classified as income from a passive activity. However, § 469(e)(1) makes it clear that portfolio income is not treated as income from a passive activity. The reason for segregating portfolio income from passive activities is explained in the legislative history as follows:

> Portfolio investments ordinarily give rise to positive income, and are not likely to generate losses which could be applied to shelter other income. Therefore, for purposes of the passive loss rule, portfolio income generally is not treated as derived from a passive activity, but rather is treated like other positive income sources such as salary. To permit portfolio income to be offset by passive losses or credits would create the inequitable result of restricting sheltering by individuals dependent for support on wages or active business income, while permitting sheltering by those whose income is derived from an investment portfolio. Tax Reform Act of 1986, Senate Finance Committee Report on H.R. 3838, 99th Cong., 2d Sess. 728 (1986).

Passive activity defined. The reach of the passive loss rule extends beyond the typical passive investment such as a limited partnership interest. It encompasses passive interests in any trade or business and investment. § 469(c)(1) and (6). However, working interests in oil and gas ventures are not subject to the limitation on the ability to deduct passive losses so that losses from such activities can offset all types of income. § 469(c)(3) and (4).

In general, a passive activity involves the conduct of any trade or business and investment where the taxpayer does not "materially participate" in the activity. § 469(c)(1)(B). An individual materially participates in an activity if he "is involved in the operations of the activity on a basis which is (A) regular, (B) continuous, and (C) substantial." § 469(h)(1). Although material participation will usually require a year-round, active involvement, the significance to be accorded each requirement, and how each requirement is to be interpreted, will vary depending on the nature of the activity. In effect, there are three factors to consider, although each factor, standing alone, is not conclusive of the presence or absence of material participation. First, is the activity a taxpayer's principal trade or business? For example, a person whose principal occupation is farming is more likely to materially participate in another farming activity than a lawyer who happens to visit his working farm every weekend. An individual can materially participate in more than one activity. At the other end an individual may be found not to materially participate in any activities. Second, how close in proximity is the taxpayer to the activity in question? Although one is more likely to be more active in an activity located in the same geographical area as his principal residence, proximity is not enough to establish material participation. Third, does the taxpayer have knowledge and experience in the enterprise? In evaluating these factors one need not be engaged in every aspect of an activity. The performance of management or supervisory functions is usually sufficient. However, a merely formal and nominal participation in management in the absence of a bona fide exercise of independent judgment or discretion is not enough. The participation of a taxpayer's spouse is taken into account in determining whether the taxpayer materially participates.

Question

Would the taxpayer who owned the farm in the Smith case at page 364 be found to satisfy the material participation standard?

In using the touchstone of material participation, the legislative history notes:

> The committee believes that, in order for tax preferences to function as intended, their benefit must be directed primarily to taxpayers with a substantial and *bona fide* involvement in the activities to which the preferences relate. The committee also believes that it is appropriate to encourage nonparticipating investors to invest in particular activities, by permitting the use of preferences to reduce the rate of tax on income from those activities; however, such investors should not be permitted to use tax benefits to shelter unrelated income.

> There are several reasons why it is appropriate to examine the materiality of a taxpayer's participation in an activity in determining the extent to which such taxpayer should be permitted to use tax benefits from the activity. A taxpayer who materially participates in an activity is more likely than a passive investor to approach the activity with a significant nontax economic profit motive, and to form a sound judgment as to whether the activity has genuine economic significance and value.

> A material participation standard identifies an important distinctin between different types of taxpayer activities. In general, the more passive investor is seeking a return on capital invested, including returns in the form of reductions in the taxes owed on unrelated income, rather than an ongoing source of livelihood. A material participation standard reduces the importance for such investors, of the tax-reduction features of an investment, and thus increases the importance of the economic features in an investor's decision about where to invest his funds.

> Moreover, the committee believes that restricting the use of losses from business activities in which the taxpayer does not materially participate against other sources of positive income (such as salary and portfolio income) addresses a fundamental aspect of the tax shelter problem. * * * [I]nstances in which the tax system applies simple rules at the expense of economic accuracy encourage the structuring of transactions to take advantage of the situations in which such rules give rise to undermeasurement or deferral of income. Such transac-

tions commonly are marketed to investors who do not intend to participate in the transactions, as devices for sheltering unrelated sources of positive income (e.g., salary and portfolio income). Accordingly, by creating a bar against the use of losses from business activities in which the taxpayer does not materially participate to offset positive income sources such as salary and portfolio income, the committee believes that it is possible significantly to reduce the tax shelter problem. Tax Reform Act of 1986, Senate Finance Committee Report on H.R. 3838, 99th Cong., 2d Sess. 716.

A limited partner's interest in a limited partnership is automatically classified as a passive activity. § 469(h)(2). However, a taxpayer cannot transfer an active business activity that produces income to a limited partnership that produces passive losses and circumvent the passive loss rule. § 469(k)(3).

Rental activity. A rental activity, as defined in § 469(j)(8), is automatically classifed as a passive activity even though a taxpayer materially participates in that rental activity. § 469(c)(2) and (4). The legislative history discusses the inadequacy of the material participation standard in the context of rental activities as follows:

> * * * [Rental] activities predominantly involve the production of income from capital. * * * Rental activities generally require less ongoing management activity, in proportion to capital invested, than business activities involving the production or sale of goods and services. Thus, for example, an individual who is employed full-time as a professional could more easily provide all necessary management in his spare time with respect to a rental activity than he could with respect to another type of business activity involving the same capital investment. The extensive use of rental activities for tax shelter purposes under [prior] law, combined with the reduced level of personal involvement necessary to conduct such activities, [made] clear that the effectiveness of the basic passive loss provision could be seriously compromised if material participation were sufficient to avoid the limitations in the case of rental activities. Tax Reform Act of 1986, Senate Finance Committee Report on H.R. 3838, 99th Cong., 2d Sess. 718 (1986).

Obviously, a line must be drawn regarding what type of rental activities are to be automatically subject to the passive loss limitation. For example, someone who materially participates in the business of renting cars under daily or short-term leases should not be subject to § 469(a). The following excerpt from the legislative history indicates that § 469(c)(2) and (4) does not apply to all rental activities.

> A passive activity is defined under the bill to include any rental activity, whether or not the taxpayer materially participates. However, operating a hotel or other similar transient lodging, for example, where substantial services are provided, is not a rental activity. An activity as a dealer in real estate is also not generally treated as a rental activity. Long-term rentals or leases of property (e.g., apartments, leased office equipment, or leased cars), on the other hand,

generally are considered to be rental activities. Tax Reform Act of 1986, Senate Finance Committee Report on H.R. 3838, 99th Cong., 2d Sess. 720 (1986).

Some relief is provided for individuals who "actively participate" in a rental real estate activity even though it is automatically classified as passive activity. An individual taxpayer who actively participates in a rental real estate activity may annually deduct against non-passive income from the other two categories up to an aggregate of $25,000 of passive activity losses from that rental real estate activity to the extent they exceed income from all passive activities. § 469(i)(1) and (2). The reason for this limited exemption from the passive loss limitation under § 469(a) is explained as follows:

> In the case of rental real estate * * * some specifically targeted relief [is] provided because rental real estate is held, in many instances, to provide financial security to individuals with moderate incomes. In some cases, for example, an individual may hold for rental a residence that he uses part-time, or that previously was and at some future time may be his primary residence. Even absent any such residential use of the property by the taxpayer, the committee believes that a rental real estate investment in which the taxpayer has significant responsibilities with respect to providing necessary services, and which serves significant nontax purposes of the taxpayer, is different in some respects from the activities that are meant to be fully subject to limitation under the passive loss provision. Tax Reform Act of 1986, Senate Finance Committee Report on H.R. 3838, 99th Cong., 2d Sess. 736 (1986).

In analyzing how a taxpayer applies the $25,000 allowance the legislative history notes:

> * * * The $25,000 allowance is applied by first netting income and loss from all of the taxpayer's rental real estate activities in which he actively participates. If there is a net loss for the year from such activities, net passive income (if any) from other activities is then applied against it, in determining the amount eligible for the $25,000 allowance.

> For example, assume that a taxpayer has $25,000 of losses from a rental real estate activity in which he actively participates. If he also actively participates in another rental real estate activity, from which he has $25,000 of gain, resulting in no net loss from rental real estate activities in which he actively participates, then no amount is allowed under the $25,000 allowance for the year. This result follows whether or not the taxpayer has net losses from other passive activities for the year. Tax Reform Act of 1986, Conference Report on H.R. 3838, 99th Cong., 2d Sess. II-141 (1986).

Since a purpose for allowing up to $25,000 of passive losses from rental real estate to offset income from the other two categories was to exempt individuals of modest means from the passive loss limitation, the $25,000 allowance is phased out for taxpayers with adjusted gross incomes in excess of $100,000. The $25,000 allowance is reduced by 50 percent of the amount by which a taxpayer's adjusted gross income exceeds $100,000. § 469(i)(3). By the time an individual has $150,000 of adjusted gross income, the allowance is completely phased out. For this purpose adjusted gross income is computed without regard to IRA contributions or other passive activity losses. § 469(i)(3)(D).

The nature of the participation necessary to satisfy the "active participation" standard is not as great as that needed to meet the "material participation" standard. The authority to specify the meaning of active and material participation has been delegated to the Commissioner. § 469(k)(1). The legislative history indicates that "active participation" is a lessor degree of involvement and can be satisfied without the regular, continuous, and substantial involvement in operations needed for material participation. The legislative history provides:

> The difference between active participation and material participation is that the former can be satisfied without regular, continuous, and substantial involvement in operations, so long as the taxpayer participates, e.g., in the making of management decisions or arranging for others to provide services (such as repairs), in a significant and *bona fide* sense. Management decisions that are relevant in this context include approving new tenants, deciding on rental terms, approving capital or repair expenditures, and other similar decisions. Tax Reform Act of 1986, Senate Finance Committee Report on H.R. 3838, 99th Cong., 2d Sess. 737–738 (1986).

However, a taxpayer cannot be treated as actively participating in a rental real estate activity if at any time his interest (including any interest of a spouse) is less than 10 percent (by value) of all interests in such activity. § 469(i)(6)(A). In addition, a limited partner, even if he owns more than a 10 percent interest, is automatically precluded from meeting the active participation standard. § 469(i)(6)(C).

Disposition of an interest in a passive activity. When a taxpayer finally disposes of his entire interest in a passive activity to someone who is not a related party, and it is found to be an arm's length sale for the fair market value of that interest, the actual economic gain (or loss) on his investment can finally be determined. If the disposition is a "fully taxable transaction," § 469(g)(1)(A), then the actual economic loss from the passive activity may be deducted against either passive income, active income or portfolio income. § 469(g)(1). Any gain recognized on the disposition of an entire interest in a passive activity is treated as passive income and any suspended losses attributable to the interest disposed of are first applied against that gain. Any suspended losses in excess of the disposition gain recognized then offsets income from other passive activities. If there are still unused suspended losses, that excess can finally be deducted against active and portfolio income. § 469(g)(1)(A). Since the passive loss rule is designed to limit deductions to real economic losses, any unused suspended credits are not allowed upon a disposition and disappear forever. An abandonment constitutes a fully taxable disposition that triggers the deduction of suspended losses attributable to the abandoned passive activity. Refer to the Arkin case at page 939. If the suspended losses triggered by the disposition are composed of capital losses, then the ability to deduct such losses is further restricted by § 1211 (discussed at page 907). § 469(g)(1)(C). The rationale for a disposition allowing suspended losses to finally be deducted is explained as follows:

> The reason for this rule it that, prior to a disposition of the taxpayer's interest, it is difficult to determine whether there has actually been gain or loss with respect to the activity. For example, allowable deductions may exceed actual economic costs, or may be exceeded by untaxed appreciation. Upon a taxable disposition, net appreciation or depreciation with respect to the activity can be finally ascertained. Tax Reform Act of 1986, Senate Finance Committee Report on H.R. 3838, 99th Cong., 2d Sess. 725 (1986).

An installment sale of a taxpayer's entire interest in a passive activity that qualifies as a fully taxable disposition also triggers the allowance of the suspended losses. However, all of the suspended losses cannot be deducted in the year of sale. Instead, the suspended losses are allocated pro rata to each year the taxpayer receives an installment payment. The suspended losses are allowed in the ratio that the gain recognized in each year bears to the total gross profit the taxpayer realized (or to be realized) when the payments are completed. § 469(g)(3).

If a taxpayer disposes of his entire interest in a passive activity by gift or at his death, he is no longer subject to the passive loss rules. However, special disposition rules apply to gratuitous dispositions.

An individual who disposes of his entire interest by gift cannot deduct his suspended losses. Instead, the donee's basis is increased by any suspended losses. § 469(j)(6). Suspended losses are thereby eliminated when added to the donee's basis in the passive activity. Therefore, a donee who later disposes of his interest in the passive activity cannot trigger the deduction of suspended losses that occurred while the interest was held by the donor. Any suspended losses that arise after the gift is made may be triggered upon a disposition by the donee. Adding suspended losses to the donee's basis has the effect of a deduction because the added basis reduces the gain realized and recognized by the donee on a subsequent disposition. However, if the donee later disposes of the passive interest at a loss, the donee's basis for purposes of determining his loss is limited to the fair market value of the interest at the time of the gift.

Under certain circumstances all or a portion of the suspended losses remaining at a taxpayer's death may be deducted on his final income tax return. The deduction allowed is the amount, if any, by which the suspended losses exceed the increase in the basis of the interest obtained under § 1014(a). § 469(g)(2)(A). Suspended losses equal to the amount of the tax-free step up in basis allowed under § 1014(a) simply disappear forever. For example, assume an individual's basis in a passive activity, valued at $150,000, is $100,000 immediately before his death. At the time of his death he has $70,000 in suspended losses. On the final income tax return $20,000 of the suspended losses may be deducted. The $50,000 in suspended losses that are not deducted are traceable to the $50,000 increase in basis.

Effective dates. The passive loss rule is fully effective for all losses generated by investments in passive activities made after December 31, 1986. However, for investments made prior to 1987, the limit on the deduction of passive losses is phased in over a five-year period. A taxpayer is allowed to deduct 65 percent of his losses from a passive activity against income from other sources in 1987, 40 percent in 1988, 20 percent in 1989, and 10 percent in 1990. § 469(l).

3. INTERRELATIONSHIP OF THE LIMITATION ON PASSIVE ACTIVITY LOSSES, THE LIMITATION ON INVESTMENT INTEREST AND OTHER CODE SECTIONS

Interest deductions attributable to passive activities constitute passive activity deductions and are not treated as investment interest. § 163(d)(3)(B)(ii). Thus, interest deductions incurred in a passive activity are subject to limitation under § 469, not under § 163(d). Furthermore, income and losses from passive activities generally are not treated as investment income or expenses in calculating the amount of the investment interest limitation. § 163(d)(4)(D). However, any passive activity losses allowed because of the phase-in of the passive loss provision (§ 469(l)) (except losses from rental real estate activities in which the taxpayer actively participates) reduce the taxpayer's investment income. § 163(d)(4)(E).

The passive activity loss limitation applies to all deductions from passive activities, including deductions under §§ 162, 163, 164, and 165. Thus, state and local property tax deductions incurred with respect to passive activities are subject to the passive loss limitation.

Mortgage interest on a principal residence or second residence is not subject to the passive loss rule even if the taxpayer rents out one of his personal residences. § 469(j)(7). However, other residence related deductions are subject to the passive loss rule.

The term "property held for investment" (§ 163(d)(5)) for purposes of the investment interest limit includes: (i) interest expense properly allocable to portfolio interest (e.g., bonds or stocks); (ii) interest expense properly allocable to an activity, involving a trade or business, in which the taxpayer does not materially participate if the activity is not treated as a passive activity under § 469; and (iii) interest expense incurred to carry an interest in a passive activity to the extent attributable to portfolio income (e.g., a real estate venture which holds stocks and bonds). Also the term "investment income" includes amounts treated as portfolio income under § 469 and income from interests in activities, involving a trade or business, in which the taxpayer does not materially participate, if that activity is not treated as a passive activity under the passive loss rule. § 163(h)(5)(A).

Question

Can taxable punitive damages received as part of a personal injury award be offset by passive activity losses? What about a taxable prize or the taxable discovery of the cash found in the piano in the Cesarini case? Examine § 469(c)(1)(A).

Problems

1. Ted Player has become a partner in his law firm and is now in the 33% marginal income tax bracket. Ted and his wife have adjusted gross income for the next three years, before the deduction from his real estate investment, of $100,000. On January 1 of the current year Ted buys a residential apartment building as an investment for $500,000, with $450,000 of the purchase price allocated to the building and $50,000 to the land. Reg. § 1.167(a)–5. Ted manages the building and makes all of the decisions regarding its operation.

(a) Ted invests $100,000 of his own money and obtains a recourse mortgage loan from a bank in the sum of $400,000 for the balance of the purchase price. The mortgage is payable over a term of 30 years. He receives gross rentals of $52,500 yearly and has yearly operating expenses and real estate taxes of $10,000. His yearly mortgage payments are $42,500, broken down as follows:

Year	Principal	Interest
1	$ 4,000	$38,500
2	5,000	37,500
3	6,000	36,500

Reconsider problem 3 at page 576.

i. What is his basis in the property (specifically, the building) when purchased?

ii. Compute the taxable income or loss generated by his rental real estate for the first three years.

iii. What is the impact of the passive loss provision contained in § 469? Consider § 469(i). What difference would it make if Ted relies on a professional management company to operate the building and that company makes all management decisions which Ted ratifies without exercising his independent judgment? What result if their adjusted gross income for the first three years was $102,000?

iv. What is Ted's income tax picture during the first three years he owns the building? Consider §§ 163(d) and (h), 164, 168(a) and § 212a. What is the impact of the at risk rule contained in § 465? What is the significance of § 163(d)(3)(B)?

v. What is Ted's adjusted basis in the building at the end of the third year? Consider § 1016(a)(2).

vi.   What is Ted's rate of return on his investment during the first three years?   His rate of return equals the sum of (1) the cash flow from the investment, and (2) the income taxes saved by being able to deduct the tax loss from his investment against his other income, divided by the amount of capital he invested in the project.

(b)   How should the financing be arranged?   Does it make any difference if the mortgage loan is recourse or noncourse?   What if Ted invested none of his own funds and borrowed the entire $500,000 purchase price?   What difference would it make if the mortgage loan was provided by the seller and it was nonrecourse?   What if there was nonrecourse seller financing and the amount of the purchase price exceeded the value of the property?

(c)   Suppose the only reason that Ted invested in this real estate was to save taxes.   What effect would that have on his ability to take deductions?   Consider § 183 and the Goldstein case at page 661.

(d)   At the beginning of year 4 Ted sells the property for $500,000, receiving $115,000 in cash because the purchaser took the property subject to the existing mortgage of $385,000.   What are the income tax consequences to Ted upon the disposition of his investment?   What are the tax consequences if Ted's adjusted gross income, before the deduction of the loss from this activity, each year was $102,000?   In evaluating an investor's rate of return while he owned the property why is it important to also consider the year of disposition?

2.   Fred's basis in his interest in a passive activity, valued at $150,000, is $100,000.   The activity is rental real estate, and Fred owns the entire building in his own name.   Fred's adjusted gross income is $200,000.   Fred gives his entire interest to his son, Sidney, as a gift.   At the time of the gift Fred had $70,000 in suspended losses under § 469.   When the gift was made the entire $70,000 in suspended losses was added to the donee's basis in the real estate.   Using his adjusted basis of $170,000 in the real estate, Sidney deducted $70,000 in depreciation, thereby generating another $70,000 in suspended losses while Sidney held the property.   Sidney then sells the property for its $150,000 value.   What are the tax consequences to Sidney upon the taxable disposition of the property?

3.   What advice would you give Fred in the above problem as to whether he should dispose of his interest in his passive activity by gift or bequest?

Vacation homes.   Taxpayers with vacation homes frequently rent them to others in order to reduce the costs of ownership.   If the vacation property is held primarily as an investment, the deductions (including depreciation) typically exceed the rental receipts, thereby generating a tax loss which, prior to the enactment of § 469, could be used to shelter income from other sources.   As the question of whether the property was held primarily for a profit is a factual determination dependent upon the taxpayer's intent, many taxpayers treated their vacation homes as investments on their income tax returns.   Often they were able to convince the Service or the courts of their profit motive.   More often they prevailed by winning the audit lottery.

Congress soon realized that the factual guidelines under § 183 were not adequate and, in 1976, added the irrebuttable presumption contained in § 280A(d)(1) to police this area of perceived abuse. If a taxpayer uses a vacation home for greater than the number of days specified in § 280A(d)(1) (the so-called 14-day rule), the property can never be treated as business or investment property and its tax treatment will then be governed by § 280A(a).

If the property is used primarily as a residence, either because the personal use exceeds the number of days proscribed in § 280A(d)(1) or because the trier of fact finds an absence of a profit motive, the tax treatment is governed by the general nondeductibility rule contained in § 280A(a). However, certain deductions may be taken up to, but not exceeding, the rental receipts. § 280A(c)(5). In effect, § 280A precludes a taxpayer from using a personal vacation residence to generate losses to be used against income from other sources, but will not require the residence to generate taxable income. The taxpayer is required by § 280A(e) to allocate his expenses between the rental use and the personal use of the vacation home. That portion of his expenses allocable to the rental use may then be used to offset the rental income, thereby reducing or eliminating any taxable income from the rental use of a personal residence. This is the same approach used for home offices and is similar to the approach § 183(b) takes with hobby farms. However, there is a de minimis exception in § 280A(g) for a personal residence rented for less than 15 days during the year. This exception allows a taxpayer to exclude his rental receipts from gross income and at the same time, precludes any deductions allowable to such minimal rental use.

If the vacation property used personally is for less than the 14-day period specified in § 280A(d)(1), then a taxpayer is allowed to treat it as a property held for a profit.[2] However, not all of the expenses are deductible. Only that portion of the expenses allocable to the rental use may be deducted against the rentals because § 280A(e) requires that the expenses be allocated between the rental and personal use. Although the taxes and interest allocable to the personal use are itemized deductions, the expenses for items, such as utilities, repairs and insurance for which no personal deduction section exists in the Code are not deductible to the extent allocable to personal use, even if the property is held for a profit.

A question arises as to how the allocation of deductions between rental and personal use is to be made for a residence covered by § 280A(a) when the combined rental and personal use is less than the entire year. For those expenses which are generally incurred only when the property is occupied, the allocation under § 280A(e) is made based on the number of days rented to the total number of days rental and personal use. But, for those deductions which occur regardless of

2. The trier of fact can still use the facts and circumstances test to find that the second home is not held primarily for profit.

the property's use (the insurance, interest and taxes), the allocation uses the number of days rented over the total days in the year. In Bolton v. Commissioner, 694 F.2d 556 (9th Cir.1982), the Commissioner argued that all expenses should be allocated using only actual use during the year. Taxpayer's victory in Bolton means that a smaller portion of the interest and taxes is allocated to the rental use so that a greater portion of the otherwise nondeductible items such as utilities and maintenance could be used to offset the rental receipts. Because the interest and taxes allocable to the personal use are itemized deductions, the taxpayer's overall deductions are greater under the Bolton case than under the Commissioner's position. The Bolton case is also a good case illustrating the mechanical application of § 280A to a vacation home used personally for 30 days and rented for 91 days.

Question

Consider the impact of §§ 163(d) and 469 on the taxpayer who owns a vacation home that is found to be held primarily for a profit.

Chapter 12

CAPITAL ASSET TRANSACTIONS

A. MECHANICS OF CAPITAL GAINS AND LOSSES

Introduction. Prior to 1987 the tax preference for capital gains was a method of reducing the graduated rates of taxation, which ranged as high as 50 percent, for certain types of income, called long-term capital gains. Long-term capital gains resulted from the sale or exchange of a capital asset held for more than six months,[1] and, prior to 1987, were subject to taxation at rates equal to 40 percent of the rates applicable to other forms of income (commonly referred to as ordinary income, § 64). Prior to 1987, when the capital gains preference was available, the maximum rate of taxation for individuals on long-term capital gains was only 20 percent instead of the 50 percent maximum applicable to ordinary income. Short-term capital gains, which arose from the sale or exchange of a capital asset held for six months or less, did not receive the 40 percent preference and were therefore taxable at the same rates as the taxpayer's ordinary income.

The Tax Reform Act of 1986 reduced the top marginal rate for individuals by instituting a simple, two-bracket system with rates of 15 and 28 percent. (For certain high-income taxpayers there is a third bracket at 33 percent because of the 5 percent phaseout of the 15 percent bracket and the personal exemption. § 1(g)). Because of the reduction in the maximum rate of taxation, Congress believed that the tax preference for capital gains was no longer necessary. Beginning in 1988 the preferential treatment of capital gains is repealed. The legislative history provides:

> The committee believes that as a result of the [Act's] reduction of individual tax rates on such forms of capital income as business profits, interest, dividends, and short-term capital gains, the need to provide a

---

1. § 1222(1)–(4). The six month holding period for long-term capital gain treatment is effective with respect to property acquired after June 22, 1984 and before January 1, 1988. A one year holding period exists for assets acquired before June 23, 1984, and after December 31, 1987.

reduced rate for net capital gain is eliminated. This will result in a tremendous amount of simplification for many taxpayers since their tax will no longer depend upon the characterization of income as ordinary or capital gain. In addition, this will eliminate any requirement that capital assets be held by the taxpayer for any extended period of time * * * in order to obtain favorable treatment. This will result in greater willingness to invest in assets that are freely traded (e.g., stocks). Tax Reform Act of 1986, Senate Finance Committee Report on H.R. 3838, 99th Cong., 2d Sess. 169 (1986).

This brief overview should help you understand why a cornerstone to tax planning was found in capital gain transactions and in the myriad of devices which sought to transform what would normally be reported as ordinary income, taxable at a maximum rate of 50 percent, into capital gains, taxable at a maximum rate of 20 percent. Although capital gains are now taxed at the same rates as ordinary income, there remain certain situations where it is necessary to determine whether or not gains or losses arise from the sale or exchange of a capital asset. For example, examine § 1031(a)(2). And, there is always the possibility that Congress will reinstate the preference for capital gains. In fact, the legislative history of the Tax Reform Act of 1986, in acknowledging the possibility of a future rate increase, retained "[t]he current statutory structure for capital gains * * * to facilitate reinstatement of a capital gains rate differential if there is a future tax rate increase." Tax Reform Act of 1986, Conference Report on H.R. 3838, 99th Cong. 2d Sess. II–107 (1986).

Prior law. The requisite tools for computing the capital gains preference available for taxable years prior to 1987 are contained in §§ 1202, 1222 and 1223. The following materials contain a brief description as to how the preference for long-term capital gains was bestowed under prior law.

Once the amount of the gain or loss from a sale or exchange was computed, the process did not end. Rather, the resulting gain or loss had to be characterized by reference to the nature of the property sold or exchanged, or otherwise disposed of, and the nature of the taxpayer's trade or business. Essentially, every transaction that produced a gain or loss was examined to determine whether the resulting gain or loss was ordinary or capital. If the item met the definition of a capital asset under § 1221, the resulting gain or loss from a sale or exchange was characterized as a capital gain or loss. It was then necessary to determine whether the gain or loss was short-term or long-term. Section 1222 defines short-term and long-term capital gains or losses by reference to the period which the taxpayer has owned the capital asset. Generally, if the taxpayer held the asset for more than six months, the capital gain or loss on its sale or exchange is characterized as long-term. § 1222(3) and (4). Conversely, if the taxpayer held the asset for six months or less, any capital gain or loss on the transaction was characterized as short-term. § 1222(1) and (2).

A noncorporate taxpayer began by aggregating all capital asset transactions in a taxable year. If all of these transactions when taken together resulted in a net gain, then the capital gain deduction under § 1202(a) came into play. First, the taxpayer separately determined the net result for long-term capital asset transactions and the net result for short-term capital asset transactions. If the aggregate of taxpayer's long-term capital asset transactions resulted in a net gain, the taxpayer had a net long-term capital gain (§ 1222(7)). Conversely, if the aggregate of taxpayer's long-term transactions resulted in a net loss, the taxpayer had a net long-term capital loss. (§ 1222(8)). The taxpayer went through a similar computation for his short-term capital transactions under § 1222(5) and (6). The special deduction under former § 1202(a) for a net capital gain applied only if the amount of the taxpayer's net long-term capital gain exceeded the amount of his net short-term capital loss. § 1222(11). A taxpayer's net capital gain was computed, pursuant to § 1222, as follows:

> Net capital gain (§ 1222(11)) = [Net long-term capital gain (§ 1222(7)) which equals "the excess of long-term capital gains [§ 1222(3)] for the taxable year over the long-term capital losses [§ 1222(4)] for such year."] *less* [Net short-term capital loss (§ 1222(6)) which equals "the excess of short-term capital losses [§ 1222(2)] for the taxable year over the short-term capital gains [§ 1222(1)] for such year."]

In other words, any net long-term capital gain remaining after deducting net short-term capital loss, if any, was called net capital gain.

If the noncorporate taxpayer had no net long-term capital gain or if his net long-term capital gain did not exceed his net short-term capital loss, he could not use the special capital gains deduction offered by former § 1202(a). Short-term capital gains were not included in the term net capital gain (§ 1222(11)) and were taxed in the same manner as ordinary income. For a taxpayer with capital losses, short-term capital gains enjoyed significant tax advantages over ordinary income. Capital losses (long-term and short-term) could be deducted dollar-for-dollar to the extent of short-term capital gains without any dollar limitation.

Taxpayers' preference for long-term capital gains was attributable to the previous preferential tax treatment afforded by the capital gains deduction of former § 1202(a), which was a deduction from gross income, rather than an itemized deduction for purposes of the computation of taxable income. The § 1202(a) deduction was available even if a taxpayer did not itemize his deductions under § 63. A taxpayer entitled to the deduction provided by former § 1202(a) included all of his capital gains in gross income and then deducted 60 percent of the net capital gain from his gross income. The following chart is helpful in defining the term "net capital gain:"

Net Capital Gain § 1222(11)

Net long-term capital gain   *exceeds*   Net short-term capital loss
     § 1222(7)   § 1222(6)

long-term	*exceeds* long-term	short-term	*exceeds* short-term
capital gain	capital loss	capital loss	capital gain
§ 1222(3)	§ 1222(4)	§ 1222(2)	§ 1222(1)

The following example may help illustrate the computations. A, an individual, had the following transactions in his tax year:

Long-term sales or exchanges:

Long-term capital gains	$10,000
Long-term capital losses	5,000
Net long-term capital gain	$ 5,000

Short-term sales or exchanges:

Short-term capital losses	$ 2,000
Short-term capital gains	1,000
Net short-term capital loss	$ 1,000

Net capital gain (excess of net long-term capital gain over net short-term capital loss)	$ 4,000

The amount of the § 1202(a) capital gain preference deduction was 60% of $4,000 (or $2,400).

When the highest marginal tax rate was set at 50 percent, the 60 percent deduction available under former § 1202(a) limited the individual's tax on his net capital gains to a maximum of 20 percent. This 20 percent maximum resulted from applying the maximum 50 percent rate of taxation to the 40 percent of the net capital gain that was effectively subject to taxation. A taxpayer who was in, for example the 38 percent marginal tax bracket paid a maximum effective rate on his net capital gain of only 15.2 percent. The elimination of the deduction for net capital gains previously available under § 1202(a), coupled with the reduction of the highest rate bracket to 28 percent, had the effect of raising the maximum rate of taxation on capital gains by 8 percent. That is why, during 1986, taxpayers were advised to sell their capital assets before the end of the year so as to report their long-term capital gains on their 1986 income tax returns, rather than defer the reporting of their capital gains to 1987 and subsequent years. Why were taxpayers advised to postpone the reporting of their short-term capital gains from 1986 to 1987? The current 28 percent rate of taxation on capital gains is a return to the maximum rate for capital gains that existed from 1978 through 1981. Prior to 1982 the higest marginal rate of taxation was 70 percent. The 60 percent deduction under former § 1202(a), combined with a 70 percent marginal tax rate, effectively taxed capital gains at a maximum of 28 percent. This resulted from applying the 70 percent rate of taxation to the 40 percent of capital gains subject to taxation. And, prior to 1978, when the deduction for net capital gains under former § 1202(a) was only 50 percent, the maximum rate on capital gains was 35 percent.

Maximum rate on capital gains. The simplification Congress intended by eliminating the preference for capital gains in the Tax Reform Act of 1986 will be delayed for at least a year because, for 1987, there is a transitional phase-in of the reduction in tax rates. § 1(h). For 1987 the maximum marginal rate on individuals is 38.5 percent. However, for 1987, the maximum rate on long-term capital gains is 28 percent and is keyed to the term "net capital gain," as defined in § 1222(11). As a result of the introduction of "net capital gain" into the computation under § 1(j), a determination of whether or not the character of a gain or loss is capital, and if capital, whether it is long-term or short-term is necessary for 1987. Section 1222(1)–(4) defines short-term and long-term capital gains and losses by reference to the period of time a taxpayer has owned a capital asset.

The elimination of the tax preference for capital gains and its intended simplification may prove to be temporary. In the event that the highest rate of taxation in § 1 ever exceeds 28 percent after 1987, Congress provided that the maximum rate of taxation on "net capital gain" will be limited to 28 percent. § 1(j)(1) and (2)(B). If Congress decides to increase the maximum rate of taxation above the 28 percent scheduled to take effect in 1988, the distinction between ordinary income and capital gain will resume its former importance and complexity. Although, for 1988 and subsequent years, there will no longer be a need to distinguish between long-term and short-term capital gains and losses, there will still be a need to determine whether or not gains and losses are capital or ordinary because of the loss limitations imposed on capital losses under § 1211(b). The limitations on capital losses will be discussed shortly. One final point should be made. While the application of § 1(j) results in limiting the maximum rate on capital gains to 28 percent, a taxpayer must take all of his capital gains and losses into account in determining whether a certain income level is reached so that the phase-out rules under § 1(g) apply.

For corporate taxpayers, beginning in 1987, the maximum rate on net capital gain is 34 percent, the same maximum rate applied to a corporation's ordinary income. §§ 11 and 1201(a). Prior to 1987, a corporation's net capital gain was taxed at a maximum of 28 percent.

Limitation on capital losses. Under certain circumstances all taxpayers, both individual and corporate, are limited in their ability to deduct all of their capital losses in the year incurred. First, as we have previously examined earlier in this book, all losses, both capital and ordinary, must satisfy the requirements imposed by § 165(b) and (c). However, § 165 is not exclusive. As discussed at page 1016, a specific category of deductible losses, nonbusiness bad debts, as defined in § 166(d)(2), are automatically characterized as short-term capital losses by § 166(d)(1). Although a capital loss may be deductible under § 165(c), § 165(f) goes on to provide that all capital losses are also subject to the restrictions imposed by §§ 1211 and 1212. These restrictions limit the ability of both corporate and individual taxpayers to currently deduct all of their otherwise allowable capital loss deductions.

For individual taxpayers, beginning in 1987, the maximum amount of ordinary income that can be offset by capital losses is limited to $3,000 each year. § 1211(b)(1). However, an individual can use his capital losses as a deduction, without limitation, to offset his capital gains. § 1211(b). If his capital losses exceed his capital gains, then only $3,000 of that excess can be deducted, effectively limiting the capital loss deduction that can offset ordinary income to $3,000 annually. Under § 1211(b) no distinction is made between short-term and long-term capital gains and losses. Any capital loss deduction not used by an individual taxpayer is merely postponed as it may be carried forward (but not back) indefinitely and is treated as a capital loss incurred in a subsequent year. § 1212(b). Under § 62(a)(3) a capital loss deduction can be taken even though the taxpayer uses the standard deduction under § 63(b). Examine § 63(d).

For a corporate taxpayer capital losses can be deducted in full to the extent of capital gains, but any excess cannot be used to offset ordinary income. § 1211(a). A corporation can also carry forward its unused capital loss deductions to subsequent years. § 1212(a).

Prior to 1987 all capital losses (long-term or short-term) incurred during a taxable year are deductible by a taxpayer to the extent of the taxpayer's capital gains (long-term or short-term) occurring during the year. The noncorporate taxpayer began by aggregating all capital asset transactions during the tax year. Only if all of these transactions, when taken together, resulted in a net loss, did the rules limiting the deductibility of capital losses come into play. The taxpayer separated the gain and loss transactions from the sale of property held for more than six months (i.e. long-term capital gains and losses) from gains and losses arising from the sale of property held for six months or less (i.e. short-term capital gains and losses). The taxpayer separately computed the net results for the long-term transactions and the short-term transactions. If all the long-term transactions produced a net gain, there was a net long-term capital gain. § 1222(7). If all the long-term transactions produced a net loss, there was a net long-term capital loss. § 1222(8). If all the short-term transactions resulted in a net gain, there was a net short-term capital gain. § 1222(5). If all the short-term transactions resulted in a net loss, there was a net short-term capital loss. § 1222(6). In sum, capital losses first offset capital gains of like term (long-term or short-term), dollar-for-dollar. The excess loss, if any, was deducted from the net gain of the other term. Thus, a net short-term loss could offset a net long-term gain, dollar-for-dollar. A net long-term loss may offset a net short-term gain, dollar-for-dollar. If the taxpayer's capital losses for the year exceeded his capital gains, former § 1211(b)(1) limited the deductibility of the excess to $3,000 per year.

Continued Importance of the Capital Asset Concept. Because capital losses offset capital gains and only a limited amount of ordinary income, the "capital asset" concept retains continued importance. It is also important for other reasons such as § 1031. Once the amount of the gain or loss from a sale or exchange has been computed, the resulting gain or loss must be characterized by reference to the nature of the property sold or exchanged and the nature of the taxpayer's trade or business. If the item meets the definition of a capital asset under § 1221, then the resulting gain or loss from a sale or exchange is characterized as a capital gain or loss.

Considerable litigation has arisen as to what is a capital asset. The impetus for this litigation is found in the exclusionary approach of § 1221, the statutory provision defining a capital asset. Although a discussion of the definition of a capital asset is found later in this chapter, it suffices to say that a careful reading of § 1221 suggests the existence of a substantial controversy in this area.

Problems

1. Len is married and has two dependent children. During the taxable year, Len and his wife received $40,000 in wages and incurred $6,000 of "itemized deductions." Len files a joint return with his wife. In each of the following situations, determine their gross income, adjusted gross income, and taxable income. Consider §§ 62, 63, 151, 1211(b) and 1222.

(a)	Capital gains	$ 4,000
(b)	Capital losses	$ 4,000
(c)	Capital gains	$10,000
	Capital losses	$ 2,000
(d)	Capital gains	$ 2,000
	Capital losses	$10,000

2. Becky has $50,000 of ordinary income from her law practice and a capital gain from the sale of stock in the amount of $10,000. Compute her adjusted gross income in each of the following, if she also has

(a) a capital loss of $17,000, or

(b) an ordinary loss of $17,000, deductible in arriving at adjusted gross income under § 62(3).

Consider §§ 1222 and 1211(b).

B. THE FAVORABLE TAX ON CAPITAL GAINS: POLICY ASPECTS

Beginning in 1988, capital gains are taxed as ordinary income. Should capital gains receive preferential treatment in comparison to receipts in the nature of ordinary income? Reconsider the tax policy criteria discussed on pp. 40–43.

Questions

1. If the goal of promoting savings is desirable, why should capital gains, one form of economic enhancement, receive preferential treatment? Is it certain that "realized" capital gains will always result in savings and in business investment, not in consumption? Would a rollover provision, such as found in § 1034, enhance the likelihood that the proceeds from capital gains would be so reinvested? Will the savings be used to finance labor-intensive activities or capital-intensive assets? Are more refined incentive techniques needed?

2. Does the tax on capital gains impair the mobility of capital and the efficient functioning of economic markets by (1) placing a tax penalty on an individual who alters his portfolio to meet changing needs and (2) creating difficulties for entrepreneurs in raising equity capital because investors face a tax cost in withdrawing from their present positions? Who are the likely sources of venture (risk) capital for entrepreneurs? Does the taxation of capital gains really contribute to a lock-in effect?

3. Should unrealized gains be taxed periodically? Reconsider Problem 3 on page 117. Should the appreciation in value of property transferred at death or by gift be taxed at the time of the gratuitous transfer? Reconsider Problem 4(c) on page 264.

4. Does the tax on capital gains impose a "double tax"? Should the increase in the value of an asset and the increase in the future revenues from an asset be viewed as two separate elements of economic enhancement, each subject to taxation only once?

5. With capital gains taxed as ordinary income, should the gains (or losses) allocable to inflation go untaxed through basis adjustments for inflation? Recall that pursuant to § 1(f), the tax tables are adjusted to reflect increases in the Consumer Price Index. Is there any correlation between changes in the value of money and the prices of particular assets? Should an inflation adjustment be limited to specified assets, such as common stock and real property? Should a bondholder be allowed to deduct the loss in value of a bond because of inflation? Is the deferral of the taxation of capital gains until realized a sufficient offset to inflation?

6. Should capital losses be deductible against ordinary income without restriction?

In thinking about these questions, consider the following excerpts:

BURNET v. HARMEL

Supreme Court of the United States, 1932.
287 U.S. 103, 106, 53 S.Ct. 74, 75, 77 L.Ed. 199, 202.

The provisions * * * for taxing capital gains at a lower rate * * *, were adopted to relieve the taxpayer from excessive tax burdens on gains resulting from a conversion of capital investments, and to remove the deterrent effect of those burdens on such conversions.

STAFF OF THE JOINT COMMITTEE ON TAXATION
General Explanation of the Revenue Act of 1978, 252 (1978).

PRIOR LAW

Under prior law, a noncorporate taxpayer could deduct from gross income 50 percent of the amount of any net capital gain for the taxable year. * * *

REASONS FOR CHANGE

The Congress believed that the present level of taxes applicable to capital gains has contributed both to a slower rate of economic growth than that which otherwise might have been anticipated, and also to the realization of fewer gains than would have been realized if the tax rates had been lower. In some instances, the taxes applicable to capital gains effectively may have locked some taxpayers into their existing investments. Moreover, the Congress believed that the present level of capital gains taxes had contributed to the shortage of investment funds needed for capital formation purposes generally, and especially for new and small businesses. * * *

The Congress believed that lower capital gains taxes will markedly increase sales of appreciated assets, which will offset much of the revenue loss from the tax cut, and potentially lead to an actual increase in revenues. In addition, the improved mobility of capital will stimulate investment, thereby generating more economic activity and more tax revenue.

In addition, the Congress believed that an increased capital gains deduction would tend to offset the effect of inflation by reducing the amount of gain which is subject to tax. However, since the deduction is constant, unlike the adjustments generally provided for in various indexation proposals, it is much simpler and should not tend to exacerbate inflation.

The Congress believed that the increased deduction, in conjunction with the Act's other capital gains tax changes and its reformulation of the minimum tax, should contribute significantly to a more favorable economic climate by increasing the mobility of capital, and by providing an incentive for taxpayers to both realize gains and to increase savings. * * *

EXPLANATION OF PROVISION

The Act [which was repealed for transactions after December 31, 1986] provides that a noncorporate taxpayer may deduct from gross income 60 percent of the amount of any net capital gain for the taxable year. The remaining 40 percent of the net capital gain is subject to tax at the otherwise applicable rates.

NORMAN B. TURE, STATEMENT—TAX POLICY, INDIVIDU-
AL INVESTORS, AND FINANCIAL MARKETS, HEAR-
INGS BEFORE THE SUBCOMMITTEE ON FINANCIAL
MARKETS OF THE COMMITTEE ON FINANCE, UNITED
STATES SENATE, FIRST SESSION ON THE IMPACT OF
INSTITUTIONAL INVESTORS IN THE STOCK MARKET

93rd Cong. 1st Sess. Pt. 2, 87, 90–94 (1973).

III. TAXATION AND INDIVIDUAL SAVING AND INVESTMENT

*   *   *

In fact, however, when the [prior preferential] tax treatment of
capital gains is viewed against the standard of equal treatment of
consumption and saving uses of income, it turns out not to be a
"loophole" but an additional tax burden on saving—a negative loophole. Perhaps an extended example will help to make this clear.

Suppose for the moment a tax-free economy. Individuals in that
society continuously make choices between the use of their current
income for consumption or for buying additional income in the future,
i. e., saving. The amount of future income which any given amount of
saving buys depends on the contribution at the margin of the additional
capital in which the savings are invested. The cost of any given
amount of future income is the amount of current consumption which
must be foregone by the saving needed to acquire it. Many considerations, of course, enter into individuals' consumption-saving decisions,
but given these considerations, those decisions depend on the relative
cost of saving and consumption.

As an example, suppose that in the tax-free economy a person
might be able to buy some given quantity of consumption goods for
$1,000 or he might use the same $1,000 instead to buy common stock in
a company earning, say $120 per share, when the market rate of
interest is 12 percent. Now suppose an income tax is levied; for ease of
illustration, suppose the tax rate is 50 percent. With the tax, the cost
of the same amount of consumption goods goes up 100 percent in the
sense that it now takes $2,000 of pretax income to buy the same $1,000
of consumption goods. But the cost of saving goes up much more. To
have $120 per year of additional income, one has to receive $240 of
pretax income. But with no change in the market rate of interest, one
must now buy $2,000 worth of the stock to get $240 per year.[9] And to
have $2,000 with which to buy the stock, $4,000 of pretax income is
needed. The 50 percent income tax, thus, has doubled the cost of
consumption, but it has quadrupled the cost of saving. Thus the tax
has doubled the cost of saving relative to the cost of consumption.

The effect of the tax on the total volume of private saving depends
on how responsive people are in their consumption-saving choices to

9. Assuming no income tax is separately levied on the corporation income.

changes in the relative cost of saving. Some economists assume that this response is zero, that personal saving decisions are unaffected by changes in the real rate of return on their saving. I find this assumption untenable on analytical grounds and unverified by actual experience. Rather, it seems to me, an increase in the real cost of saving relative to the cost of consumption will reduce the proportion of income used for saving.

To return to our example. Suppose the corporation whose stock the individual [purchases] uses the proceeds of the stock sale to buy a $1,000 machine. Suppose, to simplify the example, the machine is expected to last forever. To warrant the investment of $1,000 in the machine if there were no tax, the machine would have to add $120 per year to the company's net revenues. But if an income tax, applicable to both the corporation and the individual at a marginal tax rate of, say, 50 percent, were imposed, the machine would no longer earn $120 per year, after taxes. The corporation income tax itself would reduce the after-tax earnings to $60.00 per year. And if the corporation were to distribute the after-tax cash flow to the shareholder, he would net only $30.00 per year on his $1,000 saving.

If before the tax was imposed he required $120 per year to induce him to give up $1,000 of current consumption, he will hardly be likely to settle for $30.00. Clearly, he will reduce his saving-investing. So will others like him.

Collaterally, the corporation is hardly likely to invest $1,000 in a machine that returns only $60.00 per year after tax. With no change in the market rate of discount of future earnings, $60.00 per year is worth $500, not $1,000. If the company's objective is to maximize its profits and the net worth of its shareholders, the after-tax earnings of the machine will have to increase to $120 per year; pretax earnings, then, will have to go up to $240 per year to justify the investment, if earnings are retained. And if earnings are distributed to the shareholders, pretax earnings would have to increase still further—to about $480 per year.

Obviously, a great many capital outlays which would contribute enough to the corporation's net revenues to warrant their undertaking in the absence of the tax become unprofitable and are foregone when the tax is imposed. The reduction in saving and capital formation resulting from the tax will continue until the stock of capital falls relative to the amount of labor services used in production sufficiently to generate the required pretax and after-tax earnings.

To complete the example, suppose that after the adjustments in saving and investment are completed, the corporation retains its after-tax earnings and buys another machine which will also add $240 per year to pretax earnings, hence $120 per year to the company's after-tax earnings. The market value of the shareholders' stock in the company will go up from $1,000 to $2,000. This increase in value, of course, is exactly equal to the present or discounted value of the additional $120 per year of after-tax earnings, discounted at 12 percent as before.

Recall that every dollar of the corporation's earnings on the original machine out of which the $1,000 to buy the new machine was accumulated was taxed as it was earned. And every dollar of the earnings of the new machine will also be taxed as it is earned.

If the shareholder decides to sell his share of stock in the corporation he will realize a capital gain of $10,000. Under the present tax treatment of capital gains he'd pay an additional tax * * * on this realized capital gain. This additional tax is properly viewed as a surcharge on the tax already paid on the prior years' earnings on his initial investment or equivalently as a surcharge on the tax that will be paid over the succeeding years on the new machine's earnings. In either case, the same future earnings stream will be taxed twice, once at the 50 percent rate as the earnings are realized each year, and again * * * on the capitalized value of that future stream of earnings.

The present tax treatment of capital gains, therefore, when evaluated against the standard of equal proportionate taxation of consumption and saving uses of income, emerges not as a loophole but as an additional, heavy burden on saving. Coming as it does on top of the disproportionately heavy individual and corporate income tax load on saving, the taxation of capital gains significantly increases the relative cost of saving.

But this is not the sole effect of capital gains taxation. The tax is imposed on gains not as they accrue but only when they are realized by sale or exchange of the assets. The occasion for the tax, then, is not merely the increase in value but the transfer of the asset as well. Taxing capital gains not only increases the relative cost of saving but also increases the cost of changing the composition of the assets one owns. The interaction of these two effects of capital gains taxation is to increase the difference between the expected returns on alternative investments required to make a shift in asset holdings worthwhile.

Unless it could be established that people are utterly unresponsive to changes in transaction costs, taxing capital gains must reduce the frequency of transfers and impede prompt changes in the composition of assets in response to changes in their relative values. In turn, this clearly impedes the efficient functioning of the financial markets in providing valuations of alternative uses of saving and in allocating saving optimumly.

The present tax treatment of capital losses further burdens private saving and impedes prompt change in the composition of asset holding. Under present law, capital losses are offset against capital gains and up to [$3,000] of ordinary income. Any losses not so offset may be carried forward for an unlimited number of years, but in the case of individuals, no carryback to earlier taxable years is allowed. Since capital gains are fully subject to the additional tax in the year they are realized, the tax cushion against losses may very well be less than the additional tax burden on gains. The risk of investment is increased. In addition, where losses have accrued on an investment, the limitation on their deductibility tends to deter liquidation of that investment and its replacement by other assets. Loss treatment, therefore, accentuates the bias against saving and shifts in asset holdings imposed by the taxation of capital gains.

The weight of these tax impediments to efficient performance by the financial markets is difficult to measure in precise quantitative terms, but there can be little doubt that they are significant. There are a number of studies which show that the average length of time stocks are held is astonishingly long. And unless one attributes these very long holding periods to irrationality on the part of savers-investors, the tax treatment of gains and losses must be held largely accountable for the immobilization of huge amounts of past saving. It must, therefore, be viewed as a serious impediment to financial market efficiency.

* * *

IV. TAX CHANGES TO ENCOURAGE INDIVIDUAL INVESTMENT

Any discussion aimed at changes in the tax treatment of capital gains and losses in the interests of mitigating the existing tax bias against saving and ready transferability of assets faces a huge barrier of conventional wisdom arguing for even heavier tax burdens on capital gains. That argument is oriented primarily to so-called equity considerations. It is predicated on a concept of income deemed to be needed if the principal purpose of taxation is to equalize economic status, without regard to the impact of implementing that income concept on the neutrality of taxation with respect to the consumption-saving choice. That income concept insists that capital gains are in no wise different from any other kind of "income" for purposes of measuring economic status of various individuals, and that taxing capital gains less heavily than other income defeats the purpose of progressive taxation. The conventional wisdom is clearly based on highly circular reasoning. But it has so broadly permeated the policy forum that any proposal to alter that tax treatment of capital gains and losses in the interest of neutrality—equal treatment of saving and consumption—is more often than not received as a special pleading for "fat cats."

As an economist, I profess no expertness regarding tax equity. Both the historical record and abstract analysis strongly suggest to me that government tax and expenditure policies and programs are ineffective in redistributing income and are likely to be counterproductive. The interests of all active participants in the economy—that is, the overwhelming majority of us—rather lies in a tax system that as little as possible interferes with our private choices as to how we obtain and use our income and wealth. Such a tax system should as little as possible change the relative costs of the alternatives we face in the market place. And given the enormous requirements for additional capital we face in the coming years if we are to maintain—let alone advance—our productivity and living standards, top priority in tax policy should be given to reducing the existing heavy tax bias against saving.

The tax proposals presented following are oriented toward reducing this tax bias. In my judgment, they are also likely to make the tax laws fairer. But that judgment, just as the contrary judgments of others, should be taken as expressions of preference, not as scientifically derived truth.

It follows from my earlier argument that one important revision to reduce the existing income tax bias against saving and capital asset transactions would be to eliminate capital gains and losses entirely from the tax base. In the context of the history of the U.S. income tax, of course, this would be a drastic change. But this Subcommittee surely is aware that the income tax laws of few other advanced industrial nations apply to capital gains.

* * * [This proposal] of course, encounter the objection that they would primarily benefit the affluent. As indicated, I am highly skeptical about the relevance and validity of this objection. To the extent that such measures increase saving and business investment, their principal effect is to increase the amount of capital with which labor services are used, hence to increase the rate of advance of labor's productivity and real wages. In evaluating proposals for tax changes, it is important to look beyond their initial impact on the distribution of tax liabilities to their ultimate effects. Failure to do so is largely responsible for the existing tax bias against saving and for resistance to tax changes to reduce that bias.

But insofar as egalitarian preferences restrict the opportunities for constructive tax changes, there are a number of less drastic revisions in the tax treatment of capital gains and losses which would provide significant abatements of the existing anti-saving tax bias and encouragement for individual ownership of equity interests in American business. One of these revisions would be to allow everyone a lifetime exemption of up to, say, $50,000 or $100,000 of capital gains realized on corporate securities and perhaps other specified types of property.[11] A variation of this approach would be to exempt up to some specific amount of capital gains per year, say $5,000, realized on corporate securities. The tax abatement in this general approach would obviously be far more significant to persons of modest incomes than to those with very large portfolios.

A companion change would be to increase substantially the amount of capital losses which might be offset against ordinary income. The limit under present law is [$3,000]. This might be increased to, say, $10,000 or $20,000. Indeed, full offset of losses against ordinary income would be highly desirable and effective. And a three- or four-year

11. I.R.C. § 121 provides that an individual who has attained the age of 55 may exclude from gross income, on a one-time elective basis, up to $125,000 of gain from the sale of his or her principal residence.— Ed.

carryback of losses should be added to the present carryforward provisions for losses which cannot be offset in the current taxable year.

———

RICHARD GOODE, THE INDIVIDUAL INCOME TAX
180, 182–191, 194–201, 203–211 (Rev.Ed.1976).

The Nature of Capital Gains

* * *

The expected or unexpected character of the receipt does not afford a basis for a useful distinction. A large part of capital gains consists of the capitalization of reinvested corporate profits and other investment returns that are deliberately sought. Other capital gains are windfalls or casual income, but it is hard to see that this provides any guidance for tax policy. There is no way of discovering whether a particular gain is a windfall, and windfalls may take the form of dividends as well as capital appreciation. Nor is it clear that true windfalls, if identifiable, should be taxed more lightly than other income; heavier taxation seems at least as appropriate. Predictability and regularity of recurrence are not criteria of taxability in the American system, and—to American writers—they have no intuitive appeal as possible standards.

This line of reasoning indicates that investment and so-called speculation cannot be clearly separated. Virtually all investors are speculators in the sense that they risk their wealth in accordance with their expectations of future prices and yields. Speculative gains and losses are commonly associated with changes in asset prices but these reflect changes in yields; speculative gains and losses can be experienced without a sale.

Double Taxation?

Since capital values reflect expected earnings, an increase in the market value of an asset indicates that its yield is expected to rise in the future (on the assumption of a constant rate of discount or capitalization). To illustrate, suppose an investor owns 100 shares of stock on which current and expected annual dividends are $1 per share and the market value $16 per share. Suddenly the expected annual dividends increase to $2 per share and the market price of a share rises to $32. The investor has an accrued capital gain of $1,600, and if the expectation about yields proves correct he will receive $100 more in dividends each year for as long as he continues to hold the shares. Would it be unjust double taxation to tax both the accrued capital gain and the additional dividends? Will the answer be different if capital gains are taxed only at the time of realization?

Even though the appreciation of the shares is due solely to the expectation of increased dividends, the capital gain and the receipt of the additional dividends, in my view, may justifiably be regarded as separate taxable events. The appreciation represents an immediate increase of consumption power, resulting either from the retention of past corporate profits or from improved earnings prospects, and the receipt of the dividends represents a further gain of consumption power. There is no injustice in taxing both accretions to consumption power; failure to tax the capital gain will mean omitting part of the investor's income. The reasoning in this case is analogous to that applicable to the so-called double taxation of saving *   *. Fundamentally, whether capital gains are taxed as accrued or only at realization is irrelevant to the double-taxation point. However, when gains are taxed only at realization, even the appearance of double taxation is dispelled because it is then clear that the appreciation of the value of the asset and the additional earnings are separable. If realized gains were not taxed, an investor who sold his shares immediately after the rise in their market value and consumed the proceeds would never be taxed on the increase in his consumption power.

The argument that preferential treatment of capital gains is justifiable as a means of abating the so-called double taxation of corporate profits is also unpersuasive. Although corporate shares are an important source of capital gains, they are not the only source. Among stocks, the greatest capital gains tend to be realized on issues of corporations that retain the largest fraction of their profits and whose earnings hence are least exposed to any double taxation resulting from the application of the corporation income tax and the individual income tax on dividend income.

Price-Level Changes

Several writers who agree that certain capital gains are equivalent to ordinary investment income argue that a large proportion of nominal gains are spurious, being attributable to changes in interest rates or the price level. The point about changes in interest rates was examined [previously], where it was concluded that a rise in market value resulting from a decline in the relevant rate of interest represents a real gain to the investor and that no injustice is done in taxing him on it. The question of price-level changes was left for consideration here.

Appreciation in the price of an asset that reflects only a general rise in prices is a fictitious gain because it gives the investor no increased command over goods and services. Other income items are also affected, though in differing degrees. To illustrate, suppose the consumer price index, annual wages, dividends, and the average market price of common stocks all rise by the same percentage. Both wage earners and share holders experience a nominal increase in current income receipts but no increase in real income; the shareholders also have an accrued nominal capital gain. So long as the shareholders refrain from realizing their nominal capital gain, their taxable income will be overstated no more than that of the wage earners. If, however, the shareholders sell some of their stock, their taxable income will be further increased unless a correction for inflation is made. Under a strictly proportional tax (a flat rate with no personal exemptions) the real tax burden would not be increased on wages or dividends, but a tax would be imposed on realized capital gains solely from the inflation. With personal exemptions and graduated rates, recipients of all kinds of income will face rising effective rates of taxation during inflation unless adjustments are made to prevent this, but the impact will be heavier on realized capital gains.

The best way of removing inflation-induced capital gains from the tax base would be to calculate taxable gain as the difference between the amount realized from sale or other disposal of an asset and an adjusted basis determined by writing up the basis by a factor reflecting the increase in the price level over the holding period. An alternative procedure would be to deflate the realization proceeds by the price factor and to include in taxable income the excess of this deflated value over the basis. The latter procedure, however, would be less satisfactory because it would convert the proceeds from disposal of capital assets into the prices of an earlier period, while other receipts would be measured in current prices. The appropriate price index would be one of consumer goods and services or of all goods and services, rather than an index of the prices of capital assets, because adjustment by the latter index would eliminate genuine gains associated with increases in earnings and relative prices of capital assets. The Internal Revenue Service could publish a table of index numbers annually.

The results obtained by either of the two correction methods described above could not be approximated, even in a rough way, by two other techniques that are sometimes considered: deflation of the nominal realized gain by a price index or exclusion from taxable income of a percentage of realized gains that would increase with the length of time the asset had been held or with the size of the increase in the price level over the holding period. Both of these techniques would leave part of nominal realized gains subject to taxation but would relieve of taxation part of real gains realized on assets that had appreciated in value more than the price level had risen. They would favor the taxpayers who had the most lucrative investments and, among them, those subject to the highest marginal tax rates.[8]

A proposal to correct capital gains for inflation raises questions of fairness, administration, and economic policy. In a period of rising prices, the correction would reduce the amount of taxes paid by owners of corporate stock, unincorporated business enterprises, real estate, and other equities relative to the taxes paid by other members of the community. The persons who would obtain tax relief usually fare better during inflation than do recipients of fixed incomes and holders of money claims. Furthermore, the opportunity of deferring tax on capital gains by postponing their realization, always advantageous,

8. For a general treatment, see Roger Brinner, "Inflation, Deferral and the Neutral Taxation of Capital Gains," *National Tax Journal,* vol. 26 (December 1973), pp. 565–73; Roger Brinner and Alicia Munnell, "Taxation of Capital Gains: Inflation and Other Problems," *New England Economic Review* (September-October 1974), pp. 3–21.

becomes particularly so during inflation because payment is made in depreciated money.

Special problems would arise in the treatment of losses. Symmetrical application of the procedure for adjusting the basis of assets for inflation would turn some nominal gains into losses and would increase nominal losses realized when prices were rising. If the price level should decline—admittedly a contingency that seems far less likely than in the past—some nominal losses would be converted into gains. Such adjustments would attach even greater significance than at present to the definition and timing of realization. For example, a literal application would mean that the maturity of a bond or certificate of deposit would be the occasion for an inflation adjustment, whereas the drawing down of a savings deposit or checking account would not be. Furthermore, the logic of applying a correction to assets but not to liabilities, or to investment accounts but not to business operating accounts, is doubtful. Clearly, the adjustment of all items in balance sheets, as would be necessary to achieve fully consistent results, would be difficult, if not wholly impracticable. From the standpoint of macroeconomic policy, application of a correction for inflation to capital gains, or more broadly, would be questionable because, by reducing tax liabilities in periods of rising prices, it might lessen the stabilizing power of the income tax.

My conclusion is that under conditions of moderate inflation, * * *, the adoption of a provision for correcting nominal capital gains and losses for price-level changes would be undesirable. With more extreme inflation, however, it would become expedient at some point to adapt many features of the income tax to take account of the declining value of money. In these circumstances, the measurement of capital gains as well as income from other sources should be adjusted, together with rate schedules and personal exemptions.

Implications for Equity, Progressivity, and Administration

In the 1950s and 1960s the estimated tax on net capital gains ranged between some 2.5 percent and 9 percent of total individual income tax; the average figure was about 5 percent.[9] These percentages would have been substantially increased (but less than doubled) if capital gains had been taxed at the same rates as ordinary income.

The treatment of capital gains is far more significant for the income tax than these statistics may suggest. The progressivity and equity of the tax are greatly affected because of the concentration of gains in the hands of high-income groups and because of variations in the amounts of gains realized by persons in the same income class. The close relation of capital gains to the ownership of corporate stock and other business assets gives them strategic economic importance.

9. Treasury Department estimates for the years through 1968, from Joseph A. Pechman, *Federal Tax Policy,* rev. ed. (Brookings Institution, 1971), p. 301. The average is the unweighted arithmetic mean of the annual percentages.

Information on the distribution of net capital gains in 1968, a year of large gains, and for 1970, a year of much smaller gains * * * shows that realized capital gains were a major source of income in high brackets but a minor income source in middle and low brackets. Almost half of all reported net gains appeared on returns with AGI of $50,000 or more, which represented only 0.5 percent and 0.6 percent of all returns in 1968 and 1970, respectively. Since these returns reported only 8 percent and 6 percent of all gross income, capital gains were much more concentrated than total income.

Owing to the distribution of capital gains, the preferential tax rates for them have little effect on average effective tax rates in lower brackets but substantially reduce average effective rates at the top, thereby lessening progressivity. * * * Of course, particular individuals are affected more or less than the average for their income class depending on the composition of their income.

[The former low] rates on capital gains are favorable to investors; however, since 1924, the low rates have been accompanied by an unfavorable provision consisting of limitations on the deductibility of capital losses from ordinary income. The intention apparently is to prevent investors from timing their gains and losses so that the losses are offset against ordinary income, which is subject to higher tax rates than capital gains. Successful use of this technique would mean that the net tax attributable to the cumulative amount of net capital gains (gains minus losses) over a period of years would be even lower than the nominal rate on capital gains. The limitations, however, may work hardships on those whose gains and losses occur irregularly. These investors may be taxed on gains in certain years without ever being able to fully deduct losses incurred in other years. (Skillful investors with diversified portfolios can avoid this by careful timing of gains and losses.) A limitation on the deductibility of losses is not a suitable averaging device to correct for possible anomalies under graduated rates; the purpose of averaging would be to allow more liberal treatment than would be accorded by full deductibility in a single year.

To the extent that losses are experienced by persons who never realize equivalent gains, the favorable taxation of gains can hardly be regarded as an offset to the restrictions on loss deductibility. In the absence of continuous records of the investment experience of a representative sample of identical persons, it is not clear to what extent gains and losses are realized by different persons. Within any one year, it is unusual for certain individuals to have losses far in excess of their gains.

Even if capital gains were taxed as heavily as ordinary income, Congress, fearing manipulation, might hesitate to allow full deduction of capital losses. Full deductibility would surely encourage the realization of accrued losses. Persons with diversified portfolios might be able to schedule transactions so as to minimize their exposure to higher-bracket tax rates. But if capital losses are indeed negative income items, the chief objection to this practice is that such persons would have especially good opportunities for averaging taxable income—not a grave inequity if all capital gains, including those accrued at death, were included in gross income. Full deductibility would offer an additional incentive to claim artificial losses, but the problem of auditing such claims would not be wholly new and seems unlikely to be very difficult.

* * *

Another objection to the [former] capital gains provisions is that they allow conversion of ordinary income into capital gains in order to take advantage of the lower rate. Income from personal effort, profits from the active conduct of a business enterprise, and returns from passive investments can all be turned into capital gains in certain circumstances, but in general the ease with which the conversion can be made varies in inverse order to this listing. The history of the income tax discloses many ingenious schemes, which led to preventive legislation, which in turn prompted new efforts to qualify for [the previous preferential] long-term capital gains treatment. Several of the more transparent schemes are no longer allowed, but it will never be possible to preclude all conversions.

The fundamental method, which is perfectly legal, is to reinvest profits in a corporate business and later sell the shares at a price that reflects the earning power of accumulated profits or, better still, pass on the shares to one's heirs. This technique is suitable mainly for closely held corporations, but it can also be adapted to publicly held companies. For the latter it is facilitated by the periodic issuance of small nontaxable stock dividends.

An aspect of the capital gains problem that has received less attention than it deserves is the complexities of law, administration, and compliance that are attributable to the [former] preferential treatment of long-term capital gains. When the tax rates applicable to one form of income differ widely from those on other income, it must be expected that taxpayers will make great efforts to bring their income receipts within the preferred area while tax administrators try to protect the revenues by resisting these efforts.

One expert has summarized his views as follows:

> The income tax provisions of the 1954 Internal Revenue Code [most of which are still in effect] represent probably the most complex revenue law ever enacted in the fiscal history of any country. The subject singly responsible for the largest amount of complexity is the treatment of capital gains and losses. And the factor in that treatment which is accountable for the resulting complexity is the definition of capital gain and of capital loss.[10]

10. Stanley S. Surrey, "Definitional Problems in Capital Gains Taxation," in *Tax Revision Compendium*, Papers Submitted to House Committee on Ways and Means (1959), vol. 2, p. 1203; for an earlier version of this paper with the same title, see *Harvard Law Review*, vol. 69 (April 1956), pp. 985–1019.

He sees no escape from difficulties "formidable almost beyond belief" so long as there is a large difference between tax rates on capital gains and ordinary income, the refined and intricate definitions of the present code are followed, and Congress continues to grant relief from ordinary income tax rates by bestowing capital gains status on certain kinds of income.[11] The exclusion of capital gains from taxable income would not obliterate definitional problems, but would intensify them because it would increase the difference between the tax on capital gains and other income.

A New Method of Taxing Capital Gains and Losses

The arguments so far examined point to the conclusion that capital gains should be taxed like other income, except for a provision to alleviate the effect of the application in one year of graduated tax rates to gains that have accrued over several years. Equity also seems to call for full deductibility of capital losses from taxable income, again with a provision for correcting the effect of bunching. Bunching occurs because gains and losses are taken into account only when realized; it is in principle distinguishable from irregularities in the rate at which capital gains and losses accrue over the years.

* * *

Some method of alleviating the effects of progressive tax rates on recipients of large and irregular capital gains or losses would nevertheless be desirable. One approach would be a proration plan for gains or losses realized on assets held longer than one year. The objective would be to approximate the tax result that would have occurred if the gain or loss had been realized in equal installments over the period during which the investor held the asset. Basically, the method would be to prorate the gain or loss and to determine the tax rate applicable to the whole gain or loss by regarding the pro rata amount as a marginal addition to, or deduction from, current-year ordinary income. The total tax would be the sum of the tax on ordinary income and the (positive or negative) tax on the capital gain or loss. Where only a few transactions were involved, it might be feasible to prorate gains or losses separately for each transaction by dividing by the number of years the asset was held; but this would not be practicable for large portfolios. It would be much simpler and almost equally effective to prorate by dividing the aggregate net long-term gain or loss by an arbitrary factor of, say, 3 or 5. This would have the effect of widening the tax brackets for long-term capital gains or losses by a multiple equal to the proration factor.

Full taxation of capital gains and full deductibility of capital losses, with proration, would substantially increase the tax on income from this source and would significantly increase the progressivity of the income tax as a whole. * * *

11. Surrey, "Definitional Problems," pp. 1228–29.

A provision for constructive realization of capital gain or loss when assets are transferred by gift or at the death of the owner would be a desirable feature of any revision that increased tax rates on realized gains. Otherwise, the tax incentive for postponing the realization of gains would be unduly increased. (See the discussion of "locking-in" below.) In its capital gains tax which went into effect in 1972, Canada included constructive realization at the time of gift or death and also on the occasion of giving up residence in the country. The United Kingdom provides for constructive realization of transfers by gift, and from 1965 to 1971 realization was also deemed to occur at death.

Effects on Investment

However strong the equity argument for taxing capital gains at the same rates as other income, this will not be acceptable if there is reason to believe that the economic consequences would be highly detrimental. It has been stated that preferential taxation of capital gains is a necessary means of shielding investment from the effects of high tax rates, that the lure of lightly taxed capital gains is needed to entice investors into risky ventures.

Since the favorable treatment of capital gains applies to only one form of investment return, it does not offer general tax relief for investment. Indeed, on the assumption that total revenue is to be maintained, it requires that taxes be higher on other income, including investment income. A small general reduction in income tax rates or a substantial reduction in top-bracket rates would be possible without sacrificing revenue or overall progressivity if the differential in favor of capital gains were eliminated. Or consideration might be given to a more selective measure such as the further liberalization of depreciation allowances or operating loss offsets. On the other hand, the preferential taxation of capital gains may be supported on the grounds that the kinds of investment that benefit are especially likely to be discouraged by the income tax or have special social importance.

* * *

On the whole, it seems likely that the tax difference in favor of capital gains causes individual investors to allocate a larger fraction of their resources to risky items than they would if capital gains and losses were taxed as ordinary income and losses. The difference almost certainly encourages the retention of corporate profits and thus favors investment that can be financed from this source.

Although risk-taking is commonly regarded as wholesome, it may waste capital when carried too far. A prudent policy, therefore, might aim at neutrality toward risk assumption rather than its stimulation or discouragement. According to this standard, a tax preference for capital gains could be supported to the extent that it counterbalanced discrimination against risk-taking arising from other provisions but would be undesirable if it did more. The standard is not very helpful because its application would require more precise knowledge about investors' reactions to taxation than is now available. A further difficulty is the lack of selectivity in [the fomer preferential] capital gains tax treatment, which [was] extended to gains from land speculation and other activities that contribute little to innovation and growth as well as to gains from highly productive investments.

The consequences of a tax incentive for retaining corporate profits instead of paying dividends are debatable. Many economists argue that capital will be most efficiently allocated if profits are distributed and individual shareholders are allowed to decide whether they should be reinvested where earned or placed elsewhere. This attitude seems to be based on general confidence in the market mechanism rather than on a systematic comparison of the investment decisions of shareholders and the executives of profitable corporations. The dividend-payout ratio, moreover, may affect shareholders' consumption and thus the total amount of resources available to corporations as well as the allocation of capital among firms.

The conclusion about investment allocation must remain somewhat indefinite. On balance, the allocative effects of a tax difference in favor of capital gains may be economically desirable, but they are not unambiguously so. The capital gains potential of financial and real investments is not a reliable indicator of their social contribution, and there is much waste motion in turning investment income into capital gains.

"Locking-in"

A persistent criticism of the [former preferential] capital gains tax—which would become more powerful if the tax rate were raised—is that it "locks in" investors, making them reluctant to change their portfolios because by doing so they would incur a tax liability that could be postponed or avoided by not selling. Locking-in is said to accentuate fluctuations in security prices. At a time of rising security prices, when many investors have substantial unrealized gains, the discouragement of sales is alleged to cause the market to go still higher, ultimately provoking a greater corrective decline than would otherwise be necessary. The decline, in turn, may be accentuated if investors sell in order to take tax-deductible losses. Locking-in is also said to impair the efficiency of the capital market as a means of allocating resources. According to this view, efficiency is reduced because the capital gains tax discourages venturesome investors from selling appreciated shares and moving into unseasoned issues.

Why Locking-in Occurs

Although its extent may often be exaggerated, some locking-in will occur so long as the income tax applies to capital gains only as realized. If the tax were assessed on accrued gains without waiting for realization, locking-in would disappear. Postponing the sale of appreciated assets is now encouraged, not only by the privilege of postponing tax, but also by the opportunity of escaping tax on assets held until death.[12]

The reason locking-in occurs may be shown by a simple illustration. Suppose [during 1988] an investor owns stock bought for $50 and now selling for $100. If he sells, he will pay a tax of [$7.50 to $14.00] per share, depending on his marginal rate bracket and the size of the gain (this omits any possible liability for [the surcharge under § 1(g)] * * *). It will be advantageous to sell in order to switch investments only if the asset that can be bought with the remaining [$86.00 to $92.50] promises a greater return, in the form of appreciation and dividends or other yield, than can be obtained from $100 worth of the old shares. * * * Similar reasoning can be applied to a sale made in the expectation of a price decline and subsequent repurchase of the same asset. If the investor expects the value of an asset that he holds to decline by more than the amount of any tax liability that he avoids by not selling (plus selling expenses), he should certainly sell, because in this case a movement into cash will be advantageous. A smaller decline will justify a sale if there is an alternative investment with a positive yield.

* * *

Escape of Capital Gains Tax at Death

The possibility, which exists under present law, of escaping capital gains tax on assets held until death is an additional cause of locking-in. Certain switches that will increase the earning power of an investor's portfolio will nevertheless reduce the size of his estate. For example, a switch that is fully justified by rate-of-return calculations will reduce the estate if it involves the payment of a substantial capital gains tax and the investor dies shortly thereafter. If the deceased had held the old asset until his death, the switch could have been made by his executors or heirs without incurring a capital gains tax liability. It is difficult to decide what allowance to make for the possibility of escaping tax at death, not only because the date of death of any individual investor is unforeseeable, but also because the attitudes of investors toward the size of their estate and their heirs vary widely.

* * *

Extent and Consequences of Locking-in

* * *

Locking-in would be increased if [the former preferential] tax rates on capital gains were raised without making changes in realization

---

12. Especially enlightening analyses of the considerations that are relevant for investors can be found in Charles C. Holt and John P. Shelton, "The Implications of the Capital Gains Tax for Investment Decisions," *Journal of Finance*, vol. 16 (December 1961), pp. 559–65; Holt and Shelton, "The Lock-in Effect of the Capital Gains Tax," *National Tax Journal*, vol. 15 (December 1962), pp. 337–52; and Beryl W. Sprinkel and B. Kenneth West, "Effects of Capital Gains Taxes on Investment Decisions," *Journal of Business*, vol. 35 (April 1962), pp. 122–34. I have drawn heavily on these papers.

rules. A provision that would lessen the advantage of postponing realization of gains and that could be supported on equity grounds would be an interest charge for the privilege of deferring tax on capital gains from the time they accrued until they were realized. This could be approximated by requiring the taxpayer to write up his realized gain by a factor varying directly with the length of time the asset was held, computed to reflect interest and tax at standard rates on the assumption that the gain accrued at a steady rate over the period. This suggestion may appear strange, since it is the opposite of the common proposal that the proportion of gains included in taxable income should diminish as the holding period lengthens. The latter proposal presumably is intended as a means of adjusting for bunching or for inflation but, as shown above, is unsatisfactory for these purposes.

A less ambitious attack on locking-in would be to end the opportunity of avoiding tax on appreciated assets held until death by adopting a provision for constructive realization of gains on property held at death. Such a provision would be desirable under [the former preferential] capital gains tax rates and with higher rates would become more important for reasons of equity and economic policy.[13] Constructive realization, however, would not alleviate locking-in caused by income considerations.

The economic consequences of locking-in, as well as its extent, may be debated. Locking-in does not necessarily have any direct influence on the total volume of financial or real investment. If present holdings of appreciated securities were unlocked, funds would be transferred from the purchasers to the present holders, leaving the buyers less liquid and the sellers more liquid. In the simplest case, the sellers would use their receipts for the same purposes as the buyers would have, and the only result would be a reshuffling of the ownership of outstanding securities and new issues. Precisely this outcome does not seem likely, however, because seasoned securities and new issues are not perfect substitutes. Nevertheless, the principal effects of locking-in must be sought in the composition of portfolios and the allocation of real investment rather than in the amount of resources devoted to investment over a period of time.

Unlocking holdings of appreciated securities at a time when the stock market was rising would moderate the rise only if those who sold took part of the proceeds out of the market; to the extent that they merely switched holdings of stock, supply and demand would increase equally and prices would not be affected. Probably there would be some movement out of stocks into bonds and cash on the part of investors who felt that the general level of stock prices was too high,

13. In 1963, President Kennedy recommended a tax on gains accrued at the time of death or gift, as part of a broad reform program. See *President's 1963 Tax Message Along with Principal Statement, Technical Explanation, and Supporting Exhibits and Documents Submitted by Secretary of the Treasury*, House Ways and Means Committee Print (1963), pp. 20, 49–51, 122–34. The recommendation was not accepted by Congress.

and hence some moderating influence, but the net outward movement would surely be much smaller than the total value of sales attributable to unlocking.

Although most commentators take it for granted that locking-in impairs the efficiency of real capital allocation, there have been skeptics. Keynes, for one, thought that excessive trading in the securities markets tended to destabilize real investment and suggested that there might be grounds for making "the purchase of an investment permanent and indissoluble, like marriage, except by reason of death or other grave cause.[14] He discarded this expedient—on the grounds that the liquidity, or the illusion of liquidity, offered by the stock market calmed the nerves of investors and made them more willing to take risks—but he did not seem at all disturbed by the impediments to trading in London in the form of high brokerage charges and transfer tax. Indeed, Keynes recommended that the United States consider a transfer tax as a means of mitigating "the predominance of speculation over enterprise." [15]

* * * Locking-in does not seem to be a great economic problem, but there is a legitimate presumption that it is an undesirable side effect of the taxation of realized capital gains.

"Roll-over" Proposals

A proposal for avoiding locking-in while raising taxes on capital gains is the so-called roll-over plan. This plan would defer tax on realized gains that were reinvested but collect tax when gains were withdrawn for consumption or at the time of death of the investor. The proposal calls for an extension of the present treatment of gains on the sale of a personal residence [§ 1034].

A specific roll-over proposal includes the following provisions. The taxpayer would determine his realized net gain or loss each year without regard to the length of time he had held the assets disposed of during the year. Any net loss would be recognized immediately, and provisions for the deduction of capital losses against ordinary income would be liberalized. Tax on net gain would be deferred to the extent that it was reinvested in any capital asset, and the basis of the new asset would be reduced by the amount of untaxed gain on old assets. The adjustment of basis would be confined to assets acquired in the current year and would be apportioned among all such assets. If purchases were smaller than sales, it would be presumed that part of the gain had been withdrawn, and realized gain would be taxed dollar for dollar up to the amount of the excess of sales over purchases (with perhaps a short grace period to allow for spillovers between years). No pairing of specific sales and purchases or detailed tracing of unrecog-

---

14. John Maynard Keynes, *The General Theory of Employment, Interest and Money* (Harcourt, Brace, 1936), p. 160.

15. Ibid., pp. 159–60. In this context, Keynes defined speculation as "the activity of forecasting the psychology of the market" and enterprise as "the activity of forecasting the prospective yield of assets over their whole life" (p. 158).

nized gain would be required; all sales and purchases of any one year would be pooled. An essential part of the proposal would be that transfer of assets at death be considered a realization and tax be assessed at that time on previously unrecognized gains. The rate of tax applied to recognized gains might be the full rate for ordinary income, the full rate with provision for averaging or spreading gains over a period of years, or a preferential rate.

This plan appears to entail considerable, but not insuperable, problems of compliance or administration. Investors would be called on for more information and computations than are now required. Initially this would probably not arouse hostility since it would be part of a relief measure, but the requirements might seem more vexatious as the relief began to be taken for granted with the passage of time. The Internal Revenue Service would have more difficulty than it now does in verifying the taxpayer's representations concerning the basis of assets because of the adjustments, which would often introduce a big difference between the basis and purchase price. The basis of a listed security can now be verified from readily available publications if its purchase date is known. Under roll-over, both the government and the taxpayer would need a set of accounts showing the details of investment transactions for each year of the taxpayer's investment career.

The main objection to roll-over is that it would offer inequitable advantages to persons who realize capital gains. To illustrate, consider the unrealistic case of a person who receives all his income in the form of capital gains and reinvests all his savings in capital assets. During his lifetime, he would in effect be subject to a spending tax rather than an income tax, since he would be taxed only on gains withdrawn for consumption. On the other hand, a person who received only ordinary income would be taxed on both his consumption and his saving. The arguments that can be advanced in favor of an expenditure tax do not support roll-over because it provides tax deferral for reinvested capital gains but not for other saving.

Roll-over would allow investors maximum opportunities for timing gains so that they would be assessed at relatively low rates. Thus gains might be withdrawn in years in which tax rates were temporarily reduced or in which the investor's other income was low or negative.

* * *

The outlines of a dilemma thus emerge. Roll-over seems unfair because it would broaden tax deferral opportunities for recipients of capital gains. But even without roll-over, investors can defer tax on capital gains by postponing realization. For this privilege they pay a price in the form of forgone freedom to switch investments, and the community may suffer a loss of efficiency in allocation of real capital owing to diminished fluidity of financial capital markets. Any social cost of this nature would be increased if higher tax rates were levied on all realized capital gains. The question for policymakers is whether the economic advantages of increased capital mobility would outweigh the inequities of roll-over. In my judgment, roll-over is unjustifiable so long as capital gains enjoy a substantial degree of rate preference but would be acceptable if its adoption were necessary to clear the way for full taxation of capital gains under a proration plan.

Improvements without Fundamental Revision

Worthwhile improvements in the taxation of capital gains and losses could be effected by measures less sweeping than those discussed so far in this chapter. If for any reason a fundamental revision is not acceptable, consideration should be given to the following actions.

* * *

3. Elimination of the deferral of recognition and taxation of capital gains on owner-occupied dwellings and of the partial exclusion of such gains for persons over the age of [fifty-five]. The current taxation of all realized gains on dwellings would no doubt retard mobility to some degree, but little attention has been given to whether the economic effects would be objectionable enough to justify the special treatment. The present provision seems to have been supported mainly on grounds of equity, and by dubious logic. There is little merit in the common assertion that the sale of a dwelling in connection with a move from one neighborhood to another or from one city to another is an involuntary conversion or is not a true realization if another dwelling "must be bought." Except for condemnation proceedings, people must be presumed to decide whether to move and to buy a new house by balancing advantages and disadvantages—deliberately or impulsively, according to temperament. Decisions to sell and to replace houses seem to be essentially similar to other decisions to switch investments, even though noneconomic considerations play a bigger role in the former. The special exclusion for the elderly, which was added in 1964, is a highly discriminatory form of tax relief.

4. Adoption of the principle of constructive realization of gain or loss when capital assets are transferred by gift or at death. Existing provisions covering gifts allow appreciated assets to be transferred from owners in high tax brackets to persons in lower tax brackets without incurring an income tax liability and permit indefinite deferral of capital gains tax. Transfers at death wipe out potential capital gains tax liability. The present provisions involve an arbitrary distinction between gratuitous transfers and other transfers, and they contribute to locking-in. Assessment of both capital gains tax and gift tax or estate tax at the time of gratuitous transfer would not be unfair double taxation. The fact that income tax was assessed in prior years on current income is not considered a reason for exempting the savings built up out of that income from gift tax or estate tax. The transfer of assets would be the occasion for the assessment of both income tax and estate or gift tax only if the holder had previously enjoyed income tax deferral, unlike a person who had taken his investment return in currently taxable form. The simultaneous assessment could more accurately be viewed as evidence of a prior tax advantage than as a

hardship. The combined application of income tax and gift or estate tax would not be confiscatory since the income tax liability would be deductible from the value of the gift or estate subject to taxation.

Conclusion

Capital gains fall within a broad definition of income and are not clearly distinguishable from other kinds of income in contributing to taxpaying capacity or economic function. While special treatment of capital gains and losses is warranted because they often accrue over many years and are realized at irregular intervals, the present provisions go far beyond those required to avoid discrimination against capital gains. Realized capital gains, in fact, are taxed at much lower rates than other income. Taxpayers' attempts to convert ordinary income into capital gains and the government's efforts to prevent this are responsible for many complexities.

Realized net capital gains, though small relative to total income, are heavily concentrated in the hands of high-income investors. At very high income levels, the present capital gains provisions are the most important single factor accounting for the difference between nominal and effective tax rates and thus holding actual progressivity below apparent progressivity.

The [prior] tax provisions offer investors an inducement to seek capital appreciation in preference to other returns. The investments that are fostered include risky commitments associated with innovations but also certain routine investments and various speculative activities. The preferential tax rates for long-term capital gains are less likely to inhibit changes of investment than would higher tax rates; however, prolonged holding of appreciated assets is encouraged by the opportunity for escaping income tax on accrued gains on property transferred by bequest.

Taking into account both equity and economic effects, I believe the best solution would be to tax capital gains fully and to allow capital losses to be fully deducted, under an averaging or proration plan, relying on reasonable rates and other provisions to avoid harmful economic consequences. If agreement cannot be reached on a fundamental reform, it would still be possible to make worthwhile improvements in the taxation of capital gains.

OFFICE OF THE SECRETARY, DEPARTMENT OF THE TREASURY, TAX REFORM FOR FAIRNESS, SIMPLICITY AND ECONOMIC GROWTH

Vol. 2, 180–188 (1984).

REASONS FOR CHANGE

Measurement of Income. Tax liabilities should be imposed on the basis of real economic income. During periods of inflation, nominal gains or losses on sales of capital assets will reflect inflationary increases in the value of property which do not represent real changes in economic value. Current law, however, computes capital gains and losses by reference to historic investment cost, unadjusted for inflation, and thus overstates capital gains or understates capital losses to the extent of inflation during the period property is held before sale.

The [former] preferential tax rate for capital gains [was] often * * * justified as an allowance for the overstatement of capital gains caused by inflation. The preferential rate actually [served] this purpose only sporadically. The effects of inflation accumulate over time, yet the preferential tax rate [did] not vary with the holding period of an asset (beyond the minimum 6 months or one year) or with the actual rates of inflation during such period. As a result, the preferential rate [undertaxed] real income at low rates of inflation and [overtaxed] capital gains at higher rates of inflation; for any inflation rate, the longer an asset [was] held the greater [was] the undertaxation of real income. Moreover, the preferential rate does not prevent taxation of inflation-caused nominal gains in circumstances where the taxpayer [had] in fact suffered an economic loss.

Because the preferential tax rate [did] not account accurately for the effects of inflation, investors * * * [faced] substantial uncertainty regarding the eventual effective rate of tax on their investments. Such uncertainty [posed] unnecessary and incalculable risks for investors and thus [impaired] the capital formation needed for economic growth.

Neutrality. The preferential tax rate for capital gains also [distorted] investment decisions by providing a potentially lower effective rate of tax on assets that offer a return in the form of asset appreciation rather than current income such as dividends or interest. Along with other provisions that establish special tax treatment for particular sources and uses of income, the preferential tax rate for capital gains [was] one of an elaborate series of tax incentives for particular businesses and investments. These incentives impede the efficiency of an economy based on free market principles. This undeclared government industrial policy largely escapes public scrutiny, yet it increasingly controls the form and content of business and investment activity.

Simplification. The sharp distinction in tax rates under [prior] law between capital gains and ordinary income [was] the source of substantial complexity. Application of different tax rates to different sources of income inevitably [created] disputes over which assets are entitled to the preferential rate and [encouraged] taxpayers to mischaracterize their income as derived from the preferred source. A significant body of law, based both in the tax code and in judicial rules, * * * developed to deal with these matters. Its principles are complicated in concept and application, typically requiring careful scrutiny of the facts in each case. The taxpayer and Internal Revenue Service resources consumed in this process are substantial, yet there is little basis for confidence that the results derived in particular cases are even roughly consistent.

PROPOSAL

The preferential tax rate for long-term capital gains would be repealed. Gains and losses from sales of property would no longer be classified as either capital gains and losses (i.e., gains and losses from sales of capital assets) or ordinary gains and losses. Thus, net capital gain as defined under current law would be fully includible in taxable income and subject to tax at regular rates. Moreover, the holding period of property would no longer affect the tax treatment of gains or losses from sales.

Repeal of the preferential tax rate for capital gains would be coupled with inflation adjustment for realized gains from sales or other dispositions of property. For property other than inventory assets or debt instruments, a taxpayer's original cost basis would be indexed for inflation during the period a taxpayer holds the property. Computation of the basis adjustment for inflation is explained below. Assets required to be inventoried would not be indexed under the rules proposed here, but would be subject to inflation adjustment under the method of inventory accounting elected by the taxpayer. * * * Inflation adjustment for bonds, notes and other debt instruments would be accomplished by indexing interest payments rather than the basis in the indebtedness. * * *

* * *

Losses from sales of investment property would remain subject to limitations. Excluding personal use property, losses from sales of property other than investment property could be deducted without limitation. In general, investment property would be defined as all nonpersonal use property other than (1) property used in a trade or business, (2) inventory property and property held primarily for sale to customers in the ordinary course of business, (3) a general partnership interest, or (4) an interest in an S corporation in which the holder actively participates in management of the entity. For purposes of these loss limitation rules, investment property would generally include notes, bonds and other debt instruments. For noncorporate taxpayers, losses from sales of investment property would offset gains from such property, with any excess loss deductible up to a maximum of $3,000 in each taxable year. Investment property losses in excess of this limitation could be carried forward indefinitely. * * *

The proposal would not alter the basic realization and nonrecognition rules of current law. Thus, a taxpayer would take inflation-adjusted gains and losses into account only when realized upon a sale, exchange or other disposition of property. Current law rules regarding taxable realization events would be retained. As under current law, the donor's basis and holding period for purposes of inflation adjustment would carry over in the case of inter vivos gifts. In the case of transfers of property at death, the donor's basis would be stepped-up to fair market value and the transferee would start anew the holding period for indexing such basis.

Nonrecognition provisions of current law, which require realized gains or losses to be deferred, would also generally be retained. In particular, homeowners would be permitted, subject to existing rules, to roll over gain on the sale of a principal residence, if a new principal residence is acquired within 2 years of the sale of the prior principal residence. Moreover, subject to existing rules, homeowners who are age 55 or older would exclude permanently the first $125,000 of inflation adjusted gain upon the sale of a principal residence.

The proposal generally would retain current law rules relating to determination of the amount realized upon a sale, exchange, or disposition of property. In particular, current law rules concerning the amount realized in respect of liabilities (recourse or nonrecourse) assumed or taken subject to upon disposition of property would be retained.

The Internal Revenue Service would implement the indexing proposal by publishing inflation tables using the Bureau of Labor Statistics' Consumer Price Index for Urban Households. These tables would contain inflation adjustment factors which would be applied to the original cost basis to determine the inflation adjusted basis. The tables would specify inflation adjustment factors by calendar quarters that an asset was held. Thus, a taxpayer who bought an asset in the third quarter of 1984 and sold the asset in the second quarter of 1990 would locate in the tables a single inflation adjustment factor to be applied to the original cost basis. The tables would contain inflation adjustment factors back to January 1, 1965. Assets obtained prior to that date would be indexed as if acquired on that date.

The inflation adjustment factors would be computed using a half-quarter convention, which would allow only half the applicable quarterly inflation rate regardless of when during a quarter an asset was acquired or sold. An asset would be required to be held for one full calendar quarter in order to qualify for indexing. Assets held only for one full quarter would obtain an inflation adjustment factor only for that full quarter, and not for the partial quarters in which acquired and disposed of.

*   *   *

ANALYSIS

Effect on Saving and Investment. Under most circumstances, the proposal would either hold roughly constant or reduce effective tax rates on realized capital gains; the proposal should thus either have no or a somewhat stimulative effect on saving and investment. At current rates of inflation (four percent in 1983 and 1984), most high-bracket taxpayers would be subject to roughly the same effective tax rate on long-term capital gains as under [prior] law (i.e., a maximum rate of 20 percent on nominal gains). At rates of inflation experienced in recent years (an average annual rate of 7.9 percent between 1972 and 1982), the proposal would reduce significantly the effective tax rate on most real capital gains. *   *   *

Also, indexing would eliminate the current volatility in effective tax rates that accompanies inflation; the associated reduction in uncertainty should stimulate saving and investment. The "insurance" benefits of a tax system which guarantees an explicit inflation adjustment should not be minimized. For example, inflation averaged seven percent annually between 1971 and 1975. Over the same period, nominal capital gains on sales of corporate stock totaled $24.6 billion. Once adjusted for inflation, however, these sales actually represented a loss of $0.4 billion.

Finally, indexing capital gains for inflation would produce more accurate measurement of real losses; the associated increase in government risk-sharing should also stimulate saving and investment.

Effect on Risk-Taking. The effect of capital gains taxation on private risk-taking in the economy is of critical importance. The venture capital and associated high-technology industries seem particularly sensitive to changes in effective tax rates. Shareholders in some ventures—those which are highly successful over short periods of time—would face higher effective tax rates under the proposal. Nevertheless, more accurate measurement of economic losses and the reduction of inflation caused variations in effective tax rates would stimulate investment generally. Moreover, a maximum marginal tax rate of 35 percent on indexed gains would produce effective rates that are not substantially above those experienced during the last two venture capital booms. (Tax rates of 25 percent during the 1960s and 28 percent from 1978–81 on nominal gains were actually higher effective rates due to inflation.) In addition, all investors would continue to benefit from the deferral of tax on accrued but unrealized gains.

Also, the increase in saving stimulated by reductions in individual marginal rates * * *, as well as the elimination of many industry-specific tax preferences and the enactment of measures to reduce the advantages of investment in unproductive tax shelters, should increase the supply of capital available to high technology industries.

Housing. The indexing proposal should not, on balance, significantly affect the housing industry or the desire of individuals to invest in their own homes. Most capital gains in the housing industry have been inflationary gains that would not be subject to tax under the indexing proposal. Moreover, the proposal retains the provisions of current law permitting taxpayers to roll over realized gains on the sale of a principal residence and granting a one-time exclusion of $125,000 on the sale of a principal residence by taxpayers over the age of 55. Indeed, the one-time exclusion would be more generous under the proposal since it would apply to inflation-adjusted rather than nominal gains.

Retention of Realization Requirement. The proposal would retain the realization requirement of current law, under which gains and losses generally are not taxed until realized by sale, exchange or other disposition. One of the consequences of the realization requirement is that tax on accrued but unrealized gains is deferred, * * *. The tax advantage of deferring gains creates an incentive for taxpayers to continue to hold appreciated assets in order to avoid realizing gain. This so-called "lock-in" effect impairs capital resource allocation to the extent taxpayers are deterred from reallocating investments by the tax costs of realizing accrued appreciation.

Indexing mitigates the lock-in effect of the realization requirement by ensuring that only real gains are taxed. Under current law, unrealized inflationary gains cause a lock-in effect as much as unrealized real gains. Moreover, although the proposal eliminates the preferential tax rate for capital gains, the Treasury Department proposals include a reduction in marginal tax rates that reduces the current law distinction between capital gain and ordinary income. On balance, the relative significance of the lock-in effect under the indexing proposal versus current law depends on prospective rates of inflation. Since the lock-in effect cannot be eliminated fully in any system that retains the realization concept, the gains in certainty and measurement of income attributable to indexing and the distortions caused by a rate differential override concerns over the lock-in effect.

* * *

Scope of Loss Limitation Rules. In general, the proposal would retain the capital loss limitation rules of current law for assets held for investment and not for use in a trade or business. Such limitations are appropriately applied to investors who may selectively realize gains and losses on investment assets.

Simplification. Repealing the preferential tax rate on capital gains and taxing all inflation-adjusted income at uniform tax rates would eliminate a source of substantial complexity in [prior] law. Schemes to convert ordinary income to capital gain would be deprived of their principal tax motivation. * * *

Depreciation recapture has been necessary under ACRS and prior depreciation rules to prevent excessive depreciation deductions from being converted into capital gain. Indexing depreciation allowances and gains and losses from dispositions of property obviates the need for depreciation recapture provisions. Excessive depreciation would be "recaptured" as ordinary income, which (assuming no intervening change in the taxpayer's marginal tax rate) would substantially restore the tax benefit derived from the original deduction. Although the taxpayer would continue to receive a timing advantage where [ACRS] allowances exceed economic depreciation, taxing all recapture income as ordinary income would permit repeal of the recapture provisions for depreciable property acquired after the proposals become fully effective.

* * *

References: Waggoner, Eliminating the Capital Gains Preference: Part I: The Problems of Inflation, Bunching and Lock-In, 48 U.Colo.L. Rev. 313 (1977); Blum, A Handy Summary of the Capital Gains

Arguments, 25 Taxes 247 (1957); Slawson, Taxing as Ordinary Income the Appreciation of Publicly Held Stock, 76 Yale L.J. 623 (1967); Note, Realizing Appreciation Without Sale: Accrual Taxation of Capital Gains on Marketable Securities, 34 Stan.L.R. 857 (1982).

C. SALE OR EXCHANGE AND HOLDING PERIOD REQUIREMENTS

1. SALE OR EXCHANGE REQUIREMENT

Capital gain (or capital loss) means gain (or loss) from the "sale or exchange" of a capital asset. "Sale or exchange" is not defined in the Code.

The phrase "sale or exchange" is a judicially construed term of art. For example, C loans D $1,000 in Year 1. D gives C a note for $1,000. In Year 3, C sells the note to B for $500. In Year 5, D pays the full amount of the note to B. B realizes and recognizes $500 in ordinary income on the payment of the note as there was no sale or exchange. However, if in Year 4, B had sold the note to A for $250, B would have realized and recognized a capital loss of $250. If, in Year 6, D repaid $100 as a settlement, what is the character of A's loss? In Hudson v. Commissioner, 20 T.C. 734 (1953), affirmed 216 F.2d 748 (6th Cir.1954), the taxpayers purchased for $10,000, a $75,000 judgment from the judgment-creditor. The judgment-debtor subsequently paid the taxpayer-assignee $21,500 in cash "in full settlement." The Tax Court stated:

> Simply, the issue is whether the gain realized from the settlement of a judgment is ordinary income or capital gain when the settlement was made between the judgment debtor and the assignee or transferee of a prior judgment creditor. Petitioners contend that they are entitled to the benefits of [§ 1222], with regard to the gain from the settlement of a judgment. Respondent has determined that the gain is ordinary income and taxable as such. There is no question about the bona fides of the transaction, nor is there any disagreement about the fact that the judgment, when entered and transferred, was property and a capital asset. The parties differ, however, on the question of whether there was a "sale or exchange of a capital asset." [§ 1222]. Petitioners and respondent both adhere to the principle that the words "sale or exchange" should be given their ordinary meaning. Petitioners, citing authority, define the word "sale" as follows:
>
> > A sale is a contract whereby one acquires a property in the thing sold and the other parts with it for a valuable consideration * * * or a sale is generally understood to mean the transfer of property for money * * *.
>
> Also, "Sell in its ordinary sense means a transfer of property for a fixed price in money or its equivalent."
>
> We cannot see how there was a transfer of property, or how the judgment debtor acquired property as the result of the transaction wherein the judgment was settled. The most that can be said is that

the judgment debtor paid a debt or extinguished a claim so as to preclude execution on the judgment outstanding against him. In a hypothetical case, if the judgment had been transferred to someone other than the judgment debtor, the property transferred would still be in existence after the transaction was completed. However, as it actually happened, when the judgment debtor settled the judgment, the claim arising from the judgment was extinguished without the transfer of any property or property right to the judgment debtor. In their day-to-day transactions, neither businessmen nor lawyers would call the settlement of a judgment a sale; we can see no reason to apply a strained interpretation to the transaction before us. When petitioners received the $21,150 in full settlement of the judgment, they did not recover the money as the result of any sale or exchange but only as a collection or settlement of the judgment.

It is well established that where the gain realized did not result from a sale or exchange of a capital asset, the gain is not within the provisions of [§ 1222]. In R.W. Hale, 32 B.T.A. 356, affd. 85 F.2d 815, there was a compromise of notes for less than face value and the taxpayer claimed there was a sale or exchange of notes within the meaning of the capital gains provision of the Code. In deciding the issue against the taxpayer, we said:

> The petitioners did not sell or exchange the mortgage notes, and consequently an essential condition expressly required by the statute has not been met and no capital loss has been suffered.
>
> *   *   *

The *Hale* case was cited with approval in Pat N. Fahey, 16 T.C. 105. There, the taxpayer, an attorney, was assigned, for a cash consideration, an interest in a fee. Upon a successful settlement of the litigation, the taxpayer was paid his part of the fee. We held that his share was not capital gain because he did not sell or exchange anything.   *   *   *

Several other situations are noteworthy. A property owner who could not meet his nonrecourse mortgage payments might allow the mortgagee to foreclose on the property. A foreclosure on real property is a procedure through which the mortgagee can obtain funds to pay off the loan by selling the encumbered property. Foreclosures have long been considered as a taxable "sale" resulting in a capital gain (or loss) to the mortgagee. Helvering v. Hammel, 311 U.S. 504, 61 S.Ct. 368, 85 L.Ed. 303 (1941). Where the value of real property has declined, the owner whose adjusted basis exceeds the unpaid principal amount of a nonrecourse mortgage, may voluntarily abandon the property to the mortgages. In Rev.Rul. 78–164, 1978–1 C.B. 264, the Service ruled that a voluntary conveyance by a mortgagor to the mortgagee of property subject to a nonrecourse obligation is treated as a sale or exchange under § 1222. The ruling rejected any distinction between a situation in which a bank forecloses and those in which the owner of the property merely transfers it to the bank, thus bringing it within Helvering v. Hammel. See also Freeland v. Commissioner, 74 T.C. 970 (1980) and Yarbro v. Commissioner, 737 F.2d 479 (5th Cir.1984), cert. denied 469 U.S. 1189, 105 S.Ct. 959, 83 L.Ed.2d 965 (1985). Consider the characterization of the loss realized on the abandonment of an investment in the following case.

ARKIN v. COMMISSIONER

Tax Court of the United States, 1981.
76 T.C. 1048.

WILBUR, JUDGE: * * * Due to concessions by petitioner, the sole issues remaining for our decision are:

(1) Whether petitioner abandoned his interest in a Florida land trust in the year 1974, and if so, whether the loss sustained is ordinary or capital * * *

FINDINGS OF FACT

* * *

On his 1974 income tax return, petitioner claimed an ordinary loss deduction in the amount of $32,400 for "Acreage—Palm Beach County—Acreage Abandoned in 1974." The property referred to in the claimed loss is undeveloped real property which was acquired by a group of investors, petitioner among them, in December of 1973 through the medium of a Florida land trust. * * * The purchase price was $3,200,000, with $2,560,000 being financed by a wraparound, nonrecourse, purchase-money note and mortgage signed by Leo Rose, Jr. On December 31, 1973, Leo Rose, Jr., executed a deed conveying the property to the Florida Bank at Fort Lauderdale (the bank) to hold as trustee * * *

Also on December 31, 1973, a land trust agreement was executed between the bank and 10 named beneficiaries (investors) whereby the beneficiaries conveyed their interests in the property to the bank as trustee of the land trust. Petitioner was one of the beneficiaries and received a 5-percent interest in the land trust, which entitled him to 5 percent of any earnings or proceeds from the trust property. Petitioner paid $32,197 for his 5-percent interest in the land trust on January 8, 1974, * * *.

The purpose of the land trust was to hold title to the property until its sale. The land trust agreement provided that the beneficiaries were to have full and exclusive control over the management and operation of the trust property. The agreement also provided that the interests of the beneficiaries were rights of personality, * * *

The land trust had no value apart from the individual real estate which comprised its corpus. As an experienced real estate attorney, petitioner was aware of and sensitive to the real estate market in Florida. Petitioner purchased his interest because he believed that the market for real estate was very favorable at the time. However, during the middle of 1974, a recession halted property development and the market for real estate declined dramatically. After receiving an opinion from an outside real estate investor as to the value of the land trust property, petitioner decided in late 1974 that his interest in the property was not then worth his initial investment or any future investment.

By letter dated December 23, 1974, petitioner notified the bank and each of the other beneficiaries of his intention to abandon his interest in the land trust. * * *.

In addition to the 1973 purchase-money mortgage, there were two prior mortgages on the property. On February 7, 1975, a complaint was filed by a prior mortgagee, American Community Systems, Inc., to foreclose its mortgage. On April 19, 1977, the Circuit Court for Palm Beach County, Fla., entered a final summary judgment of foreclosure and found that the lien on the property held by American Community Systems, Inc., was prior and superior to any claim or interest held by Leo Rose, Jr., as trustee, and Florida Bank at Fort Lauderdale, as trustee, and any persons claiming through them. In May 1977, American Community Systems, Inc., purchased the property at the foreclosure sale for $1,000.

* * *

OPINION

Issue 1. Capital or Ordinary Loss

In December of 1973, petitioner purchased a 5-percent interest in a Florida land trust that held property in Palm Beach County, Fla., for $32,197. The property was first taken in the name of a partner in petitioner's law firm, as trustee, and shortly thereafter was conveyed by him and the beneficial owners to a bank to hold as trustee of a land trust. The property was taken subject to a nonrecourse mortgage of $2,560,000. It was understood among the investors that either the property would be sold within the year and they would share in the proceeds according to their proportionate interests, or that it would be held for future sale, in which case they would contribute further funds for the mortgage and taxes, again according to their proportionate shares.

According to the terms of the land trust agreement, the beneficiaries held full management and control over the property. During the middle of the following year, the real estate market in Florida collapsed and land values plunged. After consulting with a real estate expert, petitioner decided that the value of his investment was worth substantially less than his share of the outstanding nonrecourse mortgage note. Accordingly, petitioner wrote the bank and the other beneficial owners 1 week before the mortgage payment was due, informing them that he was abandoning his interest in the land trust.

The issue for our decision is whether the loss petitioner sustained on his investment is capital or ordinary. Petitioner insists that his interest was personal property, and that he effectively abandoned his interest in the land trust in 1974 and because there was no "sale or exchange," he is entitled to an ordinary loss deduction under section 165(a) and section 165(c)(2) which allow a deduction from ordinary income for losses incurred in transactions entered into for profit. Respondent characterizes petitioner's interest as ownership of encumbered real estate and argues that his abandonment of this interest in real estate constituted a sale or exchange of a capital asset under section 165(f), deductible only as a capital loss. While we agree that the interest was one of personalty, respondent nevertheless correctly concluded that the loss sustained by petitioner on his investment was a capital loss.

There is no dispute as to the amount of the loss, or that petitioner's interest in the land trust constituted a capital asset. The parties argue extensively about the character of the interest involved—whether it is an interest in personal property, or an interest in real estate. This side skirmish must be resolved for petitioner, for State statutory and judicial authority expressly provide that an interest in a Florida land trust is an interest solely in personalty. * * * Petitioner, having won this side skirmish, claims victory in the main battle, contending there was an "abandonment" rather than a sale or exchange of his interest in the land trust. We disagree.

Petitioner's interests consisted of a right to share in the management and control (including disposition) of the realty, and to receive his share of the income from, or sales proceeds of, the property. Correlative obligations of continued participation included paying a proportionate share of the taxes, mortgage, insurance, and trustees' fees. Additionally, petitioner was required to reimburse and indemnify the trustee for any liability incurred relating to the holding of the property, including "breach of contract, injury to person or property, and fines or penalties under any law." Petitioner's interest was freely alienable by a written assignment which was evidence of ownership of a beneficial interest by the assignee.

This interest was admittedly a capital asset and any gain from its sale would have been taxed as a capital gain. In determining whether a sale and exchange occurred, we are mindful that "Congress intended the words 'sale or exchange' to have a broad meaning, not to be limited to the standard transfer of property by one person to another in exchange for a stated consideration in money or money's worth." Freeland v. Commissioner, 74 T.C. 970, 980 (1980). Also, in focusing on the rights petitioner relinquished (to share in the management and control, the income from, and the proceeds of disposition) we note that the courts have tended to reject technicalities and focus on the nature of the rights relinquished; if it was a capital asset, the release of a right is generally characterized as a capital gain. Cf. Commissioner v. Ferrer, 304 F.2d 125 (2d Cir.1962).

With this background, we believe the term "sale or exchange" (as used in section 165(f)) is sufficiently resilient to encompass the circumstances before us. Petitioner abandoned or relinquished his bundle of rights comprising his interest in the land trust. In return for this relinquishment, petitioner was relieved of the obligation to bear a proportionate share of the costs of the mortgage payment, the trustees' fees, the insurance costs, and the taxes payable at the time of his relinquishment. Additionally, to the extent the abandonment was effective, he also was no longer subject to the potential liability resulting from tort or contract litigation associated with the property. We believe this is sufficient to constitute a sale or exchange for purposes of section 165(f), regardless of whether or not a technical abandonment also occurred under State law.

Our views are reinforced by our recent decision in Freeland v. Commissioner, 74 T.C. 970 (1980). In *Freeland*, we held that the reconveyance by quitclaim deed of unimproved real estate encumbered by a nonrecourse, purchase-money mortgage by the petitioner/mortgagor to the mortgagee constituted a sale resulting in a capital loss. Although no monetary consideration passed hands and although under California law petitioner's overt act of reconveyance constituted an "abandonment," we held that "*relief* from indebtedness, even though there is no personal liability, is sufficient to support a sale or exchange." 74 T.C. at 981. (Emphasis in original.) In doing so, we stated:

> We do not understand why there should be any difference between a foreclosure sale of the security property or a voluntary reconveyance of the property to the mortgagee. In either event, the mortgagor's interest in the property is terminated and title is transferred to someone else, and the mortgagor receives nothing out of the transaction. In both instances, the mortgagor is relieved of property which has a lien on it and is also relieved of the obligation to pay taxes and assessments against the property. There is no *forgiveness* of indebtedness in either case, although there is a change in the mortgagor's balance sheet or net worth. He no longer has the liability to account for, nor does he have the assets. See dissenting opinion in *Fred H. Lenway & Co. v. Commissioner,* supra. We believe the holdings of *Crane* and subsequent cases decided in the light of *Crane* mandate the conclusion that *relief* from indebtedness, even though there is no personal liability, is sufficient to support a sale or exchange. * * *
> [*Freeland v. Commissioner,* supra at 981. Emphasis in original.]

Petitioner on brief claims that his interest was "similar to that of a shareholder in a real estate corporation," and that his status was "like a minority shareholder." It may be that the land trust involved would be considered an association for tax purposes (see sec. 7701(a)(3); sec. 301.7701-2, Proced. & Admin. Regs.; Morrissey v. Commissioner, 296 U.S. 344 (1935); Strong v. Commissioner, 66 T.C. 12 (1976)), and that petitioner would be a shareholder of stock (sec. 7701(a)(7) and (8)).

However, this would be of no avail to petitioner, for the loss would then be a capital loss under the provisions of section 165(g)(1).

* * *

To reflect the foregoing,

Decision will be entered under Rule 155.

As a matter of policy, it is not clear why characterization of the gain or loss on the disposition of an asset as capital or ordinary should turn, in part, on the technical form of the disposition as well as the character of the property. Congress recognized this and, on occasion, has provided specific Code sections which artificially treat certain transactions as sales or exchanges. Let's consider two examples. First, the retirement of a corporate bond is generally deemed an exchange of the bond by the holder for payment in accordance with § 1271(a)(1). Secondly, pursuant to § 1241, amounts received by a lessee on the cancellation of a lease or by a distributor of goods on the cancellation of a distribution agreement (provided he has a substantial capital investment in the distributorship) are considered amounts received in exchange for such lease or distributorship. In contrast, note that § 1253 provides that a sale of a franchise, trademark, or trade name is not treated as the sale or exchange of a capital asset if the transferor retains any significant power, right or continuing interest (as defined in § 1253(b)(2)) with respect to the subject matter of the transferred property. Any amounts contingent on the productivity, use, or disposition of the transferred property are expressly denied capital asset status. § 1253(c).

2. HOLDING PERIOD REQUIREMENT

Prior to 1988 capital gain (or loss) treatment also requires a specified holding period. The dividing line between short-term and long-term capital gains and losses is six months with respect to property acquired after June 22, 1984 and before January 1, 1988. In 1976, in support of increasing the holding period to one year, which exists for capital assets acquired before June 23, 1984, the legislative history (H.Rep. No. 94–658, 94th Cong.2d Sess. (1976), reprinted in 1976–3 C.B. (Vol. 2) 695, 1033), indicated:

A distinction is made between short-term and long-term capital gains with respect to two major considerations ∗ ∗ ∗.

First, the special capital gains treatment is provided for long-term gains in recognition of the fact [that] the gain on the sale of an asset which is attributable to the appreciation in value of the asset over a long period of time otherwise would be taxed in one year, and, in the case of an individual, at progressive rates.

Second, it is argued that there should be special tax treatment for gains on assets held for investment but not on those held for speculative profit. The underlying concept is that a person who holds an investment for only a short time is primarily interested in obtaining

quick gains from short-term market fluctuations which is a distinctive-
ly speculative activity. In contrast, the person who holds an investment for a long time probably is basically interested fundamentally in
the income aspects of his investment and in the long-term appreciation
in value.

The legislative history (Staff of the Joint Committee on Taxation, Tax
Reform Act of 1984, 1083 (1984)) states the reasons for reducing the
holding period required for long-term capital gain treatment to six
months as follows:

> The differential tax treatment of short-term and long-term transac-
> tions creates incentives for investors not to realize short-term gains.
> Studies of capital asset sales data confirm that investors are "locked-
> in" to investments because they do not desire to realize short-term
> gains. This reduces capital market efficiency because investors hold
> assets longer than they otherwise might in the absence of tax consider-
> ations. Prior to 1977, the holding period was 6 months. By reducing
> the capital gains holding period from 12 to 6 months, the Congress
> believed that the lock-in effect and its adverse impact on capital
> market efficiency will be reduced.

What do you feel Congress will do in 1988 when the holding period
returns to one year?

For a sale or exchange prior to 1988, taxpayer must hold a capital
asset, acquired after June 22, 1984, and before January 1, 1988, for more
than six months prior to its disposition for any gain or loss to qualify as
long-term capital gain or loss. § 1222(3) and (4). A taxpayer realizes and
recognizes a short-term capital gain or loss on the sale or exchange of a
capital asset held for six months or less. § 1222(1) and (2). The taxpayer's holding period is also relevant for purposes of § 1231. In computing
the holding period, the taxpayer disregards the day of acquisition but
includes the day of sale. In addition, the taxpayer is often allowed by
§ 1223 to tack on to his holding period the time he held other property or
another taxpayer held the same property.

For gains (or losses) realized and recognized in 1988 and thereafter,
the holding period requirement is, roughly speaking, irrelevant in the
computation of a taxpayer's capital gains or capital losses. However,
where a taxpayer realizes both capital gains and capital losses in the
same taxable year and his gains exceed his losses the use of the net
capital gain concept (§ 1222(11)) in the maximum capital gains rate
calculations contained in § 1(j)(1) gives continued vitality to the holding
period requirement. In addition, the holding period requirement remains relevant for the contribution to charity of appreciated capital
gain property and the treatment of losses resulting from bad debts and
worthless securities discussed later in this chapter.

Problems

1. Father purchased stock on January 10 of Year 1 for $3,000. He
gave this stock to his son as a gift on March 10 of Year 2 when it was worth

$4,000. The son sold the stock on April 10 of Year 2 for $4,500. Can the son report a long-term capital gain even though he held the stock for only one month? Consider § 1223(2). Reconsider Problem 4(a) on page 263.

2. Father purchased stock on January 10 of Year 1 for $3,000. On March 10 of Year 1 he gave it to his son when it was worth $2,500. The son sold the stock for $2,000 on July 15 of Year 1. What is the character of the son's $500 loss? Is the donee using a carryover basis? Consider § 1223(2) and Reg. § 1.1223–1(b). Reconsider Problem 3 on page 263.

3. Father purchased stock for $3,000 on January 10 of Year 1 and died on March 10 of Year 1, when the stock was worth $3,500. He left the stock to his son. The son sold the stock on April 10 of Year 1 for $3,400. What is the character of the son's $100 loss? Consider § 1223(11). Reconsider Problem 4(b) on page 264.

4. Mack owns a truck which he uses in his business. The truck has an adjusted basis of $4,000 and a fair market value of $5,000. Mack exchanges this truck for a new truck worth $5,500, making up the difference by paying $500 in cash. Is the tacking of holding periods allowed in this situation? Consider §§ 1031 and 1223(1). Reconsider Problem 1 on page 850.

5. Bruce sold his personal residence, which originally cost him $40,000 two years ago, for $50,000. He immediately reinvested the proceeds in a new home costing $60,000. After living in his new home for only three months, he sold it for $66,000 and did not reinvest the proceeds. Bruce is 30 years old. What is the amount and character of Bruce's gain in these transactions? Consider §§ 1001(a), 1034, and 1223(7) and Reg. § 1.1223–1(g). Reconsider the problems on page 848.

D. DEFINITION OF CAPITAL ASSETS UNDER SECTION 1221 AND QUASI CAPITAL ASSETS UNDER SECTION 1231

1. WHEN GAINS AND LOSSES ARE CAPITAL: INVENTORY STOCK IN TRADE, AND OTHER ITEMS EXCLUDED FROM THE DEFINITION OF "PROPERTY"

Asset Must Be "Property." The capital gain or loss treatment described is available only with respect to the sale and exchange of capital assets and assets which are treated as capital assets under § 1231. Examine the definition of the term "capital asset" contained in § 1221 which begins by defining "capital asset" as "property held by the taxpayer (whether or not connected with his trade or business)." Note that the term "property" is not restricted to business or investment assets, and that § 1221 goes on to define property in a negative manner. Specified types of property, particularly, inventory, "property held by the taxpayer primarily for sale to customers in the ordinary course of his trade or business," and accounts receivable acquired in the ordinary course of trade or business for services rendered or from the sale of inventory, are excluded from the definition of a "capital asset."

Real property used in the taxpayer's trade or business is excluded under § 1221(2), but is eligible for capital gains treatment under § 1231(b). Section 1231 maintains noncapital asset status for inventory (§ 1231(b)(1)(A)) and property held by the taxpayer primarily for sale to customers in the ordinary course of the taxpayer's business (§ 1231(b)(1)(B)). Certain other property is excluded from the capital asset category by judicial interpretation.

Stock in Trade and Inventory Are Not Capital Assets. A number of items are specifically excluded from the definition of a capital asset under § 1221. Perhaps the most important statutory exclusion is contained in § 1221(1) which encompasses stock in trade, inventory, and property held by the taxpayer primarily for sale to customers in the ordinary course of his trade or business.

A person operating the corner grocery store may buy a can of beans for 40 cents and sell it for 65 cents. This is a sale of property; in the absence of a specific limitation under § 1221(1) the seller would receive capital gains treatment. However, because the seller is engaged in the business of retailing merchandise, it seems reasonable that the gain or loss from the sale involving an everyday business activity should be taxed to the seller as ordinary income or loss in the same way that salary, or the income of a member of a profession, is taxed. For this reason, § 1221(1) provides that the stock in trade of a taxpayer is not a capital asset. Consequently, if the taxpayer purchases raw material, converts it into a more valuable inventory item during the tax year and sells it in that period, the taxpayer will realize ordinary gain or loss in the same fashion as though the taxpayer had sold stock in trade. The same rule is applied to a class of property described in the statute as "held by the taxpayer primarily for sale to customers in the ordinary course of his trade or business;" obviously this is intended to include items arising in the course of the operation of a business which might not fall within the strict definition of stock in trade. Even where there is a bulk sale of the taxpayer's stock in trade to another, the gain realized is considered to be ordinary income. Grace Brothers v. Commissioner, 173 F.2d 170 (9th Cir.1949). In short, the items excluded under § 1221(1) are intended to produce ordinary income treatment for proceeds generated by regular business activities.

2. ENTREPRENEURS IN REAL ESTATE: WHEN DO THEY GET ORDINARY INCOME OR CAPITAL LOSS

What Constitutes Property Held Primarily For Sale to Customers in the Ordinary Course of The Taxpayer's Trade or Business So As to Create Ordinary Income or Loss. Ordinary income or loss arises from the sale or exchange of "property held by the taxpayer primarily for sale to customers in the ordinary course of his trade or business." § 1221(1). This provision seeks to distinguish a dealer, for example, a real estate subdivider or an individual who systematically buys and sells real estate, from a casual investor. For analytical purposes, the dealer-investor dichotomy turns on two questions: (1) did the taxpayer's conduct amount to a trade or business and (2) was the property held by the taxpayer primarily for sale to his customers.

From the standpoint of the policies underpinning the previous preference for capital gains, the court in Galena Oaks Corp. v. Scofield, 218 F.2d 217, 220 (5th Cir.1954), stated:

> Congress intended to alleviate the burden on a taxpayer whose property has increased in value over a long period of time. When, however, such a taxpayer endeavors still further to increase his profits by engaging in a business separable from his investment, it is not unfair that his gain should be taxed as ordinary income.

Difference Between an Investor Having Capital Gains from Investment and a Dealer Having Ordinary Income from Sale of Property. The Regulations make it clear that an individual selling real property may be a dealer who will receive ordinary income or loss treatment. Reg. § 1.1221–1(b). In the United States v. Winthrop, 417 F.2d 905, 910 (5th Cir.1969), the court set forth the following factors, which are often-mentioned judicial tests, used in determining whether a seller of real estate is a dealer or investor:

> (1) the nature and purpose of the acquisition of the property and the duration of the ownership; (2) the extent and nature of the taxpayer's efforts to sell the property; (3) the number, extent, continuity and substantiality of the sales; (4) the extent of subdividing, developing, and advertising to increase sales; (5) the use of a business office for the sale of the property; (6) the character and degree of supervision or control exercised by the taxpayer over any representative selling the property; and (7) the time and effort the taxpayer habitually devoted to the sales.

Although no single factor or circumstance is controlling, the frequency and substantiality of the sales is often preeminent. At the least, such a pattern will thwart the taxpayer from characterizing the transaction as an "isolated" sale or a passive and gradual liquidation. The presence of taxpayer activity, particularly activity involving improvements to the land, is also significant.

Mere citation of cases, whether or not accompanied by a recital of the facts involved, will be of little value to the taxpayer in planning a transaction. It is peculiarly true in this area that no two cases ever are the same, and no absolute standard exists by which the facts in a particular case can be said with reasonable accuracy to distinguish a dealer from an investor. The following case is reasonably representative with respect to the issue of whether the taxpayer's conduct constituted a business and, therefore, the taxpayer was a dealer.

BIEDENHARN REALTY CO., INC. v. U.S.

United States Court of Appeals, Fifth Circuit, 1976.
526 F.2d 409,
cert. denied 429 U.S. 819, 97 S.Ct. 64, 50 L.Ed.2d 79 (1976).

[Before the court, en banc, 13 judges; seven agreeing with the majority opinion, one concurring and five dissenting.]

GOLDBERG, CIRCUIT JUDGE:

[Taxpayer corporation, organized in 1923 to hold and manage family investments, held in the relevant years substantial investments in commercial real estate, a stock portfolio, a motel, warehouses, a shopping center, residential real property, and farm property. Among its farm property holdings was a plantation purchased for $50,000 in 1935, totaling 973 acres, which was said to have been bought for farming. The land was close to Monroe, Louisiana, and from 1939 to 1966, three basic residential subdivisions covering 185 acres were carved from the plantation. Although the plantation was named "Hardtimes," for the new owners it was a good investment and 208 lots were sold in 158 separate sales at an $800,000 profit. In a pre-1964 settlement with the government it was apparently agreed that 60 percent of the gain would be reported as ordinary income and 40 percent as then preferential capital gain for the years of the settlement. Taxpayer then reported its gains for the years 1964–66 on the same basis. The Service asserted a deficiency arguing that all the gains were ordinary income and the taxpayer filed for refund claiming all the gains to be capital.

In addition to the subdivision sales the taxpayer also sold approximately 275 other acres from the plantation in 12 separate sales starting in 1935. From other land that it owned, the company in the years 1923 through 1966 sold 934 lots, 249 before 1935 and 477 in the years 1935 through 1966.

Improvements—streets, drainage, water, sewerage, and electricity—were made in the plantation subdivisions, aggregating about $200,000.

The District Court found that the plantation was originally bought for investment and that the intent to subdivide arose later when the city of Monroe, Louisiana, expanded in the direction of the plantation. Sales by the company largely resulted from unsolicited approaches by individuals to the taxpayer corporation except that in the years 1964–66, about 75 percent of the sales were induced by independent brokers with which the company dealt. The issue before the court as to all of the 1964–66 sales from the subdivisions was whether the lots constituted property held by the taxpayer primarily for sale to customers in the ordinary course of his trade or business under § 1221(1).]

II.

* * *

The problem we struggle with here is not novel. We have become accustomed to the frequency with which taxpayers litigate this troublesome question. Chief Judge Brown appropriately described the real estate capital gains-ordinary income issue as "old, familiar, recurring, vexing and ofttimes elusive." Thompson v. Commissioner of Internal Revenue, 5 Cir.1963, 322 F.2d 122, 123. The difficulty in large part stems from ad-hoc application of the numerous permissible criteria set forth in our multitudinous prior opinions. Over the past 40 years, this case by case approach with its concentration on the facts of each suit has resulted in a collection of decisions not always reconcilable. Recognizing the situation, we have warned that efforts to distinguish and thereby make consistent the Court's previous holdings must necessarily be "foreboding and unrewarding." Thompson, supra at 127. See Williams v. United States, 5 Cir.1964, 329 F.2d 430, 431. Litigants are cautioned that "each case must be decided on its own peculiar facts. * * * Specific factors, or combinations of them are not necessarily controlling." Thompson, supra at 127; Wood v. Commissioner of Internal Revenue, 5 Cir.1960, 276 F.2d 586, 590; Smith v. Commissioner of Internal Revenue, 5 Cir.1956, 232 F.2d 142, 144. Nor are these factors the equivalent of the philosopher's stone, separating "sellers garlanded with capital gains from those beflowered in the garden of ordinary income." United States v. Winthrop, 5 Cir.1969, 417 F.2d 905, 911.

Assuredly, we would much prefer one or two clearly defined, easily employed tests which lead to predictable, perhaps automatic, conclusions. However, the nature of the congressional "capital asset" definition and the myriad situations to which we must apply that standard make impossible any easy escape from the task before us. No one set of criteria is applicable to all economic structures. Moreover, within a collection of tests, individual factors have varying weights and magnitudes, depending on the facts of the case. The relationship among the factors and their mutual interaction is altered as each criteria increases or diminishes in strength, sometimes changing the controversy's outcome. As such, there can be no mathematical formula capable of finding the X of capital gains or ordinary income in this complicated field.

Yet our inability to proffer a panaceatic guide to the perplexed with respect to this subject does not preclude our setting forth some general, albeit inexact, guidelines for the resolution of many of the § 1221(1) cases we confront. This opinion does not purport to reconcile all past precedents or assure conflict-free future decisions. Nor do we hereby obviate the need for ad-hoc adjustments when confronted with close cases and changing factual circumstances. Instead, with the hope of clarifying a few of the area's mysteries, we more precisely define and suggest points of emphasis for the major *Winthrop* delineated factors as they appear in the instant controversy. In so doing, we devote particular attention to the Court's recent opinions in order that our analysis will reflect, insofar as possible, the Circuit's present trends.

III.

We begin our task by evaluating in the light of *Biedenharn's* facts the main *Winthrop* factors—substantiality and frequency of sales, improvements, solicitation and advertising efforts, and brokers' activities—as well as a few miscellaneous contentions. A separate section follows discussing the keenly contested role of prior investment intent. Finally, we consider the significance of the Supreme Court's decision in *Malat v. Riddell.*[16]

A.   Frequency and Substantiality of Sales

Scrutinizing closely the record and briefs, we find that plaintiff's real property sales activities compel an ordinary income conclusion. In arriving at this result, we examine first the most important of *Winthrop*'s factors—the frequency and substantiality of taxpayer's sales. Although frequency and substantiality of sales are not usually conclusive, they occupy the preeminent ground in our analysis. The recent trend of Fifth Circuit decisions indicates that when dispositions of subdivided property extend over a long period of time and are especially numerous, the likelihood of capital gains is very slight indeed. See United States v. Winthrop, 5 Cir.1969, 417 F.2d 905; Thompson v. Commissioner of Internal Revenue, 5 Cir.1963, 322 F.2d 122. Conversely, when sales are few and isolated, the taxpayer's claim to capital gain is accorded greater deference. Cf. Gamble v. Commissioner of Internal Revenue, 5 Cir.1957, 242 F.2d 586, 591; Brown v. Commissioner of Internal Revenue, 5 Cir.1944, 143 F.2d 468, 470.

On the present facts, taxpayer could not claim "isolated" sales or a passive and gradual liquidation. See Gamble, supra; Dunlap v. Oldham Lumber Company, 5 Cir.1950, 178 F.2d 781, 784; Brown, supra. Although only three years and 37 sales (38 lots) are in controversy here, taxpayer's pre-1964 sales from the Hardtimes acreage as well as similar dispositions from other properties are probative of the existence of sales "in the ordinary course of his trade or business." See Levin, Capital Gains Or Income Tax on Real Estate Sales, 37 B.U.L.Rev. 165, 170 & n. 29 (1957). Cf. Snell v. Commissioner of Internal Revenue, 5 Cir.1938, 97 F.2d 891. * * * Biedenharn sold property, usually a substantial number of lots, in every year, save one, from 1923 to 1966. Biedenharn's long and steady history of improved lot sales at least equals that encountered in Thompson v. Commissioner of Internal Revenue, 5 Cir. 1963, 322 F.2d 122, where also we noted the full history of real estate activity. Supra at 124–25. There taxpayer lost on a finding that he had sold 376½ lots over a 15 year span—this notwithstanding that overall the other sales indicia were more in taxpayer's favor than in the present case. Moreover, the contested tax years in that suit involved

16. 383 U.S. 569, 86 S.Ct. 1030, 16 L.Ed. 2d 102 (1966).

only ten sales (28 lots); yet we labeled that activity "substantial." Supra at 125.

The frequency and substantiality of Biedenharn's sales go not only to its holding purpose and the existence of a trade or business but also support our finding of the ordinariness with which the Realty Company disposed of its lots. These sales easily meet the criteria of normalcy set forth in *Winthrop,* supra at 912.

Furthermore, in contrast with Goldberg v. Commissioner of Internal Revenue, 5 Cir.1955, 223 F.2d 709, 713, where taxpayer did not reinvest his sales proceeds, one could fairly infer that the income accruing to the Biedenharn Realty Company from its pre-1935 sales helped support the purchase of the Hardtimes Plantation. Even if taxpayer made no significant acquisitions after Hardtimes, the "purpose, system, and continuity" of Biedenharn's efforts easily constitute a business. See *Snell,* supra at 893; *Brown,* supra at 470. As we said in *Snell,* supra:

> The fact that he bought no additional lands during this period does not prevent his activities being a business. He merely had enough land to do a large business without buying any more.

Citing previous Fifth Circuit decisions including Goldberg v. Commissioner of Internal Revenue, 5 Cir.1955, 223 F.2d 709, 713, and Ross v. Commissioner of Internal Revenue, 5 Cir.1955, 227 F.2d 265, 268, the District Court sought to overcome this evidence of dealer-like real estate activities and property "primarily held for sale" by clinging to the notion that the taxpayer was merely liquidating a prior investment. We discuss later the role of former investment status and the possibility of taxpayer relief under that concept. Otherwise, the question of liquidation of an investment is simply the opposite side of the inquiry as to whether or not one is holding property primarily for sale in the ordinary course of his business. In other words, a taxpayer's claim that he is liquidating a prior investment does not really present a separate theory but rather restates the main question currently under scrutiny. To the extent the opinions cited by the District Court might create a specially protected "liquidation" niche,[17] we believe that the present case, with taxpayer's energetic subdivision activities and consummation of numerous retail property dispositions, is governed by our more recent decision in *Thompson v. Commissioner of Internal Revenue,* supra at 127–28. There, the Court observed:

> The liquidation, if it really is that, may therefore be carried out with business efficiency. Smith v. Commissioner of Internal Revenue, 5 Cir.1956, 232 F.2d 142, 145. But what was once an investment, or what may start out as a liquidation of an investment, may become something else. The Tax Court was eminently justified in concluding that this took place here. It was a regular part of the trade or business of Taxpayer to sell these lots to any and all comers who would meet his price. From 1944 on when the sales commenced, there is no evidence

17. See section IV infra.

that he thereafter held the lots for any purpose other than the sale to prospective purchasers. It is true that he testified in conclusory terms that he was trying to "liquidate" but on objective standards the Tax Court could equate held solely with "held primarily." And, of course, there can be no question at all that purchasers of these lots were "customers" and that whether we call Taxpayer a "dealer" or a "trader", a real estate man or otherwise, the continuous sales of these lots down to the point of exhaustion was a regular and ordinary (and profitable) part of his business activity.

See Ackerman v. United States, 5 Cir.1964, 335 F.2d 521, 524–25; *Brown,* supra at 470.

B. Improvements

Although we place greatest emphasis on the frequency and substantiality of sales over an extended time period, our decision in this instance is aided by the presence of taxpayer activity—particularly improvements—in the other *Winthrop* areas. Biedenharn vigorously improved its subdivisions, generally adding streets, drainage, sewerage, and utilities. These alterations are comparable to those in *Winthrop,* supra at 906, except that in the latter case taxpayer built five houses. We do not think that the construction of five houses in the context of *Winthrop* 's 456 lot sales significantly distinguishes that taxpayer from Biedenharn. In Barrios Estate v. Commissioner of Internal Revenue, 5 Cir.1959, 265 F.2d 517, 520, heavily relied on by plaintiff, the Court reasoned that improvements constituted an integral part of the sale of subdivided realty and were therefore permissible in the context of a liquidating sale. As discussed above, Biedenharn's activities have removed it from any harbor of investment liquidation. Moreover, the additional sales flexibility permitted the *Barrios Estate* taxpayer might be predicated on the forced change of purpose examined in section IV. Finally, in *Thompson,* supra, the plaintiff's only activities were subdivision and improvement. Yet, not availing ourselves of the opportunity to rely on a *Barrios Estate* type "liquidation plus integrally related improvements theory," we found no escape from ordinary income.

C. Solicitation and Advertising Efforts

Substantial, frequent sales and improvements such as we have encountered in this case will usually conclude the capital gains issue against taxpayer. See, e.g., *Thompson,* supra. Thus, on the basis of our analysis to this point, we would have little hesitation in finding that taxpayer held "primarily for sale" in the "ordinary course of [his] trade or business." "[T]he flexing of commercial muscles with frequency and continuity, design and effect" of which *Winthrop* spoke, supra at 911, is here a reality. This reality is further buttressed by Biedenharn's sales efforts, including those carried on through brokers.[18] Minimizing the importance of its own sales activities, taxpayer points repeatedly to its steady avoidance of advertising or other solicitation of

18. See section III. D. infra.

customers. Plaintiff directs our attention to stipulations detailing the population growth of Monroe and testimony outlining the economic forces which made Hardtimes Plantation attractive residential property and presumably eliminated the need for sales exertions. We have no quarrel with plaintiff's description of this familiar process of suburban expansion, but we cannot accept the legal inferences which taxpayer would have us draw.

The Circuit's recent decisions in *Thompson,* supra at 124–26, and *Winthrop,* supra at 912, implicitly recognize that even one inarguably in the real estate business need not engage in promotional exertions in the face of a favorable market. As such, we do not always require a showing of active solicitation where "business * * * [is] good, indeed brisk," *Thompson,* supra at 124, and where other *Winthrop* factors make obvious taxpayer's ordinary trade or business status. See also Levin, supra at 190. Plainly, this represents a sensible approach. In cases such as *Biedenharn,* the sale of a few lots and the construction of the first homes, albeit not, as in *Winthrop,* by the taxpayer, as well as the building of roads, addition of utilities, and staking off of the other subdivided parcels constitute a highly visible form of advertising. Prospective home buyers drive by the advantageously located property, see the development activities, and are as surely put on notice of the availability of lots as if the owner had erected large signs announcing "residential property for sale." We do not by this evaluation automatically neutralize advertising or solicitation as a factor in our analysis. This form of inherent notice is not present in all land sales, especially where the property is not so valuably located, is not subdivided into small lots, and is not improved. Moreover, inherent notice represents only one band of the solicitation spectrum. Media utilization and personal initiatives remain material components of this criterion. When present, they call for greater Government oriented emphasis on *Winthrop*'s solicitation factor.

D. Brokerage Activities

In evaluating Biedenharn's solicitation activities, we need not confine ourselves to the *Thompson-Winthrop* theory of brisk sales without organizational efforts. Unlike in *Thompson* and *Winthrop* where no one undertook overt solicitation efforts, the Realty Company hired brokers who, using media and on site advertising, worked vigorously on taxpayer's behalf. We do not believe that the employment of brokers should shield plaintiff from ordinary income treatment. See Gamble v. Commissioner of Internal Revenue, 5 Cir.1957, 242 F.2d 586, 592; Brown, supra at 470; Snell v. Commissioner of Internal Revenue, 5 Cir. 1938, 97 F.2d 891, 892–93; Cf. McFaddin v. Commissioner of Internal Revenue, 5 Cir.1945, 148 F.2d 570, 571. See also Levin, supra at 193–94. Their activities should at least in discounted form be attributed to Biedenharn. To the contrary, taxpayer argues that "one who is not already in the trade or business of selling real estate does not enter such business when he employs a broker who acts as an independent contractor. Fahs v. Crawford, 161 F.2d 315 (5 Cir.1947); Smith v. Dunn, 224 F.2d 353 (5 Cir.1955)." Without presently entangling ourselves in a dispute as to the differences between an agent and an independent contractor, see generally Levin, supra, we find the cases cited distinguishable from the instant circumstances. In both *Fahs* and *Smith,* the taxpayer turned the entire property over to brokers, who, having been granted total responsibility, made all decisions including the setting of sales prices. In comparison, Biedenharn determined original prices and general credit policy. Moreover, the Realty Company did not make all the sales in question through brokers as did taxpayers in *Fahs* and *Smith.*[19] Biedenharn sold the Bayou DeSiard and Biedenharn Estates lots and may well have sold some of the Oak Park land. In other words, unlike *Fahs* and *Smith,* Biedenharn's brokers did not so completely take charge of the whole of the Hardtimes sales as to permit the Realty Company to wall itself off legally from their activities.

E. Additional Taxpayer Contentions

Plaintiff presents a number of other contentions and supporting facts for our consideration. Although we set out these arguments and briefly discuss them, their impact, in the face of those factors examined above, must be minimal. Taxpayer emphasizes that its profits from real estate sales averaged only 11.1% in each of the years in controversy, compared to 52.4% in *Winthrop.* Whatever the percentage, plaintiff would be hard pressed to deny the substantiality of its Hardtimes sales in absolute terms (the subdivided lots alone brought in over one million dollars) or, most importantly, to assert that its real estate business was too insignificant to constitute a separate trade or business.[20]

The relatively modest income share represented by Biedenharn's real property dispositions stems not from a failure to engage in real estate sales activities but rather from the comparatively large profit attributable to the Company's 1965 ($649,231.34) and 1966 ($688,840.82) stock sales. The fact of Biedenharn's holding, managing, and selling stock is not inconsistent with the existence of a separate realty business. If in the face of taxpayer's numerous real estate dealings this Court held otherwise, we would be sanctioning special treatment for those individuals and companies arranging their business activities so that the income accruing to real estate sales represents only a small fraction of the taxpaying entity's total gains.

Similarly, taxpayer observes that Biedenharn's manager devoted only 10% of his time to real estate dealings and then mostly to the

---

19. Also, Henry Biedenharn stated that he kept a list of prospective buyers who had contacted him. When the Realty Company eventually hired a broker, Mr. Biedenharn provided the latter with these names.

20. This Court has repeatedly recognized that a taxpayer may have more than one trade or business for purposes of Internal Revenue Code § 1221(1). See, e.g., Ackerman v. United States, 5 Cir.1964, 335 F.2d 521, 524; Gamble v. Commissioner of Internal Revenue, 5 Cir.1957, 242 F.2d 586, 591; Fahs v. Crawford, 5 Cir.1947, 161 F.2d 315, 317.

company's rental properties. This fact does not negate the existence of sales activities. Taxpayer had a telephone listing, a shared business office, and a few part-time employees. Because, as discussed before, a strong seller's market existed, Biedenharn's sales required less than the usual solicitation efforts and therefore less than the usual time. Moreover, plaintiff, unlike taxpayers in *Winthrop,* supra and *Thompson,* supra, hired brokers to handle many aspects of the Hardtimes transactions—thus further reducing the activity and time required of Biedenharn's employees.

Finally, taxpayer argues that it is entitled to capital gains since its enormous profits (74% to 97%) demonstrate a return based principally on capital appreciation and not on taxpayer's "merchandising" efforts. We decline the opportunity to allocate plaintiff's gain between long-term market appreciation and improvement related activities. * * * Even if we undertook such an analysis and found the former element predominant, we would on the authority of *Winthrop,* supra at 907–908, reject plaintiff's contention which, in effect, is merely taxpayer's version of the Government's unsuccessful argument in that case.

IV.

The District Court found that "[t]axpayer is merely liquidating over a long period of time a substantial investment in the most advantageous method possible." 356 F.Supp. at 1336. In this view, the original investment intent is crucial, for it preserves the capital gains character of the transaction even in the face of normal real estate sales activities.

The Government asserts that Biedenharn Realty Company did not merely "liquidate" an investment but instead entered the real estate business in an effort to dispose of what was formerly investment property. Claiming that Biedenharn's activities would result in ordinary income if the Hardtimes Plantation had been purchased with the intent to divide and resell the property, and finding no reason why a different prior intent should influence this outcome,[21] the Government concludes that original investment purpose is irrelevant. Instead, the Government would have us focus exclusively on taxpayer's intent and the level of sales activity during the period commencing with subdivision and improvement and lasting through final sales. Under this theory, every individual who improves and frequently sells substantial numbers of land parcels would receive ordinary income.

While the facts of this case dictate our agreement with the Internal Revenue Service's ultimate conclusion of taxpayer liability, they do not require our acquiescence in the Government's entreated total elimination of *Winthrop*'s first criterion, "the nature and purpose of the acquisition." Undoubtedly, in most subdivided-improvement situations, an investment purpose of antecedent origin will not survive into a present era of intense retail selling. The antiquated purpose, when

21. The Government emphasizes the "unfairness" of two taxpayers engaging in equal sales efforts with respect to similar tracts of land but receiving different tax treatment because of divergent initial motives.

overborne by later, but substantial and frequent selling activity, will not prevent ordinary income from being visited upon the taxpayer. See, e.g., Ackerman v. United States, 5 Cir.1964, 335 F.2d 521; Thompson v. Commissioner of Internal Revenue, 5 Cir.1963, 322 F.2d 122; Galena Oaks Corp. v. Scofield, 5 Cir.1954, 218 F.2d 217; Brown v. Commissioner of Internal Revenue, 5 Cir.1944, 143 F.2d 468. Generally, investment purpose has no built-in perpetuity nor a guarantee of capital gains forever more. Precedents, however, in certain circumstances have permitted landowners with earlier investment intent to sell subdivided property and remain subject to capital gains treatment. See, e.g., Cole v. Usry, 5 Cir.1961, 294 F.2d 426; Barrios Estate v. Commissioner of Internal Revenue, 5 Cir.1959, 265 F.2d 517; Smith v. Dunn, 5 Cir.1955, 224 F.2d 353.

The Government, attacking these precedents, argues that the line of cases decided principally in the 1950's represented by *Barrios Estate,* supra; Goldberg v. Commissioner of Internal Revenue, 5 Cir.1955, 223 F.2d 709; Ross v. Commissioner of Internal Revenue, 5 Cir.1955, 227 F.2d 265 and including United States v. Temple, 5 Cir.1966, 355 F.2d 67, are inconsistent with our earlier holdings in *Galena Oaks Corp.,* supra; White v. Commissioner of Internal Revenue, 5 Cir.1949, 172 F.2d 629; *Brown,* supra, and the trend of our most recent decisions in *Ackerman,* supra, *Thompson,* supra and including Judge Wisdom's dissent in *Temple,* supra. Because of the ad-hoc nature of these previous decisions and the difficulty of determining in each instance the exact combination of factors which placed a case on one side or the other of the [former] capital gains-ordinary income boundary, we are loath to overrule any of these past decisions. In a sense, we adhere to our own admonitions against efforts at reconciling and making consistent all that has gone before in the subdivided realty area. But in so avoiding a troublesome and probably unrewarding task, we are not foreclosed from the more important responsibility of giving future direction with respect to the much controverted role of prior investment intent, nor are we precluded from analyzing that factor's impact in the context of the present controversy.

We reject the Government's sweeping contention that prior investment intent is always irrelevant. There will be instances where an initial investment purpose endures in controlling fashion notwithstanding continuing sales activity. We doubt that this aperture, where an active subdivider and improver receives [preferential] capital gains, is very wide; yet we believe it exists. We would most generally find such an opening where the change from investment holding to sales activity results from unanticipated, externally induced factors which make impossible the continued pre-existing use of the realty. *Barrios Estate,* supra, is such a case. There the taxpayer farmed the land until drainage problems created by the newly completed intercoastal canal rendered the property agriculturally unfit. The Court found that taxpayer was "dispossessed of the farming operation through no act of her own." Supra at 518. Similarly, Acts of God, condemnation of part of one's property, new and unfavorable zoning regulations, or other events forcing alteration of taxpayer's plans create situations making possible subdivision and improvement as a part of a capital gains disposition.[22]

However, cases of the ilk of *Ackerman,* supra, *Thompson,* supra, and *Winthrop,* supra, remain unaffected in their ordinary income conclusion. There, the transformations in purpose were not coerced. Rather, the changes ensued from taxpayers' purely *voluntary* responses to increased economic opportunity—albeit at times externally created—in order to enhance their gain through the subdivision, improvement, and sale of lots. Thus reinforced by the trend of these recent decisions, we gravitate toward the Government's view in instances of willful taxpayer change of purpose and grant the taxpayer little, if any, benefit from *Winthrop*'s first criterion in such cases.

The distinction drawn above reflects our belief that Congress did not intend to automatically disqualify from [preferential] capital gains bona fide investors forced to abandon prior purposes for reasons beyond their control. At times, the Code may be severe, and this Court may construe it strictly, but neither Code nor Court is so tyrannical as to mandate the absolute rule urged by the Government. However, we caution that although permitting a land owner substantial sales flexibility where there is a forced change from original investment purpose, we do not absolutely shield the constrained taxpayer from ordinary income. That taxpayer is not granted *carte blanche* to undertake intensely all aspects of a full blown real estate business. Instead, in cases of forced change of purpose, we will continue to utilize the *Winthrop* analysis discussed earlier but will place unusually strong taxpayer-favored emphasis on *Winthrop*'s first factor.

Clearly, under the facts in this case, the distinction just elaborated undermines Biedenharn's reliance on original investment purpose. Taxpayer's change of purpose was entirely voluntary and therefore does not fall within the protected area. Moreover, taxpayer's original investment intent, *even if* considered a factor sharply supporting capital gains treatment, is so overwhelmed by the other *Winthrop* factors discussed supra, that that element can have no decisive effect. However wide the [preferential] capital gains passageway through which a subdivider with former investment intent could squeeze, the Biedenharn Realty Company will never fit.

22. A Boston University Law Review article canvassing factors inducing involuntary changes of purpose in subdivided realty cases enumerates among others the following: a pressing need for funds in general, illness or old age or both, the necessity for liquidating a partnership on the death of a partner, the threat of condemnation, and municipal zoning restrictions. Levin, Capital Gains or Income Tax on Real Estate Sales, 37 B.U.L.Rev. 1965, 194–95 (1957). Although we might not accept all of these events as sufficient to cause an outcome favorable to taxpayer, they are suggestive of the sort of change of purpose provoking events delineated above as worthy of special consideration.

V.

The District Court, citing Malat v. Riddell, 1966, 383 U.S. 569, 86 S.Ct. 1030, 16 L.Ed.2d 102, stated that "the lots were not held * * * primarily for sale as that phrase was interpreted * * * in *Malat* * * *." 356 F.Supp. at 1335. Finding that Biedenharn's primary purpose became holding for sale and consequently that *Malat* in no way alters our analysis here, we disagree with the District Court's conclusion. *Malat* was a brief per curiam in which the Supreme Court decided only that as used in Internal Revenue Code § 1221(1) the word "primarily" means "principally," "of first importance." The Supreme Court, remanding the case, did not analyze the facts or resolve the controversy which involved a real estate dealer who had purchased land and held it at the time of sale with the dual intention of developing it as rental property or selling it, depending on whichever proved to be the more profitable. Malat v. Riddell, 9 Cir.1965, 347 F.2d 23, 26. In contrast, having substantially abandoned its investment and farming [23] intent, Biedenharn was cloaked primarily in the garb of sales purpose when it disposed of the 38 lots here in controversy. With this change, the Realty Company lost the opportunity of coming within any dual purpose analysis.

We do not hereby condemn to ordinary income a taxpayer merely because, as is usually true, his principal intent at the exact moment of disposition is sales. Rather, we refuse [preferential] capital gains treatment in those instances where over time there has been such a thoroughgoing change of purpose, see, e.g., *Thompson,* supra, as to make untenable a claim either of twin intent or continued primacy of investment purpose.[24]

VI.

Having surveyed the Hardtimes terrain, we find no escape from ordinary income. The frequency and substantiality of sales over an extended time, the significant improvement of the basic subdivisions, the acquisition of additional properties, the use of brokers, and other

23. The District Court found that Biedenharn "is still farming a large part of the land * * *." 356 F.Supp. at 1336. The record suggests neither that Biedernharn as opposed to a lessee currently farms on the Hardtimes Plantation nor that the magnitude of that lessee's farming operations is substantial. More importantly, the District Court did not find and the plaintiff does not assert that Biedenharn simultaneously held the subdivided land for sale and for farming either before or at the time of disposition. Taxpayer claims no dual purpose.

24. *Winthrop,* supra, although different from *Biedenharn* in respect to initial intent, is not contrary to our *Malat* analysis. In *Winthrop,* taxpayer inherited property, a method of acquisition which is necessarily neutral as to original purpose. We found that after receipt of his legacy, the *Winthrop* taxpayer at all times held the lots "primarily for sale." *Winthrop,* supra at 911. Although encountering original investment purpose instead of neutral intent in the present case, we conclude that Biedenharn dissipated that initial purpose by its later sales activities. This alteration resulted in Biedenharn, like Winthrop, holding retail lots over an extended period "primarily for sale to customers in the ordinary course of [his] trade or business." Thus, in both cases, taxpayers moved to and maintained a primary sales purpose over an extended period. In neither instance did they hold for dual purposes.

less important factors persuasively combine to doom taxpayer's cause. Applying *Winthrop*'s criteria, this case clearly falls within the ordinary income category delineated in that decision.[25] In so concluding, we note that *Winthrop* does not represent the most extreme application of the overriding principle that "the definition of a capital asset must be narrowly applied and its exclusions interpreted broadly." Corn Products Refining Co. v. Commissioner of Internal Revenue, 1955, 350 U.S. 46, 52, 76 S.Ct. 20, 24, 100 L.Ed. 29, 35. See also Commissioner of Internal Revenue v. Lake, 1958, 356 U.S. 260, 265, 78 S.Ct. 691, 694, 2 L.Ed.2d 743, 748. Accord, *Winthrop*, supra at 911.

We cannot write black letter law for all realty subdividers and for all times, but we do caution in words of red that once an investment does not mean always an investment. A simon-pure investor forty years ago could by his subsequent activities become a seller in the ordinary course four decades later. The period of Biedenharn's passivity is in the distant past; and the taxpayer has since undertaken the role of real estate protagonist. The Hardtimes Plantation in its day may have been one thing, but as the plantation was developed and sold, Hardtimes became by the very fact of change and activity a different holding than it had been at its inception. No longer could resort to initial purpose preserve taxpayer's once upon a time opportunity for favored treatment. The opinion of the District Court is reversed.

[Four judges joined in a dissent written by Judge Gee stating that the majority summarily discounted a critical trial court finding of fact that taxpayer was still farming a large part of the land and that neither the plaintiff nor the court claimed any dual purpose and that the majority placed preeminent emphasis on sales activities and improvements, effectively eliminating the other factors in *Winthrop*.]

* * *

In Suburban Realty Co. v. United States, 615 F.2d 171 (5th Cir. 1980), cert. denied 449 U.S. 920, 101 S.Ct. 318, 66 L.Ed.2d 147 (1980), the court held that sales of six tracts of unimproved real estate from a large property acquired more than 30 years earlier resulted in ordinary income. Because the taxpayer, over the 32 years, made 244 sales from the original acreage of both unimproved and platted land for residential development, the court concluded that the six tracts were property held primarily for sale to customers in the ordinary course of the taxpayer's

---

25. The greater percentage of realty sales income, the construction of five houses, the holding of a real estate license, the originally neutral acquisition purpose, and the slightly higher pitch of sales in the years immediately preceding suit all characteristic of *Winthrop* do not make that case significantly different from *Biedenharn* any more than the longer history of sales, additional acquisition of land, use of a business office, existence of a telephone listing, original investment purpose, or employment of brokers who advertised and actively solicited customers characteristic of *Biedenharn* materially distinguish the present suit from *Winthrop*. The cases are at bottom similar. One need not go beyond *Winthrop* in order to decide the present dispute.

real estate sales business. See also Houston Endowment, Inc. v. United States, 606 F.2d 77 (5th Cir.1979).

Question

Consider the impact of § 1031(a)(2)(A).

What Constitutes Property Held "Primarily for Sale" so as to Create Ordinary Income Rather Than Capital Gains. In addition to whether the taxpayer's conduct with respect to an asset (usually realty) amounts to a "trade or business," the tax consequences under § 1221(1) also turn on whether the property was held "primarily for sale." The "primarily for sale" problem is considered in the next case.

MALAT v. RIDDELL

Supreme Court of the United States, 1966.
383 U.S. 569, 86 S.Ct. 1030, 16 L.Ed.2d 102.

PER CURIAM.

Petitioner was a participant in a joint venture which acquired a 45-acre parcel of land, the intended use for which is somewhat in dispute. Petitioner contends that the venturers' intention was to develop and operate an apartment project on the land; the respondent's position is that there was a "dual purpose" of developing the property for rental purposes or selling, whichever proved to be the more profitable. In any event, difficulties in obtaining the necessary financing were encountered, and the interior lots of the tract were subdivided and sold. The profit from those sales was reported and taxed as ordinary income.

The joint venturers continued to explore the possibility of commercially developing the remaining exterior parcels. Additional frustrations in the form of zoning restrictions were encountered. These difficulties persuaded petitioner and another of the joint venturers of the desirability of terminating the venture; accordingly, they sold out their interests in the remaining property. Petitioner contends that he is entitled to treat the profits from this last sale as [preferential] capital gains; the respondent takes the position that this was "property held by the taxpayer primarily for sale to customers in the ordinary course of his trade or business," and thus subject to taxation as ordinary income.

The District Court made the following finding:

"The members of [the joint venture], as of the date the 44.901 acres were acquired, intended either to sell the property or develop it for rental, depending upon which course appeared to be most profitable. The venturers realized that they had made a good purchase price-wise and, if they were unable to obtain acceptable construction financing or rezoning * * * which would be prerequisite to commercial development, they would sell the property in bulk so they wouldn't get hurt.

The purpose of either selling or developing the property continued during the period in which [the joint venture] held the property."

The District Court ruled that petitioner had failed to establish that the property was not held *primarily* for sale to customers in the ordinary course of business, and thus rejected petitioner's claim to [preferential] capital gain treatment for the profits derived from the property's resale. The Court of Appeals affirmed, 9 Cir., 347 F.2d 23. We granted certiorari (382 U.S. 900, 86 S.Ct. 244, 15 L.Ed.2d 154) to resolve a conflict among the courts of appeals with regard to the meaning of the term "primarily" as it is used in § 1221(1) of the Internal Revenue Code of 1954.

The statute denies [preferential] capital gain treatment to profits reaped from the sale of "property held by the taxpayer *primarily* for sale to customers in the ordinary course of his trade or business." (Emphasis added.) The respondent urges upon us a construction of "primarily" as meaning that a purpose may be "primary" if it is a "substantial" one.

As we have often said, "the words of statutes—including revenue acts—should be interpreted where possible in their ordinary, everyday senses." Crane v. Commissioner of Internal Revenue, 331 U.S. 1, 6, 67 S.Ct. 1047, 1051, 91 L.Ed. 1301. And see Hanover Bank v. Commissioner of Internal Revenue, 369 U.S. 672, 687–688, 82 S.Ct. 1080, 1088–1089, 8 L.Ed.2d 187; Commissioner of Internal Revenue v. Korell, 339 U.S. 619, 627–628, 70 S.Ct. 905, 909, 94 L.Ed. 1108. Departure from a literal reading of statutory language may, on occasion, be indicated by relevant internal evidence of the statute itself and necessary in order to effect the legislative purpose. See, e.g., Board of Governors of Federal Reserve System v. Agnew, 329 U.S. 441, 446–448, 67 S.Ct. 411, 413–415, 91 L.Ed. 408. But this is not such an occasion. The purpose of the statutory provision with which we deal is to differentiate between the "profits and losses arising from the everyday operation of a business" on the one hand (Corn Products Refining Co. v. Commissioner of Internal Revenue, 350 U.S. 46, 52, 76 S.Ct. 20, 24, 100 L.Ed. 29) and "the realization of appreciation in value accrued over a substantial period of time" on the other. (Commissioner of Internal Revenue v. Gillette Motor Transport, Inc., 364 U.S. 130, 134, 80 S.Ct. 1497, 1500, 4 L.Ed.2d 1617.) A literal reading of the statute is consistent with this legislative purpose. We hold that, as used in § 1221(1), "primarily" means "of first importance" or "principally."

Since the courts below applied an incorrect legal standard, we do not consider whether the result would be supportable on the facts of this case had the correct one been applied. We believe, moreover, that the appropriate disposition is to remand the case to the District Court, for fresh fact-findings, addressed to the statute as we have now construed it.

Vacated and remanded.

MR. JUSTICE BLACK would affirm the judgments of the District Court and the Court of Appeals.

MR. JUSTICE WHITE took no part in the decision of this case.

———

On remand, the trial court concluded that the realty was not held primarily for sale to customers because the principal purpose of the venture was to develop the property for rental. The taxpayer was entitled to the then preferential capital gains treatment. Malat v. Riddell, 275 F.Supp. 358 (S.D.Cal.1966).

Change of purpose situations must be distinguished from dual purpose cases like Malat v. Riddell. Compare the Biedenharn Realty Co. case.

The Operation of Section 1237. Section 1237 seeks to provide objective tests for determining when sales of real property receive the previously preferential capital gain treatment. An individual who is not otherwise a real estate dealer under the general rules relating to dealers and who has held a tract of real property for five years (unless the property was acquired by inheritance) (§ 1237(a)(3)), can subdivide it and promote its sale, without being considered a dealer, if certain conditions are met. Generally, the owner must not previously have held the property or a portion of the property primarily for sale to customers in the ordinary course of his trade or business. § 1237(a)(1). In the year in which the property is sold from the tract, the taxpayer can hold no other real property for sale to customers in the ordinary course of his trade or business. § 1237(a)(1). The taxpayer must have made no substantial improvement on the tract that substantially enhances the value of the lot sold. § 1237(a)(2). The term "substantial improvement" is defined in Reg. § 1.1237–1(c)(4). Some improvements are permitted if the property has been held for ten years. § 1237(b)(3). Under § 1237(b)(1), only sales of the first five parcels receive capital gains treatment (or inclusion in § 1231). In any year in which a sixth lot is sold and thereafter, gains on all qualified lots constitute ordinary income in an amount equal to 5 percent of the sales price. The remainder of any gain is capital gains (or is covered under § 1231). § 1237(b)(1). Section 1237 is not applicable to losses. Furthermore, it is not exclusive. Reg. § 1.1237–1(a)(4). The taxpayer is free to establish his status as an investor under § 1221(1).

Problems

1. In the tax year, Terri Player, an attorney, purchased three tracts of raw land. She also sold, for a total loss of $15,000, three other parcels of land which she held, respectively, for four, five, and six years. She asks you whether she should report these transactions as capital losses or ordinary losses. List the information you need to have in order to advise her. Consider the Biedenharn Realty case.

2. Over the past three years, Owner sold 22 parcels of real property and realized a net gain of $3.4 million. In the current year, he sold seven properties for a net loss of $2.5 million. He advertised none of the seven properties for sale, nor did he list any of them with real estate brokers. All of the transactions were initiated by the purchaser or someone acting on the purchaser's behalf. None of the properties sold was subdivided. Owner neither maintained a separate real estate office nor was he a licensed real estate broker or associated with a real estate company which advertised itself. Over the last three years, the owner reported substantial amounts of rental income, but received rental income from only one of the seven properties sold in the current year. Can owner treat the $2.5 million loss as ordinary loss? Consider the Biedenharn Realty case.

3. COMPARISON OF THE TRADER IN SECURITIES AND THE SELLER OF REAL ESTATE

A basic problem with respect to investors is to determine when they are merely holders of capital assets and when they are selling inventory or stock in trade. The gains on investments in capital assets are treated differently under § 1221 than the sale of inventory or transactions by a dealer who systematically engages in buying and selling property.

Sales of Shares of Stock by Investor Create Capital Gains and Capital Losses. There has been considerable discussion with respect to activities of an investor who has, as a principal source of his total gross income, income arising from transactions in securities. Assume an investor, who makes his investment decisions, trades for his own account and takes gains with respect to such investments, but does not make any investments for others. On the securities transactions, the investor or trader, regardless of the number or the dollar volume of transactions in a year, reports his transactions as capital gains and capital losses.

VAN SUETENDAEL v. COMMISSIONER

3 T.C.M. (CCH) 987 (1944), aff'd 152 F.2d 654 (2d Cir.1945).

MEMORANDUM FINDINGS OF FACT AND OPINION

HARRON, JUDGE:

* * *

Findings of Fact

* * *

During the taxable years, and for some years prior thereto, the petitioner was primarily engaged in buying and selling securities. Approximately 90 percent of the securities purchased by him were interest-bearing bonds and the other 10 percent consisted of preferred and common stock. His income was derived principally from interest on the bonds purchased and from interest on bank deposits. He maintained an office in Yonkers and had one employee who acted as his secretary-typist and general assistant. He was not a member of any stock exchange. His name was listed in several statistical financial publications as a dealer in securities, and in the Yonkers city and telephone directories under the classification of "investments". He also listed offerings to buy or sell securities at a certain price in the National Daily Quotation Service, for which he paid an annual subscription fee. This service was circularized among investment and trading houses in the United States. Petitioner has registered with the Securities and Exchange Commission, the State of New York, and the Bureau of Internal Revenue as a broker or dealer in securities. From time to time he has advertised in a Yonkers newspaper offering to buy or sell certain securities. Occasionally, his name appeared in the advertising section of the Columbia Alumni News under the caption "Investment Securities". He has also written to individuals, banks, and insurance companies offering securities at stated prices. Over a period of years, he has occasionally distributed calendars and pocket manuals containing data on securities of companies listed on the leading stock exchanges. Prior to the taxable years, petitioner, to a small degree, had participated in selling groups for the purpose of distributing new issues of securities.

* * *

During the taxable years, petitioner maintained separate accounts with [brokerage firms having stock exchange memberships]. * * *

In reporting the transactions of the sales of securities in each year on his return, petitioner took the view that all of the securities sold were non-capital assets, * * *.

The respondent, in determining the deficiencies, held that the securities sold by petitioner were capital assets, and he therefore applied the limitations of [§ 1211(b)] computing petitioner's net income from the sale of such securities. * * *

* * *

Opinion

* * * On brief, [the petitioner] argues that the entire case resolves itself to the one question of whether he was engaged in business as a dealer in securities. That, however, is not the issue. The phrase "dealer in securities" is not defined in the statute, although it is defined in [Reg. § 1.471–5]. The only issue for determination here is whether the securities sold by petitioner during the taxable years were capital assets under [§ 1221] * * *.

Under [§ 1221], all property is to be treated as capital assets unless the taxpayer is able to bring himself within one of the stated exceptions in the definition of capital assets. As far as this proceeding is concerned, the only possible exceptions which petitioner could rely upon are that the securities sold were [described in § 1221(1)]. * * * The securities which petitioner sold during the taxable years cannot be classified as stock in trade or property subject to inventory in his hands unless they were held by him primarily for sale to customers in the ordinary course of his business. Thus, the issue turns upon whether or not the securities sold by petitioner during the taxable years were held by him primarily for sale to customers in the ordinary course of business. This is probably the reason why petitioner has placed such stress upon the contention that he was a dealer in securities since securities in the nature of stock in trade held primarily for sale to customers are held only by dealers in securities. * * * However, there may be many sales of securities by so-called dealers in securities which do not come within the exceptions set forth in the definition of capital assets. The fact that petitioner had a teletype machine, four telephones and statistical financial publications in his office, was listed as a "dealer" in certain publications, and advertised himself as willing to buy or sell securities is not determinative of the issue. The subject matter of the cited sections is property and it must be shown that the property itself comes within the exceptions stated in the definition of capital assets.

* * *

From an analysis of the schedules showing all of petitioner's transactions in securities during these years, we cannot find as a fact that petitioner held the securities sold by him during the taxable years primarily for sale to customers in the ordinary course of his business. The facts are just as consonant with the theory that petitioner held the securities for speculation or for investment. It is well established that taxpayers who buy securities for speculation or investment hold them as capital assets and not primarily for resale to customers. * * * One who holds securities in the nature of stock in trade primarily for resale to customers is regularly engaged in the purchase of securities at wholesale. * * * He is a middleman in distributing the securities and he does not resell to the same class of persons from whom he buys. * * * Here, petitioner did not make wholesale purchases of securities. The securities purchased were in relatively small quantities and were diversified. In this respect, he acted no differently from an ordinary purchaser. Most of the securities purchased by petitioner were resold to or through the same brokers from whom they were bought. Here again, petitioner acted in the same manner as an ordinary purchaser having an account with a broker. * * * These brokers or their clients cannot be considered as petitioner's customers. Over 92 percent of the securities sold by petitioner to or through [the brokers] had been previously acquired by him from the same two brokerage houses. Many of these securities were resold by petitioner at a profit on the same day in which he purchased them or a short time thereafter. * * * Petitioner could not have intended to purchase these securities for resale to "customers" as that word is used in the statute. * * * Although petitioner did make efforts to sell some of the securities through channels other than brokers and dealers, and actually did sell a small amount of the securities to other parties, we cannot find even as to those securities that they were purchased primarily for resale to customers. A mere statement in behalf of petitioner that they were purchased or held for that purpose is insufficient. * * * We think that the purchases and sales of all of the securities were engendered by the speculative advantage which might be derived by petitioner, or the income which he might receive therefrom.

Respondent points out that during the taxable years, petitioner's principal source of income was derived from interest on the bonds owned by him and that the great proportion of his losses resulted from securities which he had held for a long period of time. He argues that petitioner, during each of the taxable years, selected securities which he had held for a long time and which were then unprofitable to him and disposed of those securities at the best possible price to anyone who would buy them in order that the loss sustained thereon should offset his income from the interest-bearing bonds held by him. * * * Respondent also argues that as to the securities held for a long period, petitioner did not hold them for resale to customers, but for the income which he might derive therefrom. The facts apparently support respondent's contentions. * * *

* * *

* * * We think that a reasonable conclusion from all of the facts is that petitioner intended to sell the securities in any way he could and to any purchaser regardless of whether or not the purchaser could be deemed a "customer" within the meaning of the statute. It is therefore held that the securities sold by petitioner during the taxable years were capital assets and subject to the limitations of gain and loss set forth in [§ 1211(b)]. Respondent's determination is sustained.

* * *

Decision will be entered under Rule 50.

See also Huebschman v. Commissioner, 41 T.C.M. (CCH) 474 (1980), where the court held that a taxpayer, who bought and sold substantial amounts of stocks and bonds during the years in question was not a dealer in securities because he had no customers, was not licensed to sell securities, did not have a seat on any exchange, traded only for his own account, and all his transactions were handled through a broker.

Questions

1. What is the difference, if any, between a dealer, a trader and an investor? How did the taxpayer in Van Suetendael wish to be characterized?

2. Why did the taxpayer in Van Suetendael want ordinary loss treatment?

There has been considerable dissatisfaction because, as already stated, an individual who consistently engages for profit in the purchase and sale of real estate may not receive capital gains, as would the taxpayer dealing in securities. However, the dealer in real estate realizes ordinary losses, but not the individual dealing in securities. It is not easy to explain why different tax consequences should attach to the activities of an investor who buys and sells stocks and securities for his own account in contrast to an investor who buys and sells real estate. The legislative history of § 1221(1) indicates that the requirement that property, to avoid capital asset treatment, be held for sale "to customers," was designed to prevent a "stock speculator trading on his own account" from claiming ordinary losses. H.R.Rept. No. 1385, 73rd Cong., 2d Sess., 1939–1 C.B. (Part 2) 627, 632.

Questions

Why should there be a difference between real estate and securities for purposes of asset characterization? What is the importance of the "to customers" language contained in § 1221(1)? Is it because an investor (or a trader) who buys and sells shares to or through stock brokers is not considered to be the customer of the seller? Is it because price changes in securities occur in a single market, but real estate transactions may involve price changes in different markets?

Sales by Dealers. Normally, sales of securities by dealers, that is, individuals who hold securities primarily for sale to customers in the ordinary course of their trade or business, will generate ordinary income or loss. A person may act both as a dealer in securities for others and as an investor for his own account. Where a securities dealer is acting as an investor for his own account, the dealer may receive capital gains treatment under § 1236, provided that the security in question is clearly identified by the end of the day of acquisition as a security held for investment, the security is not at any time thereafter held by the dealer primarily for sale to customers in the ordinary course of the dealer's trade or business, and the transaction otherwise meets the requirements of the statute. For the purpose of the statute, the term "security" is defined to include notes, bonds, evidences of indebtedness or corporate shares of stock.

4. DEFINITION OF ORDINARY BUSINESS OPERATIONS: TREATMENT OF ITEMS USED IN BUSINESS

Despite the statutory exclusions from the definition of a capital asset, in some instances courts found the statutory approach insufficient. Judicial interpretations provide considerable assistance in defining the term "capital asset."

CORN PRODUCTS REFINING CO.
v. COMMISSIONER

Supreme Court of the United States, 1955.
350 U.S. 46, 76 S.Ct. 20, 100 L.Ed. 29.

MR. JUSTICE CLARK delivered the opinion of the Court.

This case concerns the tax treatment to be accorded certain transactions in commodity futures.[26] In the Tax Court, petitioner Corn Products Refining Company contended that its purchases and sales of corn futures in 1940 and 1942 were capital-asset transactions under [§ 1221]. * * *

Petitioner is a nationally known manufacturer of products made from grain corn. It manufactures starch, syrup, sugar, and their byproducts, feeds and oil. Its average yearly grind of raw corn during the period 1937 through 1942 varied from thirty-five to sixty million bushels. Most of its products were sold under contracts requiring shipment in thirty days at a set price or at market price on the date of delivery, whichever was lower. It permitted cancellation of such contracts, but from experience it could calculate with some accuracy future orders that would remain firm. While it also sold to a few customers on long-term contracts involving substantial orders, these had little effect on the transactions here involved.

In 1934 and again in 1936 droughts in the corn belt caused a sharp increase in the price of spot corn. With a storage capacity of only 2,300,000 bushels of corn, a bare three weeks' supply, Corn Products found itself unable to buy at a price which would permit its refined corn sugar, cerealose, to compete successfully with cane and beet sugar. To avoid a recurrence of this situation, petitioner, in 1937, began to establish a long position in corn futures "as a part of its corn buying program" and "as the most economical method of obtaining an adequate supply of raw corn" without entailing the expenditure of large sums for additional storage facilities. At harvest time each year it would buy futures when the price appeared favorable. It would take delivery on such contracts as it found necessary to its manufacturing operations and sell the remainder in early summer if no shortage was imminent. If shortages appeared, however, it sold futures only as it bought spot corn for grinding. In this manner it reached a balanced position with reference to any increase in spot corn prices. It made no effort to protect itself against a decline in prices.

In 1940 it netted a profit of $680,587.39 in corn futures, but in 1942 it suffered a loss of $109,969.38. In computing its tax liability Corn Products reported these figures as ordinary profit and loss from its manufacturing operations for the respective years. It now contends

26. A commodity future is a contract to purchase some fixed amount of a commodity at a future date for a fixed price. Corn futures, involved in the present case, are in terms of some multiple of five thousand bushels to be delivered eleven months or less after the contract. * * *

that its futures were "capital assets" under [§ 1221] and that gains and losses therefrom should have been treated as arising from the sale of a capital asset. In support of this position it claims that its futures trading was separate and apart from its manufacturing operations and that in its futures transactions it was acting as a "legitimate capitalist". United States v. New York Coffee & Sugar Exchange, 263 U.S. 611, 619, 44 S.Ct. 225, 227, 68 L.Ed. 475. It denies that its futures transactions were "hedges" or "speculative" dealings as covered by the ruling of General Counsel's Memorandum 17322, XV–2 Cum.Bull. 151, and claims that it is in truth "the forgotten man" of that administrative interpretation.

Both the Tax Court and the Court of Appeals found petitioner's futures transactions to be an integral part of its business designed to protect its manufacturing operations against a price increase in its principal raw material and to assure a ready supply for future manufacturing requirements. Corn Products does not level a direct attack on these two-court findings but insists that its futures were "property" entitled to capital-asset treatment under [§ 1221] and as such were distinct from its manufacturing business. We cannot agree.

We find nothing in this record to support the contention that Corn Products' futures activity was separate and apart from its manufacturing operation. On the contrary, it appears that the transactions were vitally important to the company's business as a form of insurance against increases in the price of raw corn. Not only were the purchases initiated for just this reason, but the petitioner's sales policy, selling in the future at a fixed price or less, continued to leave it exceedingly vulnerable to rises in the price of corn. Further, the purchase of corn futures assured the company a source of supply which was admittedly cheaper than constructing additional storage facilities for raw corn. Under these facts it is difficult to imagine a program more closely geared to a company's manufacturing enterprise or more important to its successful operation.

Likewise the claim of Corn Products that it was dealing in the market as a "legitimate capitalist" lacks support in the record. There can be no quarrel with a manufacturer's desire to protect itself against increasing costs of raw materials. Transactions which provide such protection are considered a legitimate form of insurance. United States v. New York Coffee & Sugar Exchange, 263 U.S. at page 619, 44 S.Ct. at page 227; Browne v. Thorn, 260 U.S. 137, 139–140, 43 S.Ct. 36, 37, 67 L.Ed. 171. However, in labeling its activity as that of a "legitimate capitalist" exercising "good judgment" in the futures market, petitioner ignores the testimony of its own officers that in entering that market the company was "trying to protect a part of [its] manufacturing costs"; that its entry was not for the purpose of "speculating and buying and selling corn futures" but to fill an actual "need for the quantity of corn [bought] * * * in order to cover * * * what [products] we expected to market over a period of fifteen or eighteen months." It matters not whether the label be that of "legitimate capitalist" or "speculator"; this is not the talk of the capital investor but of the far-sighted manufacturer. For tax purposes petitioner's purchases have been found to "constitute an integral part of its manufacturing business" by both the Tax Court and the Court of Appeals, and on essentially factual questions the findings of two courts should not ordinarily be disturbed. Comstock v. Group of Institutional Investors, 335 U.S. 211, 214, 68 S.Ct. 1454, 1456, 92 L.Ed. 1911.

Petitioner also makes much of the conclusion by both the Tax Court and the Court of Appeals that its transactions did not constitute "true hedging." It is true that Corn Products did not secure complete protection from its market operations. Under its sales policy petitioner could not guard against a fall in prices. It is clear, however, that petitioner feared the possibility of a price rise more than that of a price decline. It therefore purchased partial insurance against its principal risk, and hoped to retain sufficient flexibility to avoid serious losses on a declining market.

Nor can we find support for petitioner's contention that hedging is not within the exclusions of [§ 1221]. Admittedly, petitioner's corn futures do not come within the literal language of the exclusions set out in that section. They were not stock in trade, actual inventory, property held for sale to customers or depreciable property used in a trade or business. But the capital-asset provision of [§ 1221] must not be so broadly applied as to defeat rather than further the purpose of Congress. Burnet v. Harmel, 287 U.S. 103, 108, 53 S.Ct. 74, 76, 77 L.Ed. 199. Congress intended that profits and losses arising from the everyday operation of a business be considered as ordinary income or loss rather than capital gain or loss. The [former] preferential treatment provided by [§ 1221] applies to transactions in property which are not the normal source of business income. It was intended "to relieve the taxpayer from * * * excessive tax burdens on gains resulting from a conversion of capital investments, and to remove the deterrent effect of those burdens on such conversions." Burnet v. Harmel, 287 U.S. at page 106, 53 S.Ct. at page 75. Since this section is an exception from the normal tax requirements of the Internal Revenue Code, the definition of a capital asset must be narrowly applied and its exclusions interpreted broadly. This is necessary to effectuate the basic congressional purpose. This Court has always construed narrowly the term "capital assets" in [§ 1221]. See Hort v. Commissioner, 313 U.S. 28, 31, 61 S.Ct. 757, 758, 85 L.Ed. 1168 * * *.

The problem of the appropriate tax treatment of hedging transactions first arose under the 1934 Tax Code revision. Thereafter the Treasury issued G.C.M. 17322, supra, distinguishing speculative transactions in commodity futures from hedging transactions. It held that hedging transactions were essentially to be regarded as insurance rather than a dealing in capital assets and that gains and losses therefrom were ordinary business gains and losses. The interpretation outlined in this memorandum has been consistently followed by the courts as well as by the Commissioner. While it is true that this Court has not passed on its validity, it has been well recognized for 20 years; and Congress has made no change in it though the Code has been re-enacted on three subsequent occasions. This bespeaks congressional approval. Helvering v. Winmill, 305 U.S. 79, 83, 59 S.Ct. 45, 46, 83 L.Ed. 52. * * *

We believe that the statute clearly refutes the contention of Corn Products. Moreover, it is significant to note that practical considerations lead to the same conclusion. To hold otherwise would permit those engaged in hedging transactions to transmute ordinary income into capital gain at will. The hedger may either sell the future and purchase in the spot market or take delivery under the future contract itself. But if a sale of the future created a capital transaction while delivery of the commodity under the same future did not, a loophole in the statute would be created and the purpose of Congress frustrated.

The judgment is affirmed.

Affirmed.

MR. JUSTICE HARLAN took no part in the consideration or decision of this case.

Questions

1. Could the Supreme Court in Corn Products have reached the same result using the statutory definition of a capital asset? Consider § 1221(1).

2. Who will more often use the Corn Products doctrine, the Commissioner or the taxpayer?

In Commissioner v. Bagley & Sewall Co., 221 F.2d 944 (2d Cir.1955), the court classified what was essentially a capital asset transaction as a business transaction because of its close relationship to the taxpayer's everyday business operations. The taxpayer had purchased government bonds to post as security for a contract it had with its customer. The government bonds were purchased instead of paying a surety premium to a surety company. Since the purpose for the purchase of the bonds was entirely related to the conduct of its business and was not made as an investment, the court treated what would normally be a capital loss as giving rise to an ordinary loss.

In some situations the taxpayer's purpose for holding an asset may change or he may evidence a dual purpose. When stock initially required for business purposes is later retained solely as an investment, any gain or loss on the disposition of the stock is capital. In Gulftex Drug Co. v. Commissioner, 29 T.C. 118 (1957), affirmed per curiam 261 F.2d 238 (5th Cir.1958), the Tax Court stated "the purpose for which stock is owned and held can change, and the purpose at the time of sale is determinative of the effect of the sale for tax purposes."

W.W. WINDLE CO. v. COMMISSIONER
Tax Court of the United States, 1976.
65 T.C. 694, appeal dismissed 550 F.2d 43 (1st Cir.1977), cert. denied
431 U.S. 966, 97 S.Ct. 2923, 53 L.Ed.2d 1062 (1977).

[The taxpayer, a company engaged in wool processing, acquired 72% of the stock of another corporation, Nor-West Fabrics, Inc. for the principal purpose of obtaining a captive buyer for its supply of raw wool. The stock of Nor-West subsequently became worthless, and the taxpayer claimed an ordinary loss based on Corn Products. The Tax Court held that although "petitioner's principal motive was to acquire a captive customer, it had a substantial subsidiary investment motive, which prevented it from being entitled to an ordinary loss." (65 T.C. at 704). The court reasoned as follows (65 T.C. at 712–714):]

There are persuasive arguments on either side of the question. At first blush it appears reasonable and in line with the resolution of analogous questions in other areas that the predominant motive for acquiring the asset should determine the character of the asset in the taxpayer's hands, and that if it is a business motive, the existence of a secondary investment motive should not make the asset a capital asset. Cf. United States v. Generes, 405 U.S. 93 (1972); Malat v. Riddell, 383 U.S. 569 (1966). Such an interpretation also seemingly gives effect to the Supreme Court's admonition that exclusions from the definition of capital asset should be broadly construed. *Corn Products Refining Co. v. Commissioner,* supra at 52. * * *

On the other hand, we deal here with a judge-made addition to the statutory categories of noncapital assets, and we are not compelled by the case law to broaden such categories more than is required under a fair reading of *Corn Products* and other precedents. *Corn Products* dealt with commodity futures, not stock. Its doctrine has frequently been applied to shares of stock, and cases such as Waterman, Largen & Co. [, 419 F.2d 845 (Ct.Cl.1969), cert. denied 400 U.S. 869 (1970)] are fairly close on their facts to ours. * * *

Nor are our own precedents controlling, as in no reported decision have we yet squarely faced and ruled upon the mixed-motive situation. * * *

We are ultimately persuaded to hold that stock purchased with a substantial investment purpose is a capital asset even if there is a more substantial business motive for the purchase. There are two basic reasons for this holding. In the first place, to expand the statutory exceptions to "capital assets" into a mixed-motive case will be greatly to enlarge the far more limited category of noncapital assets which would otherwise exist. We would thereby be even more greatly expanding the "gray area" of uncertainty and controversy. Taxpayers would be presented with enlarged opportunities to claim ordinary losses on unsuccessful investments and [previously preferential] capital gains on successful ones. And they would be put to their proof by respondent with respect to their subjective intent upon claiming [previously preferential] capital gains on disposition of a wide array of successful (albeit business-related) stock investments. For example, most investments in foreign subsidiaries, which usually have an important degree of business integration with their parents, would pass into the gray area. Where given a choice, we should rule on the side of predictability.

Secondly, in the last analysis, Congress has decided what is a capital asset, and there must be limits to the liberties we can take with the statutory language of section 1221. Words are not infinitely elastic. Giving full effect to the Supreme Court's admonition in *Corn Products* that the statutory exclusion from the definition of capital assets should be broadly construed, we nevertheless must read that in light of the close relation to inventory of the assets in question in that case.

As we move from inventory-related corn futures to a more traditional form of capital asset, such as stock, we should be more reluctant to be innovative in further broadening the domain of subjective analysis and unpredictability. Accordingly, we hold that where a substantial investment motive exists in a predominantly business-motivated acquisition of corporate stock, such stock is a capital asset.

The next question is whether the subsequent effective abandonment of any investment motive as hard times befell Nor-West will change the result. We hold that it will not. To determine otherwise would put the taxpayer with mixed motives in a "heads I win, tails you lose" position, under which a successful investment would give rise to a capital gain, an unsuccessful one to an ordinary loss. The net effect would be to provide for business-related corporate stock tax treatment similar to that which Congress provided in section 1231 for assets *other* than such stock. We do not believe the *Corn Products* doctrine calls for such a result.[28]

The Internal Revenue Service announced that it would follow Windle when there is a "substantial" investment motive. Rev.Rul. 78–94, 1978–1 C.B. 58.

As the Tax Court noted in W.W. Windle, prior holdings of the Claims Court on this issue "are equivocal and recent Court of Claims authority can be cited for either [side]." (65 T.C. at 712) Compare Agway, Inc. v. United States, 207 Ct.Cl. 682, 524 F.2d 1194 (1975) (there was a substantial investment motive as well as the need to acquire a

28. In the converse situation, stock which is originally purchased for a business purpose can become a capital asset when the business motive disappears, leaving pure investment intent for continued retention. E.g., Missisquoi Corp., 37 T.C. 791 (1962). This result is not, however, inconsistent with the views we have expressed. It illustrates the fact that corporate stock is normally a capital asset, and that only where both original purpose of acquisition and the reason for continued retention are both devoid of substantial investment intent should the stock be treated otherwise.

source of supply and the court stated: " * * * Corn Products will be applied in this Court to purchases of company stock to obtain a source of supply, only if there is no substantial investment intent." 524 F.2d at 1201) with Union Pacific Railroad Co., Inc. v. United States, 208 Ct. Cl. 1, 524 F.2d 1343 (1975) (where stock in certain subsidiary railroad corporations did not constitute capital assets in the hands of the parent railroad corporation because "the acquisition of the stock can not be treated as a mere investment unrelated to the business operations of the plaintiff. It was accomplished for an operating, business purpose and the stock was held as part of the operation of plaintiff's business as a railroad." 524 F.2d at 1359).

The Windle rule was followed in Wright v. Commissioner, 756 F.2d 1039 (4th Cir.1985), where the court denied an employee an ordinary loss deduction on the sale of stock in his employer's business that he purchased to comply with his employer's desire that top management have an equity investment in the business. The court emphasized the taxpayer's testimony that he would have expected to pay taxes under the former preferential capital gain rates if the stock rose in value, as evidence of his investment purpose on the acquisition of the stock. The court also indicated that there was no evidence that the taxpayer had to buy the stock as a condition of employment, although he was urged to do so by a controlling shareholder.

Reference: LeMaster, Corporate Securities Losses: Is Corn Products Now Irrelevant?, 3 J.Corp.Tax. 141 (1976).

Question

What reasons did the court in Windle give to support its conclusion? Can you think of any other reasons in support of the court's decision?

Problems

1. Newspaper Corporation was having difficulty obtaining newsprint. To assure a supply of newsprint during a period of shortage, Newspaper Corporation purchased all of the shares of a paper manufacturer for $1,000,000.

What result:

(a) If after two years, the newsprint shortage ended and Newspaper Corporation sold the shares to a third party for $1,500,000? What if the stock was sold for $500,000? Consider the Corn Products case.

(b) If after the shortage of newsprint abated, the shares were worth $1,250,000 but Newspaper Corporation held the shares for 10 additional years and then sold the shares for $500,000? The stock was traded on a stock exchange and could have been sold at anytime.

2. You represent a bank that wants to purchase all of the shares of a corporation which now provides quick and reliable credit information to the bank and many other businesses. Business reasons exist for the purchase. Specifically, the information services are required by the bank

for its credit card program. The bank could provide funds to this corporation to automate its own operations assuring the information services needed for the bank's credit card program. After the acquisition, the bank would not only receive the credit information services more cheaply than other businesses but also have preferential access to the services. The bank also regards the shares as a good investment and foresees the possibility of a sale of the stock at a profit in three to five years. Consumer credit, an area closely related to banking, is a rapidly growing field. The bank is aware that a number of offers for this corporation's stock have been made. No dividends have been or are likely to be paid on this corporation's shares. Consider the Windle case. Can the purchase of the shares be structured to assure ordinary loss treatment?

5. PROPERTY USED IN A TRADE OR BUSINESS

Under § 1221(2) capital assets do not include real property (whether or not depreciable) used in the taxpayer's trade or business or depreciable personal property so used. These items, however, are characterized as quasi capital assets under § 1231. Non-depreciable personal property (for example, goodwill) used in a trade or business is not within the ambit of § 1221(2) and thus constitutes a capital asset.

Section 1221(2) presents two definitional questions, first, what is a trade or business and, second, when is property used in the taxpayer's trade or business. If the taxpayer owns an apartment house, the extent of the taxpayer's management activities with respect to the property can put the taxpayer in the real estate rental business. The management of an apartment house, whether or not delegated to an agent, involves finding and negotiating with tenants, collecting rents, and maintaining the property. Therefore, the apartment house is not a capital asset. Fackler v. Commissioner, 133 F.2d 509 (6th Cir.1943). See also Alvary v. United States, 302 F.2d 790 (2d Cir.1962), where two rental apartment houses managed by an agent constituted a trade or business.

But courts differ on whether the rental of a single-family dwelling constitutes a trade or business under § 1221(2). In Hazard v. Commissioner, 7 T.C. 372 (1946) (Acq. 1946–2 C.B. 3) the rental of a single-family home was held "property used in a trade or business." Yet other courts have not regarded the rental of one piece of real property as constituting a trade or business because of the lack of regular and continuous management activity. Grier v. United States, 120 F.Supp. 395 (D.Conn.1954), affirmed per curiam 218 F.2d 603 (2d Cir.1955).

6. SECTION 1231: QUASI CAPITAL ASSETS

The exclusion in § 1221(2) from the definition of capital assets for land and depreciable property used in taxpayer's trade or business seems astonishing until § 1231 is examined. Essentially, § 1231 bestows long-term capital gain treatment on gains attributable to appreciation in value of non-capital assets and on gains from capital assets that fail to satisfy the technical "sale or exchange" requirement of

§ 1222. Section 1231 may result in ordinary loss treatment on losses attributable to the decline in value of non-capital assets.

It should be noted that § 1231 only determines the character of already recognized gains and losses. Before the characterization question is reached, the taxpayer must determine whether the gain is recognized or whether the loss is allowed. Only after this recognition determination is made need a taxpayer determine the character of a gain or loss. For example, where § 267 disallows losses incurred on transactions between related taxpayers, there is no need to determine the character of that loss.

As can be seen in §§ 1231(a)(3) and 1231(b), the coverage of § 1231 extends only to recognized gains and losses in the following transactions: (1) the sale or exchange of property used in a taxpayer's trade or business, (2) the compulsory or involuntary conversion of property used in a taxpayer's trade or business, and (3) the compulsory or involuntary conversion of taxpayer's capital assets used in his trade or business or investment activity. In reading § 1231, the definition of § 1231 property in § 1231(b)(1) includes business property subject to the allowance for depreciation under § 167. A cross reference to § 167(a) is necessary to see that under § 167(a) the § 168 deduction is treated as a deduction under § 167. It should be noted that any asset held for six months or less (one year or less after 1987) is not covered by § 1231. The reason is simple. There is no need to give the capital gains preference to what would otherwise be a short-term capital gain. Prior to the 1984 legislation, § 1231 also covered transactions involving a taxpayer's personal capital assets. The characterization of a taxpayer's recognized gains and losses on his personal capital assets is now separately determined under § 165(h)(2)(B). Finally, for purposes of § 1231, § 1231(a)(4)(B) treats losses of property where there is no conversion of the property into other property or money as compulsory or involuntary conversions. See Reg. § 1.1231-1(e)(1). However, there is an exception under § 1231(a)(4)(C) for casualty losses of trade or business and investment property, automatically treating these losses and gains as ordinary if the aggregate of these casualties is a net loss.

Certain recognized gains on depreciable trade or business property are excluded from § 1231 if they are treated as ordinary income under §§ 1245 or 1250 or other recapture provisions. §§ 1245(d) and 1250(i). Gains on sales reported on the installment method under § 453 are included in § 1231 only to the extent of that portion recognized in the current tax year. The character of the gain from the installment payment depends on what other § 1231 gains and losses are reported in that year. The limitation imposed by § 1211 on the deductibility of recognized capital losses is generally ignored for purposes of § 1231. However, if § 1231 characterizes a loss as a long-term capital loss, then the taxpayer must ascertain how much of that capital loss is currently deductible under § 1211(b).

Having made a determination as to those recognized gains and losses falling within the application of the § 1231 characterization rules, the next step in the process is to determine whether the taxpayer has an aggregate net gain or net loss from all of his § 1231 transactions. If there is an aggregate net gain, then each gain is characterized as a long-term capital gain and each loss is characterized as a long-term capital loss. § 1231(a)(1). If a taxpayer's transactions are characterized as long-term capital gains and losses, they are then treated as such along with all of taxpayer's capital gains and losses (both long-term and short-term) from the sale or exchange of taxpayer's capital assets. And the usual rules for capital gains and losses described at pp. 903–908 in this chapter are applied. If the taxpayer has an aggregate net loss from all of his § 1231 transactions (or his gains equal his losses) then each transaction is considered to give rise to an ordinary gain or an ordinary loss. § 1231(a)(2). The ordinary gain on a § 1231 transaction is included in gross income, and the ordinary loss on a § 1231 transaction is taken as a deduction from gross income, the determination as to whether it is an itemized deduction being made from the nature of the underlying transaction. For example, if a taxpayer's only § 1231 transaction was the theft of a bearer bond held as an investment, the loss would be treated as an ordinary loss and a determination would have to be made whether this loss was described in § 62 so that it could be used in computing adjusted gross income.

Proper planning of the sale of trade or business assets could give a taxpayer capital gain treatment for his gains and ordinary loss treatment for his losses. A taxpayer could manipulate the mechanics of § 1231, specifically the voluntary nature of most § 1231 transactions, to give him this favorable result by bunching sales of appreciated property in one year (resulting in the characterization of the gains as long-term capital gains) and bunching his sales of trade or business property which had decreased in value into a separate taxable year (resulting in the characterization of the losses as ordinary losses).

Congress was concerned with this manipulation and added § 1231(c) in 1984 to minimize it. Under § 1231(c), the planning tool outlined in the preceding paragraph can now be taken advantage of only once every five years. Thus, if a taxpayer, who has § 1231 losses characterized as ordinary losses in any of his five preceding tax years, will have to treat a similar amount of net § 1231 gains as ordinary income in the (pre-1988) current taxable year. The effect of § 1231(c) is to ignore the annual accounting concept of looking at each year separately; however, § 1231(c) does not recharacterize gains from prior § 1231 transactions. Thus, if a taxpayer sells his loss assets in the current year and receives ordinary loss treatment, prior gains characterized as capital gains are not affected. However, any subsequent § 1231 gains must watch out for the five-year taint of § 1231(c).

Problems

1. Under § 1231, what will be the character of the gains and losses Lola incurs in each of the following (assume the land and business fixture were held for more than one year):

(a) A $4,000 gain on the sale of land used in Lola's business and a $2,000 loss from the sale of a business fixture.

(b) A $4,000 gain from the sale of land used in Lola's business and a $10,000 loss from the sale of a business fixture.

2. For the 1988 taxable year Hal, age 28, has a $50,000 operating profit from his business and is single. He had the following gains and losses from the sale of stocks and bonds, held as capital assets, during the 1988 year:

capital gain $3,000

capital loss $9,500

Hal owned a building used in his business (depreciated pursuant to the straight line method) which he sold during the 1988 year, realizing a gain of $5,000. He also sold his personal residence for a gain of $2,000 and moved into a rental unit on the bay. Some bearer bonds Hal held as an investment, having a cost of $5,000 and a fair market value of $6,000, were stolen. Hal carried no insurance on the bonds. He sold his personal airplane at a loss of $4,000. Finally, Hal sold some equipment used in his business at a loss of $7,500. Hal had other itemized deductions of $3,000.

From these facts compute Hal's gross income, adjusted gross income and taxable income for 1988. Consider §§ 1231, 1221, 1222, 1211(b), 151(b), 165(c). Assume that all the assets were held for more than one year. *Remember* that § 1231 does not include anything in gross income nor authorize a loss. Section 1231 only determines the character of already recognized and allowed gains and losses.

3. What result in "2" above if Hal also had some of his personal furniture destroyed in a fire, which cost $5,000, had a fair market value of $20,000, and was insured for $18,500. In addition, his pleasure boat was destroyed in a storm. The boat, which cost $8,000, had a fair market value of $5,000 and was insured for $4,900. Consider § 165(c)(3), (h)(1) and (h)(2)(B), and Reg. § 1.165–7(b)(1).

4. What result in "2" above if the gain realized on the sale of the building was $8,000 instead?

Exclusions from Section 1231 for "Property Used in the Trade or Business." Note the exclusions under § 1231(b)(1) include inventory, property held by the taxpayer "primarily for sale in the ordinary course of his trade or business," and copyrights held by a taxpayer described in § 1221(3). Also, the sale or exchange of a capital assets (§ 1221) results in capital gains or losses, without the need to resort to § 1231.

How is the Term "Primarily for Sale" Interpreted For Purposes of § 1231?

INTERNATIONAL SHOE MACHINE CORP.
v. UNITED STATES

United States Court of Appeals, First Circuit, 1974.
491 F.2d 157, cert. denied 419 U.S. 834,
95 S.Ct. 59, 42 L.Ed.2d 60 (1974).

[The taxpayer realized ordinary income on the sale of shoe machinery equipment. The taxpayer was willing to sell or rent its machinery depending on the preference of each customer. The taxpayer derived far less income from the sale of equipment than from the leasing of the same type of equipment. However, the sale of equipment constituted a steady source of income for the taxpayer. In concluding that the taxpayer's sales of shoe machinery were held by the taxpayer primarily for sale to customers in the ordinary course of its trade or business, the court stated:]

The case raises what has become a repeating source of difficulty in applying § 1231(b)(1)(B), which denies [the previous] highly favored capital gains tax treatment to "property held * * * primarily for sale to customers in the ordinary course of his trade or business". In particular, does the word "primarily" invoke a contrast between sales and leases, as the appellant contends, or between sales made in the ordinary course of business and non-routine sales made as a liquidation of inventory? And, if the latter, how can sales made in the ordinary course of business be distinguished from a liquidation of inventory?

In support of its contention that "primarily" refers to a contrast between sales and leases, appellant relies upon Malat v. Riddell, 383 U.S. 569, 86 S.Ct. 1030, 16 L.Ed.2d 102 (1966). There, the taxpayer purchased a parcel of land, with the alleged intention of developing an apartment project. When the taxpayer confronted zoning restrictions, he decided to terminate the venture, and sold his interest in the property, claiming a capital gain. The lower courts found, however, that the taxpayer had had a "dual purpose" in acquiring the land, a "substantial" one of which was to sell if that were to prove more profitable than development. Therefore, since the taxpayer had failed to establish that the property was not held primarily for sale to customers in the ordinary course of his business, his gain was treated as ordinary income. The Supreme Court vacated and remanded the case, stating that the lower courts had applied an incorrect legal standard when they defined "primarily" as merely "substantially" rather than using it in its ordinary, everyday sense of "first importance" or "principally". Although the Court in *Malat* was dealing with § 1221, rather than § 1231, the same clause appears in both sections. Appellant argues that the present case is analogous, since the "first" and "principal" reason for holding the shoe machinery was clearly for lease rather than for sale.

We cannot agree that *Malat* is dispositive. Even if "primarily" is defined as "of first importance" or "principally", the word may still invoke a contrast between sales made in the "ordinary course of * * * business" and those made as liquidations of inventory, rather than between leases and sales. *Malat* itself concerned the dual purposes of developing an apartment complex on the land and selling the land. Although these two possible sources of income might be characterized as income from "lease" or "sale", a more meaningful distinction could be made between on-going income generated in the ordinary course of business and income from the termination and sale of the venture. See Continental Can Co. v. United States, 422 F.2d 405, 411 (Ct.Cl.1970); Recordak Corp. v. United States, 325 F.2d 460, 463 (Ct.Cl. 1963).

We recognize that *Recordak,* invoking a contrast between "selling in the ordinary course of business and selling outside that normal course" was cited by the Supreme Court in *Malat* within a footnote which also listed the courts of appeals decisions then in conflict over the meaning of "primarily", supra, 383 U.S. at 571 n. 3, 86 S.Ct. 1030, 16 L.Ed.2d 102. Given, however, that *Recordak* was not directly included within the list, but merely cited as a case which had also addressed the question, we think that *Recordak's* interpretation of the contrast invoked by the word "primarily" remains undisturbed by the Court's opinion. Beyond semantics, an additional justification for the interpretation becomes obvious when one applies appellant's logic to a not unrealistic business situation: to rest the word "primarily" on the distinction between lease and sale income would lead to the absurd result that whenever lease income exceeded sale income on the same item, the sale income could be treated as [the former preferential] capital gain.

The real question, therefore, concerns whether or not the income from the sales of appellant's shoe machinery should have been characterized as having been generated in the "ordinary course of * * * business". Appellant contests the conclusion of the district court that selling was "an accepted and predictable part of the business" by pointing out that sales were made only as a last resort, after attempts to dissuade the customer from purchasing had failed. We think that the district court was correct in its finding. While sales were made only as a last resort, it seems clear that after 1964 such sales were expected to occur, on an occasional basis, and policies and procedures were developed for handling them. Purchase inquiries were referred to the vice president for sales, a price schedule was drawn up, and discounts were offered to good customers. Appellant may not have desired such sales. It is likely that appellant would never have developed a sales policy for its leased machines had it not been forced to do so by the pressure of competition. But it was justifiable to find that such occasional sales were indeed "accepted and predictable".

Even "accepted and predictable" sales might not, however, occur in the "ordinary course of * * * business". For example, a final liquidation of inventory, although accepted and predictable, would normally be eligible for [the former preferential] capital gains treatment. Appellant's final contention, therefore, is that the sales in question represented the liquidation of an investment. Appellant points out that the machines were leased for an average of eight and one half years before they were sold, during which time depreciation was taken on them and repairs were made. Thus, appellant seeks to bring itself within the scope of the "rental-obsolescence" decisions, which hold that the sale of rental equipment, no longer useful for renting, is taxable at [the former preferential] capital gains rates. Hilliard v. Commissioner of Internal Revenue, 281 F.2d 279 (5th Cir.1960); Philber Equipment Corporation v. Commissioner of Internal Revenue, 237 F.2d 129 (3d Cir.1956); Davidson v. Tomlinson, 165 F.Supp. 455 (S.D.Fla.1958).

In the "rental obsolescence" decisions, however, equipment was sold only after its rental income-producing potential had ended and "such sales were * * * the natural conclusion of a vehicle rental business cycle". *Philber,* supra, 237 F.2d at 132. Moreover, the equipment was specifically manufactured to fit the requirements of lessees; it was sold only when lessees no longer found the equipment useful. Id. In the present case, however, the shoe manufacturing equipment was sold, not as a final disposition of property that had ceased to produce rental income for the appellant, but, rather, as property that still retained a rental income producing potential for the appellant. Had appellant chosen not to sell the shoe machinery, the machinery would have continued to generate ordinary income in the form of lease revenue. Thus, the sale of such machinery, for a price which included the present value of that future ordinary income, cannot be considered the liquidation of an investment outside the scope of the "ordinary course of * * * business".

The Service adopted this interpretation of the word "primarily" in Rev.Rul. 80–37, 1980–1 C.B. 51.

Is the Corn Products doctrine applicable to Section 1231 assets? In Hollywood Baseball Association v. Commissioner, 423 F.2d 494 (9th Cir. 1970), cert. denied 400 U.S. 848, 91 S.Ct. 35, 27 L.Ed.2d 85 (1970) a minor league baseball club sold the contracts of its professional baseball players. The court held that the sale of player contracts produced ordinary income. The player contracts constituted property used in the taxpayer's business of providing baseball games to its customers. The taxpayer amortized the cost of each contract over the life of the contract. The contracts were, therefore, section 1231 assets. In applying the Corn Products doctrine to section 1231 assets, the court reasoned that the sale of player contracts was integrally related to the normal conduct of the business of a minor league baseball club. The court indicated:

* * * What is important is that the activities were "integral"— carried on to protect or to allow the function of the taxpayer's true business. * * *

* * *

* * * The player contracts in the case at bar were never sold because the players were no longer fit to play league baseball. Rather, the sales were generally of the more valuable players, whom the majors wanted for their own teams. We are not dealing with the replacement of an obsolete factory, old rental cars, or lost or damaged rental tools. The latter would seem to be the type of activities which the capital asset provisions were intended to cover. Rather, we are dealing with sales pursuant to an agreement which the taxpayer had to sign in order to be able to attract talented ball players—in effect, the "raw materials" or "stock in trade" of the business—in the first place. Such an activity would seem to be as "integral" as one could get. (423 F.2d at 502–503).

However, in Deltide Fishing and Rental Tools, Inc. v. United States, 279 F.Supp. 661, 666 (E.D.La.1968), the court stated that § 1231 creates a "fence of immunity" protecting property used in a trade or business from the Corn Products doctrine.

Question

Should the Corn Products doctrine apply to the sale of any depreciable property because depreciable property used in a trade or business is integral to the business?

Problems

1. The A.V. Davis Corporation, which has a history of subdivision development, has developed ten apartment buildings each with 100 units. The entire development, which is occupied by retired persons, is called Wrinkle City. In the past it has rented these apartments for periods of time running from one to five years. After holding all of the buildings for more than one year, it proposes to sell all ten buildings. What information would you like with respect to §§ 1221 and 1231, to determine whether A.V. Davis Corporation would realize ordinary loss or capital loss? Do not consider the question of depreciation recapture.

2. Sugar Corporation is engaged in the production and refining of sugar. The corporation built and rented 100 houses to its employees who operate the corporation's sugar refinery. Because the rental rate on the houses is insufficient to offset maintenance and other costs and because of charges by the employees' union that the rental of housing is "economic paternalism," the corporation is considering selling the houses and the land. Under § 1231, what is the tax treatment of the loss which will be realized on the sale? Consider the relevance of the Corn Products case.

E. TAX TREATMENT OF COPYRIGHTS

1. WHEN LITERARY INTERESTS ARE CAPITAL ASSETS: THE BASIC APPROACH

Introduction. Problems arising with respect to the treatment of copyright interests may be illustrated by the following example:

> Assume that T is a well-known public figure from the entertainment world, politics, or sports. T is not a professional writer. T prepares an autobiography at a cost of $1,000 for stenographic, typing and incidental expenses; T sells all of the rights to it for $100,000. Should the $99,000 in excess of basis represent ordinary income or capital gains? Is this gain attributable to appreciation in value?

Under § 1221(3), the sale of a copyright, a literary, musical or artistic composition, or similar property by its creator will not give rise to capital gains, but instead will create ordinary income. Proceeds from the sale of a copyright indirectly represent compensation for services. Ordinary income also results to a transferee (for example, a donee by gift or a corporation controlled by an author) on a subsequent sale of the copyright by such transferee "in whose hands the basis of such property is determined * * * by reference to the basis * * *" of the creator. § 1221(3)(C). It should be noted that a copyright, a literary, musical or artistic composition may not be a § 1231 asset, at least on a sale by the taxpayer-creator. § 1231(b)(1)(C).

But, if the author of the copyright sells it in an arm's length transaction to a third party, who does not hold the property primarily for sale to customers (§ 1221(3)) (or as depreciable property used in the purchaser's business (unless held primarily for sale to customers) (§ 1231(b))) and who pays a sum equivalent to its fair market value at the time of the purchase, the purchaser can thereafter sell the copyright and receive the previously preferential capital gains treatment or the present capital loss treatment. Because it is extremely difficult to measure the fair market value of a book, play, musical composition, libretto, or other literary composition until it has actually been placed on the market, some authors and composers have been known to sell their interests in the item they have created to members of their family in a transaction which is not tax free, in order to avoid the restrictions of § 1221(3). Thus the "purchaser" pays a minimum price, and the "purchaser" realizes capital gains (or capital losses) on a subsequent sale. This device will survive scrutiny by the Internal Revenue Service and the courts only where the price at which the item was "sold" can be established by the taxpayer as fairly representative of its fair market value at that time.

Thus, copyrights and other literary and artistic creations may be capital assets in the hands of purchasers, unless subject to §§ 1221(1) or (2) and 1231(b)(1)(A) or (B) which deny capital asset or quasi capital asset status. Whether their disposition is a sale or exchange is determined by the same tests as those applied to patents. The transfer of the exclusive right to use copyrighted material in a particular medium for the remaining term of the copyright is deemed a sale even if payments are made in the form of a royalty based on future sales, performances given, or exhibitions made, or if the "receipts are payable over a period generally coterminous with the grantee's use of the copyrighted work." Rev.Rul. 60–226, 1960–1, C.B. 26, 27.

Properties Similar to That Described in Statute. Section 1221(3) includes the phrase "property similar" to the specific items described. The Regulations interpret this term to include such items as a theatrical production, a radio program, a cartoon strip, or any other property eligible for copyright protection under statute or common law. Reg. § 1.1221–1(c). The motion picture rights to "Francis," the talking mule, were held a "literary composition," even if not subject to copyright. Stern v. United States, 164 F.Supp. 847 (E.D.La.1958), affirmed per curiam 262 F.2d 957 (5th Cir.1959), cert. denied 359 U.S. 969, 79 S.Ct. 880, 3 L.Ed.2d 836 (1959).

F. TRANSACTIONS IN DEPRECIABLE PROPERTY BETWEEN RELATED PARTIES

Section 1239 governs direct and indirect sales of depreciable property between related parties. This section covers sales or exchanges between an individual and his controlled corporation. § 1239(b)(1) and (c).

Problem

Vivian has a $750,000 capital loss carryover she has been unable to deduct because of § 1211(b). She owns an apartment building (depreciated under the straight line method) with a basis of $250,000 and a value of $1,000,000. If she sells the entire building as a whole, she will realize and recognize a $750,000 capital gain. However, if she converts the building to condominiums and sells each unit separately, she can eventually expect to receive $1,500,000 for her building. However, she is aware that by converting the building and marketing the units as individual condominiums, she faces the strong possibility of converting the building to stock in trade as discussed in Biedenharn at pp. 948–959, with the result that her entire $1,250,000 gain will be ordinary income. In order to preserve her $750,000 capital gain, she sells the building for $1 million to a corporation in which she owns 93% of the stock. The other 7% of the stock is owned by a real estate broker who will convert the building to condos and market them for sale. In this manner Vivian expects to preserve her capital gain of $750,000 and will treat the additional amount she nets over the $1 million as ordinary income. The $1 million price is to be paid out in installments as each condo is sold. Will § 1239 foil Vivian's scheme? What if, instead of a building, Vivian owned an undeveloped parcel of land? Would the result be any different if Vivian sold the building or the land to a partnership she controlled? Examine § 707(b)(2).

G. CORRELATION WITH PRIOR TRANSACTIONS

A current transaction can be correlated with the tax consequences of a related prior transaction to characterize the current year's gain (or loss) as ordinary or capital. In Year 1, assume the taxpayer recognized losses on the sale of § 1231 assets used in his business. Because the taxpayer had no gain on § 1231 assets during that year, the taxpayer deducted the losses as ordinary. In Year 5, the taxpayer received reimbursement for the losses he recognized in Year 1. The reimbursement was paid as part of a settlement of the taxpayer's claim for antitrust violations. The reimbursement constituted income to the taxpayer under the tax benefit doctrine. In Bresler v. Commissioner, 65 T.C. 182 (1975), the issue was the character of the income. The court treated the reimbursement as ordinary income in the year recovered because the taxpayer deducted the losses recognized in Year 1 as ordinary loss. The court did not permit the taxpayer to characterize the reimbursement as a § 1231 gain in the year recovered.

ARROWSMITH v. COMMISSIONER

Supreme Court of the United States, 1952.
344 U.S. 6, 73 S.Ct. 71, 97 L.Ed. 6.

MR. JUSTICE BLACK delivered the opinion of the Court.

This is an income tax controversy growing out of the following facts as shown by findings of the Tax Court. In 1937 two taxpayers, petitioners here, decided to liquidate and divide the proceeds of a corporation in which they had equal stock ownership. Partial distributions made in 1937, 1938, and 1939 were followed by a final one in 1940. Petitioners reported the profits obtained from this transaction, classifying them as [then preferential] capital gains. They thereby paid less income tax than would have been required had the income been attributed to ordinary business transactions for profit. About the propriety of these 1937–1940 returns, there is no dispute. But in 1944 a judgment was rendered against the old corporation and against Frederick R. Bauer, individually. The two taxpayers were required to and did pay the judgment for the corporation, of whose assets they were transferees. Classifying the loss as an ordinary business one, each took a tax deduction for 100% of the amount paid. Treatment of the loss as a capital one would have allowed deduction of a much smaller amount. The Commissioner viewed the 1944 payment as part of the original liquidation transaction requiring classification as a capital loss, just as the taxpayers had treated the original dividends as capital gains. Disagreeing with the Commissioner the Tax Court classified the 1944 payment as an ordinary business loss. 15 T.C. 876. Disagreeing with the Tax Court the Court of Appeals reversed, treating the loss as "capital." 2 Cir., 193 F.2d 734. This latter holding conflicts with the Third Circuit's holding in Commissioner of Internal Revenue v. Switlik,

184 F.2d 299. Because of this conflict, we granted certiorari. 343 U.S. 976, 72 S.Ct. 1075.

[Section 165(f)] treats losses from sales or exchanges of capital assets as "capital losses" and [§ 331] requires that liquidation distributions be treated as exchanges. The losses here fall squarely within the definition of "capital losses" contained in these sections. Taxpayers were required to pay the judgment because of liability imposed on them as transferees of liquidation distribution assets. And it is plain that their liability as transferees was not based on any ordinary business transaction of theirs apart from the liquidation proceedings. It is not even denied that had this judgment been paid after liquidation, but during the year 1940, the losses would have been properly treated as capital ones. For payment during 1940 would simply have reduced the amount of capital gains taxpayers received during that year.

It is contended, however, that this payment which would have been a capital transaction in 1940 was transformed into an ordinary business transaction in 1944 because of the well-established principle that each taxable year is a separate unit for tax accounting purposes. United States v. Lewis, 340 U.S. 590, 71 S.Ct. 522, 95 L.Ed. 560; North American Oil Consolidated v. Burnet, 286 U.S. 417, 52 S.Ct. 613, 76 L.Ed. 1197. But this principle is not breached by considering all the 1937–1944 liquidation transaction events in order properly to classify the nature of the 1944 loss for tax purposes. Such an examination is not an attempt to reopen and readjust the 1937 to 1940 tax returns, an action that would be inconsistent with the annual tax accounting principle.

* * *

Affirmed.

MR. JUSTICE DOUGLAS, dissenting.

I agree with MR. JUSTICE JACKSON that these losses should be treated as ordinary, not capital, losses. There were no capital transactions in the year in which the losses were suffered. Those transactions occurred and were accounted for in earlier years in accord with the established principle that each year is a separate unit for tax accounting purposes. See United States v. Lewis, 340 U.S. 590, 71 S.Ct. 522, 95 L.Ed. 560. I have not felt, as my dissent in the Lewis case indicates, that the law made that an inexorable principle. But if it is the law, we should require observance of it—not merely by taxpayers but by the government as well. We should force each year to stand on its own footing, whoever may gain or lose from it in a particular case. We impeach that principle when we treat this year's losses as if they diminished last year's gains.

MR. JUSTICE JACKSON, whom MR. JUSTICE FRANKFURTER joins, dissenting.

This problem arises only because the judgment was rendered in a taxable year subsequent to the liquidation.

Had the liability of the transferor-corporation been reduced to judgment during the taxable year in which liquidation occurred, or prior thereto, this problem, under the tax laws, would not arise. The amount of the judgment rendered against the corporation would have decreased the amount it had available for distribution which would have reduced the liquidating dividends proportionately and diminished the capital gains taxes assessed against the stockholders. Probably it would also have decreased the corporation's own taxable income.

Congress might have allowed, under such circumstances, tax returns of the prior year to be reopened or readjusted so as to give the same tax results as would have obtained had the liability become known prior to liquidation. Such a solution is foreclosed to us and the alternatives left are to regard the judgment liability fastened by operation of law on the transferee as an ordinary loss for the year of adjudication or to regard it as a capital loss for such year.

This Court simplifies the choice to one of reading the English language, and declares that the losses here come "squarely within" the definition of capital losses contained within two sections of the Internal Revenue Code. What seems so clear to this Court was not seen at all by the Tax Court, in this case or in earlier consideration of the same issue; nor was it grasped by the Court of Appeals for the Third Circuit. Commissioner of Internal Revenue v. Switlik, 1950, 184 F.2d 299.

I find little aid in the choice of alternatives from arguments based on equities. One enables the taxpayer to deduct the amount of the judgment against his ordinary income which might be taxed as high as 87% [under then applicable tax rates] while if the liability had been assessed against the corporation prior to liquidation it would have reduced his capital gain which was taxable at only 25% [under the then applicable tax preference]. The consequence may readily be characterized as a windfall (regarding a windfall as anything that is left to a taxpayer after the collector has finished with him).

On the other hand, adoption of the contrary alternative may penalize the taxpayer because of two factors: (1) [limitations on the deductibility of capital losses against ordinary income]; and (2) had the liability been discharged by the corporation, a portion of it would probably in effect have been paid by the Government, since the corporation could have taken it as a deduction, while here the total liability comes out of the pockets of the stockholders.

Solicitude for the revenues is a plausible but treacherous basis upon which to decide a particular tax case. A victory may have implications which in future cases will cost the Treasury more than a defeat. This might be such a case, for anything I know. Suppose that subsequent to liquidation it is found that a corporation has undisclosed claims instead of liabilities and that under applicable state law they may be prosecuted for the benefit of the stockholders. The logic of the Court's decision here, if adhered to, would result in a lesser return to the Government than if the recoveries were considered ordinary income. Would it be so clear that this is a capital loss if the shoe were on the other foot?

Where the statute is so indecisive and the importance of a particular holding lies in its rational and harmonious relation to the general scheme of the tax law, I think great deference is due the twice-expressed judgment of the Tax Court. June 25, 1948, * * * [which] is a more competent and steady influence toward a systematic body of tax law than our sporadic omnipotence in a field beset with invisible boomerangs. I should reverse, in reliance upon the Tax Court's judgment more, perhaps, than my own.

Questions

1. What principle does the Arrowsmith case stand for? How does the Arrowsmith principle relate to the tax benefit theory and the claim of right doctrine?

2. Assume Taxpayer reports an ordinary loss on the sale of a § 1231 asset in Year 1 and that was his only § 1231 transaction for Year 1. In Year 4, Taxpayer receives a further payment for the asset previously sold in Year 1. Consider the following alternative tax consequences:

(a) the subsequent payment inherits *all* of the characteristics of the earlier transaction so that the subsequent payment is treated as ordinary income in Year 4 regardless of Taxpayer's other § 1231 transactions in Year 4;

(b) the subsequent payment is characterized by the § 1231 hotchpot in Year 1, but only after the Year 1 hotchpot is recalculated to include the Year 4 payment;

(c) the subsequent payment is treated as a § 1231 transaction in Year 4 and goes into the § 1231 hotchpot in Year 4.

Which alternative did the court in the Bresler case adopt? Which alternative should it have adopted? Consider the Arrowsmith case, § 1231, and the annual accounting concept.

––––––––

The Arrowsmith doctrine is used to characterize the gain eventually reported by the seller in an open transaction, such as Burnet v. Logan at page 753 of Chapter 11. This was the approach used in Commissioner v. Carter, 170 F.2d 911 (2d Cir.1948). In Carter, a shareholder, in return for surrendering her stock in a corporate liquidation, received cash plus oil brokerage contracts that had no ascertainable value. The court characterized the gain eventually reported under the open transaction as a preferential capital gain using language reminiscent of Arrowsmith. It is interesting to note that the open transaction cases never quote Arrowsmith when the very definition of an open transaction is encompassed by the definition of an Arrowsmith type transaction.

In Woodward v. Commissioner, 397 U.S. 572, 90 S.Ct. 1302, 25 L.Ed. 2d 577 (1970), the Supreme Court applied an Arrowsmith approach.

The taxpayer paid legal expenses in appraisal proceedings in connection with the purchase of dissenting shareholder's stock. The Court recognized that such costs incurred in connection with the acquisition of an asset must be added to the basis. But what if the legal fees were incurred in a later year, after the initial transaction takes place? The Arrowsmith case justifies looking back to the original transaction to determine the character of the later payment.

This brings us to the cases, such as Cummings v. Commissioner, 61 T.C. 1 (1973), reversed 506 F.2d 449 (2d Cir.1974), cert. denied 421 U.S. 913, 95 S.Ct. 1571, 43 L.Ed.2d 779 (1975), where corporate insiders had to make payments constituting the repayment of insider profits for violations of § 16(b) of the Securities Exchange Act of 1934. In these cases the taxpayers made a profit dealing in their employer's stock. In Cummings, the Tax Court allowed an ordinary deduction. The appellate court reversed holding that the deduction must take its character from the transaction that generated the insider profits, a transaction in a capital asset. The better view, perhaps, would be to treat the § 16(b) payments as an adjustment to basis.

Reference: Schenk, Arrowsmith and its Progeny: Tax Characterization by Reference to Past Events, 33 Rutgers L.Rev. 317 (1981); Rabinovitz, Effect of Prior Year's Transactions on Federal Income Tax Consequences of Current Receipts or Payments, 28 Tax L.Rev. 85 (1972).

H. WHEN "PROPERTY" IS NOT "PROPERTY": SUBSTITUTES FOR ORDINARY INCOME

We have noted that a "capital asset" is defined as "property" held by the taxpayer. § 1221. Thus, "property" might include any item, tangible or intangible, to which incidents of ownership might attach. The statute does not define the term; the Regulations recite only that the term "capital assets" includes all classes of property not specifically excluded by § 1221. Reg. § 1.1221–1(a). Consider the following judicial interpretation.

HORT v. COMMISSIONER
Supreme Court of the United States, 1941.
313 U.S. 28, 61 S.Ct. 757, 85 L.Ed. 1168.

[[T]he taxpayer inherited a lot and an office building by devise from his father. The main floor and basement of the building had been leased to a bank, the Irving Trust Co., for 15 years at annual rental of $25,000. With 13 years remaining on the lease, the bank entered into negotiations with the taxpayer to cancel the lease because maintaining a branch in the taxpayer's building was unprofitable. The taxpayer agreed to cancel the lease in consideration of the payment of $140,000 in cash. The taxpayer reported a loss from the transaction of approximately $21,000 representing the difference between the present value of the future rental payments under the lease ($161,000) and the fair rental value of the space for the unexpired term of the lease (presumably $140,000). In upholding the Commissioner's determination to treat the $140,000 as ordinary income the Supreme Court stated:]

Petitioner apparently contends that the amount received for cancellation of the lease was capital rather than ordinary income and that it was therefore subject to [the provisions of the Code] which govern capital gains and losses. Further, he argues that even if that amount must be reported as ordinary gross income he sustained a loss which [§ 165(a)] authorizes him to deduct. We cannot agree.

The amount received by petitioner for cancellation of the lease must be included in his gross income in its entirety. * * * [Section 61(a)] reached the rent paid prior to cancellation just as it would have embraced subsequent payments if the lease had never been canceled. It would have included a prepayment of the discounted value of unmatured rental payments whether received at the inception of the lease or at any time thereafter. Similarly, it would have extended to the proceeds of a suit to recover damages had the Irving Trust Co. breached the lease instead of concluding a settlement. Compare Burnet v. Sanford & Brooks Co., 282 U.S. 359, 51 S.Ct. 150, 75 L.Ed. 383. That the amount petitioner received resulted from negotiations ending in cancellation of the lease rather than from a suit to enforce it cannot alter the fact that basically the payment was merely a substitute for the rent reserved in the lease. So far as the application of [§ 61(a)] is concerned, it is immaterial that petitioner chose to accept an amount less than the strict present value of the unmatured rental payments rather than to engage in litigation, possibly uncertain and expensive.

The consideration received for cancellation of the lease was not a return of capital. We assume that the lease was "property", whatever that signifies abstractly. Presumably the bond in Helvering v. Horst, 311 U.S. 112, 61 S.Ct. 144, 85 L.Ed. 75, 131 A.L.R. 655, and the lease in Helvering v. Bruun, 309 U.S. 461, 60 S.Ct. 631, 84 L.Ed. 864, were also "property", but the interest coupon in Horst and the building in Bruun nevertheless were held to constitute items of gross income. Simply because the lease was "property" the amount received for its cancellation was not a return of capital, quite apart from the fact that "property" and "capital" are not necessarily synonymous in the Revenue Act of 1932 or in common usage. Where, as in this case, the disputed amount was essentially a substitute for rental payments which [§ 61(a)(5)] expressly characterizes as gross income, it must be regarded as ordinary income, and it is immaterial that for some purposes the contract creating the right to such payments may be treated as "property" or "capital".

For the same reasons, that amount was not a return of capital because petitioner acquired the lease as an incident of the realty devised to him by his father. Theoretically, it might have been possible in such a case to value realty and lease separately and to label each a capital asset. * * * But that would not have converted into capital the amount petitioner received from the Trust Co. since [§ 102(b)(1)] would have required him to include in gross income the rent derived from the property, and that section, like [§ 61(a)], does not distinguish rental payments and a payment which is clearly a substitute for rental payments.

We conclude that petitioner must report as gross income the entire amount received for cancellation of the lease without regard to the claimed disparity between that amount and the difference between the present value of the unmatured rental payments and the fair rental value of the property for the unexpired period of the lease. The cancellation of the lease involved nothing more than relinquishment of the right to future rental payments in return for a present substitute payment and possession of the leased premises. Undoubtedly it diminished the amount of gross income petitioner expected to realize, but to that extent he was relieved of the duty to pay income tax. Nothing in [§ 165(a)] indicates that Congress intended to allow petitioner to reduce ordinary income actually received and reported by the amount of income he failed to realize. * * * We may assume that petitioner was injured insofar as the cancellation of the lease affected the value of the realty. But that would become a deductible loss only when its extent had been fixed by a closed transaction. [Reg. § 1.165–1(b)] * * *.

Note that Reg. § 1.61–8(b) provides: "An amount received by a lessor from a lessee for cancelling a lease constitutes gross income for the year in which it is received, since it is essentially a substitute for rental payments." More broadly, the sale of a carved-out interest (for example, a landlord's assignment to a third party of the rights to future rents), but not the disposition of the underlying income producing property (for example, an office building), generally gives rise to ordinary income for the seller under the substitute for future income theory.

Questions

1. Was the transaction in Hort a sale or exchange or an extinguishment of the taxpayer's lease?

2. Why does the Court in Hort cite the Horst case (page 713)? What is the significance of the fruit and tree metaphor, derived from assignment of income area, in the capital gains context?

COMMISSIONER v. McCUE BROS.
& DRUMMOND, INC.

United States Court of Appeals, Second Circuit, 1954.
210 F.2d 752, cert. denied 348 U.S. 829, 75 S.Ct. 53, 99 L.Ed. 654.

AUGUSTUS N. HAND, CIRCUIT JUDGE.

From 1928 to June 30, 1946, the taxpayer operated a retail hat store at 1294 Broadway, New York City, on the street level of the Hotel McAlpin. For the three year period February 1, 1943, to January 31, 1946, taxpayer held the premises under a lease executed with the landlord, New York Life Insurance Company. However, when that lease expired, taxpayer, under the New York Rent Control Laws which became effective January 24, 1945, Laws of New York 1945, c. 314, §§ 8, 13, McK.Unconsol.Laws, §§ 8558, 8563, had the right to remain in possession as long as it continued to pay the rent as fixed by the prior lease. Moreover, the provisions of the lease which did not conflict with the Rent Control Laws would be enforced during the statutory tenancy.

On June 27, 1945, the Jamlee Hotel Corporation, an affiliate of Crawford Clothes Inc., bought the Hotel McAlpin and formulated plans to open up a new Crawford store which would occupy part of the ground floor of the hotel including the taxpayer's store. Since the Rent Control Laws gave the taxpayer the right to remain in possession indefinitely, negotiations were entered into whereupon on May 17, 1946, the taxpayer and Jamlee signed a written agreement under which Jamlee was to pay the taxpayer $22,500 if he vacated and surrendered the store on or before June 30, 1946. The taxpayer vacated on June 28, 1946, received payment from Jamlee, and returned the $22,500 as a long term capital gain in its tax return for the fiscal year ended October 31, 1946. The Commissioner determined a deficiency on the ground that the payment represented ordinary income under [§ 61(a)]. However, the Tax Court on stipulated facts, reversed the Commissioner and held the payment to be a long term capital gain under [§ 1222].
* * *

A long term capital gain is defined as the "gain from the sale or exchange of a capital asset held for more than 6 months * * *." [§ 1222(3)] In Commissioner of Internal Revenue v. Golonsky, 200 F.2d 72, certiorari denied 345 U.S. 939, 73 S.Ct. 830, 97 L.Ed. 1366, the Court of Appeals for the Third Circuit held the payment made to a lessee by the landlord for cancelling the lease and surrendering the premises to be a capital gain. See also Commissioner of Internal Revenue v. Ray, 5 Cir., 210 F.2d 390. We agree with that decision, and, as the Tax Court found below, we consider the instant case indistinguishable from it. Whether the property is held under a lease or by virtue of the Rent Control Laws seems immaterial; in both cases the lessee or tenant has the right to the possession and use of the premises as long as he continues to pay the rent.

The Commissioner attacks the Golonsky decision on the ground that it is inconsistent with recent decisions of this court holding payments made for the release of contractual rights, such as the right to an exclusive agency, to be ordinary income. Commissioner of Internal Revenue v. Starr Bros., Inc., 2 Cir., 204 F.2d 673. In these cases no "sale or exchange" within the meaning of the statute was found because the contractual right was not transferred, but was released and merely vanished. However, we think the right of possession under a lease or otherwise, is a more substantial property right which does not lose its existence when it is transferred. If it is sold by the tenant to a third person, the gain derived therefrom is a [preferential] capital gain, Sutliff v. Commissioner, 46 B.T.A. 446, and we see no reason why a different result should be reached here. Moreover, the transaction seems closer to those cases holding that gain derived by the holder of a life interest upon sale to the remainderman is to be taxed as a [preferential] capital gain. McAllister v. Commissioner, 2 Cir., 157 F.2d 235, certiorari denied 330 U.S. 826, 67 S.Ct. 864, 91 L.Ed. 1276; Bell's Estate v. Commissioner, 8 Cir., 137 F.2d 454. The decision of the Supreme Court in Hort v. Commissioner, 313 U.S. 28, 61 S.Ct. 757, 85 L.Ed. 1168, does not require a different result. There, in holding a payment made by the lessee to the landlord to cancel the lease to be ordinary income, reliance was placed on the fact that the payment took the place of what ordinarily would be payments for rent. That argument cannot be advanced here.

In regard to the long term aspects of the payment received here, we agree with the Tax Court that the holding period commenced when the statutory right of possession attached on January 24, 1945, well beyond six months before the transaction here occurred. Accordingly we find the decision of the Tax Court correct in holding the payment received here by the taxpayer to be a [preferential] long term capital gain.

Affirmed.

The Supreme Court in Commissioner v. P.G. Lake, Inc., 356 U.S. 260, 78 S.Ct. 691, 2 L.Ed.2d 1143 (1958) held that the disposition of certain mineral payments yielded ordinary income. The Court stated (356 U.S. at 262, 265–266, 78 S.Ct. at 692–695):

> * * * Lake is a corporation engaged in the business of producing oil and gas. It has a seven-eighths working interest in two commercial oil and gas leases. In 1950 it was indebted to its president in the sum of $600,000 and in consideration of his cancellation of the debt assigned him an oil payment right in the amount of $600,000, plus an amount equal to the interest at 3 percent a year on the unpaid balance remaining from month to month, payable out of 25 percent of the oil attributable to the taxpayer's working interest in the two leases. At the time of the assignment it could have been estimated with reasonable accuracy that the assigned oil payment right would pay out in three or more years. It did in fact pay out in a little over three years.

*   *   *

We do not see here any conversion of a capital investment. The lump sum consideration seems essentially a substitute for what would otherwise be received at a future time as ordinary income. The pay-out of these particular assigned oil payment rights could be ascertained with considerable accuracy. * * * The substance of what was received was the present value of income which the recipient would otherwise obtain in the future. In short, consideration was paid for the right to receive future income, not for an increase in value of the income-producing property. (356 U.S. at 261).

———

In another case, in his concurring opinion, Judge John R. Brown in United States v. Dresser Industries, Inc., 324 F.2d 56, 61 (5th Cir.1963) stated:

Running through several of our prior opinions is the asserted concept that capital gains versus ordinary income is to be determined by the status of current earnings were the asset to have remained in the hands of the transferor. On this approach it is reasoned that if the current income would have been taxable ordinary income, then the sales price which represents the substitute for such future earnings is likewise taxable ordinary income.

I think this is both bad economics and faulty law. A person acquires property for one of two, or both reasons. The first is to receive earnings, i.e., income. The other is to hold the property for appreciation resulting from long or short range economic conditions, inflation or the like. Normally, of course, the predominant reason is to acquire the earning capacity represented by the earnings which the property will generate.

Hence it is that among those who trade in corporate securities on established national exchanges or over-the-counter markets, there are recognized rules of thumb by which the present value, hence market price, is determined for a given stock. The same is true in the contemporary, frequent practice of large-scale corporate acquisitions by one corporation of the stock or assets of another corporation. Value—market or sales price—is determined by capitalizing earnings. Whether the formula is the conservative one of 6 or 7 times earnings, or something less, or one considerably more speculative, what the buyer offers is his estimate of the present, discounted value of the future earnings of the assets or enterprise.

But although this sales price is determined by future earnings, and to the seller it takes the place of what he would have received had he continued his ownership, under no stretch of the imagination is it "ordinary income" either in the business world or in the sometimes more weird, tax world. Were this so, then every such sale for a price in excess of cost would entail this analysis and this tax consequence. There would first have to be ascertained what portion of the excess represented the present value of future earnings and what portion represented merely capital appreciation, from enhancement in value caused by inflation, scarcity or the like. Then as a second step, that portion or the excess of sales price representing future earnings would be taxed as ordinary income, the remainder as capital gains.

Conceding that Congress might compel this, that the ubiquitous and voracious tax gatherer might demand it, or that courts might ultimately sustain it, the fact is that as yet none has gone so fast so far. And that is so because of the practical economic realities which are, after all, of dominant significance in tax affairs. Income is one thing. When income, and income alone is sold or transferred, it keeps this status. But when the thing which generates the income is transferred, what is paid and received is not vicarious income, whether viewed from an economic or a tax standpoint. It is, as the economist and the businessman views it, the present, discounted value of its future earnings. If the "thing" generating such future earnings is "property" of a kind which the tax law recognizes as one entitled to capital gains or losses when used in the tax law sense, that present, discounted value is a capital gain, not ordinary income notwithstanding the economic fact that without such capacity to earn "ordinary income" in the hands of its owner the asset would be valueless.

Problem

C and D each purchase, at a cost of $25,000, identical buildings held for rental. Each building has a fair rental value of $250 per month. C and D each negotiate a 10-year lease at $250 per month. Each tenant uses the leased space for business purposes. One year later there is a depression and the fair rental value of each building drops to $200 per month. Each tenant asks his landlord to let him out of his lease. C refuses, so her tenant continues to pay the $250 monthly rental. D releases his tenant, but the tenant pays him $5,000 for the cancellation of the lease.

(a) What are the tax consequences to C and D? Has D ended his investment in any property? How is this relevant to the characterization of D's transaction? Consider the Hort and Horst (page 713 of Chapter 10) cases and Reg. § 1.61–8(b).

(b) How would D's tenant treat the payment?

Reference: Shores, Reexamining the Relationship Between Capital Gain and the Assignment of Income, 13 Ind.L.R. 463 (1980).

I. INTRODUCTION TO THE TAX CONSEQUENCES OF DEBT INSTRUMENTS: ORIGINAL ISSUE DISCOUNT, MARKET DISCOUNT AND COUPON STRIPPING

1. ORIGINAL ISSUE DISCOUNT

A debt instrument that bears no interest or interest at a rate lower than the current market rate usually is issued (sold to the public) at less than its face amount. Thus, a debt instrument with a face amount of $1,000, plus 5 percent annual interest, may be sold at $950, if the 5 percent interest rate is inadequate. This discount, which is known as original issue discount is, in essence, additional interest for the use of the borrowed funds which was not provided for in the debt instrument. In the following case, the Supreme Court dealt with the character of the income realized on the sale of an original issue discount bond. The Court concluded that the increase in the bond's value was the economic equivalent of interest.

UNITED STATES v. MIDLAND–ROSS CORPORATION

Supreme Court of the United States, 1965.
381 U.S. 54, 85 S.Ct. 1308, 14 L.Ed.2d 214.

Mr. Justice Brennan delivered the opinion of the Court.

The question for decision is whether, under the Internal Revenue Code of 1939, certain gains realized by the taxpayer are taxable as [preferential] capital gains or as ordinary income. The taxpayer bought noninterest-bearing promissory notes from the issuers at prices discounted below the face amounts. With one exception, each of the notes was held for more than six months, and, before maturity and in the year of purchase, was sold for less than its face amount but more than its issue price.[29] It is conceded that the gain in each case was the economic equivalent of interest for the use of the money to the date of sale but the taxpayer reported the gains as [preferential] capital gains. The Commissioner of Internal Revenue determined that the gains attributable to original issue discount were but interest in another form and therefore were taxable as ordinary income. Respondent paid the resulting deficiencies and in this suit for refund prevailed in the District Court for the Northern District of Ohio, 214 F.Supp. 631, and in the Court of Appeals for the Sixth Circuit, 335 F.2d 561. Because this treatment as capital gains conflicts with the result reached by other courts of appeals, we granted certiorari. 379 U.S. 944, 85 S.Ct. 441, 13 L.Ed.2d 542. We reverse.

The more favorable capital gains treatment applied only to gain on "the sale or exchange of a capital asset." [§ 1222]. Although original issue discount becomes property when the obligation falls due or is liquidated prior to maturity and [§ 1221] defined a capital asset as "property held by the taxpayer," we have held that

29. The original plaintiff, Industrial Rayon Corporation, was merged into respondent Midland-Ross Corporation in 1961. During 1952, 1953, and 1954, Industrial's idle funds were used to purchase 13 noninterest-bearing notes, varying in face amount from $500,000 to $2,000,000, from General Motors Acceptance Corporation, Commercial Investment Trust Company and Commercial Credit Company. The original issue discount in most instances was calculated to yield the equivalent of 2% to 2½% on an annual basis if the note were held to maturity, and the gains on sale approximated the discount earned to date. It is not contended that any part of the gain was attributable to market fluctuations as opposed to the passage of time.

"not everything which can be called property in the ordinary sense and which is outside the statutory exclusions qualifies as a capital asset. This Court has long held that the term 'capital asset' is to be construed narrowly in accordance with the purpose of Congress to afford capital-gains treatment only in situations typically involving the realization of appreciation in value accrued over a substantial period of time, and thus to ameliorate the hardship of taxation of the entire gain in one year." Commissioner v. Gillette Motor Transport, Inc., 364 U.S. 130, 134, 80 S.Ct. 1497, 1500, 4 L.Ed.2d 1617.

See also Corn Products Co. v. Commissioner, 350 U.S. 46, 52, 76 S.Ct. 20, 24, 100 L.Ed. 29. In applying this principle, this Court has consistently construed "capital asset" to exclude property representing income items or accretions to the value of a capital asset themselves properly attributable to income. Thus the Court has held that "capital asset" does not include compensation awarded a taxpayer as representing the fair rental value of its facilities during the period of their operation under government control, Commissioner v. Gillette Motor Transport, Inc., supra; the amount of the proceeds of the sale of an orange grove attributable to the value of an unmatured annual crop, Watson v. Commissioner, 345 U.S. 544, 73 S.Ct. 848, 97 L.Ed. 1232; an unexpired lease, Hort v. Commissioner, 313 U.S. 28, 61 S.Ct. 757, 85 L.Ed. 1168; and oil payment rights, Commissioner v. P. G. Lake, Inc., 356 U.S. 260, 78 S.Ct. 691, 2 L.Ed.2d 743. Similarly, earned original issue discount cannot be regarded as "typically involving the realization of appreciation in value accrued over a substantial period of time * * * [given capital gains treatment] to ameliorate the hardship of taxation of the entire gain in one year."

Earned original issue discount serves the same function as stated interest, concededly ordinary income and not a capital asset; it is simply "compensation for the use or forbearance of money." Deputy v. du Pont, 308 U.S. 488, 498, 60 S.Ct. 363, 368, 84 L.Ed. 416; cf. Lubin v. Commissioner, 335 F.2d 209 (C.A.2d Cir.). Unlike the typical case of capital appreciation, the earning of discount to maturity is predictable and measurable, and is "essentially a substitute for * * * payments which [§ 61(a)] expressly characterizes as gross income [; thus] it must be regarded as ordinary income, and it is immaterial that for some purposes the contract creating the right to such payments may be treated as 'property' or 'capital'." Hort v. Commissioner, supra, 313 U.S., at 31, 61 S.Ct., at 758. The $6 earned on a one-year note for $106 issued for $100 is precisely like the $6 earned on a one-year loan of $100 at 6% stated interest. The application of general principles would indicate, therefore, that earned original issue discount, like stated interest, should be taxed under § [61(a)] as ordinary income.[30]

---

30. Our disposition makes it unnecessary to decide certain questions raised at argument, as to which we intimate no view:

(1) Since each note was sold in the year of purchase, we do not reach the question whether an accrual-basis taxpayer is re-

The taxpayer argues, however, that administrative practice and congressional treatment of original issue discount under the 1939 Code establish that such discount is to be accounted for as [preferential] capital gain when realized. [Former] Section 1232(a)(2)(A) of the Internal Revenue Code of 1954 [provided] that "upon sale or exchange of * * * evidences of indebtedness issued after December 31, 1954, held by the taxpayer more than 6 months, any gain realized * * * [up to the prorated amount of original issue discount] shall be considered as gain from the sale or exchange of property which is not a capital asset," that is, it is to be taxed at ordinary income rates. From this the taxpayer would infer that Congress understood prior administrative and legislative history as extending [preferential] capital gains treatment to realized original issue discount. If administrative practice and legislative history before 1954 did in fact ignore economic reality and treat stated interest and original issue discount differently for tax purposes, the taxpayer should prevail. * * * But the taxpayer must persuade us that this was clearly the case, * * * and has not done so.

The taxpayer refers us to various statutory provisions treating original issue discount as ordinary income in specific situations, arguing that these establish a congressional understanding that in situations not covered by such provisions, original issue discount is entitled to [preferential] capital gains treatment. Even if these provisions were merely limited applications of the principle of [former] § 1232(a)(2), they may demonstrate, not that the general rule was to the contrary, but that the general rule was unclear, see Brandis, Effect of Discount or Premium on Bondholder's North Carolina Income Tax, 19 N.C.L.Rev. 1, 7 (1940), and that Congress wished to avoid any doubt as to its treatment of particular situations. Cf. S.Rep.No. 1622, 83d Cong., 2d Sess., p. 112 (1954).

* * *

For these reasons we hold that earned original issue discount is not entitled to capital gains treatment under the 1939 Code.

Reversed.

The Supreme Court, as indicated in footnote 30 of the Midland-Ross decision, did not address the timing of the accrued interest income, now covered by §§ 1271–1275. In Rev.Rul. 74–607, 1974–2 C.B., which dealt with points paid on a mortgage loan, the Service held that the interest must be accrued ratably on a straight-line basis over the period of the

quired to report discount earned before the final disposition of an obligation;

(2) Since no argument is made that the gain on the sale of each note varied significantly from the portion of the original issue discount earned during the holding period, we do not reach the question of the tax treatment under the 1939 Code of "market discount" arising from post-issue purchases at prices varying from issue price plus a ratable portion of the original issue discount, or of the tax treatment of gains properly attributable to fluctuations in the interest rate and market price of obligations as distinguished from the anticipated increase resulting from mere passage of time.

loan. Is this approach still viable after the 1984 legislation? Read § 1272(a)(1), (3), and (4).

Unstated interest may exist in any situation where a taxpayer is entitled to a future payment. Reread pp. 830–843 in Chapter 11. In Jones v. Commissioner, 330 F.2d 302 (3d Cir.1964), a taxpayer purchased a remainder interest from the beneficiary of an existing trust. Taxpayer later sold the purchased remainder interest after the life tenant of the trust died, but before the trustee distributed the trust corpus. The court characterized as ordinary income that portion of taxpayer's gain allocable to the unstated interest which had accrued during the time taxpayer owned the remainder interest.

An illustration of what the court did in the Jones case, using the 10% unisex tables in Reg. § 20.2031–7(f), is helpful. Assume that the trust corpus consisted of a $100,000 certificate of deposit paying interest at a 10% annual rate. If the life tenant was 55 when the taxpayer purchased the remainder interest, the taxpayer would pay $19,954 for the remainder interest. The present value of the right to the trust corpus was discounted because the life tenant had a remaining life expectancy of approximately 17 years. Financially, this case can be viewed as the purchase for $19,954 of an $100,000 original issue discount bond that pays no interest and will mature in 17 years. If the life tenant died five years later, there are two elements to his $80,046 gain. A portion of this gain is the interest earned on his original investment over the five year period. The remaining portion of the gain is the unexpected appreciation in value resulting from the life tenant dying prior to his life expectancy and can be justifiably treated as a capital gain. Using the 10% tables in the appendix the interest element is computed by determining how much would be on hand at the end of five years if $19,954 were invested at 10% compounded annually. [$19,954 × 1.610510 = $32,136.12]. Therefore, $67,863.88 of the gain is capital gain and $12,863.88 of the gain is the interest element reported as ordinary income.

Questions

Can the Jones decision be reconciled with Irwin v. Gavitt (page 264)?

2. MARKET DISCOUNT

A related question involves the treatment of a market discount bond. Suppose an individual purchased a corporate bond for $990 on January 1 of Year 25. This bond was originally issued for its $1,000 face amount in Year 1. This bond pays annual interest of $89 at the end of each year. The bond matures on December 31 of Year 25. The bond sold at a discount because market interest rates on January 1 of Year 25 were higher than the 8.9% return the bond provided when it was issued for $1,000. If our purchaser is looking for a 10% return on his investment of $990, he expects his investment to generate $99 in earnings. To obtain this return, the purchaser will receive an interest payment of $89 and the $1,000 in redemption proceeds at the end of Year 25. Therefore, when our investor purchased the bond its yield to maturity equalled 10%.

Although the $10 of gain realized by our investor upon redemption of the bond at maturity is the financial equivalent of an additional $10 of interest income, prior to the enactment of § 1276 in 1984, the sum of $10 was deemed to be appreciation in value resulting in a then preferential capital gain of $10. Congress recognized that from the standpoint of the purchaser the market discount is indistinguishable from the original issue discount at issue in the Midland-Ross Corporation decision. Section 1276 recognizes that the amount of the market discount is merely a substitute for stated interest. Section 1276 provides that the gain on the disposition (either by sale or redemption) of a "market discount bond," defined in § 1278(a)(1), is treated as interest to the extent of the accrued "market discount," defined in § 1278(a)(2). Interestingly, tax-exempt bonds under § 103 are not subject to the market discount rules so that the market discount interest element for their bonds is characterized as capital gain and is therefore not subject to the § 103 exclusion from gross income. § 1278(a)(1)(B). If the gain were characterized as interest, it could qualify for the exclusion under § 103.

Logically, the reporting of the interest attributable to the market discount element should follow financial reality and require the accrual of this interest each year over the remaining term of the bond. Since this would involve administrative complexity, Congress permits the taxpayer to report the entire market discount interest element in the year the bond is disposed of. § 1276(a)(1).

Any gain on the sale or other disposition of a market discount bond is ordinary income to the extent that such gain does not exceed the market discount accrued on the bond to the date of disposition. § 1276(a)(1). The accrued market discount is computed on a ratable (straight line) method. The accrued market discount equals the amount which bears the same ratio to the market discount on the bond as the number of days the investor held the bond bears to the number of days after the investor acquired the bond up to and including the date of the bond's maturity. § 1276(b)(1). The market discount is the excess, if any, of the stated redemption price of the bond at maturity over the basis of the bond immediately after its acquisition by the taxpayer. § 1278(a)(2). Any gain in excess of the accrued market discount is capital gain. The following example is helpful:

> T purchases on July 1 of Year 1 for $9,000, a $10,000 bond bearing 9% interest, which will mature in ten years. The amount of the market discount equals $1,000 because the bond was originally issued at face value. On June 30 of Year 3, T sells the bond for $9,600. Of the $600 gain, $300 (the accrued market discount, which equals $1,000 × 36/120) is treated as ordinary income and the other $300 is long-term capital gain.

Problems

1.   Tom purchased a previously issued $10,000 bond, paying interest of $600 each year, for $7,000. The bond will mature in 15 years after the purchase. Assume the bond was issued after July 18, 1984.

    a.   What are the tax consequences if Tom holds the bond to maturity? Is this a market discount bond? Consider § 1278(a)(1) and (2). If so, what are the consequences? Consider §§ 1276(a)(1) and (b) and 1278(a)(2).

    b.   What if after holding the bond for five years Tom sells the bond for $8,300?

2.   X Corporation issued a $10,000, 5–year bond on January 1, 1988, paying interest of $900 at the end of each year. The bond had a redemption date of December 31, 1992. Ike paid the X Corporation $9,620.92 for the bond on the issue date. Assume that market rates of interest at all times are 10% annual interest.

    a.   What are the income tax consequences to Ike if he holds the bond to maturity? Is this a market discount bond? Consider §§ 1272(a)(1), (3), (4) and (5); 1273(a) and (b); 1278(a)(1) and (2).

    b.   What result to Ike if he sold the bond on December 31, 1989, for $9,751.31, after holding it for only two years and collecting $1,800 in interest payments on the bond?

3.   Must a donor report accrued market discount upon disposing of the bond by gift? §§ 1276(a)(2) and (c)(1) and 7701(a)(43).

3. COUPON STRIPPING

As the preceding materials illustrate it is difficult to distinguish between the value of an asset and the income that asset generates. Most often a sale of an asset includes both the underlying property and all subsequent income that property will produce. In this simple situation, the sale of both the right to the property and its future income stream constitutes a disposition of the entire value of what the seller owned. Any gain (or loss) on the sale is treated as a capital gain (or loss) (assuming the property is a capital asset). For example, if S owns a corporate bond (having no original issue discount or market discount) with coupons attached, and S sells the bond with the coupons, any gain (or loss) is a capital gain (or loss). Economically, S has actually sold two separate property rights. The coupons represent the right to interest payments until maturity. The bond itself represents the right to the face amount of the bond at the maturity date. Assume T purchases a $10,000 bond at its issue date for $10,000, maturing in 12 years and having coupons representing the right to $1,000 a year for each of the next 12 years. If market rates are 10% (see table in appendix), the present value of the coupons (an annuity of $1,000 a year for 12 years) is $6,813.69. The present value of the bond without the coupons (the right to receive a payment of $10,000 in 12 years) is

$3,186.31. Together, the present value of the coupons and the bonds equals $10,000.

The materials discussed in connection with the Irwin v. Gavit decision at page 264 and Helvering v. Horst at page 713, indicate that the entire $10,000 basis is allocated to the bond and none to the coupons. Consequently, upon receipt of each $1,000 interest payment, the entire amount is reported as ordinary income and the entire $10,000 of redemption proceeds is treated as a return of basis.

If the owner of the bond with its coupons keeps the bond and sells all of the coupons for $6,813.69, Helvering v. Horst tells us that the carve-out principle requires the seller to treat the entire amount as an acceleration of future ordinary income currently reported in the year of sale. Furthermore, Irwin v. Gavit tells us that the entire $10,000 basis remains with the stripped bond. On the other hand, if the owner kept the coupons and sold the stripped bond for $3,186.31, he would report a $6,813.69 capital loss on the sale of the stripped bond. The buyer of the stripped bond has effectively purchased the equivalent of an original issue discount bond with no stated interest. This buyer would treat the gain realized upon redemption of the bond as ordinary income because it represents unstated interest.

Prior to the enactment of § 1286, the practice of coupon stripping gave a tax deferral to the seller of a stripped bond, who retained the coupons. The tax deferral resulted from the immediate recognition of an artificial loss on the sale of the stripped bond. Congress recognized that allocating the entire basis to the stripped bond was financially unrealistic. Congress enacted § 1286 (formerly § 1232B) which is applicable only to a disposition (by sale or by gift) which produces a separation of ownership between the bond and its coupons. Under § 1286 both the coupons and the stripped bond are treated as OID bonds issued on the date of separation. Therefore, the person who acquires the stripped bond or the coupons has the equivalent of OID instruments. And, each person must report the interest income as it accrues each year.

More importantly, the original owner of the complete bond with the coupons must allocate his original basis between the coupons and the stripped bond any time the coupons and the bond are separated. This legislative remedy effectively eliminates the artificial loss previously allowed the seller of a stripped bond. Using the facts in our illustration, the seller of the stripped bond could allocate only $3,186.31 of his $10,000 basis to the stripped bond. Since the remaining basis stays with the coupons, a portion of each coupon payment is a return of basis.

Reference: McGrath, Coupon Stripping Under § 1286: Trees, Fruits and Felines, 38 Tax Lawyer 267 (1985).

Problems

1. Ted Player, a cash method taxpayer, purchases a $10,000 corporate coupon bond from another person on January 1 Year 1 for $8,371. The bond matures on December 31 Year 15 and pays interest at a 7% annual rate. Each coupon represents the right to $350 every six months. The interest coupons are assignable.

(a) How must Ted treat the $700 in interest payments received each year? Can any of his basis in the bond be allocated to the interest payments?

(b) How will Ted treat the $10,000 received in redemption of the bond on maturity? Consider § 1276(a)(1) and (b).

(c) Assume on January 1 of Year 4 Ted sells all of the remaining interest coupons for $5,073.42, the present value of the right to receive $350 every six months for the next 12 years, discounted at 9% semiannual interest. How much of the basis in the bond is allocated to the interest coupons? Consider the Hort case, Irwin v. Gavit (pp. 264–266) (where the Supreme Court held that the life tenant is taxed on all the trust income during the term of the trust, but the remainderman includes nothing in income annually and on the termination of the trust the remainderman takes the entire basis in the trust property), and § 1286.

2. Father buys a corporate coupon bond for $10,000, with each coupon representing the right to $1000 of interest every year. The bond matures in 10 years. Consider the tax results under § 1286 in each of the following:

(a) Father gives all of the coupons to his adult son.

(i) Father retains the bond until maturity;

(ii) Father sells the bond for its present discounted value;

(iii) Son later sells all of the coupons;

(iv) Son collects each coupon payment.

(b) Father retains the coupons, but gives the stripped bond to his adult daughter.

(i) Father collects all of the coupons;

(ii) Father sells the coupons for their present discounted value;

(iii) Daughter sells the bond;

(iv) Daughter holds the bond to maturity.

(c) Father gives all of the coupons to Son and gives the stripped bond to Daughter. Consider § 1272.

(d) Father transfers all of the coupons into a trust for the benefit of his grandson who is only 10 years old. Consider § 1(i).

J. TERMINATION OF CONTRACT RIGHTS

BISBEE–BALDWIN CORP. v. TOMLINSON,

United States Court of Appeals, Fifth Circuit, 1963.
320 F.2d 929.

WISDOM, CIRCUIT JUDGE.

The question for decision is whether payments the taxpayer received for the termination of mortgage servicing contracts are taxable as ordinary income or as capital gains.[31]

This Court has recently decided three other cases concerning the tax effects of the termination of similar contracts: Nelson Weaver Realty Co. v. Commissioner, 5 Cir.1962, 307 F.2d 897; United States v. Eidson, 5 Cir.1962, 310 F.2d 111; Commissioner v. Maurice L. Killian, 5 Cir.1963, 314 F.2d 852. In Weaver, Judge Cameron, for the majority of the Court, held: "It cannot be doubted that the sum total of the ingredients of [the mortgage company's] longstanding relationship with * * * [its] clientele constitutes a property right which is the equivalent of goodwill * * * a capital asset * * * entitled to capital gain treatment" on its sale. Judge Rives dissented: The "part alloca[ble] to the right to receive service fees should be taxable as an ordinary income."[32] In Eidson Judge Tuttle, for the Court, held that it "makes no difference whether the assignment [of rights under the contract] * * * be denominated a sale"; the taxpayers assigned the right to receive "net profit of operations during the remainder of the life of the contract", which must be treated as ordinary income. Killian followed Weaver "[t]o the extent that the facts * * * established a sale of good will", but the property sold consisted of "expirations" not a bundle of rights as in Weaver, Eidson, and the case now before the Court.[33]

---

31. The tax treatment of assignment of income is examined intensively in Lyon & Eustice, Assignment of Income: Fruit and Tree as Irrigated by the P.G. Lake case, 17 Tax L.Rev. 295 (1962). See especially pages 346–353, 393–397. See also Surrey, Definitional Problems in Capital Gains Taxation, 69 Harv.L.Rev. 985 (1956); Comment, The P.G. Lake Guides to Ordinary Income: An Appraisal in Light of Capital Gains Policies, 14 Stan.L.Rev. 551 (1962).

32. Footnote 6 of the majority opinion in Weaver points out that the question of allocation according to fragments was not presented or argued before the Tax Court or this Court.

33. In Killian the Court said:

"To the extent that the facts in the case here under, review clearly established a sale of good will attendant to business, the holding of the Tax Court was in accord with this Court's opinion in Nelson Weaver Realty Co. v. Commissioner of Internal

Revenue, supra, and to this extent only is this case comparable to Nelson Weaver. We do not have in the instant case a bundle of property rights involved in a sale as did the Nelson Weaver case. There is nothing whatsoever here to be 'communicated into fragments,' with the purchase price then to be allocated among the various assets, as suggested by Judge Rives in his special concurring and dissenting opinion in Nelson Weaver. And by the same token, there are no components of sale requiring separate scrutiny as discussed in Commissioner of Internal Revenue v. Ferrer, 304 F.2d 125 (CA 2, 1962). There was no bundle sold by Killian for the $12,500 payment under review here. The property sold had one single practical and legal attribute: good will.

* * *

"We note particularly also that Killian had already received all of the commissions due him under the policies covered by

A majority of this Court conclude that they cannot bridge the gulf between Weaver and Eidson. Since we must choose between the two, we choose to follow Eidson on principle and the solution to the problem suggested by the dissent in Weaver.

I.

The facts are not in dispute.

Bisbee-Baldwin, the taxpayer, is in the mortgage banking business. Most of its loans are secured by mortgages on residential property in Jacksonville, Florida. After making a loan, the company invariably assigns the mortgage to an institutional investor. The essential profit-making element is the investor's agreement to employ the mortgage company as its agent to service the mortgages. The company receives no profit on the assignment of a mortgage but earns an annual commission of one-half of one per cent of the principal outstanding balance of the mortgages serviced. The servicing activities generate other business. For example, the company often writes fire insurance on the property mortgaged, acts as real estate broker when the property is sold, and serves as property manager when a mortgage is foreclosed. Escrow deposits by the mortgagors enhance its credit standing, a substantial benefit since the company must borrow large sums from the banks in the operation of its affairs. Thus the success of the mortgage servicing business depends upon the amount of mortgage indebtedness it services.

The taxpayer had no right to assign the servicing agreement and could not demand any payment from a successor servicing agent if the investor transferred its business to another company. The taxpayer was not the exclusive agent for any investor, even in the Jacksonville area serviced by it. Each investor had the right to enter into similar agreements with other servicing agents, and the taxpayer had the right to assign and service mortgages for other investors.

During the fiscal year ending April 30, 1957, various investors cancelled servicing agreements with the taxpayer, and gave the business to other agents. When an investor cancels such an agreement without cause, it is customary for the investor to pay a termination fee equal to one per cent of the principal balance of the mortgages then being serviced by the mortgage company. In this case, several of the

the informational date, and that he had reported them all in his tax returns and received none thereafter. This is quite distinct from the sale of anticipated renewals from, for example, life insurance policies, which pay commissions after the first year without being rewritten in a new policy. There was no service fee or other definitive accrual right here. The Tax Court was correct in its determination that the payment to Killian under these facts was not a lump sum consideration essentially a substitute for what would otherwise be regard-

ed at a future time as ordinary income. See Commissioner of Internal Revenue, et al. v. P.G. Lake, Inc., et al., 356 U.S. 260, 78 S.Ct. 691, 2 L.Ed. 743. There was nothing here which was automatic, perfunctory or legally enforceable coming to Ryan and Fry which could be equated with Killian's future income. Neither they nor Killian could do more than project, prospectively, the value of Killian's relationship with the policy holders identified on the informational data."

taxpayer's agreements with investors expressly provided for such a termination fee. The taxpayer received net termination fees of $206,454.63. The investors paid this sum to Bisbee-Baldwin, but were reimbursed by the new servicing agents for the amount of the termination fees paid to the taxpayer. In substance, therefore, the mortgage servicing was transferred from Bisbee-Baldwin to other agents for, as the district court found, the cancellations would not have taken place had the successor mortgage servicing agents not agreed to reimburse the investors in the amount of the termination fees.

The district court found that:

"Plaintiff kept extensive files containing information concerning the mortgages which it serviced. When an investor canceled an agreement the files containing information concerning the mortgages assigned to that investor were turned over either to the investor or to the new servicing agent designated by the investor. Those files were of value to the Plaintiff in obtaining the [indirect] advantages [of servicing mortgages]."

Bisbee-Baldwin reported the termination fees as a net long-term capital gain of $206,454.43. The Commissioner ruled that the sum was ordinary income and assessed a deficiency of $45,705.35 against Bisbee-Baldwin. The taxpayer paid the deficiency and then brought suit for refund. The district court, citing the "Weaver case [as] a situation very similar * * * agree[d] with the conclusion of the Tax Court that a mortgaging servicing contract is not a capital asset". The district court also held that the "termination of the mortgage servicing contracts by the various investors did not constitute sales or exchanges by the plaintiff." Bisbee-Baldwin appeals from the judgment of the district court.

II.

The fact that contractual rights in a mortgage servicing agency constitute a species of "property" under state law affords no assistance in determining whether such rights are capital assets. As the Supreme Court stated in Commissioner v. Gillette Motor Transport Co., 1960, 364 U.S. 130, 134–135, 80 S.Ct. 1497, 1500, 1501, 4 L.Ed.2d 1617:

"While a capital asset is defined in [§ 1221] as 'property held by the taxpayer,' it is evident that not everything which can be called property in the ordinary sense and which is outside the statutory exclusions qualifies as a capital asset. This Court has long held that *the term 'capital asset' is to be construed narrowly in accordance with the purpose of Congress to afford capital-gains treatment only in situations typically involving the realization of appreciation in value over a substantial period of time, and thus to ameliorate the hardship of taxation of the entire gain in one year.* * * * Thus the Court has held that an unexpired lease, * * * corn futures, * * * and oil payment rights, * * * are not capital assets even though they are concededly 'property' interests in the ordinary sense."

In Hort v. Commissioner, 1941, 313 U.S. 28, 61 S.Ct. 757, 85 L.Ed. 1168, the Court held that amounts received in cancellation of a lease were taxable as ordinary income to a lessor. The Court said:

> "Simply because the lease was 'property' the amount received for its cancellation was not a return of capital, quite apart from the fact that 'property' and 'capital' are not necessarily synonymous in the Revenue Act of 1932 or in common usage. Where, as in this case, the disputed amount was essentially a substitute for rental payments which [§ 61(2)] expressly characterizes as gross income, it must be regarded as ordinary income, and it is immaterial that for some purposes the contract creating the right to such payments may be treated as 'property' or 'capital.'" (313 U.S. 31, 61 S.Ct. 758)

This statement agrees with comparable statements in other cases that the [preferential] capital gains section is an exception from the usual requirements and must be narrowly construed. See Corn Products Co. v. Commissioner, 1955, 350 U.S. 46, 76 S.Ct. 20, 100 L.Ed. 29.

The question is, what do the mortgage servicing rights under the contracts represent. If they represent the right to earn future income in the form of commissions for services rendered, then the sum received for the cancellation of the contracts and the transfer of rights is ordinary income.

In Roscoe v. Commissioner, 5 Cir.1954, 215 F.2d 478, a sum received by taxpayers for their real-estate corporation stock in excess of the amount received by other shareholders was held to be ordinary income representing the commission which the taxpayers would have been entitled to had the land represented by the stock been sold directly. The Tenth Circuit recently reached a similar result in Wiseman v. Halliburton Oil Well Cementing Co., 10 Cir.1962, 301 F.2d 654. There the taxpayer had agreed to the termination of an exclusive license to use and to grant sub-licenses for a patented process in exchange for a non-exclusive license and one-third of the royalties received from third party licenses. The Court held that in substance the taxpayer had received the present value of income which it would otherwise have received in the future through the sublicenses. In so holding the Tenth Circuit expressly disapproved and in effect overruled Jones v. Corbyn, 10 Cir.1950, 186 F.2d 450, on which the taxpayer relies. In that case, the Court gave a broad interpretation to the terms "property" and "capital assets", and held that money received from the sale of an insurance agency represented [preferential] capital gains. Indeed, that case has long been recognized as being "in large measure a departure * * * from the general principle governing sale of the proceeds from future services." 3B Mertens, Law of Federal Income Taxation § 22.34 (Zimet ed.). See 30 Texas L.Rev. 374 (1952).

The line between contractual rights representing capital assets and those representing the right to receive future income is far from clear. Judge Friendly, for the Second Circuit, after an extremely able, thorough survey of all the relevant cases, reached the following conclusion:

"One common characteristic of the group held to come within the capital gain provision is that the taxpayer had either what might be called an 'estate' in (Golonsky, McCue, Metropolitan), or an 'encumbrance' on (Ray), or an option to acquire an interest in (Dorman), property which, if itself held, would be a capital asset. In all these cases the taxpayer had something more than an opportunity, afforded by contract, to obtain periodic receipts of income, by dealing with another (Starr, Leh, General Artists, Pittston), or by vendering services (Holt), or by virtue of ownership of a larger 'estate' (Hort, P.G. Lake)." Commissioner v. Ferrer, 2nd Cir.1962, 304 F.2d 125, 130–131.

In Judge Friendly's analysis, as in Judge Rives's analysis in Weaver, some components of the "bundle" of contractual rights held by a taxpayer are capital assets while others represent a substitute for future income. Thus in Ferrer the taxpayer's "lease" of a play and his power, incident to the lease, to prevent a disposition of motion picture, radio, and television rights until after a certain date were capital assets. Cf. Commissioner v. Ray, 5 Cir.1954, 210 F.2d 390, cert. den., 348 U.S. 829, 75 S.Ct. 53, 99 L.Ed. 654. However, that part of the taxpayer's compensation for his contractual rights representing his right to forty per cent of the proceeds from the motion picture was taxable as ordinary income. We agree with this analysis. As Judge Rives said in Weaver:

"It seems to me, however, that a substantial part of the $121,841.11 paid to the Mortgage Company was for the right to receive service fees for the remaining years of the outstanding loans. To that extent the Mortgage Company was simply converting future income into present income. Commissioner v. P.G. Lake, Inc., 1958, 356 U.S. 260, 267, 78 S.Ct. 691, 2 L.Ed.2d 743.

"The sale of 'all of the rights, title, obligations and benefits pertaining to the servicing contract,' like the sale of any going business, should, I think, be comminuted into its fragments and the 'purchase price' should be allocated among the various assets sold. Williams v. McGowan, 2d Cir., 1945, 152 F.2d 570, 572; C.I.R. v. Chatsworth Stations, Inc., 2d Cir., 1960, 282 F.2d 132, 135. I would agree that a part of the $121,841.11 represented the purchase price of capital assets."

Applying these principles to the factual situation before us, we find that the basic rights Bisbee-Baldwin sold were the annual servicing commissions on the principal balance outstanding on the mortgages. Indeed, the termination fee of one per cent of the mortgages serviced by the taxpayer was equivalent to two years gross income in commissions and was, to our minds, a substitute for the income which would have been earned by Bisbee-Baldwin had the contracts not been transferred.

This holding is, of course, in direct conflict with Nelson Weaver Realty Co. v. Commissioner, 5 Cir.1962, 307 F.2d 897. In an almost identical situation Weaver held that compensation for the assignment of a mortgage-servicing agency should be treated as [a preferential] capital gain. In reaching its decision, the Court relied heavily upon the fact that the amount paid the taxpayer "bore no convincing resemblance to the amount the purchaser would actually collect out of the service contract sold since the purchaser had to pay the cost of collection." It is equally true in the present case that the net income from commissions over a two year period would be much smaller than the sum received by Bisbee-Baldwin. But, as this Court recently stated in Eidson, "while, of course, the sum of $170,000 which [the taxpayers] received in the taxable year at issue was doubtless much larger than the income they received in any year for a current year's operation, this clearly resulted from the fact that they were assigning, * * * not a capital asset whose value had enhanced or accrued over several years, but the right to receive this net profit of operations during the remainder of the life of the contract." Since, according to undisputed testimony, the primary value of these mortgage correspondent relationships lay in the right to receive annual percentage commissions, there can be little doubt that the bulk of the sum paid to Bisbee-Baldwin was compensation for the loss of such commissions. In such a situation, the statement by the Supreme Court in Commissioner v. P.G. Lake, Inc., 1958, 356 U.S. 260, 78 S.Ct. 691, 2 L.Ed.2d 1143, is applicable.

"The substance of what was assigned was the right to receive future income. The substance of what was received was the present value of income which the recipient would otherwise obtain in the future. In short, consideration was paid for the right to receive future income, not for an increase in the value of the income-producing property."

The taxpayer seeks to distinguish between the right to *receive* future income and the right to *earn* future income. This distinction finds no support in the decisions. Indeed, in Roscoe v. Commissioner, 5 Cir.1954, 215 F.2d 478, the very fact that the taxpayer's ten per cent commissions on the sale of real estate had to be *earned* by the taxpayer's efforts caused the compensation for this right to be classified as ordinary income.

* * *

Still, some parts of the "bundle" of contractual rights transferred by Bisbee-Baldwin were capital assets. The mortgage correspondent relationships have value in addition to the rights to servicing commissions. It acts as a "feeder" for related businesses, such as insurance and real estate, frequently engaged in by mortgage bankers. The monthly escrow deposits made by the mortgagors considerably enhance the servicing agent's credit standing. Moreover, as the dissenting opinion in Nelson Weaver recognized, there *is* a sale of "good will". The mortgage portfolio of the mortgage banker tends to increase each year as both the mortgagors and the investors look to the mortgaging servicing agent for further funds and further outlets for investment. The taxpayer's extensive files and equipment are in the nature of capital assets. (Most of these were retained by the taxpayer.) These items are closely related to the everyday business operations of the taxpayer. They are not so integrally related, however, as to be insusceptible of separate valuation.

We summarize. Essentially, the contract was a management contract for the employment of personal services. The consideration received for the right to earn future servicing commissions must be regarded as a substitute for such future ordinary income. This important part of the bundle of rights sold or exchanged can be separated from the other parts and should be taxed for what it is—not for what it is not. As in Ferrer: a transaction calls for

> "In such instances, where part of a transaction calls for one tax treatment and another for a different kind, allocation is demanded, Helvering v. Taylor, 293 U.S. 507, 55 S.Ct. 287, 79 L.Ed. 623 (1935); Ditmars v. C.I.R., 302 F.2d 481 (2 Cir.1962). If it be said that to remand for this purpose is asking the Tax Court to separate the inseparable, we answer that no one expects scientific exactness; that however roughly hewn the decision may be, the result is certain to be fairer than either extreme; and that similar tasks must be performed by the Tax Court in other areas, see Webster Investors, Inc. v. C.I.R., 291 F.2d 192 (2 Cir.1961); Meister v. C.I.R., 302 F.2d 54 (2 Cir.1962) [determination of portion of purchase price attributable to good-will]." C.I.R. v. Ferrer, 2 Cir.1962, 304 F.2d 125, 135.

The case should be remanded to allow the district "Court to allocate the amount [of the purchase price] according to the realities of the transaction." Nelson Weaver Realty Co. v. Commissioner (dissent).

III.

Looking only at the form of the transaction, it might be said that the payments fail to qualify for [preferential] capital gains treatment because there was no "sale or exchange" as required in Section 1221. Thus, the Commissioner argues that on termination of the contracts, Bisbee-Baldwin's rights vanished; nothing survived to be transferred. Commissioner v. Starr Bros., 2 Cir.1953, 204 F.2d 673, 674, held that cancellation of an exclusive agency did not result in capital gain. Such release not only ended the promisor's previously existing duty but also destroyed the promisee's rights. They were not transferred to the promisor; they merely came to an end and vanished.

In General Artists Corp. v. Commissioner, 2 Cir.1953, 205 F.2d 360, 361, this rule was applied, though here the "sale" was to a third person. There the court said: "But we think the correct view is that there was a release to the obligor of a negative covenant in order to allow a new covenant to be made with the third party." See also Roscoe v. Commissioner, 5 Cir.1954, 215 F.2d 478, 482, cited and followed those cases. See, also, Leh v. Commissioner, 9 Cir.1958, 260 F.2d 489, 493–495. The district court followed these cases in holding that the "elements which normally are involved in a sale or exchange are lacking in this situation." [34]

---

34. The district court held:

"The contract provided for termination without cause by either party. Plaintiff could not have sold its rights under the contract unless the investor gave approval. Plaintiff did not assign its rights. Its contracts were terminated and the investors then entered into new contracts with other

In the fact pattern this case presents, where the "realities of the transaction" undeniably show a market value for the bundle of rights said to have vanished, we feel compelled to look through form to substance. In substance the transaction was a two-party transfer. The investors were conduits: Bisbee-Baldwin received the payments; the transferees paid through the investors. Something was transferred. What Bisbee-Baldwin transferred was a bundle of rights under its contracts to service certain mortgages. For a price, the transferees stepped into Bisbee-Baldwin's shoes. It is irrelevant that the investors' approval was required, that the consideration was fixed in the contract or by trade custom, and that instead of assignment the transfer was effected by termination of the old contracts and execution of new contracts. These circumstances do not extinguish the fact that Bisbee-Baldwin gave up mortgage servicing commissions and other profits for a consideration. See Commissioner v. McCue Bros. & Drummond, Inc., 2 Cir.1954, 210 F.2d 752.

We hold therefore that property rights passed by sale or exchange from the taxpayer to the successor agents. This holding is circumscribed by our decision that not all of the sticks making up the bundle of rights constituted capital assets. As in Ferrer, although the whole bundle was sold or exchanged, the parties set no separate price upon each stick.

We therefore affirm the judgment below in part, reverse it in part, and remand the case for the district court to determine (1) what part of Bisbee-Baldwin's compensation was a substitute for future earnings, and therefore taxable as ordinary income and (2) what part or parts, if any, were capital assets, sold or exchanged, entitled to [preferential] capital gains treatment.

GRIFFIN B. BELL, CIRCUIT JUDGE (dissenting).

I dissent. I would affirm the judgment of the District Court without reaching the capital asset question, either as presented here or in Nelson Weaver Realty Co. v. Commissioner, 5 Cir.1962, 307 F.2d 897. The sale or exchange there was undoubted. Weaver sold his mortgage banking business. The sole question was whether what was sold constituted capital assets.

Here there is a preliminary or threshold question of whether there was a sale or exchange. In fact, Bisbee-Baldwin refused to sell. Four out of several lending institutions represented by Bisbee-Baldwin shortly thereafter terminated their relationship with Bisbee-Baldwin. Two paid a termination fee required by contract. Two paid a negotiated fee in an amount customary in the trade. Three of the lending institutions

agents. This is not equivalent to an assignment of sale from plaintiff to the new agent. General Artists Corp. v. Comm., 205 F.2d 360 (2nd Cir.1953). Plaintiff had no choice in selecting the new agent. The sums received by plaintiff were determined by the termination clauses in its contracts with the investors or by trade custom. There was no bargaining as to price between plaintiff and the new agents. The elements which normally are involved in a sale or exchange are lacking in this situation."

chose the mortgage banker to represent them who had attempted to purchase their accounts from Bisbee-Baldwin, while the other chose a third mortgage banker.

The mortgage bankers reimbursed the lending institutions for the termination fees paid Bisbee-Baldwin, but by no stretch of my imagination can it be said that Bisbee-Baldwin made a sale to either of the lending institutions, or to the mortgage bankers who ended up with the accounts. Bisbee-Baldwin was simply terminated as the agent for these institutions, and continued in the mortgage banking business representing its remaining accounts.

The District Court, as did this court in United States v. Eidson, 5 Cir., 1962, 310 F.2d 111, decided the case on two grounds: there was no sale or exchange, and the subject matter of the alleged sale or exchange was not a capital asset. Nelson Weaver was decided to the contrary by our court after the District Court decision, but it does not help the taxpayer on the question of sale or exchange. And this ground remains as a sound basis in law and in fact for the decision of the District Court.

* * *

The rule that we are to look through form to substance can hardly suffice to transform the cancellation of an agency, over the protest of the agent, into a sale or exchange. The agent's rights simply came to an end. The language of the District Court set out in footnote 4 of the majority opinion, supra, amply demonstrates that there was no sale or exchange:

"The contract[s] provided for termination without cause by either party. Plaintiff could not have sold its rights under the contract[s] unless the investor gave approval. Plaintiff did not assign its rights. Its contracts were terminated and the investors then entered into new contracts with other agents. * * * Plaintiff had no choice in selecting the new agent. The sums received by plaintiff were determined by the termination clauses in its contracts with the investors or by trade custom. There was no bargaining as to price between plaintiff and the new agents. The elements which normally are involved in a sale or exchange are lacking in this situation."

Thus it is that the law, in my judgment, is duly expanded in this area by the majority opinion. That this has been done is all the more regrettable in the light of the unnecessary intra-circuit conflict that the majority establishes on the question of what constitutes a capital asset. Cf. Nelson Weaver, supra.

In my view, the judgment of the District Court should be affirmed for the reason that there was no sale or exchange. Any question as to the correctness of the Nelson Weaver capital asset rule should be postponed until a case presenting the question reaches us.

———

Nelson Weaver Realty Co. v. Commissioner, 307 F.2d 897 (5th Cir. 1962), like Bisbee-Baldwin, involved the termination of a mortgage service contract. The taxpayer entered into a contract with a life insurance company and became the exclusive mortgage sales and service agency for the company within the specified territory. After operating under the contract for eight years and developing about 1,800 mortgage accounts, the taxpayer, with the consent of the life insurance company, sold its right to service these accounts, together with the relevant records and files, to another service company. The court characterized the payment received by the taxpayer as a preferential capital gain. The court reasoned, in part, that the service agreement constituted a significant item of the taxpayer's capital structure to which was attributable "more than half of its business operations over a period of years." The court also found that the amount paid for the service contract did not bear a fixed discount relationship to the net income which the purchaser would earn, in contrast to the P.G. Lake case (page 993 of this chapter) where the right to income which was sold was certain in net amount. The purchaser would sustain the uncertain cost of performing the services required by the contract.

In Foote v. Commissioner, 81 T.C. 930 (1984), appeal pending, a university professor resigned his tenured faculty position in exchange for a lump sum to be paid in installments over two taxable years. The taxpayer's treatment of the payments as preferential long-term capital gain was denied because the Tax Court viewed the payments as consideration for the termination of a contract right to receive income for the performance of future services. Consequently, the payments were a substitute for ordinary income that would have otherwise been earned by the taxpayer had he remained employed under this contract with the university. The taxpayer argued that his right to a tenured appointment involved more than a guaranteed salary from the university. Having tenure would allow him to pursue outside consulting activities for remuneration. However, the court felt that a tenured professor's ability to consult only constitutes an opportunity to earn additional ordinary income. Therefore, the court felt it was unnecessary to distinguish between the right to ordinary income under the contract and the right to earn additional income as a result of the contract.

Is a Right of First Refusal a Capital Asset? In Anderson v. United States, 468 F.Supp. 1085 (D.Minn.1979), the taxpayer, who owned the only Holiday Inn franchise in a particular city, received a right of first refusal for any other Holiday Inn franchise in that city. A few years later the hotel chain was considering the purchase of an existing Sheraton hotel in that city. The hotel chain gave taxpayer $100,000 plus a 20% share of its management fee from this newly-acquired hotel for the taxpayer's release of his right of first refusal. For the particular tax year in question, the court characterized as capital gain the entire $132,638 received for the release of the taxpayer's contract right.

References: Chirelstein, Capital Gain and the Sale of a Business Opportunity: The Income Tax Treatment of Contract Termination Payments, 49 Minn.L.Rev. 1 (1964); Comment, The Troubled Distinction Between Capital Gain and Ordinary Income, 73 Yale L.J. 693 (1964).

Question

What are the doctrinal hurdles a taxpayer had to surmount to obtain preferential capital gains treatment in a termination of contract rights case?

The taxpayer's treatment of amounts received on the installment method under § 453 turns, in part, on whether there was a sale or exchange of property. In Billy Rose's Diamond Horseshoe, Inc. v. United States, 448 F.2d 549 (2d Cir.1971), the taxpayer-lessee leased a building pursuant to a lease which required the lessee to restore the premises at the end of the term of the lease to the same condition which existed at the beginning of the term of the lease. Lessee gave the lessor promissory notes aggregating $300,000, payable in four annual installments of $75,000 each, in return for a release of the lease restoration provisions. The court found the lessee's promissory notes constituted ordinary income to the lessor when received by the lessor. Section 453(b)(1) was held inapplicable because the release of the right to restoration was not disposition of property. The court indicated:

> * * * [C]ancellation or release of a contract right does not transfer the rights to the transferee-payor and this is not a "sale." * * * As this court stated in Starr Bros., 204 F.2d at 674:
>
> > "What the taxpayer gave in return for the cash payment was a release of United's contract obligations, chief of which was its promise not to sell its products to other dealers in New London. Such release not only ended the promisor's previously existing duty but also destroyed the promisee's rights. They were not transferred to the promisor; they merely came to an end and vanished."
>
> Similarly in this case, the release not only ended the lessee's duty under the lease restoration clause but also destroyed [taxpayer's] rights to have the property restored. These contract rights came to an end and vanished. The lessee purchased no property but merely extinguished its liabilities under the restoration clause. (448 F.2d at 551).

In another case, however, the taxpayer could report income from the sale of its loan and mortgage-servicing business where a portion of the sales price was attributable to the right to receive service fees (which constituted ordinary income) on the installment method under § 453. The mortgage servicing contracts sold were "property" eligible for installment sale treatment under § 453(b)(1). The Code and the judicial interpretation of the definition of "property" for capital gains purposes were not incorporated into the installment sale provisions which deal with the apportionment of gain. Realty Loan Corp. v. Commissioner, 478 F.2d 1049 (9th Cir.1973).

K. DEDUCTIONS AFFECTED BY CHARACTERIZATION PRINCIPLES

1. BUSINESS AND NON–BUSINESS BAD DEBTS AND WORTH-LESS SECURITIES

In General. Taxpayers receive a deduction for bad debts in computing taxable income. § 166(a)(1). A glance at § 166(b) shows that the amount of the bad debts deduction is limited to the adjusted basis of the debt as prescribed under § 1011. If the taxpayer is the original creditor, his basis equals the amount loaned. If the taxpayer acquired the debt, his basis equals the amount he paid to acquire the debt.

To qualify for a deduction under § 166, a debt must be a bona fide debt, that is, one "which arises from a debtor-creditor relationship based upon a valid and enforceable obligation to pay a fixed or determinable sum of money." Reg. § 1.166–1(c). When the loan is made, the creditor must reasonably expect repayment. A number of items specifically acknowledged to give rise to bad debts are described in the Regulations. These include notes, accounts receivable, bankruptcy claims, and claims against a decedent's estate. Reg. § 1.166–1(d)(2).

A bad debt deduction is unavailable if the taxpayer intends to make a gift. If the taxpayer's brother-in-law meets financial reverses and the taxpayer bails him out under circumstances where it is apparent that the debt will never be repaid, the Commissioner will contend that the transaction was a gift throughout; hence the bad debt deduction would be lost because no actual "debt" existed. Reg. § 1.166–1(c). Logically, transfers between relatives or close friends are presumed not to be loans. The taxpayer may, of course, rebut the presumption.

Another limitation exists with respect to the deductibility of bad debts. Assume that T, a lawyer, performs services with the reasonable value of $100 for X. X does not pay. If T is on the cash method of accounting, can T take a deduction for the bad debt which arose from the client's failure to pay? § 166(b).

Under the circumstances, T cannot take the deduction. T has no basis in the debt because T never treated the item as income. Reg. § 1.166–1(e). The net economic result of the transaction to T was that the transaction neither added to nor subtracted from T's economic worth. T did not receive the accession to wealth which he expected.

Debts Evidenced by a Security. Special rules exist for the treatment of a security which is a capital asset and which becomes worthless during the taxable year. §§ 166(e) and 165(g). A loss resulting from a worthless debt evidenced by a security (for example, a bond) gives rise to a capital loss which is treated as a loss from the sale or exchange of a capital asset on the last day of the taxable year. The term "security" is defined in § 165(g)(2). The type of capital loss (long-term or short-term) depends on whether the statutory mandated end of the year holding period together with the taxpayer's actual holding period results in a long-term or short-term holding period. A worthless security will generally generate a long-term capital loss. Thus, the tax consequences of worthless securities are less attractive than nonbusiness bad debts and considerably less attractive than business bad debts. To forestall a taxpayer's claim that a worthless security should be treated as a bad debt, § 166(e) explicitly negates the applicability of the bad debt rules under § 166 to worthless securities.

Business Bad Debts. If an individual creditor's claim is not evidenced by a security, the loss on a worthless debt is governed by § 166 which distinguishes between business bad debts and nonbusiness bad debts. A debt created or acquired in connection with the taxpayer's trade or business or a debt which was incurred in connection with the taxpayer's trade or business is a business bad debt. § 166(d)(2). And, a business bad debt is deductible as an ordinary loss against the taxpayer's income. § 165(a). The deduction for business bad debts may be taken by designating those business bad debts which have, in fact, become totally or partially worthless in the tax year. § 166(a) and (d).

Nonbusiness Bad Debts. Different rules exist for nonbusiness bad debts which are defined in § 166(d)(2). Unlike business debts, partially worthless nonbusiness debts are not deductible. Nonbusiness debts can only be deducted in the year of total worthlessness. And, under § 166(d), nonbusiness bad debts are deductible as only short-term capital losses.

Several reasons underpin the treatment of nonbusiness bad debts. In Putnam v. Commissioner, 352 U.S. 82, 91–92, 77 S.Ct. 175, 179–180, 1 L.Ed.2d 144 (1956), the Supreme Court indicated that the short-term capital loss treatment for nonbusiness bad debts was "a means for minimizing the revenue losses attributable to the fraudulent practices of taxpayers who made gifts to relatives and friends disguised as loans * * * [and] to put nonbusiness investments in the form of loans on a footing with other nonbusiness investments." But, why does the Code permit a taxpayer to deduct a nonbusiness bad debt incurred in connection with a personal activity of the taxpayer?

A taxpayer would be better off if a transaction arises out of a profit-seeking activity so as to characterize it as an ordinary loss. Under § 165(c)(2), losses in connection with profit-seeking activities are deductible in full. If the transaction arises out of the taxpayer's trade or business, a loss on a business bad debt is deductible in full. § 165(c)(1). However, the ultimate benefit of short term capital losses for individual taxpayers may not be as great as ordinary losses because capital losses offset only capital gains and a limited amount of ordinary income. § 1211(b).

Distinguishing Business and Non Business Bad Debts. Because the characterization of a bad debt has significant tax consequences, courts have attempted to set forth guidelines to delineate the business and nonbusiness bad debts of individuals. The judiciary is really trying to draw a line between trade or business activities on one hand, and investment activities on the other. The problem, as it typically arises, was litigated in Whipple v. Commissioner, 373 U.S. 193, 83 S.Ct. 1168, 10 L.Ed.2d 288 (1963), rehearing denied, 374 U.S. 858, 83 S.Ct. 1863, 10 L.Ed.2d 1082 (1963), where the taxpayer made loans to a corporation in which he was a major shareholder and chief executive officer. The corporation was one of a number of companies through which the taxpayer conducted various activities. In seeking to establish that he had an independent trade or business and thus was eligible for business bad debt status, the taxpayer argued that he furnished regular services to his corporate enterprises. The Supreme Court rejected the taxpayer's contention and viewed his shareholder-creditor activities as those of an investor. In holding that the debts, on becoming worthless, were deductible as nonbusiness bad debts, the Supreme Court stated (373 U.S. at 201–23, 83 S.Ct. at 1173–1174):

> The 1942 amendment of [§ 166] therefore, as the Court has already noted, Putnam v. Commissioner, 352 U.S. 82, 90–92, 77 S.Ct. 175, 179–180, 1 L.Ed.2d 144, was intended to accomplish far more than to deny full deductibility to the worthless debts of family and friends. It was designed to make full deductibility of a bad debt turn upon its proximate connection with activities which the tax laws recognized as a trade or business, a concept which falls far short of reaching every income or profit making activity.

* * *

> Petitioner, therefore, must demonstrate that he is engaged in a trade or business, and lying at the heart of his claim is the issue upon which the lower courts have divided and which brought the case here: That where a taxpayer furnishes regular services to one or many corporations, an independent trade or business of the taxpayer has been shown. * * *

> Devoting one's time and energies to the affairs of a corporation is not of itself, and without more, a trade or business of the person so engaged. Though such activities may produce income, profit or gain in the form of dividends or enhancement in the value of an investment, this return is distinctive to the process of investing and is generated by the successful operation of the corporation's business as distinguished from the trade or business of the taxpayer himself. When the only return is that of an investor, the taxpayer has not satisfied his burden of demonstrating that he is engaged in a trade or business since investing is not a trade or business and the return to the taxpayer, though substantially the product of his services, legally arises not from his own trade or business but from that of the corporation. Even if the taxpayer demonstrates an independent trade or business of his own, care must be taken to distinguish bad debt losses arising from his own business and those actually arising from activities peculiar to an investor concerned with, and participating in, the conduct of the corporate business.

If full-time service to one corporation does not alone amount to a trade or business, which it does not, it is difficult to understand how the same service to many corporations would suffice. To be sure, the presence of more than one corporation might lend support to a finding that the taxpayer was engaged in a regular course of promoting corporations for a fee or commission, see Ballantine, Corporations (rev. ed. 1946), 102, or for a profit on their sale, see Giblin v. Commissioner, 227 F.2d 692 (C.A.5th Cir.), but in such cases there is compensation other than the normal investor's return, income received directly for his own services rather than indirectly through the corporate enterprise, * * *. On the other hand, since the Tax Court found, and the petitioner does not dispute, that there was no intention here of developing the corporations as going businesses for sale to customers in the ordinary course, the case before us inexorably rests upon the claim that one who actively engages in serving his own corporations for the purpose of creating future income through those enterprises is in a trade or business. That argument is untenable * * * and we reject it. Absent substantial additional evidence, furnishing management and other services to corporations for a reward not different from that flowing to an investor in those corporations is not a trade or business under [§ 166(d)].

The taxpayer may, however, establish that the debt is a business bad debt which qualifies for an ordinary loss deduction if the loan arises: (1) in the taxpayer's business of loaning money; (2) in the taxpayer's business of financing or promoting corporate enterprises; (3) in the creation or protection of business relationships or the protection of the taxpayer's business reputation; or (4) in an effort to protect or advance the taxpayer's job, that is, the taxpayer's business of working as an employee of the debtor. The Supreme Court in Commissioner v. Generes, 405 U.S. 93, 92 S.Ct. 827, 31 L.Ed.2d 62 (1972), rehearing denied 405 U.S. 1033, 92 U.S. 1274, 31 L.Ed.2d 491 (1972) resolved the degree of proximity a loan by a taxpayer who wore two hats—as investor and employee—must bear to the taxpayer's business. The Court stated (405 U.S. at 103, 92 S.Ct. at 833): " * * * in determining whether a bad debt has a 'proximate' relation to the taxpayer's trade or business, as the Regulations specify, and thus qualifies as a business bad debt, the proper measure is that of dominant motivation, and that only significant motivation is not sufficient."

The business bad debt deduction is allowable only if the taxpayer establishes that his dominant motive in making the loan was connection with his business relationship with the debtor. In some cases, e.g. Anderson v. United States, 555 F.2d 236 (9th Cir.1977), the taxpayer met the heavy burden of proof requisite to establishing a loan as a business bad debt. See also Bowers v. United States, 716 F.2d 1047 (4th Cir.1983), where the court allowed a business bad debt deduction for a personal loan by the sole shareholder of a realty agency to a major client. According to the court, it would have defied logic and business reality to conclude that the loan was not made predominantly to maintain the enhanced level of his income resulting from transactions with the client. Would a better result have been to add the amount of the loan to his basis in the corporation and allow the bad debt deduction to the corporation?

How to Determine When a Debt is Worthless. One of the principal problems in claiming deductions for business debts is that they must be claimed in the year in which they become worthless. § 166(a). The taxpayer must show this fact in the same manner as he shows any other fact. The taxpayer bears the burden of proof with respect to worthlessness. Reg. § 1.166–3. There can be no accurate prediction of what factors will ultimately be controlling in a determination with respect to the time at which a debt becomes worthless. In the Regulations the Commissioner repeats the old saying that all pertinent evidence will be considered; the value of any collateral and the financial condition of the debtor are specifically mentioned. Reg. § 1.166–2(a). Of course, if the collateral is adequate to satisfy the obligation it can scarcely be said that the debt is worthless.

Legal action to collect the debt is clearly not required as long as there is a showing of worthlessness. Filing of a bankruptcy petition is generally an indication that an unsecured and unpreferred debt is at least partially worthless. LaStaiti v. Commissioner, 41 T.C.M. (CCH) 511 (1980). In many cases a debt will become worthless long before either bankruptcy or settlement with creditors, and the deduction should be taken in the earlier year. Reg. § 1.166–2(b) and (c). In short, worthlessness is determined as of the time it becomes apparent there would be no recovery from a legal action brought in a debtor-creditor relationship. One simple way of proving worthlessness is to demonstrate that the debtor is insolvent, has left the jurisdiction, and that no security for the debt exists. Other elements of proof readily come to mind: death or disappearance of the debtor leaving an insolvent estate, or the fact that the debtor has abandoned his business.

How Deduction is Available for Partially Worthless Debt. The taxpayer having a partially worthless business bad debt may deduct the worthless portion under § 166(a)(2). This deduction is only allowed for business bad debts. Close attention must be paid to Reg. § 1.166–3(a). If a business bad debt becomes one-third worthless in one year, a deduction is given to that extent. If the debt becomes totally worthless in the next year, a bad debt deduction for the remaining two-thirds of the debt is available for the second year.

Specific Charge-Off Method. The specific charge-off method allows a taxpayer to deduct bad debts as the bad debt becomes wholly or partially worthless. When a receivable is determined to be uncollectible, in whole or in part, the taxpayer reduces the receivable by the amount which is uncollectible and receives a deduction for such amount. If the taxpayer later recovers an amount charged-off as uncollectible, the taxpayer treats the recovery as a separate income item at the time of collection.

Problems

1. Ted Player purchased a registered corporate bond for $10,000 on June 1 of Year 1. What is the amount and character of his loss if:

(a) Ted sells the bond for $8,500 on October 1 of Year 1.

(b) the bond becomes worthless on October 1 of Year 1.

Consider §§ 166 and 165(g).

2. Ted Player sold his home and took back a second mortgage from the purchaser in the amount of $10,000, interest at 10%, and due in five years. Assume the note was executed on June 1 of Year 1. What is the amount and character of Ted's loss if:

(a) he sells the note for $9,500 on July 1 of Year 2.

(b) the note becomes worthless on July 1 of Year 2.

Consider § 166 and the excerpt from the Whipple case. Assume Ted does not purchase another residence and that he is under age 55 so that §§ 121 and 1034 do not apply.

3. (a) In Year 1, Uncle Ned lends his niece $1,000 so that she could open her own business, a cute little shop in a trendy section of town. By the end of Year 2 the niece is unable to pay back the loan, and Uncle Ned wishes to write it off as a bad debt. Can he take an ordinary loss because his niece used the proceeds for her business? Consider the excerpt from the Whipple case.

(b) Assume Uncle Ned claimed and was allowed a bad debt deduction for the loan in Year 2. In Year 3, the niece repays the loan the full. What are the tax consequences to Uncle Ned in Year 3? What if Uncle Ned used the standard deduction for Year 2? Consider §§ 62, 111, and the Arrowsmith case (page 985).

4. Sarah pays for an airline ticket on Comrade's Express to fly to Miami on vacation. Before the flight the airline goes bankrupt and she has to buy another ticket. Can she deduct the cost of her first ticket?

2. CHARITABLE CONTRIBUTION DEDUCTION FOR GIFTS OF APPRECIATED ASSETS

Special tax incentives exist for gifts of appreciated assets. The taxpayer receives a deduction for a contribution in the form of a gift of money or property. The donor is not deemed to have exchanged property and therefore does not realize income on the contribution of appreciated gifts in kind. Rev.Rul. 55–410, 1955–1 C.B. 297. Unless the Code otherwise provides, the amount of a charitable contribution equals the fair market value of property other than money. Reg. § 1.170A–1(c)(2) defines the term "fair market value." The taxpayer receives a deduction for the pre-contribution appreciation of property.

With the charitable deduction for the gift of an appreciated asset generally pegged to its fair market value, the determination of fair market value becomes critical. Consider the next revenue ruling.

REV.RUL. 80–69
1980–1 C.B. 55.

ISSUE

How is the fair market value of property contributed to charity determined for federal income tax purposes under the circumstances described below?

FACTS

During 1978, an individual taxpayer who was not a dealer in gems purchased an assortment of gems for $500x$ dollars from a promoter who asserted that the price was "wholesale", even though the promoter and various other dealers engaged in numerous similar sales at similar prices with individuals who were not dealers in gems. The promoter represented that if the taxpayer held the gems for over one year and then contributed them to charity the taxpayer would be entitled to a deduction of $1500x$ dollars at the time of contribution. The promoter contended that the value at the time of contribution would be at least three times as much as the price paid by the taxpayer. The taxpayer contributed the gems to a public museum 13 months after purchase, claiming a charitable contributions deduction of $1500x$ dollars. The museum is an organization described in section 170(c) of the Internal Revenue Code, contributions to which are deductible under section 170(a)(1). The museum will use the gems in a manner related to its exempt purposes.

LAW AND ANALYSIS

Section 170(a)(1) of the Code allows as a deduction any charitable contribution (as defined in section 170(c)) payment of which is made within the taxable year.

Section 1.170A–1(c)(1) of the Income Tax Regulations provides that if a charitable contribution is made in property other than money, the amount of the contribution is the fair market value of the property at the time of contribution, reduced as provided in section 170(e)(1) of the Code.

Section 1.170A–1(c)(2) of the regulations provides that the fair market value is the price at which the property would change hands between a willing buyer and a willing seller, neither being under any compulsion to buy or sell and both having a reasonable knowledge of relevant facts.

The definition of fair market value depends upon a knowledgeable willing buyer and a knowledgeable willing seller. To determine fair market value, reference is made to the most active marketplace at the time of the donor's contribution. The best evidence of fair market value depends on actual transactions and not on some artificially calculated estimate of value contrary to the prices at which the very gems at issue changed hands in the marketplace. The 500x dollars at which the promoter sold the gems to the taxpayer and others, rather than a mere speculative claim of what the gems would be worth, is the best evidence of the maximum fair market value of the gems.

HOLDING

For federal income tax purposes the fair market value of the gems was no greater than 500x dollars.

———

See also, e.g., Chiu v. Commissioner, 84 T.C. 722 (1985) (the taxpayer, who paid about $57,000 for gemstones, deducted $263,000 for donating them; the court cut the deductions back to the prices paid, "the most reliable evidence" of the value. The taxpayer's experts' valuations were not persuasive because they were not based on sales of comparable items in the collector's market and the experts had essentially no training in appraisal techniques) and Anselmo v. Commissioner, 757 F.2d 1208 (11th Cir.1985), (the deduction for donated gems was limited to the value of the gems as if sold in bulk to a jewelry manufacturer, not their retail market value).

Reference: Speiler, The Favored Tax Treatment of Purchasers of Art, 80 Columbia L.Rev. 214 (1980).

The widespread overvaluation of contributions of appreciated property was partially responsible for the enactment of § 6659. Section 6659 imposes a penalty on the underpayment of income tax for a taxable year which results from a significant overstatement of the value of property contributed in kind to a charity. The penalty is imposed only if: (1) the value of the contributed property claimed by the taxpayer exceeds 150 percent or more of the correct value of the property; and (2) the amount of the underpayment attributable to the valuation overstatement is at least $1,000. § 6659(c) and (d).

Taxpayers must maintain written documentation for each charitable contribution made. Reg. § 1.170A–13. A taxpayer making a charitable contribution of property other than money must have a receipt from the donee charitable organization and a reliable written record of specified information with respect to the donated property. Reg. § 1.170A–13(b)(2)–(4). Moreover, taxpayers who make post-1984 contributions of property valued in excess of $5,000 must comply with specified appraisal requirements. See Temp.Reg. § 1.170A–13T(b)(1) and (c).

Appreciated capital gain property (defined in § 170(b)(1)(C)(iv)), such as intangible personal property (for example, securities) and real estate held for more than the long-term holding period, may be deducted (subject to the 50 percent and 20 percent limits) only to the extent it does not exceed 30 percent of the taxpayer's contribution base in the year in which the contribution is made. § 170(b)(1)(c)(i). The amount of the capital gain property contribution allowed under the 30 percent limit is applied to the 50 percent or 20 percent limits depending on the type of charity receiving the contribution. In determining whether the taxpayer has exceeded the respective 50 percent or 20 percent limits, contributions of capital gain property are taken into account after all other contributions. § 170(b)(1)(C)(i). If the contributions of capital gain property exceed the 30 percent limit in any year, there is a carryover of such excess amount of the individual's deduction for the next five years. The carryover deduction is subject to the 30 percent limitation in each of the next five years. § 170(b)(1)(C)(i) and (ii) and (d) (1).

If the charitable donee puts tangible personal property which is a capital asset to a use unrelated to its charitable function or purpose the amount of the deduction, for an individual, is reduced by the long-term capital gain the taxpayer would have realized and recognized if the taxpayer had sold the property at its fair market value. § 170(e)(1)(B). In other words, the deduction is limited to the donor's basis in the capital asset. This limitation is not applicable if the charitable donee's use of the tangible personal property is related to its charitable function or purpose, e.g. art object given to a museum.

In case of a taxpayer's gift of appreciated property which if sold by the taxpayer for its fair market value would have produced ordinary income (for example, inventory or property held by the taxpayer primarily for sale to customers in the ordinary course of the taxpayer's business) or short-term capital gain, § 170(e)(1)(A) provides that generally the taxpayer's deduction for such property is limited to the basis of the property. No deduction is allowed for the pre-contribution appreciation on such assets even if the charity's use of the property is related to its charitable function.

Repeated charitable contributions of appreciated property may be characterized as ordinary income property. For charitable contribution purposes, individuals, because of the frequency and continuity of contributions, may be deemed to be engaged in activities substantially equivalent to those of commercial dealers. Rev.Rul. 79–256, 1979–2 C.B. 105. Thus, an individual's charitable contribution will be reduced by the amount of the appreciation in value of the assets. See also Rev.Rul. 79–419, 1979–2 C.B. 107.

Reference: Wittenbach and Milani, Charting The Current Rules On Charitable Contributions, 63 Taxes 541 (1985).

Problems

1. Terry Player owns shares of stock, which she bought several years ago, with a basis of $10,000. The stock is a capital asset. The shares are now worth $20,000. Assume the Players' adjusted gross income for the

year is approximately $100,000 and they have made no other charitable gifts in the tax year.

(a) What is the maximum charitable deduction she can get for the tax year if she gives cash to her law school? Consider § 170(b)(1)(A).

(b) Instead, she gives the stock outright to her law school. What is the maximum charitable deduction she can get for the tax year? Will she receive a charitable deduction for the full market value of the stock? Consider § 170(b)(1)(C)(i) and (iv). Will she realize any gain on the contribution of the stock? Consider § 170(e).

(c) What happens when the law school sells the stock? Consider §§ 501(a) and (c)(3), and 1015(a).

(d) What if Terri had converted the shares of stock to cash before the contribution was made? Should the taxpayer donate the appreciated shares of stock or sell the stock and give the cash proceeds to the school? Consider § 170(b)(1)(C)(i) and (e).

(e) What if her basis for the shares of stock had been $20,000 and its value $10,000? Why should she sell the shares and give the cash proceeds instead of donating the shares to the school? Reg. § 1.170A–1(c)(1). If she contributes stock has she sustained a loss under Reg. § 1.1001–1(a)? If the shares are given to the school, can the school use the loss? § 501(a).

2. What result in "1" above if the contributed property was a parcel of raw land held as an investment? Assume the land is located several miles from the campus and that the law school intends to sell the land to fund construction of a library addition.

Question

Should the charitable contribution deduction be limited to the basis of appreciated property? Or, should the donation of appreciated property result in the realization, in whole or in part, of the pre-contribution appreciation in value? Do you agree with § 170(e)(5)? Consider the following excerpt:

OFFICE OF THE SECRETARY, DEPARTMENT OF THE TREASURY, TAX REFORM FOR FAIRNESS, SIMPLICITY, AND ECONOMIC GROWTH
Vol. 2, 72–74 (1984).

REASONS FOR CHANGE

The current treatment of certain charitable gifts of appreciated property is unduly generous and in conflict with basic principles governing the measurement of income for tax purposes. In other circumstances where appreciated property is used to pay a deductible expense, or where such property is the subject of a deductible loss, the deduction allowed may not exceed the taxpayer's adjusted basis plus any gain recognized. Thus, a taxpayer generally may not receive a tax deduction with respect to untaxed appreciation in property. The current tax treatment of certain charitable gifts departs from this principle by permitting the donor a deduction for the full value of the property, including the element of appreciation with respect to which the donor does not realize gain.

The generous tax treatment for certain gifts of appreciated property also creates an incentive for taxpayers to make gifts of such property rather than gifts of cash, even though in many instances charities would prefer to receive cash rather than property of equivalent value. A taxpayer in the [33] percent bracket making a gift of $[210] in cash receives a $[210] deduction. This translates to [a $70] savings in tax, which reduces the after-tax cost of the $[210] gift to $[140]. The same taxpayer donating $[210] worth of property that is a capital asset held for the long-term capital gain holding period receives the same $[210] deduction and $[70] in tax savings. If, however, the donated property is appreciated property, the donor receives an additional tax savings by avoiding tax on the property's appreciation. Although the value of this tax savings depends on the amount of the property's appreciation and on when and how the donor otherwise would have disposed of the asset, its availability has proved to have a significant influence on the form of charitable donations.

Current law does limit the amount of the deduction for certain gifts of appreciated property, but these rules are only a partial response to the problem and require complicated inquiries concerning the donee's use of the property and the character of the property in the donor's hands. In addition, under current law it is necessary in almost all instances to value the donated property. This is a significant burden for taxpayers and for the Internal Revenue Service and leaves the system open to serious abuse through fraudulent overvaluations of contributed property.

PROPOSAL

A deduction for charitable donations of property would be allowed for the lesser of the fair market value or the inflation-adjusted basis of the property. * * *

* * *

ANALYSIS

For most income groups, charitable contributions are usually made in the form of cash, rather than property. For returns with adjusted gross incomes under $100,000, less than ten percent of contributions constitute property. Only for incomes over $200,000 does property account for as much as 40 percent of all contributions. Thus, the benefits of present law accrue to taxpayers with the [higher] marginal tax rates.

The proposal would eliminate the unwarranted tax advantages for donations of appreciated long-term capital gain property, as well as the complex rules limiting deductions for the various types of property that may be given to charity. In addition, the proposal would substantially eliminate the most serious opportunities for abuse through overvaluations of donated property.

The proposal also would eliminate the need for detailed valuations of contributed property in those cases in which the fair market value of the property clearly exceeds its adjusted basis. * * * Although valuations also would continue to be necessary for many gifts of depreciated property, taxpayers could ordinarily be expected, as under current law, to sell certain types of depreciated property and donate the proceeds of the sale in order to receive the benefit of any deductible loss. By significantly reducing the instances in which property valuations would be necessary, the proposal would ease the burden on taxpayers and the Internal Revenue Service caused by appraisal requirements.

The elimination of the current overly generous treatment of gifts of appreciated long-term capital gain property may have some adverse impact on the level of charitable giving. Some taxpayers, who are able to make gifts to charity at little or no after-tax cost under current law, may reduce their level of giving if current tax benefits are no longer available. The charitable contribution deduction, however, would still provide a significant incentive for charitable giving.

L. DEPRECIATION (ACCELERATED COST RECOVERY) DEDUCTIONS AND CAPITAL GAINS: RECAPTURE PROVISIONS

1. DEDUCTIONS UNDER THE ACCELERATED COST RECOVERY SYSTEM AND CAPITAL GAINS

When reviewing the subject of cost recovery and depreciation you should remember that the entrepreneur or investor seeks to maximize deductions which are taken dollar for dollar against ordinary income. If the depreciation deductions are greater than the decline in the value of an asset, the property's value will exceed its adjusted basis. On the sale of depreciable property held for more than six months, the amount realized over the taxpayer's adjusted basis will go into § 1231, which could have resulted in preferential long-term capital gains. The taxpayer will have converted ordinary income (more specifically, depreciation deductions which reduce ordinary income) into previously preferential long-term capital gains.

The use of this technique to obtain tax advantages became so marked that so-called recapture statutes were passed in the 1960's to block or reduce capital gains treatment on the sale of assets where the taxpayer had previously recovered all or part of the asset's basis by deductions against ordinary income. Sections 1245 and 1250 require that the taxpayer report ("recapture"), on the sale of an asset, as ordinary income all or a portion of the depreciation (cost recovery) deductions previously taken.

2. RECAPTURE UNDER SECTION 1245

The following excerpt sets forth the reasons for the depreciation recapture under § 1245.

S.REP. NO. 1881, 87th CONG. 2d SESS.
1962–3 C.B. 707, 801.

XIII. Gain From Disposition of Certain Depreciable Property

A. Reasons for provision

Under [prior] law, in the case of depreciable property the taxpayer may write off the cost or other basis of the property over the period of the useful life of the asset in his hands. This cost or other basis can be written off evenly (i.e., in a "straight line" over the asset's life), under the declining balance method, under the sum-of-the-[years] digits method, or under any other consistent method which does not during the first two-thirds of the useful life of the property exceed the allowances which would have been allowed under the declining balance method. The depreciation deduction is a deduction against ordinary income. If either the useful life of the asset is too short, or the particular method of depreciation allows too much depreciation in the early years, the decline in value of the asset resulting from these depreciation deductions may exceed the actual decline. Wherever the depreciation deductions reduce the basis of the property faster than the actual decline in its value, then when it is sold there will be a gain. Under [prior] law this gain [was] taxed as a [preferential] capital gain, even though the depreciation deductions reduced ordinary income. The taxpayer who has taken excessive depreciation deductions and then sells an asset, therefore, has in effect converted ordinary income into a [preferential] capital gain.

The President stated that our capital gains concept should not encompass the kind of income. He indicated that this inequity should be eliminated * * *. He states that we should not encourage the further acquisition of such property through tax incentives as long as the loophole remains.

Section 1245 applies to the sale, exchange or other disposition of "section 1245 property" unless expressly exempted under § 1245(b).

"Section 1245 property" includes all depreciable personal property (e.g. machinery and equipment) and certain items of depreciable real property (e.g. fixtures such as a refrigerator in an apartment building). § 1245(a)(3). Although buildings are generally excluded from the definition of "section 1245 property," certain specialized buildings are classified as "section 1245 property." Examine § 1245(a)(3)(B)–(E). In addition, if a taxpayer placed non-residential real property in service between 1981 and 1986 and depreciated that property under the 175 percent declining balance method previously permitted under former

§ 168(b)(2)(A), then under former § 1245(a)(5) that building was classified as "section 1245 property" and was subject to the recapture rules under § 1245(a)(1). Nonresidential real property covers commercial buildings such as an office or a retail store. Examine §§ 168(e)(2)(B), 167(j)(2)(B) and 167(k)(3)(C). The application of the recapture rules under § 1245(a)(1) for nonresidential real property placed in service after 1980 but before 1987 could have been avoided if the taxpayer elected, pursuant to § 168(b)(3), to depreciate the building using the straight line method. See former § 1245(a)(5)(C). By electing to use the straight line method, nonresidential real property became "section 1250 property" and was subject to the recapture rules of § 1250(a)(1). As will be explained shortly, this meant that there could be no depreciation recapture, provided the building was held for more than one year. Finally, pursuant to § 168(b)(1) and (2), a taxpayer is permitted to depreciate all personal property placed in service after 1986 using either the 200 or 150 percent declining balance method. Although a taxpayer is also permitted, under either §§ 168(b)(3)(C) or 168(g)(7), to depreciate personal property using the straight line method, such an election does not remove personal property from the reach of § 1245(a)(1). All personal property is classified as "section 1245 property" regardless of the method of depreciation used or when it is placed in service.

To the extent that a gain on the disposition of "section 1245 property" is attributable to prior depreciation or amortization deductions taken on that property (consider the effect of § 1016(a) on the basis of property), § 1245(a)(1) requires that such gain be immediately recognized as ordinary income (§ 64). The recognition of ordinary income required by § 1245(a)(1) is commonly referred to as "depreciation recapture." However, under § 1245(b) certain dispositions of "section 1245 property" are exempted from the mandatory recognition requirement of § 1245(a)(1) either because the disposition is not a taxable event (e.g. a gift, § 1245(b)(1), or a bequest, § 1245(b)(2)), or because the disposition is subject to a non-recognition provision (e.g. a like-kind exchange under § 1031, § 1245(b)(4)). Dispositions by gift and dispositions subject to a non-recognition provision are exempted from the immediate recognition requirement of § 1245(a)(1) because the recapture taint created when the property was depreciated prior to its disposition continues in the property received by gift or in the property received in a non-recognition disposition. Examine §§ 1015(a) and 1031(d). For example, a donee, by taking the donor's basis in the property under § 1015(a), will eventually characterize as ordinary income all or a part of the gain he subsequently may report to the extent the gain is attributable to depreciation deductions taken by the donor. In other words, the recapture taint created by the donor is carried over to the donee. The donee also carries over other tax attributes of the donor such as tacking of holding periods. § 1223(2). Under § 1245(a)(3), if the donor depreciated the personal property, it is "section 1245 property" in the hands of the donee even though the donee does not depreciate the property. Rev. Rul. 69-487, 1969-2 C.B.165.

As indicated in the legislative history of § 1245, depreciation recapture is primarily designed to determine the character of a gain already realized and recognized by the taxpayer. Therefore, a taxpayer is not required to report as ordinary income an amount greater than the actual gain. Gain realized and recognized on the disposition of "section 1245 property" will be treated as ordinary income to the extent of the lesser of: (1) the gain, or (2) all post-1961 depreciation deductions (regardless of the method of depreciation) on the property. More specifically, ordinary income will be recognized on the disposition of "section 1245 property" to the extent of the lesser of:

(1) the *amount realized* on a sale, exchange, or involuntary conversion or the fair market value on any other disposition *exceeds* the taxpayer's *adjusted basis* for the property, or

(2) the *recomputed basis* (§ 1245(a)(2)), that is, the taxpayer's adjusted basis of "section 1245 property" plus all deductions, allowed or allowable, for depreciation or amortization by the taxpayer or any other person (such as a donor) *exceeds* the taxpayer's *adjusted basis* for the property.

Although § 1245(a) is primarily a characterization provision, there are situations, otherwise qualifying for non-recognition treatment, where § 1245(a) will require the immediate recognition of the recapture portion of the gain. § 1245(d). If a disposition is not exempted from the reach of § 1245(a) by any of the exceptions contained in § 1245(b), then the recapture income must be immediately recognized. Examine § 453(i), discussed at page 1030.

3. RECAPTURE UNDER SECTION 1250

The following excerpt sets forth the reasons for depreciation recapture under § 1250:

S.REP. No. 830, 88th CONG. 2d SESS.
1964-1 C.B. 505, 635-636 (Part 2).

40. DISPOSITION OF DEPRECIABLE REAL ESTATE

(a) [Prior] Law—Under present law, taxpayers may take depreciation on real property (other than land) used in trade or business or held for the production of income. * * *

The depreciation is allowed as a deduction against ordinary income. As the depreciation deduction is taken the cost or other basis of the real property is reduced by a like amount. If the property subsequently is sold, any gain realized on the difference between sales price (adjusted downward for selling expenses) and the adjusted basis of the property is taxed as a [preferential] capital gain if the total transactions in depreciable property and certain other property (referred to in sec. 1231) result in a gain for the year involved. On the other hand, where the aggregate of these transactions results in a loss, the net loss is an ordinary loss.

(b) General reasons for provisions—Since the depreciation deductions are taken against ordinary income while any gain on the sale of the property is treated as a [preferential] capital gain, there is an opportunity under present law in effect to convert ordinary income into capital gain. This occurs whenever the depreciation deductions allowed reduce the basis of the property faster than the actual decline in its value.

Congress in the Revenue Act of 1962 recognized the existence of this same problem in the case of gains from the disposition of depreciable machinery and other personal property. In that act, the Congress provided that any gain realized on the sale of these assets in the future would be ordinary income to the extent of any depreciation deductions taken in 1962 and subsequent years with respect to the property.

In the case of real estate, this problem is magnified by the fact that real estate is usually acquired through debt financing and the depreciation deductions allowed relate not only to the taxpayer's equity investment but to the indebtedness as well. Since the depreciation deductions relate to the indebtedness as well as the equity in the property, this may permit the tax-free amortization of any mortgage on the property. As a result in such cases there is a tax-free cash return of a part of the investment which may in fact enable the taxpayer to show a loss for several years which he may offset against income for tax purposes. * * *

———

Section 1250 applies the recapture principle to all dispositions of "section 1250 property" unless expressly exempted from the recapture rules by § 1250(d). However, under § 1250(a) only a portion of the depreciation taken on "section 1250 property" is treated by the § 1250 recapture rules as ordinary income.

"Section 1250 property" includes all depreciable real property except those buildings governed by § 1245. § 1250(c). Under former § 1245(a)(5)(C) nonresidential real property placed in service between 1981 and 1986 and depreciated using an accelerated method was classified as "section 1245 recovery property." Both residential rental property, regardless of how depreciated, and nonresidential real property, depreciated using the straight line method, acquired between 1981 and 1986 are "section 1250 property." §§ 1250(c) and former 1250(d)(11). All real estate, both residential and nonresidential, acquired before 1981 is "section 1250 property" regardless of the method of depreciation used. Finally, all real estate acquired after 1986 is "section 1250 property."

Although a building which has been depreciated is "section 1250 property," it does not automatically follow that the recapture provisions under § 1250(a) will require the recognition of ordinary income.

Generally, recapture under § 1250 is not as stringent as under § 1245. On a disposition of "section 1250 property" the amount treated as ordinary income under § 1250(a) is limited to the amount by which the depreciation deductions taken on the building exceed the amount of depreciation that would have been taken had the straight line method been used, the so-called "additional depreciation." § 1250(b)(1). Therefore, only "section 1250 property" depreciated using an accelerated method gives rise to depreciation recapture. There will be no recapture if the building was depreciated using the straight line method. Thus, where the use of the straight line method is required for both residential rental property and nonresidential real property placed in service after 1986, § 168(b)(3), there is no recapture with respect to the depreciation deductions even though the buildings are "section 1250 property."

A series of complex rules govern recapture of pre-1976 depreciation on § 1250 residential property held for more than one year. Simply stated, for depreciation attributable to periods after 1969 but before 1976, the percentage of depreciation recaptured on the disposition of § 1250 residential property varies with the holding period. § 1250(a)(2)(B)(iii). The pre-1976 additional depreciation on § 1250 nonresidential property is subject to recapture. § 1250(a)(1)(C)(v). A special recapture rule for corporations is contained in § 291(a)(1) requiring a corporation to report more ordinary income. See § 1250(a)(4).

Note, however, that cost recovery deductions on § 1250 property held for one year or less are recaptured in full on the disposition of the property. § 1250(b)(1). Since depreciation recapture is primarily a characterization mechanism, the ordinary income recognized under § 1250 cannot exceed the taxpayer's gain, i.e. the excess of the fair market value of the property over the taxpayer's adjusted basis in the property. § 1250(a)(1)(A).

4. RELATIONSHIP OF SECTIONS 1245 AND 1250 TO SECTION 1231

Under § 1231(b) depreciable assets generally qualify for capital gain or loss treatment. However, the recognized gain treated as ordinary income by the depreciation recapture provisions comes out before the gain enters into computations under § 1231. In other words, only the recognized gain in excess of the amount subject to recapture goes into the § 1231 hotchpot. Reg. §§ 1.1245–6(a) and 1.1250–1(c)(1).

If the taxpayer sells property subject to depreciation (cost recovery) on the installment method, the recapture rules still apply. Under § 453(i), recapture income (as defined in § 453(i)(2)) arising from an installment sale of real or personal property is immediately recognized in the year of disposition of the property regardless of the amount of payments made in that year. Only the gain in excess of the recapture income is recognized on the installment method under § 453. See § 453(i)(1).

Questions

1. How is depreciation recapture a statutory application of the tax benefit principle? Why does § 1250 require ordinary income treatment only if an accelerated method of depreciation is used for § 1250 property?

2. Why are dispositions by death exempted by §§ 1245(b)(2) and 1250(d)(2)? Does death eliminate the recapture taint created by the decedent?

Problems

1. On February 1 of Year 1 Larry purchased for $10,000 a machine for use in his business. Larry sold the machine on May 1 of Year 4. The machine is seven-year recovery property and Larry used the recovery method set forth in § 168(b)(1). Over the first three years Larry held the machine, he took depreciation deductions totaling $5,626.

(a) Assume Larry sold the machine on May 1 of Year 4 for $14,000. What are the tax consequences for Larry in the year of sale? Consider §§ 1001, 1016, 1245(a)(1), (2), (3), and 1231. What is the impact of § 1245 on § 1231. Consider § 1245(d).

(b) Assume Larry sold the machine on May 1 of Year 4 for $9,000. What are the tax consequences in the year of sale?

(c) Assume Larry sold the machine on May 1 of Year 4 for $2,500. What are the tax consequences in the year of sale?

(d) Assume the machine was totally destroyed by fire on May 1 of Year 4. The machine was not insured and had a fair market value of $14,000. What are the tax consequences for Larry in Year 4? Consider § 1231(a)(4)(C).

2. (a) Merchant owns a truck used in her business. The truck, which originally cost $30,000 in 1980, has an adjusted basis of $18,000. The truck was sold in 1984 for $32,000. During 1984 Merchant also sold some vacant land used as a parking lot in her business for $6,000. The purchase price for the land was $10,000 in 1982. What is the amount and character of the gain and loss?

(b) Assume in (a) above, Merchant sold the land for $9,000. What is the amount and character of the gain and loss?

3. (a) On January 1, 1977, Merchant purchased a warehouse and land for $110,000, of which $10,000 was properly allocated to the land and $100,000 to the building. The building had a useful life of 40 years (with no salvage value). Merchant elected to use the straight line method of depreciation. On January 1, 1983, he sold the property for $150,000, allocating $40,000 of the sales price to the land. What is the amount and character of the gain on sale? Consider §§ 1250(a)(1)(B) and 1231.

(b) Assume the building in "a" above was depreciated using the 150% declining balance method. What is the amount and character of the gain on the sale? Consider § 1250(b). Assume depreciation was taken as follows:

Year	§ 167 deduction
1977	$ 3,750
1978	3,609
1979	3,474
1980	3,343
1981	3,218
1982	3,097
	$20,491 (total depreciation taken)

(c) Would the result change if Merchant purchased the real estate in 1987 and sold it in 1993? Consider §§ 168(b)(3)(A) and 1250(a)(1), (b)(1) and (c).

(d) What result in "b" above if the seller was a corporation? Consider § 291(a)(1).

4. Vicky owns a machine worth $50,000 with an adjusted basis of $21,000. She bought the machine in Year 1 at an original cost of $100,000. She has heard that she might be able to redirect income from herself to her 14-year-old daughter, who will have no other income, by giving the machine to the daughter, leasing it back and paying the highest reasonable rent to the daughter. Thus, she will get a rent deduction against her income and her daughter will have the rental income subject to her lower rates.

(a) Do you recommend this from the standpoint of § 1245 if Vicky gives this machine to the daughter as a gift in Year 4? Consider § 1245(b)(1) and Reg. § 1.1245–4(a). What tax consequences if the daughter subsequently sells the machine for $50,000, its fair market value, in Year 6? Consider § 1245(a)(2) and (3).

(b) May Vicky successfully redirect income to her daughter and deduct the rentals? How should the transaction be structures? Reconsider the problem on page 731.

M. ALTERNATIVE MINIMUM TAX

Most taxpayers, primarily middle-class taxpayers, seldom, if ever, are able to take advantage of a variety of tax preferences. Upper income taxpayers effectively utilize such preferences. Congress, in recognition of this vertical inequity, enacted the alternative minimum tax to ensure that these taxpayers pay some income tax on their income. Congress uses the alternative minimum tax to assure that after adding certain tax preference items back to the tax base and disregarding many of the itemized deductions, a taxpayer cannot reduce his taxes below a minimum statutory figure by engaging in certain activities Congress considers as an erosion of the tax base. Supposedly, every individual should shoulder the tax burden, at least to some extent.

The entire concept of a minimum tax is indeed confusing. Nevertheless, a proper understanding of the alternative minimum tax is essential for proper tax planning. An individual taxpayer who ignores the alternative minimum tax under § 55 when structuring his tax minimization and investment strategies might just as well buy a deck chair on the Titanic, for as surely as he believes he will embark on a cruise for a safe-harbor, an unexpected ice floe called the "alternative minimum tax" will strike his ship. A detailed discussion of the alternative minimum tax provision is beyond the scope of this book. What follows, however, is a brief overview of the area, which is intended to provide a conceptual framework for understanding the alternative minimum tax. Our discussion focuses on § 55 (the alternative minimum tax for noncorporate taxpayers), the related provisions of §§ 56 and 58, and § 57 (tax preference items).

The computational complexities begin with determining the taxpayer's "alternative minimum taxable income" as defined in § 55(b)(2). This is done by taking: (1) the taxpayer's taxable income (§ 63); (2) with the adjustments applicable in computing the alternative minimum tax (§ 56); (3) but with certain losses used in computing the taxpayer's regular income tax being denied (§ 58); (4) increased by the taxpayer's tax preference items (§ 57). The resulting amount, called the alternative minimum taxable income, then is reduced by a $30,000 exemption ($40,000 in the case of married taxpayers filing a joint return or a surviving spouse, and $20,000 in the case of a married taxpayer filing a separate return). § 55(d)(1). The exemption amount is subject to being phased out for taxpayers with alternative minimum taxable income above specified levels. § 55(d)(3). The resulting amount is subject to a flat rate tax of 21 percent and is then reduced by the taxpayer's alternative minimum tax foreign tax credit (as defined in § 59(a)) to arrive at the taxpayer's tentative minimum tax. § 55(b). If the tentative minimum tax is less than the taxpayer's regular income tax for the taxable year (as defined in § 55(c)(1)), the regular income tax is paid. If the tentative minimum tax is larger than the regular income tax calculation, the alternative minimum tax is paid on an amount equal to the excess of (1) the tentative minimum tax for the taxable year over (2) the taxpayer's regular income tax for the taxable year. § 55(a).

As noted above, the taxpayer's alternative minimum taxable income equals his taxable income for the taxable year determined with the adjustments provided for in §§ 56 and 58. Under § 56, the depreciation deductions with respect to any tangible property placed in service after 1986 is determined under one of two methods using the useful life set forth in § 168(g)(2)(C). The cost of § 1250 real property (as defined in § 1250(c) and other property for which the straight line method is elected (or required under § 168(g)(1)) is recovered under the straight line method. The cost of other property is recovered using the 150 percent declining balance method, switching to the straight line method. § 56(a)(1)(A). Only a special alternative tax net operating loss deduction, as defined in § 56(d), is allowed. § 56(a)(4).

Only alternative minimum itemized deductions are allowed (§ 56(b)(1)), including the deductions specified in § 67(b). Taxes allowed under § 164 are deductible, but deductions for state and local taxes are disallowed. § 56(b)(1)(A). The investment interest and personal interest limitations are not phased in. § 56(b)(1)(C). Only qualified housing interest is deductible for alternative minimum tax purposes. § 56(b)(1)(C)(i) and (e). Medical deductions are allowed only to the extent in excess of 10 percent of adjusted gross income. § 56(b)(1)(B).

Use of the installment method is not permitted on all transactions subject to the proportionate disallowance of the installment method, namely sales of trade or business property or rental property where the purchase price exceeds $150,000. § 56(a)(6). All payments from such an installment sale are deemed received in the taxable year of the disposition.

Section 58 denies a deduction for certain losses in computing the taxpayer's alternative minimum taxable income. The passive loss rules of § 469 apply without any phase in. § 58(b). Special limitations also exist on losses from passive farm losses. § 58(a).

Certain tax preference items increase the amount of the taxpayer's alternative minimum tax income. Section 57 defines these tax preference items. The major items we are familiar with are:

(1) the excess of the fair market value of stock over the option price for such shares on the exercise of an incentive stock option. § 57(a)(3)(A). The basis of stock acquired through the exercise of an incentive stock option after 1986 equals the fair market value taken into account in determining the amount of the preference. § 57(a)(3)(B).

(2) interest exempt from taxation on certain private activity bonds (§ 141) issued after August 7, 1986. § 57(a)(5).

(3) in the case of a taxpayer who makes one or more charitable contributions of appreciated capital gain property (as defined in § 170(b)(1)(C)(iv)), the amount of the untaxed appreciation. § 57(a)(6).

(4) cost recovery (or accelerated depreciation) on real property placed in service before 1987. § 57(a)(7). Specifically, the tax preference item equals the amount by which each year's cost recovery (or accelerated depreciation) deduction exceeds the amount of straight line depreciation on such property.

N. CHARACTERIZATION PRINCIPLES AND THE SALE OF A BUSINESS OR ITS ASSETS

1. SALE OF A BUSINESS

The ownership of an enterprise may be conceived of as either one property interest with various components or as the separate ownership of such items as real estate, improvements, machinery, inventory, work in process, and accounts receivable. The following materials deal with this issue.

WILLIAMS v. McGOWAN

United States Court of Appeals, Second Circuit, 1945.
152 F.2d 570.

[Williams, the taxpayer, and Reynolds engaged as partners in a hardware business. Williams had a two-thirds interest in the profits of the partnership; Reynolds, a one-third interest. On Reynolds' death, in 1940, Williams bought Reynolds' interest in the partnership. Later in 1940, Williams sold the business to the Corning Bldg. Co. Williams sustained a loss on his original two-thirds interest in the partnership, but made a small gain on the one-third interest he purchased on Reynolds' death. The taxpayer treated the loss and the gain as ordinary income items.]

L. HAND, CIRCUIT JUDGE.

* * *

* * * We have to decide only whether upon the sale of a going business it is to be comminuted into its fragments, and these are to be separately matched against the definition in [§ 1221], or whether the whole business is to be treated as if it were a single piece of property.

Our law has been sparing in the creation of juristic entities; it has never, for example, taken over the Roman "universitas facti"; [35] and indeed for many years it fumbled uncertainly with the concept of a corporation. One might have supposed that partnership would have been an especially promising field in which to raise up an entity, particularly since merchants have always kept their accounts upon that basis. Yet there too our law resisted at the price of great and continuing confusion; and, even when it might be thought that a statute admitted, if it did not demand, recognition of the firm as an entity, the old concepts prevailed. * * * And so, even though we might agree that under the influence of the Uniform Partnership Act a partner's interest in the firm should be treated as indivisible, and for that reason a "capital asset" within [§ 1221], we should be chary about extending further so exotic a jural concept. Be that as it may, in this instance the section itself furnishes the answer. It starts in the broadest way by declaring that all "property" is "capital assets," and then makes three exceptions. The first is "stock in trade * * * or other property of a kind which would properly be included in the inventory"; next comes "property held * * * primarily for sale to customers"; and finally, property "used in the trade or business of a character which is subject to * * * allowance for depreciation." In the face of this language, although it may be true that a "stock in trade," taken by itself, should be treated as a "universitas facti," by no possibility can a whole business be so treated; and the same is true as to any property within the other exceptions. Congress plainly did mean to comminute the

35. "By universitas facti is meant a number of things of the same kind which are regarded as a whole; e.g. a herd, a stock of wares." Mackeldey, Roman Law § 162.

elements of a business; plainly it did not regard the whole as "capital assets."

As has already appeared, Williams transferred to the Corning Company "cash," "receivables," "fixtures" and a "merchandise inventory." "Fixtures" are not capital because they are subject to a depreciation allowance ª; the inventory, as we have just seen, is expressly excluded. So far as appears, no allowance was made for "good-will"; but, even if there had been, we held in Haberle Crystal Springs Brewing Company v. Clarke, Collector, 2 Cir., 30 F.2d 219, that "good-will" was a depreciable intangible. It is true that the Supreme Court reversed that judgment—280 U.S. 384, 50 S.Ct. 155, 74 L.Ed. 498—but it based its decision only upon the fact that there could be no allowance for the depreciation of "good-will" in a brewery, a business condemned by the Eighteenth Amendment. There can of course be no gain or loss in the transfer of cash; and, although Williams does appear to have made a gain of $1072.71 upon the "receivables," the point has not been argued that they are not subject to a depreciation allowance.[36] That we leave open for decision by the district court, if the parties cannot agree. The gain or loss upon every other item should be computed as an item in ordinary income.

Judgment reversed.

[Dissenting opinion of Frank, J. is omitted.]

———

Under the approach of Williams v. McGowan, a portion of the total sales price of a proprietorship must be allocated to each asset according to the ratio of its fair market value to the sum of the values of all the assets sold. In making the allocation to specific items, a professional appraisal should be obtained of the items in major assets categories.

After the price allocation, the taxpayer determines (1) the amount of gain or loss realized and recognized on each asset sold and (2) the character of the gain or loss. Rev.Rul. 55-79, 1955-1 C.B. 370.

———

An allocation by parties with conflicting tax interests usually will be honored by the Service. As the following case illustrates, the allocations must, however, be reasonable and accord with economic reality.

PARTICELLI v. COMMISSIONER

United States Court of Appeals, Ninth Circuit, 1954.
212 F.2d 498.

ORR, CIRCUIT JUDGE.

Petitioner Giulio Particelli, having been engaged in the business of operating a winery in the state of California for some years, decided to

a. But see § 1231—Eds.   36. See § 1221(4)—Eds.

dispose of the winery business. Prior to making the decision to sell, petitioner had been approached by a buyer of wine, one John Dumbra, a representative of Tiara Products Company, Inc., hereafter Tiara, who made an offer to buy three or four cars of wine. Because of the then existing O.P.A. price ceilings no profit could be realized from the sale of the wine. Petitioner made a counter offer to sell the wine and winery for the sum of $350,000.[37] While Tiara had no particular desire to own or operate the winery, the demand for wine was so great and the ceiling price under which Tiara operated was such that it could afford to buy the winery in order to obtain the wine. After further negotiation the purchase price of $350,000 was agreed upon. A written contract of sale was executed wherein the sale price of the wine was fixed at $77,000 and the winery at $273,000. The subsequent escrow instructions treated the transfer of the wine and the winery as two separate sales at the prices stated in the written contract. Both buyer and seller recorded the transaction in their books in accordance with the terms of the written contract and Tiara used these cost figures in its 1943 and 1944 federal income tax returns. Petitioner and his wife treated the transaction in their 1943 federal income tax return as a sale of wine for $77,000 resulting in ordinary income of that amount, and a sale of the winery for $273,000, producing a [preferential] capital gain of $217,634.

The Commissioner of Internal Revenue assessed a deficiency of $124,445.70 against petitioner and his wife. He took the position that the real transaction was a sale of two classes of property for a lump sum price and the allocation in the written contract of the purchase price to the wine and winery was merely a subterfuge. He reallocated $302,500 of the purchase price to the wine and $47,500 to the winery. The Tax Court sustained the Commissioner's determination that the real transaction was a sale of the wine and winery for one price but reallocated the proceeds of the sale to $275,000 for the wine and $75,000 for the winery.

Petitioner is insisting that parties should not be disturbed in their right and privilege to contract as they see fit and that the terms and conditions of their contracts, as evidenced in writing, is binding for all purposes. This contention would be valid if confined to rights of the contracting parties as between themselves but is not controlling in an income tax determination. The Supreme Court of the United States has so held. In Commissioner of Internal Revenue v. Court Holding Co., 324 U.S. 331, 65 S.Ct. 707, 708, 89 L.Ed. 981, the Supreme Court said:

> "The incidence of taxation depends upon the substance of a transaction. The tax consequences which arise from gains from a sale of property are not finally to be determined solely by the means employed

37. Prior to 1942 about 80% of all wine produced in California was sold in bulk. The cost of grapes in 1943 prevented wine producers from selling unfinished wines at bulk ceiling prices and it became a common practice for the producer to sell his inventory of wine and winery in a package deal for a lump sum price. Producers could thus legally dispose of their wine at prices above the O.P.A. ceilings.

to transfer legal title. Rather, the transaction must be viewed as a whole, and each step, from the commencement of negotiations to the consummation of the sale, is relevant."

It is recognized that a taxpayer is free to employ any legal means in the conduct of his business affairs to avoid or minimize taxes, but the means employed must not be mere subterfuge or sham. Commissioner of Internal Revenue v. Tower, 1946, 327 U.S. 280, 66 S.Ct. 532, 90 L.Ed. 670.

The determination of whether the written contract reflected the real agreement between the parties was a question of fact and the Tax Court's finding with respect thereto is final if based upon substantial evidence. Commissioner of Internal Revenue v. Tower, 1946, 327 U.S. 280, 66 S.Ct. 532, 90 L.Ed. 670. We find substantial evidence in this case to support the Tax Court's conclusion that the substance of the transaction was a sale of the wine and winery for a total price of $350,000 without any bona fide agreement as to the real sales price of each piece of property involved.

The negotiations preceding the written contract disclose an intention to sell two pieces of property for a lump sum price. Petitioner expressly rejected Tiara's first offer to buy four carloads of wine. He refused to make an independent sale of wine because it cost him fifty cents a gallon to make and the ceiling price was twenty-eight cents a gallon. The free market price for the wine was slightly more than a dollar a gallon.[38] Petitioner insisted on selling the winery and the inventory of wine together. Good business judgment would not permit a sale of the wine for the stated contract price of $77,000 with its resultant financial loss, and the compelling inference to be drawn from all the facts is that petitioner did not ignore his own best interests in this transaction. We think there can be no reasonable dispute that Tiara would not and did not pay $273,000 for the winery, the price stated in the contract. At the time of the negotiations Tiara estimated that the winery itself was not worth more than $60,000 and considered that it was paying $1 to $1.12 per gallon for the wine. In fact, Tiara sold the winery a year later for $20,000.[39]

Tiara informed petitioner that it did not care how he allocated the purchase price so long as the total price did not exceed the agreed $350,000. Petitioner had been advised by his accountant that the sale of his winery would result in a [preferential] capital gains tax whereas the wine would be subject to ordinary income tax. The tax consequence of assigning a high valuation to the winery and a low valuation to the wine inventory was undoubtedly understood by petitioner. He therefore drew up the contract specifying separate prices for the wine and winery to suit his own convenience. The price allocated to the

38. During 1943 three methods were available to winery operators to legally dispose of their unfinished wines without subjecting the sale to O.P.A. ceilings.

39. The most that Tiara could have obtained for the winery was $45,000 had it sold before the market broke.

wine in the contract certainly did not represent the true value or the value contemplated by both parties and bears no resemblance to the realities of the transaction. The total purchase price was arrived at through arms length negotiation but the allocation of the selling price to the two pieces of property involved was not. Once the parties had agreed upon the purchase price it was a matter of indifference to the buyer as to how the seller allocated it. The argument that the valuation placed on the wine and the winery was of vital importance to Tiara because it necessarily affected its income tax position has no merit. That argument wholly ignores the crucial fact that the federal income tax is a graduated tax and a given transaction may have different consequences depending upon the circumstances of the particular taxpayer.[40]

Petitioner sought to explain the ridiculously low price attributed to the wine in the contract on the ground that he thought the twenty-eight cents a gallon ceiling price applied to the sale and he did not want to violate the law.[41] The Tax Court refused to credit petitioner's testimony on this point and gave weight to the testimony of witness Alberigi to the effect that petitioner told him that he, petitioner, had sold his wine at $1 a gallon and had also sold the winery in order to make it legal under the O.P.A. regulations.

The fact that Tiara charged petitioner $1,000 for 1,000 gallons of wine withdrawn by him before the sale was closed is strong evidence that the parties really intended and understood that the selling price of the wine was approximately $1 a gallon rather than the nominal price contained in the contract. Petitioner attempted to show that he was not charged $1 per gallon for the wine he retained and, among other explanations, stated that the wine retained was of higher quality than that sold to Tiara. His evidence on this point was so contradictory that the Tax Court properly rejected it. Having concluded that the contract prices for the wine and winery did not constitute the real agreement of the parties, the Tax Court determined that the wine was actually bought and sold for $1 a gallon and allocated the balance of the purchase price to the winery. Petitioner claims that it was error for the Tax Court to assign a price to the wine in excess of the O.P.A. ceiling. His argument seems to be that had the Government seized the wine under its power of condemnation it would have had to pay only twenty-eight cents a gallon, the fair market value of the wine determined by the ceiling price. Thus, petitioner says that the Government cannot place a value on the wine higher than the ceiling price because the same rule for determining the Government's liabilities in condemnation cases should be applied in determining its rights in tax cases.

40. It is suggested that any high profits realized by Tiara from the sale of the undervalued wine would be offset by high depreciation deductions based on the overvaluation of the winery or by any loss sustained from the resale of the winery. * * *

41. The O.P.A. ceiling price did not apply to the sale of wine when sold as a part of a going business.

The answer to this contention is that there was no ceiling price applicable to the sale here involved because the wine was a part of the sale of a going business. We find no merit in the contention that the sale was not exempt from the O.P.A. ceiling price because petitioner retained his bottling plant and retail store. The bottling and selling of wines is an entirely distinct and separate business from that of producing wine. The sale of the winery and all its equipment constituted the sale of petitioner's entire business as a wine producer.

* * *

Judgment affirmed.

2. SALE OF GOODWILL AND A COVENANT NOT TO COMPETE

As we have seen, courts have concluded that where the taxpayer receives something as a substitute for ordinary income, the item received will be treated as ordinary income. The concept is applied where a taxpayer "sells" a covenant not to compete to the purchaser of a business. The payment the seller receives for giving the purchaser a covenant not to compete constitutes ordinary income. In effect, the amount received for the covenant is viewed as compensation for services, the promise not to work. The buyer capitalizes the amount paid for the covenant and amortizes his basis in the covenant over the life of the covenant. The purchaser should be certain that the covenant is established for a specified number of years, so that it has a useful life of "only a limited period, the length of which can be estimated with reasonable accuracy * * *." Reg. § 1.167(a)–3.

Courts define goodwill in terms of the customer structure of the business, that is, goodwill is an asset which increases the value of a business. Goodwill is the ability to retain existing customers, resulting from a good reputation that produces greater income than the assets of a business normally generate.

The seller of a business may characterize the gain attributable to the sale of goodwill as capital gain under § 1221. If the taxpayer is a professional or is engaged in a service business, considerable controversy existed with respect to the treatment of the sale of goodwill. In Rev. Rul. 64–235, 1964–2 C.B. 18, the Service ruled that part of the sales price could be allocated to goodwill as "determined on the facts rather than by whether the business is, or is not, dependent solely upon the professional skill or other personal characteristics of the owner."

Since the payment for goodwill represents a nondepreciable asset (Reg. § 1.167(a)–3 views goodwill as not having an ascertainable useful life), the buyer can only recover his basis in goodwill when he sells the purchased goodwill (or it is destroyed; see the Rayetheon case at pp. 143–146).

The allocation of purchase price among the assets of a going business has been a troublesome area. Particular difficulties surround the valuation of goodwill. Prior to the Tax Reform Act of 1986, two methods were used to value goodwill: the residual method and the formula method. Under the residual method, the value of goodwill equals the excess of the purchase price of the business over the aggregate fair market values of the tangible assets and the identifiable intangible assets, except goodwill. Under the formula method, goodwill is valued by capitalizing the excess earning capacity of the tangible assets of the business based on the performance of the business over some period prior to the valuation date. The excess earning capacity equals the excess of the average earnings of the business during this specified period over an assured rate of return in the industry, adjusted to reflect the risk involved in the particular business, on the value of the tangible assets. The value of the unidentified intangible assets equals these excess earnings capitalized at an appropriate rate. Deficient and subjective assumptions surround both the appropriate rate of return and the capitalization rate.

Section 1060, enacted as part of the Tax Reform Act of 1986, mandates the use of the residual method, as described in Temp.Reg. § 1.338(b)–2T in any applicable asset acquisition. An applicable asset acquisition is any transfer of assets constituting a business in which the transferee's basis "is determined wholly by reference to the purchase price paid for the assets." § 1060(c). The legislative history notes: "In requiring use of the residual method, the committee does not intend to restrict in any way the ability of the Internal Revenue Service to challenge the taxpayer's determination of the fair market value of any asset by any appropriate method." Tax Reform Act of 1986, Senate Finance Committee Report on H.R. 3838, 99th Cong., 2d Sess. 255 (1986).

The Tax Reform Act of 1986 also authorizes the Treasury to require information reporting by the parties to an applicable asset acquisition. This may include, among other items, information regarding amounts allocated to goodwill. § 1060(b). Forcing the parties to allocate the purchase price and use the residual method for making allocations to goodwill should diminish inconsistent allocations by the parties for tax reporting purposes "resulting in a whipsaw of the government." Tax Reform Act of 1986, Senate Finance Committee Report on H.R. 3838, 99th Cong., 2d Sess. 254 (1986).

Where the parties to a sale of a business allocate part of the consideration to a covenant not to compete or make an allocation between a covenant not to compete and goodwill, a problem arises as to whether or not the Commissioner and the parties are bound by the allocation agreed upon in the sale contract. Whether the amounts allocated to the covenant will be respected for tax purposes turns on: the severability test and the economic reality test. The severability test focuses on whether the covenant could be segregated and valued separately from other assets transferred, particularly goodwill. See e.g., Ullman v. Commissioner, 264 F.2d 305 (2d Cir.1959). Courts applying the severability test analyze a transaction to determine if there would have been a covenant in the absence of transferable goodwill.

Increasingly, courts have applied an economic reality standard. Under the economic reality test, a covenant not to compete may have independent significance for tax purposes although it was primarily intended to preserve the transferred goodwill. As formulated in Schulz v. Commissioner, 294 F.2d 52, 55 (9th Cir.1961), affirming 34 T.C. 235 (1960), under the economic reality test the allocation of the purchase price to the covenant will be respected if the covenant had "some independent basis in fact or some arguable relationship with business reality such that reasonable men, genuinely concerned with their economic future, might bargain for such an agreement."

In applying the economic reality test, courts have generally followed the Schultz case in requiring a showing that the parties intended amounts to be paid for the covenant. In Annabelle Candy Co. v. Commissioner, 314 F.2d 1 (9th Cir.1962), the court stated that it was necessary, in addition to satisfying the economic reality test, that the buyer in claiming a deduction, in the absence of an express allocation to the covenant not to compete, show that the parties intended such an allocation.

A decision to add a covenant after the sale of a going business with the price for the entire business already determined tends to show a lack of economic reality. The purchaser has the burden of proving that notwithstanding the lack of an allocation, the parties intended to allocate some portion of the consideration to the covenant. This is a difficult burden of proof to carry. As a result courts generally will refuse to permit the purchaser to make a subsequent allocation to the covenant. See e.g., Annabelle Candy Co., supra.

The Internal Revenue Service is not bound by the parties' allocation of the purchase price. If one party is in a higher tax bracket than the other party, the parties, by contract, may give the tax benefits to the higher tax bracket party in return for other concessions by that party. The Service can challenge this type of allocation. In Dixie Finance Co. v. United States, 474 F.2d 501, 504 (5th Cir.1973) the court held that "[t]he parties cannot contractually preclude the Commissioner from attacking an allocation which has no basis in economic reality." On a challenge by the Commissioner that the allocation to the covenant not to compete is a sham, courts look to "substance over form" and may recast the economic reality of the transaction. Schulz v. Commissioner, 294 F.2d 52 (9th Cir.1961).

The next case considers the circumstances under which one of the parties to a contract may not be bound by the allocation of the purchase price.

PROULX v. UNITED STATES

United States Court of Claims, 1979.
594 F.2d 832.

OPINION

PER CURIAM:

This case comes before the court on plaintiffs' exceptions to the recommended decision of Trial Judge Lloyd Fletcher, filed November 30, 1977, pursuant to Rule 134(h), having been submitted to the court on the briefs and oral argument of counsel. Upon consideration thereof, since the court agrees with the trial judge's recommended decision, with one minor deletion by the court, it hereby affirms and adopts the recommended decision, as modified and hereinafter set forth as the basis for its judgment in this case. It is, therefore, concluded as a matter of law that plaintiffs are not entitled to recover and their petition is dismissed.

OPINION OF TRIAL JUDGE

FLETCHER, TRIAL JUDGE:

In this income tax case, the court is confronted with the complex principles of tax law which have been developed by the myriad cases dealing with the proper tax treatment to be accorded the proceeds of the sale of a business where the seller thereof agrees not to compete with the purchaser. Frequently, that problem is inextricably intertwined, as it is in this case, with the further question of whether the form given to the sale can ever govern the substance of the transaction.[42]

Unfortunately, it takes no more than a cursory examination of the case law to disclose that the decisions in this area are in bewildering disarray. This is true whether one examines the decisions of the several circuit courts of appeals, the district courts of the United States Tax Court.[43] Small wonder, then, that the author of the most recent and comprehensive study of the problem describes the area in masterful understatement as "this unruly subject."

42. This form-substance maxim has been referred to by Judge Learned Hand as an "anodyne(s) for the pains of reasoning." Commissioner v. Sansome, 60 F.2d 931, 933 (2d Cir., 1932), cert. denied 287 U.S. 667, 53 S.Ct. 291, 77 L.Ed. 575 (1932). The statement has been attributed to the late Roscoe Pound that such "maxims" should really be called "minims" since they convey a minimum of information with a maximum of pretense.

43. See, for example, the numerous studies of the covenant not to compete contained in many legal periodicals and taxation journals. Beghe, Income Tax Treatment of Covenants Not to Compete, Consulting Agreements and Transfers of Goodwill, 30 Tax.Lawyer 587 (1977) (hereinafter cited as "Beghe"); Madison, Tax Treatment of Covenants Not to Compete, 24 U. of Miami L.Rev. (1969); Messere and Davison, Goodwill or Covenants Not to Compete?, 54 Taxes 161 (1976); Barnet, Covenants Not to Compete, 18 NYU Inst. on Fed.Tax. 861 (1960); Taylor, Covenants Not to Compete, 12 NYU Inst. on Fed.Tax. 1047 (1954); Note: Tax Treatment of Covenants Not to Compete: A Problem of Purchase Price Allocation, 67 Yale L.Jour. 1261 (1958).

That this should be so is itself somewhat perplexing, for the basic underlying rules are quite simple and enjoy virtual unanimity among the courts. What a covenantor receives for his promise not to compete is taxable to him as ordinary income. Beal's Estate v. Commissioner, 82 F.2d 268 (2d Cir.1936). What the covenantee pays for that promise of non-competition may be amortized by him and deducted over the life of the covenant, provided the covenant has an ascertainable life. Commissioner v. Gazette Telegraph Co., 209 F.2d 926 (10th Cir.1954). For a comprehensive discussion of these principles, see also Schmitz v. Commissioner, 51 T.C. 306 (1968), aff'd sub nom. Throndson v. Commissioner, 457 F.2d 1022 (9th Cir.1972). These basic rules are succinctly summarized by the court in Ullman v. Commissioner, 264 F.2d 305 (2d Cir.1959) at 307–08:

> It is well established that an amount a purchaser pays to a seller for a covenant not to compete in connection with a sale of a business is ordinary income to the covenantor and an amortizable item for the covenantee unless the covenant is so closely related to a sale of good will that it fails to have any independent significance apart from merely assuring the effective transfer of that good will. [Citing cases.]

Bearing these underlying principles in mind, it is now appropriate to outline the essential facts in the case at hand.

The taxpayers, Mr. and Mrs. Arthur A. Proulx, moved from Chicago to Florida in 1958 primarily because of Mr. Proulx's failing health. At that time he was in his seventies and she in her sixties. Shortly after their move, they purchased a motel and restaurant business fronting on the Atlantic Ocean in the Sebastian area just south of Melbourne, Florida and obtained an oral commitment from their sellers that the latter would not open or operate a competing business in the area.

The trade name of their newly acquired business was the Sea Dunes Motel and Restaurant. Because of the dilapidated condition of the property, extensive renovation and improvements to both the motel units and the restaurant were necessary.

Originally, the Proulxs employed others to operate and manage the business, but after a few years they decided this arrangement was unsatisfactory. Whereupon, Mrs. Proulx personally took over all management duties [44] and thereafter ran both the motel and restaurant business during the entire period of their ownership. She built the restaurant into a noted lobster house and gradually developed the entire operation into a pleasant and popular resort. Much of the clientele were "return guests" who came from various locations in the eastern part of the country.

In addition to the oceanfront property on which was built the motel, restaurant, and their personal residence, the Proulxs owned unimproved acreage on the western side of Highway A1A. They had

---

44. Due to his continuing ill health, Mr. Proulx was unable to contribute in any substantial way to the day-by-day operation of the business.

constructed a canal on this acreage which gave it access to the Indian River, and their plans were ultimately to develop the property into residential homesites.

Mr. Proulx's health continued to deteriorate, and his doctor advised him to take no part in any business activities. He further suggested to Mrs. Proulx that her work in the management of the business was not agreeing with her. This development appears to have set the Proulxs into considering a sale of the business and its properties. Initial sales efforts by a prominent real estate agency were unsuccessful.

However, in February 1969, a local real estate broker, John Cannon, put the Proulxs in touch with Lloyd Miller and William Rose who were looking around for a motel and restaurant business in the Melbourne area. Initial negotiations seemed promising, and the Proulxs retained Frank Clark, Esq., a local criminal lawyer, to represent them.

A few days later, Cannon, on behalf of Miller and Rose, presented an offer to purchase the entire Sea Dunes property on the oceanfront side of Highway A1A for $400,000. That offer was rejected by the Proulxs whose asking price was $500,000.

Subsequently, Cannon submitted another offer on behalf of Miller and Rose to purchase the property, both east and west of Highway A1A for $465,000, with a $10,000 earnest money deposit. That offer contained a covenant not to compete and specifically allocated $50,000 of the purchase price thereto. Mrs. Proulx told Cannon that they were satisfied with the increased price and would accept such an offer, but that the contract would have to be sent over to Clark, their attorney, for his examination. The Proulxs then took the offer to Clark and left it for him to study.

Upon examining the details of the $465,000 offer, Clark found certain points unacceptable to him. He considered inadequate the earnest money deposit of $10,000, and the subordination and release clauses were unsatisfactory. Clark reviewed the covenant not to compete and while he did not understand the reason for it since he knew the Proulxs definitely intended to retire, he had no objection to its inclusion in the proposed contract. Clark also reviewed the allocation of the purchase price made to the land, buildings, personal property, liquor license, and the covenant not to compete. Clark did not know why that allocation was made, but, nevertheless, had no objection to its inclusion, Clark had no acquaintance with the tax laws, and it seems never to have occurred to him that these provisions of the proposed contract might have some tax significance to both the buyers and the sellers.

Clark told Cannon about his earnest money deposit objection and informed the attorney representing Miller and Rose, Robert T. Westman, Esq.,[45] of his objections to the subordination and release clauses.

45. Unlike Clark, Mr. Westman was not only an experienced real estate attorney but was also well-versed in the tax laws, particularly as they applied to real estate transactions.

Westman indicated that he would redraft the subject clauses in accordance with Clark's suggestions and would send those drafts to Clark. Cannon indicated that he would take care of getting an increase in the earnest money deposit. It was then agreed that the final contract would incorporate the redrafts of the subject clauses and would be typed in final draft by Clark's office. This was done. Approximately two weeks elapsed from the time that Clark received that offer from his clients for his review and the time that Clark received the redrafts from Westman and what was to become the March 17, 1969 signing. Clark was satisfied with Westman's redrafts with respect to the subordination and release clauses, and had no other legal objections to the proposed contract.

On the morning of March 17, 1969, Mrs. Proulx received a telephone call from Cannon who asked if she and her husband could be at the National Bank of Melbourne at 11:00 a.m. to sign the sales contract. After receiving assurances that all interested parties, including her attorney, would be present, Mrs. Proulx told Cannon they would be there.

Attending that meeting with the Proulxs were Cannon, Westman, Miller, Rose, and Howard Hebert, the president of the bank. Clark was not there. Despite Cannon's assurances to the contrary, apparently Clark had never been notified of the meeting. When the Proulxs arrived at the bank and noticed that Clark was not present, Mrs. Proulx became anxious and concerned. She telephoned Clark's office and was informed by Clark's secretary that he was in Titusville on a criminal matter. Mrs. Proulx returned and indicated to those present that since Clark would be unable to attend, they preferred not to continue without him. From the ensuing discussion, the Proulxs became apprehensive that the deal might fall through entirely and they went ahead and signed the contract that day. Mrs. Proulx stated that "the only reason" they did so was because they wanted to sell the Sea Dunes, and they thought Miller and Rose were able to buy it, having the money and the capabilities to operate the business.

No one present at that meeting used any physical force, pressure, threats, or abusive language designed to induce plaintiffs to sign the sales contract. In fact, it is undisputed that they were free to leave the meeting at any time they desired without signing the sales contract.

The Contract for Sale and Purchase which plaintiffs signed on March 17, 1969, provided for the sale of the Sea Dunes Motel and Restaurant business, including all real and personal property described therein to Sebastian Sea Dunes, Inc. (a Florida corporation organized and closely held by Miller and Rose) for a total price of $465,000. That contract contained a covenant not to compete and specifically allocated $50,000 of the purchase price to that covenant. It provided as follows:

> 3. Arthur A. Proulx and Babe June Proulx, his wife, jointly and severally covenant not to compete with the buyer by operating, managing, or owning, either directly or indirectly any motel, restaurant

cocktail lounge or similar facility in Brevard County or Indian River County within five (5) years from the date of closing of this transaction.

The contract also provided for the transfer of the trade name "Sea Dunes" to the purchaser of the business, as follows:

4. The sellers relinquish all right, title and interest that they may have in and to that certain trade name "Sea Dunes Motel" or "The Sea Dunes," and agree not use [sic] said name incident to any trade or business in which they may hereafter engage for a period of five (5) years from the date of closing.

No specific allocation of the purchase price was made to the trade name "Sea Dunes Motel" or the "Sea Dunes."

The sales transaction was closed on September 25, 1969. As part of that transaction, the Proulxs took back a purchase money mortgage in the amount of $365,000. Sebastian Sea Dunes, Inc. fell into default thereunder almost immediately. Since the Proulxs had no desire to retake possession of the mortgaged properties, they were very lenient in granting time extensions and mortgage modifications. Nonetheless, the buyer remained in serious default, and finally the Proulxs foreclosed on the Sea Dunes and, following a receivership, returned to operate the business for a period of several months. They were successful in reselling the property in 1971 and have not owned it since that time.

Sebastian Sea Dunes amortized the covenant not to compete and took deductions in respect thereto on its 1969 and 1970 Federal income tax returns. On their 1969 Federal income tax return, the Proulxs ignored the covenant and reported their entire gain on the sale as [preferential] capital gain. However, on audit by the Internal Revenue Service, the agent treated $50,000 of the sales proceeds as allocable to the covenant not to compete and hence taxable to plaintiffs as ordinary income. Plaintiffs contend that under the circumstances present here, this action was completely unrealistic and improper.

The case has been before the court on cross-motions by the parties for summary judgment. By Order dated October 15, 1976, (as supplemented by Order dated October 21, 1976) the court denied the cross-motions for summary judgment and remanded the case to the trial judge with instructions to hold a trial and determine "whether or not the taxpayers were induced to sign the contract of sale through fraud, duress, threats, mistake, or undue influence and whether or not the covenant not to compete is void under Florida law and, if so, whether that is material to a decision of this court, and for such other findings and proceedings as the trial judge deems proper."

In thus directing the trial judge to determine whether fraud, duress, threats, mistake, or undue influence had induced the signing of the contract with its covenant not to compete, the court is obviously reasserting its adherence to what has come to be called "the *Danielson* rule." Commissioner v. Danielson, 378 F.2d 771 (3d Cir.1967), cert. denied, 389 U.S. 858, 88 S.Ct. 94, 19 L.Ed.2d 123 (1967). There a majority of the Third Circuit Court of Appeals, sitting *en banc*, described its approach to the question of the proper tax treatment of a covenant not to compete in the following language at 378 F.2d 775:

* * * We begin by noting that the determination as to whether a covenant not to compete was actually executed is important, taxwise, both to the buyer and the seller. A tax challenge aside, the amount a buyer pays a seller for such a covenant, entered into in connection with a sale of a business, is ordinary income to the covenantor and an amortizable item for the covenantee. Ullman v. Commissioner of Internal Revenue, 264 F.2d 305 (2d Cir.1959). Indeed, the presumed tax consequences of the transaction may, as here, help to determine the total amount a purchaser is willing to pay for such a purchase. Therefore, to permit a party to an agreement fixing an explicit amount for the covenant not to compete to attack that provision for tax purposes, absent proof of the type which would negate it in an action between the parties, would be in effect to grant, at the instance of a party, a unilateral reformation of the contract with a resulting unjust enrichment. If allowed, such an attack would encourage parties unjustifiably to risk litigation after consummation of a transaction in order to avoid the tax consequences of their agreements. And to go behind the agreement at the behest of a party may also permit a party to an admittedly valid agreement to use the tax laws to obtain relief from an unfavorable agreement.

Of vital importance, such attacks would nullify the reasonably predictable tax consequences of the agreement to the other party thereto. Here the buyer would be forced to defend the agreement in order to amortize the amount allocated to the covenant. If unsuccessful, the buyer would lose a tax advantage it had paid the selling-taxpayers to acquire. In the future buyers would be unwilling to pay sellers for tax savings so unlikely to materialize.

Finally, this type of attack would cause the Commissioner considerable problems in the collection of taxes. The Commissioner would not be able to accept taxpayers' agreements at face value. He would be confronted with the necessity for litigation against both buyer and seller in order to collect taxes properly due. This is so because when the Commissioner tries to collect taxes from one party he may, as here, dispute the economic reality of his agreement. When the Commissioner turns to the other party, there will likely be the arguments that the first party, as here, received consideration for bearing the tax burden resulting from the sale and that the covenants did indeed have economic reality.

For these reasons we adopt the following rule of law: a party can challenge the tax consequences of his agreement as construed by the Commissioner only by adducing proof which in an action between the parties to the agreement would be admissible to alter that construction *or to show its unenforceability because of mistake, undue influence, fraud, duress, etc.* [Emphasis supplied.]

In a sharp dissent, the Chief Judge of the Circuit (joined by two of his colleagues) disagreed with the majority on the ground that they had disregarded the long line of decisions by the United States Supreme Court to the effect that "in determining tax liability, taxing authorities must look through form to fact and substance." [46] The dissent then goes on to remark at 378 F.2d 780:

> Although citing no authority, the majority asserts that the obliga-
> tion to ascertain the substance of a transaction does not apply in this
> case because here it is one of the parties rather than the Commissioner
> who seeks to show that the substance of the transaction differed from
> its form. This proposition does not follow from the cases; in both
> Helvering v. F. & R. Lazarus, supra, and Helvering v. Tex-Penn Oil Co.,
> supra, the victorious taxpayers had attacked the form in which the
> transactions were cast, and the Commissioner had relied on the formal
> arrangement.

In a stinging attack on the public policy underlying the majority decision, Chief Judge Staley states at 378 F.2d 782:

> The policy basis of the majority seems to be that allowance of the
> attack on the consideration allocated to the covenant may cause the
> promisee to " * * * lose a tax advantage it had paid the selling-
> taxpayers to acquire." However, as I read this, it opens the door wide
> for individuals to avoid tax consequences by artifices such as we have
> in this case. This result is an invitation to tax evasion.
>
> * * *
>
> The danger of distortion of the tax laws is particularly acute in this
> area. As noted by the majority, since the "amount allocable to a
> covenant not to compete is amortizable by the buyer and ordinary
> income to the seller, *it generally does not matter what amount is
> allocated.*" (Emphasis added.) The majority would have the Commis-
> sioner attack such an allocation only where the Government would
> suffer a net loss in revenue, apparently disregarding in all other cases
> the question whether the allocation was an artifice without "[arguable]
> independent basis in fact or arguable relationship with business reali-
> ty," the test heretofore applied by the various circuits and the Tax
> Court and the Supreme Court. The difficult burden of showing fraud,
> etc. placed upon the parties by the majority virtually insures that
> knowledgeable buyers will engage in questionable and sharp dealing to
> secure the advantages of such covenants, and the majority's rule will
> shield their agreements. I cannot condone this invitation given by the
> majority.

These lengthy quotations (perhaps unduly so) from both majority and minority opinions in the *Danielson* case have been set forth with full recognition that, under our system of *stare decisis,* it is the majority opinion that controls. It has been done here, however, to demonstrate

---

46. Helvering v. Tex-Penn Oil Co., 300 U.S. 481, 492–3, 57 S.Ct. 569, 574, 81 L.Ed. 755 (1936). Numerous other Supreme Court decisions are also discussed in the dissenting opinion including the parent case of Eisner v. Macomber, 252 U.S. 189, 40 S.Ct. 189, 64 L.Ed. 521 (1919), the landmark decision in Gregory v. Helvering, 293 U.S. 465, 55 S.Ct. 266, 79 L.Ed. 596 (1935) and Helvering v. F. & R. Lazarus & Co., 308 U.S. 252, 60 S.Ct. 209, 84 L.Ed. 226 (1939).

vividly the competing considerations which have produced the disarray in the case law referred to at the outset of this opinion.

For example, the United States Tax Court, in cases arising elsewhere than the Third Circuit, will not follow *Danielson.* See Schmitz v. Commissioner, supra, and compare a case arising from the Third Circuit, Mittleman v. Commissioner, 56 T.C. 171 (1971), aff'd per curiam, 464 F.2d 1393 (3d Cir.1972). Meanwhile, the various Circuit Courts of Appeals, mostly on appeals from the Tax Court, have been developing their own doctrines in this area.

Three distinct tests have evolved. They have been called the "severability" test, the "economic reality" test, and the "intent" test.

As noted by Beghe, the "severability" test was the first developed, and it focused on the question of whether the covenant could be segregated and valued independently from other assets transferred, particularly goodwill. See Michaels v. Commissioner, 12 T.C. 17 (1949), and Burke v. Commissioner, 18 T.C. 77 (1952). This original test now seems to have survived only in the Second Circuit. See Ullman v. Commissioner, 264 F.2d 305, (2d Cir.1959), although the case is also referred to as an example of judicial application of a rule known as the "strong proof" rule which is related to the "economic reality" test.

The general dissatisfaction with the severability test has resulted in the judicial formulation of a new test, commonly called the "economic reality" test. It seems to be the test now preferred by the Tax Court. See Wager v. Commissioner, 52 T.C. 416 (1969). The Ninth Circuit was apparently the first circuit court to articulate the doctrine clearly when it observed that to support an allocation "the covenant must have some *independent basis in fact* or some arguable relationship with *business reality* such that reasonable men, genuinely concerned with their economic future, might bargain for such an agreement." Schulz v. Commissioner, 294 F.2d 52, 55 (9th Cir.1961), aff'g 34 T.C. 235 (1960) (Emphasis supplied). See also, Bennett v. Commissioner, 450 F.2d 959 (6th Cir.1971); Wilson Athletic Goods Mfg. Co. v. Commissioner, 222 F.2d 355 (7th Cir.1955); and Balthrope v. Commissioner, 356 F.2d 28 (5th Cir.1966).

One year later, the Ninth Circuit again considered the problem and added yet another element which has become known as the "intent" test. See Annabelle Candy Co. v. Commissioner, 314 F.2d 1 (9th Cir. 1962) in which an agreement for a third party covenant did not expressly allocate any portion of the consideration to the covenant. Again rejecting the severability test, the court affirmed the Tax Court's decision disallowing the buyer's deduction, despite substantial evidence of the importance which the bargaining for the covenant had played in the negotiations. The court did this by stating that it was necessary, in addition to satisfying the economic reality test, that the buyer in claiming a deduction in the absence of an express allocation show that the parties *intended* such an allocation. Likewise, the First Circuit has held that the seller who attempts for tax purposes to repudiate an express contractual allocation to a covenant must show that there was no intent to make such an allocation. Harvey Radio Laboratories, Inc. v. Commissioner, 470 F.2d 118 (1st Cir.1972). The court appears to treat the economic reality of the allocation as irrelevant, and thus in this respect approaches the *Danielson* rule. Finally, the Fourth Circuit has adopted an approach to the problem which appears to combine both the economic reality and the intent tests. General Insurance Agency, Inc. v. Commissioner, 401 F.2d 324 (4th Cir.1968).

These disparate approaches to this complex problem leave us, to use a golfing analogy, "in the rough." [47] Fortunately, however, this court has blazed a pathway in this wilderness. On several occasions, it has referred to the rule of *Commissioner v. Danielson,* supra, with approval. A recent example is the case of Dakan v. United States, 492 F.2d 1192, 203 Ct.Cl. 655 (1974) where the court stated *per curiam:*

> The trial judge holds that in the absence of mistake, fraud, undue influence, etc., the taxpayer is bound by the allocations he made in the sales agreement, citing Commissioner v. Danielson, 378 F.2d 771 (3d Cir.1967), cert. denied, 389 U.S. 858 [88 S.Ct. 94, 19 L.Ed.2d 123] (1967). We have twice recently cited *Danielson* with approval. Davee v. United States, 444 F.2d 557, 195 Ct.Cl. 184 (1971); Eckstein v. United States, 452 F.2d 1036, 196 Ct.Cl. 644 (1971). *Danielson* involved an allocation in a selling agreement between stock and a covenant not to compete, and it was held or assumed that the assignment of any value to the covenant not to compete was not in accord with economic reality. It was also held or assumed that a polarity in the tax treatment of buyer and seller was required, i.e., one had to be a counterpart of the other. Thus to sustain the seller's position would jeopardize the buyer's enjoyment of the tax treatment it presumably had bargained and paid for. 492 F.2d 1193, 203 Ct.Cl. 657–8.

In addition to the approvals of the *Danielson* case noted above, it is entirely clear that the court has reasserted its adherence to that rule in this very case. While the court's Order of October 15, 1976, remanding this case to the trial judge does not specifically refer to the *Danielson* case, the language used in that Order very clearly adopts the Third Circuit rule and instructs the trial judge accordingly.

Nonetheless, counsel for plaintiffs continues to opt for the economic reality test as exemplified by the Ninth Circuit decisions in *Schulz* and *Annabelle Candy Co.,* supra. His position in this regard is easily understandable, for there can be little doubt on this record that the covenant not to compete as included in the plaintiffs' contract for the sale of the Sea Dunes had no significant economic reality. It is entirely clear that the Proulxs entertained no intention whatever to compete with any buyer of the Sea Dunes. For reasons of declining health and

---

47. Speaking in another context, Mr. Justice Rehnquist once said of conflicting decisions in the several courts of appeals that they "may be summarized in the language of Macduff: 'Confusion now hath made his masterpiece.'" Reid v. Immigration and Naturalization Service, 420 U.S. 619, 628, 95 S.Ct. 1164, 1170, 43 L.Ed.2d 501 (1975).

advancing age, they intended to retire with no mental reservations whatsoever.

Their intentions in this respect were well known to everyone concerned, including Miller and Rose. Both testified to that effect, although Miller did indicate a general feeling that it was "prudent" to have a covenant not to compete just in case the Proulxs should change their minds. Undoubtedly, it was this realization and knowledge of the Proulxs' intention that accounted for the failure of both sellers and buyers at any time to bargain about, or even to discuss, the proposed covenant. Such failure to negotiate for a covenant has been treated as evidence of lack of intent to allocate any sum thereto. See *General Insurance Agency, Inc. v. Commissioner,* supra. However, where early in the negotiations the buyer specified that he desired the covenant and the amount of the allocation thereto, and the seller never objected, as was true here, it has been held that there was little reason to negotiate and therefore the lack of negotiations was not critical. See Rudie v. Commissioner, 49 T.C. 131 (1967) and Levinson v. Commissioner, 45 T.C. 380 (1966).

Such discussions of the covenant as occurred here were solely between Miller, Rose, and their attorney, Westman. And even those discussions do not appear to have concerned the merits or substance of the covenant but centered instead on Westman's advice that it had substantial tax advantages to the buyer of commercial property. In contrast, neither the Proulxs, nor their attorney, had the slightest concept of the covenant's tax impact. Not that this fact in any way governs the outcome of this case, for as the Fifth Circuit of Appeals observed in *Balthrope,* supra:

> No one has to arrange his business affairs to satisfy the tax collector's appetite for revenues. But when a taxpayer has failed to arrange his affairs so as to minimize his taxes, he cannot expect the court to do it for him *nunc pro tunc.* 356 F.2d 34.[48]

See, also, Hamlin's Trust v. Commissioner, 209 F.2d 761 (10th Cir. 1954) where the court observed at 209 F.2d 765:

> It is reasonably clear that the sellers failed to give consideration to the tax consequences of the provision [a covenant not to compete], but where parties enter into an agreement with a clear understanding of its substance and content, they cannot be heard to say later that they overlooked possible tax consequences.

Even though appealing, the difficulty with plaintiffs' argument is at once apparent. While for reasons previously discussed, there is considerable merit in their contention that under the *Schulz* doctrine

---

48. In this connection, one is also reminded of Judge Learned Hand's famous dictum that "[O]ver and over again courts have said that there is nothing sinister in so arranging one's affairs as to keep taxes as low as possible. Everybody does so, rich or poor; and all do right, for nobody owes any public duty to pay more than the law demands: taxes are enforced exactions, not voluntary contributions. To demand more in the name of morals is mere cant." Commissioner v. Newman, 159 F.2d 848, 850 (2d Cir., 1947) (dissenting opinion.)

and its economic reality test the covenant here should be disregarded, they are in effect asking this trial judge to ignore the *Danielson* rule as plainly set forth in the court's order of October 15, 1976. Of course, that invitation must be declined. If the wisdom of the *Danielson* rule is in need of reexamination, that effort is for the Appellate Division of this court, not for a member of its Trial Division acting under specific instructions as outlined above.

Proceeding, then, to those specific instructions, it will be recalled that the trial judge was first directed to determine whether taxpayers were induced to sign the sales contract with its covenant not to compete through fraud, duress, threats, mistake, or undue influence. Counsel for plaintiffs vigorously asserts that by reason of their advanced ages, poor health, and general sensitivity, plaintiffs were unusually susceptible to "high pressure" tactics, and he alleges that the statements made by Westman and Hebert "in a gruff and discourteous manner" at the meeting where the sales contract was signed amounted in the case of these elderly plaintiffs to duress and undue influence. In this connection, he places great emphasis on the absence of plaintiffs' attorney. While the failure of the real estate agent to notify the attorney of the meeting was clearly inexcusable, there has not been any showing whatever that, even if present, the Proulx' attorney would have advised them not to sign the contract *because it contained a covenant not to compete,* or, indeed, for any other reason. All of the evidence of record is to the contrary and shows clearly that, once his several objections had been taken care of, he was entirely satisfied with all the contract provisions.

There is no doubt that Clark made a mistake in not recognizing the tax implications of the covenant. But, as the cases cited above show, the overlooking of possibly adverse tax consequences is simply no ground for disregarding the contract. *See Hamlin's Trust,* supra. The failure to recognize tax consequences is not the "mistake" of which *Danielson* speaks.

The court makes it clear in the *Danielson* opinion that the "mistake, undue influence, fraud, duress, etc." to which it refers is only that which in an action between the contracting parties would result in the court setting aside or reforming the contract. No such showing has been made in this case. From all the evidence in this case, it is entirely clear to me that, even if we assume that Sebastian Sea Dunes had proven to be a profitable enterprise, and if we assume further that the Proulxs had decided to compete in the area with a new motel and restaurant, a Florida court would have enforced the covenant and enjoined them from such competition. In short, plaintiffs have failed to prove that they were induced to enter into this sales contract by reason of any fraud, duress, threats, mistake, or undue influence brought to bear upon them by the buyers or their attorney.

* * *

Based upon the foregoing considerations, the plaintiffs are not entitled to recover, and their petition should be dismissed.

CONCLUSION OF LAW

Upon the trial judge's findings and the foregoing opinion, which are adopted by the court, the court concludes as a matter of law that plaintiffs are not entitled to recover, and their petition is dismissed.

———

The Tax Court has imposed a strong proof requirement on a taxpayer seeking to repudiate or alter the terms of a contract. Major v. Commissioner, 76 T.C. 239 (1981).

3. SALE OF A BUSINESS ON THE INSTALLMENT METHOD

In many instances, the only feasible way in which the purchase price of a business may be financed is through the earnings of the enterprise paid to the seller in future installments. The sale proceeds must be allocated to determine which portions qualify for installment sale treatment. Pursuant to § 453(b)(2)(B), the installment sale method is not available for the sale of inventories of personal property.

Problems

1. Marge is the sole proprietor of a soft-drink bottling business in Metroville. She uses the accrual method of accounting. The business has the following assets:

	Adjusted Basis	Fair Market Value
Building (purchased in 1983 on which a straight line depreciation is taken)	$25,000	$100,000
Land	5,000	15,000
Trucks (original cost $15,000)	2,000	8,000
Machinery (original cost $22,000)	15,000	10,000
Inventory	12,000	12,000
Accounts receivable	5,000	5,000
	$64,000	$150,000

(a) Is the sale considered to be the sale of one item, an ongoing business, or is gain or loss measured as to each item? Consider Williams v. McGowan.

(b) Determine the character of the gain or loss realized by Marge as to each item. Consider §§ 1221, 1231, 1245 and 1250.

(c) Assume that Marge agrees to sell the business to Harry for $200,000. What is Harry paying an additional $50,000 for? Consider § 1060. Why would Harry prefer to call the $50,000 an amount paid for Marge's promise not to set up a competing business in Metroville for five years? Reconsider Problem 2(b) on page 613.

(d) Consider how you would seek to allocate the $200,000 if you represented Marge. Consider the character of the gain and the recapture of depreciation.

(e) Consider how you would seek to allocate the $200,000 if you represented Harry. Consider the buyer's ability to depreciate or amortize the assets. Consider also the amount and the character of the gain on his subsequent sale of the assets.

(f) Are there limitations on freedom of the parties to allocate the purchase price? Consider § 1060.

2. Wendy offered to sell her business, including goodwill, machinery, inventory, unimproved and improved real estate for $300,000. At the conclusion of the negotiations, when it seemed probable that the parties would agree to this sum, she generously said, "Well, I want you fellows to be happy; I'll agree not to compete in this county for ten years." They then agreed on the $300,000 figure. Wendy ultimately executed a written ten year covenant, enforceable under state law.

(a) Buyer asks you to help him develop a theory to get the maximum tax advantage with respect to the covenant not to compete. Consider the Proulx case. Should the parties amend the contract?

(b) Assume that before the transaction was consummated you were asked by Buyer how the covenant should be handled. Advise him.

Appendix

10.00% ANNUAL INTEREST RATE

ANNUAL COMPOUND INTEREST AND ANNUITY TABLES

	Amount Of 1	Amount Of 1 Per Period	Present Worth Of 1	Present Worth Of 1 Per Period
	What a single $1 deposit grows to in the future. The deposit is made at the beginning of the first period.	What a series of $1 deposits grow to in the future. A deposit is made at the end of each period.	What $1 to be paid in the future is worth today. Value today of a single payment tomorrow.	What $1 to be paid at the end of each period is worth today. Value today of a series of payments tomorrow.
	$S=(1+i)^n$	$S\overline{n}\rceil=\dfrac{(1+i)^n-1}{i}$	$V^n=\dfrac{1}{(1+i)^n}$	$A\overline{n}\rceil=\dfrac{1-V^n}{i}$

YEAR				
1	1.100 000	1.000 000	0.909 091	0.909 091
2	1.210 000	2.100 000	0.826 446	1.735 537
3	1.331 000	3.310 000	0.751 315	2.486 852
4	1.464 100	4.641 000	0.683 013	3.169 865
5	1.610 510	6.105 100	0.620 921	3.790 787
6	1.771 561	7.715 610	0.564 474	4.355 261
7	1.948 717	9.487 171	0.513 158	4.868 419
8	2.143 589	11.435 888	0.466 507	5.334 926
9	2.357 948	13.579 477	0.424 098	5.759 024
10	2.593 742	15.937 425	0.385 543	6.144 567
11	2.853 117	18.531 167	0.350 494	6.495 061
12	3.138 428	21.384 284	0.318 631	6.813 692
13	3.452 271	24.522 712	0.289 664	7.103 356
14	3.797 498	27.974 983	0.263 331	7.366 687
15	4.177 248	31.772 482	0.239 392	7.606 080
16	4.594 973	35.949 730	0.217 629	7.823 709
17	5.054 470	40.544 703	0.197 845	8.021 553
18	5.559 917	45.599 173	0.179 859	8.201 412
19	6.115 909	51.159 090	0.163 508	8.364 920
20	6.727 500	57.274 999	0.148 644	8.513 564
21	7.400 250	64.002 499	0.135 131	8.648 694
22	8.140 275	71.402 749	0.122 846	8.771 540
23	8.954 302	79.543 024	0.111 678	8.883 218
24	9.849 733	88.497 327	0.101 526	8.984 744
25	10.834 706	98.347 059	0.092 296	9.077 040
26	11.918 177	109.181 765	0.083 905	9.160 945
27	13.109 994	121.099 942	0.076 278	9.237 223
28	14.420 994	134.209 936	0.069 343	9.306 567
29	15.863 093	148.630 930	0.063 039	9.369 606
30	17.449 402	164.494 023	0.057 309	9.426 914
31	19.194 342	181.943 425	0.052 099	9.479 013
32	21.113 777	201.137 767	0.047 362	9.526 376
33	23.225 154	222.251 544	0.043 057	9.569 432
34	25.547 670	245.476 699	0.039 143	9.608 575
35	28.102 437	271.024 368	0.035 584	9.644 159
36	30.912 681	299.126 805	0.032 349	9.676 508
37	34.003 949	330.039 486	0.029 408	9.705 917
38	37.404 343	364.043 434	0.026 735	9.732 651
39	41.144 778	401.447 778	0.024 304	9.756 956
40	45.259 256	442.592 556	0.022 095	9.779 051

Index

References are to Pages

A

ACCELERATED COST RECOVERY SYSTEM
See also, Depreciation, this index
Application, 570–573
Automobiles, business personal use of, 574–575
Conventions, half year and mid month, 572–573
Depreciation, contrasts with, 569–570
Depreciation methods, use of, 571
Leasehold improvements, 573
Policy aspects, 577–585
Recovery periods, 570–571
Recovery property, use of to construct long-lived, 484–486, 586–593
Tax preference item, alternative minimum tax, 1034
Tax shelters, 884–885

ACCOUNTING
See also, Claim of Right Doctrine; Installment Sale Method; Nonrecognition Transactions; Open Transaction Method
Accrual method, 226–232
  All events test, 226–230
  Economic performance test, 230–231
  Prepayment of income, 525–538
  Reserves, use of, 547–556
  Structured settlements, 156–159, 231–232
  When income is reported, 226
  When deductions can be taken, 226–232, 484
Annual accounting concept, 171–174
Cash method, 211–225
  Claim of right, 175–180
  Constructive receipt, 214–215, 217–221
  Economic benefit, 160–164, 215–216, 221–224
  Operation of, 211–212
  Payment by check, 215
  Payment by credit card, 621–622
  Prepayment of expenses, 490–495
  Receipts in kind, 212
  Valuation of obligations received in an open transaction, 753, 826–828
  When income is reported, 211–212

ACCOUNTING—Cont'd
When deductions can be taken, 225
Choice of accounting methods, 232–235
  Alternative methods to cash and accrual, 233–234
  Liberal choices available, 232
  Limitation on selection of accounting methods, 232–233
Combination of methods, 234
Financial accounting, 538–546, 830–847, 999–1001
Reserves, use of, 547–556

ACTIVE INCOME
In general, 361, 891

ACTIVE PARTICIPATION
In general, 895

ADJUSTED GROSS INCOME
In general, 12

ALIMONY
Child support payments distinguished, 629–630
Front-end loading rule, 628–629
In general, 626–629
Litigation expenses of, deduction of, 640
Property settlements distinguished, 631–637

ALTERNATIVE MINIMUM TAX
In general, 1032–1034

AMORTIZATION
Intangibles, 593–612
Start-up expenses, 503–509

AMOUNT REALIZED
Contingent payments, 803–807
Disposition of encumbered property, 765–792
In general, 752
Liabilities, impact on, 765
Open transactions, 753–756, 826–828
Valuation difficulties, 760–762

ANNUITIES
Comparison with life insurance, 291
Employee annuities, 160–164
Exclusion ratio, 152–153
In general, 152–155